T. WALTER WALLBANK
Emeritus Professor of History, University of Southern California

ALASTAIR M. TAYLOR
Professor of Political Studies and Geography, Queen's University

NELS M. BAILKEY
Professor of History, Tulane University

SCOTT, FORESMAN AND COMPANY   Glenview, Illinois   London

Civilization
past & present

SINGLE VOLUME   FOURTH EDITION

Acknowledgments for quoted matter are
included in the Footnotes, pages 867-877;
for the illustrations, in the List of
Illustrations, pages 878-883. The
Footnotes and List of Illustrations pages
are an extension of the copyright page.

ISBN: 0-673-05863-8

Library of Congress Catalog Card No. 77-139611
Copyright © 1962, 1967, 1971 by Scott, Foresman and
    Company, Glenview, Illinois 60025
Philippines Copyright 1971 by Scott, Foresman
    and Company.
All Rights Reserved.
Printed in the United States of America.
Regional Offices of Scott, Foresman are located in Dallas,
    Oakland, N.J., Palo Alto, and Tucker, Ga.

Preface

When the original planning of *Civilization Past and Present* began, well before World War II, the majority of American people had not yet fully adjusted to participation in world affairs, nor, in some respects, had college curricula. The nation clung to its isolation, seemingly insulated by two vast oceanic stretches; but in three hectic decades the United States has become totally involved in world affairs. Today in an age of global interdependence and atomic anxiety, the study of all aspects of world history has come to be viewed as essential, for only by understanding the past can one assess both the perils and opportunities of the present. *Civilization Past and Present*, first published in 1942 in two volumes, was the first text that dealt not merely with political history but with all facets—economic, artistic, intellectual, social, religious, and political—of world culture, and that treated the history of man not as a European experience nor as a western experience, but as a global experience through which all the great cultural systems have interacted to produce the present-day world.

The single-volume edition of *Civilization Past and Present*, originally published in 1956 and revised in 1962 and 1967, has continued the tradition of presenting a global survey of the significant experiences and accomplishments of mankind. This latest edition, in particular, has responded to a new, radical form of isolationism, a doctrine of complete "historical isolation." Confronted by admittedly massive current problems, its devotees see the contemporary as completely unique and the past as mainly irrelevant. This edition has sought to demonstrate that impatient as one may be to solve current difficulties, this objective is not well served by viewing them in a historical vacuum and by dismissing as irrelevant any understanding of how we got where we are. Times of upheaval and travail especially require avoidance of what has been termed "imprisonment in the present" and "being overwhelmed by the instant moment."* The maintenance of a historical perspective alone can give the comparative background indispensable for understanding the contemporary world.

This fourth edition is a thorough revision, completely redesigned and reset, with the greater part of the book having been rewritten for greater clarity and for relevance to the latest scholarship. In keeping with the objective of providing essential background to contemporary problems, material has been added on such topics as Southeast Asia and the role of the black in the Western Hemisphere. Among the special features of the book is the expanded coverage of the non-West. A new chapter has been added on the Third World during the post-World War II period. To improve the continuity of the Asian narrative, a substantial portion of the discussion of India, China, and Japan previously located in Part Three has been shifted to Part Two as a new chapter on Asia during the Middle Ages: "The Guptas and the T'ang: Two Golden Ages." A section on the historical background of the conflict in Southeast Asia has been introduced in Chapter 16, and a piece on black Africans in the new Europes has been included in Chapter 26.

The concluding part of the book has been completely revised and restructured; Part Eight contains three chapters: one on the West and Communism since 1945, the second on Asia and Africa in the same period, and the third on the intellectual and cultural ferment during the present century. Concluding the text is a rewritten Epilogue on "The Challenges Ahead." Additional features are the restructuring of the political history of each major European state from 1850 to 1914 in Chapters 23 and 24, with a final segment on World War I shifted from Chapter 28; a newly organized chapter, "New Vistas and Ominous Fears," combining the material previously found in two chapters; and the reorganization of Chapter

21 to provide a more effective presentation of both romanticism and industrialism. In addition to the black African material, Chapter 26 contains a section on the common denominators of the new Europes. Note also that to ensure better continuity the chapter "Europe's Search for Stability" has been shifted to precede "The West Takes the Offensive." Reinforcing these substantial new features, revisions have been made on nearly every page. The following topics received major revision and expansion: the Neolithic Revolution, the rise of civilization, Hellenic and Hellenistic philosophy and science, the Ottoman Turks, Muslim science and philosophy, Hebrew history, the rise of Prussia, the French Revolution, romanticism, and the dynamics of imperialism.

Brief essays by eminent specialists, the Historical Critiques, have been provided to give an extra dimension of interpretation, and a revised Prologue helps integrate these Critiques with the text. All maps have been completely redrawn in two colors; three new four-color reference maps have been added; and many maps appear in relief. In the illustration program two thirds of the pictures are new, and the color plates are mainly new and more numerous. The bibliographies have been updated, and the chronological tables have been shifted to the end of the book for more convenient reference.

The contents and organization of this revision owes much to the suggestions tendered by a distinguished group of historical specialists and to numerous comments from users. A special word of thanks to L. Gray Cowan, Director of the Institute of African Studies at Columbia University; Professor John Willis, University of California at Berkeley; and Professor Joseph D. Lewis, Central State University, for helpful comments on the African material. As in the previous edition, Franz Schulze, Professor of Art at Lake Forest College, selected the full-color illustrations, which, with his accompanying commentary, constitute a capsule history of world art.

*Daniel J. Boorstin, "A Case of Hypochondria," *Newsweek*, July 6, 1970, p. 27.

Note to the Student

This book has been developed with the dual purpose of helping you acquire a solid knowledge of past events and, equally important, of helping you think more constructively about the significance of those events for the difficult times in which we live. In the Prologue you will learn more about studying the meaning of history. This note is intended to acquaint you with the principal features of the text.

THE INTERCHAPTERS

Aid in the organization and review of your reading will be provided by the interchapters, which outline the material to be covered in each unit.

THE HISTORICAL CRITIQUES

Appearing at the end of the volume are five Historical Critiques, each contributed by a specialist. These brief essays are integrated with the text in order to provide an extra dimension of interpretation. Two of the Critiques concern themselves with the genesis and development of historical writing in the West and in China and India. Together they enable us to appreciate better how different civilizations conceptualize the purpose of history in terms of their respective culture patterns. The validity of dividing the temporal continuum into specific periods is analyzed in a third Critique which focuses upon the "Industrial Revolution." A fourth essay examines the propriety—and risks—involved in carrying over concepts from the biological sciences into human societies in an effort to explain or justify men's behavior. The final Critique brings us abreast of our own century's reinterpretations of history and society.

THE COLOR PLATES

Seven folios of full-color art reproductions appear with the interchapters. The works of art have been carefully selected and faithfully reproduced to illustrate, in every case, some facet of a culture pattern discussed in the text. These reproductions, with the accompanying commentary, constitute a capsule history of world art.

SUGGESTIONS FOR READING

In addition to the general bibliography at the end of the book, you will find in each chapter an annotated bibliography, pertaining especially to that chapter and listing special historical studies, biographies, reputable historical fiction, and some collections of source materials. As indicated in the listings, many of these works can be purchased in inexpensive paperbound editions. These bibliographies will provide you with ample readings from which to develop special reports or with which to improve your understanding of a given subject.

THE CHRONOLOGICAL CHARTS

At the end of the book is a series of eight chronological charts showing the sequence of events discussed within the eight units of the text. By studying these charts, you can fix in your mind the relationship of events in the various parts of the world.

THE MAPS

Two-color maps are liberally distributed throughout this book. Some are designed to make clear the nature of a single distinctive event or idea discussed in the text; others illustrate larger trends, as, for example, the map showing trade and cultural interchange in the ancient world (see p. 116). At the end of the book are sixteen pages of full-color reference maps, showing all the major areas of the world and virtually every town, political subdivision, and geographic feature mentioned in the text. Most of the reference maps and several of the two-color maps appear in relief.

THE PRONUNCIATION KEY

In the index the correct pronunciation is given for most proper names. Thus you will find it easy, as well as extremely helpful, to look up the correct pronunciation of the names of persons and places referred to in the text.

Contents

Prologue

Perspective on Man

If the time span of our planet—now estimated at some five billion years—were telescoped into a single year, the first eight months would be devoid of any life. The next two months would be taken up with plant and very primitive animal forms, and not until well into December would any mammals appear. In this "year" members of *Homo erectus,* the best known species of "near men," would mount the global stage only between 10 and 11 P.M. on December 31. And how has man spent that brief allotment? He has given over most of it—the equivalent of half a million years or more—to making tools and weapons out of stone. His revolutionary changeover from a food-hunting nomad to a farmer who raised grain and domesticated animals would occur in the last sixty seconds. And into that final minute would be crowded all of his other accomplishments: the use of metal, the creation of civilizations, the mastery of the oceans, the harnessing of steam, then gas, electricity, oil, and, finally, in our own lifetime, atomic energy. Thus, among man's greatest achievements on earth has been his development of tools, machines, and controlled power—in short, technology. Yet even this planet earth no longer satisfies man's technological ambitions, for he has at last succeeded in escaping his age-old bondage to the earth and is about to propel himself into the interplanetary age.

While human technology is at present moving ahead at supersonic speed, there has been no corresponding increase in man's own mental or physical capacity. He probably has no more native intelligence than his Stone Age ancestors—and undoubtedly less muscle. So we come to a fundamental question: how is twentieth-century man to cope with the ever widening disparity between what he *is* and what he *has*? How can he control and utilize his tremendous technological powers for happiness and not for nuclear self-annihilation? Today he seeks to conquer other planets before he has learned to govern his own.

Surely an indispensable step toward solving contemporary man's dilemma—technology without the requisite control and power without adequate wisdom—must be a better understanding of how man and all his works became what they are today. Only by understanding the past can mankind assess both the perils and the opportunities of the present. This accumulated experience, the memory of the race, is available for study. We call it *history.*

THE "USE" OF HISTORY

Definition of history. History is the record of the past actions of mankind, based upon surviving evidence. The historian uses this evidence to reach conclusions which he believes are valid. In this way, he becomes an interpreter of the development of mankind. History shows that all patterns and problems in human affairs are the products of a complex process of growth. By throwing light on that process, history provides a means for profiting from human experience. There would be no landmarks, no points of reference, no foundations on which to build if the individual were bereft of the knowledge of his past. The system of government under which he lives, the frontiers of his country, and its economy—such factors are meaningful because of history. In our age of global interdependence and atomic propulsion, the neglect of history would be more than folly—it could prove suicidal.

In this connection it is salutary to recall the words of the philosopher George Santayana when he declared, "Those who cannot remember the past are condemned to repeat it." Actually, history is itself a way of looking at reality, and many cultures, particularly food-collecting societies, which tend to exist on a day-to-day basis, appear to be little aware of their own past, content to live more or less in the present. As economic, social, and political activities grow more complex, however, it becomes necessary to keep records—of the grain sown, or of battles waged over disputed land. A knowledge of the past then becomes indispensable to decisions that are relevant to contemporary needs and future prospects. In such literate societies, where knowledge can be written down and preserved for future use, we find the birth and development of history and the historical method.

In this edition of *Civilization Past and Present* a number of experts have contributed special essays called Historical Critiques, concentrating on what is known as historiography—that is, the study of the philosophy and methodology of the writing of history. Some of the earliest attempts to use history for various purposes are discussed in the critiques, "The Birth of History in the West" and "Chinese and Indian Historiography." As these Historical Critiques will attest, the "use" of history means that the scribe or historian has to answer two related questions: "how" is his account to be written, and "why" has he undertaken the task?

THE "HOW" OF HISTORY

Is history a science? There is more than one way of treating the past. In dealing with the American Revolution, for example, the historian may describe its events in narrative form. Again, he may prefer to analyze its general causes or perhaps compare its stages of revolution with the patterns of revolutions in other countries. Because of these descriptive and analytical functions, historical writing has sometimes been regarded as a science. But the historian does not aim for or attain the same kind of results as the scientist. The latter can verify his conclusions by repeating his experiment under controlled conditions in his laboratory, and he also attempts to classify the phenomenon in a general group or category. The historian, on the other hand, has to pay much greater attention to the *uniqueness* of his data, because each event takes place at a particular time and in a particular place. And since that time is now past, he cannot verify his conclusions by duplicating the circumstances in which the event occurred. Moreover, since history is concerned fundamentally with the lives and actions of men, the search for causes is bound to be relatively subjective.

Nevertheless, historians insist that history be written as scientifically as possible and that evidence be analyzed with the same objective attitude employed by the scientist when he examines natural phenomena. This scientific spirit requires the historian to handle his evidence according to established rules of historical analysis, to recognize his own biases and attempt to eliminate their effects from his work, and to draw only such conclusions as the evidence seems to warrant.

Historical method. To meet these requirements, historians have evolved the "historical method." The first step is the search for what is called *sources,* without which there can be no history. These sources may consist of material remains such as bones, tools, weapons, and pottery; oral traditions such as myths, legends, and songs; pictorial data such as drawings and maps; and, of course, written records ranging from ancient manuscripts to treaties, diaries, books, and yesterday's newspaper.

Having acquired his sources, the historian must next infer from them the facts. This process has two parts. *External criticism* tests the genuineness of the source. The importance of external criticism was demonstrated dramatically in recent years by the unmasking of a hoax—Piltdown man—which had long duped scientists. Generally, however, the historian has to deal with less spectacular problems, such as checking ancient documents for errors that have crept into the text through faulty copying or translating.

The second step in the analytical process is called *internal criticism.* In evaluating written materials, the historian must ascertain the author's meaning and the accuracy of his work. To do so may require study of the language of the era or of the circumstances in which the author's statement was made. A politician's memoirs may be highly suspect because of an almost universal human tendency to present oneself in the most favorable light. Official documents must also be examined for what they may conceal as well as reveal—especially if they are documents released by governments to explain or justify a change in foreign policy or their involvement in a war.

The final step in historical method is *synthesis*. Here the historian must determine which factors in a given situation are most relevant to his purpose, since obviously he cannot include everything that occurred in the period under review. This delicate process of selection underscores the role that subjectivity plays in the writing of history. "The more complex the events dealt with, the wider their spread in time and space, the greater are the calls made upon the historian's judgment."[1]

The problem of periodization. Can we really categorize history as "ancient," "medieval," and "modern"? When we reflect upon this question, it becomes obvious that what is "modern" in the twentieth century could conceivably be considered "medieval" in the twenty-fifth century, and ultimately "ancient" in the thirty-fifth or fortieth century A.D. Yet not to break up the account would be akin to reading this book (or any other) without the benefit of parts, chapters, paragraphs, or even separate sentences. Like time itself, history would then become a ceaseless flow of consciousness and events. To simplify his task and to manage his materials more easily, the historian divides time into periods. The divisions he chooses, the lines he draws, reveal the distinctive way the historian regards the past—namely, in terms of patterns which appear to him logical and meaningful. Needless to say, no two historians see the past in an identical pattern; thus the division of the past into periods is necessarily arbitrary and, like railway or airline timetables, subject to change without prior notice.

That periodization is far from being simply a theoretical problem of interest only to the specialist can be seen from an examination of several of the Historical Critiques. The authors of "Chinese and Indian Historiography" demonstrate that those two massive societies have held very different views both of the meaning of time as a philosophical concept and of the significance of chronology as a means of dividing their respective histories into meaningful periods. Even within our own western tradition, historians do not agree as to when "medieval" history ends and "modern" history begins. Obviously, the "how" of historical method and writing raises a number of difficult, but fascinating, problems.

THE "WHY" OF HISTORY

Historical analysis. The historian seeks to describe not only *what* has happened in the past and *how* it happened but also *why* society undergoes change. Any search of this kind raises a number of fundamental questions: the roles of Providence, the individual, and the group in history; the extent to which historical events are unique and the extent to which they fit into patterns; and the problem of progress in human affairs. The answers vary with the different philosophical views of mankind.

Providence or the individual. Those who hold the teleological view see in history the guidance of a Divine Will, directing human destinies according to a cosmic purpose. This concept was accepted as self-evident in ancient theocratic societies and remained prevalent in medieval thought, but it lost ground after the Renaissance, when the spread of rationalistic doctrines and scientific triumphs seemed to forecast unlimited progress in human affairs. Yet in our own day there has been a reaction against the nineteenth century's comfortable assumption that man is a completely free agent. One distinguished historian, for example, has asserted that the only tenable interpretation of the human drama is the religious one.[2]

Others have minimized the role of Providence while exalting the role of the individual in the historical process. The nineteenth-century historian Thomas Carlyle maintained that the Alexanders, Muhammads, and Cromwells were the "Great Men" whose leadership chiefly determined the course of human events. Later historians discounted this generalization by emphasizing the impact of economic and other "impersonal" forces. With the increasing centralized control of the twentieth century, however, especially as evidenced in recent dictatorships, the rise of a leader with a strong magnetic personality, projected and "amplified" by the mass media, again underscores the power of the individual, not only to involve himself in a nation's decision making but, as in the case of Hitler, Stalin, or Mao, to affect the direction of global events.

"Laws" and "forces" in history. The opponents of Carlyle's approach often contend that history is determined by "forces" and "laws" and by the actions of entire societies. One geographer, for example, has even argued that a people's genius and progress are decided principally by climate. We can reject such an extreme claim but—as we shall see when we take up the earliest, or fluvial, civilizations—physical environment does play a significant part in the development of human societies.

Sociologists approach history primarily by analyzing the origins, institutions, and functions of groups. Some attach special importance to population factors as criteria for judging the evolution of a given society, while others analyze societies in terms of their division of labor.

Like the sociologist, the economist tends to look at the historical record from the standpoint of group action and especially the impact of economic forces such as that of, say, supply and demand or diminishing returns. Whereas historians have traditionally emphasized political and military events, sociologists and economists have brought a new dimension of interpretation to the study of history, since they are concerned with such areas as the interaction of various classes in a society, the ethics and political consequences of economic philosophies, and the impact of technology upon the living standard and economic well-being of a given society. An example of the way in which socioeconomic interpretations of historical data can enrich our understanding of the past is found in the Historical Critique, "Was There an 'Industrial Revolution'?"

Karl Marx's theory of history. The most explosive interpretation of history in modern times was made by Karl Marx. To him, irresistible economic forces governed men and determined the trend of events. Marx contended that the shift from one economic stage to another—such as from feudalism to capitalism—is attained by sporadic upheavals, or revolutions, occurring because the class controlling the methods of production eventually resists further progress in order to maintain its vested interests. Marx predicted that the proletariat would overthrow the exploiting capitalists and that the end result would be a classless society, followed by a gradual withering away of the state itself.

Many of Marx's basic assumptions, however, have been conclusively disproved by events. Contrary to his prediction, social legislation and higher productivity have enabled the living standards of the "exploited" masses in capitalist countries to become higher than ever before. And instead of the development of a classless society in the Soviet Union and other Marxist countries, the state controls all aspects of a stratified society in which a wage and privilege differential (greater than that in western societies) exists between the administrative and military elites on one hand and the masses of workers and peasants on the other. In short, although Marx claimed to have made history "scientific," events continue to attest to the presence of unpredictable factors in human affairs for which no ideological forces or laws have yet been able to account.

Theories of civilization. Numerous other attempts have been made to explain the rise and fall of civilizations according to a set of principles. The different views of modern historians are analyzed in the final Historical Critique, "Twentieth-Century Reinterpretations of History and Society." One of these historians, Oswald Spengler, a disillusioned German, maintained that civilizations were like organisms; each grew with the "superb aimlessness" of a flower and passed through a cycle of spring, summer, autumn, and winter. He declared that western civilization was in its winter period and had already entered a state of rapid decline.

Spengler influenced the English historian Arnold J. Toynbee, whose works became best sellers after World War II. To Toynbee, "challenge and response" explain the rise and fall of civilizations. Man achieves civilization "as a response to a challenge in a situation of special difficulty which rouses him to make a hitherto unprecedented effort."[3] The ancient Egyptians, for example, built their civilization by learning to control the Nile River. Toynbee holds that a civilization continues to grow as long as it is motivated by creative individuals; when they can no longer inspire the majority, social disunity brings about decline and disintegration.

Spengler was not unique in likening societies to organisms. Other thinkers have also sought to explain the life and behavior of human society in terms of biological growth and decay. In particular, the evolutionary hypothesis developed by Charles Darwin had a strong impact upon nineteenth-century intellectuals and gave rise to the concept that the principle of "survival of the fittest" must equally apply to human societies. This line of thought—known as social Darwinism—raises social and ethical questions of major importance, as the Historical Critique on that subject attests.

Is the course of history inevitable? Many eminent historians profess to find no recurring pattern in past events, seeing only, as one of them has put it, "the only safe rule for the historian [is] that he should recognize in the development of human destinies the play of the contingent and unforeseen."[4] These differences of view all lead to the question: Are men really free to choose or does history obey impersonal laws and forces—in short, is the course of history inevitable? We seem to have to accept either inevitable laws—which appear to leave no room for significant freedom of action—or the equally extreme alternative that makes every event a unique act and history merely the record of unrelated episodes.

Can this dilemma be avoided? We believe it can. Even though all events are in various respects unique, they also contain elements which invite comparison—as in the case of the origin and course of revolutions in different countries. The comparative approach permits us to seek relationships between historical phenomena and to group them into movements, or patterns, or civilizations.

The authors of this book eschew any single "theory" of history. They are eclectic in their approach because they see merit in a number of basic concepts. These include the important effects of physical environment on social organization and institutions; the powerful roles played not only by economic but also by political and religious factors; and the impact exerted upon events by various outstanding personalities occupying key positions in history.

The question of progress. Somewhere along the line, the student is likely to ask: "Are we making any progress? Is mankind getting better?" Nineteenth-century optimists confidently answered "Yes!" but our crisis-ridden century is by no means so sure. In any case, such questions are difficult to answer because of the difficulty of defining such terms as *progress* or *better*. (Better than what, for example?) Those who equate progress with material advancement might remember that the Athens of Socrates and Aristotle produced an unsurpassed galaxy of thinkers and artists without the benefit of electricity, television, or the Madison Avenue ad-man. Conversely, the advanced literacy and technology boasted by Nazi Germany did not prevent it from wallowing in the moral depravity which created concentration camps and gas chambers.

Nevertheless, our lawmakers, educators, and scientists do assume that progress can be both defined and defended on rational grounds. Various factors might be applied to test this proposition. *Material advancement* calls for improved living and health standards, increased economic production, and a distribution of goods so as to benefit the greatest number of people. *Intellectual and spiritual progress* includes educational opportunities for all and is measured in terms of creative achievements in science, the humanities, and arts. For example, Einstein's theory constitutes an advance over Newton's theory of gravitation because it can solve not only the same problems as the earlier theory but also problems that hitherto defied solution. *Social progress* covers the "pursuit of happiness" and includes such essentials as equal status for women, abolition

of conditions of servitude, and enlightened treatment of prisoners and the insane.

Yet another significant factor is *political participation*. In a democracy progress can be tested by the opportunities for the individual to assume public responsibilities and by the protection of his right to hold views at variance with those held by others, especially in the case of minorities. Finally, the growth of *international cooperation* becomes basic in any meaningful discussion of progress. This growth depends on and contributes to the maintenance of peace and security, the peaceful settlement of international disputes, and world-wide improvement in economic and social standards.

THE CULTURAL APPROACH TO HISTORY

The universal culture pattern. In the interplay of man with his environment and with his fellowmen, of which history is the written record, men have always expressed certain fundamental needs. These form the basis of a "universal culture pattern" and deserve to be enumerated.

1. *The need to make a living.* Man must have food, shelter, clothing, and the means to provide for his offspring's survival.

2. *The need for law and order.* From the earliest times communities have had to keep peace among their members, defend themselves against external attack, and protect property.

3. *The need for social organization.* In order that people may make a living, raise families, and maintain law and order, a social structure is necessary. Ideologies may differ in their concepts of the relative importance of the group and the individual within any such social organization.

4. *The need for knowledge and learning.* Since earliest times mankind has transmitted the knowledge painfully acquired from experience, first orally and then by means of language and writing systems. As societies grow more complex, there is an increasing need to preserve knowledge and to make it available through education to as many people as possible.

5. *The need for self-expression.* Man has responded creatively to his environment even before the days when he decorated the walls of Paleolithic caves with paintings of the animals he hunted. The arts appear to have a lineage as old as man himself.

6. *The need for religious expression.* Equally as old is man's attempt to answer the "why" of his existence. What primitive peoples considered

supernatural in their environment could at a later date often be explained by science in terms of natural phenomena. Yet today, no less than in prehistoric times, men continue to search for answers to the ultimate questions of existence.

These six briefly described needs have been common to men at all times and in all places. Taken together, they form the basis of a universal culture pattern. To carry this concept one step further: when a group of people behave similarly and share the same institutions and ways of life, they can be said to have a common culture. Each person born into that group will in turn derive from it his basic way of life. It follows that the basic differences between the farmers of ancient China and those of present-day Nebraska are due mainly to the fact that their culture traits are at different stages of development or that they have worked out different methods of solving the same problems of existence. In the succeeding chapters we shall be looking at a large number of different cultures, some of which are designated as *civilizations* (for a definition of this term see pp. 15 and 358).

Diffusion as a factor in culture change. Cultures are never static or wholly isolated. A particular culture may have an individuality which sets it off sharply from other cultures, but invariably it has been influenced by external contacts. Such contacts may be either peaceful or warlike, and they meet with varying degrees of resistance. The early American colonists took from the Indians the use of corn and tobacco, while the latter obtained the horse and firearms from the newcomers. On the other hand, the Second World War saw the Nazis and Japanese force their cultures upon subjugated peoples with no permanent results.

Environment and invention in culture change. While geography has profoundly influenced the development of cultures, we should not exaggerate its importance. Although riverine civilizations evolved along the Nile and the Tigris-Euphrates, for example, none emerged in the physically comparable valleys of the Jordan and the Rio Grande.[5] Moreover, environmental influences tend to become less marked as man gains increasing mastery over nature, as shown by the transformation of deserts in southwestern United States into rich citrus belts and the extension of the grain-growing belt in the Canadian prairies further north through the development of frost- and rust-resistant types of wheat.

Invention is therefore another important source of culture change. The automobile—which has revolutionized transportation, the growth of cities, and even home life—was made possible only by a host of earlier inventions, such as the internal-combustion engine and that most ancient and indispensable tool, the wheel. The study of the origins of certain basic inventions again underscores the fact that historical change is a continuous process at once dynamic and often unpredictable. The domestication of animals and grain, for example, took place in both the old and new worlds, albeit the animals and cereals were different because of the dissimilar ecological factors involved; yet so far as we know, there was no physical contact at the time between the two cultural heartlands. To what extent, then, is physical contact required in the process of invention? Or, is it possible for men in different times and places to hit upon similar solutions to the challenges posed by their respective environments —resulting in the phenomenon known as "parallel invention"?

Is race a factor in culture change? Just as no pure culture was ever developed in isolation by one group, so there is no pure race of people. Ethnic types have intermingled along with the diffusion of cultures. *Race*, a much misused term, has value only in denoting the major human divisions, each with its own distinctive physical characteristics: Caucasian (white), Mongoloid (yellow), and Negroid (black). No race has ever monopolized culture, though for a specific period one race may produce an impressive record of cultural creativity.

Unfortunately, just as ignorance has all too often led to unscientific generalizations about the differences between the "races" of *Homo sapiens* —which in turn have been employed to justify discriminatory, and even brutal, behavior toward one people by another—so the factor of race has also been employed at different times and places to "explain" the superiority which groups perceive in their own cultures as compared with those of others. Thus Caucasian peoples have been all too guilty of assuming that their particular cultural patterns and activities must be superior to the cultures which they associate with Asian and African peoples. To hold such arrogant, and demonstrably fallacious, views was more understandable, if not pardonable, in the era of western colonialism. In today's world, however, to retain such stereotyped concepts of nonwestern peoples can be dangerously explosive. New and scientifically valid images of the nonwestern world are required, and a study of history can do much to get rid of western cultural myopia.

Culture lag. Some parts of a culture pattern change more rapidly than others, so that one institution sometimes becomes outmoded in relation to others in a society. When different parts of a society fail to mesh harmoniously, the condition is often called *culture lag*. Numerous examples of this lag could be cited: the failure to enfranchise women until this century, the tragedy of hunger in the midst of plenty during the 1930's, or, in our own day, the repeated inability of the United Nations to limit atomic energy to peaceful use because of the insistence by national states to arm themselves as they wish.

In the view of some observers, culture lag has assumed its most dangerous form in the apparently widening gap in communications and outlook between science and the accelerating technological sector on the one hand and our traditional humanistic culture and values system on the other. These two major segments of our culture pattern appear to be advancing, and changing, at the speeds of a supersonic jet and of a horse and buggy respectively. Just what dynamic factors are at work which bring about different rates of speed in the processes of change? Because our modern age owes its particular world-outlook in ever growing measure to the discoveries and philosophy of science, and because the processes of change are today most apparent in our contemporary technological order, we have need to understand much more clearly than ever before the nature of the scientific revolution—not only in the way that it began in the sixteenth century, but also how it operates today and is already shaping the pattern of our culture for the decades ahead.

THE CHALLENGE

A century of conflict. The twentieth century has been phenomenally fruitful in raising economic, social, and health standards. But ours is also a century of conflict. It has been said that contemporary man is involved in three kinds of conflict: with nature, with his fellow man, and with himself. In some ways, the first can be richly rewarding. Thus the harnessing of atomic energy holds out hope for almost unlimited human advancement. But meanwhile we are depleting the earth's natural resources at an unprecedented rate, and vast areas of the globe are being ravaged by erosion.

These unresolved conflicts with nature in turn increase human tensions. Hundreds of millions in underdeveloped regions are hungry, a situation that breeds social unrest and political conflict. Today all Asia and Africa demand political freedom; but if chaos or new forms of aggression are not to follow the granting of independence, the emergent nations must be offered support in raising the living standards of the masses. This aid, however, must come from the more developed countries, which themselves are dangerously split into ideologically warring camps. Tensions abound among both the strong and the weak. Today's tensions find repercussions within man himself, as is shown by the increasing incidence of nervous and mental disorders, by the feelings of general insecurity among average people everywhere, and by a seemingly pervasive sense of rootlessness and restlessness among members of the young generation in all nations.

In short, ours is an age that is questioning all the accepted traditional concepts of what is good and permissible. The universe of Newton, with its emphasis on permanence and fixed principles, has given way to Einstein's model of a universe that is relativistic not only in its physical behavior but in the behavior of men and societies as well. Ours is an uncertain and obviously dangerous time in which to live, but at the same time it is exceedingly dynamic and challenging. In such a world it would be strange if the study of history itself were not to reflect this search for new concepts about the nature of man's involvement in his environment and his relationship to his fellow man. Understandably, then, the historians of our century have been updating the methodology of their discipline in order to take full advantage of the contributions of science and technology. Even more important, the final Historical Critique shows that twentieth-century historians are also engaged in subjecting the traditional philosophical postulates of their discipline to a searching reinterpretation in order to acquire a greater understanding of the human condition on this planet.

No time for defeatism. To many, it seems almost hopeless to try to rectify a world which, in Hamlet's phrase, seems so "out of joint." The authors disagree heartily with these prophets of doom. A study of history quickly proves that the "good old days" were actually not that good and that every age has had to bear its full burden of dire forebodings. Moreover, history teaches us that man has never yet given up his struggle for survival and the betterment of life. The authors agree with the scholar who wrote: "Others claim man will destroy himself, which is of course a political prediction. This seems to me a fate as unlikely as committing suicide by holding your breath. Man, for all his frailties, is now one of the toughest, most tenacious, most adaptable animals in the kingdom . . . and I am sure that he is here to stay."[6]

Part One

The Ancient World

■How old the universe is and how the planet earth came into being may never be known precisely, but modern scientists believe that our world has been circling the sun for four and one-half to five billion years. During that incredibly long time, the earth changed from a gaseous to a liquid state and finally solidified; waters formed on the earth's shell, and in their depths life took form. As one geological epoch succeeded another, first single-celled and then multicelled organisms evolved, and some of them learned to live on land. Eventually this ceaseless process of adaptation to environment brought forth the mammal class, of which man is a member.

Remains of the earliest manlike creatures, unearthed in Africa, may be nearly two million years old. The time span from those remote days to about 3500 B.C. is usually referred to as prehistoric, or preliterate, times. By far the greater part of that time span was taken up by man's relentless struggle for survival—a struggle in which he learned to shape crude weapons and tools from stone, make fire, and domesticate certain plants and animals. The latter achievement was of revolutionary consequence, for it freed man of the necessity to hunt the migrant beasts. And a measure of control over plants and animals meant that he could settle down in one place and become a farmer and herdsman.

The stage was now set for a progressively rapid extension of man's control over his environment. Life became more complex and more rewarding. The discovery of metallurgy, progress in arts and crafts, the organization of larger social and political units, and the invention of writing heralded a new era of existence. These momentous advances did not occur over the entire earth but were concentrated in a few great river valleys. There the well-watered, fertile soil produced abundant harvests and food surpluses supported increased populations. Cities sprang up, inhabited by men with diverse talents: priests, potters, basket weavers, tool makers, and merchants.

Along the banks of rivers, then, we must look for the first civilizations. We shall find them widely scattered: Mesopotamia straddled the Tigris and the Euphrates; Egypt stretched along the Nile; India arose along the Indus and the Ganges; and China expanded eastward from the region of the Wei and the Huang Ho. Prolific in their gifts to mankind and so dynamic that two of them have retained unbroken continuity to our own day, these civilizations possessed similarities at least as arresting as their differences. In all four, political systems were developed, crafts flourished and commerce expanded, calendars and systems of writing were invented, art and literature of extraordinary beauty were created, and religions and philosophies came into being to satisfy men's inner yearnings.

Indebted to the Egyptians and Mesopotamians, the inhabitants of Crete and Mycenaean Greece fashioned a wealthy, sophisticated, commercial culture. Much of this Aegean civilization —the first advanced culture to appear in Europe —was destroyed by the end of the second millennium B.C., but enough remained to serve as the foundation for Greek civilization. Insatiably curious about man and man's world, the Greeks enjoyed a freedom of thought and expression unknown in earlier societies. Their fierce passion to remain untrammeled, however, was too often unrestrained. The failure of the Greek city-states to find a workable basis for cooperation doomed them to political disaster. Although the conquest of the city-states by King Philip of Macedonia ended the Hellenic Age, the influence of the Greeks was destined to increase. The establishment of a vast empire in the Near East by Philip's talented son, Alexander the Great, ushered in the Hellenistic Age and the widespread diffusion of Greek culture.

Meanwhile, a new power—Rome—had been evolving on the Italian peninsula. After five centuries of modest growth, this city-state embarked upon a career of unprecedented expansion. The splendor of Roman arms was matched by skill in administration, wisdom in law, and ingenuity in the practical arts of engineering and communication. These talents and abilities enabled the Romans to erect a Mediterranean empire which survived until the fifth century A.D. Probably the greatest achievement of the Roman Empire was the skillful maintenance of a diversity of cultures within a political unity. To the Romans we owe a debt for preserving and disseminating classical culture, for the legacy of Graeco-Roman culture is the foundation of western civilization.

In the first centuries of the Christian era we enter a brief but fascinating period in which the principal civilizations of West and East were in contact, engaged in a mutually beneficial exchange of wares and ideas. Unhappily, this process of culture contact and diffusion—which, had it been allowed to continue, might have had incalculable effects for good on world history— was brought to an untimely halt, largely as a result of a crisis in the West. The Graeco-Roman world was subjected to a series of shattering invasions which will be described in the next unit. The present unit surveys the classical age of civilization in both the West and the East—a period which must always remain one of the glorious epochs in human achievement.

1. Prehistoric cave painting
(c. 15,000-10,000 B.C.). Among
the oldest known examples of
pictorial art are the animal
paintings found in caves near
Altamira, Spain. They are
products of the late Paleolithic
age. The exact purpose of
these works is not clear, but
it is often presumed that they
were part of a magic ritual intended to gain dominance
over the animals' spirits and
thus to assure success in the
hunt. They reveal a remarkable visual and formal sensi-
bility: the shapes and attitudes of the animals (note the
wounded posture of the two
bisons) have been keenly observed and conveyed with an
assured elegance of pattern
and line. At the same time the
figures are often superimposed, with little apparent
regard for their compositional
relationships, suggesting that
the act of painting them may
have been more ritualistically
important than the final
images themselves.

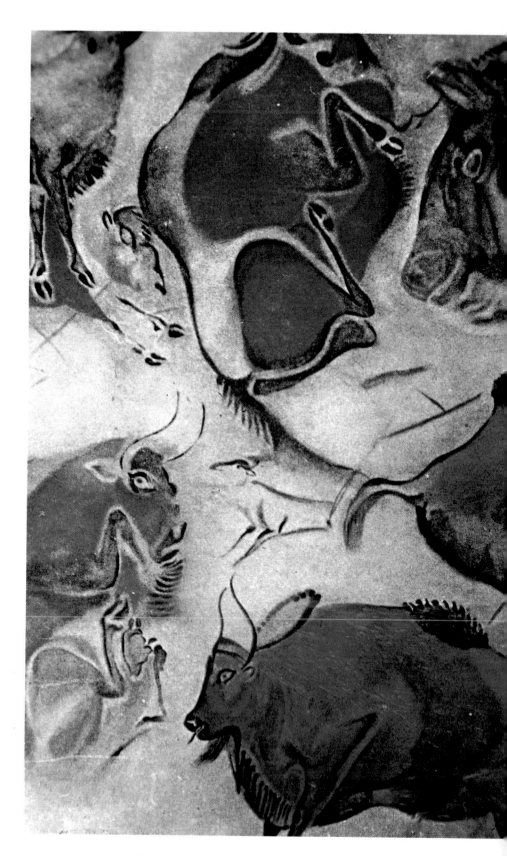

2. Egypt: Tomb of Queen Nefertari (c. 1250 B.C.). Since Egyptians believed the soul to be the counterpart of the body and the hereafter a reflection of the here-and-now, elaborate material provision was made in the tombs to assure the safe voyage of the deceased into the life after death. The pictures and hieroglyphs which adorn the richly painted New Kingdom tomb of Nefertari associate her with such Egyptian deities as Osiris, god of the dead (the standing figure on the left), and Khepri, the sun god (the seated figure with the beetle's head).

3. The Arena at Leptis Magna in North Africa (third century A.D.). The far-flung reaches of the Roman Empire were united in a complex, efficient network which infused even the cities of the provinces with the reflected glory of the capital itself. In turn, much of Rome's own splendor—at least artistically speaking—was a reflection of Greece. If the order, scale, and ambition of the buildings at Leptis Magna are Roman, their stylistic grace has its roots in the earlier Hellenic civilization which the Romans so eagerly emulated.

4. (above) **Three figures from the east pediment of the Parthenon** (c. 445-440 B.C.). The Greeks' massive contribution to the ancient world, and finally to western civilization, is graphically evident in their figure sculpture, a genre which claims no finer examples than the pedimental remains from the Parthenon. This group—probably a trio of goddesses —is treated by the Greek sculptor in so naturalistic a manner that the relative abstractness of Egyptian and Mesopotamian figures is supplanted with a vigorous immediacy and freedom of action. **5.** (below) **The Seven Steps of Buddha** (c. 500-200 B.C.). The influence of Greek culture extended not only west to Rome but east as far as Gandhara in India, where artists often echoed Alexandrian styles in the faces and clothing of their figures. In this Gandharan relief the Buddha is shown being born miraculously from his mother's right side; then, reappearing below, he immediately walks, taking seven steps in all.

Chapter 1

Along the Banks of Rivers

The Civilizations of the Ancient Near East

INTRODUCTION. Perhaps as early as two million years ago, man's ancestors first appeared on earth, naked in a world of enemies. The story of man's journey out of the darkness of ignorance and fear covers a period of hundreds of thousands of years during which he mastered the skills necessary for survival. Early man's most important achievements concern agriculture and the ways of life it engendered. Wild beasts were tamed as work animals or kept for their meat and hides. The first farmers scattered kernels of grain on the earth and waited patiently for harvest time. Because their fields and flocks could supply most of their wants, a settled existence became possible; men were no longer compelled to move on endlessly in search of food, as their food-gathering ancestors had done for countless generations. Where conditions were favorable, these ancient farmers were able to acquire more food than they needed for survival—surpluses to tide them over seasons of cold and drought. Thus, in green oases and on fertile plateaus, farming villages sprang up.

It was along the banks of great rivers that villages first grew into towns and cities. In early Egyptian picture writing a town is shown as a cross within a circle—the intersection of two pathways enclosed by a wall. The symbol is an appropriate one, for in the history of mankind the town—⊗—marks the spot where civilization as we know it began.

Within the towns the business of living took new turns. While the majority still farmed, there were now more craftsmen turning out specialized wares, merchants trading for metals and other needed raw materials, priests conducting religious ceremonies, and administrators planning and supervising the necessary cooperative effort for the common good. Time could be found also for intellectual and artistic pursuits that enriched the lives of the participants and developed a cultural heritage.

A culture can endure only if the knowledge necessary for its survival is passed on from generation to generation. Early peoples relied on information transmitted by word of mouth. But as towns and cities grew up and cultures became increasingly complex, methods for keeping records were devised and systems of writing were created. To most authorities, the development of writing is a prerequisite to civilization.

The four earliest civilizations—the Sumerian, the Egyptian, the Indian, and the Chinese—arose between c. 3500 B.C. and c. 1500 B.C., in each case in the valley of a great river system. In this chapter we shall trace the progress of civilization, including man's earliest advances in technology and his creation of written languages, in Mesopotamia and Egypt. In Chapter 4 we shall see the stirrings of civilization far to the east, in India and in China.

TOOLS AND ART OF EARLY MAN

Africa: birthplace of man? Benjamin Franklin is credited with being the first to define man as a "tool-making animal." This ability to fashion and use tools is the first evidence of man's unique faculty of reasoning out solutions to the problems of life. Since the use of stone implements, made by striking pieces of rock with other stones, was the most distinctive feature of early man's culture, the first stage in man's cultural development is known as the Paleolithic or Old Stone Age. (Paleolithic culture survives among a few primitive peoples today.) Who were the ancestors of early man and when and where tools were first fashioned are much debated questions in scholarly circles.

Until the recent discoveries in Africa, Asia was thought to have been the home of the earliest tool-making *hominids* ("near men"). Here much evidence of a group called *Homo erectus* has come to light, beginning with Java man in 1890 and Peking man in 1927. *Homo erectus* fossils, which date back at least half a million years, have also been found in Europe and Africa. Because of *Homo erectus'* brain size (c. 1000 cc.; that of modern man averages c. 1500 cc.), it

is thought probable that he knew how to speak. He was about five feet tall, had a fully erect posture, but retained heavy brow ridges and a receding forehead. *Homo erectus* was clearly a tool-maker, fashioning hand-axes by chipping hard rocks to form cutting and scraping edges. He often lived in caves and knew how to use fire.

The present consensus, which may rapidly change, is that the earliest species of hominids were the Australopithecines (Southern Apes), whose fossil remains were first unearthed in South Africa in 1925. *Australopithecus* belongs to an extinct genus and may not be in modern man's line of descent. In 1964 the British anthropologist L. S. B. Leakey discovered at Olduvai Gorge in Tanzania what he claimed was the earliest representative of the genus *Homo*. If this claim is accepted, it will push back man's age to approximately two million years. *Homo habilis* (mentally skillful man), as Leakey called his find, was about four feet tall, walked erect, had a well-developed thumb and the teeth of a meat eater. There is considerable disagreement among authorities on the significance of Leakey's discoveries. Was *Homo habilis* an advanced form of *Australopithecus* or a different genus from which man is descended? Conclusive proof is yet to be found in fossil remains still hidden in ancient strata.

In the meantime, however, numerous anthropologists, and especially Africanists, give priority to Africa as the birthplace of man and of human culture. Recent discoveries indicate that about 750,000 years ago near man began to make tools in East Africa. The earliest tools were only small pebbles shaped in a crude way, but they were gradually displaced by the "hand-ax," a more sophisticated general purpose implement and chopper. The center of this hand-ax culture was Africa, and from here this refined stone culture spread to Europe and western Asia, carried perhaps by various waves of immigrants. The discovery of these earliest tools has forced a basic reconsideration of the theory that "in the history of mankind Africa had always been the recipient, never the donor."[1]

Yet during the course of the immensely long Paleolithic Age, "Africa lost its initial pre-eminence in world history"[2] and became what has been termed "a relative backwater." No satisfactory explanation has been offered for this phenomenon. Perhaps human survival required less effort and planning in this tropical area; perhaps the growing aridity of the Sahara effectively isolated sub-Saharan Africa.

Middle and late Paleolithic cultures. From about 70,000 to 35,000 B.C.—that is, during the last half of the middle Paleolithic period—the European and western Asian landscape was inhabited by Neanderthal man, the favorite "cave man" of contemporary cartoonists. He was about five feet tall with a thick-set body (reconstructions showing him stooped are now known to be in error), and he used more specialized flake tools made from large flakes broken off from a stone block. His stone-tipped spears made him a powerful hunter.

About 35,000 B.C. the middle Paleolithic in Europe gave way to late Paleolithic cultures, a development accompanied by the displacement of Neanderthal man by modern *Homo sapiens*. By 20,000 B.C. *Homo sapiens* inhabited Europe, Asia, Africa, and Australia—and had begun to move across the Bering Strait from Asia to America. A new technique of pressure-flaking produced long, slender, sharp-edged blades which made excellent projectile points and a most useful chisel, the burin. The invention of the spear-thrower made hunting much more efficient.

To withstand the cold weather, late Paleolithic peoples fashioned garments from sewn skins and erected the first man-made buildings in areas where natural caves did not exist. The reindeer and mammoth hunters of present-day Czechoslovakia and Russia lived in tents and huts made of hides and brush or in communal houses partially sunk into the ground with mammoth's ribs for roof supports. There is also evidence that they used coal for fuel.

The first artists. One of the highest achievements of late Paleolithic culture was art. Man was an artist endeavoring to give expression to his creative imagination long before he could write or fashion a metal knife. Animated, realistic paintings of bison, reindeer, primitive horses, and other animals, colored in shades of black, red, yellow, and brown, have been found in more than a hundred caves in Spain and France (see Color Plate 1). Cave art rivals that of civilized man not only stylistically but also as an expression of significant human experience. It represents Paleolithic man's response to his complete dependence on an abundance of game animals and success in hunting them. By drawing pictures of food animals—sometimes shown pregnant or pierced by spears and arrows—he may have believed that he could wield a mystical power over their spirits, thus assuring their multiplication and his mastery over them in hunting. Like the religious art of civilized man, the magico-religious basis of Paleolithic art in no way detracts from its esthetic qualities as true art. Paleolithic man also modeled in clay and chiseled pictures on rock and bone.

Mesolithic or Transitional cultures. With the final retreat of the glaciers that had intermittently covered large portions of Europe, Asia, and North America during the million or so years before 10,000 B.C., Europe became covered with dense forests. Because of their highly specialized adaptation to cold weather, the reindeer moved north and the hairy mammoth and other animals hunted by late Paleolithic peoples became extinct.

Man himself, however, proved able to adjust to postglacial conditions by developing new cultures called Mesolithic or Transitional. Many of these Mesolithic groups lived along the coast, fishing and gathering shellfish. Others lived inland, where they made bows and arrows for hunting and devised such forms of transport as skis, sleds, and dugout canoes. Our Mesolithic forebears also domesticated the dog—the first of many animals brought into this special relationship with man.

The Neolithic revolution. While the Mesolithic peoples of Europe were adjusting to the postglacial environment by developing new food-gathering techniques, something of far greater consequence—a shift from food gathering to food producing—was taking place in the Near East. Here, on the hilly flanks of the mountains bordering what is called the Fertile Crescent (see map, p. 17), there was sufficient rainfall to nourish wild forms of wheat and barley and to provide grass for wild sheep, goats, and pigs. By 7000 B.C. men in this region had domesticated these grains and animals and were living in village communities near their herds and fields. This momentous change, the most far-reaching breakthrough in the relationship of man to his environment, ushered in the Neolithic or New Stone Age.

Between 7000 and 6000 B.C. hundreds of peasant villages arose in the foothills of northern Iraq and adjacent parts of Turkey, Syria, Iran, and Palestine. One of the oldest village sites—and the first to be excavated (after World War II)—is Jarmo in northern Iraq. The 150 people of the village lived in some twenty mud-walled houses, reaped their barley and wheat with stone sickles, stored their food in stone bowls, and possessed domesticated goats, sheep, and dogs. The later levels of settlement contain evidence of domesticated pigs and the use of clay pottery. Since many Jarmo stone tools were made of obsidian, a volcanic rock from beds more than three hundred miles to the north, a primitive form of commerce must also have existed.

The best preserved early village so far uncovered is Çatal Hüyük in southern Turkey, excavated in 1961. The large, 32-acre site, first occupied shortly before 6000 B.C., contains some of the most advanced features of Neolithic culture: pottery, woven textiles, mud-brick houses, shrines honoring a

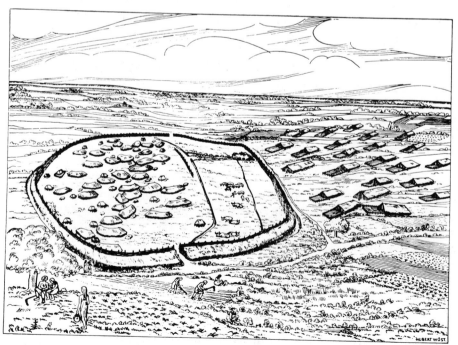

This drawing of a reconstructed Neolithic village in the Rhineland district shows, at the right, the long semisubterranean dwellings; to the left, the palisaded area containing small granaries on posts, rectangular structures probably used as communal working areas, and pasturage for cattle; and the cultivated fields surrounding the village. The two concentric circles are a common feature of Neolithic villages.

mother goddess, and plastered walls decorated with murals and carved reliefs.

In time the Neolithic revolution spread out from its original center in the Near East, reaching the Balkan peninsula of Europe by 5000 B.C., Egypt and central Europe by 4000 B.C., and the British Isles and northwest India by 3000 B.C. The Neolithic cultures of Middle America and the Andes highlands, however, are clearly independent developments, while a possible relationship between China and the Near East remains an open question.

PRIMITIVE THOUGHT AND CUSTOM

Analysis of primitive societies. Perhaps it is natural for most of us, living as we do in a highly complex machine-age society, to assume that primitive men, prehistoric or modern, would possess few laws, little education, and only the simplest codes of conduct. But this is far from true. The organization of a primitive society may be as complex as our own. Rules regarding the role of parents, the treatment of children, the punishment of the evildoer, the conduct of business, the worship of the gods, and the conventions of eating and recreation have existed for thousands of years, along with methods to compel the individual to do "the correct thing."

How can we know about those features of early man's culture which are not apparent from the remains of tools and other objects? We can glean much from the earliest myths and epics, which originated in prehistoric times before the invention of writing and which reflect early man's ideas and customs. We can also apply conclusions anthropologists have drawn from studies of present-day primitive societies. But here a word of caution is necessary. Because the general level of technological development in a modern-day primitive society appears to be similar to the level of achievement reached in a prehistoric society, it does not follow that all aspects of the two cultures are comparable. Furthermore, it is often difficult to measure

in what degree modern primitive societies have been affected by the impact of advanced civilizations like our own.

Forms of social organization. Among all peoples, past and present, the basic social unit appears to be the elementary family group—parents and their offspring. Anthropologists do not know what marriage customs were prevalent in the earliest societies, but monogamy—one husband and one wife—was probably most common.

The extended family—an individual family together with a circle of related persons who usually trace their descent through their mothers and are bound together by mutual loyalty—is often found in primitive social groupings. The extended family strengthens the elementary unit both in obtaining food and in protecting its members against other groups. Land is communally owned but allocated to separate families. Weapons, tools, and utensils are individually owned.

A third primitive social unit is the clan—a group of individuals within a community who believe that they have a common ancestor and therefore are "of one blood, or of one soul." A clan is patrilineal if its members trace their relationship through the male line, and matrilineal if through the female. Many primitive peoples identify their clans by a totem—an animal or some natural object—which is revered and made the subject for amulets of various sorts. Forms of totemism in modern-day society include military insignia, the emblems of such organizations as the Elks and Moose, and animal mascots used by college football teams.

A fourth grouping among some primitive peoples is the tribe. This term lacks a precise definition, but it may be thought of as applying to a community characterized by a common speech or distinctive dialect, a common cultural heritage, and a specific inhabited territory. Group loyalty is a strong trait among members of a tribe and is often accompanied by a contempt for the peoples and customs of other communities. Some Eskimos, for example, speak of neighboring Indians as "children of a louse's egg."

Collective responsibility in law and government. In primitive societies ethical behavior consists in not violating custom. The

The late Paleolithic Venus of Willendorf, like many similar Neolithic statues, is armless and faceless while female characteristics are emphasized. Although such figurines are usually regarded as fertility symbols, it has been suggested that they may simply be early man's equivalent of pinup girls.

close relationships that exist in extended families and clans encourage conformity.

The concept of justice among the individuals of a primitive group is synonymous with maintaining equilibrium. Thus, if one man steals another's property, the economic equilibrium has been unjustly disturbed. Such a theft constitutes a wrong against the individual; and, where modern legal procedure calls for punishment of the thief, in primitive societies justice is achieved by a settlement between the injured man and the thief. If the thief restores what has been stolen or its equivalent, the victim is satisfied and the thief is not punished. Murder and wounding are also private matters to be avenged by the next of kin on the principle of "an eye for an eye." On the other hand, certain acts are considered dangerous to the whole group and require punishment by the entire community. Treason, witchcraft, and incest are typical offenses in this category. Such acts are not settled by the payment of compensation; the punishment meted out is usually death. If a member of a clan gets into trouble too often, his fellows will regard him as a social nuisance and an economic liability; thus they may outlaw him or execute him.

As a general rule, government in primitive societies is of a democratic character. The older tribal members—the council of elders—play a dominant role in decision-making because of their greater experience and knowledge of the group's customs and lore. Serious decisions, such as going to war or electing a chief, require the consent of a general assembly of all adult males. The elected chief of the tribe, who seeks with varying success to make his position hereditary, is pledged to rule in accordance with unwritten custom and in consultation with the council of elders. Due to the strong element of representation present, this early form of government has been called "primitive democracy."

Religion and magic. Because primitive man's spear-thrower and bow incorporate the principles of the lever and of stored energy, they have been hailed as representing the beginning of science. "But this, surely, is a mistaken approach. If science is to have any real meaning, it must refer to a method derived from a mode of thought. Prehistoric men . . . possessed that part of scientific method that depends on observation. They . . . made use of what they observed. But they understood neither the processes involved nor how to make the controlled experiments that would explain them. . . . [Also] they would not expect their 'scientific' knowledge to be effective without the help of magic and religion."[3]

Religion is perhaps the strongest single force in the life of primitive people. Man's religious sensibilities apparently originated in the feeling of awe that came over him when he first became conscious of the universe about him. Awe and wonder led to the belief, usually called animism, that all things in nature—winds, stones, trees, animals, and man himself—were inhabited by spirits. Many spirits became objects of reverence, with man's own spirit being one of the first. Neanderthal man placed food and implements alongside his carefully buried dead, an indication that he believed in an afterlife and held his ancestors in awe. We know also that late Paleolithic man revered the spirits of the animals he hunted for food as well as the spirit of fertility upon which both human and animal life depended. This led to totemism and to the worship of a fertility goddess who is known to us from many carved and modeled female figures with grossly exaggerated sexual features. Neolithic farmers developed a special reverence for this embodiment of fertility in the form of the Earth Mother (or Mother Goddess).

Closely associated with primitive religion is the practice of magic. In addition to revering the spirits, primitive man wants to compel them to favor him. For this purpose he employs magic of the kind previously described in the discussion of late Paleolithic art. Primitive man also turns to medicine men to ward off droughts, famines, floods, and plagues through magical powers of communication with the spirits.

MESOPOTAMIA: THE FIRST CIVILIZATION

Prelude to civilization. About 4500 B.C., long after the agricultural revolution had begun to spread from its place of origin on the fringes of the Fertile Crescent, Neolithic farmers started filtering into the Fertile Crescent itself. Although this broad plain received insufficient rainfall to support agriculture, it was watered by the Tigris and Euphrates rivers. Known in ancient days as Mesopotamia (Greek for "between the rivers"), the lower reaches of this plain, beginning near the point where the two rivers nearly converge, was called Babylonia. Babylonia in turn encompassed two geographical areas—Akkad in the north and Sumer, the delta of this river system, in the south.

Broken by river channels teeming with fish and refertilized every year by alluvial silt laid down by uncontrolled floods, Sumer had a splendid agricultural potential—provided the environmental problems were solved. "Arable land had literally to be created out of a chaos of swamps and sandbanks by a 'separation' of land from water; the swamps . . . drained; the floods controlled; and lifegiving waters led to the rainless desert by artificial canals."[4] In the course of the several successive cultural phases that followed the arrival of the first Neolithic

farmers, these and other related problems were solved by large-scale cooperative effort. By 3500 B.C. the foundations had been laid for a type of economy and social order markedly different from anything previously known. This far more complex culture, based on large urban centers rather than simple villages, is what we associate with the term *civilization.*

Authorities do not all agree about the definition of *civilization.* Most would accept the view that "a civilization is a culture which has attained a degree of complexity usually characterized by urban life"[5]—that it is capable, in other words, of sustaining a substantial number of specialists to cope with the economic, social, political, and religious needs of a populous society. Other characteristics usually present in a civilization include a system of writing to keep records, monumental architecture in place of simple buildings, and an art that is no longer merely decorative but representational of man and his activities. Moreover, an urban environment is important because of the self-consciousness and pride which it generates.

During the millennium preceding 3500 B.C. some of the most significant discoveries and inventions in human history were achieved. By discovering how to use metals to make tools and weapons, Neolithic man effected a revolution nearly as far-reaching as that wrought in agriculture. By 4500 B.C. Neolithic artisans had discovered how to extract copper from oxide ores by heating them with charcoal. Unlike those made of stone or bone, copper implements could be formed into any desired shape, and they were less likely to break. Moreover, a stone tool had to be discarded when broken; a damaged copper implement could be recast. Soon after 3000 B.C. metalworkers discovered that copper was improved by the addition of tin. The resulting alloy, bronze, was more fusible than copper and therefore could be cast more easily; also, bronze was harder and provided a sharper cutting edge.

The farmer's first plow was probably a stick which he pulled through the soil with a rope. In time, however, the cattle that his forebears had domesticated for food and milk were harnessed to drag the hoe in place of his mate or himself. Yoked, harnessed animals pulled plows in the Mesopotamian alluvium by 3000 B.C. As a result, farming advanced from the cultivation of small plots to the tilling of extensive fields. "By harnessing the ox man began to control and use a motive power other than that furnished by his own muscular energy. The ox was the first step to the steam engine and gasoline motor."[6]

Since the Mesopotamian plain had no stone, no metals, and no timber except its soft and inadequate palm trees, there was great need of an economical means of transporting these materials from Syria and Asia Minor. Water transport down the Tigris and Euphrates solved the problem. The oldest sailing boat known is represented by a model found in a Sumerian grave of about 3500 B.C. Soon after this date wheeled vehicles appear in the form of ass-drawn war chariots. For the transport of goods overland, however, men continued to rely on the pack ass.

Another important invention was the potter's wheel, first used in Sumer soon after 3500 B.C. Earlier, men had fashioned pots by molding or coiling clay by hand, but now a symmetrical product could be produced in a much shorter time. A pivoted clay disk heavy enough to revolve of its own momentum, the potter's wheel has been called "the first really mechanical device."

The emergence of civilization in Sumer. By 3500 B.C. the population of Sumer had increased to the point where people were living in small cities and had developed a preponderance of those elements previously noted as constituting civilization. Since these included the first evidence of writing, this first phase of Sumerian civilization, to about 2800 B.C., is called the Protoliterate period.[7]

New settlers appeared in Sumer at the beginning of the Protoliterate period, and another migration occurred shortly before 3000 B.C. Scholars cannot agree on which, if either, of these newcomers were the Sumerians, whose language is not related to those major language families of mankind that later appear in the Near East—Semites and Indo-Europeans. (The original home of the Semitic-speaking peoples is thought to have been the Arabian peninsula, while the Indo-Euro-

peans migrated from the region north of the Black and Caspian seas. A third, much smaller language family is the Hamitic, which included the Egyptians and other peoples of northeastern Africa.)

How would life in Protoliterate Sumer have appeared to a visitor seeing it for the first time? As he approached Ur, one of about a dozen Sumerian cities, he would pass farmers working in their fields with ox-drawn plows. He might see some of the workers using bronze sickles. The river would be dotted by boats carrying produce to and from the city. Dominating the flat countryside would be a great ziggurat, a lofty, terraced tower, built in the shape of a pyramid and crowned by a sanctuary, or "high place." This was the "holy of holies," sacred to the local god. Upon entering the city, the visitor would see a large number of specialists pursuing their appointed tasks as agents of the community —some craftsmen casting bronze tools and weapons, others fashioning their wares on the potter's wheel, and still others, merchants, arranging to trade grain and manufactures for the metals, stone, lumber, and other essentials not available in Sumer. Scribes would be at work incising thin tablets of clay with picture signs. Some tablets might bear the impressions of cylinder seals, small stone cylinders engraved with a design. Examining the clay tablets, the visitor would find that they were memoranda used in administering the temple, which was at once the warehouse and workshop of the entire community. Some of the scribes might be making an inventory of the goats and sheep received that day for sacrificial use; others might be drawing up wage lists. They would be using a system of counting based on the unit 60, still used today, over five thousand years later, in computing divisions of time and angles.

Certain technical inventions of Protoliterate Sumer eventually made their way to both the Nile and the Indus valleys. Chief among these were the wheeled vehicle and the potter's wheel. The discovery in Egypt of cylinder seals similar in shape to those used in Sumer attests to contact between the two areas toward the end of the fourth millennium B.C. Certain early Egyptian art motifs and

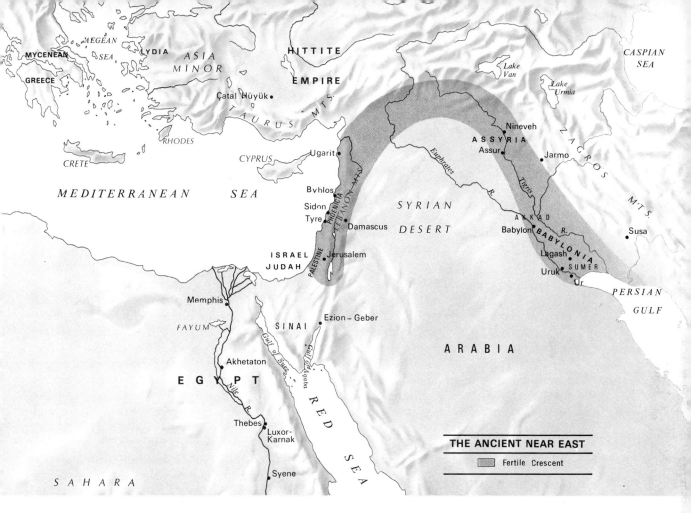

THE ANCIENT NEAR EAST

Fertile Crescent

architectural forms are also thought to be of Sumerian origin. And it is probable that the example of Sumerian writing stimulated the Egyptians to develop a script of their own. These are examples of how cultures during their most formative stages may influence one another yet continue to develop unique features which stamp them as distinctive civilizations.

Sumerian writing. As we have noted, the symbols on the oldest Sumerian clay tablets were primarily pictures. However, many matters, including thought processes, cannot be depicted conveniently by pictures. Sumerian scribes overcame this problem by arbitrarily adding marks to the picture signs to denote new meanings. During the Proto-literate period some two thousand signs were in use. This cumbersome system could have been still further enlarged and complicated by the creation of more pictures and modifying marks. Fortunately, the Sumerians adopted an alternative solution whereby the signs represented sounds rather than ob-

jects or ideas. By giving the signs a phonetic value, the Sumerians could spell out names and compound words instead of inventing new signs. The use of syllabic signs reduced the number of signs to some six hundred by 2800 B.C.

In writing, a scribe used a reed stylus to make impressions in soft clay tablets. The impressions took on a wedge shape, hence the term *cuneiform* (Latin *cuneus*, "wedge"). The cuneiform system of writing was adopted by many other peoples of the Near East, including the Babylonians, Assyrians, Hittites, and Persians.

The Old Sumerian period. By 2800 B.C. the Sumerian city-states had emerged into the light of history. This first historical age, called the Old Sumerian (or Early Dynastic) period, was characterized by incessant warfare as each city sought to protect or enlarge its land and water rights. Each city-state was a theocracy, for the local god was believed to be the real sovereign. His earthly representative was the *ensi*, the high priest and city governor, who acted as the god's steward in both religious and secular functions. Though endowed with divine right by virtue of being the human agent of the god, the *ensi* was not considered divine.

Like life on a medieval manor, early Sumerian society was highly collectivized, with the temples of the city god and subordinate deities assuming the central role. "Each temple owned lands which formed the estate of its divine owners. Each citizen belonged to one of the temples, and the whole of a temple community—the officials and priests, herdsmen and fishermen, gardeners, craftsmen, stonecutters, merchants, and even slaves—was referred to as 'the people of the god X.'"[8] That part of the temple land called "common" was worked by all members of the community, while the remaining land was divided among the citizens for their support at a rental of from one third to one sixth of the crop. Priests and temple administrators, however, held rent-free lands.

In time, priests, temple administrators, and *ensis* became venal, usurping temple

During the Old Sumerian period a boundary dispute arose between Lagash and Umma, which lasted for over two centuries. The Stele of the Vultures, erected by the *ensi* of Lagash to commemorate his victories over the Ummaites, shows the king leading his soldiers, who are marching over the prostrate bodies of the enemy.

property and oppressing the common people. This frequently led to the rise of despots called *lugals* (literally "great man" but usually translated "king") who rode to power on a wave of popular discontent. These secular rulers made the general welfare their major domestic concern. Best known is Urukagina, who usurped power at Lagash at the end of the Old Sumerian period. His reform inscriptions state that when he "had received the lugalship . . . he removed from the inhabitants of Lagash usury, forestalling, famine, robbery, attacks; he established their freedom . . . [and] protected the widow and the orphan from the powerful man."[9]

Akkadian dominance. Immediately north of Sumer lay the narrow region of Akkad, inhabited by Semites who had absorbed Sumerian culture. Appearing late in the fourth millennium B.C., the Akkadians were the earliest of the Semitic peoples who filtered into Mesopotamia from Arabia. A generation after Urukagina, Sargon I (2370-2315 B.C.), an energetic Akkadian ruler, conquered Sumer and went on to establish the world's first empire which, he claimed, extended "from the lower sea to the upper sea" (the Persian Gulf to the Mediterranean Sea).

Very proud of his lower-class origins, Sargon boasted that his humble, unwed mother had been forced to abandon him: "She set me in a basket of rushes . . . [and] cast me into the river."[10] Rescued and brought up by a gardener, Sargon rose to power through the army. As *lugal*, Sargon looked after the welfare of the lower classes and aided the rising class of private merchants. At the latter's request he once sent his army to far-off Asia Minor to protect a colony of merchants from interference by a local ruler. We are told that Sargon "did not sleep" in his efforts to promote prosperity; trade moved as freely "as the Tigris where it flows into the sea, . . . all lands lie in peace, their inhabitants prosperous and contented."[11]

Sargon's successors, however, were unable either to withstand the attacks of semibarbaric highlanders or to overcome the desire for independence of the priest-dominated Sumerian cities. As a result, the house of Sargon collapsed about 2230 B.C.

The Neo-Sumerian period. Order and prosperity were restored a century later by the *lugals* of the Third Dynasty of Ur (c. 2113-2006 B.C.). By creating a highly centralized administration in Sumer and Akkad, these rulers solved the problem of internal rebellion that had plagued Sargon and his successors. The formerly temple-dominated cities became provinces administered by governors who were watched closely by a corps of "messengers." The "church" became an arm of the state; the high priests were state appointees, and the temple economic organization was used as the state's agent in rigidly controlling the economy.

At the head of this bureaucratic state stood the now-deified ruler, celebrated in hymns as a heaven-sent messiah who "brings splendor to the land, . . . savior of orphans whose misery he relieves, . . . the vigilant shepherd who conducts the people unto cooling shade."[12] Much of what we now call social legislation was passed by these "vigilant shepherds." Such laws were called "rightings" (Sumerian *nig-si-sa*, usually translated "equity"), since their object was the righting of wrongs that were not covered by the old customary law (*nig-ge-na*, "truth"). The prologue to the law code of Ur-Nammu, founder of the dynasty, declared that it was the king's purpose to see that "the orphan did not fall a prey to the wealthy" and that "the man of one shekel did not fall a prey to the man of one mina (sixty shekels)."[13]

Disaster struck Ur about 2006 B.C., when Elamites from the highlands to the east destroyed the city. The Sumerians were never again a dominant element politically, but their culture persisted as the foundation for all subsequent civilizations in the Tigris-Euphrates valley.

For more than two centuries following the destruction of Ur, disunity and warfare again plagued Mesopotamia, along with depression, inflation, and acute hardship for the lower classes. Merchants, however, utilized the lack of state controls to become full-fledged capitalists who amassed fortunes which they invested in banking operations and in land. (These merchants used a form of double-entry bookkeeping which they called "balanced accounts." Their word for capi-

tal, *qaqqadum*, meaning "head," influenced later peoples; our word *capital* is derived from the Latin form, *caput*). The stronger local rulers of the period freed the poor from debt slavery and issued a variety of reform laws which are best illustrated by the legislation of Hammurabi.

Hammurabi and the Babylonian empire. Semitic Amorites (from *Amurru*, the "West"), under the rule of their capable king, Hammurabi of Babylon (c. 1792-1750 B.C.), again brought most of Mesopotamia under one rule by 1760 B.C.

Hammurabi is best known for his code of nearly three hundred laws whose stated objective was "to cause justice to prevail in the land, to destroy the wicked and the evil, to prevent the strong from oppressing the weak . . . and to further the welfare of the people."[14] Hammurabi's legislation reestablished a state-controlled economy in which merchants were required to obtain a "royal permit," interest was limited to 20 percent, and prices were set for basic commodities and for fees charged by physicians, veterinarians, and builders. Minimum wages were established, and debt slavery was limited to three years. Other laws protected wives and children, although a wife who had "set her face to go out and play the part of a fool, neglect her house, belittle her husband"[15] could be divorced without alimony, or the husband could take another wife and compel the first to remain as a servant. Punishments were graded in their severity; the higher the culprit in the social scale, the more severe the penalty.

In the epilogue to the code, Hammurabi eloquently summed up his efforts to provide social justice for his people.

Let any oppressed man, who has a cause, come before my image as king of righteousness! Let him read the inscription on my monument! Let him give heed to my weighty words! And may my monument enlighten him as to his cause and may he understand his case! May he set his heart at ease! (and he will exclaim): "Hammurabi indeed is a ruler who is like a real father to his people. . . ."[16]

Mathematics and science. Carrying on the work of the Sumerians, the Babylonians made advances in arithmetic, geometry, and algebra. For ease of computation with both whole numbers and fractions, they compiled tables for multiplication and division and for square and cube roots. They knew how to solve linear and quadratic equations, and their knowledge of geometry included the theorem later made famous by the Greek philosopher Pythagoras: the square of the hypotenuse of a right-angled triangle is equal to the sum of the squares of the other two sides. Perhaps their greatest achievement was the principle of place-value notation which gave numbers a value according to their position in a series.

The Babylonians achieved little that today deserves to be called science. They did observe nature and collect data, which is the first requirement of science; but in seeking intelligible explanations of natural phenomena, they did not go beyond the formulation of myths which explained things in terms of the unpredictable whims of the gods. The sun, the moon, and the five visible planets were thought to be gods who were able to influence men's lives; accordingly, their movements were watched, recorded, and interpreted.

Babylonian literature. The Babylonians took over from the Sumerians a body of literature ranging from heroic epics that compare favorably with the *Iliad* and the *Odyssey* to wisdom writings that have their counterparts in the Old Testament books of Job, Proverbs, and Ecclesiastes. Longest and most famous is the *Epic of Gilgamesh*, which recounts the exploits of a heroic ruler of Uruk who lived about 2700 B.C. The central theme of the epic is Gilgamesh's hope of immortality. This leads him to seek out and question Ut-napishtim, the Babylonian Noah who was granted eternal life because he saved all living creatures from the flood. Ut-napishtim's story has many remarkable similarities with the Hebrew account of the flood. But Gilgamesh's quest is hopeless, and he is so informed on several occasions:

Gilgamesh, whither rovest thou?
The life thou pursuest thou shalt not find.
When the gods created mankind,
Death for mankind they set aside,

Life in their own hands retaining.
Thou, Gilgamesh, let full be thy belly,
Make thou merry by day and by night.
Of each day make thou a feast of rejoicing,
Day and night dance thou and play! . . .
Pay heed to the little one that holds on to thy hand,
Let thy spouse delight in thy bosom!
For this is the task of mankind![17]

And here are a few lines from the lamentation of the Babylonian Job:

I look about me: evil upon evil!
My affliction grows, I cannot find justice. . .
Yet I thought only of prayer and supplication,
Invocation was my care, sacrifice my rule;
The day of the worship of the gods was my delight. . . . .
Who can comprehend the counsel of the gods in heaven?
The plan of a god is deep waters, who can fathom it?
Where has befuddled mankind ever learned what is a god's conduct?[18]

Fall of the Babylonian empire. The pattern of disunity and warfare, all too familiar in Mesopotamia, reasserted itself following Hammurabi's death. In 1595 B.C. the Hittites, an Indo-European people who had established themselves in Asia Minor (see p. 28), mounted a daring raid down the Euphrates, capturing and plundering Babylon. The next five centuries is a dark age about which little is known; yet it did preserve the cultural heritage left by the Sumerians and Babylonians. Meanwhile, in a neighboring river valley, another civilization had emerged.

EGYPT: GIFT OF THE NILE

Predynastic Egypt. Egypt is literally "the gift of the Nile," as the ancient Greek historian Herodotus observed. The Nile valley, extending 750 miles from the first cataract to the Mediterranean, is a fertile oasis cut out of a limestone plateau. Its soil is renewed annually by the rich silt deposited by the flood water of the river, which rises and falls with unusual precision. The rise begins early in July and continues until the banks are overrun, reaching its crest in September. By the end of October the river is once more contained within its banks.

By 4000 B.C. Neolithic villagers had begun to build dikes to catch and hold the Nile flood and to construct ditches and wells for irrigation. Population grew and social organization advanced, leading to the formation of two distinct kingdoms late in the fourth millennium: Lower Egypt comprised the broad Nile delta north of Memphis, while Upper Egypt extended southward along the narrow ten- to twenty-mile-wide valley as far as the first cataract at Syene (Aswan). Each kingdom contained about a score of districts, or *nomes*, which had formerly been ruled by independent chieftans.

The Predynastic period ended about 3100 B.C. when Menes, ruler of Upper Egypt, united the two kingdoms and founded the First Dynasty with its capital at Memphis. Because little is known of the first two dynasties, the period is called Egypt's archaic age.

The Old Kingdom (c. 2700-2200 B.C.). The pharaohs of the Third through the Sixth Dynasties—the period called the Old Kingdom or Pyramid Age—firmly established order and stability and the essential elements of Egyptian civilization. The nobility lost its independence, and all power was centered in the pharaoh (*Per-ao*, "Great House"). The pharaoh was considered a god rather than the human agent of a god, as was the rule in Mesopotamia. As the god of Egypt, the pharaoh owned all the land (although frequent grants were made to temples and private persons), controlled the irrigation system, decided when the fields should be sown, and received the surplus from the crops produced on the huge royal estates. This surplus supported a large corps of specialists—administrators, priests, scribes, artists, artisans, and merchants—who labored in the service of the pharaoh. The people's welfare was thought to rest on absolute fidelity to the god-king. "If you want to know what to do in life," advised one Egyptian writer, "cling to the pharaoh and be loyal. . . ."[19] As a consequence, the Egyptian felt a sense of security that was rare in Mesopotamia.

The belief that the pharaoh was a god led to the practice of mummification and the construction of colossal tombs—the pyramids—to preserve the pharaoh's mummy for eternity. The pyramid tombs, in particular those of the Fourth Dynasty at Gizeh near Memphis which are the most celebrated of all ancient monuments, reflect the great power and wealth of the Old Kingdom pharaohs. Their construction provided employment during the months when the land was inundated by the Nile.

Toward the end of the Sixth Dynasty the centralized authority of the pharaohs was undermined when the nobles assumed the prerogatives of the pharaohs, including the claim to immortality, and the *nomes* again became independent. For about a century and a half, known as the First Intermediate Period (c. 2200-2050 B.C.), civil war raged, and outsiders raided and infiltrated the land. The lot of the common people became unbearable as they faced famine, robbery, and oppression by petty tyrants. "The land trembled," wrote a contemporary, "all the people were in terror, the villages were in panic, fear entered into their limbs."[20]

The Middle Kingdom (c. 2050-1800 B.C.). Egypt was rescued from anarchy by the pharaohs of the Eleventh and Twelfth Dynasties, who reunited the country and ruled from Thebes. Stressing their role as watchful shepherds of the people, the Middle Kingdom pharaohs promoted the welfare of the downtrodden. One of them claimed: "I gave to the destitute and brought up the orphan. I caused him who was nothing to reach [his goal], like him who was [somebody]."[21] No longer was the nation's wealth expended on huge pyramids, but on public works. The largest of these, a drainage and irrigation project in the marshy Fayum district south of Memphis, resulted in the reclamation of 27,000 acres of arable land. Moreover, a concession that has been called "the democratization of the hereafter" gave the lower classes the right to have their bodies mummified and thereby to enjoy immortality.

Following the Twelfth Dynasty, Egypt again was racked by civil war as provincial governors fought for the pharaoh's throne. During this Second Intermediate Period (c.

1800-1570 B.C.), the Hyksos, a mixed but preponderantly Semitic people, invaded Egypt from Palestine about 1700 B.C. They easily conquered the delta and made the rest of Egypt tributary. It was probably at this time that the Hebrews entered Egypt, led by the patriarch Joseph, who rose to high position under a friendly Hyksos king.

The New Kingdom or Empire (c. 1570-1090 B.C.). The Egyptians viewed the Hyksos conquest as a great humiliation imposed on them by detestable barbarians. An aggressive nationalism emerged, promoted by the

The temple at Luxor, dedicated to Amon, was built by several New Kingdom pharaohs over a period of about two hundred years and testifies to the characteristic Egyptian love of grandiose monuments. The obelisk and massive statues were built by Ramses II, who was responsible for numerous other huge testimonials to his own power and grandeur.

native prince of Thebes who proclaimed: "No man can settle down, when despoiled by the taxes of the Asiatics. I will grapple with him, that I may rip open his belly! My wish is to save Egypt and to smite the Asiatics!"[22] Adopting the new weapons introduced by their conquerors—horse-drawn chariots, the composite bow, and weapons of bronze rather than copper—the Egyptians expelled the Hyksos and pursued them into Palestine. The pharaohs of the Eighteenth Dynasty, who reunited Egypt and founded the New Kingdom, made Palestine the nucleus of an Egyptian empire in western Asia (see Reference Map 1).

The outstanding representative of the aggressive state that Egypt now became was Thutmose III (c. 1490-1436 B.C.). This "Napoleon of Egypt" led his professional standing army on seventeen campaigns into Syria, where he set up his boundary markers on the banks of the Euphrates. Nubia and northern Sudan were also brought under his sway. The native princes of Palestine, Phoenicia, and Syria were left on their thrones, but their sons were taken to Egypt as hostages. Here they were brought up and, thoroughly Egyptianized, eventually sent home to rule as loyal vassals. Thutmose III erected obelisks—tall, pointed shafts of stone—to commemorate his reign and to record his wish that "his name might endure throughout the future forever and ever." Four of his obelisks now adorn the cities of Istanbul, Rome, London, and New York.

Under Amenhotep III (c. 1398-1361 B.C.) the Empire reached its peak. Tribute flowed in from conquered lands; and Thebes, with its temples built for the sun-god Amon across the Nile at Luxor and Karnak, became the most magnificent city in the world. The Hittites of Asia Minor and the rulers of Babylonia and Crete, among others, sent gifts, including princesses for the pharaoh's harem. In return, they asked the pharaoh for gold, "for gold is as common as dust in your land."

During the reign of the succeeding pharaoh, Amenhotep IV (c. 1369-1353 B.C.), however, the Empire went into sharp decline as the result of an internal struggle between the pharaoh and the powerful and wealthy priests of Amon. The pharaoh undertook to revolutionize Egypt's religion by proclaiming the worship of the sun's disk, Aton, in place of Amon and all the other deities. Often called the first monotheist (although, as Aton's son, the pharaoh was also a god), Amenhotep changed his name to Akhenaton ("Devoted to Aton"), left Amon's city to found a new capital (Akhetaton), and concentrated upon religious reform. Most of Egypt's vassal princes in Asia defected when their appeals for aid against invaders went unheeded. Prominent among these invaders were groups of people called the Habiru, whose possible identification with the Hebrews of the Old Testament has interested modern scholars. At home the army leaders joined with the Amon priesthood to encourage dissension. When Akhenaton died, his weak successor, Tutankhamen (c. 1352-1344 B.C.)—famed for his small but richly furnished tomb discovered in 1922—returned to Thebes and the worship of Amon.

One of the army leaders who succeeded Tutankhamen founded the Nineteenth Dynasty (c. 1305-1200 B.C.), which sought to reestablish Egyptian control over Palestine and Syria. The result was a long struggle with the Hittites, who in the meantime had pushed south from Asia Minor into Syria. This struggle reached a climax in the reign of Ramses II (c. 1290-1224 B.C.), the pharaoh of the Hebrew Exodus from Egypt. Ramses II regained Palestine, but when he failed to dislodge the Hittites from Syria, he agreed to a treaty. Its strikingly modern character is revealed in clauses providing for non-aggression, mutual assistance, and extradition of fugitives.

The long reign of Ramses II was Egypt's last period of national grandeur. The number and size of Ramses' monuments (see illustration, p. 22) rival those of the Pyramid Age. Outstanding among them are the great Hypostyle Hall, built for Amon at Karnak, and the temple at Abu Simbel, with its four colossal statues of Ramses, which has recently been raised to save it from inundation by the waters of the new High Dam at Aswan. After Ramses II, royal authority gradually declined as the power of the priests of Amon rose.

Period of Decadence (1090-332 B.C.). During the early part of the Period of Decadence the Amon priesthood at Thebes became so strong that the high priest was able to found his own dynasty and to rule over Upper Egypt. Civil war grew increasingly common, and Egypt became, in the words of the Old Testament, a "broken reed," with the result that in 671 B.C. the Assyrians made Egypt a province of their empire.

Egypt enjoyed a brief Indian summer of revived glory during the Twenty-Sixth Dynasty (663-525 B.C.), which expelled the Assyrians with the aid of Greek mercenaries. The revival of ancient artistic and literary forms proved sterile, and after attempts to regain Palestine failed, "the king of Egypt came not again any more out of his land" (II Kings 24:7). Only the commercial policies of these rulers were successful. In about 600 B.C., to facilitate trade, Pharaoh Necho ordered a canal dug between the Nile mouth and the Red Sea (it was later completed by the Persians), and he commissioned a Phoenician expedition which circumnavigated Africa in three years—a feat not to be duplicated until 1497 A.D.

Egypt passed under Persian rule in 525 B.C., and two hundred years later this ancient land came within the domain of Alexander the Great. Persian rule marked the end of thirty Egyptian dynasties which had existed for nearly three thousand years.

Egyptian society and economy. Although most Egyptians were serfs and subject to forced labor, class stratification was not rigid, and people of merit could rise to a higher rank in the service of the pharaoh. The best avenue of advancement was education. The pharaoh's administration needed many scribes, and young men were urged to attend a scribal school: "Be a scribe, who is freed from forced labor, and protected from all work. . . . he directeth every work that is in this land." Yet then as now the education of a young man was beset with pitfalls: "I am told thou forsakest writing, that thou givest thyself up to pleasures; thou goest from street to street, where it smelleth of beer, to destruction. Beer, it scareth men from thee, it sendeth thy soul to perdition."[23]

Largely because all landed property de-

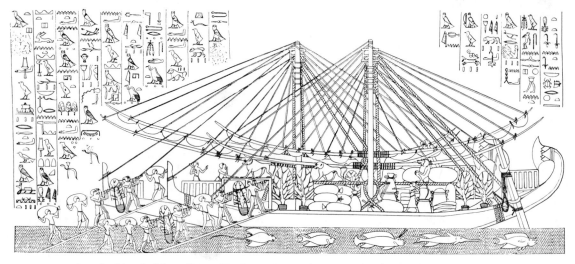

In this relief from Queen Hatshepsut's temple at Deir el-Bahri (c. 1500 B.C.), live baboons, bags of incense, exotic trees, ivory, and leopard skins are loaded on boats which will return to Egypt, via the Red Sea, from Punt, a land probably located on the Somali coast of eastern Africa. Hatsheput was the stepmother of Thutmose III.

scended from mother to daughter, the status of Egyptian women was exceptionally favorable. Upon the death of his wife a husband lost the use of the property, which was then inherited by the daughter and her husband. Brother and sister marriages often took place within the Egyptian ruling family to ensure the right of succession to the throne, which was always through the female line.

The economy of Egypt has been called "theocratic socialism" because the state, in the person of the divine pharaoh, owned the land and monopolized commerce and industry. Because of the Nile and the proximity to the Mediterranean and Red seas, most of Egypt's trade was carried on by ships. During the Old Kingdom boats plied regularly up and down the Nile, which, unlike the Tigris and the Euphrates, is easily navigable in both directions up to the first cataract. (Ships are carried downstream by the current, and the almost constant north wind enables them to sail upstream without difficulty.) Trade reached its height during the Empire, when commerce traveled along four main routes: the Nile River; the Red Sea, which was connected by caravan to the Nile bend near Thebes; a caravan route to Mesopotamia and southern Syria; and the Mediterranean Sea, connecting northern Syria, Cyprus, Crete, and Greece with the delta of the Nile. Egypt's indispensable imports were lumber, copper, tin, and olive oil, paid for with gold from its rich mines, linens, wheat, and papyrus rolls—the preferred writing material of the ancient world.

Mathematics and science. The Egyptians were much less skilled in mathematics than were the Mesopotamians. Their arithmetic was limited to addition and subtraction, which also served them when they needed to multiply and divide. They could cope with only simple algebra, but they did have considerable knowledge of practical geometry. The obliteration of field boundaries by the annual flooding of the Nile made land measurement a necessity. Similarly, a knowledge of geometry was essential in computing the dimensions of ramps for raising stones during the construction of pyramids. In these and other engineering projects the Egyptians were superior to their Mesopotamian contemporaries. Like the Mesopotamians, the Egyptians had acquired a "necessary" technology without effecting a conceptual breakthrough to a truly scientific method.

Yet, what has been called the oldest known scientific treatise was composed during the Old Kingdom. Its author described forty-eight cases requiring surgery, drawing conclusions solely from observation and rejecting supernatural causes and treatments. In advising the physician to "measure for the heart" which "speaks" in various parts of the body, he recognized the importance of the pulse and approached the concept of the circulation of the blood. This text remained unique, however, for in Egypt as elsewhere in the ancient Near East, thought failed to free itself permanently from bondage to religion.

The Old Kingdom also produced the world's first known solar calendar, the direct ancestor of our own. In order to plan their farming operations in accordance with the annual flooding of the Nile, the Egyptians kept records and discovered that the average period between inundations was 365 days. They also noted that the Nile flood coincided with the annual appearance of the Dog Star (Sirius) on the eastern horizon at dawn, and they soon associated the two phenomena. (Since the Egyptian year was six hours short of the true year, Julius Caesar in Roman times corrected the error by adding an extra day every four years.)

Egyptian religion. Early Egyptian religion had no strong ethical character. Relations between men and gods were based largely on material considerations, and the gods were thought to reward those who brought them gifts of sacrifice. But widespread suffering during the First Intermediate Period led to a revolution in religious thought. It was now believed that instead of propitiatory offerings the gods were interested in good character and love for one's fellow man: "More acceptable [to the gods] is the character of one upright of heart than the ox of the evildoer. . . . Give the love of thyself to the whole world; a good character is a remembrance."[24]

The cult of Osiris became very popular when it combined the new emphasis on moral character with the supreme reward of an attractive afterlife. "Do justice whilst thou endurest upon earth," men were told. "A man remains over after death, and his deeds are placed beside him in heaps. However, existence yonder is for eternity. . . . He who reaches it without wrongdoing shall exist yonder like a god."[25] Osiris, according to an ancient myth, was the god of the Nile, and the rise and fall of the river symbolized his death and resurrection. The myth recounted that Osiris had been murdered by Seth, his evil brother, who cut the victim's body into many pieces. When Isis, the bereaved widow, collected all the pieces and put them together, Osiris was resurrected and became immortal. Osiris was thus the first mummy, and every mummified Egyptian was another Osiris.

But only a soul free of sin would be permitted to live forever in what was described as the "Field of the Blessed, an ideal land where there is no wailing and nothing evil; where barley grows four cubits high, and emmer wheat seven ells high; where, even better, one has to do no work in the field oneself, but can let others take care of it."[26] At the time of soul testing, Osiris weighed the candidate's heart against the Feather of Truth. If the ordeal was not passed, a horrible creature devoured the rejected heart. During the Empire the priesthood of Osiris became corrupt and claimed that it knew clever methods of surviving the soul testing, even though a man's heart were heavy with sin. Charms and magical prayers and formulas were sold to the living as insurance policies guaranteeing them a happy outcome in the judgment before Osiris. They constitute much of what is known as the Book of the Dead, which was placed in the tomb.

Akhenaton's religious reformation was directed against the venal priests of Osiris as well as those of the supreme god Amon. As we have seen, Akhenaton failed to uproot Amon and the multiplicity of lesser gods; his monotheism was too cold and intellectual to attract the masses who yearned for a blessed hereafter.

Monumentalism in architecture. Because of their impressive and enduring tombs and temples, the Egyptians have been called the greatest builders in history. The earliest tomb was the mud-brick mastaba, so called because of its resemblance to a low bench. By the beginning of the Third Dynasty stone began to replace brick, and an architectural genius named Imhotep constructed the first pyramid by piling six huge stone mastabas one on top of the other. Adjoining this Step Pyramid was a temple complex whose stone columns were not freestanding but attached to a wall, as though the architect was still feeling his way in the use of the new medium.

The most celebrated of the true pyramids were built for the Fourth Dynasty pharaohs Khufu, Khafre, and Menkaure. Khufu's pyramid, the largest of the three, covers thirteen acres and originally rose 481 feet. It is composed of 2,300,000 limestone blocks, some weighing fifteen tons, and all pushed and pulled into place by human muscle. This stupendous monument was built without mortar, yet some of the stones were so perfectly fitted that a knife cannot be inserted in the joint. The Old Kingdom's eighty pyramids are a striking expression of Egyptian civilization. In their dignity, massiveness, and repose, they reflect the religion-motivated character of Egyptian society.

As the glory and serenity of the Old Kingdom can be seen in its pyramids, constructed as an act of faith by its subjects, so the power and wealth of the Empire survives in the temples at Thebes, made possible by the booty and tribute of conquest. On the east side of the Nile stand the ruins of the magnificent temples of Karnak and Luxor. The Hypostyle Hall of the temple of Karnak, built by Ramses II, is larger than the cathedral of Notre Dame. Its forest of 134 columns is arranged in sixteen rows, with the roof over the two broader central aisles (the nave) raised to allow the entry of light. This technique of providing a clerestory over a central nave was later used in Roman basilicas and Christian churches.

Sculpture and painting. Egyptian art was essentially religious. Tomb paintings and relief sculpture depict the everyday activities that the deceased wished to continue enjoying in the afterlife, and statues glorify the god-kings in all their serenity and eternity. Since religious art is inherently conservative, Egyptian art seldom departed from the traditions established during the vigorous and self-assured Old Kingdom. Sculptors idealized and standardized their subjects, and the human figure is shown looking directly ahead (see illustration, p. 22), with a rigidity very much in keeping with the austere architectural settings of the statues.

Yet on two occasions an unprecedented naturalism appeared in Egyptian sculpture. The faces of some of the Middle Kingdom rulers appear drawn and weary, as though they were weighed down by the burden of reconstructing Egypt after the collapse of the Old Kingdom. An even greater naturalism is seen in the portraits of Akhenaton and his beautiful queen, Nefertete. The pharaoh's brooding countenance is realistically portrayed, as is his ungainly paunch and his happy but far from god-like family life as he holds one of his young daughters on his knee or munches on a bone. The "heretic" pharaoh, who insisted on what he called "truth" in religion, seems also to have insisted on truth in art.

Painting in Egypt shows the same precision and mastery of technique that are evident in sculpture. However, no attempt was made to show objects in perspective, and the scenes give an appearance of flatness. The effect of distance was conveyed by making objects in a series or by putting one object above another. Another convention employed was to depict everything from its most characteristic angle. Often the head,

In contrast to conventional Egyptian art, this representation of Akhenaton is so naturalistic that it borders on caricature.

arms, and legs were shown in side view and the eye, shoulders, and chest in front view (see Color Plate 2).

Writing and literature. In Egypt, as in Sumer, writing began with pictures. But unlike the Mesopotamian signs, Egyptian hieroglyphs ("sacred signs") remained primarily pictorial. At first the hieroglyphs represented only objects, but later they came to stand for ideas and syllables. Early in the Old Kingdom the Egyptians began to use alphabetic characters for twenty-four consonant sounds. Although they also continued to use the old pictographic and syllabic signs, this discovery was of far-reaching consequence. It led to the development of the Semitic alphabet, from which our present alphabet is derived.

Egypt's oldest literature is the Pyramid Texts, a body of religious writing found inscribed on the walls of the burial chambers of Old Kingdom pharaohs. Their recurrent theme is a monotonous insistence that the dead pharaoh is really a god.

The troubled life that followed the collapse of the Old Kingdom produced the highly personal literature of the First Intermediate Period and Middle Kingdom. It contains protests against the ills of the day, demands for social justice, and praise for the romantic excitements of wine, women, and song. The universal appeal of this literature is illustrated by the following lines from a love poem, in which the beloved is called "sister":

I behold how my sister cometh, and my heart is in gladness.
Mine arms open wide to embrace her; my heart exulteth within me: for my lady has come to me. . . .
She kisseth me, she openeth her lips to me: then am I joyful even without beer.[27]

A classic of Egyptian literature is Akhenaton's *Hymn to the Sun*, which is similar in spirit to Psalm 104. A few lines will indicate its lyric beauty and its conception of one omnipotent and beneficent Creator.

How manifold are thy works!
They are hidden before men,
O sole god, beside whom there is no other.
Thou didst create the earth according to thy heart
While thou wast alone.[28]

The Rosetta Stone, discovered in Egypt in 1799 by an officer in Napoleon's army, supplied the means by which Jean Champollion was able in 1822 to decipher Egyptian writing. On the stone a decree is inscribed in three different languages, as is shown by the section reproduced here. The bottom layer of writing is Greek, which Champollion could read. Working from the Greek he was able to figure out the other inscriptions. The middle layer is Egyptian demotic, and the top layer is the more formal system of hieroglyphic writing.

By the fifth century A.D. the ability to read ancient Egyptian writing had been lost. Not until fourteen hundred years later, when the Rosetta Stone was deciphered by Jean François Champollion (1790-1832), could modern man appreciate this ancient literature.

THE HITTITES

The Hittite empire. Except for brief mention in the Bible, very little was known about the Hittites until archaeologists began to unearth the remains of their civilization in Asia Minor in 1906. By 1920 their writing had been deciphered, and it proved to be the earliest example of a written Indo-European language. The Hittites are thought to have entered Asia Minor from the north about 2000 B.C., and their superior military means—particularly the horse-drawn chariot—enabled them to conquer the native people of central Asia Minor.

After 1450 B.C. a series of energetic Hittite kings created a more centralized government and an empire that included Syria, lost by the Egyptian pharaoh Akhenaton. Pharaoh Ramses II moved north from Palestine in a vain attempt to reconquer Syria. Ambushed and forced back to Palestine after a bloody battle, Ramses agreed to a treaty of "good peace and good brotherhood" in 1269 B.C. (see p. 23). The Hittites may have been eager for peace with Egypt because of the threat posed by a new movement of Indo-European peoples. Shortly after 1200 B.C. these barbarians, chief among whom were the Phrygians, destroyed the Hittite empire. Darkness settled over Asia Minor until after 800 B.C.

Hittite civilization. The Hittite state under the empire was modeled after the older oriental monarchies of the Near East. The king claimed to represent the sun god and was deified after death. The nobles held large estates from the king and in return provided warriors armed increasingly with iron weapons. The Hittites are credited with being the first people to work iron from local deposits, which afforded them a jealously guarded monopoly. Not until after 1200 B.C. did iron metallurgy become widespread.

The Hittites adopted the Mesopotamian cuneiform script together with some works of Babylonian literature. While their law code shows some similarity to the code of Hammurabi, it differed in prescribing more humane punishments. Instead of retaliation ("an eye for an eye"), the Hittite code made greater use of restitution and compensation.

The chief importance of Hittite culture lies in the legacy it left to the Phrygians and Lydians and, through them, to the Greeks who settled along the Aegean coast of Asia Minor. The Hittite goddess Kubaba, for example, became the great Phrygian goddess Cybele, the "Great Mother" whose worship became widespread in Roman times.

After 1200 B.C., with the Hittite empire destroyed and Egypt in decline, the Semitic peoples of Syria and Palestine ceased being pawns in a struggle between rival imperialisms. For nearly five hundred years, until they were conquered by the Assyrians, these peoples were able to play an independent and significant role in history.

THE ERA OF SMALL STATES

The Phoenicians. *Phoenician* is the name the Greeks gave to those Canaanites who dwelt along the Mediterranean coast of Syria, an area that is today the state of Lebanon. Hemmed in by the Lebanon Mountains to the east, the Phoenicians turned to the sea and by the eleventh century B.C. had become the greatest traders, shipbuilders, navigators, and colonizers before the Greeks. To obtain silver and copper from Spain and tin from Britain, Gades (Cadiz) was founded on the Atlantic coast of Spain. Carthage, one of a number of Phoenician trading posts around the shores of the Mediterranean, was destined to become Rome's chief rival in the third century B.C.

Although the Phoenicians were essentially traders, their home cities—notably Tyre, Sidon, and Byblos—also produced manufactured goods. Their most famous export was woolen cloth dyed with the purple dye obtained from shellfish found along their coast. They were also skilled makers of furniture (made from the famous cedars of Lebanon), metalware, glassware, and jewelry.

Culturally the Phoenicians were not creative. They left behind no literature and little art. Yet they made one of the greatest contributions to human progress, the perfection of the alphabet, which, along with the Babylonian sexagesimal system of notation, they carried westward. The origin of the alphabet is still a moot question. Between 1800 and 1600 B.C. various Canaanite peoples, influenced by Egypt's semialphabetical writing, started to evolve a simplified method of writing. The Phoenician alphabet of twenty-two consonant symbols (the Greeks later ádded the vowel signs) is derived from the thirty-character alphabet of Ugarit, a Canaanite city on the Syrian coast opposite Cyprus.

The half-dozen Phoenician cities never united to form a strong state, and in the last half of the eighth century B.C. all but Tyre were conquered by the Assyrians. When Tyre finally fell to the Chaldeans in 571 B.C., the Hebrew prophet Ezekiel spoke what reads like an epitaph to the once great role played by the Phoenicians:

When your wares came from the seas, you satisfied many peoples; with your abundant wealth and merchandise you enriched the kings of the earth. Now you are wrecked by the seas, in the depths of the waters; your merchandise and all your crew have sunk with you. [29]

The Arameans. Closely related to the Hebrews were the Arameans, who occupied Syria east of the Lebanon Mountains. The most important of their little kingdoms was centered on Damascus, one of the oldest continuously inhabited cities of the world. The Arameans dominated the camel caravan trade connecting Mesopotamia, Phoenicia, and Egypt and continued to do so after Damascus fell to the Assyrians in 732 B.C. The Aramaic language, which used an alphabet similar to the Phoenician, became the international language of the Near East. In Judea it displaced Hebrew as the spoken language and was used by Jesus and his disciples.

The Hebrew kingdoms. In war, diplomacy, inventions, and art, the Hebrews made little splash in the stream of history. In religion and ethics, however, their contribution to world civilization was tremendous. Out of their experience grew three great religions: Judaism, Christianity, and Islam.

Hebrew experience is recorded in the Holy Writ of Israel, the Old Testament of the Christian Bible, whose present content was approved about 90 A.D. by a council of rabbis. All of us are familiar with the power and beauty of some of its many great passages. As a work of literature it remains unsurpassed; but it is more than that. "It is Israel's life story—a story that cannot be told adequately apart from the conviction that

God had called this people in his grace, separated them from the nations for a special responsibility, and commissioned them with the task of being his servant in the accomplishment of his purpose." [30]

The Biblical account of the history of the Hebrews (later called Israelites and then Jews) begins with the patriarchal clan leader Abraham. About 1800 B.C. Abraham led his people out of Ur in Sumer, where they had settled for a time in their wanderings, and eventually they arrived in the land of Canaan, later called Palestine.

About 1700 B.C., driven by famine, some Hebrews followed Abraham's great-grandson Joseph, the son of Israel (also called Jacob), into Egypt. Joseph's rise to power in Egypt, and the hospitable reception of his people there, is attributed to the presence of the largely Semitic Hyksos, who had conquered Egypt about 1700 B.C. (see p. 22). Following the expulsion of the Hyksos by the pharaohs of the Eighteenth Dynasty, the Hebrews were enslaved by the Egyptians. Shortly after 1300 B.C. Moses led them out of bondage and into the wilderness of Sinai, where they entered into a pact or covenant with their God, Yahweh. The Sinai Covenant bound the people as a whole—the nation of Israel, as they now called themselves—to worship Yahweh before all other gods and to obey his Law. In return, Yahweh made the Israelites his chosen people whom he would protect and to whom he granted Canaan, "a land flowing with milk and honey." The history of Israel from this time on is the story of the working out of this covenant.

The Israelites had to contend for Palestine against the Canaanites, whose Semitic ancestors had migrated from Arabia early in the third millennium B.C. Joined by other Hebrew tribes already in Palestine, the Israelites formed a confederacy of twelve tribes (clans of the twelve sons of Israel) and, led by war leaders called judges, in time succeeded in subjugating the Canaanites. In the meantime, however, a far more formidable foe had appeared. The Philistines, from whom we get the word *Palestine*, settled along the coast about 1175 B.C., having been uprooted from Asia Minor by the invasions that destroyed the Hittite empire (see p. 28).

Aided by the use of iron weapons, which were new to Palestine, the Philistines were well on their way to dominating the entire land by the middle of the eleventh century.

It became apparent that the loose twelve-tribe confederacy could not cope with the Philistine danger. "Give us a king to govern us," the people demanded, "that we also may be like all the nations, and that our king may govern us and go before us and fight our battles."[31] Saul, the first king of Israel (1020-1000 B.C.), died while fighting the Philistines, but his successor David (1000-961 B.C.) not only restricted the Philistines to a narrow coastal strip but became the ruler of the largest state in the ancient history of the area, stretching from the Euphrates to the Gulf of Aqaba.

The work of David was completed by his son Solomon, in whose long reign (961-922 B.C.) Israel reached a pinnacle of wordly power and splendor as an oriental-style monarchy. In the words of the Bible:

**ANCIENT ISRAEL
8TH CENTURY B.C.**

Solomon ruled over all the kingdoms from the Euphrates to the land of the Philistines and to the border of Egypt; they brought tribute and served Solomon all the days of his life. . . . And Judah and Israel dwelt in safety, from Dan even to Beer-sheba, every man under his vine and under his fig tree, all the days of Solomon. . . . And God gave Solomon wisdom and understanding beyond measure, and largeness of mind. . . . Now the weight of gold that came to Solomon in one year was six hundred and sixty-six talents of gold, besides that which came from the traders and from the traffic of the merchants, and from all the kings of Arabia and from the governors of the land. . . . The king also made a great ivory throne, and overlaid it with the finest gold. . . .[32]

But the price of Solomon's vast bureaucracy, building projects (especially the palace complex and the Temple at Jerusalem), standing army (1400 chariots and 12,000 horses), and harem (700 wives and 300 concubines) was great. High taxes, forced labor, and the loss of tribal independence led to dissension, and on the death of Solomon in 922 B.C. the realm was split into two kingdoms—Israel in the north and Judah in the south. These two weak kingdoms were in no position to defend themselves when new, powerful empires rose again in Mesopotamia. In 721 B.C. the Assyrians captured Samaria, the capital of the northern kingdom, taking 27,900 Israelites into captivity and settling foreign peoples in their place. The resulting mixed population, called Samaritans, made no further contribution to Hebrew history or religion.

The southern kingdom of Judah held out until 586 B.C. when Nebuchadnezzar, the Chaldean ruler of Babylonia, destroyed Jerusalem and carried away ten thousand captives; "none remained, except the poorest people of the land."[33] Thus began the famous Babylonian Exile of the Jews (Judeans), which lasted until 538 B.C. when Cyrus the Persian, having conquered Babylon, allowed them to return to Jerusalem where they rebuilt the Temple destroyed by Nebuchadnezzar.

Persian rule was followed by that of the Hellenistic Greeks and Romans. In 66-70 A.D. the Jews rebelled against Rome, and Jerusalem was totally destroyed in the savage fighting that ensued. The Jews were again driven into exile, and the Diaspora—the "scattering"—was at its height.

Hebrew religion. From the time of Abraham the Hebrews worshiped one god, a stern, warlike tribal deity whose name Yahweh (Jehovah) was first revealed to Moses. Yahweh differed from the many Near Eastern nature gods in being completely separate from the physical universe which He had created. This view of Yahweh as the Creator of all things everywhere was inevitably to lead to the monotheistic belief that He was the sole God in the universe.

After their entrance into Palestine, many Hebrews adopted the fertility deities of the Canaanites as well as the luxurious Canaanite manner of living. As a result prophets arose who "spoke for" (from the Greek word *prophetes*) Yahweh in insisting on strict adherence to the Sinai Covenant and in condemning the "whoring" after other gods, the selfish pursuit of wealth, and the growth of social injustice.

Between roughly 750 and 550 B.C. appeared a series of great prophets who wrote down their messages. They sought to purge the religion of Israel of all corrupting influences and to elevate and dignify the concept of Yahweh. As summed up by Micah in a statement often cited as the essence of all higher religion, "He has shown you, O man, what is good; and what does the Lord require of you but to do justice, and to love kindness, and to walk humbly with your God?"[34] The prophets viewed the course of Hebrew history as being governed by the sovereign will of Yahweh, seeing the Assyrians and the Chaldeans as "the rod of Yahweh's anger" to chastise His stubborn, wayward people. They also developed the idea of a coming Messiah, the "anointed one" from the family of King David, who would inaugurate a reign of peace and justice.

Considered the greatest of the prophets are Jeremiah and the anonymous Second Isaiah, so-called because his message was incorporated in the Book of Isaiah (chapters 40-55). Jeremiah witnessed the events that led to Nebuchadnezzar's destruction of Jerusalem and the Temple and to the Babylonian Captivity of the Jews. He prepared the people for these calamities by affirming that Yahweh would forgive their sins and restore "a remnant" of his people and by proclaiming a "new covenant." The old covenant had been between Yahweh and the nation, which no longer existed, and it had become overlaid with ritual and ceremony and centered in the Temple, which had been destroyed. The new covenant was between Yahweh and each individual; religion was now a matter of a man's own heart and conscience, and both the nation and the Temple were considered superfluous. Second Isaiah, who lived at the end of the Babylonian Captivity, capped the work of his predecessors by proclaiming Israel to be Yahweh's "righteous servant," purified and enlightened by suffering and ready to guide the world to the worship of the one, eternal, supreme God. Thus were the Jews who returned from the Exile provided with a renewed faith in their destiny and a new comprehension of their religion which would sustain them through the centuries to come.

LATER EMPIRES OF WESTERN ASIA

Assyrian expansion. By 700 B.C. the era of small states was at an end. For two hundred years the Assyrians had been bidding to translate the growing economic unity of the Near East—evidenced by Solomon's trading operations and even more by the activities of Aramean merchants—into political unity. The Assyrian push toward the Mediterranean began in the ninth century and, after a lapse, was resumed in the eighth century, during which Babylon was also subdued. By 721 B.C. the Assyrians were the masters of the Fertile Crescent.

A Semitic people long established in the hilly region of the upper Tigris, the Assyrians had been schooled for a thousand years by constant warfare. But their matchless army was only one of several factors that explain the success of Assyrian imperialism: a

The militaristic nature of the Assyrians is reflected in this relief sculpture of sling-carrying warriors.

policy of calculated terrorization, an efficient system of political administration, and the support of the commercial classes that wanted political stability and unrestricted trade over large areas.

The Assyrian army, with its chariots, mounted cavalry, and sophisticated siege engines, was the most powerful yet seen in the ancient world. Neither troops or walls could long resist the Assyrians who, in Byron's well-known phrase, "came down like a wolf on the fold." Conquered peoples were held firmly in control by systematic terrorization. "From some I cut off their noses, their ears and their fingers, of many I put out the eyes. . . . I bound their heads to tree trunks round about the city"[35] is a characteristic statement from the Assyrian royal inscriptions. In addition, mass deportations were employed as an effective means of destroying national feeling.

The well-coordinated Assyrian system of political administration was another factor in the success of the empire. Conquered lands became provinces ruled by governors

who exercised extensive military, judicial, and financial powers. Their chief tasks were to ensure the regular collection of tribute and the raising of troops for the permanent army that eventually replaced the native militia of sturdy Assyrian peasants. An efficient system of communications carried the "king's word" to the governors as well as the latter's reports to the royal court—including one prophetic dispatch reading: "The king knows that all lands hate us. . . ."[36] Nevertheless, the Assyrians must be credited with laying the foundations for the later more humane administrative systems of the Persians and Alexander the Great and his successors.

Assyrian culture. Culturally the Assyrians were not creative; their role was rather one of borrowing from the superior cultures of other peoples and unifying the best elements into a new product. This is evident in Assyrian architecture and sculpture, the work of subject artisans and artists. Both arts glorified the power of the Assyrian king. The palace, serving both as residence and administrative center, replaced the temple as the characteristic architectural form. A feature of Assyrian palace architecture was the structural use of the arch and the column, both borrowed from Babylonia. The palaces were decorated with splendid relief sculptures that glorified the king as warrior and hunter. Assyrian sculptors were especially skilled in portraying realistically the ferocity and agony of charging and dying animals.

Assyrian kings were interested in preserving written as well as pictorial records of their reigns. King Ashurbanipal (d. 631 B.C.) left a record of his great efforts in collecting the literary heritage of Sumer and Babylon, and the 22,000 clay tablets found in the ruins of his palace at Nineveh provided modern scholars with their first direct knowledge of this literature.

Downfall of the Assyrian empire. Revolt against Assyrian terror and tribute was inevitable when Assyria's strength waned and effective opposition arose. By the middle of the seventh century B.C. the sturdy Assyrian stock had been decimated by wars, and the Assyrian kings had to rely on unreliable mercenary troops and subject levies. Egypt regained its independence under the Twenty-

Sixth Dynasty, and the Medes refused further tribute. Then the Chaldeans, a new group of Semites who had filtered into Babylonia, revolted in 626 B.C. In 612 they joined the Medes in destroying Nineveh, the Assyrian capital. From one end of the Fertile Crescent to the other people rejoiced: "Nineveh is laid waste: who will bemoan her?"[37]

The Lydians and the Medes. The fall of Assyria left four states to struggle over the crumbs of empire: Chaldea and Egypt vied over Syria-Palestine, while Media and Lydia clashed over eastern Asia Minor.

After the collapse of the Hittite empire about 1200 B.C., the Lydians had followed the Phrygians, whose last king was the semi-legendary Midas (d. c. 680 B.C.), in establishing a kingdom in western Asia Minor. When Assyria fell, the Lydians expanded eastward until stopped by the Medes at the Halys River. Lydia profited from being astride the commercial land route between Mesopotamia and the Aegean and from the possession of valuable gold-bearing streams. As a result, the Lydians invented coinage (about 675 B.C.), which replaced the silver bars hitherto in general use. Lydia's most famous king was Croesus, and the phrase "rich as Croesus" is a reminder of Lydian opulence. With his defeat by the Persians (see p. 34), Lydia ceased to exist.

The Medes were an Indo-European people who by 1000 B.C. had established themselves on the Iranian plateau east of Assyria. In the seventh century B.C. they had created a strong kingdom with Ecbatana as capital and with the Persians, their kinsmen to the south, as vassals. Following the collapse of Assyria, the Medes expanded into Armenia and eastern Asia Minor, but their short-lived empire ended in 550 B.C. when they, too, were absorbed by the Persians.

The Chaldean empire. While the Median kingdom controlled the highland region, the Chaldeans, with their capital at Babylon, were masters of the Fertile Crescent. Nebuchadnezzar, becoming king of the Chaldeans in 604 B.C., raised Babylonia to another epoch of brilliance after more than a thousand years of eclipse. By defeating the Egyptians in Syria, Nebuchadnezzar ended their hopes of re-creating their empire. As we have seen

earlier (p. 30), he destroyed Jerusalem in 586 B.C. and carried several thousand Jews captive to Babylonia.

Nebuchadnezzar built Babylon into the largest and most impressive city of its day. The tremendous city walls were wide enough at the top to have rows of small houses on either side; between the rows of houses was a space wide enough for the passage of a chariot. In the center of Babylon ran the famous Procession Street, which passed through the Ishtar Gate. This arch, which was adorned with brilliant tile animals, is the best remaining example of Babylonian architecture. The immense palace of Nebuchadnezzar towered terrace upon terrace, each resplendent with masses of ferns, flowers, and trees. These roof gardens, the famous Hanging Gardens of Babylon, were so beautiful that they were regarded by the Greeks as one of the seven wonders of the ancient world.

Nebuchadnezzar also rebuilt the great

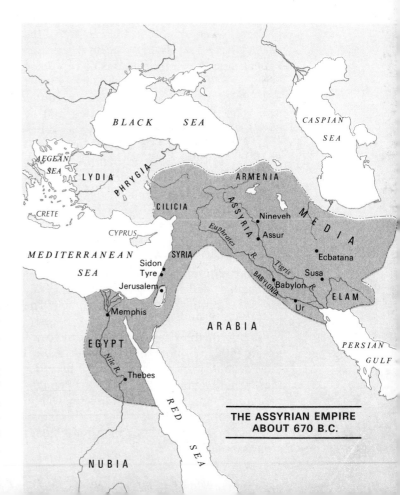

**THE ASSYRIAN EMPIRE
ABOUT 670 B.C.**

temple-tower or ziggurat, the Biblical "Tower of Babel," which the Greek historian Herodotus viewed a century later and described as

a tower of solid masonry, a furlong in length and breadth, upon which was raised a second tower, and on that a third, and so on up to eight. The ascent to the top is on the outside, by a path which winds round all the towers.[38]

Nebuchadnezzar was the last great Mesopotamian ruler, and Chaldean power quickly crumbled after his death in 562 B.C. The Chaldean priests—whose interest in astrology greatly added to the fund of Babylonian astronomical knowledge—continually undermined the monarchy. Finally, in 539 B.C., they opened the gates of Babylon to Cyrus the Persian, thus fulfilling Daniel's message of doom upon the notorious Belshazzar, the last Chaldean ruler: "You have been weighed in the balances and found wanting."

The Persian empire. Cyrus the Persian was the greatest conqueror in the history of the ancient Near East. In 550 B.C. he had ended Persian vassalage to the Medes by capturing Ecbatana and ousting the Median dynasty. The Medes readily accepted their vigorous new ruler, who soon demonstrated that he deserved to be called "the Great." When King Croesus of Lydia moved across the Halys River in 547 B.C. to pick up some of the pieces of the Median empire, Cyrus defeated him and annexed Lydia, including those Greek cities on the coast of Asia Minor which were under the nominal control of Lydia. Then he turned east, establishing his power as far as the frontier of India. Babylon and its empire, as we have seen, was next on his list. Following the death of Cyrus, his son Cambyses conquered Egypt. The next ruler, Darius I (522-486 B.C.), began a conflict with the Greeks that continued intermittently for more than 150 years until the Persians were conquered by Alexander the Great. Long before this event the Persians had forgotten Cyrus the Great's answer to the suggestion that they "leave this small and barren country of ours" and migrate to a pleasanter land:

Do so if you wish, but if you do, be ready to find yourselves no longer governors but governed; for soft lands breed soft men; it does not happen that the same land brings forth wonderful crops and good fighting men.[40]

Persian government. Although built upon the Assyrian model, the Persian administrative system was far more efficient and humane. The empire was divided into twenty provinces, or satrapies, each ruled by a governor called a satrap. To check the satraps, a secretary and a military official representing the "Great King, King of Kings" were installed in every province. Also, special inspectors, "the Eyes and Ears of the King," traveled throughout the realm.

Imperial post roads connected the important cities of the empire. Along the Royal Road between Sardis and Susa there was a post station every fourteen miles, where the king's couriers could obtain fresh horses, enabling them to cover the 1600-mile route in a week. "Nothing mortal travels so fast as these Persian messengers," wrote Herodotus. "These men will not be hindered . . . , either by snow, or rain, or heat, or by the darkness of night."[41]

The Persian empire was the first to attempt governing many different racial groups on the principle of equal responsibilities and rights for all peoples. So long as his subjects paid their taxes and kept the peace, the king did not interfere with local religion, customs, or trade. Indeed, Darius was called the "shopkeeper" because he stimulated trade by introducing a uniform system of gold and silver coinage on the Lydian model.

Persian religion and art. The humaneness of the Persian rulers may have stemmed from the ethical religion founded by the prophet Zoroaster, who lived in the early sixth century B.C. Zoroaster sought to replace what he called "the lie"—ritualistic, idol-worshiping cults and their Magi priests—with a religion centered on the sole god Ahura-Mazda ("Wise Lord"), who demanded "good thoughts of the mind, good deeds of the hand, and good words of the tongue" from those who would attain paradise (a Persian word). The new religion made little progress

THE CHALDEAN AND
PERSIAN EMPIRES

Chaldean Empire
About 586 B.C.

Persian Empire
About 500 B.C.

0   100   200   300   400   500
1" = 430 MILES

until first Darius and then the Magi adopted it. The Magi revived many old gods as lesser deities, added much ritual, and replaced monotheism with dualism by transforming what Zoroaster had called the principle or spirit of evil into the powerful god Ahriman, rival of Ahura-Mazda. The complicated evolution of Zoroastrianism is revealed in its holy writ, the *Avesta* ("The Law"), assembled in its present form between the fourth and the sixth centuries A.D. Zoroastrian eschatology—"the doctrine of final things" such as the resurrection of the dead and a last judgment—influenced Judaism. Following the Muslim conquest of Persia in the seventh century A.D., Zoroastrianism gradually died out in its homeland. It exists today among the Parsees in India.

In art the Persians borrowed largely from their predecessors in the Fertile Crescent, especially the Assyrians. Their most important work was in palace architecture, the best remains of which are at Persepolis. Built on a high terrace, the royal residences were reached by a grand stairway faced with beautiful reliefs. Instead of the warfare and violence that characterized Assyrian sculpture, these reliefs depict hundreds of soldiers, courtiers, and representatives of twenty-three nations of the empire bringing gifts to the king for the festival of the new year.

SUMMARY

This chapter has recounted the evolution of human affairs from primitive culture to civilization. The first great period in man's prehistory, during which man was a hunter and food-gatherer whose chief all-purpose tool was the hand-ax, is called the Paleolithic or Old Stone Age. Present evidence indicates that the Paleolithic cultural stage began in East Africa some 750,000 years ago. Some nine thousand years ago the Neolithic stage was initiated with the appearance of food-producing villages in western Asia.

This revolutionary change from a food-gathering to a food-producing economy, quite probably the most momentous development in human history, made possible the rise of civilization.

Civilization rose in Mesopotamia and Egypt during the second half of the fourth millennium B.C. Both these civilizations were river-made, one by the Tigris and Euphrates and the other by the Nile. In each case the complex society we call a civilization was the result of human cooperation in taming the rivers to make them work for man.

The words *monumental* and *timeless* best describe Egyptian culture. The Egyptians built colossal statues and huge tombs; their burial customs were designed to outwit time itself. The state centered upon the absolute rule of the pharaohs—god-kings who eventually extended their rule from Nubia to the Euphrates River.

The story of ancient Mesopotamia is primarily concerned with the achievements of the Sumerians and the later adoption of their civilization by various invaders. The most important of these new states was the Babylonian empire created by Hammurabi. Babylon was sacked by the Indo-European Hittites of Asia Minor, who went on to duel with Egypt over Syria and Palestine.

By 1200 B.C. the first great Near Eastern empires—Babylonian, Egyptian, and Hittite—had collapsed, allowing the small Semitic peoples of Syria and Palestine freedom to make their own contributions—the greatest being the ethical monotheism of the Hebrews. Political diversity was ended by the rise of the Assyrian empire, which unified all of the ancient Near East for the first time. After the fall of Assyria, the Chaldean Nebuchadnezzar erected a new Babylonian empire, but it was soon terminated by the expansion of Persia. Stretching from India to Europe, the Persian empire gave the Near East its greatest extension and power—which produced an inevitable conflict with the Greeks. The next major phase in the history of civilization in the West was to be centered on Greece.

SUGGESTIONS FOR READING

R. Braidwood, **Prehistoric Men**,* 7th ed., Scott, Foresman, 1967. The best short survey. Also recommended: J. Hawkes, **Prehistory**,* Mentor; A. Montegu, **Man: His First Two Million Years**, Columbia Univ., 1969; Grahame Clark and S. Piggott, **Prehistoric Societies**, Knopf, 1965; H. Bandi, **The Art of the Stone Age**, Crown, 1961.

L. Cottrell, **Digs and Diggers: A Book of World Archaeology**, World, 1964; C. W. Ceram, **Gods, Graves, and Scholars**, rev. ed., Knopf, 1967; P. Cleator, **Lost Languages**,* Mentor. Popular surveys. M. Wheeler, **Archaeology from the Earth**,* Penguin, describes the techniques of the archaeologist.

M. Covensky, **The Ancient Near Eastern Tradition**,* Harper & Row, 1966. A very brief but perceptive overview. For greater detail see Gordon Childe, **What Happened in History**,* Penguin; Sir L. Woolley, **The Beginnings of Civilization**,* Mentor; H. Frankfort, **The Birth of Civilization in the Near East**,* Anchor; S. Moscati, **The Face of the Ancient Orient**,* Anchor.

G. Roux, **Ancient Iraq**,* Penguin. An excellent detailed history of ancient Mesopotamia. See also S. N. Kramer, **The Sumerians**, Univ. of Chicago, 1963; and the same author's popular **History Begins at Sumer**,* Anchor.

C. Aldred, **The Egyptians**,* Praeger; L. Casson, **Ancient Egypt**, Time, Inc., 1965. Two brief topical surveys. Alan Gardiner, **Egypt of the Pharaohs**,* Galaxy, is a detailed political history. On the Empire period see G. Steindorff and K. Seele, **When Egypt Ruled the East**,* Phoenix; L. Cottrell, **Life Under the Pharaohs**,* Grosset & Dunlap; C. Desroches-Noblecourt, **Tutankhamen**,* Doubleday.

H. Frankfort *et al.,* **Before Philosophy**,* Penguin. A notable interpretation of Mesopotamian and Egyptian thought. John A. Wilson, **The Culture of Ancient Egypt**,* Phoenix,* is highly recommended. O. Neugebauer, **The Exact Sciences in Antiquity**,* Torchbooks, is the authoritative work on Mesopotamian and Egyptian mathematics and science.

O. R. Gurney, **The Hittites**,* Penguin; D. Harden, **The Phoenicians**,* Praeger. Authoritative surveys.

J. A. Hexter, **The Judaeo-Christian Tradition**,* Harper & Row, 1966. A succinct overview of Hebrew history and religion. Excellent longer surveys are H. M. Orlinsky, **Ancient Israel**,* Cornell; John Bright, **A History of Israel**, Westminster Press, 1959; Bernhard W. Anderson, **Understanding the Old Testament**, Prentice-Hall, 1957; O. Eissfeldt, **The Old Testament: An Introduction**, Harper & Row, 1965; Mary Ellen Chase, **Life and Language in the Old Testament**,* Norton.

A. Olmstead, **History of Assyria**, Scribner, 1923, and **History of the Persian Empire**,* Phoenix. The standard accounts. See also R. N. Frye, **The Heritage of Persia**,* Mentor; R. Zaehner, **The Dawn and Twilight of Zoroastrianism**, Putnam, 1961.

Seton Lloyd, **Art of the Ancient Near East**,* Praeger. See also H. Frankfort, **The Art and Architecture of the Ancient Orient**, Penguin, 1954; I. E. S. Edwards, **The Pyramids of Egypt**,* Penguin.

*Indicates an inexpensive paperbound edition.

Chapter 2

The Glory That Was Greece

Aegean, Hellenic, and Hellenistic Civilizations

INTRODUCTION. Scarred by time and weather, the ruins of the Athenian Acropolis stand against a vivid blue sky and overlook the trees and buildings of a modern city sprawled beneath. These ruins are striking symbols of a departed civilization—the democracy of Athens at its height.

In the fifth century B.C. the temples and statuary of the Acropolis were gleaming and new, fresh from the hands of builders and sculptors. Five hundred years later Plutarch wrote:

The works are . . . wonderful: because they were perfectly made in so short a time, and have continued so long a season. . . . [The Acropolis looks] at this day as if it were but newly done and finished, there is such a certain kind of flourishing freshness in it . . . that the injury of time cannot impair the sight thereof. As if every one of those . . . works had some living spirit in it, to make it seem young and fresh: and a soul that lived ever, which kept them in their good continuing state.[1]

Today the Acropolis bears the heavy "injury of time"; yet for us no less than for Plutarch, ancient Athens has retained a "flourishing freshness." This quality, together with a refined sense of symmetry and proportion, is characteristic of the Greek spirit and the dazzling achievements of Greek civilization. The ancient Greeks repeatedly demonstrated an ability to regard the world about them from a "young and fresh" perspective and to inject a love of proportion not only into their architecture but into almost everything they attempted. Yet in the crucial sphere of politics, their sense of proportion failed them. Instead of compromising their differences, the city-states quarreled continually, and that fervid individualism which moved them to brilliant creative efforts blinded them to the necessity of cooperation. Thus the political life of the Greeks was marked by conflicts between the city-states until they were at last subjugated by King Philip of Macedonia and his son, Alexander the Great.

Yet Alexander, out of genuine admiration of the Greek cultural achievement, strove to perpetuate the learning of the city-states as he set forth to forge a world-state. Greece's accomplishment was to prove so enduring that its magnificent legacy of knowledge and art would provide much of the cultural heritage of the West and, to a lesser extent, of the East. Thus the English poet Shelley could say with justification, "We are all Greeks." Probably no other people has made so lasting an impression on man's intellectual history.

BACKGROUND FOR GREEK CULTURE

Aegean civilization. Greek civilization was unique in so many ways that a student of history might infer that Greek culture developed in a vacuum or, free from outside influences, sprang full-blown from the rocky hills of this small land. The Greek achievement, however, was preceded by an advanced civilization located on the lands surrounding the Aegean Sea. This Aegean civilization, which came into full flower about 2000 B.C. and collapsed suddenly following 1200 B.C., developed through two major periods. The first and longer period, which ended about 1450 B.C., is called "Minoan" after the legendary Cretan King Minos. Crete was the center of Minoan civilization, which spread also to the Aegean Islands, to Troy in Asia Minor, and to Greece. The last period of Aegean civilization, the two and one half centuries following 1450 B.C. when the center of Aegean political power and culture lay on the Greek mainland, is called "Mycenaean" after its most important site at Mycenae.

The Minoans. The narrow, 160-mile-long island of Crete was a stepping stone between Europe, Asia, and Africa. Stimulated by contacts with Mesopotamia and Egypt, a brilliant civilization emerged here.

Minoan prosperity was based on large-scale trade that ranged from Troy to Egypt and from Sicily to Syria and employed the first ships capable of long voyages over the open sea. Chief exports were olive oil, wine, metalware, and magnificent pottery. This trade was the monopoly of an efficient bureaucratic government under a powerful ruler whose administrative records were written on clay tablets, first in a form of picture writing and later in a syllabic script known as Linear A. Neither script can be read, but Linear A appears to contain some borrowed Semitic words, the result of Cretan trade with the coastal cities of Syria. Our knowledge of Minoan civilization is therefore scanty and imprecise; most of it is derived from the material remains uncovered by archaeologists.

It was the epoch-making discoveries of the English archaeologist Sir Arthur Evans that first brought to light this civilization, whose existence had previously only been hinted at in Greek legends and the epics of Homer. Between 1900 and 1905 Evans unearthed the ruins of a great palace at Knossos, the dominant city in Crete after 1700 B.C. Rising at least three stories high and sprawl-

THE AEGEAN WORLD

THRACE

Byzantium

SEA OF
MARMARA

PHRYGIA

MYSIA

Hellespont

Ilium (Troy)

LESBOS

CHIOS

LYDIA

Sardis

Hermus R.

Pergamum

Maeander R.

Ephesus

Miletus

SAMOS

Halicarnassus

RHODES

SPORADES

AEGEAN

SEA

CRETAN SEA

SEA

CYCLADES

NAXOS

PAROS

IOS

CYTHERA

MELOS

THERA

Knossos

CRETE

MACEDONIA

MT OLYMPUS

THESSALY

EPIRUS

AETOLIA

ACHAIA

EUBOEA

BOEOTIA

Delphi Thebes

ATTICA

Athens

Piraeus

Corinth

Mycenae

Argos

ARCADIA

PELOPONNESUS

MESSENIA

Sparta

LACONIA

Olympia

Pylos

CYTHERA

MEDITERRANEAN

LEUCAS

CEPHALLENIA

ZACYNTHUS

CORCYRA

SAMOTHRACE

LEMNOS

75

50

25

0

Fashioned of gold and ivory, this exquisitely wrought figurine of the Cretan Mother Goddess (sixteenth century B.C.) is dressed in the Minoan style. The snake was the primary sacred symbol of this female deity.

ing over nearly six acres, this "Palace of Minos," built of brick and limestone and employing unusual downward-tapering columns of wood, was a maze of royal apartments, storerooms, corridors, open courtyards, and broad stairways. Walls were painted with elaborate frescoes in which the Minoans appear as a gay, peaceful people with a pronounced liking for dancing, festivals, and athletic contests. Women are shown enjoying a freedom and dignity unknown elsewhere in the ancient Near East or classical Greece. Furnished with running water, the palace had a sanitation system surpassing anything constructed in Europe until Roman times and, after that, until the nineteenth

century. The palace was linked to other parts of Crete by well-paved roads lined with the luxurious dwellings of the nobility.

The glory of Minoan culture was its art—gay, spontaneous, and full of rhythmic motion. Art was an essential part of everyday life and not, as in the ancient Orient, an adjunct to religion and the state. What little is known of Minoan religion also contrasts sharply with conditions in the Near East: there were no great temples, powerful priesthoods, or large cult statues of the gods. The principal deity seems to have been the Mother Goddess, and a number of recovered statuettes show her dressed like a fashionable Cretan lady with flounced skirts, a tightly laced, low-cut bodice, and an elaborate coiffure. It is also noteworthy that the later classical Greeks believed that Zeus and other deities came from Crete.

The Mycenaeans. About 2000 B.C., or shortly thereafter, the first Indo-European Greek tribes, collectively called Achaeans, entered Greece, where they absorbed the earlier settlers and ruled from strongly fortified citadels at Mycenae, Pylos, Thebes, and other sites. By 1600 B.C. the Achaeans—or Mycenaeans, as they are usually called—had evolved their own civilization, based largely on borrowings from the Minoans, and were plying the seas both as pirates and as traders.

Some of the wealth accumulated by the kings of Mycenae—the greatest single hoard of gold, silver, and ivory objects found anywhere before the discovery of Tutankhamen's tomb—was unearthed in 1876 by Heinrich Schliemann, fresh from his even more sensational discoveries at Troy (see p. 41). The royal palace on the acropolis, or citadel, of Mycenae had well-proportioned audience rooms and apartments, fresco-lined walls, floors of painted stucco, and large storerooms. Noteworthy also were the royal "beehive" tombs, constructed of cut stone and covered with earth.

The expansive force of this hitherto unimagined Mycenaean civilization led to the planting of colonies in the eastern Mediterranean (Hittite sources refer to Achaeans in Asia Minor) and to the conquest of Knossos about 1450 B.C. The latter event was made possible by the destruction of the labyrinthian palace at Knossos by fire—the after-effect, it is now conjectured, of a great tidal wave caused by the eruption of the small volcanic island of Thera (Santorini) eighty miles north of Crete. The palace at Knossos was rebuilt by the Mycenaeans (to be finally destroyed about 1380 B.C. by earthquake and fire), and the center of Aegean civilization shifted to the Greek mainland.

This story of Achaean-Cretan relations was unclear until after 1952 when a young English architect, Michael Ventris, startled the scholarly world by deciphering a type of Cretan script known as Linear B, many examples of which had been found by Evans at Knossos and by later archaeologists at Pylos, Mycenae, and Thebes. When Linear B turned out to be an early form of Greek written in syllabic characters, it followed that the rulers of Knossos after 1450 B.C. must have been Achaean Greeks who had adopted the Cretan script to write their own language.

The Linear B texts, which are administrative documents and inventories, greatly add to our knowledge of Mycenaean life. The Mycenaean centers were fortified palaces and administrative centers and not, as in Crete, true cities. The bulk of the population lived in scattered villages where they worked either communal land or land held by nobles or kings. The nobles were under the close control of the kings, whose administrative records were kept daily by a large number of scribes. Prominent in these records are details of the disbursement of grain and wine as wages and the collection of taxes in kind. The most important item of income was olive oil, the major article in the wide-ranging Mycenaean trade which was operated as a royal monopoly. Perhaps it was their role as merchant-monopolists that led the Achaean kings late in the thirteenth century B.C. to launch the famous expedition against Troy in order to eliminate a powerful commercial rival.

Troy, site of the Homeric epics. The city of Troy occupied a strategic position on the Hellespont (the straits between the Black and Aegean seas now known as the Dardanelles). From there, Troy could command both the sea traffic through the straits and the land caravans between Asia and Europe. For many years scholars thought this city existed only in the epic poems of Homer. Heinrich Schliemann (1822-1890), a German romantic dreamer and amateur archaeologist, believed otherwise. As a boy, he had read Homer's *Iliad*, and thereafter he remained firmly convinced that Troy had actually existed. At the age of forty-eight, having amassed a fortune in the California gold rush and in world-wide trade, Schliemann retired from business to put his persistent dream of ancient Troy to the test.

In 1870 Schliemann began excavations at the legendary site of Troy, where he unearthed several cities, built one on top of the other. He discovered a treasure of golden earrings, hairpins, and bracelets in the second city, which led him to believe that this was the city of Homer's epics. Excavations in the 1930's, however, showed that the seventh city, over a thousand years more recent than the second, was the one made famous by Homer.

Neither the view that Troy was the victim of commercial rivalry nor the other widely held theory that it was destroyed by Achaean pirates seeking booty corresponds to Homer's view that the Trojan War was caused by the abduction of the beauteous Helen, queen of Sparta, by the Trojan prince Paris. Led by Agamemnon, king of Mycenae, the

This vase from Mycenae, with its six helmeted soldiers carrying lances and round shields, shows both the adventurous and martial nature of the Mycenaeans.

wrathful Achaeans besieged Troy for ten long years. Homer's *Iliad* deals only with a few weeks during the tenth year of the siege.

The fall of Mycenaean civilization. About 1200 B.C., not long after the fall of Troy, a new wave of Indo-Europeans, the Dorian Greeks, materially aided by weapons made of iron instead of bronze, burst upon Greece. First of the Mycenaean strongholds to fall was Pylos, whose Linear B archives contain numerous references to hastily undertaken preparations to repel the invaders. We find orders directing women and children to places of safety; instructions to armorers, "rowers," and food-suppliers; and a report entitled "how the watchers are guarding the coastal regions."[2] The preparations were in vain, however. Pylos was sacked and burned, and the destruction of the other major Mycenaean citadels soon followed. Mycenaean refugees found a haven at Athens and in Ionia on the western coast of Asia Minor.

The next four centuries, the Greek Dark Ages, were marked by the disappearance of the major characteristics of the relatively advanced Mycenaean civilization—political centralization, wide-ranging commerce, sophisticated art forms (including monumental architecture), and writing. Yet while the Dorian invasion was an undoubted catastrophe, it was also vital to the ultimate rise of a unique Hellenic (from *Hellas*, the Greek name for Greece) civilization that was not largely an offshoot of the Near East, as was Aegean civilization.

THE RISE OF HELLENIC CIVILIZATION

The influence of geography. Geographical factors played an important part in shaping the events of Greek history. The numerous mountain ranges which crisscross the peninsula severely hampered internal communications and led to the development of fiercely independent, autonomous political units—the city-states. Furthermore, the Greeks had every incentive to go down to the sea in ships. The numerous islands and indented coastlines of the Greek peninsula and of Asia Minor stimulated seagoing trade, and the rocky soil (less than a fifth of Greece is arable) and limited natural resources encouraged the Greeks to establish colonies abroad.

The Homeric Age. Most of our information about the Greek Dark Ages (c. 1150-750 B.C.) which followed the Dorian invasion is derived from the epics composed during the last century of this period and attributed to the blind Ionian poet Homer. Controversy surrounds the problem of Homer's existence and whether he or several poets composed the *Iliad* and the *Odyssey*. The Homeric epics retain something of the material side of the bygone Mycenaean period; yet in filling in the details of political, economic, and social life, the religious beliefs and practices, and the ideals that gave meaning to life, the poet could only describe what was familiar to him in his own age.

The values that gave meaning to life in the Homeric Age were predominantly heroic values—the strength, skill, and valor of the preeminent warrior. Such was the earliest meaning of *aretē*, "excellence" or "virtue," a key term throughout the course of Greek culture. To obtain *aretē*—defined by one Homeric hero as "to fight ever in the forefront and outvie my peers"—and the imperishable fame that was its reward, men welcomed hardship, struggle, and even death. Honor, like fame, was a measure of *aretē*, and the greatest of human tragedies was the denial of honor due to a great warrior. Homer makes such a denial the theme of the *Iliad*: "The ruinous wrath of Achilles that brought countless ills upon the Achaeans" when Achilles, insulted by Agamemnon, withdraws from battle.

To the Homeric Greeks, the gods were plainly human: Zeus, the king of the gods, was often the undignified victim of the plots of his wife Hera and other deities, and he asserted his authority through threats of violence. Hades, the abode of the dead, was a subterranean land of dust and darkness, and Achilles, as Homer tells us in the *Odyssey*, would have preferred to be a slave on earth than a king in Hades.

Society was clearly aristocratic—only the *aristoi* ("aristocrats") possessed *aretē*—and the common man was reviled and beaten when he dared to question his betters. Yet the common man had certain political rights as a member of the assembly that was summoned whenever a crisis, such as war, required his participation. Two other instruments of government described by Homer were the tribal king and his council. The king was hardly more than a chief among his peers, his fellow nobles, who sat in his council to advise him and to check any attempt he might make to exercise arbitrary power. Economic conditions were those of a simple, self-sufficient agricultural system much like that of the early Middle Ages in western Europe.

The city-state: origin and political evolution. The *polis*, or city-state, the famed Greek political unit consisting of a city and its surrounding plains and valleys, did not exist in the Greek Dark Ages. The nucleus of the *polis* was the elevated, fortified site—the *acropolis*—where people could take refuge from attack. With the revival of commerce in the eighth and seventh centuries B.C., a trading center developed below the acropolis. The two parts combined, forming the *polis*, from which our word *politics* is derived.

The political development of the *polis* was so rich and varied that it is difficult to think of a form of government not experienced—and given a lasting name—by the Greeks. Four major types of government evolved: (1) monarchy limited by an aristocratic council and a popular assembly, as described in the Homeric epics; (2) oligarchy ("rule of the few"), arising when the aristocratic council ousted the king and abolished or restricted the popular assembly; (3) tyranny, imposed by one man who rode to power on the discontent of the lower classes; (4) democracy ("rule of the people"), the outstanding political achievement of the Greeks, which emerged after the tyrant was deposed and the popular assembly revived and made the chief organ of government. After dissatisfaction with democratic government became widespread in the fourth century B.C., many of the city-states returned either to oligarchy or to one-man rule.

The Age of Oligarchy. By the middle of the eighth century B.C., the nobles, who resented the power wielded by the tribal kings, had taken over the government, ushering in the Age of Oligarchy. Ruthlessly exercising their superior power, the nobles acquired a monopoly of the best land, reducing many commoners to virtual serfdom and forcing others to seek a living on rocky, barren soil.

The hard lot of the common man under oligarchy produced the anguished protest of Hesiod's *Works and Days* (c. 700 B.C.). A commoner who had been cheated out of his parcel of land by his evil brother in league with "bribe-swallowing" aristocratic judges, Hesiod was the prophet of a more exalted conception of the gods and a new age of social justice. To establish a just society, Hesiod argued, men must learn to pursue moderation (*sophrosynē*) in all things—apparently the first expression of this famous Greek ideal—and realize that "far-seeing" Zeus and the other gods punish evildoers and reward the righteous. He redefined human excellence, or *aretē*, in a way to make it attainable for the common man. Its essential ingredients were righteousness and work—honest work in competition with one's fellows being a form of strife in moderation. "Gods and men hate him who lives without work," Hesiod insisted. "His nature is like the drones who sit idle and eat the labor of the bees." Furthermore, "work is no shame, but idleness is a shame," and "esteem," "glory," and "riches" follow work.[3]

Hesiod's new ideals of moderation and justice took root slowly, and the poor found relief only by emigrating to new lands overseas. As Plato later noted, the wealthy promoted colonization as a safety valve to ward off a threatened political and economic explosion:

> When men who have nothing, and are in want of food, show a disposition to follow their leaders in an attack on the property of the rich—these, who are the natural plague of the state, are sent away by the legislator in a friendly spirit as far as he is able; and this dismissal of them is euphemistically termed a colony.[4]

From 750 to 550 B.C. the Greeks planted colonies throughout much of the Mediterranean world, a development often compared with the expansion of Europe in modern

In ancient Greece pottery was an important industrial product; today it is an invaluable source of what everyday life was like then. A detail from a cup—painted with red figures on a black background as was common in the fifth century B.C.—shows three men at a banquet.

times. Settlements sprang up along the northern coast of the Aegean and around the Black Sea. So many Greeks migrated to southern Italy and eastern Sicily that the region became known as *Magna Graecia*, or Great Greece. Colonies were also founded as far west as present-day France—at Massilia, modern Marseilles—and Spain and on parts of the African coast. Unique was Naucratis in Egypt, not a true colony but a trading post whose residents gained extraterritorial rights (their own magistrates and law courts) from the Egyptians.

In time colonization ameliorated Greece's economic and social problems. By 600 B.C. the use of coined money, learned from the Lydians, had created the beginnings of a middle class. The Greek home states gradually became "industrialized" as a result of concentrating upon the production of specialized wares—vases, metal goods, textiles, olive oil, and wine—for export in exchange for foodstuffs and raw materials. But before this economic revolution was completed, the continuing land hunger of the peasants con-

tributed to a political revolution. After 650 B.C. tyrants arose in many Greek states and, supported by the aggrieved peasantry and the rising merchant class, seized the reins of government from the nobility. These tyrants (the word meant simply "master" and did not at first have the unfavorable meaning it now possesses) not only distributed land to the peasants but, by promoting further colonization, trade, and industry, accelerated the rise of a mercantile class and the completion of the Greek economic revolution.

Athens to 500 B.C. Athens and Sparta, the city-states destined to dominate the history of Greece during the classical period (the fifth century and most of the fourth), underwent markedly different developments during the period prior to 500 B.C. While Athens' political, economic, and social evolution was typical of most other Greek states, Sparta's development produced a unique way of life that elicited the wonder and often the admiration of other Greeks.

During the course of the seventh century B.C. at Athens, the council of nobles became supreme. The popular assembly no longer met, and the king was replaced by nine aristocratic magistrates, called archons, chosen annually by the council to exercise the king's civil, military, and religious powers. The nobility acquired the good land on the plain; the peasants either stayed on as sharecroppers, who were often reduced to debt slavery, or took to the hills.

When the Athenian nobles finally realized that their failure to heed the cry for reform would result in the rise of a tyrant, they agreed to the policy of compromise advocated by the liberal aristocrat Solon. In 594 B.C. Solon was made sole archon with broad authority to reconcile the lower classes. Inspired by the new ideals of moderation and justice, Solon instituted middle-of-the-road reforms that have made his name a byword for wise statesmanship.

Solon provided a new start for the lower classes by canceling all debts and forbidding future debt bondage, but he rejected as too radical their demand for the redivision of the land. His long-range solution to the economic problem was to seek full employment by stimulating trade and industry. To achieve this goal, Solon required fathers to teach their sons a trade, granted citizenship to foreign artisans who settled in Athens, and encouraged the intensive production of olive oil for export.

Moderation also characterized Solon's political reforms—the common people were granted important political rights, but not equality. While laws continued to originate in the new aristocratic Council of Four Hundred, they now had to be ratified by the popular assembly, which Solon revived. And since property, not birth, became the qualification for membership in the Council and for the archonships, wealthy commoners acquired full political equality. Furthermore, the assembly could now act as a court to hear appeals from the decisions of the archons and to try them for misdeeds in office.

Unfortunately, Solon's moderate reforms satisfied neither party. The poor had received neither land nor political equality, while the nobles thought Solon a radical who had betrayed his class. Deeply discouraged, Solon described what is too often the lot of moderate reformers: "Formerly they boasted of me vainly; with averted eyes, now they look askance upon me; friends no more, but enemies."[5]

Solon had warned the Athenians to accept his reforms lest "the people in its ignorance comes into the power of a tyrant." He lived to see his prediction fulfilled. In 560 B.C., after a period of civil strife, Pisistratus, a military hero and champion of the commoners, usurped power as tyrant. He solved the economic problem by banishing many nobles, whose lands he distributed among the poor, and by promoting commerce and industry. Together with extensive public works and the patronage of culture—thus starting Athens on the road to cultural leadership in Greece—these reforms gave rise to a popular saying that "Life under Pisistratus was paradise on earth."

Pisistratus was succeeded by his two sons, one of whom was assassinated and the other exiled. When the nobles, aided by a Spartan army, took this opportunity to restore oligarchy, Cleisthenes temporarily seized power in 508 B.C. and put through constitutional reforms that destroyed the remaining power of the nobility. He disregarded the old noble-dominated tribes and created ten new ones, each embracing citizens of all classes from widely scattered districts. The popular assembly acquired the right to initiate legislation, while the new and democratic Council of Five Hundred, selected by lot from the ten tribes, advised the assembly and supervised the administrative actions of the archons. A final reform of Cleisthenes was the peculiar institution of *ostracism*, an annual referendum in which a quorum of six thousand citizens could vote to exile for ten years any individual thought to be a threat to the new Athenian democracy.

Sparta to 500 B.C. In sharp contrast to Athens was the rival city-state Sparta. Sparta had not joined the other Greek cities in trade and colonization but had expanded instead by conquering and enslaving its neighbors. To guard against revolts by the state slaves (helots), who worked the land for their conquerors, Sparta was forced to deviate from the normal course of Greek political development and transform itself into a militaristic totalitarian state. Aristotle called the government of Sparta a "mixed constitution"; for the small minority of ruling Spartans, it was a democracy, but for the great mass of subjected people it was an oligarchy. The government included two kings, a small Council of Elders, and a popular assembly. True power resided in five overseers, the ephors, who were elected by the assembly and wielded more influence than the dual monarchs.

The state enforced absolute subordination of the individual to its will. Throughout his life every Spartan was first of all a soldier. Sickly infants were left to die on lonely mountaintops; boys were taken from their families when they were seven years old to live under rigorous military discipline for the rest of their lives; girls were trained to become healthy mothers of warrior sons. As their men marched off to war, Spartan women bid them a laconic farewell: "Come back with your shield or on it."

While Sparta developed the finest military machine in Greece, it remained backward culturally and economically. Trade and travel were prohibited because the city fathers feared that alien ideas might disturb the status quo. A self-imposed isolation forbade those cultural contacts without which no balanced civilization can develop. Sparta is a classic example of how intellectual stagnation accompanies rigid social conformity and military regimentation.

To provide additional assurance that its helots remain uncontaminated by democratic ideas, Sparta allied itself with oligarchic parties in other Peloponnesian states and aided them in suppressing their democratic opponents. The resulting Spartan League of oligarchic states, in operation by the end of the sixth century B.C., was shortly to be faced by an Athenian-led union of democratic states (see map, p. 48).

UNITY AND STRIFE
IN THE HELLENIC WORLD

The Persian Wars. The leaders of the Greek economic and cultural revival after 750 B.C. were the Ionian Greeks, descendants of the Mycenaeans who had fled to the Aegean coast of Asia Minor and its offshore islands. Influenced by contacts with Phoenician traders (from whom they borrowed the alphabet in the eighth century), neighboring Lydia, and Egypt, the Ionians "first kindled the torch of Hellenism."

We have seen in Chapter 1 that when the Persians conquered Lydia in 547 B.C. they also annexed Ionia, which had been under nominal Lydian rule. Chafing under Persian-appointed tyrants, the Ionian cities revolted in 499 B.C., established democratic regimes, and appealed to the Athenians, who were also Ionians, for aid. Athens sent twenty ships, but to no avail. By 494 B.C. Darius I had crushed the revolt, burning Miletus in revenge.

The battle of Marathon. Darius knew that Ionia was insecure as long as Athens remained free to incite her kinsmen to revolt, and thus in 490 B.C. a Persian force of about twenty thousand men sailed across the Aegean and debarked on the plain of Marathon near Athens. Darius' aim of forcing the

Athenians to accept the exiled son of Pisistratus as a pro-Persian tyrant was frustrated when the Athenian army, half the size of the Persian, won an overwhelming victory, killing 6400 of the foe while losing only 192.

The battle of Marathon was one of the most decisive in history. It destroyed the belief in Persian invincibility and demonstrated, in the words of the Greek historian Herodotus, that "free men fight better than slaves." The victory also gave the Athenians the self-confidence that would soon make their city the leading Greek state.

End of the Persian Wars. Ten years later the Greeks were well prepared for a new Persian invasion under Xerxes, Darius' successor, whose objective was the subjection of all of Greece. Athens now had two hundred ships, the largest fleet in Greece, and Sparta had agreed to head a defensive alliance of thirty-one states.

The Persian army—reckoned by Herodotus at 1,700,000 but more likely 150,000 or so—was too huge to be transported by ship. Crossing the swift-flowing, mile-wide Hellespont on two pontoon bridges—a notable feat of engineering—the army marched along the Aegean coast accompanied by a great fleet carrying provisions. The Spartans wanted to abandon all of Greece except the Peloponnesus to the invaders but finally agreed to a holding action at the narrow pass of Thermopylae. Here three hundred Spartans and a few thousand other Greeks held back the Persians for three days, until a Greek traitor led them over a mountain path to the rear of the Greek position. The Spartans fought magnificently until all were slain, together with seven hundred other Greeks. The Spartan dead were immortalized on a monument erected at the pass: "Go tell the Spartans, thou that passeth by, / That here, obedient to their laws, we lie."

The Persians then burned Athens, whose inhabitants had fled, for they placed their faith in "wooden walls"—their fleet. Their faith was not misplaced; in the Bay of Salamis the Greek fleet, largely Athenian, turned the tide of victory with the shout: "On, sons of the Greeks! Set free your country, set your children free, your wives, the temples of your country's gods, your fathers' tombs;

now they are all at stake."[6] With 200 of his 350 ships destroyed and his lines of communication cut, Xerxes had no alternative but to retreat to Asia, although he left a strong force in Greece. The following summer (479 B.C.) the Greek army, with the Spartan contingent in the van, routed the Persian force at Plataea, and Greece was for the time being safe from invasion.

Culmination of Athenian democracy. Following the expulsion of the Persians, the Athenians "felt themselves suddenly to be 'on top of the world,' and from this in a large measure sprang the reckless confidence and boundless energy which now carried them forward to the greatest phase of their history. Athens' heyday lasted less than eighty years, and the number of her adult male citizens scarcely exceeded fifty thousand. Yet this handful of men attempted more and achieved more in a wider variety of fields than any nation great or small has ever attempted or achieved in a similar space of time."[7]

For more than thirty years (461-429 B.C.) during this Golden Age of Greece, the great statesman Pericles guided Athenian policy. In Pericles' time the actual executive power no longer resided in the archonship, which was filled by lot, but in a board of ten elected generals. This board operated much like a modern-day governmental cabinet. The generals urged the popular assembly to adopt specific measures, and the success or failure of their policies determined whether or not they would be reelected at the end of their annual term. Pericles failed of reelection only once, and so great was his influence on the Athenians that, in the words of the contemporary historian Thucydides, "what was in name a democracy was virtually a government by its greatest citizen."[8]

To enable even the poorest citizen to participate in government, Pericles extended payment to jurors (a panel of six thousand citizens chosen annually by lot) and to members of the Council. While his conservative opponents called this opportunism, Pericles insisted that it was essential to the success of democracy:

Our constitution is named a democracy, because it is in the hands not of the few but of the many.

But our laws secure equal justice for all in their private disputes, and our public opinion welcomes and honours talent in every branch of achievement, not as a matter of privilege but on grounds of excellence alone. . . . [Athenians] do not allow absorption in their own various affairs to interfere with their knowledge of the city's. We differ from other states in regarding the man who holds aloof from public life not as "quiet" but as useless; we decide or debate, carefully and in person, all matters of policy, holding, not that words and deeds go ill together, but that acts are foredoomed to failure when undertaken undiscussed.[9]

The majority of the inhabitants of Athens, however, were not recognized as citizens. Women, slaves, and resident aliens were denied citizenship and had no voice in the government. Nor did they have any standing in the law courts. If a woman desired the protection of the law, she had to seek out a citizen to plead for her in court.

Athenian imperialism. The victory over Persia had been made possible by a partial unity of Hellenic arms; but that unity quickly dissolved when Sparta, fearful of helot rebellion at home, recalled its troops and resumed its policy of isolation. Because the Persians still ruled the Ionian cities and another invasion of Greece seemed probable, Athens in 478 B.C. invited the city-states bordering on the Aegean to form a defensive alliance called the Delian League. To maintain a two-hundred-ship navy that would police the seas, each state was assessed ships or money in proportion to its wealth. From the beginning, Athens dominated the League. Since almost all of the 173 member states paid their assessments in money, which Athens was empowered to collect, the Athenians furnished the necessary ships.

By 468 B.C., after the Ionian cities had been liberated and the Persian fleet destroyed, various League members thought it unnecessary to continue the confederacy. In suppressing all attempts to secede, the Athenians were motivated by the fear that the Persian danger still existed and by the need to maintain and protect the large free-trade area so necessary for Greek—and especially Athenian—commerce and industry. The Athenians created an empire because they dared not unmake a confederation. By aiding in

GREEK POLITICAL ALLIANCES
ABOUT 431 B. C.

■ Athens and Allies
▨ Sparta and Allies
▧ Neutral Greek States

the suppression of local aristocratic factions within its subject states, Athens both eased the task of controlling its empire and emerged as the leader of a union of democratic states.

To many Greeks—above all to the members of the oligarchic Spartan League and the suppressed aristocratic factions within the Athenian empire—Athens was a "tyrant city" and an "enslaver of Greek liberties." Pericles, on the other hand, justified Athenian imperialism on the ground that it brought "freedom" from fear and want to the Greek world:

We secure our friends not by accepting favours but by doing them. . . . We are alone among mankind in doing men benefits, not on calculations of self-interest, but in the fearless confidence of freedom. In a word I claim that our city as a whole is an education to Hellas. . . .[10]

The Peloponnesian War. In 431 B.C. the Peloponnesian War broke out between the Spartan League and the Athenian empire. While commercial rivalry between Athens

and Sparta's ally Corinth was an important factor, the conflict is a classic example of how fear can generate a war unwanted by either side. According to Thucydides:

The real but unavowed cause I consider to have been the growth of the power of Athens, and the alarm which it inspired in Lacedaemon [Sparta]; this made war inevitable.[11]

Several incidents served to ignite the underlying tension, and Sparta declared war on the "aggressors."

Sparta's hope for victory lay in its army's ability to besiege Athens and lay waste its fields. Pericles, on the other hand, relied on Athen's unrivaled navy to import foodstuffs and to harass its enemies' coasts. Fate took a hand in this game, however. In the second year of the war a plague carried off a third of the Athenian population, including Pericles. His death was a great blow to Athens, for leadership of the government passed to demagogues. In the words of Thucydides:

Pericles, by his rank, ability, and known integrity, was able to exercise an independent control over the masses—to lead them instead of being led by them. . . . With his successors it was different. More on a level with one another, and each grasping at supremacy, they ended by committing even the conduct of state affairs to the whims of the multitude. This, as might have been expected in a great imperial state, produced a host of blunders. . . .[12]

Eight more years of indecisive warfare ended in 421 B.C. with a compromise peace. During the succeeding period Athenian imperialism manifested itself in its worst form through the actions of Pericles' unworthy successors. In 416 B.C. an expedition embarked for Melos, a neutral Aegean island, to force it to join the Athenian empire. Thucydides reported the specious logic the Athenians employed to justify their naked imperialism on this occasion:

We believe that Heaven, and we know that men, by a natural law, always rule where they are stronger. We did not make that law nor were we the first to act on it; we found it existing, and it will exist forever, after we are gone; and we know that you and anyone else as strong as we are would do as we do.[13]

The Athenians put all Melians of military age to death and sold the women and children into slavery.

The war was resumed in 415 B.C. with an Athenian expedition against Syracuse that was destined to end in disaster. Acting on the invitation of states that feared Syracusan expansion, the Athenians hoped to add Sicily to their empire and so become powerful enough "to rule the whole of the Greek world."[14] After two years of fighting, two great Athenian fleets and a large army were destroyed by the Syracusans, who were advised by a Spartan general. The war dragged on until 404 B.C., when Athens capitulated after its last fleet was destroyed by a Spartan fleet built with money received from Persia in exchange for possession of the Greek cities in Ionia. At home, Athens had been weakened by the plots of oligarchic elements to whom Sparta now turned over the government. The once great city was also stripped of its possessions and demilitarized.

Aftermath of the war. Anarchy and depression were the political and economic legacies of the Peloponnesian War. Having ended the "tyranny" of Athens over Greece, the Spartans substituted their own form of rule which made the Athenian empire seem mild in comparison. Everywhere democracies were replaced by oligarchies supported by Spartan troops. The bloody excesses of these oligarchs soon led to revolutions which Sparta could not suppress. As one of their generals admitted, the Spartans did not know how to govern free men. Incessant warfare filled the early fourth century as a bewildering series of shifting alliances, usually financed by Persia which wanted to keep Greece disunited and weak, sought to keep any state from predominating.

Political disintegration in turn contributed to the economic and social ills that plagued Greece during the fourth century B.C. Commerce and industry languished, and the unemployed who did not go abroad as soldiers of fortune supported demagogues and their radical schemes for the redivision of wealth. The wealthy, for their part, became increasingly reactionary and uncompromising. Even most intellectuals—including Plato and Aristotle—lost faith in democracy and joined with the wealthy in looking for "a champion powerful in action" who would bring order and security to Greece. They found him, finally, in the person of the king of Macedonia.

The Macedonian unification of Greece. To the north of Greece lay Macedonia, inhabited by hardy peasants and nobles who were related to the Greeks but were culturally inferior to them. Macedonia became a centralized, powerful state under the able and crafty Philip II (359-336 B.C.), who created the most formidable army yet known by joining the crack Macedonian cavalry of nobles with the infantry phalanx used by the Greeks. In his youth, Philip had been a hostage at Thebes, where he acquired an appreciation of Greek culture, an understanding of Greek political weakness, and a desire to win for Macedonia a place in the Hellenic world.

After unifying Macedonia—including a string of Greek colonies that had been established along its coast during the earlier centuries of Macedonia's weakness—Philip turned to the Greek city-states, whose wars afforded him the opportunity first to intervene, then to dominate. In vain did Demosthenes, the great Athenian orator and democratic leader, warn that "democracies and dictators cannot exist together" and urge the Athenians and other Greeks to stop Philip before it was too late. Belatedly, Athens and Thebes acted, but their combined forces were shattered at Chaeronea in 338 B.C. Philip then forced the Greeks into a federal league in which each state, while retaining self-government, swore to "make war upon him who violates the general peace" and to furnish Philip with men and supplies for a campaign against Persia. On the eve of setting out for Asia Minor, Philip was assassinated by a noble with a personal grudge, leaving the war against Persia as a legacy for his brilliant son Alexander.

Incapable of finding a solution to the anarchy that tore their world to shreds, the Greeks ended as political failures and at the mercy of a great outside power, first Macedonia and then Rome. They retained their cultural leadership, however, and the culture of the new Hellenistic Age and its successor, the world of Rome, was to be largely Greek.

THE GREEK GENIUS

The Greek character. The Greeks were the first to formulate many of the western world's fundamental concepts in philosophy, science, and art. How was it that a relative handful of people could bequeath such a legacy to civilization? The definitive answer may always elude the historian, but a good part of the explanation lies in environmental and social factors.

Unlike the Near Eastern monarchies, the *polis* was not governed by a "divine" ruler, nor were the activities of its citizens circumscribed by powerful priesthoods. The Greeks relished debate and argument, and one of their most striking characteristics was their

fondness for good talk. The nature of the universe and of man, man's duty to the state and to his fellow citizens, law and freedom, the purpose of art and poetry, the standards of a good life—these were a few of the numerous problems they discussed brilliantly and with pertinence for our times as much as theirs.

The Greek character was one of energy and bold experimentation tempered by the exercise of reason and clear judgment. They believed that an ideal life based on a harmony of interests and abilities should include a healthy balance of action and thought. To obtain harmony and balance, it was essential to avoid *hubris*. Meaning "pride" or "insolence," this term is a key to fathoming the Greek character. Resulting from human excesses and lying at the root of personal misfortune and social injustice, *hubris* invariably provoked *nemesis*, or retribution. According to the Greeks, an inexorable law would cause the downfall or disgrace of anyone guilty of *hubris*. The Athenian dramatists often employed this theme in their tragedies, and Herodotus attributed the Persian defeat by the Greeks to Xerxes' overweening pride, for "Zeus tolerates pride in none but himself."[15]

The Greeks exhibited human frailties and failings—they could be suspicious, vindictive, and cruel. But at their best they were guided by the ideals that permeate their intellectual and artistic legacy. The philosopher Protagoras is credited with the statement, "Man is the measure of all things"—a saying which sums up the Greek attitude toward themselves and the world of men. In short, the Greeks were humanists.

Greek religion. Early Greek religion abounded in gods and goddesses who personified physical elements. Thus Demeter was the earth and giver of grain, Apollo, the sun and giver of light, and Poseidon, who dwelled in the sea, was the ruler of the waters. Other deities had special functions, such as Aphrodite, the goddess of love, Dionysus, the god of fertility and wine, and Athena, the goddess of wisdom and the guardian of Athens. The Greeks of Homeric times believed in manlike deities, capable of malice, favoritism, and jealousy, and differing from ordinary men only in their immortality and their possession of supernatural powers. Zeus, the king of sky, earth, and men, supposedly ruled the world from Mount Olympus with the aid of lesser deities.

By the time of Hesiod, as we have seen (p. 43), a religious reformation had begun which changed the vengeful and capricious gods of Homer into austere arbiters of justice who rewarded the good and punished the wicked. Demeter and Dionysus gained prominence as the central figures of "mystery" cults whose initiates (*mystae*) were promised an afterlife of bliss in Elysium—formerly the abode of heroes only. And from the famous oracle at Delphi the voice of Zeus' son Apollo urged all Greeks to follow the ideals of moderation and reasonableness: "Nothing in excess."

Early Greek philosophy and science. Philosophy arose from the insatiable Greek curiosity about nature. As we noted in Chapter 1, the Mesopotamians were skilled observers of astronomical phenomena such as eclipses, which they attributed to magical and supernatural causes. The early Greek philosophers, beginning with Thales of Miletus (c. 636-546 B.C.), changed the course of human knowledge by insisting that the phenomena of the universe can be explained by natural causes. This rejection of the supernatural and the application of reason to discern universal principles in nature has been called the "Greek miracle." It led men to the threshold of today's world of science and technology.

Called "the father of philosophy," Thales speculated on the nature of the basic substance from which all else in the universe is composed. He concluded that it was water, which exists in different states or forms and is indispensable to the maintenance and growth of organisms. Thales' successors in Ionia proposed elements other than water as the primal substance in the universe. One called it the "boundless," apparently a general concept for "matter"; another proposed "air," out of which all things come by a process of "rarefying and condensing"; a third asserted that fire was the "most mobile, most transformable, most active, most life-giving" element. This search for a material substance as the first principle or cause of all things culminated two centuries after Thales in the atomic theory of Democritus (c. 460-370 B.C.). To Democritus, reality was the mechanical motion of indivisible atoms, which differed in shape, size, position, and arrangement but not in quality. Moving about continuously, atoms combined to create objects. Scientists have used this theory to the present day, although we are now aware that the atom is neither indivisible nor indestructible.

While these and other early Greek philosophers were proposing some form of matter as the basic element in nature, Pythagoras of Samos (c. 582-500 B.C.) countered with the profoundly significant notion that the "nature of things" was something nonmaterial—numbers. By experimenting with a vibrating cord, Pythagoras discovered that musical harmony is based on arithmetical proportions, and he intuitively concluded that the universe was constructed of numbers and their relationships. His mathematical interpretation of nature greatly influenced Plato, and modern mathematical physicists have continued along the path he was the first to trod.

An important consequence of early Greek philosophical speculation was the undermining of conventional beliefs and traditions. In religion, for example, Xenophanes ridiculed the traditional view of the gods: "If oxen and lions had hands, . . . they would make portraits and statues of their gods in their own image." The eroding of traditional views caused Greek inquiry to turn away from nature to man—to a consideration of human values and institutions. During the last half of the fifth century B.C., the Sophists —"men of wisdom" who taught public speaking and prepared men for public life— submitted all conventional beliefs to the test of rational criticism. Concluding that truth was relative, they denied the existence of universal standards to guide human actions.

Socrates, a martyr to truth. The outstanding opponent of the Sophists was the Athenian Socrates (c. 470-399 B.C.), a snub-nosed, plain man but a fascinating conversationalist. Like the Sophists, Socrates turned from cosmic to human affairs; in the words of the Roman statesman Cicero, Socrates was "the first to call philosophy down from the heavens and to set her in the cities of men, bringing her into their homes and compelling her to ask questions about life and morality and things good and evil."[16] But unlike the Sophists, Socrates believed that by asking salient questions and by subjecting the answers to logical analysis, agreement could be reached about ethical standards and rules of conduct. And so he would question passers-by in his function of midwife assisting in the birth of correct ideas (to use his own figure of speech). Taking as his motto the famous inscription on the temple of Apollo at Delphi, "Know thyself," he insisted that "the unexamined life is not worth living." To Socrates, human excellence or virtue (*aretē*) is knowledge, and evil and error are the result of ignorance.

In time Socrates' quest for truth led to his undoing, for the Athenians, unnerved by the Peloponnesian War, arrested him on the charge of impiety and corrupting youth. By a slim majority a jury of citizens condemned Socrates to die, a fate he accepted without rancor and with a last request:

When my sons are grown up, I would ask you, my friends, to punish them, and I would have you trouble them, as I have troubled you, if they seem to care about riches, or anything, more than about virtue; or if they pretend to be something when they are really nothing, then reprove them, as I have reproved you, for not caring about that for which they ought to care, and thinking that they are something when they are really nothing. And if you do this, both I and my sons will have received justice at your hands.

The hour of departure has arrived, and we go our ways—I to die, and you to live. Which is better God only knows.[17]

Plato and his Theory of Ideas. After Socrates' death, philosophical leadership passed to his most famous disciple, Plato (427-347 B.C.). Like Socrates, Plato believed that truth exists, but only in the realm of thought, the spiritual world of Ideas or Forms. Such universals as Beauty, Good, and Justice exist apart from the material world, and the beauty, good, and justice that we encounter in the world of the senses are only imperfect re-

flections of eternal and changeless Ideas. Man's task is to come to know the True Reality—the eternal Ideas—behind these imperfect reflections. Only the soul, and the "soul's pilot," reason, can accomplish this, for the human soul is spiritual and immortal, and in its prenatal state it existed "beyond the heavens" where "true Being dwells."[18]

Disillusioned with democracy, Plato expounded his concept of an ideal state in the *Republic*, the first systematic treatise on political science. The state's basic function, founded on the Idea of Justice, was the satisfaction of the common good. Plato described a kind of "spiritualized Sparta" in which the state regulated every aspect of life, including thought. The family and private property, for example, were abolished on the grounds that both bred selfishness, and marriage was controlled in order to produce strong, healthy children. Individuals belonged to one of three classes and found happiness only through their contribution to the community: workers by producing the necessities of life, warriors by guarding the state, and philosophers by ruling in the best interests of all the people.

Plato founded the Academy in Athens, the famous school which existed from about 388 B.C. until 529 A.D. Here he taught and encouraged his students, whom he expected to become the intellectual elite who would go forth and reform society.

Aristotle, the encyclopedic philosopher. Plato's greatest pupil was Aristotle (384-322 B.C.), who set up his own school, the Lyceum, at Athens. Reacting against the other-worldly tendencies of Plato's thought, Aristotle insisted that Ideas have no separate existence apart from the material world; knowledge of universal Ideas is the result of the painstaking collection and organization of particular facts. Aristotle's Lyceum, accordingly, became a center for the analysis of data from many branches of learning.

To us today, Aristotle's most significant treatises are the *Ethics* and the *Politics*. They deal with what he called the "philosophy of human affairs," whose object is the acquisition and maintenance of human happiness. Two kinds of virtue (*aretē*), intellectual and moral, which produce two types of happiness, are described in the *Ethics.* Intellectual virtue is the product of reason, and only such men as philosophers and scientists ever attain it. Much more important for the good of society is moral virtue—for example, liberality and temperance—which is the product less of reason than of habit and thus can be acquired by all. In this connection Aristotle introduced his Doctrine of the Mean as a guide for good conduct. He considered all virtues to be means between extremes; thus courage, for example, is the mean between cowardice and rashness.

In the *Politics* Aristotle viewed the state as necessary "for the sake of the good life," because its laws and educational system provide the most effective training needed for the attainment of moral virtue and hence happiness. Thus to Aristotle the viewpoint that the state stands in opposition to the individual would be unthinkable.

Aristotle's writings on formal logic, collectively known as the *Organon* ("Instrument"), describe two ways in which new truths can be acquired. The first, induction, moves from particular facts to general truths. Deductive logic, on the other hand, moves from the general to the particular. To facilitate deductive reasoning from general truths, Aristotle devised the syllogism, a logical structure requiring a trio of propositions. The first two propositions (the major and minor premises) must be plainly valid and logically related so that the third proposition, the conclusion, inevitably follows. For example, (1) all Greeks are human; (2) Socrates is a Greek; (3) therefore Socrates is human.

There has probably never been another man whose interests were so widespread or whose knowledge was so encyclopedic as Aristotle's. He investigated such diverse fields as biology, mathematics, astronomy, physics, psychology, rhetoric, logic, politics, ethics, and metaphysics. His accomplishments won him renown, and he was ultimately requested to tutor the young prince of Macedonia, who became his most famous pupil—Alexander the Great.

Medicine. Preconceived and false ideas about the human body blocked the development of medical science until 420 B.C., when Hippocrates, the "father of medicine," founded a school in which he emphasized the value of observation and the careful interpretation of symptoms. The members of this school were firmly convinced that disease resulted from natural, not supernatural, causes. Writing of epilepsy, considered at the time a "sacred" or supernaturally inspired malady, one Hippocratic writer observed:

It seems to me that this disease is no more divine than any other. It has a natural cause just as other diseases have. Men think it supernatural because they do not understand it. But if they called everything supernatural which they do not understand, why, there would be no end of such things![19]

Despite their empirical approach, the Hippocratic school adopted the theory that the body contained four liquids or humors—blood, phlegm, black bile, and yellow bile—whose proper balance was the basis of health. This doctrine was to impede medical progress until modern times.

The writing of history. History for the Hellenic Greeks was not an account of legendary events and mythical figures, nor were the forces of history attributable simply to the whims of the gods. The Greeks viewed history as a humanistic study by which historians sought to learn about the actions and characters of men. As such, history could be subjected to rational standards and critical judgment.

If history be defined as an "honest attempt first to find out what happened, then to explain why it happened," Herodotus of Halicarnassus (484?-425? B.C.) deserves to be called the "father of history." In his highly entertaining history of the Persian Wars he discerned the clash of two distinct civilizations, the Hellenic and the Near Eastern. His portrayal of both the Greeks and the Persians was eminently impartial, but his fondness for a good story often led him to include tall tales in his work.

The first truly scientific historian was Thucydides (460-400? B.C.), who wrote a notably objective chronicle of the Peloponnesian War. Although he was a contemporary of the events and a loyal Athenian, a reader can scarcely detect whether he favored

Athens or Sparta. In describing the character and purpose of his work, Thucydides probably had Herodotus in mind:

With reference to the narrative of events, far from permitting myself to derive it from the first source that came to hand, I did not even trust my own impressions, but it rests partly on what I saw myself, partly on what others saw for me, the accuracy of the report being always tried by the most severe and detailed tests possible. My conclusions have cost me some labour from the want of coincidence between accounts of the same occurrences by different eyewitnesses, arising sometimes from imperfect memory, sometimes from undue partiality for one side or the other. The absence of romance in my history will, I fear, detract somewhat from its interest; but I shall be content if it is judged useful by those inquirers who desire an exact knowledge of the past as an aid to the interpretation of the future, which in the course of human things must resemble if it does not reflect it. My history has been composed to be an everlasting possession, not the show-piece of an hour.[20]

Hellenic poetry and drama. Greek literary periods can be classified according to dominant poetic forms which reflected particular stages of cultural evolution in Greece. First came the time of great epics, followed by periods in which lyric poetry and drama flourished.

Sometime during the eighth century B.C. in Ionia, the *Iliad* and the *Odyssey*, the two great epics attributed to Homer, were set down in their present form. The *Iliad*, describing the clash of arms between the Greeks and the Trojans "on the ringing plains of windy Troy," glorifies heroic valor and physical prowess against a background of divine intervention in human affairs. The *Odyssey*, relating the adventure-filled wanderings of Odysseus on his return to Greece after Troy's fall, places less stress on divine intervention and more on the cool resourcefulness of the hero in escaping from danger and in regaining his kingdom. These stirring epics have provided inspiration and source material for generations of poets in the western world.

As Greek society became more sophisticated, a new type of poetry, written to be sung to the accompaniment of the lyre, arose among the Ionian Greeks. Its authors sang not of legendary events but of present delights and sorrows. This new note, personal and passionate, can be seen in the following examples, in which the contrast between the new values of what is called the Greek Renaissance and those of Homer's heroic age is sharply clear. Unlike Homer's heroes, Archilochus of Paros (seventh century B.C.) unashamedly throws away his shield and runs from the battlefield:

My trusty shield adorns some Thracian foe;
I left it in a bush—not as I would!
But I have saved my life; so let it go.
Soon I will get another just as good.[21]

And in contrast to the older view of an unromantic, purely physical attraction between Paris and Helen, Sappho of Lesbos (sixth century B.C.), the first and one of the greatest of all woman poets, saw Helen as the helpless victim of romantic love:

She, who the beauty of mankind
Excelled, fair Helen, all for love
The noblest husband left behind;
Afar, to Troy she sailed away,
Her child, her parents, clean forgot;
The Cyprian [Aphrodite] led her far astray
Out of the way, resisting not.[22]

Drama, which developed from the religious rites of the Dionysian mystery cult, filled a civic-religious function in Greek society. In Athens, by the fifth century B.C., two distinct forms—tragedy and comedy—had evolved. Borrowing the old familiar legends of gods and heroes for their plots, the tragedians reinterpreted them in the light of the changing spirit of the times.

By depicting man in conflict with destiny, Aeschylus (525-456 B.C.) expressed the new concern for achieving harmony and avoiding the excesses which led to suffering. In his trilogy, the *Oresteia*, for example, he concerned himself with *hubris*, as applied to the murder of the hero Agamemnon by his false queen, and then proceeded to work out its ramifications—murder piled on murder until men through suffering learn to substitute the moral law of Zeus for the primitive law of the blood feud. Like the prophets of Israel, Aeschylus taught that while "sin brings misery," misery in turn leads to wisdom:

The Persian invasion made Athens a heap of ruins, but
the withdrawal of the invaders left the Athenians free
to reconstruct the Acropolis into a treasury of temples
and statues. In the Parthenon, which housed Phidias'
huge gold and ivory statue of Athena, great care was
taken to design a structurally and visually perfect building. The tops of the Doric columns lean toward the center of each colonnade, the steps curve upward at the
center, and the columns are more widely spaced in the
middle of each row than at the ends—all these refinements create an illusion of perfect regularity which
would be lacking if the parts were actually perfectly
proportioned. The Parthenon was originally brightly
painted, and painted sculpture adorned the gables and
parts of the frieze, while another sculptured and painted
frieze ran around the walls inside the colonnade. A
reconstruction of the entire Acropolis appears at the
right.

Zeus the Guide, who made man turn
Thought-ward, Zeus, who did ordain
Man by Suffering shall Learn.
So the heart of him, again
Aching with remembered pain,
Bleeds and sleepeth not, until
Wisdom comes against his will.[23]

A generation later, Sophocles (c. 496-406 B.C.) largely abandoned the problem of how to justify the ways of god to man and concentrated upon character. To Sophocles, a certain amount of suffering was inevitable in life. No man was perfect; there was a tragic flaw in the character of the best of men which caused them to make mistakes. Sophocles dwelled mainly on the way in which men react to suffering. Like his contemporary, the sculptor Phidias, Sophocles viewed man as an ideal creature—"Many are the wonders of the world, and none so wonderful as Man"—and he displayed man's greatness by depicting him experiencing great tragedy without whimpering.

Euripides (c. 480-406 B.C.), the last of the great Athenian tragedians, reflects the rationalism and critical spirit of the late fifth century. To him, the life of man was pathetic, the ways of the gods ridiculous. His recurrent theme was "Since life began, hath there in God's eye stood one happy man?" and for this he has been called "the poet of the world's grief." Euripides has also been called the first psychologist, for he looked deep into the human soul and described what he saw with intense realism. Far more than Aeschylus or even Sophocles, Euripides strikes home to modern man.

Comedies were bawdy and spirited. There were no libel laws in Athens, and Aristophanes (c. 445-385 B.C.), the famous comic-dramatist and a conservative in outlook, brilliantly satirized Athenian democracy as a mob led by demagogues, the Sophists (among whom he included Socrates) as subversive, and Euripides as an underminer of civic spirit and traditional faith.

The Greeks as builders. In the sixth century B.C. architecture flourished in Ionia and Greece with the construction of large temples of stone, the form having developed from earlier wooden structures which had been influenced by the surviving remains of Mycenaean palaces. Architecture reached its zenith in fifth-century Athens, then at the height of its power and wealth.

The Parthenon, the Erechtheum, and the other temples on the Athenian Acropolis exhibit the highly developed features that make Greek structure so pleasing to the eye. All relationships, such as column spacing and height and the curvature of floor and roof lines, were calculated and executed with remarkable precision to achieve a perfect balance, both structurally and visually. The three orders, or styles, usually identified by the characteristics of the columns, were the Doric, which was used in the Parthenon; the Ionic, seen in the Erechtheum; and the later and more ornate Corinthian.

Located where all men could see and enjoy them, the Greek temples afford an interesting comparison with those of Egypt. Whereas the Egyptian temple was enclosed and mysterious, the Greek temple was open, with a colonnade porch and single inside room containing a statue of the god. Sacrifice and ritual took place outside the temple, where the altar was placed.

Other types of buildings, notably the theaters, stadiums, and gymnasiums, also express the Greek spirit and way of life. In the open-air theaters the circular shape of the spectators' sections and the plan of the orchestra section set a style which has survived in principle to the present day.

Sculpture and pottery. Greek sculpture of the archaic period (c. 625-480 B.C.), although crude in its representation of human anatomy, has the freshness and vigor of youth. Influenced partly by Egyptian models, the statues of nude youths and draped maidens usually stand stiffly with clenched fists and with one foot thrust awkwardly forward (see photo, p. 57). The fixed smile and formalized treatment of hair and drapery also reveal how the sculptor is struggling to master the technique of his art.

The achievement of mastery of technique by 480 B.C. ushered in the classical period of fifth-century Greek sculpture whose "classic" principles of harmony and proportion have shaped the course of western art. Sculpture from this period displays both the end of technical immaturity and the beginning of

Between the sixth and fourth centuries B.C. Greek art developed from the rigid stylization, reminiscent of Egyptian art, of the *Kourai* figure (left) to the more complex, realistic, yet idealized, Hermes, the messenger of the gods, holding the young Dionysus.

idealization of the human form which reached its culmination in the dignity and poise of Phidias' figures in the Parthenon frieze and pediments (see Color Plate 4). Carved with restraint and "calm exaltation," the frieze depicts the citizens of Athens participating in the Panathenaic procession in honor of Athena which took place every four years.

The more relaxed character of fourth-century B.C. Hellenic sculpture contrasts with the grandeur and dignity of fifth-century art. Charm, grace, and individuality characterize the work of Praxiteles, the most famous sculptor of the century. These qualities can be seen in his supple statues of the god Hermes holding the young Dionysus and of Aphrodite stepping into her bath.

The making of pottery was a highly developed art in Greece. The earliest vases were decorated with abstract geometric designs, then came paintings of scenes from mythology and daily life. From the surviving Greek pottery, we can get an inkling of what Greek painting, now lost, was like (see illustration, p. 44).

THE HELLENISTIC AGE

Alexander the Great. When Philip of Macedonia was assassinated in 336 B.C., his crown fell to his gifted twenty-year-old son, Alexander, who crushed rebellion in Greece and proved himself a resolute, ambitious king from the beginning of his reign.

Like his father, the youthful Alexander was alive to the glories of Hellenic culture, having as a youth been tutored by Aristotle. Reveling in the heroic deeds of the *Iliad*, Alexander may have seen himself as a second Achilles waging war against barbarians when he planned to revenge the Persian attacks on Greece. Two years after Philip's death, he set out with an army of 35,000 soldiers recruited from Macedonia and the Greek League that his father had organized (see p. 50). In quick succession he subdued Asia Minor, Syria, Palestine, and Egypt. Then the young leader marched into Mesopotamia and there, in 331 B.C., defeated the last powerful army of Darius III, the Persian monarch. Alexander was now master of Persia,

This mosaic from Pompeii is a copy of a fourth-century B.C. Greek painting depicting the defeat of Darius (at the right) by Alexander (at the left) at the Battle of Issus. While this mosaic can only be an imperfect realization of the original painting, the intricacy and vitality of the composition attest to the skill of the Greeks at painting, an art at which they themselves believed they excelled.

the proud empire that had controlled the Near East. He ventured as far east as the rich river valleys of India (see Chapter 4), where his weary soldiers forced him to turn back. In 323 B.C., while he was planning the circumnavigation of Arabia, Alexander died at the age of thirty-two, the victim of malaria. With the Greeks now masters of the ancient Near East, a new and distinctly cosmopolitan period in their history and culture began— the Hellenistic Age.

Alexander's legacy to political thought was the vision of a unified world and the brotherhood of mankind. Various of his military and administrative policies sought to unify the lands he conquered and to promote what he himself called "concord and partnership in the empire" between orientals and westerners. He blended orientals with Greeks and Macedonians in his army and administration; he founded numerous cities—seventy, according to tradition—in the East and settled many of his veterans in them; and he married two oriental princesses and encouraged his officers and men to take foreign wives. Finally, for reasons that remain un-

clear, Alexander ordered the Greek city-states to accord him "divine honors."

The division of Alexander's empire. For several decades following Alexander's sudden death, his generals vied for the spoils of empire. Three major Hellenistic kingdoms emerged and maintained a precarious balance of power until the Roman conquests of the second and first centuries B.C.: Egypt, ruled by Ptolemy and his successors; Asia, comprising most of the remaining provinces of the Persian empire and held together with great difficulty by the dynasty founded by Seleucus; and Macedonia and Greece, ruled by the descendants of Antigonus the One-Eyed.

While the Antigonids in Macedonia followed the model of Alexander's father Philip in posing as national kings chosen by the army, the Ptolemies ruled Egypt as divine pharaohs, and some of the Seleucids became deified "saviors" and "benefactors." Ptolemaic and Seleucid administrations were centralized in bureaucracies staffed by Greeks, an arrangement which created a vast gulf between a ruler and his native subjects.

Plagued by native revolts, dynastic troubles, and civil war, the Hellenistic kingdoms soon began to crumble. Macedonia lost effective control of Greece when Athens asserted its independence and most of the other Greek states formed two federal leagues, the Aetolian in the north and the Achaean in the Peloponnesus, which successfully resisted Macedonian domination. The eastern reaches of Alexander's empire—India, Bactria, and Parthia—gradually drifted out of the Seleucid sphere of influence. Pergamum, in northwestern Asia Minor, renounced its allegiance to the Seleucids and became an independent kingdom famous for its artists and scholars. In the year 200 B.C. the new power of Rome entered upon the scene, and by 30 B.C. Rome had annexed the last remaining Hellenistic state, Egypt.

Hellenistic economy and society. The Hellenistic Age was a time of economic expansion and social change. In the wake of Alexander's conquests, thousands of Greeks flocked eastward to begin a new era of Greek colonization. An economic union between East and West permitted the free flow of trade, and prosperity was stimulated further when Alexander put into circulation huge hoards of Persian gold and silver and introduced a uniform coinage. The result was a much larger and more affluent middle class than had hitherto existed.

By the third century B.C. the center of trade had shifted from Greece to the Near East. Largest of the Hellenistic cities, and much larger than any cities in Greece itself, were Antioch in northern Syria and Alexandria in Egypt. The riches of India, Persia, Arabia, and the Fertile Crescent were brought by sea and land to these Mediterranean ports.

Alexandria outdistanced all other Hellenistic cities as a commercial center. Its merchants supplied the ancient world with wheat, linen, paper, glass, and jewelry. Boasting a population of about a million, the city had a double harbor in which a great lighthouse, judged one of the wonders of the ancient world, rose to a height estimated at 370 feet. Its busy streets were filled with a mixture of peoples—Greeks, Macedonians, Jews, and Egyptians. As in all other Hellenistic cities in the Near East, the privileged Greeks and Macedonians were at the top of the social scale and the mass of natives at the bottom. Harsh social and economic differences separated the rich from the poor,· and the exploited workers frequently went on strike.

Hellenistic philosophy. Developments in philosophy reflected the changed environment of the Hellenistic Age. With the growing loss of political freedom and the prevalence of internal disorder, philosophers concerned themselves less with the reform of society and more with the attainment of happiness for the individual. This emphasis on peace of mind in an insecure world led to the rise of four principal schools of thought.

The Skeptics and Cynics reflected most clearly the doubts and misgivings of the times. The Skeptics achieved imperturbability by denying the possibility of finding

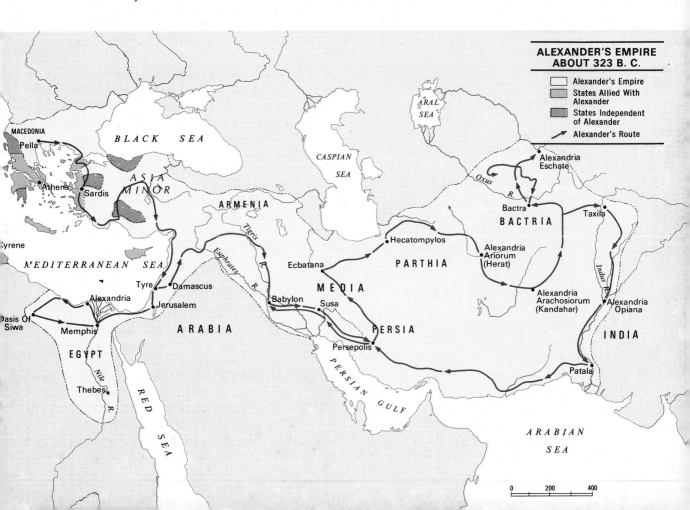

ALEXANDER'S EMPIRE ABOUT 323 B. C.

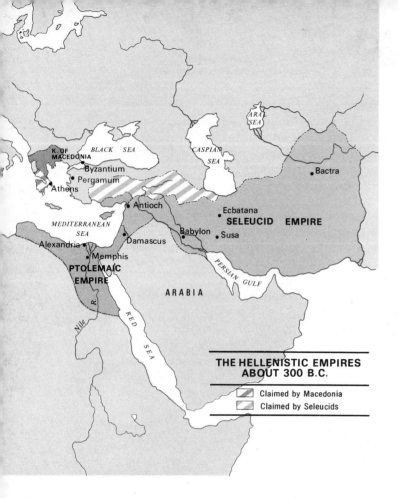

THE HELLENISTIC EMPIRES ABOUT 300 B.C.

Claimed by Macedonia
Claimed by Seleucids

fall apart at death. Thus, beyond death there is no existence and nothing to fear. Epicurus maintained that the finest pleasures were intellectual, but many of his followers later distorted his teachings so that Epicureanism appeared to be concerned only with the gratification of sensual desires.

The Stoics, followers of Zeno (c. 336-c. 264 B.C.), a Semite from Cyprus, argued in contrast to Epicureanism that the universe is controlled by some power—variously called Reason, World Soul, Fortune, and God—which determines everything that happens. Fortified by this knowledge, the Stoic wise man conforms his will to the World Will and "stoically" accepts whatever part fortune allots him in the drama of life. With its insistence on duty and on the brotherhood of man in One Great City, Stoicism was particularly attractive to the Romans.

Science and mathematics. The Greek concern for rational, disinterested inquiry reached a zenith in the Hellenistic period, particularly at Alexandria where the Ptolemies subsidized a great research institute, the Museum, and a library of more than half a million books. Emphasizing specialization and experimentation, and enriched by Near Eastern astronomy and mathematics, Greek science in the third century B.C. achieved results unmatched until early modern times.

The expansion of geographical knowledge incited scientists to make accurate maps and to estimate the size of the earth, which had been identified as a globe through observation of its shadow in a lunar eclipse. Eratosthenes, the outstanding geographer of the century, drew parallels of latitude and longitude on his map of the inhabited world and calculated the circumference of the globe with only 1 percent error by measuring the difference in the angles of the noonday sun at Aswan and Alexandria.

In astronomy, Aristarchus put forward the radical theory that the earth rotates on its axis and moves in an orbit around the sun. Most of his contemporaries adhered, however, to the prevailing geocentric theory, which stated that the earth was stationary and the sun revolved around it. This view not only was supported by the powerful authority of Aristotle, but it also seemed to ex-

truth. The wise man, they argued, will suspend his judgment and not dogmatize; he has learned that sensory experience, man's only source of knowledge, is deceptive. The Cynics carried negativism further; their ideal was nonattachment to the values and conventions of society. Cynic philosophers wandered from city to city, haranguing the public to pursue a concept of virtue that is echoed by today's hippies: "Look at me, I am without house or city, property or slave. I sleep on the ground. I have no wife, no children. What do I lack? Am I not without distress or fear? Am I not free?"[24]

More practical and popular were Epicureanism and Stoicism. The Athenian Epicurus (342-270 B.C.) taught that the wise man could achieve happiness simply by freeing his body from pain and his mind from fear—particularly the fear of death. To reach this goal, men must avoid bodily excesses, including those of pleasure, and accept the scientific teaching of Democritus that both body and soul are composed of atoms which plain all the known facts of celestial motion. This was particularly true after Hipparchus in the next century added the new idea of epicycles—each planet revolves in its own small orbit while moving around the earth. Aristarchus' heliocentric theory was not revived until the sixteenth century A.D.

Mathematics also made great advances. Euclid systematized the theorems of plane and solid geometry, and Archimedes of Syracuse, who had studied at Alexandria, calculated the value of π, invented a terminology for expressing numbers up to any magnitude, and laid the foundations of calculus. Archimedes also discovered specific gravity by noticing the water he displaced in his bath. And despite his disdain for making practical use of his knowledge, he invented the compound pulley, the windlass, and the endless screw for raising water.

The Hellenistic Greeks extended the advances in medicine made earlier by Hippocrates and his school. By dissecting bodies of dead criminals, they were able to trace the outlines of the nervous system, to understand the principle of the circulation of the blood, and to ascertain that the brain, not the heart, was the true center of consciousness.

Architecture, sculpture, and literature. The host of new cities that sprang up in Hellenistic times served as a tremendous impetus to architecture. The new cities benefited from town planning: the streets were laid out according to a rectangular plan. The great public edifices were elaborate and highly ornamented; this was an age which preferred the more ornate Corinthian to the simple Doric and Ionic orders.

Hellenistic sculptors continued and intensified the realistic, dramatic, and emotional approach that began to appear in Hellenic sculpture during the fourth century B.C. Supported by rulers and other rich patrons in Alexandria, Antioch, Rhodes, and Pergamum, they displayed their technical virtuosity by depicting violent scenes, writhing forms, and dramatic poses—all with a realism which could make stone simulate flesh. Little evidence remained of the balance and restraint of classical Greek sculpture. The famous Laocoön group (see illustration) and the frieze from the altar of Zeus at

Pergamum, with their twisted poses, contorted faces, and swollen muscles, remind one of the Baroque sculpture of seventeenth-century Europe which replaced the classical art of the Italian Renaissance.

The quality of literature from the Hellenistic Age was generally inferior to that of the Hellenic Age, although the historian Polybius, who lived in the second century B.C. and described Rome's eastward expansion, ranks second only to Thucydides (see the Historical Critique, p. 831). Scholarship flourished, and we are indebted for the preservation of much of Greek classical literature to the subsidized scholars at the Alexandrine library—"fatted fowls in a coup," as a Skeptic philosopher called them. Yet, paradoxically, these sophisticated scholars produced superb pastoral poetry extolling the simple life of shepherds. The best was written by Theocritus at Alexandria in the third

The trend toward realism and increased complexity in sculpture begun in the fourth century B.C. culminated in the art of the Hellenistic period, which produced such intricate sculptures as the contorted Laocoön group.

century B.C. The following short example, written by a contemporary, well illustrates its character and appeal:

Would that my father had taught me the craft of a
 keeper of sheep,
For so in the shade of the elm-tree, or under the
 rocks on the steep,
Piping on reeds I had sat, and had lulled my
 sorrow to sleep.[25]

The Hellenistic contribution: the East. The greatest contribution of the Hellenistic Age was the diffusion of Greek culture throughout the ancient East and the newly rising Roman West. In the East, the cities that Alexander and his successors built were the agents for spreading Hellenistic culture from the Aegean Sea to India. Literate Asians learned Greek to facilitate trade, become members of the ruling circles of the Hellenistic states, and read Hellenic classics.

For a time the Seleucid empire provided the peace and economic stability necessary to ensure the partial Hellenization of a vast area. But with an insufficient number of Greeks to colonize so large an area as the Near East, the Greek city-states remained only islands in an Asian ocean. As time elapsed, this ocean encroached more and more upon the Hellenized areas.

The gradual weakening of the loosely knit Seleucid empire eventually resulted in the creation of independent kingdoms on the edge of the Hellenistic world. Bactria achieved independence in the middle of the third century B.C. Its Greek rulers, descendants of Alexander's veterans, were remarkably successful in enlisting native cooperation; and their prosperous state, which controlled the caravan route to India, lasted for over a century (see also p. 100).

Also in the middle of the third century, a nomad chieftain founded the kingdom of Parthia, situated between the Seleucid and Bactrian kingdoms. Claiming to be the heirs of the Persians, the Parthians expanded until by 130 B.C. they had wrested Babylonia from the Seleucids. Although Parthia was essentially a native Iranian state, its inhabitants absorbed some Hellenistic culture.

The Hellenistic contribution: the West. In the history of western civilization there is little of greater significance than Rome's absorption of Greek civilization and its transferance of that heritage to modern Europe. The stage on which this story began was the cosmopolitan Hellenistic Age, which "longed and strove for *Homonoia*, Concord, between man and man . . . [and] proclaimed a conception of the world as One Great City."[26] The process by which the Roman West was Hellenized will be described in the following chapter.

SUMMARY

The two most important centers of the Aegean maritime civilization were Knossos on the island of Crete and Mycenae on the Greek mainland. Aegean civilization reached its zenith first in Crete (2000-1450 B.C.), where the island dwellers fashioned a sophisticated urban culture, synthesizing cultural elements from the Near East. After 1450 B.C. the center of Aegean culture shifted to Mycenae on the Greek mainland. The Mycenaean phase lasted until the warlike Dorians invaded the Peloponnesus and forced the Mycenaeans to flee eastward to Ionia in Asia Minor. There, by the eighth century B.C., fiercely independent city-states evolved a distinctly Hellenic culture which was to come to fruition in the Hellenic Age (the eighth to fourth centuries B.C.).

Achilles, the hero of Homer's *Iliad*, would have lived forever had not a Trojan arrow pierced him fatally in the heel, the only vulnerable part of his body. Like Achilles, the Greek city-states of the Hellenic period had one fatal defect—in their case, an inability to submerge individual differences for the sake of common survival. The city-states failed to adapt themselves to the political realities of the fifth century B.C., which had resulted from the colonial expansion and economic revolution of previous centuries and which linked the destinies of Athens and other Greek cities with those of a larger Mediterranean community. Instead of developing the Delian League into a true Greek federation, Athens placed its own interests first and converted the League into an Athenian maritime empire, thus plunging the Greeks into the disastrous Peloponnesian War.

Fortunately for the Greeks, Philip II, the Macedonian ruler who conquered the city-states sixty years after the Peloponnesian War, sincerely admired Hellenic culture—an admiration which was shared by his son, Alexander the Great. It was the ambitious and gallant Alexander who conquered the Near East and laid the boundaries for three large empires carved from his conquered lands. The Hellenistic Age, which began after Alexander's death, was a period of economic expansion, cosmopolitanism, striking intellectual and artistic achievements, and the wide diffusion of Greek culture.

What is it about the Greeks that leads us to speak so admiringly? The secret lies in the originality with which they met every situation. Free of Near Eastern superstitions and traditions, they examined each problem in a spirit of critical inquiry and sought for an explanation that accorded with the natural world rather than supernatural law. Thus their view of life, something entirely new in the world's history, tended to be secular rather than religious, rational instead of credulous. This clear-cut, straightforward approach to life may have been the most lasting contribution of the Greeks to human history.

SUGGESTIONS FOR READING

P. MacKendrick, **The Greek Stones Speak,*** Mentor; L. Cottrell, **The Bull of Minos,*** Universal. Popular accounts of the great archaeological discoveries in the Aegean area. See also R. W. Hutchinson, **Prehistoric Crete,*** Penguin; C. W. Blegen, **Troy and the Trojans,** Praeger, 1963; Alan E. Samuel, **The Mycenaeans in History,*** Prentice-Hall, 1966; E. Vermeule, **Greece in the Bronze Age,** Univ. of Chicago, 1964; John Chadwick, **The Decipherment of Linear B,*** Vintage. M. Renault, **The King Must Die,*** Pocket Books, is an absorbing novel set in Mycenaean times.

A. R. Burn, **The Pelican History of Greece,*** Penguin; M. I. Finley, **The Ancient Greeks,*** Compass; A. Andrewes, **The Greeks,** Knopf, 1967. Valuable fresh analyses. Other good surveys include M. Bowra, **The Greek Experience,*** Mentor; H. Kitto, **The Greeks,*** Penguin; H. Lloyd-Jones, ed., **The Greek World,*** Penguin. N. G. L. Hammond, **A History of Greece to 322 B.C.,** 2nd ed., Oxford, 1967, is a standard detailed history.

Chester G. Starr, **The Origins of Greek Civilization, 1100-650 B.C.,** Knopf, 1961. An illuminating survey of the formative centuries of Greek civilization. See also T. B. L. Webster, **From Mycenae to Homer,*** Norton; M. I. Finley, **The World of Odysseus,*** Compass. A. R. Burn, **The World of Hesiod,** Dutton, 1937, and **The Lyric Age of Greece,** Arnold, 1960, treat in detail the Greek renaissance of the seventh and sixth centuries B.C. On Greek colonization see A. Woodhead, **The Greeks in the West,** Praeger, 1962; J. M. Cook, **The Greeks in Ionia and the East,** Praeger, 1963. On the transition from oligarchy to democracy see A. Andrewes, **The Greek Tyrants,*** Torchbooks; W. G. Forrest, **The Emergence of Greek Democracy, 800-400 B.C.,** McGraw-Hill, 1966.

Valuable special studies on politics, economics, and society include A. R. Burn, **Persia and the Greeks: The Defense of the West, 546-478 B.C.,** St. Martin, 1962; A. de Selincourt, **The World of Herodotus,*** Little, Brown; H. Michell, **Sparta,*** Cambridge; B. W. Henderson, **The Great War Between Athens and Sparta,** Macmillan, 1927; A. E. Zimmern, **The Greek Commonwealth: Politics and Economics in Fifth-Century Athens,*** Galaxy; G. Glotz, **The Greek City and Its Institutions,** Knopf, 1930; Victor Ehrenberg, **The Greek State,** Barnes and Noble, 1960;

A. H. M. Jones, **Athenian Democracy,** Praeger, 1957; T. B. L. Webster, **Everyday Life in Classical Athens,** Putnam, 1969. Rex Warner, **Pericles the Athenian,** Little, Brown, 1962, is an absorbing biographical novel.

Edith Hamilton, **The Greek Way,*** Norton. A popular and enthusiastic appreciation of the beauty and values of Hellenic literature. A. Lesky, **A History of Greek Literature,** Crowell, 1966, is an outstanding detailed treatment. See also H. D. F. Kitto, **Greek Tragedy,*** Anchor; John B. Bury, **Ancient Greek Historians,*** Dover.

C. Seltman, **The Twelve Olympians,*** Apollo. The myths and gay stories about the Olympian gods and goddesses. See also Michael Grant, **Myths of the Greeks and Romans,*** Mentor; W. K. C. Guthrie, **The Greeks and Their Gods,*** Beacon.

Good introductions to Greek philosophy and science include W. K. C. Guthrie, **Greek Philosophers from Thales to Aristotle,*** Torchbooks; F. M. Cornford, **Before and After Socrates,*** Cambridge; R. Warner, **The Greek Philosophers,*** Mentor (contains many extracts); M. Clagett, **Greek Science in Antiquity,*** Collier. See also A. E. Taylor, **Socrates: The Man and His Thought,*** Anchor, and **The Mind of Plato,*** Univ. of Michigan; W. D. Ross, **Aristotle,*** Barnes and Noble.

Recommended for the fine arts student are J. Boardman, **Greek Art,** Praeger, 1964; G. Richter, **A Handbook of Greek Art,** Phaedon, 1960; A. W. Lawrence, **Greek Architecture,** Penguin, 1957; G. Rodenwaldt, **The Acropolis,** Argonaut, 1930; M. Robertson, **Greek Painting,** Skira, 1959.

W. W. Tarn, **Hellenistic Civilisation,*** 3rd ed., Meridian. A detailed survey. See also M. Cary, **A History of the Greek World from 323 to 146 B.C.** 2nd ed., Methuen, 1965. On the career and motives of Alexander the Great see Charles A. Robinson, **Alexander the Great: Conqueror and Creator of a New World,** Watts, 1963; W. W. Tarn, **Alexander the Great,*** Beacon; M. Wheeler, **Flames over Persepolis: Turning-Point in History,** Reynal, 1968.

*Indicates an inexpensive paperbound edition.

Chapter 3

The Grandeur That Was Rome

The Roman World: 509 B.C. to 180 A.D.

INTRODUCTION. As the Athenian saw the symbol of his city-state's democracy and culture in the rock-jutting Acropolis, so the Roman viewed the Forum as the symbol of imperial grandeur. Temples were to be found there, but in contrast to the Acropolis, the Forum was dominated by secular buildings —basilicas, the nearby Colosseum, and the great palaces of the emperors rising on the neighboring Palatine Hill. While the Acropolis was crowned with statues to Athena, the Forum gloried in triumphal arches and columns commemorating military conquests. Rome was the capital of a world-state, extending from the Rhine to the Euphrates, and its citizens were proud of their imperial mission.

Although the buildings in the Forum appear fundamentally Greek in style, they are more monumental and sumptuous. Here, then, are two clues to an understanding of the Romans: they borrowed profusely from the Greeks, and they modified what they took. *Adoption* and *adaptation* are key words in the study of Roman civilization.

Rome was the great intermediary—the bridge over which passed the rich contributions of the Fertile Crescent, Egypt, and especially Greece to form the basis of modern western civilization. The Romans replaced the anarchy of the Hellenistic Age with law and order and embraced the intellectual and artistic legacy of the conquered Greeks. As Rome's empire expanded, this legacy was spread westward throughout Europe.

Yet Rome was more than an intermediary, for it made many important and original contributions to our western culture. Throughout a history which led from a simple farming community in the plain of Latium to a strong state which became the master of the Mediterranean and finally of the entire known western world, the Romans met one challenge after another with practicality and efficiency. In the shadows of its marching legions went engineers and architects, so that today, scattered throughout the lands that once were part of the Roman world, the remains of roads, walls, baths, basilicas, amphitheaters, and aqueducts offer convincing evidence of the Romans' technical prowess (see Color Plate 3). Most lasting and far-reaching of all, their administrative institutions—the legal codes and governmental systems they developed and modified to meet changing needs —have served as the framework of western political life.

ROME TO 509 B.C.

Early settlers of Italy. The Greeks and Romans were offshoots of a common Indo-European stock, and settlement of the Greek and Italian peninsulas followed broadly parallel stages. Between 2000 and 1000 B.C., when Indo-European peoples invaded the Aegean world, a western wing of this nomadic migration filtered into the Italian peninsula, then inhabited by indigenous Neolithic tribes. The first invaders, skilled in the use of copper and bronze, settled in the Po valley. Another wave of Indo-Europeans, equipped with iron weapons and tools, followed; and in time the newer and older settlers intermingled and spread throughout the peninsula. One group, the Latins, settled in the lower valley of the Tiber River, a region that became known as the plain of Latium.

For ages history had bypassed the western Mediterranean, but it was henceforth to become an increasingly significant area. During the ninth century B.C. the Etruscans, a non-Indo-European people who probably came from Asia Minor, brought the first city-state civilization to Italy. Expanding from the west coast north to the Po valley and south to the Bay of Naples, the Etruscans organized the backward Italic peoples into a loose confederation of Etruscan-dominated city-states. After 750 B.C. Greek colonists migrated to southern Italy and Sicily, where they served as a protective buffer against powerful and prosperous Carthage, a Phoenician colony established in North Africa about 800 B.C. Yet the future was not to belong to these various invaders, but to an insignificant village on the Tiber River, then in the shadow of Etruscan expansion. This was Rome, destined to be ruler of the ancient world.

Rome's origins. According to ancient legend, Rome was founded in 753 B.C. by the twin brothers Romulus and Remus, who were saved from death in their infancy by a she-wolf who sheltered and suckled them. Virgil's *Aeneid* preserves a different tradition that the founder of the Roman race was Aeneas, a Trojan who after the fall of Troy founded a settlement in Latium. Turning from fable to fact, modern scholars believe that in the eighth century B.C. the inhabitants of some small Latin settlements on hills in the Tiber valley united and established a common meeting place, the Forum, around which the city of Rome grew. Situated at a convenient place for fording the river and protected by the hills and marshes from invaders, Rome was strategically located. Nevertheless, the expanding Etruscans conquered Rome about 600 B.C., and under their tutelage Rome first became an important city-state.

Some aspects of Etruscan culture were borrowed from the Greek colonies in southern Italy, and much of this, including the alphabet, was passed on to the conquered

Romans. (Etruscan writing can be read phonetically but not understood.) From their Etruscan overlords, the Romans acquired some of their gods and goddesses and the practice of prophesying by examining animal entrails. From the conquerors, too, the conquered learned the art of building—especially the arch. Even the name *Roma* appears to be an Etruscan word.

The Roman monarchy. Rome's political growth followed a line of development similar to that of the Greek city-states: limited monarchy of the sort described by Homer, oligarchy, democracy, and, finally, the permanent dictatorship of the Roman emperors. We shall see that in moving from oligarchy to democracy, the Romans, unlike the Greeks, succeeded in avoiding the intermediate stage of tyranny.

According to tradition, early Rome was ruled by kings elected by the people. After the Etruscan conquest, this elective system continued, although the kings chosen were usually of Etruscan origin. The king's executive power, both civil and military, was called the *imperium*, which was symbolized by an eagle-headed scepter and an ax bound in a bundle of rods (*fasces*). The *fasces* symbol is found on the United States dime, and in the 1930's it provided both the symbol and the name for Mussolini's political creed of fascism.

Although the *imperium* was conferred by a popular assembly made up of all arms-bearing citizens, the king turned for advice to a council of nobles called the Senate. Each senator had lifelong tenure, and the members of this group and their families constituted the patrician class. The other class of Romans, the plebeians, or commoners, included small farmers, artisans, and many clients, or dependents, of patrician landowners. In return for a livelihood, the clients gave their patrician patrons political support in the assembly.

EARLY REPUBLIC, 509-133 B.C. : DOMESTIC AFFAIRS

Establishment of the Republic. In 509 B.C., according to tradition, the patricians expelled the last Etruscan king, claiming that he had acted despotically, and established what they called a republic (from *res publica*, literally "public affairs"), in which they held the reins of power. The *imperium* was transferred to two new officials, called consuls. Elected annually from the patrician class, the consuls invariably exercised their power in its interest. In the event of war or serious domestic emergency, a dictator could be substituted for the two consuls, but he was given absolute power for six months only.

Struggle for equal rights. For more than two centuries following the establishment of the Republic, the plebeians struggled for political and social equality. Outright civil war was averted by the willingness, however reluctant and delayed, of the patricians to compromise. This largely explains why it was unnecessary for the plebeians to resort to tyrants to help them gain their goals, as had happened in the Greek city-states. Much of the plebeians' success in this struggle was

Cheerful artwork frequently adorned Etruscan tombs. In this painting the youth at the right is playing a double lute, an instrument the music-loving Etruscans particularly enjoyed.

also due to their tactics of collective action and to their having organized a corporate group within the state. This unofficial body, a sort of state within a state, was known as the *Concilium Plebis* and was presided over by plebeian officials called tribunes, whose job was to safeguard the interests of the plebeians and to negotiate with the consuls and the Senate. Finally, Rome's constant wars gave the plebeians, indispensable in filling the ranks of the Roman conscript army, greater bargaining power.

The advancement of the plebeians during the early Republic took two main lines: the safeguarding of their fundamental rights and the progressive enlargement of their share of political power. Because the consuls often interpreted Rome's unwritten customary law to suit patrician interests, the plebeians demanded that it be written down and made available for all to see. As a result, about 450 B.C. the law was inscribed on twelve tablets of bronze and set up publicly in the Forum. The Law of the Twelve Tables was the first landmark in the long history of Roman law, and Cicero tells us that Roman schoolchildren were required to memorize it.

The plebeians in time acquired other fundamental rights and safeguards: they secured the right to appeal a death sentence imposed by a consul and to be retried before the popular assembly; the tribunes gained a veto power over any legislation or executive act that threatened the rights of the plebeians; and marriage between patricians and plebeians, prohibited by the Law of the Twelve Tables, was legalized. Important also was the abolition of the enslavement of citizens for debt.

Little by little the plebeian class acquired more power in the functioning of the government. In 367 B.C. one consulship was reserved for the plebeians, and before the end of the century plebeians were eligible to hold other important magistracies which the patricians had in the meantime created. Among these magistracies, whose powers originally had been held by the consuls, were the praetor (in charge of the law courts), quaestor (treasurer), and censor (supervisor of public morals and the letting of state contracts). The right to hold high political offices proved to

be a stepping stone to the Senate, and some plebeians succeeded in gaining entry to that august body.

The long struggle for equality ended in 287 B.C. when the *Concilium Plebis* was recognized as a constitutional body, henceforth known as the Tribal Assembly, with the right to pass laws that were binding on all citizens, patricians as well as plebeians. The plebeians demanded this right because of the undemocratic organization and procedure of the older popular assemblies, which the patricians had been able to control. The Roman Republic was now technically a democracy, although in actual practice a senatorial aristocracy of patricians and rich plebeians continued to control the state. Having gained political and social equality, the plebeians were willing to allow the more experienced Senate to run the government during the remainder of this period of almost constant warfare down to 133 B.C.

After 287 B.C. conflict in Roman society gradually assumed a new form. Heretofore, the issue had been primarily social and political between hereditary classes. When equality was achieved, many plebeians were able to profit from new opportunities and amass prestige and wealth in the state's expanding economy. As a result, wealth instead of aristocratic descent was most important, and the old distinction between patrician and plebeian became much less fundamental than a new conflict between rich and poor which arose after 133 B.C.

The Roman citizen. The fundamental unit of early Roman society was the family. The father's power was absolute, and strict discipline was imposed to instill in children those virtues to which the Romans attached particular importance—loyalty, courage, self-control, and respect for laws and ancestral customs. The Romans of the early Republic were stern, hard-working, and practical. Man's relationship to the universe and the possibilities of immortal life did not concern them unduly, and religious practices were confined to placating the spirits (*numina*) of the family and the state. Under Etruscan influence the major spirits were personified. Thus the sky-spirit Jupiter became god of the universe; Mars, spirit of vegetation, became god of war; and Janus, whose temple doors remained open when the army was away at war, was originally the spirit of the city gate.

EARLY REPUBLIC, 509-133 B.C.: FOREIGN AFFAIRS

Roman conquest of Italy. The growth of Rome from a small city-state to the dominant power in the Mediterranean world in less than four hundred years (509-133 B.C.) is a remarkable success story. By 270 B.C. the first phase of Roman expansion was over. Ringed about by hostile peoples—Etruscans in the north, predatory hill tribes in central Italy, and Greeks in the south—Rome had subdued them all after long, agonizing effort and found itself master of all Italy south of the Po valley. Roman expansion was not deliberately planned; rather, it was the result of dealing with successive crises, caused by unsettled conditions in Italy, which the Romans considered to be threats to their security.

Rome's position was favored by geography. While the Italian peninsula has a great mountainous backbone, the Apennines, running down most of its length, the country is not so rugged as Greece. Consequently the mountains did not constitute a barrier to political unification. Also, the Alps in the north kept all but the most intrepid barbarian tribes from entering the Italian peninsula. In addition, the Latins occupied a central position on the peninsula, which made it difficult for their enemies to unite against them successfully.

Soon after ousting their Etruscan overlords in 509 B.C., Rome and the Latin League, composed of Latin peoples in the vicinity of Rome, entered into a defensive alliance against the Etruscans. This new combination was so successful that by the beginning of the fourth century B.C. it had become the chief power in central Italy. But the members of the Latin League grew alarmed at Rome's increasing strength, and war broke out between the former allies. With the victory of

Rome in 338 B.C., the League was dissolved, and the Latin cities were forced to sign individual treaties with Rome. Thus the same year which saw the rise of Macedonia over Greece (see p. 50) also saw the rise of a new power in Italy.

Border clashes with aggressive highland Samnite tribes led to three fiercely fought Samnite wars and the extension of Rome's frontiers southward to the Greek colonies in Great Greece. Fearing Roman conquest, the Greeks prepared for war and called in the Hellenistic Greek king, Pyrrhus of Epirus, who dreamed of becoming a second Alexander the Great. Pyrrhus' war elephants, unknown in Italy, twice routed the Romans, but at so heavy a cost that such a triumph is still called a "Pyrrhic victory." When a third battle failed to induce the Romans to make peace, Pyrrhus is reported to have remarked, "We are waging a war against a hydra," and returned to his homeland. The Roman army then moved into southern Italy and by 270 B.C. had subdued the Greek cities there.

Treatment of conquered peoples. Instead of slaughtering or enslaving their defeated foes, the Romans treated them fairly, in time creating a strong loyalty to Rome throughout the peninsula. Roman citizenship was a prized possession and was not extended to all peoples on the peninsula until the first century B.C. Most defeated states were required to sign a treaty of alliance with Rome which bound them to adhere to Rome's foreign policy and to supply troops for the Roman army. No tribute was required, and each state retained local self-government. Rome did, however, annex about one third of the conquered lands, establishing colonies in some parts.

The First Punic War. After 270 B.C. only Carthage remained as Rome's rival in the West. Much more wealthy and populous than Rome, with a magnificent navy that controlled the western Mediterranean and with a domain that included the northern coast of Africa, Sardinia, western Sicily, and parts of Spain and Corsica, Carthage seemed more than a match for Rome. But Carthage was governed by a commercial aristocracy which hired mercenaries to do the fighting. In the long run, the lack of a loyal body of free

ROMAN ITALY BEFORE AUGUSTUS

citizens and allies, such as Rome had, proved to be Carthage's fatal weakness.

The First Punic War (from *punicus*, Latin for "Phoenician") broke out in 264 B.C. when Rome sought to oust a Carthaginian force that had occupied Messina on the northeastern tip of Sicily just across from Roman Italy. According to Polybius, a Hellenistic Greek historian, the Romans "felt it was absolutely necessary not to let Messina fall, or allow the Carthaginians to secure what would be like a bridge to enable them to cross into Italy."[1] Rome lost 200,000 men in disastrous naval engagements before Carthage sued for peace in 241 B.C. Sicily, Sardinia, and Corsica were annexed as the first provinces of Rome's overseas empire, governed and taxed by Roman proconsuls.

The contest with Hannibal. Thwarted by this defeat, Carthage concentrated upon enlarging its empire in Spain. Rome's determination to restrict the Carthaginian sphere of influence led to the greatest and most difficult war in Roman history. While both powers jockeyed for position, a young Carthaginian general, Hannibal, precipitated the Second Punic War by attacking Saguntum, a Spanish town claimed by Rome as an ally. Rome declared war, and Hannibal, seizing the initiative, in 218 B.C. led an army of about 40,000 men, 9000 cavalry troops, and a detachment of African elephants across the Alps into Italy. Although the crossing had cost him nearly half of his men and almost all of his elephants, Hannibal defeated the Romans three times within three years.

Hannibal's forces never matched those of the Romans in numbers. At Cannae, for example, where Hannibal won his greatest victory, some 70,000 Romans were wiped out by barely 50,000 Carthaginians. On the whole Rome's allies remained loyal—a testimony to Rome's generous and statesmanlike treatment of its Italian subjects—and because the Romans controlled the seas, Hannibal received little aid from Carthage. Thus Hannibal was unable to inflict a mortal blow against the Romans.

The Romans finally found a general, Scipio, who was Hannibal's match in military strategy and who was bold enough to invade Africa. Forced to return home after fifteen years spent on Italian soil, Hannibal clashed with Scipio's legions at Zama, where the Carthaginians suffered a complete defeat (see map, p. 71). The power of Carthage was broken forever by a harsh treaty imposed in 201 B.C. Carthage was forced to pay a huge indemnity, disarm its forces, and turn Spain over to the Romans. Hannibal sought asylum in the kingdom of the Seleucids where he stirred up anti-Roman sentiment.

Roman intervention in the East. The defeat of Carthage left Rome free to turn eastward and settle a score with Philip V of Macedonia, who, fearing Roman expansion, had allied himself with Hannibal during the darkest days of the war. Now, in 200 B.C., Rome was ready to act, following an appeal from Pergamum and Rhodes for aid in protecting the smaller Hellenistic states from Philip, who was advancing in the Aegean, and the Seleucid emperor, who was moving into Asia Minor. The heavy Macedonian phalanxes were no match for the mobile Roman legions, and in 197 B.C. Philip was soundly defeated and his dreams of empire were ended when Rome deprived him of his warships and military bases in Greece. The Romans then proclaimed the independence of Greece and were eulogized by the grateful Greeks:

There was one people in the world which would fight for others' liberties at its own cost, to its own peril, and with its own toil, not limiting its guaranties of freedom to its neighbours, to men of the immediate vicinity, or to countries that lay close at hand, but ready to cross the sea that there might be no unjust empire anywhere and that everywhere justice, right, and law might prevail.[2]

A few years later Rome declared war on the Seleucid emperor who had moved into Greece, urged on by Hannibal and a few greedy Greek states that resented Rome's refusal to dismember Macedonia. The Romans forced him to vacate Greece and Asia Minor, pay a huge indemnity, and give up his warships and war elephants. The Seleucids were checked again in 168 B.C. when a Roman ultimatum halted their invasion of Egypt, which became a Roman protectorate, and a year later Rome supported the Jews in their successful revolt against the Seleucids (see p. 122).

THE ROMAN WORLD 133 B.C.

- ☐ Roman Territories
- ▨ Allies Of Rome By Treaty

Most of the East was now a Roman protectorate, the result of a policy in which Roman self-interest was mingled with idealism. But Roman idealism turned sour when anti-Romanism became widespread in Greece, particularly among the radical masses who resented Rome's support of conservative governments and the status quo in general. (The Romans, for example, helped crush a socialist revolution in Sparta.) The new policy was revealed in 146 B.C. when, after many Greeks had supported an attempted Macedonian revival, Rome destroyed Corinth as an object lesson, supported oligarchic factions in all Greek states, and placed Greece under the watchful eye of the governor of Macedonia, which was made a Roman province.

Destruction of Carthage. In the West, meanwhile, Rome's hardening policy led to suspicion of Carthage's reviving prosperity and to a demand by extremists for war—*Carthago delenda est* ("Carthage must be destroyed"). Treacherously provoking the Third Punic War, the Romans besieged Carthage, which resisted heroically for three years, destroyed the city in 146 B.C.—the same year of Corinth's destruction—and annexed the territory as a province.

Rome, supreme in the ancient world. In 133 B.C. the king of Pergamum, dying without heir, bequeathed his kingdom to Rome. Apparently he feared that the discontented masses would revolt after his death unless Rome, with its reputation for maintaining law and order in the interest of the propertied classes, took over. Rome accepted the bequest and then spent the next three years suppressing a proletarian revolution in its first Asian province.

With provinces on three continents—Europe, Africa, and Asia (see map above)—the once obscure Roman Republic was now supreme in the ancient world. But the next century, during which Rome's frontiers reached the Euphrates and the Rhine, would witness the failure of the Republic to solve the problems that were the by-products of the acquisition of an empire.

LATE REPUBLIC, 133-30 B.C.

Effects of Roman expansion. The political history of Rome thus far consists of two dominant themes: the gradual liberalization of the government and the expansion of Roman dominion over the Mediterranean world. Largely as a result of this expansion, important social and economic problems faced Rome by roughly the midpoint of the second century B.C.

One of the most pressing problems was the disappearance of the small landowner, whose energy and spirit had made Rome great. Burdened by frequent military service, his farm buildings destroyed by Hannibal, and unable to compete with the cheap grain imported from the new Roman province of Sicily, the small farmer sold out and moved to Rome. Here he joined the unemployed, discontented proletariat, so called because their only contribution was *proles*, "children."

On the other hand, improved farming methods learned from Greeks and Carthaginians encouraged rich aristocrats to buy more and more land and, abandoning the cultivation of grain, introduce large-scale scientific production of olive oil and wine, or of sheep and cattle. This trend was especially profitable because an abundance of cheap slaves from the conquered areas was available to work on the estates. These large slave plantations, called *latifundia*, were now common in Italy, while small farms were the exception.

The land problem was further complicated by the government's earlier practice of leasing part of the territory acquired in the conquest of the Italian peninsula to anyone willing to pay a percentage of the crop or animals raised on it. Only the patricians or wealthy plebeians could afford to lease large tracts of this public land, and in time they treated it as if it were their own property. As early as the fourth century B.C. plebeian protests had led to an attempt to limit the holdings of a single individual to 320 acres of public land, but the law devised for that purpose was never enforced.

Corruption in the government was another mark of the growing degeneracy of the Roman Republic. Provincial officials seized opportunities for lucrative graft, and a new class of Roman businessmen scrambled selfishly for the profitable state contracts to supply the armies, collect taxes in the provinces, and lease mines and forests. Although in theory the government was a democracy, in practice it remained a senatorial oligarchy, as we have seen (p. 67). The tribunes, guardians of the people's rights, had become mere yes-men of the Senate.

Thus by the middle of the second century B.C., the government was in the hands of the wealthy, self-seeking Senate, which was unable to cope with the problems of governing a world-state. Ordinary citizens were for the most part impoverished and landless; and Rome swarmed with fortune hunters, imported slaves, unemployed farmers, and discontented war veterans. The poverty of the many, coupled with the opulence of the few, hastened the decay of the old Roman traits of discipline, simplicity, and respect for authority.

The next century (133-30 B.C.) saw Rome convulsed by civil war, even while engaged in occasional foreign wars. The Senate was noticeably inefficient in carrying on foreign conflicts, but its most serious weakness was its inability to solve the economic and social problems following in the wake of Rome's conquests. This led to the establishment of a dictatorship and the end of the Republic.

Reform movement of the Gracchi. An awareness of Rome's profound social and economic problems led to the reform program of an idealistic young aristocrat named Tiberius Gracchus. Supported by a few liberal Senators, Tiberius was elected tribune for the year 133 B.C. at the age of twenty-nine. His reforming zeal was the product of the newly imported liberal learning of Greece and an awareness that the old Roman character and way of life was fast slipping away. He sought to arrest Roman decline by restoring the backbone of the old Roman society—the small landowner.

Tiberius proposed to the Tribal Assembly that the act limiting the holding of public land to 320 acres per person be reenacted.

Much of the public land would in the future be held by the present occupants and their descendants as private property, but the surplus was to be confiscated and allotted to landless Roman citizens. In his address to the assembly Tiberius noted that

it is with lying lips that their commanders exhort the soldiers in their battles to defend sepulchres and shrines from the enemy; . . . they fight and die to support others in wealth and luxury, and though they are styled masters of the world, they have not a single clod of earth that is their own.[3]

Although the Tribal Assembly adopted Tiberius' proposal by a wide majority, the Senate induced one of the other tribunes to veto the measure. On the ground that a tribune who opposed the will of the people thereby forfeited his office, Tiberius took a fateful—and, the Senate claimed, unconstitutional—step by having the assembly depose the tribune in question. The agrarian bill was then passed.

To ensure the implementation of his agrarian reform, Tiberius again violated custom by standing for reelection after completing his one-year term. On the pretext that he sought to make himself king, partisans of the Senate murdered Tiberius and three hundred of his followers. The Republic's failure at this point to solve its problems without bloodshed stands in striking contrast to its previous development by peaceful means.

Tiberius' work was taken up by his younger brother, Gaius Gracchus, who was elected tribune for 123 B.C. In addition to the reallocation of public land, Gaius proposed establishing Roman colonies in southern Italy and on the site of Carthage. To protect the poor against speculation in the grain market (especially in times of famine), Gaius committed the government to the purchase and storage of wheat and to its subsequent distribution to the urban masses at about half the former market price. Unfortunately, what Gaius intended as a relief measure later became a dole, whereby free food was distributed—all too often for the advancement of astute politicians—to the entire proletariat.

Another of Gaius' proposals would have granted citizenship to Rome's Italian allies, who were now being mistreated by Roman officials. This proposal cost Gaius the support of the Roman proletariat, which did not wish to share the privileges of citizenship or endanger its control of the Tribal Assembly. Consequently, in 121 B.C. Gaius failed to be reelected to a third term and the Senate was emboldened to resort to force again. Martial law was declared and three thousand of Gaius' followers were arrested and executed, a fate Gaius avoided by committing suicide.

The Senate had shown that it had no intention of initiating needed domestic reforms, or of allowing others to do so, and the Gracchi's deaths were ominous portents of the manner in which the Republic was henceforth to decide its internal disputes.

In foreign affairs, too, the Senate soon demonstrated its incapability. Rome was forced to grant citizenship to its Italian allies after the Senate's failure to deal with their grievances goaded them into revolt (99-88 B.C.). Other blunders led to the first of the civil wars that destroyed the Republic.

The first civil war: Marius vs. Sulla. Between 111 and 105 B.C. Roman armies, dispatched by the Senate and commanded by senators, failed to protect Roman capitalists in North Africa and to prevent Germanic tribes from overrunning southern Gaul, now a Roman province, and threatening Italy itself. Accusing the Senate of lethargy and incompetence in directing Rome's foreign affairs, the people elected Gaius Marius to the consulship in 107 B.C., and the Tribal Assembly commissioned him to raise an army and deal with the foreign danger. Marius first pacified North Africa and then crushed the first German threat to Rome. In the process he created a new-style Roman army that was destined to play a major role in the turbulent history of the late Republic.

In contrast to the old Roman army, which was composed of conscripts who owned their own land and who thought of themselves as loyal citizens of the Republic, the new army created by Marius was recruited from landless citizens for long terms of service. These professional soldiers identified their own interests with those of their commanders, to whom they looked for bonuses of land or money, and were ready to follow them in any undertaking. Thus the character of the army changed from a militia to a career service in which loyalty to the state was no longer paramount. Aspiring generals would soon use their military power to seize the government.

In 88 B.C. the ambitious king of Pontus in Asia Minor, encouraged by the growing anti-Roman sentiment in Asia Minor and Greece caused by corrupt governors and tax collectors, declared war on Rome. The Senate ordered Cornelius Sulla, an able general and a staunch supporter of the Senate's prerogatives, to go east. As a countermove, the Tribal Assembly chose Marius for the eastern command. In effect both the Senate and the Tribal Assembly, whose power the Gracchi had revived, claimed to be the ultimate authority in the state. The result was a series of civil wars between rival generals, each claiming to champion the cause of either the Senate or the Tribal Assembly. The first of the civil wars ended in a complete victory for Sulla, who in 82 B.C. had himself appointed dictator for an unlimited period with power to "issue edicts and reorganize the Republic."

Sulla set out to restore the preeminence of the Senate. He drastically curtailed the powers of the tribunes and the Tribal Assembly, giving the Senate the control of legislation which it had enjoyed two hundred years before. Convinced that his work would be permanent, Sulla voluntarily resigned his dictatorship in 79 B.C. His reactionary constitutional changes were not to last.

The second civil war: Pompey vs. Caesar. The first of the civil wars and its aftermath increased factionalism and discontent and nursed the ambitions of individuals eager for personal power. The first to come forward was Pompey, who had won fame as a military leader. In 70 B.C. he was elected consul, and, though he was a former partisan of Sulla, courted the populace by repealing Sulla's laws against the tribunes and the Tribal Assembly. Pompey then put an end to anarchy in the East caused by piracy, the protracted ambitions of the king of Pontus, and the death throes of the Seleucid empire. New Roman provinces and client states brought order eastward to the Euphrates and southward through Palestine.

Still another strong man made his appearance in 59 B.C., when Julius Caesar allied himself politically with Pompey and was elected consul. Following his consulship, Caesar spent nine years conquering Gaul, where he accumulated a fortune in plunder and trained a loyal army of peerless veterans. During his absence from Rome, he cannily kept his name before the citizens by publishing a lucidly written account of his military feats, *Commentaries on the Gallic War.*

Caesar's conquest of Gaul was to have tremendous consequences for the course of western civilization, for its inhabitants quickly assimilated Roman culture. Consequently, when the Roman Empire collapsed in the West in the fifth century A.D., Romanized Gaul—or France—emerged before long as the center of medieval civilization.

Jealous of Caesar's achievements in Gaul and fearful of his growing power, Pompey conspired with the Senate to ruin him. When the Senate demanded in 49 B.C. that Caesar disband his army, he crossed the Rubicon, the river in northern Italy which formed the boundary of Caesar's province. By crossing the Rubicon—a phrase employed today for any step that commits a person to a given course of action—Caesar in effect declared war on Pompey and the Senate. He marched on Rome while Pompey and most of the Senate fled eastward. Pompey was soon killed in Egypt where he sought refuge, but the last Pompeian army was not defeated until 45 B.C.

Caesar assumed the office of dictator for life, and during his brief period of autocratic rule he initiated far-reaching reforms. He granted citizenship liberally to non-Italians and packed the Senate with many new provincial members, thus making it a more truly representative body as well as a rubber stamp for his policies. In the interest of the poorer citizens, he reduced debts, inaugurated a public works program, established colonies outside Italy, and decreed that one third of the laborers on the slave-worked estates in Italy be persons of free birth. As a result, he was able to reduce from 320,000 to 150,000 the number of people receiving free grain. His most enduring act was the reform of the calendar in the light of Egyptian knowledge; with minor changes, this calendar of 365¼ days is still in use today.

Caesar realized that the Republic was, in fact, dead. In his own words, "The Republic is merely a name, without form or substance." He believed that benevolent despotism alone could save Rome from continued civil war and collapse. But Caesar incurred the enmity of many, particularly those who viewed him as a tyrant who had destroyed the Republic. On the Ides (the fifteenth) of March, 44 B.C., a group of conspirators, led by ex-Pompeians whom Caesar had pardoned, stabbed him to death in the Senate, and Rome was once more plunged into conflict.

Caesar's assassins had been offended by his trappings of monarchy—his purple robe, the statues erected in his honor, the coins bearing his portrait—and they assumed that with his death the Republic would be restored to its traditional status. But the people of Rome remained unmoved by the conspirators' cry of "Liberty! Freedom! Tyranny is dead!" The majority of them were prepared to accept a successor whose power and position stopped just short of a royal title. The real question was: Who was to be Caesar's successor?

The third civil war: Antony vs. Octavian. Following Caesar's death, his eighteen-year-old heir, Octavian, allied himself with Caesar's chief lieutenant, Mark Antony, against the conspirators and the Senate. Although he was not a conspirator, Cicero, the renowned orator and champion of the Senate, was put to death for his hostility to Antony, and the conspirators' armies were routed. Then for more than a decade Octavian and Antony exercised dictatorial power and divided the Roman world between them. But the ambitions of each man proved too great for the alliance to endure.

Antony, who took charge of the eastern half of the empire, became infatuated with Cleopatra, the last of the Egyptian Ptolemies. He even went so far as to transfer Roman territories to her dominions. Octavian took advantage of this high-handedness to arouse Rome and Italy against Antony. When Octavian's fleet met Antony's off Actium in Greece, first Cleopatra and then Antony deserted the battle and fled to Egypt. There

Antony committed suicide, as did Cleopatra soon afterwards when Alexandria was captured in 30 B.C. At the end of a century of civil violence Rome was at last united under one ruler, and the Republic gave way to the Empire. Two centuries of imperial greatness, known as the *Pax Romana* (the Roman peace), followed.

THE PAX ROMANA: 30 B.C. TO 180 A.D.

Reconstruction under Augustus. Following his triumphal return to Rome, Octavian in 27 B.C. announced that he would "restore the Republic." But he did so only outwardly by blending republican institutions with strong personal leadership. He provided the Senate with considerable authority, consulted it on important issues, allowed it to retain control over Italy and half of the provinces, and gave it the legislative functions of the nearly defunct Tribal Assembly. The Senate in return bestowed upon Octavian the title *Augustus* ("The Revered," a title previously used for gods), by which he was known thereafter.

Augustus never again held the dictatorship, and he seldom held the consulship. Where, then, did his strength lie? Throughout his career he kept the power of a tribune (which gave him the right to initiate and to veto legislation) and the governorship of the frontier provinces, where the armies were stationed. Augustus' control of the army meant that his power could not be successfully challenged. From his military title, *imperator* ("victorious general"), are derived our modern terms of *emperor* and *empire*.

Augustus thus effected a compromise "between the need for a monarchical head of the empire and the sentiment which enshrined Rome's republican constitution in the minds of his contemporaries."[4] He preferred the modest title of *princeps*, "first citizen" or "leader," which he felt best described his position, and his form of disguised monarchy is therefore known as the Principate. At the beginning of the Empire, then, political power was divided between the Senate and the *princeps*, and this *dyarchy* ("rule of two") lasted for more than two centuries, although the Senate slowly faded into the background.

Augustus faced the problems of curing a sick society and removing the scars resulting from a century of civil strife. The aristocracy was too decadent to be patriotic, and in the cities an unemployed mob favored with free bread and circuses had long since lost interest in hard work. Accordingly, Augustus concentrated on internal reform, although he did extend the Roman frontier to the Danube as a defense against barbarian invasions while failing in an attempt to conquer Germany up to the Elbe River (see map, p. 77). His thorough reconstruction of government and society laid the foundation for two centuries of order and prosperity. For example, he created a professional civil service, open to all classes—which greatly reduced the corruption and exploitation that had flourished in the late Republic—and a permanent professional army, stationed in the frontier provinces and kept out of politics. By means of legislation and propaganda, he also sought with some success to check moral and social decline and to revive the old Roman ideals and traditions. Augustus' reforms engendered a new optimism and patriotism which

The Gemma Augustea celebrates some of the great events of Augustus' reign. Holding the imperial staff, Augustus and the goddess Roma rest their feet on the weapons of conquered peoples. The emperor is receiving a laurel crown, the symbol of civilization. Tiberius, Augustus' successor, steps from a chariot at the left. Victorious Roman soldiers occupy the lower panel.

were reflected in the art and literature of the Augustan Age (discussed later in chapter).

The Julio-Claudian and the Flavian emperors. Augustus was followed by four descendants of his family, the line of the Julio-Claudians, who ruled from 14 to 68 A.D. Tiberius, Augustus' stepson whom the Senate accepted as his successor, and Claudius were fairly efficient and devoted rulers; in Claudius' reign the Roman occupation of Britain began in 43 A.D. The other two rulers of this imperial line were of a different stripe: Caligula was a madman, who demanded to be worshiped as a god and made his favorite horse a senator; Nero was infamous for his immorality, the murder of his wife and his mother, and his persecution of Christians in Rome.

During Nero's reign, in 64 A.D., a great fire raged for nine days, destroying more than half of the capital. The Roman historian Tacitus has left us a vivid account of how Nero made the unpopular Christians scapegoats for the fire:

> . . . large numbers . . . were condemned—not so much for incendiarism as for their anti-social tendencies. Their deaths were made farcical. Dressed in wild animals' skins, they were torn to pieces by dogs, or crucified, or made into torches to be ignited after dark. . . . Nero provided his Gardens for the spectacle, and exhibited displays in the Circus . . . . Despite their guilt as Christians, and the ruthless punishment it deserved, the victims were pitied. For it was felt they were being sacrificed to one man's brutality rather than to the national interest.[5]

The Julio-Claudian line ended in 68 A.D. when Nero, faced by army revolts, committed suicide. In the following year four emperors were proclaimed by rival armies, with Vespasian the final victor. For nearly thirty years (69-96 A.D.) the Flavian dynasty (Vespasian followed by his two sons) provided the Empire with effective, if autocratic, rule. The fiction of republican institutions gave way to a scarcely veiled monarchy as the Flavians openly treated the office of emperor as theirs by right of conquest and inheritance.

The Antonines: "five good emperors." An end to autocracy and a return to the Augustan principle of an administration of equals—emperor and Senate—characterized the rule

THE GROWTH OF THE ROMAN EMPIRE
44 B.C. TO 180 A.D.

Acquired before the Death of Caesar, 44 B.C.
Acquired before the Death of Augustus, 14 A.D.
Acquired before the Death of Marcus Aurelius, 180 A.D.

of the Antonine emperors (96-180 A.D.), under whom the Empire reached the height of its prosperity and power. Selected on the basis of proven ability, these "good emperors" succeeded, according to Tacitus, in "reconciling things long incompatible, supreme power and liberty." Two of these emperors are especially worthy of notice.

Hadrian reigned from 117 to 138 A.D. His first important act was to stabilize the boundaries of the Empire. He gave up as indefensible recently conquered Armenia and Mesopotamia and erected protective walls in Germany and Britain, the latter an imposing structure of stone and turf twenty feet high. Hadrian traveled extensively, inspecting almost every province of the Empire. New towns were founded, old ones restored, and many public works were constructed, among them the famous Pantheon in Rome (see illustration, p. 83).

The last of the "five good emperors," Marcus Aurelius, who ruled from 161 to 180 A.D., approached Plato's ideal of the "philos-opher king" and preferred the quiet contemplation of his books to the blood and brutality of the battlefield. Yet, ironically, he was repeatedly troubled by the invasions of Germanic tribes across the Danube. While engaged in his Germanic campaigns, he wrote his *Meditations*, a philosophical work notable for its lofty Stoic idealism and love of humanity.

The "immense majesty of the Roman peace." In the finest period of the Empire, a vast area stretching from Britain to the Euphrates and from the North Sea to the Sahara and containing upwards of 100 million people was welded together into what Pliny the Elder, in the first century A.D., termed the "immense majesty of the Roman peace." Non-Romans were equally conscious of the rich benefits derived from Roman rule. To a Greek writer of the second century, it was

a world every day better known, better cultivated, and more civilized than before. Everywhere roads are traced, every district is known, every country opened to commerce. . . . There are now as many cities as there were once solitary cottages. . . . Wherever there is a trace of life there are houses and human habitations, well-ordered governments and civilized life.[6]

This quotation throws significant light upon the period known as the *Pax Romana.* While the economy remained predominantly agricultural, the Empire became progressively more urban in character as cities increased in number, particularly in the frontier provinces (see Color Plate 3). The cities formed vital nerve centers linked together by a vast network of roads and waterways. The Empire lay secure behind natural frontiers guarded by well-trained armies, the roads cleared of brigands and the seas of pirates. The *Pax Romana* also witnessed the creation of a cosmopolitan world-state where races and cultures intermingled freely.

The Graeco-Roman cultural synthesis. Writing during the rule of Augustus, the Roman poet Virgil was the spokesman for what enlightened Romans felt to be the mission of the Empire:

Others, doubtless, will mould lifelike bronze with greater delicacy, will win from marble the look of life, will plead cases better, chart the motions of the sky with the rod and foretell the risings of the stars. You, O Roman, remember to rule the nations with might. This will be your genius —to impose the way of peace, to spare the conquered and crush the proud.[7]

By "others," Virgil was referring to the Greeks, to whom the Romans willingly acknowledged a cultural debt. The Romans learned the Greek language, copied Greek architecture, employed Greek sculptors, and identified their gods with Greek deities. Although Greek ways of life introduced sophisticated habits which were often corrupting to the Roman virtues of self-reliance, personal integrity, family cohesion, and discipline, Greek influences made the Romans on the whole less harsh and insensitive. Largely because of their admiration for Greek culture, the Romans helped perpetuate the legacy of Greece. The *Pax Romana* was the acme of Graeco-Roman civilization.

Governing the diverse state. At the head of this huge world-state stood the emperor, its

defender and symbol of unity as well as an object of veneration. The major theme of the many encomiums written to celebrate the enlightened, beneficent government of the Principate was that liberty had been exchanged for order and prosperity. The Empire was said to represent a new kind of democracy—"a democracy under the one man that can rule and govern best." "The whole world speaks in unison, more distinctly than a chorus; and so well does it harmonize under this director-in-chief that it joins in praying this Empire may last for all time."[8] Nevertheless, during the Principate the cities of the Empire continued to exercise a large measure of self-government, and although the central government increasingly intervened in their affairs, this was usually the result of the failure of city authorities to solve local problems.

Economic prosperity. Rome's unification of the ancient world had far-reaching economic consequences. The *Pax Romana* was responsible for the elimination of tolls and other artificial barriers, the suppression of piracy and brigandage, and the establishment of a reliable coinage. Such factors, in addition to the longest period of peace the West has ever enjoyed, explain in large measure the great expansion of commerce that occurred in the first and second centuries A.D. Industry also was stimulated, but its expansion was hindered since wealth remained concentrated and no mass market for industrial goods arose. Industry remained organized on a small-shop basis with producers widely scattered, resulting in local self-sufficiency.

Although the cities were the centers of political and cultural life, most of them, particularly in the West, were of secondary importance economically. They consumed much more than they produced and flourished only because the economy of the Empire remained prosperous enough to support them. Most were like Rome itself, into which so much revenue poured from the provinces that its citizens had the necessary purchasing power to buy immense quantities of goods from other parts of the Empire and even from regions far beyond the imperial frontiers.

The economy of the Empire remained basically agrarian, and the huge estates, or *latifundia*, prospered. On these tracts, usually belonging to absentee owners, large numbers of *coloni*, free tenants, tilled the soil as sharecroppers. The *coloni* were gradually replacing slave labor, which was becoming increasingly hard to secure with the disappearance of the flow of captives from major wars.

Despite the general prosperity, the Empire under the Antonines had already entered upon its "Indian summer." Once the Empire had ceased to expand geographically, its economy in turn became progressively more static. Late in the first century A.D. Italian agriculture began to suffer from the loss of its markets in the western provinces, which were becoming self-sufficient in the production of wine and olive oil. To aid the wine producers the Flavian emperor Domitian created an artificial scarcity by forbidding the planting of new vineyards in Italy and ordering the plowing under of half the existing vineyards in the provinces. This was followed by a program of state subsidies, inaugurated by the Antonine emperors. Loans at 5 percent interest were made to ailing landowners, with the interest to be paid into the treasuries of declining Italian municipalities and earmarked "for girls and boys of needy parents to be supported at public expense." This system of state subsidies to both producers and consumers was soon extended to the provinces. Also contributing to Roman economic stagnation was the continuing drain of money into the oriental luxury trade (see p. 117). This early evidence of declining prosperity foreshadowed the economic crisis of the third century A.D., when political anarchy and monetary inflation caused the economy of the Empire to decline rapidly (see Chapter 5).

Rome, imperial capital. At the hub of the sprawling Empire was Rome, with about a million inhabitants. Augustus boasted that he had found a city of brick and had left one of marble. Nonetheless, Rome presented a striking contrast of magnificence and tawdriness, of splendid public buildings and squalid tenements which often collapsed or caught fire. The crowded narrow streets, lined with apartment houses and swarming with all manner of people, are described by the satirist Juvenal early in the second century A.D.:

. . . Hurry as I may, I am blocked
By a surging crowd in front, while a vast mass
Of people crushes onto me from behind.
One with his elbow punches me, another
With a hard litter-pole; one bangs a beam
Against my head, a wine-cask someone else.
With mud my legs are plastered; from all sides
Huge feet trample upon me, and a soldier's
Hobnails are firmly planted on my toes.[9]

Social life. At the top of the social order were the old senatorial families who lived as absentee owners of huge estates and left commerce and finance to a large and wealthy middle class. In contrast to the tenements of the poor, the homes of the rich were palatial, as revealed by excavations at Pompeii, which was buried by the eruption of Vesuvius in 79 A.D. These elaborate villas contained courts and gardens with fountains, rooms furnished with marble walls, mosaics on the floors, and numerous frescoes and other works of art. An interesting feature of Roman furniture was the abundance of couches and the scarcity of chairs. People usually reclined, even at meals—a custom which may have had its value during the sumptuous dinners served by the wealthy gourmands, who were not above administering emetics to permit disgorging and starting afresh on more food and wine.

The lower classes in the cities found a refuge from the dullness of their existence in social clubs, or guilds, called *collegia*, each comprising the workers of one trade. The activity of the *collegia* did not center on economic aims, like modern trade unions, but on the worship of a god and on feasts, celebrations, and decent burials for members.

The living conditions of slaves varied greatly. Those in domestic service were often treated humanely, and their years of efficient service frequently rewarded by emancipation. Nor was it uncommon for freed slaves to rise to places of eminence in business, letters, and the imperial service. On the other hand, conditions among slaves on the large estates could be indescribably harsh. Beginning with Augustus, however, numer-

The Colosseum, built by the Flavian emperors, uses arch construction both to light the interior and to disperse weight. Largest of the Roman amphitheaters, it was used for gladiatorial combats, animal fights, and even for naval exhibitions—water pipes for flooding still exist in some arenas.

ous enactments protected slaves from mistreatment; Hadrian, for example, forbade private prisons and the killing of a slave without judicial approval.

Recreation played a key role in Roman social life. Both rich and poor were exceedingly fond of their public baths, which in the capital alone numbered eight hundred during the early days of the Empire. The baths served the same purpose as our modern-day athletic clubs. The larger baths contained enclosed gardens, promenades, gymnasiums, libraries, and famous works of art as well as a wide variety of types of baths. An old Roman inscription expresses an interesting

philosophy: "The bath, wine, and love ruin one's health but make life worth living."

Foot races, boxing, and wrestling were minor sports; chariot racing and gladiatorial contests were the chief amusements. The cry for "bread and circuses" reached such proportions that by the first century A.D. the Roman calendar had 159 days set aside as holidays, 93 of which were given over to games furnished at public expense. The most spectacular sport was chariot racing. The largest of six race courses at Rome was the Circus Maximus, a huge marble-faced structure seating about 150,000 spectators. The games, which included upwards of twenty-four races each day, were presided over by the emperor or his representative. The crowds bet furiously on their favorite charioteers, whose fame equaled that of the all-American football heroes of our own day.

Scarcely less popular, but infinitely less civilized, the gladiatorial contests were also organized by the emperors as a regular feature on the amusement calendar. These cruel spectacles, which have no exact counterpart in any other civilization, were held in arenas, the largest and most famous of which was the Colosseum. The contests took various forms. Ferocious animals were pitted against armed combatants or occasionally even against unarmed men and women who had been condemned to death. Another type of contest was the fight to the death between gladiators, generally equipped with different types of weapons but matched on equal terms. It was not uncommon for the life of a defeated gladiator who had fought courageously to be spared at the request of the spectators. Although many Romans decried these blood-letting contests, there persisted a streak of cruelty in Roman public amusements which can scarcely be comprehended, far less condoned, today.

THE ROMAN CONTRIBUTION

The Roman spirit. The Roman spirit was compounded of many factors. Never completely lost was the tradition of plain living. Geography was another factor; for centuries the Romans were faced with the need to conquer or be conquered, and they had to stress discipline and duty to the state. But the Roman spirit also had another side. It could be arrogant and cruel, and its deep-rooted sense of justice was too often untempered with mercy.

By and large, the Romans lacked the creative fire of the Greeks, but they knew superbly well how to preserve, adapt, and disseminate civilization. Therefore we might characterize the Romans as synthesists rather than innovators—and at the same time pay respect to their recognition of cultural indebtedness. For all their limitations, the Romans had greatness as a people. The *Pax Romana* could have been fashioned and maintained only by a people grave in nature, mature in judgment, and conscious of their responsibilities to others.

Contributions in government. Roman political thinkers such as Cicero contributed the germinal ideas for many governmental theories destined to be influential in later centuries. Some of these deserve mention: the social-contract theory (that government originated as a voluntary agreement among citizens); the idea of popular sovereignty (that all power ultimately resides with the people); and the concept that law must be the paramount rule in government. Although the growing despotism of the Roman emperors corroded these concepts, they were never lost sight of and ultimately were transmitted to modern times. Important, too, was the Roman tradition of unity and order within a great imperial structure. As we will see in later chapters, this concept was to play an important role in the politics of medieval Europe.

The Romans laid the foundations for the political framework of modern Europe in still other ways. Many current administrative divisions, such as the county and province, are derived from Roman practice. In some instances European boundaries are little altered from those existing under the Caesars. The medieval Church also modeled its organization, administrative units, and much of its law after that of the Empire.

Evolution of Roman law. Of the contributions made by the Romans in government and politics, Roman law is preeminent. Two great legal systems, Roman law and English common law, are the foundation of jurisprudence in most modern western nations. Roman law is the basis for the law codes of Italy, France, Scotland, and the Latin American countries. Where English common law is used, as in the United States, there is also a basic heritage of great legal principles originated by ancient Roman jurists. In addition, Roman legal principles have strongly affected the development of the canon law of the Roman Catholic Church; and international law has borrowed principles inherent in the Roman system.

Roman law evolved slowly over a period of about a thousand years. At first, when Rome was a struggling city-state, the law was unwritten, mixed with religious custom, and harsh in its judgments. In the fifth century B.C., as we have seen (p. 67), the law was written down in the Law of the Twelve Tables. During the remainder of the Republic the body of Roman law (*jus civile*, "law of the citizen") was enlarged by legislation passed by the Senate and the assembly and, equally important, by judicial interpretation of existing law to meet new conditions. By the second century A.D. the emperor had become the sole source of law, a responsibility he entrusted to scholars "skilled in the law" (*jurisprudentes*). Holding to the idea of equity ("follow the beneficial interpretation"), and influenced by Stoic philosophy with its concept of a "law of nature" common to all men and ascertainable by means of human reason, these jurists humanized and rationalized Roman law to meet the needs of a world-state. Finally, in the sixth century A.D., the enormous bulk of Roman law from all sources was codified (see p. 151) and thus easily preserved for posterity.

Roman engineering and architecture. The Empire's needs required a communication system of paved roads and bridges as well as huge public buildings and aqueducts for the cities. Pride in the Empire led also to the erection of ostentatious monuments symbolizing Rome's dignity and might.

As road builders, the Romans surpassed all previous peoples. Constructed of layers of stone according to sound engineering principles, their roads were planned for the use of armies and messengers and were kept in constant repair. The earliest and best known main Roman highway was the Appian Way, running from Rome to the Bay of Naples, which was built about 300 B.C. to facilitate Rome's expansion southward. It has been said that the speed of travel possible on Roman highways was not surpassed until the early nineteenth century.

In designing their bridges and aqueducts, the Romans placed a series of stone arches next to one another to provide mutual support. At times several tiers of arches were used, one above the other. Fourteen aque-

ducts, stretching a total of 265 miles, supplied some fifty gallons of water daily for each inhabitant of Rome. The practical nature of the Romans and their skill and initiative in engineering were demonstrated also in the many dams, reservoirs, and harbors they constructed.

At first the Romans copied Etruscan architectural models, but later they combined basic Greek elements with distinctly Roman innovations. The structural simplicity of Hellenic buildings was too restrained for the Romans who, by utilizing brick and concrete as new building materials, developed new methods for enclosing space. The static post and lintel system of the Greeks was replaced with the more dynamic techniques of vaulting.

The barrel vault, basically a series of adjoining arches forming a structure resembling a tunnel, was a new method of enclosing space. In the barrel vault the piers, or supports, of the arches became heavy masonry walls to bear the weight of the vaulted roof. The Romans next developed the cross vault by intersecting two barrel vaults at right angles. Cross vaults were employed to great effect in public baths and basilicas.

Another important advance in architectural engineering was the Romans' success in constructing concrete domes on a magnificent scale. The weight of the dome was transferred directly to the walls, and since there was no sidewise thrust, no other support was necessary. The largest of the domed structures was the Pantheon (temple of "all

In the barrel vault, essentially a Roman contribution, the walls support the sideways and downward pressure of the material above. The walls of the cross vault, an advance in architectural engineering, did not need to be as thick as those of a barrel vault, because the weight of the material was spread over a larger area. Also, openings in the supporting walls furnished window space.

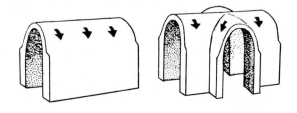

the gods"), which still stands (see illustration).

The standard type of Roman public building was the basilica, a colonnaded structure that became a model for early Christian churches (see illustration, p. 127). Rows of columns divided the interior into a central nave and side aisles, with the roof over the nave raised to admit light, creating a clerestory like those found in Egyptian temples. Perhaps the most famous Roman edifice is the Colosseum (see illustration, p. 80), a huge amphitheater about one quarter of a mile around on the outside and with a seating capacity of about 45,000. Its three stories of arches are decorated with Doric, Ionic, and Corinthian columns.

Roman buildings were built to last, and their size, grandeur, and decorative richness aptly symbolized the proud imperial spirit of Rome. Whereas the Greeks evolved the temple, theater, and stadium, the Romans contributed the triumphal arch, bath, basilica, amphitheater, and the multistoried apartment house. Many modern public buildings show the influence of Rome's bold new architecture.

Sculpture and painting. After the conquest of Greece thousands of statues and other art pieces were brought to Rome. Many Romans acquired a passion for art, and the homes of the wealthy were filled with all kinds of Greek art.

Although strongly influenced by Etruscan and Greek models, the Romans developed a distinctive sculpture of their own which was remarkably realistic, secular, and individualistic. Lifelike portraiture flourished particularly during the Republic, probably originating in the early practice of making and preserving wax images of the heads of important families. During the Principate, on the other hand, portraiture and relief sculpture tended to idealize the likenesses of the emperors (see illustrations, pp. 76, 84). Portraits on coins also served to glorify the Empire and particular emperors. Equestrian statues, sculptured coffins, or sarcophagi, and the reliefs found on imperial monuments were exceptionally fine works of art. The Romans developed a great fund of decorative motifs, such as cupids, garlands of

The Pantheon, shown in an eighteenth-century painting by the Italian Giovanni Paolo Pannini, is the most impressive surviving example of the Roman dome. It was built by the emperor Hadrian.

flowers, and scrolls of various patterns, which are still used today.

What little Roman painting has been preserved clearly reflects the influence of Hellenistic Greek models. The Romans were particularly skilled in producing floor mosaics—often copies of some Hellenistic painting (see p. 58)—and in painting frescoes. The frescoes still to be seen in Pompeii and elsewhere show that the artist drew the human figure accurately and showed objects in clear though imperfect perspective.

Literary Rome. In literature as in art the Romans turned to the Greeks for their models. Roman epic, dramatic, and lyric poetry forms were usually written in conscious imi-

Roman skill at portraiture is illustrated by the individuality of these busts of various emperors and their families. Augustus, crowned with laurel and somewhat idealized, appears in the foreground.

ed from Hellenistic Greek originals but with many Roman allusions, colloquialisms, and customs added. Plautus' comedies are bawdy and vigorously humorous, and their rollicking plots of illicit love and stock characters of the shrewish wife, henpecked husband, lovelorn youth, clever slave, and swashbuckling soldier reveal the level of culture and taste in early Rome. The works of Plautus suggest many of the types that modern comedy has assumed—the farce, burlesque, and the comedy of manners. From him Shakespeare got ideas for his *Comedy of Errors* and *The Merry Wives of Windsor*.

The Golden Age of Latin literature. Latin literature entered its first great period of creative activity in the first century B.C., when an outpouring of intellectual effort coincided with the last years of the Republic. This period marks the first half of the Golden Age of Latin literature, known as the Ciceronian period because of the stature of Marcus Tullius Cicero (106-43 B.C.), the greatest master of Latin prose and perhaps the outstanding intellectual influence in Roman history.

Acclaimed as the greatest orator of his day, Cicero found time during his busy public life to write extensively on philosophy, political theory, and rhetoric. Some nine hundred of his letters still exist, and these, together with his speeches, give us insight into Cicero's personality, as well as into the problems and manners of republican Rome. Much of the value of Cicero's letters lies in the fact that most were not intended for publication and thus he spoke his mind freely. Cicero also made a rich contribution to knowledge by passing on to later ages much of Greek thought—especially that of Plato and the Stoics—and at the same time interpreting it from the standpoint of a Roman intellectual and practical man of affairs. He did more than any other Roman to make Latin a great literary language.

The Ciceronian period also produced the personal lyrical poetry of Catullus (c. 87-54 B.C.), a young man about town who wrote intensely of his loves and hates:

I hate and love—the why I cannot tell,
But by my tortures know the fact too well.[10]

tation of Greek masterpieces. Hence Latin writing was less creative than Greek, but it remains one of the world's great literatures largely because of its influence upon medieval, Renaissance, and modern culture.

Formal Latin literature did not begin until late in the third century B.C. when a Greek slave named Livius Andronicus translated Homer's *Odyssey* and several Greek plays into Latin. By the end of the same century the first of a series of Latin epics dealing with Rome's past was composed.

The oldest examples of Latin literature to survive intact are the twenty-one comedies of Plautus (c. 254-184 B.C.), which were adapt-

Catullus' contemporary, Lucretius (99-55 B.C.), found in the philosophy of Epicurus an antidote to his profound disillusionment with his fellow citizens who, he wrote, "in their greed of gain . . . amass a fortune out of civil bloodshed: piling wealth on wealth, they heap carnage on carnage. With heartless glee they welcome a brother's tragic death."[11] His long philosophical poem, *On the Nature of Things*, will be discussed later in this chapter.

Augustus provided the Roman world with a stability that was conducive to a further outpouring of literary creativeness. The second phase of the Golden Age of Latin literature, the Augustan Age, was notable particularly for its excellent poetry. Virgil (70-19 B.C.) was probably the greatest of all Roman poets. His masterpiece, a great national epic called the *Aeneid*, glorifies the work of Augustus and eloquently asserts Rome's destiny to conquer and rule the world (see quotation, p. 78). Using Homer's *Iliad* and *Odyssey* as his models, Virgil recounted the fortunes of Aeneas, the legendary founder of the Latin people, who came from his home in Troy to Italy. The *Aeneid* breathes Virgil's deep and enthusiastic patriotism and is as much a piece of imperial symbolism as Rome's triumphal arches.

Horace (65-8 B.C.) was famous for both lyrical odes and satirical verse. Succeeding generations have turned to Horace because of his urbane viewpoint and polished style:

Happy the man, and happy he alone,
He, who can call to-day his own:
He who secure within, can say,
To-morrow do thy worst, for I have lived to-day.[12]

Quite a different sort was Ovid (43 B.C.-17 A.D.), a poet akin to Catullus in spirit and personal life, who combined a predilection for themes on sensual love with first-rate storytelling. In fact, it is largely through his *Metamorphoses*, a collection of Greek stories about the life of the gods, that classical mythology was transmitted to the modern world.

The Silver Age. The literature of the so-called "Silver Age," the period between the deaths of Augustus and Hadrian (14-138 A.D.), substitutes a more critical and negative spirit for the patriotism and optimism of the Augustan Age. Despite a great emphasis upon artificial stylistic devices, the Silver Age was memorable for its moral emphasis (seen in Tacitus, Plutarch, and Seneca) and its brilliant satirical poetry which reached its peak in Juvenal (55?-130 A.D.). This master of poetic invective flayed the shortcomings of contemporary Roman society (see also quotation, p. 79):

Whatever passions have the soul possessed,
Whatever wild desires inflamed the breast
(Joy, Sorrow, Fear, Love, Hatred, Transport, Rage),
Shall form the motley subject of my page.
For when could Satire boast so fair a field?[13]

The writing of history. Two Roman historians produced notable works during the Golden and Silver Ages. The first, Livy (59 B.C.-17 A.D.), was a contemporary of Virgil; his immense *History of Rome*, like the latter's *Aeneid*, is of epic proportions and glorifies Rome's conquests and ancestral ways. By assembling the legends and traditions of early Roman history and welding them into a continuous narrative, Livy, like Virgil, sought to advance Augustus' program of moral and social regeneration. He glorified the virtues of the ancient Romans—their heroism, patriotism, and piety—and sought to draw moral lessons from an idealized past.

Tacitus (55-117 A.D.), like his contemporary Juvenal, was concerned with improving society, but he used history rather than poetry to serve his ends. In his *Germania* Tacitus contrasted the life of the idealized, simple Germanic tribes with the corrupt and immoral existence of the Roman upper classes. In the *Annals* and *Histories* he used his vivid, epigrammatic prose to depict the shortcomings of the emperors and their courts from the death of Augustus to 96 A.D. Some of his brief, trenchant statements have been quoted for centuries; for example, "Tyrants merely procure infamy for themselves and glory for their victims"; "The more corrupt the state, the more numerous the laws"; and (in his description of Roman conquest) "They make a solitude and call it peace." Tacitus suffered from the bias of his own senatorial class; he looked upon the emperors as tyrants and thus could not do justice to the positive contributions of imperial government.

The most famous Greek author in the Empire was Plutarch (46?-120? A.D.). He lectured on philosophy at Rome before retiring to his small hometown to pursue research on the outstanding figures in Roman and Greek history in order to discover what qualities make men great or ignoble. His *Parallel Lives*, containing forty-six biographies of famous Greeks and Romans arranged in pairs for the purpose of comparison, is one of the eminently readable classics of Greek literature. Because many of the sources Plutarch used have been lost, his *Lives* is a mine of invaluable information for the historian.

Stoicism and Epicureanism. The Romans contributed no original philosophical theories, preferring to adapt existing Greek systems of thought to suit their needs. As men of action with grave governmental responsibilities, the Romans paid scant attention to such abstract problems as the nature of the universe and of human knowledge. But the corrupting effects of life in the late Republic on the old Roman virtues and traditions caused thoughtful Romans to be concerned over problems of behavior. As a consequence, they were attracted to the two chief Hellenistic ethical philosophies, Epicureanism and Stoicism.

Epicureanism made its greatest impact during the last days of the Republic, since men found its tenets comforting in a period of political upheaval when no one knew what the morrow would bring. As young men, Virgil and Horace embraced Epicureanism, but Lucretius was the most important Roman interpreter of this philosophy. In his *On the Nature of Things*, Lucretius followed Epicurus (see p. 60) in basing his explanation of the "nature of things" on materialism and atomism. He called on men to free themselves from the superstitious fears of the gods and of death, which were causing them to become converts to the emotional mystery religions of Greece and the East. Lucretius exhorted his readers to "make the most of today," but to seek pleasure in philosophical serenity, rather than in sensuous gratification, and to have no fear of death since souls, like bodies,

are composed of atoms that fall apart when death comes:

What has this bugbear Death to frighten man,
If souls can die, as well as bodies can? . . .
So, when our mortal frame shall be disjoin'd,
The lifeless lump uncoupled from the mind,
From sense of grief and pain we shall be free;
We shall not feel, because we shall not be.[14]

More enduring, especially in the days of the Empire, was the appeal of Stoicism to the Roman ruling classes. It had a humanizing effect on Roman law by introducing such concepts as the law of nature (see p. 82), the brotherhood of men—including slaves—and the view that a man is innocent until proved guilty. The main emphasis of Roman Stoicism was on a just life, constancy to duty, courage in adversity, and service to humanity.

One of the outstanding Roman Stoics was Seneca (4 B.C.-65 A.D.), Nero's tutor and a writer of moral essays and of tragedies meant to be read rather than performed. He was regarded with high favor by the leaders of the early Christian Church, for his Stoicism, like that of the ex-slave Epictetus (d. 135 A.D.) and the emperor Marcus Aurelius, was a kind of religious creed. He stressed an all-wise Providence, or fatherly god, and the immortality of the soul. Seneca occupies an important place in the development of moral theory in Europe because his essays enjoyed a wide reputation among thinkers during the Middle Ages and the Renaissance.

Science in the Roman Empire. The Romans had little scientific curiosity, but by putting the findings of Hellenistic science to practical use, they became masters in engineering, applied medicine, and public health.

The Romans pioneered in public health service and developed the extensive practice of hydrotherapy—the use of mineral baths for healing. Beginning in the early Empire, doctors were employed in infirmaries where soldiers, officials, and the poor could obtain free medical care. Great aqueducts and admirable drainage systems also indicate Roman concern for public health.

Characteristic of their utilitarian approach to science was the Romans' predilection for amassing immense encyclopedias. The most important of these was the *Natural History* compiled by Pliny the Elder (23-79 A.D.), an enthusiastic collector of all kinds of scientific odds and ends. In writing his massive work, Pliny is reputed to have read more than two thousand books. The result is an intriguing mixture of fact and fable thrown together with scarcely any method of classification. Nevertheless, it was the most widely read work on science during the Empire and the early Middle Ages.

Pliny was well aware of the lack of creative scientific activity in his day. "In these glad times of peace," he wrote, "no addition whatever is being made to knowledge by means of original research, and in fact even the discoveries of our predecessors are not being thoroughly studied." To Pliny, the cause of this state of affairs was "blind engrossment with avarice," and he cited this example: ". . . now that every sea has been opened up . . . , an immense multitude goes on voyages—but their object is profit not knowledge."[15] Pliny himself was suffocated by a rain of hot ashes while he was studiously observing the eruption of Mount Vesuvius at Pompeii.

The last great scientific minds of the ancient world were two Greeks, Claudius Ptolemy and Galen, both of whom lived in the second century A.D. Ptolemy resided at Alexandria, where he became celebrated as geographer, astronomer, and mathematician. His maps show a comparatively accurate knowledge of a broad section of the Old World, and he used an excellent projection system (see illustration, p. 367). But he exaggerated the size of Asia, an error which influenced Columbus to underestimate the width of the Atlantic and to set sail from Spain in search of Asia. His work on astronomy, usually called the *Almagest* ("the great work") from the title of the Arabic translation, summed up the geocentric, or earth-centered, view of the universe that was to rule men's minds until the sixteenth century. In mathematics, Ptolemy's work in improving and developing trigonometry became the basis for modern knowledge of the subject.

Born in Pergamum in Asia Minor, Galen was a physician for a school of gladiators. His fame spread and he was called to Rome where he became physician to Marcus Aurelius. Galen was responsible for notable advances in physiology and anatomy; for example, he was the first to explain the mechanism of respiration. Forbidden by the Roman government to dissect human bodies, Galen experimented with animals and demonstrated that an excised heart can continue to beat outside the body and that injuries to one side of the brain produce disorders in the opposite side of the body. The most experimental-minded of ancient physicians, he once wrote: "I confess the disease from which I have suffered all my life—to trust . . . no statements until, so far as possible, I have tested them for myself."[16] His medical encyclopedia, in which he summarized the medical knowledge of antiquity, remained the standard authority until the sixteenth century.

SUMMARY

The story of how Rome rose from an insignificant muddy village along the banks of the Tiber to the mighty ruler of the Mediterranean world will always remain one of the most fascinating stories in world history. Emerging from obscurity about the middle of the eighth century before Christ, the Latin people who clustered about Rome and its seven hills succeeded in 509 B.C. in ousting their Etruscan overlords and establishing a republic. The history of the Roman Republic can be divided into two distinct periods. During the first, from 509 to 133 B.C., two themes are dominant: the gradual democratization of the government and the conquest of the Mediterranean.

By 287 B.C., thanks to the reluctant willingness of the patricians to compromise, the plebeians had succeeded in breaking down the privileged position of the patricians by obtaining recognition of their fundamental rights as citizens and by acquiring a progressively more important share of political power. Having achieved these gains, the rank and file of the citizens allowed the aristocratic Senate to continue exercising full control of the Republic.

The other theme in the early history of the Roman Republic was the conquest of the Mediterranean. Between the years 509 and 270 B.C. the Romans crushed all resistance to their rule in Italy. They then clashed with Carthage, and after a herculean struggle, Carthage surrendered in 201 B.C. Having conquered the West, the Romans found themselves drawn to the East, and by 133 B.C. Macedonia and Greece were ruled by Roman governors, the Seleucid emperor in Asia had been defeated and humbled, and Rome had acquired its first province on the Asian continent. But as the Mediterranean world succumbed to the Roman legions, the Republic itself faced civil war and degeneration.

The second and last period in the history of the Roman Republic, from 133 to 30 B.C., began with the attempts of the Gracchi brothers to persuade the senatorial oligarchy to allow the enactment of necessary reforms, but to no avail. Marius, Sulla, Pompey, and Julius Caesar mark the appearance of one-man rule and the end of the Republic. Augustus, the heir of Caesar, ruled Rome wisely and well. On the surface the old republican institutions, such as the Senate, were preserved, but Augustus wielded the real power in the new government, which is called the early Empire, or Principate. For two hundred years, during the *Pax Romana,* many millions of people in Italy and the Empire's provinces enjoyed peace and prosperity.

Through the Roman achievement of a single empire and a cosmopolitan culture, the Greek legacy was preserved, synthesized, and disseminated—and the Romans were able to make important contributions of their own. The Romans excelled in political theory, governmental administration, and jurisprudence. While the Greeks were individualistic, the Romans put a higher value on conformity, and their essentially conservative and judicious attitude of mind compensated for their lack of creativity. Primarily synthesists rather than innovators, the Romans willingly admitted their cultural indebtedness and by doing so exhibited a magnanimity characteristic of the Roman spirit at its best.

SUGGESTIONS FOR READING

D. H. Lawrence, **Etruscan Places,*** Compass. An enthusiastic appraisal of the Etruscan way of life. See also H. Pallotino, **The Etruscans,*** Penguin; Emeline Richardson, **The Etruscans: Their Art and Civilization,** Univ. of Chicago, 1964. On Rome's other neighbors see B. Warmington, **Carthage,*** Penguin; T. G. E. Powell, **The Celts,** Praeger, 1958.

R. Bloch, **The Origins of Rome,** Praeger, 1960. An examination of the archaeological, historical, and legendary evidence. For an instructive survey of archaeological discovery in Italy, see P. MacKendrick, **The Mute Stones Speak,*** Mentor.

Alexander H. McDonald, **Republican Rome,** Praeger, 1966. See also H. Scullard, **History of the Roman World from 753 to 146 B.C.,** 3rd ed., Methuen, 1969; F. B. Marsh, **History of the Roman World from 146 to 30 B.C.,** 3rd ed., Methuen, 1963.

H. Scullard, **From the Gracchi to Nero,** 2nd ed., Methuen, 1964. The transition from the late Republic to the early Empire. E. Salmon, **History of the Roman World from 30 B.C. to A.D. 138,** 4th ed., Methuen, 1968, details the history of the early Empire.

Recommended special studies: F. E. Adcock, **Roman Political Ideas and Practices,*** Univ. of Mich.; L. Homo, **Roman Political Institutions,** Barnes and Noble, 1962; G. P. Baker, **Hannibal,** Barnes and Noble, 1967; Richard E. Smith, **The Failure of the Roman Republic,** Cambridge, 1955, and **Cicero the Statesman,** Cambridge, 1966; R. Syme, **The Roman Revolution,*** Oxford; G. Ferrero, **The Life of Caesar,*** Norton; Lily R. Taylor, **Party**

Politics in the Age of Caesar,* Univ. of Cal.; J. Buchan, **Augustus,** Verry, 1947; B. W. Henderson, **Five Roman Emperors,** Barnes and Noble, 1969; T. Africa, **Rome of the Caesars,*** Wiley.

D. R. Dudley, **The Civilization of Rome,*** Mentor. An excellent general survey. See also R. Barrow, **The Romans,*** Penguin; M. Grant, **The World of Rome,*** Mentor; H. Mattingly, **Roman Imperial Civilization,** St. Martin, 1957; C. G. Starr, **Civilization and the Caesars,*** Norton.

W. Fowler, **Social Life at Rome in the Age of Cicero,*** St. Martin; S. Dill, **Roman Society from Nero to Marcus Aurelius,*** Meridian; M. Johnston, **Roman Life,** Scott, Foresman, 1957; J. Balsdon, **Roman Women,** Day, 1963; E. R. Pike, **Love in Ancient Rome,** Muller, 1965; H. J. Rose, **Ancient Roman Religion,** Hutchinson, 1958.

Martin L. Clarke, **The Roman Mind: Studies in the History of Thought from Cicero to Marcus Aurelius,** Harvard, 1956; M. Grant, **Roman Literature,*** Penguin; Edith Hamilton, **The Roman Way,*** Norton; G. Highet, **Poets in a Landscape,** Knopf, 1957; M. Wheeler, **Roman Art and Architecture,*** Praeger.

Recommended historical novels: W. Bryher, **The Coin of Carthage,*** Harvest; T. Wilder, **The Ides of March,*** Signet; R. Graves, **I, Claudius,*** Vintage; M. Yourcenar, **Memoirs of Hadrian,*** Noonday.

*Indicates an inexpensive paperbound edition.

Chapter 4

The Asian Way of Life

Ancient India and China to 220 A.D.

INTRODUCTION. Civilization had its genesis in four Afro-Asian regions: Egypt, Mesopotamia, and the valleys of the Indus and the Huang Ho. For some two thousand years these areas charted the path for the onward march of civilization. By 500 B.C. western peoples began to join this procession, making rapid progress in the civilized arts of life; and for a thousand years both great segments of the human race were roughly in equilibrium.

One of the basic themes of world history, therefore, may be called the Afro-Asian strand. The early chapters relating to this theme are largely concerned with the origins, growth, and flowering of the Afro-Asian cultures from the fifth century B.C. to the fifteenth A.D. During their classical period great civilizations emerged in Asia and northern Africa. Imbued with massive political power and economic opulence and graced with cultural magnificence, these civilizations of the East were not only comparable to those of the West, but from time to time, in important respects, superior. Although isolated sub-Saharan Africa suffered from inertia and a certain amount of cultural stagnation during this period, the accomplishments of its peoples were not trivial, and their worth has recently been rediscovered and truly appreciated.

An Indian scholar has written: "All that India can offer to the world proceeds from her philosophy."[1] Indian philosophers have consistently held a fundamental belief in the unity of life—a unity within which has been assimilated and synthesized a variety of beliefs and customs from both native and foreign cultures. Thus a basic concept dominates the life and thought of both ancient and modern India—unity in diversity. India's intricate religious philosophy developed in ancient times, along with a unique social pattern, the caste system.

Whereas religion has dominated the customs and attitudes of India's people, the Chinese have been more humanistic and worldly. Their attitude toward life has led to a concern for natural science, the art of government, the keeping of historical records, and the formulation of down-to-earth ethical standards. But despite the great differences in their cultures, these two Asian nations have much in common. Weighed down by poverty, both can look back to days of ancient glory; striving to direct their own affairs, both can remember foreign conquerors; hemmed in by age-old tradition and custom, both find themselves in a world of nuclear power and space science. The course that these countries follow in the future will inevitably be conditioned by all that they have experienced in the long centuries since their birth.

INDIA: UNITY IN DIVERSITY

Geography of India. We can think of India* as a gigantic triangle, bounded on two sides by ocean and on the third by the mountain wall of the Himalayas. Through the passes to the northwest came the armed conquerors, restless tribes, and merchants and travelers who did much to shape the turbulent history of this land.

For purposes of discussion, the land can be divided into four parts: Baluchistan, Hindustan, the Deccan, and Tamil Land (see map, p. 91). Our interest lies principally in Hindustan, for in the alluvial plain watered by the upper Indus and its tributaries (called the Punjab) and in the territory along the lower Indus (called Sind), India's earliest civilization developed.

In recent years scholars have come to the conclusion that the ancient Near East should not be considered as isolated from the Asian lands to the east. Rather, we should conceive of a "Greater Near East" which extended beyond the Fertile Crescent through Iran and Baluchistan to the Indus valley. By taking this larger western Asian setting as the subject for investigations, archaeologists are discovering significant trade and cultural relationships between Mesopotamia, Iran,

and prehistoric India. Scholars now emphasize that the transition from food gathering to food production, the all-important agricultural revolution, did not emerge independently in India. Food production began in Mesopotamia, then radiating in several directions, diffused eastward across the Iranian plateau into Baluchistan and hence into the Indus valley. In this northwestern area of India the new farming became the economic basis for India's first civilization.

The Indus civilization. How old is the Indus valley culture, the first Indian culture to reach a level of achievement that can be described as civilization? Unknown before 1920 when its remains were first uncovered, its pictographic script could not be read and its historical background was largely conjectured. In 1969, however, Finnish scientists claimed to have deciphered this ancient tongue and to have thereby discovered new insights into the origin of the Hindu caste system. Most scholars date the Indus civilization approximately 2300 to 1800 B.C.

The Indus civilization eventually extended

---

*Until the text deals with the creation of the separate states of India and Pakistan in 1947, the word *India* will refer to the *entire* subcontinent.

some 950 miles along the valley from the Himalayan foothills in the north to the coast, embracing an area estimated to have been twice the size of the Old Kingdom in Egypt and some four times the size of Sumer and Akkad. Harappa and Mohenjo-Daro, the two largest cities that have been excavated, were the political capitals and commercial centers of this region.

The Indus civilization comprised numerous cities and small towns, and although Harappa and Mohenjo-Daro were four hundred miles apart, the Indus River made possible the maintenance of a strictly organized, uniform administration and economy over the large area. In this stretch of territory, containing some three dozen settlement sites, houses were built of uniform-sized baked bricks. The people used stamp-seals, engraved with a uniform script, and a standard system of weights. They cultivated grains, domesticated cattle and sheep, worked metals, made textiles, and carried on trade. There is evidence that considerable trade existed between the Indus cities and those of Sumer. While revealing characteristics typically Indian, the Indus valley civilization was based upon techniques and crafts similar to earlier Sumerian and Egyptian methods, indicating some possible borrowing of culture.

For centuries the people of the Indus valley pursued a meticulously regulated, efficient, but relatively static way of life. At Mohenjo-Daro, however, excavations show clearly the decline of the city in its latter days. Street frontages were no longer strictly observed, the brickwork was becoming shoddy, and residential areas were degenerating into slums. Finally, groups of skeletons huddled together in their dwellings suggest that this city and perhaps the civilization came to a sudden end. We can only speculate on what great disaster—a plague or a flood, perhaps—may have overtaken these people.

The Aryan invasions. About 1500 B.C. a group of Aryans migrating from the shores of the Black and Caspian seas began to invade India, coming into conflict with the native Dravidians, described as a short, dark people. In a few hundred years the Aryans conquered and settled the upper Indus valley and began penetrating the Ganges region. A tall people with fair skins and long heads, the Aryans fought readily and knew neither writing nor city life. The number of cattle a man owned was the measure of his wealth, and the word for war meant "a desire for more cows." Each tribe was headed by a rajah, women had a high social status, and marriage was monogamous and confined to the group.

Overcome by the storm of invasion from the north, the native Dravidians were enslaved or driven southward, much as the North American Indians were pushed back by the pioneers. As time passed, the Aryans contemptuously referred to the people they conquered as *Dasyu*, or slaves. The *Dasyu*, however, possessed a culture superior in some respects to that of the Aryans; and the invaders borrowed many customs and ideas from the conquered people, including their system of land tenure and taxation and their

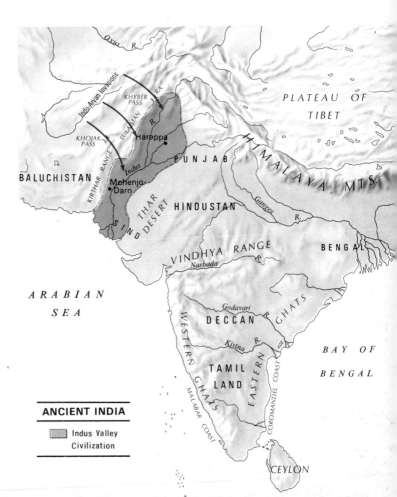

ANCIENT INDIA

Indus Valley Civilization

village community. The native people of India also influenced the development of the Indo-Aryan tongue, Sanskrit.

Early Vedic Age (c. 1500-900 B.C.). Aside from the rajah, his tribal assembly, and the common tribesmen, there were few social gradations in the Aryan tribal structure prior to the invasion of India. In the process of subjugating and settling among the dark-skinned natives, the Aryans realized that they would be absorbed racially unless they took steps to prohibit intermarriage. Class division now took on a new purpose—that of preserving purity of race. This concept is intrinsic in the Vedic Sanskrit word for class, *varna*, which means "color." (It was translated later by Portuguese travelers as *casta*, from the Latin *castus*, meaning "pure"; hence, the term *caste*.)

The oldest examples of Sanskrit literature are the *Vedas*, collections of hymns, epic chants, and ritual formulas. The earliest—the *Rig-Veda*—reflects the events, religious beliefs, and heroic interests of the period of Aryan conquest. The *Vedas* also show that after the conquest the invaders in time settled down to village life and agricultural pursuits. In many ways village life was simi-lar to that of modern India, although complexities of later Indian life such as the restriction of women's rights and the prohibition against eating cattle did not exist at this time. The most important figure of the village was the headman, sometimes elected and at other times holding his position by hereditary right. The village was composed of a group of families, and the villagers worked as farmers or artisans or both.

Later Vedic Age (c. 900-500 B.C.). About the beginning of the ninth century B.C., the center of power and culture shifted eastward from the upper Indus valley to the upper Ganges valley. There the Aryans created small, isolated city-states, each sovereign unto itself. The epic poems describing these times tell of constant warfare and shifting military alliances among the city-states.

The cities of the Later Vedic Age were surrounded by moats and walls, and their streets were well planned. Usually occupying a palace located at the center of a city, the rajah possessed powers greater than those of the village headman of the Early Vedic Age. He had his own retinue of followers and was advised by a royal council com-

Excavations at Mohenjo-Daro have unearthed mother-goddess figurines and seals which may have had religious significance. The seals bear Indus writing, essentially a pictographic script employing about 250 symbols and 400 characters, which is still undeciphered. Such seals have been found along the Iranian plateau trade routes and on an island in the Persian Gulf, indicating that trade existed between the Indus civilization and western civilizations. This seven-inch-high statue of a man also suggests contacts between the Mesopotamian and Indus valley civilizations because of its heavy beard, a common feature of contemporaneous Sumerian sculpture.

posed of his relatives and nobles. He received taxes and was probably, in theory at least, the owner of all land. In cities a tradesman class existed, and unskilled, menial tasks were performed by slaves. Trade contacts with Mesopotamia were renewed during this period, and merchants may have brought back from the West the use of coinage and the notion of an alphabetic system of writing that was eventually adapted to Sanskrit.

The village, caste, and family. In the Later Vedic period the three pillars of traditional Indian society—the autonomous village, caste, and the joint-family—were established. India has always been primarily agricultural, and its countryside is still a patchwork of thousands of villages. As we mentioned, the village in early times was made up of family groups who possessed certain rights and duties and were governed by the headman. An elected council of villagers, on which women were allowed to serve, distributed the land and collected taxes. Villages within a city-state enjoyed considerable autonomy, with the rajah's government hardly interfering at all as long as it received its quota of taxes. This system of self-governing villages continued until government became more centralized under British rule.

If the earliest caste division had been inaugurated to separate the Aryans from the *Dasyu*, by the Later Vedic period caste became more sharply defined and complex as the Aryans themselves split into castes. The four castes recognized at this time were ultimately ranked: (1) the Brahmins, or priests; (2) the Kshatriyas, or warriors; (3) the Vaisyas, or traders, merchants, and bankers; and (4) the Sudras, or farm workers and serfs. In addition there was a group of outcastes, or Pariahs, called "untouchables" because their touch was considered defiling to the upper castes. The non-Aryan population remained at the bottom of the social scale, as Sudras and outcastes.

At first the Kshatriyas had a higher social rank than the Brahmins; but as time went on, warfare declined while religion increased in importance. As educators, historians, and intermediaries between the gods and men, the priests assumed the dominant position which they have successfully maintained into the twentieth century. Eventually the four castes were subdivided into thousands of groups with special social, occupational, and religious significance. The definition and order of importance of the four castes have remained much the same, however, throughout India's history.

The third pillar of Indian society was the joint-family. "Joint in food, worship, and estate," the family was made up of descendants of a common ancestor. The joint-family was governed by the patriarch during his lifetime; after his death, authority was transferred to the eldest son. All males of the group had to be consulted on serious matters, since the property belonged to the family as a whole. Everything earned by individuals in the group went into a common fund, from which was drawn what was needed to supply each member. It was possible for a man to acquire property and to live in his own residence, but he had to show that his holdings had been obtained without use of the family patrimony.

The joint-family was not only a cooperative economic unit but also a powerful instrument for social cohesion. It encouraged a strong family life in which the individual was made to feel his subordination to the group. Marriage was all-important in protecting family ties, and the individual member's desires were considered less important than the family's interests. For thousands of years the joint-family concept dominated the socioeconomic life of the large majority of India's people.

The emphasis placed on the interests and security of the group rather than on the individual is a common denominator of the three pillars of Indian society—the autonomous village, the caste system, and the joint-family. Thus Indian society has always been concerned with stability rather than with progress in the western sense, and the individual Indian has tended to acquire a more passive outlook toward life than his western counterpart. This traditional emphasis upon the group also helps explain the socialistic approach of Nehru and his successors toward contemporary economic and social issues.

Language and literature. The Aryans were part of the huge Indo-European linguistic group and therefore bequeathed to India a language related to Persian, Greek, Latin, and most modern European languages, including English. The various dialects of the invading bands, mixed with the speech of the natives, developed into Sanskrit. By the fourth century B.C. Sanskrit had evolved in such a fashion that the vernacular differed from the traditional Sanskrit of the priests and bards. The chief modern Indian language, Hindi, is derived from the speech of this period.

After the composition of the *Vedas*, which passed orally from generation to generation, a series of prose commentaries on them were produced, including the famous *Upanishads* ("session," at which a teacher gave instruction). Written between 800 and 600 B.C., the *Upanishads* extend and replace the old Vedic concepts with profound speculations about the ultimate truths of life.

A different, and originally secular, Indian tradition produced two great epic poems. The *Mahabharata*, similar to the Greek *Iliad*, glorifies the Kshatriyan, or warrior, caste, as it recounts the struggle between two Aryan tribes. The most famous section of the *Mahabharata* is a philosophical poem called the *Bhagavad-Gita (The Lord's Song)*, which emphasizes that men must never shirk their duty or fear death. Some modern Indians have found in this ancient poem a justification for righteous warfare; others, notably Gandhi, have used it to support nonviolence and passive resistance.

The other magnificent epic, the *Ramayana*, has been likened to the Greek *Odyssey* because it tells of a hero's wanderings and his faithful wife's long vigil. Where the *Mahabharata* is a vigorous glorification of war and adventure, the *Ramayana* shows the growth of chivalric ideals among the Aryans. Both epics have provided all subsequent Indian literature with a vast supply of stories.

Religion in India. The power of religion in Indian life has always been extraordinarily strong. From this ancient land have come some of the most novel and complex religious ideas. These concepts constitute one of India's unique contributions to world civilization. Its religious values and philosophical tradition were not fully known to western scholars until the late eighteenth and mid-nineteenth century, when the *Rig-Veda* and the *Bhagavad-Gita* were translated into English by Max Muller and Sir Edwin Arnold. Throughout the nineteenth century Hindu philosophical and spiritual thought intrigued numerous western literary and intellectual figures, such as Thoreau, Emerson, Goethe, Wordsworth, and Tolstoi; and the founding of the famous Theosophical Society in the 1870's was a mark of the wide appreciation of the Hindu spiritual tradition.

What was to become one of the world's most complex religious and philosophical systems, touching upon all facets of life, had

The Kailasa Temple at Ellora, the largest and most elaborate of the Indian temples carved out of solid rock, contains intricate carvings of incidents and characters from the great epics, the *Mahabharata* and the *Ramayana*.

the most simple beginnings. The early Aryans had unsophisticated religious views; they worshiped various gods with sacrificial rites. The most popular deity was Indra, a boisterous god who wielded the thunderbolt, ate bulls by the score, and quaffed lakes of wine. The earliest Vedic philosophy was not complicated. After death the human soul experienced either eternal punishment or everlasting bliss. Gradually, however, there evolved the idea that Something existed beyond the everyday acts of both gods and men, Something which underlay all life, a Moral Law governing even the gods themselves. The *Vedas* show the evolution of Indian religion from a simple belief in many gods toward a complete pantheism, a conception of the universe and everything in it as God.

The Upanishads: core of Indian theology. The pantheistic conception was subsequently developed with great subtlety in the *Upanishads*, which form the core of all subsequent Indian religious thought and are the foundation on which Hinduism was built. The main teachings of the *Upanishads* may be summarized as follows:

1) Brahman is the Absolute, the eternal universal essence, the all-pervading force permeating the universe.

2) As part of this world force is its Atman, the Universal Soul, to which all individuals belong.

3) As individual souls living in a world of the senses, we think we exist apart from the One Soul—but this is *maya*, or illusion. As long as individuals exist in this world, they are kept from the desired goal of absorption into the Absolute, into Brahman.

4) While living in this state of illusion, of separateness from the One Soul, the individual places his faith in things that are meaningless, transitory, and unsatisfying. As long as such earthly goals as pride, power, and material success are sought, the result must be pain and sorrow. Deliverance and emancipation can only be attained by *moksha*, the ultimate absorption and loss of self into Brahman. The essence of *Upanishadic* thought is escape from illusion.

5) This release from the meaningless state of earthly existence and its attendant *maya* is part of a cosmic and complicated process of reincarnation. The individual soul must go through a long series of wanderings— of earthly reincarnations from one body to another. A man's status at any particular point in time is not the result of fortuitous lot but depends on his soul's actions in previous existences.

6) Gradually Hinduism gave the caste system a religious significance by linking it to the process of reincarnation. In effect, caste became the essential machinery for the educative process of the soul as it went through the infinitely long succession of rebirths from the lowest categories in caste to that of the Brahmin, who presumably is near the end of the cycle.

7) *Karma* is the inexorable law of caste and salvation. A man must accept whatever caste he is born into. There is no favoritism in the universe, for a man brings his *karma* into the world and everything that happens to him springs from this fact. "Just as he acts, just as he behaves, so he becomes." If and as long as *karma* is defied, the soul is condemned to an infinite number of earthly existences and denied escape from the sufferings of *maya*. Central to *Upanishadic* teaching is the belief that death is only a single, essential incident in the foreordained cycle of rebirth. In the *Bhagavad-Gita* the Lord loftily proclaims:

Just as a man, having cast off old garments, puts on other, new ones, even so does the embodied one, having cast off old bodies, take on other, new ones.[2]

Hinduism: a religious synthesis. The philosophy of the *Upanishads* permeates Hinduism. Although the main tenets of Hinduism can be summarized, as in the preceding section, it has been said that Hinduism is less a religion than a way of life because it possesses no canon, such as the Bible or the Koran, no single personal founder, such as Christ or Muhammad, and no precise body of authoritative doctrine of belief.

In time literally thousands of deities, demigods, and lesser spirits came to be added to Indra and the early Aryan gods, forming the Hindu pantheon. Early Aryan and Dravidian gods merged, evolved, and acquired new characteristics and new names for many centuries. In this process of evolution any god accepted by Hinduism became identified with the central Reality. Hindus, therefore, do not think of their religion as polytheistic, for all gods and various spirits are manifestations of the Absolute Reality, Brahman, which pervades everything.

Gradually Hinduism acquired a trinity consisting of Brahma, the creator; Vishnu, the preserver; and Shiva, the destroyer. These names and others have often been used interchangeably for the Absolute Reality. In popular worship Vishnu and Shiva achieved special importance, a position they continue to maintain. Vishnu is a benevolent deity, working continually for the welfare of the world; his followers believe that he has appeared in some ten incarnations to save the world from disaster. The other great god, Shiva, personifies the Life Force and is worshiped as embodying power, in both its constructive and destructive aspects. Some representations portray Shiva in terrifying guise, garlanded with skulls; others show him as the Lord of Dancers, whose activities are the source of all movement within the cosmos. Although the basic teachings of the *Upanishads* remained constant, Hinduism from its earliest origins exhibited an unusual organic quality of growth and adaptation (see Chapter 7).

The simplicity of Gautama Buddha. During the time of the later *Vedas* and the *Upanishads* (900-500 B.C.), religious rites were supervised by the Brahmins. They kept strict control over the people and stressed religious ceremonies, costly sacrifices, and the passive acceptance of Brahmin dogmas. But many individuals criticized or even rejected Brahminic caste requirements and claims for special prerogative. Some would-be religious reformers sought to make the goals of *Upanishadic* thought available without priestly apparatus and sacrificial ritual. None did this more simply and effectively than Gautama, who became the Buddha ("The Enlightened One"). The Buddha (563?-483 B.C.) stands out as one of the most profound influences in the history of mankind because of two principal factors: the beauty and simplicity of his own life and the philo-

sophical depth and ethical purity of his teaching.

Gautama was the son of the ruler of a kingdom located at the foot of the Himalayas. As a privileged youth, he led a happy life and married his beautiful cousin, who bore him a son. One day, according to traditional Indian literature, Gautama was deeply shocked by the misery, disease, and sorrow that he saw as he walked through the streets of his native city. The happiness that his wife and son offered him only made the world's suffering appear more unbearable by contrast. He determined to abandon palace life and seek an answer to his questions about life and death in the outside world. For seven years he dwelt in a forest, practicing the self-mortification rites of the ascetics he found there. Gautama almost died from fasting and self-torture and at last concluded that these practices did not lead to wisdom.

One day, while sitting beneath a large tree meditating on the problem of human suffering, he received "enlightenment." From this insight, he constructed a religious philosophy that has affected the lives of millions of people for 2500 years. He soon attracted disciples, the most devoted being the faithful Ananda, who occupies the same position in Buddhist stories as the disciple John in the New Testament. Dressed always in a simple yellow robe, with begging bowl in hand, the Buddha wandered through the plains of the Ganges, preaching to the villagers who flocked to hear him. He spoke with everyone, regardless of caste, and, like Jesus, who congregated with sinners and publicans instead of the "respectable" Pharisees, the Buddha would decline the sumptuous banquets of nobles to partake of the simple hospitality of peasants and social outcasts.

At last, when eighty years old and enfeebled by his constant travels, the Buddha was invited by a poor blacksmith to a meal. According to legend, the food was tainted, but Gautama ate it rather than offend his host, although he forbade his disciples to follow his example. Later in the day the Buddha was taken with severe pains, and he knew death was near. Calling his disciples together, he bade them farewell. Ananda burst into tears, and the master gently reproved him, saying, "Enough, Ananda! Do not let yourself be troubled; do not weep!"

Buddhist teachings. The fundamental teachings of the Buddha, briefly stated, consist of the Four Noble Truths, which were revealed to the Buddha in the Great Enlightenment:

"1. 'the truth of pain,' as manifest in 'birth, old age, sickness, death, sorrow, lamentation, dejection, and despair';

"2. 'the truth of the cause of pain,' viz., craving for existence, passion, pleasure, leading to rebirth;

"3. 'the truth of cessation of pain,' by ceasing of craving, by renunciation; and

"4. 'the truth of the way that leads to the cessation of pain,' viz., the Middle Path, which is the Eight-fold Path consisting of 'right views, intention, speech, action, livelihood, effort, mindfulness, and concentration.'"[3]

In addition to these teachings, the Buddha set forth certain moral injunctions: not to kill, not to steal, not to speak falsely, not to be unchaste, and not to drink intoxicating liquors. Nonviolence and respect for all life were strongly enjoined.

Buddhism should not be thought of as a completely new religion, for its founder's teachings were aimed at reforming an existing system, not at completely repudiating it. Buddhist and *Upanishadic* philosophies, though, differ in important aspects. Gautama taught that a man's caste, whether Brahmin or Sudra, had no bearing on his spiritual stature. Only by living the true philosophy could one win deliverance from illusion (*maya*). Nor was the Buddha interested in rituals or ceremonies or priestly mediation between gods and man. As a consequence, Buddhism (unlike Hinduism) has no trinity, nor does it even postulate the existence of a God or First Cause. When the whole cosmos attains its ideal state, all beings will be in perfect harmony.

According to the Buddha, the individual cannot hope to attain an ideal state so long as he remains attached by transitory desires to the wheel of birth and rebirth. Reincarnation is a necessary doctrine in Buddhism, for only by repeated lives can the individual come to realize that the world of the senses is but a spiritual illusion. Once this is learned, the path by which sorrow is removed opens to the seeker. The strict rules of the Eightfold Path will free him from the bondage of rebirth and make possible a reabsorption into the Universal Soul, the "slipping of the dewdrip into the Silent Sea"—the entry into *nirvana*. And unlike Hinduism, the process of rebirth could be long or short, depending upon the degree of morality of an individual's everyday life. Man, therefore, was essentially a free agent despite *karma*.

What is *nirvana*? Does it constitute the total annihilation of the individual or rather the end of the illusion of separateness from the One Soul? According to one Indian scholar, "*nirvana* is incommunicable, for the Infinite cannot be described by finite words. The utmost that we can do is to throw some light on it by recourse to negative terms. *Nirvana* is the final result of the extinction of the desire or thirst for rebirth . . . it is the incomparable and highest goal . . . [The] Buddha purposely discouraged questions about the reabsorption of the individual soul, as being of no practical value in the quest for salvation."[4]

A temple wall painting shows the many-armed Hindu god Shiva as the Lord of the Dancers. In his hands he holds symbols of the various aspects of his divine power.

The Buddha and later Buddhism. The Buddha reformed Indian religion. He censured the rites and dogmas of Brahmins, broke with the rules of caste, taught that all men are equal, and gave the world a code of morals whose purity is universally recognized. He founded orders of monks, and the monasteries gradually developed into important academic centers. During his lifetime his teachings were disseminated through central India. The beauty and nobility of his thought can be appreciated from the following excerpts from Buddhist literature:

Hatred does not cease by hatred at any time; hatred ceases by love.

All men trouble at punishment, all men love life. Remember that you are like unto them, and do not cause slaughter.

Not by birth does one become an outcaste, not by birth does one become a Brahmin. By deeds one becomes an outcaste, by deeds one becomes a Brahmin.[5]

Though the Buddha was a reformer, after his death many of the evils that he had attacked crept, ironically enough, into Buddhism itself. In spite of Buddha's denigration and rejection of deities, in time men prayed to him as a god who could assure their salvation. Subsequently his teachings were elaborated into metaphysical beliefs, and Buddhism in its new form spread throughout eastern Asia.

INDIA UNDER THE MAURYAS AND THE KUSHANS

Alexander the Great in India. By the sixth century B.C. nearly a score of royal states or tribal republics had been established in northern India. Of these the most important was Magadha (see map, p. 99), along the lower Ganges. In 326 B.C. Alexander of Macedon, continuing his conquest of the former Persian empire (see p. 57), brought his phalanxes into the easternmost Persian satrapy in the Indus valley, defeating local Punjab rulers. He turned back from a contemplated attack into the Ganges valley be-cause of the near mutiny of his travel-weary troops. After Alexander died, the empire he had built in such meteoric fashion quickly disintegrated; by 321 B.C. his domain in the Punjab had completely disappeared. But from the towns he had founded in Bactria, beyond the northwest passes, were to come important Hellenistic influences on India in later times.

Chandragupta Maurya. By 322 B.C. a new era was at hand for India. In that year Chandragupta Maurya, who apparently had served as a Magadhan soldier, gathered an army and seized the Magadha state from an unpopular sovereign. In the next twenty-four years Chandragupta conquered much of north India and founded the Maurya dynasty, which endured until about 185 B.C.

The emergence of this Mauryan empire stemmed from three significant factors. First, by the sixth century B.C. important advances in agriculture, trade, and general prosperity in north India led to the emergence of a new merchant class whose interests were menaced by constant feuds and wars between numerous petty kingdoms. This middle class sought law and order and naturally favored the creation of large stable governments. Second, Alexander's invasion had broken the power of numerous small kingdoms, leaving behind a debris of weakness and confusion. Into this vacuum intruded the third factor: a new type of ruler who by force and craft created the "new kingship in India."

Chandragupta may be considered the first emperor of India, even though his power did not extend to the southern regions of the subcontinent. The Magadhan maintained contacts with the Greeks after he became emperor and fostered a friendly exchange of information between the Seleucid empire and his own. He lived in great splendor; his court included Greek courtiers and was run according to Persian ceremonial, factors which scarcely endeared him to his Indian subjects. So great was the danger of conspiracy that Chandragupta lived in strict seclusion, surrounded by a bodyguard of women who cooked his food, served his wine, and in the evening lulled him to sleep with music.

Life in the Mauryan empire. In its structure and the hierarchy of administrative divisions, the Mauryan empire was remarkably advanced. It was divided into a small number of provinces, each governed by a viceroy and a staff of officials. The emperor was not limited by any law, and the central government maintained a tight rein over the distant provinces. Over all, there were some thirty imperial departments overseeing such affairs as markets, canal irrigation, public works, and revenues. The municipal organization of the capital was amazingly comprehensive. Comprising six boards, it provided for the treatment of foreigners, birth and death statistics, retail trade, manufacturing, and the collection of a sales tax. Excellent roads connected the many villages and towns; and a postal service was maintained by royal couriers.

Practically the only work on statecraft in India that has survived from ancient times is the *Arthasastra*, written by Chandragupta's able chief minister, Kautilya. From this book we learn that justice was dispensed sternly but fairly in both civil and criminal cases. Under the supervision of a well-organized war office, the large army was fed, trained, and led. Apparently like the later Renaissance Italian author on statecraft, Machiavelli, Kautilya believed in deception or unscrupulous means to attain any desired end. The *Arthasastra* comments that "intrigue, spies, winning over the enemy's people, siege and assault" are the five means of capturing a fort. The main pillar of the government was the pervasive and dreaded secret service, which employed a large number of spies.

All land belonged to the state, and agriculture was the chief source of wealth. Irrigation and crop rotation were practiced, and famines were almost unknown. Trade was cosmopolitan; in the bazaars of Pataliputra, the splendid capital city known today as Patna, were displayed goods from southern India, China, Mesopotamia, and Asia Minor. Indian ships sailed the Indian Ocean to the head of the Persian Gulf and to Arabia, and from these points caravans carried Indian goods overland toward markets as distant as the cities of Greece. Manufactur-

ing was also important in the Mauryan empire. Greek accounts refer to the making of arms and agricultural implements and the building of ships; northwestern India was famous for cotton cloth and silk yarn.

About 297 B.C. Chandragputa was succeeded by his son Bindusara. A charming story about Bindusara indicates the close cultural relations which existed at this time between the Mauryan and Seleucid rulers. Writing to Antiochus, Bindusara asked for a sample of Greek wine, some raisins, and a Sophist. In his reply Antiochus stated that he was sending the wine with pleasure, but that "it isn't good form among the Greeks to trade in philosophers."[6]

Ashoka, propagator of Buddhism. Ashoka, a son of Bindusara, reigned from 273 B.C. to 232 B.C. He was one of the few early kings who pursued the arts of peace more diligently than the arts of war; his first military campaign was also his last.

In 262 B.C. Ashoka attacked the state of Ka-

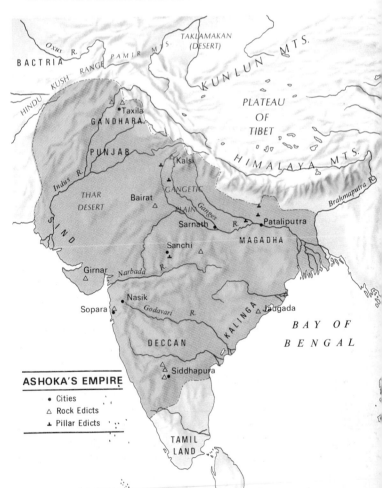

linga to the south, whose inhabitants stubbornly resisted his invasion. In the war of extermination that followed, victory fell to Ashoka, and at least 200,000 Kalingans were killed or captured. Thus Ashoka extended the Mauryan empire so that it included nearly all of India into the northern area of Tamil Land (see map, p. 99). But the cruelty of the campaign horrified him, and he resolved never again to permit such acts of butchery. Soon after this war, Ashoka was converted to Buddhism, whose gentle teachings increased his aversion to warfare.

As the years passed, Ashoka became even more deeply religious. Throughout his empire he had his imperial edicts carved on rocks and stone pillars. Some of the latter still stand today. These huge, polished sandstone pillars, thirty to forty feet high, together with a series of Rock Edicts, give little or no information concerning political events, but their inscriptions are invaluable for appreciating the spirit and purpose of Ashokan rule. Stressing compassion, kindness to all living things, truth, purity, and liberality, the edicts were a practical application of the teachings of Buddha. The inscriptions on Ashoka's pillars show not only that the art of calligraphy was highly developed but also that writing was commonly used for practical purposes throughout the empire.

Although a devout Buddhist, Ashoka believed in complete religious toleration; he did not persecute the Brahmins, who upheld Hindu tradition. A strong believer in the doctrine of *ahimsā*, or noninjury to men or animals, he forbade the sacrifice of animals in the capital, substituted royal pilgrimages to Buddhist shrines for hunting expeditions, and did away almost entirely with the slaughter of animals for meat at the palace. Ashoka ate no meat himself and probably encouraged vegetarianism among his subjects.

Termed "the first royal patron of Buddhism," Ashoka has been likened to St. Paul and Constantine—a successful propagator of his faith. Ashoka sent Buddhist missionaries to many lands—the Himalayan regions, the Tamil kingdoms, Ceylon, Burma, and even as far away as Syria, Egypt, and Macedonia—to teach the gospel of salvation and equality. Thus transformed from a small Indian sect to a powerful religion, Buddhism began to make its influence felt beyond its homeland. Ashoka's missionary efforts had enduring success in neighboring Asian lands, particularly in Ceylon, where Buddhism is found today in nearly its original form.

Fall of the Mauryan empire. Almost immediately after Ashoka's death in 232 B.C., the Mauryan empire began to disintegrate. The last emperor was assassinated in 185 B.C., and the state was then invaded by a ruler from southern India and also by Demetrius, the fourth Bactrian king (see p. 62), who overran the Punjab in northwest India.

Although the Mauryan state had once been powerful, it crumbled almost overnight. So dramatic was the collapse and so grave the consequences that, like the decline and fall of the Roman empire, it has provoked much scholarly speculation. Whatever the reasons for the fall of the Mauryan empire, its contribution to world civilization survived, for "the moral ascendancy of Indian culture over a large part of the civilized world, which Ashoka was mainly instrumental in bringing about, remained for centuries as a monument to . . . [India's] glory. . . ."[7]

The Graeco-Bactrian kingdom. When Demetrius invaded India, he occupied Gandhara (see map, p. 99), whose inhabitants had been converted to Buddhism by Ashoka. The Bactrians organized the chief Gandharan town as a Hellenistic city and even fashioned an acropolis there. Demetrius also acquired Taxila (an administrative center of the Mauryan empire) and Pataliputra, the Mauryan capital. Thus he ruled an area stretching from the Persian desert to the middle of the Ganges valley.

Demetrius organized his domain much as a Seleucid kingdom. In keeping with Alexander's ideal of bringing East and West together on a basis of equality, Demetrius issued a bilingual coinage bearing Greek inscriptions on one side and Indian on the other. "His realm was to be a partnership of Greek and Indian. He was not to be a Greek king of Indian subjects, but an Indian king no less than a Greek one, head of both races."[8]

During the period of the Graeco-Bactrian kingdom, a prolific Graeco-Roman Buddhist school of art evolved from the fusion of Greek and Buddhist elements in Gandhara. Because of the Buddha's prohibitions against idolatry, artists had for centuries refrained from portraying the Buddha in human form, depicting instead only symbols of his life and teaching. In the capital from one of Ashoka's pillars, for example, the lion suggests Buddha's majesty and power while the wheel below is the Wheel of Law which was set in motion through his teachings. With the growth of the *Mahayana* school, however, artists began to create figures of the Buddha. Dating from the fifth century A.D., the head of Buddha from Gandhara shows Hellenistic influence in the modeling of the features and hair, while the elongated ear lobes, heavy-lidded eyes, mark on the forehead, knot of hair, and expression of deep repose are Indian. Eventually the *Mahayana* school of Buddhism and Graeco-Roman Buddhist art spread together throughout eastern Asia.

His general, Menander, who subsequently ascended the throne, continued the concept of partnership. Whereas in the West the Seleucid rulers had endeavored to create a basically Greek empire filled with Greek settlements, it was not possible to found Greek cities on any such scale in India. Thus Menander's kingdom was essentially Indian with a small Greek ruling class. The kingdom of Bactria attained a high state of culture before being crushed by the nomadic tribes that swept out of Central Asia about the close of the second century B.C.

The Kushan empire. A turbulent period followed the fall of the Bactrian kingdom. But by the first century A.D. the most important of the invading clans, the Kushans, had established themselves as masters of a large part of northwestern India and had founded another of the great empires in Indian history.

Kanishka, the most outstanding of the Kushan rulers, became king sometime between 78 and 128 A.D. (probably closer to the former date). All of northwest India, perhaps as far south as the Narbada River, and much of present Afghanistan to the north were under his sway. This enlightened monarch took over the civilization of the people he conquered. During his reign the arts and sciences flourished, imposing buildings were constructed, and advances were made in the field of medicine.

Mahayana and Hinayana Buddhism. Whereas Gautama Buddha had concerned himself primarily with the removal of individual suffering through a life of purity and self-denial, later Buddhists added to this central doctrine more emotional and less purely philosophical concepts, together with myths and rituals. By the time of Kanishka this less austere approach with its great mass appeal had aroused the opposition of many Buddhists, who viewed it as a corruption of the original Buddhism.

In an effort to heal the growing split in Buddhism, Kanishka convened a great council of five hundred monks. But unity was not restored, and henceforth two major forms of Buddhism flourished: the more popular *Mahayana*, or "Great Vehicle," and the more orthodox *Hinayana*, or "Lesser Vehicle." The *Mahayanists* viewed the Buddha as a Bodhisattva, an exalted being who renounced *nirvana* in order to save mankind, and they claimed that their doctrine, less rigorous and more easily adapted to the needs of the common man, was the great vehicle by which enlightenment might be more easily achieved. With its message of hope and salvation for the masses, *Mahayana* Buddhism spread rapidly along the trade routes to Nepal, Tibet, China, Korea, and Japan. The *Hinayana*—which remained primarily an ethical philosophy, austere and rational— became the southern branch of Buddhism, spreading from India and Ceylon to Burma, Thailand, Cambodia, Vietnam, the Malay peninsula, and Indonesia.

Like Ashoka, Kanishka was a Buddhist convert who was instrumental in helping make Buddhism a world religion. Hinduism, however, still had a strong hold on the Indian people. While the Buddhists had disregarded caste and accepted both the Greeks and the Kushans, the Hindus rejected the foreign invaders as outcastes. Gradually, the Indians came to consider Hinduism a more characteristically Indian movement than Buddhism. Therefore, although Kanishka helped spread Buddhism to other countries, in the long run his support probably lessened its popularity within India.

Trade with the West. At the tip of the Indian peninsula lay the Tamil country, peopled by Dravidians who had long been absorbing elements of Hindu culture from the lands to the north. These states enjoyed commercial ties with the Hellenistic Greeks, particularly those in Egypt, and the vigor of the commercial contact is shown by some interesting examples of linguistic influences: the Hebrew term for peacock and the Greek words for ginger, cinnamon, and rice come from the Tamil language.

In Roman times trade with the Tamil kingdoms and that with the Kushans expanded. When Augustus became head of the Roman world, the Kushan and Tamil rulers sent him congratulatory embassies, an honor never before paid a western prince. The ambassadors took about four years en route and bore such gifts as "a gigantic python, huge tortoises, and an armless boy who could shoot arrows and throw darts with his feet!" In the period from Augustus' rule to the reign of the first Constantine, at least nine other embassies from India visited the Roman emperors to arrange for the protection and well-being of Indian ships and traders at Roman ports.

Roman merchants dwelt in Tamil seaports, and through them precious metals, coins, wine, pottery, glassware, silverware, and even craftsmen and masons were brought to India. Tamil poets described Roman ships that carried a guard of archers to ward off pirates, while the Tamil kings themselves employed bodyguards of Roman soldiers, whose habit of wearing long coats aroused much comment in a land where comparative nudity was the rule. For its part, India was exporting drugs, pearls, silks, muslins, and spices. In view of the magnitude of the Roman-Indian trade, we can understand why Ptolemy showed considerable knowledge of the geography of India (see illustration, p. 367).

Soon after 220 A.D. the Kushan empire collapsed, and northern and central India entered a chaotic period. In Chapter 7 we will continue the story of India. Now let us trace the development of civilization in the secluded land of China.

CHINA: THE FORMATIVE CENTURIES

The checkerboard land. Chinese civilization arose and developed in a vast land of over four million square miles which was for centuries almost completely isolated from the other centers of civilization by mountains, deserts, and ocean. This isolation helps explain the great originality of China's culture. For example, of all the world's writing systems today, only the Chinese and its derivatives are not based ultimately on the alphabet developed in West Asia.

Geographically, China looks like a vast checkerboard divided by mountain ranges and river systems. Two mountain chains cross the country from southwest to northeast, and three more extend from west to east, forming three great river valleys. The Yellow River (Huang Ho), traditionally known as China's Sorrow because of the misery caused by its periodic flooding, traverses the North China Plain; here was the original homeland of Chinese culture. This valley was eventually superseded by the Yangtze River valley in Central China as the most important economic and cultural region. The shorter rivers and valleys converging on present-day Canton form the third major river system.

These rivers were of crucial importance in the development of Chinese civilization. They provided water for irrigation and served as a cheap and efficient transportation system. As in Egypt, the beginning of political organization was linked with geography: governing bodies were needed to construct and control irrigation systems and to prevent ruinous flooding. The complex system of mountain ranges and river systems has, throughout China's history, created problems of political and military unity. At the same time, the great river valleys were suited to the growth of a homogeneous civilization extending over a greater land area than any other culture in the world.

The Shang dynasty: China enters history. The first Chinese state for which we possess written historical evidence, the Shang dynasty, flourished in the region of An-yang, a site in the Yellow River valley, from about 1500 to 1027 B.C. An-yang was a crossroads of influence from North and Southeast Asia as well as from West Asia and had long been a culture center. The remarkably advanced Shang civilization was distinguished from its predecessors by three important developments: bronze metallurgy, a writing system, and the emergence of a state organization in an urban environment.

Carrying bronze metallurgy, which probably originated in West Asia, to heights never surpassed in world history, the Shang people cast elaborate bronze ceremonial vessels and weapons, intricately decorated with precisely incised or high-relief designs. Different from anything found in prehistoric China or the West, Shang design may be the earliest example of a unique Pacific Basin style, characterized by frontal views of animal heads, in contrast to animal profiles which predominated in the West. The cere-

monial bronze vessels were required for religious rituals, which also fostered sacred dancing and music.

The Shang people invented or perfected a distinctive writing system, unquestionably Chinese in both language and form. They possessed sufficient written words, over two thousand, to express themselves with considerable facility. Some are still in use today. These characters, or glyphs, representing individual words, rather than sounds, consisted of three types: pictographs, recognizable as pictures of observable objects; ideographs, representing ideas; and characters, formed in part on phonetic principles.

Shang society appears to have centered on a city-state and its surrounding settlements, ruled by hereditary kings. Shang kings and aristocrats lived in imposing buildings, went to battle in horse-drawn chariots, conducted human sacrifices, and buried live servants with their dead masters. In contrast, the common people lived in primitive pit dwellings and went to war on foot. Warfare was frequent, and the chariot, a new weapon, facilitated the spread of Shang power through large parts of the Yellow River valley. Both military and administrative inventions made

Shang artisans produced bronze vessels by a casting process as sophisticated as any ever devised. This three-legged wine cup was used in religious ceremonies by the earliest emperors. The swallow on the lid was their emblem.

possible the emergence of a recognizable state by the late Shang period. Political and social authority rested on the aristocrats' monopoly of bronze metallurgy, their possession of expensive war chariots, and the king's religious functions.

Shang religion centered around the worship of deities, spirits, ancestors, natural phenomena such as the wind and the earth, and the cardinal points of the compass. Animal sacrifices were usual, and sometimes libations of a beerlike liquor were poured on the ground. One of the deities worshiped was Shang Ti (Supreme Ti). In Chinese mythology the Five Ti were early Chinese rulers, and Shang Ti was probably worshiped as a "supreme ancestor."

In the nascent urban centers people made a living in specialized occupations and trade. The majority of the population, however, consisted of peasants who grew wheat, millet, and rice and raised cattle, sheep, pigs, and horses. Farming methods were primitive; for a plow, farmers used a stick dragged through the soil.

Chou: the classical period. In 1027 B.C. (or 1122 B.C., according to some sources), the Chou people conquered the Shang. With their capital at Hao, near modern Sian, the Chou lived on the edge of Shang civilization and authority, sharing its culture and language. The Chou undoubtedly benefited from their proximity to nomadic tribes in the north and west, from whom they may have learned some of the martial skills that made their conquest of Shang possible.

The Chou kings conquered most of the North China Plain, but the lack of efficient communications made the development of a unified state impossible. Consequently, the kings delegated local authority, particularly in the east, to relatives or military chieftains and social magnates. These vassal lords, whose power was hereditary, recognized the suzerainty of the Chou kings and were responsible for supplying the kings with military aid. As the vassal states grew in size and developed their own bureaucratic and military organizations, they became virtually independent, and the Chou kings continued to reign only on the sufferance of the feudal lords.

The remnants of Chou royal power disappeared completely in 771 B.C., when an alliance of dissident vassal states and "barbarians" seized the capital and killed the king. Part of the royal family managed to escape eastward to Lo-yang, however, where the dynasty, now known as the Eastern Chou, survived for another five centuries. At Lo-yang, Chou royal functions were largely confined to performing state religious rituals and arbitrating differences among the feudal lords. As the stronger feudal states gradually absorbed their weaker neighbors, the domains of the Eastern Chou kings themselves diminished in size and strength in comparison with their vassals'. Warfare between the feudal states was incessant, particularly in the "Period of Warring States" (403-221 B.C.).

The interstate system. The disappearance of Chou influence over the vassal states during the Eastern Chou period led not only to rapidly increasing interstate warfare but to a decline in adherence to the traditional rules of the proper conduct of warfare and the establishment of legitimacy. Particularly in the fourth and third centuries B.C., many state rulers took the title *wang*, or king, formerly reserved for the Chou ruler alone. Enemy states sought to exterminate each other and to annex each other's territory. As the states grew in size, the scale of warfare grew too. In the latter years of the Chou some states could throw thousands of chariots and tens of thousands of peasant foot soldiers into battle. Interstate conferences were held to consider and conclude treaties and alliances and to develop disarmament proposals. Alliances were established and cemented through royal marriages, and hostages were exchanged to ensure loyalty.

The formation of leagues and alliances, the exchange of ambassadors, political marriages, and the holding of interstate conferences all resemble the interstate system that developed in Europe in late medieval and early modern times. By 221 B.C., however, the Period of Warring States ended when the state of Ch'in conquered all its rivals; and while Europe, after the fall of the Roman Empire, was never again to achieve political or administrative unity, China was never again permanently disunited.

Chou culture. The Chou destruction of Shang did not result in any sharp break in the development of Chinese culture. The writing system became more complex and sophisticated, and the Chou continued to produce bronze vessels, but with less elaborate designs than the Shang. During the sixth century iron was introduced and came into general use by the end of the Chou, when China had drawn abreast, if not ahead, of technological developments in the rest of the world. Iron weapons made warfare more efficient, and iron plows contributed to the expansion of agriculture.

The Eastern Chou is unrivaled by any later period in Chinese history for its energy and dynamic creativity. The ox-drawn iron-tipped plow, together with the growth of large-scale irrigation and water-control projects, led to population growth based on increased agricultural yields. Canals were constructed to facilitate the moving of commodities over long distances. Commerce and wealth grew rapidly, and a merchant and artisan class emerged. Cowrie shells, bolts of silk, and ingots of precious metals were the media of exchange, and by the end of the Chou period copper cash, small round coins with square holes, were being minted and used in general circulation. They remained the basic coinage of China into the late nineteenth century. Chopsticks and lacquer, today universally considered as symbols of Chinese and East Asian culture, were also in use by the end of the period.

The art of horseback riding, which was developing among the nomads of Central and West Asia, deeply influenced Chou China. The horse contributed to the ease and growth of communications between east and west, and technological and intellectual developments in India and West Asia were gradually carried to China. In design, for instance, the typical western profile replaced the Shang highly stylized frontal view. Central Asian horsemen threatened China militarily, and in response the Chinese began constructing defensive walls, later joined together to become the Great Wall of China. Inside China itself, cavalry replaced the chariot in warfare, and the use of the horse improved internal communications, contrib-

uting to the process of political centralization. All these developments led to a growing self-consciousness on the part of the Chinese who, while divided into states fighting among themselves, began to distinguish between their own high civilization and the barbarian peasants and nomads. This sense of unique superiority of their own civilization became a lasting characteristic of Chinese culture.

The classes. Class divisions and consciousness were highly developed during the Chou and have remained so down to modern times. The king and the aristocracy were sharply separated from the mass of people on the basis of land ownership and family descent. The nobility were members of a territorially dispersed clan system, and the clans in turn were divided into families, each with a male head. Until the later stages of Chou, the nobility held the chief posts in the army and administration. The fact that the aristocrats' inherited privileges depended

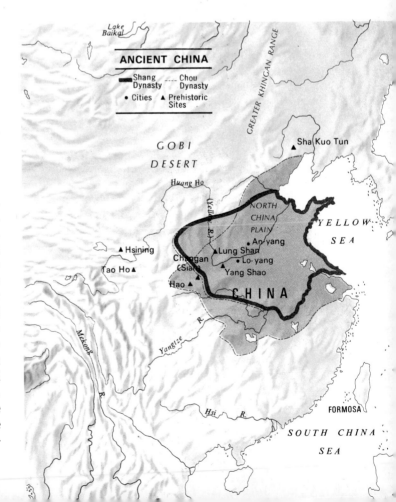

on proof of their noble ancestry was at least partly responsible for the great emphasis which the Chinese placed on ancestor worship.

The feudal nobles lived a far different life from that of farmers. Their customs can be compared in a general way to those of Europe's feudal nobility (see Chapter 8). Underlying the feudal structure was a code of chivalry, practiced in both war and peace. The intricate and complex code became so important to the nobility as a symbol of gentility that nobles devoted years to its mastery. Arrayed in breastplate and helmet, the Chinese noble waged war from his chariot and, to display his martial skill and social grace, "would come to the court of his seigneur to take part in tournaments of the noble sport of archery which was accompanied by musical airs and interspersed with elegant salutations, the whole regulated like a ballet."[9]

Village life. Agriculture, of course, was the occupation of the overwhelming proportion of the population. Large-scale irrigation, fertilizer, and the ox-drawn iron-tipped plow modified the traditional feudal land system, stimulating a gradual changeover to private land ownership based on increased productivity. But the masses generally had no political rights and, until the end of the Chou, little or no land. The peasants cultivated their fields as the tenants of nobles or landlords, paid taxes, and served as common soldiers. Families lived together in villages clustered about the residence of a noble or, after feudal times, a landlord. Eventually, the village community included members not related by blood to the original family group.

Despite increased agricultural productivity and changes in property structure, the farm population still had difficulty eking out an existence. A major problem in the Chinese economy has been that the majority of farmers worked fields so small that they could not produce a crop surplus to tide them over periods of scarcity. This problem, evident as early as 400 B.C., became especially acute from the eighteenth century on, when population pressures led to a marked decline in in the size of peasant holdings.

The rise of philosophical schools. By the fifth century B.C. rapid economic, social, political, and technological change, coupled with increasing warfare between the states, destroyed the apparent stability that had characterized Chinese society internally during the Shang, Western Chou, and early Eastern Chou dynasties. Educated Chinese became aware of the great disparity between the traditions inherited from their ancestors and the reality in which they themselves lived. Moreover, the nascent bureaucratic class had no place in the traditional scheme of Chinese society, with its two classes: the aristocracy and the peasants.

The tension between inherited tradition and existing reality led directly to the birth of social and personal consciousness in China on the eve of the Period of Warring States. Many scholars have noted with excitement the parallel between the flourishing intellectual life of fifth-century B.C. China and the Golden Ages of Greek philosophy and Indian religious thought at the same time. More than Indian and Mediterranean thinkers, Chinese philosophers concerned themselves primarily with man's control of himself and his society in an age when it appeared that he could no longer control either.

Although they often disagreed violently among themselves, most of the schools of Chinese philosophy in the Eastern Chou shared certain characteristics. Dismayed with the present state of man and society, they looked to the past for models on which to base the construction of a meaningful ethical system for man and the reconstruction of Chinese society. This led to a greater consciousness of history in China than in other world cultures. From this time on, the writing of history was a major literary activity, and down to the end of the nineteenth century all intellectual innovations sought their justification in historical examples and classical writings (see the Historical Critique, p. 834). These influences are even present in Communist China today. All schools of Chinese thought also shared a common interest in the achievement of order in society and of a proper balance between man and man, and man and nature.

Master K'ung, the sage. The first, most famous, and certainly most influential professional Chinese philosopher and teacher was K'ung-fu-tzu, Master K'ung, known in the West by the Latinized form of his name, Confucius (551-479 B.C.). His teachings had a greater and longer-lasting influence in China and the rest of East Asia than those of any other philosopher and became the official school of thought in Japan, Korea, the Ryukyu Islands, and Vietnam, as well as in China. He is still venerated as the official philosopher of the Nationalist Chinese government on Taiwan. The teachings of the sage and his most famous disciple, Mencius, are written down in a group of books known as the Thirteen Classics. In the West the best known of these is the Analects, a collection of Confucius' responses to his disciples' questions. In this work, each of Confucius' statements begins with the phrase, "The Master said," the original of the English expression, "Confucius say. . . ."

Confucius was born in the small state of Lu, in modern Shantung province, into what was evidently a family of the lower aristocracy that had sunk into poverty. Orphaned as a child, he obtained an education and became a member of the new bureaucratic class. Tradition has it that he found employment for a while as an official in his native state, but he never achieved the prominent public position he sought. Dissatisfied with the conditions of Chinese social and moral life, he spent at least ten years wandering around the country advising princes and teaching young men, who, he hoped, might succeed where he had failed. Confucius was evidently a teacher of rare ability, and it is said that he had more than three thousand students. Confucius said of himself, "I am a transmitter and not a creator. I believe in and have a passion for the ancients." Living in an age of social, political, and moral turmoil, Confucius was probably the first Chinese to be conscious of tradition as tradition, and he sought to revive it by organizing it into a system of thought.

Confucianism is a social and moral philosophy, not a religion. While accepting the existence of Heaven (*T'ien*) and spirits, Confucius was fundamentally an agnostic who

Courtesy, Museum of Fine Arts, Boston, Bigelow Collection

Buddha, Lao-tzu, and Confucius were three of the great leaders of East Asian thought. In this Japanese painting from the Kano period (1336-1558) they are depicted conversing together. Although the three philosophers were not contemporaries, their discussion symbolically represents the interaction of the three philosophical schools.

believed that the basic concern of man is man. "We don't know yet how to serve men, how can we know about serving the spirits?" he said. And, "We don't know yet about life, how can we know about death?" "Devote yourself to the proper demands of the people, respect the ghosts and spirits but keep them at a distance—this may be called wisdom."

Confucius' home state of Lu was known for its conservatism, and the Master believed that the social and political problems of his day could be solved only if men would return to the traditions of the founders of the Chou dynasty. Society would be stable if only each man would play his assigned role: "Let the ruler be a ruler and the subject a subject; let the father be a father and the son a son." He advocated a paternalistic form of government in which the ruler made himself responsible for the welfare of his people and the family was the model for the state.

Government, according to Confucius, was primarily a problem of ethics. While he did not challenge the hereditary rights of the rulers, he insisted that their primary responsibility was to serve as an example of correct ethical conduct for the people. The cultivation of virtue depended on *li*, "propriety," which characterized proper conduct for those in a ruler's court; *li*, in turn, depended on education. Each man would play his proper role in society if he performed the rituals proper to his station. "By nature men are pretty much alike; it is learning and practice that set them apart."

The ideal man, according to Confucius, was the *chün-tzu*, the cultivated man. The primary virtues were integrity, righteousness, conscientiousness or loyalty toward others, altruism, and love for one's fellow man. Etiquette or decorum were essential expressions of virtue. Confucius said, "Courtesy without decorum becomes tiresome. Cautiousness without decorum becomes timidity, daring becomes insubordination, frankness becomes effrontery." The ruler who possessed the essential virtues and behaved with decorum, Confucius insisted, would be able to rule by example rather than force.

Taoism: intuitive mysticism. While Confucianism stressed reason and social cohesiveness, Taoism, the most important school of Chinese thought next to Confucianism, emphasized the individual man and insisted that man's greatest problem was to conform to nature, not to society. Taoism often represented the revolt of the man of sensibilities and the common man against the social and moral rigidity of orthodox Confucianism.

The *Tao te ching*, or the *Classic of the Way and Power*, is the most important Taoist work, and though attributed to Lao-tzu, apparently a mythical figure who tradition says was slightly older than Confucius, it probably dates only to the third century B.C. Because the *Tao te ching* is cryptic and overly concise, it has been subject to many different interpretations, and no two western translations agree on its precise meaning. Taoism's second most important book, the *Chuang-tzu*, was also written in the third century B.C., though it is attributed to a fourth-century philosopher of the same name. One of the most beautiful works of Chinese literature, it contains stories and passages of great poetic delight and philosophical insight.

Popular Taoism quickly degenerated into a religion of spirits and magic, but philosophical Taoism sought to define the "true nature" of man in abstract terms. The word *tao*, meaning "road" or "way," in Confucianism stood for the ideal society which that school advocated. The Taoists defined it to mean the scheme of nature to which man should conform. Man could live in harmony with nature only if he turned his attention inward and experienced oneness between himself and the universe. In the Tao there are no distinctions. Everything is relative. The Taoists' highest ideal was the state of original and complete simplicity, and they advocated a society in which man lived simply, without law or machinery, without striving to be more than a harmonious part of nature.

The Taoists believed that the only way to achieve union with nature was through inaction, doing nothing: "Do nothing and nothing will not be done." Spontaneity, not conscious planning, was the key to correct behavior. The ideal political system, according to Taoism, would be "a small country with a few inhabitants."[10] In the early history of Chinese thought Taoism represented a strain of romanticism in contrast to Confucian rationalism.

Mencius and the "Mandate of Heaven." The most significant transmitter of Confucian doctrine was Mencius (372-289 B.C.), who like Confucius, failed to achieve a high position in government and became a wandering teacher. Mencius added important new dimensions to Confucian thought. He taught that man's nature was fundamentally good and could be developed by self-cultivation through education and a kind of spontaneous inner search resembling Taoist mystical experiences. Government should be guided not by opportunism but by ethical standards, he claimed. A moral ruler will behave benevolently toward his people, providing for their well-being. A true king must have the support of his people. Heaven manifests itself through the people, and if the people accept and support their ruler, he has the "Mandate of Heaven" to rule over them. If they overthrow their ruler, he has lost Heaven's mandate and his right to leadership. This rationalization of revolution had originally been used by the Chou to justify their revolt against the Shang. But Mencius now developed it into a full justification of revolution.

Modern commentators, both Chinese and western, have seen in Mencius' concept of the Mandate of Heaven a form of protodemocratic thought. Mencius evidently believed that all men were morally equal and that the good ruler needed the consent of his people. But it would perhaps be more accurate to define Mencius' political theories as advocating benevolent autocracy rather than popular democracy.

The school of law. Following the end of the Period of Warring States, a non-Confucian school of philosophy, the School of Law or Legalists, developed. The Legalists taught that man is by nature selfish and evil and that moralists like the Confucians contributed to evil by encouraging human desires. According to the Legalists, people primarily want security and social order, and this can be achieved only in a society where the uneducated citizen, living in a kind of Taoist primitive state, blindly follows an absolute ruler and is subordinate to the state. To achieve this kind of society, harsh punishments and the strictest laws would be necessary. People were to be mutually responsible for the enforcement of the law, and anyone who had knowledge of a crime but did not report it was considered as guilty as the criminal himself. The ruler, by nature, would seek to create a strong and secure state, and therefore only his desires would be right.

Chinese art and literature. In general the Chinese arts are marked by restraint, a quality probably derived from Chinese conservatism and serenity. For example, a poem seldom employs a great deal of highly ornate language, nor is it effusive in its effect.

During the Shang and Chou periods the Chinese were already skillful craftsmen and sensitive artists. Jade ornaments have been found in the earliest Chinese graves. From Shang times the Chinese cut jade into forms of fishes to use as "sound stones" which, when struck, emitted a clear tone for a considerable length of time. Strikingly beautiful ceremonial bronzes were produced during the Shang period and for the next 1500 years (see illustration, p. 103).

Taoism made a profound impression upon Chinese art. The Taoist and the Chinese artist alike are deeply introspective and intuitive in approach, seeking to understand the processes of nature that create the landscape. Painting to express his reaction to a scene is more important to the Chinese artist than depicting the landscape realistically. Unfortunately almost no examples survive of the earliest Chinese painting, but literary references indicate that it was an established art centuries before the birth of Christ.

In the Chinese spoken language, differences in meaning are achieved through the uses of tones, of which there are from four to nine for each word sound depending on the dialect. While the spoken language has split into various dialects, the written language has remained comparatively unchanged. Under the Chou dynasty it assumed the form which, with some modifications, it possesses today. The historic continuity of the written language has advantages, for a literate Chinese today can read works written twenty centuries ago. The difficulty, however, is to become a literate Chinese; the language never developed beyond a primitive form of expressing each idea with a different character, so that today it includes forty thousand separate characters, rather than the small alphabet of letters used in other languages.

During China's formative centuries literature flourished. Although most poetry written prior to the age of Confucius has unfortunately been lost, 305 poems have been preserved in the *Shih Ching*, or *Book of Odes*. From this book we see that the age-old problems of living affected the ancient Chinese much as they affect us. We can sympathize deeply with soldiers engaged in a conflict they did not create:

O thou distant and azure Heaven!
When shall all this end? . . .
What leaves have not turned purple?
What man is not torn from his wife?
Mercy be on us soldiers—
Are we not also men?[11]

CHINA: THE FIRST EMPIRES

Rise of Legalist Ch'in. As we recall, China was experiencing significant growth despite, or perhaps because of, its division into many petty, warring states. No state strove more for internal centralization and wielded increasingly autocratic power than the state of Ch'in, which embraced the ruthless philosophy of Legalism (see p. 109). Bearing

strong resemblances to modern totalitarian thought, Legalism contributed greatly to Ch'in's eventual success in conquering and unifying all China. Although it disappeared as a legitimate philosophical school with the fall of the Ch'in empire about 206 B.C., its advocacy of a strong ruler and a universal criminal code were important additions to Chinese statecraft and strongly influenced the orthodox philosophy, founded on the teachings of Confucius and Mencius, that was to dominate China for over two thousand years.

Ch'in, a frontier state located in the far northwestern part of China in what is now Kansu and Shensi provinces, was less bound by tradition and more innovative than states in the central region. The other Chinese states considered Ch'in a country of barbarians, uncivilized and ignorant. Gradually, however, Ch'in was more and more influenced by Chou culture, and in 352 B.C. Shang Yang, a scion of the ruling house of a small

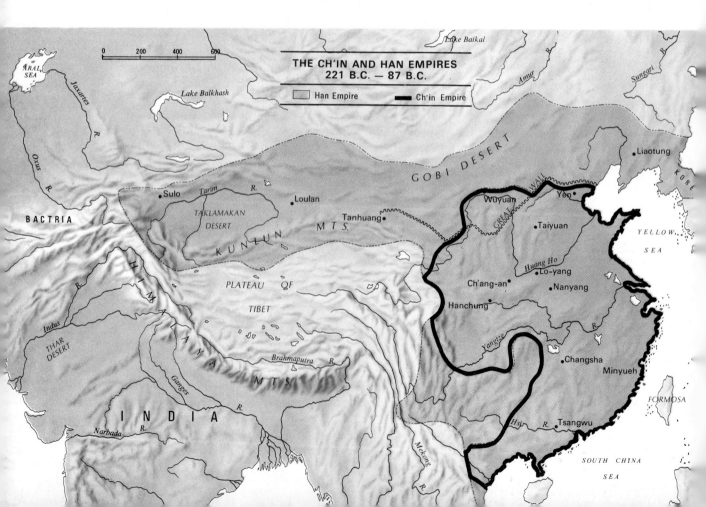

THE CH'IN AND HAN EMPIRES
221 B.C. — 87 B.C.

Han Empire   Ch'in Empire

Chou state, became chancellor of Ch'in, ruling until 338 B.C.

Shang Yang instituted far-reaching changes in Ch'in government and society. Recognizing that the growth of Ch'in's strength and power depended on a more efficient and centralized bureaucratic structure than could exist under feudalism, Shang Yang suppressed the old nobility and created a new aristocracy based on military merit. He divided the population into five- and ten-family units ruled directly by officials of the state and introduced a universal draft beginning at approximately age fifteen. Soldiers distinguishing themselves in battle were awarded with the services of five peasant families, and all noble ranks and access to a life of luxury were based on military accomplishment. Based on this new system, Ch'in eventually fielded and supported an army of one million men.

Economically, Shang Yang encouraged agricultural development and for the first time in the state's history levied direct state taxes on land in the place of the older system of communal work. Commerce, too, was encouraged, under a system of laws that protected merchants and their property.

These reforms made Ch'in the most powerful state of the time; and after Shang Yang's death Ch'in began to conquer the other states of Chou China, extending to the entire country the institutional innovations and social changes that had taken place in Ch'in as well as those that had occurred in the states it had conquered—for example, regulation of weights and measures, price control, state monopolies in the salt and iron mines.

Ch'in unites China. In the middle of the third century B.C. the Legalist Li Ssu, one of the most remarkable statesmen in Chinese history, helped the king of Ch'in conquer the other states of Chou China, establishing the first unified empire in Chinese history by 221 B.C. The king then assumed the title *Shih Huang-ti*, "First Emperor," taking for his title two terms that referred to the gods (Shang Ti) and the sage-emperors of the mythical age (the Three Huang and the Five Ti).[12] *Huang-ti* remained the title of Chinese emperors until the end of the imperial system in 1911.

Men of immense drive, skill, and imagination, Shih Huang-ti and Li Ssu carried out a revolution in Chinese society that went far beyond the unification of the country through centralization of bureaucratic administration. In effect, they created a precursor of the modern totalitarian state, particularly its fascist variety, in a premodern society. They gathered the complete aristocratic class— some 120,000 families, according to tradition—at the capital and replaced them with their own bureaucratic administrators in the provinces. With the exception of the imperial soldiers, the entire population had to surrender its weapons to the state. Shih Huang-ti standardized weights, measures, coinage, and axle lengths throughout the empire. The standardization of axle lengths was particularly important, for it permitted the creation of a unified road system radiating out from the capital, thus contributing to the ease of imperial control.

A single harsh legal code replaced all local laws and went far toward shattering long-standing traditions; the entire realm was divided into provinces, administrative units drawn to obliterate traditional feudal units and to facilitate direct rule by the emperor's own centrally controlled civil and military appointees. To destroy the source of the aristocracy's power and to permit the emperor's agents to tax every farmer's harvest, private ownership of land by peasants was allowed.

Vast public works of both a civilian and a military nature were undertaken for the greater security of the state and glory of the emperor. Shih Huang-ti's most spectacular public work was repairing the remnants of walls built in earlier times and joining them into the Great Wall, extending from the sea into Central Asia for a distance of over 1400 miles. The wall was both a line of defense against the barbarians who habitually raided China and a symbol of distinction between China's sedentary agricultural civilization and the nomadic animal-husbandry societies of Central Asia. It was meant to keep the nomads out and, at the same time, to keep the Chinese in.

One of the most important keystones of Ch'in imperial policy was intellectual control and enforced conformity. Li Ssu standardized the Chinese writing system, giving it essentially its modern form, thus facilitating written communication and inhibiting heterodox thought by destroying regional scripts. Furthermore, he tried to enforce intellectual conformity and make the Ch'in imperial system appear to be the only natural political order by attempting to destroy the historical memory of the intellectuals. In 213 B.C. he instituted the first literary inquisition in history, known as the "Burning of the Books." The Confucian classics, all works of history that did not support the Ch'in, and any other books that appeared to be of a subversive nature were destroyed; scholars who protested were banished from the empire or killed. The only exceptions were works of a utilitarian nature, according to Legalist philosophy: books on medicine, agriculture, divination, Ch'in history, and certain government libraries and documents. These measures, strongly resembling Hitler's purge of German literature in the twentieth century, dealt a blow to Chinese thought from which it never fully recovered.

When Shih Huang-ti died in 210 B.C., his inept son was unable to control the rivalry among the First Emperor's chief aides. As the court sank into intrigue, anarchic popular rebellion swept the land; by 206 B.C. the Ch'in dynasty, which claimed that it would endure for "ten thousand generations," had completely disappeared. But the Chinese empire, which Ch'in created, lasted for more than two thousand years, evolving eventually into Communist China today. Although Ch'in itself disappeared, it created the longest-lived political institution in world history.

The Han dynasty: the Legalist state survives. In 202 B.C., the year in which the Romans defeated the Carthaginians at the battle of Zama, Liu Pang, better known under his posthumous title Kao Tzu (High Ancestor), won control of China and established the Han dynasty, with its capital at Ch'ang-an (see map, p. 110). The Han dynasty is traditionally divided into two parts: the Earlier Han, from 206 B.C. to 8 A.D., and the Later Han, from 23 A.D. to 220 A.D. It was interrupted by a short-lived dynasty under a usurper of the throne. The Han corresponded in the East to the Roman Empire in the West in time, significance, power, and prestige. Chinese today still call themselves "Men of Han," and the Japanese call the Chinese characters they use in writing their own language "Han characters," much as we speak of the "Latin alphabet."

Although the anti-Ch'in rebellions were characterized in part by a nostalgia for Chou society, the clock could not be turned back; the Legalist imperial state had become a permanent feature of the Chinese political landscape. Kao Tzu and his successors succeeded where the Ch'in had failed because they retained the Legalist state in all its essentials but tempered their approach to the intellectuals and the people with moderation. At first Kao Tzu and his immediate successors, faced with the problem of ruling a vast empire without efficient means of communications, reestablished some of the vassal kingdoms in distant regions, but they spent the first century and a half of their rule subjugating their own creations, returning to Legalist political institutions. Although the dynasty constantly faced internal threats and external danger, the population grew dramatically. A "census" of 2 A.D. listed the population of the empire as almost sixty million, a greater number of people than ever recognized Rome's rule.

In accord with Legalist principles, which were tempered by Confucian ideas, the Han emperors established complex administrative organs staffed by a salaried bureaucracy to rule their vast empire. Periodic searches were made for men of talent, chosen through a primitive examination and recommendation system and promoted by merit. By the first century B.C. the government employed more than 130,000 bureaucrats, or one for every 400 to 500 people in the empire. Relatively small by modern standards, the Han bureaucracy set the pattern for all subsequent periods of Chinese history down to 1949.

Although the examinations were theoretically open to all Chinese except merchants, the bureaucrats were drawn largely from the landlord class, because wealth was needed to obtain the education to pass the examinations. Consequently, the earlier division of Chinese society between aristocrats and peasants was now transformed into a division between landowner-bureaucrats and peasants.

Wu Ti, the "Martial Emperor." After sixty years of consolidation, the Han empire reached its greatest extent and development during the long reign of Wu Ti, from 141-87 B.C., who embarked on a policy of territorial expansion. He justified his conquests in terms of self-defense against the threat of attacks by nomads, but desire to control the trade routes of Central Asia may also have been a major factor. In the north, he drove the nomads into and beyond the Gobi Desert. In the west, he extended the Great Wall out into the desert of the Tarim Basin and settled some 700,000 Chinese on the borders of this barren region, conquering it for China forever. His armies conquered parts of what is now Russian Turkestan, and under one of his successors Han armies reached beyond this point, extending Chinese power farther from the capital than Roman power reached out from Rome at any time. In the east, Wu Ti conquered southern Manchuria and northern Korea, bringing these areas once and for all under the sway of Chinese culture. And to the south, he extended his empire along the coast well into North Vietnam.

Wu Ti's great conquests were based on far-reaching economic and financial reforms aimed at providing the government with revenue to administer the growing empire. The emperor increased taxes, made the laws more stringent, established state monopolies on such vital products as salt and iron, and used conscript and slave labor in constructing public works. As costs increased, taxes increased, until the government's fiscal situation grew precarious and the peasants' burdens led to revolt. This in turn increased the government's need for revenue to pay for the suppression of the rebellions its policies had caused. Moreover, as the government at the center grew weaker, it had to rely more and more on local military commanders and magnates for control of the population, giving them greater power and prestige at its own expense. This vicious circle of decline after an initial dynastic

period of increasing prosperity and power has been the pattern of most Chinese dynasties since the Han; western historians of China call it "the dynastic cycle." In the Han this eventually led to the temporary usurpation of the throne that divided the Earlier from the Later Han.

The Later Han dynasty never reached the heights of its predecessor. Warlords in the provinces seized more and more power for themselves, and widespread peasant rebellions sapped the state's resources. Reduced to a political fiction for the last three decades of its reign, the dynasty finally collapsed completely in 220 A.D. when the throne was usurped by the son of a famous general. But China succeeded where Europe failed: after three and a half centuries of disunion, China

Built as a defense against the barbarians, the Great Wall symbolizes China's self-enforced and militant isolation. The wall remains today one of the greatest monuments to man's engineering skill in the pre-industrial age and one of the wonders of the world.

once again was united and, with minor exceptions, has remained united to this day. In Europe, unification remains, even now, a dream.

Han intellectual developments. In his political style and policies, Wu Ti was almost as much a Legalist as the Ch'in First Emperor, and yet his court was strongly oriented toward Confucianism. While neither Wu Ti nor Kao Tzu, the founder of the dynasty, wasted affection on scholars, they recognized that a literate and educated bureaucracy was necessary for governing so vast an empire. Consequently the way was open for a revival of the intellectual life that had been suppressed under the Ch'in. In 191 B.C. the Han lifted the Ch'in ban on Chou literature, and some older men were apparently able to write down from memory texts they had memorized in their youth, before the Ch'in dynasty was established. Legend has it that other texts were found hidden in the walls of houses, where they had been put by scholars to escape the Ch'in book burning.

Han thought included ideas drawn from a variety of schools, which were woven into a new synthesis that was very different from Chou philosophy. The primary interest of scholars during the first century of Han was the recovery of Chou literature. Their understanding of the old texts was at times vague, however, and it was Confucius as the ideal image of the sage rather than Confucianism as a political and social philosophy that eventually triumphed during the Han. While Legalism as a philosophical school was anathema to the Han scholars, Legalist statecraft was redefined in Confucian terms (as understood by the Han scholars), and Chou ethical concepts tempered the harshness of Legalist practice. The result was a philosophy of benevolent imperial despotism, a far cry from Confucius' feudal concept of the *chün-tzu* and Mencius' doctrine of the Mandate of Heaven.

The Han dynasty witnessed many other important intellectual developments. The Five Classics were established as the primary Confucian canon and the basis of education. In 124 B.C. an imperial university was established, and by the latter half of the first century B.C. it was said to have had three thousand students. In the Later Han this increased tenfold. By 1 A.D. one hundred men a year entered government service through official examinations based on the Confucian classics, and Han Confucianism became the orthodox philosophy of the state in 58 A.D., when regular sacrifices to Confucius were ordered performed in all government schools.[13]

In Wu Ti's reign, Ssu-ma Ch'ien, a court astrologer, wrote the *Shih chi*, or *Historical Records*, which set the pattern for all subsequent Chinese historical writing up to the twentieth century. Ssu-ma Ch'ien was an unusually sophisticated historian, and his work included annals, chronological tables, essays on such subjects as music, astronomy, rivers and canals, and economics; over half the book is made up of biographies (see the Historical Critique, p. 834). In the Later Han, Pan Ku wrote the *History of the [Earlier] Han*, and thereafter it was customary for each dynasty to write the official history of its immediate predecessor. Chiang Kai-shek's Nationalist government has recently published the official history of the Manchu dynasty. It remains to be seen if the Chinese Communists will write an official history of Chiang Kai-shek. The world's first modern dictionary, the *Shuo wen* (*Explanation of Writing*), was also published during Wu Ti's reign.

Technological advancement. During the Han period China equaled and even surpassed the level of scientific and technological development in the rest of the world. Advances were particularly notable in the fields of mineralogy, alchemy and chemistry, pharmacology, zoology, and botany. The Han Chinese invented a primitive seismograph, knew of sunspots, invented the water-powered mill, paper, and porcelain, and reckoned accurately the length of the year as early as 28 B.C. In textiles they were far ahead of the West. Although little remains of it, tradition indicates that the capital at Ch'ang-an must have rivaled Rome in wealth and splendor.

Buddhism and Buddhist art enter China. In Central Asia, where the Han had recently extended the *Pax Sinica*, the Chinese were in close contact with the Kushan empire in northwest India. This contact facilitated the spread of Buddhism from northwest India into China during the later Han dynasty, for Buddhist missionaries made their way through the heart of Asia along the same protected routes as the silk caravans. Transported to China along with the Buddhist faith were the Gandharan Graeco-Indian artistic techniques and the stupa architecture, from which the style of the Chinese pagoda is derived.

A first-century Han emperor gave Buddhism official recognition and so initiated its spread within China, although its impact was not felt strongly until after the Han period. At first progress was hindered by the suspicions of the Chinese that Buddhist monasticism did not fit into the country's family tradition. But much of Buddhist mysticism was like that of Taoism, and the resemblance facilitated its eventual approval by many of the Chinese. Both *Hinayana* and *Mahayana* Buddhism were imported into China, but the latter, with its acceptance of Bodhisattvas and even local Chinese gods, gained the ascendancy. Today there are about ten separate Buddhist sects in China, and in general their teachings have diverged widely from the doctrines taught by the Buddha.

THE MEETING OF EAST AND WEST

Beyond the Roman frontiers. During its period of greatest prosperity, the Graeco-Roman world-state, centered in the Mediterranean basin, maintained trade contacts extending far beyond the imperial boundaries. In the market quarter of imperial Rome, Chinese silk was sold, and Indian merchants frequented the streets of Alexandria. During the four centuries after 334 B.C. (the year when Alexander the Great entered Asia), the frontiers of civilization were progressively enlarged until finally a great chain of intercommunicating states stretched across Eurasia from the Atlantic to the Pacific.

The eastward drive of Hellenism was ac-

Constructed with remarkable precision, this Chinese sundial from the Han period was superior to any devised in the West until the thirteenth century A.D. The base and vertical shaft have been reconstructed for this photograph.

companied by a marked increase in economic activity throughout western Asia and in the exchange of goods between East and West. The trade between India and the West took several routes (see map, p. 116). From northern India, caravans proceeded across Parthia, while ships from southern Indian ports sailed to meet overland routes across Mesopotamia, Arabia, and Egypt.

Monsoons encourage sea traffic. After Egypt and other Hellenistic areas had succumbed to Roman conquest, the Romans took over the rich trade with the East. From the Roman standpoint, the routes from India that centered on Syria had serious disadvantages: they led through Parthian territory, and the caravans were subject to heavy tolls by the Parthian government. The high profits that caravan merchants made as middlemen also boosted costs. Therefore Augustus and his successors encouraged the use of the southern sea route to India.

About 100 B.C. a most important discovery had been made when a Greek mariner found how to use the monsoon winds that blow from the southwest across the Arabian Sea from May to October. Eliminating the tedious journey along the coasts, sailors could now voyage from Aden to the west coast of India across the open sea. Furthermore, ships could return from India by using the countermonsoon blowing from the northeast between November and March. Thus round-trip voyages could be made in less than a year, and Strabo, the Greek geographer during the time of Augustus, stated that 120 ships sailed to India every year from Egyptian ports. This improvement in the sailing route encouraged western merchants to strike still farther east by ship, and they subsequently rounded the southern points of India and Ceylon.

The silk trade. The first move to pierce the land barrier separating China from the West was made by the Chinese rather than the Europeans. In 138 B.C. the Chinese emperor Wu Ti dispatched an ambassador into west Central Asia to seek allies against the Huns. Although the ambassador failed to secure

alliances, he aroused Wu Ti's curiosity by describing the lands beyond the Pamirs and by showing his ruler the alfalfa and grape seeds he had carried back with him to China. Wu Ti resolved to open up trade relations with the peoples to the west. Thus, as a result of Chinese initiative, the use of silk spread to the Mediterranean during the early part of the first century B.C.

The silk caravans from northwest China which passed through Turkestan and Parthia before reaching the Roman dominions were also subject to heavy tolls. By diverting the caravans around Parthia to Indian ports and by transporting goods in Roman ships from there to the Red Sea and Egypt, the price of silk was reduced. As a result of this seaborne competition, the silk trade became highly developed; the reduction of prices made this commodity available for more than just the wealthiest people in the West.

Severance of East-West contacts. Unfortunately for the cause of international relations,

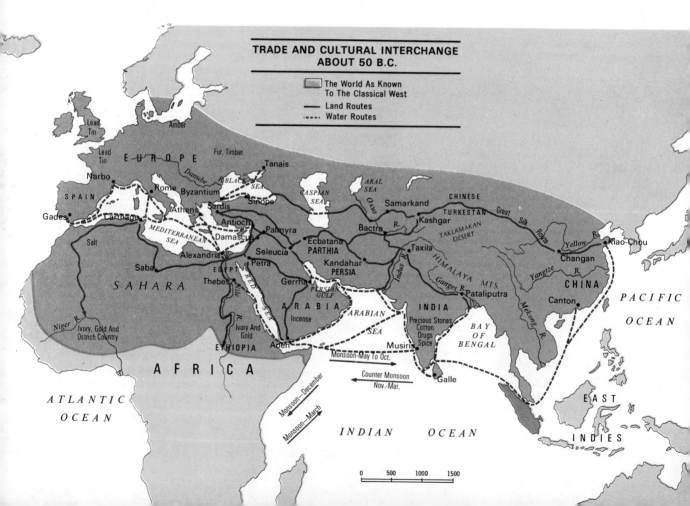

commercial and cultural interchange among the three great civilizations of classical times was interrupted more and more frequently after the beginning of the third century A.D. With the overthrow of the Han dynasty in 220 A.D., China's power and prestige dwindled in Central Asia. By coincidence, at the same time the Kushan empire in northeast India succumbed, and Indian civilization also underwent a process of change and transition. About the same time, and probably most significant in the disruption of Eurasian relations, came the political and economic decline of the Graeco-Roman world (see Chapter 5).

An economic consequence of East-West trade. The volume of the Graeco-Roman world's oriental trade had been surprisingly large. Because Roman exports to the East did not match in quantity or value the empire's imports of silk, spices, perfumes, gems, and other luxuries, the West had suffered seriously from an adverse balance of trade. Thus precious metals were continually being exported to Asia. Pliny declared that India, China, and Arabia drained away annually at least 100,000,000 sesterces (about $5,000,000 at a time when dollars had more purchasing value than today)—"that is the sum which our luxuries and our women cost us."[14] The discovery of vast hoards of Roman coins in India supports Pliny's statement.

One scholar has estimated that between 31 B.C. and 192 A.D. alone, Rome's trade with the Orient cost Rome a net money loss of about $500,000,000. This serious drain, which took place at a time when the empire's known sources of gold and silver were being exhausted, was a prime cause of the deterioration of the imperial coinage and one of the factors in the general economic decline of the Roman world in the third century A.D.

The influence of West upon East. Roman contact with the East was made largely through trade with India and China and substantially increased the knowledge of both sections of the world about each other. But Greek influence was even more consequential.

There is little doubt that the strongest Greek influence on Indian civilization was in the field of sculpture, as demonstrated by the results of the Graeco-Buddhist school at Gandhara, which in turn affected art forms in China and even in Japan. For a time, Indian coinage also bore the strong imprint of Hellenistic influence. Indian astronomy, which made many significant advances in its own right, also benefited from Greek learning.

The influence of East upon West. The trade with both India and China made a powerful impact on the economy of the Graeco-Roman world, as we have pointed out, and those Romans and Greeks who could afford luxuries enjoyed a variety of spices, muslins, silks, and other goods.

Whatever the immediate impact upon the West may have been, the long-range consequences of its meeting with the East were quite significant. With the contact once established, cultural exchange was going to continue, even though sometimes at a slow pace and by indirect means. Medieval Europe was to benefit from the success of the classical civilizations in establishing contact with each other. For example, "Chinese technological inventions poured into Europe in a continuous stream during the first thirteen centuries of the Christian era, just as later on the technological current flowed the other way."[15] No longer can an educated westerner assume the attitude that the meeting of East and West has always demonstrated the superiority of the West.

SUMMARY

From about 2300 to 1800 B.C. the counterpart of the civilizations that developed along the Nile and the Tigris-Euphrates emerged along the Indus in India. Then about 1500 B.C. Aryan nomads invaded India, and as a result a new culture developed. During this Vedic Age the foundations of the unique socio-religious system of Hinduism were laid, and the three pillars of Indian society— the autonomous village, the caste system, and the joint-family—evolved. In the sixth century B.C. Gautama Buddha gave India a philosophy which has endured in Asia until the present.

During the fourth century B.C., shortly after the Hellenic Age in the West, the Mauryan emperors in India, especially the pious and gentle Ashoka, presided over a progressive and prosperous realm in India. This ruler sent missionaries throughout southern and eastern Asia, carrying the civilizing tenets of Buddhism. In turn the great Kushan monarch Kanishka further advanced Indian culture and encouraged the penetration of Buddhism into China.

The formative centuries of Chinese civilization began under the Shang dynasty about the end of Indus culture in India. Building on this advance, the Chou period (1027 or 1122-256 B.C.) was one of remarkable dynamism and creativity in technology and commerce. Its greatest achievement was the contribution to philosophy by Confucius, Mencius, and Lao-tzu. In the third century B.C. Ch'in, which embraced the philosophy of Legalism, established the first unified empire in Chinese history. While the Ch'in dynasty was short-lived, the imperial form of government it created was to endure for more than two thousand years. Its successor, the great Han dynasty (202 B.C. to 220 A.D.), gave China one of its most illustrious eras. Corresponding in time to the Roman Empire in the West, it carved out an extensive empire, especially in Central Asia.

During the centuries immediately preceding and following the birth of Christ, the great civilizations of the world—Graeco-Roman, Indian, and Chinese—were connected by tenuous routes of commercial and cultural exchange. Although this contact between East and West was eventually cut off, it continued long enough to establish a durable tradition in both the Orient and the Occident that beyond the mountains and the deserts to the east or to the west lay other great civilizations. This tradition incited adventurous spirits many centuries later to bring the "halves" of world civilization together once again.

SUGGESTIONS FOR READING

S. Piggott, **Prehistoric India,** * Penguin. Describes the archaeological evidence for the Indus civilization. See also M. Wheeler, **Early India and Pakistan,** Praeger, 1962; and Bridget and Raymond Allchin, **The Birth of Indian Civilization,** * Penguin. B. G. Gokhale, **Asoka Maurya,** Twayne, 1966, and R. Thapar, **Asoka and the Decline of the Mauryas,** Oxford, 1961, are two significant works on India's first empire. A. L. Basham, **The Wonder That Was India,** * Evergreen, is a comprehensive study of Indian culture prior to the coming of the Muslims in the eleventh century.

S. Radhakrishnan, **The Hindu View of Life,** Macmillan, 1927. Today's foremost Indian philosopher compares Hinduism with western philosophy. W. T. De Bary, *et al.,* eds. **Sources of Indian Tradition,** Columbia Univ., 1958, contains significant selections from Vedic and Upanishad texts, with illuminating introductions. Excellent translations of Hindu religious texts are S. Prabhavananda and F. Manchester, trans., **The Upanishads: Breath of the Eternal,** * Mentor; and S. Prabhavananda and C. Isherwood, trans., **The Song of God—The Bhagavad-Gita,** * Mentor.

C. Humphreys, **Buddhism,** * Penguin. Describes the life of the Buddha and the rise of the major branches of Buddhism, as does Edward Conze, **Buddhism,** * Torchbooks. E. A. Burtt, ed., **The Teachings of the Compassionate Buddha,** * Mentor, contains excerpts from Buddhist writings, including Chinese and Japanese.

John H. Marshall, **The Buddhist Art of Gandhara,** Cambridge Univ., 1960; I. D. Lyons and H. Ingholt, **Gandharan Art in Pakistan,** Pantheon, 1957. Two recent books on the relationship of Indian and Graeco-Roman art. See also A. Coomaraswamy, **History of Indian and Indonesian Art,** * Dover, and **The Dance of Shiva,** * Noonday; H. Zimmer, **Art of Indian Asia,** 2 vols., Pantheon, 1955.

W. Watson, **China Before the Han Dynasty,** Praeger, 1961. A good nontechnical survey. L. Cottrell, **The Tiger of Ch'in,** Holt, Rinehart & Winston, 1962, is a rapid history to the third century B.C. M. Granet, **Chinese Civilization,** * Meridian, comes down to Han times. T. Chêng, **Chou China,** Univ. of Toronto, 1964, is a re-creation of this dynasty's culture.

Fung Yu-lan, **A Short History of Chinese Philosophy,** * MacMillan; Liu Wu-Chi, **A Short History of Confucian Philosophy,** * Penguin. Two excellent introductions. A. Waley, **Three Ways of Thought in Ancient China,** * Anchor, 1956, is a concise introduction to Confucianism, Taoism, and Legalism.

W. T. De Bary, *et al.,* eds., **Sources of Chinese Tradition,** Columbia Univ., 1960. An outstanding collection of translations with valuable introductions and commentaries.

J. Needham and Wang Ling, **Science and Civilisation in China,** 4 vols., Cambridge Univ. A major work.

On Chinese art see R. Grousset, **Chinese Art and Culture,** * Evergreen; and L. Sickman and L. Soper, **Art and Architecture of China,** Penguin, 1956.

M. Wheeler, **Rome Beyond the Imperial Frontiers,** * Penguin. A well-illustrated study of Rome's foreign trade.

E. C. Bagchi, **India and China: A Thousand Years of Cultural Relations,** Philosophical Lib., 1951. A stimulating study.

*Indicates an inexpensive paperbound edition.

Part Two

The Middle Ages

■ When we speak of the "fall" of Rome, perhaps we forget that the great classical tradition was carried on for another thousand years without interruption in Constantinople, or "New Rome." Until it fell in 1453 the Byzantine empire acted as a buffer for western Europe, staving off attack after attack from the east. The culminating series of attacks, resulting in the collapse of the empire, was launched by the adherents of Islam—a dynamic way of life developed by the followers of Muhammad, an eloquent prophet who instilled in his people a vital sense of their destiny to rule in the name of Allah. With unbelievable swiftness, the followers of the Prophet became rulers of the Near East, swept across North Africa and surged into Spain, and expanded eastward to the frontiers of China. The Muslims, the great middlemen of medieval times, shuttled back and forth across vast expanses, trading the wares of East and West and acting as the conveyors of culture. Throughout most of the Middle Ages, the East outshone the West even as Constantinople and Baghdad outdazzled in material magnificence and intellectual and artistic triumphs any capital in western Europe.

In Europe, after the inundation of the Roman Empire by Germanic tribes in the fifth century brought disorder and fragmentation, a painful search for stability began. Centuries of confusion followed until Charlemagne established a new "Roman" empire. This ambitious and laudable experiment was premature, however, and after its collapse a new system had to be created—one which would offer at least a minimum of security, political organization, and law enforcement. This was feudalism. Under this system, the landed nobility acted as police force, judiciary, and army. Accompanying feudalism was the manorial system—an economic order which provided food and life's necessities and divided men into two great classes: the fighters or nobles and the workers or serfs.

Crude as it was, feudalism served to mitigate the chaos which followed the fall of Charlemagne's empire. Yet feudalism and the manorial system were inherently rural and rigid, and by the eleventh century new forces were at work. Shadowy outlines of new kingdoms—Germany, England, France, and Spain—began to emerge under the direction of vigorous monarchs. Europe went on the offensive, ejecting the Muslims from the southern part of the Continent, breaking Muslim control of the Mediterranean, and launching crusades to capture Jerusalem from the infidel. The "closed" economy of the feudal countryside gave way before the revival of trade and communications, the growth of towns, the increased use of money as a medium of exchange, and the rise of a new class in society—the bourgeoisie.

The greatest stabilizing force in Europe during the medieval period was the Church. The Middle Ages has sometimes been characterized as the Age of Faith; to an extent greater than in classical or modern times, the attention of men living in those days was directed toward a religious goal —the salvation of the soul—and the Church was the great arbiter of human destiny. With the authority that stemmed from its vital spiritual service, the Church provided the nearest approach to effective and centralized supervision of European life. All men were born, lived, and died under its protection. In the thirteenth century, when popes such as Innocent III bent proud monarchs to their will, the Church reached the zenith of its influence as a kind of international government as well as the focus of medieval society, arts, and scholarship. The Church was the chief patron of poets and artists; its monasteries were repositories for precious manuscripts; and it fostered a new institution of learning— the university.

During the ten centuries commonly referred to as the medieval period in the West, great civilizations in India and China experienced their golden ages while Europe was struggling to build a new and viable civilization on the debris of the defunct Roman Empire. In Gupta India the government was stable, and science and the arts flourished. Under the rule of the T'ang and Sung dynasties, Chinese life was enriched by notable creativity. Later, Mongol conquerors, symbolized by Genghis Khan, put together the largest empire in the world, stretching west from China as far as Russia and Mesopotamia. And influenced greatly by China, the proud and independent Japanese developed a unique culture pattern characterized best by the *samurai*, the knight, and the *bushido*, the code of the warrior.

6. (preceding page) **Hagia Sophia, Istanbul** (532-537 A.D.). By the sixth century the gradual decline of the Roman Empire had emptied the Graeco-Roman classical tradition of nearly all its strength. The imperial capital had been moved from Italy to Constantinople in 330. Christianity was now the state religion and already showing signs of becoming what it was destined to be: a primary force in shaping the world of the next 1000 years. Europe was on the brink of the Middle Ages. At this moment of climactic transition in western history, Hagia Sophia was erected, an immense stone symbol linking past and future. The grandeur of its construction —it is one of the greatest domed vaults of all time—recalls the glory of Rome, while its almost mystical il-

lumination and spiritualized atmosphere prefigure the coming dominance of the Christian faith. After Constantinople was captured by the Turks in 1453, Hagia Sophia became an Islamic mosque, serving in this capacity until recently, when it was converted into a museum. **7.** (above) **Muhammad Ascending to Paradise** (sixteenth century). Islam's meteoric rise to power and subsequent hegemony in the whole Middle East were attended by notable, often superb, achievements in the arts. This manuscript page from Persia was executed at a time when influences from both Christianity and the Far East relaxed the abhorrence Muslims traditionally felt toward making images of Muhammad. Note, however, that the Prophet's face is blank.

8. A Temple on a Clear Day in the Mountains, by Li Ch'eng (c. 960-990 A.D.). Li Ch'eng was one of the greatest exponents of the monumental style in Chinese landscape painting. The twofold goal of this art is to discover the unity and harmony that underlie nature and to incorporate man—both artist and viewer—into that harmony. Li Ch'eng's landscapes are among the most exquisitely wrought and deeply felt objects from the whole vast range of Chinese art.

9. The French town of Conques, with the Church of Ste. Foy (eleventh century). By the eleventh century a wave of religious fervor swept across the Continent. Hosts of pilgrims traveled set routes to sacred sites, and along these routes towns sprang up. The towns erected churches, which were grander than ever before, and whose complex floor plans could more readily accommodate the traffic of the pilgrims. Christianity began to belong to the masses, and the flowering of the Middle Ages grew increasingly evident in the stately towers and arches of the monumental Romanesque style.

Chapter 5

The City
of
God

The Rise of Christianity and the Fall of Rome

INTRODUCTION. To the inhabitants of the Graeco-Roman world, Rome was the "Eternal City"—a proud designation which is still used today. When, therefore, in 410 A.D. the barbarian Visigoths responded to its magnetic lure by entering Italy and sacking the city, a cry of anguish reverberated throughout the crumbling Empire. In distant Bethlehem St. Jerome cried, "The lamp of the world is extinguished, and it is the whole world which has perished in the ruins of this one city."[1]

This chapter completes the history of Rome—it tells of the fall of the City of the Caesars and the emergence, like the phoenix arising from the ashes, of the "City of God." It was St. Augustine who, in the wake of the Visigoths' capture of Rome, devised that phrase to represent the rise of a new Christian society on the ruins of paganism and a once invincible Empire—and to assure Christians that the "community of the Most High" would endure, although the greatest city on earth had fallen.

This period in history has several facets.

One concerns the national history of the Jews, the coming of Jesus in the midst of their turbulent relations with the Romans, and the eventual triumph of his teachings. Another is the story of the progressive decline of the Roman Empire during the time of Christianity's triumph. A third element is the migration of the Germanic peoples and their settlement in Europe—a movement which completed the disintegration of the western half of the Roman Empire. A final aspect (to be discussed in the next chapter) is the shift in civilization's center of gravity —from the West, overrun by barbarians, to the eastern shores of the Mediterranean and even beyond.

THE RISE AND TRIUMPH OF CHRISTIANITY

Post-exilic Jewish nationalism. At the very time when the Principate of Augustus was laying the foundations of Rome's imperial greatness, events were taking place in the distant Roman province of Judea that would one day alter the course of western history. Following the conquests of Alexander the Great in the Near East, Palestine was ruled first by the Ptolemies and then by the Seleucids. Since their return from exile in Babylonia in 538 B.C. (see p. 30), the Jews in Palestine had created a theocratic community, based upon the Torah, God's Law, originally revealed to Moses and contained in the Pentateuch (the first five books of the Old Testament), and later supplemented by the teachings of the prophets and the writings of scholars. Religious life centered on the Temple at Jerusalem, which echoed with the cry "Hallelujah" ("Praise ye Yahweh") in thanksgiving for Yahweh's gracious dealing with his people. The most powerful figure was the high priest, assisted by the Sanhedrin, the high court for the enforcement of the Law. Since there was no distinction between civil and religious law, the jurisdiction of the Sanhedrin covered all aspects of Jewish life.

The Hebrews, the "People of God," were tightly knit; even the Jewish groups outside Palestine were linked by spiritual bonds to the Temple and to a law which they believed to be divinely inspired. But, being unable to participate in the services of the Temple at Jerusalem, the Jews of the Diaspora met in local synagogues (from the Greek word for "assembly") for informal worship and instruction in the Scriptures. In the long run, the synagogue, which probably first arose during the Babylonian Exile, outlived the Temple to become the heart of Judaism. It also influenced the forms of worship in the Christian church and the Muslim mosque.

During the Hellenistic Age, Greek influences were constantly at work among the Jews. Most Jews outside Palestine spoke Greek, and a Greek translation of the Hebrew Scriptures became a necessity. Called the Septuagint (Latin for "seventy") from the tradition that it was the work of seventy scholars whose independent translations were miraculously identical, it was produced at Alexandria in the third century B.C.

Greek influences contributed to factionalism among the Jews in Judea. Eventually, one extremely pious group came to blows with the aristocratic pro-Greek Sadducees, as they came to be called, who were favored by the Seleucid rulers of Palestine. The internal conflict gave the Seleucid king an opportunity to intervene, and in 168 B.C., seeking to completely Hellenize the Jews, he ordered the Temple dedicated to the worship of Zeus. Viewing this decree as a blasphemous defilement, the Jews rebelled. Under their leader, Judas Maccabaeus, they rededicated the Temple to Yahweh and in 142 B.C. won their independence from the Seleucids.

Although Judas and his immediate successors contented themselves with the title of high priest, later members of the family were known as kings. In time these rulers became worldly and corrupt, and factionalism again flared up, resulting in persecution and bloodshed. It was in the midst of a civil war that the Roman legions appeared on the scene.

Roman occupation of Palestine. Adopting the practice habitually followed by eastern Mediterranean states, one Jewish faction appealed to Rome for aid. Pompey, who was then completing his pacification of Asia Minor and Syria (see p. 74), ended the civil war in 63 B.C. by making Judea subject to the governor of Syria.

Eventually, Herod the Great, a half-Jewish, half-Arab leader from Edom just south of Judea, rose to power as a tool of the Romans. Appointed by Mark Antony, Herod served as king of Judea from 37 to 4 B.C. He erected a magnificent palace, a theater, a hippodrome, and rebuilt the Temple on a lavish scale. To the Jews, however, Herod remained a detested usurper who professed Judaism as a matter of expediency. Soon after his death, Judea was made into a minor Roman province ruled by governors called procurators, the best known of whom is Pontius Pilate (26-36 A.D.), under whom Jesus was crucified.

The Jews themselves remained unhappy and divided. During centuries of tribulation the prophets had taught that God would one day create a new Israel when righteousness prevailed under a God-anointed leader, the Messiah. In time, many Jews lost hope in a political Messiah and an earthly kingdom and instead conceived of a spiritual Messiah who would lead all the righteous, including the resurrected dead, to a spiritual kingdom. But a group of ardent Jewish nationalists, called Zealots, favoring the use of force to drive the hated foreigner out of God's land, precipitated a fatal clash with Rome.

Destruction of Jerusalem. In 66 A.D. violence erupted when the Roman garrison at Jerusalem was massacred. After a five-year siege, Titus, son of the emperor Vespasian, laid waste the city. What came to be called the "Wailing Wall," a small part of the Temple complex, remained standing. The story is that it was protected by angels whose tears cemented the stones in place forever. It was later prophesied that a third Temple would be erected on the site when the Messiah came. (The Dome of the Rock, a mosque built by the Muslims, has occupied the site since the eighth century A.D.) The wholesale destruction of Jerusalem in 70 A.D. spelled the end of the ancient Hebrew state. The Jewish dream of an independent homeland was to remain unrealized for almost nineteen centuries, until the republic of Israel was proclaimed in 1948.

Development of Jewish religious thought. The destruction of Jerusalem did not destroy the most important single aspect of Jewish culture—its religion. Through centuries of suffering, captivity, and subjugation, the Jews had been taught by a succession of prophets to cleave to their covenant with Yahweh and to safeguard their religious inheritance.

In the centuries just preceding and following the birth of Christ, Judaism exhibited vigor and strength. While the aristocratic Sadducees, who controlled the office of high priest, stood for strict adherence to the written Law or Torah, the more numerous Pharisees believed that, with divine guidance, men could modify and amend the Law. For example, they accepted the belief in personal immortality and the Kingdom of Heaven. From their ranks came the rabbis, scholars who expounded the Law and applied it to existing conditions. The "oral law" propagated by the Pharisees became the core of the later Talmud. Moreover, following the destruction of the Temple and the end of the high priesthood, the rabbinical schools of the Pharisees did much to ensure that Judaism would endure.

The Dead Sea Scrolls. In recent years the discovery of the Dead Sea Scrolls has added greatly to our knowledge of another Jewish sect, the Essenes. While exploring caves about the desolate western shore of the Dead Sea in 1947, two Bedouin boys came across several clay jars containing long manuscripts wrapped in linen. Later, many more scrolls were found in other caves. Nearby were the ruins of a monastery built by the Essenes "to separate themselves," as the scrolls state, "from the abode of perverse men." Occupied between the second century B.C. and 68 A.D., the monastery was destroyed by the Romans during the great Jewish revolt. Prior to its destruction the Essenes hid their manuscripts in the caves.

Some scrolls are portions of the Old Testament dating from the first century B.C. and

The partially unrolled Thanksgiving Scroll, one of the Dead Sea Scrolls preserved at the Hebrew University in Jerusalem, is composed of religious hymns which poetically develop the Essenes' theological doctrines.

thus are centuries older than the earliest text previously known. Jewish and Christian scholars alike have been thrilled to read the Book of Isaiah in such ancient manuscript and to discover that the version we have been using, although based on much later sources, has been accurate except in some details.

Those scrolls which describe the Essene sect in the first century B.C.—that is, just prior to the appearance of Christianity—have been said to constitute "a whole missing chapter of the history of the growth of religious ideas between Judaism and Christianity."[2] Some scholars have attached much significance to common elements in the beliefs and practices of the Essenes and early Christians. The Essenes' founder, a shadowy figure known as the Teacher of Righteousness, suffered persecution and perhaps martyrdom late in the second century B.C. The sect considered itself the true remnant of God's people, preached a "new covenant," and waited patiently for the time when God would destroy the powers of evil and inau-

gurate His Kingdom. Similar views concerning the transition from the "Old Age" to the "New Age" were held by many other Jews as well as by Christians. For the Christians, however, the gap had been bridged. The Messiah had come, and his resurrection was proof that the New Age had arrived. "The New Testament faith was not a new faith, but the fulfillment of an old faith. . . . Lines of continuity between Moses and Jesus, Isaiah and Jesus, the Righteous Teacher and Jesus, John the Baptist and Jesus should occasion no surprise. On the contrary, a biblical faith insists on such continuities. . . . [The Bible is] a history of God's acts of redemption."[3]

The life of Jesus. Whatever its parallels with the Essene sect—including baptism and a communal meal—Christianity bears the unmistakable imprint of the personality of its founder, Jesus of Nazareth. According to the Biblical account, he was born in Bethlehem during the reign of Herod; therefore he may have been born by the time of Herod's death (4 B.C.) rather than in the year which traditionally begins the Christian era. After spending the first years of his life as a carpenter in the village of Nazareth, Jesus began his brief mission, preaching a gospel of love for one's fellow man and urging people to "Repent, for the kingdom of heaven is at hand" (Matthew 4:17).

The fame of Jesus' teaching and holiness spread among the Jews as he and his twelve disciples traveled from village to village in Palestine. When he came to Jerusalem to observe the feast of the Passover, he was welcomed triumphantly by huge crowds as the promised Messiah. But Jesus was concerned with a spiritual, not an earthly, kingdom, and when the people saw that he had no intention of leading a nationalistic movement against the Romans, they turned against him. His enemies then came forward—the moneylenders whom he had denounced, the Pharisees who resented his repudiation of their minute regulations of daily behavior, the people who considered him a disturber of the status quo, and those who saw him as a blasphemer of Yahweh. Betrayed by Judas, one of his disciples, Jesus was condemned by the Sanhedrin for blasphemy "because he claimed to be the Son of God" (John 19:7). Before the procurator Pontius Pilate, however, Jesus was charged with treason for claiming to be the king of Jews.

"Are you the king of Jews?" he [Pilate] asked him. Jesus answered, . . . "My kingdom does not belong to this world; if my kingdom belonged to this world, my followers would fight to keep me from being handed over to the Jews. No, my kingdom does not belong here. . . . You say that I am a king. I was born and came into the world for this one purpose, to speak about the truth. Whoever belongs to the truth listens to me." "And what is truth?" Pilate asked.[4]

Jesus was condemned to the death that Rome inflicted on criminals—crucifixion.

With Jesus' death it seemed as though his cause had been exterminated. No written message had been left behind, and his few loyal followers were disheartened. Yet in the wake of his martyrdom the Christian cause took on new impetus. Reports soon spread that Jesus had been seen after his crucifixion and had spoken to his disciples, giving them solace and inspiration. At first there were few converts within Palestine itself, but the Hellenized Jews living in foreign lands, in contact with new ideas and modes of living, were less firmly committed to traditional Jewish doctrines. The new religion first made real headway among the Jewish communities in such cities as Damascus, Antioch, Corinth, and Rome.

Paul's missionary work. As long as the followers of Jesus regarded him exclusively as a Messiah in the traditional Jewish sense, requiring his followers to observe the Jewish Law, the new religion could have no universal appeal. Largely through the missionary efforts of Paul, this obstacle was removed.

Born Saul, of strict Jewish ancestry, and raised in a Hellenistic city in Asia Minor, this Christian saint possessed a wide knowledge of Greek culture. Saul was also a strict Pharisee who considered Christians to be blasphemers against the Law and took an active part in their persecution. One day, on the road to Damascus—in Saul's own words:

And as I was traveling and coming near Damascus, about midday a bright light suddenly flashed from the sky around me. I fell to the ground and heard a voice saying to me, "Saul, Saul! Why do you persecute me?" "Who are you, Lord?" I asked. "I am Jesus of Nazareth, whom you persecute," he said to me. The men with me saw the light but did not hear the voice of the one who was speaking to me. I asked, "What shall I do, Lord?" and the Lord said to me, "Get up and go into Damascus, and there you will be told everything that God has determined for you."[5]

Saul, henceforth known as Paul, turned from being a persecutor into the greatest of Christian missionaries.

Paul taught that Jesus was the Christ (from *Christos*, Greek for "Messiah"), the Son of God, and that He had died to atone for the sins of mankind. Acceptance of this belief guaranteed salvation to Jews and gentiles alike. The Law, with its strict dietary regulations and other requirements that discouraged the conversion of gentiles, was unnecessary:

A man is put right with God only through faith in Jesus Christ, never by doing what the Law requires. . . . So there is no difference between Jews and Gentiles, between slaves and free men, between men and women: you are all one in union with Christ Jesus.[6]

Tradition states that after covering eight thousand miles teaching and preaching, Paul was beheaded at Rome about 65 A.D. (as was also Peter, founder of the church at Rome) during the reign of Nero. By this time Christian communities had already been established in all important cities of the Roman Empire.

Persecution of Christians. The Roman government tolerated any religion that did not threaten the safety or tranquility of the Empire. Christianity, however, clearly appeared to be a subversive danger to society and the state. The Christians refused to participate in the worship of the emperor which, although not an official state religion, was considered an essential patriotic rite uniting all Roman subjects in common loyalty to the imperial government. To Christians there was only one God; no other could share their loyalty to Him. In the eyes of the Roman officials this attitude branded them as traitors. In addition, the Christians seemed a secret, unsociable group forming a state within a state—"walling themselves off from the rest of mankind," as a pagan writer observed. Many were pacifists who refused to serve in the army, and all were intolerant of other religious sects and refused to associate with pagans or take part in social functions that they considered sinful or degrading.

During the first two centuries A.D. persecution was only sporadic and local, like that at Rome under Nero (see p. 76). But during the late third and early fourth centuries, when, as we shall see, the Empire was in danger of collapse, three organized empire-wide efforts were made to suppress Christianity. By far the longest and most systematic campaign against the Christians, who now comprised perhaps one tenth of the population, was instigated by the emperor Diocletian from 303 to 311. But the inspired defiance of the Christian martyrs, who seemed to welcome death—"The blood of the martyrs is the seed of the Church" are the words of a third-century Christian[7]—could not be overcome.

Official recognition and acceptance. In 311 the emperor Galerius recognized that persecution had failed and issued an edict of toleration making Christianity a legal religion in the East. In the following year the emperor Constantine was swayed toward Christianity during a desperate battle with the army of a rival for the throne. At the height of the conflict, tradition has it that he saw emblazoned across the sky a cross with the words *In hoc signo vinces* ("By this sign thou shalt conquer"). Constantine won the battle, and in 313 he issued the Edict of Milan, which legalized Christianity throughout the Empire and put it on a par with all the pagan cults. Constantine favored Christianity by granting many privileges to the Church, but he waited until he was on his deathbed before receiving baptism. His successors, with one exception, were Christians.

In his brief reign (361-363) the scholarly emperor Julian, Constantine's nephew, who had been raised a Christian, renounced his faith and sought to revive paganism; as a result, he was branded the Apostate. Julian did not persecute the Christians ("Those who are in the wrong in matters of supreme importance," he wrote, "are objects of pity rather than of hate"[8]), and his efforts to revive paganism failed dismally. On his deathbed he is supposed to have said, "Thou hast conquered, O Galilean."

From the time that Constantine legalized Christianity, representations of Jesus became numerous throughout the Roman Empire and in converted areas. These images changed in accord with the temper of the time and the people creating them. A bas-relief from a late fourth-century sarcophagus shows a mild, youthful Jesus (left) speaking with the apostle Peter. Both are dressed in traditional Roman robes.

The final step in the triumph of Christianity was taken during the reign of Theodosius I (379-395), who made Christianity the official religion of the Empire. Henceforth paganism was persecuted, and even the Olympic games were suppressed.

Reasons for the spread of Christianity. In its rise to preeminence Christianity competed with the philosophies and religions of the day. The philosophies were becoming more religious and other-worldly, however, which made it easy for their adherents to accept a Christianity whose doctrines, as we shall see, were becoming more philosophical. During the early Empire most Roman intellectuals had embraced Stoicism which, unlike Epicureanism with its unyielding materialism, had room for God (see p. 86). The dominant philosophy of the third century, Neo-Platonism, rejected human reason and taught that the only reality is spirit and that the soul's principal objective is to escape from the material world and, by union with God, return to its spiritual home.

There were also the popular mystery religions such as the worship of the Phrygian Great Mother (Cybele), the Egyptian Isis, the Greek Dionysus, and the Persian Mithras, god of light who fought against darkness (Mithras was especially popular with soldiers). All of these cults presented the comforting idea of a divine savior and the promise of everlasting life. Their followers found Christian beliefs and practices sufficiently familiar so as to make conversion easy.

But Christianity had far more to offer than did the mystery religions. Its founder was not a creature of myth, like the gods and goddesses of the mystery cults, but a real historic personality whose lofty ethical teachings and whose death and resurrection as the divine incarnation of God were preserved in detail in a unique record—the New Testament. Also unique was the Christian God—the omnipotent, jealous yet loving God of the Hebrew Scriptures now universalized as the God of all mankind. Moreover, Christianity was a dynamic, aggressive faith. It upheld the equality of all men—Jesus' ministry was chiefly to the poor and downtrodden—taught that a loving Father had

The Church of St. Apollinare in Classe, outside Ravenna, is an early basilica (from the Greek, *basilikos,* meaning "kingly") which Justinian erected on the site of a temple of Apollo. Strong Byzantine influence is especially apparent in the remarkable mosaics in the apse.

sent His only Son to atone for men's sins, and offered a vision of immortality and an opportunity to be "born again" cleansed of sin. Its converts displayed enthusiasm and zeal, and the courage with which they faced death and persecution impressed even their bitterest enemies. In time, also, a Church organization was created that was far more united and efficient than any possessed by its competitors.

Church organization. The years immediately following Christ's death had passed with little organization in the Christian movement. Viewing the present world as something that would end quickly with the imminent Second Coming of their Lord, the earliest converts saw no necessity for organization. But after it became clear that the Second Coming had been postponed, a definite Church organization began to emerge.

At first there was little or no distinction

between laity and clergy. Traveling teachers visited Christian communities, preaching and giving advice where needed. But the steady growth in the number of Christians made necessary special Church officials who could devote all their time to religious work, clarifying the body of Christian dogma, conducting services, and caring for the funds. The earliest officials were called presbyters (elders) or bishops (overseers). By the second century the offices of bishop and presbyter had become distinct. Churches in the villages adjacent to the mother Church, which was usually located in a city, were administered by priests (a corruption of *presbyter*) responsible to a bishop. Thus evolved the diocese, a territorial administrative division under the jurisdiction of a bishop. Furthermore, the bishops were recognized as the successors of the apostles and, like them, the guardians of Christian teaching and tradition.

A number of dioceses made up a province; the bishop of the most important city in each province enjoyed more prestige than his fellows and was known as an archbishop or metropolitan. The provinces were grouped into larger administrative divisions called patriarchates. The title of patriarch was applied to the bishop of such great cities as Rome, Constantinople, and Alexandria.

Primacy of the bishop of Rome. A development of outstanding importance was the rise of the bishop of Rome to a position of preeminence in the hierarchy of the Church. At first only one of several patriarchs, the Roman bishop gradually became recognized as the leader of the Church in the West with the title of pope—from the Greek word meaning "father."

Many factors explain the emergence of the papacy at Rome. As the largest city in the West and the capital of the Empire, Rome had an aura of prestige that was transferred to its bishop. When the Empire in the West collapsed in the fifth century, the bishop of Rome emerged as a stable and dominant figure looked up to by all. The primacy of Rome was fully evident during the pontificate of Leo I, called the Great (440-461), who provided both the leadership that saved Italy from invasion by the Huns (see p. 135) and

the major theoretical support for papal headship of the Church—the Petrine theory. This doctrine held that since Peter, whom Christ had made leader of the apostles, was the first bishop of Rome, his authority over all Christians was handed on to his successors at Rome. The Church in the East, insisting on the equality of all the apostles, has never accepted the Petrine theory.

Foundations of Christian doctrine and worship. While the administrative structure of the Church was being erected, Christian beliefs were being defined and systematized. This process of fixing the dogma began with Paul, who stressed the divinity of Jesus and interpreted his death as an atonement for man's sins.

In time differences of opinion over doctrinal matters caused clashes. One of the most important controversies was over Arianism. At issue was the relative position of the three persons of the Trinity—God the Father, God the Son, and God the Holy Spirit. The view that the Father and the Son were equal was vigorously denied by Arius (256-336), a priest of Alexandria, who believed that Christ was not fully God because he was not of a substance identical with God and, as a created being, was not coeternal with Him. The controversy became so serious that in 325 the emperor Constantine convened the first ecumenical Church council, the Council of Nicaea, to resolve the problem. With Constantine presiding, the council branded the Arian belief a heresy—an opinion or doctrine contrary to the official teachings of the Church—and Christ was declared to be of the same substance as God, uncreated, and coeternal with Him. This mystical concept of the Trinity, without which the central Christian doctrine of the incarnation would be undermined, received official formulation in the Nicene Creed. Despite persecution, Arianism continued to flourish throughout the fourth century, and we shall see that some of the German tribes had been converted to this Christian heresy before they invaded the Empire.

The liturgy in the early churches was plain and simple, consisting of prayer, Scripture reading, hymns, and preaching. The early Christian worshiped God and sought salvation largely through his own efforts. Following the growth of Church organization and dogma, however, the Church was believed to be the indispensable intermediary between God and man. Without the Church the individual could not hope to approach God.

The development of the Church's dogma owed much to the Church Fathers of the second through fifth centuries. Since most of them were intellectuals who came to Christianity by way of Neo-Platonism and Stoicism, they maintained that Greek philosophy and Christianity were compatible. Because reason (*logos* in Greek) and truth come from God, "philosophy was a preparation," wrote Clement of Alexandria (d. 215), "paving the way towards perfection in Christ,"[9] the latest and most perfect manifestation of God's reason. Thus Christianity was viewed as a superior philosophy which could supersede all pagan philosophies and religions.

In the West three Church Fathers stand out. The scholarship of St. Jerome (340-420) made possible the famous Vulgate translation of the Bible into Latin, which in a revised form is still the official translation of the Roman Catholic Church. St. Ambrose (340-397) resigned his government post to become bishop of Milan, where he employed his great administrative skills to establish a model bishopric. By reproving the actions of the strong emperor Theodosius I and forcing him to do public penance, St. Ambrose was the first to assert the Church's superiority over the state in spiritual matters. St. Augustine (354-430) was probably the most important of all the Church Fathers. At the age of thirty-two he found in Christianity the answer to his long search for meaning in life, as he relates in his *Confessions*, one of the world's great autobiographies. As bishop of Hippo in North Africa, he wrote more than a hundred religious works which became the foundation of much of the Church's theology.

The regular clergy. So far we have discussed the secular clergy, who moved through the world (*saeculum*) administering the Church's services and communicating its teachings to the laity. But another type of churchmen also arose—the regular clergy, so called because they lived by a rule (*regula*) within monasteries. These monks sought seclusion from the distractions of this world in order to prepare themselves for the next.

The monastic way of life was older than Christianity, having existed in Judaism, for example, among the Essenes (see pp. 123–124). Christian ascetics, who had abandoned the worldly life and become hermits, could be found in the East as early as the third century A.D. Some went so far as to denounce even beauty as evil and, in pursuit of spiritual perfection by subordinating their flesh, tortured themselves and fasted to excess. In Syria, for example, St. Simeon Stylites lived for thirty-seven years on top of a pillar sixty feet high.

As a more moderate expression of asceticism, Christians in Egypt developed the monastic life, wherein men seeking a common spiritual goal lived together under a common set of regulations. St. Basil (330-379), a Greek bishop in Asia Minor, drew up a rule based on work, charity, and a communal life in which, however, each monk retained most of his independence. The Rule of St. Basil became the standard system in the eastern Church.

In western monasticism the work of St. Benedict (c. 480-543) paralleled St. Basil's efforts in the East. About 529 St. Benedict led a band of followers to a hill between Rome and Naples, named Monte Cassino, where they erected a monastery on the site of an ancient pagan temple. There he composed a rule which gave order and discipline to western monasticism. Benedictine monks took the three basic vows of poverty, chastity, and obedience to the abbot, the head of the monastery. Unlike eastern monks, the daily activities of the Benedictine monks were closely regulated: they participated in eight divine services, labored in field or workshop for six or seven hours, and spent about two hours studying and preserving the writings of Latin antiquity at a time when chaos and illiteracy had overtaken the western half of the Roman Empire. Benedictine monasticism was to be the most dynamic civilizing force in western Europe between the sixth and the twelfth centuries.

DECLINE AND DIVISION IN THE ROMAN WORLD

The crisis of the third century. In the third century A.D., while Christianity was spreading throughout the Roman world, internal anarchy and foreign invasion drastically transformed the nature of the Empire. What can be called the constitutional monarchy of the first and second centuries (see p. 75) changed to a despotic absolute monarchy in which the emperors made no attempt to hide the fact that they were "army made." By the late third century the emperor was no longer addressed as *princeps*, meaning first among equals, but as *dominus et deus*, "lord and god." The Principate had been replaced by absolute rule known as the Dominate.

The transformation of the Roman Empire in the third century was foreshadowed by the reign of Commodus, who succeeded his father, Marcus Aurelius, in 180 A.D. Commodus was an incompetent voluptuary whose dissipations, cruelties, and neglect of affairs of state motivated a group of conspirators to have him strangled in 192 A.D. Civil war followed as rival armies fought for the imperial throne—on one occasion troops holding Rome sold the throne to the highest bidder—until Septimius Severus emerged on top and established a dynasty that provided some measure of order.

The Severan dynasty (193-235), like the reign of Commodus and its aftermath, marks the approaching end of the Principate. The Senate was ignored and the army pampered and enlarged. Septimius Severus' dying words to his sons, "Enrich the soldiers and scorn all others," reflect the trend of the times.

The dire effects of this toadying to the soldiery became apparent after 235, when the last member of the Severan dynasty was murdered by mutinous troops. During the next fifty years the Empire was rent from within by bloody civil wars and lashed from without by foreign invaders. The imperial scepter was dragged in the gutter by generals who murdered emperors with no compunction, intimidated all opposition, and put themselves or their puppets on the throne. Of the twenty-six who claimed the title of emperor during this long period of military anarchy, only one died a natural death.

Meanwhile, German tribes breached the imperial frontiers: the Franks devastated Gaul and Spain, the Saxons attacked Britain, and the Goths occupied Dacia (modern Rumania). For the first time since Hannibal's invasion five centuries earlier, it was felt necessary to protect Rome itself with a wall twenty feet high and twelve feet wide, which still stands. In Asia a powerful new menace appeared after 226—a reinvigorated Persia under the rule of the Sassanid dynasty, which proceeded to attack Syria.

Economic decline. As deadly to the well-being of the Empire as military anarchy and foreign invasions was prolonged economic decline. The Empire was no longer expanding; the economy had become static. In the past military expansion had paid off in rich booty, and the tapping of new sources of wealth had justified a large army. Now, however, wars were defensive, and the army had become a financial liability rather than an asset. Gold and silver were also being drained away because of the one-sided trade with India and China (see pp. 116-117).

The trend toward the concentration of land ownership in a few hands was greatly accelerated by the turbulent conditions of the third century. Small farmers abandoned their lands, which were then bought up cheaply by large landowners, and the emperors added to their vast estates through confiscation. The number of tenant farmers, or *coloni* (see p. 79), increased as small farming decreased and men fled the insecurity of city life to find jobs and protection on the large estates with their fortified villas. There they cultivated their patches of land, paying rent to the landowner and providing him with free labor at sowing and reaping time. The condition of the *coloni* worsened as they fell behind in their rents and taxes and, by imperial order, were bound to their tenancies until they had discharged their debts. This was a first step toward serfdom and the social and economic pattern of the Middle Ages.

To make matters worse, the monetary system became extremely confused. In order to meet their military and administrative expenses, the emperors repeatedly devalued the coinage by reducing its silver content. Ultimately the amount of alloy reached 98 percent, and prices soared as people gradually lost confidence in the debased currency. Even the government eventually refused to accept its own money for taxes and required payment in goods and services. Civil war also disturbed trade and thus helped undermine the prosperity of the cities, whose population decreased correspondingly.

Diocletian. A much-needed reconstruction of the Empire was accomplished by Diocletian (285-305), a rough-hewn soldier and administrative genius whose work of stabilization is often compared to that of Augustus after a similar period of turmoil. But while Augustus had established a form of constitutional monarchy, Diocletian founded an undisguised oriental despotism.

To increase the strength of the government, Diocletian completed the trend toward autocracy. The Senate was relegated to the status of a mere city council, while the person of the emperor was exalted. Adorned in robes laden with jewels, the emperor surrounded himself with all the splendor of an oriental despot. An imperial etiquette was established which transformed the emperor into a veritable god; rigid ceremonial demanded that men bow low before him and address him as "the most sacred lord."

The imperial administration was greatly enlarged. Diocletian realized that the Empire's problems had become too great for one man. He divided the Empire, retaining the eastern half for his own administration. In the West he created a coemperor who, like himself, was designated an Augustus. Each Augustus in turn was to entrust the direct rule of half his realm to an assistant, termed Caesar. Since each Caesar would succeed his Augustus when the senior official died or retired, the problem of succession was supposedly solved.

Next, Diocletian greatly increased the number and variety of administrative units

Diocletian and his co-Augustus, each with his appointed Caesar, are shown in an embrace symbolic of the unity which Diocletian hoped to maintain despite administrative division of the empire. This sculpture now adorns St. Mark's Cathedral in Venice.

within the four divisions of the Empire. The provinces were reduced in size and more than doubled in number. (Italy lost its hitherto favored position and was divided into provinces.) The 120 provinces were grouped into thirteen dioceses, each under a vicar. The dioceses in turn were grouped into four prefectures, each under a prefect who served directly under one of the four emperors. Paralleling this civil administration was a separate hierarchy of military officials. Finally, a large secret service was created to keep close watch over this vast bureaucracy. Even the Christian Church did not escape the spreading tentacles of the new regimented state, as Diocletian's ruthless persecution of Christianity demonstrates.

Diocletian also made strenuous efforts to arrest economic decay in the Empire. He gradually restored confidence in the debased currency by issuing new standard silver and gold coins. In the meantime, in an effort to stem the runaway inflation, he issued an edict fixing maximum prices for all essential goods and services, ranging from peas to beer, and from haircuts to freight rates. The following selection from the preamble of the edict reflects the paternalistic social philosophy of the new age:

If the excesses perpetrated by persons of unlimited and frenzied avarice could be checked by some self-restraint—this avarice which rushes for gain and profit with no thought for mankind . . . ; or if the general welfare could endure without harm this riotous license by which, in its unfortunate state, it is being seriously injured every day, the situation could perhaps be faced with dissembling and silence. . . . But the only desire of these uncontrolled madmen is to have no thought for the common need. . . . Therefore we who are the protectors of the human race, are agreed, as we view the situation, that decisive legislation is necessary. . . .[10]

Constantine. After Diocletian and his fellow Augustus retired in 305, his scheme for the succession collapsed, and civil war broke out once again. Within a few years Constantine (306-337), the only one of five rival emperors who favored Christianity (see p. 126), forged to the front, and after sharing the Empire for a few years with an eastern rival, became sole emperor in 324.

Constantine carried on Diocletian's work of reconstructing and stabilizing the Empire. We have already noted his solution of the Christian problem. To stabilize the manpower situation, necessary for the production of essential goods and services as well as the collection of taxes, Constantine issued a series of decrees which froze people to their occupations and places of origin. Henceforth no *colonus* could leave the soil, and the children of a *colonus* had to accept the same status as that of their father. In the cities the same restrictions were applied to members of those guilds whose activities were essential to the state, such as baking and transportation. Born into and bound to their occupations, members had to marry within the guild and train their sons to carry on the same line of work. Thus, to serve the interests of the state and to arrest further economic decline, a veritable caste system was established.

Division of the Empire. The Roman world's center of gravity shifted eastward during the age of Diocletian and Constantine. The administrative reforms swept away Italy's former primacy, and Rome even ceased to be a seat of imperial authority. Diocletian's coemperor in the West ruled from Milan, while Diocletian himself chose to govern the eastern half of the Empire and set up his court at Nicomedia in northwestern Asia Minor. His was a logical choice; the East had declined less than the West, and the greatest dangers to the Empire came from beyond the Danube River and from Persia. But even more strategic than Nicomedia was the old Greek colony of Byzantium, across the straits, selected by Constantine for a new capital. Reached only through a narrow, easily defended channel, Byzantium possessed a splendid harbor at the crossroads of Europe and Asia. Constantine dubbed his capital New Rome, but it soon became known as Constantinople.

The establishment of an eastern capital foreshadowed the impending division of the Empire into two completely separate states, the East and the West. For about fifty years following the death of Constantine in 337, the unity of the Empire was preserved, although there were often two joint emperors, one in the East and the other in the West. But after Theodosius I divided it between his two sons in 395, the Empire was never again governed as a single unit. Henceforth we can speak of a western Roman empire, which soon fell, and of an eastern Roman—or Byzantine—empire, which endured for another thousand years during which it adhered to the paternalistic and authoritarian pattern laid down by Diocletian and Constantine.

UPHEAVAL IN THE WEST

The Germanic tribes. Weakened by economic, social, and political decline, Rome had turned to the most extreme forms of absolutism in an effort to ride out the storm that threatened to engulf it. But its internal crisis was compounded by mounting external pressures that threatened to stave in its far-flung frontiers. The greatest danger lay to the north, the home of restless bands of fierce barbarians—the Germans. From the Franks on the Rhine to the Goths on the Black Sea, they were grouped into tribes (whose names will appear in the text as each makes its bid for the spoils of a tottering empire). Semi-nomads, the Germans were at a cultural stage midway between a pastoral and an agricultural economy. They engaged in so little commerce that cattle, rather than money, were sufficient as a measure of value.

According to the Roman historian Tacitus, the Germans were notorious as heavy drinkers and gamblers. On the other hand, Tacitus praised their courage, respect for women, and freedom from many Roman vices. A favorite amusement was listening to the tribal bards recite ancient tales of heroes and gods.

Each warrior leader had a retinue of followers, who were linked to him by personal loyalty. According to Tacitus:

On the field of battle it is a disgrace to the chief to be surpassed in valour by his companions, to the companions not to come up to the valour of their chief. As for leaving a battle alive after your chief has fallen, *that* means lifelong infamy and shame. To defend and protect him, to put down one's own acts of heroism to his credit—that is what they really mean by "allegiance". The chiefs fight for victory, the companions for their chief.[11]

This war band—called *comitatus* in Latin—had an important bearing on the origin of medieval feudalism, which was based on the personal bond between knights and their feudal lords. The heroic virtues associated with the *comitatus* also continued into the Middle Ages where they formed the basis of the value system of the feudal nobility.

In an effort to eliminate blood feuds, the Germanic system of justice was based on the principle of compensation. For the infliction of specific injuries a stipulated payment termed a *bot* was required. The amount of compensation varied according to the severity of the crime and the social position of the victim. For example, it cost forty times as much to kill a man of rank as a common man. Some crimes were botless—that is, so grave in character that compensation could not be paid. A person charged with such a crime had to stand trial and produce oath-helpers who would swear to his innocence. If unable to obtain oath-helpers, he was subjected to trial by ordeal, of which there were three kinds. In the first, the defendant had to lift a small stone out of a vessel of boiling water; unless his scalded arm had healed within a prescribed number of days, he was judged guilty. In the second, he had to walk blindfolded and barefooted across a floor on which lay pieces of red-hot metal; success in avoiding the metal was a sign of innocence. In the third, the bound defendant was thrown into a stream which had been blessed; only if the holy water accepted him and he sank was he believed innocent. Trial by ordeal, which was employed only where a strong presumption of guilt existed, lasted until the thirteenth century, when it was outlawed by Pope Innocent iii and various secular rulers.

Roman-German contacts. During the many centuries that the Romans and Germans faced each other across the Rhine-Danube frontier, there was much contact—peaceful as well as belligerent—between the two peoples. Roman trade reached into Germany, and Germans entered the Empire as slaves. During the troubled third century many Germans were invited to settle on vacated lands within the Empire or to serve in the Roman legions. By the end of the fourth century the Roman army and its generals in the West had become almost completely German.

The Germans beyond the frontiers were kept in check by force of arms, by frontier walls, by diplomacy and gifts, and by employing the policy of playing off one tribe against another. In the last decades of the fourth century, however, these methods proved insufficient to prevent a series of great new invasions. A basic factor behind Germanic restlessness seems to have been land hunger. Their numbers were increasing, much of their land was forest and swamp, and their methods of tillage were inefficient.

Wholesale barbarian invasions. Meanwhile another restless people were on the move. The Huns, superb Mongolian horsemen and fighters, were nomads from Central Asia who had for centuries plundered and slain their Asian neighbors. In 372 they

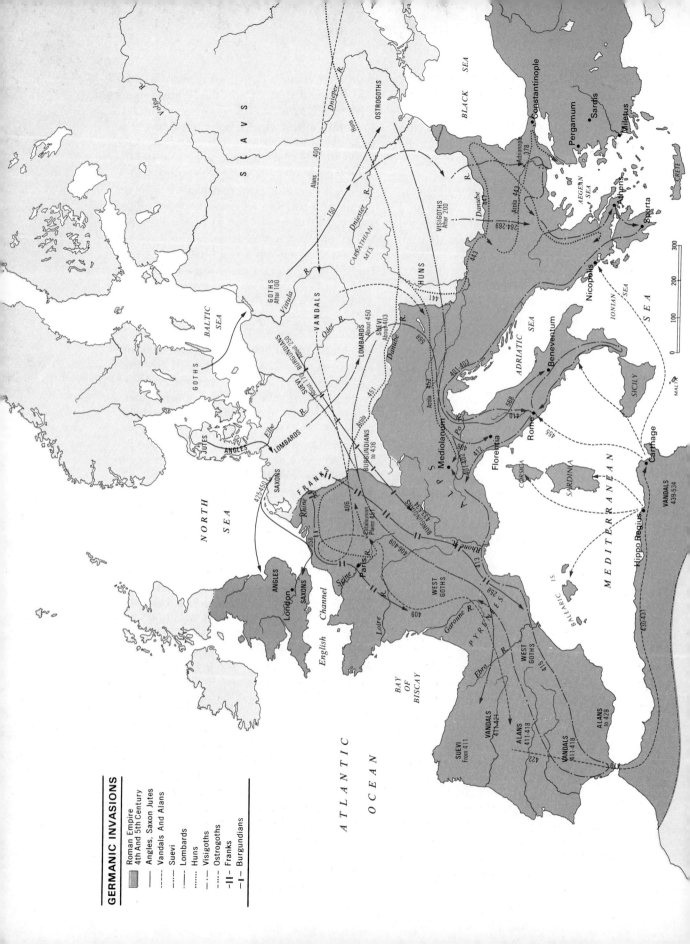

GERMANIC INVASIONS

Roman Empire
4th And 5th Century

Angles, Saxon Jutes

Vandals And Alans

Suevi

Lombards

Huns

Visigoths

Ostrogoths

Franks

Burgundians

crossed the Volga and soon subjugated the easternmost Germanic tribe, the Ostrogoths. Terrified at the prospect of being conquered in turn by the advancing Huns, the Visigoths petitioned the Romans to allow them to settle as allies inside the Empire. Permission was granted, and in 376 the entire tribe crossed the Danube into Roman territory. But soon corrupt Roman officials cheated and mistreated the Visigoths, and the proud barbarians went on a rampage. The inept East Roman emperor sought to quell them, but he lost both his army and his life in the battle of Adrianople in 378.

Adrianople has been described as one of history's decisive battles: it destroyed the legend of the invincibility of the Roman legions and ushered in a century and a half of chaos. For a few years the capable emperor Theodosius I held back the Visigoths, but after his death in 395 they began to migrate and pillage under their leader, Alaric. He invaded Italy, and in 410 his followers sacked Rome. The weak West Roman emperor ceded southern Gaul to the Visigoths, who soon expanded into Spain. Their Spanish kingdom lasted until the Muslim conquest of the eighth century.

To counter Alaric's threat to Italy, the Romans had withdrawn most of their troops from the Rhine frontier in 406 and from Britain the following year. The momentous consequence of this action was a flood of Germanic tribes across the defenseless frontiers. The Vandals pushed their way through Gaul to Spain and, after pressure from the Visigoths, moved on to Africa, the granary of the Empire. In 455 a Vandal raiding force sailed over from Africa, and Rome was sacked a second time. Meanwhile the Burgundians settled in the Rhone valley, the Franks gradually spread across northern Gaul, and the Angles, Saxons, and Jutes invaded Britain. Although each of these several tribes set up a German-ruled kingdom within the confines of the Empire, only the Franks in Gaul and the Angles and Saxons in Britain managed to perpetuate their kingdoms longer than a few centuries.

While the Germans were taking over the western part of the Empire, the Huns pushed farther into Europe. Led by Attila, the "scourge of God," the mounted nomads crossed the Rhine in 451. The remaining Roman forces in Gaul, joined by the Visigoths, defeated the Huns near Troyes. Atilla then plundered northern Italy and planned to take Rome, but disease, lack of supplies, and the dramatic appeal of Pope Leo I— which was to give the papacy great prestige —caused him to return to the plains of Hungary. The Hunnic hordes disintegrated after 453, when Attila died on the night of his marriage to a Germanic princess whom legend immortalized as Krimhild of the *Nibelungenlied* (see p. 256).

The fall of Rome. What was happening to the imperial throne in the West during this turbulent period? As we have mentioned (p. 132), after the death of Theodosius I in 395, the Empire was divided between his two sons. Roman rule in the West grew increasingly impotent as a series of incompetent emperors sought safety behind marshes at Ravenna. The leaders of the mercenary soldiers, whose ranks were now mainly German, wielded the real power.

In 475 Orestes, the Germanic commander of the troops, forced the Senate to elect his young son Romulus Augustulus ("Little Augustus") as emperor in the West. In the following year another Germanic commander, Odovacar, slew Orestes and, seeing no reason for continuing the sham of an imperial line, deposed Romulus Augustulus and proclaimed himself head of the government. The deposition of the boy, who by a strange irony bore the names of the legendary founder of Rome and the founder of the Empire, marks the traditional "fall" of the Roman Empire.

Actually, no single date is accurate, for the fall of Rome was a long and complicated process. Yet 476 at least symbolizes the end of the Roman Empire in the West, for in this year the long line of emperors inaugurated by Augustus ended and the undisguised rule of Italy by Germanic leaders began.

Theodoric's kingdom in Italy. The disintegration of the Hunnic empire following the death of Attila freed the Ostrogoths to migrate as other tribes were doing. Under their energetic king, Theodoric (c. 454-526), who had spent some years as a hostage at Constantinople, the Ostrogoths were galvanized into action.

Theodoric accepted a commission from the emperor in the East to reimpose imperial authority over Italy, now in Odovacar's hands. In 488 he led his people into the Italian peninsula, where, after hard fighting, Odovacar sued for peace and was treacherously murdered. Theodoric then established a strong Ostrogothic kingdom in Italy with its capital at Ravenna. Because he appreciated the culture he had seen at Constantinople, Theodoric pursued a successful policy of maintaining classical culture on a high level. Following his death without a male heir in 526, civil war broke out in Italy, paving the way for a twenty-year war of reconquest (535-555) by the armies of the East Roman emperor Justinian. Italy was ravaged from end to end by the fighting, and the classical civilization that Theodoric had carefully preserved was in large part destroyed.

The Lombards. In 568, only three years after Justinian died, the last wave of Germanic invaders, the fierce Lombards, poured

Reminiscent of the classical architecture which the Ostrogothic king admired, Theodoric's tomb in Ravenna is remarkable for its dome, which is one enormous slab of stone, 35 feet in diameter and weighing 470 tons.

into Italy. The Eastern emperor held on to southern Italy, as well as Ravenna and Venice, and the pope now became the virtual ruler of Rome. Not until the late nineteenth century would Italy again be united under one government. The Lombard kingdom in Italy, weakened by the independent actions of many strong dukes, did not last long. In 774 it was conquered by the Franks, who, as we shall see in Chapter 8, had in the meantime established the most powerful and longest lasting of all the Germanic kingdoms that arose on the territory of the western empire.

The problem of the fall of Rome. The shock and dismay felt by contemporaries throughout the Roman world on learning of Alaric's sack of the Eternal City in 410 were to echo down the centuries, leaving the impression that the fall of Rome was a major calamity, one of the greatest in history.

Pagan writers attributed the sack of Rome to the abandonment of the ancient gods. In *The City of God* St. Augustine argued against this charge and put forth the theory that history unfolds according to God's design. Thus Rome's fall was part of the divine plan—"the necessary and fortunate preparation for the triumph of the heavenly city where man's destiny was to be attained."[12] This view was challenged in the eighteenth century by Edward Gibbon, author of the famous *Decline and Fall of the Roman Empire*, who saw Rome's fall as the "triumph of barbarism and religion." Christianity, he argued, had played an important role in undermining the imperial structure: "The clergy successfully preached the doctrines of patience and pusillanimity; . . . the last remains of the military spirit were buried in the cloister."[13]

In our time some explanations of Rome's fall have been rooted in psychological theories. For example, the basic cause has been attributed to a weakening of morale in the face of difficulties, to a "loss of nerve." Or it has been argued that the ultimate failure of Rome came from its too complete success. The easy acquisition of power and wealth and the importing of ready-made cultures from conquered peoples led to "a changed attitude of men's minds" and indo-

lence and self-gratification among the ruling classes. Such subjective theories can scarcely be proven, however, or even fairly assessed.

Most historians account for Rome's decline in terms of a variety of interacting forces. On the political side, the failure of civil power to control the army following the death of Marcus Aurelius resulted in military anarchy, the disintegration of central authority, and the weakening of Rome's ability to withstand external pressures. Diocletian and his successors had to increase the military establishment despite a growing manpower shortage. "Hence they found themselves on the horns of a dilemma. Either they could conscript Roman civilians for military service and so decrease still further production and the state revenues, or they could . . . make up the deficit with barbarians."[14] The decision they felt called on to make led to the barbarization of the army and to wholesale barbarian colonization within the empire.

On the economic side, the small farmer class disappeared, and more and more land was consolidated into huge *latifundia*; civil war and barbarian attacks disturbed trade relations; a debased currency and a crushing tax burden undermined the confidence of the people. Eventually the rigid economic and social decrees of Diocletian and Constantine created a vast bureaucracy which only aggravated the existing ills in the western half of the Empire, already far gone along the road to decline.

Western Europe in the sixth century. In the West the Empire was no more than a memory by the sixth century. In its place were new states that foreshadowed the major political divisions of modern Europe: Visigothic Spain, Anglo-Saxon England, Frankish Gaul, and a divided Italy ruled by Lombard dukes, the Eastern emperor, and the pope.

Vast tracts of formerly cultivated land were left untilled, and the failure of communications and transportation, coupled with the flight of the labor force from the cities to the country, had brought on a progressive decentralization of the economy. With much industry transferred from cities to large country estates, scores of once flourishing towns near the frontiers ceased to exist, while those closer to the Mediterranean shrank in size and importance. "Roman civilization had been essentially urban; medieval civilization was to be essentially rural. With the decline of the towns the general level of civilization was lowered and western Europe began to assume its medieval aspect."[15]

Yet the Germanic invasions were not as cataclysmic as was once thought. True, the invaders pillaged ruthlessly, and in certain sections of the Empire, especially in Britain, Roman civilization was entirely wiped out. The Germans also seized a great deal of land, but most of this was either vacant or belonged to the emperors; few private landowners were displaced. In most areas the invaders still represented a minority of the population, and a gradual blending and fusing of the cultures and the blood of the two peoples began. Thus the barbarians in time lost their Germanic customs, religion, and speech; that is why hardly a trace of the Germanic languages remains in Italy, France, and Spain. The Church, under the dual leadership of Benedictine monasticism and the papacy, assisted the fusion between German and Roman.

By the sixth century the foundations for the spiritual and political power of the papacy, which would lead to the Church-state rivalry of the Middle Ages, had been laid. We have seen how Pope Leo the Great acquired the moral leadership of the West by successfully protecting Italy from the Huns, and how the Lombard conquests in Italy gave the papacy its opportunity to achieve independence. In addition, ready for future use was the doctrine of the supremacy of the Church over the state in spiritual matters, a doctrine implied by St. Augustine in his *City of God* and clearly expressed by St. Ambrose during his clash with the emperor Theodosius I.

By the sixth century, then, the three elements that were to create the pattern of western civilization in the Middle Ages were being interwoven: Graeco-Roman culture, the Christian Church, and the Germanic peoples and their institutions. Here, in a sense, were the mind, spirit, and muscle that were to work together in western man during the next thousand years.

Survival in the East. In our study of history thus far it is apparent that the most westerly focus of civilization was Rome, which was not only far removed from the "heartland" of civilization in the Fertile Crescent and Egypt but was also the cultural area most exposed at this time to counterforces. As a consequence, the western half of the Roman Empire was overwhelmed by those forces, while the eastern half, though seriously threatened, managed to ride out the storm.

Until 1453 the eastern—or Byzantine—empire maintained the Roman imperial tradition and administrative structure. Equally important was the preservation of Greek language and learning. The East also evolved its own Orthodox Church, which was to play a vital role in shaping the course of civilization in Russia and the Slavic world. For these reasons we must redirect our steps toward the East, where the Graeco-Roman legacy endured and from where it would one day be transmitted back to the West.

SUMMARY

Christianity's roots extend back into Jewish history long before the birth of Christ, and it is there that we find the concept of the Messiah, the divinely appointed leader who would create a new Israel. Under the rule of the Hellenistic Seleucid empire and later of Rome, many Jews hoped for such a Messiah to lead them to political independence; but when Jesus attacked the shortcomings of the established religion and refused to head a political revolt against the Romans, his enemies brought about his condemnation and execution. Yet his teachings did not die with his crucifixion. Interpreted through the efforts of St. Paul and the Church Fathers, they spread rapidly throughout the Roman Empire. Despite persecution, converts flocked to the new faith, and finally, with the Edict of Milan in 313, the emperor Constantine made Christianity a legal religion. Thereafter the Church grew and flourished, with an organization based on the imperial Roman pattern and a hierarchy of officials culminating in the pope at Rome.

From the death of Marcus Aurelius in 180 A.D., the Roman Empire declined as its rulers became pawns of the army. Only Diocletian and Constantine were able to check the downward trend, and in the long run their system of despotism failed to save the western half of the Empire from further deterioration. When the Visigoths, pushed by the Huns, defeated Roman forces at the battle of Adrianople in 378, the gates of the Empire burst open before the barbarian tribes. The date of the final collapse of Rome may be set at 476, when the last Roman emperor in the West was deposed.

The fall of Rome—one of the great dramatic developments in history—has been explained in a variety of ways by later historians. No single cause can be given; the collapse appears to have been the result of various interacting factors. Following the devastating invasions which overwhelmed the western half of the Empire, the gap left by the Caesars was filled by a powerful new agency, the Christian Church.

As the Roman Empire crumbled in the West, a new center of imperial strength arose in the East at Constantinople. To this city and its Byzantine civilization—a continuation of the Graeco-Roman but with original contributions of its own—we shall now turn.

SUGGESTIONS FOR READING

J. A. Hexter, **The Judaeo-Christian Tradition,*** Harper & Row, 1966. Brief but highly valuable survey of the evolution of ancient Judaism and Christianity. On the late ancient history of the Jews see also E. Bickermann, **From Ezra to the Last of the Maccabees: Foundations of Post-Biblical Judaism,*** Schocken, 1962; R. Herford, **The Pharisees,*** Beacon; D. S. Russell, **The Jews from Alexander to Herod,** Oxford, 1967.

Edmund Wilson, **The Scrolls from the Dead Sea,*** Meridian, and **Dead Sea Scrolls, 1947-1969,** Oxford, 1969. The most readable introduction to a fascinating subject. See also M. Burrows, **The Dead Sea Scrolls,*** Compass; Frank M. Cross, **The Ancient Library of Qumran and Modern Biblical Studies,*** Anchor; G. Vermes, **The Dead Sea Scrolls in English,*** Penguin.

Albert Schweitzer, **The Quest of the Historical Jesus,*** Macmillan. Surveys the attempts of scholars to discover the Jesus of history. See also E. J. Goodspeed, **A Life of Jesus,*** Torchbooks; H. Daniel-Rops, **Jesus and His Times,*** 2 vols., Image; M. Enslin, **Christian Beginnings,*** Torchbooks; R. Bultman, **Primitive Christianity in Its Contemporary Setting,*** Meridian; H. Kee and F. Young, **Understanding the New Testament,** Prentice-Hall, 1957.

J. G. Davies, **The Early Christian Church,*** Anchor; H. Chadwick, **The Early Church,*** Penguin. Excellent surveys of the first five centuries of Church history. See also A. Powell Davies, **The First Christian: A Study of St. Paul and Christian Origins,*** Mentor; Cyril Richardson, **Early Christian Fathers,** Westminster, 1953; H. Mattingly, **Christianity in the Roman Empire,*** Norton; E. R. Dodds, **Pagan and Christian in an Age of Anxiety,** Cambridge, 1965; C. N. Cochrane, **Christianity and Classical Culture: A Study of Thought and Action from Augustus to Augustine,*** Galaxy; A. H. M. Jones, **Constantine and the Conversion of Rome,*** Collier.

On early monasticism see H. Waddell, **The Desert Fathers,*** Ann Arbor; E. Duckett, **The Gateway to the Middle Ages: Monasticism,*** Ann Arbor.

S. Katz, **The Decline of Rome and the Rise of Medieval Europe,*** Cornell. A concise, clear account. A. H. M. Jones, **The Decline of the Ancient World,*** Holt, Rinehart and Winston, is a recent detailed survey. See also F. Lot, **The End of the Ancient World and the Beginning of the Middle Ages,*** Torchbooks; J. C. Burckhardt, **The Age of Constantine the Great,*** Anchor; R. MacMullen, **Constantine,** Dial, 1969.

Edward Gibbon, **The Decline and Fall of the Roman Empire,*** Dell, ed. by F. C. Bourne, is an abridgment of this eighteenth-century classic. For modern scholarly opinion on Rome's decline see Lynn White, Jr., ed., **The Transformation of the Roman World: Gibbon's Problem after Two Centuries,** Univ. of Cal., 1966; F. Walbank, **The Awful Revolution: The Decline of the Roman Empire in the West,** Liverpool Univ., 1969; R. M. Haywood, **The Myth of Rome's Fall,*** Apollo; D. Kagan, ed., **Decline and Fall of the Roman Empire: Why Did It Collapse?,*** Heath (Problems in European Civilization).

J. B. Bury, **The Invasion of Europe by the Barbarians,*** Norton. The best general work on the nature and effect of the Germanic invasions. See also H. Moss, **The Birth of the Middle Ages, 395-814,*** Galaxy; E. A. Thompson, **The Early Germans,** Oxford, 1965.

W. Bryher, **The Roman Wall,*** Vintage. A novel which gives a vivid picture of the last days of the Roman empire in the West.

*Indicates an inexpensive paperbound edition.

Chapter 6

Citadel and Conqueror

The Byzantine Empire, Early Russia, and Muslim Expansion

INTRODUCTION. When we speak of the fall of the Roman Empire, we sometimes forget that in fact only the western portion of that empire succumbed to the German invaders and entered into what has been described as its "Dark Ages." In the East, despite many vicissitudes, the east Roman or Byzantine empire stood for a thousand years as a citadel protecting an unappreciative West slowly emerging from semibarbarism.

Furthermore, the Byzantine empire made great contributions to civilization: Greek language and learning were preserved for posterity; the Roman imperial system was continued and Roman law codified; the Greek Orthodox Church converted the Slavic peoples and fostered the development of a splendid new Graeco-oriental art that was dedicated to the glorification of the Christian religion. Situated at the crossroads of East and West, Constantinople acted as the disseminator of culture for all peoples who came in contact with the empire. Called with justification "The City," this rich and turbulent metropolis was to the early Middle

Ages what Athens and Rome had been to classical times. By the time the empire collapsed in 1453, its religious mission and political concepts had borne fruit among the Slavic peoples of eastern Europe and especially among the Russians. The latter were to lay claim to the Byzantine tradition and to dub Moscow the "Third Rome."

The only rival of Byzantine civilization close at hand was the culture developed by followers of the Prophet Muhammad, who united the Arabian peninsula under the banner of his new religion, Islam, with its fundamental teachings of monotheism. The dynamic faith of Muhammad spread so rapidly that within a hundred years after the Prophet's death his followers had established a vast empire stretching from the Pyrenees to the Indus. This breathtaking religious and political expansion was followed by a flowering of Islamic culture that rivaled the achievements of the Byzantine empire and far surpassed those of western Europe at this time. The Muslims share with the Byzantines chief credit for preserving and disseminating learning in the Middle Ages.

THE PRECARIOUS FORTUNES OF THE EASTERN EMPIRE

Constantine's city. At the southern extremity of the Bosporus stands a promontory that juts out from Europe toward Asia, with the Sea of Marmora to the south and a long harbor known as the Golden Horn to the north. On this peninsula stood the ancient Greek city of Byzantium, which Constantine enlarged considerably and formally christened "New Rome" in 330 A.D.

Constantine had chosen his site carefully. The city commanded the waterway connecting the Mediterranean and the Black seas and separating Europe and Asia. Moreover, the site favored defense; it enabled Constantinople not only to become the great warehouse for East-West commerce but above all to be a buffer protecting Europe from attack.

In Chapter 5 we saw how, during the fourth and fifth centuries, both the eastern and western provinces of the Roman Empire were beset by dangers from beyond the northern frontier. Storming into the Empire, Visigoths, Huns, and Ostrogoths pillaged the Balkans and threatened Constantinople. But the more populous eastern provinces, with their greater military and economic strength, were saved from the fate that befell Rome.

As the western half of the Roman Empire crumbled, Constantinople turned eastward for its livelihood and culture, becoming gradually less Roman and western and more Greek and oriental. A panorama of triumphs and defeats, Byzantine history for the next one thousand years can be divided into four main periods—expansion, peril, recovery, and disintegration.

Justinian's reconquests. The history of the empire in the sixth century focuses upon the reign of Justinian (527-565), whose ambition was to restore the Roman Empire to its ancient scope and grandeur. Much of his success he owed to his wife, Theodora, who had been a dancer and was said to be the daughter of a circus animal trainer. Theodora proved to be a brave empress and a wise counselor. In 532, early in Justinian's reign, occurred the Nike rebellion (named after the victory cry of the rioters), the most famous of many popular revolts that have led historians to characterize Byzantine history as a despotism tempered by revolution. Theodora's coolness and bravery inspired her hard-pressed husband to remain in the capital and crush the rebellion:

May I never be separated from this purple, and may I not live that day on which those who meet me shall not address me as mistress. If, now, it is your wish to save yourself, O Emperor, there is no difficulty. For we have much money, and there is the sea, here the boats. . . . as for myself, I approve a certain ancient saying that royalty is a good burial-shroud.[1]

To carry out his plan for recovering the lost half of the Roman Empire from the Germans, Justinian first bought off the Persian

Sassanid kings, who threatened Syria and Asia Minor (see p. 130). Then in 533 he seized North Africa and the islands of the western Mediterranean from the Vandals. But it took twenty years of exhausting warfare for his generals to regain Italy from the Ostrogoths. Rome and other great Italian cities lay in ruins, and the classical civilization that the Ostrogothic king Theodoric had taken care to preserve was virtually annihilated. Justinian also wrested the southeastern portion of Spain from the Visigoths. Yet his empire was still much smaller than the Roman Empire at its height. Only a small part of Spain was his; nor had he recovered Gaul, Britain,

This oldest known view of Constantinople, drawn in 1420, shows both its wealth of monumental architecture and its outstanding fortifications—two attributes which particularly impressed contemporaries. With the sea on two sides, a sixty-foot-wide moat on another, and thirteen miles of very thick triple walls, the city was impregnable for many centuries. The largest domed building on this map is Hagia Sophia.

or southern Germany. Furthermore his reconquests had been accomplished at the price of exhausting the empire, both militarily and financially. Nor were Justinian's reconquests permanent; three years after his death most of devastated Italy fell to the Germanic Lombards, and the Persians made inroads into Syria.

In domestic affairs as in warfare, Justinian sought to restore the dignity and splendor of the Roman Empire. In this area are found his greatest accomplishments—the codification of Roman law and the erection of the great Church of Hagia Sophia, both described later in this chapter.

Three centuries of peril, 565-867. With Justinian's death, the first and perhaps the greatest period of Byzantine history ended. The exhausted empire now entered an era of peril lasting from the middle of the sixth to the middle of the ninth century. By the time Heraclius (610-641) ascended the throne, the empire was in a desperate position. Slavic tribes had invaded the Balkans, a new wave of Asiatic nomads, the Avars, were being kept beyond the Danube only by the payment of tribute, and the Persians were in the process of conquering Syria, Palestine, and Egypt. Jerusalem fell in 614, and various sacred relics, including what was reputed to be the Holy Cross, were carried off to the Persian capital. While one Persian army conquered Egypt, another advanced to a point in Asia Minor opposite Constantinople. In three brilliant campaigns Heraclius virtually destroyed the Persian empire and regained Syria, Palestine, and Egypt, along with the Holy Cross.

Although the centuries-old menace of the Persians had now been removed, the Eastern empire was soon confronted with a new danger. The early part of the seventh century saw in Arabia the birth of a new faith—Islam. With fanatical zeal the Arabs attacked the weakened Persian and Byzantine empires, and by the middle of the century they had subjugated Palestine, Syria, Persia, Egypt, and much of North Africa (see map, p. 159). An Arab fleet even besieged Constantinople annually for several years, and the distracted empire was also threatened by a new Hunnish menace, the Bulgars, who in 680 settled

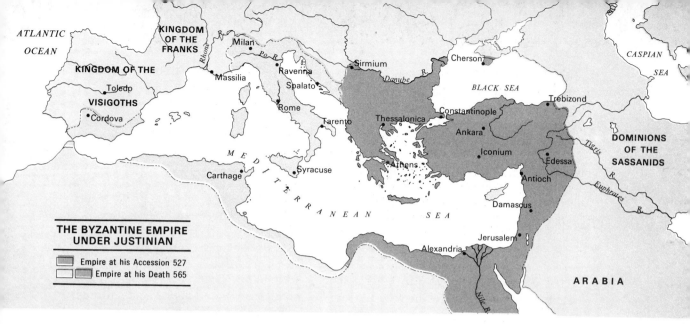

THE BYZANTINE EMPIRE UNDER JUSTINIAN

Empire at his Accession 527

Empire at his Death 565

in what is now Bulgaria. By 700 the Eastern empire stood on the brink of disintegration. In the Middle East it held only Asia Minor, while in the West it maintained a precarious hold on Sicily, southern Italy, Venice, and the exarchate of Ravenna, which extended from Ravenna southward through Rome.

The able Emperor Leo III (717-741) saved the hard-pressed empire. With the aid of a secret weapon, Greek fire (see p. 146), Leo repulsed the last great Arab assault on Constantinople in 718. He then turned to administrative and military reform. Civil and military authority in the provinces, separated by Diocletian (see p. 131), were reunited in the hands of provincial generals. Land was granted to the peasants in exchange for military service, and these free soldier-farmers, led by the powerful provincial generals, became the backbone of the Byzantine army. In contrast to the West, where the peasants were fast becoming serfs, a free peasantry continued to exist in the Eastern empire. Leo's religious policy, however, produced the iconoclastic controversy (see p. 147), which for over a hundred years caused widespread dissension.

Last days of grandeur, 867-1057. A little more than a century after Leo III's reforms had restored order to the hard-pressed empire, the strong Macedonian dynasty (867-1057) ushered in the third period of Byzantine history during which the empire went on the offensive. South Italy, which along

with Sicily had recently been lost to the Muslims, was regained. The powerful Bulgarians, now Christianized and seeking to possess all the Balkans, were conquered, and the power of the Muslims in the East was shattered as the Byzantines regained the island of Cyprus and Antioch in Syria, both lost since the seventh century. It is also noteworthy that during this period of resurgence the emperors forged a new sphere of Byzantine influence in Russia.

The empire reached a high level of power under the energetic Basil II (976-1025). Byzantine military forces finally crushed their Bulgarian foes with great severity. On one occasion fifteen thousand Bulgars were blinded and only a handful, each with a single eye, were left to guide the rest home. The Bulgarian king is said to have died of shock when this sightless multitude returned. Basil the "Bulgar-slayer" incorporated the Bulgarian kingdom into the empire and the Byzantine frontier again reached the Danube.

Basil II was friendly with Vladimir, the prince of Kiev in southern Russia, and was instrumental in bringing about that ruler's conversion to Christianity. Other Russians also began to adopt Christian beliefs and various aspects of Byzantine culture. Trade augmented these relations.

Four centuries of decline: Part I, 1057-1204. At the end of the Macedonian dynasty in 1057, the Byzantine empire entered its last tempestuous period, one of decline, at times obvious and rapid, then again imperceptible and gradual. During these four centuries the foundations of Byzantine strength—a strong government, a prosperous economy, and a stable social order—suffered irreparable damage, and the weakened empire was shattered by both Christian and Muslim invaders.

During the tenth century a powerful landed nobility had begun to threaten the emperor's power. By absorbing the lands of the free peasants and reducing them to dependency, these landed magnates, whose interests were usually opposed to those of the central government, greatly increased their wealth and power. Since the free peasants had been the state's best taxpayers and the backbone of its armies, the empire's revenues and defenses became seriously undermined. At the end of the century Basil II twice had to repress the revolts of generals who represented the hostile aristocracy. Basil's successors held the great magnates in check until 1081, when one of them usurped the imperial throne.

In the meantime, within the orbit of Byzantine commerce a dangerous rival was emerging—the city of Venice, founded in the fifth and sixth centuries by refugees who fled the barbarian invasions of northern Italy and found safety on a cluster of small islands off the northern Adriatic coast. The island city of Venice was relatively safe from the barbarian hordes and thus remained under Byzantine sovereignty when most of the Italian peninsula was overrun. As subjects of the Byzantine empire, the Venetians enjoyed access to the eastern Mediterranean trade, but they were far enough away from Constantinople to run their own affairs. By the eleventh century Venice had acquired undisputed supremacy in the Adriatic, and ambitious Venetian merchants were dreaming of supplanting Byzantine commercial supremacy over all the eastern Mediterranean.

In the eleventh century also, the Byzantines were confronted with two new foes. The formidable Seljuk Turks (see p. 161) threatened Asia Minor; and the adventurous Normans, led by Robert Guiscard (see p. 207), began to carve out possessions for themselves in southern Italy. The Byzantine army was defeated by the Turks at the critical battle of Manzikert in 1071, and all of Asia Minor was soon lost. By an unfortunate coincidence, Bari, the empire's last stronghold in southern Italy, was captured by the Normans in the same year that the battle of Manzikert took place.

In 1081, when the empire stood deprived of rich possessions, sapped by growing commercial rivalry, and torn by the struggle with the landed aristocracy, a powerful landowner, Alexius Comnenus, became emperor by a coup d'état. Soon afterwards, in 1096, the first crusaders from the West appeared on the scene. Hoping to obtain some European mercenary forces to help defeat the

THE BYZANTINE EMPIRE
ABOUT 814

THE LATIN EMPIRE
ABOUT 1214 A.D.

Latin Empire
Venetian Possessions

Seljuk Turks, Alexius had appealed to Pope Urban II for assistance, but he was dismayed to find a host of crusaders, including the dreaded Normans, approaching the capital. The western response to Urban's appeal to save the Eastern empire and the Holy Land from the Seljuks was met with suspicion on the part of the Byzantines, who viewed the pope as heretical and the crusaders as potentially dangerous to the Eastern empire. Adroitly, Alexius encouraged the crusaders to forgo his hospitality as quickly as possible and attack his Seljuk enemies. The successful weakening of Muslim power by the First Crusade enabled Alexius to recover valuable portions of Asia Minor.

With the Fourth Crusade (1202-1204), the envy and enmity which had been building up for decades in the West against the Byzantine empire were converted into violence. Dependent upon the Venetians for ships and money, the crusaders were persuaded to attack first the Christian city of Zara in Dalmatia, a commercial rival of Venice, and then Constantinople. The Venetian goal was to obtain a monopoly on Byzantine trade.

Constantinople was so rent by factional strife that the crusaders had little trouble in capturing it. A French noble among the crusaders described the resulting sacking of the city:

[I saw] . . . the great churches and the rich palaces melting and falling in, and the great streets filled with merchandise burning in the flames. . . . The booty gained was so great that none could tell you the end of it: gold and silver, and vessels and precious stones, and samite, and cloth of silk, and robes vair [squirrel] and grey, and ermine, and every choicest thing found upon the earth . . . . never, since the world was created, had so much booty been won in any city.[2]

Priceless works of art were destroyed, yet many art treasures and sacred relics did find their way to the West.

The Fourth Crusade irreparably weakened the Byzantine empire. A tiny empire in exile held out around Nicaea in Asia Minor, while a Latin emperor ruled at Constantinople and Venice took over islands and coastal ports which enabled her to monopolize the eastern trade.

Four centuries of decline: Part II, 1204-1453. The Latin empire of Constantinople, hated by the native population upon whom it imposed the Roman Church, lasted only until 1261. In that year Michael Palaeologus of Nicaea, allying himself with Genoa, which was jealous of Venetian commercial supremacy in the eastern Mediterranean, reconquered Constantinople. Amid the rejoicing of the populace, a Greek patriarch was reinstated in Hagia Sophia.

The rule of the Palaeologi lasted until the demise of the Byzantine empire—a span of two centuries of decline. Internally, the empire lost strength and resiliency. A form of feudalism developed in which the great landed magnates resisted the authority of the emperor and the imperial bureaucracy. Taxes and customs duties diminished, coinage was debased, and the military and naval forces, composed increasingly of mercenaries, grew fatally weak. Bitter religious disputes arose between the clergy and the emperors who sought western aid in return for a promise to unite the Eastern and Roman churches.

Externally, the situation was critical. The empire held only a small portion of its former territory and was surrounded by ambitious rivals and foes. The Latins still retained southern Greece; the Venetians and Genoese each possessed coastal cities and island territories of the empire; and in the fourteenth century a powerful Serbian kingdom developed in the Balkans and menaced Constantinople.

In the meantime a new and ultimately fatal menace had arisen across the Straits in Asia Minor. In the late thirteenth century the Ottoman or Osmanli Turks, named after their early leader Osman, had received from the Seljuk sultan at Ankara a military fief along the Byzantine border south of Nicaea. The prospect of booty from raids across the border attracted swarms of recruits, with the result that Nicaea was taken in 1331. In 1356 the Ottomans crossed over to Europe and

soon captured Adrianople, which became their capital. By 1390 they had overrun Bulgaria and Serbia and reached the Danube. The Ottoman Turks also expanded eastward in Asia Minor, until they were defeated in 1402 by the Mongol marauder Timur the Lame, or Tamerlane (see p. 173).

This defeat and the lack of a strong navy delayed the Turkish conquest of Constantinople. The end came in 1453. After a heroic defense of seven weeks, in which Constantine XI confronted the Turkish army of nearly 160,000 soldiers with only 9000 fighting men (half of whom were foreign mercenaries), the great eastern bulwark of Christian civilization collapsed before the might of Islam. As the Turks stormed the walls of the city, the emperor rushed to meet them, crying out as he was cut down: "God forbid that I should live an Emperor without an Empire! As my city falls, I will fall with it."[3]

The fall of Constantinople reverberated throughout the contemporary world. The last direct link with the classical era was shattered. First Rome had perished, now New Rome; an epoch that had seemed eternal had passed into history.

Reasons for endurance of the Byzantine empire. As the preceding résumé of Byzantine history attests, the empire's political life had always been stormy. During its thousand years of existence it experienced some sixty-five revolutions and the abdications or murders of more than sixty emperors. How did the empire manage to survive for such a long period?

One reason lay in its continuous use of a money economy, in contrast to the primitive barter economy then prevailing in the West. The use of money facilitated trade and the payment of taxes and enabled the empire to maintain standing military and naval forces. Until the latter days of the empire Byzantine military science was relatively advanced and the armed forces effective. Surviving military manuals indicate the efficiency of army organization, which included engineering and medical units. Also, the Byzantines had a secret weapon called "Greek fire," an inflammable chemical mixture whose main ingredient, saltpeter, made it a forerunner of gunpowder. As from a modern flamethrower,

As heirs of the Romans, the Byzantines were fierce and disciplined fighters. The navy coupled its battle prowess with a secret weapon, Greek fire.

Greek fire was catapulted out of tubes onto the decks of enemy ships.

Of great significance for the endurance, as well as the character, of the empire was the wholesale loss of African, Italian, and eastern territory by the year 700. The lands still under the emperor's control were now more homogeneous; most of the population was Greek. Thus historians speak of the seventh century as the period when the eastern Roman empire was transformed into the "Byzantine" empire—that is, transformed into a Hellenized civilization, taking its name appropriately from the original Greek settlement on which Constantinople had been built.

Another reason for the empire's endurance was its centralized system of administration. Where the West was broken up into numerous feudal principalities, the Byzantines were governed by a strong monarchy, aided by a well-trained bureaucracy. The emperor was the supreme military commander, the highest judge, the only legislator, and the protector of the Church. His authority rested on the claim that he was chosen by God to rule the Christian empire entrusted to him by God. So absolute was the emperor's control that his title *Autokrator* has been carried over into the English word *autocracy*, meaning "absolute supremacy." Only a successful revolution could depose him.

The Orthodox Church was another factor in the endurance of the empire. Linked closely to the state, the Church usually was the staunchest ally of the throne.

THE ORTHODOX CHURCH

Collaboration between Church and state. The Byzantine, or Orthodox, Church not only dominated religious and cultural life in the empire but was also interwoven with the political fabric. Whereas the Roman Church did not identify itself with the Roman Empire or any other state in the West but became an international body, the Orthodox Church was a state church ruled by God's vicar on earth—the king-priest who, surrounded by splendid pomp and ceremony, ruled the By-

zantine empire. In essence, the Church was a department of the state, and the emperor at times even intervened in spiritual matters. In many respects the patriarch of Constantinople had a position analogous to that of the pope in Rome, but with a significant difference—the patriarch, although elected by the bishops, was nominated by the emperor. Such blending of authority over Church and state in the office of emperor has been termed *Caesaropapism* (combining the functions of Caesar and pope).

The iconoclastic controversy. Relations between the eastern and western branches of the Church, continually undermined by what Constantinople viewed as Rome's excessive claims of primacy (see p. 128), deteriorated sharply in the eighth century as a result of the policies of the emperor Leo III. Although Leo had no use for Islam as a religion, he agreed with its contention that the employment of images and pictures in worship eventually led to idolatry. Therefore, in 726 Leo issued an edict forbidding the use of images (icons) of the sacred personages of Christianity, including Christ and all the saints. Statues were removed from churches, and church walls were whitewashed to cover all pictures.

In Constantinople rioting in protest against iconoclasm, or image breaking, broke out immediately. The demonstration was put down by troops, who killed some of the rioters. When the patriarch of Constantinople objected, he was replaced by another man more agreeable to the emperor's will. Riots continued to break out in Greece and Italy, and the pope at Rome, Gregory II, called a council of bishops who read out of the Church all those who had accepted iconoclasm. This caused an open breach between the papacy and the Eastern emperor.

Final separation of the churches. In 843 the iconoclastic controversy was finally settled by the restoration of images, but other sources of friction made permanent reunion of the Byzantine and Roman churches impossible. Exactly when the final breaking point was reached is difficult for scholars to determine. The traditional date is 1054, when doctrinal and liturgical disputes (the use of leavened vs. unleavened bread in the communion service, for example) caused the pope and the patriarch of Constantinople to excommunicate each other, thus creating a schism that was never to be healed. The important fact is that for centuries the papacy in the West and the Orthodox Church in the East steadily grew apart until they came to maintain distinctly separate existences, each viewing the other with suspicion and intolerance.

Missionary activity of the Church. The credit for converting many Slavic tribes to Christianity goes to the Orthodox Church. About 863 two monks who were also brothers, Cyril and Methodius, set out from Constantinople to bring the gospel to the pagan Moravians, a Slavic group living in what is now Czechoslovakia. They took with them translations of the Bible and the divine service written in an alphabet of modified Greek characters adapted to the Slavic languages. (The Cyrillic alphabet, used even now in Bulgaria, Serbia, and Russia, is named after Cyril, who invented it.) Although the Moravians and others of the westernmost Slavs eventually came under the sway of the Roman Church, the work begun by the two brothers triumphed among the Slavs to the east and south, so that ultimately the Orthodox Church extended throughout eastern Europe.

BYZANTINE ECONOMY, SOCIETY, AND CULTURE

Byzantine prosperity. During the early Middle Ages, Constantinople was called "The City"—with good reason. Visitors were fascinated by the pomp and pageantry of the court and Church, the scholarly and artistic endeavors, and the wealth, which far surpassed anything to be found in the West.

The complex urban civilization of the Byzantine world rested upon a foundation of strong and well-diversified economic activities. For centuries a stable agricultural system provided city and country folk with adequate food, and a varied industrial and commercial economy successfully supported large urban populations. The decline of population which had contributed to the collapse of the Roman Empire in the West did not occur in the East.

Geography was another major factor responsible for Byzantine prosperity. Constantinople stood at the crossroads of Europe and Asia, and its site ensured its being a port of transit for a great marine trading basin extending from the Adriatic to southern Russia. The merchants of Constantinople exported luxury goods, wines, spices, and silks to Russia and in turn imported furs, fish, caviar, beeswax, honey, and amber. Metalwork, leather goods, and other products manufactured in the empire went to India and China, while back to Constantinople came spices, precious stones, costly woods, and perfumes, some of which were transported on to the few western Europeans who could afford the luxuries of the Orient.

Trade supported, and was in turn stimulated by, the existence of a sound gold currency. In the West a decline in commerce had been attended by a shrinkage in the supply and use of money. The Byzantine empire, on the other hand, retained a currency of such excellence that its gold bezant was a medium of international exchange, remaining free of debasement until the eleventh century—far longer than any other coinage in history.

Besides being the greatest trading center of the early Middle Ages, Constantinople had industries that supplied Christendom with many products. The city specialized in luxury goods, and was famous for the manufacture of armor, weapons, hardware, and textiles. Until the time of Justinian, all raw silk for manufacturing fabrics had been imported from China, but after silkworms were smuggled out of China about 550 A.D., silk production began to flourish within the empire. Silken fabrics embroidered with gold and silver thread and fashioned into costly vestments for Church services or court attire were eagerly sought all over Europe. The silk industry was a profitable state monopoly.

The state controlled the economy through a system of guilds to which all tradesmen and members of the professions belonged. Wages, profits, hours of labor, and the price of foodstuffs—all were controlled "so that," as stated in a Byzantine handbook detailing such regulations, "men, being well directed thereby, should not shamelessly trample upon one another and the stronger should not do violence to the weaker."[4]

Constantinople, city of contrasts. The colorful social life of the empire was concentrated in Constantinople. The city itself had three centers: the imperial palace, the Church of Hagia Sophia, and the giant Hippodrome.

Court ceremonial was arranged to impress both foreigners and Byzantines with the emperor's exalted nature and his remoteness from mundane matters. An envoy to the palace was escorted through great lines of uniformed guards and dignitaries into a resplendent hall. At the appointed time a curtain was raised, disclosing the emperor clad in his imperial robes on his throne. Golden lions flanked the throne and golden birds perched in pomegranate trees. While the envoy prostrated himself, the throne would be raised aloft, symbolizing the unapproachability of the heir of the Caesars. During the audience the emperor remained motionless, silent, and aloof, while a court official spoke in his name.

Seating perhaps eighty thousand spectators, the Hippodrome was the scene of hotly disputed chariot races between the two major factions of the populace, the Blues and the Greens. Organized for political purposes as well as for sports, these factions used the Hippodrome as a forum to voice their opinions. The Blues tended to reflect the views of the great landowners, the Greens those of the merchants and the bureaucracy. In the Nike rebellion (see p. 141), Blues and Greens united in opposition to Justinian's costly policies.

Byzantine art: a unique synthesis. While Byzantine art was basically Roman in character during the reigns of the first Constantine and his immediate successors, the new capital's eastern location could not fail to bring additional artistic forces into play. Greek tradition had persisted in Alexandria and Antioch, and Constantinople was exposed also to influences from Persia. By the sixth century these elements were fused with the strong Christian spirit that had motivat-

The synthesis of Graeco-Roman and oriental styles is apparent in this ivory carving of a Byzantine empress. She is flanked by Roman eagles and degenerated Corinthian columns, but her stiff, frontal pose and jewels are oriental.

ed New Rome since its inception; the result was a new style of a uniquely Byzantine character (see illustration, p. 119).

Byzantine painting, for example, displays a synthesis of different—and even conflicting—cultural influences. The Greek tradition provided a graceful and idealistic approach; art historians point out, however, that while classical elements remained in Byzantine art, oriental influences—with their emphasis upon a more abstract and formalized style, vivid coloring, and ornamentation—eventually predominated.

Church architecture. The first great age of Byzantine art was associated with Justinian, who commissioned the magnificent Church of Hagia Sophia (Holy Wisdom), as well as many other churches and secular buildings. No other Byzantine church equaled Hagia Sophia in size or magnificence. According to Procopius, the historian of Justinian's reign, it was "a church, the like of which has never been seen since Adam, nor ever will be" (see Color Plate 6). The effect of light playing upon its multicolored marbles and bright mosaics moved Procopius to declare:

On entering the church to pray one feels at once that it is the work, not of man's effort or industry, but in truth the work of the Divine Power; and the spirit, mounting to heaven, realizes that here God is very near and that He delights in this dwelling that He has chosen for Himself.[5]

The dome is the crowning glory of Hagia Sophia both because of its beauty and because it represents a major advance in architecture. With forty windows piercing its base, Procopius described it as

marvellous in its grace, but by reason of the seeming insecurity of its composition altogether terrifying. For it seems somehow to float in the air on no firm basis, but to be poised aloft to the peril of those inside it.[6]

The Romans had been able to construct a huge dome in the Pantheon but had erected it upon massive circular walls which limited the shape of the building. The dome of Hagia Sophia was supported by pendentives, four triangular segments which received the weight of the dome and distributed it to four supporting piers. The use of pendentives made it possible to place a dome over a square area.

Over the centuries many other fine structures employed the pendentive principle. A favorite design, with symbolic appeal, was a church in the shape of a cross, surmounted by a dome. A still further development was the five-domed church, which was cross-shaped, with a central dome at the crossing and a smaller dome on each of the four arms. The most famous existing example of this design is St. Mark's in Venice, constructed in the eleventh century.

Vivid mosaics and decorative arts. The second outstanding period of Byzantine art began in the middle of the ninth century with the settling of the iconoclastic controversy and lasted until the sack of Constantinople in 1204. This age is notable for producing the finest examples of Byzantine decorative art.

In the decoration of churches, Byzantine artists made extensive use of mosaics—small pieces of multicolored glass or stone cemented into patterns to form brilliant decorations. Not only did the rich colors of the mosaics increase the splendor of the church interiors and heighten the emotional appeal of the rituals, but the representations also served as useful teaching devices by presenting the viewer with scenes from the Bible and with images of Christ, the Virgin, and the saints.

With their penchant for vivid colors and elaborate detail, Byzantine artists also excelled in such decorative arts as carving in ivory, the illumination of manuscripts, and the decoration of book covers, chests, thrones, and altars. Constantinople was renowned for its cloisonné technique, by which enamel was inlaid between thin gold bands to form the design.

Wall and panel painting. The third important period of Byzantine artistic activity took place during the fourteenth and fifteenth centuries when Byzantium was no longer wealthy. This revival expressed itself in brilliant paintings on walls and panels, a form of art necessitated in some measure by

In this late tenth-century mosaic over the south door of Hagia Sophia, Constantine is offering his city and Justinian is presenting his church to the Virgin. The combination of oriental style and Christian subject matter is characteristic of Byzantine art.

the need to find cheaper substitutes for expensive mosaics and enamels.

Like mosaics, Byzantine wall paintings were employed to decorate churches. In addition, icons—panel paintings of sacred personages—were used in daily worship. As in mosaics, the subject matter of Byzantine painting was treated symbolically rather than realistically: "like much of the art of today, which is not easy to understand at first glance, its significance lies below the surface; it is an art of the spirit rather than of the flesh, and must be approached from that point of view."[7]

The preservation of classical learning. The official adoption of the Greek language in the formative centuries of the Byzantine empire proved a stimulus to the preservation of classical works in philosophy, literature, and science. The scholars who perpetuated the Greek tradition were not clerics, as in the West, but members of the civil service; Byzantine monasteries produced many saints and mystics but showed little interest in learning or teaching. Byzantine scholars, concerned chiefly with recovering and classifying Hellenic and Hellenistic learning, were imitative rather than creative, and their own contributions tended to be a rehash of classical works. Yet when in the twelfth century the West began absorbing Greek science and Aristotelian philosophy from the Muslims in Spain, it was to Byzantine scholarship that the latter were indebted. Moreover, most of the West's knowledge of Greek literature and Platonic philosophy came from Constantinople in the fourteenth and fifteenth centuries.

One of the great achievements of Byzantine scholarship was the codification of Roman law. In 528 Justinian convoked a commission of scholars to gather and classify the vast, disorganized, and often contradictory mass of law that had accumulated during centuries of Roman government. The result was a great legal work popularly known as the Justinian Code and formally titled the *Corpus Juris Civilis*. It organized the imperial law of the last four centuries into the *Codex* and included as well the *Digest* of the writings of republican and imperial jurists, and the *Institutes*, a commentary on the principles

As objects of veneration, icons followed strict formal rules. Painted in the thirteenth century, "Madonna Enthroned" follows a pattern developed several hundred years earlier.

underlying the laws. Appended to the main text were the *Novels*, the laws promulgated by Justinian and written in Greek, now the dominant language of the empire.

By this codification, Rome's priceless legal heritage was preserved and passed on to posterity. In holding that the will of the emperor is the source of law, that the judge is the emperor's representative in interpreting law, and that equity is the basic principle of law, Justinian's Code stands in sharp contrast to Germanic folk law (see p. 133). The Code was unknown in the West during the early Middle Ages, but in the twelfth century it slowly began to have a notable influence on the improvement of medieval justice and the emergence of strong monarchs, who borrowed for their own use the Roman doctrine of imperial autocracy.

EARLY RUSSIA

The Slavs. While the fortunes of the Byzantine empire had been ebbing and flowing, its culture had exercised continuous and substantial influence upon the development of Russia in its formative centuries.

The ancestors of the Russians were the Slavic tribes, whose original home is thought by some scholars to have been the wooded area of the Pripet Marshes (see map, p. 153). Moving into the lands vacated by the migrating Germans, in time three main groups developed. The Western Slavs—Poles and Bohemians—reached the Elbe and came under Latin Christian influences. Both the Southern Slavs, who moved into the Balkans, and the Eastern Slavs, the ancestors of the Russians who occupied the lands between the Carpathians and the Don, were subjected to Greek Christian influences.

Founding of a Russian state. About the time when their Viking brethren from Denmark and Norway were plundering and conquering throughout western Europe (see p. 194), Swedish Norsemen, called Varangians by the Byzantines, combined piracy with trade and began to venture along the waterways from the eastern Baltic to the Black and Caspian seas. The Slavic settlements along the rivers often hired the fierce Varangians as protectors. In 862 the people of Novgorod employed one such warrior, the half-legendary Rurik, who became prince of the city. His brothers and companions established themselves in other cities, one being Kiev.

By the late ninth century the Varangian ruler of Kiev had succeeded in establishing his supremacy over a large area which gradually became known as Russia, a name derived from *Rus* (meaning "seafarers"), by which the Slavs knew the Norse. The Kievan state operated as a loose confederation, with the prince of Kiev recognized as senior among his kinsmen who ruled the other Russian city-states. By the end of the tenth century the Norse minority had merged with the Slavic population.

Kievan Russia was less a political entity than a commercial entity, a coordinated group of princely states with a common interest in maintaining trade along the river routes. Kievan military expeditions against Constantinople itself began as early as 860, partly as typical Viking raids for plunder and partly to extort treaties which opened up a profitable Russian-Byzantine trade. Every spring after the ice had melted on the Dnieper, cargoes of furs, wax, honey, and slaves were floated down to Kiev. From there a great flotilla would descend the Dnieper and proceed along the Black Sea shore to Constantinople. Returning with silks, spices, jewelry, wines, and metalwares, the Kievans would pass these goods on to northeastern Europe via Novgorod and the Baltic.

Christianity in Kievan Russia. The official conversion of the Russians to Christianity took place about 989 under Prince Vladimir of Kiev. According to an early Russian chronicle, Vladimir shopped around before making his choice of religions. He rejected Islam because of its injunctions against the use of strong drink, Judaism because the God of the Jews could not be considered very powerful since He had allowed them to be ejected from their Holy Land, and Roman Christianity because the pope entertained dangerous ideas about his superiority to all secular rulers. There remained the Orthodox Church of the Byzantines, which was presented to Vladimir's subjects as his choice.

From the outset the Kievan princes followed the Byzantine example and kept the Church dependent on them, even for its revenues, so that the Russian Church and state were always closely linked. The Russians also copied the Byzantines in Church ritual, theology, and such practices as monasticism.

Apogee and decline of Kiev. Kiev reached its greatest splendor in the reign of Yaroslav the Wise (1019-1054 A.D.), who issued Russia's first law code (based on the customary law of the Eastern Slavs) and was a patron of art and learning. Byzantine architects and artists were brought to Kiev to build the cathedral of Hagia Sophia, named after its prototype in Constantinople. Yaroslav negotiated marriage alliances for his children with the royal families of Poland, Norway, Hungary, and France.

Following the death of Yaroslav, however, the princes of the various cities fought increasingly among themselves for possession of the Kievan state; and to these disruptions was added the devastation of the nomads who roamed uncomfortably close to the capital and cut the trade route to Constantinople. The trading and farming population around Kiev could not sustain such hardships, and they sought refuge in flight. Many fled northeastward to city-states in the neighborhood of present-day Moscow. When the Asiatic Mongols destroyed Kiev in 1240 (see p. 277), it had already lost much of its power, wealth, and population.

Byzantine aspects of Kievan culture. The commercial contacts between Constantinople and Kiev and the power of the Orthodox Church during the Kievan period were the chief factors responsible for the Byzantine influences in Russia. Architecture, for ex-ample, came within the province of the Church. The outstanding churches built at Kiev, Novgorod, and other cities show strong Byzantine influence. In time architects developed a distinctly Russian style, including the characteristic "onion dome," which is merely a fanciful "helmet" covering the dome. The decoration of churches also followed Byzantine models. In fact, the earliest mosaics, as well as mural and icon paintings, appear to have been the work of Byzantine artists who were brought to Russia. At Hagia Sophia in Kiev, some of these wall paintings still remain.

The adaptation of the Greek alphabet to the Slavic tongue and the translation of Church liturgy into Slavic stimulated the growth of Russian literature. Although at first Kievan literature consisted of translations of Byzantine works—chiefly sermons, saints' lives, and condemnations of Roman Catholicism—in time a literature of the Russian people emerged, as epics of their strug-

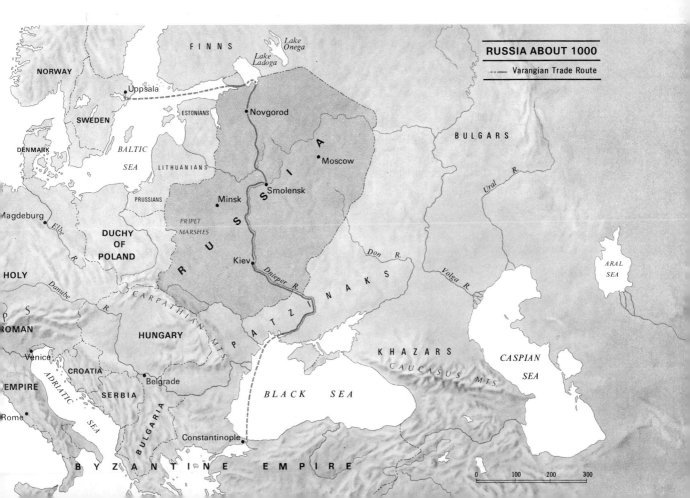

RUSSIA ABOUT 1000

----- Varangian Trade Route

FINNS

Lake Onega

Lake Ladoga

NORWAY

Uppsala

SWEDEN

ESTONIANS

Novgorod

Moscow

BULGARS

DENMARK

BALTIC SEA

LITHUANIANS

PRUSSIANS

Minsk

Smolensk

Ural R.

R U S S I A

Magdeburg

Elbe R.

DUCHY OF POLAND

PRIPET MARSHES

Kiev

Dnieper R.

Don R.

Volga R.

ARAL SEA

HOLY

Danube R.

CARPATHIAN MTS.

P A T Z I N A K S

ROMAN

HUNGARY

KHAZARS

CASPIAN SEA

Venice

CROATIA

Belgrade

CAUCASUS MTS.

EMPIRE

ADRIATIC SEA

SERBIA

BLACK   SEA

Rome

B U L G A R I A

Constantinople

B Y Z A N T I N E   E M P I R E

0   100   200   300

The Byzantine influence on Russian architecture is evident in Hagia Sophia in Kiev, originally built in the eleventh century by Yaroslav the Wise.

gles to resist the barbaric nomads from the steppes appeared. But the use of Slavic in the Church caused many churchmen to remain ignorant of Latin and to lack even a good knowledge of Greek; hence the majority of the learned had no direct contact with the literature in those two languages. Much of Russia's cultural isolationism in the past has been ascribed to this factor.

By the eleventh century, however, and particularly during the reign of Yaroslav the Wise, Kievan Russia could boast of a culture and an economy that were superior to what then existed in western Europe; for these achievements Kiev was primarily obligated to the Byzantine empire, which at the time enjoyed the highest cultural level in Christendom. In the wake of the fall of Constan-

tinople in 1453, the Russians would appropriate even more of the Byzantine tradition, dubbing the new Russian center of Moscow the "Third Rome."

MUHAMMAD AND HIS FAITH

Pre-Islamic Arabia. In our examination of the Byzantine empire, we had occasion to mark the swift rise of a rival religious culture, Islam, imbued with expansionist aims. In 1453, adherents of that faith succeeded in conquering the eastern citadel of Christianity. We shall now trace the genesis and meteoric expansion of Islam, together with the splendid civilization it fostered.

The term *Islam*, meaning "submission to God," is derived from the Muslim holy book, the Koran. The followers of Muhammad, the founder of the faith, are known as Muslims. (This faith is often referred to as Muhammadanism, but Muslims frown on this term, which implies the worship and deification of Muhammad.)

The story begins in Arabia, a quadrangular peninsula with an area of about 1,200,000 square miles. Much of it is desert, and rainfall is scarce in the rest of the peninsula. Thus vegetation is scant and very little land is suitable for agriculture. Throughout much of Arabia, particularly in the interior, nomadism was the only way of life.

The nomads, or Bedouins, lived according to a tribal pattern; at the head of the tribe was the sheik, elected and advised by the heads of the related families comprising the tribe. Driven from place to place in their search for pastures to sustain their flocks, the Bedouins led a precarious existence. Aside from their flocks, they relied on booty from raids on settlements, on passing caravans, and on one another. The Bedouins worshiped a large number of gods and spirits, many of whom were believed to inhabit trees, wells, and stones. Each tribe had its own god, symbolized generally by a sacred stone which served as an altar where communal sacrifices were offered.

Although the Bedouins of the interior led a primitive and largely isolated existence, some parts of Arabia were influenced by neighboring—and more advanced—cultures. By the latter half of the sixth century Christian and Jewish groups were found throughout the Arabian peninsula. Their religious convictions and moral principles had a strong effect on the indigenous population, and their monotheistic beliefs were later incorporated into Islamic doctrine.

Mecca. Several of the more advanced cities were in Hejaz, among them Mecca, destined to be the key city in the Islamic religion. Fifty miles inland from the port of Jiddah, Mecca was favorably located for trade. Its merchants carried on business with southern Arabia, with Abyssinia across the Red Sea, and with the Byzantine and Persian empires. Mecca was controlled by the Quraysh, an Arab tribe whose members formed trading companies that cooperated in dispatching large caravans north and south.

The Quraysh merchants were also concerned with protecting a source of income derived from the annual pilgrimage of tribes to a famous religious sanctuary at Mecca. Known as the Kaaba (cube), this square temple contained the sacred Black Stone, by legend brought to Abraham and his son Ishmael by Gabriel. According to tradition, the stone was originally white but had been blackened by the sins of those touching it. The Kaaba supposedly housed the images of some 360 local deities and fetishes.

Muhammad, founder of Islam. Into this environment at Mecca was born a man destined to transform completely the religious, political, and social organization of his people. Muhammad (570-632) came from a family belonging to the Quraysh tribe. Left an orphan in early life, he was brought up by an uncle and later engaged in the caravan trade. Muhammad's formative years are known to us by legend only, but his first biographer relates that he was influenced by a monotheist named Zayd, who may have been either a Jewish or a Christian convert. When he was about twenty years old, Muhammad entered the service of a wealthy widow, Khadija, whose caravans traded with Syria. In his twenty-fifth year he married his employer, who was some fifteen years his senior. Despite the difference in their

ages, the marriage was a happy one; and they had four daughters.

According to tradition, Muhammad frequently went into the foothills near Mecca to meditate. One night he dreamed that the archangel Gabriel appeared with the command, "Recite!" When Muhammad asked, "What shall I recite?" he was told:

Recite in the name of thy Lord who created
Man from blood coagulated.
Recite! Thy Lord is wondrous kind
Who by the pen has taught mankind
Things they knew not (being blind).[8]

This was the first of a series of visions and revelations.

Far from regarding himself as a prophet, Muhammad was at first afraid that he had been possessed by a spirit, and he even contemplated suicide. During his periods of doubt and anguish Muhammad was comforted by Khadija, and finally he became certain that he was a divinely appointed prophet of Allah, "*The* God." He became convinced that Allah was the one and only God—the same God worshiped by the Jews and Christians—who had chosen him to perfect the religion revealed earlier to Abraham, Moses, the prophets, and Jesus.

At first Muhammad had little success in attracting followers. His first converts were his wife, his cousin Ali, and Abu Bakr, a leading merchant of the Quraysh tribe who was highly respected for his integrity. Abu Bakr remained the constant companion of the Prophet during his persecution and exile and eventually became the first caliph of Islam. Most other early converts were slaves or oppressed persons. Opposition came from the leading citizens ("Shall we forsake our gods for a mad poet?"), who either ridiculed Muhammad's doctrine of resurrection (pre-Islamic Arabs had only vague notions concerning the afterlife) or feared that his monotheistic teaching might harm the city's lucrative pilgrimage trade to the Kaaba.

The Hijra and triumphal return to Mecca. The first encouraging development occurred when a group of pilgrims from Medina, a prosperous town supported by agriculture and handicrafts, accepted the Prophet's teachings. Meanwhile, increased persecu-

Every year thousands of Muslims make a pilgrimage to Mecca to worship at the Kaaba, a cube-shaped temple housing the sacred Black Stone that the angel Gabriel, according to legend, gave to Abraham and his son.

tion of the Muslims in Mecca encouraged the Prophet to migrate with his band to Medina.

Carried out in secrecy, this move took place in 622 and is known as the *Hijra*, which means "flight" or, in this context, "the breaking of old ties." The Hijra was such a turning point in Muhammad's career that the year in which it occurred is counted as the first in the Muslim calendar. In Mecca, Muhammad's own kinsmen had persecuted him, but in Medina he came to be acknowledged as a leader with divine authority in spiritual and temporal matters. He commanded the Muslims to turn toward Mecca when praying. This practice served to recognize the city as the spiritual capital of Islam and also emphasized the need for its conquest from the pagan trading oligarchy that governed it.

In the year 630 Muhammad marched on Mecca with an army. His old enemies were forced to surrender to the Prophet, who acted with magnanimity toward them. His first act was to cast out of the Kaaba its multitude of idols and fetishes; but the temple itself, together with the Black Stone, was preserved as the supreme center of Islam, the "Mecca" to which each devout Muslim should make a pilgrimage during his lifetime.

With Mecca and Medina both under his control, Muhammad became the undisputed master of Hejaz. In the two remaining years of his life tribe after tribe of Bedouins throughout Arabia offered him their loyalty. Upon his death in 632 the Prophet left behind a faith which had united Arabia and which was to astound the world with its militant expansion.

The Koran, the Muslim bible. Muslims believe that the Koran contains the actual word of God as revealed to Muhammad. The Prophet's revelations occurred over a period of more than twenty years, and before his death many of the messages had been written down. Abu Bakr, Muhammad's successor as head of the community, ordered the compilation of all these materials, including the passages that had only been committed to memory. Twenty years after the death of the Prophet, an authorized version was promulgated, which has remained the official text to the present day.

Because the Koran must never be used in translation for worship, the spread of Islam created a great deal of linguistic unity. Arabic supplanted many local languages as the language of daily use, and that part of the Muslim world which stretches from Morocco to Iraq is still Arabic-speaking. Furthermore, this seventh-century book remains the last word on Muslim theology, law, and social institutions and is therefore still the most important textbook in Muslim universities.

Theology of Islamic faith. Within the Koran one finds the central tenet of Islam— monotheism. There is only one God, Allah; this is proclaimed five times daily from the minaret of the mosque as the faithful are called to prayer:

God is most great. I testify that there is no God but Allah. I testify that Muhammad is God's Apostle. Come to prayer, come to security. God is most great.[9]

While Allah is the only God, many other supernatural figures are acknowledged, as in Christianity. Islamic angels, for example, are similar to those described in the Bible. In addition, there exist *jinn*, who are spirits midway between angels and men. Some *jinn* are good, while others are evil. Islam recognizes the existence of prophets who preceded Muhammad. The Koran mentions twenty-eight, of whom four are Arabian, eighteen are found in the Old Testament, three in the New Testament (including Jesus), and one of the remainder has been identified as Alexander the Great. But to Muslims the greatest prophet is, of course, Muhammad. He is ascribed no superhuman status, although he was chosen to proclaim God's message of salvation. That message included the belief in the Last Judgment and the existence of paradise and hell.

Geography played an important role in the Prophet's concepts of heaven and hell: both are described in terms that incite an immediate reaction in people living in the desert. Those who have submitted to Allah's rule—the charitable, humble, and forgiving —and those who have fought for His faith, shall dwell in a Garden of Paradise, reposing in cool shades, eating delectable foods, attended by "fair ones with wide, lovely eyes like unto hidden pearls," and hearing no vain speech or recrimination but only "Peace! Peace!" This veritable oasis is far different from the agonies of the desert hell that awaits the unbelievers, the covetous, and the erring. Cast into hell with its "scorching wind and shadow of black smoke," they will drink of boiling water.

Islam imposes on all Muslims five obligations, known as the "Pillars of Faith"—belief in only one God and in Muhammad as His Prophet, prayer, almsgiving, fasting, and a pilgrimage to Mecca. Prayers are said five times a day, and each occasion calls for a sequence of recitations coordinated with a sequence of postures. They are to be repeated either alone or, preferably, in a mosque. The Muslim is required to give alms, a practice regarded as expressing piety and contributing to one's salvation. During the month of Ramadan, the ninth month of the lunar year, Muslims fast. Since food and drink are prohibited between sunrise and sunset, this is a very strenuous observance, although sick persons and travelers are exempted providing they fast for an equal length of time later. The second chapter of the Koran commands Muslims to make a pilgrimage to Mecca, where they go through traditional ceremonies, such as kissing the Black Stone in the Kaaba. Each Muslim should make the pilgrimage to Mecca at least once during his lifetime if he has the means.

The Koran also provides Muslims with a body of ethical teachings. Idolatry, infanticide, usury, gambling, the drinking of wine, and the eating of pork are all prohibited. Similarly, Islam encouraged the humane treatment of slaves and regulated such matters as the guardianship of orphans and divorce. Muslim men were allowed four wives (and an unspecified number of concubines), but if he could not treat them all with equal kindness and impartiality, a husband should retain but one.

Pervading Islam was the principle of religious equality. There was no priesthood— no intermediaries between man and God. There were leaders of worship in the mosques as well as the *ulema,* a class of learned experts in the interpretation of the Koran; but they were all laymen. In this way Islam was spared the priestly tyranny such as arose in India, where the Brahmins considered themselves superior to all other classes in the rigid caste system.

Islamic law. In addition to being a religion, Islam offered a system of government, law, and society. The Islamic community was an excellent example of a theocratic state, one in which all power resides in God in whose behalf political, religious, and other forms of authority are exercised.

Especially in the period of expansion after the Prophet's death, the Islamic state required detailed rules covering a variety of new situations. The code that was developed was based partly on pre-Islamic legal customs. Before Muhammad's time each tribe had its own *sunna*, or body of custom, which served as a law code. After the Prophet's death his followers prepared a Sunna based upon the "traditions" (*hadith*) of what he had said and done. Using the Koran and the Sunna as their sources, Islamic jurists developed a body of religious law which regulated all aspects of Muslim life. Its development and interpretation were in the hands of the *ulema*. Agreement among these scholars set the seal of orthodoxy on questions of text and doctrine, with the result that Islamic law became progressively authoritarian and static.

THE SPREAD OF ISLAM

Expansion under the first four caliphs. Upon the Prophet's death in 632 the question arose as to who should direct the fortunes of Islam. This was a dangerous moment. Muhammad left no son to succeed him; and, even if he had, neither his unique position as the Prophet nor Arab custom permitted any such automatic succession. Acting swiftly, Muhammad's associates selected the Prophet's most trusted friend and advisor, Abu Bakr, as his official successor, the caliph (from *khalifa*, meaning "deputy"). The second caliph was also one of Muhammad's companions, while the fourth was his cousin and son-in-law.

During the reigns of the first four caliphs (632-661) Islam spread rapidly. Their wars of conquest were aided by the Prophet's belief that any Muslim dying in battle for the faith was assured entrance into paradise. This concept of holy war (*jihad*) bred in the Arabs, already a fierce fighting people, fanatical courage. Moreover, the prospect of rich and fertile territory, as well as plunder, proved a strong incentive to a people who had been eking out a bare existence from the desert.

The Islamic cause was also aided by political upheavals occurring outside of Arabia. The Muslim triumphs in the Near East can be partly accounted for by the long series of wars between the Byzantine and Persian empires. The Byzantine victory in 628 had left both sides exhausted and open to conquest. Moreover, the inhabitants of Syria and Egypt, alienated by religious dissent, were anxious to be free of Byzantine rule. In 636 Arab forces conquered Syria. The Muslims then wrested Iraq from the Persians and, within

ten years after Muhammad's death, subdued Persia itself. The greater part of Egypt fell with little resistance in 640 and the rest shortly afterward. Thus, by the end of the reigns of the first four caliphs, Islam had vastly increased its territory (see map, p. 159).

The imposition of a head tax on all non-Muslims encouraged many to become converts to Islam. Contrary to exaggerated accounts in the West of the forceful infliction of Islam upon conquered peoples, the Jews and Christians outside of Arabia enjoyed toleration because they worshiped the same God as the Muslims.

Islam is one of the most effective religions in removing barriers of race and nationality. Apart from a certain privileged position allowed the Arabs, distinctions were mostly those of class. The new religion converted and embraced peoples of many colors and cultures. This egalitarian feature of Islam undoubtedly aided its expansion.

Arab domination under the Umayyads. The expansion of Islam under the first four caliphs produced a new type of claimant to the caliphate—powerful generals and governors of provinces. In 661 the governor of Syria proclaimed himself caliph, made Damascus his capital, and founded the Umayyad dynasty which lasted until 750. Thus the caliphate became in fact, although never in law, a hereditary office, not, as previously, a position filled by election.

The Umayyad navy held Cyprus, Rhodes, and a string of Aegean islands, which served as a base for annual sea-borne attacks on Constantinople from 674 to 678. With the aid of Greek fire, Constantinople was saved, and the Arab advance was checked for the first time. Westward across North Africa, however, the Umayyad armies had great success. The Berbers, a warlike Hamitic-speaking people inhabiting the land between the Mediterranean and the Sahara, resisted stubbornly until converted to Islam. The next logical jump was across the Strait of Gibraltar into the weak kingdom of the Visigoths in Spain. The governor of Muslim North Africa sent his general, Tarik, and an army across the Strait into Spain in 711. Seven years later the kingdom of the Visigoths had completely crumbled. The Muslims swept across the

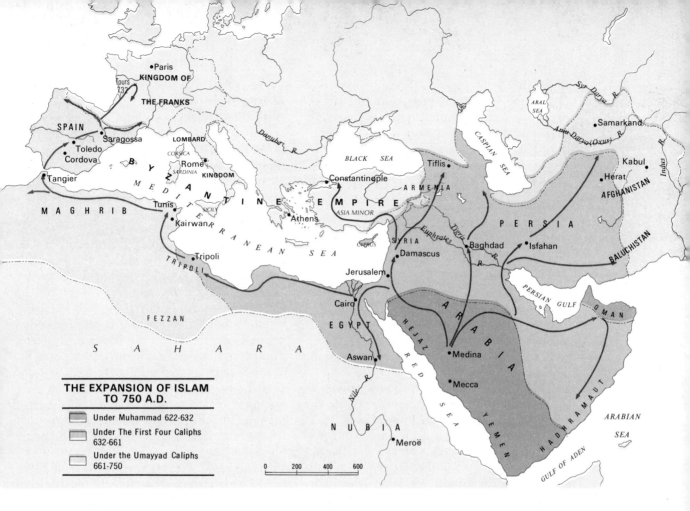

Pyrenees and gained a foothold in southwest France, where they carried out a major raid to explore the possibility of a further northward advance. However, they were defeated by Charles Martel near Tours in 732 (see p. 190), in a battle which, together with their defeat by the Byzantine emperor Leo III in 718 (see p. 143), proved decisive in halting their westward expansion. Meanwhile the Muslims had been expanding eastward into Central Asia, and by the eighth century they could claim lands as far as Turkestan and the Indus valley.

The mainstay of Umayyad power was the ruling class of Arabs, who formed a privileged aristocracy greatly outnumbered by non-Arabic converts to Islam—Egyptians, Syrians, Persians, Berbers, and others. Many of these possessed cultures much more advanced than that of the Arabs, and the economic and cultural life of the Arab empire depended on these people. But because they were not Arab by birth, they were treated as second-class Muslims. They were not per-

mitted to marry Arab women, and as soldiers they received less pay and booty than the Arabs. Resentment grew among the non-Arabic Muslims and eventually helped bring about the downfall of the Umayyads.

Shia movement against the ruling group. This resentment also found expression in the religious sphere, where large numbers of the non-Arabic Muslims joined the sect known as the Shia, formed when Ali, Muhammad's son-in-law and fourth caliph, was deposed by the Umayyads. The Shia continued to regard Ali and his descendants as the rightful rulers of the Islamic community. They believed that in every age an infallible leader with superhuman qualities would appear and that he must be obeyed. The Shia rejected the Sunna, the body of traditions concerning Muhammad, but in time they developed their own body of elaborate religious knowledge not contained in the Koran. Though originally an Arab party, the Shia in time became a general Islamic movement that stood for opposition to the ruling dynasty. The Shia evolved into one of the two major groups in Islam. The majority, named Sunnites because they were the "orthodox" perpetuators of Muhammad's Sunna, or tradition, upheld the principle that the caliph owed his position to the consent of the Islamic community. The numerical superiority of the Sunnites has continued to this day.

The Abbasids, high tide of Islamic civilization. In 750 the Umayyad dynasty was crushed by rebels, and a new dynasty, the Abbasid, ruled most of the Muslim world from 750 to 1258. The city of Baghdad was built in 762 as the capital of the new dynasty. The Abbasids owed their success to the discontent of the non-Arabic Muslims, who were the chief elements in the towns and in the Shia.

The fall of the Umayyad dynasty marked the end of Arab predominance; henceforth all Muslims were treated as equals. The Arab aristocracy had led the forces of conquest during the great period of Islamic expansion, but with the advent of more stable political conditions, the important status thus far held by the Arab soldier was given to non-Arab administrators and merchants. The traditional Arabic patterns of nomadism and tribal war were giving way before economic prosperity, the growth of town life, and the rise of a merchant class. The Abbasid caliph who built Baghdad forecast that it would become the "most flourishing city in the world"; and indeed it rivaled Constantinople for that honor, situated as it was on the trade routes linking West and East. Furthermore, Abbasid patronage of scholarship and the arts produced a rich and complex culture far surpassing that then existing in western Europe.

The location of a new capital at Baghdad resulted in a shift of Islam's center of gravity to the province of Iraq, whose soil, watered by the Tigris and Euphrates, had nurtured man's earliest civilization. Here the Abbasid caliphs set themselves up as potentates in the traditional style of the ancient East—and more particularly of Persia—so that they were surrounded by a lavish court that contrasted sharply with the simplicity of the Prophet.

The Abbasid dynasty marked the high tide of Islamic power and civilization. The empire ruled by these caliphs was greater in size than the domain of the Roman Caesars; it was the product of an expansion during which the Muslims had assimilated peoples, customs, cultures, and inventions on an unprecedented scale. This Islamic state, in fact, drew on the resources of the entire known world.

Trade, industry, and agriculture. From the eighth to the twelfth centuries the Muslim world enjoyed a prosperity such as post-Roman Europe did not experience until early modern times. In close contact with three continents, the Muslims could shuttle goods back and forth from China to western Europe and from Russia to central Africa. Trade was facilitated also by the absence of tariff barriers within the empire and by the tolerance of the caliphs, who allowed non-Muslim merchants and craftsmen to reside in their territories and carry on commerce with their home countries. The presence of such important urban centers as Baghdad, Cairo, and Cordova stimulated trade and industry throughout the Muslim world.

The cosmopolitan nature of Baghdad was evident in its bazaars, which contained goods from all over the known world. There were spices, minerals, and dyes from India; gems and fabrics from Central Asia; honey and wax from Scandinavia and Russia; and ivory and gold dust from Africa. One bazaar in the city specialized in goods from China, including silks, musk, and porcelain. In the slave marts the Muslim traders bought and sold Scandinavians, Mongolians from Central Asia, and Africans. Joint-stock companies flourished along with a system of branch banking, and checks drawn on a bank in one city could be cashed elsewhere in the empire.

Muslim textile industries turned out excellent muslins, silks, cottons, and linens. The steel of Damascus and Toledo, the leather of Cordova, and the glass of Syria became world famous. Agriculture under the Abbasids was both extensive and profitable. Vast irrigation projects in Iraq resulted in an increase of cultivable land which yielded large crops of fruits and cereals. Wheat came from the Nile valley, cotton from North Africa, olives and wine from Spain, wool from eastern Asia Minor, and horses from Persia.

The opulent reign of Harun al-Rashid.

Just as the Abbasid was the most brilliant of Muslim dynasties, so the rule of Harun al-Rashid (786-809) was the most spectacular of the Abbasid reigns. He was the contemporary of Charlemagne, who had revived the Roman Empire in the West (see Chapter 8), and there can be no doubt that Harun was the most powerful ruler of the two and the symbol of the more highly advanced culture. The two monarchs were on friendly terms, based on self-interest. Charlemagne wanted to exert pressure on the Byzantine emperor to recognize his new imperial title. Harun, on the other hand, saw Charlemagne as an ally against the Umayyad rulers of Spain, who had broken away from Abbasid domination. The two emperors exchanged embassies and presents. The Muslim sent the Christian rich fabrics, aromatics, and even an elephant named Abu-Lababah, meaning "the father of intelligence." An intricate water clock from Baghdad seems to have been looked upon as a miracle in the West.

Relations between the Abbasid caliphate and the Byzantine empire were never very cordial, and conflicts often broke out along the constantly shifting border that separated Christian and Muslim territories. Harun al-Rashid once replied to a communique from the Byzantine emperor in the following terms:

In the name of God, the Merciful, the Compassionate. From Haroun, Commander of the Faithful, to Nicephorus, the dog of the Greeks. I have read your letter, you son of a she-infidel, and you shall see the answer before you hear it.[10]

Whereupon the irate caliph sent forth expeditions to ravage Asia Minor.

In the days of Harun al-Rashid, Baghdad's wealth and splendor equaled that of Constantinople, and its chief glory was the royal palace. With its annexes for eunuchs, officials, and a harem, the caliph's residence occupied a third of Baghdad. Resplendently furnished, the caliph's audience chamber was the setting for an elaborate ceremonial which continued that of the Byzantines and Persians.

Disintegration of the Abbasid empire.

Despite the unprecedented prosperity of the far-flung Islamic world, the political unity of Islam began to disappear soon after the accession of the Abbasid dynasty. The first sign of political disintegration appeared in 756 when a member of the deposed Umayyad family founded his own dynasty at Cordova in Spain; in 929 his descendant assumed the title of caliph. Also in the tenth century the Fatimids—Shiites who claimed descent from Muhammad's daughter Fatima who had married Ali, the fourth caliph—proclaimed themselves the true caliphs of all Islam. From their capital at Cairo, which they founded, their rule eventually extended from Morocco to northern Mesopotamia.

Meanwhile, in the latter part of the tenth century Turkish nomads, called Seljuks, had migrated from Central Asia into the Abbasid lands, where they accepted Islam. After annexing most of Persia, the Seljuks gained control of Baghdad in 1055 and absorbed Iraq. Subsequently they conquered Syria and Palestine at the expense of the Fatimids and proceeded to annex most of Asia Minor from the Byzantines. It was the Seljuk's great advance that prompted the First Crusade in 1095. The Seljuks permitted the Abbasids to retain nominal rule, but a new and terrible enemy was now to appear and change everything.

Early in the thirteenth century Genghis Khan succeeded in uniting the nomads of Mongolia; he and his successors conquered eastern and central Asia (see Chapters 7 and 10) and swept into Persia and Iraq. In 1258 a grandson of Genghis Khan captured Baghdad and had the caliph put in a sack and trampled to death. Not only did the Abbasid dynasty come to an end, but so did most of the vast irrigation system that had supported the land since the beginning of civilization; Iraq was not to recover until modern times. The dynasty established by the Mongols survived for only a short time, and the Mongol ruling class was eventually absorbed into the native population of Persia and Iraq.

Meanwhile, in 1260, an army of foreign-born slaves in Egypt called Mamluks saved Muslim Egypt from the Mongol advance. The Mamluks took over Palestine and Syria, ejecting the last of the crusaders in 1291. Ultimately they fell before the onslaught of another offshoot of the once great Seljuk empire, the Ottomans.

The Ottoman Turks. Having settled in northwestern Asia Minor in the thirteenth century as vassals of the Seljuks, the Ottoman Turks had organized their own aggressive state of Muslim frontier fighters by the end of the century (see p. 146). The Ottomans pitted their strength against the crumbling power of the Byzantines, and after capturing Constantinople in 1453 they pressed on into southeastern Europe. Driving as far as Vienna, they were turned back with difficulty in 1529 and again in 1683. Meanwhile, in 1517, the Ottomans had conquered the Mamluk territories, and within a few years they had added Iraq, much of Arabia, and all of the North African coastal belt to the borders of Morocco.

We have reviewed the expansion of Islam into western Asia and areas around the Mediterranean. In Chapter 7 we shall trace its expansion as a missionary faith into South and Southeast Asia, and Chapter 10 will describe the medieval Afro-Muslim kingdoms of equatorial Africa. Although political solidarity was not maintained in the Islamic world, a form of unity was perpetuated by a common religion and culture. As a result, that world emerged in modern times as an almost solid ribbon of peoples stretching from Morocco in the west through Indonesia in the east. Today about one seventh of the world's population is composed of Muslim peoples, whose religious solidarity and cultural heritage provide the basis for a program of political resurgence.

ISLAMIC CULTURE

Borrowing the best from other cultures. The high attainment of the Muslims in the intellectual and artistic fields can be primarily attributed not to the Arabs, who as a group remained concerned with religion, politics, and commerce, but rather to those peoples who had embraced Islam in Persia, Mesopotamia, Syria, Egypt, North Africa, and Spain. Muslim learning benefited primarily from Islam's ability to synthesize the best in other cultures rather than from native genius. The cosmopolitan spirit permeating the Abbasid dynasty supplied the tolerance necessary for a diversity of ideas, so that the science and philosophy of ancient Greece and India found a welcome in Baghdad. Under Harun al-Rashid and his successors the writings of Aristotle, Euclid, Ptolemy, Archimedes, Galen, and other great Greek scientific writers were translated into Arabic. This knowledge formed the basis of Muslim learning, which in turn was later transmitted to scholars in western Europe (see p. 252). In addition to being invaluable transmitters of learning, the Muslims also made some original contributions of their own to science.

Advances in medicine. The two hundred years between 900 and 1100 can be called the golden age of Muslim learning. This period was particularly significant for advances made in medicine. In spite of a ban against the study of anatomy and a few other limitations imposed on Muslims by their religion, their medical men were in most ways far superior to their European contemporaries. Muslim cities had excellent pharmacies and hospitals, and both pharmacists and physicians had to pass state examinations to be licensed. Physicians received instruction in medical schools and hospitals.

Perhaps the greatest Muslim physician was the Persian al-Razi (d. 925), better known to the West as Rhazes. He wrote more than a hundred medical treatises in which he summarized Greek medical knowledge and added his own acute clinical observations. His most famous work, *On Smallpox and Measles*, is the first clear description of the symptoms and treatment of these diseases. The most influential Muslim medical treatise is the vast *Canon of Medicine* of the Persian scholar Avicenna (d. 1037), in which all Greek and Muslim medical learning is systematically organized. In the twelfth century the *Canon* was translated into Latin and was so much in demand in the West that it was issued sixteen times in the last half of the fifteenth century and more than twenty times in the sixteenth. It is still read and used in the Orient today.

Progress in other sciences. Muslim physicists were no mere copyists. Alhazen (d. 1039) of Cairo developed optics to a remarkable degree and challenged the view of Ptolemy and Euclid that the eye sends visual rays to its object. The chief source of all medieval western writers on optics, he interested himself in optic reflections and illusions and examined the refraction of light rays through air and water.

Although astronomy continued to be astrology's handmaiden, Muslim astronomers built observatories, recorded their observations over long periods, and achieved greater accuracy than the Greeks in measuring the length of the solar year and in calculating eclipses. Interest in alchemy—the attempt to transmute base metals into precious ones and to find the magic elixir for the preservation of human life—produced the first chemical laboratories in history and an emphasis on the value of experimentation. Muslim alchemists prepared many chemical substances (sulphuric acid, for example) and developed methods for evaporation, filtration, sublimation, crystallization, and distillation. The process of distillation, invented around 800, produced what was called *al-kuhl*, a new liquor that has made Geber, its inventor, an honored name in some circles. Others claim that "Geber" became the etymological root of "gibberish."

In mathematics the Muslims were indebted to the Hindus as well as to the Greeks. From the Greeks came the geometry of Euclid and the fundamentals of trigonometry which Ptolemy had worked out. From the Hindus came arithmetic and algebra and the nine signs, known as Arabic numerals, whose value depends on their position in a series. The Muslims invented the all-important zero, although some scholars assign this honor to the Indians. Two Persians deserve mention: al-Khwarizmi (d. about 840), whose *Arithmetic* introduced Arabic numerals and whose *Algebra* first employed that mathematical term; and Omar Khayyám (d. 1123?), whose work in algebra went beyond quadratics to cubic equations. Other scholars developed plane and spherical trigonometry.

Muslim scholars devoted themselves to the study of science and medicine. In an observatory in Constantinople some astronomers make mathematical computations with the assistance of a variety of instruments, while others gather around a globe showing Asia, Africa, and Europe.

In an empire that straddled continents, where trade and administration made an accurate knowledge of lands imperative, the science of geography flourished. The Muslims added to the geographical knowledge of the Greeks, whose treatises they translated, by producing detailed descriptions of the climate, manners, and customs of many parts of the known world.

Islamic literature and scholarship. To westerners, whose literary tastes have been largely formed by classical traditions, Arab literature may seem strange and alien. Where we are accustomed to restraint and simplicity, "the Muslim writer excels . . . in clothing the essential realism of his thought with the language of romance."[11] Consequently, Arabic poetry abounds in elegant expression, subtle combinations of words, fanciful and even extravagant imagery, and witty conceits.

Westerners' knowledge of Islamic literature tends to be limited to the *Arabian Nights* and to the hedonistic poetry of Omar Khayyám. The former is a collection of often erotic tales told with a wealth of local color; although it professedly covers different facets of life at the Abbasid capital, it is in fact often based on life in medieval Cairo. The fame of Omar Khayyám's *Rubáiyát* is partly due to the musical (though not overaccurate) translation of Edward Fitzgerald. The following stanzas indicate the poem's beautiful imagery and gentle pessimism:

A Book of Verses underneath the Bough,
A Jug of Wine, a Loaf of Bread—and Thou
　　Beside me singing in the Wilderness—
Oh, Wilderness were Paradise enow!

Some for the Glories of This World; and some
Sigh for the Prophet's Paradise to come;
　　Ah, take the Cash, and let the Credit go,
Nor heed the rumble of a distant Drum! . . .

The Moving Finger writes; and, having writ,
Moves on: nor all your Piety nor Wit
　　Shall lure it back to cancel half a Line,
Nor all your Tears wash out a Word of it.

And that inverted Bowl they call the Sky,
Whereunder crawling coop'd we live and die,
　　Lift not your hands to *It* for help—for It
As impotently moves as you or I.[12]

The same rich use of imagery is found in much Islamic prose. As the first important prose work in Arab literature, the Koran set the stylistic pattern for Arabic writers even down to modern times. The holy book was designed particularly to be recited aloud; anyone who has listened to the chanting of the Koran can testify to its cadence, melody, and power.

Muslim philosophy, essentially Greek in origin, was developed by laymen and not, as in the West, by churchmen. Like the medieval Christian philosophers (see Chapter 11), Muslim thinkers were largely concerned with reconciling Aristotelian rationalism and

This map, made for Roger II of Sicily (note the size of Sicily in comparison to the rest of Europe), represents a direct contact between medieval Arab and European cartography. Arabia was placed near the top of the world; thus for clarity the map should be viewed upside down. Based on classical Ptolemaic models, the map uses a grid system of horizontal and vertical lines to divide the world into seventy geographical areas, thus producing a forerunner of the modern rendering of longitude and latitude.

religion. The earlier Muslim thinkers, including Avicenna, the physician with many talents, sought to harmonize Platonism, Aristotelianism, and Islam. Avicenna's work was widely read in the West, where it was translated in the twelfth century. The last great Islamic philosopher, Averroës (d. 1198), lived in Cordova where he was the caliph's personal doctor. In his commentaries on Aristotle's works, which gave the Christian West its knowledge of Aristotle long before the original Greek texts were obtained from Constantinople, Averroës rejected the belief in the ultimate harmony between faith and reason along with all earlier attempts to reconcile Aristotle and Plato. Faith and reason, he argued, operate on different levels; a proposition can be true philosophically but false theologically. On the other hand, Moses Maimonides, Averroës' contemporary who was also born in Muslim Spain, sought, in his still influential *Guide to the Perplexed*, to harmonize Judaism and Aristotelian philosophy. When St. Thomas Aquinas in the next century undertook a similar project for Christianity, he was influenced by these earlier attempts to reconcile faith and reason.

Islamic historiography found its finest expression in the work of ibn-Khaldun of Tunis (d. 1406), who has also been called "a father of sociology." Despite his busy life in public affairs, he found time to write a large general history dealing particularly with man's social development, which he held to be the result of the interaction of society and the physical environment. Ibn-Khaldun defined history as follows:

It should be known that history, in matter of fact, is information about human social organization, which itself is identical with world civilization. It deals with such conditions affecting the nature of civilization as, for instance, savagery and sociability, group feelings, and the different ways by which one group of human beings achieves superiority over another. It deals with royal authority and . . . with the different kinds of gainful occupations and ways of making a living, with the sciences and crafts that human beings pursue as part of their activities and efforts, and with all the other institutions that originate in civilization through its very nature.[13]

Artistry and precise observation combine to make this illustration from a thirteenth-century Islamic natural history text both graceful and accurate. Not only the doe and stag but also the willow tree and the various small grasses and shrubs are carefully rendered.

Ibn-Khaldun conceived of history as an evolutionary process, in which societies and institutions change continually.

Art and architecture. Religious attitudes played an important part in Muslim art. Because the Prophet inveighed strongly against idols and their worship, there was a prejudice against pictorial representation of human and animal figures. The effect of this prejudice was to encourage the development of stylized and geometrical design. Muslim art, like Muslim learning, borrowed from many sources. Islamic artists and craftsmen followed chiefly Byzantine and Persian models and eventually integrated what they had learned into a distinctive and original style (see Color Plate 7).

The Muslims excelled in two fields—architecture and the decorative arts. That Islamic architecture can boast of many large and imposing structures is not surprising, because it drew much of its inspiration from the Byzantines and Persians, who were monumental builders. In time an original style of building evolved; the great mosques

With its arches, decoration, domes, minarets, and formal gardens, the Taj Mahal is a fine example of Islamic architectural traditions.

embody such typical features as domes, arcades, and minarets, the slender towers from which the faithful are summoned to prayer. The horseshoe arch is another graceful and familiar feature of Muslim architecture.

On the walls and ceilings of their buildings, the Muslims gave full rein to their love of ornamentation and beauty of detail. The Spanish interpretation of the Muslim tradition was particularly delicate and elegant (see p. 208). Other outstanding examples of Islamic architecture are to be found in India; the Taj Mahal, for example, is based largely on Persian motifs.

Being restricted in their subject matter, Muslim craftsmen conceived beautiful patterns from flowers and geometric figures. Even the Arabic script, the most beautiful ever devised, was used as a decorative motif. Muslim decorative skill also found expression in such fields as carpet and rug weaving, brass work, and the making of steel products inlaid with precious metals.

SUMMARY

We have examined two rival but equally fascinating civilizations: first, the Byzantine, a citadel of classical and Christian culture; second, a dynamic Islam, conqueror alike of kingdoms and of the spiritual allegiance of populations stretching from Gibraltar to Java. With the conquest of Constantinople in 1453, this second civilization overwhelmed its rival.

When Constantine chose the site for New Rome, he picked a location that was geographically excellent for defense and trade. Constantinople's tradition as the eastern capital of the Roman empire encouraged Justinian to attempt to recover the western territory that had been under Roman rule; but these efforts failed, and in the long run Byzantium had to fight continually against invasions that diminished its empire on all sides. In 1453 the Ottoman Turks conquered "The City," and the empire of a thousand years was destroyed.

For a millennium the empire had acted as a buffer state, repulsing attacks while the weak, divided West grew in strength. And while learning was all but lost in medieval western Europe, the Byzantine world remained the custodian of classical knowledge and ideals until a resurgent West was able to assimilate its classical heritage. But Constantinople did much more than all this. Roman, Greek, and oriental elements were fused into a distinct and original culture; Slavic peoples were converted to Christianity; and the benefits of civilization were brought to Russia and neighboring lands.

The Norsemen who founded Kievan Russia also set up trade with Constantinople which continued for centuries. Through this medium, culture and religion were imported into Russia from the Eastern empire. While Constantinople itself fell, its heritage was in many ways maintained in the new Slavic state that was spreading across the vast Russian plain.

Muhammad (570-632), the founder of the Islamic religion, was born into a desert area populated by nomadic Bedouins and a few scattered groups of townsmen. Soon after Muhammad's death, his monotheistic teachings were compiled in the Koran, the Muslim bible.

During the reigns of the first four caliphs and the century of the Umayyad dynasty (661-750), great strides were made in annexing new territories and peoples. But the Umayyad dynasty was based on a ruling hierarchy of Arabs, and the resentment of the non-Arabs produced a revolution which set the Abbasid dynasty (750-1258) on a new throne in Baghdad.

During the early Abbasid period Islam reached the high point of its geographical expansion and cultural achievements, and a ribbon of Muslim peoples extended from Spain across three continents to the Far East. Unparalleled prosperity evolved from a combination of successful trade, industry, and agriculture. But the Muslims were not able to maintain an integrated empire; despite a religious unity, which still exists (though without formal organization), politically the empire broke up into smaller Muslim states.

The Muslims were especially gifted in science, literature, and philosophy. Muslim intellectual life was in good part the product of a genius for synthesizing varying cultures, and their diffusion of this knowledge was a tremendous factor in the revival of classical learning and the coming of the Renaissance in Europe.

Ironically, while the arts and learning were beginning to thrive in the West, Islamic civilization itself entered a period of cultural decline. Various reasons have been advanced for this phenomenon, including the influx of semibarbarous peoples into Islamic lands, intellectual stagnation resulting from too rigid interpretation of the Koran, and the despotic and eventually corrupt rule of such Muslim dynasties as the Ottomans in Turkey, who destroyed all progressive political and economic movements.

SUGGESTIONS FOR READING

Charles Diehl, **Byzantium: Greatness and Decline**,* Rutgers. Highly recommended as a brief introduction. Also brief is R. Guerdan, **Byzantium: Its Triumphs and Tragedy**,* Capricorn. For greater detail see G. Ostrogorsky, **History of the Byzantine State**, Rutgers, 1957; Romilly Jenkins, **Byzantium: The Imperial Centuries, A.D. 610-1071**,* Vintage; **The Cambridge Medieval History**, Vol. IV, rev. ed., **The Byzantine Empire**, Pt. I, **Byzantium and Its Neighbors**, 1966; Pt. II, **Government, Church and Civilization**, 1967.

D. A. Miller, **The Byzantine Tradition**,* Harper & Row, 1966. A brief perceptive survey of Byzantine civilization. See also J. Hussey, **The Byzantine World**,* Torchbooks; S. Runciman, **Byzantine Civilization**,* Meridian.

John W. Barker, **Justinian and the Later Roman Empire**, Wisconsin, 1966. Clear, lively, and recent. See also G. Downey, **Constantinople in the Age of Justinian**, Oklahoma, 1960; Dean A. Miller, **Imperial Constantinople**,* Wiley, 1969.

Charles M. Brand, **Byzantium Confronts the West, 1184-1204**, Harvard, 1968; D. Queller, ed., **The Latin Conquest of Constantinople**,* Wiley, 1970. Describe the events marking the beginning of the disintegration of the Byzantine empire.

H. Magoulias, **Byzantine Christianity: Emperor, Church and the West**,* Rand McNally, 1970; T. Ware, **The Orthodox Church**,* Penguin. Two good surveys. S. Runciman, **The Eastern Schism**, Oxford, 1955, disentangles fact from legend.

D. Talbot Rice, **Art of the Byzantine Era**,* Praeger; A. Grabar, **Art of the Byzantine Empire**, Crown, 1966. For superb color reproductions of Byzantine mosaics, see H. Newmayer, **Byzantine Mosaics**,* Crown, and A. Grabar, **Byzantine Painting**, Skira, 1953.

F. Dvornik, **The Slavs in European History and Civilization**, Rutgers, 1962. Emphasizes Byzantine influences. G. Vernadsky, **Kievan Russia**, Yale, 1948, is detailed and authoritative. M. Florinsky, **Russia: A History and an Interpretation**, Vol. I, Macmillan, 1954, is excellent on early Russia. See also G. Fedotov, **The Russian Religious Mind: Kievan Christianity, the Tenth to the Thirteenth Centuries**,* Torchbooks.

P. K. Hitti, **The Arabs: A Short History**,* Gateway. An abridgment of a scholarly general history of the Arabs. See also C. Brockelmann, **History of the Islamic Peoples**,* Capricorn.

W. Montgomery Watt, **Muhammad: Prophet and Statesman**,* Oxford. Short and excellent. See also T. Andrae, **Mohammed: The Man and His Faith**,* Torchbooks. For an interpretation and translation of the Koran, see M. Pickthall, **The Meaning of the Glorious Koran**,* Mentor. H. A. R. Gibb, **Mohammedanism: An Historical Survey**,* Galaxy, is outstanding.

H. Pirenne, **Mohammed and Charlemagne**,* Barnes and Noble. Propounds the thesis that the expansion of Islam, and not the Germanic invasions, brought about the economic disintegration of the western Roman world. See also A. Havighurst, ed., **The Pirenne Thesis: Analysis, Criticism, Revision**,* Heath.

P. Coles, **The Ottoman Impact on Europe**,* Harcourt, Brace & World, 1968. A lucid, profusely illustrated survey. See also S. Runciman, **The Fall of Constantinople, 1453**,* Cambridge.

R. A. Nicholson, **A Literary History of the Arabs**,* Cambridge, 1969. Traces the growth of Arab thought and culture through its literature. See also P. Hitti, **Makers of Arab History**, St. Martin's, 1968; G. von Grunebaum, **Medieval Islam**,* Phoenix; D. Talbot Rice, **Islamic Art**,* Praeger.

*Indicates an inexpensive paperbound edition.

Chapter 7

The Guptas and the T'ang: Two Golden Ages

India, China, and Japan: 200-1450

INTRODUCTION. The span of little more than a thousand years from the fifth to the fifteenth century was characterized in most parts of the world by numerous ethnic migrations and significant intercultural impacts. Later chapters will describe the ebb and flow of peoples—Vikings, Mongols, Magyars, and Germanic tribes—in medieval Europe; this chapter discusses the movement of peoples and cultural diffusion in Asia. During this period Indian culture expanded throughout Southeast Asia, enriching indigenous societies in what are now Burma, Indochina, the Malay peninsula, and Indonesia, while Buddhism exerted a profound influence upon China and Japan. Similarly, there was a continuous flow of Chinese culture eastward to the Korean peninsula and Japan. In the later part of this period, Muslim conquest appreciably influenced Indian society, and the repeated invasions by the Mongols and other nomadic peoples wrought important political and social changes in China.

The events related in this chapter point up a significant theme in history—the important role played by restless, nomadic peoples in the rise and fall of civilizations. In the decline of the Roman Empire, as treated in Chapter 5, we witnessed a classic example of this recurring phenomenon—nomad tribes pressing and probing "softer," more civilized, less dynamic groups, discovering the weak spots in their defenses, and finally overwhelming them. Again, in Chapter 6, we saw Byzantium assailed continuously for a thousand years until it at last fell victim to inexorable outside pressures. Perhaps the most awesome of all the nomads were the Mongols ruled by Genghis Khan, who led his hordes into China in search of booty and went on to create the greatest empire the world had yet seen—a vast realm extending all the way from the China Sea to eastern Europe. But if the assault of nomads is an important concern of this chapter, a corollary is how, once victorious, the predatory invader usually becomes respectable and sedentary, ceasing to be a menace to neighboring peoples.

In spite of these seemingly confused migrations and confrontations between peoples—or perhaps in part because of them—Asian civilizations reached a high peak during this period. In India the Gupta rulers came to power, and the subcontinent bene-fited from their enlightened government. Hindu culture entered a period of flourishing growth marked by important advances in mathematics, medicine, chemistry, textile production, and imaginative literature. In fact, in the realm of culture diffusion and creative thought, India played the major role in Eurasia during the four centuries from 200 to 600 A.D. In the following period, from the seventh through the tenth centuries, the T'ang dynasty held sway in China, reviving the greatness of Chinese civilization after a period of disorder and division. For the most part, the Chinese enjoyed prosperity and good government, and there was a flowering of scholarship and the arts. It was during the T'ang and Sung dynasties that such revolutionary inventions as printing, explosive powder, and the compass were devised. The Japanese archipelago, after being occupied by ancestors of the present inhabitants, was never successfully invaded until the twentieth century. Influenced greatly by China, the proud and independent Japanese gradually developed a unique culture pattern best symbolized by the *samurai*, the knight, and *bushido*, the code of the warrior. Here, too, was a development which centuries later affected world history.

INDIA: THE IMPERIAL GUPTAS

The Gupta empire. As we recall from Chapter 4, the Kushan dynasty, which had witnessed one of the richest periods in Indian civilization, crumbled about 220 A.D. Subsequent events in northern India followed a pattern that has recurred time and again in the history of the subcontinent: an epoch of distinction followed by an era of political disintegration and comparative cultural darkness.

With the advent of the Gupta empire in the fourth century, northern India came out of its dark era and entered upon another epoch of greatness. In about 320 A.D., the first ruler of the Gupta dynasty, Chandragupta I (not related to Chandragupta Maurya, p. 98), established himself as monarch of the Ganges valley; and his successor ex-tended the imperial boundaries in all directions. As a result, much of northern India from the Himalayas south to the Narbada River was included within the Gupta empire, thus making it the most extensive and powerful Indian state since the days of Ashoka six centuries earlier. Nor had its limits been reached. The grandson of the dynasty's founder, Chandragupta II, extended the empire still farther west until it stretched from sea to sea (see map, p. 171). During his reign (c. 380-c. 413), the Gupta empire reached its zenith. In all its long history before the British conquest India probably came closest to political unity during the reigns of Ashoka, Chandragupta II, and the Mughuls (see Chapter 16).

Under the Gupta dynasty, India exhibited

a state of cultural integration and social harmony such as it has never since achieved. By comparison with the Roman Empire, which was nearing its demise, and China, which was enduring a troubled interim period between the two great eras of the Han and the T'ang, India was probably the most civilized region of the world at this time.

Dominance of Hinduism. Although religious tolerance was characteristic of the Gupta period, the Gupta rulers preferred Hinduism to Buddhism, and the Brahmin caste enjoyed imperial patronage. While Buddhism as a distinct faith became practically extinct, certain of its teachings—for example, *ahimsā*, nonviolence and respect for life—were incorporated into Hinduism. From about 185 B.C. to about 800 A.D., Hinduism not only became dominant in India but also gradually crystallized into its present form.

By recognizing all varieties of religious experience, Hinduism is capable of absorbing different and often even contradictory points of view—a factor that helps account for its tremendous tenacity. Names mean very little; God may be worshiped in many forms and by many names. Hinduism stresses conduct and ceremony rather than rigid belief. To be a Hindu it is only necessary to accept the leadership of the Brahmins and one's status in caste, thereby implying acceptance of the belief of reincarnation.

Notwithstanding the many invasions into India, all of the intruders—excluding the Muslims and later the British—were absorbed and found a place in Hinduism.

The caste system. By the Gupta period the caste system was rapidly assuming its basic features. Each caste was usually related to a specific occupation, was endogamous (a man was expected to select his bride from within his own group), and had its own *dharma*—rules regulating the types of food eaten, the manner of consumption, and with what other castes there could be social contact. The untouchables, the lowest rung in the caste ladder, had a degraded status.

In the light of modern democratic ideology, caste is a reprehensible system and indeed is so regarded by many of India's present leaders. Defenders of the institution, however, point out that a caste forms a kind of brotherhood in which all members are equal. Furthermore, within his caste the Hindu enjoys a sense of security that makes him feel part of a cosmic process in which no mistakes are made.

Achievements in Sanskrit literature. The Gupta period has been called the golden age of Sanskrit, the classical language of India. Court poetry was zealously produced, and the kings were generous patrons of many writers. The most famous writer, Kalidasa (c. 400-455), excelled as both a lyric and an epic poet and has been termed the "Indian

The best examples of Gupta painting are found in the caves at Ajanta in the Deccan. Hollowed out of solid rock and adorned with sculpture and murals, these twenty-nine worship halls and dwelling places served as a hermitage for Buddhist monks. Some of the paintings, which depict scenes from the life of Buddha and from Buddhist stories, date from the second century B.C.; the finest, however, were painted during the Gupta period. Presenting a brilliant panorama of contemporary life, the murals portray beggars, princes, peasants, women, children, beasts, and birds. This painting depicts the temptation of Buddha.

Shakespeare" because of his superb dramas. Characterized by a lack of action unfamiliar to western audiences, his plays abound in splendid imagery.

India presented an unusually fertile soil for the creation of fables and folklore. Since its religions stressed the unity of all life and the cycle of transmigration, it was not difficult for storytellers to reverse the positions of the animal and human kingdoms and to conceive of beasts acting like men and vice versa. Many Indian stories were eventually carried to Europe by the Muslims. Perhaps the most famous is the story of Sindbad, which found its way into the *Arabian Nights*. Boccaccio, Chaucer, La Fontaine, the Grimm brothers, and Kipling have all been indebted to Indian folklore.

Gupta science and technology. Scholarship and science were of a very high caliber during Gupta times. Students from all over Asia came to India's foremost university, situated at Nalanda. The most famous scientist was the astronomer and mathematician Aryabhata, who lived in the fifth century. In verse he discussed quadratic equations, the value of π, solstices and equinoxes, the spherical shape of the earth, and the earth's rotation. Other Indian astronomers predicted eclipses accurately, calculated the moon's diameter, and expounded on gravitation.

In astronomy and mathematics (except for geometry) the Hindus surpassed the achievements of any ancient western people. The Arabic numerals and the decimal system we use today appear to have come originally from India. Even the zero may have come from Indian rather than Arabic sources.

The Hindus were also remarkably advanced in chemistry; they discovered how to make soap and cement and were the finest temperers of steel in the world. Indian industry was famous for its superior dyes and fine fabrics; the methods of production were taken over by the Arabs, and from them by Europeans. The Arabs named one Indian cloth *quittan*—hence the word *cotton*. *Calico*, *cashmere*, *chintz*, and *bandanna* are also of Indian origin.

The development of Indian medicine was due to various factors, including an interest in physiology which resulted from Yoga. Some Gupta physicians were surprisingly modern in their techniques; they prepared carefully for an operation and sterilized wounds by fumigation. Caesarean operations, bone setting, and plastic surgery were all attempted. The Indians also used many drugs then unknown in Europe.

A period of instability. By 413, when Chandragupta II died, the Gupta empire had reached the zenith of its power. In the last half of the fifth century, while their kinsmen were ravaging Europe under Attila, "The Scourge," Huns invaded the Punjab. They soon gained control of northwestern India but were prevented from advancing into eastern India by a confederacy of Hindu princes.

In the seventh century the various states in the Ganges valley fought constantly with one another until at last a strong man arose. In the short space of six years (606-612) Harsha, rajah of one of the northern kingdoms, mastered much of the territory formerly

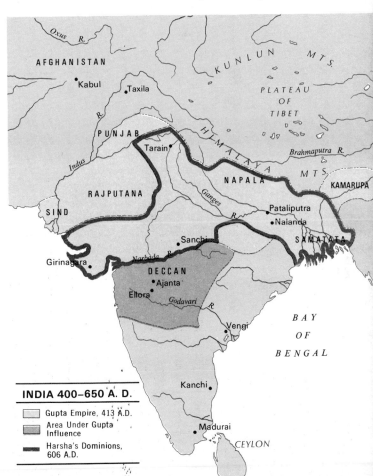

INDIA 400–650 A.D.

Gupta Empire, 413 A.D.
Area Under Gupta Influence
Harsha's Dominions, 606 A.D.

ruled by the Guptas. With his death in 647, northern India reverted to confusion and warfare which lasted for centuries.

Particularly warlike were the descendants of Central Asian peoples who had followed the Huns into northwest India in the fifth century and had intermarried with the local population. In time these people assumed the privileges of "blue-blooded" Hindus, haughtily called themselves Rajputs (Sons of Kings), and carved out kingdoms for themselves in parts of north India, especially in what became known as Rajputana, a strategic area between the Indus and Ganges valleys. The Rajputs possessed a code of chivalry not unlike that which existed in medieval Europe. Youths were brought up with the privileges and obligations of the warrior caste (the Kshatriya) and taught to respect women, spare the fallen, and demand fair play.

Expansion of Indian culture. For nearly one thousand years India sent her art, religious ideas, literature, and traders to many parts of Asia. The diffusion of *Mahayana* Buddhism into Central Asia, China, Korea, and finally Japan during this period was the most striking sign of the dynamic power of Indian culture. The relationship between India and China was especially strong, and many Chinese scholars made pilgrimages to the former. The most celebrated was Hsüan-tsang (or Yuan-chuang), who spent thirteen years (630-643) in Buddha's holy land. Returning to his native land, Hsüan-tsang brought back 657 manuscripts, together with many Buddhist relics, and devoted the remainder of his life to translating his treasures. His journal is one of the most valuable sources of information on medieval India.

Resulting mainly from peaceful trading activities, Indian cultural expansion in what has been called "Greater India" in Southeast Asia began about the second century A.D. and continued until the ninth or tenth century. The impact of Indian culture was not equally strong or enduring over all sections. One scholar has divided Greater India into two segments: the western zone (including Ceylon, Burma, the central part of Siam, and the Malay peninsula) received the full force of Indian colonizing activity and conse-quently developed a culture that was largely a colonial imitation of the original; the eastern zone (comprising mainly Java, Cambodia, and Champa in Indochina) experienced Indianization that was very definite but not strong enough to prevent the indigenous peoples from developing their own distinctive cultures and ways of life.

From the second century A.D. on, the kingdoms established in Greater India were ruled by monarchs with Indian names. Some of these kingdoms endured more than a thousand years, persisting, in fact, after India itself had been overwhelmed by foreign invaders. Two monuments attest to the splendor of these states.

About 1100 one of the greatest architectural edifices in history was erected in Cambodia —Angkor Wat (see Color Plate 15). Long forgotten and swallowed up by the jungle, this vast complex was accidentally discovered by a French naturalist in 1861. It is surrounded by a stone enclosure measuring half a mile from north to south and two thirds of a mile from east to west. Nearby lay the Cambodian capital city, which may have had a population of close to one million.

In central Java one of the most imposing Buddhist shrines in the world is located: the immense monument of Borobudur. Erected on the top of a hill in nine successive terraces, Borobudur is covered with images of the Buddha, sculptures illustrating Buddhist texts, and carved scenes of everyday life. The art of Southeast Asia was unmistakably influenced by Indian styles and techniques, but in Angkor Wat and Borobudur the works created were larger than anything found in India itself.

THE MUSLIM CONQUEST OF INDIA

The Muslim invasions. In 711, the same year in which they invaded Spain, Arabs appeared in India. They made the southern valley of the Indus a province of the vast Umayyad empire, but the Rajput princes soon halted further Arab penetration of India.

At the end of the tenth century more Muslim invaders swept through the northwest passes. The newcomers were Turks and Afghans who, in 1022, annexed the Punjab. Despite destructive forays by various Muslim sultans, the Rajput and other Hindu kingdoms of the interior remained independent. Not until the closing years of the twelfth century did the Muslims establish a large Indian dominion.

The Delhi sultanate. The first important Muslim ruler was a former general who in 1206 established himself as sultan at Delhi, ruling a strong Muslim kingdom covering much of north India. The Delhi sultanate existed until the early years of the sixteenth century, and during the period of its greatest power (1206-1388), it gave northern India political unity. The early Delhi sultans also pushed Muslim authority and religion southward into the Deccan and in the first decades of the fourteenth century reached southernmost India. The Delhi sultanate, however, soon lost control in southern India to a rival sultanate in the Deccan and to other Muslim and Hindu states.

Tamerlane. In 1398 the Punjab was invaded by a Mongol who had already conquered Central Asia—Timur the Lame (Tamerlane). Defeating all armies sent against him, Timur looted wealthy Delhi, killing perhaps 100,000 prisoners. Afterwards, he departed westward for Samarkand, leaving Delhi's few surviving inhabitants to perish of famine and plague. After Timur's terrible visitation, nearly all semblance of political unity was destroyed in north India, and Muslim sultans maintained independent principalities in defiance of the ineffectual authority at Delhi.

Effects of Muslim rule. The Muslim conquest of India was unusually ruthless. To the Muslims, Hinduism with its many deities, elaborate ritual, powerful priestcraft, and fondness for images was the opposite of all that Islam held sacred. Hindu forces desperately resisted their Muslim conquerors and, after defeat, often suffered wholesale massacre. Many people clung tenaciously to their Hindu faith—the upper classes in particular—but a fairly large number of Hindus were converted to Islam. In some cases it was a choice between Allah or the sword; in others it was a voluntary matter: poor men sought to avoid the heavier taxes levied on infidels, low-caste Hindus became Muslims to escape their degraded status, and ambitious administrators accepted Islam in order to succeed in the official service of the Muslim rulers. One result of the Muslim intrusion was the emergence of a common spoken language—Urdu. This language was a combination of Persian, Turkish, and Arabic words which utilized the grammatical constructions of the Hindu languages. Urdu and the native Hindi became the languages most commonly used in northern India, and they are today the dominant languages of Muslim Pakistan and Hindu India.

The injection of the Islamic way of life into the pattern of Hindu society was to have profound effects upon the history of the Indian subcontinent. Fiercely proud of their own faith, and disdainful of Hinduism, the Muslims jealously retained their religion and ways of life. After the establishment of the powerful Delhi sultanate in 1206, therefore, the life of India was divided into two streams, the Hindu and the Muslim, which mingled only superficially and never really united. This division was to have momentous consequences in the twentieth century, when India, freed from British rule, split into two nations, India and Pakistan.

CHINA: THE MEN OF T'ANG

An age of political division. After the fall of the Han empire in 220 A.D., China was destined to suffer three and a half centuries of disorder and division before another great dynasty arose and reunited the country. The internal collapse of the Han empire —as with the breakdown of the Mauryan and Gupta regimes in India and of Rome in the West—allowed various nomadic peoples to penetrate the frontiers and raid and pillage. In North China these barbarians set up various petty states, especially after the opening of the fourth century.

Central and South China escaped these

barbarian intrusions and were now more intensively developed than before, especially by émigrés from the north. Hence the literate classical tradition was preserved in the south; and a sequence of regimes, with capitals at Nanking, kept alive the notion of a unified state under a "Son of Heaven."

Buddhism adapts itself. Although Buddhism had been introduced into China during Han times, this religion made its most important gains from the third century A.D. on. As the sober, balanced social order inculcated by Confucianism came to make less sense in a world run by warlords, all classes of Chinese were touched by Buddhism. Part of Buddhism's appeal resembled that of the mystery religions and of Christianity in the decaying Roman world: the assurance of inner consolation through faith and of salvation in a glorious afterlife even for humble folk. The monastic aspects of Buddhism appealed to many thousands of Chinese seeking seclusion and protection in the face of contemporary social chaos.

Political and economic conditions under the T'ang. After internal collapse and barbarian invasion, neither the Indian nor the Graeco-Roman world-state was ever able fully to regenerate itself politically. But in the late sixth and early seventh centuries the Chinese did just that, re-creating and improving on the Han model. After a short-lived and unpopular dynasty, the T'ang emperors (618-906) provided a long period of stable growth and cultural flowering, giving China renewed preeminence in all East Asia. As the Gupta empire represents the golden age of Hindu culture, the T'ang dynasty represents the golden era of China. Even today many Chinese like to consider themselves not only "Sons of Han" but also "Men of T'ang."

The second emperor (and real founder) of the T'ang dynasty—T'ai Tsung—reigned from 627 to 650 and is considered one of China's greatest emperors. After defeating the northern Turks decisively in 630, he took advantage of internal dissension in Turkestan to reestablish Chinese dominance over the Tarim Basin. Under his son, a successful war was undertaken against Korea, which was made a tributary vassal state. At this point China stood at the zenith of its power. The T'ang empire extended from Korea and Manchuria through Tibet and Central Asia to the borders of India and Persia (see map, p. 175).

A statesman as well as a great soldier, T'ai Tsung was energetic in instituting reforms. One of his major reforms was to strengthen the administrative system of the country. The emperor governed the center of his empire by means of a bureaucracy recruited through a civil service program rooted in Han precedent but now more elaborated. T'ang innovations also extended to land reform; laws were passed to curb the growth of large estates and to ensure equitable amounts of land for the peasants. Economic prosperity resulted from these reforms as well as from the more efficient transportation system which the T'ang developed by completing the canal system. A thriving foreign commerce also contributed to the economic boom. Caravans arrived frequently from West and Central Asia; and great quantities of luxury goods were exported to such far-distant points as Jerusalem and Cairo.

T'ang scholarship. The T'ang period was outstanding in scholarly achievements. Two encyclopedias were compiled to assist bureaucrats in their work, and Buddhist scholars translated sacred texts into Chinese. T'ai Tsung ordered the publication of an elaborate edition of the Thirteen Classics of Confucianism and also stressed the value of historical writings:

. . . by using a mirror of brass you may see to adjust your cap; by using antiquity as a mirror, you may learn to foresee the rise and fall of empires.[1]

Li Po and Tu Fu, masters of T'ang poetry. An eighteenth-century anthology of T'ang poetry included dozens of volumes containing 48,900 poems by 2300 poets. The astonishing literary output of the T'ang era would almost appear to justify the remark: "[At this age,] whoever was a man was a poet."[2]

The two greatest poets of this era, Li Po (701?-762) and Tu Fu (712-770), were good friends who occasionally twitted each other in their works. Tu Fu summed up his fellow poet—a true Bohemian spirit who was notorious for his heavy drinking—in this fashion:

As for Li Po, give him a jugful of wine,
And he will write a hundred poems.[3]

And Li Po once addressed these witty lines to Tu Fu:

Here! is this you on the top of Fan-Ko
  Mountain,
Wearing a huge hat in the noon-day sun?
How thin, how wretchedly thin, you have
  grown!
You must have been suffering from poetry
  again.[4]

The poetry of Li Po exerted a great appeal for his countrymen. But the majority of Chinese scholars and poets today consider Tu Fu the greater poet, perhaps China's greatest.

T'ang artistic endeavors. The T'ang dynasty was the formative period of Chinese painting. The great Wu Tao-tzu furthered the development of a national school independent of foreign influences. The story is told that his last painting was a landscape to serve as a wall decoration for the emperor. As Wu and the emperor stood admiring the lifelike scene, the artist clapped his hands, a door in the painting opened, and Wu disappeared within, never to be seen again.

Sculptors used Buddhist subject matter, but their work bore the impress of indigenous artistic standards rather than those of India. *Mahayana* religious figures evinced a distinctively Chinese interpretation, with strong humanistic emphasis.

The invention of printing. In the first century A.D. the Chinese had discovered how to make paper, and in the fifth century they put ink stampings on documents by using seals fashioned from metal and stone. These

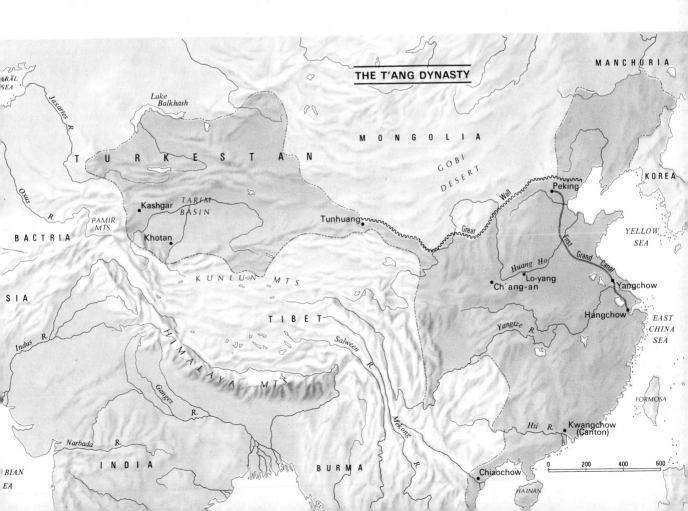

THE T'ANG DYNASTY

The Chinese invented block printing in about 600, and the earliest existing book printed by this method is the *Diamond Sutra,* dating from about 868.

technical discoveries paved the way for the culminating invention—printing.

Evidence would indicate that the process of block printing—printing from an image cut in a wooden block—was invented in China by about 600, although the earliest surviving examples come from Japan and date from 764 to 770. The first extant printed book is the *Diamond Sutra,* which was discovered in a cave in northwestern China. Printed in 868, the *Diamond Sutra* consists of six sheets of text pasted together to form a roll some sixteen feet long; the sheets are each two and a half feet by almost one foot in size and must have been printed from very large blocks.

Because the Chinese language is written not by means of an alphabet but by means of separate characters that represent entire words, the Chinese found block printing satisfactory. Nevertheless, they were the first to invent movable type, probably in the first half of the eleventh century.

T'ang decline: the end of an epoch. In the seventh century the T'ang dynasty still enjoyed a suzerainty that stretched from the Pamir Mountains in the west into Korea in the east, but during the next century divisive political forces arose. From mid-century on, the imperial boundaries contracted, and within the empire, decadence and disorder held sway. In 755 a revolt broke out, and the emperor was forced to flee, abdicating in

favor of his son. When the rebellion was finally put down, the weakened dynasty survived for a century and a half; in 906 the T'ang dynasty came to an end.

The Sung dynasty. The fall of the T'ang dynasty left China vulnerable to external attack and in another of its periods of internal disorder. This upheaval was followed by the founding of the Sung dynasty (960-1279). Early in the eleventh century the Sung emperors adopted the practice of "buying protection" by paying the Khitan Tatars in North China an annual tribute of 100,000 ounces of silver and 200,000 pieces of silk. In time the Sung were forced to increase these amounts and to begin paying tribute to other border kingdoms. Even though such payments did not represent a large percentage of the total state revenues, they were a drain on the imperial finances.

The unprecedented development of large estates whose owners managed to evade paying their share of taxes resulted in an increasingly heavy burden of taxation falling on the small farmers. The drop in the state revenues, a succession of budget deficits, and widespread inflation caused the emperor to seek advice from one of China's most fascinating statesmen and economists, Wang An-shih (1021-1086).

Wang An-shih believed that the ruler was responsible for providing his subjects with the necessities of life. He expressed his social philosophy thus:

The state should take the entire management of commerce, industry, and agriculture into its own hands, with a view to succoring the working classes and preventing them from being ground into the dust by the rich.[5]

To this end, he initiated an agricultural loans measure to relieve the farming peasants of the intolerable burden of interest which callous moneylenders exacted from them in difficult times and to ensure that lack of capital would not hinder the work of agriculture. To destroy speculation and break up the monopolies, he initiated a system of fixed commodity prices; and he appointed boards to regulate wages and plan pensions for the aged and unemployed. Wang An-shih also revamped the state examination system so that less emphasis was placed on literary style and memorization of the classics and more on practical knowledge.

In the next generation opposition from vested interests, difficulties in maintaining reforming zeal and efficiency among officials, the impracticality of some reform projects, and renewed foreign crises led to the victory of the conservative opposition and to the rescinding of most of Wang's "new laws." It is remarkable, nonetheless, to see how modern his theories were; the concepts of the welfare state and a planned economy are apparently not quite so new as we may have supposed.

The Neo-Confucian synthesis. Under the impact of Buddhist thought, many of Wang's opponents were interested in finding a better philosophic basis for the Confucian ethical system; consequently there developed, from elements of the old classic literature and Buddhist scriptures, a metaphysics that did not depend on the Buddhist church for ultimate explanations. This conservative reinterpretation of tradition we call Neo-Con-

fucianism. Its most important advocate was Chu Hsi (1130-1200), a brilliant scholar, famous historian, and the greatest commentator on the Chinese classics. Neo-Confucianism, while indebted both to Buddhism and Taoism, essentially represented a resurgence of Confucian thought. Its central and most pervasive influence was upon political and ethical institutions. Stressing the importance of good government in the hands of a benevolent ruler, it also advocated a bureaucratic state administered by intelligent and morally dedicated officials chosen by a rigorous examination system based on the classics.

Neo-Confucianism, as shaped particularly by Chu Hsi, became the dominant intellectual force down to the twentieth century. As such, it has been described as an "intellectual strait jacket," making China culturally stable but inimical to innovation. It was this rigidity that rendered the country so defenseless against the dynamic West in the nineteenth century.

The empirical sciences. Chu Hsi contended that self-cultivation required the extension of knowledge, best achieved by the "investi-

During the T'ang and Sung dynasties Chinese science and technology were far in advance of European science of the same era. One of the most complicated Chinese mechanical and scientific creations, this astronomical observatory, dating from about 1090, used a water-powered clock to rotate the instruments in time with the motion of the stars. Until very recently it was thought that the mechanical clock was a western achievement of the fourteenth century.

gation of things." As a consequence, Neo-Confucianism was accompanied by significant advances in experimental and applied sciences. The Sung period witnessed the production of large numbers of works concerning chemistry, zoology, and botany. Algebra was developed until it was the most advanced in the world. In medicine, inoculation against smallpox was introduced. Progress was also notable in astronomy, geography, and cartography; at this time, the earliest relief maps were constructed. By the end of the eleventh century the magnetic compass was employed as an aid to navigation. Another major development was the use of explosive powder—first in fireworks, then in warfare.

Excellence in Sung art. Many critics assert that "at its best Chinese painting is one of the outstanding expressions of man's ability to create beauty."[6] The Chinese painter believed that only days spent in meditation of a vista would reveal to him the scene's essential mood. When he had observed nature as long as he thought necessary, he would then paint the scene without looking at it. The awe and love felt for nature by Chinese painters was the force behind much of their work (see Color Plate 8).

Chinese paintings were not publicly displayed but were mounted on heavy paper and kept hidden away. Only on special occasions were they taken out for a short period of concentrated esthetic enjoyment. The painter was highly esteemed, for his techniques required years of intensive training. The use of ink on silk meant that he had to be sure of every line, for once the brush stroke had been made, no changes were possible. The use of the brush in writing the intricate Chinese word symbols gave the painters excellent training. In fact, calligraphy could be considered a branch of painting.

Sung pottery—especially porcelain—was also of unsurpassed excellence. Perhaps the best known is the green celadon.

Early modern China. During the eleventh century a group of people from Manchuria took northern China, ruling as the Chin dynasty (not related to the earlier Ch'in, p. 110). From 1127 on, the Sung had no control over northern China. They established a capital in the south of China, first at Nanking and then at Hangchow, and for the next one hundred years China was thus divided into two empires, the Sung and Chin.

Although militarily weak, the Southern Sung was economically and socially one of the greatest periods in Chinese history. Society was transformed to such an extent that we may speak of this period as the beginning of the modern period in Chinese history. Increased population, together with marked improvements in production, led to vastly increased internal and external trade. Commerce broke out of the controlled marketplaces, and shops began to line the streets of the towns and cities. As Chinese foreign trade grew, large communities of foreign merchants settled inside China.

The growth of commerce required a more efficient monetary system. At first copper cash was used, but the advance of trade created such a money shortage that bank drafts and other forms of commercial paper were introduced in the ninth century. By 1024 the government began to issue paper money. This commercial revolution strongly resembled that which was to take place in Europe several centuries later. In the latter, however, feudalism was too rigid to develop within itself the new institutions required by commerce. In China commerce developed within the framework of a highly bureaucratic empire that could accommodate the new commercial activity with no challenge to the basic social structure.

During the Southern Sung the bureaucracy, recruited more and more by examination and from the Yangtze valley, began to replace the northern aristocracy as the main support of dynastic power. This professionalization of government service was an important factor in the early modernization of Chinese society. The power of the aristocracy and great landholders was further weakened by a change in the tax system that emphasized commercial tax revenues and permitted the appearance of small- and medium-sized landholdings. Although still based largely on landownership, the new "gentry" class exerted its influence through the government bureaucracy, which drew most of its members from this class.

THE BARBARIAN CHALLENGE TO CIVILIZATION

China and the "barbarians." At the end of the twelfth century, with China split between the rule of the Chin and the Southern Sung, East Asian civilization faced a new threat from the north, greater than any in its previous history. By this time a recognizable pattern had emerged in China's relations with the nomadic peoples who surrounded her from the northeast to the southwest. Dynastic weakness encouraged "barbarian" invaders. The "barbarians" usually obtained the advice of Chinese administrators and military specialists, and they had superior military power based on the cavalry of the Central Asian steppe and the stirrup, which enabled an archer to shoot from the back of his horse without falling off. The stirrup was the thirteenth-century equivalent of today's atomic bomb.

Recognizing that nomadic institutions would not work in ruling a village-dwelling people, the "barbarians" usually adopted Chinese government institutions and frequently employed the conquered Chinese in administration and tax collection. They also often employed other foreigners in their administration, feeling they could be trusted more than the Chinese.

All "barbarian" dynasties faced two great problems in their relationship with the Chinese. First, they sought to maintain their own identity by keeping their original homeland separate and by preserving their own language and customs. Always a small minority, they constantly faced the problem of losing their "barbarian" vigor by adopting the sedentary and "cultured" ways of the Chinese. Second, they had to control their new territories and alien population by military means. This meant stationing their forces at strategic locations throughout the country and defending major urban centers and economic regions from other "barbarians" and from internal revolt. Their resources were often not sufficient to accomplish this.

Genghis Khan and the Mongol onslaught. Up to the middle of the twelfth century the Mongol peoples had no national organization or identity but lived in scattered tribes spread over large areas. The majority lived as pure nomads, depending on animals instead of land for all their needs. The "barbarian" nomads were never wholly independent from the sedentary civilizations like the Chinese, because they could not themselves produce the grains, metal goods, and luxury items they needed or desired. These they customarily obtained by trade or raid.

At the time of Genghis Khan's birth (c.

This silk painting of barbarian royalty worshiping Buddha gives some indication of the extent of Chinese interaction with the outside world during the T'ang and Sung periods. Notice the many different kinds of dress and facial expression among the foreigners and the quality of caricature in their depiction, as compared with the portrayal of the serene and very Chinese Buddha with his disciples and guardians.

1162) no one leader had yet emerged to unite the Mongols as a whole. During his youth his father was killed in a blood feud, and Genghis and his mother were forced to hide from enemies. Brought up in a spirit of revenge, he slowly built up a personal following and overpowered his own overlord and other clans and tribes. At last, at a great meeting of the Mongol tribes in 1206, he was recognized as the ruler of all the Mongols and given the title by which he is known to history, Genghis Khan, which probably meant "ocean ruler" or "universal ruler."

Genghis was one of the greatest organizational geniuses of all time. Out of a population of a little over a million Mongols, he fashioned a war machine based on units of ten and trained in the most sophisticated cavalry techniques. With this machine he and his people conquered most of the known world from the Pacific to the Danube and the Mediterranean, terrorized the rest, and established a *Pax Tatarica* in eastern Europe, the Middle East, Central Asia, and the Far East that permitted the greatest development of travel and trade between the continents that the world was to witness before the seventeenth century.

Leading his magnificent army, Genghis campaigned against the Chin empire. In 1215 the Chin capital near Peking was sacked and its inhabitants massacred. Following this victory, the attack on the Chin slowed down because Genghis sent much of his army westward on a campaign through Central Asia and on into Russia. But the conquest of northern China was later renewed, and city after city was subdued. The Great Khan himself was killed, probably by assassination, in 1227. A Mongol legend claims that he will return one day to lead the Mongols to world conquest once more.

Genghis' death did not slow down the Mongol war machine. By 1234 the last remnants of the Chin empire were extinguished by his son, who then embarked on the slow process of conquering the Southern Sung. After years of heroic resistance the Chinese were vanquished by the new Mongol dynasty, the Yüan—the first "barbarian" dynasty in history to rule all China.

Although China was now incorporated into an empire that stretched across the world, it did not lose its separate identity. On the death of Genghis, portions of the empire had been administered by his sons and grandsons under the general leadership of one son elected as khan of all the Mongols. After 1260 the unity of an empire divided into a suzerain khanate and four vassal khanates was becoming a fiction, and Mongol China was a distinct state. The unity of the empire weakened after Kublai Khan, who from 1260 to 1294 held the suzerain khanate comprising China and Mongolia, moved his capital to Peking.

China under the Mongols. Instead of turning all North China into one vast pasture land, Genghis taught the khans the art of governing the sedentary Chinese and the advantages of maintaining a stable society in China from which the Mongols might obtain great benefits through taxation. While separating themselves from the Chinese by custom and law, the Mongols adopted most of the T'ang and Sung administrative institutions and even instituted an examination system to recruit bureaucrats. The Yüan also employed many foreigners in high positions, including Marco Polo. They set up a hierarchical system in which they were at the top and the Southern Chinese, the most numerous group, were at the very bottom.

The arts flourished during this "barbarian" dynasty. The drama, which was probably influenced by Central Asian dance performances, was popular, and what we now know as the "Chinese opera," a combination of singing, dancing, and acting accompanied by music, achieved its classical development during the Yüan. Growing out of the prompting books used by professional storytellers, the novel also developed rapidly.

The reign of Kublai Khan. For knowledge of Kublai Khan's reign, we are indebted to the famous Venetian traveler Marco Polo, author of probably the world's outstanding travelogue and what has been called the finest European account of Chinese civilization at this time. As a youth, Marco Polo accompanied his father and uncle, two Venetian merchants, eastward to Kublai Khan's court, arriving there about 1275. Received with honor and given posts in the imperial service, the Polos remained seventeen years in China. Marco Polo reported that the Great Khan maintained order throughout his dominions, improved the roads, constructed canals, revised the calendar, built granaries to store food surpluses, and aided the sick, orphans, and old scholars by means of state care.

After Marco Polo returned to Italy, he wrote of his travels. But his fellow Venetians were so incredulous of the figures he used in describing the wealth and power of China, whose civilization was superior to that of thirteenth-century Europe, that they dubbed him "Messer Millions." His account of black stones (coal) used for heating purposes and the people's habit of taking frequent baths seemed fabulous to them, since coal was unknown in medieval Europe and Europeans in the Middle Ages seldom, if ever, took baths.

Pax Tatarica: relinking of East and West. In the first centuries of the Christian era the West had been linked with India and China by the spice and silk trades. The subsequent centuries of mutual isolation were broken during the T'ang dynasty when its court attracted such diverse groups as Muslims, Christians, and Persians. With the advent of the nomadic Mongols, East and West were again linked together along the ancient silk routes. The resumption of this trade had permanent consequences. By making the trade routes across Asia safe and by tolerating diverse religions, the Mongol dynasty attracted European traders and missionaries to China.

With the unification, however temporary, of almost all Asia and the restoration of roads, communication was restored to the point where the Polos were far from being the only travelers to cross the great spaces separating East and West. One monk, from a Christian community in Peking, traveled in the thirteenth century as an envoy of Mongol Persia to the pope and also met the kings of England and France. The papacy sent various missions to the Far East in the same century, with the result that in the early fourteenth century a Roman Catholic community of several thousand persons existed in China.

Cultural interchange between China and the West was also considerable during medieval times. One authority believes that the Mongols and other Central Asian peoples conveyed gunpowder to Europe, and we know that the Muslims transmitted westward such invaluable Chinese inventions as the arts of papermaking and printing and the magnetic compass. China itself was enriched by its imports. One of the most important was a new food, sorghum, which was brought to China by way of India in the thirteenth century. By that time the abacus, a familiar sight in Far Eastern shops today, had also made its appearance. Ceramics and bronzes were affected by influences from civilizations to the west, especially Persia, while the cloisonné technique was undoubtedly borrowed from the Byzantines.

These are but random examples of a cultural interchange which certainly enriched East and West alike. Yet the profound psychological effect created in Europe by the accounts of Marco Polo and other travelers was perhaps even more far-reaching in the evolution of world history. Travelers' accounts had revealed that the Far East not only equaled but exceeded Europe in population, wealth, and luxury. Europeans now realized that the Mediterranean was neither the central nor the most important area of the world, and they began to develop new attitudes to fit this knowledge.

Decline of Mongol China. Actually, the prosperous appearances which Marco Polo described were largely deceptive. Kublai Khan's ambitious foreign wars and domestic works necessitated heavy government spending. Tax rates rose, and many peasants were dispossessed of their land and forced to work for greedy landowners of vast estates. Large issues of paper money depreciated in value, while hard currency diminished. Kublai Khan's projected invasion of Japan was a disastrous failure (see p. 184).

The seven other Yüan emperors who succeeded Kublai Khan all proved to be inadequate rulers. The Mongols allowed their armed strength to lapse; and the exclusion of Chinese from the imperial administration continued to fan the resentment of the people against the rule of foreigners. By 1368, less than a century after Kublai's final conquest of the Sung, rebellious forces from South China, led by an ex-Buddhist novice, took Peking and founded the Ming dynasty.

The nomad challenge of the Mongols was thus rebuffed in East Asia, but its scourge was longer felt elsewhere. Remnants of West Asian Mongols, converted to Islam, were part of continuing steppe-world invasions into India. Older Muslim centers in Mesopotamia never fully recovered. That segment of Mongols who had settled as overlords in southern Russia continued for more than two centuries to affect and condition Russian development.

THE EVOLUTION OF JAPAN

The geography of Japan. In the mountainous Japanese archipelago of over three thousand islands, only four are relatively large: Honshu, Hokkaido, Shikoku, and Kyushu (see map, p. 183). The oceanic sides of Kyushu and Honshu receive abundant rain and are warmed by the Japan Current (the Pacific's analog to the Gulf Stream); here have been the centers of Japanese life, past and present. Earthquakes, typhoons, and tidal waves are frequent catastrophes; yet the Japanese in all ages have expressed love for their native land and a sensitive appreciation of its scenic beauties.

Japan's distance from the major centers of older continental cultures has meant that while there have been crucial periods of close cultural borrowing (usually based on Japanese initiative), there have also been long periods of relatively isolated development. Japanese culture has been notably homogeneous, partly because in historic times there were no notable additions of new peoples—nothing equivalent to the British Isles' successive experience of Romans, Angles, Saxons, Danes, and Normans.

Origins of the Japanese people. In prehistoric times there must have been many strands of migration, particularly from Northeast Asia and the Asian mainland by way of Korea and from Southeast Asia and its adjacent islands by way of the island chain south of Japan. No precise theories concerning the origins of the Japanese people are possible, but the evidence points to a mixed origin. In time there developed a common ethnic community—predominantly Mongoloid though darker and hairier than Mongoloid types on the Asian mainland—with a single basic language belonging to the same Altaic family as Korean.

Early Japanese society. In ancient times the mountainous islands of Japan facilitated the growth of numerous small tribal states, each ruled by a hereditary chieftain who claimed descent from a tribal deity. According to Japanese folklore, the first emperor of Japan—Jimmu Tenno—descended from the Sun Goddess and became emperor in 660 B.C. Ever since, the same family has reigned in Japan, and thus the Japanese claim with justice to have the oldest unbroken dynastic line in the world. Historians believe that the ruling family of Japan originated with the most important tribal group—the Yamato clan—which occupied a fertile plain on Honshu.

The religion of the Japanese, known as *Shinto*, or "Way of the Gods," included the worship of forces and objects of nature and of ancestral spirits. With the growth of Yamato power, Shinto centered primarily on the Sun Goddess as the divine ancestress of the Yamato and, eventually, of all the Japanese people.

Agriculture was the foundation of the economy, with the clan rulers and nobles controlling the land. With the clans engaged in constant struggles for land, warfare was the order of the day. The rigid social structure was well suited for purposes of warfare; the subservient lower orders had to cater to the warrior nobles and their divinely descended chieftain. Thus the warrior in Japan has from earliest times tended to enjoy a social position and political power greater than that of his Chinese counterpart.

During the first few centuries A.D. the Yamato clan extended its power in central Japan. Its chieftain began to regard himself as a kind of emperor, while the chieftains of clans brought under the control of the Yamato attached themselves to the imperial court. Still, however, the Yamato had only nominal suzerainty over some of the more powerful clans.

Influence of China. While the Japanese archipelago is sufficiently removed from the Asian mainland to make invasion extremely difficult, it is close enough to allow commercial and cultural contacts. Thus much of Japan's history is the story of the influx of external ideas and institutions and adaption by the Japanese to form a unique culture pattern. During the Han dynasty (202 B.C.-220 A.D.) Chinese rule was extended to part of Korea, and elements of Chinese culture were transmitted from there to Japan. In the succeeding centuries the influx of Chinese and Korean artisans, potters, weavers, painters, and farmers enriched Japanese culture. In addition, Chinese medicine and military science were introduced and the Chinese calendar adopted. Educated scribes brought to Japan the Chinese language with its character script and also the riches of Chinese literature. Transplanted from Korea in the

sixth century A.D., Buddhism was promoted by the rulers both as a means of weakening the clans with their allegiance to native Shinto and as a vehicle for the importation of Chinese ways and ideas.

The Taika reform: emulation of China. Faced by continued clan power and strife, the emperor and his advisers turned to T'ang China, probably the world's best-governed state in the seventh century, as a model for reforms that would change Japan from a clan and tribal society to a strongly centralized state. Inaugurated in 646, this "Great reform" (Taika) created a centralized bureaucracy and adopted the T'ang system of landholding and taxation (see p. 174), preferring, however, hereditary aristocratic privilege to the social mobility found in China. Also, unlike the Chinese model, the emperor of Japan was claimed to be a divine personage, so that rebellion against the throne constituted a religious crime. Belief in the emperor's divinity continued deeply entrenched until

JAPAN

after World War II, even though centralized government in Japan had collapsed by the eleventh century.

The Fujiwara regents (857-1160). In 784 the capital was removed from Nara, where a Chinese-type court had been established in 710, and ten years later settled upon Kyoto—then called Heian-kyo—where it remained until 1868. The early centuries at Kyoto are identified politically as the Fujiwara period.

The Fujiwara family had been prominent in the government at Nara and soon rose to dominate the imperial government at Kyoto. Holding vast provincial estates, this family acquired so much power that the emperors were reduced to the status of puppet rulers whose wives were chosen for them from Fujiwara women. Once a royal son had been born, the emperor would frequently be forced to abdicate and retire to a Buddhist monastery, leaving a Fujiwara grandfather or uncle to rule the country as regent for the new infant emperor. Between the ninth and twelfth centuries, the tradition was thus established that the emperor reigned but did not rule, for his powers were delegated to hereditary officials of an aristocratic civil bureaucracy.

At Kyoto, Japanese culture, hitherto an unashamed imitation of Chinese culture, began to develop its own distinctive character. A refined appreciation of beauty in all its forms emerged from the gay, sophisticated ceremonial of Fujiwara court life, in which women played a major role. This preoccupation with the esthetic inspired a sudden flowering of literature and art that established the classic canons of Japanese artistic tradition.

In time the hereditary bureaucracy of the Fujiwara grew inefficient and the government became impoverished. Taxable property steadily decreased, due to the exemption of temple lands and of estates that originally had been given to officials as payment for their services and which then remained hereditary. Eventually most of the land in the kingdom ceased to be a source of revenue for the imperial government.

The bankruptcy of the government finances was accompanied by an increase of disorder and lawlessness in the provinces.

To protect their estates, the provincial lords hired bands of professional soldiers, and a feudal society began to develop. By the twelfth century, power and authority had shifted from the civil aristocracy to a military nobility, who were destined to dominate Japanese history for the next seven centuries.

The Kamakura shogunate and the samurai. After the two leading military clans had battled from one end of the country to the other—a brutal struggle celebrated in present-day Japanese movies, television series, and historical fiction—one of Japan's outstanding soldier-statesmen, Yoritomo of the Minamoto clan, emerged victorious in 1185. He soon forced the emperor to grant him the office of *shogun* (generalissimo) and effectively ruled Japan through a feudal hierarchy of warrior nobility. From his residence at Kamakura, Yoritomo appointed constables and stewards in every province to prevent rebellion. Although he continued to pay the utmost respect to the emperor and governed at a discreet distance from the imperial court at Kyoto, the shogun, not the emperor, was the real ruler in Japan.

Following Yoritomo's death in 1199, control passed to the leaders of the Hojo clan who, copying the Fujiwara technique of rule, governed in the name of puppet shoguns. The outstanding event in the Hojo period was the repulse of invasions by Kublai Khan of Mongol China in 1274 and 1281, the only such external attacks the Japanese experienced until World War II. On both occasions nature in the form of a typhoon (thenceforth called *Kamikaze*, or "the Divine Wind") aided the Japanese by shattering the invading armadas.

The establishment of the shogunate gave prominence to the growing strength and importance of the *samurai* or *bushi*, the warrior nobility. Official recognition was now given to *Bushido* ("The way of the warrior"), the unwritten *samurai* code of conduct that resembled the western code of chivalry, but lacked its religious inspiration and idealization of women. This stern code was instilled in childhood with such injunctions as:

What a coward to cry for a little pain! What will you do when your arm is cut off in battle, or when, for the sake of honor, you must rip your stomach open with your sword?[7]

Stressing courage, fortitude, loyalty, and discipline, the code of *Bushido* approved the custom of ceremonial suicide—*seppuku*—which is generally known to westerners as *hara-kiri*. By means of *seppuku*, a warrior could atone for his crimes, escape disgrace if he had "lost face," or prove his loyalty to his lord.

The *samurai* spirit infused and strengthened the tightly knit system of noble privilege, military government, and national loyalty. It persisted long after the overthrow of the shogunate in 1868—until, in fact, the defeat of Japan in World War II.

Joined with the *samurai* spirit was Shinto's glorification of the nation and the emperor's sacred position, together with Zen Buddhism's stress on strict mental and physical discipline as the means of achieving enlightenment. Imported from China late in the twelfth century, the Zen sect discarded not only emphasis on ritual and learning but also the simple piety and devotionalism of the savioristic sects of Buddhism that were followed by the humbler folk.

The Ashikaga shogunate. In 1333 Kamakura, the seat of the shogunate since its establishment in 1192, was destroyed by the Ashikaga family, which succeeded in founding a new shogunate five years later with headquarters at the imperial city of Kyoto. The Ashikaga shoguns failed to establish effective control over the other great barons (*daimyos*) and the *samurai* retainers, and the whole country drifted into disorder. By 1500 Japanese society was completely feudalized in a fashion comparable to western Europe during the same period.

A feudal society began to develop in Japan about the same time that feudal institutions were evolving in western Europe. Power soon passed to the mounted warriors, the *samurai*, who corresponded in status to the medieval knights. This *samurai* battle scene is a detail from a Kamakura painting, "The Burning of the Sanjō Palace."

SUMMARY

At the very time when Europe was beset by the tribulations following the collapse of the Graeco-Roman world, Asia was being enriched by what were probably its most splendid centuries of cultural development. The first of these centuries saw the emergence of a golden age in India. With the Guptas, the zenith of Hindu culture was reached. Artists produced paintings of contemporary life and sculpture characterized by dignity and restraint; the Gupta poet Kalidasa wrote dramas which have been compared favorably with those of Shakespeare. In mathematics, the so-called Arabic numerals, the decimal system, and many of the basic elements of algebra came into use; and there were important discoveries in chemistry and medicine. So powerful was Gupta civilization that it diffused to many parts of Asia, thereby raising the cultural level of a large segment of mankind.

The Gupta age was followed in India by a period of internal dissolution and external invasion, culminating in the subjugation of the country by the forces of an uncompromisingly antagonistic religious culture, Islam. The consequences of that impact were in our own century to split the Indian subcontinent into two separate states: India and Pakistan.

China's outstanding achievement was the successful re-creation of a unitary centralized state on classical lines that had no analogy in India or the West. Barbarians were domesticated in the T'ang period, which also saw a rich flowering of poetry, painting, and sculpture, and the invention of printing.

The Sung period, despite its weakness in dealing with barbarian states, brought to perfection the bureaucratic civil service system, saw Buddhism lose ground to a secular Neo-Confucian philosophy among the upper classes, and refined many traditional arts and crafts, especially painting and ceramics. The invention of explosive powder for warfare, the magnetic compass, and paper money bear witness to the range of Chinese creative ability.

The short period of Mongol rule in China, through briefly uniting China with the West by trade routes, confirmed the growing Chinese tendency to be contemptuous of foreign ways and to accept despotic rule. Economic disorders and popular rebellion ended the Mongols' regime in China sooner than in other parts of their far-flung empire.

Japan was brought within the world of civilized communities by impulses radiating from the T'ang. The Japanese blended continental forms of government, social organization, religion, and the arts with their own native traits. They preferred patterns of hereditary aristocratic privilege to the social mobility found in China. Embracing Buddhism, they also retained their native Shinto in both public life and popular cult. While China was perfecting its centralized civilian administrative system, Japan was increasingly divided by the controls and ideals of a hereditary feudal military nobility.

SUGGESTIONS FOR READING

H. Wales, **The Making of Greater India**, B. Quaritch, 1951. A stimulating discussion of the expansion of Indian culture into Southeast Asia from the second to the tenth centuries A.D. For well-illustrated accounts of the influence of India's art on neighboring countries, see B. Rowland, **The Art and Architecture of India**, Penguin, 1953; and R. Mukerjee, **The Culture and Art of India**, Praeger, 1959.

R. C. Majumdar and A. D. Pulsaker, eds., **The Classical Age**, Paragon, 1954, Vol. III of **The History and Culture of the Indian Peoples**, is the most comprehensive history of the Gupta period. See also B. G. Gokhale, **Samudra Gupta**, Asia, 1962.

For the Islamic impact upon India the following are authoritative: K. S. Lal, **Twilight of the Sultanate**, Asia, 1963; S. M. Ikram, **Muslim Civilization in India**, ed. by A. T. Embree, Vol. VII of **The History and Culture of the Indian Peoples**.

G. Coedes, **The Indianized States of Southeast Asia**, East-West Center Press, 1968. The basic work.

Three excellent biographical studies of leading personalities under the T'ang are C. P. Fitzgerald, **Son of Heaven: A Biography of Li Shih-min, Founder of the T'ang Dynasty**, Cambridge, 1933; by the same author, **The Empress Wu**, Cresset, 1956; and A. Waley, **The Real Tripitaka, and Other Pieces**, Macmillan, 1952.

C. P. Fitzgerald, **China: A Short Cultural History**,* Praeger, 1954. Contains an excellent brief account of the intellectual and artistic activities of the T'ang and Sung periods.

The lives and works of the two greatest T'ang poets are treated authoritatively in A. Waley, **The Poetry and Career of Li Po: 701-762 A.D.**, Macmillan, 1950; and W. Hung, **Tu Fu, China's Greatest Poet**, 2 vols., Harvard, 1952.

T. F. Carter, **The Invention of Printing in China and Its Spread Westward**, Ronald, 1955. The best detailed study.

E. Kracke, **Civil Service in Early Sung China, 960–1067**, Harvard, 1953. Useful for an understanding of the Chinese political system.

H. D. Martin, **The Rise of Genghis Khan and His Conquest of North China**, Johns Hopkins, 1950. Relates the life-and-death struggle of the Chinese with the neighboring Mongols.

Jacques Gernet, **Daily Life in China on the Eve of the Mongol Invasion**,* Stanford. Vivid description of all facets of life.

L. Olschki, **Marco Polo's Asia**, Univ. of Calif., 1960. An exhaustive study of the life and times of Marco Polo. See also the same author's **Marco Polo's Precursors**, Johns Hopkins, 1943; and M. Collis, **Marco Polo**,* New Directions.

John Meskill, **Wang An-Shih; Practical Reformer?*** Heath. An introduction, through readings and discussion, to the greatest premodern Chinese social theorist.

Michael Loewe, **Imperial China**, Praeger, 1966. Incisive background.

G. B. Sansom, **A History of Japan**, 3 vols., Stanford Univ., 1958-1963. The best history in English. Also extremely valuable is E. O. Reischauer and J. K. Fairbank, **East Asia: The Great Tradition**, Houghton Mifflin, 1960. Malcolm Kennedy, **A Short History of Japan**,* Mentor, is useful. E. O. Reischauer, **The United States and Japan**,* Compass, is a synthesis of modern scholarship on Japanese history and culture. The relinking of East and West under the *Pax Tatarica* is treated in G. F. Hudson, **Europe and China: A Survey of Their Relations from the Earliest Times to 1800**,* Beacon.

*Indicates an inexpensive paperbound edition.

Chapter 8

Europe's Search for Stability

**The Rise and Fall of the Carolingian Empire;
Feudalism and the Manorial System (500-1050)**

INTRODUCTION. We last surveyed the fortunes of Europe at a crucial turning point in western civilization—the fifth century (see Chapter 5). The mighty Roman Empire in the West was breaking apart under the pressure of incoming Germanic tribes, and unity and stability gave way to fragmentation and disorder. What was the future of western Europe to be?

The first indication of the new forms that life and politics would take in the West came from the Germanic Franks in alliance with the Church. In the single century from 714 to 814, covering the reigns of the Frankish rulers from Charles Martel to Charlemagne, the Carolingian House of the Franks gave Europe an interim of stability and progress. A great empire was fashioned, Christianity was extended to barbarian tribes, and law and order were maintained.

This accomplishment of the Carolingians was premature, however. Charlemagne's empire could not endure, partly because it lacked the economic basis that had supported the Romans. By the ninth century

Muslim conquests had cut off what remained of European trade in the Mediterranean; inland trade shriveled up and urban life almost disappeared. In addition, the empire had no strong administrative machinery to compensate for the weak Carolingian rulers who followed the dominating figure of Charlemagne on the throne; the empire disintegrated amid civil wars and invasions.

Out of the ruins of the Carolingian empire emerged a new form of government known as feudalism. Based on local authority, feudalism was a poor and primitive substitute for a powerful, comprehensive central government; but it was better than no authority at all, and it survived for several hundred years. Also appropriate to the times was the rural, self-sufficient economy known as the manorial system. In sum, the poverty and localism of western Europe in the tenth century contrasts sharply with the contemporary societies of Byzantium and Islam.

NEW EMPIRE IN THE WEST

The Franks under the Merovingians. In the blending of the Roman and Germanic peoples and cultures, the Franks played an especially significant part. The kingdom of the Franks was not only the most enduring of all the Germanic states established in the West, but it became, with the active support of the Church, the center of the new Europe that arose upon the ruins of the western Roman empire.

Before the Germanic invasions the several tribes that made up the Franks lived along the east bank of the Rhine close to the North Sea. Late in the fourth century the Franks began a slow movement south and west across the Rhine into Gaul. By 481 they occupied the northern part of Gaul as far as the old Roman city of Paris, and in this year Clovis I of the Merovingian House became ruler of one of the petty Frankish kingdoms. By the time of his death in 511, Clovis had united the Franks into a single kingdom that stretched southward to the Pyrenees.

Clovis achieved his goal with the aid of an arsenal of weapons that included marriage alliances, treachery, assassination, and religion. As a first step, Clovis allied himself with other petty Frankish kings to dispose of Syagrius, the last Roman general in Gaul. The victor then turned against his Frankish allies and subdued them.

According to the sixth-century Gallo-Roman bishop and historian Gregory of Tours, whose *History of the Franks* is the fullest account of any Germanic people, Clovis became converted to Christianity in 496 as a result of a battle against the Alemanni, a pagan Germanic tribe whose name became the French word for Germany, *Allemagne*. On the verge of being defeated, Clovis called upon Christ for help:

"For I have called on my gods, but I find they are far from my aid. . . . Now I call on Thee. I long to believe in Thee. Only, please deliver me from my adversaries."[1]

Clovis won the battle and was baptized together with his whole army. He became the only orthodox Christian ruler in the West, for the other Germanic tribes were either pagan or embraced the heretical form of Christianity known as Arianism (see pp. 128, 242).

The conversion of the Franks must be considered a decisive event in European history. Ultimately it led to an alliance of the Franks and the papacy, and immediately it assured Clovis the loyalty of the Gallo-Roman bishops, the leaders of the native Christian population of Gaul. This was a political advantage not open to the heretical Arian Visigothic and Burgundian kings. Thus with the help of the native population of Gaul, Clovis was able to expand his realm in the name of Christian orthodoxy.

In 507 Clovis attacked the Visigoths, who ruled Gaul south of the Loire River and all of Spain (see map, p. 137). "Verily it grieves my soul," Clovis told his troops, "that these Arians should hold a part of Gaul."[2] The Visigothic king was killed, and his people abandoned most of their Gallic territory. Clovis died four years later at the age of forty-five—a ripe old age for a barbarian. Although never hardly more than a Germanic chieftain, he had created France.

Decline of the Merovingians. Clovis' sons and grandsons conquered the Burgundian kingdom and extended the Frankish domain to the Mediterranean and further into Germany. At the same time, however, the Merovingian House began to decay from inner weaknesses. The Germanic practice of treating the kingdom as personal property and dividing it among all the king's sons resulted in constant and bitter civil war. The royal heirs plotted murders and became adept at intrigue and treachery. The Merovingian princes also engaged in all manner of debaucheries, the least unpleasant of which was excessive drinking. Soon the Frankish state broke up into three separate kingdoms; in each, power was concentrated in the hands of the chief official of the royal household, the mayor of the palace, a powerful noble who desired to keep the king weak and ineffectual. The Merovingian rulers were mere puppets, the *rois fainéants* ("do-nothing kings").

A dark age. By the middle of the seventh century western Europe had lost most of the essential characteristics of Roman civilization. The Roman system of administration and taxation had completely collapsed, and the dukes and counts who represented the Merovingian king received no salary and usually acted on their own initiative in commanding the fighting men and presiding over the courts in their districts. International commerce had ceased except for a small-scale trade in luxury items carried on by adventurous Greek, Syrian, and Arab traders, and the old Roman cities served mainly to house the local bishop and his retinue. The virtual absence of a middle class meant that society was composed of the nobility, a fusion through intermarriage of aristocratic Gallo-Roman and German families who owned and exercised authority over vast estates, and, at the other end of the social scale, the semi-servile *coloni*, who were bound to the land. These serfs included large numbers of formerly free German farmers.

The abstract transfigured Christ carved on a seventh-century Frankish tomb shows Jesus holding a spear. Even in a spiritual image, a militant rather than a meek Savior may have seemed most appropriate to the warlike Franks.

Only about 10 percent of the peasant population of France maintained a free status.

Coinciding with Merovingian decay, new waves of invaders threatened. A great movement of Slavic people from the area that is now Russia had begun about 500 A.D. (see p. 152). From this nucleus the Slavs fanned out, filling the vacuum left by the Germanic tribes when they pushed into the Roman Empire. By 650 the western Slavs had reached the Elbe River, across which they raided German territory. Another danger threatened western Europe from the south; in the late seventh century the Muslim Moors prepared to invade Spain from North Africa.

Charles Martel and the rise of the Carolingians. A new period dawned when Charles Martel became mayor of the palace in 714. His father, one of the greatest Frankish landowners, had eliminated all rival mayors, and Charles ruled a united Frankish kingdom in all but name. For the time being, however, the Merovingian kings were kept as harmless figureheads at the court.

Charles is best remembered for his victory over the Muslim invaders of Europe, which earned him the surname Martel, "The Hammer." In 711 an army of Moors from North Africa had invaded Spain, and by 718 the weak kingdom of the Visigoths had collapsed. With most of the peninsula under control, the Muslims began making raids across the Pyrenees. In 732 Charles Martel met them near Tours, deep within the Frankish kingdom. Muslim losses were heavy, and during the night they retreated toward Spain.

A major military reform coincided with the battle of Tours. For some time before this conflict, the effectiveness of mounted soldiers had been growing, aided by the introduction of the stirrup, which gave the mounted warrior a firm seat while wielding his weapons. To counteract the effectiveness of the quick-striking Muslim cavalry, Charles recruited a force of professional mounted soldiers whom he rewarded with sufficient land to enable each knight to maintain himself, his equipment, and a number of war horses. Such grants of land later became an important element in feudalism.

KINGDOM OF CLOVIS I

NORTH SEA

Elbe R.

Cologne
Tournai
Rhine R.
Seine R.
Paris
Strasbourg
Danube R.
Loire R.
Tours
Rhone R.
Bordeaux
Garonne R.
Po R.
Toulouse
PYRENEES

MEDITERRANEAN SEA

Pepin the Short. Charles Martel's son, Pepin the Short, who ruled from 741 to 768, was a worthy successor to his father. To legalize the regal power already being exercised by the mayors of the palace, he requested and received from the pope a ruling which stipulated that whoever had the actual power should be the legal ruler. In this maneuvering, St. Boniface (p. 242) was the intermediator, and in 751 Pepin was elected king by the Franks and crowned by St. Boniface. The last Merovingian was quietly shelved in a secluded monastery. In 754 the pope reaffirmed the usurpation by crossing the Alps and personally anointing Pepin, in the Old Testament manner, as the Chosen of the Lord.

Behind the pope's action lay his need for a powerful protector. In 751 the Lombards had conquered the exarchate of Ravenna, the seat of Byzantine government in Italy, and were demanding tribute from the pope and threatening to take Rome. Following the coronation, the pope secured Pepin's promise of armed intervention in Italy and his pledge to give the papacy the exarchate of Ravenna, once it was conquered. In 756 a Frankish army forced the Lombard king to relinquish his conquests, and Pepin officially conferred the exarchate of Ravenna upon the pope. Known as the "Donation of Pepin," the gift made the pope a temporal ruler over the Papal States, a strip of territory that extended diagonally from coast to coast (see map, p. 235).

The alliance between the Franks and the papacy affected the course of politics and of religion for centuries. It accelerated the separation of Latin from Greek Christendom by providing the papacy with a dependable western ally in place of the Byzantines, hitherto its only protector against the Lombards; it created the Papal States which played a major role in Italian politics until the late nineteenth century; and, by the ritual of anointment, it provided western kingship with a religious sanction that would in time contribute to the rise of monarchs strong enough to pose a threat to the papacy.

Charlemagne: the man and his conquests. Under Pepin's son, Charlemagne (Charles the Great), who ruled from 768 to 814, the

Frankish state and the Carolingian House reached the summit of their power. Einhard, in his famous biography of Charlemagne, pictured his king as a natural leader of men— tall, physically strong, and a great horseman who was always in the van of the hunt. Although he was preeminently a successful warrior-king, leading his armies on yearly campaigns, Charlemagne also sought to provide an effective administration for his realm. In addition, he had great respect for learning and was proud of the fact that he could read Latin.

Taking advantage of feuds among the Muslims in Spain, Charlemagne sought to extend Christendom southward into that land. In 778 he crossed the Pyrenees with indifferent success. As the Frankish army headed back north, it aroused the antagonism of the Christian Basques, who attacked its rear guard. In the melee the Frankish leader, a gallant count named Roland, was killed. The memory of his heroism was later enshrined in the great medieval epic, the *Chanson de Roland (Song of Roland)*. On later expeditions the Franks drove the Muslims back to the Ebro River and established a frontier area known as the Spanish March, or Mark, centered around Barcelona. French immigrants moved into the area, later called Catalonia, giving it a character distinguishable from the rest of Spain.

Charlemagne conquered the Bavarians and the Saxons, the last of the independent Germanic tribes. It took thirty-two campaigns to subdue the staunchly pagan Saxons, who lived between the Rhine and Elbe rivers. Charlemagne divided Saxony into bishoprics, built monasteries, and proclaimed harsh laws against paganism. Eating meat during Lent, cremating the dead (an old pagan practice), and pretending to be baptized were offenses punishable by death.

Like his father before him, Charlemagne intervened in Italian politics. Expansionist ambition drove the Lombard king to invade again the territories of the papacy. At the behest of the pope, Charlemagne defeated the Lombards in 774 and proclaimed himself their king. While in Italy, he cemented his father's alliance with the Church by confirming the Donation of Pepin.

This picture of Charlemagne's coronation, from a fourteenth-century illuminated manuscript, reflects the Church's later view of this event. Earlier representations had shown Charlemagne and the pope as coequals. In this picture, however, Charlemagne, kneeling at the pope's feet, seems to be little more than a vassal of the Church.

The empire's eastern frontier was continually threatened by the Avars, Asiatic nomads related to the Huns, and the Slavs. In six campaigns Charlemagne decimated the Avars and then set up his own military province in the valley of the Danube to guard against any possible future plundering by eastern nomads. Called the East Mark, this territory later became Austria.

Charlemagne's coronation in Rome. One of the most important single events in Charlemagne's reign took place on Christmas Day in the year 800. The previous year the unruly Roman nobility had ousted the pope, charging him with moral laxity. Charlemagne came to Rome and restored the pope to his office. Then, at the Christmas service while Charlemagne knelt before the altar at St. Peter's, the pope placed a crown on his head amid the cries of the assembled congregation: "To Charles Augustus crowned of God, great and pacific Emperor of the Romans, long life and victory!"

This ceremony demonstrated that the memory of the Roman Empire still survived as a vital tradition in Europe and that there was a strong desire to reestablish political unity. Implicit also in this coronation was another great theme of medieval history, the

CHARLEMAGNE'S EMPIRE
- At His Accession, 768
- At His Death, 814

struggle between the revived empire and the papacy. Charlemagne was crowned not only by, but presumably with the consent of, the pope. He was emperor by the grace of God, with heaven and its earthly agency, the Church, on his side. But it was not all gain for the ruler; the pope could claim superiority as the maker of emperors. The collapse of both the empire and the papacy in the ninth and tenth centuries postponed the inevitable clash between the imperial and papal powers.

Charlemagne's administration. The extent of Charlemagne's empire was impressive. His territories included all of the western area of the old Roman Empire except Africa, Britain, southern Italy, and most of Spain (see map). Seven defensive provinces, or marks, protected the empire against hostile neighbors.

The Carolingian territories were divided into some three hundred administrative divisions, each under a count (*graf*) or, in the marks along the border, a margrave (*mark graf*). In addition, there were local military

officials, the dukes. In an effort to solve the problem of supervising the local officials, a problem that plagued all German rulers, Charlemagne issued an ordinance (capitulary) creating the *missi dominici*, the king's envoys. Pairs of these itinerant officials, usually a bishop and a lay noble, traveled throughout the realm to check on the local administration. To make the *missi* immune to bribes, they were chosen from men of high rank, were frequently transferred from one region to another, and no two of them were teamed for more than one year.

The Carolingian Renaissance. Charlemagne also fostered a revival of learning and the arts. His efforts in this area were destined to be far more lasting than his revival of the Roman Empire in the West, and they have prompted historians to speak of this period as one of cultural rebirth.

In 789 Charlemagne decreed that every monastery must have a school for the education of boys in "singing, arithmetic, and grammar." As he stated in a letter to the abbot of Fulda, Charlemagne was greatly concerned over the illiteracy of the clergy:

Since in these years there were often sent to us from divers monasteries letters in which . . . , owing to neglect of learning, the untutored tongue could not express [itself] without faultiness. Whence it came that we began to fear lest, as skill in writing was less, wisdom to understand the Sacred Scriptures might be far less than it ought rightly to be.[3]

At Aix-la-Chapelle, his capital, the emperor also sponsored a palace school for the education of the royal household and the stimulation of learning throughout the realm. Alcuin, an Anglo-Saxon scholar in charge of the school, began the arduous task of reviving learning by undertaking the first step of writing textbooks on grammar, spelling, rhetoric, and logic. "Ye lads," Alcuin exhorted his students, "whose age is fitted for reading, learn! The years go by like running water. Waste not the teachable days in idleness!"[4]

The reform of handwriting and the preservation of classical manuscripts were significant achievements of the Carolingian revival. Copyists labored in monasteries to preserve the classics of pagan and Christian thought with the result that the oldest manuscripts of most of the Latin classics that have come down to us date from the age of Charlemagne. The corrupt and almost illegible script of the Merovingian period was replaced by a more legible style of writing, known as Carolingian minuscule—"little letters," in contrast to the capitals used by the Romans—which became the foundation for the typeface still used in present-day printing.

At Aix-la-Chapelle Charlemagne also strove to recapture something of the grandeur of ancient Rome by building a stone palace church modeled after a sixth-century church in Ravenna. Its mosaics were probably the work of Byzantine artisans, and its marble columns were taken from ancient buildings in Rome and Ravenna.

Charlemagne's work on balance. Charlemagne must be considered one of the great constructive figures of world history. He extended Christian civilization in Europe, set up barriers against incursions of the Slav and Avar, and created a new Europe whose center was in the north rather than on the Mediterranean and in which a measure of law and order was again enforced after three centuries of disorder. Furthermore, his patronage of learning left a cultural heritage that later generations would build upon in producing a European civilization distinct from the Byzantine to the east and the Muslim to the south.

Charlemagne's empire afforded no more than a breathing space, however, for its territories were too vast and its nobility too powerful to be held together under existing conditions after the dominating personality of its creator had passed from the scene. Charlemagne had no standing army; his foot soldiers were essentially the old Germanic war band summoned to fight by its war leader, and his mounted warriors served him, as they had Charles Martel, in return for grants of land. Nor did Charlemagne have a bureaucratic administrative machine comparable to that of Roman times. The Frankish economy was agricultural and localized, and there was no system of taxation adequate to maintain an effective and permanent administration. Under Charlemagne's weak successors the empire disintegrated amid the confusion of civil wars and devastating new invasions. Progress toward an advanced civilization in the new Europe founded by Charlemagne was delayed for two centuries.

The division of the empire. Before his death in 814, Charlemagne himself, ignoring the pope, placed the imperial crown on the head of his only surviving son, Louis the Pious. Louis subsequently partitioned his realm among his sons, and bitter rivalry and warfare broke out among the brothers and their father. In 840 Louis the Pious died, a well-meaning man who was loved by the clergy, ignored by the nobility, and mistreated by his sons.

Strife continued among Louis' three surviving sons. Lothair, the elder, was opposed by the two younger—Louis the German and Charles the Bald. In 842 the younger brothers joined forces in the famous Strasbourg Oaths. The text of these oaths is significant in that one part was in an early form of French, the

NORTH
SEA

THE
DANELAW

ENGLISH
KINGDOMS

ENGLISH CHANNEL

Aix-la-Chapelle
(Aachen)

Paris

Verdun

Strasbourg

Loire R.

WEST
FRANKS

KINGDOM
OF
CHARLES

UMAYYAD
EMIRATE
OF
CORDOVA

Ebro R.

CORSICA

MEDITERRANEAN   SEA

Rhine R.

Elbe R.

Vistula R.

EAST

KINGDOM
OF
LOUIS

TRIBUTARY

FRANKS

Danube R.

SLAVIC

STATES

KINGDOM   OF   LOTHAIR

Rhone R.

BYZANTINE   EMPIRE

both Latin and Teutonic cultures, and although it was divided in 870 between Charles and Louis, the area was disputed for centuries. Lorraine remained one of the cockpits of Europe, a land drenched with the blood of countless French and German peoples.

The rival Carolingian houses produced no strong leaders worthy of being called "Hammer" (Martel) or "Great"; instead, we find kings with such revealing names as Charles the Fat, Charles the Simple, Louis the Child, and Louis the Sluggard. The last of the East Frankish Carolingians died in 911. In West Frankland the nobles, ignoring the eighteen-year-old Carolingian prince, chose Odo, the count of Paris, as king in 887.

The new invasions. During the ninth and tenth centuries the remnants of Charlemagne's empire were also battered by new waves of invaders. Scandinavians attacked from the north, Muslims from the south, and a new wave of Asiatic nomads, the Magyars, struck from the east. Christian Europe had to fight for its life against these plundering and murdering raiders, who did far more damage to life and property than the Germanic invaders of the fifth century.

From bases in North Africa, Muslim corsairs in full command of the sea plundered the coasts of Italy and France. In 827 they began the conquest of Byzantine Sicily and southern Italy. From forts erected in southern France they penetrated far inland to attack the caravans of merchants in the Alpine passes. What trade still existed between Byzantium and western Europe, except for that of Venice and one or two other Italian towns, was now almost totally cut off, and the great inland sea became a Muslim lake.

The most widespread and destructive raiders came from Scandinavia. During the ninth and tenth centuries Swedes, Danes, and Norwegians—collectively known as Vikings—stormed out of their remote forests and fiords. The reason for this expansion is not clear. Some historians stress overpopulation and a surplus of young men. Other scholars view these raiders as defeated war bands expelled from their homeland by the gradual emergence of strong royal power. Still others see a clue in the fact that the Vikings had developed seaworthy ships ca-

other in German. The first could be understood by Charles' followers, who lived mainly west of the Rhine; the other by Louis' followers, who lived east of the Rhine. These oaths are evidence that the Carolingian empire was splitting into two linguistic parts—East Frankland, the forerunner of modern Germany, and West Frankland, or France.

In 843 the brothers met at Verdun, where they agreed to split the Carolingian lands three ways. Charles the Bald obtained the western part and Louis the German the eastern; Lothair, who retained the title of emperor, obtained an elongated middle kingdom which stretched a thousand miles from the North Sea to central Italy (see map).

The importance of the Treaty of Verdun is that it began the shaping of modern France and Germany by giving political recognition to the cultural and linguistic division shown in the Strasbourg Oaths. Lothair's middle kingdom soon collapsed into three major parts, Lorraine in the north and Burgundy and Italy in the south. Lorraine encompassed pable of carrying a hundred men and powered by long oars or by sail when the wind was favorable. Viking sailors also had developed expert sailing techniques; without benefit of the compass, they were able to navigate by means of the stars at night and the sun during the day.

The range of Viking expansion was amazing. The Vikings went as far as North America to the west, the Caspian Sea to the east, and the Mediterranean to the south. Few areas seemed immune from their lightning raids, which filled civilized Europeans with a fear that is reflected in a new prayer in the litany of the Church: "From the fury of the Northmen, O Lord deliver us."

Three main routes of Viking expansion can be identified. The outer path, which was followed principally by the Norwegians, swung westward to Ireland and the coast of Scotland. Between 800 and 850 Ireland was ravaged severely. Monasteries, the centers of the flourishing culture attained by the Irish Celts, were destroyed. By 875 the Norwegians were beginning to occupy remote Iceland, and it was here rather than in their homeland that the magnificent Norse sagas were preserved, little affected by either classical or Christian influences. During the tenth century the Icelandic Norsemen ventured on to Greenland and, later, to North America (see p. 367).

Another route, the eastern line, was followed chiefly by the Swedes, who went down the rivers of Russia as merchants and soldiers of fortune and, as has been described in Chapter 6, forged the nucleus of a Russian state.

The Danes took the middle passage, raiding England and the shores of Germany, France, and Spain. By the 870's they had occupied most of England north of the Thames. Also in the middle of the ninth century their fury broke upon the Continent, where their long boats sailed up the Rhine, Scheldt, Seine, and Loire. In particular the Danes devastated northwest France, destroying dozens of abbeys and towns. Unable to fend off the Viking attacks, the weak Carolingian king Charles the Simple arranged an epoch-making treaty with a Norse chieftain named Rollo in 911. This agreement created

a Viking buffer state, later called Normandy, and recognized Rollo as duke and vassal of the French king. Like Viking settlers elsewhere, these Northmen, or Normans, soon adopted Christian civilization. By the eleventh century, as we shall see later, Normandy was a powerful duchy, and the Viking spirit of the Normans was producing the most vigorous crusaders, conquerors, and administrators in Europe.

Europe in 900. Europe's response to the invasions of the ninth and tenth centuries was not uniform. In England by 900 Viking occupation initiated a strong national reaction which soon led to the creation of a united English kingdom. Similarly, Germany in 919 reacted to the Magyar danger by installing the first of a new and able line of kings who went on to become the most powerful European monarchs since Charlemagne. The response to the invasions in France, however, is a different story.

The Viking attacks on France had the effect of accelerating the trend toward politi-

The people of Scandinavia first began to use sails during the Viking period. The huge, square-rigged sails, traditionally patterned with intersecting diagonals, were raised or furled by means of an intricate system of ropes. The Vikings in this stone carving, which dates from the tenth century, are under full sail and are ready for battle, dressed in pointed helmets, their round shields overlapping the side of the ship.

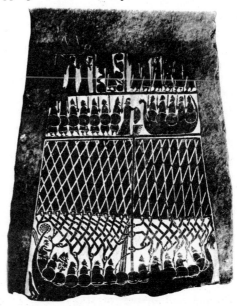

cal fragmentation that began under the Merovingians but was temporarily halted by the strong personal leadership provided by the Carolingians. When Charlemagne's weak successors were unable to cope with the incessant Viking assaults, people increasingly surrendered both their lands and their persons to the many counts, dukes, and other local lords in return for protection. The decline of trade further strengthened the aristocracy, whose large estates, or manors, became economically self-sufficient. In addition, the old Germanic levy of foot soldiers, who provided their own arms when called to battle, was dying out in favor of a professional force of heavily armed mounted knights, who received land grants from the king in return for military service.

Out of all these elements—the disintegration of central power, the need for protection, the decrease in the class of freemen, the rise of a largely independent landed aristocracy, and the creation of the mounted knight—new patterns of society, feudalism and the manorial system, took shape. Reaching their height in France during the tenth and eleventh centuries, feudalism and manorialism were the culmination of earlier trends that had been accelerated by the Viking attacks.

FEUDALISM

Nature and origins of feudalism. Feudalism can be defined as a type of government in which political power is exercised locally by private individuals rather than by the agents of a centralized state. It is often a transitional stage which follows the collapse of a unified political system; it serves as a stopgap until conditions permit the emergence of a centralized government. Feudalism has appeared in various areas and times in world history—in ancient Egypt and in modern Japan, for example—but the most famous of all feudal systems emerged in France following the collapse of Charlemagne's empire.

Fully developed feudalism was a fusion of three basic elements: (1) the personal element, called lordship or vassalage, by which one nobleman, the vassal, became the loyal follower of a stronger nobleman, the lord or suzerain; (2) the property element, called the fief (usually land), which the vassal received from his lord in order to enable him to fulfill the obligations of vassalage; and (3) the governmental element, meaning the private exercise of governmental functions over vassals and fiefs. The roots of these three elements run back to late Roman and early Germanic times.

By the fifth century the ability of the Roman emperor to protect his subjects had disappeared, and citizens had to depend on the patronage system, by which a Roman noble organized a group of less fortunate citizens as a personal bodyguard and in return looked after their wants and interests. A similar arrangement existed among the Germans—the war band or *comitatus*, described by Tacitus (see p. 133). Vassalage, the personal element in feudalism, arose from the combination of patronage and the *comitatus*.

The roots of the property element in feudalism, the fief, go back to Roman practices mainly. In the late Roman Empire the owners of great estates (*latifundia*) were steadily adding to their already extensive holdings. Unable to manage their tracts, the nobles granted the temporary use of portions to other people in exchange for dues and services. Such land was called a *beneficium*, or benefice (literally, a "benefit"). In late Merovingian times, when mounted warriors rather than old-style foot soldiers were needed to deal effectively with Muslim raiders from Spain, Charles Martel granted numerous benefices to compensate his mounted followers for this added expense. During the civil wars and foreign invasions of late Carolingian times, the competition among Charlemagne's successors for the available supply of mounted knights led not only to the wholesale granting of benefices but also to making the benefice hereditary. On the death of the vassal, the benefice now passed to his heir instead of reverting to the king. Hereditary benefices were commonly called fiefs.

The third basic element in feudalism, the exercise of governmental power by private individuals, also had antecedents in late Roman times. As the imperial government weakened, the powerful Roman landowners organized their own private armies to police their estates and fend off governmental agents, particularly tax collectors. The emperors also favored certain estates with grants of immunity from their authority, a practice which the Germanic kings often followed and which became the rule with Charlemagne's successors in their competitive efforts to fill their armies with mounted fief-holding vassals. And where immunity from the king's authority was not freely granted, it was often usurped.

With the coalescing of these three elements, feudalism can be said to have emerged as a definable—although highly complex and variable—governmental system in France by the end of the ninth century. To a greater or less degree the feudal system spread throughout most of western Europe, but our description of it applies particularly to the form it took in northern France.

The feudal hierarchy. In theory feudalism was a vast hierarchy. At the top stood the king, and theoretically all the land in his kingdom belonged to him. He kept large areas for his personal use (royal or crown lands) and, in return for the military service of a specified number of mounted knights, invested the highest nobles—such as dukes and counts (in England, earls)—with the remainder. Those nobles holding lands directly from the king were called tenants-in-chief. They in turn, in order to obtain the services of the required number of mounted warriors (including themselves) owed to the king, parceled out large portions of their fiefs to lesser nobles. This process, called *subinfeudation*, was continued until, finally, the lowest in the scale of vassals was reached—the single knight whose fief was just sufficient to support one mounted warrior.

Subinfeudation became a problem when a conflict of loyalties arose. Since the Count of Champagne, for example, was vassal to nine different lords, on whose side would he fight should two of his lords go to war against one another? This dilemma was partially solved by the custom of liege homage. When a vassal received his first fief, he pledged liege or prior homage to that lord. This obligation

was to have top priority over services that he might later pledge to other lords.

Except for the knight with a single fief, a nobleman was usually both a vassal and a lord. Even a king might be a vassal; John of England was vassal to King Philip of France for certain French lands, yet he in no way thought himself inferior to Philip.

By maintaining a king at the head of the hierarchy, feudalism kept intact the vestiges of monarchy, which would in time reassert itself and restore centralized government. As one historian put it, feudalism "contained in its bosom the weapons with which it would be itself one day smitten."[5]

Relation of lord and vassal: the feudal contract. Basic to feudalism was the personal bond between lord and vassal. In the ceremony known as the act of *homage*, the vassal knelt before his lord, or suzerain, and promised to be his "man." In the oath of fealty which followed, the vassal swore on the Bible or some other sacred object that he would remain true to his lord. Next, in the ritual of *investiture*, a lance, glove, or even a bit of straw was handed the vassal to signify his jurisdiction (not ownership) over the fief.

The feudal contract thus entered into by

Warfare was a normal occupation for gentlemen during the feudal age, and even the more brutal aspects of combat were not considered ignoble subjects for art.

lord and vassal was considered sacred and binding upon both parties. Breaking this tie of mutual obligations was considered a felony, because it was the basic agreement of feudalism and hence of early medieval society. The lord for his part was obliged to give his vassal protection and justice. The vassal's primary duty was military service. He was expected to devote forty days' service each year to the lord without payment. In addition, the vassal was obliged to assist the lord in rendering justice in the lord's court. At certain times, such as when he was captured and had to be ransomed, the lord also had the right to demand money payments, called *aids*. Unusual aids, such as defraying the expense of going on a crusade, could not be levied without the vassal's consent.

The lord also had certain rights, called feudal *incidents*, regarding the administration of the fief. These included *wardship*—the right to administer the fief during the minority of a vassal's heir—and *forfeiture* of the fief if a vassal failed to honor his feudal obligations.

Feudal warfare. The final authority in the feudal age was force, and the general atmosphere of the era was one of violence. Recalcitrant vassals frequently made war upon their suzerains. But warfare was also considered the normal occupation of the nobility, for success offered glory and rich rewards. If successful, warfare enlarged a noble's territory; and, if they produced nothing else, forays and raids kept a man in good mettle. To die in battle was the only honorable end for a spirited gentleman; to die in bed was a "cow's death."

The Church and feudalism. Another unhappy result of feudalism was the inclusion of the Church in the system. The unsettled conditions caused by the Viking and Magyar invasions forced Church prelates to enter into close relations with the only power able to offer them protection—the feudal barons in France and the kings in Germany. Bishops and abbots thus became vassals, receiving fiefs for which they were obligated to provide the usual feudal services. The papacy fared even worse; during much of the tenth and early eleventh centuries the papacy fell into decay after becoming a prize sought after by local Roman nobles.

On the positive side, however, the Church in time sought to influence for the better the behavior of the feudal warrior nobility. In addition to attempting to add Christian virtues to the code of knightly conduct called chivalry, which will be described later in this chapter, the Church sought to impose limitations on feudal warfare. In the eleventh century bishops inaugurated the Peace of God and Truce of God movements. The Peace of God banned from the sacraments all persons who pillaged sacred places or refused to spare noncombatants. The Truce of God established "closed seasons" on fighting: from sunset on Wednesday to sunrise on Monday and certain longer periods, such as Lent. These peace movements were generally ineffective, however.

Class structure. Medieval society conventionally consisted of three classes: the nobles, the peasants, and the clergy. Each of these groups had its own task to perform. The nobles were primarily fighters, belonging to an honored society distinct from the peasant workers—freemen and serfs. In an age of physical violence, society obviously would accord first place to the man with the sword rather than to the man with the hoe. The Church drew on both the noble and the peasant classes for the clergy. Although most higher churchmen were sons of nobles and held land as vassals under the feudal system, the clergy formed a class that was considered separate from the nobility and peasantry.

THE MANORIAL SYSTEM

The manor in relation to feudalism. Having discussed feudalism, the characteristic political system of the ninth, tenth, and eleventh centuries, let us turn to the economic organization of the period, the manorial system. The feudal system was the means whereby protection was obtained for society; the manor was the agency that provided the necessary food for society's members. Feudalism and the manorial system evolved independently, but they were intimately connected.

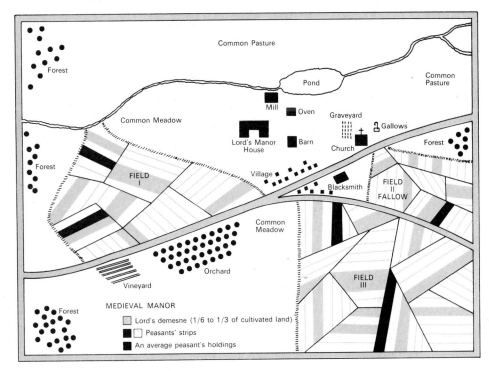

As the self-contained economic unit of early medieval life, the manor operated on a system of reciprocal rights and obligations based on custom. In return for protection, strips of arable land, and the right to use the nonarable common land, the peasant paid dues and worked on the lord's demesne. Under the three-field system, one third of the land lay fallow so that intensive cultivation did not exhaust the soil.

The term manorial system refers to the economic and social system that centered on the manors, the great estates whose origins go back to the Roman *latifundia* with their *coloni* workers (see p. 79). In Gaul, in particular, these estates survived the Germanic invasions. During the early Middle Ages they were held either by the descendants of their Roman owners or by Frankish kings, nobles, and the Church. The medieval serf was the direct descendant of the Roman *colonus* who worked the land, paid rent in kind, and could not leave the estate without the owner's permission.

Agriculture, the chief function of the manor. The manor varied in size from one locality to another. A small one might contain only about a dozen households. Since the allotment to each family averaged about thirty acres, the small manors probably included about 350 acres of tillable land, not counting the meadows, woods, wasteland, and the lord's demesne land. A large manor might contain fifty families and a total area of 5000 acres.

The center of the manor was the village, with the thatched cottages of the peasants grouped together along one street. Around each cottage was a space large enough for a vegetable patch, chicken yard, haystack, and stable. An important feature of the landscape was the village church, together with the priest's house and the burial ground. The lord's dwelling might be a castle or a more modest manor house.

Distribution of the land. Every manor contained two types of land, arable and nonarable. Part of the arable land, called the *demesne*, was reserved for the lord and was cultivated for him by his serfs. The remainder of the arable land was held by the villagers. The nonarable land, consisting of meadow, wood, and wasteland, was used in common by the villagers and the lord.

From one third to two fifths of the arable land was given over to the lord's demesne. The demesne might be either sharply set off from the tenures of the villagers or distributed among the lands of the tenants. The land not held in demesne was allotted among the villagers under the open-field system, whereby the fields were subdivided into strips. The strips, each containing about an acre, were separated by narrow paths of uncultivated turf. The serf's holding was not all in one plot, for all soil throughout the manor was not equally fertile, and a serious attempt was made to give each of the villagers land of the same quality.

Each tenant was really a shareholder in the village community, not only in the open fields but also in the meadow, pasture, wood, and wastelands. His rights in these common lands were determined by the number of acres he held in the open fields.

The wooded land was valuable as a place to graze pigs, the most common animal on the manor. Again the tenant was limited in the number of pigs that he might turn loose there. The tenant could also gather dead wood in the forest, but cutting down green wood was prohibited unless authorized by the lord.

Medieval farming methods. It is dangerous to generalize too sweepingly about agricultural methods, because differences in locality, fertility of soil, crop production, and other factors resulted in a variety of farming methods. But if we study farming as practiced in northwestern Europe, we can discover some common factors. The implements which the peasants used were extremely crude; the plow was a cumbersome instrument with heavy wheels, often requiring as many as eight oxen to pull it. (By the twelfth century plow horses were common.) There were also crude harrows, sickles, beetles for breaking up clods, and flails for threshing. Inadequate methods of farming soon exhausted the soil. It has been estimated that the average yield per acre was only six to eight bushels of wheat, a fourth of the modern yield.

In classical times farmers had learned that soil planted continually with one crop rapidly deteriorated. To counteract this, they employed a two-field system, whereby half of the arable land was planted while the other half lay fallow to recover its fertility. Medieval farmers learned that wheat or rye could be planted in the autumn as well as in the spring. As a result, by the ninth century they were dividing the land into three fields, with one planted in the fall, another in the spring, and the third left lying fallow. This system not only kept more land in production but also required less plowing in any given year.

Administration of the manor. Though the lord might live on one of his manors, each manor was administered by such officials as the steward, the bailiff, and the reeve. The steward was the general overseer who supervised the business of all his lord's manors and presided over the manorial court. It was the bailiff's duty to supervise the cultivation of the lord's demesne, collect rents, dues, and fines, and inspect the work done by the peasants. The reeve was the "foreman" of the villagers, chosen by them and representing their interests.

In status and function the various social classes that made up the manor community differed not only from locality to locality but from period to period. However, they can be roughly divided into three major categories: the lord and his officials, the free peasants, and the semifree peasants.

There often were freemen on the manor, however small a proportion of its population they may have represented. They possessed personal freedom and were not subject to the

In this fourteenth-century illumination peasants reap grain under the direction of the reeve.

same demands as the semifree people. The freeman did not have to work in the lord's fields himself but could send substitutes. He paid rent for his holding and, if he wanted to leave, could locate a new tenant for the land, provided the transfer took place in open court and the new man was acceptable to the lord. Aside from these privileges, however, the freeman was little different from the semifree man. His strips in the open field adjoined those of the servile worker, and he lived in a cottage in the same village.

The semifree persons, the serfs, were bound to the manor and could not leave without the lord's consent. Serfdom was a hereditary status; the children of a serf were attached to the soil as their parents were. The lord of the manor was bound by the force of custom to respect certain rights of his serfs. So long as they paid their dues and services, serfs could not be evicted from their hereditary holdings. Although a serf could not appear in court against his lord or a freeman, he could appeal to the manor court against any of his fellows.

Whereas the peasants found their economic, political, legal, and social life in the manor, to the lord the manor was essentially a source of income from three obligations imposed on the peasantry: (1) services in the form of labor, (2) dues levied on the peasant, and (3) manorial monopolies.

The most important service was *weekwork*. The peasant had to donate two or three days' work each week to the lord. The weekwork included such jobs as repairing roads or bridges or carting manure to the fields. Because the lord's demesne "had always to be plowed first, sowed first, and reaped first," the peasant also had to perform extra *boon-work* at these times.

Various dues or payments—usually in produce, in money if it was available—were made to the lord. The *taille* (or tallage), a tax on whatever property a peasant managed to accumulate, was the most common. It was levied on all peasants one or more times a year. Another burdensome tax was imposed when a peasant died; before a son could inherit his father's cottage and strips, the lord claimed the best beast or movable possession as inheritance tax.

In addition to services and dues, the lord profited from certain monopolies. He operated the only grain mill, oven for baking bread, and wine and cider press on the manor, and he collected a toll each time these services were needed.

The weary round of peasant life. On the manors of the Middle Ages the margin between starvation and survival was narrow, and the life of the peasant was not easy. Famines were common; warfare and wolves were a constant threat; grasshoppers, locusts, caterpillars, and rats repeatedly destroyed the crops. Men and women alike had to toil long hours in the fields. A medieval poem vividly describes the life of a peasant family:

I saw a poor man o'er the plough bending. . . .
All befouled with mud, as he the plough followed. . . .
His wife walked by him with a long goad, . . .
Barefoot on the bare ice, so that the blood followed.
And at the field's end lay a little bowl,
And therein lay a little child wrapped in rags,
And twain of two years old upon another side;
And all of them sang a song that sorrow was
  to hear,
They cried all a cry, a sorrowful note,
And the poor man sighed sore, and said 'Children, be still.'[6]

The difficulties of the peasant's life were reflected in his home, a cottage with mud walls, clay floor, and thatched roof. The fire burned on a flat hearthstone in the middle of the floor; and unless the peasant was rich enough to afford a chimney, the smoke escaped through a hole in the roof. The windows had no glass and were stuffed with straw in the winter. Furnishings were meager, consisting usually of a table, a kneading trough for dough, a cupboard, and a bed, often either a heap of straw or a box filled with straw, which served the entire family. Pigs and chickens wandered about the cottage continually, while the stable was frequently under the same roof, next to the family quarters.

The peasant, despite his hard, monotonous life, was not without a few pleasures. Wrestling was exceedingly popular, as were cockfighting, a crude type of football, and fighting with quarterstaves, in which both the con

Into this medieval print the artist has crowded the whole life of the manorial village. A hunting party is shown in the foreground, the ladies riding behind the knights. The castle, with its moat and drawbridge, dominates the countryside. In the midst of the village houses, which are surrounded by a fence, stands the church. Note also the mill and the millrace at the left and what appears to be a wine or cider press to the right of the mill. In the upper right corner a serf is using the heavy plow common to northwestern Europe (the artist has shown only two draft animals). The nets were apparently set to catch hares, and below them stands a wayside shrine. Visible on the horizon is a gibbet with buzzards wheeling over it.

testants stood an excellent chance of getting their heads bashed in. Around the porch of the parish church the peasants often congregated to dance and sing on the numerous holy days. The Church preached in vain against "ballads and dancings and evil and wanton songs and such-like lures of the Devil." The peasants refused to give up these amusements, a small enough compensation for the constant exploitation they suffered. Yet medieval serfs also possessed a large degree of economic security, and in this respect they were perhaps better off than the factory workers of the early nineteenth century.

THE AGE OF CHIVALRY

Chivalry in feudal society. One of the most interesting and significant legacies of the Middle Ages is its concept of chivalry, a code which governed the behavior of all truly perfect and gentle knights. Such a paragon was Sir Galahad—"the gentlest man that ever ate in hall among the ladies." Early chivalry, however, which emerged during the heyday of feudalism in the eleventh century, was rough and masculine. It stressed the warrior virtues that were essential in a feudal society: prowess in combat, courage, and loyalty to one's lord and fellow warriors. The virtues of early chivalry are best expressed in early medieval epics, such as the eleventh-century *Song of Roland*, where they are summed up in the words of the hero who, surrounded by foes, cries: "Better be dead than a coward be called."

The later chivalry of the twelfth and thirteenth centuries contained new virtues which the Church and the ladies sought to impose upon the generally violent and uncouth behavior of feudal warriors. The chivalric romances that began to be written in the twelfth century mirror these new influences. In Chrétien de Troyes' *Perceval*, for example, the hero's mother sends him off to be dubbed a knight with these words of advice:

Serve ladies and maidens if you would be honored by all. If you capture a lady, do not annoy her. Do nothing to displease her. He has much from a maiden who kisses her if she agrees to give a kiss. You will avoid greater intimacy if you wish to be guided by me. . . . Above all I wish to beg you to go to churches and abbeys and pray to our Lord so that the world may do you honor and you may come to a good end.[7]

In sum, fully developed chivalry was a combination of three elements: warfare, religion, and reverence toward women. It required the knight to fight faithfully for his lord, champion the Church and aid the humble, and honor womankind. Unfortunately, practice often differed from theory. The average knight was more superstitious than religious, and he continued to fight, plunder, and abuse women, especially those of the lower class. The ideals of chivalry, however, have affected manners in later eras, and even today they color our concept of a gentleman.

Women in general shared the characteristics of the menfolk. They lived in a crude and often brutal age devoid of many of our modern refinements. Like their husbands, medieval women were heavy drinkers and eaters. It is said that a common compliment to a member of the fair sex was that she was "the fairest woman who ever drained a bottle."

Training for knighthood. From the time they were boys, men of the nobility underwent a rigid training for knighthood. At the age of seven, a boy was sent to the household of a relative, a friend, or the father's suzerain. There he became a page, learning the rudiments of religion, manners, hawking, and hunting. When about fifteen or sixteen, he became a squire and prepared himself seriously for the art of war. He learned to ride a war horse with dexterity and to handle the sword, the shield, and the lance correctly. The squire also waited on his lord and lady at the table and learned music, poetry, and games.

If not already knighted on the battlefield for valor, the squire was usually considered eligible for knighthood at twenty-one. By the twelfth century the Church claimed a role in the ceremony, investing it with impressive symbolism. The candidate took a bath to symbolize purity and watched his weapons before the altar in an all-night vigil, confessing and making resolutions to be a worthy knight. During the solemn Mass that followed, his sword was blessed on the altar by a priest. The climax of the ceremony came when the candidate, kneeling before his lord, received a light blow on the neck or shoulder (the *accolade*), as the lord pronounced these words: "In the name of God, Saint Michael, and Saint George, I dub thee knight. Be valiant." The ceremony was designed to impress upon the knight that he must be virtuous and valiant, loyal to his suzerain and to God.

Heraldry. With its unique decorative designs, worn proudly by each noble family on its armor, heraldry was one of the more colorful aspects of chivalry. The popularity of heraldry began to sweep through Europe in the twelfth century. The use of the closed helmet, which hid the face, required that some means of identification be developed. Ingenious feudal artists devised 285 variations of the cross and decorated the nobles' shields with such real and fictitious animals as the lion, leopard, griffin, dragon, unicorn, and a host of others in fanciful postures. A man's social position was evident in his coat of arms, for its quarterings, or divisions, showed to which noble families its owner was related.

Castles as fortresses and homes. The life of the nobles centered about the castle. The earliest of these structures, mere wooden blockhouses, were built in the ninth century. Not until the twelfth and thirteenth centuries were massive castles constructed entirely of stone.

The donjon, or central tower, was the focal point of the castle; it was surrounded by an open space that contained storerooms, workshops, and a chapel. The outside walls of the castle were surmounted by turrets from which arrows, boiling oil, and various missiles might be showered upon the attackers. Beyond the wall was the moat, a steep-sided ditch filled with water to deter the enemy. The only entrance to the castle lay across the drawbridge. The portcullis, a heavy iron grating which could be lowered rapidly to protect the gate, was a further barrier against unwanted intrusion.

A French manuscript illumination of a knight entering the lists to fight in a tournament gives some idea of the splendor with which such contests were frequently invested. These often brutal battles were considered suitable entertainment for noble ladies and gentlemen.

Life in the castle was anything but comfortable or romantic. The lord at first dwelt in the donjon, but by the thirteenth century he had built more spacious quarters. Because the castle was designed for defense, it possessed no large windows; and the rooms were dark and gloomy. The stone walls were bare except for occasional tapestries to allay the draft and dampness, and a huge fireplace provided the only warmth.

Amusements of the nobles. The average noble derived his pleasures primarily from outdoor sports, among which he included warfare. In peacetime the joust and tournament substituted for actual battle. The joust was a conflict between two armed knights, each equipped with a blunted lance with which he attempted to unseat the other. The tournament was a general melee in which groups of knights attacked each other. Often fierce fighting ensued, with frequent casualties.

The nobles were very fond of hunting, and the constant demand for fresh meat afforded a legitimate excuse for galloping over the countryside. Most hunting was done in the nearby forests, but at times an unlucky peasant's crops might be ruined during the chase.

A similar outdoor pastime, which lords, ladies, and even high church dignitaries delighted in, was falconry, a method of hunting with predatory birds. The hawks were reared with the utmost care, and large companies of lords and ladies spent many afternoons eagerly wagering with one another as to whose falcon would bring down the first victim. Nobles often attended Mass with hooded falcons on their wrists.

Indoor amusements included the universally popular diversions of backgammon, dice, and chess. The long, monotonous nights were sometimes enlivened by the quips of jesters. At other times a wandering minstrel entertained his noble hosts in exchange for a bed and a place at the table.

The decline of chivalry. The development of national governments under strong kings who enforced tranquility and order changed the whole basis of feudal society (see Chapter 10). Knights were no longer needed to fight for their lords, to rush to the succor of helpless maidens, or to take the law into their own hands in defense of personal honor. Yet chivalry continued on as an ideal, reaching its culmination in the fourteenth and fifteenth centuries. By the sixteenth century its code had become fantastic and even ridiculous, as is pointed out so cleverly in Cervantes' *Don Quixote*. Some knights continued to live in the past and obtained their excitement by becoming robbers, picking needless quarrels with their neighbors, or inventing imaginary females who had to be rescued from a fate worse than death.

SUMMARY

This chapter has surveyed the political, economic, and social history of the early Middle Ages (500-1050), during which the axis of European civilization was centered in France. The conversion of Clovis to Christianity and the subsequent Frankish alliance with the papacy meant that the most energetic of the Germanic tribes had united with the greatest existing force for civilization in western Europe—the Christian Church. The foundation of the new Europe whose center was no longer the Mediterranean was completed by Charlemagne, but his empire depended too heavily on the forceful personality of its founder and did not survive his inferior successors. After the Carolingian collapse, new political and economic patterns evolved to meet the turbulent conditions of the time.

Feudalism was a bridge between the centralized governments of the Romans and Carolingians and the national states of modern Europe. Like so many things in medieval civilization, feudalism was a blend of German and Roman customs, enriched and humanized by the ideals of Christianity. The people who held land under feudal tenure were a privileged caste of landed aristocrats whose main function was military service. Set apart from the feudal nobles but forming the backbone of economic life was the vast majority of the people—the peasants. On the manors, the economic units of early medieval life, the unfree peasants or serfs grew the food for all medieval people and performed the heavy labor needed. They were politically inarticulate, tied to the soil, and seldom masters of their own destinies.

One aspect of feudalism which has come down to the twentieth century as a highly romanticized tradition is chivalry. Although its practice in the Middle Ages fell far beneath its principles, its idealism became part of the medieval legacy to the twentieth century.

SUGGESTIONS FOR READING

The Cambridge Medieval History, 8 vols., Cambridge 1924-1936. Best used for reference, these volumes include extensive bibliographies. B. Lyon, **The Middle Ages in Recent Historical Thought,*** American Historical Assoc. (Service Center for Teachers of History), 2nd ed., 1965, summarizes the principal scholarly interpretations and debates on selected topics in medieval history. L. Genicot, **Contours of the Middle Ages,** Barnes and Noble, 1967, is a superb synthesis of the three divisions of the Middle Ages—"dawn," "noon," and "dusk." For other works which survey the history of the Middle Ages, see the List of Readings, p. 862.

J. Wallace-Hadrill, **The Barbarian West, 400-1000,*** Torchbooks; Richard E. Sullivan, **Heirs of the Roman Empire,*** Cornell; A. R. Lewis, **Emerging Medieval Europe, A.D. 400-1000,*** Knopf. Excellent brief surveys of the early Middle Ages. For greater detail see F. Lot, **The End of the Ancient World and the Beginnings of the Middle Ages,*** Torchbooks; H. Moss, **The Birth of the Middle Ages, 395-814,*** Oxford; C. Dawson, **The Making of Europe,*** Meridian; M. Deanesley, **History of Early Medieval Europe, 476-911,*** Barnes and Noble. C. Delisle Burns, **The First Europe: A Study of the Establishment of Medieval Christiandom, A.D. 400-800,** Verry, 1948, is a novel and stimulating presentation.

H. Fichtenau, **The Carolingian Empire: The Age of Charlemagne,*** Torchbooks. The best work on the subject. See also R. Winston, **Charlemagne: From the Hammer to the Cross,*** Vintage; S. Easton and H. Wieruszowski, **The Era of Charlemagne: Frankish State and Society,*** Anvil. On the Carolingian Renaissance see E. Duckett, **Alcuin, Friend of Charlemagne: His World and His Work,** Macmillan, 1951, and M. Laistner, **Thought and Letters in Western Europe, A.D. 500 to 900,** Cornell, 1957.

J. Bronsted, **The Vikings,*** Penguin; Gwyn Jones, **A History of the Vikings,** Oxford, 1968. Outstanding on Viking activities. G. Turville-Petre, **The Heroic Age of Scandinavia,** Hutchinson Univ. Library, 1951, describes the Norse way of life as reflected in their heroic legends.

Carl Stephenson, **Mediaeval Feudalism,*** Cornell. A clear introduction. See also F. Ganshof, **Feudalism,*** Torchbooks; M. Bloch, **Feudal Society,*** 2 vols., Phoenix. S. Painter, **French Chivalry,*** Cornell, is a delightful essay on the feudal, religious, and courtly aspects of chivalry. English castle architecture is interestingly described and superbly illustrated in W. D. Simpson, **Castles from the Air,** Scribner, 1949.

R. Latouche, **The Birth of Western Economy: Economic Aspects of the Dark Ages,*** Torchbooks. Throws new light on the economic history of Europe from the fourth through the eleventh centuries. On rural life and the manorial system see **The Agrarian Life of the Middle Ages (The Cambridge Economic History of Europe,** Vol. I), 2nd ed., Cambridge, 1967; G. G. Coulton, **Medieval Village, Manor, and Monastery,*** Torchbooks; H. S. Bennett, **Life on the Medieval Manor,*** Cambridge; E. Power, **Medieval People,*** Barnes and Noble.

*Indicates an inexpensive paperbound edition.

Chapter 9

The West Takes the Offensive

The Crusades and the Rise of Trade, Towns, and a New Society: 1050-1300

INTRODUCTION. Following the collapse of Charlemagne's empire, Europeans probably felt that the future held little promise. No longer was there an effective central government to maintain peace and enforce laws over large territories, and with political fragmentation had come economic localism in the form of the self-sufficient manorial system.

In this chapter we shall trace the rise of a new Europe—a Europe which in the eleventh century was to emerge from what is sometimes called the "dark ages." With the ejection of the Muslims from Sicily and the successful challenge to Muslim control of the Mediterranean, Christian Europe ceased to be on the defensive and took the offensive instead.

In northern Spain a few bands of Christians sparked a long struggle against the Muslims in a movement known as the *Reconquista*, meaning "reconquest"; but the most dramatic manifestation of Europe's new dynamism was the crusades. Spurred on by religious fervor, love of adventure, and hopes of personal gain, the crusaders set out to drive the Muslims from the Holy Land and free Jerusalem from the infidel. These expansive movements helped the recovery of international trade and the rise of flourishing towns. New markets stimulated the growth of industry and crafts; and the development of banking and the use of money, which superseded the old exchange by barter, made everyday business transactions more efficient. At the same time, men cleared and drained forests and swamps, and new lands went under the plow. All these factors—particularly the revival of urban life—sounded the death knell for the manorial system in western Europe.

Above all, the forces transforming the western world led to the growth of a new class in society—townsmen, the bourgeoisie or middle class. The status of a member of the middle class was based not on ancestry or ownership of large estates, as was the case with the feudal aristocrat, but on possession of goods and money. Gradually the bourgeoisie gained influence as well as wealth and began to exert a growing impact on history.

EUROPE AGAINST THE MUSLIMS

Norman conquests in Italy and Sicily. About the year 1000 southern Italy was a battleground for rival Lombard dukes, the Byzantine empire, and the Muslims. The Lombards ruled several duchies; the Eastern empire controlled the "heel and toe" of the peninsula, all that remained of Justinian's reconquest of Italy; and across the Strait of Messina Muslim princes ruled the island of Sicily.

In 1016 adventurers of Viking ancestry from Normandy plunged into this maelstrom of continual warfare. At first the Norman knights fought for hire, but soon they began to carve out large estates for themselves. The obscure house of Tancred of Hauteville was burdened with twelve husky sons, all of whom made their way to southern Italy. One blond giant of this family, Robert Guiscard, established his authority over his fellow Normans and by 1071 extinguished the last Byzantine foothold in southern Italy (see p. 144). Meanwhile Robert had allied himself with the pope, and in return the papacy recognized him as the ruler of southern Italy and of Sicily, still in Muslim hands. Under the leadership of Robert and his brother Roger, the Normans crossed the Strait of Messina and gained a footing in Sicily just a few years before another Norman, William the Conqueror, crossed the Channel to invade England. In 1072 they captured Palermo, and twenty years later the entire island of Sicily had fallen.

Venice, Genoa, and Pisa battle the Muslims. While the Normans had been ejecting the Muslims from Sicily, similar offensives had been going on elsewhere in the Mediterranean. Venice, still nominally a part of the Byzantine empire, had cleared the Adriatic Sea and in 1002 had won a great naval victory over a Muslim fleet. This enhanced Venetian trade with Byzantium. Genoa and Pisa also began to fight the Muslims, and by 1090 the western Mediterranean had been cleared of Muslim pirates and traders. The crusades to the Holy Land would shortly do the same for the eastern Mediterranean.

Muslim civilization in Spain. Although the offensive of the West had cleared the Muslims from the waters of the western Mediterranean, Muslim power remained in Spain. We will recall that with the fall of Rome in the fifth century, Visigothic tribes had settled in Spain; but they in turn had fallen to the Muslim invasion (see p. 190). Muslim Spain was ruled from Damascus until 756, when it became an independent Muslim state under the last remaining member of the Umayyad dynasty.

From their center at Cordova, the ancient capital of Roman Spain, the Umayyad rulers (756-1031) inaugurated a brilliant era. The Caliphate of Cordova, as Muslim Spain was called after 929, made many economic and cultural advances. Water power was harnessed to drive mills, new crops such as rice and sugar cane were introduced, and

The Great Mosque at Cordova is a fine example of the Islamic art that flourished in Spain during the Muslim rule of that country.

grain cultivation flourished. Other important products included wine, olive oil, leather goods, weapons, glass, and tapestries. Cordova itself far outshone contemporary European cities.

The Muslims of Spain were the most cultured people of the West. Literature and art became their glories, and learning flourished when the rulers, often men of letters themselves, invited some of the best scholars of the Muslim East to settle in Spain. By the twelfth century scholars from northern Europe were flocking to Spain to study, and through them much of the learning of the Arabs passed to Christian Europe.

The lot of the conquered Christians was not especially bad. Christian worship continued, and, generally speaking, tolerance was granted to all people—including Christians and Jews. The latter, who had been persecuted under the Visigoths, flourished in the professions and as officials of the state. Many Jews came from Christian Europe and the East, and the Talmudic school at Cordova became a leading center of Hebrew learning. Christians were converted to Islam, there was much intermarriage, and many of the later Muslim leaders were of Gothic or Hispano-Roman descent.

Politically, Muslim Spain was usually weak and disunited. Spain had been conquered by a medley of Arabs, Syrians, and Berbers who were often in discord and outnumbered by the native population. The Caliphate reached the height of its power in the tenth century but thereafter the caliphs were a mediocre lot, unable to withstand the pressures of factionalism. In 1031 the Umayyads were overthrown, and the Caliphate of Cordova was replaced by twenty-three small, warring states.

Early Christian victories in the Reconquista. During the period of Muslim dominance the following Christian states survived in the north of Spain (see map, p. 233): the county of Barcelona, nucleus of later Aragon, in the east; Leon in the west; and in between, Navarre, peopled by the fiercely independent Basques whom neither the Romans nor the Visigoths had wholly subdued.

Slowly gathering strength and resolution, these Christian states expanded south through the hills, with Leon leading the way. An offshoot of Leon was the county of Castile, named after the many castles built to defend it. In the mid-tenth century Castile became strong enough to throw off the rule of the king of Leon. The disintegration of the Caliphate of Cordova into small Muslim states after 1031 opened the way for further Christian advances: Castile captured a large part of what was to become Portugal, and the southern border of Castile was pushed from the Douro to the Tagus River. In 1063, a generation before the first crusade to the Holy Land, the pope proclaimed the *Reconquista* to be a holy crusade, and the first of many northern knights flocked to Spain to fight the Muslims. In 1085 the mighty bastion of Toledo fell to the king of Castile, and the end of the Muslim occupation seemed in sight. Yet the *Reconquista* continued for nearly five hundred years more, and militant expansion in the name of Christianity colored the formative years of the two modern nations of Spain and Portugal.

THE CRUSADES: "GOD WILLS IT!"

The call to a crusade. The most dramatic expression of Europe on the offensive was the crusades. For hundreds of years peaceful pilgrims had been traveling from Europe to worship at the birthplace of Christ. By the tenth century bishops were organizing mass pilgrimages to the Holy Land; the largest of these, which set out from Germany in 1065, included about seven thousand pilgrims.

During the eleventh century, however, Christian pilgrims began to be persecuted, and when the Seljuk Turks, new and fanatical converts to Islam, came sweeping and plundering into the Near East, the situation became especially aggravated. The Seljuks seized Jerusalem from their fellow Muslims and then swept north into Asia Minor. Byzantine forces desperately tried to bar the invader, but at the battle of Manzikert (1071) the eastern emperor was captured and his army scattered. Within a few years Asia Minor, the chief source of Byzantine revenue and troops, was lost, and the emperor was writing to western princes and to the pope seeking mercenaries with which to regain lost territories. In addition, tales of alleged Turkish mistreatment of Christian pilgrims circulated throughout Europe, and though there is evidence that these stories were propaganda, men's minds became inflamed.

In 1095 Pope Urban II proclaimed the First Crusade to regain the Holy Land. Preaching at the Council of Clermont in that year, he exhorted Christians to take up the cross and strive for a cause that promised not merely spiritual rewards but material gain as well:

For this land which you inhabit . . . is too narrow for your large population; nor does it abound in wealth; and it furnishes scarcely food enough for its cultivators. Hence it is that you murder and devour one another. . . . Enter upon the road to the Holy Sepulchre; wrest that land from the wicked race, and subject it to yourselves.[1]

At the end of his impassioned oration the crowd shouted "God wills it"—the expression which the crusaders later used in battle.

Yet the primary impetus behind the crusades was undoubtedly religious; they constituted in effect a holy war, and following Pope Urban's appeal, there was a real and spontaneous outpouring of religious enthusiasm. The word *crusade* itself is derived from "taking the cross," after the example of Christ. (On the way to the Holy Land, the crusader wore the cross on his breast; on his journey home, he wore the cross on his back.) Urban promised the crusaders that they would enjoy indulgence from purgatorial sufferings for their past sins. He also hoped that the religious enthusiasm following in the wake of the crusades would strengthen his claim to the moral leadership of Europe. Furthermore, the pope saw in the crusades an outlet for the restless, pugnacious nobles—their warring energies would be channeled for the glory of God.

The First Crusade gains the Holy Land. From the end of the eleventh century to the end of the thirteenth, there were seven major crusades, as well as various small expeditions which from time to time tried their hands against the Saracen.

The First Crusade, composed of feudal nobles from France, parts of Germany, and Norman Italy, proceeded overland to Constantinople. Having expected the help of European mercenaries against the Seljuks, the emperor Alexius Comnenus was taken aback when confronted by an unruly horde of what Pope Urban himself had called "aforetime robbers." He hastily directed the crusaders out of Constantinople to fight the Turks. The First Crusade was the most successful of the seven; with not more than five thousand knights and infantry, it overcame the resistance of the Turks, who were no longer united. Above all, it captured the Holy City—Jerusalem. A contemporary account of the Christian entrance into Jerusalem reads:

But now that our men had possession of the walls and towers, wonderful sights were to be seen. Some of our men . . . cut off the heads of their enemies; others shot them with arrows, so that they fell from the towers; others tortured them longer by casting them into the flames. Piles of heads, hands, and feet were to be seen in the streets of the city. It was necessary to pick one's way over the bodies of men and horses. But these were small matters compared to what happened at the Temple of Solomon [where] . . . men rode in blood up to their knees and bridle reins. Indeed it was a just and splendid judgment of God that this place should be filled with the blood of the unbelievers, since it had suffered so long from their blasphemies.[2]

The First Crusade conquered a long strip of territory along the eastern coast of the Mediterranean and created the feudal Latin kingdom of Jerusalem, which lasted until its last remnant fell to the Muslims in 1291.

When the kingdom of Jerusalem became endangered, St. Bernard of Clairvaux organized the Second Crusade in 1147. It met with many misfortunes in getting to the Near East, and ended when its forces were routed at Damascus.

The "Crusade of Kings." The fall of Jerusalem in 1187 to the Muslims, reinvigorated under the leadership of Saladin, the Kurdish sultan of Egypt and Syria, served to provoke the Third Crusade (1189). Its leaders were three of the most famous medieval kings— Frederick Barbarossa of Germany, Richard the Lion-Hearted of England, and Philip Augustus of France. Frederick was drowned in Asia Minor; and, after many quarrels with Richard, Philip returned home. Saladin and Richard remained the chief protagonists.

To keep the Muslims united, Saladin proclaimed a *jihad*, or holy war, against the Christians, but he remained a patient statesman and chivalrous warrior. "Abstain from the shedding of blood," he once said, "for blood that is spilt never slumbers."[3] His commonsense approach to a settlement was evidenced when he proposed that Richard should marry his sister and be given Palestine as a wedding present, a proposal which shocked the Europeans.

Richard and Saladin finally agreed to a three-year truce and free access to Jerusalem for Christian pilgrims. Since Saladin would have granted this concession at any time, the truce scarcely compensated for the cost of such an expensive crusade.

The Fourth Crusade. The Fourth Crusade is an example of the degradation of a religious ideal. The few knights who answered Pope Innocent III's call were unable to meet the outrageous shipping charges demanded by the Venetians (see p. 145). The Venetians persuaded them to pay off the sum by capturing the Christian town of Zara on the Adriatic coast, which had long proved troublesome to Venetian trading interests. Then, in order to absorb all Byzantine commerce, the Venetians pressured the crusaders into attacking Constantinople. After conquering and sacking the greatest city in Europe, the crusaders set up the Latin empire of Constantinople (see map, p. 145) and forgot about recovering the Holy Land.

In this manuscript illumination Saladin wrests the cross, symbol of Christianity, from one of the leaders of the crusades.

Later crusades fail. The thirteenth century saw other crusades. The youngsters of the ill-fated Children's Crusade in 1212 fully expected the waters of the Mediterranean to part and make a path to the Holy Land, which they would take without fighting, but thousands of them were sold into slavery by Marseilles merchants. The Fifth Crusade in 1219 failed in its attack on Egypt, the center of Muslim power in the Near East. The unique Sixth Crusade in 1228 was organized and led by the excommunicated enemy of the pope, the emperor Frederick II, who by skillful diplomacy succeeded in acquiring Jerusalem, Bethlehem, and Nazareth from the sultan of Egypt without striking a blow. This arrangement ended in 1244 with the Muslim reconquest of the Holy City. The loss inspired the saintly Louis IX of France to organize the Seventh Crusade in 1248, but despite his zeal it ended in a fiasco when Louis was captured in Egypt and forced to pay an enormous ransom. This was the last major attempt to regain Jerusalem, and the era of the crusades ended in 1291 when Acre, the last stronghold of the Christians in the Holy Land, fell to the Muslims.

The crusader states. Altogether four crusader principalities, with the kingdom of Jerusalem dominant, had been established along the eastern Mediterranean coast. By the time Jerusalem fell to Saladin in 1187, however, only isolated pockets of Christians remained, surrounded by a vast hinterland of hostile Muslims. They were able to survive only by reason of frequent transfusions of strength from Europe in the form of supplies and manpower. It was natural for the European nobles who sought a permanent home in the Holy Land to adopt the customs of their Muslim neighbors and dress in light, flowing robes and turbans. Their houses were like Moorish villas, decorated and furnished with divans of brocade, Persian rugs, mosaic floors, and silk hangings. These transplanted Europeans became tolerant and easygoing, trading and even hunting with Muslims. Frequently there was bad blood between them and the visiting nobles who had merely come for a short visit and a dash against the infidel.

The crusader states were protected by the semi-monastic military orders: the Templars, or Knights of the Temple, so called because their first headquarters was on the site of the old Temple of Jerusalem; the Hospitalers, or Knights of St. John of Jerusalem, who were founded originally to care for the sick and wounded; and the Teutonic Knights, exclusively a German order. Combining monasticism and militarism, these orders had as their aims the protection of all pilgrims and perpetual war against the Muslims. These men of the cross could put five hundred armed knights into the field, and their great castles guarded the roads and passes against Muslim attack. For two centuries the uniforms of these orders were a common sight in the crusader states; the Templars wore a white robe decorated with a red cross, the Hospitalers a black robe with a white cross, and the Teutonic Knights a white robe with a black cross.

The crusades evaluated. Even though the crusades failed to achieve their specific objective permanently, they cannot be written off as mere adventures. On the contrary, their influence extended over a much wider geographical field than just the Holy Land. Much of the crusading fervor carried over to the fight against the Muslims in Spain and the pagan Slavs in eastern Europe. Politically the crusades weakened the Byzantine empire and accelerated its fall (see Chapter 6). Although the early crusades strengthened the moral leadership of the papacy in Europe, the ill-success of the later crusades, together with the preaching of crusades against Christian heretics (see p. 248) and political opponents (see p. 238), lessened both the crusading ideal and respect for the papacy.

The contact with the East widened the scope of the Europeans, ended their isolation, and exposed them to a vastly superior civilization. Although it is easy to exaggerate the economic effects of the crusades, they did complete the reopening of the eastern Mediterranean to western commerce, which in turn stimulated the rise of cities and the emergence of a money economy in the West. The crusades as a movement were a manifestation of the dynamic vitality and expansive spirit of Europe, evident in many fields by the end of the eleventh century.

THE RISE OF TRADE AND TOWNS

Revitalized trade routes. Although scholars have long debated the extent of trade and urban life that existed during the early Middle Ages, there is general agreement that fresh trade activity was evident even before the crusades. With the ending of Viking and Magyar attacks in the tenth century, a northern trading area developed which extended from the British Isles to the Baltic Sea. Closely related to this northern trade area was the route established by the Vikings as early as the ninth century, when they settled in Russia and created the lucrative Varangian route from the eastern Baltic down the rivers of Russia to the Black Sea and Constantinople (see p. 152).

The center of this northern trade system was the county of Flanders. By 1050 Flemish artisans were producing a surplus of woolen cloth of such fine quality that it was in great demand. Baltic furs, honey and forest products, and British tin and raw wool were exchanged for Flemish cloth. From the south by way of Italy came oriental luxury goods—silks, sugar, and spices.

Equally important as a catalyst of the medieval commercial revolution—whose impact on the Middle Ages deserves to be compared to that of the Industrial Revolution on the modern world—was the opening up of the Mediterranean trading area. In the eleventh century the Normans and Italians broke the Muslim hold on the eastern Mediterranean and the First Crusade inaugurated trade with the Near East. Arab vessels brought luxury goods from the East to ports on the Persian Gulf and Red Sea. From there they were shipped by caravan to Alexandria, Acre, and Joppa, and from those ports the merchants of Venice, Genoa, and Pisa transported the goods to Italy on their way to the markets of Europe. Other trade routes from Asia came overland, passing through Baghdad and Damascus and on to ports, such as Tyre and Sidon, in the crusader states. The easiest route north from the Mediterranean was via Marseilles, up the Rhone valley.

Early in the fourteenth century two more major trade lanes developed within Europe. An all-sea route connected the Mediterranean with northern Europe via the Strait of Gibraltar. The old overland route from northern Italy through the Alpine passes to central Europe was also developed. From Venice and other north Italian cities, trade flowed through such passes as the Brenner, sharply reducing the business of the Rhone valley route and the famous fairs of Champagne.

Fairs, centers of European trade. Along the main European trade routes, astute lords set up fairs, where merchants and goods from Italy and northern Europe met. During the twelfth and thirteenth centuries the fairs of Champagne in France (see Reference Map 4) functioned as the major clearing house for this international trade.

Fairs were important and elaborate events held either seasonally or annually in specified areas of each European country. The feudal law of the region was set aside during a fair, and in its place was substituted a new commercial code called the "law merchant." Special courts, with merchants acting as judges, settled all disputes which arose. In England such courts were called "pie-powder courts," from the French *pied-poudré*, meaning "dusty foot." Fairs also greatly stimulated the revival of a money economy and early forms of banking and credit.

Factors in the rise of towns. The resurgence of trade in Europe was the prime cause of the revival of towns. Trade and towns had an interacting effect on each other; the towns arose because of trade, but they also stimulated trade by providing greater markets and by producing goods for the merchants to sell.

In the revival of cities, geography played a significant role. Rivers, which were important in the evolution of ancient civilizations, were also important in the development of medieval towns. They were natural highways on which articles of commerce could be easily transported. Many communities developed at the confluence of two important streams; others arose where a river might be easily crossed by a ford or bridge, "Oxford" or "Cam-bridge," for example.

Often at a strategic geographic location a feudal noble had already erected a fortified castle, or *burg* (*bourg* in French, *borough* in English). Such a stronghold offered the merchants a good stopping place. The inhabitants of the burg were likely to buy some of the merchant's wares, and the castle offered him protection. In time a permanent merchant settlement, called a *faubourg*, grew up outside the walls of the burg. Frequently, too, merchants settled at an old Roman episcopal city like Cologne (Colonia Agrippina) or a fortified abbey or cathedral. Munich grew up around a monastery, and Durham was "half cathedral and half fortress against the Scot."

Another factor contributing to the rise of towns was the growth of population. In England, for example, the population more than tripled between 1066 and 1350. The reasons for this rapid increase in population are varied. The ending of bloody foreign invasions and, in some areas, the stabilization of feudal society were contributing factors. More important was an increase in food production brought about by the cultivation of wastelands, the clearing of forests, and the draining of marshes. Technological innovations such as the three-field system of crop rotation also increased production.

Interacting with the growth of towns was the decline of serfdom. Many serfs escaped from the manors and made their way to the towns. After living a year and a day in the town, a serf was considered a freeman.

The Hanseatic League. Sometimes a group of towns joined forces for mutual protection and to win special privileges. This was particularly true in Germany where by the thirteenth century a strong state capable of maintaining order ceased to exist. Most famous was the Hanseatic League, whose nucleus was Lübeck, Hamburg, and Danzig, but which by the fourteenth century comprised more than seventy cities. The League built up a lucrative monopoly on Baltic and North Sea trade. Its wealth came primarily from its control of the Baltic herring fisheries, its corner on Russian trade, and its rich business with England and Flanders. It established permanent trading stations in such leading European centers as London, Bruges, and Novgorod. Until the fifteenth century, when it began to lose its privileges and

A guild warden examines the work of an apprentice mason and carpenter before their admission as master craftsmen.

monopolies, the Hanseatic League remained the great distributor of goods to northern Europe. Its navy safeguarded its commerce from pirates and even waged a successful war with the king of Denmark when he threatened its Baltic monopoly.

Merchant and craft guilds. In each town the merchants and artisans organized themselves into guilds, which were useful not only for business but also for social and political purposes. There were two kinds of guilds: merchant and craft.

The merchant guild ensured a monopoly of trade within a given locality. All alien merchants were supervised closely and made to pay tolls. Disputes among merchants were settled at the guild court according to its own legal code. The guilds also tried to make sure that the customers were not cheated: they checked weights and measures and insisted upon a standard quality for goods. To allow only a legitimate profit, the guild fixed a "just price," which was fair to both producer and consumer.

When guilds first appeared, there was no adequate central government to protect merchants as they carried on their trading activities throughout the land. As a result the guilds assumed some functions which would otherwise have been governmental. If a merchant was imprisoned in another town, the guild tried to secure his release at its own expense. If a merchant of a London guild refused to pay a debt owed to a merchant of a guild in Bristol, the merchant guild in the latter town would seize the goods of any London merchant coming to Bristol.

The guild's functions stretched beyond business and politics into charitable and social activities. If a guildsman fell into poverty, he was aided. The guild also provided financial assistance for the burial expenses of its members and looked after their dependents. Members attended social meetings in the guildhall and periodically held processions in honor of their patron saints.

The increase of commerce brought a quickening of industrial life in the towns so that, as early as the eleventh century, the artisans began to organize. Craftsmen in each of the medieval trades—weaving, cobbling, tanning, and so on—joined forces. The result was the craft guild, which differed from the merchant guild in that membership was limited to artisans in one particular craft.

The general aims of the craft guilds were the same as those of the merchant guilds—the creation of a monopoly and the enforcement of a set of trade rules. Each guild had a monopoly of a certain article in a particular town, and every effort was made to prevent competition between members of the same guild. The guild restricted the number of its members, regulated the quantity and quality of the goods produced, and set prices. It also enforced regulations to protect the consumer from bad workmanship and inferior materials.

The craft guild also differed from the merchant guild in its recognition of three distinct classes of workers—apprentices, journeymen, and master craftsmen. The apprentice was a youth who lived at the master's house and was taught the trade thoroughly. Although he received no wages, all his physical needs were supplied. His apprenticeship commonly lasted seven years. When his schooling was finished, the youth became a journeyman (from the French *journée*, meaning "day's work"). He was then eligible to receive wages and to be hired by a master.

When about twenty-three, the journeyman sought admission into the guild as a master. To be accepted he had to prove his ability. Some crafts demanded the making of a "master piece"—for example, a pair of shoes that the master shoemakers would find acceptable in every way.

In the fourteenth century, when prosperity began to wane, the master craftsmen drastically restricted the number of journeymen who were allowed to become masters. The guilds either admitted only the relatives of masters or imposed excessively high entrance fees. When the journeymen then set up their own journeyman organizations, they were crushed by the wealthy guild masters, who usually controlled the town governments. By the fifteenth century most journeymen could not hope to become more than wage earners, and they bitterly resented the restrictions of the guild system.

Acquiring urban freedom. The guilds played an important role in local government. Both artisans and merchants, even though freemen, were subject to the feudal lord or bishop upon whose domain the city stood. The citizens of the towns resented the fact that their overlord collected tolls and dues as though they were serfs. The townsmen demanded the privileges of governing themselves—of making their own laws, administering their own justice, levying their own taxes, and issuing their own coinage. Naturally the overlord resented the impertinent upstarts who demanded self-government. But the towns won their independence in various ways.

One way was to become a commune, a self-governing town. The merchant guilds took the lead in acquiring charters of self-government for the towns. Often a charter had to be won by a revolt; in other circumstances it could be purchased, for a feudal lord was always in need of money. By 1200 the Lombard towns of northern Italy, as well as many French and Flemish towns, had become self-governing communes.

Where royal authority was strong, we find "privileged" towns. In a charter granted to the town by the monarch, the inhabitants won extensive financial and legal powers. The town was given management of its own

The horses pulling grain uphill in this illumination are wearing improved horseshoes which permit greater traction and collars which, by relieving pressure on their windpipes, greatly increase their pulling power.

finances and paid its taxes in a lump sum to the king. It was also generally given the right to elect its own officials. The king was glad to grant such a charter, for it weakened the power of his nobles and won him the support of the townsmen.

Founding new towns was still another way in which feudal restrictions were broken down. Shrewd lords and kings, who recognized the economic value of having towns in their territories, founded carefully planned centers with well-laid-out streets and open squares. As a means of obtaining inhabitants, they offered many inducements in the form of personal privileges and tax limitations. Among such new towns were Newcastle, Freiburg, and Berlin.

Technological advances. While in ancient societies men and animals were almost the only source of power, our medieval ancestors succeeded in greatly maximizing the muscle power of draft animals by three major developments. First, for the traditional horse collar which fastened around the animal's neck and choked him when pulling a heavy load, they substituted a harness fitted so that the shoulders bore the weight. Second, they developed a tandem harness in order to utilize the strength of several horses; and finally, they improved traction with a new type of horseshoe. These inventions are said to have done for the eleventh and twelfth centuries what the steam engine did for the nineteenth. In addition, our medieval forebears increased the number of

prime movers beyond sheer human and animal muscle power. They developed watermills (known but little used in the ancient world) and invented windmills for use in flat lands where waterfalls did not exist. Useful not only for grinding grains, these water- and windmills provided power for draining marshlands, for reclaiming areas from the sea (as in the Low Countries), and for fulling woolen cloth, which the West exported in quantity to the Byzantine and Muslim East.

The use of money, banking, and credit. All the aspects of Europe's expansion—the crusades, and the revival of trade, cities, and industry—had far-reaching effects on the financial structure. The first big change came with the reappearance of money as a medium of exchange. Coins were made from silver dug from old and new mines throughout Europe, but during the whole of the Middle Ages silver bullion was in short supply. In the thirteenth century silver coins were superseded in international trade by gold, especially the florin of Florence, which became a monetary standard for Europe.

When the English king Henry III invaded France in 1242, he carried with him thirty barrels of money, each containing 160,000 coins, to defray the expenses of the expedition. This incident graphically illustrates the need for instruments of credit and other forms of banking. All-important was the technique of "symbolic transfer." By this system a man deposited his money in a bank

Representative of the burgeoning trade and commerce of the fourteenth century, this miniature depicts a Genoese moneylender bargaining with men who have come to pawn items similar to those hanging at the back of the shop, while a second moneylender enters accounts in a ledger.

and received in return a letter of credit which, like a modern check, could later be cashed at any of the offices of the same bank. Letters of credit were common at fairs and very useful during the crusades, when the Templars arranged a system whereby crusaders could deposit money in the Paris office and withdraw it from the office in the Holy Land.

Banking also sprang from the activities of moneychangers at fairs and other trading centers. In addition to exchanging the coin of one region for another, these moneychangers would also accept money on deposit for safekeeping. The most important bankers, however, were Italian merchants from Florence and the Lombard cities, who by the middle of the thirteenth century were loaning their accumulated capital to kings and prelates. They found various ways of circumventing the Church's disapproval of all interest as usury. For example, if a sum was not repaid by a certain date, a penalty charge was levied.

THE EMERGENCE OF A NEW SOCIETY

The typical town. Medieval towns, which by the twelfth century were centers of an advanced culture as well as of trade and industry, were not large by modern standards. Before 1200 no town contained 100,000 inhabitants, and one of 20,000 was a metropolis. Since the area within the walls was at a

premium, medieval towns were more crowded than the average modern city. Shops were even built on bridges (as on the Ponte Vecchio, which still stands in Florence), and buildings were erected to a height of seven or more stories. The houses projected over the street with each additional story so that it was often possible for persons at the tops of houses opposite one another to touch hands.

The streets below were dark and narrow and almost invariably crooked, although they were often designed to be wide enough "to give passage to a horseman with his lance across his saddle-bows." The streets were full of discordant sounds—drivers yelled at pedestrians to get out of the way of the horses and oxen; dogs, pigs, and geese added their alarms; merchants bawled out their wares; people of every description jostled past one another, and unoiled signs above inns and shops creaked ominously in the wind, constantly threatening to crash down on some innocent passerby.

The bourgeoisie. The triumph of the townsmen in their struggle for greater self-government meant that a new class had evolved in Europe, a powerful, independent, and self-assured group, whose interest in trade was to revolutionize social, economic, and political history. The members of this class were called burghers or the bourgeoisie. Kings came to rely more and more on them in combating the power of the feudal lords, and their economic interests gave rise to a nascent capitalism. Also associated with the rise of towns and the bourgeoisie were the decline of serfdom and the manorial system and the advent of modern society.

A medieval townsman's rank was based on money and goods rather than birth and land. At the top of the social scale were the great merchant and banking families, the princes of trade, bearing such names as Medici, Fugger, and Coeur. Then came the moderately wealthy merchants and below them the artisans and small shopkeepers. In the lowest slot was the unskilled laborer, whose miserable lot and discontent were destined to continue through the rest of the Middle Ages and most of modern history.

The decay of serfdom. Attracted by the freedom of town life, many serfs ran away from their manors and established themselves in a town. As a result the remaining serfs became unreliable. Sometimes they secured enough money to buy their freedom by selling food surpluses in the towns, but often the lords freed their serfs and induced them to remain on the manor as tenants or hired laborers. As a first step in the emancipation of the serfs, the lords accepted a money payment from them as a substitute for their old obligations of labor and produce. The final step was for the lord to become a landlord in the modern sense, renting the arable land of the manor to free tenants. Thus former serfs became satisfied tenants or, on occasion, members of the yeoman class who owned their small farms. Serfdom had largely died out in England and France by 1500, although in the latter country many of the old and vexatious obligations, such as payment for the use of the lord's mill and oven, were retained. In eastern Europe serfdom persisted until the nineteenth century.

Peasant revolts. The improvement in the status of the peasants did not necessarily mean that life was pleasant and untroubled. The twelfth and thirteenth centuries were almost a boom period; but economic depression, unrest, and tension followed in the period from 1350 to 1450. The Black Death, a bubonic plague from Asia carried by fleas on rats, struck western Europe in 1347, decimating and demoralizing society. It is estimated that about one third of the population was wiped out. Hardest hit were the towns; the population of Florence, for example, fell from 114,000 to about 50,000 in five years. Coupled with this blow was the destruction and death caused by the Hundred Years' War between France and England (1337-1453).

One of the symptoms of economic setback was the revolt of urban workers and peasants during the course of the fourteenth century. Textile workers in the Flemish cities and in Florence waged class war against guild masters and rich merchants, while peasant unrest flamed into revolt in France and England. A famous example of the latter was the Wat Tyler uprising in England in 1381. The decimation of the peasant population by the Black Death caused a rise in the wages of the day laborers and an increased demand for the abolition of serfdom. Parliament tried to legislate against the pay raise but succeeded only in incurring the anger of the peasants. This resentment was fanned by the sermons of a priest, John Ball, known as the first English socialist:

Ah, ye good people, the matter goeth not well to pass in England, nor shall not do so till every-

In this representation of the Wat Tyler uprising, John Ball is shown at the head of a well-disciplined group of helmeted peasants bearing the banners of England and St. George.

thing be common, and that there be no villains [serfs] or gentlemen, but that we may be all united together and that the lords be no greater masters than we be. What have we deserved or why should we be thus kept in serfdom; we be all come from one father and one mother, Adam and Eve.[4]

As in the case of other revolts, this uprising was crushed amid a welter of blood and broken promises.

Depression and economic stagnation began to be eased by the middle of the fifteenth century. The period of strong and efficient monarchies was at hand; and Europe was on the verge of a new period of expansion, this time over the face of the globe.

SUMMARY

Constructive forces fashioning a new Europe became apparent in the period between 1050 and 1300. The great achievement of the eleventh century was expansion and offensive action by the forces of western Europe. The Muslims lost naval supremacy in the Mediterranean, and a Christian reconquest was initiated in Spain. Above all, a great movement, the crusades, was initiated in 1095. While the objective was to push the Muslims out of the Holy Land and particularly from Jerusalem, the crusades opened new doors for the narrow, ingrown Europeans.

During the eleventh century Europe was transformed by new forces: increased food production and population, revitalized trade, new towns, expansion of industry, and a money economy. A new society began to take shape; the bourgeoisie emerged and serfdom declined. (From 1350 to 1450, however, economic depression produced unrest among peasants and urban workers.) In the political realm, the tradition of kingship persisted in spite of feudalism with its many local sovereignties. Aided substantially by the new economic forces, the kings were to impose their will on the nobles and become masters of new nations. The beginnings of this movement, which were contemporary with the developments described in this chapter, will be set forth in Chapter 10.

SUGGESTIONS FOR READING

C. H. Haskins, **The Normans in European History**,* Norton; David C. Douglas, **The Norman Achievement**, California, 1969. Excellent studies of the remarkable explosion of Norman power.

S. Runciman, **A History of the Crusades**,* 3 vols., Cambridge. Highly recommended for both its literary and historical merit. R. A. Newhall, **The Crusades**,* Holt (Berkshire Studies), is a brief, lucid introduction to the subject. D. C. Munro, **The Kingdom of the Crusaders**, Appleton-Century, 1935, is an absorbing account of the crusades as well as of the kingdom of Jerusalem. Also recommended are Zoé Oldenbourg, **The Crusades**,* Ballantine; Gertrude Slaughter, **Saladin**, Exposition, 1955; R. Dozy, **Spanish Islam: A History of the Moslems in Spain**, Barnes and Noble, 1969. **The Cornerstone**,* Ballantine, by Zoé Oldenbourg, is a good historical novel dealing with the Crusades.

R. M. Smail, **Crusading Warfare (1097-1193)**, Cambridge, 1967. Describes the weapons, organization, and tactics of both the Latin and Muslim armies together with the nature and function of the crusaders' castles. C. Oman, **The Art of War in the Middle Ages: A.D. 378–1515**,* Cornell, is the standard work.

H. Pirenne, **Economic and Social History of Medieval Europe**,* Harvest, and **Medieval Cities**,* Princeton. Two small classics on the revival of trade and growth of cities. F. Rörig, **The Medieval Town**,* California, treats urban life from the eleventh to the sixteenth centuries. See also R. Latouche, **The Birth of Western Economy**,* Torchbooks; A. R. Lewis, **Naval Power and Trade in the Mediterranean, A.D. 500-1100**, Princeton, 1951; S. Baldwin, **Business in the Middle Ages**, Cooper Square, 1968; **Trade and Industry in the Middle Ages** (The Cambridge Economic History of Europe, Vol. I), Cambridge, 1954. Good reading on the careers of early capitalists includes I. Origo, **The Merchant of Prato, Francesco di Marco Datini, 1335-1410**, Knopf, 1957; T. B. Costain, **The Moneyman**,* Permabooks, a popular historical novel on the spectacular rise and fall of the fifteenth-century French capitalist Jacques Coeur; and the last two chapters in E. Power, **Medieval People**,* Barnes and Noble.

D. M. Stenton, **English Society in the Early Middle Ages (1066-1307)**,* Penguin. A brief, comprehensive, and readable account of the life of the rich and the poor, the economy, church affairs, and government. See also A. Luchaire, **Social France at the Time of Philip Augustus**,* Torchbooks; and P. Ziegler, **The Black Death**, Day, 1969.

*Indicates an inexpensive paperbound edition.

Chapter 10

Nations in the Making

Medieval Political History: 1050-1300

INTRODUCTION. Between 1050 and 1300, a period sometimes called the High Middle Ages, political as well as economic and social change was manifest in Europe. Not only did trade revive, cities grow, and a new bourgeois social class emerge, but kings developed their power at the expense of the feudal nobility. Inadequate to meet the demands of a new and progressive society in the making, feudalism was on the wane.

Perhaps the greatest weakness of feudalism was its inability to guarantee law and order. Too often feudalism meant anarchy in which robber barons, in the words of a twelfth-century observer, "levied taxes on the villages every so often, and called it 'protection money'" (see p. 224). Feudalism provided no consistently effective agency to deal with such ruffians. As a result, confusion, inefficiency, and injustice often prevailed.

The inefficiency inherent in the feudal system also hindered economic progress. Trade and commerce spread over ever larger areas, but the boundaries of many tiny feudal principalities acted as barriers to this expansion. Along the Seine River, for example, there were tolls every six or seven miles. Only by welding the confusing multiplicity of fiefs and principalities into a large territorial unit—the nation—could the irritating tolls and tariffs imposed by local barons be removed, trade advanced, the lack of a uniform currency be remedied, and justice established. In other words, the ills of feudalism could be cured only by the creation of unified and centralized national states. We shall see in this chapter how monarchs in England and France expanded their power and improved the machinery of government, thus laying the foundations for such states. In Germany and Italy, however, efforts to create a national state ended in failure, and in Spain unification was retarded by the formidable task of ousting the Muslims.

THE GENESIS OF MODERN ENGLAND

Britain after the Romans. When the Roman legions withdrew from Britain to Italy at the beginning of the fifth century, they left the Romanized Celtic natives at the mercy of the Anglo-Saxon invaders. These Germanic tribes devastated Britain so thoroughly that little remained of Roman civilization other than a splendid system of roads. Proof of the force with which the invaders struck is the fact that almost no traces of the Celtic language remain in modern English. Not only did the Anglo-Saxons push most of the Celts out of Britain, but they also fought among themselves. At one time there were more than a dozen little tribal kingdoms, all jealous and hostile, on the island.

The Anglo-Saxon monarchy. Gradually peace and a semblance of order came to the distracted island as rivalries among the kingdoms diminished and the overlordship of the island was held in turn by the different rulers. In the ninth century the kingdom of Wessex (see map, p. 192) held the dominant position. The famous Wessex king, Alfred the Great (871-899), was confronted with the task of turning back a new wave of invaders, the Danes, who overran all the other English kingdoms. After a series of disheartening reverses, Alfred defeated the Danes and forced them into a treaty whereby they settled in what came to be called the Danelaw (see map, p. 194) and accepted Christianity.

In addition to being a successful warrior, Alfred the Great made notable contributions in government in order, as he wrote, that he "might worthily and fittingly steer and rule the dominion that was entrusted to me."[1] He reorganized the militia of freemen (*fyrd*) so that part was always ready for battle while the rest tilled the soil, and the ships he built to repel future Viking attacks have won him the title of founder of the English navy. He also issued a set of laws, which reflect his desire to see the average man protected from wrongdoing and violence.

Following the example of Charlemagne, Alfred also advanced the intellectual life of his country. He invited learned men from abroad and founded a palace school. Since Latin was virtually unknown in England, Alfred urged the bishops to have translated into English the books "which are most necessary for all men to know." He also encouraged monks to keep an account of current affairs, the *Anglo-Saxon Chronicle*, which continued to be written for hundreds of years afterward.

Alfred's successors were able rulers who conquered the Danelaw and created a unified English monarchy. Danes and Saxons intermarried, and soon all differences between the two people disappeared. After 975, however, a decline set in. The power of the central government lagged and with it the ability to keep order at home and repel outside attacks. The impotence of the kingdom is well illustrated in the unhappy reign of Ethelred the Unready (978-1016), who was unable to keep a firm hand on the great nobles or to cope with a new attack by the Danes.

In its political structure, the major defect

of Anglo-Saxon England was the weakness of its central government: the inability of the king to control the great nobles, the earls, who were the king's deputies in their districts. But as a positive contribution to political history, the Anglo-Saxons developed local government to a strong degree. They left us a valuable legacy: the tradition of the people's participation in their government. In the local political divisions—the shires and their subdivisions, the hundreds—numerous assemblies or courts (moots) existed. Presided over by a royal official, the reeve, and composed of freemen of the area, the moots dispensed justice according to local custom and helped administer the realm. Here was one of the seeds of later democratic government. It is an interesting carry-over that American law students call their trial cases "moot court cases" and that our modern title of sheriff is derived from the shire's most important official, the shire reeve.

Following the reign of Ethelred, the Anglo-Saxons were again overrun by the Danes, and King Canute of Denmark ruled England as well as Norway. Canute proved to be a wise and civilized king and was well liked by his Anglo-Saxon subjects because he respected their rights and customs. Canute's empire fell apart after his death in 1035, and in 1042 the English crown was secured by Ethelred's son, Edward the Confessor. So pious that he remained a virgin all his life, Edward was a weak ruler who had little control over the powerful earls who had usurped most of the king's authority in their regions. This decline in government was reversed after the Normans conquered the island in 1066.

The Norman Conquest. The Norman Conquest of England really began in the reign of Edward the Confessor. Edward had spent most of his early life in Normandy, and as king of England he showed a strong pro-Norman bias. On his death without heir in 1066 the *Witan*—the council of the kingdom —selected Harold Godwinson, a powerful English earl, as the new ruler. Immediately William, duke of Normandy, claimed the English throne, basing his demand on a flimsy hereditary right and on the assertion that Edward had promised him the crown.

An outstanding statesman and soldier, William as duke of Normandy had subdued the rebellious nobles and established a new kind of centralized feudal state. William effectively controlled his vassals, and his feudal army of one thousand knights made him the most powerful ruler west of Germany. His centralized authority in Normandy contrasted sharply with the situation in England, where the powerful earls were continually embarrassing the king.

By promising to promote Church reform in England, William secured the sanction of the pope, which gave his invasion the flavor of a crusade. His well-equipped army of hard-fighting Norman knights and landless nobles from Brittany and Flanders looked upon the conquest of England as an investment that would pay them rich dividends in the form of lands and serfs.

The cross-Channel maneuver was hazardous; five thousand knights, bowmen, and supporting infantry, as well as many horses, had to be transported in open boats. On October 14, 1066, at Hastings, William's mounted knights broke the famed shieldwall of the English infantry, and resistance ceased when King Harold was slain. The defeat ended Anglo-Saxon rule and brought a new pattern of government that would make England the strongest state in Europe.

William the Conqueror's centralized feudal monarchy. As king of England, William directed all his policies at a single goal—the increase of his own power within the context of feudalism. And, sensibly, he utilized some of the institutions existing in England. He retained the Anglo-Saxon shires and hundreds as administrative divisions, along with the system of local courts and sheriffs. But the long arm of royal power also reached the local level through the king's commissioners, who occasionally toured the shires, and the sheriffs, who became the effective local agents of the king in collecting the feudal dues and in presiding over the shire courts.

Most important, William introduced the Norman system of centralized feudalism into England. As owner of all England by right of conquest, William retained some land as his royal domain and granted the remainder as fiefs to royal vassals called tenants-in-chief, among whom were bishops and abbots. In return for their fiefs, the tenants-in-chief provided William with a stipulated number of knights to serve in the royal army. To furnish the required knight service, the great vassals—most of whom were French-speaking Normans—subinfeudated parts of their fiefs among their own vassals. But from all the landholders in England, regardless of whether or not they were his immediate vassals, William exacted homage and an oath that they would "be faithful to him against all other men." Hence, both the tenants-in-chief holding fiefs directly from the king and the lesser tenants holding fiefs as vassals of the tenants-in-chief swore loyalty to the king, their feudal suzerain. This meant that a disgruntled noble could not call out his own vassals against the king, because every man owed his first allegiance to William.

William did not depend solely upon feudal levies, however; he retained the old Anglo-Saxon militia, in which every freeman was required to serve, and he hired mercenaries.

Thus the king had in readiness an independent fighting force to crush a rebellious baron. Furthermore, private feudal warfare was forbidden, and no castle could be built without royal permission.

The Domesday Survey is another example of the energetic and methodical manner in which William took over full control of England. Because William, like all medieval kings, constantly needed money, he ordered an accurate census of the property and property holders in his realm as a basis for collecting all the feudal "aids" and "incidents" (see p. 198) owed to him. Royal commissioners gathered testimony from local groups of older men who were put under oath and questioned. The complaints and even riots which the inventory caused are reflected in the *Anglo-Saxon Chronicle*:

So very narrowly did he cause the survey to be made that there was not a single hide nor a rood of land, nor—it is shameful to relate that which he thought no shame to do—was there an ox or a cow or a pig passed by that was not set down in the accounts. . . .[2]

The Bayeux tapestry, actually a woolen embroidery on linen, dates from the eleventh century. Over 230 feet long and 20 inches wide, it both depicts and narrates (in Latin) the events of the Norman Conquest of England in 1066. This section shows the English shield wall being attacked by the mounted French knights.

This seal was struck during the reign of William the Conqueror. The Latin inscription on the face reads "Know by this sign William, chief of the Normans"; the reverse reads "By this sign know the same William, king of the English."

In line with his policy of controlling all aspects of the government, William revamped the old Anglo-Saxon *Witan*, which had elected and advised the kings. The new Norman ruler changed its title to the Great Council—also called *curia regis*, the king's council or court—and converted it into a feudal body composed of his tenants-in-chief. The Great Council met at least three times a year as a court of justice for the great barons and as an advisory body in important matters. At other times a small permanent council of barons advised the king.

William also dominated the English Church. He appointed bishops and abbots and required them to provide military service for their lands. Although he permitted the Church to retain its courts, he denied them the right to appeal cases to the pope without his consent. Nor could the decrees of popes and Church councils circulate in England without royal approval.

Thus William formed the conquered island into one of Europe's most advanced states. In his determination to be master of his own house, he ruthlessly oppressed any opposition to his will. The nobility and the Church were burdened with feudal services, and the Anglo-Saxon freemen, oppressed by the exactions of their Norman lords, were in time reduced to serfdom. William advanced political feudalism and the manorial system and fused the two into a highly centralized feudal structure.

William's sons. William II, who succeeded his father in 1087, was a disappointing namesake. Utilizing his father's methods, but without his ability, William II stirred up several baronial revolts before being shot in the back—accidentally, it was said—while hunting. Succeeding him was his brother, Henry I (1100-1135), a more able and conciliatory monarch who met with only one baronial revolt.

While the Great Council, made up of the chief nobles, occasionally met to advise the king, the small permanent council of barons grew in importance. From it now appeared the first vague outlines of a few specialized organs of government. The exchequer, or treasury, supervised the collection of royal revenue, now greatly increased with the revival of a money economy. Notable was *scutage* or "shield money," a fee which the king encouraged his vassals to pay in lieu of personal military service. The well-trained "barons of the exchequer" also sat as a special court to try cases involving revenue. At times members of the small council were sent throughout the realm to judge serious crimes which endangered what was called the King's Peace.

Henry I's achievements in strengthening the monarchy were largely undone by the nineteen years of chaos that followed his death. Ignoring their promise to recognize Henry's only surviving child, Matilda, wife of Geoffrey Plantagenet, count of Anjou in France, many barons supported Henry's weak nephew Stephen. During the resulting civil war the nobility became practically independent of the crown and, secure in their strong castles, freely pillaged the land. According to the *Anglo-Saxon Chronicle:*

They levied taxes on the villages every so often, and called it "protection money." . . . If two or three men came riding to a village, all the villagers fled, because they expected they would be robbers. The bishops and learned men were always excommunicating them, but they thought nothing of it. . . .[3]

Henry II. Anarchy ceased with the accession of Matilda's son, Henry II (1154-1189), the founder of the Plantagenet, or Angevin, House in England. As a result of his inheritance (Normandy and Anjou) and his marriage to Eleanor of Aquitaine, the richest heiress in France, Henry's possessions stretched from Scotland to the Pyrenees. The English holdings in France far exceeded the land directly ruled by the French kings, who eyed their vassal rival with jealousy and

These faces looking down from the capital of a medieval pillar, found today in the Cloisters Museum in New York City, are believed to represent Henry II (right) and his queen, Eleanor of Aquitaine. During their stormy married life, Henry was once forced to imprison Eleanor because she incited their sons to rebel against him. As Richard I and John I, two of these sons later ruled England; one daughter became queen of Sicily, and another became queen of Castile.

fear. Henry's reign marks the outbreak of the strife between England and France, which runs like a red thread throughout the tapestry of medieval and modern history.

Stephen, Henry's weak predecessor, had left a sorry heritage. The judicial system was confused and corrupt. The royal courts administered by the king's justices faced strong competition from both the baronial courts, run independently by feudal lords, and the Church courts, which threatened to extend their supremacy over the whole realm.

Henry's chief contribution to the development of the English monarchy was to increase the jurisdiction of the royal courts at the expense of the feudal courts. This produced three major results: a permanent system of circuit courts presided over by itinerant justices, the jury system, and a body of law common to all England.

Itinerant justices on regular circuits were sent out once each year to try breaches of the King's Peace. To make this system of royal criminal justice more effective, Henry employed the method of inquest used by William the Conqueror in the Domesday Survey. In each shire a body of important men were sworn (*juré*) to report to the sheriff all crimes committed since the last session of the king's circuit court. Thus originated the modern-day grand jury which presents information for an indictment.

Henry's courts also used the jury system as a means of settling private lawsuits. Instead of deciding such civil cases by means of oath-helpers or trial by ordeal (see p. 133), the circuit judges handed down decisions based upon evidence sworn to by a jury of men selected because they were acquainted with the facts of the case. This more attractive and efficient system caused litigants to flock to the royal courts, a procedure facilitated by the sale of "writs," which ordered a sheriff to bring the case to a royal court. Not only was the king's income greatly increased by fees from the sale of writs, but the feudal courts of the nobility were greatly weakened.

This petit or trial jury eventually evolved into the modern trial jury whose members, no longer witnesses, determine guilt or innocence. Trial by jury became the most characteristic feature of the judicial system of all English-speaking nations and was carried to the far corners of the earth as a hallmark of justice.*

Henry's judicial reforms promoted the growth of the common law—one of the most important factors in welding the English people into a nation. The decisions of the royal justices became the basis for future decisions made in the king's courts, superseded the many diverse systems of local justice in the shires, and became the law common to all Englishmen.

Thomas à Becket, victim of Church-state rivalry. While Henry skillfully diminished the activities of the baronial courts by making the royal courts more powerful, he was not so successful against his other legal rival—the Church courts. When he appointed Thomas à Becket archbishop of Canterbury, the king assumed that his former boon companion and royal chancellor could easily be persuaded to cooperate, but Becket proved to be stubbornly independent, stoutly upholding the authority of the Church.

In 1164 Henry stipulated that clergymen found guilty by a Church court of committing heinous crimes, such as murder and grand larceny, were to be unfrocked and handed over to a royal court where punishments were more severe than in the Church courts. Henry's idea was to prevent the abuses resulting from "benefit of clergy"— the principle that the Church alone had legal jurisdiction over its clergy, among whom were included all who claimed to be students, crusaders, and even servants of clergymen. Becket refused to yield, claiming that clergymen would suffer unjust "double punishment" for a crime—unfrocked by the Church and punished by the state.

When Becket received no support from the English clergy, he fled to France and

Henry II was king, feudal suzerain, and vassal—all in one. He was king of England, feudal overlord of Scotland, Wales, Ireland, and Brittany, and vassal to the French king for the English holdings in France (although he held more territory there than the French monarch).

appealed to the pope for aid. After a few years the pope patched up the quarrel, and the archbishop returned to England. His first act, however, was to excommunicate the bishops who, in his absence, had crowned the eldest prince heir to the throne. When this news reached Henry, in a fit of passion he roared: "What a pack of fools and cowards I have nourished in my house, that not one of them will avenge me of this turbulent priest."[5] Responding to this tirade, four knights went to Canterbury and murdered Becket before the high altar of the cathedral. An eyewitness wrote that Becket "fell on his knees and elbows, offering himself a living victim, and saying in a low voice, 'For the name of Jesus and the protection of the church I am ready to embrace death.'"[6]

The resulting uproar destroyed all chance of reforming the Church courts. Becket be-

*The workings of Roman law offer an interesting contrast. "Under Roman law, and systems derived from it, a trial in those turbulent centuries, and in some countries even today, is often an inquisition. The judge makes his own investigation into the civil wrong or the public crime, and such investigation is largely uncontrolled. The suspect can be interrogated in private. He must answer all questions put to him. His right to be represented by a legal adviser is restricted. The witnesses against him can testify in secret and in his absence. And only when these processes have been accomplished is the accusation or charge against him formulated and published. Thus often arise secret intimidation, enforced confessions, torture, and blackmailed pleas of guilty."[4]

came a martyr and, after miracles were reported to have occurred at his tomb, was canonized a saint. For the remainder of the Middle Ages, benefit of clergy remained an obstacle to the royal ambitions for equal justice for all Englishmen.

Richard the Lion-Hearted, knight-errant. As was the case after William the Conqueror's reign, the good beginning made by Henry II was marred by the mistakes of his successors. Having no taste for the prosaic tasks of government, Richard the Lion-Hearted wasted his country's wealth in winning a great reputation as a crusader (see p. 210) and in fighting the king of France. Richard spent only five months of his ten-year reign (1189-1199) in England, which he regarded as a source of money for his overseas adventures. The royal bureaucracy worked so well, however, that the king's absence made little difference.

John's powers limited by Magna Carta. Richard's successor, his brother John (reigned 1199-1216), was an able ruler who worked hard to promote his father's governmental system but who lacked his brother's chivalrous qualities. His cruelty and unscrupulous-

A detail from a medieval illuminated manuscript depicts the murder of Thomas à Becket.

ness cost him the support of his barons at the very time he needed them most in his struggles with the two ablest men of the age, Philip II of France and Pope Innocent III. As feudal overlord for John's possessions in France, Philip found the occasion to declare John an unfaithful vassal and his fiefs forfeit. John put up only feeble resistance, and after losing more than half his possessions in France he became involved in a struggle with Innocent III in which he was forced to make abject surrender (see pp. 245-246). In the meantime, John had completely alienated the English barons by attempting to collect illegal feudal dues and committing other infractions of feudal law. The exasperated barons rebelled and in 1215 forced John to affix his seal to Magna Carta, which bound the king to observe all feudal rights and privileges. People in later centuries, however, looked back upon Magna Carta as one of the most important documents in the story of human freedom.

To Englishmen of the time, this document did not appear to introduce any new constitutional principles. It was merely an agreement between the barons and the king, the aristocracy and the monarchy. But the seeds of political liberty were to be discovered in Magna Carta. Certain provisions were later used to support the movement toward constitutional monarchy and representative government:

Clause XII. [Taxation or feudal aids except those sanctioned by custom] . . . shall be levied in our kingdom only by the common consent of our kingdom [i.e., by the king's Great Council].

Clause XXXIX. No free man shall be taken or imprisoned or dispossessed, or outlawed, or banished, or in any way destroyed . . . except by the legal judgment of his peers or by the law of the land.

Clause XL. To no one will we sell, to no one will we deny, or delay right or justice.[7]

In 1215 these limitations upon the king's power applied only to freemen—that is, to the clergy, the barons, and a relatively small number of rural freeholders and burghers—not to the majority of the population, who were still serfs. As serfdom gradually disappeared, however, the term *freeman* came to include every Englishman.

The importance of Magna Carta does not lie in its original purpose but rather in the subsequent use made of it. Two great principles were potential in the charter: (1) the law is above the king; and (2) the king can be compelled by force to obey the law of the land. This concept of the rule of law and the limited power of the crown was to play an important role in the seventeenth-century struggle against the despotism of the Stuart kings; Clause XII was interpreted to guarantee the principle of no taxation without representation and Clause XXXIX to guarantee trial by jury.

The origins of Parliament. The French-speaking Normans commonly used the word *Parlement* (from *parler*, "to speak") for the Great Council, or *curia regis*, composed of the king's feudal tenants-in-chief. Anglicized as *Parliament*, the term was used interchangeably with Great Council and *curia regis*. Modern historians, however, generally apply the term to the Great Council only after 1265, when its membership was radically enlarged.

The first meeting of Parliament—the enlarged Great Council—took place in the midst of a baronial rebellion against Henry III, the son of King John. In an effort to gain the widest possible popular support, Simon de Montfort, the leader of the rebellion, summoned not only the barons but also two knights from every shire and two burghers from every borough to the Great Council in 1265.

Parliament gains stature. Parliament first became important during the reign of Henry III's son, Edward I (1272-1307), one of England's half-dozen outstanding monarchs. Beginning with the "Model Parliament" of 1295, Edward followed the pattern set by Simon de Montfort in summoning representatives of shires and towns to meetings of the Great Council. Two years later he agreed that certain taxes could not be levied without the assent of Parliament, a principle which assured that body of being summoned from time to time.

From Edward's reign on, Parliament became more and more essential to English

Probably the earliest authentic view of Parliament in session, this picture shows a meeting called by Edward I. The dignitaries occupying the center benches are Church officials and secular lords. In the center are members of the judiciary seated on woolsacks to remind them that wool was vital to the English economy. Just below them are representatives from the towns and shires.

government. In calling Parliaments, the English kings had no idea of making any concession to popular government. Their main objective was revenue. As recognition of the growing wealth and influence of the bourgeoisie and as a means of obtaining another source of revenue, the English kings, along with other European monarchs, began the practice of including representatives of the bourgeoisie in their feudal councils.

Early in the fourteenth century the representatives of the knights and the burghers, called the "Commons," adopted the practice of meeting separate from the lords spiritual and temporal. Thus arose the divisions of Parliament that came to be called the House of Commons and the House of Lords.

Parliament, particularly the Commons, soon discovered its power as a major source of money for the king. It gradually became the custom for Parliament to exercise this "power of the purse" by withholding its financial grants until the king had redressed grievances, made known by petitions. Parliament also presented petitions to the king with the request that they be promulgated as statutes, as the laws drawn up by the king and his council and confirmed in Parliament were called. Gradually the right to initiate legislation through petition was obtained. Again, Parliament's "power of the purse" turned the trick.

Edward I's statutes. Edward issued through Parliament a series of great statutes, many aimed at curtailing the power of the nobility that had greatly increased during the baronial revolts of his father's reign. The statute known as *Quo Warranto*, which demanded of a lord that he prove "by what warrant" he exercised certain rights and privileges, led to the recovery of lost royal rights. Another statute established the entail system which enabled a landowner to will his entire estate to his eldest son on condition that the property remain forever undivided. The younger brothers were thus forced to shift for themselves in governmental service, in the professions, or in commerce. By contrast, estates on the Continent were usually divided among all the sons in a family, a practice which encouraged the growth of a large and parasitic class of landowners. Edward also restricted the power of the Church, grown exceedingly rich through gifts of land. The Statute of Mortmain forbade the giving of more land to the Church without royal approval.

Widening the boundaries of the realm. Edward I was the first English king who was determined to be master of the whole island of Britain—Wales, Scotland, and England. In 1284, after a five-year struggle, English law and administration were imposed on Wales. As a concession to the Welsh, Edward gave his oldest son the title of Prince of Wales.

A dispute over the succession to the Scottish throne in the 1290's gave Edward his opportunity to intervene in the land to the north. After calling upon Edward to settle the dispute, the Scots accepted him as their overlord. Then Edward unwisely demanded that the Scots furnish him with troops to fight in England's wars. Under the courageous William Wallace, rebellion quickly flared up. After winning several victories against the English, Wallace was defeated and hanged as a traitor. But the fires of Scottish nationalism continued to burn despite numerous attempts to put out the flames. Edward II, the next English king, attempted to humble the Scots, but at the battle of Bannockburn (1314) the Scots, led by Robert Bruce, won their independence. The two peoples remained bitter enemies, with the Scots often joining the French in their wars against the English. Not until 1603 were the two kingdoms united under a common monarch.

THE BEGINNINGS OF THE FRENCH NATIONAL STATE

Political fragmentation. At the time William the Conqueror set sail, the monarchy in France barely existed. As we saw in Chapter 8, the later Carolingian rulers were generally weak and unable to defend the realm from Viking incursions. This task fell to the local counts and dukes, who built castles to protect the countryside and exercised the powers of the king in their territories. In France by the beginning of the tenth century there were more than thirty great feudal princes who were nominally vassals of the king but who gave him little or no support. Nevertheless, except for the short reign of Odo (see p. 194), the Carolingian kings maintained their precarious grasp on the throne. When the last Carolingian, Louis the Sluggard, died in 987, the nobles elected as his successor Hugh Capet, count of Paris and descendant of Odo.

The "kingdom" that Hugh Capet theoretically ruled was roughly comparable to, but smaller than, modern France. The territory Hugh actually controlled was a small feudal county extending from Paris to Orléans. It was almost encircled by rivers—hence, perhaps, its name: the Ile de France. The royal domain was surrounded by many independent duchies and counties, such as Flanders, Normandy, Anjou, and Champagne, which were a law unto themselves.

The early Capetians. Starting with little power and limited territory under their direct rule, the Capetian monarchs gradually extended their control over the great magnates. France was literally made by its kings, for ultimately the royal domain, in which the king's word was law, came to coincide with the boundaries of the realm.

In the late tenth and eleventh centuries, however, there was little tangible evidence that the Capetian kings would fulfill their destiny. They were weaker than many of their own vassals, and they had no hand in the stirring events of their time. While they remained historical nonentities, one of their vassals, the duke of Normandy, seized the throne of England; another, the count of Flanders, became a leader of the First Crusade and ruler of the kingdom of Jerusalem; and another vassal became the founder of the kingdom of Portugal.

The major accomplishment of the first four Capetian kings was their success in keeping the French crown within their own family. The nobles who elected Hugh Capet to the kingship had no thought of giving the Capetian family a monopoly on the royal office. But the Capetian kings, with the support of the Church, which nurtured the tradition of kingship as a sacred office, cleverly arranged for the election and coronation of their heirs. Before the king died, the young prince was crowned by the Church and became "associated" with his father in his rule. For three hundred years the House of Capet never lacked a male heir, and by the end of the twelfth century the hereditary principle had become so ingrained that French kings no longer took the precaution of crowning their sons during their own lifetime.

Louis the Fat pacifies the Ile de France. The advent of the fifth Capetian king, Louis VI (1108-1137), also known as Louis the Fat, heralded the end of Capetian weakness. Louis' pacification of the royal domain, the Ile de France, paralleled on a smaller scale the work of William the Conqueror in England.

With the support of the Church (which supplied him with able advisers), Louis determined to crush the lawless barons who were defying royal authority in the Ile de France. According to Abbot Suger, his chief adviser and biographer:

A king, when he takes the royal power, vows to put down with his strong right arm insolent tyrants whensoever he sees them vex the state with endless wars, rejoice in rapine, oppress the poor, destroy the churches, give themselves over to lawlessness which, and it be not checked, would flame out into ever greater madness. . . .[8]

In the end the castles of the defiant vassals were captured and in many cases torn down. "And this," writes Abbot Suger, "they deserved who had not feared to raise their hand against the Lord's anointed."[9] Louis had made his word law in the Ile de France, established a solid base from which royal power could be extended, and so increased the prestige of the monarchy that the great duke of Aquitaine deigned to marry his daughter Eleanor to Louis' son. Unfortunately, Eleanor's behavior so scandalized Louis' pious son ("I thought I married a king," Eleanor

FEUDAL FRANCE ABOUT 1000

Ile de France

once exclaimed, "but instead I am the wife of a monk") that he had the marriage annulled, and Aquitaine passed to Eleanor's second husband, Henry II of England.

Philip Augustus extends royal rule. The first great expansion of the royal domain was the work of the next Capetian, Philip II Augustus (1180-1223), during whose reign the French king for the first time became more powerful than any of his vassals and France replaced Germany as the strongest monarchy in continental Europe.

Philip Augustus' great ambition was to wrest from the English Plantagenets the vast territory they held in France. Philip made little headway against Henry II, except to make Henry's life wretched by encouraging

The *Très Riches Heures du Duc de Berry* is a devotional book containing prayers for each day of the year. The months are illustrated by full-page miniatures. This one, of October, depicts peasants sowing grain in fields on one bank of the Seine, while on the far bank is the Louvre as it appeared in the time of Philip II, who built the fortress as a storage place for his records and money.

his faithless sons, Richard the Lion-Hearted and John, to revolt. As we have seen, Philip took Normandy, Maine, Anjou, and Touraine from John, thereby tripling the size of the royal domain.

Philip also greatly strengthened the royal administrative system by devising new agencies for centralized government and tapping new sources of revenue, including a money payment from his vassals in lieu of military service. New salaried officials, called bailiffs, performed duties similar to those carried out in England by itinerant justices and sheriffs. A corps of loyal officials, like the bailiffs recruited not from the feudal nobility but from the ranks of the bourgeoisie, was collected around the king. As in England, special administrative departments were created: the *parlement*, a supreme court of justice (not to be confused with the English Parliament, which became primarily a legislative body); the chamber of accounts, or royal treasury; and the royal or privy council, a group of advisers who assisted the king in the conduct of the daily business of the state.

In this early phase of consolidation of royal power, the papacy, which was struggling with the German emperors, usually allied itself with the French monarchy. As in England and Germany, however, the kings sometimes collided with the popes. Philip II defied Innocent III by having French bishops annul his marriage; but when the pope imposed an interdict on France, Philip backed down, and his wife again became his queen.

On the other hand, the Church inadvertently helped expand the royal domain. In southern France, particularly in Toulouse, the heretical Albigensian sect flourished. Determined to stamp out this sect, Innocent III in 1208 called the Albigensian Crusade, discussed in Chapter 11. Philip, faced with the enmity of King John and the German emperor, did not take part, but he allowed his vassals to do so. After Philip's death his son Louis VIII led a new crusade to exterminate the remnants of Albigensian resistance. Later in the century Toulouse escheated to the French crown when its count died without heir. The royal domain now stretched from the chilly coast of the

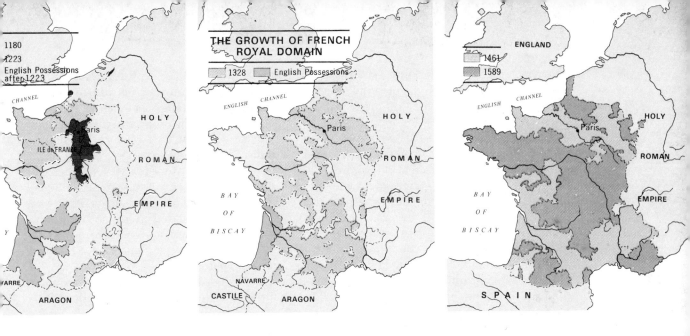

English Channel to the warm shores of the Mediterranean.

Louis IX dignifies the throne. After the brief reign of Louis VIII, France came under the rule of Louis IX (1226-1270), better known as St. Louis because of his piety and noble character. In contrast to the cunning opportunism of his grandfather, St. Louis' ideal was to rule justly, and he made some sacrifices to that end. For example, special officials were created to check on the bailiffs, who were forbidden to encroach on the feudal rights of the nobility. On the other hand, St. Louis believed himself responsible only to God, who had put him on the throne to lead his people out of a life of sin. Accordingly, St. Louis was the first French king to issue edicts for the whole kingdom without the prior consent of his council of great vassals. He also ordered an end to trial by battle and the time-honored feudal right of private warfare. Certain matters, such as treason and crimes on the highways, were declared to be the exclusive jurisdiction of the royal courts. Furthermore, St. Louis insisted on the right of appeal from the feudal courts of his vassals to the high royal court of *parlement* at Paris.

St. Louis' passion for justice impressed his contemporaries. He endeavored to hear personally his subjects' problems and complaints, and Joinville, his friend and biographer, whose *St. Louis, King of France* is a medieval masterpiece, has left us this sketch:

Many a time it happened that in summer time he would go and sit down in the wood at Vincennes, with his back to an oak, and make us take our seats around him. And all those who had complaints to make came to him without hindrance from ushers or other folk. Then he asked them with his own lips: "Is there any one here who has a cause?" Those who had a cause stood up when he would say to them: "Silence all, and you shall be dispatched [judged] one after another."[10]

Just, sympathetic, and peace-loving, St. Louis convinced his subjects that the monarchy was the most important agency for assuring their happiness and well-being.

Climax of Capetian rule under Philip IV. The reign of Philip IV, the Fair (1285-1314), climaxed three centuries of Capetian rule. The antithesis of his saintly grandfather, Philip was a man of craft, violence, and deceit. He took advantage of the growing anti-Semitism that had appeared in Europe with the crusades to expel the Jews from France and confiscate their possessions. (Philip's English contemporary, Edward I, had done the same.) Again, heavily in debt to the Knights Templars, who had turned to banking after the crusades, Philip had the order suppressed on trumped-up charges of heresy.

Philip's need of money also caused him to clash with the last great medieval pope. As we shall see in Chapter 12, Pope Boniface VIII refused to allow Philip to tax the French clergy and made sweeping claims to supremacy over secular powers. But the national state had reached the point where such leaders as Philip IV would not brook interference with their authority no matter what the source. The result of this controversy was the humiliation of Boniface, a blow from which the medieval papacy never recovered.

In domestic affairs the real importance of Philip's reign lies in the increased power and improved organization of the royal government. Philip's astute civil servants, recruited mainly from the middle class, concentrated their efforts on exalting the power of the monarch. Trained in Roman law, and inspired by its maxim that "whatever pleases the prince has the force of law," they sought to make the power of the monarch absolute.

Like Edward I in England, Philip enlarged his feudal council to include representatives of the third "estate" or class—the townsmen. This Estates-General of nobles, clergy, and burghers was used as a means of obtaining popular support for Philip's policies, including the announcement of new taxes. Significantly, Philip did not need to ask the Estates-General's consent for his tax measures, and it did not acquire the "power of the purse" that characterized the English Parliament. Philip had sown the seeds of absolutism in France, but their growth was to be interrupted by the Hundred Years' War between France and England, which broke out twenty-three years after his death (see Chapter 12).

CHRISTIAN RECONQUESTS IN SPAIN

The Reconquista. The unification of Spain was a more complex process than that of either France or England. The customary rivalry between the feudal aristocracy and the royal authority was complicated by another significant element—a religious crusade. Unification required the ejection of the Muslims, with their alien religion and civilization. Unity also called for the integration of several distinct Christian states.

In Chapter 9 we noted the beginning of the *Reconquista*, or reconquest of Spain, up to the year 1085, when the Muslim strong-hold of Toledo was captured. During this long struggle a mounting patriotism blended with a fanatical religious spirit. As early as the ninth century northern Spain became suffused with a religious zeal centering around Santiago de Compostela, reputed to be the burial site of the apostle St. James. His bones were enshrined in a great cathedral which thousands of pilgrims visited. Banners were consecrated there, and the battle cry of the Christian soldiers became "Santiago" (a contraction of *Sante Iago*, St. James' name in Spanish).

The Poem of My Cid. Another symbol of national awakening was an eleventh-century soldier of fortune, El Cid (Arabic for "lord"). His exploits against the Muslims thrilled Europe, and he became the hero of the great Spanish epic, *Poema de Mio Cid*. In the epic El Cid appears as a perfect Christian knight, although in reality he was an adventurer seemingly more interested in booty and power than in religion. The following characteristic lines begin with a reference to a victory over the Moors near Valencia:

His fame goes re-echoing even beyond the sea;
My Cid rejoiced, and all his company,
because God had given him aid and he had routed
   them there.
He sent out raiders, all night they rode; . . .
They destroyed the lands of the Moors as far as
   the seashore. . . .
Seizing and despoiling, riding at night,
sleeping in the daytime, taking those towns,
My Cid spent three years in the lands of the
   Moors. . . .
He sent forth a herald to Aragón and Navarre;
he sent his messages to the lands of Castile:
"Whoever would leave his toil and grow rich,
let him come to My Cid, whose taste is for battle.
He would now lay siege to Valencia to give it to
   the Christians."[11]

In 1212, at Las Navas de Tolosa, the Christians achieved one of the decisive victories of the Middle Ages. A few years later they captured first Cordova, whose great mosque was reconsecrated as a cathedral (see illustration, p. 208), and then Seville. By the end of the thirteenth century, when the reconquest halted until the latter part of the fifteenth century, Moorish political control was confined to Granada.

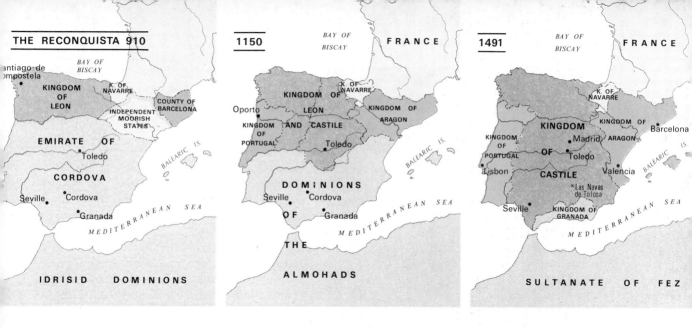

THE RECONQUISTA 910 / 1150 / 1491

It was usual for the Christian victors to allow their new Muslim subjects to enjoy their own religion and traditions. Muslim traders and artisans were protected because of their economic value, and Muslim culture—art in particular—was often adapted by the Christians.

FAILURES OF THE NATIONAL STATE: GERMANY AND ITALY

German tribal duchies. Following the collapse of the Carolingian empire, the tribal consciousness of its people kept Germany from falling into the extreme political fragmentation that characterized feudal France. When the successors of Louis the German, who received East Frankland in the Treaty of Verdun in 843 (see p. 194), proved incapable of coping with the attacks of savage Magyar horsemen in the late ninth and early tenth centuries, the task was taken over by the tribal leaders of the Saxons, Bavarians, Swabians, and Franconians who assumed the title of duke. The dukes of the five German duchies —including Lorraine, which Louis the German had acquired on the breakup of Lothair's middle kingdom—usurped the royal power and crown lands in their duchies and also took control over the Church.

When the last Carolingian, Louis the Child, died in 911, the dukes elected the weakest among them, Conrad of Franconia, to be their king. The new monarch ruled just eight years and proved himself incapable of meeting the menace of the Magyar raids. On his deathbed he recommended that the most powerful of the dukes, Henry the Fowler, duke of Saxony, be chosen as his successor. Henry founded the illustrious Saxon dynasty, which ruled until 1024 and made Germany the most powerful state in western Europe.

Henry the Fowler. After some initial opposition, Henry I (919-936) obtained recognition of his kingship from the other dukes. He exercised little authority outside of his own duchy, however, and his kingdom was hardly more than a confederation of independent duchies.

Against Germany's border enemies, Henry was more successful. He pushed back the Danes and established the Dane Mark as a protective buffer. Inroads were also made against the Slavs across the Elbe, where in 928 Brandenburg was set up as another defensive mark. Thus began the *Drang nach Osten* ("push to the East"), which became a permanent feature of German history. Further to the southeast, in Bohemia, Henry forced the Slavic Czechs to recognize his overlordship.

More spectacular was Henry's great victory over the Magyars in 933, following his refusal to pay the annual tribute demanded by these marauders. By this victory Henry

The crown of Otto I, probably made for his coronation in Rome, consists of eight gold plaques held together by hinges which open or close by means of pearl-headed pins. The crown was constructed in this portable fashion because Otto traveled a good deal and needed to have his crown with him for state occasions in various countries. Four of the plaques consist of pearls and gems held together by gold filigree. The other four plaques contain enamel panels showing God, David, Hezekiah with Isaiah, and (in the plaque visible here) Solomon. The upper part of the crown is an eleventh-century addition.

earned the gratitude of the German people, and when he died no one disputed the election of his son Otto to succeed him.

Otto the Great. Realizing that the great hindrance to German unity was the truculence of the dukes, Otto I, the Great (936-973), initiated a policy of gaining control of the unruly duchies by setting up his own relatives and favorites as their rulers. As an extra precaution he appointed, as supervising officials, counts who were directly responsible to the king. This policy was only temporarily successful, however, for both the counts and Otto's relatives and favorites proved unreliable. Even Otto's son, who was made duke of Swabia, rebelled against his father.

In the long run it was by means of an alliance with the Church that Otto constructed a strong German monarchy. The king protected the bishops and abbots and granted them a free hand over their vast estates; in return the church prelates furnished him with the officials, the income, and the troops that he lacked. Otto appointed the bishops and abbots, and since their offices were not hereditary, he could be sure that their first obedience was to his royal person. These prelates replaced the counts as the chief agents of the king in the duchies and furnished as much as three quarters of his military forces.

This alliance of crown and Church was a natural one at the time. At his coronation at Aachen, Otto had insisted on being anointed *rex et sacerdos* ("king and priest"), thus reviving the Carolingian concept of the theocratic ruler and the alliance between crown and Church. Furthermore, both partners feared the unruly and arrogant dukes whose usurpations included the right to appoint bishops and abbots in their duchies.

Otto also put an end to the Magyar menace, thereby enhancing his claim that the king, and not the dukes, was the true defender of the German people. In 955 Otto crushed the Magyars at Lechfeld, near Augsburg (see map, p. 235), another decisive battle of the Middle Ages. The people of the time compared Lechfeld to the battle of Tours; and Otto the Great, like Charles Martel, was hailed as the savior of Europe. The remaining Magyars settled quietly in Hungary, and by the year 1000 they had accepted Christianity.

The eastward movement. Otto continued German expansion eastward against the Slavs, and the region between the Elbe and the Oder became more and more Germanized. Like Charlemagne earlier, Otto relied on the Church to Christianize the stubborn heathens, and Magdeburg and other bishoprics were established in the conquered lands.

This expansion has been called the greatest achievement of the medieval Germans. Had it not been for this move eastward, modern Germany would have been a narrow strip of land wedged in between the Rhine and the Elbe; it has been estimated that 60 percent of German territory before the First World War had been taken from the Slavs. On the other hand, because the borders between the German colonists and the Slav natives were never clearly defined, pockets of Slavs and Germans intermingled. This ethnic admixture has caused serious disputes and conflicts in modern times.

The German empire. Like so many men of the Middle Ages, Otto the Great tended to revere the past, and he regarded the Roman and Carolingian empires as golden ages. As one historian succinctly put it: "His objective was Empire, and his model was Charlemagne." This pursuit of an empire characterized the German monarchy until the middle of the thirteenth century and was a major factor in its collapse.

Italy in the tenth century, having split into warring fragments, was a tempting field for an invader. In the north the old Lombard realm, which had been a part of Lothair's middle kingdom, became the object of various rival contenders. In central Italy were the Papal States, ruled by the pope. During this century, however, the popes were appointed and controlled by the Roman nobility, and the power and prestige of the papacy was at its lowest ebb. Further south were two Lombard duchies; and, finally, at the extreme tip of the peninsula, the Byzantine empire retained a shaky foothold on the Italian mainland. Dotted here and there were cities, such as Venice, which had never become completely depopulated.

In deciding to invade Italy, Otto the Great was initially motived by defense. The dukes of the south German duchies of Swabia and Bavaria were hopeful of seizing Burgundy and Lombardy, and Otto believed that his position as German king would be endangered if those large remnants of Lothair's old middle kingdom fell into the hands of his German rivals. He first placed Burgundy and its weak ruler under his "'protection." Then he turned to Italy, where not only politics but, as chivalrous contemporary accounts explained it, romance also beckoned. Queen Adelaide, the widow of the former king of Lombardy, had been imprisoned by a usurper. Her plight suited Otto's political ambitions. In 951 he crossed the Alps, met Adelaide, who had escaped, and married her. He then dethroned her captor and proclaimed himself king of Italy.

On his second expedition to Italy in 962, Otto was crowned emperor by the pope, whose Papal States were threatened by an Italian duke. No doubt Otto thought of himself as the successor of the imperial Caesars and Charlemagne; and, in fact, his empire later became known as the Holy Roman Empire. But Otto also needed the imperial title to legitimatize his claim to Lombardy, Burgundy, and Lorraine, which had belonged to the middle kingdom of Lothair, the last man to hold the imperial title. Otto's coronation was a momentous event that brought Italy and Germany, pope and emperor, into a forced and unnatural union.

The distracting, even malevolent, effect of the German pursuit of empire in Italy is demonstrated by the reign of Otto III (983-1002), who eagerly promoted his grandiose scheme for "the renewal of the Roman Empire." Ignoring Germany, the real source of his power, he made Rome his capital, built a palace there, and styled himself "emperor of

GERMANY ABOUT 1000

☐ Holy Roman Empire

the Romans." As the "servant of Jesus Christ," another of his titles, Otto installed non-Italian popes in Rome and conceived of the papacy as a partner in ruling an empire of Germans, Italians, and Slavs. But notwithstanding Otto's love for Italy, the fickle Roman populace revolted and forced him to flee the city. He died a year later while preparing to besiege Rome.

Despite the distractions in Italy, the Saxon rulers were the most powerful in Europe. They had permanently halted Magyar pillaging and, by utilizing the German Church as an ally, had curbed the divisive tendencies toward feudalism. Economically, too, there was progress. German eastward expansion had begun, and the Alpine passes had been freed of Muslim raiders and made safe for the Italian merchants who by the year 1000 were ready to act as middlemen linking western Europe with the eastern Mediterranean.

The Salian emperors vs. the papacy. Pioneers in nation-making, the Saxon kings were succeeded by a new royal line, the Salian House (1024-1125), whose members set about with increased vigor to establish a centralized monarchy. To the dismay of many nobles, a body of lowborn royal officials was recruited; and the power of the dukes was weakened further when the crown won the allegiance of the lesser nobles.

The reign of Henry IV (1056-1125) was a watershed in German history. The monarchy reached the height of its power, but it also experienced a major reversal. For a century the Ottonian system, by which the king had governed his kingdom through the clergy, whom he appointed, had functioned smoothly. Under Henry IV, however, the revival of a powerful papacy led to a bitter conflict, centering on the king's right to appoint Church officials who were at the same time his most loyal supporters. This conflict, known as the Investiture Struggle (see p. 244), resulted in the loss of the monarchy's major sources of strength: the loyalty of the German Church, now transferred to the papacy; and the chief material base of royal power, the king's lands, which were dissipated by grants to loyal nobles.

The real victors in the Investiture Struggle were the German nobles, many of whom allied themselves with the papacy and continued to wage war against the monarchy long after the reign of Henry IV. From the time of Henry's death in 1106 until the accession of Frederick Barbarossa in 1152, the Welfs of Bavaria and the Hohenstaufens of Swabia, along with other noble factions, fought over the throne, which they made elective rather than hereditary. The outcome was that the structure of a strong national state was wrecked and Germany became extensively feudalized. The great nobles usurped royal rights, built strong castles, and forced lesser nobles to become their vassals. On the other hand, the great nobles acknowledged no feudal relationship to the king. Many free peasants, in turn, lost their freedom and became serfs. The evil effects of this period were to hinder the development of a unified Germany until modern times.

Prosperity in divided Italy. Italy was even less unified than Germany. Jealous of one another and of their independence, the prosperous city-states in northern Italy joined the struggle between the German emperors and the papacy. The Welf-Hohenstaufen rivalry in Germany was reflected in Italy, where the rival factions were known as Guelphs and Ghibellines—the latter name derived from Waiblingen, the chief Hohenstaufen stronghold in Swabia. The former were usually pro-papal; the latter strongly favored the German monarchy's imperial claims in Italy. Yet, amidst the turmoil, the vitality, wealth, and culture of the northern Italian cities increased.

A brilliant civilization also flourished on the island of Sicily. By 1127 the Norman conquests (see p. 207) resulted in the establishment of the kingdom of Naples and Sicily which, under the able rule of Roger II (1130-1154), became one of the strongest and wealthiest states in Europe. Scholars from all over the East and Europe traveled to Roger's court, which ranked next to Spain's in the translation of Arabic documents. Life and culture in the Sicilian kingdom, which included Norman, Byzantine, Italian, and Arabic elements, was diverse and colorful. In the thirteenth century the history of Naples and Sicily became fatally entwined with the history of the German empire and hinged on the rise and fall of the powerful royal house of Hohenstaufen.

Frederick Barbarossa. The second Hohenstaufen emperor, Frederick I Barbarossa ("Red-beard"), who reigned from 1152 to 1190, realistically accepted the fact that during the preceding half century Germany had become thoroughly feudalized; his goal was to make himself the apex of the feudal pyramid by forcing the great nobles to acknowledge his overlordship. Using force when necessary, he was largely successful, and Germany became a centralized feudal monarchy not unlike England in the days of William the Conqueror.

To maintain his hold over his German tenants-in-chief, Frederick needed the resources of Italy—particularly the income from taxes levied on wealthy north Italian cities, which, encouraged by the papacy, joined together in the Lombard League to resist him. Frederick spent about twenty-five years fighting intermittently in Italy, but although some of the cities submitted to his authority, the final result was failure. The opposition from the popes and the Lombard League was too strong. Frederick did score a diplomatic triumph, however, by marrying his son to the heiress of the throne of Naples and Sicily. The threat of Hohenstaufen encirclement made it vital to the papacy that this royal house be destroyed.

Frederick Barbarossa died in Asia Minor while en route with the Third Crusade, and in time he became a folk hero in Germany. It was believed that he still lived, asleep in a cave in the mountains near Berchtesgaden in Bavaria. Some day, awakened by a flight of ravens, he would emerge and bring unity and strength back to Germany. "In the late nineteenth century, the artists of the Prussian court delighted to paint pictures of his last, and joyful, awakening in 1871, when the sky was full of ravens since a second German Empire had been called into existence. Statues of Frederick Barbarossa and Kaiser Wilhelm I were placed side by side to symbolize the 'fact' that where one had left off, the other had begun."[12]

Frederick II, a brilliant failure. It fell to the lot of Frederick Barbarossa's grandson,

The proud and handsome Frederick Barbarossa, to whom is credited the title "Holy Roman Empire" for the lands he claimed in Germany and Italy, sought to centralize royal power in his empire. He is remembered as one of Germany's great national heroes.

Frederick II (1194-1250), to meet the pope's challenge to the threat of Hohenstaufen encirclement. Orphaned at an early age, Frederick was brought up as the ward of the most powerful medieval pope, Innocent III. During Frederick's minority the empire fell on evil days; the Welf and Hohenstaufen factions resumed their struggle over the throne, and the strong feudal monarchy created by Frederick Barbarossa collapsed. In 1215, one year before Innocent died and with his support, Frederick was elected emperor. Faced by a resurgent nobility in Germany, he soon turned his attention to wealthy Italy.

The papacy and the north Italian cities successfully defied Frederick throughout his reign, and in the end he experienced the same failure as had Frederick Barbarossa. Frederick also clashed with the papacy in another sphere. Embarking on a crusade at the pope's insistence, he turned back because of illness and was promptly excommunicated. A few months later Frederick resumed his crusade and was again excommunicated, this time for crusading while excommunicated. When Frederick acquired Jerusalem by negotiation (see p. 211) and agreed to allow Muslims to worship freely in the city, the pope called him "this scorpion spewing poison from the sting of its tail" and excommunicated him a third time.

Frederick sacrificed Germany in his efforts to unite all Italy under his rule. He transferred crown lands and royal rights to the German princes in order to keep them quiet and to win their support for his inconclusive Italian wars. Born in Sicily, he remained at heart a Mediterranean monarch. He shaped his kingdom of Sicily into a modern state. Administered by paid officials who were trained at the University of Naples, which he founded for that purpose, his kingdom was the most centralized and bureaucratic in Europe. Economically, too, it was far in advance of other states; Frederick minted a uniform currency and abolished interior tolls and tariffs, and his powerful fleet promoted and protected commerce.

As long as he lived, this brilliant Hohenstaufen held his empire together, but it quickly collapsed after his death in 1250. In Germany his son ruled ineffectively for four years before dying, and soon afterward Frederick's descendants in Sicily were killed when the count of Anjou, brother of St. Louis of France, was invited by the pope to annihilate what remained of the "viper breed of the Hohenstaufen."

Significance of the fall of the Hohenstaufens. The victory of the papacy was more apparent than real, for its struggle against the emperors lost it much of its prestige. Men had seen popes using spiritual means to achieve earthly ambitions—preaching a crusade against Frederick II and his descendants, for example. More and more, popes acted like Italian princes, playing the game of diplomacy amid shifting rivalries. This involvement in worldly concerns and the accompanying decay in ideals helps explain the revolt against papal authority—one of the themes of Chapter 14.

Italy might have found the nucleus of a centralized government in the kingdom of Naples and Sicily. However, the count of Anjou's seizure of the kingdom initiated a long period of bitter rivalry between Spaniards of the House of Aragon, who had married into the Hohenstaufen family, and Frenchmen representing Anjou. Beset by this interference, southern Italy and Sicily precipi-

tously declined amid alien rule, corruption, and, at times, horrible cruelty.

The Holy Roman Empire never again achieved the brilliance it last enjoyed during the reign of Frederick Barbarossa. The emperors usually did not try to interfere in Italian affairs, and they ceased going to Rome to receive the imperial crown from the pope. In German affairs the emperors no longer even attempted to assert their authority over the increasingly powerful nobles. After the fall of the Hohenstaufens, Germany lapsed more and more into the political disunity and ineffectual elective monarchy that remained characteristic of its history until the late nineteenth century.

SUMMARY

During the period from 1050 to 1300, England and France arose as pioneers in national unification and centralization. The essential pattern of historical development was similar in both nations, although each had its distinctive problems. (1) At first the kings were faced with serious competitors to their royal authority, the feudal nobility and the Church; (2) the kings became more powerful than their competitors, first by strengthening their power within the context of the feudal system, then by gradually establishing some of the military, judicial, and administrative agencies of a modern state; (3) the kings in effect made alliances with the rising middle class in the cities against their common enemy, the nobility. From the middle class came most of the money that the king needed to maintain a professional civil service, including a standing army that gradually replaced the often unreliable feudal levies.

In England William the Conqueror secured a unified kingdom in 1066 as a result of the Conquest, and successive English kings managed to keep their competitors under control and build up the machinery of royal administration. English development is also noteworthy for its legal and constitutional achievements: the common law, the jury system, circuit judges, and the first steps in the creation of representative government through Parliament.

In France the movement toward the consolidation of royal power started from a small area—the minuscule Ile de France. Each of the many counties and duchies that constituted feudal France had to be subordinated and brought within the framework of royal authority. It took the French kings three centuries to accomplish what William the Conqueror had done in one generation.

Nation-making in Spain was unique, since it was suffused with the religious fervor of a crusade. In the mid-eleventh century the Christian Spanish states began the *Recon-*

quista in earnest, but not until the end of the fifteenth century would the task be completed.

Although they had initial success in building a strong state at home, the German kings dissipated their energies by seeking the prize of empire over the Alps. For hundreds of years German rulers pursued this imperial phantom in Italy. In the face of resistance from the Italian cities, the treachery of the German nobles, and the opposition of the papacy, the German kings failed to achieve their goal. In both Germany and Italy after 1250, disunity and weakness prevailed; national unification was delayed until the nineteenth century.

SUGGESTIONS FOR READING

F. Heer, **The Medieval World: Europe, 1100-1350,** * Mentor; S. Painter, **The Rise of the Feudal Monarchies,** * Cornell. Excellent syntheses. See also C. Brooke, **Europe in the Central Middle Ages, 962-1154,** * Holt, Rinehart and Winston; C. Previté-Orton, **A History of Europe from 1198 to 1378,** 3rd ed., Barnes and Noble, 1951.

H. Cam, **England before Elizabeth,** * Torchbooks; G. Sayles, **The Medieval Foundations of England,** * Perpetua; C. Brooke, **From Alfred to Henry III, 871-1272,** * Norton. Valuable surveys of English history during the period covered in this chapter.

F. Stenton, **Anglo-Saxon England,** 2nd ed., Oxford, 1947. The standard account. See also D. Kirby, **The Making of Early England,** Schocken, 1968.

R. Allen Brown, **The Normans and the Norman Conquest,** Crowell, 1969; H. Loyn, **The Norman Conquest,** * Torchbooks; D. Whitelock **et al., The Norman Conquest: Its Setting and Impact,** Scribner, 1966; D. Matthew, **The Norman Conquest,** Schocken, 1966. Recent outstanding treatments. H. Muntz, **The Golden Warrior,** * Scribner, is a first-rate novel dealing with the Norman conquest.

Works on English leaders of the period include E. Duckett, **Alfred the Great: The King and His England,** * Phoenix; Amy Kelly, **Eleanor of Aquitaine and the Four Kings,** * Vintage; S. Painter, **The Reign of King John,** * Johns Hopkins; K. Norgate, **Richard Lion Heart,** Macmillan, 1924; R. Winston, **Thomas Becket,** Knopf, 1967; Thomas M. Jones, ed., **The Becket Controversy,** * Wiley, 1970; L. Salzman, **Edward I,** Praeger, 1968.

On English constitutional history see J. C. Holt, **Magna Carta,** * Cambridge; G. L. Haskins, **The Growth of English Representative Government,** * Perpetua; B. Lyon, **A Constitutional and Legal History of Medieval England,** Harper & Row, 1960; A. Pollard, **The Evolution of Parliament,** 2nd ed., Russell, 1964.

R. Fawtier, **The Capetian Kings of France, 987-1328,** * St. Martin. The best account. See also C. Petit-Dutaillis, **The Feudal Monarchy in France and England: From the Tenth to the Thirteenth Centuries,** * Torchbooks. Z. Oldenbourg, **The World Is Not Enough,** * Ballantine, is an historical novel set in twelfth-century France.

R. Merriman, **The Rise of the Spanish Empire in the Old World and in the New,** Vol. 1, Macmillan, 1918. The standard work on medieval Spain. See also R. Menendez Pidal, **The Cid and His Spain,** Murray, 1934.

J. Bryce, **The Holy Roman Empire,** * Schocken. An old masterpiece; should be supplemented by G. Barraclough, **The Origins of Modern Germany,** * Capricorn, and F. Heer, **The Holy Roman Empire,** * Schocken. See also the diverse scholarly opinions presented in R. Herzstein, ed., **The Holy Roman Empire in the Middle Ages: Universal State or German Catastrophe?,** * Heath. P. Munz, **Frederick Barbarossa: A Study in Medieval Politics,** Cornell, 1969, and E. Kantorowicz, **Frederick the Second,** Ungar, 1957, are instructive biographies.

William F. Butler, **The Lombard Communes: A History of the Republics of North Italy,** Haskell, 1969. Reprint of a standard work. L. Salvatorelli, **A Concise History of Italy,** Oxford, 1939, is a good general survey.

*Indicates an inexpensive paperbound edition.

Chapter 11

To the Glory of God

Faith, Thought, and Art in Medieval Europe

INTRODUCTION. In Paris, on a small island in the Seine, stands an edifice of weather-beaten stone, the Cathedral of Notre Dame. Dedicated to the glory of God and the veneration of Our Lady, this cathedral offers a fascinating glimpse into the life and spirit of medieval Europe. Notre Dame de Paris was built by cooperative community action between 1163 and 1235, during some of the most epoch-making years of the Middle Ages. While workmen were supporting the cathedral's vault with flying buttresses and carefully fitting the multicolored windows into place, churchmen and students lolled on the Petit Pont, a bridge that led to the Left Bank. The students wrangled over theology, accused one another of heresy, and occasionally composed blasphemous poems that parodied the sacred liturgy. Some of these students were one day to occupy episcopal thrones as princes of the Church; one of the mightiest occupants of the papal throne, Innocent III, once studied in Paris.

The underlying difference between our medieval ancestors and ourselves would appear to be one of perspective. To them theology was the "science of sciences," whereas today there are those who say that we have made science our theology. Yet this difference is not due exclusively to the extension of knowledge during the intervening centuries. It also lies in the fundamental premise governing the lives of our medieval forefathers. They believed in a world order, divinely created and maintained. For them, the universe possessed an inner coherence and harmony, which it was the function of the theologian and the scientist alike to discover. Revelation and knowledge, faith and reason, Church and state, spirit and matter—these dualities could be reconciled in a great spiritual and social synthesis.

In this chapter we will examine the methods by which medieval men sought to realize this synthesis and the measure of their success. As a first step, we shall trace the institutional growth of the one universal organization of medieval Europe, the Church. Next we shall watch its progressive assumption of secular powers, culminating in the triumphs of Innocent III. Finally, we shall see how, under the sponsorship of the Church, scholars and philosophers, scientists and inventors, and artists and artisans labored for the glory of God and the salvation of man.

THE CHURCH IN THE EARLY MIDDLE AGES

Gregory the Great and the early medieval papacy (600-1050). While Europe gradually recovered from the shock of the Roman Empire's demise, the Church—the papacy and Benedictine monasticism in particular—became the mainstay of European civilization. During the pontificate of Gregory I, the Great (590-604), the medieval papacy began to take form. Gregory's achievement was to go beyond the claim of papal primacy in the Church (see p. 128) to establish the actual machinery of papal rule, temporal as well as spiritual.

A Roman aristocrat by birth, Gregory witnessed and commented on the devastation of Rome as the city changed hands three times during Justinian's long struggle to retake Italy from the Ostrogoths:

Ruins on ruins. . . . Where is the senate? Where the people? All the pomp of secular dignities has been destroyed. . . . And we, the few that we are who remain, every day we are menaced by scourges and innumerable trials.[1]

Concluding that the world was coming to an end, Gregory withdrew from it to become a Benedictine monk. In 579 the pope drafted him to undertake a fruitless mission seeking Byzantine aid against the Lombards, who had invaded Italy a few years before. After the people of Rome elected Gregory pope in 590, he assumed the task of protecting Rome and its surrounding territory from the Lombard threat. Thus Gregory was the first pope to act as temporal ruler of a part of what later became the Papal States.

Gregory the Great also laid the foundations for the later elaborate papal machinery of Church government. He took the first step toward papal control of the Church outside of Italy by sending a mission of Benedictine monks to convert the heathen Anglo-Saxons. The pattern of Church government Gregory established in England—bishops supervised by archbishops, and archbishops by the pope—became standard in the Church.

The task of establishing papal control of the Church and extending the pope's temporal authority was continued by Gregory the Great's successors. In the eighth century English missionaries transferred to Germany and France the pattern of papal government they had known in England; and the Donation of Pepin (see p. 190), by creating the Papal States, greatly increased the pope's temporal power. The papacy's spiritual and temporal power suffered a severe setback, however, with the onset of feudalism. Beginning in the late ninth century, the Church, including the papacy, fell more and more under the control of feudal lords and kings.

Missionary activity of the Church. The early Middle Ages was also a vital period of missionary activity. By disseminating Christianity, the missionaries aided in the fusion of Germanic and classical cultures. Monasteries served as havens for those seeking a contemplative life, as repositories of learning for scholars, and often as progressive farming centers.

One of the earliest Christian missionaries to the Germans was Ulfilas (c. 311-383), who spent forty years among the Visigoths and translated most of the Bible into Gothic. Ulfilas and other early missionaries were followers of Arius, and thus the heretical creed of Arianism (see p. 128) came to be adopted by all the Germanic tribes in the empire except the Franks and Anglo-Saxons. As we saw in Chapter 8, the Franks' adoption of official Roman Catholic doctrines as espoused by the pope had momentous consequences for European statecraft.

Another great missionary, St. Patrick, was born in Britain about 389 and later fled to Ireland to escape the Anglo-Saxon invaders. As a result of his Irish missionary activities, monasteries were founded and Christianity became dominant. From these monasteries in the late sixth and seventh centuries a stream of monks went to Scotland, northern England, the kingdom of the Franks, and even to Italy. The Irish monks eagerly pursued scholarship, and their monasteries were repositories for priceless manuscripts.

Beginning with the pontificate of Gregory the Great, the papacy joined forces with Benedictine monasticism to become very active in the missionary movement. Gregory, as we saw, sent a Benedictine mission to England in 596. Starting in Kent, where an archbishopric was founded at Canterbury ("Kent town"), Roman Christianity spread through England, and finally even the Irish Church founded by St. Patrick acknowledged the primacy of Rome.

The English Church in turn played an important part in the expansion of Roman-controlled Christianity on the Continent. St. Boniface, the greatest missionary from England in the eighth century, spent thirty-five years among the Germanic tribes. Known as the "Apostle to the Germans," he established several important monasteries, bishoprics, and an archbishopric at Mainz before he turned to the task of reforming the Church in France. There he revitalized the monasteries, organized a system of local parishes to bring Christianity to the countryside, and probably was instrumental in forming the alliance between the papacy and the Carolingian house. Roman Catholic missionaries also worked among the Scandinavians and the Western Slavs.

The monks as custodians of knowledge. One of the great contributions of the monasteries was the preservation of learning. Writing in the sixth century, Bishop Gregory of Tours lamented:

A monk copies a manuscript in the *scriptorium,* surrounded by other manuscripts and such tools of his trade as inkpots, pens, and brushes.

In these times . . . there has been found no scholar trained in the art of ordered composition to present in prose or verse a picture of the things that have befallen.[2]

Learning did not entirely die out in western Europe, of course. Seeing that the ability to read Greek was fast disappearing, the sixth-century Roman scholar Boethius, an administrator under the Ostrogothic king Theodoric, determined to preserve Greek learning by translating all of Plato and Aristotle into Latin. Only Aristotle's treatises on logic were translated, and these remained the sole works of that philosopher available in the West until the twelfth century. Unjustly accused of treachery by Theodoric, Boethius was thrown into prison, where he wrote *The Consolation of Philosophy* while awaiting execution. This little classic later became a medieval textbook on philosophy.

Cassiodorus, a contemporary of Boethius who had also served Theodoric, devoted most of his life to the collection and preservation of classical knowledge. By encouraging the monks to copy valuable manuscripts, he was instrumental in making the monasteries centers of learning. Following his example, many monasteries established scriptoria, departments concerned exclusively with copying manuscripts.

During the early Middle Ages most education took place in the monasteries. In the late sixth and seventh centuries, when the effects of the barbarian invasions were still being felt on the Continent, Irish monasteries provided a safe haven for learning. There men studied Greek and Latin, copied and preserved manuscripts, and in illuminating them produced masterpieces of art. *The Book of Kells* is a surviving example of their skill.

The outstanding scholar of the early Middle Ages, the Venerable Bede (d. 735), followed the Irish tradition of learning in a northern England monastery. Bede described himself as "ever taking delight in learning, teaching, and writing." His many writings, which included textbooks and commentaries on the Scriptures, summed up most knowledge available in his age. Through Alcuin later in the century, Bede's learning influenced the Carolingian Renaissance (see p. 192). Bede's best known work, the *Ecclesiastical History of the English People*, with its many original documents and vivid character sketches, is our chief source for early English history.

THE CHURCH MILITANT

The Church-state rivalry. In the last quarter of the eleventh century a resurgent and militant papacy entered into a bitter and prolonged struggle with what was then Europe's strongest state, the German or Holy Roman Empire. By 1200 the papacy had emerged triumphant; under Pope Innocent III, the most powerful man ever to sit on St. Peter's chair, the theory and the practice of papal power coincided.

Medieval political theory begins with the concept of a universal community divided into two spheres, the spiritual and the temporal—a view based upon Christ's injunction to "Render therefore to Caesar the things that are Caesar's, and to God the things that are God's" (Matthew 22:21). As Pope Gelasius I declared in the fifth century, God had entrusted spiritual and temporal powers to two authorities—the Church and the state—each supreme in its own sphere. At first the question of ultimate superority between these authorities did not arise, although Gelasius had implied that the Church was superior to the state in the same way that the soul was superior to the body. The issue could not be permanently shelved, however; a fight for supremacy was in the long run inevitable.

When the German king Otto the Great revived the Roman empire in the West in 962 (see p. 235), his act reemphasized the concept of the dual leadership of pope and emperor. Otto claimed to be the successor of Augustus, Constantine, and Charlemagne, although his actual power was confined to Germany and Italy. At first the papacy looked to the German king for protection against the unruly Italian nobles who for a century had been making a prize of the papacy. From the Church's viewpoint, however, this ar-

During the fourteenth century the Church-state struggle produced a great amount of rival political theory, with the Church making much use of symbolism and allegory. In this illumination Christ hands the sword of temporal power to a worldly king, while St. Peter, as pope, receives the key to heaven, symbol of spiritual power. Christ's gaze is fixed on St. Peter, thus indicating that the Church was more important than the state.

rangement had its drawbacks, for the German kings continued to interfere in ecclesiastical affairs—even in the election of popes.

During the eleventh century the controversy between Church and state centered on the problem of lay investiture. Theoretically, on assuming office a bishop or abbot was subject to two investitures; his spiritual authority was bestowed by an ecclesiastical official and his feudal or civil authority by the king or a noble. In actual fact, however, feudal lords and kings came to control both the appointment and the installation of church prelates. As noted earlier (p. 234), this practice was most pronounced in Germany, where control of the Church was the foundation of the king's power. The German Church was in essence a state Church.

The Cluniac reform. A religious revival—often called the medieval reformation—began in the tenth century and reached full force in the twelfth and thirteenth. The first far-reaching force of the revival was the reformed Benedictine order of Cluny, founded in 910. From the original monastery in Burgundy, there radiated a powerful impulse for the reform of the feudalized Church. The Cluniac program began as a movement for monastic reform, but in time it called for the enforcement of clerical celibacy and the abolition of simony, the purchase or sale of a Church office. (The term *simony* comes from Simon the magician, who tried to buy the gift of the Holy Spirit from the apostles.) The ultimate goal of the Cluniac reformers was to free the entire Church from secular control and subject it to papal authority. Some three hundred Cluniac houses were freed from lay control, and in 1059 the papacy itself was removed from secular interference by the creation of the College of Cardinals, which henceforth elected the popes.

Gregory VII. The most ambitious proponent of Church reform was Pope Gregory VII (1073-1085), who claimed unprecedented power for the papacy. Gregory held as his ideal the creation of a Christian commonwealth under papal control. Instead of conceding equality between the Church and the state, he drew from the Gelasian theory the conclusion that the spiritual power was supreme over the temporal. In the *Dictatus Papae* ("Dictate of the Pope") Gregory claimed:

That the Roman pontiff alone can with right be called universal.
That he alone may use the imperial insignia.
That of the pope alone all princes shall kiss the feet.
That it may be permitted to him to depose emperors.
That he himself may be judged by no one.
That he who is not at peace with the Roman Church shall not be considered catholic.
That he may absolve subjects from their fealty to wicked men.[3]

The Investiture Struggle. In 1075 Gregory VII formally prohibited lay investiture and threatened to excommunicate any layman who performed it and any ecclesiastic who submitted to it. This drastic act virtually declared war against Europe's rulers, since most of them practiced lay investiture. The climax to the struggle occurred in Gregory's clash with the emperor Henry IV. The latter was accused of simony and lay investiture in appointing his own choice to the archbishopric of Milan and was summoned to Rome to explain his conduct. Henry's answer was to convene in 1076 a synod of German bishops which declared Gregory a usurper and unfit to occupy the Roman See:

Wherefore henceforth we renounce, now and for the future, all obedience unto thee—which indeed we never promised to thee. And since, as thou didst publicly proclaim, none of us has been to thee a bishop, so thou henceforth wilt be Pope to none of us.[4]

In retaliation Gregory excommunicated Henry and deposed him, absolving his subjects from their oaths of allegiance.

At last, driven to make peace with the pontiff by a revolt among the German nobles, Henry appeared before Gregory in January 1077 at Canossa, a castle in the Apennines. Garbed as a penitent, the emperor is said to have stood barefoot in the snow for three days and begged forgiveness until, in Gregory's words: "We loosed the chain of the anathema and at length received him into the favor of communion and into the lap of the Holy Mother Church."[5]

This dramatic humiliation of the emperor did not resolve the quarrel, nor do contemporary accounts attach much significance to the incident—public penance was not uncommon in those days even for kings. Yet the pope had made progress toward freeing the Church from interference by laymen and toward increasing the power and prestige of the papacy. The problem of lay investiture was settled in 1122 by the compromise known as the Concordat of Worms. The Church maintained the right to elect the holder of an ecclesiastical office, but only in the presence of the king or his representative. The candidate, such as a bishop, was invested by the king with the scepter, the symbol of his administrative jurisdiction, after which he performed the act of homage and swore allegiance as the king's vassal. Only after this ceremony had taken place was the candidate consecrated by the archbishop, who invested him with his spiritual functions, as symbolized by the ring and pastoral staff. Since the kings of England and France

had earlier accepted this compromise, the problem of lay investiture waned.

The struggle between Church and empire continued for another century, sparked by the papacy's resentment at the emperors' continued interference in Italian affairs. We have already seen (p. 237) how the prosperous cities of northern Italy formed the Lombard League, defeated Frederick Barbarossa, and achieved the pope's aim of keeping the emperor out of Italy.

THE CHURCH TRIUMPHANT

The papacy's zenith: Innocent III. Aided by the success of the papal-proclaimed First Crusade, the papacy emerged in the twelfth century as potentially the most powerful office in Europe—a papal monarchy. In the hands of a strong leader, the papacy could overshadow all secular monarchs. Such a leader was Pope Innocent III (1198-1216), a new type of administrator-pope. Unlike Gregory VII and other earlier reform popes, who were monks, Innocent and other great popes of the later twelfth and thirteenth centuries were trained as canon lawyers. Innocent was like Gregory VII, however, in holding an exalted view of his office:

The successor of Peter is the Vicar of Christ: he has been established as a mediator between God and man, below God but beyond man; less than God but more than man; who shall judge all and be judged by no one.[6]

Innocent III told the princes of Europe that the papacy was as the sun, whereas the kings were as the moon. As the moon derives its light from the sun, so the kings derived their powers from the pope. So successful was the pontiff in asserting his temporal as well as spiritual supremacy that many states, both large and small, formally acknowledged vassalage to the pope. In the case of King John of England, a struggle developed over the election of the archbishop of Canterbury, and Innocent placed England under interdict and excommunicated John. Under attack from his barons, John capitulated to Innocent by becoming his vassal, receiving England back as a fief, and paying him an annual monetary tribute. Innocent forced Philip Augustus of France to comply with the Church's moral code by taking back as his queen the woman he had divorced with the consent of the French bishops. As for the Holy Roman Empire, Innocent intervened in a civil war between rival candidates for the throne, supporting first one, then the other. In the end Innocent secured the election of his ward, the young Hohenstaufen heir Frederick II, who promised to respect papal rights and to go on a crusade.

Within the Church itself, nothing better illustrates the power of the papal monarchy under Innocent III than the Fourth Lateran Council, which he called in 1215 to confirm his acts and policies. More than four hundred bishops, some eight hundred abbots and priors, and representatives of all leading secular rulers answered Innocent's call. The Council dealt with a wide range of subjects; for example, it outlawed trial by ordeal, required Jews to wear distinctive yellow badges, declared clergymen exempt from state taxation, and formally defined the Christian sacraments, setting their number at seven.

The sacramental system. Christian theology held that salvation was won only with the grace of God, and that God bestowed His grace on man by means of sacraments through the Church and its officials. Thus the Church was the necessary intermediary between God and man, a position strengthened when the Fourth Lateran Council decreed that every adult Christian must confess his sins and attend communion at least once a year.

The sacraments have been defined as outward or visible signs instituted by Christ to signify and to give grace. Until fixed at seven by the Fourth Lateran Council, as many as eleven sacraments had been accepted.

In the first of the seven sacraments, Baptism, the taint of original sin was washed away, and the person was given a Christian name, hence "christening." Confirmation strengthened the character of the recipient and confirmed his membership in the Church. The sacrament of Matrimony was instituted to give the married couple spiritual help—although celibacy was prescribed for those who entered the Church as a career. Holy Orders, or ordination into the priesthood, was administered by a bishop. This sacrament conferred the power and grace to perform the sacred duties of the clergy; the ordained priest was capable of administering all sacraments except Confirmation and Holy Orders. Penance enabled sins committed after Baptism to be forgiven through the absolution of the priest. Extreme Unction was administered when death appeared imminent; it forgave remaining sins and bestowed grace and spiritual strength on the dying Christian.

The most important and impressive sacrament was the Holy Eucharist, defined as "both a sacrament and a sacrifice; in it Our Savior, Jesus Christ, body and blood, soul and divinity, under the appearance of bread and wine, is contained, offered, and received." The significance of this sacrament as the core of Christian worship can be fully appreciated only when the doctrine of transubstantiation is understood. According to this doctrine—a subject of dispute until formally defined by the Fourth Lateran Council—when the priest performing the mass pronounces over the bread and wine the words Christ used at the Last Supper, "This is My Body . . . . This is the chalice of My Blood . . . ," a miracle takes place. To all outward appearances, the bread and wine remain unchanged, but in "substance" they have been transformed into the very body and blood of the Savior.

Church administration. The universality and power of the Church rested not only upon a systematized, uniform creed but also upon the most highly organized administrative system in the West. At the head was the pope, or bishop of Rome (see Chapter 5). He was assisted by the Curia, the papal council or court, which in the twelfth and thirteenth centuries developed an intricate administrative system. Judicial and secretarial problems were handled by the papal Chancery, financial matters by the Camera, and disciplinary questions by the Penitentiary.

Special emissaries called legates, whose powers were superior to those of local prelates, carried the pope's orders throughout Europe.

The Church was ahead of secular states in developing a system of courts and a body of law. Church or canon law was based on the Scriptures, the writings of the Church Fathers, and the decrees of Church councils and popes. In the twelfth century the Church issued its official body of canon law, which guided the Church courts in judging perjury, blasphemy, sorcery, usury (the medieval Church denounced the taking of interest), and heresy. Heresy was the most horrible of all crimes in medieval eyes. A murder was a crime against society, but the heretic's disbelief in the teachings of Christ or His Church was considered a crime against God Himself.

The papacy's chief weapons in support of its authority were spiritual penalties. The most powerful of these was excommunication, by which people became anathema, "set apart" from the Church and all the faithful. "They could not act as judge, juror, notary, witness, or attorney. They could not be guardians, executors, or parties to contracts. After death, they received no Christian burial, and if, by chance, they were buried in consecrated ground, their bodies were to be disinterred and cast away. If they entered a church during Mass, they were to be expelled, or the Mass discontinued. After the reading of a sentence of excommunication, a bell was rung as for a funeral, a book closed, and a candle extinguished, to symbolize the cutting off of the guilty man."[7]

Interdict, which has been termed "an ecclesiastical lockout," was likewise a powerful instrument. Whereas excommunication was directed against individuals, interdict suspended all public worship and withheld all sacraments other than Baptism and Extreme Unction in the realm of a disobedient ruler. Pope Innocent III successfully applied or threatened the interdict eighty-five times against refractory princes.

In the last analysis the Church's effectiveness depended upon the parish priest, whose importance was enhanced by the required confession and communion decreed by the Fourth Lateran Council. Although the priest

This detail from a fifteenth-century manuscript of Chaucer's *Canterbury Tales* shows the good parson.

was very likely of humble birth and little education, he was father confessor, social worker, policeman, and recreation director, all rolled into one. In most cases he was a credit to his Church. The "poor town Parson" in Chaucer's *Canterbury Tales* is a sympathetic portrayal.

He was a kind man, full of industry,
Many times tested by adversity
And always patient. . . .
Wide was his parish, with houses far asunder,
But he would not be kept by rain or thunder,
If any had suffered a sickness or a blow,
From visiting the farthest, high or low,
Plodding his way on foot, his staff in hand.
He was a model his flock could understand.
For first he did and afterward he taught.[8]

From the reign of Innocent III until the end of the thirteenth century, the Church radiated power and splendor. It possessed perhaps one third of the land of Europe, and all secular rulers and Church prelates acknowledged the power of Christ's vicar. Innocent III and his successors could and did "judge all and be judged by no one."

Yet while the Church's wealth enabled it to perform educational and charitable functions that the states were too poor and weak to provide, this wealth also encouraged abuses and worldliness among the clergy. Cracks were appearing in the foundation even while the medieval religious structure received its final embellishments. Weaknesses were evident in the lessening of religious zeal in the later crusades, in the need for renewed internal reform, and in the growth of heresy.

New monastic reforms. The medieval reformation gained momentum late in the eleventh century with a second movement of monastic reform brought on by the failure of the Cluniac reform to end laxity in monastic life. Among the new orders were the severely ascetic and hermit-like Carthusians and the very popular Cistercians.

The Cistercian movement received its greatest impetus from the zealous efforts of St. Bernard of Clairvaux in the twelfth century. The abbeys were situated in solitary places, and their strict discipline emphasized fasts and vigils, manual labor, and a vegetarian diet. Their churches contained neither stained glass nor statues, and the puritanical Bernard denounced the beautification of churches in general:

Oh! vanity of vanities! but not more vain than foolish. . . . What has all this imagery to do with monks, with professors of poverty, with men of spiritual minds? . . . In fact, such an endless variety of forms appears everywhere that it is more pleasant to read in the stonework than in books, and to spend the day in admiring these oddities than in meditating on the Law of God.[9]

Spurred on by this militant denouncer of wealth and luxury in any form, the Cistercian order had founded 343 abbeys in western Europe by the time of Bernard's death in 1153 and more than double that number by the end of the century. Yet in one important sense these austere new monastic orders were failures. Being exclusively agricultural and dwelling apart from society, these orders were unfitted to cope with religious discontent in the towns and the consequent rise of heresy.

Heresies. Heresy, defined as "the formal denial or doubt by a baptized person of any revealed truth of the Catholic faith,"[10] flourished particularly in the towns, where an increasing consciousness of sin and a demand for greater piety went largely unheeded by old-style churchmen. This fertile ground produced many heresies, among which the Albigensian and Waldensian were major ones.

Harking back to an early Christian heresy, the Cathari ("Pure") or Albigensians—so called because Albi in southern France was an important center—went to extremes in thinking of the world as the battleground of the opposing forces of good and evil. The Albigensians condemned many activities of the state and the individual, even condemning marriage for perpetuating the human species in this sinful world.

The Waldensians derived their name from Peter Waldo, a merchant of Lyons who gave his wealth to charity and founded a lay order, the Poor Men of Lyons, to serve the needs of the people. He had parts of the New Testament translated into French, held that laymen could preach the Gospel, and denied the efficacy of the sacraments unless administered by worthy priests. Because the Waldensian church still exists today in northern Italy, it has been called the oldest Protestant sect.

For ten years Innocent III tried to reconvert these heretical groups. Failing, in 1208 he instigated a crusade against the prosperous and cultured French region of Toulouse, where the Albigensian heresy was widespread. The crusade began with horrible slaughter to the cry of "Kill them all, God will know His own." Soon the original religious motive was lost in a selfish rush to seize the wealth of the accused. In time the Albigensian heresy was destroyed, along with the flourishing culture of southern France, and the Waldensians were scattered. The time was to come, however, when the popes could not suppress heresy so successfully.

The Inquisition. In 1233 a special papal court called the Inquisition was established to cope with the rising tide of heresy and to bring about religious conformity. The accused was tried in secret without the aid of legal counsel. If he confessed and renounced his heresy, he was "reconciled" with the Church on performance of penance. If he did not voluntarily confess, he could be tortured. If this failed, the prisoner could be declared a heretic and turned over to the secular authorities, usually to be burned at the stake.

In any evaluation of the Inquisition, it should be remembered that the soul was considered incomparably more important than the body—therefore torturing a suspected heretic was justifiable if confession could save his soul from the greater torments of hell. Furthermore, the use of torture, secret testimony, and the denial of legal counsel prevailed in all courts that followed Roman law procedure.

The Franciscans and Dominicans. As a more positive response to the spread of heresy and the conditions which spawned it, Innocent III approved the founding of the Franciscan and Dominican orders of friars ("brothers"). Instead of living a sequestered existence in a remote monastery, the friars moved among their brother men, ministering to their needs and preaching the Gospel.

The Franciscans were founded by St. Francis of Assisi (1182?-1226), who, like Peter Waldo, rejected riches and spread the gospel of poverty and Christian simplicity. Love of one's fellow men and all God's creatures, even "brother worm," were basic in the Rule of St. Francis, which was inspired by Jesus' example:

Jesus called the twelve disciples together and gave them power and authority to drive out all demons and to cure diseases. Then he sent them out to preach the Kingdom of God and to heal the sick. He said to them: "Take nothing with you for your trip: no walking stick, no beggar's bag, no food, no money, not even an extra shirt. . . ." The disciples left and traveled through all the villages, preaching the Good News and healing people everywhere.[11]

The second order of friars was founded by St. Dominic (1170-1221), a well-educated Spaniard whose early career had been spent fighting the Albigensian heresy in southern France. There he decided that to combat the strength and zeal of its opponents, the Church should have champions who could preach the Gospel with apostolic fervor. Dominic's order of friar-preachers dedicated themselves to preaching as a means of maintaining the doctrines of the Church and of converting heretics.

The enthusiasm and sincerity of the friars in their early years made a profound impact upon an age which had grown increasingly critical of ecclesiastical worldliness. But after they took charge of the Inquisition, became professors in the universities, and served the papacy in other ways, the friars lost much of their original simplicity and freshness. Yet their message and zeal had done much to

The simple piety preached by St. Francis is reflected in this altarpiece, painted only nine years after his death, which shows the characteristically austere saint surrounded by six scenes from his life. The marks on St. Francis' hands and feet are stigmata—symbolic wounds representing his identification with Christ—which he received after a period of prayer and meditation.

provide the Church with moral and intellectual leadership at a time when such leadership was badly needed.

Veneration of saints and relics. Neither the Church's concern for theology nor its claims to universal authority appealed to ordinary men; they wanted solace on this earth and assurance of salvation in the next life. Such concerns enhanced the veneration of the Virgin Mary, one of the most potent forces in the medieval reformation. In an age when even the most educated persons believed that thunderstorms, plagues, and famines were the devil's work and that hell loomed perilously close, it seemed natural to pray to the Mother of Christ for protection and comfort. As an earthly mother supplicates for mercy on behalf of her erring child, so the Virgin Mary would supplicate her Son in heaven for her children on earth. Many magnificent Gothic cathedrals, such as Notre Dame (Our Lady) in Paris, were dedicated to Mary as symbols of the people's devotion.

Medieval people believed that relics of saints had miraculous powers. The bone of a saint, for example, supposedly would halt disease or create abundant harvests. The manner in which unscrupulous venders of fake relics sometimes duped Christians has been vividly recounted by Chaucer in his description of the Pardoner:

No pardoner could beat him in the race,
For in his wallet he had a pillow case
Which he represented as Our Lady's veil;
He said he had a piece of the very sail
St. Peter, when he fished in Galilee
Before Christ caught him, used upon the sea.
He had a latten cross embossed with stones
And in a glass he carried some pig's bones,
And with these holy relics, when he found
Some village parson grubbing his poor ground,
He would get more money in a single day
Than in two months would come the parson's way.
Thus with his flattery and his trumped-up stock
He made dupes of the parson and his flock.[12]

The crusades, and especially the sack of Constantinople in 1204, so flooded the West with relics that the Fourth Lateran Council prohibited, with little effect, the sale of relics and required papal approval of all new relics.

THE INTELLECTUAL SYNTHESIS

The medieval renaissance. "The meeting of Roman decrepitude and German immaturity was not felicitous."[13] This concise commentary on the character of early medieval civilization is especially relevant to the intellectual side of the period, and it remains a moot question among modern scholars whether the seventh century or the tenth was "the darkest of the Dark Ages." By the close of the sixth century even the most influential of early medieval popes, Gregory the Great, was contributing to the growing intellectual murkiness by voicing strong disapproval of secular literature, insisting that "the same mouth cannot sing the praises of Jupiter and praises of Christ." So feeble had the light of learning become by the end of the eighth century that Charlemagne found it necessary to order the monasteries to revive their schools and resume instruction in the rudiments of "singing, arithmetic, and grammar" (see p. 192).

In sharp contrast to the fate of his political achievements, Charlemagne's modest educational revival survived his death. At least partly as a result of this stimulus, western Europe by the late eleventh century was on the threshold of one of the most productive and energetic periods in the history of western thought—the medieval renaissance.

What was revived first of all during the medieval renaissance was intellectual curiosity, plainly evident from contemporary accounts, such as the following concerning an eleventh-century scholar from Liège:

Olbert was not able to satiate his thirst for study. When he would hear of some one distinguished in the arts he flew there at once, and the more he thirsted the more he absorbed something delightful from each master. At Paris he worked at Saint-Germain and studied the Holy Faith which glowed there. In Troyes he studied for three years, learning gratefully many things. . . . He felt obliged to listen to Fulbert of Chartres who was proclaimed in the liberal arts throughout France. Afterwards just like the bees among flowers, gorged with the nectar of learning, he returned to the hive and lived there studiously in a religious way, and religiously in a studious manner.[14]

Scholasticism. Living "religiously in a studious manner" aptly characterizes the scholars of the medieval renaissance and points up an essential difference between medieval thought on the one hand and early Greek philosophy and modern scientific thought on the other. With but few exceptions, medieval man did not think of truth as something to be discovered by himself; rather, he saw it as already existing in the authoritative Christian and pagan writings handed down from antiquity. Spurred on by a new zest for employing reason (called logic or dialectic), medieval scholars of the twelfth and thirteenth centuries succeeded in understanding and reexpressing those elements in the Christian and pagan heritage that seemed significant to them. Since this task was carried out largely in the schools, these scholars are known as schoolmen—or scholastics—and the intellectual synthesis they produced is called scholasticism.

Each scholar formed his own judgments and earnestly sought to convince others. This led to much debate, often uncritical but always exuberant, on a wide range of subjects. Most famous was the argument over universals known as the nominalist-realist controversy.

Nominalists and realists battled over the problem of universal Ideas, basing their arguments on indirect evidence, transmitted by Boethius and others, that Plato and Aristotle did not agree on the subject. Plato had argued that Ideas had reality apart from their existence in men's minds. A specific object was *real* only insofar as it represented the nature of its Idea (see p. 52). Thus Plato himself, for example, was real inasmuch as he partook of the Idea of Man. Aristotle, taking an opposite view, maintained that individuals existed as individuals—a human being was a real entity, not just a reflection of the universal Idea of Man. To the realists in the Middle Ages, only universal Ideas could be real and exist independently. To the nominalists, abstract concepts such as universal Ideas were only names (*nomina*) and had no real existence.

Both realism and nominalism—if carried to their logical extremes—resulted in principles equally abhorrent to the Church. Realism became pantheism (the universe as a whole is God), and nominalism became materialism (the universe is composed solely of matter).

The contribution of Abélard. The extreme views of nominalists and realists, along with other examples of the sterile use of logic ("whether the pig is led to the market by the rope or by the driver"), outraged a brilliant young student named Pierre Abélard (1079-1142), later a popular teacher at the cathedral school of Notre Dame in Paris. Like many bright students in all ages, Abélard succeeded in antagonizing his teachers, both realist and nominalist. "I brought him great grief," he wrote of one, "because I undertook to refute certain of his opinions." Another teacher was mercilessly ridiculed:

> He had a miraculous flow of words, but they were contemptible in meaning and quite void of reason. When he kindled a fire, he filled his house with smoke and illumined it not at all. He was a tree which seemed noble to those who gazed upon its leaves from afar, but to those who came nearer and examined it more closely was revealed its barrenness.[15]

Abélard's great contribution to medieval thought was freeing logic from barrenness and rerouting it to become again a means to an end rather than an end in itself. Conceptualism, his common-sense solution to the nominalist-realist controversy, held that universals, while existing only in the mind as thoughts or concepts, are nevertheless valid (real) since they are the product of observing the similar qualities that exist in a particular class of things. Thus, by observing many chairs and sitting in them, we arrive at the universal concept "chair."

In addition to redefining the purpose of scholastic thought, Abélard perfected the scholastic method. Like others before him, Abélard emphasized the importance of understanding, but whereas the former had begun with faith, Abélard started with doubt. We must learn to doubt, he insisted, for doubting leads us to inquire, and inquiry leads us to the truth. Abélard's intellectual skepticism was not that of modern experimental science, however; he never transcended superimposed authority. He aimed to arouse intellectual curiosity in his students and turn it into useful channels, bringing reason to bear on inherited truths in order to achieve understanding.

In an epoch-making work, *Sic et Non* (*Yes and No*), Abélard demonstrated his method. Listing 158 propositions on theology and ethics, he appended to each a number of statements pro and con taken from the authoritative writings of the Church. Abélard did not go on to reconcile these apparent contradictions, but he urged his students to do so by rational interpretation. Abélard's methodology was used by his successors to assimilate and reexpress the pagan as well as the Christian heritage of the past. The resulting scholarly compilations, which bear such apt titles as *concordantia* (concordance), *speculum* (mirror), and *summa* (sum total), constitute the crowning achievement of the medieval intellectual synthesis.

Abélard is remembered as a great lover as well as a great scholar—a rather uncommon combination. His ill-starred romance with his pupil, the learned and beautiful Héloïse, niece of the canon of Notre Dame, cut short his promising career as a teacher. The two lovers were married in secret, but Héloïse's uncle, falsely believing that Abélard planned to abandon Héloïse, hired thugs who attacked and emasculated the scholar. Both Abélard and Héloïse then sought refuge in the Church—Pierre as a monk and Héloïse as the abbess of a nunnery.

The new material and the task of reconciliation. In the twelfth century the study of Greek learning with its Muslim additions was undertaken by western scholars who flocked to Spain and Sicily and there translated Muslim editions of ancient writings. As a result of these translations a host of new ideas, particularly in science and philosophy, were introduced to western scholars. Western knowledge was expanded to include not only Arabic learning but also such important classical works as Euclid's *Geometry*, Ptolemy's *Almagest*, Hippocrates' and Galen's treatises in medicine, and all of Aristotle's extant writing except the *Poetics* and the *Rhetoric*.

As his works became known, Aristotle became, in Dante's words, "the master of those who know," and his authority was generally accepted as second only to that of the Scriptures. But because the Church's teachings were considered infallible, Aristotle's ideas, as well as those of other great thinkers of antiquity, had to be reconciled with religious dogma. Using Abélard's methodology, the scholastic thinkers of the thirteenth century succeeded in this task of reconciliation.

Scholasticism reached its zenith with St. Thomas Aquinas (1225?-1274). In his *Summa Theologica* this brilliant Italian Dominican dealt exhaustively with the great problems of theology, philosophy, politics, and economics. After collecting the arguments pro and con on a given problem—for example, "Whether it is lawful to sell a thing for more than its worth?"—he went on to draw conclusions. (His answer to the problem cited reflects the great influence of Christian ethics upon medieval economic thought: "I answer that, it is altogether sinful to have recourse to deceit in order to sell a thing for more than its just price, because this is to deceive one's neighbour so as to injure him."[16])

St. Thomas' major concern was to reconcile Aristotle and Church dogma—in other words, the truths of natural reason and the truths of faith. There can be no real contradiction, he argued, since all truth comes from God. In case of an unresolved contradiction, however, faith won out, because of the possibility of human error in reasoning. St. Thomas was so convincing in settling this conflict—the first clash between science and religion in the history of our western civilization—that his philosophy still has its followers today.

The decline of scholasticism. Having reached its zenith, scholasticism declined rapidly. The assumption that faith and reason were compatible was vigorously denied by two Franciscan thinkers, Duns Scotus (d. 1308) and William of Occam (d. c. 1349), who elaborated on Aquinas' belief that certain religious doctrines are beyond discovery by the use of reason. They argued that if the human intellect could not understand divinely revealed truth, it could hope to comprehend only the natural world and should not intrude upon the sphere of divine truth. Such a position tended to undermine the Thomistic synthesis of faith and reason. Realism and nominalism revived, the one promoting an increase in mystical, nonrational religion, the other contributing to the growing scientific spirit and to individualism and worldly concerns in general. For better or for worse, this trend toward the emancipation of human knowledge and action from the unifying authority of religion and the Church became a characteristic feature of western civilization.

After the thirteenth century scholasticism increasingly became a term of reproach, for its adherents were obsessed with theological subtleties, discouraged independent thought, and in general lost touch with reality. But it should be remembered that the scholastics sought to appropriate and make subjectively their own the store of Christian and pagan knowledge left to them by a more advanced civilization. In terms of their needs and objectives—an intelligible and all-embracing synthesis of faith, logic, and science—the scholastics were eminently successful, and people of our own age should not look askance at their accomplishments. Ironically, we today increasingly recognize the importance of reconciling science and faith in an age which has so much of the former and so little of the latter.

Medieval science. Because of the emphasis upon authority and the all-pervasive influence of the Church, the medieval atmosphere was not conducive to free scientific investigation. Those who studied science were churchmen, and their findings were supposed to illuminate rather than contradict the dogmas of the theologians. During the early Middle Ages scientific knowledge was limited to such compilations as the *Etymologies* of Isidore, bishop of Seville. Written in the seventh century, this naive and uncritical scrapbook of information remained a standard reference work in the West for three centuries. Isidore believed that the real nature of a thing was to be found in its name, and so he usually introduced each item with an often fanciful etymological explanation:

The liver [*iecur* in Latin] has its name because there is resident the fire [*ignis*] which flies up into the brain. . . . and by its heat it changes into blood the liquid that it has drawn from food, and this blood it supplies to the several members to feed and nourish them.[17]

The *Etymologies* has been called "the fruit of the much decayed tree of ancient learning."

When Greek and Arabic works were translated in the twelfth century, the West inherited a magnificent legacy of mathematical and scientific knowledge. Algebra, trigonometry, and Euclid's *Geometry* became available, and Arabic numerals and the symbol *zero* made possible the decimal system of computation. Leonard of Pisa (d. 1245), the greatest mathematician of the Middle Ages, made a great original contribution to mathematics when he worked out a method to extract square roots and to solve quadratic and cubic equations. On the other hand, Ptolemy's belief that the earth was the center of the universe—a fallacious theory destined to handicap astronomy for centuries—was commonly accepted.

Physics was based on Aristotle's theory of four elements (water, earth, air, and fire) and on his theories of dynamics—doctrines which took centuries to disprove. Some fourteenth-century nominalists were the first to challenge Aristotle's theory that a heavy object falls faster than a light one. Chemistry was based on Aristotelian concepts, mixed with magic and alchemy. Like the Muslim alchemist, his European counterpart tried in vain to transmute base metals into gold and silver and to obtain a magic elixir that would prolong life; in both cases the attempts did much to advance chemistry.

Frederick II and Roger Bacon. Two notable exceptions to the medieval rule of subservience to authority were the emperor Frederick II (see also p. 237) and the English Franciscan Roger Bacon. Frederick had a genuine scientific interest in animals and was famed for his large traveling menagerie, which included elephants, camels, panthers, lions, leopards, and a giraffe. He wrote a remarkable treatise, *The Art of Falconry*, which is still considered largely accurate in its observations of the life and habits of various kinds of hunting birds. "We discovered by hard-won experience," he wrote, "that the

In this picture from a fifteenth-century manuscript the university students oppose one another in "disputation," the class debates which went on for hours.

deductions of Aristotle, whom we followed when they appealed to our reason, were not entirely to be relied upon."[18] At his Sicilian court Frederick gathered about him many distinguished Greek, Muslim, and Latin scholars (including Leonard of Pisa), and he wrote to others in distant lands seeking their views on such problems as why objects appear bent when partly covered by water. He indulged in many experiments; one was a test to determine what language children would speak if raised in absolute silence. The experiment was a failure because all the children died.

Roger Bacon (1214-1292) also employed the inductive scientific method—he coined the term "experimental science"—and boldly criticized the deductive syllogistic reasoning used by scholastic thinkers. His *Opus Maius* contains this attack on scholasticism:

There are four principal stumbling blocks to comprehending truth, which hinder well-nigh every scholar: the example of frail and unworthy authority, long-established custom, the sense of the ignorant crowd, and the hiding of one's ignorance under the show of wisdom.[19]

Bacon never doubted the authority of the Bible or the Church—his interest lay only in natural science—yet his superiors considered him a dangerous thinker because of his criticism of scholastic thought.

Medieval medicine. By the thirteenth century learned Muslim commentaries on Galen and Hippocrates and on Aristotle's biology were available in the West. This knowledge, coupled with their own discoveries and improved techniques, made medieval doctors more than just barbers who engaged in bloodletting. Yet the overall state of medical knowledge and practice was, by our standards at least, still primitive. This can be seen in the prevalence of superstitious beliefs and the resort to magical practices, the general lack of concern for public sanitation, the periodic decimation of entire populations by epidemics such as the Black Death, and that significant indicator of the state of public health—the infant mortality rate, which was staggeringly high.

Origin of universities. Roman schools had a curriculum of seven liberal arts, separated into two divisions: a *trivium* consisting of grammar, rhetoric, and dialectic; and a *quadrivium* of arithmetic, music, geometry, and astronomy. When the Roman empire in the West fell, the task of education went to the Church; and the liberal arts were adapted to prepare youths for the ministry. Through the work of Cassiodorus in the sixth century (see p. 243), monasteries became important centers of learning. By 1200, however, monastic schools were overshadowed by the more dynamic cathedral schools established by bishops in such important centers as Paris, Chartres, Canterbury, and Toledo.

The renaissance of the twelfth century, with its revival of classical learning, its unprecedented number of students flocking to the schools, and its development of professional studies in law, medicine, and theology, led to the rise of organized centers of learning—the universities, which soon eclipsed the monastic and cathedral schools. Originally the word *university* meant a group of persons possessing a common purpose. In this case it referred to a guild of learners, both teachers and students, analogous to the craft guilds with their masters and apprentices. In the thirteenth century the universities had no campuses and little property or money, and the masters taught in hired rooms or religious houses. If the university was dissatisfied with its treatment by the townspeople, it could migrate elsewhere. The earliest universities—Bologna, Paris, and Oxford—were not officially founded or created, but in time the popes and kings granted them and other universities charters of self-government. The charters gave legal status to the universities and rights to the students, such as freedom from the jurisdiction of town officials.

Two systems: Bologna and Paris. Two of the most famous medieval universities were at Bologna in northern Italy and at Paris. The former owed its growth to the fame of Irnerius (d. 1130), who taught civil law. Because of his influence, Bologna acquired a reputation as the leading center for the study of law. The students soon organized a guild for protection against the rapacious townspeople, who were demanding exorbitant sums for food and lodging. Because the guild went on to control the professors, Bologna became a student paradise. In the earliest statutes we read that a professor requiring leave of absence even for one day first had to obtain permission from his own students. He had to begin his lecture with the bell and end within one minute of the next bell. The material in the text had to be covered systematically, with all difficult passages fully explained. The powerful position of the students at Bologna developed as a result of the predominance of older students studying for the doctorate in law.

At the university in Paris conditions developed differently. This university, which had grown out of the cathedral school of Notre Dame, specialized in liberal arts and theology and became the most influential intellectual center in medieval Europe. Its administration was far different from Bologna's. The chancellor of Notre Dame, the bishop's officer who exercised authority over the cathedral school, refused to allow the students or the masters to obtain control of the burgeoning university. Charters issued by the French king in 1200 and by the pope in 1231 freed the university from the bishop's authority by making it an autonomous body controlled by the masters.

The collegiate system. Universities owned no dormitories, and students lived in rented rooms or pooled their resources to obtain housing on a cooperative basis. With masters' fees and living expenses to pay, the impoverished student labored under decided handicaps. A philanthropic patron, however, sometimes provided quarters where poor scholars could board free of charge. One such patron was Robert de Sorbon, the royal chaplain to the saintly Louis ix. About 1257 Robert endowed a hall for sixteen needy students working for their doctorates in theology, thus founding the College de Sorbonne; the University of Paris is still popularly known by the name of its great benefactor.

As more colleges were established, the large universities became collections of colleges in which the students lived and studied. Although organization by colleges finally disappeared in the University of Paris where the system originated, at both Oxford and Cambridge the collegiate system has remained an integral part of the university to this day.

Curriculum and degrees. The degrees available at medieval universities were similar to those offered today. The bachelor's degree, which could be obtained after studying from three to five years, was not considered very important. For a master of arts degree, which admitted the holder into the guild of masters and was a license to teach, particular emphasis was placed on the works of Aristotle. In theology, law, and medicine the master's degree was commonly called a doctorate. It was no easy matter to get a master's degree (or doctorate) from a medieval university; many years of preparation were required, and at the final examination the candidate had to defend his thesis publicly for hours against the learned attacks of the masters. If successful in his defense, the candidate then stood the cost of a banquet for his examiners.

Latin literature. During the entire Middle Ages Latin served as an international means of communication. This common tongue provided much of the cohesion of the Middle Ages, for virtually all the crucial communications of the Church, governments, and schools were in Latin. Undoubtedly the most splendid medieval Latin is found in the Church liturgy, which was chanted by the priest.

Any misconception that the Middle Ages were simply "other-worldly" and long-faced will be rudely shattered by glancing at the Latin poetry written during the twelfth and thirteenth centuries by students. Known as Goliardic verse because its authors claimed to be disciples of Goliath, their synonym for the devil, it unhesitatingly proclaimed the pleasures of wine, women, and song:

'Tis most arduous to make
   Nature's self-surrender;
Seeing girls, to blush and be
   Purity's defender!
We young men our longings ne'er
   Shall to stern law render,
Or preserve our fancies from
   Bodies smooth and tender. . . .

In the public house to die
   Is my resolution;
Let wine to my lips be nigh
   At life's dissolution:
That will make the angels cry,
   With glad elocution,
"Grant this toper, God on high,
   Grace and absolution!"[20]

The Goliardic poets were brilliant at parodying and satirizing the ideals of their elders. They substituted Venus for the Virgin, wrote masses for drunkards, and were guilty of other blasphemies. Yet many of these poets later became respected officials in the Church.

In contrast, the great Latin hymns such as the *Dies Irae* and the *Stabat Mater Dolorosa* show the genuineness of the religious spirit of the twelfth and thirteenth centuries. The latter hymn movingly describes the Virgin Mary standing beside the cross:

By the cross, sad vigil keeping,
Stood the mournful mother weeping,
While on it the saviour hung;
In that hour of deep distress
Pierced the sword of bitterness
Through her heart with sorrow wrung.[21]

Vernacular literature. A rising tide of literature in the vernacular tongues began to appear by the twelfth century, with the epic as the earliest form. The greatest of the French epics, or *chansons de geste* ("songs of great deeds"), is the late eleventh-century *Song of Roland*, which recounts the heroic deeds and death of Count Roland in the Pyrenees while defending the rear of Charlemagne's army (see p. 191). The great Spanish epic, the *Poema del Mio Cid* (see quoted selection, p. 232), is a product of the twelfth century. These stirring epic poems, with their accounts of prowess in battle, mirror the masculine warrior virtues of early chivalry (see p. 202).

By the twelfth century in the feudal courts of southern France, poets called troubadours were composing short, personal lyrics dealing mainly with romantic love. "The delicacy and romanticism of the troubadour lyrics betoken a more genteel and sophisticated nobility than that of the feudal north—a nobility that preferred songs of love to songs of war. Indeed, medieval southern France was the source of the entire romantic-love tradition of Western Civilization, with its idealization of women, its emphasis on male gallantry and courtesy, and its insistence on embroidering the sex drive with an elaborate ritual of palpitating hearts, moonlight, and sentimental ties."[22] Typical are these lines written in adoration of the lovely Eleanor of Aquitaine:

When the sweet breeze
Blows hither from your dwelling
Methinks I feel
A breath of paradise.[23]

Nothing comparable to these lines exists in the *chansons de geste*, but during the last half of the twelfth century this new interest in love fused with the purely heroic material of the early epics. The result was the medieval romance, an account of love and adventure, to which was often added a strong coloring of religious feeling. Examples are Chrétien de Troyes' *Perceval* (see p. 202) and the tales concerning King Arthur and his Round Table of chivalrous knights who variously pursue adventure, charming ladies, and the Holy Grail. In Germany about the beginning of the thirteenth century, the old saga material dealing with Siegfried, Brunhild, and the wars against the Huns was recast into the *Nibelungenlied* (*Song of the Nibelungs*).

All the foregoing literary types were written for the aristocracy. The self-made burgher preferred more practical and shrewd tales. His taste was gratified by the bawdy *fabliaux*, brief, humorous tales written in rhymed verse; and the animal stories about Reynard the Fox, the symbol of the sly bourgeois lawyer who easily outwits King Lion and his noble vassals. In England during the fourteenth century the Robin Hood ballads celebrated robbing the rich to give to the poor and *Piers the Plowman* condemned the injustices of a social system that had brought on the peasant revolt in England (see p. 217 and quoted selection, p. 201).

Dante Alighieri. The vernacular was also used by two of the greatest writers of the period—Dante and Chaucer. Combining a profound religious sense with a knowledge of scholastic thought and the Latin classics, the Italian Dante (1265-1321) produced one of the world's greatest narrative poems. The *Divine Comedy*, which Dante said described his "full experience," is an allegory of medieval man (Dante) moving from bestial earthiness (hell) through conversion (purgatory) to the sublime spirituality of union with God (paradise). Dante describes how

Midway this way of life we're bound upon,
    I woke to find myself in a dark wood,
    Where the right road was wholly lost and gone.[24]

Dante then accepts the offer of Virgil, symbol of pagan learning, to be his "master, leader, and lord" to guide him through hell and purgatory. But it is Beatrice, the lady whom he had once loved from afar and who is now the symbol of divine love, who guides him through paradise. At last Dante stands before God, and words fail him as he finds peace in the presence of the highest form of love:

Oh, how fall short the words! . . .
The Love that moves the sun and every star.[25]

The wit of Chaucer. In the *Canterbury Tales*, Geoffrey Chaucer (1340?-1400), one of the greatest figures in medieval literature, reveals a cross section of contemporary English life, customs, and thought (see quoted selections, pp. 247, 250). The twenty-nine

pilgrims who assembled in April 1387 at an inn before journeying to the shrine of St. Thomas à Becket at Canterbury were a motley group. The "truly perfect, gentle knight," just returned from warring against the "heathen in Turkey," was accompanied by his son, a young squire who loved so much by night that "he slept no more than does a nightingale." The clergy was represented by the coy prioress who "would weep if she but saw a mouse caught in a trap,"[26] the rotund

The compelling interest which Dante's *Divine Comedy* has held for centuries of readers is aptly demonstrated by this engraving from an edition of the *Comedy* published and illustrated by William Blake, the English poet and artist of the late eighteenth and early nineteenth centuries. Shown is the marsh of the River Styx, the abode of the wrathful ("all naked and with brows in anger bent") and the sullen ("who gloom and blacken in the mire").

monk who loved to eat fat swan and ride good horses, the friar who knew the best taverns and all the barmaids in town, and the poor parish priest who was a credit to his faith. Also included in the group were the merchant who could talk only of business, the threadbare Oxford student, the miller with a wart on his nose, and the worthy wife of Bath, who had married five times and was now visiting Christian shrines in search of a sixth husband.

Chaucer's fame rests securely upon his keen interest in human nature and his skill as a storyteller. The Midland dialect he used was the linguistic base for the language of future English literature, just as Dante's use of the Tuscan dialect fixed the Italian tongue.

Rebirth of drama. Like Greek drama, medieval drama developed out of religious ceremonies; it was used by churchmen to instruct the faithful. The earliest forms were the mystery plays, which naively but forcefully dramatized Biblical stories, and the miracle plays, which described the miraculous intervention of saints in human affairs. At first the plays supplemented the regular service and were performed inside the church proper. As their popularity grew, they were presented either on the church steps or on a separate stage. By the fourteenth century another type, the morality play, had become popular. The actors personified virtues and vices, and the plot of the drama usually centered on a conflict between them. *Everyman*, an excellent example of a morality play, is still occasionally produced.

THE ESTHETIC SYNTHESIS

Artistic correlation. The *Summa Theologica* of St. Thomas Aquinas and the *Divine Comedy* of Dante represent the best intellectual expressions of the medieval spirit. Similarly, the Gothic cathedral is the ultimate artistic expression of the age. Each of these masterpieces represents a different aspect of the attempt to organize everything into an overall pattern that would glorify God.

The order and form of scholastic thought find their counterparts in the structure and style of the Gothic edifices. A scholastic treatise was systematically arranged in logical parts; the cathedral was similarly articulated in space. The main sections, the nave, transept, and apse, were individually distinctive yet integrated into a coherent structure.

Early Christian churches. Early Christian churches imitated the plan of the Roman basilicas. In this design a rectangle is divided into three aisles: a central aisle, or nave, ending in a semicircular apse, and a lower-ceilinged aisle on each side. Parallel rows of columns separated the nave from the side aisles. The roof over the nave was raised to provide a clerestory—a section pierced by windows to illuminate the interior (see illustration, p. 127). In the fourth century the basilica plan was modified by the addition of a transept across the aisles between the apse and the nave. This essentially "T" shape added Christian symbolism to the basic plan of the pagan-style building. Graceful bell-towers were erected separate from the church building; the "leaning tower" of Pisa is a famous later example.

Romanesque architecture. In the eleventh century occurred a tremendous architectural revival, marked by the recovery of the art of building in stone rather than in wood, as was common during the early Middle Ages. At a much later date the name *Romanesque* came to be applied to this new style, because, like early Christian architecture, it was based largely on Roman models. Although details of structure and ornamentation differed with locality, the round arch was a standard Romanesque feature (see Color Plate 9). Both barrel and cross vaults were used, particularly in northern Europe, where the need to build fireproof churches made it impractical to follow the common Italian practice of using flat wooden roofs. While there was often one long barrel vault over the nave, the aisles were divided into square areas or bays with a cross vault over each bay. Thick outside walls and huge interior piers were necessary to support the heavy stone barrel and cross vaults. (In time diagonal ribs were built along the groins of the cross vault, transforming it into the ribbed-groin vault; see diagram.) Because the walls would be weakened by large window apertures, the clerestory windows were small or nonexistent. Thus the northern Romanesque interior was dark and gloomy, the exterior massive and monumental.

Gothic architecture. Actually, no clear-cut cleavage exists between Romanesque and Gothic. There was a gradual evolutionary process, which reached its culmination in the thirteenth and fourteenth centuries. The architects of the Gothic-style cathedral developed ribbed-groin vaults with pointed rather than round arches. This enabled them to solve the technical problem of cross-vaulting the nave, which, being wider than the aisles, could not easily be divided into square bays covered by Romanesque cross vaults (see diagram of floor plan, p. 261). Thus light ribbed-groin vaults, whose sides were of different length to fit the rectangular bays of the nave, replaced the heavy barrel vault, and the roof of the nave could be raised to permit the use of large clerestory windows. The thrust of the vaults over both the nave and the aisles was concentrated on a few strong structural supports. Part of the weight was carried down to the ground by columns within the building, and part by flying buttresses at points along the walls. With such vaulting and buttresses, the weight of the roof was largely shifted off the walls (see diagram of cross section, p. 261). Large stained-glass windows were set into the walls between the buttresses. The dark, somber interior of the Romanesque churches gave way to the jeweled light of the Gothic interiors.

Sculpture and stained glass. Most Romanesque and Gothic sculpture served an archi-

The Gothic age was the culmination of the Middle Ages, and the cathedral was the concrete synthesis of Gothic ideals. With his knowledge of weights and thrusts, the Gothic architect was able to raise his building to unprecedented heights and open it dramatically to light. The result, as evident in the cathedral at Cologne, is one of the most compelling unities of form and feeling in all of architecture.

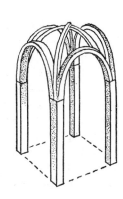

The ribbed-groin vault developed by Romanesque architects derived from the Roman intersecting vaults. The ribbed vault is made up of arches which span the sides of a square bay, with groin arches crossing diagonally from corner to corner.

tectural function by being carved to fit into the total composition of a church. To use sculpture to the best architectural advantage, the subject was often distorted to achieve a particular effect. Yet many thirteenth-century Gothic statues are masterpieces both in their fully developed craftmanship and the grace and nobility of their content (see photos, pp. 261, 224). The relationship of the earlier Romanesque sculpture (see photo, p. 260) to the later Gothic reduplicates in large part that of archaic and classical sculpture in ancient Greece (see pp. 56-57).

Like sculpture, medieval painting in the form of stained-glass windows was an integral part of architecture. Composed of small pieces of colored glass held together in a

At the bottom of this detail of the "Last Judgment" scene at Autun Cathedral the dead rise from their graves in fear; at the top their souls are weighed in the balance. While the saved cling to the angels, the damned are seized by grinning devils and thrown into hell.

massive castles. By the thirteenth century castle building in Europe reached a high point of development. The towers were rounded, and bastions stood at strategic points along the walls. The castle as a whole was planned in such a skillful manner that if one section was taken by attackers, it could be sealed off from the remaining fortifications. Whole towns were fortified in the same way, with walls, watchtowers, moats, and drawbridges.

Toward the end of the Middle Ages there was less need for fortified towns and castles. At the same time the wealth accruing from the revived trade and increased industry encouraged the development of secular Gothic architecture. Town and guild halls, the residences of the rich, and the chateaux of the nobles all borrowed the delicate Gothic style from the cathedrals.

SUMMARY

The traditional division of history into "ancient," "medieval," and "modern" is fundamentally arbitrary and artificial in that history is a continuous process. Applying the same common denominator—"medieval" —to the thousand turbulent years between the fifth and fifteenth centuries obscures the wide variations that existed during the period. For five centuries after the fall of Rome, western civilization was on the defensive against invading barbarians from the east and north. The Church took the lead in fusing classical, barbarian, and Christian elements and nurtured such intellectual activity as existed. By the eleventh century Europe had shifted to the offensive, and its resurgence was reflected in the Church's militant drive to political triumph in the thirteenth century.

Emerging out of feudal decentralization ahead of the state, the Church developed the first unified system of law and administration in medieval Europe and intimately affected the life of every person. It gave man a sense of security against the dangers on earth and those beyond. To perform its historical mission, the Church required a hierarchy of clergy and an elaborate doctrine,

pattern by metal strips which both braced the glass and emphasized the design, stained glass was an art whose excellence has not been duplicated in modern times. By adding various minerals to molten glass, thirteenth-century craftsmen achieved brilliant hues. Details such as hair were painted on the glass. The object, however, was not realism but the evoking of a mood—to shine with the radiance of heaven itself.

Secular architecture. What the cathedral was to religious life, the castle was to everyday living. Both were havens, and both were built to endure. The new weapons and techniques of siege warfare, which the crusaders brought back with them, necessitated more

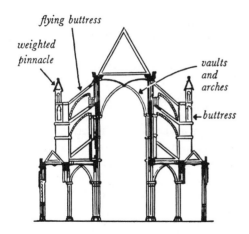

weighted pinnacle

flying buttress

vaults and arches

buttress

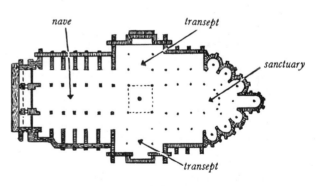

nave

transept

sanctuary

transept

By Ewing Galloway, N.Y.

The fusing of sculpture and architecture is apparent in this detail of one of the doorways of Amiens Cathedral. Medieval cathedrals were rich in sculptures of saints and great men of antiquity, episodes from history and the Old and New Testaments, and allegorical representations of science, philosophy, and theology. The unified effect of the fully developed Gothic style is one of awesome, but ordered, intricacy, as the photograph of the entire front of Amiens Cathedral demonstrates. Above is a drawing of the cross section and floor plan of the same cathedral. Vaults, arches, buttresses, and weighted pinnacles were important structural elements in the Gothic style of architecture.

accompanied by methods for enforcing its will. We have followed the areas of reform, watched the Church's power reach its apex in the age of Innocent III, and noted signs of its eventual decline.

Within the Church, thinkers wrestled with philosophical issues, such as the realist-nominalist controversy. In the thirteenth century such famous scholastics as St. Thomas Aquinas made herculean attempts to reconcile faith and reason, Church authority and classical thought.

Stimulated by the acquisition of Greek and Arabic knowledge, education established new frontiers. The earliest universities grew from unorganized groups of scholars and students to important centers of learning. Bologna and Paris, in particular, directly affected other universities. In literature, Latin, the international language of the educated, slowly gave way to the vernacular tongues. Chaucer and Dante, giants in the literary field, both wrote in their native languages and did much to develop modern English and Italian respectively.

Evolving from Romanesque patterns, the splendid Gothic cathedrals were the greatest artistic achievement of the medieval period. The rounded arches and massive walls of Romanesque architecture were replaced by pointed arches, ribbed-groin vaults, and the flying buttresses of the soaring Gothic cathedrals. This style carried over from churches to castles, town halls, and urban dwellings.

SUGGESTIONS FOR READING

R. W. Southern, **The Making of the Middle Ages,*** Yale. A brilliant topical treatment of the eleventh and twelfth centuries. F. Heer, **The Medieval World,*** Mentor, vividly pictures the society of the twelfth and thirteenth centuries.

M. W. Baldwin, **The Mediaeval Church,*** Cornell. A perceptive essay on Church development through the pontificate of Innocent III. See also Jeffrey Russell, **A History of Medieval Christianity: Prophecy and Order,** Crowell, 1968; M. Deanesly, **A History of the Medieval Church, 590-1500,*** 9th ed., Barnes and Noble, 1969; H. Daniel-Rops, **The Church in the Dark Ages, 406-1050,** Dutton, 1959.

G. Barraclough, **The Medieval Papacy,*** Harcourt, Brace & World, 1968. Brief and lavishly illustrated S. R. Packard, **Europe and the Church Under Innocent III,** Russell, 1927, is short and admirable. For greater detail see W. Ullmann, **The Growth of Papal Government in the Middle Ages,** 3rd ed., Barnes and Noble, 1970. On Church-state political theory see K. Morrison, **Tradition and Authority in the Western Church, 300-1140,** Princeton, 1969; W. Ullmann, **A History of Political Thought: The Middle Ages,*** Penguin; C. McIlwain, **The Growth of Political Thought in the West,** Macmillan, 1932.

D. Knowles, **The Monastic Order in England,** 2nd ed., Cambridge, 1963. Considered to be the best introduction to medieval monasticism. See also H. Workman, **The Evolution of the Monastic Ideal,*** Beacon; E. Duckett, **The Wandering Saints of the Early Middle Ages,*** Norton.

H. C. Lea, **The Inquisition of the Middle Ages,*** Torchbooks; A. Turberville, **Medieval Heresy and the Inquisition,** Shoe String, 1964. Standard accounts. Religious radicalism, particularly that inspired by the love ethic, is treated in N. Cohn, **The Pursuit of the Millennium,*** Torchbooks. On the Albigensian heresy see S. Runciman, **The Medieval Manichee,** Cambridge, 1947.

C. Brooke, **The Twelfth Century Renaissance,*** Harcourt, Brace & World, 1969. A brief introduction, copiously illustrated. The basic study is C. H. Haskins, **The Renaissance of the Twelfth Century,*** Meridian.

D, Knowles, **The Evolution of Medieval Thought,*** Vintage. An excellent introduction. Recommended for greater detail are G. Leff, **Medieval Thought: St. Augustine to Ockham,*** Penguin; R. Bolgar, **The Classical Heritage and Its Beneficiaries,*** Cambridge; F. Artz, **The Mind of the Middle Ages,** 3rd ed., Knopf, 1958; J. Sikes, **Peter Abailard,** Russell, 1965; F. Copleston, **Aquinas,*** Penguin; A. C. Crombie, **Medieval and Early Modern Science,*** 2 vols., Anchor.

C. H. Haskins, **The Rise of the Universities,*** Cornell. A brief survey. See also G. Leff, **Paris and Oxford Universities in the Thirteenth and Fourteenth Centuries,*** Wiley, 1968.

William T. Jackson, **The Literature of the Middle Ages,** Columbia, 1960, and **Medieval Literature: A History and a Guide,*** Collier. Recommended surveys. Outstanding also are Helen Waddell, **Mediaeval Latin Lyrics,*** Penguin; C. S. Lewis, **The Allegory of Love,*** Galaxy (on the literature of romantic love); E. Curtius, **European Literature and the Latin Middle Ages,*** Torchbooks.

H. Focillon, **The Art of the West in the Middle Ages,** 2 vols., Phaidon, 1963. Excellent on Romanesque and Gothic art. Also recommended are C. Morey, **Christian Art,** Norton, 1942; O. von Simson, **The Gothic Cathedral,*** Torchbooks; A. Temko, **Notre-Dame of Paris,*** Compass.

Stimulating interpretations of the interrelationship of medieval art, thought, and spirit are Henry Adams, **Mont-Saint-Michel and Chartres,*** Anchor; E. Mâle, **The Gothic Image,*** Torchbooks; and E. Panofsky, **Gothic Architecture and Scholasticism,*** Meridian.

*Indicates an inexpensive paperbound edition.

Part Three

The Transition to Modern Times

■ So far in our study of history, we have encountered a number of societies which emphasized the group at the expense of the individual—societies such as that of ancient Egypt, for example, or of medieval Europe. In other societies, such as that of classical Greece, individualism counted for more than collectivism. During the period which historians speak of as early modern times, the interests and rights of the individual were again in the ascendant. In the political sphere, this emphasis upon individualism was manifested by the creation of nation-states; in the realm of thought and art, it produced the Renaissance; in the area of religion, it split Christendom through the Reformation; and in the field of exploration, it resulted in the discovery and colonization of the Americas and the reopening of the East to western trade.

By the end of the fifteenth century the medieval ideal of universal political unity had been shattered as national monarchies gained supremacy in England, France, and Spain. Despite opposition from popes and nobles alike, vigorous monarchs in these countries succeeded in their attempts at nation-making—a process that fostered and was in turn supported by a growing national consciousness among the common people. In Germany and Italy, however, unification was hampered by many obstacles, and in eastern Europe nation-making proceeded slowly, though Russia emerged as a powerful state after throwing off the Mongol yoke.

In the realm of thought, Italian scholars known as humanists discovered in the manuscripts of ancient Greece and Rome the same emphasis on individual freedom which was rapidly gaining momentum in their own day, and with this spirit of individualism sprang up an unashamed delight in the beauties and joys of life. Heeding Protagoras' ancient maxim that "Man is the measure of all things" and revolting against medieval authority and asceticism, Renaissance man was impelled by a new spirit of independence, a new hunger for experience. The creative vigor of the Italian Renaissance in literature, thought, and the fine arts surged throughout Europe, resulting in one of the most fruitful epochs in the cultural history of mankind.

Carried into the religious sphere, the resurgence of individualism shattered the universal supremacy of the Church and gave rise to the religious diversity of the modern western world. The followers of Luther, Calvin, and Zwingli substituted the authority of the Scriptures for that of the Roman Church and interposed no priestly mediator between the individual and his God. The Roman Church, which launched a vigorous reform movement of its own, nevertheless continued to be a potent force.

Finally, the economic structure of western Europe was transformed radically in early modern times. The quickening of town life abetted the rise of a new and forceful middle class, whose members were the chief supporters and benefactors of the system of economic individualism known as capitalism. Furthermore, overseas expansion stimulated trade, increased wealth, and introduced to European markets an abundance of products previously scarce or unknown. So important was the new trade and its many influences on European life and manners that it is referred to as the Commercial Revolution. The barter economy of the Middle Ages was superseded by one of money, banks, and stock exchanges; and Europe rapidly became the economic center of the world.

Up to the fifteenth century, Asia had been equal or superior to Europe in military power and cultural attainments. But as the West advanced, China and India declined in power and creativity. The European scramble for empire had serious consequences. In Asia, important trading concessions were wrung from the natives; in the New World, indigenous peoples were decimated and their cultures all but erased; in tropical Africa, the Europeans established a lucrative slave trade and reaped rich profits from this callous exploitation of human lives. From the mid-point of the seventeenth century to our own day, European civilization—the most creative, expansive, and aggressive on earth—was to be the dominant and pervasive influence in world history.

10. Masaccio: "St. Peter Healing the Sick" (c. 1427). One of the most innovative contributors to the transformation of western culture during the Renaissance was the young Masaccio, whose painting reveals a profound new understanding of the natural world. The figures in this fresco have weight and conviction, and they move easily through deep space which is consistently illuminated by a single light source and organized rationally according to the laws of perspective. No trace remains of the decorative abstraction of Gothic painting. Masaccio's monumental realism did much to shape the painting of the next 450 years.

11. (above) **Michelangelo Buonarroti: "Pieta"** (c. 1498). The High Renaissance, more than any other period, developed the idea of artistic genius—of great creative, even "divine" talent—in a single individual who, by its possession, stood above the rules of ordinary men. No one represented this concept more convincingly than Michelangelo—sculptor, painter, architect, and poet, who bestrode his time like a colossus. The nobility of sentiment and classic rectitude of the High Renaissance are clearly evident in this early work,

executed when the sculptor was in his twenties. 12. (right) **Jan van Eyck: "Madonna of Chancellor Rolin"** (c. 1434). Northern Europe's cultural pulse quickened at the same time as Italy's, but the northerners held to the ancient medieval vision more tenaciously, for they possessed scarcely any memories of the classical past. Nonetheless, within a framework of transcendent Christian piety, Flemish artists like Van Eyck achieved an intimate, detailed realism which was as compelling as the grander scale of the Italians.

13. Peter Paul Rubens: "The Abduction of the Daughters of Leucippus" (c. 1617).
Significant differences between northern and Italian art persisted into the seventeenth century but were then greatly resolved by the ascendancy of the Baroque
style, a powerful form of dramatic realism which began, expectably enough, in
Italy but quickly spread throughout Europe. Among the first painters to assimilate
the Italian manner, and perhaps the most effective in popularizing it throughout
northern Europe, was the great Flemish painter Peter Paul Rubens, whose surging
compositions, dazzling color, and exuberantly sensual mood comprise an unsurpassed exemplar of the Baroque ideal.

Chapter 12

Europe in Transition

Religion and Politics: 1300-1500

INTRODUCTION. In Europe the fourteenth and fifteenth centuries were marked by a decline of those institutions and ideas which we think of as typically "medieval" and which had reached their high point during the preceding two centuries. In thought and art an empty formalism replaced the creative forces which had given the Middle Ages such unique methods of expression as scholasticism and the Gothic style. Economic and social progress gave way to depression and social strife, with peasant revolts a characteristic symptom of instability.

The universal Church experienced a disintegration similar to that which had already fatally weakened its great medieval rival, the Holy Roman Empire. The Church's prestige was gravely weakened from within by the reformers and heretics, while external factors, chiefly political and economic, undermined its power and authority. By the sixteenth century these forces would be strong enough to bring about the Protestant and Catholic reformations.

Despite crises and setbacks—the Hundred Years' War came close to wiping out the gains made earlier by French and English monarchs—the process of nation-making continued during the fourteenth and fifteenth centuries. In western Europe the contrasting political trends clearly evident at the end of the thirteenth century—unification in England, France, and Spain, and fragmentation in Germany and Italy—reached their culmination. And in Slavic eastern Europe significant progress in nation-making was made in Russia. In much of Europe by the end of the fifteenth century, the conflicting aims of what are sometimes called the "new monarchies" were superseding the quarrels of feudal barons.

THE DECLINE OF THE MEDIEVAL CHURCH

Dangers facing the papacy. The history of the medieval Church divides roughly into three periods—dissemination, domination, and disintegration. In the initial period, which lasted from about the fifth through the eleventh centuries, Roman Christianity spread throughout the West—even into Slavic and Scandinavian lands. The Church's administrative apparatus was disrupted by feudalism, but by the end of the eleventh century the Church had become the most powerful propertied and political institution in the West. The period of domination—the twelfth and thirteenth centuries—reached its zenith in the pontificate of Innocent III, who made and deposed temporal princes at will. The Church then seemed unassailable in its prestige, dignity, and power. Yet that strength had already begun to wane, and during the next two centuries the processes of disintegration were to run their course.

Papal power was threatened by the growth of nation-states, which challenged the Church's temporal pretensions. Joined by some of the local clergy, rulers opposed papal interference in state matters and favored the establishment of general Church councils to curb papal power. In addition, the papacy was criticized by reformers, who had seen the medieval reformation and the crusades transformed from their original high-minded purposes to suit the ambitions of the pontiffs, and by the bourgeoisie, whose realistic outlook was fostering growing skepticism, national patriotism, and religious self-reliance. During the fourteenth and fifteenth centuries these factors took their toll, and papal influence rapidly declined.

Boniface VIII. A century after the papacy's zenith under Innocent III, Boniface VIII (1294-1303) was forced to withdraw his fierce opposition to taxes levied on the great wealth of the Church by Edward I in England and Philip IV in France. Emulating Innocent, Boniface threatened to depose the "impious king," as he termed Philip, but he gave way when Philip with the support of the Estates-General prohibited the export of money to Rome.

A final and more humiliating clash with the French king had long-range implications for the papacy. When Boniface boldly declared, in the most famous of all papal bulls, *Unam Sanctam* (1302), that "subjection to the Roman pontiff is absolutely necessary to salvation for every human creature," Philip demanded that the pope be tried for his "sins" by a general Church council. In 1303 Philip's henchmen broke into Boniface's summer home at Anagni to arrest him and take him to France to stand trial. Their kidnaping plot was foiled when the pope was rescued by his friends. Shocked and humiliated, Boniface died a month later.

The Avignon papacy. The success of the French monarchy was as complete as if Boniface had been dragged before Philip. Two years after Boniface's death, a French archbishop was chosen pope. Taking the title of Clement V, he not only exonerated Philip but praised his Christian zeal in bringing charges against Boniface. Clement never went to Rome, where feuding noble families made life turbulent, but moved the papal headquarters to Avignon in France, where the papacy remained under French influence from 1305 to 1377. During this period, the so-called "Babylonian Captivity" of the Church, papal prestige suffered enormously. All Christendom believed that Rome was the only rightful capital for the Church. Moreover, the English, Germans, and Italians accused the popes and the cardinals, who were also French, of being instruments of the French king.

The Avignon papacy added fuel to the fires of those critics who were attacking Church corruption, papal temporal claims, and the apparent lack of spiritual enthusiasm. Deprived of much of their former income from England, Germany, and Italy, and living in splendor in a newly built fortress-palace, the Avignon popes expanded the papal bureaucracy, added new Church taxes, and collected the old taxes more efficiently. This produced denouncements of the wealth of the Church and a demand for its reformation.

The Great Schism. When the papacy took heed of popular opinion and returned to Rome in 1377, it seemed for a time that the fortunes of the Roman Church would improve. But the reverse proved true. A papal election was held the following year, and the College of Cardinals, perhaps influenced by a shouting mob milling around the Vatican, elected an Italian pope. A few months later the French cardinals declared the election invalid and elected a French pope, who returned to Avignon.

The Church was now in an even worse state than it had been during the Babylonian Captivity. During the Great Schism, as the split of the Church into two allegiances was called, there were two popes, each with his college of cardinals and capital city, each claiming universal sovereignty, each sending forth papal administrators and taxing Christendom, and each excommunicating the other. The nations of Europe gave allegiance as their individual political interests prompted them. In order to keep that allegiance, the rival popes had to make concessions to their political supporters and largely abandoned the practice of interfering in national politics.

The Great Schism seemed to be permanent after the original rival popes died and each camp elected a replacement instead of working to heal the breach in the Church. Reli-gious life suffered, for "Christendom looked upon the scandal helpless and depressed, and yet impotent to remove it. With two sections of Christendom each declaring the other lost, each cursing and denouncing the other, men soberly asked who was saved."[1] Heresy flourished as doubt and confusion caused many to break away from the Church.

The Conciliar Movement. Positive action came in the form of the Conciliar Movement, a return to the early Christian practice of solving Church problems by means of a general council of prelates (see p. 128). In 1395 the professors at the University of Paris proposed that a general council, representing the Universal Church, should meet to heal the Schism. A majority of the cardinals of both camps accepted this solution, and in 1409 they met at the Council of Pisa, deposed both pontiffs, and elected a third man. But neither of the two deposed popes would give up his office, and the papal throne now had three claimants.

Such an intolerable situation necessitated another Church council. In 1414 the Holy Roman emperor assembled at Constance the most impressive Church gathering of the period. For the first time voting took place on a purely national basis. Instead of the traditional assembly of bishops, the Council included lay representatives and was organized as a convention of "nations" (German, Italian, French, and English, the Spanish entering later). Each nation had one vote. The nationalistic structure of the Council was highly significant as an indication that the new tendency toward such alignments was being recognized by the Church's hierarchy. Finally, through the deposition of the various papal claimants and the election of Martin v in 1417, the Great Schism was ended, and a single papacy was restored at Rome.

Failure of internal reform. The Conciliar Movement represented a reforming and democratizing influence in the Church, aimed at transforming the papacy into something like a limited monarchy. But the movement was not to endure, even though the Council of Constance had solemnly decreed that general councils were superior to popes and that they should meet at regular intervals in the future. Taking steps to preserve his posi-

In this contemporary sketch of John Huss being led to execution, the reformer wears the headgear which branded him as a heretic condemned by the Council of Constance in 1415.

tion, the pope announced that to appeal to a Church council without having first obtained papal consent was heretical. The restoration of a single head of the Church, together with the inability of later councils to bring about much-needed reform, enabled the popes to discredit the Conciliar Movement by 1450. It was almost a century before the great Council of Trent met in 1545 to reform a Church which had already irreparably lost many countries to Protestantism.

Unfortunately, while the popes hesitated to call councils to effect reform, they failed to bring about reform themselves. The popes busied themselves not with internal problems but with Italian politics and patronage of the arts. Thus, "the papacy emerged as something between an Italian city-state and a European power, without forgetting at the same time the claim to be the vice-regent of Christ. The pope often could not make up his own mind whether he was the successor of Peter or of Caesar. Such vacillation had much to do with the rise and success . . . of the Reformation."[2]

Heresy: Wycliffe and Huss. Throughout the fourteenth century the cries against Church corruption became louder at the same time that heretical thoughts were being voiced. In England *Piers the Plowman* (see p. 257) mercilessly upbraided the corruption, ignorance, and worldliness of the clergy, and a professor at Oxford named John Wycliffe (1320?-1384) assailed not only Church abuses but Church doctrines. Because of his beliefs that the Church should be subordinate to the state, that salvation was primarily an individual matter between man and God, that transubstantiation as taught by the Church was false, and that outward rituals and veneration of relics were idolatrous, Wycliffe has been called the dawn-star of the Protestant Revolt. He formed bands of "poor priests," called Lollards, who taught his views; and he provided the people with an English translation of the Bible, which he considered the final authority in matters of religion. Although Wycliffe's demands for reform did not succeed, the Lollards, including the famous John Ball (see p. 217), spread a more radical version of Wycliffe's ideas until the movement was driven underground early in the next century.

In Bohemia—where a strong reform movement, linked with the resentment of the Czechs towards their German overlords, was under way—Wycliffe's doctrines were propagated by Czech students who had heard him at Oxford. In particular, his beliefs influenced John Huss (1369?-1415), an impassioned preacher in Prague and later rector of the university there. Huss' attacks on the abuses of clerical power led him, like Wycliffe, to conclude that the true Church was composed of a universal priesthood of believers and that Christ alone was its head. But Huss, who was more preacher and reformer than theologian, did not accept Wycliffe's denial of the validity of transubstantiation.

Huss' influence became so great that he was excommunicated. Later the emperor gave him a safe-conduct to stand trial for heresy at the Council of Constance. Huss refused to recant his views, and the Council ordered him burned at the stake in spite of his safe-conduct. This action made Huss a martyr to the Czechs, who rebelled against both the German emperor, who was also king of Bohemia, and the Catholic Church. The Czechs maintained their political and religious independence for more than a generation before they were crushed. In the sixteenth century the remaining Hussites merged with the Lutherans.

Reasons for Church decline. The reasons for the Church's decline during the fourteenth and fifteenth centuries can be divided into those that existed within the Church itself and those that were weakening it from the outside. By the early sixteenth century these forces were strong enough to bring about the Reformation.

As we have seen, trenchant criticisms of the clergy had come from a variety of sources, and the Conciliar Movement had gone so far as to challenge the supreme power of the pope himself. And while criticisms increased, the Church continued to decline in spiritual leadership. The worldly concerns of the fourteenth- and fifteenth-century popes—including their deep involvement in Italian politics—pushed the Church further in the direction of secularization.

Among the outside pressures that led to the Church's decline, the new spirit of inquiry encouraged by the Renaissance (see Chapter 13) resulted in a new critical attitude toward religious institutions. And the newly invented printing press provided the means for the rapid dissemination of ideas. In the socioeconomic field, the medieval Church was slow in adapting itself to the new environment of the towns. The problems arising from town life too often went unanswered by the Church, which failed to provide enough parish priests to keep pace with the growth of urban population. It is no accident that the towns became centers of heresy. Finally, the development of nationalism and the growing reluctance of kings to obey any opposing institution, including the Church, were evident in the encounters between Boniface VIII and the French ruler Philip IV.

CRISIS IN ENGLAND AND FRANCE

The Hundred Years' War. Nation-making in both France and England was greatly affected by the long conflict that colored much of their history during the fourteenth and fifteenth centuries. In both lands the crisis of war led to a resurgence of feudalism. Another deterrent to the rise of royal power was the increase in the power of the representative assemblies, Parliament and the Estates-General. Nevertheless, in the long run the increasing anarchy and misery of the times stimulated nationalistic feelings and a demand for strong rulers who could guarantee law and order. Thus by the late fifteenth century the French and English kings were able to resume the task of establishing the institutions of the modern nation-state.

The Hundred Years' War sprang from a fundamental conflict between the aims of the English and the French monarchies. The English kings wanted to regain the large holdings in France that had been theirs in the days of Henry II. The French kings, on the other hand, were determined not only to keep what had been taken from John of England but to expand further. Their ultimate goal was a centralized France under the direct rule of the monarchy at Paris.

Another factor was the clash of French and English economic interests in Flanders. This region was coming more and more under French control, to the chagrin of the English wool growers who supplied the great Flemish woolen industry, and of the English king whose income came in great part from duties on wool.

The immediate excuse for the Anglo-French conflict was a dispute over the succession to the French throne. In 1328, after the direct line of the Capetians became extinct, Philip VI of the House of Valois assumed the throne. The English king, Edward III, maintained that he was the legitimate heir to the French throne because his mother was a sister of the late French king. The

French nobility disputed this claim, which became a pretext for war. Interrupted by several peace treaties and a number of truces, the conflict stretched from 1337 to 1453. At the naval battle of Sluys (1340) the English gained command of the Channel and thus were able to send their armies to France at will. Thereafter England won a series of great victories—at Crécy (1346), Poitiers (1356), and Agincourt (1415), where the French lost some 7000 knights, including many great nobles, and the English only 500.

The English armies were much more effective than those of the French. With no thought of strategy, the French knights charged the enemy at a mad gallop and then engaged in hand-to-hand fighting. The English learned other methods. Their secret weapon was the longbow, apparently taken over from the Welsh. Six feet long and made of special wood, the longbow shot steel-tipped arrows which were dangerous at four hundred yards and deadly at one hundred. The usual English plan of battle called for the knights to fight dismounted. Protecting them was a forward wall of bowmen just behind a barricade of iron stakes planted in the ground to slow down the enemy's charge. By the time the enemy cavalry reached the dismounted knights, only a few remained to be taken care of; the "feathered death" had done its work.

English military triumphs stirred English pride and what we now think of as nationalism—love of country, identification with it, and a sense of difference from, and usually superiority to, other peoples. However, patriotism was stirring in France also. The revival of French spirit is associated with Joan of Arc, who initiated a series of French victories.

Impelled by inward voices which she believed divine, Joan persuaded the timid French ruler to allow her to lead an army to relieve the besieged city of Orléans. Clad in white armor and riding a white horse, she inspired confidence and a feeling of invincibility in her followers, and in 1429 Orléans was rescued from what had seemed certain conquest. But Joan met a tragic end. Captured by the enemy, she was found guilty of bewitching the English soldiers and was burned at the stake, while the French king remained indifferent to her fate.

The martyrdom of the Maid of Orléans was a turning point in the long struggle. The French army was reorganized: a strong force of artillery was developed, and the soldiers were well paid and sternly disciplined. English resistance crumbled as military superiority now turned full circle; the English longbow was outmatched by French artillery. Of the vast territories they had once controlled in France, the English retained only Calais when the war ended in 1453.

Aftermath of war in England. The Hundred Years' War exhausted England, and discontent was rife in Parliament and among the peasants. (On the peasants' revolt of 1381, see p. 217.) Richard II (1377-1399), the last Plantagenet king, was unstable, cruel, and power hungry, and he foreshadowed modern absolute monarchs in believing that the king should control the lives and property

This illumination depicts a scene of late medieval warfare typical of the Hundred Years' War. Note the suits of armor, crossbows, longbows, and the early form of cannon.

of his subjects. His seizure of the properties of Henry, the duke of Lancaster, led to a revolt in which Henry was victorious.

Henry IV established the House of Lancaster, which ruled England from 1399 to 1461. He had the support of Parliament, which had deeply resented Richard's autocratic reign and was determined that its authority should not again be slighted. Hard-pressed for money to suppress revolts at home and carry on the war in France, the Lancastrian kings became more and more financially dependent upon Parliament. In return for money grants, Parliament acquired such gains as the guarantee of freedom of debate, the right to approve the appointment of the king's chief officials and members of his council, the stipulation that money bills must originate in the House of Commons, and the rule that the king's statutes should duplicate exactly petitions presented by the Commons. Not until 1689, when England became a constitutional monarchy, would Parliament again exercise such powers.

Baronial rivalry to control both Parliament and the crown flared up during the reign of the third Lancastrian king, and when he went completely insane in 1453, the duke of York, the strongest man in the kingdom, became regent. Two years later full-scale civil war broke out between the House of York and the partisans of the Lancaster family. The struggle became known as the Wars of the Roses; the white rose was the badge of the House of York, and the red rose that of the House of Lancaster. In 1461 the Yorkists managed to have their leader, Edward IV, crowned king. Ten years later Edward had succeeded in cowing the nobles and in winning the support of the middle class, who saw a strong monarchy as the only alternative to anarchy. Edward's power became practically absolute, foreshadowing the strong rule of the Tudors that soon followed.

The promise of the House of York ended in 1483 when Edward IV died, leaving two young sons as his heirs. Their uncle, Richard, bribed and intimidated Parliament to declare his nephews illegitimate and took the throne. The two boys were imprisoned in the Tower of London, where they were secretly murdered. The double murder was too much for

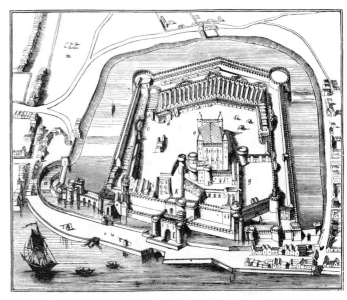

A sixteenth-century engraving of the Tower of London, long used as a prison for those accused of crimes against English monarchs, shows the complex network of walls, towers, living quarters, and fortress which was continually added to and modified from the time of William the Conqueror until well into modern times.

the nation, and support was thrown to the cause of Henry Tudor, who, in his lineage and later marriage to Edward IV's daughter, united the Houses of Lancaster and York. At Bosworth Field in 1485 Richard died fighting as his army deserted him. According to tradition, his crown was found in a bush on the battlefield and placed on the head of Henry VII, the first of the Tudor line, which ruled England from 1485 to 1603.

Beginning of Tudor rule. Under Tudor rule England achieved the full status of a national state. During the reigns of the shrewd Henry VII (1485-1509) and his successor, Henry VIII (1509-1547), strong, almost absolute government was reintroduced into England, with the people supporting the monarchy because it held the nobility in check. The Court of Star Chamber, established by Edward IV, was the most effective royal instrument in suppressing the unruly barons; it bypassed the established common law courts, whose judges and juries were too often intimidated and bribed by powerful nobles, and operated secretly and swiftly without benefit of juries. Because the Tudor rulers restored order and promoted trade at home and abroad, they won the support of the people of middle rank—the burghers and landed gentry—and upon this support their power was primarily built. Though often high-handed, Tudor kings always worked through Parliament.

France after the Hundred Years' War: Louis XI. The Hundred Years' War left France with a new national consciousness and a royal power that was stronger than ever before. In 1438 the king had become the virtual head of the church in France by decreeing that it be run by a council of French bishops whose appointment was to be controlled by the monarch. Furthermore, the *taille*, a land tax voted during the war to support a standing army, became permanent, making the king financially independent of the Estates-General. Thus the purse strings, which the English Parliament used to gain concessions from the king, were kept firmly under royal control in France.

After the war the process of consolidating royal power was continued by Louis XI (1461-1483), son of the king aided by Joan of Arc. Physically unattractive and completely lacking in scruples, Louis earned himself the epithet, the "universal spider." In his pursuit of power he used any weapon—violence, bribery, and treachery—to obtain his ends. When the French nobles rose in revolt, dignifying themselves as the League for the Public Welfare, Louis outfoxed them by agreeing to their Magna Carta-like demands and then ignoring his pledged word.

Louis XI's most powerful antagonist was the duke of Burgundy, Charles the Bold, whose possession of Flanders and the other Low Countries or Netherlands (modern Holland, Belgium, and Luxemburg) made him one of Europe's richest rulers. After Charles' death in 1477, Louis seized most of Burgundy, while the remainder of the duke's possessions passed to his daughter Mary. When she married the German emperor Maximilian I, the Netherlands came into the hands of the House of Hapsburg (see map, p. 327). Like Henry VII of England, Louis XI was one of the "new monarchs" who created the absolute states which were to dominate Europe in the early modern period.

THE POLITICAL UNIFICATION OF SPAIN AND PORTUGAL

Ferdinand and Isabella: "One king, one law, one faith." Another "new monarchy" emerged in 1479 when Isabella of Castile and Ferdinand of Aragon, who had married ten years earlier, began a joint rule that united the Iberian peninsula except for Granada, Navarre, and Portugal. The "Catholic Sovereigns," to use the title the pope conferred on Ferdinand and Isabella, set out to establish an effective royal despotism in Spain. The Holy Brotherhood, a league of cities which had long existed for mutual protection against unruly nobles, was taken over by the crown, and its militia was used as a standing army and police force. The powerful and virtually independent military orders of knights, which had emerged during the *Reconquista*, were also brought under royal control.

Ferdinand and Isabella believed that the Church should be subordinate to royal government—a belief they shared with the other "new monarchs" of Europe. By tactful negotiations, the Spanish sovereigns induced the pope to give them the right to make Church appointments in Spain and to establish a Spanish Court of Inquisition, largely free of papal control. The Inquisition confiscated the property of most Jews and Muslims and terrified the Christian clergy and laymen into accepting royal absolutism as well as religious orthodoxy. Although the Inquisition greatly enhanced the power of the Spanish crown, it also caused many talented people to flee the land of persecution. About 150,000 Spanish Jews, mainly merchants and professional people, fled to Holland, England, North Africa, and the Ottoman empire. Calling themselves Sephardim, these exiles retained their Spanish language and customs into the twentieth century.

A final manifestation of Spanish absolutism, defined by Isabella herself as "one king, one law, one faith," was the virtual ignoring of the Cortes of Castile and Aragon. These representative assemblies had emerged in the twelfth century and were thus older than the English Parliament.

The most dramatic act of the Catholic Sovereigns was the conquest of Granada in 1492, the same year that Columbus claimed the New World for Spain. Before Ferdinand died in 1516, twelve years after Isabella, he seized that part of Navarre which lay south of the Pyrenees Mountains. This acquisition, together with the conquest of Granada, completed the national unification of Spain.

Results of Spanish unification. Royal absolutism and unification, coupled with the acquisition of territory in the New and Old Worlds, made Spain the strongest power in sixteenth-century Europe. But the process of unifying Spain had some unfortunate results: (1) Centuries of fighting against the Muslims left a legacy of warlike spirit and inordinate national pride. (2) Religious enthusiasm was whipped up as a means to an end, and the sequel was a heritage of religious bigotry and the death of that tolerance, intellectual curiosity, and sense of balance which had been characteristic of Muslim culture in Spain. (3) Spanish contempt for the Muslims created a scorn for those activities in which the unbelievers had engaged—trade, crafts, manual labor, and agriculture. This attitude hampered Spanish economic development in subsequent centuries.

Portugal. The nucleus of the area which eventually became Portugal was a part of Castile until 1095. In that year the king of Castile gave his daughter to Count Henry of Burgundy, one of many French knights who had helped take Toledo (see p. 208). Her dowry was the county of Portugal, named after its chief town Oporto ("The Port") at the mouth of the Duero River. The son of this marriage organized a revolt against his overlord, the king of Castile, and in 1139 proclaimed himself king of Portugal.

Attempts by Castile to regain Portugal ended in 1385 when John I, aided by English archers, decisively defeated the invader. The following year John signed an alliance with England which has been reaffirmed down the centuries and remains the oldest alliance in existence. In 1415 John took Ceuta in North Africa (see Reference Map 7), thus initiating Portuguese overseas expansion. Carried on by his son, Henry the Navigator, this policy eventually led to the creation of a great overseas empire (see Chapter 17).

DISUNITY IN GERMANY

The early Hapsburgs and the Golden Bull. Between 1254 and 1273 the German monarchy was made virtually nonexistent by the election of two rival foreign princes, neither of whom received wide recognition. Then in 1273 the imperial crown was bestowed upon the obscure Count Rudolf (1273-1291) of the House of Hapsburg—from Habichtsburg (Castle of the Hawk), their home in northern Switzerland. During the remainder of the Middle Ages and in modern times, the Hapsburgs had amazing success in adding to their ancestral lands. Rudolf himself acquired Austria through marriage, and thereafter the Hapsburgs ruled their holdings from Vienna. In the sixteenth century they obtained Bohemia and part of Hungary (see p. 276).

For the time being, however, the Hapsburg hold on the imperial crown proved to be brief. After Rudolf's reign it was passed from one family to another. Then in 1356 the nobility won another significant victory. The Golden Bull, a document which served as the political constitution of Germany until early in the nineteenth century, laid down the procedure for election of the emperor by seven German dignitaries—three archbishops and four lay princes. The electors and other important princes were given rights that made them virtually independent rulers, and the emperor could take no important action without the consent of the imperial feudal assembly, the Diet, which met infrequently. It has been said that the Golden Bull "legalized anarchy and called it a constitution"; in reality it stabilized the political situation in Germany by recognizing the independence of the princes, thereby encouraging them to emulate the new national monarchs and create stable governments in their principalities. It also ended disputed elections and civil wars over the succession. But with the emperor virtually powerless, people thereafter commonly referred to the welter of duchies, counties, bishoprics, and free cities as the Germanies, not Germany.

The imperial crown of Germany was returned to the Hapsburg family in 1438. From this time until 1806, when the Holy Roman Empire disappeared, the Hapsburgs held the imperial crown almost without a break. Maximilian I (1493-1519) helped make the Hapsburgs the most potent force in sixteenth-century Europe by taking as his wife Mary of Burgundy (see p. 272), heiress of the rich Low Countries, and by marrying his son to the heiress of Spain.

Inspired by the rise of the "new monarchies," Maximilian attempted to strengthen his power. His program for a national court system, army, and taxation was frustrated by the German princes who insisted on jealously guarding what they called "German freedom." The emperor continued to be limited in power; nor did the empire have

an imperial treasury, an efficient central administration, or a standing army. And so the phantom Holy Roman Empire lived on as Voltaire later characterized it: "Neither Holy, nor Roman, nor an Empire."

ITALY: WEALTHY BUT DIVIDED

The northern city-states. The virtual ending of German imperial influence after 1250 left the three major divisions of Italy—the city-states of northern Italy, the Papal States, and the Kingdom of Naples (see map, p. 283)—free to follow their own devices. Such city-states as Venice, Florence, Milan, Genoa, and Pisa had grown wealthy from their thriving industries, lucrative trade, and banking houses that handled papal revenues and made loans to European monarchs.

Within each city there were intense rivalries and feuds. Unlike the situation in northern Europe, where the bourgeoisie inhabited the towns and the nobles lived on country manors, the Italian nobility had city houses as well as country villas. In some Italian cities arcaded streets enabled the townsmen to go about their business safe from the arrows which from time to time flew between the towered houses of feuding nobles.

In both the intracity rivalries and the struggles between city-states, mercenary soldiers under the command of leaders called *condottieri* were employed. Coming from all over Europe, these adventurers sold their swords to the highest bidder, but, in order to live and fight another day, they carried on their fighting with a minimum of bloodshed. Far different from the twentieth-century wars of annihilation, these petty conflicts did not hinder the spectacular progress in art and learning called the Italian Renaissance (see Chapter 13).

Civic patriotism advanced rapidly under the influence of the prosperous burghers, who finally succeeded in ousting the restless feudal aristocrats from positions of power. Ingenious city charters and civic constitutions were drafted, and there was much trial

In the early 1400's goods from many parts of the world flowed into Italy to be sold side by side in the marketplaces, such as this drapers' market in Bologna.

and error in the art of government. Until the end of the thirteenth century the prevailing political trend in the cities was toward republicanism and representative government.

Two city-state republics were of unusual interest. Venice, the "Pearl of the Adriatic," was one of the richest cities of its time, controlling an empire of ports and islands in the eastern Mediterranean and carrying much of Europe's maritime trade in its great fleets. The government of this rich republic had been in the hands of a doge (duke), together with a popular assembly, but beginning in the thirteenth century the rich merchants gradually took over the reins of power. They alone sat in the Great Council, which replaced the popular assembly. This oligarchic council appointed the doge and the members of smaller councils which administered the government. Most famous among the smaller councils was the secret Council of Ten, which dealt swiftly with suspected enemies of the government. The merchant oligarchy of Venice provided good government and, unlike other city-states, resolutely squashed internal strife.

Florence—the center of flourishing wool, leather, and silk industries—boasted merchants and bankers who were among the most prosperous in Europe, and its gold florin circulated in many lands as a standard coin. With its many checks and counterchecks of power, the Florentine constitution was bewilderingly complex. For example, the head of the state held office for two months only, and all measures needed a two-thirds majority in five different committees or assemblies to become laws. In theory Florence was a democracy but, as in Venice, real political power was wielded by wealthy businessmen.

During the fourteenth century republicanism declined and most Italian city-states came under the rule of despots. Conspiracy, confusion, and incompetence caused many citizens to welcome a strong leader as political boss or despot. Although Venice maintained the benevolent oligarchy of its merchants with the doge as a figurehead, Florence went under the thumb of the Medici family, and its republican institutions became largely empty forms. The Medici had

no aristocratic antecedents; their status was based on commerce and finance. The significance of the family emblem—six red balls on a field of gold—is unknown, but we are all familiar with the later modification of this insigne—the three balls of the pawnbroker.

The Papal States and the Kingdom of Naples. The Papal States, extending from fifty miles south of the mouth of the Tiber to the northeast across Italy as far as the mouth of the Po River, were poorly organized. The popes found it difficult to force their will upon various petty despots who defied their political authority. Although they headed the great international Church, in Italy the popes acted little differently from the rulers of the other states in the matter of hiring troops, waging wars, and making treaties.

The Kingdom of Naples covered the southern half of the Italian peninsula as well as Sicily. After 1250 the houses of Aragon and Anjou disputed over the kingdom (see p. 238) until Aragon won out early in the fifteenth century. Impoverished by the warfare of foreign armies, with its powerful nobles rebellious, and with brigandage rampant, southern Italy and Sicily sank into a backwardness that was to continue into the twentieth century.

EASTERN EUROPE

German eastward expansion. Since the early tenth century German barons and churchmen had been founding bishoprics and colonizing the land east of the Elbe. The German settlements, however, remained precariously isolated in the midst of large Slavic populations. Then, shortly after 1200, a new development occurred. The Teutonic Knights, a military-religious order founded at the time of the Third Crusade, transferred their operations to eastern Europe. Within fifty years the Knights had conquered the pagan Slavs in Prussia, and by 1350 they ruled the Baltic coastlands as far north as the Gulf of Finland. Assuming the role of a colonial aristocracy, the Knights built castles and towns, and a steady stream of German settlers moved into the conquered lands.

Poland and Lithuania. To the south of Prussia lived the Slavic Poles. They were first united into a state late in the tenth century, but the Polish nobility seldom allowed their monarch to exercise much power. Also in the late tenth century the Poles were converted to Roman Christianity, thus linking Poland to western European culture.

The continued threat of the aggressive Teutonic Knights caused the Polish nobles in 1386 to offer the Polish crown to the king of the neighboring Lithuanians, a pagan people who had expanded into a Russia weakened and fragmented by the Mongol conquest (see p. 277). Converted to Latin Christianity, the Lithuanians joined with the Poles in defeating the Teutonic Knights in the great battle of Tannenberg in 1410. The Knights never regained their former power, and in 1466 they turned West Prussia over to the Poles, retaining East Prussia as a fief of the Polish crown. This settlement was a great blow to German expansion, for the Poles obtained control of the Vistula River and a corridor north to the Baltic Sea, including the important port of Danzig. East Prussia was now cut off from the rest of Germany. In the history of modern Europe, the Polish corridor and Danzig have played an important role.

The Polish state, united with Lithuania in 1386 under a common sovereign, was the largest in Europe, but its promise was never realized. The nobility succeeded in keeping the monarchy elective and weak, and the middle class, composed largely of German settlers and Jewish refugees from persecution in western Europe, remained small and powerless. Above all, Poland faced the hostility of the ambitious tsars of Moscow who sought to rule over all Russians, including those in the huge Polish-Lithuanian state.

Bohemians and Magyars. Two other peoples appeared in the east European family in the Middle Ages. During the ninth and tenth centuries the Slavic Czechs established a kingdom on the Bohemian plain. German influence became strong in Bohemia, which was a part of the Holy Roman Empire, and the Golden Bull of 1356 made the Bohemian king one of the seven imperial electors. Living southeast of Bohemia in the wide and fertile plain known as Hungary were the Magyars, an Asiatic people. Originally the terror of eastern Europe because of their brutal raids (see p. 233), they became civilized, adopted Christianity, and in the eleventh century expanded their state.

The promise of both these rising nations— Bohemia and Hungary—was blighted by a common disaster. The king of Hungary, who was also king of Bohemia, met his death fighting against the Turks in 1526. Terrified at the prospects of Muslim rule, both the Czechs and Hungarians elected the same man to their vacant thrones—Ferdinand, the Hapsburg archduke of neighboring Austria. The Turks, however, occupied most of Hungary (which they would hold until the end of the seventeenth century), leaving Ferdinand only a narrow strip along the western border (see map at left). This intertwining of national fortunes explains how the Haps-

CENTRAL AND EASTERN EUROPE 1526
— Hungary

burgs at Vienna came to rule a polyglot empire of Bohemians, Hungarians, and German Austrians.

South Slavs and Turks in the Balkans. The outstanding political development in southeastern Europe at the close of the Middle Ages was the disappearance of the Byzantine empire and the emergence of the Ottoman Turks as a threat to Europe. Before the end of the fifteenth century the Turks had extended their control over the Balkans and were pushing on toward Vienna. This huge new empire, with its center at Constantinople, was in no sense a national state but rather a bewildering mixture of Turks, Serbs, Hungarians, Bulgarians, Rumanians, Armenians, Greeks, and Jews.

Turkish rule delayed the rise of national states in southeastern Europe until the nineteenth century. The multiplicity of small countries in the Balkans in modern times and the resultant tensions and conflicts have made the peninsula a European danger zone, a source of constant worry to diplomats, and, as in 1914, the direct or indirect cause of wars.

The Mongol conquest of Russia. In Chapter 7 we followed the amazing career of Genghis Khan, who united the unruly tribesmen of Mongolia and then launched them like a thunderbolt on a campaign of world conquest. By 1240 the Mongols had conquered the various Russian principalities, and in 1242 they penetrated to the outskirts of Vienna. Western Europe seemed theirs for the taking, but the death of the great Khan in far-off Mongolia caused the Tatar, or Mongol, armies to return to the lower Volga pending the election of a new khan.

Central Europe was not molested again, but the Mongols continued to dominate Russia from their capital at Sarai on the Volga not far from the modern city of Volgograd. The various Russian principalities were allowed to govern themselves as long as they paid tribute to the Golden Horde, as the Tatars in Russia were called. The khanate of the Golden Horde was only one of the Mongol states, however; the successors of Genghis Khan ruled an empire stretching from Korea on the east to Poland on the west. On the south their holdings included Persia and Afghanistan, as well as the area north of what is now India and Burma. Only since the Second World War has an empire arisen—that of Soviet Russia and its satellites—which could rival the vast expanse of contiguous territory controlled by the Mongols. In fact, the Russian empire together with Communist China not only rivals but nearly duplicates that of the Mongol khanates.

Mongol domination changed the whole course of Russian history; it completed the break between Russia and western European civilization initiated by the decline of Kiev. Asian cultural influences were strong—the status of women was lowered as they accepted the veil and oriental seclusion. Mongols and Russians intermarried freely; hence the saying, "Scratch a Russian and you will find a Tatar." Many authorities believe that the Mongol conquest was a wholesale calamity. Russia was cut off from Europe, and a new Russia north and east of Kiev began to develop. Its nucleus was the grand duchy of Moscow.

Alexander Nevski: pioneer of Russian greatness. Following the Mongol conquest, the most important Russian leader was the prince of Novgorod, Alexander Nevski, who later became the ruler of Vladimir. In the 1240's, before the Mongol onslaught, this staunch warrior had won great victories over the Swedes and the Teutonic Knights. To the Orthodox Church and most princes, the westerners seemed a greater threat to the Russian way of life than the Mongols. Indeed, Nevski obtained Mongol protection and assistance in fighting invaders from the west, who, hoping to profit from the Russian collapse under the Mongol impact, tried to annex territory. Meanwhile, Nevski may have looked forward to the day when his successors would be strong enough to challenge Tatar rule.

Moscow, challenge to Tatar rule. Daniel, the youngest son of Nevski, founded the grand duchy of Moscow, which eventually expelled the Tatars from Russia. Well situated in the central river system of Russia and surrounded by protective forests and marshes, Moscow was at first only a vassal of Vladimir, but it soon absorbed its parent

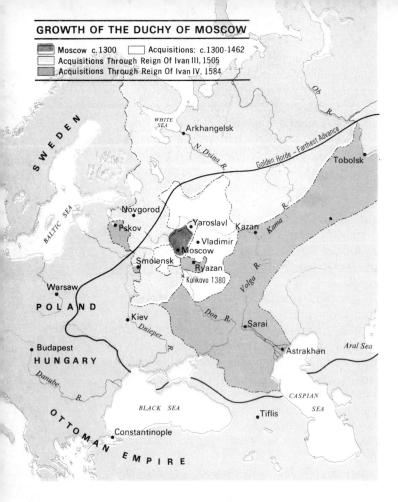

GROWTH OF THE DUCHY OF MOSCOW

- Moscow c. 1300
- Acquisitions: c. 1300-1462
- Acquisitions Through Reign Of Ivan III, 1505
- Acquisitions Through Reign Of Ivan IV, 1584

Ivan the Great. The Muscovite prince who laid the foundations for a Russian national state was Ivan III, the Great (1462-1505), a contemporary of the Tudors and other "new monarchs" in western Europe. Ivan more than doubled his territories by placing most of north Russia under the rule of Moscow, and he proclaimed his absolute sovereignty over all Russian princes and nobles by taking the title of "Great Prince and Autocrat of All Russia." Refusing further tribute to the Tatars, Ivan initiated a series of attacks that opened the way for the complete defeat of the declining Golden Horde, now divided into several khanates.

Ivan married Sophia Palaeologus, the niece of the last Byzantine emperor, and she brought with her to Moscow a number of gifted Italians. Among them were architects who designed an enormous walled palace called the Kremlin. Ivan not only adopted the double-headed eagle and court ceremonies of the Byzantine emperors but also claimed to be their legitimate successor. Thus Ivan sometimes used the title of *tsar*, derived from "Caesar," and he viewed Moscow as the Third Rome, the successor of New Rome (Constantinople).

"Two Romes have fallen, and the third stands." The doctrine that the Russian tsar was the successor of the Byzantine emperors was expressed by the monk Philotheos of Pskov late in the fifteenth century. "Two Romes have fallen," he wrote, "and the third stands, and a fourth one there shall not be." On the basis of the conviction that they were heirs of the Byzantine tradition, Russian rulers were later to press claims to the Dardanelles and parts of southeastern Europe. Moreover, as in the idea expressed by Philotheos when he said, "you are the only tsar for Christians in the whole world,"[3] the Russian tradition would henceforth encompass a great imperial mission.

Some historians see this Russian sense of destiny still operating in a new manifestation—communism—with the same fervor of the earlier Russian dedication to Orthodox Christianity. "Five centuries ago the words of Philotheos of Pskov may have sounded arrogant and foolhardy; but for us today, in the new constellation of world-

state. A major factor in the ascendency of Moscow was the cooperation of its rulers with their Mongol overlords, who granted them the title of Grand Prince of Russia and made them agents for collecting the Tatar tribute from the Russian principalities. Moscow's prestige was further enhanced when it became the center of the Russian Orthodox Church. Its head, the metropolitan, fled from Kiev to Vladimir in 1299 and a few years later established the permanent headquarters of the Church in Moscow.

By the middle of the fourteenth century the power of the Tatars was declining, and the Grand Princes felt capable of openly opposing the Mongol yoke. In 1380, at Kulikovo on the Don, the khan was defeated, and although this hard-fought victory did not end Tatar rule of Russia, it did bring great fame to the Grand Prince. Moscow's leadership in Russia was now firmly based, and by the middle of the fifteenth century its territory had greatly expanded through purchase, war, and marriage (see map).

forces after 1945, they echo through the centuries as the prophetic expression of the most momentous consequence of the fall of Constantinople . . . . on the wider stage of world-history the effects of the events of 1453 are only now making themselves felt."[4]

Ivan the Terrible. The next great ruler of Moscow was Ivan III's grandson, Ivan IV (1547-1584), called "the Terrible." Russia became more despotic as Ivan ruthlessly subordinated the great nobles to his will, exiling or executing many on the slightest pretext. With no consideration for human life, Ivan ordered the destruction of Novgorod, Russia's second city, on suspicion of treason. Another time, in a rage, he struck and killed his gifted eldest son. Yet Ivan was also a farseeing statesman who promulgated a new code of laws, reformed the morals of the clergy, and built the fabulous St. Basil's Cathedral that still stands in Moscow's Red Square.

During Ivan's reign eastern Russia was conquered from the Tatars, and Cossack pioneers then crossed the Ural Mountains in their push to the Pacific—a movement which can be compared with the simultaneous expansion of western Europe across the Atlantic. Ivan's efforts to reach the Baltic and establish trade relations with western Europe were forcibly stopped by Sweden and Poland. Later, however, he was able to inaugurate direct trade with the West by granting English merchants trading privileges at the White Sea port of Archangel (Arkhangelsk) in the far north.

Ivan's death in 1584 was followed by the Time of Trouble, a period of civil wars over the succession and resurgence of the power of the nobility. Both Poland and Sweden intervened in Russian affairs, and their invasions across an indistinct frontier which contains no major natural barriers demonstrated again the danger from the West and contributed to Russia's growing tendency to withdraw into her own distinctive heritage. Order was restored in 1613 when Michael Romanov, the grandnephew of Ivan the Terrible, was elected to the throne by a national assembly that included representatives from fifty cities. The Romanov dynasty ruled Russia until 1917.

SUMMARY

The medieval ideal was unity—a Europe united as a Christian commonwealth and ruled by dual powers, the universal Church and an all-embracing Holy Roman Empire. In theory the emperor would rule in the temporal or earthly realm, and the pope in the affairs of the spirit. Because papal authority was not constricted to national boundaries, the Church was nearly all-encompassing. By contrast, the emperor's authority was limited for the most part to Germany and Italy, and even there imperial power was intermittent.

During the fourteenth and fifteenth centuries, forces were at work which threatened and ultimately undermined the medieval

The moody Ivan the Terrible alternated between acts of political terrorism and prayer. His last act, while on his deathbed, was the taking of monastic vows.

ideal and the edifices stemming from it. The Church was badly weakened from within as a result of the Babylonian Captivity, the Great Schism, and the demands of reformers. And despite continuous opposition from both the Church and the feudal nobles, the national state had become a reality in Europe by the end of the period discussed in this chapter.

Influencing nation-making in both France and England was the Hundred Years' War, which stimulated nationalism in the hearts of Englishmen and Frenchmen alike. Other significant changes resulted from that conflict: in England, the power of Parliament was increased, and the upsurge in the power of the nobility led to the Wars of the Roses, which ended finally with the accession of the Tudors; in France, royal power was consolidated under Louis XI, and further progress in national unification was made. Ferdinand and Isabella completed the creation of a national state in Spain and laid the foundations for its future greatness. On the other hand, Germany and Italy continued divided and weak; their day of national unification would not arrive until the nineteenth century.

Eastern and southern Europe were on the periphery of most of the dynamic currents of change that were transforming western Europe. There was much movement of peoples, and the rise and fall of states culminated in the emergence of Poland, Lithuania, Bohemia, and Hungary. Russia, effectively isolated on its frozen plains, languished for years under the rule of the Mongols. But when the dukes of Moscow assumed leadership of the Russians, a long campaign was initiated against the alien Mongols—a historical movement somewhat similar to the *Reconquista* in Spain.

Truly, the late Middle Ages was an era of nation-making. The nation-states this period produced—in particular England, France, and Spain—would assume new roles in the stirring international drama that is the story of Europe from about 1500 to 1650, a story which will be taken up in Chapter 15.

SUGGESTIONS FOR READING

W. K. Ferguson, **Europe in Transition, 1300 to 1520,** Houghton Mifflin, 1963. A comprehensive work of synthesis. See also D. Hay, **Europe in the Fourteenth and Fifteenth Centuries,** Harcourt, Brace & World, 1967; and E. Cheyney, **The Dawn of a New Era, 1250-1453,*** Torchbooks. R. E. Lerner, **The Age of Adversity: The Fourteenth Century,*** Cornell, and Jerah Johnson and W. Percy, **The Age of Recovery: The Fifteenth Century,*** Cornell, are lively interpretative essays. M. Aston, **The Fifteenth Century: The Prospect of Europe,*** Harcourt, Brace & World, 1968, is a well-illustrated popular introduction.

Good accounts of Church history during this period are: L. Elliott-Binns, **History of the Decline and Fall of the Medieval Papacy,** Shoe String, 1967; and L. von Pastor, **The History of the Popes from the Close of the Middle Ages,** Vol. I, Herder, 1923. See also G. Mollat, **The Popes at Avignon,** Nelson, 1962; G. Leff, **Heresy in the Later Middle Ages,** 2 vols., Barnes and Noble, 1967; K. McFarlane, **John Wycliffe and the Beginnings of English Nonconformity,** Verry, 1952; M. Spinka, **John Hus: A Biography,** Princeton, 1968.

E. Perroy, **The Hundred Years' War,*** Capricorn. The standard account.

A. R. Myers, **England in the Late Middle Ages,*** Penguin; George Holmes, **The Later Middle Ages, 1272-1485,*** Norton. Excellent surveys of English history during the period. See also J. R. Lander, **The Wars of the Roses,*** Capricorn; and Faith Thompson, **A Short History of Parliament, 1295-1642,** Minnesota, 1953.

P. S. Lewis, **Later Medieval France,** St. Martin's, 1967. Government and society in the late Middle Ages. Also recommended are J. Michelet, **Joan of Arc,*** Michigan; and Paul M. Kendall, **Louis XI,** Norton, 1969. The France of Louis XI is the setting of Sir Walter Scott's famous novel, **Quentin Durwood** (many editions).

J. Mariéjol, **The Spain of Ferdinand and Isabella,** Rutgers, 1961. A gracefully written history of the emergence of Spain. A popular account is Townsend Miller, **The Castles and the Crown,*** Capricorn. See also J. H. Elliott, **Imperial Spain, 1469-1716,*** Mentor; and C. Roth, **The Spanish Inquisition,*** Norton.

G. Barraclough, **The Origins of Modern Germany,*** Capricorn. The best account of this period of German history. J. A. Symonds, **The Renaissance in Italy,** Vol. I, **The Age of the Despots** (many editions), is a celebrated account of Italian politics in the fourteenth and fifteenth centuries.

Good introductions to Slavic eastern Europe are O. Halecki, **Borderlands of Western Civilization: A History of East Central Europe,** Ronald, 1952; and F. Dvornik, **The Slavs in European History and Civilization,** Rutgers, 1962. See also P. Coles, **The Ottoman Impact on Europe,*** Harcourt, Brace & World, 1968.

N. Riasanovsky, **History of Russia,*** 2nd ed., Oxford, 1969; G. Vernadsky, **History of Russia,*** rev. ed., Yale, 1961. Excellent surveys. See also Vols. III-V of G. Vernadsky's detailed **History of Russia,** Yale, 1953-1969; I. Grey, **Ivan III and the Unification of Russia,*** Collier; J. Koslow, **Ivan the Terrible,** Hill and Wang, 1962.

*Indicates an inexpensive paperbound edition.

Chapter 13

Man Is the Measure

The Renaissance: 1300-1600

INTRODUCTION. To the historians who viewed the Middle Ages as the "dark ages" —a time of stagnation and ignorance—the epoch of European history that followed seemed to spring to life suddenly like Minerva from the brow of Jove, resplendent in beauty and wisdom. They looked on the new age as an awakening from centuries of lethargy, and they labeled it *Renaissance*, meaning "rebirth."

Today many historians deny that the Renaissance brought any distinct break in the development of European culture. As we have already noted, the Middle Ages made rich intellectual and artistic contributions to civilization. In what ways, then, can the Renaissance be said to signify a "rebirth"?

First of all, there was an intense renewal of interest in the literature of classical Greece and Rome—a development known as the Revival of Learning. No longer were scholars confined to medieval translations of the famous writers of ancient Greece; many began to read the works of Plato, Aristotle, and others in the original Greek. In addition, they searched the monasteries for old Latin manuscripts and translated hitherto unknown works from Greek antiquity into Latin. Thus the humanists, as these scholars were called, reintroduced classical learning into the mainstream of western thought. Second, while the scholars rediscovered classical thought, artists in Italy were stimulated and inspired by their study and imitation of classical architecture and sculpture.

But the spirit of the Renaissance was not characterized by a mere cult of antiquity, a looking backward into the past. The men of the Renaissance were the harbingers of the modern world, energetically and enthusiastically engaged in reshaping their political, economic, and religious environment, in pushing back geographical boundaries and extending the limits of human knowledge. Renaissance culture strikingly exhibits belief in the worth of man and his desire to think and act as a free agent and a well-rounded individual. The Renaissance spirit was admirably summed up by a versatile genius of the fifteenth century, Leon Battista Alberti, when he declared, "Men can do all things if they will."[1]

In some respects every age is an age of transition, but it may be fair to state that the Renaissance marks one of the turning points in western civilization. The dominant insti-

tutions and thought systems of the Middle Ages were becoming devitalized; scholasticism, Church authority, and conformity were on the wane, and a more modern culture which depended on individualism, skepticism, and ultimately on science was taking its place.

We must be cautious in our analysis, however. The Renaissance did not burst forth simultaneously in all parts of Europe, and some medieval habits and institutions persisted for a long time; throughout the Renaissance the vast majority of illiterate common people clung to the ways of their forefathers.

The Renaissance originated with a relatively small, educated group dwelling in the cities of central and northern Italy. We shall begin with the Revival of Learning and the flowering of art in this locality and conclude with a discussion of other facets of the Renaissance as its ideas crossed the Alps to France, Germany, and England. It was in England that the underlying optimism and dynamism of the entire Renaissance period was epitomized by Shakespeare when he said:

> O, wonder!
> How many goodly creatures are there here!
> How beauteous mankind is! O brave new world,
> That has such people in't![2]

THE ITALIAN RENAISSANCE: THE BACKGROUND

The waning of the Middle Ages. By the fourteenth century there was a marked decline in medieval institutions and ideas. The feudal social structure was weakening before the growing power of the middle class, which sided with the new monarchs and thrived on the revival of trade and the growth of towns. The threat of armies using gunpowder was revolutionizing warfare at the expense of armor-clad knights. Heresy and schism racked the Church, and its temporal power was increasingly being challenged by aggressive national monarchs.

An empty formalism replaced the creativeness that had given the twelfth and thirteenth centuries their unique forms of ex-

pression. Although asceticism remained a pious ideal, it gained few adherents among the acquisitive townspeople and was openly flouted by many of the clergy. Scholars still held learned disputations at the universities, but scholasticism was unable to satisfy the growing interest in man and society. In art the Gothic style of the twelfth and thirteenth centuries, superb in its balance and restraint, had given place to exaggeration and flamboyance. Decoration and ornamentation became ends in themselves.

Meanwhile, sophisticated Italian urban society no longer found medieval ideals of other-worldliness and asceticism satisfactory. Pious religious themes were not so engaging as satires directed against a sometimes corrupt clergy and the outworn conventions of chivalry. Searching for new modes of expression, thinkers and artists found what they wanted in the classical legacy of Greece and Rome.

Individualism and tradition in the Renaissance. In a sense, the Renaissance is the history of individual men expressing themselves brilliantly, and often tempestuously, in art, poetry, science, religion, and exploration. While the medieval way taught the unimportance of this life, stressed its snares and evils, and smothered the individual with a host of confining rules and prohibitions, the Renaissance beckoned man to enjoy beauty, to savor the opportunities of this world, and to be himself, regardless of restraints. Above all, the new spirit called upon its followers to adopt the concept of *l'uomo universale* ("the universal man" or "the complete man"). Life was best lived when the human personality showed its versatility by expression in many forms: ad-

vancement of the mind, perfection of the body, cultivation of the social graces, and appreciation and creativity in the arts.

Like any other movement, however, individualism had its negative aspects and its excesses. The lawlessness and political confusion of the Italian Renaissance and the strongly amoral character of its society were due in no small measure to the tendency of men to regard themselves as above the law.

Despite the prevalence of individualism, however, most men continued to share in the corporate life of the Church and the guilds, and many medieval customs and habits of thought persisted for centuries. In the case of humanism, as we shall see, no sudden revolution of philosophical doctrines occurred to set the Renaissance apart from the Middle Ages. Similarly, the artists of the Renaissance, who found inspiration in antiquity and whose works reflected a renewed interest in classical mythology and in the beauties of the human body, did not break completely with the subject matter and

RENAISSANCE EUROPE
ABOUT 1500

Northward Spread
of Renaissance

artistic techniques of their medieval predecessors. Although their interest in rendering secular subjects increased, Renaissance artists still looked to the Church as their greatest single patron. Building churches, sculpturing saints and Madonnas, and painting religious murals continued to occupy the genius of hundreds of artists during this period.

Renaissance patrons. In the Italian cities the newly wealthy class of traders, bankers, and manufacturers conspicuously displayed their wealth and bolstered their social importance by patronizing artists and scholars. While leading commissions for artists in the fifteenth century were still obtained from such communal bodies as guilds and churches, individual patronage began to play a more important role.

Among the most famous patrons were members of the Medici family who, by acting as champions of the lower classes, ruled Florence for sixty years (1434-1494) behind a facade of republican forms. Lorenzo de' Medici, who was first citizen of Florence from 1469 until his death in 1492, carried on

his family's proud traditions and added so much luster to Florence that he became known as Lorenzo the Magnificent. His career signifies the zenith of Florentine leadership in the arts.

Other princes and despots of Italian city-states patronized the arts, and the popes were eager to sponsor artists. In the sixteenth century the popes outdid secular rulers in the splendor of their court. Pope Alexander VI (1492-1503), the father of the unscrupulous poisoners Cesare and Lucrezia Borgia, was a target for criticism because he devoted more time and thought to furthering the fortunes of his family than he did to religious matters. Wealthy families actively sought to control the papacy, and the Medici succeeded in placing two of their members, Leo X (1513-1521), son of Lorenzo, and Clement VII (1523-1534), nephew of Leo, in this office. Leo's pontificate, in particular, was one of great activity in the arts and learning in Rome.

A Renaissance artist had the benefit of the security and protection offered by his patron and enjoyed a definite advantage from working exclusively on commission. The artist knew where his finished work would repose, in cathedral, villa, or city square; this situation contrasts with some later periods, when artists painted when and as they wished and then attempted to sell the work to anyone who would buy it.

Manners and morals. During the Renaissance the newly wealthy citizens of the Italian cities sought refinement in every aspect of their culture. Believing that the mark of nobility was an elegance of manner as well as a cultivated mind, they eagerly read etiquette books to learn the rules of correct social behavior.

The most famous book on Renaissance manners, published in 1528, was *The Courtier* by Baldassare Castiglione (1478-1529), which established a model for the Renaissance gentleman. To Castiglione, good manners and deportment were essential to the ideal courtier, but his central idea was that a courtier's true worth was more commensurate with his strength of character and excellence of intellect than with his hereditary social position. The courtier should be a well-

The popes' building program was in large measure responsible for Rome superseding Florence as the center of artistic activity during the High Renaissance. The greatest builder, Julius II (1503-1513) commissioned Bramante to begin the new St. Peter's and had Michelangelo paint the Sistine Chapel while Raphael decorated adjoining rooms in the Vatican.

Leonardo da Vinci, who had a wide knowledge of many fields besides painting, typifies the Renaissance ideal of the "universal man." In his "Virgin of the Rocks" (National Gallery, London), from which the head of an angel (below) is a detail, Leonardo established himself as a master of the High Renaissance in form and style. Another version, now in the Louvre, was painted twenty-five years earlier and was originally intended for an altar panel. Throughout his life Leonardo carried a sketchbook which he would fill with drawings and notes in his unusual handwriting, written inverted from right to left and best deciphered with a mirror. Unfortunately, approximately two thirds of his original writings have been lost. He never organized his extensive work, and the *Treatise on Painting*, compiled after his death by one of his closest friends, and a few fragments are all that remain. Although he had a distinct ideal of beauty (as in the angel), Leonardo was also fascinated by ugliness, and he would often follow grotesque-looking people, making numerous caricatures and studies, like those in the sketch at right. His interest in anatomy was more than a passing one; his drawings of embryos (far right) and other anatomical subjects are amazingly accurate.

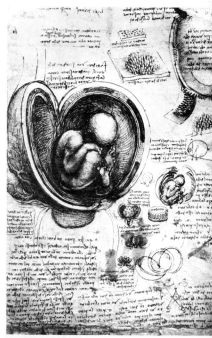

rounded individual, capable in the arts both of war and of peace.

The *Autobiography* of Benvenuto Cellini (1500-1571) gives us a vivid insight into Renaissance manners and morals, but it is no book of etiquette. Cellini was a bold and worldly adventurer, constantly embroiled in excitement and adventure—duels, love affairs, and prison terms. But he was also a sculptor of repute (see p. 408). Vigorous and energetic, Cellini possessed *virtù,* a term used in the Renaissance to characterize a man of natural ability and abounding vitality. *Virtù* should not be confused with virtue; in fact, a man possessing *virtù* often appeared to be singularly deficient in virtue, as Cellini's life story reveals. Possession of *virtù* enabled a man to be considered *l'uomo universale*, the Renaissance ideal of greatness. While Cellini approximated this ideal, geniuses like Leonardo da Vinci and Michelangelo attained it in a greater measure.

THE REVIVAL OF LEARNING

Humanism and the classical revival. During the Middle Ages, Virgil, Cicero, and Caesar were popular authors; Aristotle was venerated much as though he were a Church Father; and Roman law greatly influenced Church, or canon, law. But in medieval times the writers of antiquity had been interpreted within the framework of the Christian religion and often cited as authorities to bolster Church dogma. Although many aspects of antiquity were avoided because of their disturbingly pagan quality, churchmen did make use of pagan literature for allegorical narratives which were Christian in character. Consequently, the true nature of the classical world was often distorted or obscured.

In fourteenth-century Italy, however, a new perspective was attained and a fresh appreciation of classical culture emerged. Successors to a small group of medieval teachers of grammar and rhetoric, the representatives of this new movement called themselves humanists, a name derived from the *studia humanitatis*, or "humanities,"

which Roman authors had used in the sense of a liberal or literary education.

Medieval scholastic education had emphasized the sciences and professional training in law, medicine, and theology at the expense of the "arts," or literary side of the curriculum. Hence the scholastics had centered their attention on Aristotle's scientific writings and other ancient works on astronomy, medicine, and mathematics. Stimulated by a rebirth of men's interest in the problems and values of human living, the humanists reversed this medieval emphasis and called attention to the importance of an education in the humanities—history, grammar, rhetoric, poetry, and moral philosophy. The humanists disdained the sciences because, as Petrarch—the first of the Italian humanists—wrote:

. . . they help in no way toward a happy life, for what does it advantage us to be familiar with the nature of animals, birds, fishes, and reptiles, while we are ignorant of the nature of the race of man to which we belong, and do not know or care whence we come or whither we go?[3]

Thus, despite the fact that both the humanist and the scholastic looked to the past and venerated its heritage, they differed widely in their choice of the ancient material to be revered.

Humanists and scholastics also differed in the manner in which they saw themselves in relation to the writers of ancient times. While the scholastic always felt himself inferior to the ancients and looked up to them as son to father or pupil to teacher, the typical humanist in his exultant individualism saw himself equal to the ancients and boldly hailed them as man to man and friend to friend. At the beginning of his *Divine Comedy* Dante described medieval man's reliance upon the authority of the ancients in allegorical terms. Dante (medieval man) is lost in the "dark wood" which is this life until he is rescued by Virgil (a favorite medieval symbol of ancient wisdom), who thereafter guides him along the right path. "Losing me," Virgil is made to say to Dante, "ye would remain astray."

The noticeably different attitude of the humanists was well expressed by one of their few medieval forerunners, John of Salisbury (d. 1180): "Most delightful in many ways is the fruit of letters that, banishing the irksomeness of intervals of place and time, bring friends into each other's presence. . . ."[4] It was in this spirit that Petrarch wrote his *Letters to Ancient Authors*, addressing Homer, Plato, Cicero, and others in familiar terms and sharing with them his own thoughts and experiences. This feeling of equality with ancient authors was also behind the humanists' practice of stuffing their own writings with apt quotations from the classics. The humanists' purpose, however, differed from that of the scholastics, who also quoted extensively from the ancients; as the humanist Montaigne explained in his essays (see p. 300), he quoted the ancients not because he agreed with them but because they agreed with him!

Petrarch, the "father of humanism." The "father of humanism" is a title that has been given to Francesco Petrarca, better known to us as Petrarch (1304-1374). Resentful as a youth of his father's desire to have him become a lawyer, he turned to reading Virgil and Cicero for consolation; and though he studied law at Bologna, he dreamed constantly of the glories of the classical age.

In 1327 he met the lady Laura and fell in love with her. Little is known of Laura or of the true nature of her relationship to Petrarch. But inspired by his love of her, Petrarch wrote sonnets which made him one of the greatest lyric poets of all time. In the love poetry of the age, his portrayal of Laura represents a fresh approach. Earlier poets had woven about their heroines an air of courtly love and religious idealization which made the characters quite unreal. Petrarch's Laura was a flesh-and-blood creature whom all readers could recognize as human.

The ancients wrote of the joys of this world, and their attitude toward life struck a sympathetic chord in Petrarch. In his *Secret* Petrarch has an imaginary conversation with St. Augustine which forcibly brings out the conflict between new ideas and those of medieval times. Petrarch concluded that, despite the importance of the world to come, the world of here and now held many delights which should not be shunned.

This inner conflict between his love of earthly things and his loyalty to the traditional medieval ideal of self-denial and other-worldliness exemplifies the transitional position Petrarch occupied in western culture. A product of medieval beliefs and attitudes, he nevertheless could not accept a depreciation of man's importance in the scheme of things or a constriction of his mental horizons. And thus he condemned the rigidity and arid logic of scholasticism and the extent to which medieval education was governed by dead tradition. He himself was not a careful scholar and never learned Greek, yet this versatile rebel had a profound influence upon his contemporaries and gave humanism its first great impetus.

Boccaccio and the Decameron. Another celebrated humanist was Giovanni Boccaccio (1313-1375), who began his career as a writer of poetry and romances. In 1348 the calamitous Black Death struck—a disaster which wiped out nearly two thirds of Florence's population. Boccaccio used this event to establish the setting of his masterpiece, the *Decameron*. To escape the pestilence, his characters—three young men and seven young women—sought seclusion in a country villa, where they whiled away the time by telling each other stories. Boccaccio suffused the hundred tales of the *Decameron*, based on the old *fabliaux* (see p. 257) and on chivalric accounts, with a new and different spirit. Recounted by sophisticated city dwellers, the tales satirize the follies of knights and other medieval types and express clearly the contempt which had developed for the old, and by then threadbare, ideals of feudalism. Many tales are bawdy and even scandalous—a charge which Boccaccio undertook to refute:

Some of you may say that in writing these tales I have taken too much license, by making ladies sometimes say and often listen to matters which are not proper to be said or heard by virtuous ladies. This I deny, for there is nothing so unchaste but may be said chastely if modest words are used; and this I think I have done.[5]

Nevertheless, the *Decameron* offers a wealth of anecdotes, portraits of flesh-and-blood characters, and a vivid (although one-sided) picture of Renaissance life.

The *Decameron* closed Boccaccio's career as a creative artist. Largely through the influence of Petrarch, whom he met in 1350, Boccaccio gave up writing in the Italian vernacular and turned to the study of antiquity. He attempted to learn Greek, wrote an encyclopedia of classical mythology, and went off to monasteries in search of manuscripts. By the time Petrarch and Boccaccio died, the study of the literature and learning of antiquity was growing throughout Italy.

The search for manuscripts. The search for manuscripts became a mania, and before the middle of the fifteenth century works by most of the important Latin authors had been found. The degree of difference between humanist and scholastic is indicated by the ease with which the early humanists recovered the "lost" Latin literary masterpieces: they were found close at hand in monastic libraries, covered by the undisturbed dust of centuries. The books had always been there; what had been largely lacking was a mature and appreciative audience of readers. In addition to these Latin works, precious Greek manuscripts were brought to Italy from Constantinople during the fifteenth century.

Individual scholars had their favorite classical authors, both Greek and Roman, but the highest universal praise was reserved for Cicero. Compounded of moral philosophy and rhetoric, his work displayed a wide-ranging intellect which appealed to many humanists. The revival of the art of writing classical Latin prose was due largely to the study and imitation of Cicero's graceful, eloquent, and polished literary style.

Revival of Platonism. As a result both of their rebellion against the Aristotelian emphasis upon natural science and of their search for a classical philosophy that stressed moral purpose and religious and mystical values, many humanists gravitated to Platonism during the fifteenth century. A factor in this revival was the study of Plato in the original Greek, particularly at Florence where Cosimo de' Medici, one of the great patrons of the Renaissance, founded the informal club that came to be known as the Platonic

Academy. Its leader, Marsilio Ficino (1433-1499), who always kept a candle burning before a bust of Plato, made the first complete Latin translation of Plato's works.

Ficino also sought to synthesize Christianity and Plato, much as St. Thomas Aquinas had done with Aristotle. In his principal work, *Theologia Platonica*, Ficino viewed Plato as essentially Christian and Plato's "religious philosophy" as a God-sent means of converting intellectuals. He coined the expression "Platonic love" to describe an ideal, pure love, and this concept found its way into much of Renaissance literature.

Aristotelianism. Despite its great attraction for many humanists, Platonism still had a formidable rival in Aristotelianism. Concerned chiefly with natural philosophy, logic, and metaphysics, Aristotelian commentators still dominated teaching in the Italian universities.

The most influential Aristotelians were the Latin Averroists, followers of the Muslim philosopher Averroës (see p. 165). The Averroists followed Aristotle in teaching that matter is eternal and in denying the immortality of the soul. Since such views were contrary to the Biblical story of creation and the belief in personal immortality, the Averroists advocated the doctrine of "double truth"—a truth in philosophy need not be valid in religion.

By the fifteenth century Padua had become the center of Aristotelianism, which reached its peak in the next century. By championing a secular rationalism that kept philosophy separate from theology, its adherents helped create an environment necessary for the triumph of scientific thought in the seventeenth century. As we shall see in Chapter 18, the new developments that Aristotelianism encouraged were to overthrow Aristotle's own brilliant but outmoded theories in physics and other fields of science.

Evaluation of humanism. We owe the humanists a debt of gratitude for reintroducing the whole of Latin and Greek literature into the mainstream of western thought. From their reading of the classics, humanists came to understand the classical world in a true historical perspective and corrected many misconceptions about ancient times which had existed in the Middle Ages. Medieval scholars, for example, had pictured Alexander the Great's soldiers as knights, but Renaissance historians no longer made such naive mistakes.

On the other hand, although the humanists condemned medieval restrictions, they themselves were often subservient to the authorities of antiquity. Indeed, theirs was a closed culture whose boundaries had been set by ancient Greece and Rome, so that the only course open to them was to retravel the ground, not to explore uncharted territory. Intent on returning to antiquity, so to speak, the humanists resented the centuries separating them from the golden days of Greece and Rome. Unfortunately, this viewpoint resulted in their disparagement of the best works produced in the Middle Ages.

The cult of classical letters gave rise to other defects. Humanist scholars were so dominated by Roman and Greek forms that they tended to imitate rather than to create for themselves. Their passion for Ciceronian Latin became pernicious; too often their writings were rich in form but barren in content. Worse still, their preoccupation with classical authors retarded the growth of a much more vital vernacular literature—as in the case of Boccaccio, who gave up writing prose and poetry in Italian to devote himself to Latin studies.

The humanists' contributions to philosophy were not extensive; they did little original thinking. Nevertheless the spread of humanistic influence resulted in a renewed and valuable emphasis upon the freedom and dignity of man as an individual and the importance of his place in the cosmos. This interest was manifested not only in literature but also in the fine arts.

ITALIAN RENAISSANCE ART

Transitional period in sculpture and painting. North of the Alps during the fourteenth and fifteenth centuries there was a continuation of "Gothic" art—in painting and sculpture, the same emphasis on realistic detail (see illustrations, pp. 230, 261); in architecture, an elaboration of the Gothic style. Fourteenth-century Italy, however, produced innovations in painting and sculpture that mark the beginnings of Renaissance art. Influenced by the humanistic spirit in thought and religion, a new society centered in rich cities, and a revived interest in antique art, Italian Renaissance art reached its zenith early in the sixteenth century.

The greatest figure in the transitional art of the fourteenth century was the Florentine painter Giotto (1266-1336), who, it was said,

Renaissance artists presented traditional subject matter in novel ways. Giotto's "Lamentation over the Dead Christ," one of thirty-eight frescoes painted for the Arena Chapel in Padua, lends a new drama and a new credibility to a familiar Biblical story.

"achieved little less than the resurrection of painting from the dead." While earlier Italian painters had copied the unreal, flat, and rigidly formalized images of Byzantine paintings and mosaics, Giotto observed from life and painted a three-dimensional world peopled with believable human beings dramatically moved by deep emotion (see illustration, p. 289). He humanized painting as St. Francis humanized religion.

Quattrocento painting. The lull in painting that followed Giotto, during which his technical innovations were retained but the spirit and compassion that make him one of the world's great painters were lost, lasted

until the beginning of the *quattrocento* (Italian for "four hundred," an abbreviation for the 1400's). In his brief lifetime the Florentine Masaccio (1401-1428) completed the revolution in technique begun by Giotto. As can be seen in "St. Peter Healing the Sick with His Shadow" (see Color Plate 10), Masaccio largely mastered the problems of perspective, anatomical naturalism of flesh and bone, and the modeling of figures in light and shade rather than by sharp line. Masaccio was also the first to paint nude figures whose counterparts can be found in classical, but not in medieval, art.

Inspired by Masaccio's achievement, most *quattrocento* painters constantly sought to improve technique. This search for greater realism culminated in such painters as Andrea Mantegna (1431-1506), whose "St. James on the Way to His Execution" well shows the results of his lifelong study of perspective.

While Masaccio and his successors were intent upon giving their figures a new solidity and resolving the problem of three-dimensional presentation, a later Florentine painter, Sandro Botticelli (1447-1510), proceeded in a different direction, abandoning the techniques of straightforward representation of people and objects. Botticelli used a highly sensitive, even quivering, line to stir the viewer's imagination and emotion and to create a mood in keeping with his subject matter, frankly pagan at first but later deeply religious (see illustration, p. 263). Movement and the patterning of hair and drapery in such allegorical and mythological works as the "Primavera" are particularly sensitive (see illustration, p. 291).

Quattrocento sculpture. In the meantime progress was being made in sculpture, and it, like painting, reached stylistic maturity at the beginning of the *quattrocento*. In his two sets of bronze doors for the baptistery in Florence, on which he labored for forty-four years, Lorenzo Ghiberti (1378-1455) achieved the goal he had set for himself: "I strove to imitate nature as closely as I could, and with all the perspective I could produce." These marvels of relief sculpture (p. 292), which drew from Michelangelo the declaration that they were worthy to be the gates of

"St. James on the Way to His Execution," a fresco by Andrea Mantegna, is innovative in its perspective and use of classical models. St. James, at the left, is shown blessing a Roman soldier and healing a paralytic. Mantegna's interest in historical detail is obvious in both the classical buildings and the costumes of the soldiers.

As a master of line, Botticelli is probably unsurpassed in the western world. His "Primavera," which centers on the figure of Venus, is an allegorical painting depicting the return of spring. It has been called a *quattrocento* love-in.

paradise, depict skillfully modeled human figures—including some classically inspired nudes—which stand out spatially against architectural and landscape backgrounds.

Although Ghiberti was a superb craftsman, he was less of an innovator than his younger contemporary in Florence, Donatello (1386-1466), who visited Rome to study the remains of antique statuary. Divorcing sculpture from its architectural background, Donatello produced truly freestanding statues based on the realization of the human body as a functional, coordinated mechanism of bones, muscles, and sinews, maintaining itself against the pull of gravity. His "David" is the first bronze nude made since antiquity, and his equestrian statue of Gattamelata the *condottiere* is the first of its type done in the Renaissance. The latter clearly reveals the influence of classical models and was probably inspired by the equestrian statue of Marcus Aurelius in Rome.

More dramatic than either of these equestrian statues is that of the Venetian *condottiere* Bartolomeo Colleoni (see p. 293), the creation of Andrea del Verrocchio (1435-1488). A versatile Florentine artist noteworthy as a sculptor, painter, and the teacher of Leonardo da Vinci, Verrocchio designed the statue of Colleoni to permit one of the horse's forelegs to be unsupported—a considerable achievement. The posture and features of the *condottiere* convey dramatically a sense of the supreme self-confidence and arrogance usually associated with Renaissance public figures.

Quattrocento architecture. Renaissance architecture, which far more than sculpture reflects the influence of ancient Roman models, began with the work of Filippo Brunelleschi (1377-1446). As a youth Brunelleschi

The first set of bronze doors Ghiberti made for the baptistery in Florence have twenty-eight panels depicting New Testament scenes which, with their Gothic frames, reflect the artist's debt to the realistic style of his medieval predecessors. By contrast, the second set of doors, done twenty years later, contain ten larger New Testament scenes which, in their modeled figures and space effects, reflect a new Renaissance style strongly influenced by classical sculpture and architecture. This panel from the second set of doors is a scene from the Old Testament story of Joseph.

accompanied Donatello to Rome where he employed measuring stick and sketchbook to master the principles of classical architecture. Returning to Florence, Brunelleschi constructed the lofty dome of the cathedral, the first to be built since Roman times. Although strongly influenced by classical architecture, Brunelleschi's buildings in Florence, which include churches and palaces, were not just copies of Roman models. Employing arcades of Roman arches, Roman pediments above the windows, and engaged Roman columns and other decorative motifs, Brunelleschi re-created the Roman style in a fresh and original manner.

The High Renaissance, 1500-1530. During the High Renaissance the center of artistic activity shifted from Florence to Rome and Venice, where wealthier patrons lived and where consequently greater opportunities were available to artists. The popes were lavish patrons, and the greatest artists of the

period worked in the Vatican at one time or another. It did not seem inconsistent to popes and artists to include representations of pagan mythological figures in the decorations of the papal palace, and thus the Vatican was filled with secular as well as religious art.

The great architect of the High Renaissance was Donato Bramante (1444-1514) from Milan. Bramante's most important commission came in 1506 when Pope Julius II requested him to replace the old basilica of St. Peter, built by the emperor Constantine, with a monumental Renaissance structure. Bramante's plan called for a centralized church in the form of a Greek cross surmounted by an immense dome. The exterior of St. Peter's exemplifies the spirit of High Renaissance architecture—to approach nearer to the monumentality and grandeur of Roman architecture. In Bramante's own words, he would place "the Pantheon on top of the Basilica of Maxentius." Bramante died when the cathedral was barely begun, and it was left to Michelangelo and others to complete the work (see illustrations, p. 294).

High Renaissance architects also produced magnificent palaces and other secular buildings. Their decorative features show how classical details blended in a new fashion resulted in an impressive and refined structure. From the sixteenth century on, all Europe began to take to the new architecture.

The painters of the High Renaissance inherited the solutions to such technical problems as perspective space from the *quattrocento* artists. But whereas the artists of the earlier period had been concerned with movement, color, and narrative detail, painters in the High Renaissance strove to eliminate nonessentials and concentrated on the central theme of a picture and its basic human implications. By this process of elimination, many High Renaissance painters achieved a "classic" effect of seriousness and serenity and endowed their works with idealistic values.

Leonardo da Vinci. The great triad of High Renaissance painters consists of Leonardo da Vinci, Raphael, and Michelangelo. An extraordinary man, Leonardo da Vinci (1452-1519) was proficient in a variety of fields: engineering, mathematics, architecture, geology, botany, physiology, anatomy, sculpture, painting, music, and poetry. He was always experimenting, with the result that few of the projects he started were ever finished.

A superb draftsman, Leonardo was also a master of soft modeling in full light and shade and of creating groups of figures perfectly balanced in a given space. One of his most famous paintings is the "Mona Lisa," a portrait of a woman whose enigmatic smile has intrigued art lovers for centuries. Another is "The Last Supper," a study of the moment when Christ tells his twelve disciples that one will betray him. When he painted this picture on the walls of the refectory of Santa Maria delle Grazie in Milan, Leonardo was experimenting with the use of an oil medium combined with plaster, and, unfortunately, the experiment was unsuccessful. The painting quickly began to disintegrate and has had to be repainted several times. Last of the great Florentine painters, Leonardo combined an advanced knowledge of technique with deep psychological insight into many facets of human nature (see p. 285).

Raphael. The second of the great triad of High Renaissance painters was Raphael (1483-1520). By the time he was summoned to Rome to aid in the decoration of the Vatican, Raphael had absorbed something of Leonardo's intellectuality and Michelangelo's "body dynamics" and grandeur. His Stanze frescoes in the Vatican display a magnificent blending of classical and Christian subject matter and are imbued with a clarity and breadth of vision expressive of the High Renaissance at its best. Considered by some critics as unrivaled in the mastery of space composition, Raphael was equally at home in handling a single figure or in grouping masses (see illustration, p. 296).

Michelangelo. The individualism and idealism of the High Renaissance have no greater representative than Michelangelo

In Verrocchio's "Monument to Colleoni" the spirit of the great military leader is captured in the face, which is individual and very human rather than classical.

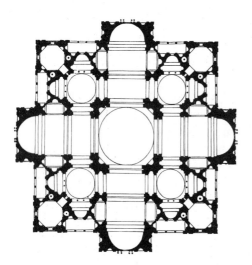

Bramante designed St. Peter's in the shape of a Greek cross with a dome similar to that of the Pantheon (see his architectural drawing). After his death, however, his plan was modified. Michelangelo redesigned the dome—which has been called the greatest achievement of Renaissance architecture—and later a long nave was added to the front of the church, giving it the form of a Latin cross rather than of a Greek cross. The courtyard view of the Palazzo Farnese in Rome shows the classical simplicity and symmetry which marked late Italian Renaissance palaces. The even spacing of the windows, the equal height of the three stories, and the repetition of decorative motifs all contribute to a feeling of unity in design.

Buonarroti (1475-1564). Stories of this stormy and temperamental personality have helped shape our ideas of what a genius is like. Indeed, there is something almost superhuman about both Michelangelo and his art. His great energy enabled him to complete in four years the entire work of painting the ceiling of the Vatican's Sistine Chapel, an area of several thousand square yards, and his art embodies a superhuman ideal of man. With his unrivaled genius for rendering the human form, he devised a wealth of expressive positions and attitudes for his figures in scenes from Genesis. Their physical splendor is pagan, but their spirit is Christian (see p. 296).

Michelangelo considered himself first and foremost a sculptor, and this *uomo universale*, who also excelled as poet, engineer, and architect, was undoubtedly the greatest sculptor of the Renaissance. The glorification of the human body, particularly the male nude, was Michelangelo's great achievement. Fired by the grandeur of such newly discovered pieces of Hellenistic sculpture as the Laocoön group and strongly influenced by Platonism, he expressed in art his idealized view of man's dignity and majesty (see Color Plate 11). Succeeding Bramante as chief architect of St. Peter's, Michelangelo designed he great dome (see p. 294), and was in the midst of creative activities when he died, almost in his ninetieth year, in 1564. He had long outlived the High Renaissance.

The Venetian school. Venice offered a congenial environment to artists. A prosperous merchant-prince could well afford to play the role of patron of the arts; trade with the East provided Venetians with luxuries and comforts which added splendor and color to daily life; and the beauty of the city itself would attract the eye of any artist.

This wealthy, sophisticated milieu produced a secular rather than a devotional school of painting. Most Venetian artists were satisfied with the here and now; they were not overly concerned with antiquity or classical canons. While they sometimes painted exquisite Madonnas, they more often painted wealthy merchants and proud doges, attired in rich brocades, jewels, and precious metals and grouped with beautiful young women who scarcely looked like Madonnas. There is a sensuousness in the Venetian painting of this period which is evident in the artists' love of decoration, rich costumes, radiant light and color, and striking nude figures.

Giorgione (1478-1511), like Botticelli, used classical themes and idyllic landscapes in his paintings. But unlike the Florentine master, who made his mythological figures imaginative and idealized, Giorgione's muses and Venuses were lovely Venetian models.

The pictures of Titian (1485?-1576) contain sensuous beauties of color and atmosphere. During his long working life he proved himself a master of a wide variety of subjects ranging from religion to pagan mythology. His portraits, which earned him the greatest fame among his contemporaries, show the Venetian love of color and texture of rich fabrics (see p. 296).

High Renaissance music. In contrast to the single-voiced or homophonic music—called plain song or Gregorian chant—of the early Middle Ages, the late medieval composers wrote many-voiced, many-melodied, or polyphonic music. Polyphony often involved a shuttling back and forth from one melody to another—musical counterpoint. By the fifteenth century as many as twenty-four voice parts were combined into one intricately woven musical pattern. The composers of the High Renaissance continued to produce complicated polyphonic music, but in a calmer and grander manner. Compared with the style of his predecessors, that of Josquin des Près (d. 1521), the founder of High Renaissance music, "is both grander and more simple. All stark intervals of early polyphony are ruled out; few dissonances are used, and the rhythms and forms used are based on strict symmetry and mathematically regular proportions. Josquin handled all technical problems of complicated constructions with the same ease and sureness one finds in the drawings of Leonardo and Raphael."[6] During the sixteenth century, also, instruments such as the violin, spinet, and harpsichord developed from more rudimentary types.

The Renaissance in Italy stimulated many

Michelangelo's "Creation of Adam" (top), one of the major scenes on the ceiling of the Sistine Chapel, depicts God, with Eve protected under His left arm, instilling life in Adam by merely pointing His finger. The frescoed figures have a sculptural quality that creates an illusion of roundness and depth. While Michelangelo used the human figure as an expression of spirituality and sublime beauty, Raphael's works stressed the earthly qualities of natural human beauty. Although the subject matter is religious, his "Madonna of the Chair" (bottom left) is endowed with a warm, human quality. This painting also demonstrates Raphael's concern for form and equilibrium within a composition. Titian's paintings are marked by their sensuousness and intense, jewel-like colors. His "Young Woman at Her Toilet" (bottom right) typifies his favorite theme of warm feminine beauty.

new forms of secular music, especially the madrigal, a love lyric set to music. The madrigal found favor in England, while French *chansons* and German *lieder* added to the growing volume of secular music.

THE NORTHERN RENAISSANCE

The northward spread of the Renaissance. The Italian Renaissance had projected man once more into the center of life's stage and permeated the intellectual and artistic environment with humanistic values. In time the stimulating ideas current in Italy spread to other areas and combined with indigenous developments to produce a French Renaissance, an English Renaissance, and so on.

While the wealthy burghers of the northern cities patronized the work of artists and scholars, the prime sponsors of the Renaissance north of the Alps were often the kings of the new national states. By importing artists and learned men from Italy or supporting native geniuses, the rulers added brilliance to their courts.

The influence of printing. Perhaps even more important in the diffusion of the Renaissance and later in the success of the Reformation was the invention of printing in Europe. The essential elements—paper and movable type—had long been known in non-European cultures. As early as the second century the Chinese had made paper from rags and other materials. In the eighth century the Muslims had created a cotton paper which, along with its linen counterpart, entered Europe through Spain. By the eleventh century the enterprising Chinese had invented movable type, but the system was not put to use in Europe until 1448. In his printing shop at Mainz, Germany, John Gutenberg used movable type to print papal documents and the first published version of the Bible (1454).

Within fifty years after Gutenberg's Bible had been published, all the major countries of Europe possessed the means for printing books. It is said that the prices of books soon sank to one eighth of their former cost, thus placing books within the reach of a multitude of people who formerly had been unable to buy them. In addition, pamphlets and controversial tracts soon were widely circulated, and new ideas reached a thousand times more people in a relatively short span of time. In the quickening of Europe's intellectual life, it is difficult to overestimate the effects of the printing press.

Erasmus and northern Humanism. The intellectual life of the first half of the sixteenth century was dominated by Desiderius Erasmus (1466?-1536). Born in Rotterdam, he passed most of his long life elsewhere—in Germany, France, England, Italy, and especially Switzerland. The most influential and cosmopolitan of the northern humanists, he corresponded with nearly every prominent writer and thinker in Europe and knew

Although printing was a far superior system of reproducing books than hand copying, it still was a slow, tedious, and expensive process. A copy of the Gutenberg Bible cost forty-two gulden, a price equivalent to that of fourteen oxen. Although large books were beyond the means of most common people, the presses turned out small books, pamphlets, and circulars in large quantities for common consumption.

The high level of European portraiture in the sixteenth century reflected the man-centered outlook of the time. The traditional meticulous realism of the north was employed by Hans Holbein the Younger, who recorded the likeness of the humanist Erasmus—as well as other famous contemporaries—with jewel-like accuracy and brilliance.

personally popes, emperors, and kings. He was *the* scholar of Europe, and his writings were read eagerly everywhere.

Perhaps the most famous and influential work by Erasmus was *In Praise of Folly*, a satire written in 1511 at the house of the English humanist Sir Thomas More. The book concerns a female character called Folly, Erasmus' conception of human nature, who is represented as delivering a lecture to university students. A historian has described the work in these words: "At first the book makes kindly and approving fun of the ways of action and the foibles and weaknesses of mankind. It is not mordant, only amused. But gradually from fools innocent and natural and undebased, it passes to those whose il-

lusions are vicious in their setting and results."[7] Among such are merchants ("they lie, swear, cheat, and practice all the intrigues of dishonesty"), lawyers ("they of all men have the greatest conceit of their own abilities"), scholastic philosophers ("that talk as much by rote as a parrot"), and scientists ("who esteem themselves the only favourites of wisdom, and look upon the rest of mankind as the dirt and rubbish of the creation"). Most roughly handled are churchmen, in particular monks, who are "impudent pretenders to the profession of piety," and popes, cardinals, and bishops, "who in pomp and splendour have almost equalled if not outdone secular princes." While his satire is indeed harsh, Erasmus was himself balanced, moderate, and intolerant only of bigotry, ignorance, greed, and violence.

In Praise of Folly points up a significant difference between the northern humanists and their Italian predecessors. While both were repelled by much that seemed to them wrong in the life of their day, their reactions took different forms. The typical Italian humanists followed the course set by Petrarch: "In order to forget my own time I have constantly striven to place myself in spirit in other ages. . . ."[8] Disdaining such escapism, the great majority of northern humanists faced up to reality and became reformers of their society's ills. They also went further in broadening their interest in ancient literature to include early Christian writings—the Scriptures and the works of the Church Fathers. This led them to prepare new and more accurate editions of the Scriptures (Erasmus' Greek edition of the New Testament became famous and was used by Luther) and to compare unfavorably the complexities of the Church in their own day with the simplicity of primitive Christianity. Since the northern humanists held that the essence of religion was morality and rational piety—what Erasmus called the "philosophy of Christ"—rather than ceremony and dogma, it is not surprising that the Church became a major target of their reforming zeal.

Sir Thomas More's Utopia. The most significant figure in English humanism was Sir Thomas More (1478-1535), the friend of Erasmus. More is best known for his *Utopia*, the first important description of the ideal state since Plato's *Republic*. In his epoch-making work More criticized his age by using as his spokesman a fictitious sailor who contrasts the ideal life he has seen in Utopia (The Land of Nowhere) with the harsh conditions of life in England. More's denunciations centered on the new acquisitive capitalism, which he blamed for the widespread insecurity and misery of the lower classes. More felt that governments

are a conspiracy of the rich, who, in pretence of managing the public, only pursue their private ends, . . . first, that they may, without danger, preserve all that they have so ill acquired, and then, that they may engage the poor to toil and labor for them at as low rates as possible, and oppress them as much as they please.[9]

In Utopia, by contrast, no man is in want because the economy is planned and co-operative and because property is held in common. Utopia is the only true commonwealth, concludes More's imaginary sailor:

In all other places, it is visible that while people talk of a commonwealth, every man only seeks his own wealth: but there, where no man has any property, all men zealously pursue the good of the public. . . . in Utopia, where every man has a right to every thing, they all know that if care is taken to keep the public stores full, no private man can want any thing; for among them there is no unequal distribution, so that no man is poor, none in necessity; and though no man has anything, yet they are all rich; for what can make a man so rich as to lead a serene and cheerful life, free from anxieties; neither apprehending want himself, nor vexed with the endless complaints of his wife?[10]

More was the first of the modern English socialists, but his philosophy should not be considered a forerunner of the socialism of our day. His economic outlook was a legacy from the Middle Ages, and his preference for medieval collectivism over modern individualism was of a piece with his preference for a Church headed—medieval style—by popes rather than by kings, a view that prompted Henry VIII to execute him for treason (see p. 315).

Rabelais. One of the best known of the French humanists was François Rabelais (1494-1553). A brilliant, if coarse, lover of all life from the sewers to the heavens, Rabelais is best remembered for his work *Gargantua and Pantagruel* (published 1533-1552). Centering on figures from French folklore, this work relates the adventures of Gargantua and his son Pantagruel, genial giants of tremendous stature and appetite, to whom were ascribed many marvelous feats.

In the course of his pungent narrative, Rabelais inserted his views on educational reform and his humanistic belief in man's inherent goodness and ability to solve his problems by reason. He made vitriolic attacks on the abuses of the Church and the shortcomings of scholastics and monks, but he had little patience with overzealous Protestants either. What Rabelais could not stomach was hypocrisy and repression; and for those guilty of these tendencies, he reserved his choicest invective. In the following excerpt he bids his readers to flee from that

rabble of squint-minded fellows, dissembling and counterfeit saints, demure lookers, hypocrites, pretended zealots, tough friars, buskin-monks, and other such sects of men, who disguise themselves like masquers to deceive the world. . . . Fly from these men, abhor and hate them as much as I do, and upon my faith you will find yourself the better for it. And if you desire . . . *to live in peace, joy, health, making yourselves always merry*, never trust those men that always peep out through a little hole.[11]

Von Hutten: German humanist and patriot. One of the outstanding German humanists was Ulrich von Hutten (1488-1523). In him was blended a hatred of ecclesiastical abuses with romantic nationalist feelings. This scion of an aristocratic family, who wanted to unite Germany under the emperor, led a tumultuous life as a wandering Greek scholar and satirist. He supported Luther as a rallying point for German unity against the papacy, to which Von Hutten attributed most of his compatriots' ills. Although he neither reconciled his humanistic philosophy with Luther's theology nor formulated a practical political program, Von Hutten reflected the tensions and aspirations of the German people in the early years of the sixteenth century.

The vividness of the characters Shakespeare created is illustrated by this engraving of Sir John Falstaff by the famed nineteenth-century caricaturist, George Cruikshank, who credits his work as "drawn by William Shakespeare, etched by Geo. Cruikshank."

Montaigne. The last notable northern humanist was the French skeptic Michel de Montaigne (1533-1592). At the age of thirty-eight he gave up the practice of law and retired to his country estate and well-stocked library, where he studied and wrote. Montaigne developed a new literary form and gave it its name—the essay. In ninety-four essays he set forth his personal views on many subjects: leisure, friendship, education, philosophy, religion, old age, death, and so forth. He did not pretend to have the final answer to the subjects he discussed. Instead, he advocated open-mindedness and toleration—rare qualities in the sixteenth century, when France was racked by religious and civil strife.

Montaigne condemned the pedantry into which humanism and humanistic education had largely degenerated by the end of the sixteenth century, arguing that "To know by heart is not to know; it is to retain what we have given our memory to keep."[12] Even today's student may have cause to listen sympathetically to the following words:

Our tutors never stop bawling into our ears, as though they were pouring water into a funnel;

and our task is only to repeat what has been told us. I should like the tutor to correct this practice . . . I want him to listen to his pupil speaking in his turn.[13]

Montaigne's final essay, entitled "Of Experience," which developed the thought that "when reason fails us we resort to experience," is an acknowledgment of the bankruptcy of humanism and a foreshadowing of the coming triumph of science.

Cervantes, creator of Don Quixote. The transition from feudal knight to Renaissance courtier finds its greatest literary expression in a masterpiece of Spanish satire, *Don Quixote de la Mancha*, the work of Miguel de Cervantes (1547-1616). By Cervantes' day knighthood had become an anachronism, though its accompanying code of chivalry still retained its appeal. It remained for a rationalist like Cervantes to show up the inadequacies of chivalric idealism in a world that had acquired new, and intensely practical, aims. He did so by creating a pathetic but infinitely appealing character to serve as the personification of an outmoded way of life.

Don Quixote, the "knight of the woeful countenance," mounted on his "lean, lank, meagre, drooping, sharp-backed, and raw-boned" steed Rozinante, sets out in the Spanish countryside to right wrongs and uphold his lady's and his own honor. In his misadventures he is accompanied by his squire, the much less gallant but infinitely more realistic Sancho Panza, whose peasant adages and hard-grained common sense serve as a contrast to the unpractical nature of his master's chivalric code. Tilting at windmills, mistaking serving wenches for highborn ladies and inns for castles, and lamenting the invention of gunpowder as depriving ardent knights of a chance to win immortality, Don Quixote is, on the surface at least, a ridiculous old man whose nostalgia for the "good old days" is a constant source of grief to him. Thus the story represents a superb satire directed against the outworn ideology of the Middle Ages; in particular, it laughed the ideal of chivalric romance into the world of make-believe.

And yet *Don Quixote* is still more. Cervantes instilled in his main character a pathos born in large measure of the author's own career of frustrated hopes and ambitions. As a result, Don Quixote becomes more than a romantic lunatic; he serves to embody that set of ideals which each of us would like to see realized but which we must compromise in a world that has other interests to serve.

Secular drama appears. Like Greek drama, medieval drama developed out of religious ceremonies (see p. 258). A complete divorce of the Church and stage did not occur until the middle of the fifteenth century when the Renaissance era of drama began in Italian cities with the performance of ancient Roman comedies. In the following century appeared the *commedia dell'arte*, reflections of everyday life in vulgar and slapstick fashion usually improvised by the players from a plot outline.

As secular dramas grew in popularity, theaters were built as permanent settings for their presentations. Great ingenuity was shown in the design of elaborate, realistic stage scenery as well as in lighting and sound effects. Theaters embodying these innovations only gradually appeared outside Italy. Not until 1576 was the first public theater erected in London; three years later, a similar theater was constructed in Madrid.

Imitating the ancient models they admired, French and Italian writers followed what they believed were the rigid conventions of the classical drama and, to a large extent, catered to the aristocracy. By contrast, Spanish and English playwrights created a theatrical environment that was at once more socially democratic, more hospitable to national themes, and less concerned with classical models.

William Shakespeare. The spring of lyric song that bubbled up in the England of Henry VIII formed a veritable stream of verse that sparkled through his daughter Elizabeth's countryside. Her reign (1558-1603) climaxed the English Renaissance and produced such a galaxy of talented writers that some scholars have felt it necessary to go back as far as Athens in the fifth century B.C. to find an age as prodigal of literary genius. Strongly influenced by the royal court, which served as the busy center of intellectual and artistic as well as of economic and political life, their writings were highly colored, richly romantic, and often wildly extravagant in spite of all their poetic allusions to classical times.

The supreme figure in Elizabethan literature and perhaps in all literature is William Shakespeare (1564-1616). We can only touch briefly upon a few facets of this versatile genius. His rich vocabulary and poetic imagery were matched only by his turbulent imagination. He was a superb lyric poet, and numerous critics have judged him the foremost sonnet writer in the English language.

Shakespeare wrote thirty-eight plays—histories, comedies, and tragedies. His historical plays reflected the patriotic upsurge experienced by Englishmen as their country grew stronger and more prosperous. For his comedies and tragedies, Shakespeare was content in a great majority of cases to borrow plots from earlier works. His forte lay in his creation of characters—perhaps the richest and most diversified collection conceived by the mind of one man—and in his ability to translate his knowledge of human nature

A print from an early German edition of Cervantes' *Don Quixote de la Mancha* shows the knight on an adventure with his faithful squire, Sancho Panza.

Northern Renaissance painting, with its original Gothic realism (see Color Plate 12), began to be affected by the Italian tendency toward naturalism and secularism at the end of the fifteenth century. One of the first German painters influenced by the Italian style was Albrecht Dürer. His engraving "Knight, Death, and Devil" is typical of his combination of the new style (compare with Verrocchio's "Monument to Colleoni") with medieval subject matter. In "Landscape with the Fall of Icarus" (detail, above) Pieter Brueghel the Elder has depicted an ancient myth as though it occurred in contemporary Flanders. Icarus (lower right) plunges into the water unnoticed by the herdsman and farmer, who continue their work.

into dramatic speech and action. Today his comedies are played to enthusiastic audiences: *The Taming of the Shrew, As You Like It, The Merchant of Venice, Merry Wives of Windsor,* to mention but a few. But it is in his tragedies that the poet-dramatist runs the gamut of human emotions and experience. Shakespeare possessed in abundance the Renaissance concern for man and the world about him. Hence his plays deal first and foremost with man's personality, passions, and problems. In such works as *Romeo and Juliet, Measure for Measure,* and *Troilus and Cressida,* the problems of love and sex are studied from many angles. Jealousy is analyzed in *Othello,* ambition in *Macbeth* and *Julius Caesar,* family relationships in *King Lear,* and man's struggle with his own soul in *Hamlet.* Shakespeare's extraordinary ability to build every concrete fact and action upon a universal truth makes his observations as applicable today as they were when first presented in the Globe Theater. Small wonder that next to the Bible, Shakespeare is the most quoted of all literary sources in the language.

Developments in painting. Before the Italian Renaissance permeated the artistic circles of northern Europe, the painters of the Low Countries had been making significant advances on their own. Outstanding was Jan van Eyck (1385?-1440), whose work has been called "the full flowering of the spirit of the late Middle Ages,"[14] for he continued to paint in the realistic manner developed by medieval miniaturists (see manuscript illuminations, pp. 215, 230). Van Eyck also perfected the technique of oil painting, which enabled him to paint with greater realism and attention to detail (see Color Plate 12).

The first talented German painter to be influenced deeply by Italian art was Albrecht Dürer (1471-1528) of Nuremberg. Dürer made more than one journey to Italy, where he was impressed both with the painting of the Renaissance Italians and with the artists' high social status—a contrast with northern Europe, where artists were still treated as craftsmen. Because he did not entirely lose many of the medieval qualities of the milieu in which he worked, his own work is a blend of the old and the new; but among German artists he went farthest in adopting the rational standards of Italian art. His "Knight, Death, and Devil" fuses the realism and symbolism of the Gothic with the nobility of Verrochio's statue of Colleoni (compare p. 293). In the long run Dürer became better known for his numerous engravings and woodcuts than for his paintings.

Another German painter, Hans Holbein the Younger (1497-1543), was less imaginative than Dürer; but whereas the latter lived principally in Germany and interpreted its spirit, the younger artist worked abroad, especially in England, and as a result his painting acquired a more cosmopolitan character. In his portraits of Erasmus and Henry VIII (pp. 298, 328), northern realism and concern for detail continues evident.

While many Flemish painters lost their northern individuality in the rush to adopt Italian techniques, Pieter Brueghel the Elder (1525?-1569) retained a strong Flemish flavor in his portrayal of the faces and scenes of his native land. He painted village squares, landscapes, skating scenes, peasant weddings and dances just as he saw them, with a reporter's eye for detail. He also took Biblical or mythological themes and depicted them as if the events were taking place in the Flanders of his own day. The depiction of everyday scenes in realistic fashion is known as *genre* painting; and in this medium, Pieter Brueghel and the Flemish school as a whole remained unexcelled.

SUMMARY

In the Middle Ages man had thought and acted primarily as a member of a community —a manor, a guild, or, above all, the universal Christian community represented by the Church and the Holy Roman Empire. But gradually, for a variety of reasons, he began to attach importance to himself as an individual and to develop an interest in worldly things for their own sake without relation to the divine. This new individualistic and secular spirit, the period in which it became prominent, and the ways in which it manifested itself in art, literature, and learning we call the Renaissance.

The change took place earliest in Italy and first expressed itself in the great intellectual movement known as humanism. In its early stages humanism was a revival of classical learning. Scholars eagerly searched for ancient manuscripts and introduced the literature of Greece and Rome into schools and universities. This reverence for antiquity led to the copying of classical literary and artistic forms, and many humanists wasted on such imitation talents which might better have been employed in creating original literature in their native language.

But humanism was much more than sterile imitation. It provided the West not only with a comprehensive knowledge of classical literature and thought but also with a more accurate historical perspective. The humanists absorbed classical ways of thinking, as well as classical modes of expression, and fostered an appreciation of the studies we know today as the "humanities." Above all, humanism reintroduced into western culture a much-needed emphasis on the dignity of man as an individual and on his place in the cosmos.

In its broader ramifications humanism stimulated a vital concern for the problems and challenges of the contemporary world. As we saw in this chapter and the one preceding, there was a progressive quickening of social life, resulting in sweeping changes in politics and economics and in men's minds. The common denominator of these changes was individualism.

Individualism manifested itself no less in the way in which the artist related his esthetic canons to the new man-centered view of the world. The extent to which the Renaissance sculptor, architect, and painter succeeded remains one of the glories of western civilization.

SUGGESTIONS FOR READING

J. Russell Major, **The Age of the Renaissance and Reformation,*** Lippincott, 1970. A brief interpretive synthesis. W. K. Ferguson, **The Renaissance,*** Holt, Rinehart & Winston, is an excellent brief survey of the Italian and Northern Renaissances. G. Sellery, **The Renaissance: Its Nature and Origins,*** Wisconsin, concentrates on leading personalities and movements.

J. C. Burckhardt, **The Civilization of the Renaissance in Italy,*** Mentor. The classic study; should be read in conjunction with W. K. Ferguson, **The Renaissance in Historical Thought: Five Centuries of Interpretation,** Houghton Mifflin, 1948, and T. Helton, ed., **The Renaissance: A Reconsideration of the Theories and Interpretations of the Age,*** Wisconsin, 1961.

P. O. Kristeller, **Renaissance Thought: The Classic, Scholastic, and Humanist Strains,*** Torchbooks. An excellent analysis of Italian humanism. See also J. H. Whitfield, **Petrarch and the Renascence,** Haskell, 1943.

G. Brucker, **Renaissance Florence,*** Wiley, 1969. Much information in a short space. See also C. Ady, **Lorenzo de' Medici and Renaissance Italy,*** Collier; and P. Laven, **A Comprehensive History of Renaissance Italy, 1464-1534,*** Capricorn.

Margaret M. Phillips, **Erasmus and the Northern Renaissance,*** Collier. A valuable introduction. Preserved Smith, **Erasmus: A Study of His Life, Ideals, and Place in History,*** Dover, is a first-rate biography. Outstanding studies of other Northern Renaissance figures include R. W. Chambers, **Thomas More,*** Michigan; J. H. Hexter, **More's Utopia: The Biography of an Idea,*** Torchbooks; D. B. Lewis, **Doctor Rabelais,** Greenwood, 1969; M. Chute, **Shakespeare of London,*** Everyman. **The New Cambridge Modern History,** Vol. I, **The Renaissance, 1493-1520,** Cambridge, 1957, is a detailed scholarly work.

J. Huizinga, **The Waning of the Middle Ages,*** Anchor. An influential study of "fading and decay" in the culture of northern Europe during the fourteenth and fifteenth centuries.

On printing and its effect on culture see P. Butler, **The Origin of Printing in Europe,** Univ. of Chicago, 1940; and Marshall McLuhan, **The Gutenberg Galaxy,*** Univ. of Toronto.

F. B. Artz, **From the Renaissance to Romanticism: Trends in Style in Art, Literature, and Music, 1300-1830,*** Phoenix. A valuable overall view of the arts through six centuries, with a comprehensive bibliography.

E. Newton, **European Painting and Sculpture,*** Penguin. Brief and particularly valuable on the Renaissance. Also recommended are Creighton Gilbert, ed., **Renaissance Art,*** Torchbooks, 1970; and A. Hauser, **A Social History of Art,** Vol. II, **Renaissance to Baroque,*** Vintage.

B. Berenson, **Italian Painters of the Renaissance,*** Meridian; H. Wölfflin, **The Art of the Italian Renaissance,*** Schocken. Two classics of art history. On northern painting see O. Benesch, **The Art of the Renaissance in Northern Europe,** Phaidon, 1965; F. M. Simpson, **History of Architectural Development,** Vol. IV, **Renaissance Architecture,** McKay, 1961.

D. Merejkowski, **The Romance of Leonardo da Vinci,*** Modern Library; I. Stone, **The Agony and the Ecstasy,*** Signet. Two noted historical novels, the latter on Michelangelo.

On music see Alfred Einstein, **A Short History of Music,*** Vintage; G. Reese, **Music in the Renaissance,** Norton, 1959.

*Indicates an inexpensive paperbound edition.

Chapter 14

Here I Take My Stand

The Protestant and Catholic Reformations

INTRODUCTION. On October 31, 1517, a professor of theology named Martin Luther nailed some papers on the door of the castle church in Wittenberg, Germany. It was the custom of the day for a man who wanted to engage in a scholastic debate with another to post his propositions publicly. In this respect Luther's action was not unusual, yet the forces he set in operation altered the entire religious and intellectual pattern of the western world. A religious movement was launched that split Christendom into numerous factions and sects.

Until his death in 1546, Luther believed that it might be possible to reform Catholicism to the conditions existing in early Christian times. From this standpoint the religious upheaval which he did so much to set in motion can be logically designated as the Reformation. On the other hand, because the struggle shattered western Christendom permanently, it might be described from a broader historical viewpoint as a revolution or, alternatively, as the Protestant Revolt. The sixteenth century also witnessed a significant revival of Catholicism itself. This renewal of the traditional faith was not solely a Counter Reformation in the sense that it represented a belated response to the challenge of Protestantism. As modern scholars have demonstrated, a strong Catholic Reformation had been gathering momentum even before Luther posted his theses.

The Reformation had both its negative and its positive aspects. In the name of God, men persecuted and killed their fellow men. Rulers anxious for absolute power used the conflicts engendered by the religious upheaval to serve their own political ends. Yet, much as in the early centuries of Christianity, when the blood of the martyrs became the seed of the Church, so the struggles of the sixteenth century, led by men afire with conviction and ready to sacrifice their lives for what they believed, renewed and stimulated the religious consciousness of western Europe. Luther declared: "Here I take my stand"; and in a broad sense this affirmation was echoed by Zwingli in the Swiss cantons, by Calvin at Geneva, and by the Catholic Church at the Council of Trent. Such staunch and uncompromising assertions of honest differences of doctrine gave institutionalized Christianity the new religious vitality and intellectual diversity that were to leave their mark on almost every phase of life in the West and bequeath us a rich legacy of values.

THE PROTESTANT REFORMATION

Passing of the medieval order. The Church's dominant position in European society depended on the continuance of the medieval world order; during the late Middle Ages, however, forces were slowly modifying every aspect of that order. The spirit of the Middle Ages was fundamentally one of faith, devotion to established institutions— the feudal order, the guild, and the Church— and the subordination of the individual's interests to those of the group. It was this spirit which fed the power of the Church. When the Renaissance changed this spirit, the universalities of the Middle Ages were shattered. Man became assertive. He began to rebel against all institutions which prevented him from acting as he wished.

Broadly speaking, the ideal of the Middle Ages was other-worldliness; the ideal of the Renaissance was present-worldliness. The Church represented the older ideal. Thus it was not simply that the Church's financial and moral abuses stood in need of correction, but that the Church's ideals no longer commanded the same respect and allegiance among all the population. The European townsman, for example, found himself increasingly out of sympathy with the Church's economic concepts of the "just price" and anti-usury statutes, for they conflicted with the new capitalism.

The Church itself embodied a dangerous contradiction at this time. In dogma it was medieval, yet its highest officials, including the popes, were patrons of a Renaissance culture deriving its inspiration from pagan Greece and Rome. The Church might denounce usury, but at the same time it utilized the services of powerful moneylending families.

As we have seen in Chapter 13, the northern humanists directed searching criticisms against the Church, though for the most part they wished to remain within it. But because it was primarily an intellectual movement, humanism could not create the dynamic drive necessary to inspire widespread reform. Having laid the intellectual groundwork for the pending religious revolt, the humanists left to other men—the militant and the martyrs alike—the task of arousing action. The time was ripe for the rise of a religious leader who would employ as his weapon not the conflict of Renaissance ideology with that of the Church, for that was a philosophical problem of which few were conscious, but rather the financial and moral abuses of the Church, which were common knowledge.

Religious ferment in Germany. The religious issue first came to a head in Germany. Aided by the invention of printing, devout

Germans had been studying the Scriptures carefully and censuring the behavior of many of the German clergy. Whereas in Italy familiarity bred a tolerance and rationalization of papal corruption, the Germans fiercely resented papal abuses and expected practice and theory to coincide.

The political situation also had a bearing on the religious question. Divided into hundreds of states, Germany lacked unity except for the nominal rule of the elected emperor of the Holy Roman Empire. The failure of imperial administrative reform (see p. 274) encouraged the many German states to imitate the new nationalism of countries to the west. With the religious affairs of each principality increasingly under the control of its ruler, a greater diversity of religious opinion could exist in fragmented Germany than in a state ruled by a centralized authority.

Nor must economic factors be overlooked. Trade and banking flourished, and the German burgher found no conflict between piety and profits. On the other hand, his piety and profits were both affected by the draining of German revenues by the Roman Church, especially when unscrupulous means were used to gather them. In short, Germany was ripe for religious revolt.

Martin Luther. The son of a German peasant who by virtue of thrift and hard work had become a petty capitalist, Martin Luther was born on November 10, 1483. Young Martin received a sound education which included university studies, but he accepted as a matter of course the prevalent beliefs in witchcraft and other superstitions. To the end of his life Luther believed vividly in the existence of devils and witches. The story goes that he once threw an inkpot at a devil whom he thought he saw leering at him. In 1505 he became a member of the mendicant order of Augustinian monks, a move which met with scant favor from his practical father, who wanted his son to study law. In 1508 Luther received a temporary appointment as a lecturer at the new University of Wittenberg, and a few years later he became professor of theology.

In the meantime Luther had struggled with

The deterioration of monasticism was responsible for much disenchantment with the Church. Monks were accused of every possible vice, from drunkenness and adultery to the frequenting of brothels. Such charges fostered the contempt vividly illustrated in this early sixteenth-century woodcut.

and solved for himself the spiritual problem that confronted many people in his time: In view of God's absolute power and man's powerlessness, how can man be certain of salvation for his soul? For many years Luther probed deeply this problem of eternal salvation. Finally, in 1515, while contemplating St. Paul's Epistle to the Romans (1:17), he came upon these words: "For therein is the righteousness of God revealed from faith to faith: as it is written, The just shall live by faith." Luther believed that his quest for spiritual certainty had been solved:

Night and day I pondered until I saw the connection between the justice of God and the statement that "the just shall live by his faith." Then I grasped that the justice of God is that righteousness by which through grace and sheer mercy God justifies us through faith. Thereupon I felt myself to be reborn and to have gone through open doors into paradise.[1]

Man was saved only by his faith in the validity of Christ's sacrifice, which alone could wash away sin and save him from the grasp of the devil. Luther had come to his famous doctrine of justification by faith, as opposed to the Roman Church's doctrine of justification by faith and good works—the demonstration of faith through virtuous acts, acceptance of Church dogma, and participation in Church ritual. Later, in a hymn that reflects his vigorous style of expression, Luther described his spiritual journey from anxiety to conviction:

In devil's dungeon chained I lay
  The pangs of death swept o'er me.
My sin devoured me night and day
  In which my mother bore me.
My anguish ever grew more rife,
I took no pleasure in my life
  And sin had made me crazy.

   . . .

Thus spoke the Son, "Hold thou to me,
  From now on thou wilt make it.
I gave my very life for thee
  And for thee I will stake it.
For I am thine and thou art mine,
And where I am our lives entwine,
  The Old Fiend cannot shake it."[2]

The implications of Luther's doctrine were enormous. If salvation could come only through a personal belief in Christ's sacrifice, then an interceding priesthood became superfluous, for each man would then be his own priest. But Luther himself had no idea as yet where his views would eventually lead him and half of Christendom. It required a financial abuse by the Church to bring on the religious revolt.

Tetzel and the indulgences. Leo X, a cultured scion of the Medici family, "who would have made an excellent Pope if he had only been a little religious,"[3] wanted to complete the magnificent new St. Peter's in Rome, but he lacked money for the costly enterprise. Several papal agents were sent out to sell indulgences as a means of raising money. One of these agents, named Tetzel, discharged his mission "in the German archbishopric of Mainz in a manner which would be recognized in America to-day as high-pressure salesmanship."[4]

The Church's position in regard to indulgences has often been misunderstood. Although the sacrament of Penance absolved the sinner from guilt and eternal punishment, some temporal punishment remained. An indulgence was a type of good work, to be compared with praying, visiting shrines, and contributing to worthy causes, and like all good works it was a means of remitting or pardoning the temporal penalty for sins. Theologically, the concept of indulgences rested on the theory of a "treasury of merits," which held that Christ and the saints had won merit far in excess of their own needs and had thereby created a vast storehouse of good works. By means of indulgences the Church was able to draw upon and distribute this surplus to help those who felt they had not rendered sufficient penance to extinguish the punishment which they deserved.

It was the abuse attending the sale of indulgences to raise money that was chiefly responsible for the growing tide of resentment. The common folk did not understand theology and thought that a payment of money would buy God's grace and insure their salvation. Tetzel did nothing to enlighten the populace as to the true nature of indulgences but rather exhorted them to give liberally for themselves and for their dead relatives in purgatory who were "crying to them for help." Luther's case against indulgences rested on both moral and theological grounds.

Development of Luther's ideas. On October 31, 1517, Luther, following a university custom, posted ninety-five propositions (theses) on the subject of indulgences on the church door at Wittenberg, at the same time challenging anyone to debate them with him. The following are typical:

6. The pope has no power to remit guilt, save by declaring and confirming that it has been remitted by God; ...

21. Therefore those preachers of indulgences are in error who allege that through the indulgences of the pope a man is freed from every penalty.

36. Every Christian who is truly contrite has plenary remission both of penance and of guilt as his due, even without a letter of pardon.[5]

An anonymous caricature of Johann Tetzel, the German hawker of indulgences, entitled "Johann Tetzel and His Indulgence-Junk." The last two lines of the notorious jingle here ascribed to Tetzel read: "As soon as coin in the coffer rings, Right then the soul to Heaven springs."

Luther wrote the ninety-five theses in Latin for the edification of his fellow theologians, but they were soon translated into the common tongue and six months later were well known throughout Germany. At first the Church at Rome did not seriously trouble itself. Heresy was anything but new, as the history of the Waldensians, Albigensians, and the followers of Wycliffe and Huss showed. But this particular "squabble among monks," as Leo x dismissed the matter, did not subside.

In 1519 Luther debated with the eminent Catholic theologian John Eck at Leipzig. Luther maintained that the pope ruled by virtue of human rather than divine authority and was not infallible; that Church councils did not exist by divine right either and could also err; and that Scripture constituted the sole authority in matters of faith and doctrine. When Eck pointed out that such views were similar to those of Wycliffe and Huss, Luther boldly declared that "among the opinions of John Huss and the Bohemians many are certainly most Christian and evangelic, and cannot be condemned by the universal church."[6] Yet in spite of these wide theological divergences, Luther continued to speak with affection of his "mother Church," which he hoped could be reformed

and remain unified. By basing his position squarely on the doctrine of justification by faith alone, however, Luther found himself propelled by its implications to a position far removed from that of the Church.

Following the Leipzig debate, Eck initiated proceedings at Rome to have Luther declared a heretic. Luther in turn decided to put his case before the German people by publishing a series of pamphlets. In his *Address to the Nobility of the German Nation*, Luther called on the princes to reform ecclesiastical abuses, to strip the Church of its wealth and worldly power, and to create, in effect, a national German Church. Among numerous other proposals contained in this influential treatise, Luther urged a union with the Hussites, claiming that Huss had been unjustly burned at the stake.

The Babylonian Captivity of the Church summarized Luther's theological views. He attacked the papacy for having deprived the individual Christian of his freedom to approach God directly by faith and without the intermediation of the priesthood, and he set forth his views on the sacramental system. To be valid, a sacrament must have been instituted by Christ and be exclusively Christian. On this basis Luther could find no justification for making a sacrament of matrimony, which was also observed by non-Christians, or for any of the other sacraments except Baptism and the Lord's Supper (his term for the sacrament known to Roman Catholics as the Holy Eucharist). Luther rejected the doctrine of transubstantiation on the grounds that a priest could not perform the miracle of transforming bread and wine into the Body and Blood of the Lord. Nevertheless, he believed in the real presence of Christ in the bread and wine of the sacrament. In Luther's view, the bread and wine coexist with the Body and Blood without a change of substance.

Luther's third pamphlet, *The Freedom of a Christian Man*, which was dedicated to the pope in the slight hope that reconciliation was still possible, set forth in conciliatory but firm tones Luther's views on Christian behavior and salvation. He did not discourage good works but argued that the inner spiritual freedom which comes from the certainty found in faith leads to the performance of good works. "Good works do not make a man good, but a good man does good works."[7]

The breach made complete. In June 1520 Pope Leo x issued the bull *Exsurge Domine* ("Arise, O Lord, . . . Arise all ye saints, and the whole universal Church, whose interpretation of Scripture has been assailed"[8]), which gave Luther sixty days to turn from his heretical course. When Luther publicly burned the bull amid the applause of students and townsmen, he propelled himself into the center of German politics and brought about a showdown with Rome. In January 1521 Leo x excommunicated Luther.

Meanwhile, Charles v, who had recently been crowned emperor, found himself in a difficult situation. He was aware of popular German feelings and was not anxious to see papal power reconsolidated in his domains, yet he was bound by his oath to defend the Church and extirpate heresy. Moreover, Charles was orthodox in his own religious beliefs. It was decided that Luther should be heard at the emperor's first Diet, which was held at Worms. Summoned under an imperial safe-conduct, Luther was asked whether he intended to stand by everything he had written. He stood before the assembly and replied firmly:

In this workroom in Wartburg castle Luther completed his translation of the New Testament into German.

Your Imperial Majesty and Your Lordships demand a simple answer. Here it is, plain and unvarnished. Unless I am convicted of error by the testimony of Scripture or (since I put no trust in the unsupported authority of Pope or of councils, since it is plain that they have often erred and often contradicted themselves) by manifest reasoning I stand convicted by the Scriptures to which I have appealed, . . . I cannot and will not recant anything, for to act against our conscience is neither safe for us, nor open to us.

On this I take my stand [*Hier stehe Ich*]. I can do no other. God help me. Amen.[9]

In May 1521 the Diet declared Luther a heretic and outlaw. He was, however, given protection by the elector of Saxony, in whose strongest castle he lived for almost a year under the guise of "Knight George."

During this period Luther began the construction of an evangelical church distinct from Rome. He wrote incessantly, setting forth his theological views in a collection of forceful sermons for use by preachers, in correspondence with friends and public figures, and in a treatise condemning monasticism. (In 1525 Luther married an ex-nun who had left the cloister after reading this treatise.) Luther also translated the New Testament into German, a monumental job accomplished in only eleven weeks. Later he translated the Old Testament. Luther's Bible was largely responsible for creating a standard literary language for all Germany.

Luther and the Peasants' War. Luther's teachings spread quickly through central and northern Germany. Pious persons who wanted the Church reformed embraced the new cause. Worldly individuals who believed that it would afford an opportunity to appropriate Church property also aided the movement, as did ardent nationalists like Von Hutton (see p. 299), who saw in it a means of uniting Germany. The emperor, meanwhile, was too deeply involved in a struggle with the French and the Turks to stamp out the new heresy (see p. 329).

Encouraged by Luther's concept of the freedom of a Christian man, which they applied to economic and social matters, the German peasants revolted in 1524. Long ground down by the nobles, the peasants included in their twelve demands the abolition of serfdom "unless it should be shown us from the Gospel that we are serfs"; a reduction of "the excessive services demanded of us, which are increased from day to day"; the fixing of rents "in accordance with justice"; and an end to "the appropriation by individuals of meadows and fields which at one time belonged to a community."[10] Luther recognized the justice of these demands, but when the peasants began to employ violence against established authority he turned against them. In a virulent pamphlet, *Against the Thievish and Murderous Hordes of Peasants*, Luther called on the princes to "knock down, strangle, and stab . . . and think nothing so venomous, pernicious, or Satanic as an insurgent."[11]

The revolt was stamped out in 1525 at a cost of an estimated 100,000 peasant dead, and the lot of the German peasant for the next two centuries was probably the worst in Europe. Luther had become a false prophet to the peasants, who either returned to Catholicism or turned to more radical forms of Protestantism. Politically and economically conservative, Luther believed that the equality of all men before God applied in spiritual but not in secular matters. This philosophy alienated the peasants but made allies of the princes, many of whom became Lutheran in part because it placed them in control of the church in their territories, thereby enhancing their power and wealth.

Local religious autonomy in Germany. At a meeting of the Diet of the Empire in 1529, the Catholic princes, with the emperor's support, pushed through a decree that the Mass must not be interfered with anywhere. This meant that while Lutheran activities were restricted in Catholic regions, those of the Catholics could be carried on even in Lutheran areas. In answer, the Lutheran leaders drew up a protest, and from this incident the word *Protestant* derives. The next Diet, meeting at Augsburg in 1530; was presented with a statement of Christian doctrine from the Lutheran viewpoint designed to conciliate the two parties. The Catholics refused to accept this statement, known as the Augsburg Confession, which became the official creed of Lutheranism.

The emperor now made public his intention to crush the growing heresy. In defense, the Lutheran princes banded together in 1531 in the Schmalkaldic League, and between 1546 and 1555 a sporadic civil war was fought. A compromise was finally reached in the Peace of Augsburg (1555), which allowed each prince to decide the religion of his subjects, gave Protestants the right to keep all Church property confiscated prior to 1552, forbade all sects of Protestantism other than Lutheranism, and ordered all Catholic bishops to give up their property if they turned Lutheran.

The effects of these provisions on Germany were profound. The Peace of Augsburg confirmed Lutheranism as a state religion in large portions of the Empire. Religious opinions became the private property of the princes, and the individual had to believe what his prince wanted him to believe, be it Lutheranism or Catholicism. Furthermore, by formally sanctioning state religion and thus enhancing a prince's power, the Peace of Augsburg added to Germany's political disintegration.

The death of Luther. In 1546, during the Schmalkaldic War, the founder of the new faith died. Martin Luther had been a born leader, genius, and zealot. His life had been molded by an absolute conviction of the rightness of his beliefs, which goes far to explain both his driving power and his limitations. "His weaknesses were manifest: intransigency in theological views, proneness to vehemence, narrowness of social concepts. . . . But Luther also had qualities to offset these: sincere desire for the truth, courage, determination, power of organization, an outstanding gift for identifying himself with the language and thought of the simple man. These were the qualities that permitted him to carry through what he had begun." [12]

In closing this account of Luther and the momentous movement which he set rolling, we might append an ironic footnote. The same sale of indulgences which furnished the money to build a fitting capital for a universal Church (St. Peter's in Rome) at the same time provided the occasion for destroying the unity of western Christendom.

Lutheranism in Scandinavia. In 1525 the Grand Master of the Teutonic Knights who ruled Prussia (see p. 275) turned Lutheran, dissolved the order, secularized its lands, and declared himself duke of Prussia. With this exception, outside Germany Lutheranism permanently established itself as a state religion only in the Scandinavian countries. Here emerging modern monarchs welcomed the opportunity to obtain needed wealth by confiscating church property and needed power by filling church offices with Lutherans who preached obedience to constituted authority. This was particularly the case in Sweden where Gustavus Vasa led a successful struggle for Swedish independence from Denmark. In 1523 he was elected king, and soon thereafter he declared himself a Lutheran and filled his empty treasury from the sale of confiscated Church lands. A century later his descendant, Gustavus Adolphus, would intervene in the religious wars in Germany and be instrumental in saving German Protestantism from extinction. In Denmark, which also ruled Norway, the spread of Lutheranism was encouraged by the king. In 1537 an ordinance, approved by Luther, established a national Lutheran church with its bishops as salaried officials of the Danish state.

Zwingli in Switzerland. Meanwhile, Protestantism had taken firm root in Switzerland.

Some of the giants of the Protestant Reformation are shown in this picture painted about 1530 by Lucas Cranach the Elder. At the far left is Luther, and at the far right his associate Melanchthon, who wrote the Augsburg Confession. Next to Melanchthon is Zwingli. In the center of the picture is John Frederick the Magnanimous, elector of Saxony, whose family supported Luther, John Frederick's uncle, Frederick III, once sheltered Luther in his Wartburg castle.

In the German-speaking area of that country —particularly in Zurich—the Reformation was led by Ulrich Zwingli (1484-1531). Like Luther, who was the same age, Zwingli repudiated papal in favor of scriptural authority, preached justification by faith, attacked monasticism and clerical celibacy, and drastically revised the sacramental system. But the differences between the two leaders proved irreconcilable when they met in 1529 at the University of Marburg, founded two years earlier as the first Protestant university in Europe. Whereas Luther looked on baptism as a means of helping to regenerate the individual, Zwingli considered it only a means of initiating a child into society. Nor did he believe with Luther that the real presence of Christ was found in the Lord's Supper. To Zwingli, who had been trained as a humanist and was therefore more of a rationalist than Luther, the bread and wine symbolized Christ's body and blood and the service was a commemoration of the Last Supper.

Zwingli was an ardent Swiss patriot who had once served as chaplain with Swiss mercenaries in Italy. The Swiss Confederation, comprising thirteen cantons, was a by-product of the weakness and disunity of the Holy Roman Empire. Originating in 1291 as a defensive union of three cantons, the confederation expanded and repulsed all attempts of the emperors to exercise jurisdiction over it. Switzerland's independence was won by the valor of its hardy peasant pikemen, whose prowess became so famed that foreign rulers and popes eagerly sought their services. Garbed in colorful Renaissance costumes, Swiss mercenaries still guard the Vatican.

In 1531 war broke out between Protestant and Catholic cantons, and Zwingli was slain in battle. The war ended in the same year with an agreement that anticipated by a quarter of a century the Peace of Augsburg in Germany—each canton was allowed to choose its own religion. This settlement was largely responsible for keeping Switzerland from taking sides in the great religious wars that subsequently engulfed Europe. Furthermore, it helped set the policy of neutrality which the Swiss have followed to our own day.

These pen and ink sketches of John Calvin in his later years were drawn by one of his students.

John Calvin. The most famous sixteenth-century Protestant leader after Luther was John Calvin (1509-1564). A Frenchman of the middle class, Calvin studied theology and law at Paris, where he became interested in Luther's teachings. About 1533 he had what he called a "conversion," whereby he abandoned Catholicism and fled to the Protestant city of Basel in Switzerland. Here in 1536 he published the first edition of his great work, the *Institutes of the Christian Religion*, unquestionably one of the most influential books of systematic theology ever written. His capacity for creative thinking was overshadowed by his ability as an organizer and synthesist. Influenced by his legal training as well as by humanistic scholarship and the doctrines of Luther, Calvin set forth a system that was a masterpiece of logical reasoning.

Whereas Luther's central doctrine was justification by faith, Calvin's was the sovereignty of God. "Both Calvin and Luther had an overwhelming sense of the majesty of God, but whereas for Luther this served to point up the miracle of forgiveness, for Calvin it gave rather the assurance of the impregnability of God's purpose."[13] God was omnipotent and for His own purposes had created the world and also man in His image. Since Adam and Eve had fallen from a state of sinlessness, man was utterly depraved and lost.

Carrying these doctrines to their logical conclusions, Calvin defined man's relation to God in his famous doctrine of predestination. Since God is omniscient, He knows the past, present, and future. Consequently, He must always know which men are to be saved and which men are to be damned eternally. Man's purpose in life, then, is not to try to work out his salvation—for this has already been determined—but to honor God. While Calvin did not profess to know absolutely who were to be God's chosen—the elect—he believed that the following three tests constituted a good yardstick by which to judge who might be saved: participation in the two sacraments, Baptism and the Lord's Supper; an upright moral life; and a public profession of the faith.

Calvin's emphasis upon the sovereignty of God led him to differ with Luther on the relationship of church and state. To Luther the state was supreme, but to Calvin the church and its ministers, as representatives of the sovereignty of God, must dominate. Calvinist church government in turn was democratically oriented in that it was based on the authority not of bishops but of synods or presbyteries, elected bodies composed of ministers and elders. Although Calvin upheld lawful political authority, he also approved of rebellion against a tyranny "which overrides private conscience." Thus, wherever Calvinism spread it carried with it the seeds of representative government and of defiance against despotism.

Calvinist Geneva. In 1536 the Protestants of Geneva invited Calvin to become their leader, and there he put his ideas on government into effect. Calvin believed it was the duty of the elect to glorify God by establishing a theocracy that would be governed according to scriptural precept. Although the Bible was the supreme authority, the chief instrument of government was the Consistory, or Presbytery, a council of ministers and elders which made and enforced the laws. Calvin in turn dominated the Consis-

tory, which showed great zeal in disciplining the community and punishing or removing any person found guilty of unseemly behavior. Although the regime was high-minded, it carried its zeal to ridiculous lengths. Penalties were inflicted for being absent from sermons or laughing during the church service, for wearing bright colors, for swearing or dancing, for playing cards, or for having one's fortune told by gypsies.

In regard to more serious offenses, especially in the religious sphere, Calvin and his associates acted with a severity common to the Reformation age. They used torture to obtain confessions and banished citizens for heresy, blasphemy, witchcraft, and adultery. When the Spanish physician Servetus sought refuge in Geneva, having fled from Catholic persecution because he was a Unitarian who denied the doctrine of the Trinity, Calvin had him burned for heresy. "Because the Papists persecute the truth," Calvin explained, "should we on that account refrain from repressing error?"

The spread of Calvinism. From Geneva, Calvinism spread far and wide, imbued with its founder's spirit of austerity and a self-righteousness born of confidence in being among the elect of God. Many of its leaders studied at the Academy (today the University of Geneva), which trained students from other countries in Calvin's theology. In France, Calvinism made influential converts among both the bourgeoisie and the nobility. Known as Huguenots, the French Calvinists remained a minority but, as we shall see in the next chapter, their importance far outweighed their numbers. In Scotland the fiery Calvinist John Knox successfully challenged the authority of the Roman Church (see p. 316), and in Germany and the Netherlands Calvin's teachings formed the basis for the German and Dutch Reformed churches.

Henry VIII's quarrel with Rome. In Germany the revolt against the Church was primarily religious in nature, although it possessed political implications; in England the situation was reversed. There the leader was a monarch, Henry VIII (1509-1547), not a priest. Henry broke with Rome not for theological reasons but because the pope would not annul his marriage to Catherine of Aragon, daughter of Ferdinand and Isabella of Spain, whom he had married for dynastic reasons.

Catherine had given Henry a daughter, Mary, but no son, and Henry was convinced that a male heir was necessary if the newly established Tudors were to endure as a dynasty and England kept from reverting to anarchy. Catherine was the widow of his brother, and Church law forbade a man to marry his brother's widow. A special papal dispensation had been granted for the marriage, but Henry claimed the dispensation was not valid and in 1527 asked Pope Clement VII to revoke it.

Normally the pope might have acquiesced to Henry's wishes, for other popes had granted similar favors to monarchs and Henry had been loyal to the Church. In answer to Luther he had written a *Defense of the Seven Sacraments* (1521), in which he castigated Luther as a "poisonous serpent," the "wolf of hell," and the "limb of Satan." The pope gratefully bestowed on Henry the title "Defender of the Faith"—a title which English monarchs still possess. But much as he might have wished, the pope could not support Henry in his desires. There were two good reasons. First, the pope felt it would be dangerous for one pontiff to reverse the judgments of a predecessor. Second, the emperor Charles V, the most powerful monarch in Europe, was a nephew of Catherine and threatened the pope if he declared the marriage null and void. Clement decided to wait before giving his answer, hoping that in the meantime events would resolve themselves.

But Henry would not wait. He obtained from Parliament the power to appoint bishops in England without papal permission, designating Thomas Cranmer as archbishop of Canterbury—a willing tool who was sure to do his master's bidding. In 1533 Cranmer pronounced the king's marriage to Catherine invalid and legalized Henry's marriage to coquettish Anne Boleyn, whom he had secretly married three months earlier. At last goaded into action, Clement VII excommunicated Henry and maintained that Catherine alone was the king's true wife.

Establishment of the Anglican Church. In 1534 Henry severed all connections with Rome. A compliant Parliament passed the famous Act of Supremacy, which stated that the king "justly and rightfully is and ought to be supreme head of the Church of England." It also enacted the Treason Act, which declared liable to the death penalty anyone who called the king a "heretic, schismatic, tyrant, infidel, or usurper." Turning on his old friend, Henry had Sir Thomas More beheaded because he would not acknowledge the sovereign as head of the English Church. In recent years More has been canonized by the Catholic Church not only for his saintly life but also for his martyrdom in opposing Henry VIII's divorce and break with the Church.

To replenish the royal coffers and to gain popular support, Henry, working through Parliament, dissolved the monasteries and sold their lands to the nobles and gentry. Thus Henry acquired accomplices, in a sense, in his conflict with Rome. It must be remembered that Henry and Parliament could not perhaps have effected such sweeping changes if many Englishmen had not been anticlerical.

In the same year (1539) in which Parliament acted to dissolve the monasteries, it also passed the Six Articles, which reaffirmed the main points of Catholic theology. By this act, both the Catholic who denied the supremacy of the king and the Protestant who denied the validity of transubstantiation were to be punished severely. Thus England threw off the supremacy of the pope without at that time adopting the Protestant faith; the elements of Protestantism in the English Church crept in after the break with Rome.

After Henry's death in 1547, his frail ten-year-old son mounted the throne as Edward VI. During his reign the growing Protestant party in England became ascendant. The Six Articles were repealed; priests were no longer held to their vows of celibacy; and the old Latin service was replaced by Cranmer's Book of Common Prayer, written in English, which brought the service much closer to the people and exerted a powerful influence on the development of the language. In 1553 the Forty-Two Articles defined the faith of the Church of England along Protestant lines.

Under the devoutly Catholic Mary (1553-

In this contemporary illustration John Knox sounds his trumpet of reform in the ears of Mary, Queen of Scots. The text accompanying the picture reads, "No Queen in her kingdom can or ought to sit fast, if Knox's . . . books blow any true blast."

1558), the unfortunate daughter of the still less fortunate Catherine of Aragon, Catholicism was reinstated, and three hundred Protestants, including Archbishop Cranmer, were burned at the stake. But with the accession to the throne of Anne Boleyn's red-headed and fiery-tempered daughter, Elizabeth I (1558-1603), the Anglican Church took on a strong Protestant character. Realizing the political necessity for religious peace, Elizabeth worked hard to achieve a compromise settlement. Although the Church of England remained a state church under the control of the monarch, Elizabeth astutely changed her title from "Supreme Head" to the more modest "Supreme Governor." In accepting the Bible as the final authority, and in recognizing only Baptism and Holy Eucharist as Christ-instituted sacraments, Elizabeth's Thirty-Nine Articles (1563) were essentially Protestant, although many articles were ambiguously phrased in an effort to satisfy both parties. Much Catholic ritual was preserved, along with the ecclesiastical government of bishops in apostolic succession.

Presbyterianism in Scotland. The religious revolt in Scotland was largely the work of the zealous reformer John Knox (1505?-1572), who had become a disciple of Calvin in Geneva, which he called "the most perfect school of Christ that ever was on earth since the days of the Apostles." After returning to his native Scotland in about 1559, Knox became the leader of a group of Protestant nobles who wished to overthrow both the jurisdiction of the Roman Catholic Church and the monarch—Queen Mary Stuart, whose husband was king of France (see p. 333). In 1560 the Scottish Parliament severed all ties with Rome and accepted Knox's Articles of the Presbyterian Church, modeled after Calvin's views on theology and church government. When the beautiful but ill-fated queen returned from France one year later she found her bleak kingdom alienated from her own Catholic views. Her scandalous behavior (see p. 333) and her steadfast Catholicism led the Scots to depose her in 1567 in favor of her Protestant son James.

The Anabaptists. The most radical among those who rejected the religious establishment of the time were the Anabaptists ("rebaptizers"), so called because they denied the efficacy of infant baptism. They formed many sects led by self-styled "prophets" who carried to extreme Luther's doctrines of Christian liberty, priesthood of all believers, and return to primitive Christianity. Centered in Germany and the Netherlands, Anabaptism was predominantly a lower-class movement; many of the peasants whose hopes for economic and social reform had been crushed by the Peasants' War turned from Luther to the Anabaptists. In communities of their own, they shared their worldly goods with one another and lived as they thought the primitive Christians had lived, working and praying together. On occasion they employed force to purify society and establish a New Jerusalem. Mainly, however, they believed in the separation of church and state and advocated pacifism and the love-ethic. Today some portion of their spirit lives on among such groups as the Mennonites, the Amish, and the Quakers.

THE CATHOLIC REFORMATION

The background. The Catholic Reformation should not be viewed as only a retaliatory movement or a series of measures taken to stem the rising tide of Protestantism. The Roman Church had always retained latent forces of recuperation and strength which it could draw upon in challenging times. Before Luther had posted his ninety-five theses, evidence of renewed vitality and internal reform was visible in the Roman Church.

One of the prime examples of this resurgence occurred in Spain under Ferdinand and Isabella, ardent Catholics as well as autocrats. To deal with Moors, Jews, and heretics, the "Catholic Sovereigns" requested and got papal permission for a separate Spanish Inquisition under their control (see p. 272). The Inquisition soon came to dominate the Spanish Church, making it virtually a state church, and moved on to the problem of religious reform. Under the able Grand Inquisitor, Cardinal Ximenes (d. 1517), both the secular clergy and the monastic orders were invigorated by a renewal of spirit, discipline, and education—the latter including the scholarly study of the Bible at the University of Alcala, founded by Ximenes as a means of training able bishops. Thus Spain became a model Catholic state, where Protestantism would make few converts.

In a category of his own was the Dominican friar Savonarola (1452-1498), an ardent puritan, mystic, and reformer of Church and society. In 1496, when the Medici were expelled from Florence, Savonarola emerged as master of the city. For four years he ruled the Kingdom of God, as he called Florence, invoking the wrath of God upon worldly living and sinful luxuries. Bands of teenagers were organized to go about the city collecting and burning "vanities"—fashionable clothes, wigs, ornaments, and secular books and paintings. Savonarola also bitterly denounced the iniquities of the Borgia pope, Alexander VI, and called for a general council to reform the Church. But he lacked the power to reform the papacy and the Church, or even to maintain his hold on the fickle Florentines. Publicly humiliated by having his Dominican garb torn from him in the great square of Florence, Savonarola was hanged and burned, a victim of political intrigue. He was later hailed by Luther and the Protestants as a forerunner of their movement.

By the middle of the sixteenth century the Church had rallied its forces and was ready to take the offensive against the inroads of Protestantism. This renewal of strength, known as the Catholic Reformation—or, as some prefer, Counter Reformation—penetrated all areas of the Church. New monastic orders adapted monastic life to the needs of the time, the papacy headed a program of vigorous reform, and the Church regained much ground lost to the Protestants. Climaxing the whole movement was the Council of Trent, where the Church boldly reaffirmed its traditional doctrines and flatly refused to compromise in any way with the Protestants.

Reformist monasticism. In response to the same forces that had produced monastic reform during the earlier medieval reformation (see Chapter 11), a number of new monastic orders sprang up in the first half of the sixteenth century. Prominent among them were the Theatines, a body of devoted priests who undertook to check the spread of heresy by concentrating upon the regeneration of the clergy; the Capuchins, an offshoot of the Franciscan order inspired by the original spirit of St. Francis, who became notable for their preaching and for the care of the poor and the sick; and the Ursulines, whose special task was the education of girls. Reflecting both the reforming zeal of the new orders and the mystical reaffirmation of faith that characterized most reformers, Protestant as well as Catholic, was the order of barefoot Carmelites and their founder, the Spanish nun St. Theresa. These devout sisters slept on straw, ate no meat, and lived on alms. Quietistic mysticism, which teaches that spiritual peace can be attained by losing the sense of self in passive contemplation of God and His works, is well reflected in St. Theresa's written accounts of her ecstasies and visions.

Loyola and the Jesuits. The Society of Jesus, better known as the Jesuits, founded

Bernini's Baroque sculpture for a side altar in a small Roman church depicts a vision of St. Theresa. Describing her mystical experiences, St. Theresa once told of a moment of ecstasy and pain in which an angel pierced her heart with a flaming arrow. As the saint ascends to heaven on a cloud, the angel approaches her and she swoons.

by the Spanish nobleman and ex-soldier Ignatius Loyola (1491-1556), played a vital role in the Catholic Reformation. While recovering from a severe battle wound, Loyola experienced a mystical religious conversion and vowed to become a soldier of Christ and "serve only God and the Roman pontiff, His vicar on earth." His "Company [*Societas*] of Jesus," founded in 1534 and given papal authorization in 1540, was organized along military lines with Loyola as "general." Members were carefully selected, rigorously

trained, and subjected to an iron discipline. One of the classics in the field of religious literature, Loyola's *Spiritual Exercises*, a work of great psychological penetration based on his own mystical religious experience, was used to inculcate disciplined asceticism and absolute obedience to superior authority. In addition to the usual monastic vows of chastity, obedience, and poverty, the Jesuits took a special vow of allegiance to the pope. As preachers, confessors to monarchs and princes, and educators, the Jesuits had remarkable success in stemming and even reversing the tide of Protestantism, particularly in Poland, Bohemia, Hungary, Germany, France, and the Spanish Netherlands (modern Belgium). In addition, the Jesuits performed excellent missionary work in America and Asia.

Papal reform: Paul III. A new era was at hand for the Church when Paul III, who reigned from 1534 to 1549, ascended the papal throne. He chose outstanding men as cardinals and appointed a commission to look into the need for reform. Their report listed the evils requiring correction, including the appointment of worldly bishops and priests, the traffic in benefices and indulgences and other financial abuses, the venality of some cardinals, and the absence of others from the papal court. Ignoring the opposition of some high churchmen, Paul made plans to call a general council to carry out needed reforms.

The Council of Trent. The Catholic Reformation came to a climax in the Council of Trent, which met in three sessions between 1545 and 1563. Rejecting all compromise with Protestantism, the Council restated the basic tenets of Catholic doctrine. It declared salvation to be a matter of both faith and good works, and it affirmed the source of doctrine to be not only the Bible, as interpreted by the Church, but also the "unwritten traditions, which were received by the Apostles from the lips of Christ himself, or, by the same Apostles, at the dictation of the Holy Spirit, and were handed on and have come down to us...."[14] The Council also reaffirmed the seven sacraments, with special emphasis on transubstantiation, decreed that only Latin be used in the Mass, and approved the spiritual usefulness of indulgences, pilgrimages, veneration of saints and relics, and the cult of the Virgin.

At the same time, the Council sought to eliminate abuses by ordering reforms in Church discipline and administration. Such evils as simony, absenteeism, the abuse of indulgences, and secular pursuits on the part of the clergy were strictly forbidden. Bishops were ordered to supervise closely both the regular and the secular clergy, appoint reputable and competent men to ecclesiastical positions, and establish seminaries to provide a well-educated clergy. The clergy, in turn, were requested to preach frequently to the people.

In addition to freeing the Church of its worst abuses and formulating its doctrines clearly and rigidly, the Council of Trent strengthened the authority of the papacy. The pope's party in the Council, ably led by Jesuit theologians, defeated all attempts to revive the theory that a general council was supreme in the Church. And when the final session of the Council voted that none of its decrees were valid without the consent of the Holy See, the Church became more than ever an absolute monarchy ruled by the pope.

EFFECTS OF
THE RELIGIOUS UPHEAVAL

Religious division but renewed faith. By 1550 Christendom was composed of three divisions—Greek Orthodox, Roman Catholic, and Protestant. With Protestantism predominant in northern Europe, the unity of western Christendom was split irreparably. The Catholics placed their faith in the authority of the pope and the need for a mediatory priesthood. The Protestants placed their faith in the authority of the Bible and held that every Christian could win salvation without priestly mediation. But since they differed among themselves in their interpretation of the Bible and the methods of church organization, in time hundreds of separate Protestant sects arose.

Although the religious upheaval fostered the religious diversity of modern times, it also represented in some aspects a return to medievalism. It was a great religious revival, a renewal of faith. Renaissance emphasis on free and secular thought gave way again to authority—for Protestants it was the Bible; for Catholics, the Church. The Renaissance movement, having fostered doubt and criticism of medieval values, was now engulfed in a return to some of those values. Thus, temporarily at least, the Renaissance spirit was stifled. But it was to prove stronger than this intense religious revival and in time was to profit from the passing of the single religious authority of the universal Church.

Another by-product of the religious upheaval was a new interest in education, already broadened by the intellectual and moral concerns of the humanists. Each faith wanted its youth to be properly trained in its teachings. As part of its campaign to win Protestants back to the fold, the Jesuits in particular developed a school system so superior and so attractive that many Protestant as well as Catholic youths attended. One feature of Protestantism eventually stimulated education a great deal. Its emphasis upon the importance of Bible reading encouraged the promotion of universal education; Luther, for example, insisted not only that the state should establish schools but that "the civil authorities are under obligation to compel the people to send their children to school."[15]

On the debit side the Reformation era witnessed an intensification of religious intolerance. There seems little choice between Catholics and Protestants in the degree of their detestation for one another and for religious liberty in general. Each religious sect assumed that salvation came through it alone, and all were equally intolerant when they had the power to be so. In the words of Sebastian Castellio (d. 1563), a one-time follower of Calvin who wrote a protest against the execution of Servetus:

Although opinions are almost as numerous as men, nevertheless there is hardly any sect which does not condemn all others and desire to reign alone. Hence arise banishments, chains, imprisonments, stakes, and gallows and this miserable rage to visit daily penalties upon those who differ from the mighty about matters hitherto unknown, for so many centuries disputed, and not yet cleared up.[16]

How can we call ourselves Christians, Castellio asked in effect, if we do not imitate Christ's clemency and mercy?

O Creator and King of the world, dost Thou see these things? Art Thou become so changed, so cruel, so contrary to Thyself? When Thou wast on earth none was more mild, more clement, more patient of injury. . . . O blasphemies and shameful audacity of men, who dare to attribute to Christ that which they do by the command and at the instigation of Satan![17]

Unfortunate, too, was the break between the humanists and the Protestants, which began when Luther broke with the Church.

Although both groups wanted to reform the Church by removing its abuses and returning to the practices and faith of early Christianity, Erasmus could say of Luther's revolt: "I laid a hen's egg: Luther hatched a bird of quite different breed."[18] The humanists, in other words, desired reform, not revolution. Furthermore, because they exalted the rationality and innate goodness of man, the humanists disagreed with the strong Protestant emphasis on man's depravity and the necessity of salvation by superhuman means. As Luther saw it, "The human avails more with Erasmus than the divine."[19]

Protestantism and capitalism. The Renaissance had encouraged a new individualism in economic matters, which contributed to a breakdown of the guild system and to the rise of the individual entrepreneur. While

Both Catholics and Protestants were guilty of incredible atrocities in their respective attempts to achieve religious conformity. Processions such as this became common in French cities as members of a "holy league" paraded through the streets seeking out Huguenots to execute for heresy.

Luther continued to accept the medieval concept of the "just price" and the ban against usury (receiving interest on money loaned), with the Calvinists investment of capital and loaning of money became respectable. Calvinism especially encouraged enterprise; some Calvinists regarded prosperity as a sign of election to grace and poverty as evidence of damnation. Indeed, it has been asserted that:

Calvin did for the bourgeoisie of the sixteenth century what Marx did for the proletariat of the nineteenth, . . . the doctrine of predestination satisfied the same hunger for an assurance that the forces of the universe are on the side of the elect as was to be assuaged in a different age by the theory of historical materialism. He set their virtues at their best in sharp antithesis with the vices of the established order at its worst, taught them to feel that they were a chosen people, made them conscious of their great destiny in the Providential plan and resolute to realize it.[20]

The business classes were among those that encouraged the revolt from Rome; we can now see that they were also among those that gained most by it.

Union of religion and politics. In many cases the religious division of Europe followed political lines. In Germany the Peace of Augsburg gave the ruler of each state the right to decide the faith of his subjects, thus controlling the church in his realm. Similarly, rulers of other countries, both Catholic and Protestant, developed national churches, so that Europe was divided religiously into an Anglican Church, a Dutch Church, a Swedish Church, and so on.

In many countries one effect of such division was to strengthen the hand of the king in building a unified state. The authority and prestige of the Protestant monarch was increased as he became the spiritual as well as the political ruler of his subjects. Even in Catholic countries, though the pope remained the spiritual ruler, the Church became national in sentiment, and it was the king rather than the pope who enforced religious conformity among his subjects. Conversely, where the split between Protestants and Catholics was deep, as in the Holy Roman Empire, the power of the central ruler was limited and national unity impeded.

Freedom of religion, as we have noted, was still far from a reality. Persecution flourished, partly because the clash between faiths engendered intolerance but even more because religious uniformity was the ideal of the rulers of the rising national states. Just as he sought to create a uniform system of law and justice throughout his realm, so the strong monarch endeavored to establish a single faith to which his subjects owed complete obedience. An incidental result of this policy was the emigration of religious minorities to areas where they could worship freely, as in the New World.

Political and religious developments continued to be closely related throughout the sixteenth and early seventeenth centuries. In the Religious Wars to be described in the next chapter political duels were superimposed on religious quarrels, resulting in some of the bloodiest and most prolonged warfare in human history. The founder of the Christian religion had given as a primary command, "Thou shalt love thy neighbor as thyself." But there was no brotherhood between Catholic and Protestant nor between political rivals who played on religious antagonisms to serve their own ends.

SUMMARY

The Renaissance represented a new emphasis on man's individuality, an outlook which could not fail eventually to have its impact on religion. An appeal for religious reform came from the northern humanists who criticized ecclesiastical abuses and called for a Christianity based closely upon the New Testament. By means of the printing press, which vastly increased the number of books available, the new ideas spread rapidly throughout Europe. Already beginning to revolt against all institutions which hampered them in their new economic freedom, many men of the middle class were sympathetic to the cry for Church reform. The new spirit also found an ally in the new nationalism and in the growing power of the kings, who were reluctant to be thwarted by any force, even the Church. When a leader appeared with a religious message in keeping with the spirit of the age, the long bottled-up forces of reform exploded.

Luther's open breach with the Church encouraged such Protestant leaders as Zwingli, Calvin, and other reformers to form their own churches. The essence of the new movements was an emphasis on Biblical authority, a denial of the need for priestly mediation for salvation, and a repudiation of the pope as head of organized religion. After the Protestant Revolt, churches were firmly tied to the political administration of the states. Thus Calvin and Zwingli established theocracies in Geneva and Zurich in Switzerland. In Germany each prince chose between Lutheranism and Catholicism for the religion of his subjects. In the Scandinavian countries the national churches were Lutheran. Without repudiating the basic elements of Catholicism, the English king broke with Rome and assumed the headship of the Anglican Church.

The challenge flung at the Church did not remain unanswered. As the medieval Church had arrested decline by new zealous orders of monks, so once again the Church was invigorated by various new religious brotherhoods and a resurgence of mysticism and morality. Pope Paul III and his successors carried out an energetic program to excise the abuses which had plagued the Church for centuries. Without any compromise with the Protestants, the Council of Trent reaffirmed the fundamental doctrines of the Church. But there was no possibility of the Church reuniting Europe.

Europe was plunged into an epoch of intolerance and bigotry from which it slowly emerged when, after the prolonged and bloody struggles to be described in the next chapter, it became apparent that no one faith could exterminate the others. But if the clock was set back in some ways, in other ways the religious upheaval furthered the transition from a medieval to a modern pattern of life. The revolt from the universal Church shattered the medieval ideal of unity and gave us the religious diversity of the modern world.

SUGGESTIONS FOR READING

G. L. Mosse, **The Reformation,*** 3rd ed., Holt, Rinehart & Winston; E. H. Harbison, **The Age of Reformation,*** Cornell; Philip Hughes, **A Popular History of the Reformation,*** Image; H. J. Hillerbrand, **Men and Ideas in the Sixteenth Century,*** Rand McNally; A. G. Dickens, **Reformation and Society in Sixteenth-Century Europe,*** Harcourt, Brace & World. Good brief surveys; the last volume cited contains many illustrations. J. Hurstfield, ed., **The Reformation Crisis,*** Torchbooks, contains brief, perceptive essays by noted scholars on major aspects of the Reformation era. More detailed are G. R. Elton, **Reformation Europe, 1517–1559,*** Torchbooks; and H. Grimm, **The Reformation Era, 1500–1650,** rev. ed., Macmillan, 1965. See also John P. Dolan, **A History of the Reformation: A Conciliatory Assessment of Opposite Views,*** Mentor.

J. Huizinga, **Erasmus and the Age of the Reformation,*** Torchbooks. Excellent on the northern humanists' criticisms of the Church. See also E. H. Harbison, **The Christian Scholar in the Age of the Reformation,*** Scribner.

R. H. Bainton, **Here I Stand: A Life of Martin Luther,*** Mentor. The most readable account. See also E. Erikson, **Young Man Luther,*** Norton; F. Lau, **Luther,** Westminster, 1963; E. Schwiebert, **Luther and His Times,** Concordia, 1950.

Williston Walker, **John Calvin: The Organiser of Reformed Protestantism,*** Schocken. Probably the best introduction. G. Harkness, **John Calvin: The Man and His Ethics,*** Abingdon, and J. T. McNeill, **The History and Character of Calvinism,*** Scribner, are standard works. See also W. Monter, **Calvin's**

Geneva,* Wiley, 1967; and J. Ridley, **John Knox,** Oxford, 1968.

A. G. Dickens, **The English Reformation,*** Schocken; T. M. Parker, **The English Reformation to 1558,*** 2nd ed., Oxford. Excellent surveys. C. Parmiter, **The King's Great Matter,** Barnes and Noble, 1967, describes Henry VIII's efforts to annul his marriage.

On the "left wing" of Protestantism, see F. Littell, **The Anabaptist View of the Church,** Beacon, 1958, and N. Cohn, **The Pursuit of the Millennium,*** Torchbooks.

A. G. Dickens, **The Counter Reformation,*** Harcourt, Brace & World, 1969. Brief and richly illustrated. Sympathetic Catholic accounts are H. Daniel-Rops, **The Catholic Reformation,** 2 vols., Image, and P. Janelle, **The Catholic Reformation,** Bruce, 1949. See also R. Ridolfi, **The Life of Girolamo Savonarola,** Knopf, 1959; J. Broderick, **The Origin of the Jesuits,** Longmans, 1949.

On the effects of the religious upheaval see W. Pauck, **The Heritage of the Reformation,*** rev. ed., Galaxy, 1968; R. H. Tawney, **Religion and the Rise of Capitalism,*** Mentor; R. Kingdon and R. Linder, eds., **Calvin and Calvinism; Sources of Democracy?*** Heath, 1970; H. Kamen, **The Rise of Toleration,*** McGraw-Hill, 1967; E. Troeltsch, **Protestantism and Progress: A Historical Study of the Relation of Protestantism to the Modern World,*** Beacon; E. W. Monter, **European Witchcraft,*** Wiley, 1969.

*Indicates an inexpensive paperbound edition.

Chapter 15

The Strife of States and Kings

**Power Politics and the New Diplomacy:
1500-1650**

INTRODUCTION. By acquiring a historical perspective we can do much to illuminate today's events and problems and bring them into focus. The period from 1500 to 1650 is particularly significant; it can serve as a laboratory in which we can watch the genesis and development of the statecraft of modern times.

The central factor in this troubled period was the rise of the competitive state system, involving the actions of independent and sovereign nations. These budding nations exhibited three fundamental features that contrasted sharply with the characteristics the same territories had possessed in earlier, feudal times: they had strong and effective central governments, their citizens displayed increased national consciousness, and their rulers claimed sovereignty—that is, supreme power within the boundaries of their own states. As we shall see in this chapter, these states were expansionist and aggressive, taking every opportunity to grow more powerful at the expense of weaker nations.

The decline of the medieval Church and the religious revolt in the sixteenth century ended the Church's role as the arbiter of right and justice in disputes between secular rulers. The rulers of the sovereign states were thus completely free and untrammeled in the arena of international politics. Would one state be able to dominate all the rest? Would there be varying degrees of power among states without any one becoming supreme? Would these independent and sovereign nations be able to establish a pattern of cooperation, ensuring thereby a measure of peace and political amity in the western world? These fundamental questions were answered in Europe between 1500 and 1650. And the way in which they were answered set the pattern of international relations from that day to this.

The one hundred fifty years following 1500 are among the bloodiest and most complex in European history. The story of these years is chiefly one of battles, alliances, and treaties —in a word, drum-and-trumpet history. Yet running through the wars and complexities of this period two major threads can be discerned: the emergence of the modern diplomatic technique of the "balance of power" as a means of providing some degree of equilibrium to the new European state system, and the rise and fall of Spain as the dominant power in Europe.

THE COMPETITIVE STATE SYSTEM EMERGES

Sovereignty replaces suzerainty. Both the medieval ideal of universal empire and Church and the medieval actuality of decentralized feudalism were undermined by the rise of strong monarchs who defied popes and put down rebellious nobles. The century before 1500 had witnessed much disorder, civil conflict, and war; more and more, people looked to their kings to provide the state with a measure of stability and security. Rulers also took an active part in stimulating the economy of their nations, and in return they obtained from the bourgeoisie larger revenues which they used to expand administrative bureaus and government services. Of great importance was the fact that kings could now afford to hire soldiers for standing armies—monarchs were no longer dependent upon the irregularly available feudal forces. Moreover, the king's army could easily squelch the retainers of a rebellious noble. Thus the power once distributed throughout the feudal pyramid was concentrated in the hands of the ruler.

The theory of centralized unchallenged authority—that is, sovereignty—was given its first comprehensive expression by a French lawyer and university professor, Jean Bodin (1530-1596). Dismayed by the disorders of the religious wars in France (see p. 335), Bodin attacked both the feudal idea of contract and the universalism of empire and Church in his work *Concerning Public Affairs*. He supported the power of the monarch and his right of sovereignty, which he defined as "unlimited power over citizens and subjects, unrestrained by law."[1] According to Bodin, the king was free of all restraint save some rather shadowy limitation exercised by God and divine law.

The advent of power politics. Equipped with a standing army, royal courts, and new sources of revenue and backed by the growing support of the bourgeoisie, a European monarch was master in his own nation by the beginning of the sixteenth century. And, equally significant, he was his own master in foreign affairs. The Church was no longer an international arbiter, and the factionalism of the Protestant Reformation was soon to reduce appreciably the Church's claim to universal influence. The international arena now consisted of a number of free agents who could keep what they could defend and take what they wanted if they had sufficient force. A nation-state depended for survival on the exercise of its power, and war was the chief instrument at hand. Thus statecraft became the politics of power, and the competitive state system emerged.

The rise of modern diplomacy. The development of the competitive state system gave rise to the practice of modern diplomacy. Rulers needed to be informed about the plans and policies of their rivals; states fearful of attack from stronger foes had to seek out allies; and, after wars had been fought, agreements between victor and vanquished required negotiations.

Medieval popes customarily sent envoys to reside at royal courts, but modern diplomatic practice had its real birth among the fiercely independent city-states of northern Italy. The republic of Venice—"the school and touchstone of ambassadors"—was particularly active; its authorities maintained diplomatic archives and sent their representatives throughout Europe with elaborate instructions. To act as a safeguard against poisoning, trusted cooks were part of a diplomat's retinue, but ambassadors' wives were forbidden to accompany their husbands on diplomatic missions for fear they might divulge state secrets. About 1455 the first permanent embassy in history was sent to Genoa by the duke of Milan. Within a short time most of the important nations of the day followed suit and posted representatives in European capitals.

On many occasions the new diplomacy encouraged negotiation and prevented war. Diplomatic methods so often involved deceit and treachery, however, that negotiations often fanned rather than diminished the fires of international hostility. A seventeenth-century Englishman defined an ambassador as "an honest man sent to lie abroad for the commonwealth."[2] Diplomacy during the past three hundred years often has done little to refute this definition.

Balance-of-power politics. One of the most important achievements of the new diplomacy was the technique known as the "balance of power," whereby a coalition of states could checkmate the swollen power of one or more rival states and thereby restore equilibrium. Balance-of-power politics then and later aimed not so much at preventing war as at preserving the sovereignty and independence of individual states from threatened or actual aggression. Yet as international relations more and more took the form of alignments aimed at preserving the balance of power, a sense of the interdependence

of the European state system developed. The strong movement toward European unity in our day is the latest manifestation of this sense of interdependence.

The sixteenth century was the formative period for the behavior pattern of modern nations in international affairs. Unrestrained by religious or ethical scruples, the sovereign governments were about to begin an era of international strife with the quest for power as their only guide to success. With disunited Italy as a pawn in the game, the counters on the chessboard began to move.

ITALY: CASE STUDY IN POWER POLITICS

Charles VIII and the Italian Wars. Because of Louis XI's success as a statemaker (see p. 272), his son Charles VIII (1483-1498) entertained grandiose notions of imitating the exploits of Hannibal and Charlemagne by invading Italy, conquering Naples, and eventually wresting Constantinople from the Turks. In 1494 Charles crossed the Alps at the head of thirty thousand well-trained troops and initiated the Italian Wars that were to last intermittently until 1559. At first the expedition was little more than a holiday for the French. Charles' cavalry, pikemen, and light, quick-firing cannon won easy victories, and he soon took possession of Naples.

This quick conquest alarmed the rulers who had previously acquiesced to Charles' plan. Ferdinand of Spain suspected that Charles might next try to conquer the Spanish possession of Sicily, and the Holy Roman emperor became uneasy at the prospect of French dominance in Italy. In addition, Venice feared for its independence and took the lead in forming a league which also included the Papal States, the Holy Roman Empire, and Spain. Called the Holy League, it was the first important example of a coalition of states formed to preserve the balance of power in Europe. Its armies drove Charles out of Italy in 1495, thus halting French designs on the peninsula for the moment.

Machiavelli's works, which were translated into several different languages, had tremendous impact all over Europe.

End of the first phase of the Italian Wars. Following the death of Charles VIII in 1498, his successor, Louis XII, invaded Italy. The counters again moved on the chessboard: alliances were made and then broken, pledges went unhonored, and allies were deserted. Ferdinand of Spain offers a particularly good example of duplicity and treachery. Louis XII accused Ferdinand of cheating him on at least two occasions. Hearing this, Ferdinand scoffed: "He lies, the drunkard; I have deceived him more than ten times."[3]

In the first phase of the Italian Wars—which ended in 1513 with the French again ejected from Italy—one can see the new power politics at work, without benefit of rules and indeed without benefit of any moral or religious scruples. The only important objectives were glory, power, and wealth. In attaining these objectives "necessity knows no law," as Renaissance lawyers liked to observe. The conflict over Italy clearly prophesied the mode of future relations among modern sovereign states.

Machiavelli and Machiavellian politics. The primer for diplomacy and power politics was written by Niccolò Machiavelli (1469-1527), historian, playwright, and official in the Florentine republic. Outraged at the cavalier manner in which invaders had smashed their way into his beloved Italy, Machiavelli mourned his native land as being

more a slave than the Hebrews, more a servant than the Persians, more scattered than the Athenians; without head, without government; defeated, plundered, torn asunder, overrun; subject to every sort of disaster.[4]

Machiavelli's wide acquaintance with the unprincipled politics of the early Italian Wars produced his cynical and ruthless attitude toward men and politics. *The Prince*—one of a half-dozen volumes that have helped form western political thought—was written as a guide for an audacious leader who would use any means to win and hold power, free Italy from invaders, and end Italian disunity. A realist who wanted his leader-statesman to understand the political facts of life as they had been operating in Europe, Machiavelli wrote:

A prudent ruler . . . cannot and should not observe faith when such observance is to his disadvantage and the causes that made him give his promise have vanished. If men were all good, this advice would not be good, but since men are wicked and do not keep their promises to you, you likewise do not have to keep yours to them. Lawful reasons to excuse his failure to keep them will never be lacking to a prince.[5]

Machiavelli did not, of course, invent the precepts of ruthlessness in politics. Rulers had dishonored treaties and used force to attain their ends before *The Prince* was written. What Machiavelli did was to accept the politics of his day without any false illusions. He gave his prince many suggestions for survival and conquest in the brutal world of unrestrained power.

In the actions of all men, and especially those of princes, where there is no court to which to appeal, people think of the outcome. A prince needs only to conquer and to maintain his position. The means he has used will always be judged honorable and will be praised by everybody, because the crowd is always caught by appearance and by the outcome of events, and the crowd is all there is in the world. . . .[6]

Although "Machiavellian politics" is generally a term of condemnation, it should be noted that Machiavelli had an idealistic end in view: to "bring good to the mass of the people of the land" of Italy.[7]

EUROPEAN EMPIRE OR SOVEREIGN STATES?

Charles V. The manner in which the rulers of Europe practiced power politics is shown clearly by the events in Europe during the first half of the sixteenth century, a period often referred to as the Age of Charles V.

Charles' grandfather, Maximilian I, Archduke of Austria and Holy Roman emperor, had added the Netherlands and Franche-Comté to his realm by marrying Mary of Burgundy. (Franche-Comté was that part of Burgundy not seized by Louis XI; see p. 272). Maximilian's son (Charles' father) had married a daughter of Ferdinand and Isabella of Spain. Thus, by a calculated policy of dynastic marriages, the Austrian Hapsburgs enjoyed a position no ruler since Charlemagne had held. Following his father's death in 1506, Charles became ruler of the Netherlands; in 1516 his maternal grandfather, Ferdinand, bequeathed him Spain and its overseas empire and Naples and Sicily. The death of his other grandfather, Maximilian, gave him Austria and left vacant the throne of the Holy Roman Empire, to which Charles was elected in 1519 as Emperor Charles V.

Charles' efforts in protecting his dispersed territories, together with his dream of restoring royal authority and religious unity in Germany, led many of his contemporaries to believe that he sought to dominate all of Europe. Although he was essentially conservative and moderate, Charles found himself with too many irons in the fire; he was constantly frustrating plots, crushing rebellions, and repelling invasions in his many dominions.

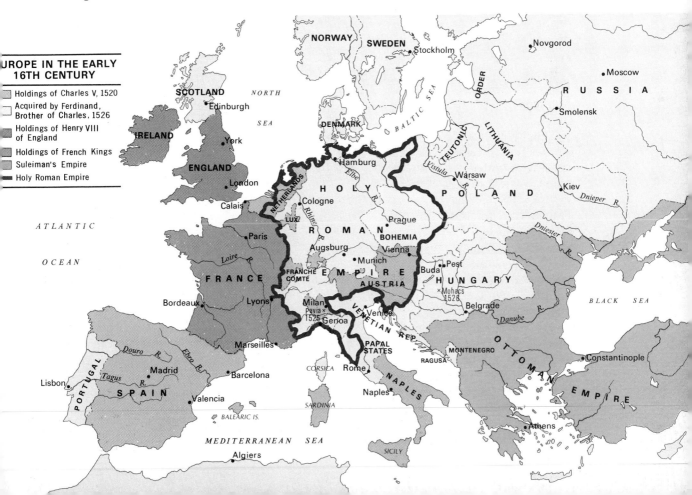

EUROPE IN THE EARLY 16TH CENTURY

Holdings of Charles V, 1520
Acquired by Ferdinand, Brother of Charles, 1526
Holdings of Henry VIII of England
Holdings of French Kings
Suleiman's Empire
Holy Roman Empire

Two prominent kings on the European chessboard were Francis I (left, portrait by Jean Clouet) of France and Henry VIII (right, portrait by Hans Holbein).

Charles' problems were inextricably connected with the activities of Francis I of France, Henry VIII of England, and Suleiman, ruler of the Ottoman empire. Out of the interplay of their rivalries unfolded the bloody drama of the first half of the sixteenth century.

New moves on the chessboard. The basic cause of Franco-Hapsburg rivalry was the fact that Charles' possessions encircled the realm of Francis I (1515-1547). In 1515, just before Charles V came into his inheritance, Francis invaded Italy, occupied Milan, and so set the stage for the renewal of the Italian Wars. Across the English Channel, Henry VIII followed the events closely, aiming to use his state, with its small population of 2,500,000, as a counterweight in the Franco-Hapsburg rivalry. Believing Francis to be militarily stronger than Charles, Henry allied himself with the Hapsburg emperor in order to check French power.

The test of strength began as Charles' forces drove the French from Milan. Francis soon recaptured it, but at the battle of Pavia (1525) the French were defeated and Francis was taken prisoner. Realizing that he had

miscalculated, Henry VIII executed a sudden about-face, deserting Charles and supporting France and a coalition of lesser powers against the Hapsburgs. This use of England's power to equalize the strength of Continental rivals is a spectacular example of what now became the cornerstone of English foreign policy. Time and again in modern history, England has employed balance-of-power diplomacy to maintain European equilibrium.

Suleiman, ruler of the Turks. The Ottoman empire, which reached the height of its power under Suleiman the Magnificent (1520-1566), was far stronger than any European state. The outstanding feature of its efficient administrative and military system was the dominant role played by slaves. Although Christians were granted a separate religious and civil status under the leadership of their bishops, every five years between 2,000 and 12,000 Christian boys from the ages of ten to fifteen were enslaved and brought to Constantinople. There they were converted to Islam and trained to enter the administration, where even the post of grand vizier was open to them, or the army. In the latter instance they served as Janissaries, the elite 12,000-man core of the Turkish standing army, who were fanatical in their devotion to Islam.

The powerful Ottoman empire was still expanding. Suleiman's predecessor had given Europe a respite by turning eastward to conquer Syria and Egypt, but Suleiman resumed the advance westward. With the European states politically and religiously at odds, Suleiman faced no concerted resistance. In 1521 he captured Belgrade, the key fortress of the Hungarian frontier, and in 1526 on the plain of Mohacs the Janissary infantry crushed the cavalry of the Hungarian magnates. The Hungarian king and many of his magnates were killed, and Suleiman moved on to plunder Buda without organized resistance.

The king who perished at Mohacs had ruled both Hungary and Bohemia. Terrified by the prospect of new Turkish attacks, both the Bohemians and the Hungarians offered their vacant thrones to Ferdinand, brother-in-law of the dead king and brother of Charles v. Since most of Hungary had been occupied by the Turks, Ferdinand's rule extended only over the northwest portion of that country. Thus a Turkish victory placed the destiny of both Hungary and Bohemia in the hands of the Hapsburgs and established the Turks as a threat on Charles' Austrian borders.

Religion and politics on the chessboard. Following his release from captivity in 1526, after making promises he had no intention of keeping, Francis I decided upon an alliance with Suleiman. The enemies of the French king protested loudly against this "unholy alliance," but power politics took precedence over religion in both Paris and Constantinople.

Indirectly, the Turks aided the Protestant cause in Germany. In 1529 Suleiman's armies besieged Vienna, but supply difficulties and Hapsburg resistance forced the attackers to retire. To deal with the Turkish threat, Charles, who had been planning measures against the Lutherans, was forced to arrange a truce with the Protestant princes to gain their support against the Turks.

Suleiman now turned to the Mediterranean where Tunisia and Algeria became Ottoman vassal states and bases for Turkish pirates, known as corsairs, who preyed on Christian shipping and raided the coasts of Spain and Italy. The strength that Charles might have amassed to crush the French monarchy was diverted to his besieged lands bordering on the Mediterranean. A truce in 1544 halted the French-Hapsburg struggle, and Charles could at last concentrate his efforts on the German states, where in 1546 the Lutheran struggle flared into civil war. With France aiding the Lutherans and the Catholic princes

This allegorical portrait of Charles v, painted after his campaign against Suleiman in 1532, depicts the "Protector of Christiandom" riding triumphant over the prostrate body of the vanquished Turkish sultan.

giving only half-hearted support to Charles lest he become powerful enough to dominate them, the Schmalkaldic War ended in 1555 with the compromise Peace of Augsburg (see p. 311). The Lutheran faith received official sanction, and Charles was thwarted in his cherished aim of restoring religious unity to Germany.

In 1556, five months after the Peace of Augsburg, the weary and discouraged emperor retired to a monastery. He turned over the Hapsburg possessions in central Europe to his brother Ferdinand, who was elected emperor, and gave Spain, the Netherlands, and his Italian possessions to his son Philip. Thereafter two Hapsburg dynasties, one Spanish and the other Austrian, ruled in Europe. A legend has it that Charles spent the two remaining years of his life trying to make several clocks keep exactly the same time—apparently an allegory suggesting that he was faced with so many problems that he could never settle all of them.

Significance for modern times. The eventful Age of Charles v had laid down much of the political and religious foundation for modern Europe:

1) It had been decided by force of arms that no single state was to dominate all of Europe. The balance of power was maintained.

2) German and Italian national growth was further stunted. Italy had been a battleground since 1494, and when the Italian Wars finally ended in 1559, Milan and Naples were Spanish possessions and Spain was to dominate Italy for nearly two hundred years.

3) Charles' wars with France and the Turks prevented him from applying pressure on the Lutherans and so saved the Reformation in Germany.

4) The Peace of Augsburg confirmed France's hold on the bishoprics of Metz, Toul, and Verdun in Lorraine, which the French had occupied during the Schmalkaldic War. French expansion toward the Rhine had begun, with momentous consequences for the future.

5) The advance of Ottoman power in Europe meant that Turkish control over the Balkans was handed down to later European statesmen as an explosive legacy. The alliance of France with Turkey, which also gave the French trading rights and a protectorate over the Holy Places in the Near East, became an enduring though irregular factor in European diplomacy.

6) The history of the first half of the sixteenth century made it quite clear that diplomacy a la Machiavelli was to be the order of the day. Deceit, treachery, surprise attacks, and broken promises were written into the record.

FAITH AND NATIONALITY IN WESTERN EUROPE

Era of the Religious Wars. While the threat of Hapsburg domination of Europe had been lessened after Charles v divided his lands, the Continent was still to witness convulsive rivalries and a century more of warfare. The period from roughly the middle of the sixteenth century to the middle of the seventeenth century is often referred to as the Era of the Religious Wars, for the religious issues which flamed forth from the Protestant upheaval—particularly that most international form of Protestantism, Calvinism—colored every political conflict.

Zenith of the Spanish state. The Era of the Religious Wars began in 1556 when Philip II, the son of Charles v, became king of Spain. Several factors made it seem that Philip's future would be impressive and successful. First, when his uncle Ferdinand received the Hapsburg Austrian lands together with the imperial crown of the Holy Roman Empire, Philip was freed of the political and religious complexities in middle Europe; that is, he had no "German problem." Second, the end of the Franco-Hapsburg wars over Italy in 1559 was followed by religious wars in France (see p. 335), leaving Spain without a rival on the Continent. Third, Philip inherited a new empire overseas which was more lucrative and more easily administered than his father's empire in the Germanies had been. From the New World came untold treasure to enrich the Hapsburg coffers at Madrid (see Chapter 17).

In addition to the riches of the Americas

and the Spanish possessions in Europe—the Netherlands, Franche-Comté, Naples, Sicily, and Milan—Philip had the best army of the time. The mercenary armies employed by other states could not rival the training and discipline of the native Spanish infantry. The dread of Spanish power caused people to say, as they had under Charles v, that "When Spain moves, the whole world trembles."

During his long reign (1556-1598) Philip sought three basic goals: to make his royal power absolute in all his possessions, to combat heresy and strengthen Catholicism, and to extend Spain's influence. Under Charles v the traditional parliaments, or Cortes, of Castile and Aragon had been largely superseded by a number of royal councils staffed by a well-trained civil service. Building on this foundation, Philip erected a centralized system of government in which every decision rested with the king and in which all agencies of government were subordinate to his will.

Philip was extremely devout and saw no distinction between the good of the Church and the interest of the Spanish state. At home the Spanish Inquisition both ferreted out heretics and strengthened royal power. Abroad, by championing the Counter Reformation Philip also justified his interference in the political and religious conflicts of other European nations.

One of Philip's great achievements was the uniting of the Iberian peninsula under the Spanish crown. In 1580 the direct line of the Portuguese royal family died out, and Philip claimed the throne through his mother, a Portuguese princess. When the Portuguese refused to accept him as their ruler, Philip invaded the country and seized the throne. The annexation of Portugal and its vast colonial empire brought new riches to Madrid from Brazil, Africa, and the East Indies.

Crusade in the Mediterranean. After Suleiman's death in 1566 the Turkish advance in the Mediterranean continued, and in 1570 the Turks captured the Venetian island of Cyprus, the last Christian outpost in the area. At the pope's urging, Christian Europe turned to Philip, the champion of the Catholic faith, to block Turkish expansion.

A Holy League was formed to raise a great fleet and destroy Ottoman naval power in the Mediterranean. Spanish and Venetian warships, together with the smaller squadrons of Genoa and the Papal States, made up a fleet of over two hundred vessels which was joined by volunteers from all over Europe. In 1571 the League's fleet and the Turkish navy clashed at Lepanto, on the western side of Greece. The outcome was a decisive victory for Christian Europe; Ottoman sea power was crushed, never to be restored as a major threat to Christendom. Lepanto is often considered the last crusade.

Unrest and revolt in the Netherlands. The conquest of Portugal and the defeat of the Turks were signal victories for Philip, but the specter of failure stalked him in the Netherlands. The seventeen provinces of the Low Countries (which included today's Holland, Belgium, and Luxemburg) had been restive under Charles v, who had imposed heavy taxes to help finance his wars. Yet he had continued to enjoy the confidence of the Netherlanders, who regarded him as one of themselves because he had been born in the city of Ghent. But the Netherlanders did not feel the same about Philip, whom they distrusted as a foreigner. Seeking to make his rule absolute in the Netherlands, Philip excluded the local nobility from the administration, maintained an army of occupation, and introduced the Inquisition to stop the advance of Calvinism.

Calvinism continued to spread, however, and in 1566 a series of violent anti-Catholic and anti-Spanish riots broke out. "The Council of Troubles"—soon dubbed "The Council of Blood"—was set up to stamp out treason and heresy. During the ensuing reign of terror some 8,000 were slain, 30,000 were deprived of their property, and 100,000 fled the country. At the same time Philip proposed new and oppressive taxes, including a 10 percent sales tax, which antagonized most Netherlanders, Catholic as well as Protestant. Under the Dutch leader, William the Silent of the House of Orange, discontent flared into open revolt in 1568.

In the first years of the revolt the puny forces commanded by the tenacious William the Silent were dispersed again and again.

The Dutch turned to the sea to outfit privateers to prey on Spanish shipping. Then in 1576 the incident of the Spanish Fury electrified the entire Netherlands. Usually well-disciplined, the badly fed and unpaid Spanish soldiers mutinied and marched on Antwerp where they burned public buildings and murdered seven thousand citizens. The calamity settled the local differences between the seventeen provinces that had prevented them from making a concerted effort against Spanish tyranny. The Pacification of Ghent, which the provincial representatives signed in 1576, declared that all Spanish soldiers must be expelled from the land, after which the representative body, the Estates-General, would govern the country.

Unfortunately for the rebels' cause, the seventeen provinces did not long maintain the unity manifested in the Pacification of Ghent. The Spaniards were able to take advantage of the differences between the Protestant provinces in the north and the predominantly Catholic provinces in the south. Employing a combination of diplomacy and force, the Spanish succeeded in reuniting the ten southern provinces with Spain in 1579. The Dutch in the north, however, continued to fight on, and in 1581 the Estates-General of the Dutch United Provinces (also called Holland because of the preeminence of that province with its flourishing city of Amsterdam) issued a declaration of independence. One of its provisions stated:

The people were not created by God for the sake of the Prince . . . but, on the contrary, the Prince was made for the good of the people.[8]

The declaration of 1581 set the model for later declarations justifying revolution in England, France, and the English colonies in America. It also established another landmark in modern history by decreeing freedom of worship for the large Catholic minority in the new nation. The stability of the state had become a greater concern than religious conformity.

Three years later the cause of Dutch freedom was placed in serious jeopardy when William the Silent was assassinated by a young Catholic fanatic and the Spanish stepped up their efforts to destroy the new republic. At this critical moment Elizabeth I of England, fearing that Philip planned to use the Netherlands as a base for an invasion of England, rushed troops to the aid of the United Netherlands. The destruction of Philip's Armada by England in 1588 (see p. 344) further weakened Spanish ability to crush the Dutch.

In 1609 a twelve years' truce was signed, which recognized the partition of the Netherlands along the line where the fighting had stopped. Not until the end of the Thirty

The 1566 rioting in the Netherlands was instigated by mobs of Calvinists who invaded Catholic churches, toppling images, smashing windows, and looting valuable articles. The Spanish reacted to such riots with ferocity.

Years' War in 1648 did the Dutch gain from the Spanish formal recognition of their independence. For more than two hundred years the southern provinces remained in the hands of the Hapsburgs, first as the Spanish Netherlands and then as the Austrian Netherlands. In 1830 they achieved independence as the state of Belgium.

The English throne: Protestant or Catholic? On more than one occasion during the reign of Philip II, it seemed that England would come under Spanish domination. In 1554, two years before he ascended the throne of Spain, Philip had married Mary Tudor, the older daughter of Henry VIII. Mary adored her husband, and as queen she was strongly influenced by him, although he had no official status in the governing of England. After a brief reign Mary died, and in 1558 her half-sister, Elizabeth I, assumed the throne.

Elizabeth's disputed succession provided the next occasion for possible Spanish domination of England. The daughter of Henry by his second wife, Anne Boleyn, Elizabeth was considered illegitimate by English Catholics, who recognized only Henry's first marriage as valid. Furthermore, in the eyes of Catholic Europe, the rightful heir to the throne was the great-granddaughter of Henry VII, Mary Stuart, Queen of Scotland.

Brought up in France as a Catholic, Mary had wed the heir to the French throne and reigned for two years as queen of France. After the death of her husband, she returned to her native Scotland, where her French mother had been ruling as regent with the aid of French troops. Mary found Scotland in the hands of rebellious nobles and vigorous Protestant preachers under the Calvinist reformer John Knox (see p. 316). A widow of eighteen, famous for her charm, beauty, and grace, Mary proceeded to alienate her subjects by a series of blunders: she was too frivolous for her straitlaced Calvinistic subjects, she was unsuccessful in concealing her pro-Catholic sympathies, and, finally, she was accused of being involved in the sordid murder of her weakling husband, Lord Darnley. The Scottish Presbyterians revolted, and in 1568 Mary was forced to seek refuge with her cousin Elizabeth in England. There,

During the brief marriage of Philip II of Spain and Queen Mary of England, it appeared that Spain might come to dominate the island kingdom.

her Catholicism and her good claim to Elizabeth's throne made her an unwelcome guest, potentially dangerous to the Tudor monarch and to English Protestantism.

For his part, Philip had no compunctions about plotting to place Mary on the throne of England. Philip's ambassador in London became the center of a web of intrigue.

The island fortress: obstacle to Spanish hegemony. As Philip became the chief enemy of Protestant England, Elizabeth gradually emerged as the foremost obstacle to Spanish power. Unlike the impetuous Mary Stuart, who was often the blind instrument of her emotions, Elizabeth was realistic, calculating, and thoroughly Machiavellian. As the Spanish ambassador wrote to Philip:

. . . what a pretty business it is to treat with this woman who I think must have a hundred thousand devils in her body, notwithstanding that she is forever telling me that she yearns to be a nun and to pass her life in prayer.[9]

Elizabeth resorted to every subterfuge and trick available to her in the duel with Philip of Spain. Using her sex as a diplomatic weapon, she carried on long flirtations with the brothers of the French king, thereby helping to prevent an alliance between France and Spain. In addition she sent covert assistance to the Dutch, aware that their rebellion was sapping Spanish strength.

Elizabeth also secretly encouraged her sea captains to prey upon Spanish shipping and to attack the rich Spanish settlements in the New World. The most famous of Elizabethan Sea Dogs, Sir Francis Drake, sailed into the Pacific, plundered the western coast of Spanish America, and, after circumnavigating the globe, arrived in England with a hold full of gold and silver.

Aware of Elizabeth's duplicity, Philip planned to gain control over England by placing Mary Stuart on the English throne. But a plot against Elizabeth's life, in which Mary was obliquely implicated, was discovered. Parliament was convinced that as long as Mary lived, Elizabeth's life would

be endangered, and therefore, in 1587, Elizabeth signed Mary's death warrant. But in a sense Mary had not failed. She had left behind in Scotland a son, James, who was destined to become the common monarch of England and Scotland, not by conspiracy or force but by common consent.

Philip and Elizabeth at war. After the discovery of the plot against her life, Elizabeth sought to hinder Philip's plans by openly sending arms and soldiers to the Netherlands, by aiding the Protestant cause during the French religious wars, and by authorizing Drake to destroy Spanish shipping. Philip meanwhile was planning his "great enterprise"—an invasion of England, blessed by the pope, to gain the kingdom for himself and wean its people from heresy.

Philip's strategy was to have a fleet of 130 ships, called by contemporaries the "Invincible Armada," join a large Spanish army in the Netherlands and then land this force on the coast of England. The Dutch, however, prevented the rendezvous by blocking the main ports in the Low Countries, and Philip's designs were ruined completely when the Elizabethan Sea Dogs trounced the Armada in the English Channel. The small, swift English ships outmaneuvered the bulky Spanish galleons, and a severe storm, the famed "Protestant wind," completed the debacle. The Armada limped home after losing a third of its ships.

The defeat of the Armada meant that England would remain Protestant, that it would soon emerge as a dominant sea power, and that the Dutch rebellion against Spain would succeed. By building new ships, Spain quickly recovered from the material effects of the defeat of the Armada, but it never overcame the psychological effects of that disaster. The Spanish people had been told that the Armada was "the most important [enterprise] undertaken by God's Church for many hundreds of years. . . . we are defending the high reputation of our King and lord, and of our nation; . . . and simultaneously our peace, tranquility and repose."[10] The optimism engendered by Spain's great past achievements soon vanished; in the words of a modern scholar, "If any one year marks the division between the triumphant

With the threat of Spanish invasion, Elizabeth gave the English people an example of courage and resolution. This portrait was painted during her reign.

In July 1588 the English completely routed Spain's "Invincible Armada."

Spain of the first two Hapsburgs and the defeatist, disillusioned Spain of their successors, that year is 1588."[11]

The Wars of Religion in France. Soon after France and Spain ended their long conflict over Italy in 1559, France underwent one of the most terrible civil conflicts in its history. Persecution of Protestants had been sporadic under Francis I (d. 1547) and his son Henry II (d. 1559), who were more fearful of the Hapsburgs than of heresy, but by 1560 the Calvinist Huguenots numbered about one million out of a population of sixteen million. Huguenots were numerous in the cities, except in Paris, but the most influential element was the 40 to 50 percent of the nobility that had been attracted to Calvinism. The French nobility had long been restless; its numbers were increasing and it was frustrated by the loss of its former military and political preeminence.

Because the three weakling sons of Henry II had no heirs, the Valois line that had ruled France since 1328 (see p. 269) was nearing its end. This situation led to ruthless factional rivalry between two noble houses in France, both of which aspired to the throne. The Bourbons, who espoused Protestantism, had the better claim because they traced their descent from St. Louis, the revered Capetian king of the thirteenth century. Champions of Catholicism were the powerful Guises, who claimed descent from Charlemagne. This was the setting for the series of civil wars, partly religious and partly political, that broke out in 1562.

During this period and until her death in 1589, the most powerful individual in France was Catherine de' Medici, the queen mother. Like her contemporary in London, Queen Elizabeth, Catherine was completely cynical and ruthless in statecraft. Even her youngest son referred to her as "Madame la Serpente." No matter how cruel or base, no technique was beneath her use; one of Catherine's political weapons was "'a flying squadron' of twenty-four maids of honor of high rank and low principles to help her seduce the refractory nobles on both sides."[12]

Determined to maintain the power of her sons, Catherine attempted to steer a middle course and to play one party off against the other. But as the Huguenots grew stronger, she resolved to crush them. Thus Catherine is blamed for the terrible Massacre of St. Bartholomew's Day. At dawn on August 24, 1572, with a signal from the bell of the Palace of Justice in Paris, the Catholics fell upon their Protestant rivals, and ten thousand Huguenots were slain.

The massacre did not destroy Huguenot power, however, and civil conflict continued. A new phase began in 1585, when Philip II entered the war on the side of the Catholics. He hoped first to extirpate Protestantism in France and then to control French policy, thereby gaining valuable support in crushing the Dutch revolt and in conquering England. In 1589, after assassins had eliminated both the Guise pretender and the last weakling Valois ruler, the Protestant Bourbon prince Henry of Navarre became King Henry IV of France by right of succession. Philip determined to crush the new king before he could consolidate his power. At this critical moment Queen Elizabeth intervened by sending Henry five thousand troops which turned the tide in his favor. Realizing that most Frenchmen were Catholic and sensing

that all were weary of civil war, Spanish intervention, and anarchy, Henry decided to place the welfare of France ahead of his own conscience and accepted the faith of Rome. "Paris is well worth a mass," he is supposed to have said, and soon Paris and other cities opened their gates to him. By 1595 the civil war was over and Philip was forced to withdraw his troops.

The Edict of Nantes. Although Henry IV changed his own faith, he sought to protect the liberties of the Huguenot minority in the Edict of Nantes (1598). When both Catholic and Protestant extremists denounced the measure, Henry refused to be intimidated: "I insist upon being obeyed. It is time that we all, having had our fill of war, should learn wisdom by what we have suffered."

The Edict of Nantes followed the example first set by the Dutch Republic of recognizing that more than one religion could be maintained within a state. To guarantee their religious freedom, Henry allowed the Protestants to fortify about a hundred French towns and garrison them with their own troops. As a result, the Huguenots in France constituted virtually a state within a state.

The failure of Philip II. Philip's failure in France was the last of his many setbacks. His final opponent, Henry IV, provided some fitting last words on Philip's hopes for Spanish dominance in Europe: while witnessing the departure of Spanish troops from Paris, Henry called out, "Gentlemen, commend me to your master, but do not come back."

While in the eyes of his Spanish subjects Philip was a wise, moderate, pious, and hardworking monarch, his enemies singled him out as a detestable example of trickery, cruelty, and religious intolerance. Yet Philip was not equal to Elizabeth in duplicity and diplomatic cunning, and it must be remembered that nearly all sixteenth-century European monarchs believed that the relentless persecution of noncomformists was essential to the welfare of the state. Philip's failures cannot be attributed to defects ingrained in his nature but to the fact that, in general, he was less skillful than his opponents in the game of power politics.

Most important, perhaps, is that Philip unwittingly pitted himself against the grow-

The belief that Spain was the greatest power in Europe is illustrated by this contemporary map showing Spain as the head and crown of Europe.

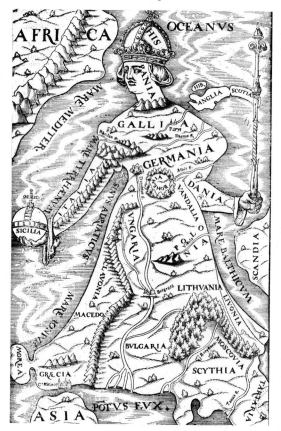

ing feelings of nationalism. Patriotism thwarted Philip's ambitions in the Netherlands and in England, and it also contributed to the failure of his intervention in the French religious wars.

Despite Philip's failures, Spain still enjoyed the reputation of being the first power in Europe. Spanish soldiers were the best on the Continent, and Spain's wealth from its vast overseas possessions seemed inexhaustible. Moreover, Spanish writers, scholars, and painters were outstanding; in fact, the last half of the sixteenth century and the first half of the seventeenth are usually regarded as the zenith of Spanish culture.

In the seventeenth century, however, Spanish power rapidly declined. Bad economic policies (see Chapter 17) coupled with continued overexertion in the game of power politics proved too great a burden for a nation of only eight or nine million people. The last of the so-called religious conflicts, the Thirty Years' War (1618-1648), accelerated the decline of Spain and left France the dominant state in Europe.

The issues of the Thirty Years' War. The Peace of Augsburg (see p. 311) failed to bring about a satisfactory religious settlement in the Germanies, and friction continued after 1555. The higher clergy and the princes who thereafter turned Protestant continued to take over Church lands within their jurisdiction. Furthermore, religious toleration for rapidly spreading Calvinism was now a burning issue, since the Peace of Augsburg had recognized only Lutheranism and Catholicism. A final religious factor was the progress being made by the Catholic Counter Reformation in the empire under the leadership of the Jesuits and the Jesuit-educated emperor, the Hapsburg Ferdinand II.

In addition to his deep antipathy toward heretics, Ferdinand wanted a united and subservient empire to strengthen his position in Europe. His desire to reassert imperial authority was opposed by the princes whose own power would remain strong with Germany divided and weak. Even the Catholic princes, who willingly supported Ferdinand as a Catholic leader against the Protestants, were opposed to any strengthening of imperial power. The papacy, too, was often

lukewarm in its support, regarding a strong emperor as a threat to the freedom of the Church in Germany and fearing that a too close association with the Hapsburgs would alienate the rulers of other states. Ferdinand could hope for unquestioned support only from his cousin, the Hapsburg king of Spain, who was still considered the most powerful ruler in Europe.

The varied religious and political issues in the empire created an atmosphere of tension in which one slight incident might upset the precarious peace. A prelude to the contest of arms was the formation of a Protestant League of German princes in 1608 and a similar Catholic League in 1609.

Phases of the Thirty Years' War. The complexities of the Thirty Years' War, which soon became an international struggle, can be divided into four phases: (1) Bohemian, (2) Danish, (3) Swedish, and (4) French.

The first battleground was Bohemia, preponderantly Protestant and strongly nationalistic, which had enjoyed a large measure of toleration under its Catholic Hapsburg kings. When Ferdinand withdrew that tolerance on mounting the throne of Bohemia in 1617, he precipitated a rebellion in 1618 which became a general religious war when the Bohemians invited the Calvinist head of the Protestant League to rule them. By the end of the following year Ferdinand had crushed the Bohemians, and his kinsmen, the Spanish Hapsburgs, had defeated the German Protestants supporting the Bohemian insurrection. Protestantism was stamped out in Bohemia, and the Protestant League in Germany was dissolved.

The second phase of the conflict began in 1625 when the Lutheran king of Denmark, who as duke of Holstein (see Reference Map 5) was also a prince of the empire, invaded Germany. The Danes sought not only to champion hard-pressed Protestantism but also to gain additional German territory and to thwart Hapsburg ambitions. However, the Hapsburg armies soon crushed the Danes.

This second defeat of the Protestants threatened to undo the work of the Protestant Reformation and to create a unified Hapsburg-ruled Germany. This prospect drew the leading Lutheran power, Sweden, into the fight in 1630. King Gustavus Adolphus told his people that "the papal deluge is approaching our shores"; he also hoped to acquire territories along Germany's Baltic coast as "guarantees against the emperor." The Swedish king was the founder of a new technique of warfare which stressed discipline, mobility, and morale; in Germany his well-drilled, hymn-singing veterans and mobile cannon quickly scored a series of brilliant victories. But after Gustavus Adolphus was killed in battle, a compromise peace was arranged in 1635.

The peace never went into effect, however, for Cardinal Richelieu, the chief adviser of the French king and the actual head of the government, decided that France would be secure only when the Hapsburgs of Austria and Spain, whose lands ringed France on three sides, had been defeated. Richelieu earlier had given secret aid to the German Protestants, the Danes, and the Swedes; now, in 1635, he came out in the open and the struggle became primarily a dynastic contest between Bourbons and Hapsburgs. The Swedes and the German Protestants kept the Austrian Hapsburg armies busy in Germany while French arms were concentrated against the Spanish Hapsburgs. In 1643 at the battle of Rocroi in the Spanish Netherlands the legend of the invincibility of the Spanish infantry came to an end, and the French turned to the Germanies. Although Richelieu had died in 1642, his successor, Cardinal Mazarin, continued his designs for weakening the power of the Hapsburgs.

The Peace of Westphalia. Peace negotiations began in 1644 without a cease-fire agreement, but they proceeded slowly. The delegates wrangled endlessly over such questions of protocol as who was to enter the conference room first and where they were to sit, and the fortunes of war frequently altered the bargaining power of the rival diplomats. Finally, in 1648, the longest peace negotiation on record ended in a series of treaties collectively known as the Peace of Westphalia. (Spain, however, stubbornly refused to make peace with France until 1659.)

A recapitulation of the various provisions of the peace would be very complex; suffice it to say that France moved closer to the Rhine with the acquisition of much of Alsace; Sweden and the Protestant state of Brandenburg made important territorial gains along Germany's Baltic coast; and Holland and Switzerland—the latter having successfully resisted its Hapsburg overlords since 1291—were granted independence. The Calvinists were given recognition in Germany, and Protestants were allowed to retain the Church lands they had taken before 1624.

The Peace of Westphalia permanently ended Hapsburg dreams of reviving the authority of the emperor in Germany. The sovereignty of the more than three hundred German states was recognized, with each state having the right to coin money, make war, maintain armies, and send diplomatic representatives to foreign courts. Henceforth the Hapsburg emperors worked to form a strong Danubian monarchy out of their varied Austrian, Bohemian, and Hungarian possessions.

The great significance of the Peace of Westphalia was that it symbolized the emergence and victory of the sovereign state which acknowledged no authority higher than its own interests and was prone to assume what Thomas Hobbes three years later called "the position of gladiators." More specifically, the conference established the basic principle underlying the modern state system—the essential equality of all independent sovereign states. It also instituted the diplomatic procedure of convening international congresses in order to settle the problems of war and peace by negotiation.

Thus the struggle against the Hapsburg encirclement of France begun by Francis I against Charles V early in the sixteenth century ended more than a century later. Changes had been wrought in the relative powers of nations. Both England and Holland had become great sea powers, and their commercial prosperity was increasing rapidly. The golden age of Spain was over, and France emerged as the greatest power in Europe. Although reports of devastation, population decline, and cultural retrogression in the Germanies have perhaps been exaggerated, the Thirty Years' War left a grievous legacy and thwarted German progress for a century. But by demonstrating that Protestants and Catholics were unable to exterminate each other, the Thirty Years' War—indeed, the entire Era of the Religious Wars—greatly promoted the cause of religious toleration in Europe.

THE CONTINUING SENSE OF EUROPEAN INTERDEPENDENCE

Proposals for keeping the peace. The irresponsible use of power was the outstanding feature of international politics in the late sixteenth and early seventeenth centuries. But gradually powerful rulers and diplomats realized that frequent wars threatened the growth of European trade and commerce and menaced even the existence of civilized society in the West. We have seen some of the early steps taken to improve international relations—the establishment of consular and diplomatic services, the formation of alignments to preserve the balance of power, and the first use of a general European peace congress to adjust conflicting interests after a great war. In addition, trade agreements and treaties formed the crude beginnings of a system of international law. Although these varied measures all too often had a negligible effect on the continued use of war as the means of settling disputes among nations, they reflect a continuing sense of the interdependence of the European state system—the Concert of Europe, as it would later be called.

The increased destructiveness of modern warfare had aroused the protests of many sixteenth-century humanists—Erasmus, for example, asserted that "war is sweet only to the inexperienced." In the early seventeenth century students of international affairs made some specific recommendations that are of particular interest today.

In 1623, Emeric Crucé, an obscure French monk, published a plan to eliminate war by means of an international organization which, he claimed, would be "useful to all nations, and agreeable to those who have

some light of reason and the sentiment of humanity." The central idea in his work was that all wars were harmful and their abolition would allow governments to devote themselves to the arts of peace. To this end he proposed that a permanent corps of ambassadors from all over the world be maintained at Venice as an international assembly for the settlement of all disputes through negotiation and arbitration. Crucé acknowledged that his plan for a seventeenth-century "United Nations" was in advance of his time, but added:

I have wished, nevertheless, to leave this testimony to posterity. If it serves nothing, patience. It is a small matter to lose paper and words. I have said and done what was possible for the public good, and some few who read this little book will be grateful to me for it, and will honor me, as I hope, with their remembrance.[13]

Either the first Bourbon monarch, Henry IV, or his chief minister, the Duke of Sully, devised the plan known as the Grand Design, which called for the establishment of a European federal union headed by a council of representatives from all states. The council was to secure disarmament and to control an international police force which would back its decisions by force. Each state was to contribute troops and money according to its strength. Despite its theoretical and utopian character, the Grand Design "shows that at the very moment when the modern national state, centralized within and dividing Europe into mutually hostile camps, emerged from the ruins of medieval unity, the ablest minds realized that eventually a new unity would have to be built out of these distinct entities, a United States of Europe. . . ."[14]

Grotius and international law. A number of European scholars were also at work laying the foundation for a science of international law by developing the principle that the nations formed a community based upon natural law. The first to obtain a hearing outside scholarly circles was Hugo Grotius (1583-1645), a gifted Dutch historian, theologian, practicing lawyer, and diplomat. In 1625 appeared *On the Law of War and Peace,* the work which gained Grotius instant fame and lasting recognition as the founder of international law. "Such a work," he declared, "is all the more necessary because in our day, as in former times, there is no lack of men who view this branch of law with contempt as having no reality outside of an empty name." And he continued:

> I have had many and weighty reasons for undertaking to write upon this subject. Throughout the Christian world I observed a lack of restraint in relation to war, such as even barbarous races should be ashamed of; I observed that men rush to arms for slight causes, or no cause at all, and that when arms have once been taken up there is no longer any respect for law, divine or human; it is as if, in accordance with a general decree, frenzy had openly been let loose for the committing of all crimes.[15]

War and Peace are reconciled in the allegorical title page from the 1689 edition of Grotius' *De Jure Belli ac Pacis.* Four years before he wrote this great work, Grotius had escaped from a Dutch prison, where he had been sentenced to life imprisonment as a result of his campaign for religious toleration between Protestant and Catholic and for a more liberal regime in his own country, Holland.

Grotius endeavored to set forth a new code of international conduct based not upon the authority of the Church but on what he termed the fundamental idea of the law of nature. The law of nature was in turn founded on the dictates of reason, morality, and justice. If civilization was to endure, Grotius argued, humane considerations should prevail in the councils of the mighty, and rules of conduct binding all men should be established.

More realistic than his contemporaries Cruce and Sully, Grotius did not propose to eliminate war entirely. He sought instead to outlaw "unjust" wars and limit the effects of "just" wars. Wars were justified only to repel invasion or to punish an insult to God. Grotius' appeal fell largely upon deaf ears. Machiavelli's *The Prince* enjoyed more popularity in European palaces than *On the Law of War and Peace.*

SUMMARY

By the middle of the seventeenth century the pattern of politics in western Europe had changed significantly. Gone was the ideal of unity, whether based on empire or on universal Church; sovereignty had replaced suzerainty. The new monarchies were largely absolute in authority within their own frontiers and free agents in the domain of international affairs. Following the principles of political behavior systematized by Machiavelli, these sovereign states pursued power, prestige, wealth, and security. No moral or religious scruples were allowed to interfere with these objectives. It was considered axiomatic that a nation had no permanent enemies or friends—only permanent interests. This maxim was illustrated by the manner in which alliances based on the new diplomatic technique of balance of power were formed on the European chessboard. We shall see in our study of later eras how the great powers have continued to alter their alliances in deference to the exigencies of the balance of power. It is also noteworthy that since balance-of-power diplomacy was the product of a felt need to preserve the security and independence of the new sovereign states, it reflected an early recognition of the interdependence of the European state system. The present-day movement toward European unity can be viewed as the latest expression of this recognition.

Power politics between 1500 and 1650 developed amid complex happenings, especially the so-called Religious Wars. Just what was religion and what politics was often difficult to determine, especially since religion was often used as a cover for political intrigue. With Philip II of Spain, for example, Catholic conviction appropriately coincided with Spanish national interests; to champion the Catholic Church was, in Philip's mind, to build a strong Spain. In other instances expediency, not religious principles, governed international politics: witness Francis I's alliance with the Turks and Richelieu's support of the German Protestants.

The revolt of the Dutch from Spain was the first large-scale example before 1650 of a successful countertrend to the increasing centralization of the monarch's power. The establishment of the Dutch Republic in the name of people's rights foreshadows the later and more famous revolts against absolutism which would establish constitutional government in England during the last half of the seventeenth century and in North America and France by the end of the eighteenth.

In the survey of European affairs in this chapter, two opposing principles were discussed: one, the right of a state to conduct its foreign affairs—even to waging war—without hindrance; the other, the concept that nations should accept some limitation of their freedom of action in international affairs. Ever since the early seventeenth century, when scholars began to think of limiting wars and the need for international law, national sovereignty and internationalism have been in competition. Sovereignty has gotten the best of it by far. But we will see that since Grotius' time, much effort has been devoted to a study of averting conflicts and subordinating disputes to the rule of law.

SUGGESTIONS FOR READING

The following are crisp, purposeful, and readable political surveys of all or part of the century and a half following the beginning of the Protestant Reformation (see also the works cited for Chapters 14 and 19): M. L. Bush, **Renaissance, Reformation and the Outer World, 1450-1660,** * Torchbooks; H. Koenigsberger and G. Mosse, **Europe in the Sixteenth Century,** Holt, Rinehart & Winston, 1969; J. H. Elliott, **Europe Divided, 1559-1598,** * Torchbooks; T. Aston, ed., **Crisis in Europe: 1560-1660,** * Anchor; C. J. Friedrich, **The Age of the Baroque, 1610-1660,** * Torchbooks; A. Moote, **The Seventeenth Century: Europe in Ferment,** * Heath, 1970.

J. H. Whitfield, **Machiavelli,** Russell, 1947. A sympathetic account. The older, unfavorable view is well presented in H. Butterfield, **The Statecraft of Machiavelli,** * Collier. S. Anglo, **Machiavelli: A Dissection,** Harcourt, Brace & World, 1970, is a perceptive study with new insights. See also the brilliant study by G. Mattingly, **Renaissance Diplomacy,** * Penguin; John W. Allen, **A History of Political Thought in the Sixteenth Century,** * Barnes and Noble; J. N. Figgis, **The Divine Right of Kings,** Peter Smith, 1945.

J. Lynch, **Spain Under the Hapsburgs,** Vol. I, **Empire and Absolutism, 1516-1598,** Oxford, 1964. The latest authoritative treatment. Also recommended are J. H. Elliott, **Imperial Spain, 1469-1716,** * Mentor; R. Trevor Davies, **The Golden Century of Spain, 1501-1621,** * Torchbooks; K. Brandi, **Emperor Charles V: The Growth and Destiny of a Man and a World,** * Humanities, 1965; R. B. Merriman, **Suleiman the Magnificent,** Cooper Square, 1944.

P. Geyl, **The Revolt of the Netherlands, 1555-1609,** * Barnes and Noble. The best short account. C. Wedgwood, **William the Silent,** * Norton, is a beautifully written biography.

G. Mattingly, **The Armada,** * Sentry. The classic account. Popular and profusely illustrated is Jay Williams, **The Spanish Armada,** Harper and Row, 1966.

Elizabeth Jenkins, **Elizabeth the Great,** * Capricorn. Short and lively. J. Neale, **Queen Elizabeth I,** * Anchor, is the most authoritative biography. Antonia Fraser, **Mary Queen of Scots,** Delacorte, 1969, is a best seller. See also J. Hurstfield, **Elizabeth I and the Unity of England,** * Torchbooks; A. L. Rowse, **The England of Elizabeth,** * Collier; S. Bindoff, **Tudor England,** * Penguin; R. Wernham, **Before the Armada: The Emergence of the English Nation, 1485-1588,** Harcourt, Brace & World, 1966.

J. Neale, **The Age of Catharine de' Medici,** * Torchbooks. The religious and political troubles of sixteenth-century France. For a briefer account see F. Palm, **Calvinism and the Religious Wars,** Fertig, 1932.

C. V. Wedgwood, **The Thirty Years' War,** * Anchor. A vigorous account. See also H. Holborn, **A History of Modern Germany,** Vol. I, **The Reformation,** Knopf, 1959, the standard survey of Hapsburg Germany to 1648.

*Indicates an inexpensive paperbound edition.

Chapter 16

Old Worlds Beyond the Horizon

India, China, Japan (1500-1650), Southeast Asia (100-1650), Africa (1000 B.C.-1650 A.D.), and Native Cultures in the Americas (1000 B.C.-1500 A.D.)

INTRODUCTION. Europe's isolation from Asia and its ignorance of sub-Saharan Africa and the Americas ended in the fifteenth century when a multitude of European explorers, traders, conquerors, and missionaries secured footholds in territories far from their homelands. Reaching out to trade, to conquer, and to spread the gospel of Christianity, they encountered civilizations and ways of life which dramatically revealed the limitations of their own knowledge and experience. The story of their explorations and discoveries will be taken up in Chapter 17; this chapter is concerned with the civilizations in the Far East, Africa, and the Americas prior to the arrival of Europeans.

In recounting the histories of India, China, and Japan up to the middle of the seventeenth century, we shall be continuing a story we began much earlier. But in describing early times in Southeast Asia, sub-Saharan Africa, and the Americas, we shall be introducing to the stage of world history peoples we have not previously encountered. In a number of instances we shall be taking a giant step backward to the dawn of civilization, for both Africa and the Americas had inhabitants who, in 1650, were not so advanced as some of their European and Asian brothers had been two thousand years before. Yet both continents had fascinating cultures, some of which were to make important contributions to the civilization we know today. The variety of these contributions—from cotton, coffee, and Indian corn to the rhythms upon which jazz is based and sculpture which strongly influenced the development of modern art—reflects the remarkable diversity of the peoples of these lands, peoples who hunted, farmed, built cities, worshiped gods, and waged wars for centuries while Europeans remained totally ignorant of their existence.

Today a significant aspect of our world is the reawakening of old centers of civilization in the Americas, Africa, and the Far East. Nationalistic fervor and brave hopes for the future have been built on pride in the past. Even in Communist China, where many Confucian traditions are being super-seded by Marxist practices, inspiration is still drawn from past days of glory. The people of present-day India and Pakistan also seek inspiration from bygone years, particularly from the era of power, grandeur, and wealth enjoyed under the Guptas and the Mughuls. African nationalist leaders look back to their native roots; for example, the former British colony known as the Gold Coast adopted the name of a long-dead African empire, Ghana, when it was granted independence in 1957. In the New World, Mexican artists take their themes and motifs not from their Spanish colonial heritage but from the pre-Spanish Indian cultures.

Thus, if we are to understand the new dynamic spirit that now moves many Afro-Asian regions, we must know something of the sources of inspiration upon which their people draw. Such sources are outlined in the history of the non-European world in the centuries covered by this chapter and the next.

THE GLORY OF THE MUGHULS IN INDIA

Babur, founder of the Mughul empire. At the end of the twelfth century Hindu power in India was eclipsed by invading Muslims who established a powerful dynasty in Delhi. By 1500, however, a new Muslim force from the north was preparing to invade India. Two years after Columbus sailed westward toward what he hoped would be India, a descendant of Genghis Khan and Tamerlane mounted the throne of a little principality in Turkestan (see map, p. 175). The youthful ruler was Babur (the Tiger), an able general with the strength of a giant, who was to be the founder of the Mughul empire in India. In his memoirs Babur says that he used to think ceaselessly of the capture of Hindustan. At length he set out with an army of no more than twelve thousand men to achieve his goal. Defeating the large forces of the sultan of Delhi, who then ruled all Hindustan, Babur made himself sultan in 1526. A year later he subdued the Rajputs, who were trying to restore Hindu supremacy in northern India. The submission of the Rajputs placed the Mughul dynasty securely on the Delhi throne. (The name *Mughul* is a corruption of *Mongol*, a word much dreaded in India because of its association with Tamerlane, the ruthless destroyer of Delhi.) Babur himself did not live long to enjoy the fruits of his victory; worn out by his campaigns and adventures, he died in 1530.

Akbar, conqueror and administrator. Babur's grandson was Akbar, meaning "Very Great." In 1560 Akbar's empire consisted of a strip of territory some three hundred miles wide, extending from the northwest frontier eastward to Bengal. Sixteen years later Akbar had extended his rule over all of India north of the Vindhya Mountains, the natural boundary between Hindustan and the Deccan. Continuing southward, Akbar invaded part of the Deccan. When he died in 1605, his dominions ran from Kashmir in the far north well into the Deccan in the south, and his heirs were to extend them even farther.

Akbar's greatness should not be measured

In this contemporary painting the great Mughul ruler, Akbar, is depicted superintending the construction of his new capital at Fathpur Sikri.

by his military conquests alone, however. He instituted innovations and reforms in the government and fostered cultural growth and religious toleration. As an administrator he had few equals. He divided his empire into twelve provinces (later increased to fifteen), ruled by governors whom he appointed and who were paid monthly salaries from the imperial treasury. Each province was divided into districts, and each district into smaller units.

Law was similarly well administered. In each village the headman was responsible for keeping law and order, while in the larger cities special officials were in charge of the administration of justice. Akbar himself often acted as a judge, for everyone in

his domain had the right to appeal to him personally. The practice of *suttee* (burning a wife on her husband's funeral pyre), which had come into use during the Gupta age, was forbidden, and widows were permitted to remarry. Akbar prohibited child marriages and trial by ordeal, although he permitted such tortures as impalement, amputation, and death by elephant dragging. Nevertheless, in contrast to the barbaric punishments permitted in Europe at this time, the Mughul emperor probably had the most enlightened criminal code in the sixteenth century.

Despite the Mughul dynasty's allegiance to the Muslim faith, Akbar allowed complete freedom of religious belief in his empire, because he realized that religious strife made for political and social disintegration. Akbar's views were not based simply on political expediency, however; his own temperament was the chief reason for his enlightened policy. He felt that every faith had something of truth to offer but that all were untrue when they denied each other's sincerity of purpose. Every Thursday, Muslims, Brahmins, and members of smaller sects congregated in his Hall of Worship for religious debates which often lasted far into the night. When the Jesuits arrived in India, Akbar had them stay at his court for periods of several years and treated them with every courtesy.

But the sultan never accepted any one religion completely; instead he created his own religion, called *Din Ilahi*, the "Divine Faith," which incorporated what he considered the best features of the other existing religions. By promulgating this new faith, he hoped to bring all India into common agreement on religious matters. But the older faiths were too strongly entrenched, and Akbar's religious theories died with him.

Monuments of Mughul architecture. At the crest of their power in the reigns of Akbar and his immediate successors, the Mughuls displayed one of the most magnificent civilizations of their time. In military strength, government efficiency, and patronage of the arts, they had few equals. Above all, they were great builders.

The Indo-Islamic style of architecture which the Mughuls developed for tombs, mosques, forts, and palaces was a blend of

Indian and Persian elements characterized by a lavish use of mosaics, bulbous domes, cupolas, and lofty vaulted gateways. The Mughuls were also fond of formal gardens in which pools and fountains, architecture and greenery were carefully harmonized.

The Mughul style began with Akbar, an avid builder. Not far from the modern city of Agra, he erected a new capital, Fathpur Sikri, which he occupied for only fourteen years before abandoning it for Lahore. Fathpur Sikri is still preserved intact today, and a tourist strolling through its splendid buildings can feel the power of the great empire that made this city possible.

During the reign of Shah Jahan, Akbar's grandson, Mughul architecture reached its zenith. Shah Jahan had the red sandstone buildings of Akbar at Delhi demolished and erected a huge capital of marble containing fifty-two palaces. The famous Hall of Private Audience had ceilings of solid silver and gold and a Peacock Throne encrusted with costly gems. On the walls can still be seen the inscription by a Muslim poet: "If anywhere on earth there is a Paradise, it is here, it is here, it is here." Besides making Delhi a site of unrivaled splendor, Shah Jahan erected at Agra the famous Pearl Mosque and the Taj Mahal, the marble mausoleum built as a final resting place for himself and his favorite wife (see illustration, p. 166).

Signs of Mughul decline. The blend of Hindu-Islamic cultural elements under the Mughuls brought civilization in India to the highest point yet achieved there. It is unfortunate for world culture that the union of Muslim and Hindu genius could not continue to flower. But Akbar's tolerance and wisdom were lost in the fanaticism of his successors.

Shah Jahan, who came to the throne in 1628, held none of Akbar's views on religious toleration. He officially promoted the Muslim faith, destroyed Hindu temples, and forcibly opposed the spread of Christianity. In 1630 Shah Jahan began the conquest of the Deccan; eventually it was subjugated and divided into four provinces. After Shah Jahan's health began to fail in 1657, a ruinous civil war broke out among his four sons,

each of whom became an almost independent ruler. The last eight years of Shah Jahan's life (d. 1666) were spent as a prisoner of his son and successor, Aurangzeb. Despite his ignominious end, the reign of Shah Jahan marked the summit of the Mughul empire. During the reign of Aurangzeb the forces which eventually destroyed the Mughuls began to manifest themselves.

CHINA CLOSES ITS DOORS

Establishment of the Ming dynasty. As we recall from Chapter 7, the Sung rulers were not equal to the task of protecting China from neighboring barbarian tribes. The Mongols finally conquered the entire country and early in the thirteenth century established the Yüan dynasty. Following the reign of Kublai Khan (1260-1294), a succession of weak rulers led to the overthrow of this alien regime. The Chinese drove the Mongols back into Central Asia and established the Ming dynasty (1368-1644).

Under the first emperor, Hung-wu, and his able successor, Yung-lo (1403-1424), the Ming sought to reestablish such Chinese traditions as the examination system and rule by scholar-bureaucrats. They aided education, compiled a great law code based on T'ang and Sung precedents, rebuilt the country's defenses, and repaired the irrigation systems. While officially espousing Neo-Confucianism, the Ming dynasty was far more despotic than any of its Chinese predecessors. The emperor's personal rule was strengthened by the abolition of the office of prime minister and by the improvement of such institutions as the censorate and the growth of the palace eunuchs, both personally loyal to the emperor himself. Moreover, harsh punishments for both the people and the bureaucracy became a major characteristic of Ming rule, despite Confucian teachings that the emperor should rely on the virtuous to rule the empire.

China in isolation. Political stability and economic prosperity in Ming China encouraged the growth of antiforeignism, which had originally developed in reaction to

Mongol rule. Chinese antagonism to foreign influence and concentration on the unique qualities and superiorities of Chinese civilization eventually grew into an attitude of indifference to all things foreign. In philosophy this was accompanied and encouraged by a new Confucian school of thought which taught that knowledge was intuitive and should be sought through meditation.

The antiforeignism and intellectual introspection of Ming China did not, however, lead to the physical isolation of China. Contacts with the outside world, particularly with Japan, and foreign trade increased considerably. Yung-lo strenuously tried to extend China's influence beyond her borders by encouraging other rulers to send ambassadors to China to present tribute. The most remarkable venture, during the reigns of Yung-lo and his successors, was the dispatch of seven spectacular naval expeditions, which ranged far and wide through the Indian Ocean and the Southeast Asian archipelago. The first expedition, in 1405, consisted of 62 ships and 28,000 men, the largest naval expedition and greatest feat in seamanship the world had witnessed to that date. While the expeditions brought China knowledge and items of material culture from exotic lands, they did not contribute to the economic well-being of the state and were stopped after the seventh venture. By the next century imperial edicts forbade Chinese ships to sail beyond China's own coastal waters. Thus after an initial adventure into international maritime activity, China shut itself off from the era of expansion that began at approximately the same time to spread European influence across the globe.

As we shall see in Chapter 17, the ruthless activities of the Portuguese traders who arrived in China in the sixteenth century hampered the development of cordial East-West trade relations. Unpleasant experience with outsiders encouraged China to isolate itself, a development which in the long run had stultifying effects on its civilization.

Ming decay. Although the most powerful dynasty in China since the T'ang, the Ming did not fulfill its promise. The energy of the dynasty dried up and the empire shrank.

Ming sea power became so restricted that pirates from offshore islands preyed on passing ships and raided mainland ports.

In 1592 the Japanese attempted to conquer Korea, a vassal of the Ming empire, and through it, China. Following a successful landing in Korea, the Japanese won victories over both Chinese and Korean armies, but Korean sailors thwarted Japanese hopes by defeating the invading fleets. Cut off from supplies from their island home, the Japanese were forced to withdraw, leaving the Ming dynasty still on the Chinese throne.

This victory did not halt Ming decay, however. More and more, the Chinese became convinced of the superiority of their culture, and their experiences with outsiders intensified their desire to isolate themselves. Chinese citizens were forbidden to travel abroad, and the country was almost completely sealed tight against foreign influences. Complacent and static, the empire rapidly lost its strength. By the early part of the seventeenth century China was in a state of dissolution: the court was a center of corruption, taxes had become exorbitant, and the plight of the peasants was pitiable. Peasant uprisings broke out throughout the land.

At the same time that rebellions began to break out against the Ming regime, new invaders—the Manchus—were launching assaults in the north. In 1644 they captured the Ming capital at Peking and a few weeks later proclaimed their rule; China once again was under an alien emperor.

Ming art and scholarship. Whether the Ming dynasty deserved its name, which means "brilliant," depends on how one would evaluate its achievements. Many excellent works of art were produced, but few were as original as those from earlier periods. Ming artisans tried to duplicate the standards of the classic Sung pottery, but instead of emphasizing the beauty of the form of the vessel, they concentrated on brilliant coloring and elegant decoration.

The Forbidden City, the imperial family's area of palaces and temples at Peking, was constructed in the early years (1403-1424) of the Ming dynasty. With its series of courtyards, brilliant lacquer work, and tile, marble, and alabaster decorations, it is typical of a period of richly ornamented architecture.

When the Ming reestablished the traditional competitive examination system, scholarship was stimulated and histories, encyclopedias, dictionaries, and other important scholarly works appeared. Civil service examinations, based upon a thorough knowledge of the classics, were given every three years. In use until 1904, the examination system preserved Chinese traditions remarkably well but kept China excessively conservative and intellectually sterile.

JAPAN'S SELF-IMPOSED ISOLATION

Ashikaga state and culture. The decline of the Kamakura shogunate resembled the end of a dynasty in China. It was accompanied by economic difficulties, political and military strife, and the erosion of the bonds of feudal loyalty. Although the successors to the Kamakura shogunate, the Ashikaga, retained the shogunal office from 1338 to 1573, their government was so different from that of its predecessor that it represented a new stage in the history of Japanese feudalism. The local lords called *daimyo* ("great names"), not the shoguns, were the key figures during this period, and effective Ashikaga rule did not extend far from the capital. The warrior class had broken up into separate groups of lords and retainers, and Japan, like feudal Europe, was almost constantly involved in warfare between various feudal lords.

Despite warfare and political decentralization, the Ashikaga period was one of important economic growth. The feudal lords encouraged trade and commerce in their own domains, and as the money economy grew, various merchants and even some Buddhist monasteries began to play the role of bankers. Merchants organized themselves into a kind of guild system to protect their interests and encourage trade across feudal boundaries, and towns began to develop at important geographical points and around castles and monasteries.

The Ashikaga period was also a period of great cultural developments. With ancient Kyoto as their capital, the shoguns promoted a distinctive new culture, fusing the once separate courtier and warrior cultures. Zen Buddhism, dominated both the imperial and the shogunal courts, and Japanese culture came to be pervaded by an urbane taste for things elegantly simple: the restrained and quiet contemplation of the tea ceremony, new architectural styles, monochrome painting, and landscape gardening, which eventually influenced western gardening. The *No* drama, which combined stately mimetic dancing, music, and song, was the most important literary development.

With the arrival of the Portuguese in Japan in 1542, western influence began to make itself felt. Francis Xavier, a Jesuit missionary, began to preach Christianity in western Japan and Kyoto in 1549, and by the end of the century Japan may have had as many as 300,000 Christians, including some of the feudal lords in Kyushu, who converted in order to gain commercial advantages and advanced military technology from their relations with the westerners.

Changes toward unification. Warfare among Japanese feudal lords sharpened as they adopted improved European firearms. This led to the fall of some feudal houses and the rise of new ones and a general blurring of class lines towards the end of the Ashikaga period. It also meant increasing economic burdens on the peasants and townfolk, so that riots and local uprisings became frequent. Between 1560 and 1600, however, three able leaders in sequence progressively established a single military power over all the *daimyo*. At first this drive for unification was conducted in the name of the last Ashikaga shogun, but he was driven out of Kyoto by his own supporter, Nobunga, in 1573 and no successor was chosen, bringing the line to an end.

The second of these leaders, Hideyoshi, son of a peasant soldier, created a dictatorial power unique in Japanese history. Although theoretically the chief minister of the emperor, Hideyoshi ruled Japan through the feudal institution of vassalage. In attempting to create stability by halting social change,

東海道五拾三次之内
府中

As a defense measure, the Tokugawa shogunate banned the building of bridges across major rivers where they intersected important roads. The people were thus forced to cross the rivers by palanquin or on the backs of coolies, as shown in this contemporary painting.

he tried to define more sharply than before the various social classes and to prevent people from changing their class status. He also disarmed the populace, banned foreign missionaries, and began persecuting Japanese Christians. Hideyoshi regarded both foreign and Japanese Christians as possible agents for change in Japanese society. His large-scale invasion of Korea in 1592 may have been in response to his increasing megalomania as well as to dispose of some of Japan's surplus of professional soldiery, always a danger to internal peace and stability. Korea appealed to China as suzerain; Chinese armies were slowly thrown into the peninsular war, which reached such a stalemate that, on Hideyoshi's death in 1598, his field commanders completely withdrew.

The Tokugawa shogunate. Now was the moment of opportunity for the third leader, Tokugawa Ieyasu, who, as Hideyoshi's agent, had been lord of eastern Japan. By cautious maneuvering and a minimum of fighting, he brought all the barons and their fighting men under his allegiance. Without purporting to establish a national government, he revived the devices of ancient feudalism. He required the emperor to bestow upon him the title of shogun, took the best lands for himself and his family, and assigned the rest to lesser lords in accordance with his view of their loyalty to him. From his

personal headquarters at Edo (Tokyo), he set up a rigid system of laws and institutions designed to perpetuate his family's position indefinitely. Fear of developments that might threaten the status quo led the regime to question European missionary activity and ultimately to ban Christianity altogether; to expel European missionaries and traders; to execute large numbers of native Christians; and finally to exclude all foreigners except the nonproselyting Dutch, who were allowed limited and rigidly controlled trade at Nagasaki. At the same time, all Japanese were forbidden to go abroad or even to build ships capable of navigating beyond coastal waters. This was the beginning of Japan's "centuries of isolation."

SOUTHEAST ASIA: BACKGROUND OF CONFLICT

The geographical foundations of disunity. At the southern tip of the Asian mainland, wedged between India and China and including a multitude of islands in both the Indian and Pacific oceans, lies Southeast Asia. Stretching over a combination of land and sea far greater in size than the United States, Southeast Asia is geographically, culturally, and politically one of the most complex regions in the world.

The Irrawaddy, Salween, and Mekong rivers, which flow south from the Tibet-Burma-China border region, provided avenues for the southward migration of distinctive ethnic groups from South China. North-south mountain chains, which divide Burma from Thailand and Thailand from Vietnam, provided barriers to communication that further emphasized the cultural and political differentiation between the peoples occupying the river valleys. Moreover, later migrants pushed earlier inhabitants out of the valleys and into the mountainous regions, making for further ethnic complexities. Unlike China, where some form of political unity and cultural homogeneity developed, Southeast Asia has always been characterized by political and cultural balkanization. The thousands of islands that make up the Philippine and Indonesian archipelagoes were also subject to natural division rather than unity. Pervasive influences exerted by the great civilizations of India and China added to the confusion.

Chinese, Islamic, and Christian influences in Southeast Asia. In addition to Hindu cultural penetration (discussed in Chapter 7), Chinese influence and on occasion political sovereignty has been a factor in Southeast Asia. During the past five hundred years especially, Chinese settlers migrated to urban centers in this region, where as merchants they came to dominate both local and foreign trade.

The spread of Islam to the Far East started only after the conquest of India by Turkish Muslims during the eleventh and twelfth centuries. As Muslim political and military power began to become dominant, many local rulers found it to their political and commercial advantage to become Muslims. During the fifteenth century, as Hindu rulers were driven from their thrones, Java was completely converted to Islam, which also spread to Sumatra, the Malay peninsula, and the other islands of the Indonesian archipelago. The one exception was the fabled island of Bali, which became the refuge of the former ruling family and has retained its basically Hindu culture into modern times.

In the fifteenth and sixteenth centuries Malayan and Indonesian merchants and settlers carried Islam into the Philippines particularly to the large southern island of Mindanao. But its influence was too late and too weak to spread further north, where Christianity was beginning to make significant inroads.

Spain began a concerted attempt to occupy the Philippines in the middle of the sixteenth century and established its colonial capital at Manila in 1571. By 1581, when Manila was made a bishopric, no fewer than four Catholic orders were active in the islands, and the Catholic university of Santo Tomàs was founded in 1611. By 1622 there were half a million Catholic converts in the Philippines, and this number increased to almost a million within a century. With the exception of Mindanao and some minor peripheral islands, the Philippines were destined to become the only Christian country in Southeast Asia.

The birth of nationhood. The heritage of geographical and ethnic complexity, of conflict between lowland immigrants and older settlers in the hills, and the waves of distinctive cultural influences from outside Southeast Asia, all made for uneven political development throughout the area in the centuries before the arrival of the West, and it is almost impossible to make any generalizations that are valid for the entire region.

What is now Burma was occupied in successive waves and regions by various ethnic groups. Constantly at war with each other and with the neighboring Thais, and often in conflict with the Chinese to the north, the Burmese never succeeded in developing a unified kingdom with a centralized bureaucracy. There was often little continuity in succession from king to king, and though often successful in war, the Burmese kings were more given to raids and brief occupations than to the painstaking business of nation-building and statecraft.

The Thai, or Siamese, on the other hand, early developed a sense of nationhood and a durable administrative system. Furthermore, the Thais were culturally more homogeneous than the Burmese. By the early seventeenth century the Thai monarchs were already in active contact with the West, sending embassies to Holland and the court of Louis XIV. They were also in early contact with China, whose merchants purchased rice in Thailand. Chinese merchants and their families settled in Thailand early and in such numbers that they became a significant part of Thai society and were not even considered foreigners. Because the Chinese community was an important source of attractive women for the royal harem, many Thai monarchs were at least half Chinese, and the present dynasty and its capital, Bangkok, were founded by a half-Chinese general in the latter part of the eighteenth century.

Laos, lying in the northwestern part of the Indochinese peninsula, was a congeries of petty princedoms fought over by the Thais, Vietnamese, and Cambodians. The modern Cambodians are largely descended from the Khmer builders of the great empire which centered on Angkor Wat. Indonesia and Malaya remained the realm of petty Muslim princes and European colonies, which fought to control the rich resources of these lands and the trade routes between eastern and southern Asia.

In the islands of the Indonesian archipelago, one kingdom and empire succeeded another on the great islands of Sumatra and Java. The sea was their thoroughfare, and the important Strait of Malacca, which controlled the trade routes between the Indian Ocean and the Far East, was a major prize of war. But the successive waves of cultural influence that traveled along the trade routes were not a sufficient basis for unification when faced with the geographical and ethnic divisions that plagued both continental and island Southeast Asia. The religious and political thought and institutions of *Hinayana* Buddhism, superimposed on early Brahminic Hindu influence, dominated, and continue to dominate today, Burma, Thailand, Laos, and Cambodia. Islam today pervades Indonesia, the southern Philippines, and the Malay peninsula.

The only region in Southeast Asia to come under Chinese cultural and political domination was what today constitutes North and South Vietnam. The Vietnamese people

are the product of the integration of early migrants from South China with local populations, and their language, closely resembling Chinese, has marked Khmer and Thai elements. Spending over a thousand years of their history, beginning with the Han dynasty, under Chinese rule, and even longer under Chinese influence, Vietnam so closely resembled China culturally and politically that it has been called "The Lesser Dragon." Adopting *Mahayana* Buddhism, Confucian political thought, Chinese institutions, and the Chinese written language, the Vietnamese constructed a Confucian state on the Chinese model, complete with an emperor, a civil service bureaucracy recruited through the traditional Confucian examination system, a mandarin class, and court records and a literature in the Chinese style. Even the imperial palace at the capital at Hue in central Vietnam was built on the Chinese model. Sometimes more conservative than the Chinese themselves, the Vietnamese held onto tradition longer. For instance, Confucian examinations which were abolished in China in 1905, remained in force in Vietnam until the mid-1920's. But despite the amazingly strong Chinese influence on Vietnam and its culture, the Vietnamese throughout their history remained strongly conscious of themselves as Vietnamese. They constantly struggled for independence from China and, once independence was achieved, for the continuity and integrity of their own state.

AFRICA: THE NEGLECTED CONTINENT

Reconstructing Africa's past. Extending from the fringes of the Sahara Desert south to the Cape of Good Hope is sub-Saharan Africa. The terms *Africa* and *Africans* are often used to refer solely to this part of the African continent and its native inhabitants. While the Nile valley was one of the original cradles of civilization and North Africa was an integral part of the Graeco-Roman classical world, it is one of history's ironic touches that sub-Saharan Africa, despite its proximity to both regions, was one of the last areas to come to the attention of the outside world. Only after 1500 A.D. did European traders, missionaries, and explorers progressively penetrate the so-called "Dark Continent."

This outside impact came at a time when the West was experiencing remarkable advances in technology and the arts stemming from the Renaissance, geographical exploration, and the scientific and the industrial revolutions. To the intrusive Europeans, Africa south of the Sahara appeared static, and its people primitive. Above all, the absence of writing in African societies colored western stereotypes. Preliterates were considered barbaric, a people without records of their past and therefore without history. Since 1945, however, a new school of African studies has become established, dedicated to demonstrating that there is "a recoverable African past," notwithstanding the paucity of written materials. Its advent as an integral part of world history is one of the most exciting and rewarding happenings in contemporary historical studies.

The progressive rediscovery of the African past has been aided by the newly independent sub-Saharan states' interest in archaeological and historical research. Greatly expanded archaeological and anthropological activity has led to the discovery of many new prehistoric sites and to the possibility that manlike creatures may actually have originated in Africa (see Chapter 1). Mainly, however, the rediscovery of Africa's past has been made possible by the development of new research techniques.

In the new types of research methods now being utilized, specialists from other fields collaborate with historians. Botanists' study of the introduction and diffusion of food crops has illuminated significant features of Africa's pre-European past. The utilization of oral tradition is promising to be a significant technique where no records are available. Another research approach, called glotto-chronology, involves the use of linguistics to trace the routes and times of migrations as well as the diffusion of various culture items. These new methods used in

recovering the African past are collectively known as ethnohistory. With them, the badly needed chronology of African history is slowly being pieced together.

Peoples of Africa. Between the Sahara and the Mediterranean, North Africa has been peopled for at least five thousand years by the Hamitic-speaking Berbers. In addition, this area has a prominent Semitic element, introduced through the immigration of both Jews and Arabs during the period of the Roman Empire and the later era of Muslim expansion. Southward, a wide variety of physical types are found: the so-called "true Negro" living along the west coast; the tall, slender Nilo-Sudanic people in the northeast; the congeries of Bantu-speaking peoples dominant in the center and south of the continent; the Pygmies living in the deep rain forest of central Africa; and the Bushmen and Hottentots of southern Africa.[1]

Continent in isolation. The key to an understanding of the history of sub-Saharan Africa has been its geographic isolation. To the north stretches the huge barrier of the Sahara, which for centuries prevented easy contact with the dynamic civilizations fringing the Mediterranean. The African coastline is forbidding, with few bays or inlets to serve as harbors; and most of the rivers are blocked by rapids and sandbanks. Miasmal swamps and dense jungles in some areas are other obvious obstacles to communication. Added to these barriers is the threat of tropical disease.

But the geographical picture is not completely negative. Sub-Saharan Africa also has cool highlands, broad grassy plains, fertile valleys, valuable mineral reserves, and abundant animal resources. The coast of western Africa has been successfully farmed since early times, supporting a comparatively dense population. The largest rivers of western Africa have been useful for communication—the Niger for most of its 2600 miles, the Senegal for 560 miles, and the Gambia for 350 miles.

Even so, the isolation of much of sub-Saharan Africa must be considered a major factor in its history. It not only helps explain the remarkable continuity and distinctiveness of the African way of life; it is also a key to sub-Saharan retardation, especially in technology.

Africa: the formative period. It is now believed that during the Old Stone Age, Africa was the most advanced area in the world, a leader in the slow march toward civilization. In addition to developing the hand-ax, Africa produced the first true weapon of attack, the bolas, and its tool-making techniques may have been diffused to other continents by streams of migration.

In contrast to some other areas in the world, Africa suffered a culture lag after 8000 B.C. The technique of plant domestication had spread from western Asia to North Africa, and under the pharaohs, farming flourished in the lower Nile valley at least by the fifth millennium B.C. Unfortunately, farming and other adjuncts of civilization did not diffuse rapidly southward into the African continent, and it is now generally held that there was no independent invention of agriculture in sub-Saharan Africa. The people of the savanna region of the Sudan, directly south of the Sahara and north of the forests, probably did not begin to cultivate crops until after 2000 B.C. In fact, the earliest important Neolithic farm culture

Near the junction of the White and Blue Nile in the Sudan, the Kushites founded their fabulous capital, Meroë, building massive monuments, palaces, and sculptured gods. Their remains give a vivid impression of the city's former grandeur.

yet identified dates from 800 B.C. to 200 A.D. Known as the Nok culture, it originated in northern Nigeria. Its people had begun to work iron and tin, and their most distinctive accomplishment was the production of strikingly beautiful terra-cotta sculpture.

During the first millennium B.C. the tempo in Africa began to quicken. Iron was introduced, and its use spread over much of Africa between 300 B.C. and 900 A.D. In West Africa (in the area of Nigeria) Bantu-speaking peoples who farmed and worked iron began to increase in numbers. This "population explosion" led to an historic migration southward into the rain forest regions. At the outset, the Bantu migrants needed crops that could thrive in the wet and excessively hot forests. Such new crops as bananas and varieties of yams became available when Asian immigrants brought them to East Africa in the early centuries A.D. The Bantus increased rapidly, and as they pushed southward, they absorbed most of the Pygmy and Bushmen types they encountered. By the eighth century A.D. they had reached the area of present-day Rhodesia and by the sixteenth century were nearing the tip of South Africa.

Africa's contacts with the earliest civilizations. The vast coastline of sub-Saharan Africa was touched only here and there by sailors and traders in ancient times. In general the contacts were spasmodic and not very important. By about 300 B.C. merchants from southern Arabia began trading with the peoples on the east coast of Africa, and merchants from India may have ventured inland as far as the Great Lakes in central Africa in their search for ivory and for slaves. Certainly the ancient Egyptians sailed far up the Nile and sent their mariners down the east coast. The most famous expedition was sent by Queen Hatshepsut in about 1470 B.C. to the legendary land of Punt, which probably was located in what is now Somaliland (see illustration, p. 24). Of all the ancient peoples who approached sub-Saharan Africa, the most successful were the Phoenicians. The most famous of their several voyages was that of a fleet of sixty ships which in 520 B.C. was sent by the Phoenician colony at Carthage to explore north-

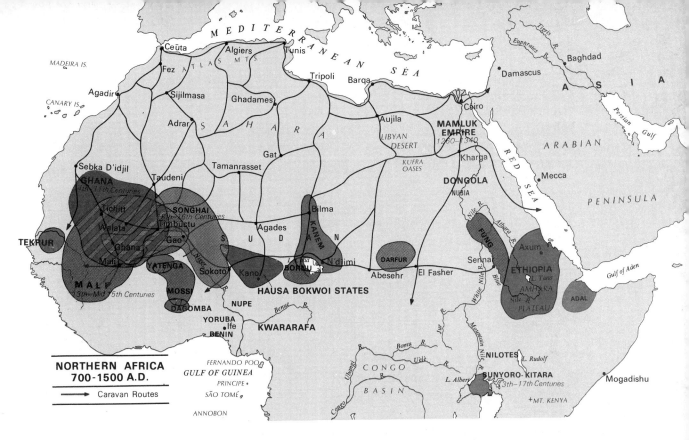

NORTHERN AFRICA
700-1500 A.D.
→ Caravan Routes

western Africa and to establish trading posts there. The expedition sailed as far south as the modern nation of Sierra Leone, some three thousand miles from its home port in the Mediterranean.

Along the valley of the Nile, the pharaohs had extended their control well into Upper Egypt by 2000 B.C., and five hundred years later they gained mastery of the area known as Kush in the northern part of the modern state of the Sudan. The Kushites became thoroughly Egyptianized, but about 1000 B.C., when Egyptian power had begun to wane, they set up an independent kingdom.

Waxing strong and prosperous, the Kushites soon conquered Egypt, which they ruled from about 725 B.C. to 600 B.C., when they were pushed out of Egypt back into the Sudan. Not far from the modern city of Khartoum the Kushites founded their capital of Meroë. From 250 B.C. to the beginning of the Christian era Meroë enjoyed its golden age. The Kushite dynasty, ruling over a mixed white and black population, encouraged trade, accumulated wealth, and produced great architecture—Egyptian-inspired. The Meroitic kingdom was undoubtedly a center for iron smelting and manufacturing, as proved by the many slag heaps that still can be identified. In fact, Meroë can be called the Pittsburgh of ancient Africa. While scholars do not all agree, Meroë may have been an important channel of culture diffusion, mainly Egyptian, into central Africa. Knowledge of iron working may also have spread from this center to other parts of the continent. Although generally not appreciated, Meroë can be considered, along with Carthage and Egypt, as one of the great civilizations of ancient Africa.

Africa and the classical world. While the Greeks and Romans were setting the pattern for western culture and the Han in China and the Guptas in India were supporting highly civilized societies, little was known about Africa south of the Sahara, and its advancement was hindered by its relative isolation. The Phoenicians and Greeks had dotted the African Mediterranean coast with colonies and trading posts, and, with the rise of the Roman Empire, the entire region had become part of the realm of the Caesars. Imperial North Africa flourished and great cities gradually developed. After

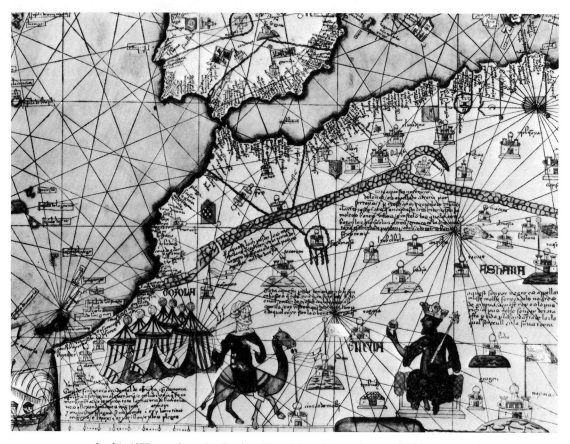

In this 1375 map from the Catalan Atlas, Mansa Musa, the wealthy king of Mali, awaits the arrival of a Muslim trader. Although both are West Africans, the Arab is from the Sahara Desert, while the Negro king is from the western Sudan. The system of trade within the African continent was highly organized in the precolonial era.

about 100 A.D. the Romans made a few Sahara crossings, and the classical geographer Ptolemy, in the second century A.D., apparently learned of the junction of the Blue and the White Nile and their source in the inland lakes. But after the decline of Rome, what little knowledge had been gained about the great continent was forgotten or lay hidden in unread manuscripts.

At the time of the Roman Empire the kingdom of Axum (in present-day Ethiopia) became prominent. We have only fragmentary knowledge of this kingdom, which flourished from the first to the seventh centuries A.D. Its people were a mixture of Hamitic stock and Semitic-speaking immigrants who came from Arabia about 1000 B.C. Their kings traced their lineage from Menelik, (the son, according to Ethiopian tradition, of King Solomon and the Queen of Sheba).

Christianity, which had spread down into most of northeastern Africa, became the official religion in Axum in the fourth century A.D. Led by powerful kings, Axum armies subdued surrounding territory as far as the Nile valley, but their expansion was eventually halted by the victorious force of Islam in Egypt and the entire Red Sea area. Thereafter the Ethiopians remained isolated and stagnant in their highlands, and this part of Africa was cut off from the rest of Christendom (and, in fact, from any contact with Europe) until 1500.

Afro-Muslim empires in the Sudan. Between the fourth and sixteenth centuries A.D. a series of large empires rose, flourished, and disappeared in the western Sudan. The first such imperial state was Ghana, located in the upper areas of the Niger and Senegal rivers (see map, p. 353). In the fourth century a group of immigrants from North Africa, probably Hamitic Berbers, established their control over the indigenous peoples. Gradually the more numerous Negroes absorbed their conquerors and, in the late eighth century, seized control and created their own dynasty.

After the amazingly rapid spread of the Islamic Arabs across North Africa in the eighth century, a new and more potent alien influence traversed the Sahara. Muslim Berber tribes, together with Arab adherents of the Prophet, began to filter into the Sudan—a huge grassy plain stretching from the Atlantic to the Nile valley. The Sudan became an area of racial mixture, where Negroid peoples came under the influence of Muslim culture.

Many of these North African Muslims settled in the capital city of Ghana as merchants and officials, making it the first great commercial center of the Sudan. Arabic became the official language of the empire, and the Islamic way of life and religion made numerous converts. Ghana attained a remarkable degree of control of the western trans-Saharan trade route. Gold and slaves from the south were traded for salt from northern desert areas and for goods from Morocco.

From the revenues from this trans-Saharan trade, the Ghanian rulers were able to maintain a sumptuous royal court, and their empire enjoyed stable government for more than two hundred years. Their wealth, however, attracted the cupidity of Muslim neighbors, desert Berbers who had embraced a form of militant Islam. Ostensibly crusaders pledged to extirpate the paganism of the Ghanian rulers, these invaders captured Ghana in 1076 (just ten years after the Norman victory at Hastings in England), forcing many of its inhabitants to accept Islam. Thus the conquerors conveniently mixed religious zeal with a desire to enjoy the profits of the trans-Saharan trade.

Several centuries later Ghana became part of a new empire—that of Mali. This most famous Afro-Muslim kingdom stretched for fifteen hundred miles in the western Sudan. Ruled by Mandingos, a Negro people whose chiefs had been converted to Islam in the eleventh century, Mali attained greatness in the thirteenth century. Its major commercial city, Timbuktu, succeeded Ghana as the main point of convergence for the north-south caravan routes (see map, p. 353) and became a great metropolis. Under Mandingo rule, Timbuktu boasted a great mosque and a university for Koranic studies.

Mali at its height controlled an area as large as western Europe, but it enjoyed only a century of greatness and after 1350 rapidly dwindled in extent and power. It was replaced by another great empire—Songhai—which reached its height in the fifteenth and sixteenth centuries. Its capital was Gao, a commercial center on the Niger. At the end of the sixteenth century the Songhai empire was destroyed by a Moroccan army whose superior firearms were new to the Sudan. The period of greatness of the Sudanese kingdoms was over.

These Sudanic empires had a number of common features that made them relatively short-lived. Their boundaries were ill defined and embraced a variety of ethnically and culturally diverse peoples. Often established by conquest, these empires depended

No European ever saw Timbuktu until 1828, when René Caillé, disguised as a Muslim pilgrim, made the journey. The mixture of Muslim and native architecture is apparent in his drawing of the city. Caillé was most impressed by the difficulties the builders must have encountered in setting up a great city "in the midst of the sands."

upon military force and personal leadership for their perpetuation, and they lacked stable systems of succession to the throne. But despite their built-in forces of disunity, these empires are rightly regarded as important political achievements in sub-Saharan history.

Some historians deny the importance of external influences in West African political development. There is, however, evidence that Islamic traders and settlers from North Africa played a significant role in the rise of the Sudanic empires. As Muslim schools were founded in the Sudan, a class of educated and literate scholars was produced whose services were indispensable in setting up and running imperial administrations. Arabic was also the lingua franca of diplomacy and trade. It has been said that "Without losing their distinctive 'Sudanic' character, the great states and cities of the western Sudan became definitely part of the Islamic world."[2]

Impact of Islam in East Africa. The impact of Islam was also strongly felt along the East African coast. From the seventh century A.D.

The ruins in the valley of Zimbabwe, meaning "the sacred graves of the chiefs," are dominated by the massive stone wall of the temple.

Arab traders came in growing numbers for gold, ivory, and slaves. Permanent settlements sprang up until the entire east coast was dotted with small Muslim states. These urban trading centers, such as Lamu, Kilwa, Mombassa, and Zanzibar, were never effectively united and controlled from any one point, and there was continuous rivalry among them.

One of the results of this active coastal trade was the emergence of an important, prosperous African state in what is now Rhodesia. The rulers of this kingdom built the great stone city of Zimbabwe over a long time period from as early as the fifth to the eighth century until the early eighteenth. Constructed of granite blocks without mortar or cement, the massive walls of its temple ruins measure from ten to fifteen feet thick and from twenty to thirty feet high. The remains of the acropolis—built to be an impregnable fortress—can be seen on a nearby hill. Close by is the Valley of the Ruins, probably the site of a flourishing tribal administrative center.

The various Arab settlements along the eastern coast made up the Zenj empire, and the entire coastal strip was called Zenjibar, meaning "black coast." Made wealthy by trade, the Zenj empire attracted merchants from as far east as Malaya and China, and numerous Chinese coins and many fragments of Chinese porcelain have been found along the coast. The empire endured for nearly five hundred years, until the arrival of the Portuguese in 1497. In the last half of the seventeenth century Arabs from Oman ejected the Portuguese from the East African coast north of Mozambique, but Mozambique is still under Lisbon's control today.

European contact and the slave trade. For some eight hundred years, beginning about 700 A.D., Islam had been the most important outside influence in Africa and the main agency of communication with the outside world. This Islamic contact had been mainly by land across the Sahara Desert and by sea along the east coast. With the coming of the Europeans in the fifteenth century, the pattern of outside contact was revolutionized, for now it was to come mainly from the west and by sea to both the east and west coasts. Trans-Saharan trade dwindled as European ships came to the coasts to trade for gold, ivory, and especially slaves. Their arrival marked the beginning of the European period of African history, which lasted for about five hundred years.

Domestic slavery had been practiced in Africa since ancient times, but the slave trade was first organized by the Arabs mainly along the east coast. The Arabs used East African slaves themselves and exported thousands across the Indian Ocean. After the European trade began, West African slaves, possibly more than thirty million in all, were brought to the Americas. Furthermore, it is said that for every slave sold to a colonial plantation, another lost his life in the cruel roundup in Africa or on the crowded slave ships.

The African slave trade has been called the greatest crime in history; and some Negro leaders blame this nefarious trade for Africa's failure to keep up with European progress in early modern times. Europeans cannot be absolved from their part in the slave trade; at the same time it should be understood that both Europeans and Africans accepted the trade and cooperated with it. Slaves were captured in the hinterland by Africans who then delivered the victims to the slave ships on the coast. It was a very lucrative enterprise. On the basis of this traffic in human beings, new West African states, such as Benin, Dahomey, Oyo, and Ashanti, rose to power and wealth. Although they compared in artistic development and territorial influence with the earlier empires of the western Sudan, these states of the Guinea forest quickly declined as a result of tyrannical, greedy rulers and wars with their African trade rivals.

Historians continue to study and debate the long-term effects of the slave traffic. There is a consensus on the unmitigated evils of the slavers in East Africa, but authorities are reluctant to make sweeping generalizations about its effects in West Africa. Granting the stimulus to intertribal wars, the depopulation of raided areas, and its ultimate inhumanity and cruelty, the slave traffic did result in a new type of contact with the outside world that was not com-

This bronze relief was fashioned by artisans of the ancient city-state of Benin in present-day Nigeria. The king in the center, wearing coral necklaces up to his jowl, is flanked by pages and guards. Plaques like these decorated the walls and square pillars of the Royal Palace of Benin.

pletely evil. New medicines and tools became known. Above all the introduction of new crops, such as maize, cassava, and the sweet potato, made a revolutionary difference to food supplies. Depopulation caused by the slave trade was in some instances more than offset by an increase in population made possible by these more productive crops.

Indigenous culture of Black Africa. What can be said of the collective achievement of the African before the European impact? Certainly Africans lagged behind Europe and America in their control over nature. There was no science, mathematics, or technology worthy of the name; no sails for ships, no animal-drawn plows, no use of the wheel, and above all no alphabet or forms of writing. But aside from these aspects of material culture, African society in its law, government, education, and codes of social conduct was as complex and efficiently regulated as our own. Rules and conventions regarding the role of parents, worship of the gods, education of children and customs relating to eating, recreation, and the like were carefully worked out, and effective methods were at hand to compel the individual to conform.

In political organization the basic unit was the tribe. In Africa there are still hundreds of these tribal units, microscopic or large. And while Africans did not develop the highly centralized and bureaucratically organized nations that emerged in late medieval Europe, they did establish a number of important kingdom states. Moreover, African rulers were not usually despots; they had to govern within the framework of accepted custom and seek the advice of their council of elders.

Religion touched every phase of African life—births, marriage, death, war, rainmaking, and harvest. While religious practices varied from tribe to tribe, three basic essentials could usually be recognized: "spiritism," which includes ancestor worship and the propitiation of such spirits of nature as lightning and rain; belief in some kind of supreme being or highest power; and the practice of magic.[3] This last element may be defined as a technique directed at obtaining the aid of supernatural powers and forces. On its positive side it is definitely protective. But there is also "black magic" and witchcraft, the magic that has been most feared by Africans.

The most distinctive African art form has been music, which plays an integral part in everyday life. "The African sings about work, about hunting, about money, about women, about canoeing, about planting, about war—in short about all the things that men dwell naturally upon in their minds."[4] Unlike music in the western world where there are usually two parties—the artist and the audience—all Africans participate in the rendering of music. Their music is communal, not individual.

African visual art par excellence is sculpture. While it is sometimes called "primitive," it follows complex traditions. The sculpture is usually carved of wood, but ivory, terra cotta, and bronze have also been used. Some bronze work has been compared to the best produced by Renaissance artists. A naturalistic bronze head found at the site of the ancient city-state of Ife in Nigeria has been pronounced the finest surviving example of African art.

Indigenous African culture cannot be summarily dismissed as uncivilized. To be sure, the term *civilization* has traditionally referred to a stage of human culture characterized by writing and an urban base in which there is considerable use of technology, the operation of economic specialization, and a complex infrastructure of law and government. In recent years, however, there has been substantial rethinking on this matter as social scientists, particularly anthropologists, have learned more about the culture of people usually referred to as primitive. A spokesman for this new viewpoint has written:

This magnificent bronze head was found at the site of the city-state of Ife in Nigeria.

The term civilization refers literally to a city-state, at the least to a state that encourages urbanization and industrialization. But in its more general usage it implies a system of living where law and order are maintained with justice and equality, human conflicts both inside and outside the group are resolved with a minimum of violence, and where there is a moral code which people keep, more because they believe in it than because they are afraid of the consequences of breaking it.[5]

Seen in this light, Africa has indeed a long tradition of civilization. In fact, while African culture was certainly deficient in technology and writing it could boast outstanding sculpture, complicated and vital music, functional and well-organized political forms, and significant religious systems. Some tribes paid careful attention to family planning and population control. Capital punishment was rare; only the habitual murderer or thief was put to death. The rights of a wife—in relation to property, custody of children, and protection from abuse from the husband—were often more carefully spelled out than in western societies until very recent times. One of the most admirable traits of African society was the prevalence of the idea of community. A built-in system of social security took care of the needy, the old, the orphan, or the widow. Unlike the westerner with his emphasis on individual advance (often at the expense of the group), the African always had to think of the group and family interests rather than his own.

The new image of Africa. The advent of European explorers marked the beginning of a new era in Africa, one which, while it created new problems, also removed age-old handicaps. With the end of its isolation, a more accurate knowledge of African cultures spread to the outside world; and increasingly, a new value was placed upon some of the qualities of pre-European African societies. Shortly after 1900 the artistic worth of African sculpture was discovered by the Paris school of avant-garde painters, among them Picasso and Matisse. This so-called primitive art, long considered grotesque and infantile, provided artists with a sought-for channel to revolt against the naturalistic conventions that had dominated western art for two thousand years. African sculpture soon came to be recognized as one of the world's major art forms and was a source of inspiration for Cubism (see Color Plate 31) as well as the general vogue of abstract art in the western world. African music also made an important contribution. It is the major ultimate source of American spirituals and of jazz. Similarly, the rumba of Cuba, the calypso of Trinidad, and the samba of Brazil reveal their debt to the rhythmic figures of African music.

During the past two decades—building on the growing appreciation of Negro artistic gifts, the widening vista of African history, and the amazing postwar emergence of more than forty independent nations—a new ideology has developed among African intellectuals. Known as *Négritude*, it asserts the Negro's distinctiveness from other races and proudly champions his unique qualities, including blackness. It has been tersely defined as the "positive affirmation of the values in African culture."[6]

Négritude seeks to rediscover the long-forgotten African past and to make it the foundation for group dignity and aspirations. It endeavors to find cultural antecedents which have been forgotten or minimized. Believing that Europeans have downgraded African achievements, it passionately denies the still dominant idea of the long history of barbarism in Africa before the advent of European colonial rule. It calls attention to early African achievements in art, folk literature, music, and dance forms and to the virtues in African religious and social systems. Undoubtedly these claims have an element of idealization, but on the whole they are a long-needed corrective.

OLD CIVILIZATIONS IN THE NEW WORLD

The earliest American immigrants. The question of when the Western Hemisphere was first settled remains uncertain. It is generally agreed that man did not originate in the Americas, for no bones of humans earlier than *Homo sapiens* have been found there. Man was already fully developed when he became the earliest immigrant to seek his fortune in the New World.

Making their way from Asia to Alaska via the Bering land bridge, nomadic groups spread out in various directions on the American continents. Until the 1920's it was thought that the Amerinds (American Indians) came to the Western Hemisphere as recently as three thousand years ago. The date of their arrival, however, has been pro-

MEXICO

Mayapán • Chichén Itzá

MAYA
Uxmal

YUCATAN
PENINSULA

AZTEC
Tula • • Teotihuacan
• Tenochtitlán

Rio Las Balsas

BRITISH
HONDURAS

Tikal

MAYA
GUATEMALA HONDURAS
• Copan

EL
SALVADOR NICARAGUA

COSTA RICA
PANAMA

PACIFIC

OCEAN

AZTEC AND MAYAN CIVILIZATIONS

gressively modified. Significant research in the 1960's has dated the Bering crossing as far back as 15,000 B.C. The most spectacular claim, not yet fully substantiated, is the discovery in central Mexico of crude tools dating back 40,000 years ago. It is apparent that the chronology of the Amerind migrations will be substantially rewritten in the near future.

The cultural levels achieved by different groups of Amerinds before the arrival of the Europeans varied. Most of the Indians of North America and of the Amazon region never progressed further than the Neolithic stage, with its dependence upon hunting, primitive agriculture, and village life. By contrast, the Mayas and the Aztecs in Mexico and Central America and the Incas in the Andes of Peru created advanced civilizations on a par with those which arose in Asia and the Near East. Perhaps the major reason for the more advanced cultures of the Mayas, Aztecs, and Incas was the efficient domestication of the all-important maize, or Indian corn, known as the "food of the gods." This former wild grass, skillfully bred into a basic crop, was capable of supporting large populations.

Unfortunately, we probably know less about these remarkable civilizations than about any great civilization of the Old World. In their fanatical zeal, many early Spanish *conquistadores* and missionaries destroyed libraries, dismantled cities, and suppressed as much of the native tradition as possible. The historical record of the Americas was damaged beyond repair.

The splendid culture of the Mayas. At its height, Mayan civilization was much more advanced than any other on the western continents. At least a thousand years before the birth of Christ, the Mayan Indians migrated into northern Central America. At the time that the Roman Empire and the classical civilization of the Mediterranean were collapsing, the Mayas had built wonderful cities in the southern part of their territory. Later, the southern cities of what is called the Mayan classical period sank into decay, and the center of the Mayan civilization shifted northward to the Yucatán peninsula. From about 980 to 1200 a confederacy of independent city-states held sway; and during that period there occurred a splendid Mayan renaissance in architecture and art.

Within the city-states strict social stratification existed: the highest classes were the priests and nobles; below them were the farmers, craftsmen, and merchants; the last two levels included the lowest freemen and the slaves making up the bottom rank. The slaves performed the drudgery and heavy work; their lot was especially arduous, for until the arrival of the Spaniards there were no beasts of burden or wheeled vehicles in North and Central America.

Most of the populace labored in the fields surrounding the cities. The rich soil laid bare when the jungle was cleared away was made more productive by irrigation. The Mayas raised squash, pumpkins, chili peppers, and many grains and vegetables. But maize—the mainstay of their civilization—was the chief crop, supplying 80 percent of their food.

Religion permeated all phases of Mayan life. Dominated by a powerful priesthood, the government was a form of theocracy. Education was concerned primarily with religion, and reading and writing were the private domain of the clergy. The numerous gods of the Mayas were divided into three general groups: the deities of the sky, the earth, and the underworld. To maintain an accurate schedule of religious observances, which were intimately linked to their agricultural way of life, the Mayas constructed a calendar which approaches our own in accuracy. They also built several observatories, which were run by the priests; exactness in astronomical calculations was possible because of the excellent numerical system the Mayas devised.

Of all the Amerinds, the Mayas came the closest to developing an efficient system of writing. They used an advanced system of pictographs rather than alphabetic letters or a syllabic system, but no Rosetta Stone has yet been discovered to give us a key to the hieroglyphics which adorned their monuments, buildings, jewelry, pottery, and books.

In architecture and sculpture the Mayas produced work of the highest quality. In the plaza of a Mayan city was a terraced mound or pyramid, topped by a temple. The highly stylized sculpture which decorated the temple terraces is regarded by some art experts as among the world's best, despite the fact that Mayan sculptors did their intricate carving without the aid of anything better than stone tools. Almost completely religious in inspiration, Mayan art depicted the deities and the animals connected with them— snakes, frogs, jaguars, and hummingbirds. Minor arts such as weaving, jade sculpture, ceramics, and gold and silver work were also highly developed and showed an extremely sophisticated sense of design which compares favorably with the best of Egyptian art.

Eventually the Mayan cities fell victim to internal strife, in which petty chieftains fought for supremacy. In addition to civil war, inroads were made by Toltec and Aztec invaders, who eventually conquered the Mayas. After the conquest, the Mayan popu-

Tikal, located in what is now northern Guatemala, is the oldest and one of the largest of the Mayan temple centers. The Mayas lived close to their fields and only came to their cities for religious ceremonies and to work on necessary construction.

lation and culture declined. When the *conquistadores* came upon the scene, the country was in chaos; and the Spaniards found it a simple matter to subdue the Mayan peoples.

The warlike Aztecs. In the early centuries A.D. the peoples of the Mexican plateau were also advancing in civilization. They built cities, pyramids, and temples, which can be seen at Teotihuacán, near Mexico City. As warlike peoples came in from the north, empires arose, for example, the Toltec empire. The last and best known migrants, the Aztecs, entered central Mexico and, about 1325, founded a lake settlement called Tenochtitlán on the site of the present Mexico City. Then, allying themselves with other Mexican Indian tribes, they created a confederacy which in the fifteenth century ruled an area extending across Mexico from the Gulf of Mexico to the Pacific Ocean. Like the ancient Assyrians, the Aztecs glorified war, maintained a superb fighting force, and plundered the lands of their neighbors. However, Aztec power lasted less than a century, for the arrival of Cortés in 1519 brought about its collapse.

Scholars have held different opinions concerning the Aztec form of government. Earlier writers looked upon it as an empire, ruled by an absolute king. Many historians today feel that the Aztec government was essentially a democracy. In Aztec society the main controller of rank was ability. As in our own society, a man could rise to any position if he had the requisite ability. Thus, through personal talent and initiative, a craftsman or farmer might become a priest or a member of the tribal council. Among the soldiers, rank was determined mainly by success in war. Chiefs were elected from powerful families and could be removed; sons or brothers of chieftains succeeded them only if they were capable.

While the Aztecs worshiped a pantheon of gods, their devotion to the sun was particularly important and unusually barbaric. In every city of their domain, great pyramids were built, topped by temples to the sun and rain. There, stone altars were set up, on which thousands of people were sacrificed to Uitzilopochtli, the god of war and the sun. Victims included men, women, and children, who were stretched out on a sacrificial stone where the priests tore out their hearts as offerings to the god. Aztec military superiority assured a large number of captives for these sacrifices.

Like the Romans, the Aztecs borrowed many aspects of their culture from their predecessors or captives. In fact, a fair analogy may be drawn between the Mayas and Aztecs in the New World and the ancient Greeks and Romans. Generally speaking, the Mayas were more artistic and intellectual than the Aztecs and remind us somewhat of the Greeks. The brusque and brutal characteristics of the Aztecs can be likened to the tendencies which the Romans sometimes displayed.

The Incas. About the eleventh century some people known as Incas (children of the sun) settled in the heartland of the Andes. Some archaeologists believe that they wandered northward from the Lake Titicaca region until they came to the valley of Cuzco. From there they began to extend their dominion over the mountain peoples and the coastal dwellers. From 1438 until the arrival of the *conquistador* Pizarro in 1532, a vast Inca empire flourished, extending for about 2700 miles along the western coast of the continent and including an estimated population of ten million at the time of the Spanish conquest. Even today the bulk of the peoples on the Peruvian coast and in the highlands are descended from Inca stock.

The Inca form of government was a hereditary absolute monarchy, ruled by a king called the Inca, who exercised the power of life and death over his subjects. Actually, it was a true theocracy, for the people were sun worshipers who believed that the Inca was an offspring of the sun.

The power of the ruler depended largely on an excellent military organization based on compulsory and universal military training. Another source of power was control by the Inca of all the food throughout the empire. If any district produced more than it needed, he had the surplus stored for future use or transferred to a district which through drought or other misfortunes had failed to produce enough food.

The absolute control which the Inca exercised over his subjects made possible the magnificent construction projects in the empire. Immense slabs carved out of the mountain sides were trimmed at the quarry to fit exactly into a specific niche in a temple or fortress wall; no mortar was used by the Incas. Despite their lack of wheeled vehicles, the Incas transported the giant blocks for miles through the mountains. A splendid system of roads and trails radiated from Cuzco to every part of the Inca realm.

Why did the wealthy, powerful Inca and Aztec empires fall so easily before a handful of European conquerors during the sixteenth century? A primary reason is that both the great Indian empires of the Western Hemi-

A natural fortress, Machu Picchu was built by the Incas probably after 1440 on a narrow ridge between two mountain peaks. It appears to have been the residence and stronghold of the last Incan ruler after the Spanish conquest had begun. When the ruler died, the city was abandoned and lost until it was rediscovered in 1911.

sphere were weakened by internal strife; the tribes ruled by the Incas and the Aztecs were restive under the control of their conquerors. Thus the Spanish with their firearms—weapons completely unknown to the Indians—were able to hasten a process of political dissolution perhaps already under way.

SUMMARY

Most of the Indians of North America never achieved what can be called "civilization," but in Mexico and Central and South America a number of brilliant civilizations emerged—those of the Aztecs, Mayas, and Incas. The Aztecs have been compared to the Romans: they were practical, martial people, skillful at conquest and at governing subject peoples. By contrast, the Mayas have been likened to the Greeks: they were great builders and artists, and they were also scholars and scientists who invented a remarkable calendar, studied astronomy, and pursued mathematics. Of all the American Indians, the Incas should be remembered for developing one of the first totalitarian states in history.

During the many centuries covered by this volume, little has been seen of Africa south of the Sahara. This vast region lay on the periphery of great world movements; and the key to its past has been its isolation. Much of African history, therefore, was unknown, and the achievements of its people usually dismissed as inconsequential. A more accurate evaluation, however, has developed in recent decades. Scholars, while recognizing that Africans did not attain the achievements of Europeans and Asians in the mechanical arts and in the sciences, point out the Africans' significant advances in social organization and in the arts.

Far more advanced than societies in the Americas or in Africa were the civilizations of India, China, Japan, and Southeast Asia.

They seemed to reach their height in the period corresponding to Europe's Middle Ages; then they began to decline. The alien Mughuls gave India its most brilliant period, surpassing the glories of the Guptas. The Mughul ruler Akbar is regarded as one of the greatest statesmen of all time. All facets of culture flourished under Mughul rule, but the noblest legacy was in architecture.

Conditions in India were reversed in China, for here the alien Mongol rulers were ousted and a native dynasty set about developing the country. A bright period of prosperity, expansion, and cultural activity followed. But the Ming suffered from a serious psychological handicap. The essence of their rule was restoration of the old and suspicion of the strange and new. China became self-satisfied and impervious to new ideas. The inevitable result was decline and, ironically, conquest by another foreign dynasty, the Manchu.

Under the Tokugawa shoguns, the Japanese were even more determined to cut themselves off from the outside world. Like the Ming, they had no use for foreign ways. But new forces, mainly economic, were at work, which would end isolation and abolish forever the institution of the shogunate.

Although strongly influenced by Indian and Chinese cultures, the incredible political and ethnic complexities that characterized Southeast Asia inhibited the growth of the kind of cultural and national self-consciousness that marked China and Japan. Moreover, geographical divisions contributed to the peoples' inability to develop political unity and stability. These factors were to make Southeast Asia a relatively easy prey for Europe's expanding empires.

In following the events in Europe and in European colonies, we must not lose sight of these peoples of the other continents, who far outnumbered Europeans and who, in the centuries ahead, would move ever closer to the center of the stage of world history.

SUGGESTIONS FOR READING

G. A. Lensen, **The World Beyond Europe,*** 2nd ed., Houghton Mifflin. The best brief introduction. The best large-scale general survey of the Far East is E. O. Reischauer, J. K. Fairbank, and A. Craig, **History of East Asian Civilization,** Vol. I, **East Asia: The Great Tradition,** Houghton Mifflin, 1960. See also W. Bingham *et al.,* **A History of Asia,** 2 vols., Allyn and Bacon, 1964–1965; and D. Lach and C. Flaumenhoft, eds., **Asia on the Eve of Europe's Expansion,*** Prentice-Hall (documentary readings).

M. Biardeau, **India,** Viking, 1960. A well-illustrated introduction. V. Smith, **Akbar the Great Mogol,** Chand, 1958, is an important biography of Akbar. See also S. M. Ikram, **Muslim Civilization in India,** Columbia, 1964.

Dun J. Li, **The Ageless Chinese: A History,*** Scribner. A well-written full account. On Sino-European contacts see G. F. Hudson, **Europe and China,*** Beacon; and K. Panikkar, **Asia and Western Dominance, 1498–1945,** Allen & Unwin, 1959.

E. O. Reischauer, **Japan: The Story of a Nation,** Knopf, 1970. Lucid and authoritative. G. B. Sansom, **A History of Japan,** 3 vols. Stanford, 1958–1963, is a detailed account. See also G. B. Sansom, **The Western World and Japan,** Knopf, 1950.

Excellent general surveys on Southeast Asia are D. G. E. Hall, **A History of South-East Asia,** 2nd ed., St. Martin's, 1964; J. F. Cady, **Southeast Asia: Its Historical Development,** McGraw-Hill, 1964; B. Harrison, **Southeast Asia,** St. Martin's, 1954.

Basil Davidson, **Africa: History of a Continent,** Macmillan, 1966. A superbly illustrated survey. R. Oliver and J. D. Fage, **A Short History of Africa,*** Penguin, is the best introductory general history. R. Oliver, ed., **The Dawn of African History,*** Oxford, covers the Middle Age of African history. For additional facets of African history see D. P. Mannix and M. Cowley, **Black Cargoes,** Viking, 1962; R. Hallett, **The Penetration of Africa,** Routledge & Kegan Paul, 1965; R. and C. Oliver, eds., **Africa in the Days of Exploration,** Prentice-Hall, 1965 (documentary readings); J. S. Trimingham, **A History of Islam in West Africa,** Oxford, 1962; G. Hamilton, **In the Wake of Da Gama,** Skeffington, 1965. E. Elisofan and W. Fagg, **The Sculpture of Africa,** Praeger, 1958, contains some 300 photos of the masterpieces of African art. See also P. Wingert, **The Sculpture of Negro Africa,** Columbia, 1950.

J. D. Page, ed., **Africa Discovers Her Past,*** Oxford. Essays evaluating the "new African history." For an analysis of *Négritude* consult Colin Legum, **Pan-Africanism,** Praeger, 1962. Basil Davidson, **The African Genius,** Little Brown, 1970 is a sympathetic and scholarly analysis of indigenous cultures.

S. G. Morley, **The Ancient Maya,** Stanford, 1956. The best general survey. V. W. von Hagen, **The World of the Maya,*** Mentor, is a rapid survey.

F. Peterson, **Ancient Mexico,*** Capricorn. A valuable survey. Brief, lucid surveys of Aztec civilization are V. W. von Hagen, **The Aztec,*** Mentor; and G. C. Vaillant, **The Aztecs of Mexico,*** Penguin. See also J. Soustelle, **Daily Life of the Aztecs on the Eve of the Spanish Conquest,*** Stanford.

J. A. Mason, **The Ancient Civilizations of Peru,*** Penguin. An anthropological history of the culture and peoples of pre-Columbian Peru. See also V. W. von Hagen, **Realm of the Incas,*** Mentor; and B. Flornoy, **The World of the Inca,*** Anchor.

* Indicates an inexpensive paperbound edition.

Chapter 17

Seek Out, Discover, and Find

**Exploration and Colonization (1450-1650);
the Commercial Revolution (1450-1750)**

INTRODUCTION. One of the most potent forces molding modern world history was the thrust of European political power, commerce, and culture over the globe. Before 1500 the people of Europe existed largely on their own resources, supplemented by a slender trade with Africa and Asia. But within the next 150 years the picture was dramatically altered through the discoveries of new continents and trade routes. The riches of the entire world were funneled into Europe's economy, and the horizons of Europe's people were immensely widened— socially and intellectually as well as geographically. The discovery of hitherto unknown and unsuspected parts of the globe was probably more revolutionary than the space explorations of our own day.

Who wrought this miracle? First, there were the sea captains—da Gama, who made the first ocean voyage from Europe to India; Columbus, who introduced Europe to a New World; and Magellan, whose expedition ventured ever westward until its weary survivors had sailed completely around the world and dropped anchor once more in their home port. Close on the heels of such captains came the *conquistadores*—the "conquerors"—resourceful and ruthless soldiers like Cortés and Pizarro, who laid the foundations for a vast European empire by overwhelming flourishing native cultures in the New World.

Then came the task of exploiting what had been found and won. The European powers took advantage of the claims of their discoverers and explorers in one of two basic ways—through trade or by colonization. In Africa and Asia the emphasis was on trade; Europeans carried on their business from forts, acting as foreign merchants rather than as settlers. While in Africa their dealings were mostly with tribal peoples, in the Far East they faced venerable civilizations and urban cultures. There, they were the barbarians, and when their activities proved offensive by native standards, reprisals could be swift and severe.

The story of European expansion in the New World, on the other hand, is largely that of colonization, of the transplanting of European civilization to a new and exotic environment. Politically, the territories in the Americas were treated as extensions of the mother countries. The Spanish colonies, for example, were ruled directly by the king of Spain; the colonial economy was geared to supplement that of the homeland; and the Spanish priests set out to bring the Indians into the spiritual fold with their Spanish masters. Similarly, the English and French who settled in North America brought with them the economic, political, and social institutions they had known at home.

For the native peoples of the New World, the arrival of the Europeans was cataclysmic. And the impact of the New World on the Old, while obviously quite different, was no less significant. As new stores of wealth were tapped by the immensely lucrative transatlantic trade, Europe's economic center of gravity shifted from the Mediterranean to the Atlantic seaboard; and the rapid influx of gold and silver made possible an unprecedented expansion of the economy. Nor was the revolution confined to economics: new medicines, foods, and beverages became available to Europeans, and even styles of dress were altered. Thus a handful of adventurers, ranging beyond the horizon in quest of El Dorado, the legendary city of gold which symbolized their hopes and dreams, set in motion a train of events which brought significant changes to European society and which ultimately influenced the very history of civilization.

CAPTAINS AND CONQUISTADORES

Medieval maps and adventurers. Early medieval maps were curiosities rather than documents of fact. They included lands which no man had ever seen; the oceans were shown abounding in sea dragons, while drawings of elephants and more fanciful animals were used to fill up empty land spaces, thereby adding to the picturesqueness of the map as well as conveniently concealing the ignorance of the map maker. Arabic works on astronomy and geography, acquired in the thirteenth century, proved that the earth was a sphere and greatly expanded geographical knowledge. Of greatest significance for the development of scientific geography, however, was the recovery in 1409 of Claudius Ptolemy's *Geography* (see p. 87) with its elaborate map of the world. Although this second-century work added greatly to current knowledge, it contained a number of errors, two of which encouraged Columbus and other fifteenth-century explorers to sail boldly across the uncharted oceans. Ptolemy exaggerated the size of the known continents so that the distance between western Europe and eastern Asia appeared much smaller than it really is, and he underestimated the circumference of the world by five thousand miles.

Medieval adventurers also contributed to geographical knowledge, much of which influenced Columbus and his fellow explorers. The earliest prime examples were the Norsemen, who reached Iceland in the last half of

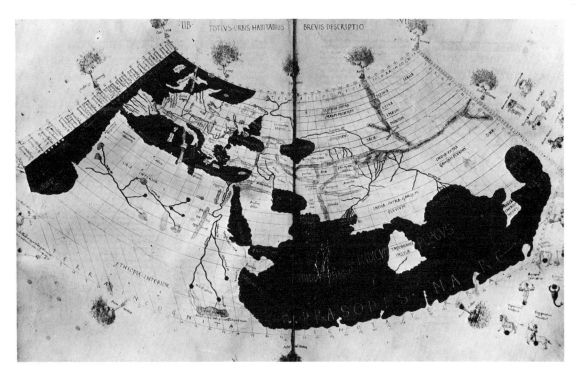

This map, published in the fifteenth century but based on one designed by Ptolemy in the second century, represents the first attempt to project the curved surface of the earth on a flat surface. The outline of the European continent (upper left) is fairly accurate.

the ninth century (see p. 195). In about 982 Eric the Red, son of a Norwegian noble, was banished from the Norse settlements in Iceland and sailed west to Greenland, which may have been discovered earlier in the century by Celtic refugees from Ireland, fleeing Viking raids on their homeland. Eric founded two settlements on the western coast of Greenland, which existed until about 1500 when they mysteriously vanished. It now appears that the first European to set foot on the North American coast was Bjarni Herjolfson. In 985 Bjarni was blown off course while sailing from Iceland to Greenland and made a landfall in Newfoundland. About fifteen years later Leif, son of Eric the Red, retraced Bjarni's route and named the country *Vinland* (Wineland) because of its wooded, vine-covered shore. A number of other voyages were made to Vinland, whose lumber was highly prized in treeless Greenland. Apparently no permanent settlement was made in Vinland, although archaeologists have recently discovered what appears to be the remains of a Viking camp in New-

foundland at L'Anse au Meadow.[1] But monumental as these voyages were, their implication were lost on contemporary Europeans, and they added little or nothing to European knowledge of geography.

In the thirteenth and fourteenth centuries a number of Europeans, many of them Christian missionaries, journeyed overland to the Far East. The most famous of these travelers was Marco Polo (see p. 180). But these exploits had little permanent effect because of political changes in Asia in the last decades of the fourteenth century. The Mongol dynasty in China, which had been friendly to European missionaries and merchants, was overthrown, and the succeeding Ming rulers proved anti-Christian. Meanwhile, the belligerent heathen Turks stood astride the eastern Mediterranean. These two developments put an end to further European penetration into the Orient, although trade continued at certain terminals controlled by the Muslims.

The search for new routes. The three major routes by which trade flowed from the

Far East to Europe had existed since Roman times (see map, p. 116). The northern one cut across Central Asia and the Caspian and Black seas to Constantinople (Byzantium); the middle route went by sea along the coasts of India and Persia through the Persian Gulf and the Euphrates valley to Antioch; and the southern route utilized the monsoon winds to strike across the Indian Ocean and up the Red Sea to Alexandria in Egypt. During the fifteenth century the commerce that flowed westward to Europe was rich indeed, even though the expansion of the Turks greatly reduced the importance of the northern route across Asia. The most important imports into Europe were spices—pepper, cinnamon, nutmeg, ginger, and cloves—highly valued as condiments and preservatives for food. Also in great demand were Chinese silk, Indian cotton cloth, and various precious stones.

The Mediterranean carrying trade in oriental goods was in the hands of Venice and other Italian city-states, which wielded an extensive and lucrative monopoly. Since the Arabs held a similar monopoly east of the Mediterranean, oriental goods were sold in the West at many times their price in India. As the demand for the products of the East increased during the latter half of the fifteenth century, the rulers of the new nations of western Europe became aware that an adverse balance of trade was draining their coined money away to Italy and the East. They determined to find new trade routes of their own, and, as rulers of powerful nation-states, they had the resources to support the stupendous feats of discovery and conquest that were needed.

Prince Henry the Navigator. It was the Portuguese who spearheaded the drive to find oceanic routes that would provide cheaper and easier access to oriental products. The man who set in motion the brilliant Portuguese achievements in exploration and discovery was Prince Henry the Navigator (1394-1460), whose goal was the circumnavigation of Africa. For more than forty years Henry sent forth expedition after expedition to unravel the secrets of the African coastline.

Henry employed skilled cartographers and navigators to construct accurate maps, and under his direction the caravel, the finest vessel afloat for long voyages, was developed. By utilizing the lateen rig, the triangular sail developed by the Arabs, the caravel revolutionized sailing by being able to tack into the wind. Augmenting Henry's innovations were other navigation aids. In the twelfth century the Europeans set their course with the aid of a magnetic needle floating on a straw in a bowl of water. By the time Henry's sailors were setting sail, the compass consisted of a needle which pivoted on a card showing the points of the compass. During the fifteenth century another great aid to navigation came into general use— the astrolabe, a graduated brass circle by which the altitude of stars could be estimated and latitudes more accurately measured.

The African voyages. Although Henry died before any of the numerous expeditions he sent forth had explored the entire length of Africa, his mariners did not fail him. In 1488 Bartholomew Diaz rounded the southern tip of Africa, from which point he noticed that the coast swung northeast. But his disgruntled crew forced him to turn back. Pleased with the prospect of soon finding a direct sea route to India, King John II of Portugal named the great cape rounded by Diaz "Cape of Good Hope."

Vasco da Gama commanded the first Portuguese fleet to reach India. Three ships left Lisbon in 1497 and, after rounding the Cape, crossed the Indian Ocean to Calicut in twenty-three days. The Arab merchants in Calicut sought to preserve their trading monopoly by delaying the return voyage, and it was not until 1499 that da Gama dropped anchor in Lisbon. He had lost two of his ships and one third of his men through scurvy and other misfortunes, but his one cargo of pepper and cinnamon was worth sixty times the cost of the expedition.

Lured by such fantastic profits another expedition set sail the following year and established a permanent base south of Calicut at Cochin. The Portuguese soon acquired a monopoly over trade in the Indian Ocean, and by 1516 their ships had reached Canton in China. The king of Portugal assumed the impressive title "Lord of the Conquest,

VOYAGES OF DISCOVERY

NORTH

AMERICA

Cabot

EUROPE

A S I A

ATLANTIC

CANARY IS.

Columbus

CHINA

JAPAN

PACIFIC

INDIA

OCEAN

Magellan

WEST INDIES

CAPE VERDE IS.

OCEAN

P A C I F I C

PANAMA

AFRICA

Dias

da Gama

ST. LAZARD
(PHILIPPINES)

SUMATRA

BORNEO

SOUTH

AMERICA

O C E A N

ZANZIBAR

I N D I A N

da Gama

MADAGASCAR

OCEAN

O C E A N

Cape of Good Hope

Magellan's Crew

Magellan

TO SPAIN

Str. of Magellan

TO PORTUGAL

Treaty of Tordesillas – 1494   →| Pope's Line of Demarcation – 1493   Treaty of Saragossa – 1529

Navigation, and Commerce of Ethiopia, Arabia, Persia, and China.''

Columbus discovers the New World. Meanwhile, Spanish ambitions for riches and prestige were realized through the exploits of a Genoese sailor named Christopher Columbus (1451?-1506). Influenced by Marco Polo's overestimate of the length of Asia and Ptolemy's underestimate of the size of the world, Columbus believed that Japan was less than 3000 miles from Europe (the actual distance is 10,600 nautical miles) and that it could be reached in one or two months by sailing westward. He tried unsuccessfully to interest the rulers of Portugal, England, and France in his enterprise before Queen Isabella of Castile agreed to sponsor his voyage. On August 3, 1492, Columbus set sail from Spain with three small ships and ninety men. On October 12 he landed on a small island in the West Indies. After he returned to Spain, Columbus announced that he had found the route to Asia, and the Spanish monarchs proclaimed him ''Admiral of the

Ocean Sea, Viceroy and Governor of the Islands that he has discovered in the Indies.''

Even after da Gama's voyage had opened up the eastward route to India, Columbus steadfastly refused to acknowledge that what he himself had discovered was in fact a massive obstacle on the route to the Far East. Although he made three more voyages to the New World in a vain attempt to find a direct opening to the Asian mainland, Columbus had already changed the course of history, though he did not know it. A New World had been revealed; old geographical views had been shattered; and the entire history of Europe was soon to be affected by the discovery of the new lands.

Spain and Portugal divide the new lands. An immediate repercussion of Columbus' first voyage was the destruction of Portugal's monopoly over discovery. Some sort of compromise had to be worked out between the two countries, and the Spanish monarchs invited the pope to define the pagan areas which Spain and Portugal might claim. In

1493 the pope issued the Bull of Demarcation, which drew a line from north to south running one hundred leagues west of the Azores and proclaimed that all heathen lands west of this line as far as the Indies were reserved for Spain. The Portuguese protested, claiming that this arrangement would confine their operations too closely to the African coast. By the Treaty of Tordesillas (1494) Spain agreed to have the line moved farther west. This new demarcation later enabled Portugal to claim Brazil after Pedro Cabral's sighting of South America in 1500 while sailing to the Indies. In 1529 another treaty fixed a similar demarcation line in the Eastern Hemisphere.

Balboa and Magellan. The search for riches drove the Spaniards to organize many expeditions to chart the coastlines and to penetrate the interior of the New World. One such enterprise was particularly successful. Having heard from Indians of a vast ocean only a short distance to the west, Vasco de Balboa led a band of 190 Spaniards across the Isthmus of Panama. On September 25, 1513, Balboa climbed to the summit of a hill from

The Spanish troops, aided by Indian allies, storm the main gate of Tenochtitlán in this illustration from a sixteenth-century Aztec manuscript.

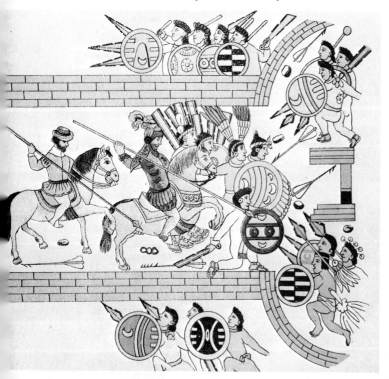

which he beheld the Pacific Ocean—and in that act paved the way for European exploration of the largest single portion of the world's surface.

Ferdinand Magellan, a Portuguese navigator in the service of Spain, found a sea route into the Pacific. Encouraged by Balboa's discovery of the short distance between the two oceans, Magellan believed it was possible to sail around South America just as Diaz had rounded Africa. In August 1520 Magellan made his memorable discovery of the strait which bears his name. His five small ships made their way between huge ice-clad mountains and through tortuous passages. After a terrifying thirty-eight days they sailed out upon the western ocean, which looked so calm after the stormy straits that Magellan termed it "Pacific." Then followed a harrowing ninety-nine day voyage across the Pacific to Guam, during which rats had to be eaten for food. Magellan was slain by natives in the Philippine Islands, and only one of his ships returned to Spain in 1522 by way of India and the Cape of Good Hope. Its cargo of spices paid for the cost of the entire expedition. Magellan's tiny vessel had taken three years to circumnavigate the world, but henceforth no one could doubt that the earth was round and that the Americas constituted a New World.

Cortes conquers Mexico. While the Portuguese soon profited from their hold on the rich oriental trade, the Spaniards found that the islands and coasts of the New World did not immediately produce the harvest of riches which they had eagerly sought. Such wealth was not to be found along the seashore but in the unknown hinterland, where rich indigenous cultures flourished. Penetration of inland areas was the work of the *conquistadores*, the courageous but independent-minded and often brutal conquerors who looted whole native empires and planted the Spanish flag from California to the tip of South America.

In the same year that Magellan set forth (1519), the Spanish governor of Cuba dispatched Hernando Cortés on an expedition to Mexico, from which had come rumors of a great Aztec empire, flowing with gold. Montezuma, ruler of the Aztecs, had thousands of warriors, while Cortés had about six hundred men. But the Spaniards were equipped with horses, armor, and gunpowder, all unknown to the Aztecs. Two other factors aided the Europeans: the discontent of many subject tribes, which looked for a chance to break the Aztec rule; and an ancient Mexican legend which prophesied that the Aztecs would one day be conquered by the white-skinned descendants of an ancient god-king who had been repudiated by their ancestors.

Having made the fateful decision to march inland on the Aztec capital, Tenochtitlán, Cortés destroyed his ships to prevent his men from turning back. Crossing the coast lands and the mountains, the Spaniards entered the valley of Mexico. Cortés treacherously made a virtual prisoner of Montezuma and through his cooperation ruled peacefully until a popular uprising gave the Spaniards an excuse to plunder and destroy the capital. Yet Cortés was more than a plunderer; he built a new City of Mexico on the site of Montezuma's capital and demonstrated administrative skills in adapting the former Aztec confederacy to Spanish rule.

Pizarro in Peru. The conquest of the Incas in Peru was carried out with less skill and more enduring ill effects than Cortés' exploit in Mexico. Obsessed by tales of a rich and mighty empire in South America, a tough, illiterate peasant's son named Francisco Pizarro determined to explore and conquer it. In 1531 Pizarro sailed from Panama with 180 men and 27 horses. Landing on the Peruvian coast, the small band made its way across the barren mountains into the interior, where they seized the Incan monarch Atahualpa.

Attempting to buy his freedom by paying a huge ransom, Atahualpa offered to have a room measuring seventeen by twelve feet filled to a height of some seven feet with plates and vessels of gold and to have it filled twice over with silver. Despite this magnificent ransom, the Spaniards did not release the emperor but instead sentenced him on trumped-up charges to be burned to death. In the end, because Atahualpa accepted Christian baptism, he was merely strangled. The imprisonment and death of its ruler

rendered the highly centralized Incan government incapable of effective, organized resistance; and Pizarro soon captured the capital.

Within a decade civil war broke out among the conquerors, and Pizarro was murdered. When the Spanish royal government sought to protect the oppressed Indians from their colonial masters, Gonzalo Pizarro, a brother of Francisco, set up a government independent of Spain. But Madrid dispatched officials and soldiers to arrest the unruly *conquistadores* and to pacify the area so that silver could be mined for Spain and conversion of the natives to Christianity could proceed. Not until near the end of the sixteenth century was Spanish authority securely established over Peru. In time Spanish dominions in South America formed a huge, uninterrupted semicircle, while the Portuguese took possession of the vast hinterland of Brazil (see Reference Map 6).

Spanish penetration into North America. Using Mexico and the West Indies as bases, the Spanish explorers searched what is now the southern part of the United States for the treasures which rumors planted there. That the expeditions failed to find gold or other riches does not detract from the tremendous progress they made in opening up new and potentially wealthy areas. Not only mythical treasure but an equally mythical Fountain of Youth attracted Spanish *conquistadores*. In 1521 Juan Ponce de León lost his life trying to find the Fountain of Youth in Florida.

Eighteen years later Hernando de Soto, whose participation in the conquest of Peru had gained him a fortune, landed in Florida with a company of some six hundred adventurers. His search for treasure took him through the southern United States, and De Soto was possibly the first white man to sight the Mississippi River. He died without finding any treasure, and his followers buried him in the Mississippi.

Marvelous tales had persisted of a fabled land north of Mexico containing seven cities with golden towers, and in 1540 Francisco de Coronado set out from Mexico with a large band to find them. But the fabled cities turned out to be only adobe pueblos. In his vain search Coronado appears to have penetrated as far as Kansas, becoming the first European to behold the vast herds of buffalo roaming the American plains. The adventurer returned embittered by failure, and the Spanish authorities concluded that there was little to be gained in occupying the area north of the silver mines of Mexico.

English search for the Northwest Passage. The division of the overseas world between Spain and Portugal, as set forth by the Bull of Demarcation and the Treaty of Tordesillas, aroused little enthusiasm among other European powers, and it was not long before France, England, and Holland encroached on the private preserves of both Portugal and Spain.

In 1497—the same year in which da Gama embarked for India—John Cabot, an Italian mariner financed by the merchants of Bristol in England, sailed across the North Atlantic in a small ship manned by only eighteen men. After a turbulent six weeks' voyage, the expedition dropped anchor off the northern coast of the New World. When Cabot returned to England, Henry VII rewarded him with £10, the title of Grand Admiral, and the

Drawn by Sir Humphrey Gilbert in 1582, this polar map shows a clear northwest route to the East. The belief in the existence of such a route helped stimulate the exploration of North America.

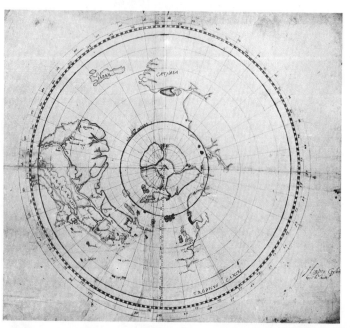

right to make another voyage. Cabot made his second voyage in 1498, coasting along the eastern shore of America in a vain attempt to find a passage to the Orient.

Cabot was the first European after the hardy Norse sailors to land on the mainland of North America; and, what was most important, his discovery laid the foundation for England's claim to the whole rich continent. Thus for £10 and a title England eventually acquired all of Canada and the territory along the Atlantic coast which constituted the thirteen American colonies—certainly an excellent business transaction.

For the next hundred years English seamen tried in vain to reach China through the illusive Northwest Passage, a sea route believed to exist north of Canada. Although similar expeditions trying to reach China by way of the Northeast Passage above Russia also failed, one of them reached Archangel and was granted trading privileges by Tsar Ivan the Terrible (see p. 279).

French explorations of inland America. France also joined in the search for the Northwest Passage. In 1523 Francis I commissioned the Florentine mariner Giovanni da Verrazzano to investigate the coast from North Carolina to Newfoundland. Eleven years later Jacques Cartier was sent on the first of two voyages that explored the St. Lawrence River as far as the present city of Montreal. These expeditions gave France its claim to sovereignty over eastern North America, a claim which duplicated England's.

Not until after its Wars of Religion did France resume its activities in the St. Lawrence region. Sponsored by the energetic first Bourbon ruler, Henry IV, Samuel de Champlain not only founded the first successful French overseas colony at Quebec (1608) but also journeyed over the lake which bears his name and westward to the Great Lakes. In 1673 Louis Joliet, a fur trader, and Father Marquette, a Jesuit missionary, reached the Mississippi River and followed it as far south as Arkansas in the hope of finding a short route to the Pacific. Nine years later René de La Salle explored the Mississippi to its mouth, taking possession of the entire territory and naming it *Louisiana* in honor of Louis XIV.

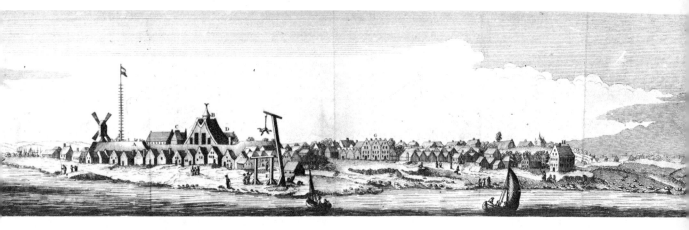

Pictured above is New Amsterdam (New York) as it appeared around 1640. In the center foreground are the gallows, to the right the West India Company stores (G), and to the left the governor's house (D), a church (B), the jail (C), and the fort (A).

The Dutch in America. Dutch interest in the New World coincided with the rise of the United Provinces (Holland) to a position of political independence and great economic strength during the first half of the seventeenth century. Dutch ambitions to find a shorter route to the Far East caused them to hire the English explorer Henry Hudson, who in 1609 sailed up the river that now bears his name. In 1621 the Dutch West India Company was founded for the purpose of trading in western Africa and the Americas. As part of its work, the company founded New Amsterdam on Manhattan Island in 1624 and permanently colonized Guiana, Curaçao, and Aruba in the Caribbean area.

EUROPE INVADES THE EAST

Portugal's eastern empire. Before the exciting era of exploration began to wane, the Europeans were faced with the problem of exploiting their newly found territories. In virtually every case, the natives suffered. Only in a few instances, notably in the Far East, were the indigenous people able to enforce their own policies. In most extreme contrast was Africa, where millions of natives were enslaved.

To ensure their toehold in Africa, the Por-

tuguese built fortified posts along the coast, began to develop a colony in Angola, and settled traders on the island of Zanzibar. Early in the sixteenth century Afonso de Albuquerque, the greatest of all Portuguese viceroys (1509-1515), resolved to consolidate his country's position in Africa and in the East. As a realist, he saw that Portugal could wrest commercial supremacy from the Arabs only by force, and he therefore devised a plan to establish forts at strategic sites which would dominate the trade routes and also protect Portuguese interests on land. The western end of the Arab trade routes was partially sealed off: Ormuz at the mouth of the Persian Gulf (see Reference Map 6) was captured, but the attempt to close the entrance to the Red Sea at Aden was only temporarily successful. To obtain a major base for a permanent fleet in the Indian Ocean, Albuquerque in 1510 seized Goa on the coast of India, which the Portuguese held until 1961. From Goa the Portuguese dominated the Indian ports that had supplied the Arab traders.

Albuquerque next set about securing control of the trade with the East Indies and China. His first objective was Malacca, which controlled the narrow strait through which most Far Eastern trade moved. Captured in 1511, Malacca became the springboard for further eastward penetration. The first Portuguese ship reached Canton on the south coast of China in 1516, but it was not until 1557 that the Portuguese gained a permanent base in China at Macao, which they still hold. About 1516, also, the first trading post was established in the rich Moluccas, or Spice Islands, source of the finest spices.

Thus Portugal, through its control of most of the traffic between India and Europe as well as the trade between India and the Far East, developed the first European commercial empire. Portugal's greatest poet, Luis de Camoëns, in 1572 celebrated his compatriots' overseas achievements in a memorable epic poem, *The Lusiads* ("The Portuguese"):

In golden treasures rich, distant Cathay,
And all the farthest Islands of the East,
And all the seas, to them shall homage pay.[2]

An already lucrative trade was vastly augmented when the Portuguese began to export slaves from Africa in 1541. Envying the rich profits, other nations—England, Holland, France, and Sweden—began to send in rival expeditions, and Portugal was forced on the defensive. In 1642 the Dutch drove the Portuguese out of the Gold Coast, and this rich trade and slaving area was left to other Europeans, especially the Dutch and English.

Dutch inroads in the East. Portugal's star was destined to set for many reasons, not the least of which was attacks on their commercial empire launched by the Dutch and the English—the beginning of a world-wide struggle over empire that lasted until 1763. Two events facilitated Dutch encroachment on the Portuguese monopoly of oriental trade. One was the Netherlands revolt against Spanish rule, and the other was the Spanish acquisition of Portugal. The Dutch looked on Spain's trade and colonies as fair game, and when the two crowns of the Iberian peninsula were joined in 1581, they felt free to attack Portuguese territory in eastern waters. Furthermore, the Dutch had previously enjoyed a rich trade carrying oriental goods from Lisbon to the ports of northern Europe; this traffic ceased when Spain took control of Portuguese ports. If Dutch trade was to survive, the Hollanders had to capture its source in the East.

In the 1590's a number of Dutch companies were formed to finance trading expeditions to the Far East. Because competition lowered their profits, in 1602 the companies amalgamated into the Dutch East India Company which received from the government the right to trade and rule in the area stretching from the Cape of Good Hope eastward to the Strait of Magellan. It was the Dutch East India Company that broke the power of the Portuguese in the islands of the Malay archipelago.

The governor-general of the East Indies who was appointed in 1618, Jan Pieterszoon Coen, laid the foundations for the Dutch empire in the East Indies. Whereas Albuquerque had felt that it was sufficient to occupy strategic points along the sea routes, Coen believed that the Dutch had to control the actual areas of production as well. He built a fortified trading station at Batavia on Java, a site which eventually became the capital of the Dutch East Indies, including Sumatra and the Moluccas. Dutch monopoly of the spice trade became complete after they drove the Portuguese from Malacca (1641) and Ceylon (1658), the latter the main source of cinnamon. In 1652 the Dutch established a colony at Cape Town on the southern tip of Africa as a port of call on the long journey to the Far East.

The English gain a foothold in India. The English meanwhile were staking out claims in India at the expense of the Portuguese. In 1600 Queen Elizabeth incorporated the English East India Company, granting it a monopoly of trade from the Cape of Good Hope eastward to the Strait of Magellan. By 1622 the company had put the Portuguese posts on the Persian Gulf out of business, and in 1639 it acquired Madras on the east coast of India. Through political stratagems, bribes, diplomacy, and exploitation of weak native rulers, the company prospered in India, where it became the most powerful political force in the subcontinent.

Europeans unwelcome in China. When the Portuguese first arrived in Canton in 1516, they were given the same privileges that Arab merchants had enjoyed for centuries. In response, the Portuguese behaved very badly, scorning the customs of the sophisticated inhabitants, and treating the "heathen" with arrogance and cruelty.

However, because trade was mutually profitable to both Chinese and foreign merchants, in 1557 the Portuguese were granted the right to trade at Macao. There, under close surveillance and subject to many strict regulations, the "ocean devils" conducted business. Stemming from this period is the mutual suspicion and hostility which characterized Sino-European relations in the nineteenth and early twentieth centuries.

A somewhat friendlier contact occurred when Jesuit missionaries arrived in China during the second half of the sixteenth century. They converted many important persons at the imperial court and in the provinces, thereby gaining protection for Christians generally.

Japan rejects European contacts. About 1542 three Portuguese ships from Macao were driven far off their course and landed at one of the southern Japanese islands. Before long, others visited the islands and began trading. Hearing about Japan after he had sailed from Lisbon for the Far East, St. Francis Xavier went there and started to convert the inhabitants. After Xavier's death, his work was carried on by other Jesuit missionaries. Within thirty years Japanese converts to Christianity numbered about 150,000.

Suspicion on the part of the Japanese rulers that Christianity was merely a cloak for political usurpation was reinforced by the bigotry of many Christians and by economic exploitation on the part of various unscrupulous Portuguese merchants. As we have seen (p. 348), the Japanese began persecuting the

Portuguese ships are shown anchored at the port of Macao on the Chinese coast in this sixteenth-century engraving.

AMACAO.

Jesuits and their converts, and in 1638 Japan cut itself off from the outside world:

> For the future, let none, so long as the Sun illuminates the world, presume to sail to Japan, not even in the quality of ambassadors, and this declaration is never to be revoked on pain of death.[3]

Except for a small, closely watched Dutch post at Nagasaki, the islands were closed to western contact until 1853.

The Philippines. In the Far East, Spanish energies were concentrated primarily on the Philippine Islands. After 1565, cargoes of Chinese goods were transported from the Philippines to Mexico and from there to Spain. By this complicated route, Spain enjoyed some of the oriental commerce about which Columbus had dreamed. Spanish officials and missionaries brought Christianity and a degree of European civilization to the islands, which were henceforth a corner of the Far East fundamentally oriented toward the West, in contrast to Japan and China.

Renewal of the East-West contact. The remarkable series of geographical discoveries beginning in the fifteenth century which carried intrepid European explorers, soldiers, traders, and missionaries to the ends of the earth recalls a similar movement in the second and third centuries A.D. when rich contacts in commerce and culture existed among three intercommunicating empires— the Graeco-Roman, the Indian, and the Chinese. But the decline of Rome and other factors (discussed in Chapter 4) weakened and ultimately destroyed the lines of contact. For nearly a thousand years there was little exchange or communication between East and West.

Until the fifteenth century civilizations in the Near East, India, and China had been fully as advanced as those in Europe; and in some eras and in some aspects of culture they had surpassed the West. In the late Middle Ages, however, western Europe began to experience an astonishing resurgence —a "rebirth" which was reflected in the rise of powerful and well-administered nation-states, the increase of wealth and trade, the growing importance of the bourgeoisie, and the intellectual and artistic achievements of humanist scholars and artists. In contrast to the energetic West, the empires of India and China (as we saw in Chapter 16) were less dynamic both culturally and politically. And in Japan, isolation was the keynote of the Tokugawa shogunate—a regime no longer dynamic. Therefore, when the contact between East and West was renewed in the fifteenth century, it was not a meeting of equals. The discrepancies in effective political organizations, in disciplined armies, in energy and ambition prevented the resumption of East-West contacts on the same equal footing as had prevailed a thousand years earlier.

Europe's dominance begins. The same imbalance was readily apparent in both Africa and the Americas. In the Western Hemisphere promising civilizations among the Incas, the Aztecs, and the Mayas were no match for armed invaders. African potentialities had been restricted by isolation and harsh environmental forces, so that the natives fell an easy prey to the Europeans. Progress in sub-Saharan Africa was probably cut short by the effects of the slave trade.

The natural result of the impact of the strong upon the weak was that Europe took advantage of the other continents; the wider world became the servant of the West. The expansion of Europe and its mastery of much of the world is generally referred to as imperialism. Many of the conflicts and tensions in modern world politics find their source to a large degree in the imperial systems created by the West.

VICEROYS AND COLONISTS IN THE NEW WORLD

Spain consolidates its empire in the Americas. The *conquistadores* who carved out a mighty Spanish empire in the New World had been allowed to embark on their expeditions only after having secured royal permission. The crown's ultimate purpose was to replace these brilliant but erratic men of action with staid but reliable civil servants who would consolidate the territorial gains into a centralized colonial regime.

In theory, all overseas dominions were the personal property of the king, who made the major administrative decisions aided by one of his advisory councils, the Council of the Indies. Holding almost unrestricted power during the reigns of weak monarchs, the Council of the Indies formulated legislation, appointed colonial officials, and heard important colonial law cases. Before the end of the sixteenth century Spain possessed an American empire twenty times its own size, comprising in 1574 some 200 towns and about 160,000 Spanish settlers. For most of the colonial period the Spanish empire in the Americas was divided into two kingdoms: New Spain, which was made up of the West Indies, Venezuela, and the lands north of the Isthmus of Panama; and Peru, which consisted of all Spanish territory south of those lands.

Each kingdom had a viceroy who lived in splendor in Mexico City or Lima. Although the viceroys were the kings' representatives in America, they enjoyed only the appearance of great power. The Council of the Indies kept a tight rein on imperial affairs, judging the viceroys chiefly by their effectiveness in sending back treasure to Madrid. Under orders from the Spanish crown, the colonial regimes sharply restricted self-government. In the ten largest cities of the empire lawyers sent from Spain were in charge of courts called *audiencias*, which not only heard appeals against the decisions of viceroys and governors but also advised them in administrative matters. The crown levied head taxes, customs on imports, and excise charges on goods exchanged within the colonies, as well as demanding one fifth of all the gold and silver mined. The colonists were left no voice in the taxation. Membership in town councils was the only regular political outlet for the Spanish settlers, and there only the richest could participate. The Spaniards born in the Americas (Creoles) were regarded as potential rebels against the mother country, as indeed they proved to be in the nineteenth century.

For three centuries Spain was a potent agent in transmitting European culture and institutions to the New World. Its most important contributions were its language and literature. Also of lasting significance was the establishment of schools of higher learning. In 1551, eighty-five years before the founding of Harvard College, the first two universities in the New World—one at Lima, the other at Mexico City—were established. By the end of the seventeenth century no less than seven universities had been founded in Spanish America.

Mercantilism guides economic life. The economic theory current in the nation-states of Europe during this period was mercantilism, a doctrine which stressed the need of governmental intervention to increase the wealth and power of the state. Mercantilism had ramifications for the colonies as well as for the mother country. It postulated that a nation should be as economically self-sufficient as possible and that the colonies should be exploited for the gain of the ruling country. Each European nation wanted to export more than it imported, and the colonies provided ready-made markets for the finished products of the homeland. Thus Spain sent wines and finished goods to the New World but forbade the colonists to produce goods that would compete with those produced in Spain.

Under the mercantile system a nation's wealth was measured by the amount of precious metal it had accumulated, and the New World was a source of fantastic riches for Spain. Transporting the silver and gold to Spain was a perilous business. Each spring two well-guarded fleets left Seville or Cádiz, one heading for Mexico and the other for Panama. Laden with silver from the Andes and Mexico, the convoys returned to Spain in the autumn at great risk. After a rendezvous at Havana the combined fleets ran the gantlet back to Spain. Pirates and buccaneers were ever ready to swoop down on stragglers, as were warships of rival powers. Yet most of the treasure usually reached Spain, where the crown received its royal fifth.

In return for exploiting the virgin wealth of the New World, the Spanish introduced new products and methods which revolutionized agriculture, the mainstay of the American economy. To obtain farms, settlers often banded together to found a town in exchange for a royal grant of land, which was apportioned among the citizens. On the large estates of the aristocrats and the clergy, the forced labor of Indians and, later, African slaves was employed in the cultivation of cotton, vanilla, indigo, cacao, and other crops for export. The Spanish brought with them wheat, barley, rye, and rice, as well as coffee, sugar cane, and a variety of fruits. The importation of cattle and other livestock not only drastically modified the native diet but also stimulated such valuable new industries as breeding animals and exporting their hides. Originally the Indians had been their own pack animals, for the New World lacked beasts of burden except for the llamas domesticated by the Incas. The *conquistadores* introduced horses and mules and further revolutionized transportation by the introduction of the wheel. Through these imports and many more, the cultural state of certain areas in the Americas was abruptly jerked from a Neolithic level to a position approaching that of the Old World.

Indian plight eased by the Church. The desire to extend Christianity among the heathen had been one of the avowed objectives of every *conquistador*, but it was generally overlooked in the mad scramble to acquire gold and silver, jewels and slaves. In the islands of the Caribbean the forced labor and even enslavement of the Indians on the plantations proved so injurious that most of them died off. They were replaced by African slaves, who were imported to the islands about 1503 and to the American mainland a few years later. From the middle of the sixteenth century to the middle of the eighteenth century, some three thousand African slaves were imported annually, eventually transforming the racial composition of the Caribbean islands.

The work of the Church in establishing missions and persuading the crown to enact safeguards enabled the natives to survive in other areas of Spanish America. Early in the sixteenth century some clerics began to upbraid the Spaniards for their cruelties in exploiting the labor of the Indians. The most famous of these reformers was a Dominican friar, Bartolomé de Las Casas (1474-1566),

who insisted that the Indians, as subjects of the Spanish king, enjoyed the same rights as the Spaniards. He obtained royal permission to establish missions and settlements where the Indians and Spaniards could live on civilized terms. Las Casas' efforts also led to the promulgation of the New Laws of the Indies, directed at the greed of the plantation owners. But the attempt to improve the lot of the Indians was a losing battle, since the reforms ran counter to the economic interests of the settlers.

In order both to convert and to protect the Indians, a number of religious orders established mission towns. There, a few friars shielded the natives from white exploitation and taught them Christianity along with European habits and skills. The missionaries followed Las Casas in believing that the Indians should be converted not by force but by patient persuasion, "as rain and snow falls from heaven, not impetuously, not violently, not suddenly like a heavy shower, but gradually, with suavity and gentleness, saturating the earth as it falls."[4]

Portuguese activity in South America. Already burdened by its sprawling African and Asian interests, Portugal managed to establish a local administration in Brazil by the middle of the sixteenth century. In the 1570's Brazil's surge forward began as great numbers of African slaves were imported to cultivate sugar. This forced immigration continued for almost three centuries. During this period the crown imposed a highly centralized control on Brazil through its own officials, and a mercantilist policy was pursued in economic affairs.

After the Spanish king acquired control over Portugal, the Dutch and English regarded Portuguese possessions as lawful prizes to be won from their Spanish enemies. The Dutch took over land north of the mouth of the Amazon and founded Dutch Guiana. Subsequently, the English and French gained control over other parts of Guiana.

French colonization of North America. In 1608, as we noted earlier in this chapter, the city of Quebec was founded by Samuel de Champlain. To exploit the infant colony, a joint-stock company headed by Cardinal Richelieu was formed about twenty years

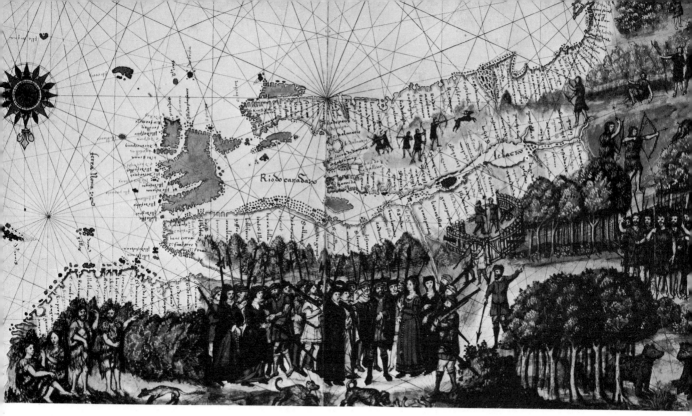

An early drawing shows the arrival of the first French colonists, brought by Cartier on his third voyage in 1541, against a map of the St. Lawrence estuary. The colony soon failed. The map is drawn so that north is at the bottom of the drawing rather than at the top.

later. In return for a perpetual monopoly on the fur trade and the title to certain lands, this company was supposed to bring several thousand settlers to Canada. But the company was unable to attract colonists. Stories of the severe Canadian winters frightened away most potential settlers; and the Huguenots, who would have been glad to escape religious restrictions, were not allowed to leave France.

By the middle of the seventeenth century New France had survived the initial, dangerous stages of an infancy marked by parental neglect. After La Salle in 1682 had explored the Mississippi River to its mouth, France also claimed the entire Mississippi valley. The French were at last firmly established in North America, ready to do battle with the English for the northern half of the continent and the Mississippi basin and prepared to resist any encroachment by the Spaniards from the Gulf of Mexico.

English colonies on the Atlantic seaboard. Like France, England was slow in following up the valuable work of its explorers. Cabot had given it the means of claiming an entire continent, yet it was not until the days of Queen Elizabeth that Englishmen began to interest themselves in the potentialities of the New World. The defeat of the Spanish Armada in 1588 and the building of a strong English navy ensured safer passage from the Old World to the New. Reports of the wealth garnered by the Spaniards whetted the appetites of Englishmen to look for El Dorado. More important, the economic difficulties accompanying the spread of the enclosure movement—the diverting of land from food growing to sheep raising—brought unemployment and with it the desire by many to try their luck overseas. Added to these factors was the religious question. Although the Spanish and French governments forbade nonconforming religious elements to move to the New World, the English government saw emigration as an excellent means of getting rid of dissident sects. For their part, these strong-willed, God-fearing people were eager to migrate to a new land where they could worship freely.

Actually, the first successful English settlement was founded by a joint-stock company, called the London Company, whose shareholders hoped for substantial profit. (They were told that the lands to be developed were so rich that pots and pans were made of solid gold.) The company's charter, issued by James I, permitted it to act as a miniature government, even to the extent of coining money, levying taxes, and annexing territory.

In 1607 the London Company landed its first colonists at Jamestown in Virginia. For a number of years the colonists suffered from lack of food and other privations, but they were tided over this initial period by the dauntless Captain John Smith, whose motto was "It is less perilous to go forward than to go backward," and whose romantic rescue by the beautiful Pocahontas is one of the legends most cherished by Americans. Recent scholarship suggests that this story, like other of Smith's improbable tales, may have a basis in fact.

The first example of the transplantation to the New World of English common law and representative government is found in the royal charter to the London Company:

All and every the Persons, being our Subjects, which shall dwell and inhabit within every and any of the said several Colonies and Plantations, and every of their children . . . shall have and enjoy all Liberties, Franchises and Immunities within any of our Dominions . . . as if they had been abiding and born within this our Realm of England.[5]

In 1619 the governor of the Jamestown colony called a representative assembly to assist in the tasks of government. This body, which later became the legislature of the state of Virginia, is one of the oldest representative assemblies in existence.

Another great landmark in American history was the landing of the Pilgrims at Plymouth in 1620, after James I had granted them permission. This momentous royal decision in effect opened English North America to settlement by religious dissenters. Ten years later another Puritan group,

organized as the Massachusetts Bay Company, settled around Boston. Both groups had secured royal charters which allowed them to be virtually self-governing.

Between 1629 and 1642, as a result of increased hostility toward religious dissenters in England, some 25,000 Puritans migrated to New England. This movement, called the Great Migration, had important consequences for the future. It brought to the New World a number of educated and responsible people whose courage and intellectual attainments greatly stimulated the process of colonization. By the middle of the seventeenth century the English language and law and the religious and cultural institutions of England had become firmly rooted in North American soil.

THE COMMERCIAL REVOLUTION

The transformation of Europe's economic life. In the period between 1450 and 1750 Europe underwent a great economic transformation which is associated with the rise of capitalism and the shift from the town to the territorial state as the center of the economy. The period is often termed the Commercial Revolution because commerce and the activities of merchants were central to the great economic progress of the age.

The nature of capitalism. Capitalism is commonly defined by economists as an economic system in which capital, or wealth, is put to work to produce more capital. A more comprehensive explanation would include other important factors—private ownership of property, the presence of large amounts of capital (money, land, raw materials, equipment), and the existence of specialized business techniques such as banking, credit, and insurance. But whatever the definition, the driving force behind capitalism is the securing of profits.

Four phases of capitalism. Much of the history of the five hundred years between the midpoint of the fifteenth century and the present day is concerned with the virtues and sins of capitalism, its defense and condemnation, and its development (as in the United States) or rejection (as in the Soviet Union). Its history can be traced in four distinct stages.

The first stage—commercial capitalism—is associated with geographical discoveries, colonization, and the astounding increase in overseas trade. These early capitalists, protected and encouraged by governmental controls, subsidies, and monopolies, made most of their profits from the buying and selling of goods.

Beginning about 1750, the second phase—industrial capitalism—was made possible by the accumulation of vast amounts of capital and its investment in machinery and the factory system of manufacturing. During the resulting Industrial Revolution the industrialist replaced the merchant as the dominant figure in the capitalistic system.

In the last decades of the nineteenth century, when the ultimate control and direction of large areas of industry came into the hands of financiers, industrial capitalism gave way to finance capitalism. The establishment of mammoth industrial empires and the ownership and management of their assets by men completely divorced from production were the dominant features of this third phase.

Since the great world depression of the 1930's, the state has played an increasingly dominant role in the capitalistic system, one well-known manifestation in the United States being the New Deal and its successor programs. This fourth phase is commonly known to economists as state capitalism and to its opponents by such terms as "creeping socialism."

Mercantilism. The body of economic theory and practice that accompanied commercial capitalism is called mercantilism. As previously noted (p. 377), mercantilism was a system of governmental regulation of economic matters in order to increase the wealth of the nation. In the words of Francis Bacon, its purpose was "the opening and well-balancing of trade; the cherishing of manufactures; the banishing of idleness; the repressing of waste and excess by sumptuary laws; the improvement and husbanding of the soil; the regulation of prices. . . ."[6] A similar program of stimulation and regimentation had characterized the economic life of medieval towns; now, under mercantilism, the new territorial state superseded the town and its guilds as the regulator of the economy.

Among the major tenets of mercantilism was bullionism, a doctrine which stressed the importance of accumulating precious metals. Mercantilists emphasized state power as the chief objective of economic policy, and "money," they liked to say, "is the sinews of war."

A second and corollary tenet of mercantilism was that a nation should maintain the most favorable balance of trade possible: it should export more than it imported so that foreign nations would have to pay the difference in precious metals. Only raw materials that could not be obtained at home were to be imported; after these materials had been manufactured into finished articles, they were then to be exported. Government subsidies, such as the granting of monopolies and the use of protective tariffs, encouraged the home production of manufactured goods.

Mercantilists believed that when raw materials were native, the profit to the home country was 100 percent. Therefore, if a country could not supply its own materials, it should acquire colonies from which they could be procured. Furthermore, colonies constituted not only sources of supply for raw materials but also markets for finished products. Because the mother country did not want competition for its infant industries, colonies were prevented from engaging in manufacturing. In addition, the colonies were prohibited from trading with foreign powers.

Mercantilism declined after 1750, when a new group of economic theorists challenged such basic mercantilist doctrines as the belief that the amount of the world's wealth remains constant and a nation can increase its wealth only at the expense of another. The more backward economic powers such as Russia and Prussia, however, still favored mercantilism long after other nations had turned to newer doctrines.

Decline of the early commercial centers. During the Middle Ages the central agency of European trade was the city-state. In northern Europe trade had been dominated by the confederacy of towns in the Baltic area known as the Hanseatic League. After the fifteenth century, however, the League rapidly declined, a victim of mercantile rivalry from the rising nation-states of Denmark, Sweden, and Russia. The absence of a strong central government in Germany left the League without adequate protection.

In southern Europe the merchants of the Italian city-states, with Venice in the lead, had for centuries acted as the great middlemen of Europe because they controlled the lucrative Asiatic trade. But the Portuguese smashed the Italian monopoly by discovering a new sea route to India and by obstructing the Red Sea and Persian Gulf routes that led to the Mediterranean ports. In addition, the Italian Wars of the sixteenth century had a disastrous effect upon the prosperity of the Italian city-states.

Portugal, temporarily paramount. With its limited population, Portugal could not permanently administer and protect an empire scattered over three continents. During the sixteenth century emigration, plague, and famine reduced the country's population from one and a half million to less than one, and the Portuguese were unable to man their ships and fortresses adequately. In 1580 Portugal came under the Spanish crown, and when it regained its independence in the following century, it retained only a few small possessions in the Far East, some islands in the mid-Atlantic, Brazil, and Mozambique and Angola in Africa. The economic power of Portugal ebbed away, not from lack of initiative so much as from lack of resources to support so great a task.

The economic decay of Spain. The decline of Spain's commercial might cannot be explained so simply. This nation apparently had everything—and failed. During the sixteenth century Spain had far more gold and silver than any of its rivals; and to this wealth was added that of Portugal and its possessions. Yet the wealth and power lavishly displayed during the reign of Philip II (1556-1598) were only surface deep. Farming was neglected, and industry was overburdened with governmental regulations. Religious

persecution and the expulsion of the Jews and Moors had deprived Spain of many of its skilled financiers and craftsmen. Since the Church and the upper classes were exempt from certain forms of taxation, the tax burden fell disproportionately on the classes engaged in trade, commerce, and industry.

An outward symbol of wealth, the rich flood of bullion from the Americas wreaked havoc in the Spanish economy by causing inflation. From 1500 to 1600 Spain experienced a fivefold rise of prices, a condition which attracted a stream of lower-priced products from Holland, France, and England, to the detriment of Spanish manufacturers. Spain's riches were drained off to purchase foreign manufactured goods—and even grain—and to pay the costs of Philip II's wars.

Antwerp's period of glory. As Spain and Portugal declined, the commercial center of Europe moved northward to Antwerp. To this great Flemish port came Europe's merchants and bankers. Antwerp was made a toll-free port, and the city fathers set up a merchants' exchange—the bourse—which, unlike the medieval fairs, operated continuously as an international commercial and financial center. It was said that Antwerp did as much business in one month as Venice in two years. Various institutions of modern capitalism evolved at Antwerp. Its bourse developed into the first stock exchange, trading in the shares of joint-stock companies. Life and property insurance came into use. But the spectacular prosperity of Antwerp was short-lived; in 1576, during the wars of the Netherlands against Spain, the city was sacked, and in 1585 the Dutch occupied the mouth of the Scheldt River and cut off the city's access to the sea. Henceforth Antwerp's trade and finances were largely appropriated by the Dutch city of Amsterdam.

Holland's golden age. During most of the seventeenth century Holland was the principal commercial, financial, and manufacturing country in Europe. Both the Dutch East India Company and the West India Company were markedly successful. The Dutch built better ships than their rivals and operated them more efficiently; their lower freight rates gained for them a monopoly on the carrying trade of Europe. The Dutch policy of religious toleration attracted artisans from abroad, and Holland became the leading industrial nation of Europe. Dutch exports included textiles, salted herring, glazed pottery, fine jewelry, and printed books. Trade, in turn, made Amsterdam the center of banking and credit.

Nevertheless, like Portugal, Holland was a comparatively small nation, and larger neighbors were presently to overtake it. Rivalry with England and France led to a series of wars during the latter half of the seventeenth century, and the Dutch lost much of their carrying trade to the English. Yet Dutch skill, together with the retention of the East Indies, enabled Holland to remain a significant factor in world commerce and finance.

France's rise and decline. With a population of about fifteen million in the seventeenth century, France was the premier nation of Europe. Its abundant economic resources were assiduously cultivated by Colbert (1619-1683), Louis xiv's astute minister of finance, who sponsored colonization, expanded colonial trade, and encouraged manufacturing. But although his aggressive mercantilist policies appeared to work well at first, the merits of his program were gradually offset by evils inherent in the system. Many industries, such as textiles, porcelains, and tapestries, were subsidized by the government, but the numerous official decrees controlling them became in the long run a handicap to economic development. Also, the court life at Versailles created a market for luxury goods limited to the upper classes, while the needs of the common people were ignored.

After the death of Colbert in 1683, his mercantilistic system began to develop creaks and strains. Lacking Colbert's guiding genius, his followers added all kinds of minute and irksome regulations. The system's weaknesses also became apparent when, in retaliation for Colbert's restrictions against foreign imports, other nations refused to purchase French farm products and wines. Furthermore, the big governmental monopolies were increasingly unpopular with businessmen, who demanded the removal of governmental regulations and of controls by the old medieval guilds.

In addition, it has been estimated that between 1685 and 1715 France lost a million subjects through warfare, the surrender of colonies, and the drain of emigration. The revocation of the Edict of Nantes in 1685 resulted in the flight from France of a large group of industrious Huguenots, who took their capital and skills as artisans to neighboring countries. And the rivalry between France and England during the Seven Years' War (see Chapter 19) culminated in French disaster. Thus France lost to England the commercial supremacy which it might have had.

Rise of England's sun. Although England was inferior to France in area, fertility of soil, and population, this island kingdom had many factors in its favor which more than compensated for its disadvantages. Geographical isolation discouraged military conquest from the Continent—the last successful invasion by a foreign power had taken place in 1066—and the English economy had not been burdened by the cost of maintaining large standing armies. After the union of England and Scotland in 1707, internal trade flourished in the largest customs-free area in western Europe. The aristocracy and middle class which controlled Parliament also controlled the principal trading and banking companies so that the growth of new enterprises was more peaceful and steady than anywhere else in Europe. The gradual control of the seas, the establishment of trading posts in exotic lands, and the shrewd policy of taking overseas territory as its booty from successful European wars enabled England to gain commercial benefits and to build the world's largest empire.

An important step in the rise of England's sun came in 1651 with the passage of the first Navigation Act forbidding the importation of goods into England or its dependencies except in English ships or in ships of the country producing the goods. The act was aimed at the Dutch carrying trade, and it provoked the first of three maritime wars with Holland noted previously. England soon outstripped Holland and by 1750 had laid the

The New World provided Europe with many valuable raw materials. From Potosi, in the Andes mountains, came enough silver to triple Europe's silver supply. A 1584 painting shows relays of llamas carrying ore down from the "mountain of silver" to the primitive Spanish refinery.

foundation for its economic domination of the world in the nineteenth century.

We shall see that England's textile industry was no small factor in accounting for its overall growth. Daniel Defoe, the author of *Robinson Crusoe*, maintained that the woolen industry in England was "the richest and most valuable manufacture in the world,"[7] of greater value to England than the rich mines of Peru and Mexico were to Spain.

More imports in Europe's markets. The discovery of sea routes to both Asia and the Americas provided an unparalleled impetus to the expansion of Europe and its commerce. The spice trade was especially profitable because there was no refrigeration for foods at this time, and slightly spoiled food could be made palatable by seasoning it with cloves, cinnamon, or pepper. Cloths from the East— calicoes, chintzes, and ginghams—became popular. The textile workers of England became so incensed at the foreign competition that they demanded a prohibition on the import of these inexpensive cotton fabrics, which they maintained were "made by a

parcel of heathens and pagans that worship the Devil and work for 1/2*d.* a day."[8] Among other imports from Asia were silks, carpets, and rugs, precious stones, porcelain, brassware, and the all-important beverages tea and coffee.

From the New World came a variety of products which revolutionized the eating and drinking habits of the Europeans. The food supply of Europe was greatly improved by the addition of potatoes, maize (Indian corn), and tomatoes. From the Caribbean came sugar, which soon became so popular that it supplanted honey. An abundant supply of fish, primarily cod, came from Newfoundland's Grand Banks; and warm furs were obtained by trappers penetrating the interior of North America. The sacred beverage of the Aztecs, cocoa, found its way to Spain and thence throughout Europe.

The use of one commodity—tobacco— spread rapidly among rich and poor alike. It was used mainly in the form of snuff or for smoking in pipes. The medicinal qualities of tobacco were strongly recommended; even schoolchildren were forced to smoke during the Great Plague in London. Seventeenth-century claims for tobacco were as extravagant as some we hear today:

Divine Tobacco! which gives Ease
To all our Pains and Miseries;
Composes Thought, makes Minds sedate,
Adds Gravity to Church and State . . .[9]

Gold and ivory came to Europe from Africa, but the most important African export enriched the European powers indirectly. This export was that most misery-ridden produce —slaves. To obtain slaves to labor in the mines and on the plantations of the New World, slavers sailed to the Guinea coast, where they bought or stole their human freight. "A woman slave might change hands for a gallon of brandy, six bars of iron, two small guns, one keg of powder, and two strings of beads; a man slave might cost eight guns, one wicker-covered bottle, two cases of spirits, and twenty-eight sheets."[10] The voyage across the Atlantic to America cost the lives of from 10 to 25 percent of the Africans—inhumanly packed as they were in evil-smelling, suffocating quarters below deck—but the remainder were profitably disposed of at their destination. One authority estimates that in three centuries some twenty million Africans were brought to the Americas.

The influx of precious metals. The gold and silver brought into the European market from the colonies in enormous quantities may have had a more direct effect on Europe's economy than any of the other products of Africa, Asia, or the Americas. By the middle of the fifteenth century Europe had been confronted with a severe shortage of gold and silver, caused both by the depletion of European mines and by increasing demands for currency to finance the new standing armies and navies and to pay for spices and other luxury commodities. But the critical situation was partially relieved by the development of new European mines, by imports of gold from West Africa, and, above all, by the unprecedented quantities of precious metals from the mines of Spanish America. The bonanza of bullion upset price levels throughout western Europe; between 1500 and 1650 commodity prices more than tripled. This price revolution affected all classes. Merchants were benefited, but laborers were harmed because wages lagged behind prices.

Banking becomes big business. One indicator of the resurgence of commerce was the growth of banking and related business practices. The word *bank* derives from the Italian *banca*, meaning "bench," on which medieval Italian moneylenders sat in the marketplace to carry on their business. When a man failed, the people broke his bench, and from this custom came the word *bankrupt*, or "broken bench." During the late Middle Ages moneylending became indispensable to the administration of both national monarchies and the Church so that the traditional prohibition on usury was often ignored.

Large-scale banking was first developed in Italian cities, where merchant bankers arranged bills of exchange and negotiated loans. By 1350 some eighty banking houses were in business in Florence alone. In the fifteenth century the most illustrious of these families was the Medici, who established branch offices all over western Europe and acted as financial agents for the popes. The Medici represented a new capitalist class which treated money as a commodity. Whereas in medieval economic theory money was only a means of exchange and was justified only to the extent that it reflected both honest labor and a "just price" concept, early capitalist speculators like the Medici valued and traded in currencies and bullion for their own sake. Many loans were made to rulers who were continually in need of funds to carry on their wars.

The greatest of the sixteenth-century bankers were the Fuggers of Augsburg in Germany. They repeated the pattern set by the Medici, loaning money to the Church (half of the money collected by Tetzel from the sale of indulgences went to repay a Fugger loan), to Charles V to finance his election as emperor, and to the Spanish and Austrian Hapsburgs. The Hapsburg loans were secured by mining concessions, and the Fuggers gained a virtual monopoly on silver and copper mining in central Europe and silver and mercury mining in Spain. For decades the Fuggers realized an average yearly profit of over 30 percent, but they went bankrupt in 1607 when Spain for the third time defaulted on its loans.

By the seventeenth century the resources of banking families like the Fuggers were inadequate to meet the needs of the time, and private banks were superseded by public banks chartered by the government. The first of these great public institutions was the Bank of Amsterdam, chartered in 1609. Its main purpose was to facilitate trade by the conversion of various currencies into credits called bank money, which because of its standard value came to be preferred to coins. In 1694 the Bank of England was chartered as a means of financing England's wars. In return for a large loan to the government at 8 percent, the bank was granted a monopoly on such banking operations as issuing paper bank notes and marketing the government's securities.

With banking there naturally evolved new financial techniques. Despite the increase in precious metals after 1500, the supply could not keep pace with the increase in trade, and the Bank of Amsterdam began the practice of issuing loans against its deposits. Because it found that it could safely loan larger sums than had been deposited, the Bank of Amsterdam thus initiated a new and effective means of expanding credit. Likewise, bank notes came to replace gold and silver currency, and merchants developed the method of raising ready money known as discounting. Instead of waiting months to cash a bill of exchange owed to them, they sold it before its due date for something less than its face value. Banks in particular offered this service, holding the discounted bills until they matured at full value.

Progress was also made in commercial arithmetic and in bookkeeping. Simple single-entry bookkeeping had been developed as early as the thirteenth century. Soon afterwards, double-entry bookkeeping came into use; it was well known in Italy by 1500 and in western Europe a century later. By listing a transaction either as a *debit* (meaning, "he owes") or a *credit* ("he believes" a promiser will carry out his promise), a businessman could readily determine his status in terms of profit and loss.

New methods of financing companies. Not only banks but also modern corporations were developed in response to needs arising from the expanded commerce of early modern times. Unprecedented difficulties resulted from trading at long distances overseas in strange lands. It was natural that those engaged in overseas trade should seek to combine their efforts both to provide mutual protection and to share losses as well as profits.

The companies were of two main types—regulated and joint-stock—and both were chartered, regulated, and granted monopolies by the state. In the regulated company individuals financed their own businesses and abided by the rules the group had accepted to protect the trade in which the members had a mutual interest. The earlier companies were of this nature.

The joint-stock companies involved an association of capital as well as of men. The members put their money into a common fund and gave over the management to a board of directors. Because of its advantages, the joint-stock company became almost universal. It had a permanent legal personality that did not expire, whereas the regulated company was not a legal entity, and in case of damages each member had to sue or be sued individually. As many people as wanted could contribute capital. Stock might be transferred as the owner saw fit, and at the same time, the company's policy underwent no serious change. The vast corporations of today grew out of this early type of business organization.

Stock exchanges and insurance. The creation of joint-stock companies gave impetus to the growth of stock exchanges, because the shares could be easily transferred from one person to another like any other commodity. A stock exchange made it easier to accumulate capital from many different sources, thereby enabling very large commercial companies to be formed. We have seen that the first stock exchange, the bourse at Antwerp, was primarily a commodity exchange. Later the two functions were separated.

Another method of sharing losses besides the joint-stock company was insurance. Since the loss of his vessel might well ruin an individual merchant, it came to be the practice to distribute losses among a group of traders by means of insurance. Interested merchants drew up an agreement by which each was responsible for a percentage of any possible loss. Because the merchants signed their names at the bottom of this document, the practice came to be known as underwriting.

The most famous of all marine insurance groups, Lloyd's of London, came into being about 1688. Lloyd's was not a stock company but an association of shipowners, merchants, and underwriters who first met together in a London coffee house owned by Edward Lloyd. Since its modest beginnings, Lloyd's has grown steadily and branched out into other forms of insurance. Today it is the world authority on matters of ship classification, and it publishes *Lloyd's List*, a daily paper which indicates the whereabouts of all registered vessels.

After the disastrous London fire of 1666,

fire insurance companies were started, and in the same period companies specializing in life insurance were also formed. In 1684 the Friendly Society was organized. This society was the first mutual company—an association in which policyholders received a share of the company profits.

Speculation and business bubbles. Toward the end of the seventeenth century, the accumulation of capital brought about a mania for speculation in the shares of joint-stock companies in England, France, and Holland. One authority comments on the fantastic nature of the wildcat schemes, "which promised to earn great dividends by trading in human hair, making square cannon balls, getting butter from beech trees, marketing an air pump for the brain, perfecting a wheel for perpetual motion, searching for rich wrecks off the Irish coast, or importing jackasses from Spain."[11] The two most notorious speculative companies were the South Sea Company in England and the Mississippi Company in France.

The financiers of the South Sea Company assumed the British national debt of about £9,000,000 in return for a 6 percent annual interest payment and a monopoly of British trade with South America and the islands in the South Seas. The price of company stock rose rapidly until it was far above the value of the company's earnings. In 1720, with a £100 share selling for £1,060, the huge speculative bubble burst when shareholders lost confidence and began to sell. Many lost not only their savings but also property they had mortgaged in the hope of getting rich quickly.

The Mississippi Company had a similar history. Formed to promote trade with France's Louisiana territory, where it founded New Orleans in 1718, the company soon acquired a monopoly on all French colonial trade. In addition, the company assumed the national debt and was granted the right to collect all indirect taxes in France and to establish a central bank with the privilege of issuing paper money. Speculative fever combined with currency inflation to bid up the company's stock to fantastic heights. Thousands suffered losses when shareholders began to unload and the company went bankrupt in 1720.

The demoralizing failure of these schemes left a legacy in both countries. In England Parliament passed the "Bubble Act," which drastically restricted the right of incorporation. In France distrust of paper money and the government's credit and solvency continued for generations.

The domestic system. In the Middle Ages manufacturing had been carried on under the guild system. The impetus of commercial expansion caused an important change in the organization of industry. The domestic, or putting-out, system evolved in the sixteenth century and reached its widest application in the textile industry of England. It operated in this fashion: a merchant capitalist would buy raw materials, assign them to artisans to be worked on in their own homes, take the finished product, and sell it to his customers. Thus, between producer and customer, a middleman intervened—an entrepreneur who accumulated capital by selling his goods at a profit. Because work was no longer planned and conducted by master and apprentice under one roof, this

The famous insurance association known as Lloyd's of London took its name from Lloyd's coffee house, where the insurance underwriters used to meet with merchants and shipowners. This satirical scene at Lloyd's dates from the late eighteenth century.

system widened the gulf between employer and employee, capitalist and worker.

The domestic system had many advantages. The accumulation of capital in the hands of the entrepreneur made possible the purchase of raw materials in greater bulk and allowed for marketing of finished products on a larger scale than had been possible under the guild system. The domestic system also contributed to an increased specialization of skills within an efficient system of overall production; an employer could have his raw wool sent to spinners, then to weavers, and finally to dyers. From the workers' point of view, it was now possible for agricultural tenants to augment the bare subsistence they eked from the soil by working at home. The capitalist employer, on the other hand, could operate without the restrictions imposed by the urban guilds.

The domestic system persisted for two hundred years in England, although in some trades workers were brought together in central shops long before the beginning of the machine age and the factory system proper. On the Continent, however, where the guilds were retained as agents of the mercantilist state in controlling industry, the guild system remained strong. Hence industrial production on the Continent lagged behind that in England, where industry was less restricted by guild practices.

Innovation in agriculture. The condition of agriculture was a basic socioeconomic factor in the life of the period, for agriculture provided the majority of Europeans with their livelihood. In England, especially, the advent of commercial capitalism wrought significant changes. The profit-making potentialities in farming attracted enterprising entrepreneurs, who bought up large tracts of land. Because the possession of land had always been the mark of nobility, the *nouveaux riches* consolidated their position in polite society by acquiring estates and marrying into the landed gentry. The alliance between land and trade created a powerful new group in Parliament—a class which promoted legislation favorable to its own needs and desires, often at the expense of the national good. But the satisfaction of the profit motive had a beneficial effect upon agriculture; the

new commercial landowners applied efficient business methods to the management of their estates. They encouraged the use of new tools and crops and were sympathetic to new ideas in stock breeding and soil development.

A pioneer agronomist was Jethro Tull (1674-1741), who advocated careful plowing of the land, planting seeds in neat rows by the use of a drill he invented, and keeping the plants well cultivated as they grew to maturity. By mixing clay and lime into the soil, Viscount Charles Townshend (1674-1738) restored the fertility of land that had once been worthless swamp and sand. He also suggested crop rotation as a method of soil restoration superior to the wasteful custom of allowing good farm land to lie fallow. He was so enthusiastic over turnips, his pet crop for livestock feed, that he was nicknamed "Turnip Townshend."

Robert Bakewell (1725-1795) was responsible for attacking the problem of livestock breeding. Haphazard breeding had resulted in sheep weighing only from twenty-five to forty pounds and cattle of about four hundred pounds. Through the select breeding of choice animals, Bakewell raised larger livestock, improved the quality of the meat, and increased the quantity of milk available from his dairy cattle. His methods attracted attention, especially from the wealthy farmers, but most of the rank and file were suspicious of his innovations and too poor to adopt them.

While the tempo of agricultural reform was much faster and more general in England than on the Continent, there was evidence of some progress in farming methods there also. In fact, the great advances in English agriculture owed much to Continental techniques and improved seeds, but these achievements were applied much more systematically in England.

The enclosure movement. The practice of enclosing open lands, a development which had begun in England even before Tudor times, was accelerated by the changes in farming methods. Aided by special acts of Parliament, members of the new commercial landowning class seized the opportunity to enclose the common lands, where for hundreds of years English villagers had grazed their cattle, and to purchase and fence in the small farms owned and operated by the sturdy, independent yeomen. These lands were consolidated into holdings which were, in effect, large-scale business enterprises requiring substantial capital for operation and upkeep. The demand for wool in the textile industry resulted also in the enclosure of large tracts of arable land for sheep raising.

The controversy over the enclosure movement reached its climax between 1750 and 1810. The advocates of enclosure justified amalgamation of small agricultural holdings by claiming that new methods of stock breeding and crop rotation could not be practiced on unfenced land. From an economic standpoint, enclosure was inevitable, and some historians believe that the enclosure movement resulted ultimately in a more careful use of a greater amount of land than had been available before. Better and more food was thus made available for a population on the verge of rapid increase. Like most drastic economic changes, however, the enclosure movement spelled misery and dislocation to a large number of countryfolk. The destruction of the yeoman class and the depopulation of many villages was ruefully pondered by Oliver Goldsmith in his poem, "The Deserted Village":

Ill fares the land, to hastening ills a prey,
Where wealth accumulates, and men decay.
Princes and lords may flourish, or may fade;
A breath can make them, as a breath has made;
But a bold peasantry, their country's pride,
When once destroyed can never be supplied. . . .
Ye friends to truth, ye statesmen, who survey
The rich man's joy increase, the poor's decay,
'Tis yours to judge how wide the limits stand
Between a splendid and a happy land.

The saga of the yeoman's misfortunes did not end with their departure from the villages; its finale took place in the cities. When the story of industrial capitalism is taken up in Chapter 21, we will view the bleak and harsh environment of displaced rural people as they labored long and hard in grimy factories and lived as best they could in ugly, disease-ridden slums.

SUMMARY

Braving the terrors of uncharted seas and the dreadful hardships of long voyages, a few daring sea captains opened up rich trade routes to the East and discovered new lands in the Western Hemisphere. In the New World the feats of the explorers were followed by the bold, and often cruel, exploits of the *conquistadores*, who carved out vast empires for their homelands.

Meanwhile, various European countries had erected forts on the African coast for the purpose of exploiting the slave trade. In the teeming lands of Asia, European penetration was secured only by the establishment of strongly fortified trading settlements at strategic sites. Using this system, the Portuguese controlled trade in the East during the 1500's but gradually lost out to the English and Dutch, who garnered most of the profits in the next century. While the Dutch concentrated more and more on the East Indies, the English East India Company built up a commercial stronghold in India. In China and Japan the behavior of the Portuguese caused native officials to restrict the westerners to a narrow theater of operations. In the East, European standards were successfully and permanently imposed only in the Philippines.

In sharp contrast to their failures in Japan and China, the western European powers were able to transplant not only their authority but also their institutions and culture to the sparsely populated lands of the Americas. The government and economics of the Spanish and Portuguese colonies were directly—and minutely—controlled by royal decrees and officials, whereas the development of the French, English, and Dutch colonies was left largely to private companies.

The impact of the New World upon the Old was so far-reaching as to intensify the Commercial Revolution, the name given to the first phase of our capitalistic economic system. The capitalism of this period, during which the economy in western Europe became nation-centered instead of town-centered, is called commercial capitalism because of the dominant part played by commerce as a producer of wealth. With the spectacular outburst of geographical discoveries and the creation of new trade routes, the areas which had thrived on the Mediterranean trade lost their leading roles to those along the Atlantic seaboard. The first great colonial empires were built up by Portugal and Spain, only to be superseded through the dynamism of Holland and later England and France. New products poured into Europe to augment diet, clothing, and the general standard of living, while the influx of gold and silver completed the change from a barter to a money economy and produced a price revolution.

This era also saw the development of large-scale banking and commercial practices. By the seventeenth century important banking institutions had been founded throughout western Europe. Because overseas trading ventures required large amounts of capital and entailed great risks, merchants pooled their resources by forming companies, the earlier ones of the regulated type, the later and more successful ones joint-stock companies—forerunners of present-day corporations. To serve as marketplaces for stock that could change hands readily, stock exchanges developed.

The geographical, political, and commercial expansion of Europe between the years 1450 and 1650 was so immense that it transformed the basic pattern of global existence. With it we enter the formative period of modern times. For the next three centuries the civilization of western Europe—carried to the four corners of the earth and stimulated by new and dynamic forces—was to dominate world culture.

SUGGESTIONS FOR READING

C. Nowell, **The Great Discoveries and the First Colonial Empires**,* Cornell; J. H. Parry, **The Establishment of the European Hegemony: 1415-1715**,* Torchbooks, and **The Age of Reconnaissance**,* Mentor. Excellent brief coverage of most of the material discussed in this chapter. See also Robert L. Reynolds, **Europe Emerges: Transition Toward an Industrial World-Wide Society, 600-1750**,* Wisconsin, 1961. D. Lach, **Asia in the Making of Europe**, Vol. I: **The Century of Discovery**, Univ. of Chicago, 1965, describes what Europe had learned about Asia by 1600.

J. Brebner, **The Explorers of North America, 1492-1806**,* Meridian. An engrossing survey. The best book on Columbus is S. E. Morison, **Admiral of the Ocean Sea**, Little, Brown, 1942, condensed as **Christopher Columbus, Mariner**,* Mentor. On exploration in America before Columbus see H. Holand, **Norse Discoveries and Explorations in North America**,* Dover, 1969, and Carl Sauer, **Northern Mists**,* California, 1968.

E. Prestage, **The Portuguese Pioneers**, Barnes and Noble, 1967. The standard work. See also Jean Anderson, **Henry the Navigator, Prince of Portugal**, Westminster, 1969.

F. A. Kirkpatrick, **The Spanish Conquistadores**,* Meridian. A colorful treatment. See also J. Bannon, ed., **The Spanish Conquistadores: Men or Devils?**,* Holt, Rinehart & Winston, and Carl Sauer, **The Early Spanish Main**,* California. W. H. Prescott, **History of the Conquest of Mexico**,* Phoenix, and **The Conquest of Peru**,* Mentor, both abridged, are historical classics. See also S. de Madariaga, **Hernán Cortés: Conqueror of Mexico**,* Anchor; C. M. Parr, **Ferdinand Magellan: Circumnavigator**, Crowell, 1964.

C. Boxer, **Four Centuries of Portuguese Expansion, 1415-1825**, Dufour, 1961. See also A. Toussaint, **History of the Indian Ocean**, Univ. of Chicago, 1966.

C. Boxer, **The Dutch Seaborne Empire, 1600-1800**, Knopf, 1965; G. Masselman, **The Cradle of Colonialism**, Yale, 1963. Valuable surveys of Dutch expansion.

C. H. Haring, **The Spanish Empire in America**,* Harbinger. The best introduction. See also J. H. Parry, **The Spanish Seaborne Empire**, Knopf, 1966; L. Hanke, **The Spanish Struggle for Justice in the Conquest of America**,* Little, Brown.

A. L. Rowse, **The Expansion of Elizabethan England**, St. Martin's, 1955. A highly readable account. C. Bridenbaugh, **Vexed and Troubled Englishmen, 1590-1642**, Oxford, 1968, describes the factors influencing English migration to America. Also recommended are Grace Woodward, **Pocahontas**, Oklahoma, 1969, and G. D. Langdon, Jr., **Pilgrim Colony: A History of New Plymouth, 1620-1691**,* Yale.

H. See, **Modern Capitalism: Its Origin and Evolution**, Ben Franklin, 1928. A useful introduction. The following are excellent detailed studies: R. De Roover, **The Rise and Decline of the Medici Bank, 1397-1494**,* Norton; R. Ehrenberg, **Capitalism and Finance in the Age of the Renaissance: A Study of the Fuggers and their Connections**, Kelley, 1928; V. Barbour, **Capitalism in Amsterdam in the Seventeenth Century**,* Michigan.

A. P. Thornton, **Doctrines of Imperialism**,* Wiley, 1965; Raymond Betts, **Europe Overseas: Phases of Imperialism**, Basic Books, 1968. Contain good short accounts of early modern imperialism and mercantilism. On other aspects of the Commercial Revolution see Earl J. Hamilton, **American Treasure and the Price Revolution in Spain, 1501-1650**, Octagon, 1965; J. Pope-Hennessy, **Sins of the Fathers: A Study of the Atlantic Slave Traders, 1441-1807**, Knopf, 1968; R. H. Tawney, **The Agrarian Problem in the Sixteenth Century**,* Torchbooks.

*Indicates an inexpensive paperbound edition.

Part Four

Charting
the Present

■ The story of Europe and the New World in the period from 1650 to 1815 forms one of the most complex chapters in world history. Following the challenge to the ideas and institutions of the Middle Ages posed by the Renaissance, the Reformation, and the great religious wars, the search for principles of order became a consistent theme in the writings of scientists as well as in literature and the fine arts. This search for order also played an important role in the ambitious domestic and foreign ventures of autocratic rulers.

A succession of fresh concepts about the universe (in the seventeenth century), about society (in the eighteenth century) and about man (in the nineteenth century) called into question and in some cases overthrew long-established beliefs and institutions. The first major advance was the development in the seventeenth century of the scientific method, which relied upon deductive reasoning. Other new ideas, many stemming from the spread of the scientific method, began to develop in the social and natural sciences.

In politics the late seventeenth century witnessed the high-water mark of absolutism under Louis XIV of France. But new political concepts rose rapidly to challenge royal prerogatives everywhere. The eighteenth century was the period of revolutions that established the precedents and voiced the ideology that were to become the inspiration for the whole liberal-democratic movement of modern times.

These political advances were accompanied, and indeed only made possible, by comparably important progress in thought. Outmoded ideas in economics and politics were attacked. So pervasive were the transformations in thought that they constituted an intellectual revolution known as the Enlightenment. Under the spell of the remarkable achievements of science—capped by the work of Newton—thinkers, writers, artists, and members of polite society sought to express a truly scientific, or at least rational, point of view. For many intellectuals, religion lost its emotional fervor and became a philosophical creed. Literature, in this Age of Reason, was guided by the mind rather than by the heart. Most painting and architecture was restrained and balanced in both form and spirit. In Paris, where the cult of reason reached its height, the salon was the temple of cultivated society. Here Europe's cosmopolitan intellectuals gathered to exchange views on all aspects of life; the result was witty, well-informed, and often brilliant conversation. The liberal tenets of the Enlightenment touched even the autocrats of the Continent; in Prussia, Austria, and Russia, benevolent despots made at least superficial attempts at reform.

The present owes much to the period from 1650 to 1815. That period provided us with the heart of our liberal political beliefs; it encouraged religious tolerance and freedom of inquiry; and, above all, it made man the focus of attention—his happiness, his freedom, his potentialities. All these developments made this period a time of hope for the future of mankind.

There was, however, a disquieting feature. The liberalism and rationalism we have discussed operated *within* but not *between* states. Humanitarianism did not touch international affairs. These were dominated by the competitive state system, in which each nation was a law unto itself and any weak neighbor was a potential victim. In this state of international anarchy the nations of Europe evolved the balance of power to check the grandiose ambitions of national rulers whose only law was force and to achieve some order in the relations between rival states. Thus a coalition of rival powers thwarted the plans of Louis XIV, of the French revolutionary leaders, and finally of the brilliant and unscrupulous Napoleon, who sought to control all of Europe under the pretex of spreading the ideals of equality and liberty. The discrepancy between benevolence and liberalism, on the one hand, and force and autocracy, on the other, was to become increasingly a paradox of modern civilization.

14. (preceding page) **Moronobu: "Gay Life in Early Edo"** (seventeenth century). The impact of the commercial class was felt in Japanese art of the late seventeenth century. At that time the country's merchants were gaining rapidly in power and influence, and cities like Edo (today's Tokyo) were growing at a brisk rate. Edo in fact was the center of an unprecedented new art which found its subject matter in the activities of everyday life. This screen painting shows local merchants providing a variety of pleasures to feudal lords who had lately moved to the city and were enjoying its delights with great relish. **15.** (above) **Angkor Wat, Cambodia** (early twelfth century). Indian art styles spread far beyond the borders of India and in many cases not only retained vitality but gained in it. Many critics consider Angkor Wat, the immense temple city of the Khmers in Cambodia, to be the most perfectly realized example of Indian architectural technique. The gigantic size of the complex (its moat is two and one half miles long and one of its courtyards contains a half mile of sculptured reliefs) is matched by the brilliant spatial ordering of its profusion of galleries, sanctuaries, pavilions, and towers.

16. Mural painting at Bonampak (c. sixth century). This fresco from the classic period of Mayan culture represents Central American antiquity at its most sophisticated. Although no historical link has been established, Mayan painting looks curiously like that of ancient Egypt, in that it deals with the facts of daily life and is rendered in flat color, linear contour, and horizontal registers. Here a group of captives, surrounded by victorious Mayas, are shown waiting in fear to learn the role they will play in a sacrificial ceremony.

17. J. F. Goya: "Shooting of the Rebels of May 3, 1808" (1814). Romanticism, a product of the immensely complex forces at work in the late eighteenth and early nineteenth centuries, has deeply affected the spirit of the modern world ever since. Characteristic of romantic thinking is the element of strong, even violent, feeling, and no less typical is the artist's new assertion of the personal freedom to evoke such feeling. In this sense, then, the Spaniard Goya was a romantic, as he amply proves in this stark depiction of an execution. He has spared no formal means to produce a shudder of empathic horror in the viewer. Just as important, he has felt no compunction about protesting against a brutal authority which he, as an individual, abhors.

Chapter 18

New Dimensions of the Mind

Science, Thought, and the Arts in the Age of Reason: 1600-1800

INTRODUCTION. The first phase of the transition from medieval to modern times in the western world ended about 1600, to be followed by an even more epochal period of intellectual change. So important were the changes in this latter period that the intellectual movement they comprised is identified as the Enlightenment and the time span in which they occurred is known as the Age of Reason. In the broadest sense, the Age of Reason can be thought of as comprising the seventeenth and eighteenth centuries. The spirit and purpose of the Enlightenment were eloquently expressed by one of its spokesmen, the *philosophe* Baron d'Holbach, who wrote: "Let us then endeavor to disperse those clouds of ignorance, those mists of darkness, which impede Man on his journey, which block his progress, which prevent his marching through life with a firm and steady step. Let us try to inspire him . . . with respect for his own reason—with an inextinguishable love of truth . . . so that he may learn to know himself . . . and no longer be duped by an imagination that has been led astray by authority . . . so that he may learn to base his morals on his own nature, on his own wants, on the real advantage of society . . . so that he may learn to pursue his true happiness, by promoting that of others . . . in short, so that he may become a virtuous and rational being, who cannot fail to become happy."[1]

This message indicates how rapidly the heritage of the Middle Ages was being left behind. No longer was reason to serve faith, mind to obey authority, and man to spend his life in preparation for the next world. The thinkers of the Age of Reason believed in happiness and fulfillment in this world; they regarded mind rather than faith as the best source of guidance and were suspicious of emotion, myth, and supernaturalism. The chief support of the cult of reason was science, with its new laws and methods. The great age of science initiated by Copernicus in 1543 reached its climax in 1687 with Newton's explanation of the law of gravitation. The supreme achievement of the Enlightenment, however, was not in discovering additional scientific laws but rather in translating the advances of science into a new philosophy and world view.

Exaltation of science, faith in reason, and belief in humanitarianism led writers and thinkers of the Enlightenment to carry on a strenuous campaign of reevaluation of all aspects of society. They were positive that reason could solve all human problems. All thought was colored by a belief in progress and by a vigorous optimism regarding mankind's improvability. In religion a movement known as Deism, reflecting these views, sought to establish a "rational" faith; and in the study of mankind, the foundations were laid for the systematic disciplines of the social sciences.

Literature, music, and the fine arts were affected profoundly by the cult of reason. Everywhere there was supreme confidence in logic, a tendency to minimize spirit and emotion, and a close attention to the forms and rules which had characterized the classical era in Greece and Rome, when the splendor of human reason had first been extolled. In literature and music this emphasis on reason culminated in Neoclassicism, and in art it led from the grandiose Baroque and the more dainty Rococo styles to the pure Neoclassical style.

THE SCIENTIFIC REVOLUTION

From "authority" to "facts." The transition from the Middle Ages to early modern times represents a shift in emphasis from "authoritative" truth to "factual" truth. Medieval thought had enthroned theology as the "queen of the sciences" because the scholastics sought to relate human knowledge to ultimate divine purposes. Hence they made little distinction between a "fact" and a theological "truth." In their world view man was seen to be dependent upon a divine order in which God was responsible for mankind's origin and destiny alike. The medieval mind had also associated this earthly life with the loss of Eden and the physical world with the works of Satan. In order to justify modern man's extension of his environmental powers, it was first necessary to adopt a new attitude, namely, that God had revealed His

divine purpose both in scripture and in nature. As a consequence, interest shifted progressively to discovering the processes and laws governing the natural world. Instead of concentrating their attention on *why*, or final cause, men concerned themselves with *how*, or the manner of causation.

Important consequences derived from this conceptual shift. Men continued to regard scriptural revelation as providing certainty in the subjective world of faith and ethics. But increasingly they employed their reasoning powers to discover in the objective world of nature the principles of causation—and to do so in terms that were both mathematical and mechanical. Eventually this rationalistic emphasis upon the scientific method was to affect virtually every area of human activity, including the evolution of religious thought into Deism (see p. 401). Yet this view of a mathematical and mechanical nature was purchased at a high price: it threatened to drain the universe of all spiritual content and meaning and to reduce man himself to the status of an automaton. One day he would rebel against such a world view.

Progress of the scientific method. The birth of modern science is often regarded as marked by the publication in 1543 of Copernicus' heliocentric theory which denied that the earth was the center of the cosmos. This revolutionary theory challenged the teachings of religion and the traditional ideas concerning the nature of the universe and man's place in it. By the last half of the seventeenth century the Copernican system and the progress made in other branches of science besides astronomy had produced a change in man's outlook upon the world that is considered one of the greatest revolutions in the history of human thought. When Charles Darwin in the nineteenth century wrote that "science and her methods gave me a resting place independent of authority and tradition," he was describing what has been frequently called the fundamental faith of modern western man.

Basic to the growth of science was the development of the scientific method, a systematic and logical way of seeking truth. In the search for facts, this new servant relied on curiosity, healthy skepticism, and reason rather than faith. The foundations of the new method were laid in the first half of the seventeenth century by Francis Bacon in England and René Descartes in France.

Bacon's attack on unscientific thinking. Sir Francis Bacon (1561-1626) attacked humanism and scholasticism and derided Plato and Aristotle, maintaining that they had managed to survive for centuries only because of their shallowness, which had given them the necessary buoyancy to ride down the stream of time. In his *Novum Organum* (*The New Instrument*), published in 1620, Bacon described the course which science and a scientifically oriented philosophy should take. First, man must cope with four major prejudices (in Bacon's famous term, *Idols*) which had so far obstructed human progress. The Idols of the Tribe are the prej-

udices inherent in human nature itself; in particular, they represent the tendency to see only those facts which support an opinion one wishes to entertain. The Idols of the Cave are prejudices fostered in the individual by his particular environment—the circumstances of his birth, childhood, education, and so forth. The Idols of the Market Place are false opinions which spread when men consort together. Lastly, there are the Idols of the Theater, resulting from men's tendency to become attached to particular theories, schools of thought, and philosophies and to hold on to them long after the logical basis for their continuance has disappeared.

If better results were to be obtained, new ways of thinking and of approaching the world of nature had to be devised. Here we come to Bacon's famous method of induction, by which he advocated a systematic recording of facts derived from experiments. These facts would lead to tentative hypoth-

Sir Francis Bacon urged the need for experiment, because "men have been kept back . . . from progress in the sciences by reverence for antiquity, by the authority of men accounted great in philosophy, and then by general consent."

eses which could then be tested by fresh experiments under different conditions. Eventually it should prove possible for men to arrive at universal principles and scientific laws.

Bacon himself was an indifferent scientist. The significance of his work lies in the fact that he set forth a program to direct the course of scientific and philosophical inquiry at the time when the traditional modes of thought were crumbling. In his own words, "he rang the bell which called the wits together." Bacon also forecast the vast importance of the new science in enabling man to conquer his environment. In his *New Atlantis* (1627)—his description of a utopian society—emphasis is centered on a research institute called "Solomon's house," where experimentation and invention were subsidized and directed toward the goal of "the enlarging of the bounds of Human Empire, to the effecting of all things possible."[2]

Descartes, champion of the deductive method. As an advocate of the inductive method, Bacon undervalued the role of mathematics and deduction. Experimentation is not the only approach to scientific knowledge, as the mathematical approach attests. The mathematical approach is to begin with a self-evident axiom and then, by logical reasoning, to deduce various inferences. Applied to scientific investigations as a whole, this type of approach—known as the deductive method—advances by logical steps from simple self-evident truths to more complex truths. As we saw earlier, Aristotle had employed the syllogism to point out fallacies in human reasoning. It was the achievement of René Descartes (1596-1650) to make brilliant use of this method of reasoning in his attempt to extend the mathematical method to all fields of human knowledge.

Like Bacon, Descartes maintained that the first step in the search for truth was for men to rid themselves of preconceived notions and to take nothing for granted. Bacon had called for "minds washed clean of opinions," and Descartes began by being prepared to doubt everything except the fact of his own doubting. And if he doubted, he must in fact exist—hence his famous expression *Cogito, ergo sum* ("I think, therefore I am").

For Bacon, experiment was the next step in the quest for truth. Although Descartes by no means rejected the value of experimentation, he placed reliance above all on the attainment of knowledge through reason. By logical deduction, Descartes built up a concept of a unified, mathematically ordered universe which operated like a perfect mechanism; in this universe, supernatural phenomena were impossible and everything could be explained rationally, preferably in mathematical terms.

Some scientists criticized Descartes for not having made sufficient use of experiment, even as he had criticized Bacon for weakness in mathematics. As we well know, the experimental and mathematical methods are complementary. Before the mid-point of the seventeenth century, the two methods had been combined by Kepler and Galileo. ("Sense must be accompanied by reason"[3] was the way in which Galileo described the union of induction and deduction.) Thus a revolution in scientific thinking had been effected, and the foundation of modern science and modern philosophy had been firmly laid.

Science takes to the heavens. It was in astronomy that science made its first spectacular advance. For over a thousand years western Europe had accepted the view of Ptolemy, a Greek scholar of the second century A.D., that the earth was stationary. Rotating around it were concentric, impenetrable, crystalline spheres to which were attached the sun, planets, and fixed stars. The Ptolemaic system as expressed in the geocentric (earth-centered) theory was incorporated into the scholastic system of the Church. By the middle of the seventeenth century, however, a revolution in man's conceptions of the heavens had been attained through the labors of a Pole, Copernicus; a Dane, Tycho Brahe; a German, Kepler; and an Italian, Galileo.

Copernicus (1473-1543) was a contemporary of Martin Luther and Michelangelo. During visits to Italy for study, he read widely in the classical authors and was much impressed by the Platonist philosophy that beauty was supreme and that mathematics was the ideal science. As a mathematician, Copernicus found parts of the Ptolemaic

The 1559 engraving at right illustrates Ptolemy's system of the universe. Surrounding the earth are spheres containing the moon, sun, planets, and fixed stars. An additional sphere provides the system's motion. Beyond that is the Empyrean, where God dwells. The diagram above, illustrating the heliocentric theory of the universe, appeared in the first edition of Copernicus' *Concerning the Revolutions of the Heavenly Spheres* (1543). It places the sun in the center, surrounded by the first six planets in their correct order. The outer sphere was thought to be the home of all fixed stars.

theory "not sufficiently pleasing to the mind" and began to seek a more pleasing combination of circles to express the motions of the planets. He obtained such a model by assuming that the earth moves "like any other planet," while the sun stands still in the middle of the planetary orbits. Near the end of his life, he was persuaded to publish his views under the title *Concerning the Revolutions of Heavenly Spheres* (1543). In this work he refuted the theory that the earth remained stationary in the middle of the universe, contending instead that it rotated every twenty-four hours upon its axis from west to east and that it made an annual movement around the sun. As early as 1539 Luther attacked Copernicus' views as contrary to the truth of the Bible. Not until 1616, however, did the Catholic Church place Copernicus' book on the *Index of Prohibited Books* "until corrected," from which it was removed in 1620 after only minor revisions.

By brilliant mathematical and analytical reasoning, based on a slender body of facts, Copernicus had been able to bring one epoch in scientific thought to a close and to open

the door for another. However, the truth of his theory could be demonstrated beyond doubt only after a great number of accurate observations of the heavens had been charted. This need was in large part supplied by Tycho Brahe (1546-1601), although he himself never fully accepted the Copernican theory. For twenty-one years Brahe carried on accurate daily observations and carefully plotted the positions of hundreds of celestial bodies. He tracked the planets through the whole of their courses instead of contenting himself with picking them out at different points in their orbits. Thus in painstaking fashion he carried the science of observation as far as it could go prior to the invention of the telescope.

Brahe's data was used by his one-time assistant, Johann Kepler (1571-1630), a brilliant German mathematician. As a mathematician with a strong leaning toward Platonic idealism, Kepler quickly adopted the Copernican theory. While working with Brahe's data on the movements of Mars, Kepler had to account for the apparent irregularities in that planet's perplexing orbit.

After patiently applying one mathematical hypothesis after another, he was able to verify that the planet did not move in a circular orbit but described an ellipse. He then proceeded to assume that the other planets also traveled in elliptical orbits. Another planetary law discovered by Kepler was that the pace of a planet accelerated as it approached the sun. After reading Gilbert's book on magnetism (see p. 407), Kepler concluded that the sun emitted a magnetic force that moved the planets in their courses—an idea that formed a valuable basis for Newton's theory of gravitation.

A contemporary of Kepler, Galileo Galilei (1564-1642), discovered new facts to verify the Copernican theory but, as he wrote to Kepler:

. . . I have not dared to make [it] known, as I have been deterred by the fate of our teacher Copernicus. He, it is true, won undying fame amongst some few, but amongst the multitude (there are so many fools in the world) he was only an object of scorn and laughter.[4]

In 1609 Galileo made a telescope, and with it he discovered mountains on the moon, sunspots, the satellites of Jupiter, and the rings of Saturn. Thrilled with these discoveries, Galileo publicized his findings and beliefs. In 1616 he was constrained by the Church to promise that he would not "hold, teach, or defend" the heretical Copernican doctrines, and in 1633 he was forced to make a public recantation of his heretical doctrine. A legend has it that Galileo, upon rising from his knees after renouncing the idea that the earth moved, stamped on the ground and exclaimed, "Eppur si muove!" ("But it does move!")

Galileo was also the first to establish the law of falling bodies, proving that, irrespective of the weight or the size of the bodies, their acceleration is constant (the increase of velocity being thirty-two feet per second). Thus another entrenched belief inherited from the ancients was refuted: Aristotle's contention that bodies fall to earth at speeds proportional to their weight.

Newton and the law of gravitation. Great as the contributions of Brahe, Kepler, and Galileo had been to astronomy, their indi-

vidual discoveries had yet to be united into one all-embracing principle or law which would explain the motion of all bodies in the planetary system and present the universe as one great unity operating according to unalterable principles. This goal was realized by Isaac Newton (1642-1727), the most illustrious scientist in the Age of Reason.

At the age of only twenty-four, Newton had made all his important discoveries: the law of gravitation, the principles of calculus, and the compound nature of light. At twenty-seven, the youthful genius was given a professorship in mathematics at Cambridge University. Although he had already discovered the principle of gravitation, he was not able to prove it mathematically until 1685. Two years later his momentous work was published in Latin under the title *Philosophiae Naturalis Principia Mathematica* (*Mathematical Principles of Natural Philosophy*). By this work all laws of motion, both celestial and terrestrial, were synthesized in a master principle for the universe, the law of gravitation, which was expressed in a concise, simple, mathematical formula:

Every particle in the universe attracts every other particle with a force varying inversely as the square of the distance between them and directly proportional to the product of their masses.[5]

The publication of the *Principia* climaxed the near century and a half in which scientists had struggled against static tradition and intolerant authority.

Advances in mathematics and scientific instruments. Meanwhile, mathematicians had been keeping abreast of the work of the astronomers and physicists and providing them with new tools. Indeed, as Galileo pointed out, mathematics was the language of science; of necessity these two fields had to progress hand in hand. Mathematical calculation was greatly simplified by the invention of time-saving devices and by the development of new forms of mathematical analysis. Decimals were introduced in 1585 and logarithms in 1614. Eight years later the slide rule was invented, followed in 1645 by the first adding machine. The degree to which these devices speeded up computation is indicated by the saying that John

Napier, the Scotsman who invented logarithms, doubled the lives of his fellow mathematicians by halving the time involved in solving intricate problems.

Two new branches of mathematical analysis helped make the seventeenth century the great age of science. Descartes "discovered the foundations of a wonderful science" (the words of his enthusiastic announcement) by uniting algebra and geometry into a unified discipline. The result, analytic geometry, permitted relationships in space to be translated into algebraic equations—a development of obvious value to astronomers, for example, since it helped them to represent astronomical phenomena in mathematical symbols and formulas.

Algebra was next applied to motion. The result was calculus, the greatest mathematical achievement of the seventeenth century, worked out independently by Newton and a German philosopher of remarkable versatility, Gottfried Leibnitz. This new calculus enabled scientists to consider quantitatively such problems as the movement of heat and the motion of stars, to compute quickly the content of circles, and to calculate stresses. Newton himself used it to arrive at and to prove his law of gravitation.

The work of science was no less dependent upon the development of new and more precise instruments. At the beginning of the seventeenth century the telescope and microscope appeared in Holland. We have already seen the invaluable use to which the first of these instruments was put by Galileo. After 1650, microscopic examinations of the lungs and other organs of the body were yielding vital information regarding their structure and functions. At this time also, Galileo and others were constructing crude thermometers; and a Dutchman, Christian Huygens, invented the pendulum clock and brought accuracy to the measurement of time. The micrometer, the barometer, and the air pump are other examples of seventeenth-century inventions that arose to serve science. The eighteenth century contributed the centigrade and the Fahrenheit thermometers, the chronometer, the sextant, and the anemometer, a device for measuring the force of wind.

A woodcut from Tycho Brahe's works shows the astronomer and his assistants plotting the positions of the planets by means of the precision instruments he designed.

Another important factor in the progress of science was the establishment of scientific societies. The first, the Academy of Experiments, was founded at Florence in 1657. In 1662 the Royal Society of London received its charter from Charles II, and four years later the French Academy of Science was established in Paris. These societies concentrated upon the promotion of experimentation and the collection of scientific data.

THE CRISIS IN THE EUROPEAN CONSCIENCE

The spiritual crisis. In the latter half of the seventeenth century much of western Europe was undergoing a revolution—not in the realm of politics but in the minds of men. As a result of the impact of the scientific revolution, with Newton's discoveries as its crowning achievements, a new concept of a universe without supernatural or miraculous forces came into being. This universe could be understood; it was a smooth-running machine with all parts fitting into a harmonious whole. Scientists now were inclined to regard God not as a personal deity but as the embodiment of scientific natural law which operates the universe and holds the stars in their courses. "The ideal of a clockwork universe was the great contribution of seventeenth-century science to the eighteenth-century age of reason."[6]

By contrast to the harmony and reasonableness of the natural world revealed by the scientists, society and its institutions seemed more and more archaic and the world of man seemed one governed by intolerance, prejudice, strife, and unreasoning authority. But in the face of the teachings of science, many men were convinced that their world of religion, law, and government could also be brought under the control of reason.

The problem of how to reconcile old faiths with new truths had become, in the words of a noted French scholar, the "crisis in the European conscience."[7] Scholars and thinkers, therefore, set about seeing what could be reconciled between the old and new, what faiths if any might be left intact, and what should be completely discarded.

The dualism of Descartes. We must now return briefly to Descartes, for in addition to his many other endeavors this pioneer thinker sought to reconcile medieval religious faith with a mechanistic world in which supernatural phenomena were impossible and in which everything had to be explained rationally. According to Descartes, reason was the chief source of knowledge. By logical methods of thought, the nature of reality, the existence of God, and the existence of the human self could be demonstrated. Descartes' proof of the existence of God was based on his assertion that, since existence must be an attribute of perfection and since the Deity must by definition be the all-perfect Being, a God must perforce exist.

Descartes divided ultimate reality into two substances: mind and matter. He argued that there was no connection between the two realms except by God's intervention. The first was the realm of faith and theology, impenetrable and unknowable to science; the second was that of reason and the laws of nature, subject to the understandable processes of science. Thus Descartes, a loyal Catholic, sought to reconcile the old and the new by his system of philosophical dualism.

Spinoza and pantheism. Born in Holland to well-to-do Jewish refugees who had fled from the Inquisition in Portugal, Baruch Spinoza (1632-1677) was another thinker who sought to reconcile spirit and matter. Following the methods of Descartes, Spinoza strove to build a mathematical philosophy: his *Ethics* (1663) is filled with geometric axioms, postulates, and theories. But Descartes' dualistic system was rejected by Spinoza, to whom mind and matter were manifestations of one substance—nature, or God. In other words, the universe and God are one. While Spinoza was alive, both Jews and Christians persecuted him, but his true spirituality later was better understood. He has been called "the God-intoxicated man."

Locke and empiricism. In the main, the Continental philosophers were rationalists who believed that knowledge is gained through reasoning. By contrast, English thinkers tended to believe that knowledge came only from sensory experience, a school of thought known as empiricism. Its founder was John Locke (1632-1704), who felt that there was too much abstruse and flighty thought in Europe.

In 1690 Locke published *An Essay Concerning Human Understanding*, which sought to analyze the human mind. According to him, the mind at birth is like a blank tablet (*tabula rasa*), and the experience gained through the senses is recorded on this tablet. Unlike the rationalists on the Continent, Locke maintained that, of itself, the mind has no innate power to grasp reality. In acquiring knowledge, however, the mind is not completely passive. Locke believed that reflection also played a role: by the process of association, the mind combines new and old impressions to form a new idea.

Locke's empiricism was of fundamental importance in the cultural development of modern Europe. A true son of the Age of Reason, Locke believed that investigation of such basic philosophical questions as the existence of God and the fundamentals of morality would lead men to a state of universal reasonableness and thereby free them from the necessity of relying blindly on authority.

Deism: a solution to the spiritual crisis. By the end of the first quarter of the eighteenth century the crisis in the European conscience had eased. After this time most intellectuals pegged their faith to the new science and the new philosophy.

Upon this rationalistic, scientific basis they built their religion. Known as Deism, it stripped Christianity of most of its traditional dogmas. God—thought of as an impersonal force—became in their eyes the First Cause, the custodian of the world machine, the master "clockwinder" of the universe. God had been necessary to create the universe, but once the universe had been set in motion, its immutable laws could not be altered. It was regarded as useless to invoke the intercession of God to bring about a deviation from the laws of nature. Men must rely upon reason, not miracles, to solve the problems of society.

The Deistic concept of a "natural" religion included only a few basic beliefs: the existence of God as master of the universe, the necessity of worshiping God, the atonement by man for his sins, the doctrine of immortality, and the view that the aim of religion is virtue, or sensible living. All religions were to be based on these simple and rational essentials; anything additional was extraneous and not worth squabbling about. Deists maintained that if all creeds would give up or at least minimize their "extraneous" dogmas, religious intolerance and bigotry would cease. The God of Deism was universal and acceptable to all. It mattered little what He was called. In the words of Alexander Pope:

Father of all! in every age,
In every clime adored,
By saint, by savage, and by sage,
Jehovah, Jove, or Lord![8]

The philosophes, critics of society. By 1750 France was so decidedly the intellectual center of Europe that it has been said "an opinion launched in Paris was like a battering ram launched by thirty millions of men."[9] Here a group of thinkers and writers known as the *philosophes* brought the Age of Reason to its climax.

The term *philosophes* cannot be translated as "philosophers," because they were not philosophers in any strict sense but rather students of society who analyzed its evils and advocated reforms. Foremost among these *philosophes* were Voltaire and Diderot, whose influence will be noted in this chapter, and Rousseau and Montesquieu, whose importance in political reform will be discussed in Chapter 19.

Voltaire, prince of the philosophes. More than any other thinker, Voltaire (1694-1778) personified the skepticism of the eighteenth century toward traditional religion and the evils of the time. He enjoyed exercising a caustic pen, soon ran afoul of the law, twice was imprisoned in the Bastille, and finally was banished to England for three years. Upon his return to France, Voltaire again championed tolerance, popularized the science of Newton, fought for personal liberty and freedom of the press, and acted as an influential propagandist for Deism. He turned out a prodigious number of works: histories, plays, pamphlets, essays, and novels. In his correspondence—estimated at ten thousand letters—he wittily spread the gospel of rationalism and scathingly attacked the abuses of his day.

Voltaire achieved his greatest fame as the most relentless critic of the established churches, Protestant and Catholic alike. He was sickened by the intolerance of organized Christianity and disgusted by the petty squabbles which seemed to monopolize the time of many priests and clergymen. Yet, in spite of his vituperation against Christianity, Voltaire did not wish to wreck religion. He once said that if a God did not exist, it would be necessary to invent one.

Voltaire's short fictional satire *Candide* (1759) was a biting attack on the easy optimism of some *philosophes* and the view that this world is "the best of all possible worlds." As his hero, Voltaire used a naive young man, Candide, who learns after many hair-raising and comic adventures that the "best of all possible worlds" is rent by earthquakes, famines, plagues, greed, war, and injustice. The story ends with Candide advising his former tutor, Dr. Pangloss, that we must "cultivate our garden" (instead of concerning ourselves with unanswerable philosophical questions)—a succinct expression of Voltaire's common-sense approach to life.

Diderot and the Encyclopédie. Voltaire had many disciples and imitators, but his only rival in spreading the gospel of rationalism and Deism was a set of books—the famous French *Encyclopédie*, edited by Denis Diderot (1713-1784). The *Encyclopédie* constituted the chief monument of the *philosophes*, declaring the supremacy of the new science, championing tolerance, denouncing superstition, and expounding the merits of Deism. Its seventeen volumes contained articles whose authors—tradesmen as well as scientists and philosophers—criticized in a moderate tone unfair taxation, the slave trade, and the cruelty of the existing criminal code.

The Pietist reaction. In the middle of the eighteenth century there developed a reaction against both the rational approach of Deism and the cold formality of much organized religion. This new religious movement, known as Pietism, developed to restore faith, emotion, and the spirit as the mainsprings of worship.

Pietism was foreshadowed by the teachings of George Fox (1624-1691), the founder of the religious sect called the Quakers, or the Society of Friends. Fox believed that the external aspects of Christianity—dogma, organization, and ritual—were unimportant compared to the spiritual experience of the individual (the "inner light"). The Quakers criticized religious intolerance severely and condemned warfare.

The surge of Pietism got under way in England in 1738, when the brothers John and Charles Wesley began to preach to the people in a new way, discarding the formalism of the established church for a glowing

The French *philosophes* were not only acquainted with each other's ideas, but were also personal friends. In this eighteenth-century engraving some prominent *philosophes* are gathered for dinner and conversation—among them Voltaire, with his hand in the air, and Diderot, to the right of Voltaire.

emotionalism. Instead of stilted sermons, the Wesleys offered extemporaneous appeals charged with religious fervor. *Methodist*—at first a term of derision—came to be the respected and official name of the movement. After John Wesley's death in 1791, the Methodists officially broke away from the Anglican Church, and the new denomination became one of the most important religious forces in England's national life.

On the European continent, Pietists stressed "the religion of the heart" rather than that of unimportant externals. In some Catholic countries a religious movement similar to Pietism arose—Quietism—but it was quickly crushed by the alliance of Church and state.

Kant and the Critique of Pure Reason. The German philosopher Immanuel Kant (1724-1804) symbolized the revival of the heart and of faith. Thoroughly aroused by the exaggerated skepticism and materialism of the age, he determined to shift philosophy back to a more sensible position without giving up too much of its "rational" basis. Kant's answer, contained in the *Critique of Pure Reason* (1781), marked the end of eighteenth-century natural philosophy and ushered in philosophical idealism, so important in the first part of the nineteenth century.

To resolve the conflict between mind and matter, Kant resorted to dualism. Beyond the physical world, which is the legitimate realm of science or "pure reason," lies the world of "things-in-themselves," he believed, where science can never penetrate and which is the legitimate realm of faith or "practical reason." Kant agreed that the existence of God could not be demonstrated scientifically but declared that man's moral sense compels him to believe in the immortality of the soul and in the presence of God. Thus Kant put as the basis of religious faith not reason, which is subject to experience, but an absolute innate moral sense, a conscience which is independent of experience yet able to distinguish between right and wrong. On this basis, Kant believed that free will and the existence of God could be proven. Reason cannot prove that there is a just God behind the world as it is, but our moral sense demands such a belief. Thus there are truths of the heart above and beyond those of the head.

The new humanitarianism. Pervading the thought of the Enlightenment was a deep concern for the welfare of mankind. Belief in the helplessness of man and the depravity of human nature was superseded by recognition of man's mental and moral dignity. Intolerance and undue emphasis upon dogma and form were giving way to the practical application of Christ's teachings and to religious tolerance.

"It was the special function of the Eighteenth Century," wrote the English historian Trevelyan, "to diffuse common sense and reasonableness in life and thought, to civilize manners and to humanize conduct."[10] Notable among its humanizing functions was the emergence of the antislavery movement in England, spearheaded by the Quakers and the Methodists. A court case in 1772 in effect ended slavery in England itself, and the insistence that the black man anywhere should by law be considered as a human being rather than as property alone was prominent in litigation of the 1780's. The agitation against slavery found its foremost champion in William Wilberforce (1759-1833), who, beginning in 1789, introduced motions in the House of Commons to end trafficking in human misery, until in 1807 the slave trade in British territories was legally abolished. Not content with this victory, Wilberforce carried on his crusade to free all slaves in the British empire, a goal that was reached in 1833, the year in which he died.

One of the outstanding characteristics of the eighteenth century was its cosmopolitanism. This quality was so strong that even war did not necessarily breed extreme national hatreds. During the long period in which France was at war with most of Europe, English thinkers and their *philosophe* friends in Paris could fraternize with no difficulty. Proud of belonging to the European "republic of letters," the intellectuals of the time were gravely concerned with the problem of war. As we have seen, Voltaire made a scathing attack on war in *Candide*, and several works were written urging the creation of machinery to enforce peace.

TOWARD A NEW
SCIENCE OF MAN

Birth of the social sciences. One of the great achievements of the eighteenth century was the application of the methods of science to the better understanding of man. The *philosophes* believed that by such application the laws governing society could be discovered. As one of them observed:

I believed that morals should be treated like all other sciences, and that one should arrive at a moral principle as one proceeds with an experiment in physics.[11]

This spirit of inquiry led to important innovations in the writing of history and the creation of those studies known today as the social sciences—political science, economics, anthropology, and psychology. In addition, important advances were made in criminology and education.

The ideas of progress and human perfectibility—concepts basic to the temper of the eighteenth century—were expressed most clearly by the Marquis de Condorcet, a member of the circle of *philosophes* around Voltaire. In his famous *Progress of the Human Mind* (1794) Condorcet asserts that there are no limits to human perfectibility and declares that progress will come by abolishing inequalities between nations, by securing equality for all men within nations, and by improving the human race in mind and body.

The writing of history. The greatest historian of this period was an Englishman, Edward Gibbon (1737-1794). The prose of this master craftsman was polished again and again until it emerged in glittering and sonorous sentences that carry the reader along with their majestic cadence. Gibbon shared the rational spirit of his day, and his *Decline and Fall of the Roman Empire* (1776-1787) was a vehicle for his ideas. He exposed the evils of tyrannical rulers and attacked the "barbarism and religion" that in his view had weakened the greatness of classical Roman culture.

Voltaire was also a historian of no mean merit, creating a new form, or school, of history, one that forsook the old reliance on wars and the foibles of rulers. He was interested in capturing "the spirit of the times" and in describing the progress and influence of ideas; in short, Voltaire approached history as an account of the evolution of civilization.

Men like the Italian Giovanni Battista Vico studied the "philosophy" of history—not the "what happened" so much as the "why." In his important *Principles of a New Science* (1725) Vico discussed the operation of laws in history, stressing the idea that every age is imbued with a certain "psychology," mood, or point of view and that each age is not only the product of the one preceding but also the creator of the next.

Other social sciences. The eighteenth century witnessed notable advances in political science, the study of government. In Chapter 19 we shall read of the writings of Hobbes, Bossuet, and Locke, and note the work of the *philosophes* Rousseau and Montesquieu as they analyzed the machinery and purposes of government.

Economics as a distinct subject for study emerged in the last half of the seventeenth century, much of it justifying the policy of mercantilism. Later, the Scotsman Adam Smith (see p. 445) and a number of the French *philosophes* known as the physiocrats made important contributions to economic theory by attacking the prevailing mercantilistic philosophy and initiating economic principles that were dominant down to the twentieth century.

As efforts were made to classify human races and to make comparative studies of various groups of people, the first halting steps were taken toward a science of anthropology. Much of the information used for these studies was provided by the writings of explorers, traders, and missionaries.

The science of criminology was established by the Italian Cesare Beccaria, whose *Essay on Crimes and Punishments* (1764) contained the plea that prison terms should be deterrents to crime rather than punishments for crime. Shortly thereafter, John Howard in England stressed the need for efficient prison administration and maintained that the chief aim of imprisonment should be reformation of the criminal.

New attitudes toward education. Until the eighteenth century education was almost unattainable for common people, the subjects taught often bore no relation to the needs of actual life, and the prevailing idea seemed to be that schoolchildren needed frequent beatings. In that century, however, educational thought began to reflect the humanitarianism of the age.

The scientific basis for the psychology of learning as well as for modern psychology in general was laid by the versatile British thinker John Locke at the end of the seventeenth century. His conception of the mind as a *tabula rasa* (blank tablet) at birth, and of the adult mind as one formed by experience through sensation and refined and tempered by reflection, memory, and judgment, was basic to the development of the discipline of psychology. One of the most important influences in education was that exerted by Jean Jacques Rousseau (1712-1778), whose novel *Émile* (1762) stated that the aim of education should be self-expression, not repression. Education must be many-sided to appeal to different children; and the pupil, not the subject matter, is most important.

Pietism, along with rationalism, entered into the motivation of education. In England the Sunday School movement, sponsored mainly by the Methodists, was a pioneer attempt to bring the rudiments of learning to the poor.

SCIENTIFIC PROGRESS CONTINUES

The dawn of modern medicine. We have seen the spectacular discoveries made in astronomy and mathematics and their profound impact on thought and religion. Meanwhile, scientific progress was being made in other branches of knowledge, with medicine being one of the first to be placed upon a scientific foundation.

Paracelsus (1493-1541), a contemporary of Copernicus, was an egotistical, opinionated German-Swiss physician who was so annoyed with the tyranny of tradition in his field that he advocated instead the value of experimental science. The gist of his teachings was that since the human body was basically chemical in its construction, the prescription of chemicals was in turn required to cure disease. He appears to have been the first to use such drugs as silver nitrate, copper vitriol, and arsenic and antimony compounds and to introduce the zinc oxide ointment commonly used today for treatment of skin diseases. One of his most original books dealt with the peculiar ailments of miners—the poisonous effects of metallic dusts that penetrated their skin, lungs, and mucous membranes.

Another scientist to find himself at odds with the followers of Galen and Hippocrates was Andreas Vesalius (1514-1564), a native of Brussels. Although he did not deny the merits of the Greek authorities, Vesalius contended that in medical schools, attention should first be given to the actual dissection of human bodies. At the age of twenty-three, Vesalius became a professor at the famous University of Padua. He was perhaps the first professor to perform dissection in the classroom. In 1543, within a few weeks of the appearance of Copernicus' masterpiece, Vesalius published his treatise *The Fabric of the Human Body*. This work exposed the errors made by classical scholars, showed the true structure of the human body, and by its revolutionary approach achieved for anatomy what Copernicus' book did for astronomy.

A commensurate advance in physiology (without which there could be no science of internal medicine) was made by the Englishman William Harvey (1578-1657), who had studied at Padua. Becoming interested in the problem of how the blood travels, Harvey plunged into painstaking research. Aristotle had declared that the blood was carried from the liver to the heart and thence sent by veins to the various parts of the body, and Galen believed that the arteries also contained blood. In Harvey's time doctors thought that the blood moved in the body, but they knew nothing of the functions of the heart nor did they know that the blood travels in a continuous stream, returning to its source. Harvey's description of the circulation of the blood,

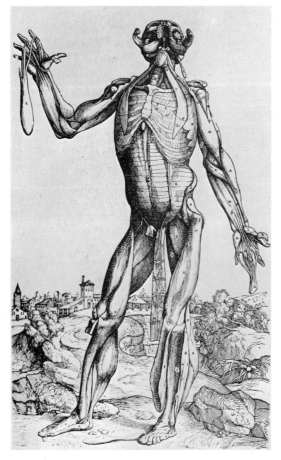

This weird figure, a cadaver with its jawbone split and its muscles cut away, appears in an illustration from Vesalius' book on anatomy.

published in 1628 and entitled *Anatomical Exercise on the Motion of the Heart and Blood*, was a kind of master key to unlock the many doors leading to an understanding of how the human body functions.

In the eighteenth century, the most noteworthy advance in medicine was the introduction of inoculation against smallpox, then a fatal and widespread disease. About 1798 a perfected method, called vaccination, was introduced by the English physician Edward Jenner. A great step forward in the advance of medical diagnosis was the invention of the stethoscope, through which the sounds of the heart and respiratory organs could be heard. Still another advance was the study of blood pressure, one of the most important means of discovering disease. Although the method

employed was crude, it led to the making of modern-day apparatus.

Foundations of modern chemistry. The science of chemistry suffered from arrested development in the sixteenth and early seventeenth centuries as men followed the will-o'-the-wisps of alchemy and magic. Then appeared the son of an Irish nobleman, Robert Boyle, who is considered the father of modern chemistry. In 1660 he formulated the law that "at constant temperature, the volume of a gas varies inversely as the pressure upon it" (Boyle's law). And in his influential book *The Sceptical Chemist* (1661) he struck out against alchemy and urged the use of inductive inquiry in chemistry.

Joseph Priestley, an English chemist, isolated ammonia, the gas which in modern times plays an important role in the refrigeration process; and in 1774, he discovered the gas later named oxygen. His last important experiment in 1799 was the production of carbon monoxide gas. Much of the gas used in our homes for cooking and heating purposes is made by the method first devised by Priestley.

Through Boyle and Priestley, chemistry had come a long way from medieval alchemy, but it would not become an exact science until the phlogiston theory of combustion could be disproved. This theory contended that in all inflammable things there existed a combustible substance called phlogiston (from the Greek "to set on fire"), which was "a principle of fire, but not fire itself." Destruction of the phlogiston theory was the remarkable achievement of the eighteenth-century French scientist Antoine Lavoisier.

Supporters of the old theory maintained that phlogiston was removed during combustion. By using chemists' scales in his experiment, Lavoisier proved that nothing was given off, that, on the contrary, something was added. From this evidence Lavoisier reasoned that burning is a process in which the "dephlogisticated air" (oxygen) discovered by Priestley is taken from ordinary air and unites with the substance consumed. By decomposing the red powder he had obtained by burning mercury, Lavoisier conclusively proved his thesis; the loss of weight of the powder was exactly equivalent to the weight of the dephlogisticated air given off. To the element so essential in combustion Lavoisier gave a new name—*oxygen.*

In his experiments on combustion Lavoisier also discovered the law of the conservation of matter—that matter cannot be created or destroyed. With the knowledge that weight is a constant and that the scientist, aided by his balance, can accurately determine by weight the substances in any compound, measurements in chemistry could be made with the precision required of an exact science.

Beginnings of electricity. Only three hundred years ago practically nothing was known of electricity and its seemingly magical potentialities. The scientist William Gilbert was the first to use the term *electricity*, which he derived from the Greek word for amber (*elektron*). In his work *De Magnete* (1600) Gilbert described the attraction between magnets as well as the forces which are created when bodies such as amber are rubbed.

The next important step in the history of electricity was the creation of a crude machine to produce it. A device consisting of a globe of sulfur set in a glass sphere mounted on a revolving axis was invented in 1660. When rubbed by a cloth, it produced both sound and light. With this device an electric current could be sent from one end of a thread to the other—the first hint of possibilities for the transmission of electricity. The discovery in 1745 of the Leyden Jar at the University of Leyden in the Netherlands made possible the accumulation in a glass phial of the electricity which was produced by friction.

The next important advance is credited to Benjamin Franklin, who was America's first great name in science. Believing that lightning was identical with the static electricity in the Leyden Jar, Franklin in June 1752 carried out his famous kite experiment during a thunderstorm. Holding the kite string with a key tied to it, he soon felt the tingle of electricity in the key, through which electricity was freely conducted as the rain soaked the string. Franklin's experiment provided a rational explanation for what had been an awe-inspiring and terrifying phenomenon for thousands of years. The experiment led

to the invention of the lightning rod, which soon became standard equipment on all important buildings.

Another great name in electricity is that of Alessandro Volta. In 1800 Volta, an Italian physicist, found a new way of generating electricity; he was able to make it flow continuously instead of discharging itself in one spark as was the case with the Leyden Jar. Volta's apparatus consisted of a set of glass tumblers containing water and a little sulfuric acid. In each solution two plates, one copper and one zinc, were immersed. The copper plate of one glass was wired to the zinc of the next. Electricity flowed through the connecting wires; the free copper plate carried a positive charge and the free zinc plate, a negative charge. Thus Volta's machine—the direct ancestor of modern electric cells and batteries—produced electricity simply but effectively. Volta's name has been immortalized in the term used for a unit of electrical measurement, the volt.

Advances in other sciences. Another science which made remarkable advances during the eighteenth century was geology. Here the most important figure was a Scottish gentleman farmer, James Hutton. His two-volume work, *Theory of the Earth* (1795), completely overthrew the catastrophic theory then current, which taught that the earth's surface was the result of sudden catastrophic action. In brief, Hutton maintained that behind all the various formations of the earth's surface two fundamental processes are at work in a constant and relatively imperceptible manner. The two processes are disintegration, or decay, and reconstruction, or repair. Through the action of water and wind and chemical decomposition, the former continually wears away the earth's surface. The process of reconstruction takes place as the material carried off and deposited on ocean, lake, and valley floors constantly forms new strata. By changing the concept of the earth as a static thing and stressing the immensity of geological time, Hutton gave the world an entirely new time perspective.

Exploration and scientific investigations in the seventeenth and eighteenth centuries brought to light a vast body of new information on plant and animal life which had to be classified. The old, unscientific method, which had designated all living things as fish, birds, beasts, trees, herbs, or shrubs, was inadequate to cope with the wealth of new data. The eighteenth-century Swedish naturalist Carolus Linnaeus worked out a logical system of plant classification, dividing the plant kingdom into classes, orders, genera, and species—still the basis of modern nomenclature. In the field of zoology the French scientist Georges Buffon performed the same function Linnaeus had performed in botany.

THE ARTS IN EARLY MODERN TIMES

The "anti-Renaissance" style: Mannerism. In Italy, where the Renaissance had initially burst forth, a countermovement in art appeared in the sixteenth century. There artists —who so often act as barometers to register sensitive changes in the cultural atmosphere

During the Renaissance renewed interest in classical antiquity resulted in the frequent use of subjects from Greek and Roman mythology. Benvenuto Cellini's salt-cellar represents Neptune, god of the sea, and Tellus, goddess of the earth. A virtuoso study in the technique of the goldsmith, it is less a utilitarian object than a piece of fine art. The boat in the foreground served as a salt receptacle, while an arch of triumph on the opposite side was designed to hold pepper.

—responded to the stresses of the Protestant and Catholic Reformations. The result was the development in Italian painting of a new, "anti-Renaissance" style called Mannerism. No longer was the artist working in that spirit of calm and balance, of harmony and proportion, which had prevailed in Renaissance art at its finest. The Mannerist artist lived instead in a state of doubt and indecision, and his work reflected those tensions. Technically speaking, Renaissance painters had mastered the problems of space and perspective, so that the artist placed his figures in balanced relationships enriched by vigorous and harmonious colors. By contrast, Mannerist painters such as Tintoretto (1518-1594) often defied the rules of perspective in order to obtain an oblique and even twisted point of view; their lines might be agitated, their designs asymmetric. They did not hesitate to distort the human figure in order to achieve emotional intensity (see illustration, p. 409).

Among the sculptors of the Mannerist period was the boastful Benvenuto Cellini (see p. 285), whose overelaborate compositions are typical of the extreme individualism and experimentation of the period. Some Mannerist architects sought to develop a more lavish classical style. The exaggerated magnificence of the Villa Rotunda near Venice, designed by Andrea Palladio (1518-1580), was achieved by grouping four identical temple facades on the sides of a square domed building. The Palladian style so impressed later generations that Thomas Jefferson used the Villa Rotunda as a prototype for his own Monticello.

Outside Italy the Mannerist style found its greatest achievements in the works of El Greco ("the Greek"). Born in Crete as Domenico Theotocopuli, El Greco (1547-1614) studied in Italy and later settled in Toledo in Spain. He was not concerned with depicting nature realistically but distorted space and perspective to create an often eerie world of the imagination. To achieve dramatic effects, he used *chiaroscuro* (strong contrasts of light and shade) and abrupt transitions in color. El Greco's paintings are easily recognizable for their elongated figures (see illustration, p. 410). To us he appears amazingly "modern," and his works have had a decided influence upon twentieth-century painting.

Triumph of the Baroque style. Meanwhile, other developments had been pushing aside the doubts characteristic of Mannerism and were helping create a style expressing the varied facets of the seventeenth century: its intellectual zest, religious exaltation, sensuality, and violence. By announcing its regeneration with majestic voice, the Church of the Catholic Reformation indirectly exerted a powerful influence on the development of a new style of artistic expression—one that would proclaim the message of the revived Church with pomp and circumstance. This new style was the Baroque.

The Baroque style sought to synthesize two major traditions, one derived from the Middle Ages, the other from the Renaissance. The medieval esthetic tradition was transcendental in its purpose and marked by religious intensity, while the Renaissance was more natural in its conception and technically brilliant. In his synthesis the Baroque artist sought by the skill and grandeur of his treatment to arouse the strongest possible emotions in the beholder. As a result, by an emphatic use of color, gesture, ornamentation, and movement, he developed a style that tended to be grandiose and exaggerated. In keeping with the spirit of the times, moreover, the Baroque gave expression to two new forces in Europe: the Catholic Reformation and royal absolutism (see Chapter 19). "In its sacred branch it discharged the mighty task of realizing and consolidating a Catholic reform of art, of emphasizing the aesthetic and emotional side of religion. In the secular field it ministered to the pomp and pride of princes. To both church and throne it lent effulgence." [12]

The Baroque style merged painting, sculpture, and architecture in new, large-scale combinations marked by heroic proportions and dramatic arrangements of light and space. One of the creators of the Baroque in painting whose influence permeated western Europe was the Flemish artist Peter Paul Rubens (1577-1640). An artist of prodigious gifts, Rubens chose dramatic themes from both pagan and Christian literature. Truly Baroque is his sensuous use of rich textures,

Tintoretto, an early apprentice of Titian, soon fell out with his master and developed his own style. In his "Abduction of the Body of St. Mark" his taste for intensive drama is expressed in the lighting, and the tension is compounded by the asymmetrical design. This is in sharp contrast to the balanced and classical mood of High Renaissance paintings.

as shown in his painting of flesh, satin, armor, and the hides of horses (see Color Plate 13).

The cool and objective point of view displayed by the canvases of the Spanish court painter Diego Velázquez (1599-1660) seem static alongside the sensuous exuberance of Rubens and the mannerisms of El Greco. Velázquez painted exactly what he saw in a style essentially his own, an unaffected and unadorned naturalism. He did not paint forms or surfaces so much as the movement of light over those surfaces, which produced an effect of the utmost reality. This preoccupation with light explains his "modernity" and especially his influence upon the French Impressionists of the nineteenth century.

The Dutch masters: Hals, Vermeer, Rembrandt. The first half of the seventeenth century was a golden age for Holland. Prosperous and comfortable, the burghers often acted as patrons of the arts. Their tastes in paintings differed greatly from those of kings, prelates, and aristocrats. These Dutch merchants and bankers favored familiar scenes of the flat lush countryside, seascapes in all seasons, and comfortable household interiors. A horde of competent Dutch painters arose in response to the demands of this republican art, and their overproduction soon depressed prices and created the image of the starving artist. Among the Dutch painters, the names of Hals, Vermeer, and Rembrandt stand out.

The robust Frans Hals (1580-1666) possessed a vigorous style that enabled him to catch with particular success the spontaneous, fleeting expressions of his portrait sub-

El Greco, the master of the Mannerist style, was deeply influenced by Tintoretto. Carrying the revolt against Renaissance style even further, El Greco distorted his figures to obtain the desired emotional intensity. In "St. Martin and the Beggar" the elongation gives the beggar's body a suggestion of weightlessness.

jects (see illustration, p. 411). His canvases provide us with an interesting gallery of types—from cavaliers to fishwives and tavern denizens. As for Jan Vermeer (1632-1675), the subtle delicacy with which he handled the fall of subdued sunlight upon interior scenes has never been equaled (see illustration, p. 411). His few canvases raised *genre* painting to perfection, and today each commands a king's ransom.

The finest of Dutch painters—and one who ranks with the outstanding artists of all time—was Rembrandt van Rijn (1606-1669). His straightforward and realistic works gained him fame at an early age, but his later work declined in popularity as his style became more subtle. He concentrated progressively in his portraits on psychological and emotional qualities, and his work exhibits a strong element of the dramatic, which links Rembrandt to the mainstream of Baroque style (see illustration, p. 411).

Baroque architecture. The Baroque style endowed architecture with a new emotional significance, dynamism, and fluidity. Where the architecture of the Renaissance is severe and self-contained and emphasizes symmetry and "squareness," the Baroque sweeps us off our feet by subjecting us to an almost physical pull. It is a magnificent stage set, full of visual illusions intended to arouse an emotional response.

The capital of the new Baroque architecture was Rome, and the most renowned seventeenth-century architect of the Baroque school was Giovanni Lorenzo Bernini (1598-1680). He designed the colonnades outside the Basilica of St. Peter's, and his plan is typical of the Baroque use of vast spaces and curving lines. Besides being an accomplished architect and painter, Bernini was also a magnificent sculptor (see his "St. Theresa," p. 318), as were many other artists of the Baroque. In fact, the architect acted also as a sculptor, painter, and interior decorator, for the integration of Baroque art reached the point where it was difficult to see where one art left off and another began (see illustration, p. 412).

After 1600 the Baroque style spread over much of Europe, being favored both by the Catholic Church and by rulers whose palaces

Seventeenth-century Dutch artists preferred portraits of the citizens themselves and scenes of daily life to religious subjects and grandiose display. Within these confines, however, they used various techniques and created different effects. The ostensibly rough-hewn, yet deft, brushstrokes of Franz Hals' "Malle Babbe" (left) contrast vividly with the delicate line and subtle play of light in Jan Vermeer's "The Lacemaker" (bottom left), while Rembrandt van Rijn seems to combine the subdued, centralized lighting of Vermeer with the ruggedness of Hals to offset the unswerving realism of "Jan Six" (bottom right).

were designed to serve as symbols of power and magnificence. The Baroque features of the luxurious palace of Louis XIV at Versailles (see p. 423), an ideal which nearly every European prince hoped to attain, include the sweeping composition of its vast facade as well as its formal gardens with their imposing fountains, formal statuary, and elegant rows of hedges. In the interior, the silk and velvet draperies, rich marbles, and gilded carving created a background for profuse painted decoration. Although the Baroque won little favor in England or its colonies, Sir Christopher Wren's St. Paul's Cathedral, completed in 1710, blends the classical and the Baroque. Its Baroque features include the lantern atop its imposing dome and the two turrets flanking the facade.

The Rococo style. In France early in the eighteenth century a variation on the Baroque, called Rococo, appeared as a reaction to the Baroque's robustness and exuberance. Manifested chiefly in interior decoration and

in painting, the Rococo is an intimate, gay, and dainty style. In the designing of interiors, the grandiose features of the Baroque are replaced by an almost effeminate delicacy (see below). The Rococo paintings of Jean Antoine Watteau (d. 1721) delicately blend fantasy with acute observation of nature and reflect the grace, ease, luxuriousness, and gentle artificiality of eighteenth-century French court life.

Classicism and the arts. Even during the heyday of the Baroque in the seventeenth century, many of the arts continued to follow the tenets of classicism often reinforced by the cultivation of reason. This was generally true of all the arts in England and of some of the arts, particularly literature, in France (see illustration, p. 422).

By the eighteenth century a great classical revival, usually called Neoclassicism, was under way in all the fine arts as well as literature. Inspired in part by the order and symmetry of the world as revealed by science,

The influence of the Roman Baroque on aristocratic French interiors is evident in the Appartement du Roi in Cheverny, built before 1634 (right). Representative of the extravagant yet delicate Rococo style of interior decoration is the music room in the Potsdam palace of Frederick II (left).

and in part by a reaction against the Baroque and the Rococo, the creative artists of the Age of Reason were noteworthy for their rationalism, sophistication, balance, and self-control. Furthermore, the Enlightenment was a continuation of Renaissance humanism and its revival of antiquity, coupled with the new scientific outlook. In literature and the arts there was a respect for definite rules and conventions. The men of the time felt spiritually akin to Rome's Augustan Age and strove to exhibit the same stability, refined polish, and control over emotion. In consequence, every work of art tended to have a cold, rational aspect, whether it was a philosophical poem by Pope or a dainty symphony by Haydn. Inspiration sprang from the intellect, not the heart; from reason, not emotion. Generally speaking, classical forms were slavishly imitated; to writers the style of expression was considered so all-important that many of them were content to express old ideas so long as they were elegantly phrased.

French classical drama. The veneration for order and restraint was reflected in seventeenth-century French drama, with its emphasis on the rules of classical tragedy as first defined by Aristotle. His strictures had been expanded and redefined in the Renaissance as the three unities: unity of action (a single plot line shorn of irrelevant subplots), unity of time (confinement of a play's action to a single day), and unity of place (restriction of setting to one locale). It was believed that the illusion of reality, so essential to the success of the drama, would be destroyed if the unities were ignored. "Reason leads us to accept these rules," stated a French critic, truly a man of his times.

The works of the two greatest writers of tragedy in the seventeenth century—Pierre Corneille and Jean Racine—are important not so much for their scrupulous adherence to rigid conventions, however, as for their psychological insights and polished beauty of language. For plots, they relied on tales from Greek and Roman mythology or events of antiquity; for heroes and heroines, they drew idealized characterizations of the courtiers of their own day.

With its immensity, statuary, and ornate dome, the Sta. Maria della Salute in Venice, designed by Baldassare Longhena, is an outstanding example of the power and magnificence exuded by Baroque architecture.

The wittiest comedies of the period were those of Molière. As a true voice of the Age of Reason, he believed that moderation and good sense were the keynotes of life and that any deviation from reasonable behavior was fair game for comedy. With rapier-like wit, he spoofed the pretensions of learned females and the aspirations of the social-climbing bourgeoisie. But like all great writers, Molière created characters that were universal figures as well as individuals of his own time.

Alexander Pope. The foremost exponent of Neoclassicism in English literature was the poet Alexander Pope (1688-1744). An imitator of the classical satirists Horace and Juvenal, Pope ridiculed those who did not conform to the standards of the age:

Pains, reading, study are their just pretense,
And all they want is spirit, taste, and sense.[13]

Shying away from the robust heavy-handedness of the Baroque period, Watteau aspired to a more graceful, gentle art form. His "Réunion en Plein Air" displays the quick, supple line and light, sensitive brushwork characteristic of the Rococo style.

In his most famous poem, *An Essay on Man* (1733), Pope reduced to a series of epigrams the philosophy of his day. Reflecting the strong note of optimism so characteristic of the Enlightenment, Pope accepted the cosmos thus:

All are but parts of one stupendous whole,
Whose body nature is, and God the soul. . . .
All nature is but art, unknown to thee;
All chance, direction, which thou canst not see.
All discord, harmony not understood;
All partial evil, universal good;
And, spite of pride, in erring reason's spite,
One truth is clear: *Whatever is, is right.*[14]

The English novel. In conformity with the emphasis on clarity and simplicity in an age of science and reason, the eighteenth century was in general an age of prose. This contributed to the growth of a new literary form —the novel. Daniel Defoe's *Robinson Crusoe* (1719) is sometimes called the forerunner of the modern novel, but the title is probably better deserved by Samuel Richardson's *Pamela* (1740-1741), written in the form of letters. In line with the rationalistic temper of the age, Richardson's servant-girl heroine succeeds in holding her lecherous employer at bay with lectures on moral philosophy until virtue at length has its reward and the reformed rake proposes marriage.

With Henry Fielding the novel achieved full stature. Disgusted with Richardson's "goody-goodness," Fielding achieved fame by parodying the latter's smug sentimentality and, as the author of *Tom Jones* (1749), by composing one of the great novels in English literature. The hero Tom is a high-spirited, good-hearted young man who is continually being exploited by self-seeking worldlings and led astray by designing females. Finally, after many comic adventures, he learns eventually that he must check his natural impulsiveness with good sense and reasonable behavior.

In keeping with the Age of Reason's attack on irrational customs and outworn institutions, this period produced masterpieces of satire, such as Voltaire's *Candide*. One of England's outstanding satirists was Jonathan Swift, whose *Gulliver's Travels* (1726) ridicules the pettiness of man's quarrels, wars, and vices. For example, in the fictitious country of Lilliput, Captain Gulliver finds two opposing factions: the Big-endians, who passionately maintain that eggs must be opened at the big end, and the Little-endians, who are equally vehement that the small end should be used. This absurd quarrel satirizes a petty religious dispute then raging in England. It is ironic that a satire such as *Gulliver's Travels*, because of its absorbing adventures and strange characters, should have become (in adapted form) a favorite book for children.

The Neoclassical style in architecture. About midway in the eighteenth century, a reaction set in against both Baroque and Rococo, manifesting itself in a return to the intrinsic dignity and restraint of what a contemporary called "the noble simplicity and tranquil loftiness of the ancients." Too often, however, the Neoclassical imitations and adaptations of the antique were cold and pedantic. The Madeleine in Paris (see below) is a faithful copy of a still-standing Roman temple, and the Brandenburg Gate in Berlin is modeled after the monumental entrance to the Acropolis in Athens. In England, where the classical style had resisted Baroque influences, the great country houses of the nobility now exhibited a purity of design which often included a portico with Corinthian columns. Outstanding as examples of

Neoclassicism in colonial America are Mount Vernon and the stately mansion of Thomas Jefferson at Monticello. Interest in the classical style carried over through the nineteenth century, and today in the United States many libraries and government buildings are classical in derivation.

Painting and sculpture. The arts of painting and sculpture in the Age of Reason were dominated by the tastes of the aristocracy. Watteau's successors in France—Boucher and Fragonard—mirrored the artificiality and idleness in which the aristocrats at Versailles, sometimes thinly disguised as Greek gods and goddesses, spent their lives. In England the most famous beauties of the day and many prominent men sat for portraits painted in the "grand manner" by Sir Joshua Reynolds or Thomas Gainsborough.

Two great nonconformist painters, William Hogarth in England and Francisco de Goya in Spain, strove to reproduce realistically the

Modeled after a Roman Corinthian temple, the Church of the Madeleine in Paris has columns sixty-three feet tall, a height which surpasses that of the temple of antiquity. The church has no windows in the walls; light is furnished by rounded windows in the roof.

life around them in the gutter, the tavern, and the royal court, sometimes using their art to draw attention to the evils of the day. In his series of paintings called "The Harlot's Progress," "The Rake's Progress," and "Marriage à la Mode," Hogarth showed himself to be a pictorial pamphleteer, shrewdly exposing the vices of London life (see p. 417). Goya's portraits of the Spanish royal family and the nobility display his keen insight into character. In the early years of the nineteenth century his art reached its peak in a series of etchings of the Napoleonic invasion and occupation of Spain. Called "The Disasters of War," they portrayed in powerful, shocking fashion the bestiality and misery wrought by war. Typical of Goya's abhorrence of brutality is his stark depiction of an execution in the "Shooting of the Rebels of May 3, 1808" (see Color Plate 17).

In sculpture the works produced in the eighteenth century were mostly imitations of classical forms and personages, such as Venus. Houdon's "Portrait of Voltaire" (see illustration, p. 391) is a well-known example of Neoclassical sculpture at its best.

Developments in music. As we saw in Chapter 13, late medieval religious music was polyphonic, not homophonic, in form. By the sixteenth century many-voiced polyphonic music had become so excessively complicated that some Church reformers at the Council of Trent demanded an end to polyphonic music and a return to the homophonic Gregorian chant of the early Middle Ages. The results of the Council's compromise decision were best expressed in the sacred music of Giovanni Palestrina (d. 1594), who greatly simplified the prevailing style by uniting homophony with polyphony. The restrained yet powerful effect of Palestrina's music has earned him the honor of being called the "first Catholic Church musician."

In the seventeenth century the Baroque spirit was manifested in music by the development of new forms of expression and by experiments in harmony which moved away from the calm and exalted manner of Palestrina. For the first time instrumental music—in particular that of the organ and the violin family—became of equal importance with

vocal music. Outstanding among Baroque innovations was opera, which originated in Italy at the beginning of the seventeenth century and quickly conquered Europe. With its opulence, highly charged emotional content, and sweep of expression, opera was almost the perfect musical expression of the Baroque style. Here again we find an integration of the arts: dramatic literature, music, and acting, with the skills of the painter employed for elaborate stage settings.

The elaboration of polyphonic music during the Baroque era culminated in the sumptuous effects of the deeply religious music of Johann Sebastian Bach (d. 1750), the prolific German organ master and choir director. Bach's equally great contemporary, the German-born, naturalized Englishman George Frederick Handel (1685-1759), is known for his large, dramatic, and mostly homophonic operas, oratorios, and cantatas; he is best known today for his religious oratorio *Messiah* (1742).

To composers living in the latter half of the eighteenth century, the style of the Baroque masters Bach and Handel seemed too heavy and complex. Like the other arts of the Age of Reason, music now exhibited greater clarity and simplicity of structure and a strict adherence to formal rules and models. Emphasis was placed on a homophonic style and on simple, often folklike, melodies, and most compositions followed the sonata-form with its three clearly defined thematic sections—exposition, elaboration, and recapitulation.

New musical forms reflected new trends in instrumental music. As symphonies, sonatas, concertos, and chamber music appeared, music became more than the mere accompaniment to religious services and operatic performances. The chamber music played in courts and salons was written for wood winds and brasses as well as strings. Thus the modern orchestra developed along with the symphonic form.

The music of the latter half of the eighteenth century, with its emphasis on technical perfection of form, melody, and orchestration, was summed up in the work of the Viennese composers Franz Joseph Haydn and Wolfgang Mozart. The prolific Haydn

In "The Marriage Contract," a painting from Hogarth's series "Marriage à la Mode," a wealthy but low-born merchant is arranging the marriage of his daughter to the son of an impoverished but high-born noble. While the fathers talk business, the daughter listens to the blandishments of a young lawyer, and the son, a silly fop, takes snuff and stares into space. Typical of Hogarth's method of putting satirical meaning into every detail of his work are the two chained dogs (left corner) who represent the plight of the young couple.

wrote over one hundred symphonies in addition to numerous other works. For his part, Mozart, a child prodigy who at the age of six was composing minuets, wrote forty-one symphonies, climaxing his career with a trio of famous operas, *The Marriage of Figaro, Don Giovanni,* and *The Magic Flute.*

SUMMARY

The Age of Reason was a vigorous and productive period in the history of western culture. The promise of science initiated by Copernicus was fulfilled in Newton's brilliant postulation of the law of gravitation. New sciences, such as chemistry, electricity, and geology, were founded; and other sciences, such as astronomy, physics, and medicine, were put on a scientific foundation. Meanwhile, a system of scientific method, or investigation, was established. Two thinkers, especially, investigated the problem of developing new methods of inquiry.

Francis Bacon placed chief reliance upon the inductive method, in which facts drawn from experimentation are used to formulate hypotheses and eventually to reach universal principles and scientific laws. A younger contemporary in France, Descartes, was more interested in deduction and used the mathematical method to reason his way to the concept of a mechanically run universe. Actually, the mathematical and experimental methods were complementary and were soon combined to promote the further advancement of science.

By the mid-point of the seventeenth century it was apparent that respect for science and scientific attitudes was to be the keynote of the culture of the new era. To many of the intellectuals, little seemed left of faith and traditional Christianity; and as men ceased to believe in miracles and denominational theology, what has been termed the "crisis in the European conscience" arose. Some met the crisis by turning to a new form of rational, scientific religion in which faith became a matter of logic and intellect. And as science came to modify religion substantially, so it also came to be applied to the affairs of men in society, to what we now term the social sciences. A start was made in organizing systematic studies in history, government, economics, and criminology.

In the field of literature and the arts, no less than in religion and the social sciences, scientific law and the vogue of rule played their part. Writing had to be faultlessly phrased, witty, and elegant. This polished, sophisticated, classical style reached its acme in the verses of Pope. While poetry and drama, on the whole, were not of a high order, the eighteenth century was one of great prose. The novel (which largely escaped the bonds of Neoclassical restriction) came of age in this period.

Preceded by a style of painting known as Mannerism—the best example of this troubled, distorted style is the work of El Greco—Baroque art and music captured the imagination and allegiance of seventeenth-century Europe. This exuberant and grandiloquent style gave way, in the eighteenth century, to the lighter Rococo and Neoclassical styles.

The portraits of Reynolds, the landscapes of Watteau, and the elegant musical patterns of Haydn served to embellish the essentially aristocratic culture of the Age of Reason. There are some critics of twentieth-century culture who look back with nostalgia to the aristocratic culture of the age. These critics see contemporary culture, dominated by the machine and by the mass mind, as vulgarized. The essence of history, however, is change and not permanence. In the latter half of the eighteenth century there were important signs that the primacy of the aristocracy and the dominance of rationalism were coming to an end. New currents and forces were being released that would produce sweeping changes and mold the nineteenth century into another distinct age in the history of western civilization.

SUGGESTIONS FOR READING

Short but meaty treatments of European culture, with valuable bibliographies, are contained in the following volumes in The Rise of Modern Europe series,* Torchbooks: C. J. Friedrich, **The Age of the Baroque, 1610–1660;** F. L. Nussbaum, **The Triumph of Science and Reason, 1660–1685;** J. B. Wolf, **The Emergence of the Great Powers, 1685–1715;** P. Roberts, **The Quest for Security, 1715–1740;** W. L. Dorn, **Competition for Empire, 1740–1763;** and L. Gershoy, **From Despotism to Revolution, 1763–1789.**

Intellectual developments are the focus of attention in Preserved Smith, **A History of Modern Culture, 1543–1776,*** 2 vols., Collier; and J. Bronowski and B. Mazlish, **The Western Intellectual Tradition from Leonardo to Hegel,*** Torchbooks. See also another well-known work, J. H. Randall, **The Making of the Modern Mind,** Houghton Mifflin, 1940.

H. Butterfield, **The Origins of Modern Science, 1300–1800,*** Free Press; and A. R. Hall, **The Scientific Revolution, 1500–1800,*** Beacon. Two highly recommended books on the formation of the modern scientific attitude. Two well-written volumes in Harper & Row's Rise of Modern Science series are Marie Boas, **The Scientific Revolution: 1450–1630,** 1962, and A. R. Hall, **From Galileo to Newton: 1630–1720,** 1963. For a condensed account by these same authors see **A Brief History of Science,*** Signet. On applied science see Thomas P. Hughes, ed., **The Development of Western Technology Since 1500,*** Macmillan. T. S. Kuhn, **The Structure of Scientific Revolutions,*** Phoenix, discusses the dynamic factors involved in major conceptual changes in science. See also W. D. D. Dampier-Whetham, **A History of Science and Its Relations with Philosophy,** Cambridge, 1929.

A. Koestler, **The Sleepwalkers: A History of Man's Changing Vision of the Universe,*** Penguin, Parts 3–5. A stimulating study of cosmological reconceptualization in early modern times—involving Copernicus, Brahe, Kepler, and Galileo. For a skillful recapitulation of the climate of opinion in which the heliocentric theory emerged, see T. S. Kuhn, **The Copernican Revolution,*** Vintage. A. Armitage, **The World of Copernicus,*** Mentor, is a popular study. See also A. Koyré, **From the Closed World to the Infinite Universe,*** Torchbooks. G. de Santillana, **The Crime of Galileo,*** Phoenix, is an exciting account of the scientist's struggle against censorship. Z. de Harsanyi, **The Star-Gazer,*** is a biographical novel about Galileo and his times.

H. Sigerist, **Great Doctors,*** Anchor. A notable biographical history of medicine. Also recommended are two books by C. Singer: **From Magic to Science,*** Dover; and **A Short History of Anatomy and Physiology from the Greeks to Harvey,*** Dover.

F. B. Artz, **From the Renaissance to Romanticism,*** Phoenix. Highly valuable view of the arts through six centuries. B. Willey, **The Seventeenth Century Background: Studies in the Thought of the Age in Relation to Poetry and Religion,** Chatto & Windus, 1967, is an excellent study. On art see W. Sypher, **Four Stages of Renaissance Style,*** Anchor; R. Wilenski, **Introduction to Dutch Art,** Faber, 1929; and V. Tapié, **The Age of Grandeur: Baroque Art and Architecture,*** Praeger. On music see M. Bukofzer, **Music in the Baroque Era,** Norton, 1947.

*Indicates an inexpensive paperbound edition.

Chapter 19

L'Etat, C'est Moi

**Absolutism and the Politics of Power:
1650-1775**

INTRODUCTION. The century following
the Peace of Westphalia (1648) was a vitally
important period in European politics. In the
weighing scales of power and military might,
the modern hierarchy of nations was being
established. Some of the old political structures were decaying: the Holy Roman Empire,
Poland, and the empire of the Ottoman Turks.
Such powerful nations as Spain and Sweden
were passing their golden ages and slipping
into a tranquil state of ineffectuality in the
realm of international affairs. In contrast,
France and England were dynamic and aggressive; Prussia, Russia, and Austria had
achieved stability and were advancing rapidly into the category of first-class powers.

What might be called the natural rise and
fall of nations was accelerated by the deliberate policies of strong powers operating in
the political climate termed the competitive
state system. In the perpetual competition
between nations, the decisive weapon was
military force. No one nation, however, was
allowed to become too strong; competitive
states manipulated the balance of power to
try to prevent the rise of a paramount nation

—France of Louis xiv in particular. Yet the prevalence of warfare during this age of absolutism should not blind us to the fact that the absolute monarchs provided the strong governments needed to achieve civil order after a long period of internal strife.

Offering a contrast to the pattern of growing absolutism on the Continent were the events taking place across the Channel. The Revolution of 1688 thwarted the growth of royal power in England and hastened its decline on the Continent. The system of government begun by that revolution—aristocratic liberalism—was an important step toward ultimate democratic parliamentary government.

THE SYSTEM OF ROYAL ABSOLUTISM

Architecture of absolutism. In the period from 1650 to 1775 the royal architects of the national state system reached the height of their power. During this age of absolutism the king was in theory and in fact an autocrat responsible to God alone. The outstanding example of the absolute monarch was Louis xiv of France, who is said to have once exclaimed to his fawning courtiers, "L'état, c'est moi" ("I am the state").

Under the system of absolutism the king's power touched every aspect of his subjects' existence. He was the supreme and only lawgiver—the fountain of justice. As head of the church he decided what religion his subjects were to follow and persecuted those who dissented. The worship of God was a matter of state, not the preserve of the individual conscience. The king regulated every phase of economic life, from the establishment of new industries to working conditions and standards of quality. In addition, he was the arbiter of manners and fashion, the patron of arts and letters, and the personification of national glory. An obedient bureaucracy and a powerful royal army enforced his will.

Although such a system of all-pervasive absolutism is abhorrent to us today, in the seventeenth century it was generally unquestioned and often very popular. A powerful king stood for order, efficiency, security, and prosperity—values willingly exchanged for the uncertainties of upheaval and bloodshed such as had been experienced during the turmoil of the preceding era of religious wars.

Bossuet and Hobbes: defenders of absolutism. The new absolute state was explained and rationalized by a number of political theorists. Jacques Bossuet (1627-1704) was a prominent French churchman who had been entrusted with the education of Louis xiv's son and was finally elevated to the position of bishop. Utilizing the doctrine of the divine right of kings, Bossuet composed a brilliant justification of absolute monarchy:

It appears . . . that the person of the king is sacred, and that to attack him in any way is sacrilege . . . the royal throne is not the throne of a man, but the throne of God himself. . . . Kings should be guarded as holy things, and whosoever neglects to protect them is worthy of death. . . . the royal power is absolute . . . [and] the prince need render account of his acts to no one. . . . Where the word of a king is, there is power. . . . Without this absolute authority the king could neither do good nor repress evil.[1]

In the long run, it was Thomas Hobbes (1588-1679) who composed the most penetrating and influential justification of absolutism. To this English student of the new scientific thought, absolutism was not to be defended by resort to religion. In the *Leviathan* (1651) Hobbes drew upon science and its servant, psychology. From the excesses of the religious wars in France, the Thirty Years' War in Germany, and the Civil War in England (see p. 427), Hobbes discovered what he believed to be the essential nature of man when not restrained by law. A pessimistic, cynical observer of human conduct, Hobbes saw man "as a wolf to his fellow man" and mankind as essentially selfish and cruel. Before law and authority came into existence men lived under the adverse conditions of the state of nature, in which there is no place for industry . . . no culture of the earth . . . no arts; no letters; no society; and which is worst of all, continual fear, and danger of violent death; and the life of man, solitary, poor, nasty, brutish, and short.[2]

To create a workable society and escape from the intolerable evils of the state of nature, men had gladly surrendered all their rights and powers to a sovereign government, an action which bound them to an irrevocable contract. Hobbes did not actually believe that there had once existed a "state of nature" and that at some specific date in world history mankind had decided to create, by contract, a despotic, all-powerful government. But if not demonstrable by experience, his argument was natural in terms of rational thought as an explanation of the nature of government.

Hobbes' Leviathan, the sovereign state, could be any one of a number of forms of government. But, to Hobbes, monarchy was the most effective and desirable, for only thus could peace and security be maintained. There was no right of revolution, even against tyranny.

LOUIS XIV: THE EPITOME OF ABSOLUTISM

Inheritance of Louis XIV. The best example of political absolutism is offered by France in the days of Louis XIV, who reigned from 1643 to 1715. This proud Bourbon monarch inherited a realm which had been made powerful during the preceding fifty years. The previous century, the sixteenth, had been a sorry period in France's history. Wars with the Hapsburgs had been followed by religious civil wars that almost destroyed the nation. The reign of Henry IV (1589-1610), however, brought peace and laid the foundations of the great nation which was to enjoy economic, military, and intellectual leadership in the seventeenth century.

The death of Henry left Louis XIII, a boy of nine, on the throne, with the queen mother as regent. During the next fourteen years Henry IV's achievements were slowly under-mined, until in 1624 Cardinal Richelieu, the clever protégé of the queen mother, became the real power behind the throne. For eighteen years the biography of Richelieu was truly the history of France. As chief advisor to Louis XIII, the "grim cardinal" set about restoring and furthering the accomplishments of Henry IV. He strove to exalt the power of France in Europe and of royal authority within the state. Richelieu himself loved power; while he made his royal master the first man in Europe, he made the king the second man in France.

Under Richelieu's direction the structure of absolutism quickly took shape. Castles of the nobility were torn down, officials of the central government called *intendants* replaced the nobility as the chief administrators in the provinces, and the Estates-General—a body that might have challenged the power of the king—was not summoned. In foreign affairs Richelieu was equally decisive and crafty. As we have already noted (p. 338), his intervention in the Thirty Years' War struck a staggering blow against the Hapsburgs and helped make France the greatest power in Europe.

After the deaths of Richelieu in 1642 and Louis XIII in 1643, the throne of France was again occupied by a child, Louis XIV, who was less than five years old. Richelieu had anticipated this emergency, however, by grooming a promising young Italian, Cardinal Mazarin, to be adviser to the regent. Mazarin governed France with a firm and efficient hand during the minority of the king, although the royal authority was seriously challenged by civil outbreak. For six years (1648-1653) France was convulsed by disorder. This civil war—a reaction against the excesses of the now powerful royal administration, known as the Fronde—had no effect in tempering absolutism. In fact, the violence of the struggle served to convince many Frenchmen that the only alternative to royal absolutism was anarchy.

Following the death of Mazarin in 1661, Louis XIV, then twenty-three years old, took over the personal management of state affairs. He found his people obedient and docile; Henry IV, Richelieu, and Mazarin had done their work efficiently.

France's rise to power in Europe was accompanied by the rise of French painting to a position of world leadership. The rulers of Bourbon France regarded art as a means of glorifying the monarchy, and they patronized the arts liberally. Philippe de Champaigne's "Triple Portrait of Richelieu," painted with keen precision and sophisticated use of colors, conveys the cool intellect, the poised manner, and the iron will of Richelieu. It is, moreover, a typical example of the classical realism of seventeenth-century French painting.

Louis XIV: the Sun King. Believing implicitly in the divine right of kings, Louis chose the sun as the symbol of his power. His courtiers dubbed him *Le Roi Soleil* (the Sun King), and he was also known throughout Europe as the Grand Monarch. Louis labored to enhance the power and prestige of the crown, which he frequently defended in haughty style:

All power, all authority, resides in the hands of the king, and there can be no other in his kingdom than that which he establishes. The nation does not form a body in France. It resides entire in the person of the king.[3]

The palace of the Louvre in Paris had been good enough for his predecessors, but Louis wanted a more magnificent symbol for his greatness. On barren marshland a few miles from Paris, Louis ordered the construction of the palace of Versailles. The total cost of construction probably exceeded one hundred million dollars. The marshland was transformed into a beautiful park surrounding the palace, whose facade was more than a quarter mile in length. The symmetry in the design of formal gardens and surroundings for the palace reflected the orderliness that Louis XIV, throughout his long reign, tried to impose on the society of his age.

Today the palace of Versailles is merely a historical monument, a symbol of royal elegance and glittering court life that has no place in our modern world. But two hundred years ago it was the most fashionable spot in Europe. During the day the French nobles promenaded with their king among the groves, terraces, and fountains of the park or hunted and hawked in the nearby woods and meadows. At night lords and ladies in powdered wigs, silks, and laces attended balls, masquerades, and concerts.

Just as science followed the rule of law, so life and manners conformed to the rules of etiquette. Studied elegance, formal manners, extravagant expressions of courtesy, and witty but superficial conversation all too often constituted the base of polite society, and manners were more important than morals. The aristocratic life of elegance, leisure, and polished deportment is well symbolized by the graceful minuet—a dance which "was a school for chivalry, courtesy and ceremony. . . ."[4]

Palace etiquette was carried to ridiculous extremes; the "cult of majesty" resulted in the king's being treated practically like a god. Louis was surrounded by fawning sycophants and servile courtiers, and his every action was made a regal ceremony based on the strictest precedent. For example, a nobleman of designated rank was required to dry the king after his bath, and only a very illustrious noble could hand the king the royal shirt or breeches during the public ceremony of dressing.

Louis' absolutism: the balance sheet. During the late seventeenth century France was the premier nation of Europe. In nearly every aspect—the splendor and formality of Versailles, the functioning of the central government, the organization of the military services—the absolute state of Louis xiv was the model.

Louis worked hard at what he called "the business of being king." He increased the powers of the *intendants* instituted by Richelieu; reorganized the army, making it the largest (nearly 400,000 men by 1703) and most modern in Europe; and instituted a wide variety of economic reforms to strengthen the French economy and increase revenue. Louis was fortunate in having as his finance minister the able Colbert, whose aggressive mercantilist practices (see p. 383) enabled a surplus to be accumulated in the royal treasury.

The positive side of Louis' reign—his own administrative zeal and the financial genius of Colbert—was counterbalanced by some unfortunate manifestations of Louis' lofty concept of the dignity of his office. The pomp and ceremony of Versailles is an example; Louis moved in a world of glitter and luxury, isolated from his people.

One extremely unwise act was the revocation of Henry iv's Edict of Nantes, which had guaranteed religious freedom for the Protestant Huguenots. To an absolute monarch like Louis, complete uniformity within his state was a cherished ideal, and legal toleration of religious nonconformity was a serious flaw in the system of absolutism. Therefore, in 1685, Louis revoked the Edict and caused thousands of industrious Huguenots to flee to other lands, taking with them

The symmetry and order of the palace and surrounding lands are evident in this bird's-eye view of Versailles as it looked in 1668, before it received extensive changes at the hands of Louis xv. Preceded by a large cavalry guard, the king is arriving in a carriage drawn by six horses, while the queen follows in the next carriage.

the principles which governed that science until the twentieth century.

Possessing the strongest army and the most capable generals of the age, Louis embarked on a series of wars to attain for France her "natural boundaries" by extending French territory eastward to the Rhine at the expense of the Spanish and Holy Roman empires (see Reference Map 5). Louis' chief motive was not security for France but prestige for the monarchy.

France threatens the balance of power. Taking advantage of Spain's decline, Louis in 1667 marched in and laid claim to the rich Spanish Netherlands (modern Belgium). The Dutch, alarmed by the loss of a buffer state between themselves and France, formed an alliance with England and Sweden and forced Louis to renounce his claim and withdraw. To eliminate this obstacle to his plans, Louis bought off Holland's allies and in 1672 invaded the Dutch provinces. The Dutch were in desperate straits until the inspired leadership of William of Orange (great-grandson of William the Silent who had led the revolt against Spain) and the aid of their old enemies, the Spanish and Austrian Hapsburgs, enabled them to checkmate Louis. Weak Spain paid the price of the peace by ceding Franche-Comté to France (see Reference Map 5).

Louis precipitated a third war in 1688 by laying claim to various Rhineland districts, mainly in Alsace and Lorraine. William of Orange, who with his English wife Mary had replaced James II on the throne of England in 1689, became the vigorous leader of a new anti-French coalition consisting of England, Holland, Austria, Spain, Sweden, and a few German states. With England for the first time playing the part of a major power in European affairs, Louis again was held in check and in 1697 signed a compromise peace in which he gained little.

War of the Spanish Succession. The death of the childless king of Spain left the Spanish throne open to the conflicting claims of distantly related princes of both Hapsburg Austria and Bourbon France. In his will the dying king left this great prize to Louis XIV's grandson, Philip. All Europe realized that, with his grandson as king of Spain, Louis

Louis XIV was not merely the architect of an era, he was also its product. This engraving, dating from 1676, depicts Louis (plumed hat) visiting the French Academy of Science. His own special enthusiasms—architecture and landscape gardening—are symbolically represented in the scene outside the window of the Academy.

skills and knowledge which were to enrich the enemies of France.

Finally, and most important of all, Louis squandered the resources of his realm in his passion for military conquest. War had become an all-important function of the state which required efficiency, organization, and discipline. Important changes were made in tactics and weapons: the improvement of firearms and the introduction of the bayonet eliminated the pike as the main infantry weapon; artillery and fortification methods were improved and so, in turn, were siege methods for the reduction of fortresses. Indeed, the tactics for siege warfare devised by Vauban, Louis' military engineer, established would have an empire rivaling in its extent and power the possessions of Charles V in the sixteenth century. Louis defied the Austrian claim and European sentiment by accepting the Spanish throne for Philip.

In answer to Louis' menacing move to dominate Europe, England organized another coalition against him. From 1702 to 1713 French armies fought the combined forces of this Grand Alliance in Spain, Italy, France, Germany, and the Low Countries. The allies were blessed with a remarkable English commander, John Churchill, the duke of Marlborough, an ancestor of Winston Churchill. Marlborough's most famous victory was the battle of Blenheim (1704); not until the French Revolution would French armies again terrorize Europe.

Treaty of Utrecht. In 1713 the War of the Spanish Succession ended with the forces of France considerably weakened and the Grand Alliance split by petty rivalries. Comparable in importance to the Peace of Westphalia, which had ended the Thirty Years' War, was the series of treaties signed at Utrecht between France and the members of the alliance. As a result of this peace settlement, a fairly satisfactory balance of power was maintained on the Continent for nearly thirty years without any major wars.

The most important terms of the Utrecht settlement were as follows: (1) Louis' grandson, Philip V, was permitted to remain king of Spain so long as the thrones of France and Spain were not united. (2) France was allowed to retain all of Alsace. (3) The Spanish empire was divided: Philip V retained Spain and Spanish America, while Austria obtained Naples, Milan, Sardinia, and the Spanish Netherlands (Belgium)—thereafter called the Austrian Netherlands. (4) England gained important colonies from France and Spain: Nova Scotia, Newfoundland, and the Hudson Bay territory, and valuable Mediterranean naval bases in the Balearic Islands and at Gibraltar. (5) As a reward for joining the Grand Alliance, the duke of Savoy was given Sicily and the title of king, and the Hohenzollern elector of Brandenburg was recognized as "king in Prussia." (In 1720 Savoy ceded Sicily to Austria in exchange for Sardinia.)

The significance of several provisions in this peace should be noted. The accession of the Bourbons to the throne of Spain after almost two centuries of Hapsburg rule marked the end of an era. The long-standing French-Spanish rivalry was now replaced by a strong French-Spanish family alliance since Bourbons occupied the two thrones. The English acquisition of important colonies and naval bases marked an important stage in the rise of Great Britain to world power. The treaty also gave recognition to two aggressive ruling families, the House of Savoy and the House of Hohenzollern. In the nineteenth century the House of Savoy would succeed in unifying Italy, and the Hohenzollerns Germany.

Consequences of Louis' wars. In 1715 Louis XIV died, leaving behind him a kingdom demoralized and debilitated by costly wars. France continued to be a first-class power and French culture was universally admired and imitated, but in retrospect we can see that Louis' reign did much to discredit the system of absolutism. He left behind a record of misery and discontent that paved the way for the French Revolution and the bloody downfall of his dynasty.

Louis' four wars strengthened the guiding principle of international diplomacy in modern times—the concept of the balance of power (see Chapter 15). To prevent France from dominating Europe, coalition after coalition had been formed. England was the balance wheel in the maintenance of this delicate equipoise, throwing support from one side to the other in order to maintain the balance of power on the Continent.

EVOLUTION OF CONSTITUTIONAL MONARCHY IN ENGLAND

Background for the English Civil War. The victory of England over France involved more than just the matter of English superiority in arms or diplomacy. It was the triumph of a system of government set in a mold different from that of Louis XIV's absolutism. This new political form has been termed *aristocratic liberalism* and defined as "government in accordance with the agreed decisions of bodies which were drawn from a limited class but acted after free discussion and with some degree of tolerance and of consideration for the governed."[5]

The revolution in England that produced aristocratic liberalism in the eighteenth century grew out of English experience with divine-right monarchy in the seventeenth century. The English Civil War (1642-1648), which was followed by the interim of the Commonwealth and Protectorate (1649-1660), was a complex blend of politics and religion. But unlike the Thirty Years' War, for example, the English Puritan Revolution was a domestic duel between groups fundamentally opposed in viewpoint—traditionalists who upheld the power of the monarchy and those who favored a government more representative of the people. The religious implications of the Civil War were important, but they have been overshadowed by the constitutional results stemming from the struggle. The outcome strongly influenced the development of constitutional governments and the growth of democracy in modern times.

For hundreds of years English institutions had been developing slowly in the direction of constitutional, representative government. During the Wars of the Roses, which followed the Hundred Years' War, constitutional progress was almost submerged in feudal disorder. Then, largely with the cooperation of Parliament and the approval of the English people, Tudor monarchs had restored law and order to England, broken with the Church of Rome, and ruled with a strong hand. No consistent breach of opinion developed between the crown on the one hand and Parliament and the people on the other to raise constitutional issues or to challenge the royal power so skillfully wielded by the Tudors.

If the growth of constitutional government had been temporarily placed in cold storage, it had not been frozen. During most of Elizabeth I's reign the House of Commons was content to improve its procedures and gain parliamentary experience. Following the defeat of the Spanish Armada, however, Parliament began to reassert itself. On questions of taxation it became increasingly independent, and unpopular measures presented by the queen's advisors were occasionally rejected.

James I and Parliament. Elizabeth's successor was James Stuart, king of Scotland and the son of Mary Stuart. As James I of England, he reigned from 1603 to 1625. Scotland and England remained separate states, and not until 1707 did the Scots consent to the Act of Union which created the United Kingdom of Great Britain.

James had scholarly interests which led him to appoint a commission to make a new English translation of the Bible—the King James Version (1611), a masterpiece of English prose. But notwithstanding his erudition, the new king was totally unfitted for his position. He lacked common sense and tact; small wonder that the French dubbed him "the wisest fool in Christendom."

James' initial unpolitic move was to advocate the divine right of kings in his first address to Parliament:

The state of monarchy is the supremest thing upon earth, for kings are not only God's lieutenants upon earth and sit upon God's throne, but even by God himself they are called gods. . . . That as to dispute what God may do is blasphemy, . . . so is it sedition in subjects to dispute what a king may do in the height of his power . . . I will not be content that my power be disputed upon. . . .[6]

Disregarding the temper of his new English subjects and their institutions, James made it plain that he meant to be an absolute monarch. In 1611 he dissolved Parliament and ruled without it until 1621.

The religious issue. The constitutional issue of king against Parliament was complicated by religious issues. Some Englishmen were content with the Anglican Church as it then was. Others hoped to reintroduce more of the ritual and tenets of Roman Catholicism, although they had no desire to return to papal control. Still others took an extreme reformist position.

The most important members of the latter group were known as Puritans because they wished to "purify" the Anglican Church of its "papal rites" and ecclesiastical hierarchy. They were against any priest or ceremony standing between them and God. They also considered James overfriendly with Catholic sovereigns abroad and inclined to favor and protect Catholics at home.

Many of the Puritans were members of the urban middle class. Engaged in trade and commerce, they resented James' arbitrary taxation and wanted to secure laws for the protection and expansion of English commercial interests. Puritan lawyers supplied historical precedents as ammunition against the growing absolutism of the throne.

Charles I and Parliament. James' mistakes were repeated by his son Charles I (1625-1649)—and to an even greater degree. Like father, the son espoused the divine right of kings, was contemptuous of the rights of Parliament, and supported the pro-Catholic or High Church faction in the Anglican Church.

Insisting on absolute royal power, Charles opened his reign with stormy debates with Parliament; but in return for revenue grants he agreed in 1628 to the famous Petition of Right—a reenactment of the "ancient rights of Englishmen." The most important provisions denied the monarch the right to tax without parliamentary consent or to imprison a freeman without just cause.

Charles' capitulation was only temporary, and from 1629 to 1640 he ruled England without calling Parliament. During this period he resorted to methods of taxation which alarmed all property owners and which the supporters of Parliament considered illegal. In addition, Charles punished those who opposed his efforts to promote High Church Anglicanism.

Royalists vs. Parliamentarians. When Charles attempted to force his brand of High Church Anglican religion on the Presbyterian subjects of his Scottish kingdom, they promptly took up arms against their king. Faced by a hostile army and without sufficient funds to put a force of his own into the field, Charles was forced to convene Parliament.

When Parliament refused to vote any money until Charles had redressed certain grievances, Charles promptly dissolved it. But riots in London and a Scottish invasion compelled him to recall Parliament. Sensing the weakness in the king's position, Parliament immediately set to work to make its powers at least coequal with his. This session became known as the "Long Parliament" because it lasted nearly twenty years.

As the tension between the crown and Parliament increased, two bitterly antagonistic groups quickly developed: the Royalist "party" and the Parliamentary "party." While both groups included all classes, the Parliamentarians attracted most of the merchants and the Royalists most of the younger men—the latter apparently reacting to their elders' puritanism. The Parliamentarians were divided between Independents and Presbyterians, who differed over questions of church government but agreed in holding generally to a Calvinistic system of religion and in demanding further reductions in the political and religious prerogatives of the monarch.

The Royalists, whose leaders came mainly from the great landowners, opposed the extreme reforms urged by the Puritans. While agreeing with the Puritans in opposing royal despotism, they were unwilling to see the monarchy stripped of all its powers. This party also included a substantial number of clergy and laymen who, like their monarch, were believed by the Puritans to be pro-Catholic, ready to return the Anglican Church to the fold of Rome.

Civil war. Civil war erupted in 1642; within four years the Parliamentarians—by virtue of control of the sea, greater economic resources, superior generalship, and an alliance with the Scots—defeated the king's armies. A major factor in their triumph was Oliver Cromwell, a country gentleman and a military genius of the first order. Cromwell instilled in his troops a sense of discipline and religious mission and sent them into battle singing hymns. His God-fearing irresistible force became known as Cromwell's Ironsides.

By the end of 1646 the king had surrendered, and for the next two years he tried to play off his enemies—the Scots; the Presbyterians, who dominated Parliament; and the

Independents, who dominated the army—against each other. He actually succeeded in splitting Parliament and making a secret alliance with the Scots. The upshot was the rise of fierce resentment against the king in the ranks of the Independent army, and in 1648 the civil war resumed. The allies of the king were defeated, and in December 1648 all Presbyterian members of the House of Commons were purged from that body by the victorious Independent army. Following a brief trial, Charles I was executed in January 1649.

The Protectorate and Cromwell. Abolishing the House of Lords, the House of Commons proclaimed England a republic—the Commonwealth. But in 1653 the army, still distrusting Parliament, overthrew the Commonwealth and set up a new form of government, the Protectorate, in which Oliver Cromwell held the office of Lord Protector, assisted by a new Parliament. The structure and operation of the government was based on a constitution called The Instrument of Government, the first written constitution of modern times.

Now virtual dictator of England, Cromwell endeavored to achieve a religious settlement for the nation. Amid the rivalries between Independents, Presbyterians, Royalists, Scots, and others, he had been forced to assume the role of dictator, but at heart Cromwell was a moderate, believing in religious toleration for all Protestants and constitutional government. It was impossible, however, to reconcile the Independents, the Presbyterians, the High Church party, and other religious factions. The last three years of Cromwell's life were filled with disappointment and trouble. Although he did not favor it, his more extreme Puritan colleagues muzzled the press and foisted on a pleasure-loving folk hateful prohibitions which closed the theaters and stamped out wholesome as well as unwholesome popular amusements.

Cromwell died in 1658 amid rising discontent with his rule. One contemporary observer claimed: "it was the joyfulest funeral I ever saw for there were none that cried but dogs . . . ."[7] Seemingly, Cromwell's work had been a failure; yet his firm opposi-

tion to royal despotism and his advocacy of religious toleration were priceless legacies from the kingless decade. The Civil War and the Commonwealth had also generated a substantial body of liberal and democratic thought.

The magniloquent John Milton (1608-1674), author of the great Puritan epic, *Paradise Lost* (1667) and a member of Cromwell's administration, espoused political freedom in opposition to tyranny. Arguing that men are born free, that kings are elected deputies without power except that given by their subjects, Milton maintained that a republic is "held by wisest men of all ages the noblest, the manliest, the equallest, the justest government. . . ."[8] One of his best known tracts is *Areopagitica* (1644), an impassioned plea for freedom of the press:

Who kills a man kills a reasonable creature, God's image; but he who destroys a good book, kills reason itself, kills the image of God, as it were in the eye. Many a man lives a burden to the earth; but a good book is the precious life-blood of a master-spirit, embalmed and treasured up on purpose to a life beyond life. . . . We should be wary therefore . . . how we spill that seasoned life of man, preserved and stored up in books; since we see a kind of homicide may thus be committed . . . whereof the execution ends not in the slaying of an elemental life, but strikes at that ethereal and fifth essence, the breath of reason itself, [and] slays an immortality rather than a life. . . .[9]

A group known as the Levellers—made up of small merchants, farmers, and artisans, many of whom were in Cromwell's army—advocated democracy and a written constitution guaranteeing equal rights to all. Another group, known as the Diggers, deplored the existence of private property and unequal wealth. Such groups as the Levellers and Diggers eventually died out, but the slow ferment of their ideas influenced English political life.

Ironically enough, the Puritans—champions of liberty against the Stuarts—ruled England in more autocratic fashion than had Charles I. Oliver Cromwell was succeeded as Lord Protector by his son, who lost control of the army and resigned in less than a year. To most Englishmen the restoration of the monarchy seemed the only solution.

The serious and scholarly James I (left), with his close-cropped hair and relatively conservative clothing, contrasts sharply with the debonair elegance of his grandson, the Restoration king, Charles II (right).

Restoration of Charles II. When the exiled Charles Stuart, son of the late king, returned to England as Charles II in 1660, it was with the implicit understanding that he should rule through Parliament. Thus the English monarchy was made responsible to a representative body, in sharp contrast to the pattern of absolutism on the Continent.

However, the king still wielded considerable power. He could veto laws; he commanded the militia; and unless he committed a breach of law serious enough to warrant his deposition, Parliament had no weapon other than its control of the national pocketbook to compel him to do its will.

Behind the backs of his anti-French subjects, the king in 1670 negotiated a secret treaty with Louis XIV of France—the Treaty of Dover. In return for an annual subsidy from the French government, which made him more financially independent of Parliament, Charles agreed to become a Catholic, make England a Catholic nation, and support Louis in his war against Holland (p. 424) After collecting a substantial sum from Louis, Charles had the effrontery to persuade Parliament to grant him money for waging war against the French king, his secret ally. No ruler has ever been able to give a better performance of running with the hare and hunting with the hounds.

In 1672 Charles suspended the operation of laws directed against English Catholics and Protestant Dissenters. Since the English had come to associate Catholicism with the menace of strong foreign foes and with despotic government, a political crisis resulted. One year later Parliament passed the Test Act, which excluded all Catholics and Dissenters from public office. Among its victims was the king's brother James, a staunch Catholic.

Monarch vs. Parliament. One notable consequence of the controversy between Charles and Parliament was the gradual rise of amorphous, but recognizable, political groupings that were forerunners of political parties as we define such groups today. To thwart Charles' pro-Catholic tendencies, some members of the House of Commons formed the Whig "party," which stood for the supremacy of Parliament, Protestantism, and the interests of the business classes. The Whig motto was "life, liberty, and property." Similarly, a group drawing heavily upon the landed gentry for support began to form, championing "the king, the church, and the land"—the Tory "party." Such vague associations to support particular Parliamentary interests did not function as a two-party system, however, before the end of the Stuart dynasty (1714).

A second important consequence of the conflict between king and Parliament was the passage of the Habeas Corpus Act in 1679. Anyone believing himself unjustly imprisoned could obtain a writ of *habeas corpus*, which compelled the government to explain why he had lost his liberty. Later this safeguard against arbitrary imprisonment became part of the Constitution of the United States.

James II and the Revolution of 1688. When Charles II died in 1685 and his brother James ascended the throne, the Whig opposition, and many Tories, soon came to believe that the cause of popular liberty and the Anglican Church were in serious danger. James adjourned Parliament after it refused to repeal the Test and Habeas Corpus acts and by royal order suspended all laws against Catholics and Dissenters. He also appointed many Catholics to important positions.

When James' second wife, a Catholic, unexpectedly gave birth to a son in 1688, the threat of a Catholic succession cost James his remaining Tory support. An invitation from both Whigs and Tories was extended to William of Orange, ruler of the Dutch, to assume the English crown. This choice was dictated by two factors: William was the husband of Mary, the older daughter of James II and the Protestant next in line to the throne; he was also considered the champion

In this anti-Catholic cartoon about the Glorious Revolution, fruit from the orange tree (representing the new ruler, William of Orange) knocks the crown from the head of James II and fells one of his officials. At the far right "the whole Heard of Papists and Jesuists" flee precipitately from the new Protestant king.

of Protestantism in Europe. In November 1688 William set sail for England and landed without opposition. The discouraged James, forsaken by his army, fled to France.

The Bill of Rights. Parliament offered the crown to William and Mary as joint sovereigns—an offer contingent on their acceptance of a declaration of rights, later enacted as the Bill of Rights. This declaration provided (1) the king could not suspend the operation of laws; (2) no taxes were to be levied or standing army maintained in peacetime without the consent of Parliament; (3) sessions of Parliament were to be held frequently; (4) freedom of speech in Parliament was to be assured; (5) subjects were to have the right of petition and were also to be free of excessive fines, bail, and cruel punishment; and (6) the king must be a Protestant. The Bill of Rights has exercised a tremendous influence on the development of constitutional government. The first ten amendments to the Constitution of the United States show their debt to the English declaration of 1688.

Results of the Glorious Revolution. The events which placed William and Mary on the English throne are referred to by Englishmen as the Glorious, or Bloodless, Revolution. Without bloodshed Parliament had deposed the old line of kings and laid down the conditions under which future English sovereigns were to rule. The theory of divine right was discredited, and Parliament was on the road to becoming the dominant element in government. In foreign affairs the events of 1688 resulted in a switch from the pro-French policy of Charles II and James II. Acting as the champion of Protestantism on the Continent, William used England's resources to check the designs of Louis XIV (see p. 424).

The Revolution was consolidated by other actions supplementing the Bill of Rights. The Toleration Act of 1689 gave Protestant Dissenters the right of public worship, although they remained excluded from public office. In 1693 Parliament refused to pass the customary licensing act which former governments had used to muzzle the press. Given freedom of expression, the press thus became an increasingly important aid to representative government. Another act made judges irremovable and led to a more independent judiciary.

Significant as they were, the achievements of the Revolution were limited. The Bill of Rights and subsequent legislation guaranteed certain fundamental rights to the common people, but the nation was now governed by a small, wealthy minority of merchants, gentry, and landed nobility. However, the development of such concepts as popular sovereignty and the right of revolution which were established in England by the Revolution of 1688 were later to have a profound influence on the world's governments and peoples.

Locke's justification of the Revolution of 1688. John Locke, as we have seen (pp. 400, 405), was one of the most eminent thinkers of his day. In his "Of Civil Government," the second essay in *Two Treatises of Government*, published in 1690, Locke justified the overthrow of James II by expounding the following ideas:

Before government was established, all men, living in a state of nature, possessed certain natural rights. These rights consisted principally of the rights to life, liberty, and property. While life in a state of nature was not frighteningly ruthless, as Hobbes supposed, it was unsatisfactory because society was handicapped in many ways by the absence of government. There was no superior agency to enforce the law of nature, which is a body of rules ensuring the equality of all men and every man's enjoyment of his natural rights. Since men in a state of nature arrived at different interpretations of natural law, uncertainty and conflict often resulted.

Therefore, by common consent, an agreement, or contract, was entered into by which a sovereign was set up with power to govern and enforce the laws of nature. Through this contract the people give up some of their rights to the government, but their basic natural rights are in no way surrendered. Finally, the social contract is bilateral, or binding upon both parties. The government, for its part, can demand the obedience of the people, but the people may also expect that the government will keep its part of the contract by not in any way abridging the natural rights of the people. If these rights are violated, if the government rules unwisely and tyrannically, the people have a perfect right to overthrow their rulers. In short, the people are the real rulers, the custodians of popular sovereignty, which gives them the right of revolution. Thus, unlike Hobbes, Locke used the social contract theory to challenge rather than to support absolutism. His ideas were to find new expression in the American and French revolutions a century later.

Genesis of cabinet government. During the century following the Revolution of 1688 there slowly evolved what is known today as cabinet government—government by an executive committee, headed by a prime minister, which rules in the king's name but in reality is the instrument of the majority party in the House of Commons. A unique British contribution to the art of government, the cabinet system has spread to many parts of the world.

The evolution of cabinet government be-

Sir Robert Walpole, the first prime minister, dominated the British government from 1721 to 1742.

gan during the reign of William III and Mary (1689-1702). King William selected his own ministers and controlled their policies. Because Parliament and the king agreed on fundamentals, a clash did not arise. Politics in England were now controlled by an oligarchy of great landed nobles and country squires plus wealthy commercial and banking families often related to the nobility. The loyalties of these groups were divided between the Tories and the Whigs who, although they quarreled about particular issues, usually agreed on broad political principles.

William soon discovered that only when all his ministers were of the same party as the majority in Commons did the government function smoothly. Decisions were still frequently made by the monarch, sitting in conference with his ministers, but by 1714, at the end of the reign of William's successor, Queen Anne, the cabinet—as it was now known—was a distinct factor in policy-making.

The Hanoverians and the prime minister. By the Act of Settlement (1701), Parliament had provided for a Protestant succession through a granddaughter of James I (the Electress Sophia of Hanover), since neither William III nor Anne had surviving children to accede to the English throne. The accession in 1714 of the Hanoverian dynasty from the German state of Hanover stimulated the growth of cabinet government. The first Hanoverian, George I, was over fifty years old and thoroughly German in speech, habits, and interests. He so remained and could converse with his English chief minister only in French or in poor Latin. England interested him solely because its resources strengthened his hand in the game of petty politics in Germany.

Not much of an improvement as king was George II, also German-born, whose only claim to fame was that he was the last English monarch to lead his troops on the field of battle. Fortunately for English constitutional development, George's queen was a devoted friend of the chief minister, Robert Walpole, and through her influence the king was easily managed. Walpole served from 1721 to 1742 as leader of the Whig party and the House of Commons and real head of the government. In effect, he was the first prime minister.

Walpole established the principle that the entire cabinet had to act as the single administrative instrument of the House majority and that cabinet unanimity was a necessity. If any member refused to support the official policy, he had to resign. When Walpole eventually lost his majority in the Commons, he resigned. This act confirmed the principle that the executive branch of government—in theory the king but in practice the prime minister and cabinet—must resign when its policies are no longer supported in the Commons.

After the fall of Walpole, the next dominating figure in British politics was William Pitt the Elder (1708-1778), who was determined to cleanse British politics of corruption. Unfortunately, his health steadily declined, and his prestige and influence were cleverly reduced by a new power in politics. This was, surprisingly, the king.

Pretensions of George III. George III, who had come to the throne in 1760, was determined to "be a king," as his mother had long urged, and restore to the crown the power lost since the days of William III. In short, his object was to destroy the cabinet system by becoming his own chief minister. George III did not aspire to be a tyrant or to rule as a divine-right monarch; rather, he wished to rule as a "Patriot King," above political parties and in accordance with his own ideas.

It took George III only a few years to destroy the power of the Whigs and to secure control of Parliament. By 1770 all effective opposition to the king had been swept away, for George had filled the Commons with supporters known as the "King's Friends," bought by royal favors and pensions. For twelve fateful years George III was the effective head of the government. In this period Great Britain's thirteen North American colonies waged their successful war for independence.

Restoration of cabinet government. The disaster to British arms in America dealt the king's policies and methods a crushing blow. In a sense, by gaining their liberty, the Americans helped the Britons gain theirs. In 1780 the House of Commons resolved "that the influence of the crown has increased, is increasing, and ought to be diminished."[10] By 1782 George III had to dismiss Lord North, his subservient prime minister, and employ ministers who were willing to make concessions to public opinion.

In 1783 George III called the twenty-four-year-old son of the great war leader William Pitt (see p. 440) to be prime minister. Undoubtedly the king expected to control the youthful statesman, but he more than met his match. A new Tory party, reinvigorated by Pitt's leadership, took firm control of the affairs of state. The king was no longer consulted on the day-to-day details of government and only occasionally tried to intervene. When the king's mental instability and final insanity removed royal influence from governmental affairs, the prime minister and his cabinet colleagues assumed full control.

From the Glorious Revolution of 1688 until another great peaceful revolution in 1832, England was the perfect example of aristocratic liberalism. Ingrained in this English system was a habit of political thought that gave room for reform to take place very gradually, until ultimately the narrow oligarchical liberalism of the late seventeenth century broadened into the full democracy of the late nineteenth century.

THE RISE OF RUSSIA

Peter the Great and his objectives for Russia. In 1682 a new era in Russian history began with the accession of Peter I, who soon showed himself to be master of his unruly state, which was still a world apart from western Europe. The fourth member of the Romanov dynasty that had secured the throne in 1613 at the end of Russia's "Time of Trouble" (see p. 279), Peter grew up without benefit of discipline or formal education. But this six-foot-nine-inch giant possessed an excellent mind and such great stores of energy that his contemporaries contended that "he works harder than any *muzhik* [peasant]." Having a sound appreciation of what was essential for Russian progress, Peter

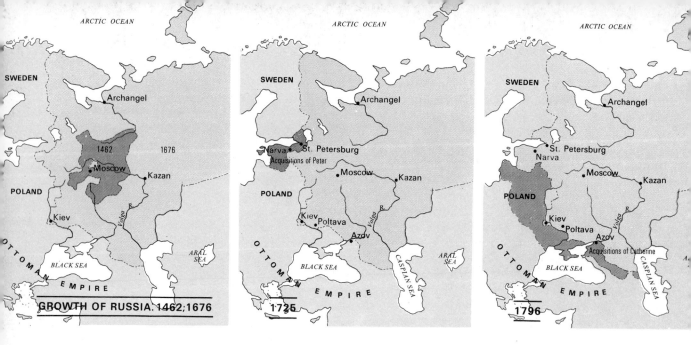

GROWTH OF RUSSIA 1462-1676   **1725**   **1796**

pursued three basic policies during his long reign: (1) to Europeanize his people, (2) to obtain an outlet, "a window on the sea," and (3) to make his power absolute.

Peter's Grand Embassy. Peter first turned his attention to the Turks, who blocked Russia's way to the Black Sea. It took two expeditions to conquer Azov from the Turks, and Peter realized that he must learn from the West how to modernize his army and build a navy. He organized a Grand Embassy whose dual object was to secure allies against the Turks and to observe the most advanced European methods of warfare, government, industry, and education. Traveling as plain Peter Mikhailov, Peter visited Holland, England, and Germany. He astonished the rulers of western Europe by his curiosity as well as by his carousing and pranks. In Holland Peter worked as a common ship carpenter in order to learn Dutch methods of shipbuilding at first hand.

During his return trip to Russia Peter learned that his palace guard had revolted. He hurried back to Moscow and crushed the rebellion with savage cruelty, executing the leaders with his own hand. Peter then engaged European officers to build a western-type conscript army which in time numbered 100,000 men.

Peter obtained some seven hundred technicians from the West but no allies against the Turks. He therefore decided to direct his energies away from the Black Sea to the Baltic.

The Great Northern War. Peter's ambitions for a "window on the sea" led him in 1699 to make a secret alliance with Poland and Denmark against Sweden, which controlled most of the Baltic shores. Peter hoped to take advantage of the inexperience of Charles XII of Sweden, a youth of eighteen. Without waiting to be attacked, however, Charles launched the Great Northern War with an invasion of Denmark and quickly brought the Danes to their knees. The "Swedish Meteor" next landed at the other end of the Baltic, crushed Peter's army at Narva, and turned aside to deal with the Poles. Six years later, when Charles invaded Russia, the Swedish army was first weakened by Peter's "scorched earth" withdrawal into the heart of the Ukraine, then annihilated at Poltava (1709). The battle of Poltava amazed westerners and made them conscious for the first time of Russia's power.

Charles XII escaped to Sweden by way of Turkey—where he induced the sultan to attack Russia and regain Azov—only to be killed in 1718 in a skirmish with the Norwegians. The Great Northern War ended in 1721 when an exhausted Sweden sued for peace with the last of its foes, Russia. Sweden's days as a great power, inaugurated by Gustavus Adolphus, were over; except for Finland, almost nothing remained of its Baltic empire. Peter acquired four provinces situated south and east of the Gulf of Finland, thus securing his coveted access to the sea.

At tremendous cost in treasure and human life, western architects built the new capital of St. Petersburg as "a window opened upon Europe," replacing Moscow, the center of Russia's old way of life. Meanwhile Peter had bestowed on himself the titles "Father of the Country" and "the Great."

Attempts to westernize Russia. Peter resolved to change the age-old customs of his people in spite of their own opinions and desires. He instructed his male subjects to cut off their long beards, encouraged the adoption of European breeches instead of the flowing oriental robes which many men wore, and attempted to end the seclusion of women. Crude as he was, Peter endeavored to introduce the manners of polite European society into his country.

Responsible for the revision and simplification of the old Russian alphabet, Peter also established printing presses, promoted the study of foreign languages, sent many young men to western Europe to study, and started new schools for advanced training in engineering, navigation, and accounting. In the economic field he was a staunch mercantilist who sought to make his country as nearly self-sufficient as possible. Some of Peter's reforms, such as the establishment of new industries, failed shortly after his death. In addition, his aggressive program of westernization provoked much hostility, including that of the Church. Furthermore, Peter did nothing to alleviate the arduous lot of the Russian peasants, more than half of whom had been reduced to serfdom by their landlords with the consent of earlier Romanov tsars.

Absolutism of Peter the Great. Peter the Great accelerated the molding of Russia into an absolutist state. All vestiges of local self-government were removed, and Peter continued and intensified his predecessors' requirement of state service for all nobles. They were compelled to serve in the army, in the government, or in industry, and to send their sons abroad for study. In return, this "service nobility" was granted a free hand in dealing with their serfs.

The Church also became a tool of the state when Peter abolished the office of patriarch and appointed a Holy Synod of bishops to govern the Church. The new body was dominated by a layman called the procurator, who represented the tsar. For the next two hundred years the Church served as one of the most powerful agents and supporters of Russian absolutism.

Worn out from his exertions in politics and his excesses in drinking and brawling, Peter died in 1725 at the age of fifty-three. He had firmly established absolutism in Russia and ended its isolation from the West. Russia was now ready to play an important part in European history, but nearly forty years were to pass before an equally ambitious and ruthless monarch appeared on the Russian throne.

Catherine the Great. Catherine II was a German princess who married the Russian heir to the crown. Finding him half insane— "a moronic booby"—Catherine tacitly consented to his murder. It was announced that he died of "apoplexy," and in 1762 she became the ruler.

Catherine contributed to the resurgence of the Russian nobility that began after the death of Peter the Great. State service had been abolished, and Catherine delighted the

A contemporary woodcut by a Russian artist lampoons the cutting off of beards in Russia following Peter the Great's decree banning them.

nobles further by turning over most governmental functions in the provinces to them. The condition of the serfs, on the other hand, became so bad—for example, Catherine legalized the selling of serfs separate from the land—that in 1773 a terrifying peasant uprising occurred. Inspired by a Cossack named Pugachev ("Hang all the landlords!"), the rebels threatened to take Moscow before they were dispersed. Catherine had Pugachev drawn and quartered in Red Square, but his specter continued to haunt her and her successors.

Catherine served both her own interests and those of the Russian state with craft, shrewd diplomacy, and utter lack of conscience. She imitated the best features of the culture of Versailles and equaled its vices. In her own private life she was frankly immoral, and stories of her misconduct were common all over Europe. Just as the mistresses of Louis XIV graced the French court, so the male favorites of Catherine were openly paraded in her palaces.

This brilliant and unscrupulous monarch waged war successfully against the decaying Ottoman empire and advanced Russia's southern boundary to the Black Sea (see p. 542). Then, as we shall see later in this chapter, by plotting with the rulers of Prussia and Austria she annexed half of Poland and pushed the Russian frontier westward into central Europe. By the time of her death in 1796, Catherine's expansionist policy had made Russia a major European power.

THE EMERGENCE OF PRUSSIA

Rise of the House of Hohenzollern. If the rise of Russia was remarkable, the development of Prussia was even more amazing. History has scarcely a parallel example of the manner in which one royal house, the Hohenzollern, expanded its territory and exalted its power by fair means or foul.

The earliest Hohenzollerns were unimportant nobles occupying a castle on the heights of Zollern in south Germany. In 1417 a member of the family, who was one of the seven German electors (see p. 273), was made

ruler of the unpromising Mark of Brandenburg, one of the border provinces carved out of Slavic lands east of the Elbe during the Middle Ages. By turning Lutheran during the Reformation, the Hohenzollerns gained wealth from seized Church properties, and the elector increased his authority as head of the new church in Brandenburg.

In the first decades of the seventeenth century the Hohenzollerns made further gains in territory, the most important being the acquisition of East Prussia. We saw earlier (pp. 276, 312) how the Teutonic Knights ruled East Prussia until the Protestant Reformation when the Grand Master, who was a member of the Hohenzollern family, turned Lutheran, dissolved the order, and ruled thereafter as hereditary duke of Prussia. In 1618, when the duke of Prussia died without immediate heirs, the duchy passed to the elector of Brandenburg.

Just four years before this windfall the elector had secured the lands of Cleves, Mark, and Ravensberg on the lower Rhine. (These territories were relatively unimportant until the Industrial Revolution of the early nineteenth century made the Ruhr valley a great industrial center.) Thus by the early seventeenth century the Hohenzollerns held territory as far east as the Niemen River and as far west as the Rhine, with Brandenburg and the small provincial town of Berlin located in the center. The policy of future electors was to bridge the gap between their detached lands and to forge a united state.

Creating the Prussian state. The Hohenzollerns were threatened with ruin during the Thirty Years' War, when Brandenburg was occupied by the Swedes from 1630 to 1643. The first of the four creators of the Prussian state was Frederick William (1640-1688), known as the Great Elector, who returned from exile in Holland determined to build a strong monarchy that would prevent such humiliations in the future. This meant the creation of a modern standing army and centralized bureaucracy, and the elimination of opposition from the nobility.

Frederick William's small but effective army cleared his lands of foreign troops and made good his claim to eastern Pomerania (along the Baltic coast) at the Peace of Westphalia. After the war he increased the army to 30,000 men and laid the foundations for a civil service which governed the scattered Hohenzollern possessions directly from Berlin. The bureaucracy and the army remained the two main pillars of the Prussian state down to modern times.

The Prussian nobility (Junkers) were encouraged to accept the new powerful state in return for important concessions—a monopoly of the key positions in the army and the bureaucracy, freedom from taxation, and a free hand in dealing with their peasants. As a result the rural masses of Prussia—as well as Russia and Austria, where a similar policy was followed—were forced deeper into serfdom at a time when the peasantry of western Europe had long been emancipated.

The Great Elector also promoted economic progress in his domains. Immigrants were brought in—diligent Dutch farmers, harassed Jews, and (after Louis XIV revoked the Edict of Nantes) thousands of skilled Huguenots.

The Great Elector's son, Frederick I (1688-1713), added lustre to the dynasty by obtaining the title "King in Prussia" as a reward for his support of the alliance against Louis XIV in the War of the Spanish Succession. He also took advantage of Sweden's defeat in the Great Northern War to annex western Pomerania. By the opening of the eighteenth century Prussia, as the combined lands of the Hohenzollerns now came to be called, had almost reached a position where it could embark on more ambitious and aggressive programs of expansion. The contribution of the next Hohenzollern was necessary, however, before this new phase in Prussian history could begin.

Like his grandfather, the Great Elector, Frederick William I (1713-1740) firmly believed that the destiny of Prussia, an artificial combination of lands without defensible frontiers, lay with its army. During his reign the army increased to 83,000 men—in size the fourth army in Europe and without a

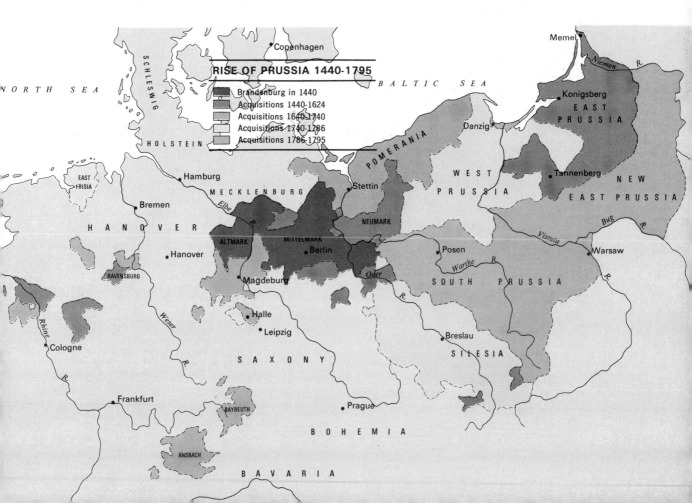

RISE OF PRUSSIA 1440-1795

Brandenburg in 1440
Acquisitions 1440-1624
Acquisitions 1640-1740
Acquisitions 1740-1786
Acquisitions 1786-1795

doubt the most efficient. As his contemporaries put it: "Prussia is not a State which possesses an army, but an army which possesses a State."[11]

King Frederick William also completed the task of creating a modern centralized government, run by a trained and efficient civil service and obeyed by a docile citizenry, who were told by their crusty king: "No reasoning, obey orders." He has well been dubbed "the Potsdam Führer," for it was through this ruler, with his maxims of "order, discipline, and work" and "Salvation belongs to the Lord, everything else is my business," that Germany developed its tradition of subordination to the state and blind confidence in the military point of view.

Frederick William I had high hopes for his son Frederick, who was subjected to a Spartan training. But Frederick loved music, art, and philosophy, and at eighteen he attempted to flee to France. Caught, he was forced to witness the beheading of his accomplice and best friend and was then subjected to more years of severe training and discipline. As the old king neared his last days he is supposed to have said: "O my God, I die content, since I have so worthy a son and successor." Frederick William was correct; his son was eventually to become the greatest soldier of his day and a master of Machiavellian diplomacy. Frederick II (1740-1786), known as Frederick the Great, brought Prussia fully into the arena of European politics (see p. 439). He also continued his predecessors' work of building a powerful Prussian state at home. The remarkable rise of Prussia is illustrated by the chart below.

The Rise of Prussia

	1648	1740	1786
Population	750,000	2,500,000	5,000,000
Army	8,000	83,000	200,000
Annual revenue in thaler	?	7,000,000	19,000,000
Stored treasure in thaler	0	8,000,000	51,000,000

Adapted from S. B. Fay, *The Rise of Brandenburg-Prussia to 1786* (New York: Henry Holt and Co., Inc., 1937), p. 141.

POWER POLITICS AND THE DUEL FOR WORLD EMPIRE

Seeds of conflict. In 1740 Europe had not seen a major war for a generation—not since the Peace of Utrecht in 1713 had brought the War of the Spanish Succession to a close. Political and economic forces were at work, however, which would in 1740 plunge the Continent into war, and the third quarter of the eighteenth century was to witness a series of destructive conflicts. France and Britain were becoming bitter rivals over commerce and colonies; Prussia under Frederick the Great was well armed and eager to secure additional territory; Russia under Catherine the Great was in a position to renew the expansionist policy of Peter the Great; and a fifth great power, Austria, had emerged along the middle Danube as the Hapsburgs, having failed as Holy Roman emperors, concentrated upon organizing their family lands into a monarchy capable of holding its own in the competitive state system.

As the vigor and acquisitive appetites of the five major powers mounted, three once great states were lapsing into impotence. Spain was no longer a power to be reckoned with, and the Ottoman Turks no longer inspired fear. Following the death of Suleiman the Magnificent in 1566, the Ottoman empire had begun a gradual decline marked by the defeat at Lepanto in 1571 and the loss of Hungary to Austria in 1699. It was now caught in a net of intrigue woven by Russia and Austria. Poland still loomed large on the map of Europe (see Reference Map 5), but it lacked strong government and natural boundaries and was to become the most notable victim of aggression by powerful neighbors.

From 1688 to 1713, during the last three of Louis XIV's wars, England had not only been pitted against France on the Continent but the two states had also begun a long duel on a world-wide stage for colonial possessions in North America, the West Indies, and India. As the eighteenth century progressed, this colonial rivalry became increasingly intense. In line with the philosophy of mercantilism, one London merchant expressed the clash of economic interests in this fashion: "Our trade will improve by the total extinction of theirs."[12]

England came to realize that it could best checkmate French ambitions in Europe by destroying French commerce and sea power in North America and India. When war resumed on the Continent in 1740, the English had perfected the practice of obtaining and subsidizing allies to keep the French occupied in Europe while the bulk of British troops, especially naval forces, concentrated on the task of conquering the colonies and destroying the commerce of the French overseas, where distance served to neutralize France's advantages as a land power. The French, on the other hand, divided their energies by trying to play the game of power politics in Europe and at the same time endeavoring to compete with England over colonies. The result was to spell failure for France in both areas.

War of the Austrian Succession. It was the Austrian emperor who set the stage for a renewal of war on the Continent. Foreseeing the difficulties his young daughter, Maria Theresa, would have coping with greedy neighboring monarchs, he had drawn up in 1713 a document called the Pragmatic Sanction. The rulers who signed this document, including Frederick the Great's father, agreed to respect the territorial boundaries of Austria upon Maria Theresa's accession to the throne; but when the emperor died in October 1740, Frederick the Great, who had become king in Prussia in May of that year, had no intention of honoring the Pragmatic Sanction. He trumped up spurious claims to Maria Theresa's rich province of Silesia. On examining the document containing his demands, Frederick exclaimed to his advisers:

Bravo! This is the work of an excellent charlatan. If there is anything to be gained by honesty, then we shall be honest; if we must dupe, then let us be scoundrels.[13]

In December 1740 Frederick began the War of the Austrian Succession by occupying Silesia. France, Spain, Bavaria, and Saxony then threw in their lot with him to obtain a share of the loot. But having secured Silesia, Frederick had no desire to continue fighting so that his allies also could filch territory from Austria. Thus in 1741 he withdrew from the conflict.

At first England was content to send subsidies to Maria Theresa, but in 1742 it entered the fray allied with Austria, Holland, and Hanover against the Franco-Spanish coalition. Meanwhile Frederick had reentered the war, and in 1745 his army roundly defeated the Austrians. Prussia and Austria then withdrew from the conflict, but fighting continued and the war broadened into a world-wide conflict involving the European colonial possessions. Thus it was, as the famous English historian Macaulay observed, "Because a monarch robbed a neighbor he had promised to defend, red men scalped each other by the Great Lakes of America, while black men fought on the [Indian] coast of Coromandel."[14]

The French triumphed in India, seizing the British outpost of Madras, but the British took the offensive in North America by capturing the French fortress of Louisburg, a stronghold guarding the entrance to the Gulf of St. Lawrence. On the seas, the British fleet successfully held off the French.

The war dragged on until 1748, when a general peace was signed at Aix-la-Chapelle. Louisburg was returned to the French and Madras to the English, and Frederick was confirmed in his possession of Silesia. The Peace of Aix-la-Chapelle—called "the peace without victory"—settled nothing. The rivalries that had ignited the conflagration continued to smolder, and in less than a decade they were to blaze forth in another major war.

The Diplomatic Revolution. The duel for world empire between England and France reached a decisive stage in the Seven Years' War (1756-1763), known in American history as the French and Indian War. The war was preceded in North America and India by preliminary skirmishes between English and French forces, and in Europe by a very significant regrouping of alliances in which two sets of traditional enemies became allies.

Thirsting for revenge against Frederick the Great, Maria Theresa turned to her country's hereditary enemy, France, and suggested to Louis xv that an alliance be formed against

A major British victory in the Seven Years' War, the taking of Quebec in 1759, is depicted in an eighteenth-century engraving.

Frederick. The determining factor in Louis' decision to accept the Austrian offer was his realization that the English had replaced the Hapsburgs as France's most dangerous enemy. In the spring of 1756 Louis signed a pact whereby France joined Russia, Sweden, and various states in the Germanies as allies of Austria. (Five years later Spain was to join this coalition by declaring war on Great Britain.)

To check French ambitions on the Continent, England in the meantime had made an alliance with its recent foe, Prussia. So thoroughly had the traditional alignment of powers been reversed that this new grouping of nations—Austria and France vs. England and Prussia—is referred to as the Diplomatic Revolution of the eighteenth century.

Frederick opens the Seven Years' War. Frederick the Great applied the match to the international powder keg in 1756, making the droll observation: "If Austria is pregnant with war, I shall offer the service of the midwife."[15] Quickly attacking the coalition, he aimed heavy blows at Austria before France

and Russia could threaten him. But he soon was attacked on all sides. With brilliant strategy Frederick marched and wheeled his forces, winning battles but despairing of ever winning the war.

William Pitt's "system." In the colonial phase of the Seven Years' War, Great Britain at first suffered severe defeats. But the crisis ended when a remarkable statesman, William Pitt the Elder, came to power in 1757 (see p. 433) and, like Winston Churchill in 1940, gave England new heart and a new war strategy.

Pitt had supreme confidence in his own abilities, once saying: "I am confident that I can save the country and that no one else can." He developed a successful global strategy of war, known as his "system," which consisted of (1) providing large subsidies of money to Prussia, (2) destroying French sea power and thus preventing men and supplies from reaching the French possessions overseas, and (3) dispatching well-equipped English forces to the colonies to conquer the isolated French armies.

In 1759 one French fort after another fell in North America: Duquesne, Louisburg, Niagara, and Ticonderoga; and the defeat of France in North America was sealed when General Wolfe vanquished Montcalm's forces and captured Quebec. In India there was a similar chronicle of victories, the most decisive resulting from the infamous incident concerning the Black Hole of Calcutta. The ruler of Bengal, fearful of English influence, captured Calcutta and cruelly forced 146 English captives into a small dungeon, where during the night all but twenty-three died of suffocation and thirst. British forces commanded by Robert Clive avenged this act by defeating the ruler of Bengal in the decisive battle of Plassey (1757). Clive's victory laid the foundation for nearly two hundred years of British rule in India.

Survival of Prussia. The victories won by Great Britain contrasted markedly with the ordeals suffered by Prussia. In spite of Frederick's tactical victories, which made him a great hero and symbol for later Germans, Prussia lacked the necessary manpower to defeat the combined forces of Austria, France, and Russia. Attacked on all sides, Frederick compared himself to a man assaulted by flies:

When one flies off my cheek, another comes and sits on my nose, and scarcely has it been brushed off than another flies up and sits on my forehead, on my eyes and everywhere else.[16]

Frederick was saved by the narrowest of margins when a new tsar, the "moronic booby" whose wife Catherine was later called "the Great," recalled his armies from the gates of Berlin and withdrew from the war in 1762. Unable to continue without Russian support, Austria sued for peace in 1763. Prussia's hold on Silesia was confirmed, and the Continental phase of the war ended.

Treaty of Paris. In 1763 peace was also concluded between Great Britain and France and Spain. The Treaty of Paris provided for French cession to England of Canada and all the territory east of the Mississippi River. Spain ceded Florida to England and, as compensation, received from France the Louisiana territory including New Orleans. This marked the end of French rule in North America. France regained its trading posts in India as well as Martinique and other rich islands in the West Indies. The British also returned Havana and Manila to Spain.

By the Treaty of Paris, Great Britain became the greatest colonial, commercial, and naval power in the world. That a country of 6.5 million should triumph over a nation such as France, with a population of 23 million, was remarkable. As one Englishman wrote:

I shall burn my Greek and Latin books. They are the histories of little people. We subdue the globe in three campaigns, and a globe as big again as it was in their days.[17]

Partition of Poland. The eighteenth century offers many illustrations of the callous and cold-blooded manner in which wars were precipitated, promises broken, and allies deserted. Yet today, in an age accustomed to accepting the right of national self-determination, the most shocking example of completely unprincipled statecraft was the ruthless partition of Poland by Prussia, Russia, and Austria.

Without natural barriers to aid in its defense, Poland was a handicapped nation. In addition, it was dominated by a reactionary nobility whose insistence on retaining its feudal "liberties" rendered the central government virtually powerless. The monarchy was elective, and as the Poles usually could not agree on the choice of a king from among their own factions, only two native-born Poles had been elected to the throne in two hundred years. The Diet, composed solely of nobles, was completely impotent; by the *liberum veto* any single member could force the dissolution of this body. Such action was called "exploding the Diet," and during the century preceding 1764 forty-eight of fifty-five Diets were "exploded." This was not government but anarchy.

The first partition of Poland, in 1772, came about as a result of international tensions produced by the decline of the Ottoman empire. Austrian opposition to Russian designs on the Crimea and Moldavia (see Reference Map 7) brought the two states close to war. Frederick the Great, fearing that Prussia

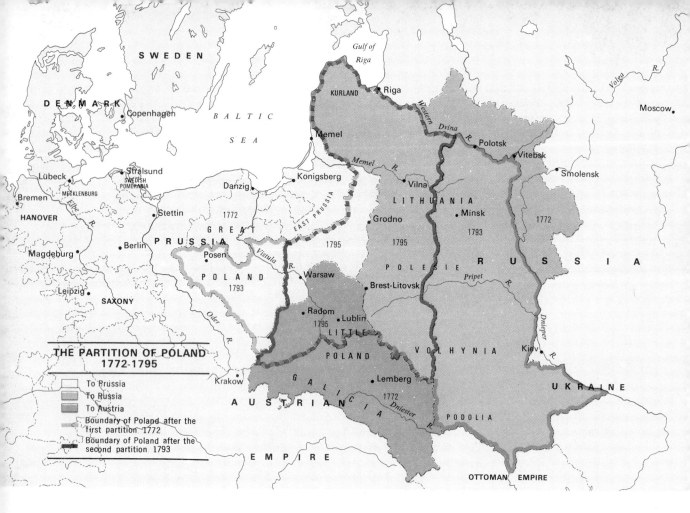

THE PARTITION OF POLAND
1772-1795

To Prussia
To Russia
To Austria
Boundary of Poland after the
first partition 1772
Boundary of Poland after the
second partition 1793

would be drawn into the conflict, then persuaded Catherine the Great to satisfy her territorial ambitions at the expense of helpless Poland. Frederick also aimed at annexing West Prussia (the Polish Corridor) in order to link East Prussia with the main body of Hohenzollern possessions. Maria Theresa of Austria reluctantly agreed to participate in the partitioning. In a wry comment on Maria Theresa's action, Frederick epitomized the ruthlessly competitive nature of international relations: "She wept, but she kept on taking."

In 1793, and again in 1795, while the rest of Europe was distracted by the French Revolution, Poland was again partitioned, Austria abstaining from the second operation. By the third partition Poland ceased to exist as an independent state. Under the alien rule of three different governments, the Poles continued to hope for the resurrection of their nation. Their faith was not rewarded until after the First World War.

SUMMARY

The concentration of power in the hands of absolutist kings resulted in a succession of wars that convulsed Europe between 1650 and 1775: the War of the Spanish Succession, the Great Northern War, the War of the Austrian Succession, and the Seven Years' War. Declining states, such as Turkey, and temporarily weakened states, such as Austria at the accession of Maria Theresa, were susceptible to the designs of their aggressive neighbors. In Poland's case, Prussia, Russia, and Austria joined in territorial banditry or, as it is more politely described, the "collective partition" of this helpless state.

By 1700 commercial and colonial rivalry added to the intense competitive spirit existing in Europe and culminated in the worldwide duel for empire between France and Great Britain. Great Britain, as the leader of various coalitions and the self-appointed caretaker of the Continental balance of power, emerged victorious over France and the monarchical despotism it symbolized. In England the successful Revolution of 1688 heralded the triumph of aristocratic liberalism—the rule of Parliament and of law. The most wealthy and influential elements in society controlled the government, and their support made for a stronger and more united government than that operating from Versailles. The English government thus proved fit to achieve victory in foreign diplomacy and warfare.

The interplay of international rivalries during the last half of the seventeenth century and the first three quarters of the eighteenth century had many significant implications for modern times. In this period it was determined that North America would be mainly Anglo-Saxon in culture; British rule was firmly established in India; and Britain's sea power gained the world-wide supremacy it was to hold well into the twentieth century. This period also saw the rise of the Prussian type of absolutism—the militaristic state—and the birth of the Russian policy of securing access to the Baltic and Mediterranean seas.

SUGGESTIONS FOR READING

Brief general introductions to the history of this period include J. M. Thompson, **European History, 1494-1789,*** Torchbooks; John B. Wolf, **Toward a European Balance of Power, 1620-1715,** Rand McNally, 1970; M. Beloff, **The Age of Absolutism, 1660-1815,*** Torchbooks; C. J. Friedrich and C. Blitzer, **The Age of Power,*** Cornell; F. Manuel, **The Age of Reason,*** Cornell; M. S. Anderson, **Eighteenth-Century Europe, 1713-1789,*** Galaxy; A. Cobban *et al.,* **The Eighteenth Century: Europe in the Age of Enlightenment,** McGraw-Hill, 1969 (contains almost six hundred illustrations).

The following are more detailed surveys: D. Maland, **Europe in the Seventeenth Century,** St. Martin's, 1966; A. Moote, **The Seventeenth Century: Europe in Ferment,** Heath, 1970; David Ogg, **Europe in the Seventeenth Century,*** Collier; J. Stoye, **Europe Unfolding, 1648-1688,*** Torchbooks; Matthew S. Anderson, **Europe in the Eighteenth Century,** Holt, Rinehart & Winston, 1961; David Ogg, **Europe of the Ancien Régime, 1715-1783,*** Torchbooks. Also valuable are the pertinent volumes in the **Rise of Modern Europe** series* (Torchbooks) cited in Chapter 18.

On the eighteenth-century power struggle see L. Dehio, **The Precarious Balance: Four Centuries of the European Power Struggle,*** Vintage; and A. Sorel, **Europe under the Old Régime,*** Torchbooks.

L. B. Packard, **The Age of Louis XIV,*** Holt, Rinehart & Winston; M. Ashley, **Louis XIV and the Greatness of France,*** Free Press; David Ogg, **Louis XIV,*** Oxford. Brief and excellent. John B. Wolf, **Louis XIV,** Norton, 1968, is the latest detailed study. See also William F. Church, ed., **The Impact of Absolutism in France: National Experience under Richelieu, Mazarin, and Louis XIV,*** Wiley, 1969; C. V. Wedgwood, **Richelieu and the French Monarchy,*** Collier.

W. H. Lewis, **The Splendid Century: Life in the France of Louis XIV,*** Anchor. A popular account, beautifully written. P. Erlanger, **The Age of Courts and Kings: Manners and Morals, 1558-1715,*** Anchor, is witty and charming. R. Hatton, **Europe in the Age of Louis XIV,*** Harcourt, Brace & World, 1969, is a profusely illustrated social history. See also O. Ranum, **Paris in the Age of Absolutism,*** Wiley, 1968.

R. Lockyer, **Tudor and Stuart Britain, 1471-1714,** St. Martin's, 1964; Dorothy Marshall, **Eighteenth Century England,** McKay, 1962. Excellent general surveys. M. Ashley, **England in the Seventeenth Century, 1603-1714,*** Penguin, and G. Aylmer, **A Short History of Seventeenth-Century England,*** Mentor, are brief and first rate. The classic survey of the Stuart period is G. M. Trevelyan, **England under the Stuarts,*** Barnes and Noble.

On the English constitutional crisis see Philip Taylor, ed., **The Origins of the English Civil War: Conspiracy, Crusade, or Class Conflict?*** Heath; Christopher Hill, **The Century of Revolution, 1603-1714,*** Norton; M. Ashley, **The Greatness of Oliver Cromwell,*** Collier; C. V. Wedgwood, **Oliver Cromwell,*** Collier; C. H. Firth, **Oliver Cromwell and the Rule of the Puritans in England,** Oxford, 1958; G. M. Trevelyan, **The English Revolution, 1688-1689,*** Galaxy. On the Levellers and Diggers see M. Walzer, **The Revolution of the Saints: A Study of the Origins of Radical Politics,*** Atheneum.

B. Sumner, **Peter the Great and the Emergence of Russia,*** Collier; L. J. Oliva, **Russia in the Era of Peter the Great,*** Spectrum; G. S. Thomson, **Catherine the Great and the Expansion of Russia,*** Collier. Good brief accounts. Good reading also are K. Waliszewski, **The Romance of an Empress: Catherine II of Russia,** Shoe String, 1968; I. Grey, **Catherine the Great,** Lippincott, 1962. On the plight of the Russian peasant see J. Blum, **Lord and Peasant in Russia from the Ninth to the Nineteenth Centuries,** Princeton, 1961.

S. B. Fay, **The Rise of Brandenburg-Prussia to 1786,*** rev. ed., Holt, Rinehart & Winston. An admirable introduction. See also H. Holborn, **A History of Modern Germany, 1648-1840,** Knopf, 1963; Walter H. Wilson, **The Soldier Kings: The House of Hohenzollern,** Putnam, 1969; R. Ergang, **The Potsdam Führer, Frederick William I,** Columbia, 1941; H. Rosenburg, **Bureaucracy, Aristocracy, and Authority: The Prussian Experience, 1660-1815,*** Beacon; G. A. Craig, **The Politics of the Prussian Army: 1640-1945,*** Galaxy.

*Indicates an inexpensive paperbound edition.

Chapter 20

The Rights of Man

Revolution in the Western World: 1776-1815

INTRODUCTION. The political changes that occurred during the last quarter of the eighteenth century and the first quarter of the nineteenth were world-shaking. John Locke's justification of the Glorious Revolution as a revolt against tyranny was a forerunner of the eighteenth-century attacks on the existing order. Physiocrats condemned the oppressive restraints of mercantilism, and *philosophes* attacked the irresponsible despotism of absolutism. Some monarchs heard the voice of reform and tried to uproot the evils of the Old Regime, but the momentous reforms that made the period from 1776 to 1815 a watershed in western political history were not imposed by authoritative decree from above but by revolutionary action from below.

In this chapter we shall follow the actions of the thirteen colonies as they successfully defy Britain and achieve their independence, we shall witness the overthrow of an ineffectual French king and watch a new republic rising from the bloodshed of revolution, and we shall observe the struggle of colonials in Latin America to throw off the shackles of repressive Old World regimes.

The rise of republican France was a challenge to despotic regimes throughout Europe, and the result was intermittent warfare on the Continent from 1792 to 1815. In the midst of this troubled era Napoleon came to power. Turning the new-born republic into a tool for conquest, this self-styled "man of destiny" threatened all Europe until defeat at Waterloo finally crushed his dreams of empire.

Before this period from 1776 to 1815, little is heard of the rights of the people; after it, representative government is in the ascendancy. Ever stronger voices speak forth for the rights of citizens, for bills of rights and constitutions—political concepts which have had an immeasurable influence on the course of western civilization.

THE INTELLECTUAL ASSAULT ON ABSOLUTISM

Criticism of existing governments. As we have seen in Chapter 18, eighteenth-century thought was characterized by the belief that all aspects of civilization should be based on reason, the ultimate touchstone of perfection. Faith in reason led the *philosophes* of the Enlightenment to reevaluate all aspects of society. These intellectuals were positive that reason could solve all human problems and that mankind's ability to improve itself was limitless.

The middle class, too, found much that was irrational and indefensible in the institutions of the day. Perhaps the most important factor in middle-class discontent was the government-controlled economy of mercantilism (see p. 381). Convinced that capitalism had outgrown the need for state assistance with its accompanying controls, the bourgeoisie were ready for a system of free enterprise. As early as the seventeenth century English merchants had denounced the hoarding of bullion, advocating instead that "the exportation of our moneys in trade of merchandise is a means to increase our treasure."[1] This growing concern for freedom of trade led the middle class to support the physiocrats, eighteenth-century economic thinkers who, as their name indicates, shared with *philosophes* the viewpoint that all human activity—economic, social, and political—was subject to natural laws similar to those governing the physical universe.

The physiocrats, laissez faire, and Adam Smith. The physiocrats believed that money should circulate naturally, much as the blood does in the human body, and that all economic activity should be freed from artificial restrictions. They believed in a "free market," the concept which implies that natural forces of supply and demand should be allowed to regulate the conduct of business. In sum, governments should adopt the policy of laissez faire (letting business alone).

The most influential advocate of laissez-faire economics was a Scottish professor of moral philosophy, Adam Smith (1723-1790). In 1776 his systematic formulation of the new science of economics, *An Inquiry into the Nature and Causes of the Wealth of Nations*, was published.

Smith was indebted to the physiocrats for his views of personal liberty, natural law, and the position of the state as a mere "passive policeman." He argued that increased production depends largely on division of labor, with each individual—and each nation—performing the work for which he is best fitted. By a wise division of labor, each member of society will perform quickly and efficiently the tasks for which he has an aptitude and will have a large field in which to exchange the results of his own labor for commodities produced by the labor of others. Smith maintained that every individual is and ought to be motivated by self-interest:

It is not from the benevolence of the butcher, the brewer, or the baker, that we expect our dinner, but from their regard to their own interest. We address ourselves, not to their humanity but to their self-love, and never talk to them of our own necessities but of their advantages. . . . Every individual is continually exerting himself to find out the most advantageous employment for whatever capital he can command. It is his own advantage, indeed, and not that of society, which he has in view.[2]

Smith looked on all fixing of wages, guilds and trade unions that limit apprenticeship, and tariffs and other governmental interference as injurious to trade, and he scoffed at the mercantilists' view that the wealth of a nation depends on achieving a surplus of exports, amassing bullion, and crippling neighboring countries. He insisted that trade works for the benefit of all nations the world over and that a country cannot thrive and its trade flourish if its neighbors are not prosperous.

Philosophes urge political reforms. Working with the physiocrats as they sought to remove outworn economic abuses, the *philosophes* carried on an offensive against tyranny, misgovernment, and unjust laws. The reform movements of the physiocrats and the *philosophes* were inseparably connected, for only by obtaining efficient and rational government could essential economic reforms be carried through.

The *philosophes* militantly advocated the end of arbitrary government and the adoption of such rights as civil liberty, trial by jury, and freedom of expression—freedoms which they construed as implicit in natural law. By expressing the belief that laws and institutions could be based on a natural law as immutable as Newton's laws of physics, they helped undermine the edifice of absolutism. Preeminent for their intellectual assault on absolutism were Montesquieu and Rousseau, whose theories rank in importance with those of John Locke (see pp. 400 and 431).

Montesquieu and The Spirit of Laws. Montesquieu (1689-1755), a French nobleman, was the most systematic and comprehensive student of government during the first half of the eighteenth century. His famous *Persian Letters* (1721), purporting to be the correspondence of two oriental gentlemen writing their friends in the East while traveling about France, was a devastating satire on French customs and institutions. The sophisticated French bourgeoisie were delighted as they read such comments as:

It is by sitting on chairs that nobility is acquired. A great noble is a man who sees the King, speaks to his ministers, and who possesses ancestors, debts, and pensions.[3]

Montesquieu's most important work was *The Spirit of Laws* (1748), a massive study of the salient features of numerous governments. Widely discussed in the French salons, it later became the political bible of important statesmen in England and colonial America. Unlike the English philosopher Locke and many of the *philosophes*, Montesquieu did not use the deductive method of analysis. He began not with the universal principles or natural laws but with facts. His method was to describe and analyze actual governments, both past and present, and then to show how they reflected the environment in which they functioned.

In *The Spirit of Laws* Montesquieu concluded that all governments conformed to certain specific factors of geography, economics, and race, which varied from country to country. Since the value of any governmental system depended on its relation to these specific factors, there could be no single "best" form of government.

Montesquieu was a relentless critic of tyranny and a champion of liberty. Although he did not endorse any one form of government, he admired the limited parliamentary monarchy of England. In the separation of executive, legislative, and judicial powers, he found the bulwark of liberty. Actually, Montesquieu misinterpreted the operation of the unwritten English constitution, for with its cabinet system of government England was moving toward unity of powers. However, this concept of separation of powers greatly influenced the planners of the American Constitution.

Rousseau and the Social Contract. Jean Jacques Rousseau (1712-1778) was one of the most enigmatic and significant persons of his time. Although believing in the general objectives of the *philosophes*, Rousseau distrusted reason and science. He gloried in impulses and intuitions, trusting emotions rather than thoughts, the heart rather than the mind. His early hand-to-mouth existence and the rebuffs and ridicule he suffered from polite society contributed to his hatred of the Old Regime and the status quo. He was also influenced by the ideal of the "noble savage" who lived "without faith . . . law . . . [with] neither king, nor judge, nor priest . . . nor taxes, nor prisons."[4] It was not surprising, then, that Rousseau excoriated the society that had refused to open its doors to him, urged the overthrow of artificial modes of life, and encouraged men to listen to their hearts and to the voice of nature rather than to their minds and the postulates of formal philosophy.

Rousseau's most important work and indeed one of the most influential books on political theory in modern times was his *Social Contract* (1762), which opens with the stirring statement: "Man is born free, but is everywhere in chains." In this work Rousseau endeavored to construct a theory of government based on the consent of the governed while reconciling the conflicting demands of individual liberty and social organization. In Rousseau's ideal society an individual surrenders all his natural rights—as envisaged by Locke—to the group and yet retains his freedom if the government follows what is called the "General Will." The General Will is defined as any action that is right and good for all; hence by obeying the General Will the individual is really obeying what is in his own best interest. Rousseau never made clear how the General Will was to be determined, except to imply that in an ideal society it would coincide with the will of the majority. In such a society the majority is always right, and the individual must obey its commands.

Rousseau defined the social contract in a way that emphasized the sovereignty of the people. By means of the social contract each individual surrenders his natural rights to the state, meaning the people as a whole. The people and the state are therefore identical, but the government is something quite different—it is merely the executive agent of the people's will:

. . . the depositories of the executive power are not the people's masters, but its officers; . . . it can appoint and dismiss them at pleasure; . . . for them there is no question of contract, but of obedience.[5]

Rousseau was hailed as the champion of democracy. But it is also true that his doctrine of the General Will later came to be used by ambitious despots. Claiming that he alone knew what constituted the General Will, a shrewd leader could justify his seizure of power. It is one of history's ironies that the *Social Contract*, written to justify democracy, was used later on to justify dictatorship.

Faith in enlightened despotism. The majority of the *philosophes* believed that the most logical way to attain desirable reforms was through the rule of an "enlightened despot": secure a well-meaning, intelligent monarch imbued with the philosophy of the Enlightenment and all would be well. In a sense, this theory of government was akin to the Platonic ideal of a society where philosophers would be kings.

A few eighteenth-century monarchs were progressive, sincerely believing in the ideas of the *philosophes*. Major figures who were touched by the Enlightenment and became (or seemed to become) enlightened despots were Frederick the Great of Prussia, Catherine the Great of Russia, and the Austrian emperor Joseph II.

Enlightened despotism in Prussia, Russia, and Austria. Dedicated to the improvement of the Prussian state, Frederick the Great expressed his concept of the enlightened monarch's role thus:

The monarch is only the first servant of the State, who is obliged to act with probity and prudence, and to remain as totally disinterested as if he were each moment liable to render an account of his administration to his fellow-citizens. . . . As the sovereign is properly the head of a family of citizens, the father of his people, he ought on all occasions to be the last refuge of the unfortunate.[6]

"Old Fritz," as his subjects affectionately called him, traveled about his kingdom a great deal, studying its problems and hearing complaints from his people. No aspect of government escaped his attention. His reforms included a law code and the most efficient courts in Europe, a system of primary education, and equal status for his Catholic subjects. In economic matters Frederick remained a mercantilist, seeking to

The reforming rationalism of the *philosophes* spread to many of the royal courts of Europe. In this engraving Catherine the Great talks with Diderot.

make Prussia self-sufficient by subsidizing and controlling industry and commerce and by improving agricultural techniques. Although he admitted that serfdom was wrong he did nothing about it, not wishing to antagonize the Junker landowners. Until he died in 1786 at the age of seventy-four, Frederick worked diligently as the "first servant" of the state, aware that he had made Prussia a great European power.

In the early part of her reign Catherine II of Russia prided herself on being a patron of learning and the arts, a friend to the *philosophes*, and an exponent of the Enlightenment in government. The *philosophes* applauded her writings and her publicly announced policy of reform. They were the first to hail her as "the Great." But Catherine only posed at being a reformer, and little or nothing came of the changes she contemplated: the secularization of Church lands, the codification of the law, and the reform of local government.

The most sincere of the enlightened despots was Joseph II, the son of Maria Theresa. Joseph's reforms included the abolition of serfdom, toleration for Protestants and Jews, advancement of public education, equality of taxation, and centralization of the administrative and court systems.

Failure of enlightened despotism. Enlightened despotism was incapable of rooting out the deep-seated evils of the Old Regime. No matter how sincere and devoted to reform, an enlightened ruler such as Joseph of Austria could not achieve success against the entrenched power of the nobility and Church and the ignorance of the peasantry. Many of Joseph's reforms were hastily conceived and premature, and most of them died with him.

In most cases enlightened absolutism was nothing but a facade, a mere playing at reform because it was fashionable. "The Enlightenment was a fashion in Russia," it has been observed, "never a fact." Before her death in 1796, Catherine no longer quoted her "dear *philosophes*" or proclaimed their ideas. She had repressed a widespread peasants' rebellion with savage cruelty, and she had been frightened by the French Revolution, "the enemy of God and of the Thrones," as she called it.

Even half-hearted benevolent despotism was better than no benevolence at all, however. But the evils inherent in an all-powerful monarchy tainted the system. As the last phase of authoritarian absolutism, enlightened despotism more often aimed at strengthening the power of the state than at increasing the public welfare. Reforms were imposed from above on people who had not been educated to political realities. In the words of the British ambassador in Berlin:

The Prussian Monarchy reminds me of a vast prison in the centre of which appears the great keeper, occupied in the care of his captives.[7]

The successful reform movements were to come from below, from the revolutionary action of the people. It is noteworthy that in 1789, one year before Joseph II died a broken-hearted failure; a bourgeois revolution with a program in large part similar to Joseph's exploded in France. This French Revolution, inspired in part by the American Revolution, would end absolutism in France and sound its death knell throughout Europe.

THE AMERICAN REVOLUTION

Opposition to mercantilism. In 1776, with George III in full command of the British government (see p. 433), there began the stirring revolt that created in the western world a new nation, based on the political ideas espoused by Locke and Montesquieu. Many historians believe that the American Revolution was not so much a revolt against the tyranny of George III as a revolt of the American middle class against England's mercantilistic economic policy. In accord with the prevailing view that colonies existed for the benefit of the mother country, English navigation laws and other restrictive acts required the colonists to trade only with England and prohibited them from competing with English manufactured goods. For about a century these acts were not rigidly enforced, but finally the day of reckoning came.

After the Seven Years' War, England was saddled with a debt of nearly $700 million. The added expense of maintaining a strong force of British regulars in America, made necessary by a serious uprising of Indians in the Northwest in 1763, was therefore especially troublesome. The prime minister, George Grenville, having decided that the colonists should bear some of the expense of their own defense, induced Parliament to enact a series of acts designed for this purpose. A storm of protest arose in America, especially to the Stamp Act (1765), which levied duties on dice, playing cards, and—to the chagrin of newspaper publishers, lawyers, and merchants—on newspapers and legal and commercial documents. The Americans raised the constitutional principle of "no taxation without representation"; the British countered with the argument that Americans were indeed represented in Parliament because the members of that body represented not only the kingdom but the entire empire.

A revolution in minds and hearts. Although England's taxation measures precipitated the rebellion, it would be a mistake to interpret the American Revolution as resulting solely or even primarily from economic causes. Like all great historical movements, the American Revolution was a complex phenomenon. While admitting that the new taxes were ill timed, that they came too rapidly, and that the British government followed a confused policy of advance and then retreat under pressure, many historians deny that British mercantilism discriminated heavily against the colonists. The American colonies enjoyed a high degree of prosperity.

Agreement is growing among historians that the American Revolution was not so much brought about by a "cause" as by "conditions." As John Adams wrote in 1818:

But what do we mean by the American Revolution? Do we mean the American War? The Revolution was effected before the war commenced. The

American opposition to British taxation found violent expression as early as 1773. In this eighteenth-century British engraving of the Boston Tea Party the king's tax collector is shown being forced to drink the health of the royal family after being tarred and feathered. In the background other rebels pour tea into Boston Harbor.

Revolution was in the minds and hearts of the people. . . . This radical change in the principles, opinions, sentiments, and affections of the people, was the real American Revolution.[8]

It has been said that the separation movement really began when the first Englishman set foot on the soil of America. Many colonists had suffered religious persecution in the mother country and felt little love for their homeland. Many other colonists never had any connection with England. In 1775, out of a population of nearly three million, almost 40 percent were of non-English stock, mainly from Ireland and southern Germany. "To many Americans England had been an arbitrary and unkind mother; to a greater number she had never been a mother."[9] Of course, many other colonists considered themselves loyal Englishmen and opposed the break with the mother country.

The English colonial majority, however, prided themselves on their rights as Englishmen, rights stemming back to the Magna Carta. They had read the political writings of Montesquieu and Voltaire, and they accepted Locke's contract theory and the concept of the sovereignty of the people. .

In summary, these were the conditions which predisposed the colonies to revolution: a fierce spirit of freedom, experience in self-rule in the colonial assemblies, the impact of liberal political ideas from the writings of the French *philosophes*, and the lessons of the Puritan Revolution and the Revolution of 1688 in England.

The war against England. Following the imposition of the stamp tax, events moved rapidly toward open hostilities. Colonial boycotts of British goods and English retaliatory measures, skirmishes at Lexington and Concord between British troops and colonial militia, and the well-organized movement for independence, led by such radicals as Samuel Adams and Patrick Henry, heightened sentiment against the mother country. On July 4, 1776, the revolt of the American colonies was formally proclaimed in the Declaration of Independence.

With the outbreak of war, Britain's state of unpreparedness was quickly exposed. After its victory in the Seven Years' War,

Britain had failed to build up any alliance system to offset the enmity of its vanquished enemies, Spain and France. The British armies and fleets were woefully neglected; commanders found it impossible to put fifteen thousand regulars in the field in America.

Even if Britain had been better prepared, the military situation was very difficult. Britain had to subdue a people now numbering almost one third of its own population on a battlefield three thousand miles distant. And unlike the situation today, when only highly industrialized powers are able to manufacture the complicated weapons of war, the colonists could make most of the gunpowder and muskets they needed as well as a substantial amount of artillery.

The struggle dragged on for seven years. Colonial forces were puny and colonial supplies inadequate, but the revolutionary cause was immensely strengthened by the courage, determination, and skill of its leaders—Washington, patient patriot and dedicated commander; Franklin, sage diplomat and famous scholar; Madison, skilled student of government; Jefferson, ardent and courageous champion of freedom; and Hamilton, adept politician and Washington's wartime aide. The defeat of the British general Burgoyne in October 1777 and the alliance with France in the following year turned the scales in favor of the colonies.

The participation of France, seconded by Spain and Holland, widened the conflict into another European colonial war. In essence, this conflict was a great world struggle, with England, devoid of allies, fighting in the West Indies, the North Atlantic, West Africa, and India as well as in North America. Faced with the active coalition of France, Spain, and Holland—plus a league of neutrality composed of Russia, Sweden, and Denmark—England granted independence to the thirteen colonies in 1783. They were now free to make their own destinies, unhampered by constraints from Europe.

In meeting the challenge of the great European alliance intent on destroying its empire, Britain was more successful than it had been in its attempt to crush the far weaker forces of the American colonists. Regaining mastery of the seas, Britain still maintained its world position.

Constitutional government. Just before the conflict with Great Britain ended, the American colonies ratified the Articles of Confederation (1781), setting up a loose league of independent states under a weak central government. This system produced civil strife and confusion, and tariff and boundary disputes raged between the states.

At this juncture a group of public-spirited men, including Hamilton, Madison, and Washington, urged the establishment of a strong central government. Their efforts led to the Constitutional Convention, which met at Independence Hall in Philadelphia from May to September 1787. After much debate between the advocates of a strong central government and those favoring sovereign states, a brilliant compromise was reached— the Constitution of the United States— which assured the supremacy of the federal government without making puppet governments of the states. In April 1789 George Washington took the oath of office as first president under the Constitution.

The American Constitution represented a clean break with the past and a promise of complete democracy in the near future. Manhood suffrage was not realized under the Constitution for several decades, but this delay does not detract from the importance of the advanced democratic philosophy which became the law of the land.

The American Constitution embodied certain fundamental principles. The first was the doctrine of popular sovereignty—all power ultimately resides in the people. Constitutional provisions required the participation of the people in amending the Constitution and denied this right to the national government acting alone. Another principle, revolutionary in its day, was that of limited government, which safeguards the rights of the people by setting up definite bounds and restraints on the actions of their public officials. A third important feature was the principle of federalism. In most countries all power resided in the central government, but in the United States power was divided between the state governments and the national government. The principle of strong federalism became one of America's greatest contributions to government.

Separation of powers was a fourth fundamental aspect of the new Constitution. The powers and duties of legislature, judiciary, and executive were carefully defined. Thus Congress makes the laws, the president applies and enforces them, and the courts interpret them. However, by a fifth feature— checks and balances—careful provision was made so that no one of the three governmental departments could become too independent or too powerful. The president, for example, can veto laws passed by Congress. But the legislature can by a two-thirds vote pass bills over the president's veto. In like manner, the Supreme Court stands as an ultimate safeguard because it can declare any law unconstitutional.

Finally, the Constitution contains a sixth basic principle, the protection of the rights of the individual, although in reality this principle appears in the first ten amendments to the Constitution—the Bill of Rights —instead of in the Constitution proper. No laws can be made encroaching upon freedom of religion, press, and speech, and all persons are safeguarded from arbitrary arrest and imprisonment.

THE FRENCH REVOLUTION

The Old Regime in France. In the eighteenth century France suffered greatly from the indifference and incompetence of its rulers. The century had opened with the costly wars of Louis xiv; and Louis xv, who reigned from 1715 to 1774, was preoccupied with personal pleasure and indifferent to matters of state. The next monarch, Louis xvi, was well meaning, but ill educated, indolent, and shy; he spent his happiest hours in a workshop tinkering with locks. Lack of uniformity in legal codes, tariff boundaries, weights and measures, and taxation added to the confusion and inefficiency of government.

Discrimination and injustice prevailed in the social structure; birth, not intelligence or achievement, assured success and social position. Of France's total population of 25,000,000 people, only 200,000 belonged to the privileged classes—the clergy and the nobility. These two groups controlled nearly half of the nation's land, monopolized the best positions in the Church, army, and government, and evaded much of the taxation. The peasants—80 percent of the population—were saddled with intolerable burdens. The *taille*, a land tax; the tithe, levied by the Church; the *gabelle*, a tax on salt; and various other taxes took nearly half of a peasant's income. In addition, while the practice of serfdom had practically disappeared, peasants suffered from many vestiges of medieval social discrimination. Fishing, hunting, and keeping pigeons were activities reserved exclusively for the nobility, and peasants were forbidden to molest the deer and rabbits that destroyed their crops. Fields were often trampled underfoot by hunting parties of nobles, and swarms of pigeons gobbled up newly planted seed. Many nobles were absentee landlords who squandered their income from peasant tenant farmers and sharecroppers in ostentatious expenditures at Versailles.

The French middle class had wealth without responsibility, intelligence without authority, and ability without recognition. Practical and businesslike, they resented playing second fiddle to a parasitic nobility and were disgusted at the inefficiency of government. The extravagance of the royal court, the unfair methods of tax collection, the absence of a sound system of national bookkeeping, and the continuance of mercantilistic controls especially called forth censure. The middle class sought economic freedom and above all a constitutional monarchy in which they would be dominant.

Conditions in France were not the worst in Europe. France had the most prosperous middle class outside of England, and the peasants were better off than in any other Continental country. The revolution came to France because the middle class was keenly aware of the evils of the Old Regime.

As we shall see, the impending national bankruptcy, coupled with the selfishness of the nobles, finally brought on the crisis precipitating revolution. But in the background were the ideas of the *philosophes* and physiocrats. By criticizing the evils of the times, stimulating discontent—especially among the bourgeoisie—and offering a logical picture of what a well-ordered society might be, they created a widespread atmosphere of grievance and supplied political and economic philosophies for the future.

Effect of the American Revolution. In France the impact of the American Revolution was deep and widespread; the Americans showed the French how an antiquated government could be removed. War makes strange bedfellows. In France the government of a monarch who opposed freedom at home gave its support to American independence and painted an idyllic picture of the brave new republic. Many aristocrats who espoused the doctrines of the *philosophes* sympathized with the colonists. But, as one of them observed, "None of us stopped to think of the danger of the example which the New World set to the Old."

The financial crisis. Whatever its effect on the climate of opinion in France, the most immediate influence of the American Revolution upon France was acceleration toward bankruptcy. Participation in the American Revolution had cost France nearly $400 million. The credit of the government became so poor that it had to pay an interest rate of 20 percent on its loans, whereas England paid only 4 percent. By 1789 the government was faced with an annual deficit of $27 million, and interest payments on the national debt took half of the total national revenues.

When Louis XVI and his advisers proposed a program of tax equalization that would have put French finances in order, the nobility flatly turned it down. They insisted that the king convene the Estates-General, which they expected to dominate and thereby regain the power they had lost to the monarchy during past centuries. Thus by paralyzing the royal power and forcing the summoning of the Estates-General, the French nobility can be said to have initiated the Revolution. In the words of a nineteenth-century Frenchman, "The patricians began the Revolution; the plebians finished it."

The Estates-General, inactive since 1614 (see p. 421), was composed of representatives of the First Estate (the clergy), the Second Estate (the nobility), and the Third Estate (the middle class and the peasants). As a gesture to the bourgeoisie, the Third Estate was granted twice the number of representatives allowed each of the other two estates.

The National Assembly. The calling of the Estates-General in 1789 precipitated a demand for reform all over France. For the guidance of the delegates to the assembly, the people prepared *cahiers* (lists) of grievances. The *cahiers* included demands for personal liberty, a national legislature to make the laws, a jury system, freedom of the press, and abolition of unfair taxation. Thus the *cahiers* presented a program of wide but moderate social and economic reform.

On May 5 the Estates-General was formally convened. The delegates of the Third Estate consisted of some six hundred deputies; half were lawyers, the remainder merchants, bankers, governmental officials, and farmers. According to custom the three estates were expected to vote by orders—that is, by estates rather than as individuals. This would mean that any scheme of reform formulated by the Third Estate could always be defeated by a two-to-one vote at the hands of the two privileged estates.

After six weeks of wrangling on the question of whether voting should be by order or by head, the members of the Third Estate assembled at an indoor tennis court and solemnly took the Tennis Court Oath, declaring that they would not disband until a constitution had been drawn up. A royal official sent to order the Assembly to disband was told by the defiant leader Mirabeau, "Sir, go tell your master that nothing but bayonets will drive us out of here." Louis weakly yielded, and the Third Estate, augmented by a few members of the other orders, declared itself the National Constituent Assembly of France.

Collapse of absolutism. All over France millions followed the events at Versailles. Peasants and city workers grew bold at the capitulation of the king, and in July 1789, disorders and riots broke out throughout the land. In the cities, houses of the nobility were sacked; in the country, peasants demolished the castles of their lords. Every-

Social stratification under the Old Regime in France is bitterly satirized in this cartoon which shows the First Estate and the Second Estate—the clergy and the nobility—riding on the back of the Third Estate, represented here by an aged, toilworn peasant.

where it was manifest that royal government in France was collapsing.

Following a rumor that the king was concentrating troops at Versailles as a means of browbeating the Assembly, a Parisian mob attacked the Bastille, a grim fortress and the hated symbol of the Old Regime. Although on that fateful day of July 14, 1789, the Bastille contained only seven prisoners (four counterfeiters, one habitual drunkard, and two lunatics), the mob stormed the fortress and slew its defenders. King Louis is said to have remarked, "This is a revolt." "No, Sire," was the reply, "it is a revolution."

Renunciation of the Old Regime. The National Constituent Assembly was in session from June 1789 until October 1791. During this period the Assembly passed more than two thousand laws and effected a peaceful and moderate revolution. In the words of one historian, "No other body of legislators has ever demolished so much in the same brief period."[10]

One of the most important and dramatic

acts of the Assembly took place in the critical days of August 1789. The Bastille had just fallen, and peasants all over France, frightened by false rumors that brigands employed by nobles were burning peasant homes and fields and determined to destroy the records listing the surviving manorial obligations they owed to the lords, fell upon their hated oppressors. They killed some lords and destroyed the châteaux of others.

As the frightening news reached Paris, the deputies in the Assembly realized that immediate action had to be taken. During the night of August 4, noble after noble arose to renounce his feudal dues and privileges. By these proclamations, known as the August Decrees, serfdom was abolished (there were still some serfs in Alsace and Lorraine), old game laws were repealed, manorial courts were swept away, and tithes and all other fees of the Church were ended. It was declared that from that time on taxes were to be collected from all citizens irrespective of rank, the sale of judicial and municipal offices was to cease, justice was to be freely dispensed, and all citizens, regardless of birth, were eligible for any office.

The Constituent Assembly passed other important reforms. It abolished the old provinces and replaced them with eighty-three equal administrative divisions called "departments." It ended restrictions on the conduct of business and encouraged individual enterprise by abolishing guilds and prohibiting trade unions.

The Assembly also substantially changed the status of the Church. Monasteries were dissolved and all Church property confiscated. The former Church lands were used as collateral for paper money called *assignats*. By the Civil Constitution of the Clergy, the Church was secularized. Bishops and priests were now elected by the people, paid by the state, and required to swear allegiance to the new constitution of France.

The Declaration of the Rights of Man. Before drawing up the new constitution, the Assembly produced a document which summarized the principles upon which the new regime should be based—the Declaration of the Rights of Man. Its most important provisions were:

1. Men are born and will remain free and endowed with equal rights. . . .

2. The end and purpose of all political groups is the preservation of the natural and inalienable rights of Man. These rights are Liberty, the Possession of Property, Safety, and Resistance to Oppression. . . .

4. Liberty consists in being able to do anything which is not harmful to another. . . .

6. The Law is the expression of the will of the people. . . . the Law must be the same for all. . . .

9. Every individual . . . [is] presumed innocent until he has been proved guilty. . . .

10. None is to be persecuted for his opinions, even his religious beliefs, provided that his expression of them does not interfere with the order established by the Law.

11. Free communication of thought and opinion is one of the most precious rights of Man. . . .

17. The possession of property being an inviolable and sacred right, none can be deprived of it, unless public necessity, legally proved, clearly requires the deprivation, and then only on the necessary condition of a previously established just reparation.[11]

The Declaration of the Rights of Man embodied the spirit of constitutional government and political liberalism underlying the Glorious Revolution in England and the revolt of the thirteen colonies in America. This French pronouncement appealed immediately to reform groups in all European nations, and during the nineteenth century it inspired many peoples to throw off the yoke of their own old regimes.

The Legislative Assembly. By September 1791 the National Constituent Assembly had formulated a new constitution which made France a limited monarchy. The chief organ of government was an elected single-chamber legislature called the Legislative Assembly. Louis XVI was given only a suspensive veto over legislation, a device which could retard action by the Assembly but could not block its will indefinitely. No longer could the king use the formula of Louis XIV, *L'état, c'est moi*; the monarch was now "Louis by the grace of God and the Constitution, King of the State."

Despite the rights guaranteed in the Declaration of the Rights of Man, the suffrage was given to only a minority of "active" citizens—those who paid a specified minimum amount of direct taxes. Thus one of the striking features of the French constitution of 1791 was its reflection of the interests of the influential bourgeosie.

This first phase of the French Revolution has been called the Bourgeois Revolution. After relatively little violence France had become a constitutional monarchy with the upper middle class in control. Their concern now was to "stabilize" the Revolution by blocking further change.

Opposition to the Legislative Assembly. The peasants were among the many elements in France that were discontented with the new government. Although the Constituent Assembly in the August Decrees had ruled that many privileges, such as possession of serfs, labor service, and hunting and fishing rights, were to be abolished without compensation, other old manorial dues and obligations were to be commuted into money payments. Most peasants, however, defied the government and refused to make the payments. Hatred against men of property and their agents in the Legislative Assembly grew.

Instead of accepting the moderate changes brought about between 1789 and 1791 and thus helping consolidate and strengthen the moderate revolution, Louis XVI tried to weaken the new regime. He apparently did not understand that if the Legislative Assembly failed, the Revolution would take a radical turn and the monarchy would be swept away. In June 1791 Louis and his family attempted to escape from the country, an act which increased the suspicion that he was an enemy of the Revolution.

The Civil Constitution of the Clergy had been condemned by Pope Pius VI, and consequently about half of the clergy refused to take the oath of fidelity to the constitution. These nonjuring priests told the people that sacraments administered by priests who had accepted the Civil Constitution of the Clergy were ineffectual. In the country districts the peasants supported their nonjuring priests, and serious disorders broke out. Thus, from the outset, the Legislative Assembly was faced with the enmity and opposition of a determined Catholic group.

The common people of the cities were especially disgruntled. The cost of living and

The idealization of the French Revolution is epitomized in Francois Rude's romantic "La Marseillaise" from the Arc de Triomphe in Paris. Classically garbed soldiers march forward dauntlessly under the guidance of the spirit of Liberty.

unemployment were increasing, and they saw no hope of relief in a government from which they were excluded. Largely illiterate and motivated by emotion, these urban workers could be aroused to wild passions of frenzy by eloquent leaders, and as time passed they became increasingly dangerous.

Factions in the Legislative Assembly. The division of opinion in the country at large was mirrored by factionalism in the Assembly itself. About one third of the deputies were conservatives; they made up the party of the Right, which supported the king and was satisfied with the achievements of the moderate revolution. Seated in the middle of the Assembly was the party of the Center, made up of representatives who had no particular program or principles. Next to the apathetic Center were the deputies of the Left, dynamic and aggressive young radicals who distrusted the king, were dissatisfied with the constitution of 1791, and wished the Revolution to continue. From the very start the enemies of the constitution assumed the leadership of the Legislative Assembly and worked for its downfall.

Leaders of the Jacobin movement. The enthusiastic radicals who were determined to advance the Revolution formed various clubs in Paris that were centers of agitation and revolutionary propaganda. The most important of these organizations met in an abandoned Jacobin (Dominican) monastery and took the name "Society of the Friends of the Constitution Meeting at the Jacobins in Paris." Their program was the overthrow of the monarchy and greater justice and opportunity for the masses. Soon, Jacobin Clubs sprang up all over France.

Most prominent in Jacobin circles were Jean Paul Marat, Georges Jacques Danton, and Maximilien Robespierre. As champion of the masses, Marat founded the newspaper *L'Ami du Peuple (Friend of the People)* and carried on a campaign for direct action by the people until 1793 when he was struck down by an assassin's dagger. Robespierre was deeply influenced by the works of Rousseau and became a fanatical reformer who quietly bided his time until he possessed the necessary power to establish an ideal republic based on virtue and justice. Danton, unlike the theorist Robespierre, was a practical republican who had little use for utopias.

Opposition to the Legislative Assembly outside France. Also plotting against the Assembly were many reactionary émigré nobles who had fled France when the Revolution wiped out their ancient privileges. Most of them had taken refuge in various states along the Rhine, where they found receptive ears for their conspiracies against the French government. Many German bishops and princes who possessed lands in French Alsace were indignant over the abolition of feudal dues and services. Furthermore, many German nobles feared that the abolition of the seigneurial privilege in France would lead to insurrections on their own estates.

Although they were uneasy about the trend of events in France, the rulers of the large European states adopted a wait-and-see policy, hoping that factionalism in France would weaken the nation and perhaps reduce it to a state of impotency. However, Leopold II of Austria, brother of the French queen, became concerned over her safety and, with the king of Prussia, issued the Declaration of

A group of revolutionaires—ragged *sans culottes* (that is, those who did not wear knee breeches like the aristocrats but trousers instead)—celebrate a military victory by dancing around a Liberty Tree decorated with emblems of the Revolution.

Pillnitz (August 1791), which declared that the restoration of absolutism in France was of "common interest to all sovereigns of Europe."

France vs. Austria and Prussia. Opposed from without and weakened from within, the moderate constitutional monarchy was doomed to failure. The shock of foreign war precipitated its downfall.

Nearly all the factions in France favored war—each for a different reason. The king and his supporters, as well as the émigré nobles, favored war because they believed the government would be defeated, discredited, and then overthrown. The radicals, especially a faction called the Girondists, who at first formed part of the Jacobin organization, were eager to involve France in a conflict because, in their opinion, war would discredit the monarchy and give them a chance to rise to power and establish a republic. Egged on by the Girondists, France declared war on Austria in April 1792. Prussia shortly afterward entered the conflict as an ally of Austria.

Yet, while eager for war, the French were utterly unprepared for it. During the summer of 1792, fortress after fortress fell to the invaders. On July 27 the Duke of Brunswick, commander of the allied forces invading France, issued a manifesto declaring that his object was "to restore to the king . . . the legitimate authority which belongs to him." He added that he would destroy Paris if the royal family was harmed. The actual result of the manifesto, however, was to bolster the position of the most radical groups, discredit the king completely, and end the monarchy in France.

Insurrection in Paris. The reply to the manifesto was the insurrection of the ninth and tenth of August instigated by radical Jacobin leaders. They set up a revolutionary "Commune" which controlled Paris and intimidated the Legislative Assembly into deposing Louis XVI and calling for the election, by universal male suffrage, of a National Convention to draw up a new constitution. As head of the Paris Commune, Danton became dictator of France.

The September Massacres. On September 2, news reached Paris that the fortress of

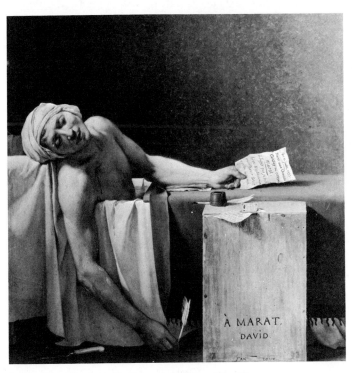

Stabbed by Charlotte Corday, a supporter of the Girondist faction, the Jacobin leader Marat lies dead in his bath in this famous Neoclassical painting by Jacques Louis David (1793).

Verdun had fallen to the invaders. As reinforcements were sent off to the front, the Paris Commune took care that no traitors were left behind at home. Many citizens believed that counterrevolutionists, in league with the enemy, would try to seize power. All suspected of sympathy for the monarchy were butchered. The prisons were emptied of nonjuring priests and nobles, who were then executed without trial. During the next five days nearly two thousand suspected royalists were killed.

Inauguration of the Republic. While the frenzy engendered by the September Massacres was spreading throughout France, the election of representatives to the National Convention quickly took place. The Legislative Assembly came to an end on September 20, 1792, when the National Convention held its first meeting. The following day the Convention abolished monarchy in France and proclaimed September 22, 1792, as beginning Year 1 of the Republic. France was now a republic, the former king Louis XVI a prisoner in fear for his life, and the first phase of the French Revolution—that of moderate reform—a failure.

Problems facing the National Convention. The National Convention remained in session three years. At the outset it was faced with serious problems: (1) foreign armies had to be driven out of France; (2) a vital decision had to be made as to what should be done with the king; (3) revolts throughout the country had to be suppressed; (4) a republican constitution had to be framed; and (5) the social and economic reforms initiated between 1789 and 1791 had to be completed and put into action.

Danton proceeded with alacrity to increase the armed forces and give them new spirit. During the autumn of 1792 the tide of foreign invasion receded as French armies took the offensive. They occupied the Austrian Netherlands (Belgium), the Rhineland, and Nice and Savoy.

Trial and execution of Louis XVI. The fate of Louis XVI was soon settled. The Girondists, now more moderate in their views and split from the Jacobins, wished to postpone the king's trial for treason until after the war, but the radical Jacobins demanded his death. A follower of Robespierre declared:

The death of the tyrant is necessary to reassure those who fear that one day they will be punished for their daring, and also to terrify those who have not yet renounced the monarchy. A people cannot found liberty when it respects the memory of its chains.[12]

The execution of Louis XVI was carried out on January 21, 1793. On the scaffold the king acted with quiet dignity and splendid fortitude. A French historian has declared: "he was greater on [the scaffold] . . . than ever he had been on his throne."[13]

European opinion turns against the Revolution. During the first years of the French Revolution a strong body of European opinion had acclaimed its reforms. Liberals cheered the news of the fall of the Bastille. The English romantic poet William Wordsworth described his feelings during those stirring days:

Bliss was it in that dawn to be alive,
But to be young was very Heaven! O times,

In which the meagre, stale, forbidding ways
Of custom, law, and statute, took at once
The attraction of a country in romance![14]

But there also had been voices raised in warning. In 1790 the influential English statesman Edmund Burke published his *Reflections on the Revolution in France.* A conservative, Burke feared the effect of the Revolution on English radicals and predicted that it would lead to mob violence and dictatorship in France. He likened the Revolution to "a strange chaos of levity and ferocity, and of all sorts of crimes jumbled together with all sorts of follies."[15] To Burke, the rule of the mob was as terrifying and as unjust as the rule of a capricious absolute monarch; stability, gradual change, and respect for the old as well as receptivity for the new were the basis of the good society.

Is it in destroying and pulling down that skill is displayed? . . . The shallowest understanding, the rudest hand, is more than equal to that task. Rage and frenzy will pull down more in half an hour than prudence, deliberation, and foresight can build up in a hundred years. . . . People will not look forward to posterity, who never look backward to their ancestors. . . . A disposition to preserve, and an ability to improve, taken together, would be my standard of a statesman.[16]

While the Legislative Assembly was in power and Louis XVI was on the throne, most observers thought Burke's arguments exaggerated; but they began to think differently after the September Massacres, the acquisition of territories outside of France, and the execution of Louis XVI.

In November 1792, after its armies had reached the Rhine, the National Convention declared that "France will grant fraternity and assistance to all peoples who shall desire to recover their liberty." This announcement in essence proclaimed an international revolution. In December the Convention stated that "it considered itself called to give liberty to the human race and to overthrow all thrones" and declared war on tyrants. It was also announced that in all countries conquered by the French, the inhabitants had to accept the principles of the Revolution; property belonging to counterrevolutionaries and to the Church was to be seized.

England as the leading anti-French power. In the face of French aggression—which, at the least, threatened the balance of power in Europe—England, Spain, Holland, and Sardinia joined Prussia and Austria in the First Coalition to wage war on the French Republic. Of all France's foes, England became the most implacable. From 1793 to 1815 England and France were at war almost continuously.

The prime minister in England at this time was William Pitt the Younger. Something of a liberal at the beginning of his career, Pitt wanted no war with France and considered Burke's dire warnings about the Revolution exaggerated. After the French occupied Belgium and threatened Holland, Pitt changed his opinions; he now believed that war with France was inevitable.

Pressures inside and outside France. In the spring of 1793 the armies of the First Coalition converged on France. The Revolution was again in peril. In addition to this foreign menace, France was rent by internal strife as moderate and radical factions fought for control of the National Convention. More representative of the bourgeois moderate revolution and of provincial support for federalism, the Girondists feared mob violence and radical reforms; to them the Revolution had gone far enough. By contrast, the Jacobins were tough realists who sided with the urban masses, welcomed more bloodletting, and were determined to advance the Revolution. The Jacobins finally ousted their rivals from the Convention and placed them under arrest. Some of the Girondists, however, escaped to the country, where they organized a rebellion against the tyranny of the radicals in Paris. Meanwhile, royalist Catholics rose again in rebellion. These disorders weakened the economy of the country, and bread riots broke out in Paris.

The Reign of Terror. To deal with the internal and external dangers, the National Convention entrusted its power to twelve men known as the Committee of Public Safety. It also passed a decree making liable to arrest every person of noble birth, anyone who had any contact with an émigré, and anyone who could not produce a certificate of citizenship.

The Committee of Public Safety inaugu-

The excesses of the French Revolution are typified by the guillotine, the instrument used during the Reign of Terror to behead thousands of Frenchmen, including Louis XVI, whose head is being displayed to the crowd. Ironically, the guillotine was first recommended by a Paris physician, Joseph Ignace Guillotin, who wanted a more humane method of punishment instead of the feudal tortures used to execute criminals. Before the Revolution only the nobility were allowed the relatively painless death of decapitation.

rated the Reign of Terror. Thousands of suspected royalists were arrested and thrown into prison. After a summary trial, many of them were thrown into carts—the tumbrels —and taken to the public square to be guillotined. Perhaps as many as five thousand persons were executed in Paris; in the provinces the number was probably twenty thousand.

The "nation in arms." With subversive activity crushed on the home front, the leaders of the Republic turned their attention to the foreign danger. To meet its enemies, France forged a new weapon, the "nation in arms." Compulsory military service was introduced. In February 1793 the Convention passed a decree calling 300,000 men to the colors and making all men between eighteen and forty liable for military service. Military seniority was discarded, and brilliant young generals were given the highest commands. Results were demanded from these officers; it was victory or the guillotine.

In August 1793 the Convention decreed a general mobilization of the country. Scientists were enlisted to help the war effort, and workmen were conscripted and shifted from nonessential to war work. In Paris alone, 258 forges were set up out in the open to make 1000 gun barrels a day. Business was organized to produce vast quantities of medicines, shoes, and uniforms.

During 1794 and 1795 the new French armies carried out a series of great campaigns. The citizen armies of the Republic were motivated by a spirit not found in the professional and mercenary armies of their opponents. The French citizen-soldier believed he was fighting for his own liberty and for the right to enjoy the fruits of the Revolution.

By 1795, with Spain and Prussia no longer offering effective resistance to the French, the First Coalition had almost been dissolved. Holland was allied with France, Belgium was annexed outright, and French troops controlled all the territory up to the Rhine. In three years the Republic had gained the "natural frontiers" that Louis XIV had dreamed about. By 1795 only England, Austria, and Sardinia remained at war with France.

Social and economic changes. Among the significant reforms achieved during the period of the National Convention (also known as the Jacobin Republic) were the plan for a national system of education, abolition of slavery in French colonies, final eradication of manorial dues and obligations without compensation, and the establishment of a metric system of weights and measures. The welfare of the lower classes was promoted by placing ceilings on prices and by selling the confiscated estates of the émigrés. As a result of the latter measure, France became a land of small proprietors, and the once radical French peasant became a conservative.

The everyday life of the people was transformed in numerous ways. A strong anti-Christian movement was initiated; churches were closed and religious images destroyed. Everything that smacked of royalty and privilege was discarded. Knee breeches, a symbol of the aristocracy, were declared unpatriotic. In their place were substituted long trousers, the *sans culottes* (literally, "without short breeches"), which "made all legs equal by concealment." Titles were discarded; the proper form of address became "citizen" and "citizeness." Both men and women gave up aristocratic wigs and powdered hair, and men adopted mustaches as a symbol of virility and patriotism. Streets formerly named for kings or nobles were renamed to commemorate revolutionary events or heroes. And men changed their names, especially if their Christian name was Louis. Even the name of the queen bee was changed to "laying bee."

The Terror continues. In the autumn of 1793 the Reign of Terror reached its height. The Girondists who had been expelled from the National Convention were executed, and the guillotine also claimed the queen, Marie Antoinette. By controlling the all-powerful Committee of Public Safety, Robespierre was now the dominant force in the government.

By the spring of 1794 there was no longer any justification for continuance of the Terror. But to the fanatical Robespierre, a "republic of virtue" had to be achieved, in which there would be no excesses of wealth, where every citizen would serve the public good, and where justice and love would prevail. To attain this utopian Jacobin commonwealth, Robespierre believed that "the people's prejudices must be destroyed . . . its habits altered, its vices eradicated, and its desires purified."[17] While a bewildered Paris looked on, many courageous leaders of the Revolution who dared to disagree with his fanatical views were executed. Among them was Danton, who wished to end the policy of terror. Disgusted at the bloodshed, the members of the Convention finally arrested Robespierre and sent him to the guillotine.

Reaction against the Terror. Frenchmen now hoped that the long period of excesses was over and that the nation could bind up its wounds and settle down to a period of tranquility and repose. Thousands of suspects were freed, the Paris Commune was dissolved, and the extraordinary powers of the Committee of Public Safety were swept away. In Paris gangs of young men attacked Jacobins, and in the provinces there was a veritable "White Terror" against the radicals. The Jacobin Clubs were closed and the Catholic churches were reopened. Conservatism was now the order of the day. It was not that the people wanted to go back to the old days. They wanted to see the gains of the Revolution safeguarded and perpetuated, but they were tired of extremists and fanatics.

THE NAPOLEONIC PERIOD

The Directory. The National Convention now drafted a new republican system of government, the Directory, which was composed of two legislative chambers and a weak executive body of five members called directors. The right to vote was restricted to some twenty thousand property owners.

Assuming power in 1795, the Directory faced opposition from extremists on the right and on the left. The royalists were so bold as to foment an insurrection in Paris, which an obscure young general named Napoleon Bonaparte dispersed with a "whiff of grapeshot." In the spring of 1796 a radical working-class leader named "Gracchus" Babeuf plotted to seize the government and introduce a socialist economy. He ended as a guest of "Madame Guillotine"—and a martyr for modern Communists to honor—while the workers continued to suffer from inflation and unemployment.

Determined to smash the remnants of the First Coalition, the Directory commissioned three armies to invade Austrian territory. Two of these forces failed, but the one led by Napoleon Bonaparte crossed the Alps in 1796 and crushed the Sardinians and the Austrians. With a French army at the gates of Vienna, the Austrians were forced to accept the Treaty of Campo Formio (1797). Only Great Britain, protected by its fleet, remained at war with France.

Napoleon rises to power. Following his triumph over Austria, Napoleon obtained the consent of the Directory to invade Egypt in order to menace English interests in India. He is reputed to have said, "This little Europe does not supply enough glory for me." Evading the English fleet, Napoleon and his army landed in Egypt and were at first victorious. Efforts to crush Turkish forces were not successful, however, and in the meantime the English Admiral Nelson in 1798 destroyed Napoleon's Mediterranean fleet in the battle of the Nile. Aware that the Directory was becoming more and more incapable of coping with the problems of France, Napoleon in 1799 deserted his army and returned to France, where he was wildly acclaimed.

The France to which Napoleon returned was again in a state of crisis. A newly formed Second Coalition threatened to invade the country, and inflation threatened the economy. Faced with financial ruin and invasion, the French turned to the one man they believed could save the day—Napoleon. Sensing the mood of the nation, Napoleon in 1799 swept the Directory from power and established a new government called the Consulate—ostensibly a republic but with nearly all power centralized in the thirty-year-old First Consul, Napoleon. The new constitution was approved by the people in a plebiscite; the vote was 3,011,007 to 1,526.

Napoleon's genius for leadership. What manner of man was this "savior" of France?

Born in Corsica in 1769, the young Napoleon was a member of the Corsican lower nobility of Italian origin. Educated in a French military school, he joined the French army at the beginning of the Revolution. His "whiff of grapeshot," which saved the Directory from a royalist coup, and his marriage to the morally lax Josephine de Beauharnais, who was influential with the directors, gained him his first big chance—command of the army of Italy.

Napoleon liked to describe himself as a "man of destiny." He also once remarked: "I am no ordinary man, and the laws of propriety and morals are not applicable to me." He had a great reservoir of energy which enabled him to be in the saddle all day and to pore over his maps most of the night. For fifteen years the Little Corporal amazed and confounded his opponents by his brilliant tactics and strategy and by the élan he inspired in his troops.

After becoming First Consul, Napoleon quickly scattered the forces of the Second Coalition. The Austrians were compelled to sign the Treaty of Lunéville (1801), and although Great Britain was not defeated, France and England arranged a truce in 1802.

Napoleon's domestic reforms. The First Consul then turned his attention to domestic reforms. The system of local government was reorganized to provide a completely centralized governmental structure. Prefects appointed by the central government were given almost complete charge of local affairs, an arrangement which made for efficiency at the expense of liberty. Next, Napoleon grappled with the financial problem. Graft and inequality in tax collection were ended, economies in public expenditures were effected, and most important, the Bank of France was established. It still exists today as a model of banking stability.

While irreligious himself, Napoleon shrewdly realized that the people demanded the reestablishment of the Church. In the

NAPOLEONIC EUROPE

- France in 1789
- Acquisitions of Napoleon to 1810
- Dependent States of Napoleon
- Allies of Napoleon
- → Napoleon's Campaigns

Concordat of 1801 with the Vatican, the pope was granted the right to approve of bishops appointed by Napoleon. In addition, seminaries were again permitted, and the state agreed to pay the salaries of the clergy. The Catholic Church was now restored in France, but without its former power and wealth.

Before 1800 scarcely 25,000 children in France were attending elementary school. To remedy this situation, Napoleon created a system of public education which provided an educational pyramid of public elementary schools, secondary institutions (*lycées*), special schools for technical training, and the University of France. The latter was not a teaching body but an administrative one; its function was to regulate and control the entire educational system.

Napoleon believed in rewarding ability and in opening the way for talent. In 1802 he created the order of the Legion of Honor to honor citizens who made outstanding contributions to society. Napoleon told his advisers that men "have one feeling—honour. We must nourish that feeling: they must have distinctions."[18]

Napoleon's most famous accomplishment was his codification of the numerous laws and decrees of the Revolution and some 360 local law codes. Completed in 1804, the great Civil Code was written with precision and clarity; it guaranteed many achievements of the French Revolution, such as religious toleration and the abolition of privilege. The Code Napoléon, as it was renamed in 1807, has exerted a marked influence upon the law of other countries, and Napoleon later claimed that he was prouder of it than of his forty battles.

When Napoleon declared himself emperor in 1804, a grateful and contented people overwhelmingly approved his action in another plebiscite. The First French Republic was now no more.

Napoleon at the height of his power. Just before Napoleon assumed the crown of emperor, war between Great Britain and France broke out once more. Napoleon welcomed war. His meteoric rise from a nonentity to the first citizen of France had not satisfied his lust for glory. During 1803 and 1804 he directed extensive preparations for an invasion of England, but the inability of Napoleon's naval forces to gain control of the approaches to England and the formation of the Third Coalition (composed of Great Britain, Russia, Austria, and Sweden) compelled him to march eastward against his Continental enemies in 1805.

Meanwhile Napoleon's hopes of securing control of the seas and invading or at least starving out Britain were ended rudely in the smoke of Trafalgar (October 1805). In this decisive naval battle Lord Nelson defeated the combined French and Spanish fleets. Undaunted, Napoleon crushed the armies of Austria and Russia at Austerlitz, the most brilliant of his victories. In 1806 he occupied Berlin after the Prussians, still basking in the reflected glory of Frederick the Great, declared war. Napoleon organized the territory seized by Prussia in the partitions of Poland into a French dependency. In 1807, at Tilsit, after suffering a third defeat in two years, the Russian tsar agreed to assist France in disposing of the emperor's stubborn antagonist—England.

By 1808 Napoleon ruled over a France which extended from the North Sea to the Pyrenees and included much of Italy. He had placed several of his relatives on the thrones of nearby countries. Prussia and Austria were impotent before French power, and Russia appeared to be only a Napoleonic satellite.

Napoleon was now at the height of his great powers. Few men in history have possessed his gifts and achieved such amazing results. He was the dynamo and the brain of his "Grand Empire." But, as we shall shortly see, the load was too much for one man. The powers of Napoleon began to decline while his problems continued to increase.

Importance of British sea power. By 1808 it was apparent that British sea power was the all-important obstacle standing in the way of Napoleon's mastery of Europe. Safe behind warships, English factories turned out more and more war goods. British commerce and wealth increased, while French trade declined. Great Britain imposed a naval blockade against Napoleonic Europe. Seeking to crush England's economy by imposing a counterblockade, Napoleon prohibited the

In 1804 Napoleon declared himself emperor of France; in 1815 he was exiled to St. Helena. In Jacques Louis David's painting of the coronation Napoleon, who is crowning Josephine, wears a laurel wreath. In this ceremony, which was presided over by the pope, the allusions to the Roman and Carolingian empires were intentional. A romanticized painting by the Scottish artist Orchardson shows the defeated emperor brooding on the deck of the British ship, the H.M.S. Bellerophon, which carried him to his final exile.

entry of British vessels into countries under his control, a policy known as the Continental System. Fundamentally, the war was now a struggle between the sea power and industrial superiority of England and French military power on the Continent.

Reaction against French imperialism. Ostensibly "liberators" of subject people in Europe, Napoleon's armies disseminated the French revolutionary ideals of "liberty, equality, fraternity." But as Napoleon became more and more imperialistic, the people he had "emancipated" realized that they had merely exchanged one despotism for another. In posing as the champion of the Revolution, Napoleon had sown the seeds of nationalism and liberty which were to prove his undoing.

The occupation of Portugal (1807) and Spain (1808), in order to shore up in the Continental System, proved to be the first crack in the facade of Napoleon's Grand Empire. In both nations guerrilla warfare soon broke out, and a British expeditionary force joined the fighting against the French invaders.

All over Germany a wave of nationalism stirred the people to prepare for a war of liberation. Prussia in particular underwent a regeneration which caused German patriots to look to it for leadership. Liberal ministers began a program of social reform that included the abolition of serfdom, land for the peasants, and a degree of self-government in the cities. Although Napoleon had limited the Prussian army to 42,000 men, the Prussians undermined this provision by a subtle subterfuge: as soon as one army was trained, it was placed on reserve and a new army was called up for training. In this way Prussia managed to prepare a potential army of 270,000 men. Prussian intellectuals used education as a means of nationalistic propaganda. Founded in 1810, the University of Berlin became a center of strong nationalistic movements.

Invasion and retreat in Russia. Napoleon made a major misstep when, after a quarrel with Alexander I of Russia, he launched an invasion of the tsar's realm in 1812. The campaign was a catastrophe. Although Napoleon's Grand Army fought its way to

Moscow, the enemy forces remained intact, and the Russians' scorched-earth strategy prevented the invaders from living off the country. While the French occupied Moscow, fires broke out, destroying three fourths of the city. After spending thirty-three days in the empty shell of Moscow vainly waiting for the tsar to agree to a peace, Napoleon gave the order to retreat.

As the Grand Army marched west along the frozen Russian roads, it rapidly disintegrated. Guerrilla forces hovered about the retreating columns, continually pouncing on stragglers. In the bitterly cold weather, campfires were inadequate, shoes soon wore out, and thousands died in the snow. Out of the 611,000 men who had crossed the Russian frontiers in June, a tattered fragment of about 100,000 was able to make a wintry escape from Russia to Germany.

Downfall of Napoleon. Prussia and Austria now joined Russia in the "War of Liberation." English troops commanded by the Duke of Wellington, "The Iron Duke," cleared French armies out of Spain, and in 1813 at Leipzig the allies inflicted a disastrous defeat upon Napoleon in the Battle of the Nations. Napoleon, however, spurned a peace offer:

What is it you wish of me? That I should dishonour myself? Never. I shall know how to die, but never to yield an inch of territory. Your sovereigns, who were born on the throne, may get beaten twenty times, and yet return to their capitals. I cannot. For I rose to power through the camp.[19]

After Leipzig the empire of Napoleon tumbled like a house of cards. In March 1814, allied forces entered Paris. Two weeks later the French emperor abdicated his throne, receiving in return sovereignty over Elba, a little island between Corsica and Italy. Nearly one year later, in February 1815, Napoleon eluded the British fleet, landed in France, and after a tumultuous welcome entered Paris and raised another army. In haste, the allies dispatched the British and Prussian armies toward France.

At the Battle of Waterloo in Belgium (June 18, 1815), Napoleon was outgeneraled and defeated by Wellington and soon thereafter sought asylum with the British. He hoped to live in exile either in England or the United States, but the British, taking no more chances, shipped him off to the bleak mid-Atlantic island of St. Helena, five thousand miles from Paris. Here, in 1821, he died of cancer at the age of fifty-one.

Why did the French empire, which appeared invincible under Napoleon, collapse? When Napoleon's physical vigor and mental brilliance began to flag after the destruction of the Third Coalition, his empire—the creation of one man's military and administrative genius—began to fall apart. A tired man, Napoleon fast became corpulent and lethargic. And if the emperor was tired, the French people were also suffering from war weariness. In addition, the resurgence of nationalism in Europe was bound to destroy any dictator who first stimulated it by prating about liberty, equality, and fraternity and then enslaved those he had "liberated."

Students of warfare point out that the defeat of Napoleon is explained chiefly by the relative importance in that day of sea power on the one hand and land power on the other. These military historians maintain that British command of the sea finally led to the Napoleonic collapse. Finally, some historians see Napoleon's greatest blunder in his invasion of Russia, which boomeranged and ended with the disastrous retreat from Moscow.

Accomplishments of Napoleon. Napoleon's rise to power is one of the most remarkable stories in all history, and his significance in history cannot be dismissed with only a negative verdict. It is true that his wars killed perhaps as many as six million people, but his interference throughout Europe spread French revolutionary ideals and kindled nationalism. In Germany, in addition, he contributed toward ultimate unification by allowing the larger principalities to annex their smaller neighbors, thus reducing the number of German states from more than three hundred to thirty-nine. He also did away with the hoary old Holy Roman Empire.

Napoleon is especially important because he preserved and disseminated many of the results of the French Revolution. In France

he firmly established and safeguarded the social and economic gains of the Revolution, most of which benefited the middle class. The same can be said of French-occupied Europe: "the sale of sequestrated properties, the sweeping away of old feudal enclaves and immunities, the opening of careers to men of talent, . . . the liberation of the internal market from restrictive tolls and guilds . . . all helped to promote the growth and raise the social status of the bourgeoisie."[20] Outside of France after 1815 the Old Regime was restored, but the seeds planted by Napoleon in his self-styled role as "the son of the Revolution" could not be uprooted. During the nineteenth century they would come to flower as the middle-class movement called liberalism.

DISCONTENT AND REVOLUTION IN LATIN AMERICA

Climate for revolution. The wars for independence in Spanish America during the first quarter of the nineteenth century were another manifestation of the cycle of revolutions initiated by the Glorious Revolution in England in 1688 and followed by the American Revolution in 1775 and the French Revolution in 1789. All these movements sprang from the same body of political ideals.

During the eighteenth century the main intellectual and political currents in Europe penetrated to the colonies of the New World. One effect of the diffusion of liberal and reformist ideas was a partial rejuvenation of the Spanish and Portuguese empires in America. Colonial administration was made more efficient, the power of the Church in the colonies to suppress new ideas and censor educational activities was curbed, and greater prosperity was enjoyed.

Despite such progress, a good deal of discontent existed. The Creoles (Spaniards born in the colonies) resented the haughty *peninsulares* (the Spaniards sent from the homeland) who monopolized all the highest governmental positions. The rising young Creole generation feasted on the ideas of Montesquieu, Voltaire, and Rousseau. Although such works were banned after 1790, they were smuggled into the country in great numbers.

While government policy was reformist, it could not keep pace with the growth of liberal ideas, especially after the American and the French revolutions. The high degree of censorship and control infuriated the young intellectuals. There was, of course, no hint of the government giving people a greater voice in politics. While not so rigid, mercantilism was still in force, the courts were often corrupt, and the *peninsulares* dominated the Creoles and *mestizos* (those of mixed Spanish and Indian blood).

Thoughts of independence were in the air as the eighteenth century came to a close. Uprisings increased, and on occasion the English were asked for help. The most active of the so-called Precursors of Revolution was Francisco de Miranda (1750-1816), who spent thirty years traveling in the United States and Europe. His plans for emancipating the colonies from Spain intrigued English leaders, who gave him some support, but his incursion into Venezuela in 1806 ended in failure.

Toward independence. Only a spark set off by the Napoleonic wars was needed to ignite the revolutionary flame in Spanish America. When the news reached the colonies that Napoleon had unceremoniously removed the Bourbons and placed his brother Joseph on the throne, deep resentment stirred in Spanish America. The colonial authorities proclaimed their loyalty to Ferdinand VII, the former king, who was now interned in France. In a number of colonies liberal Creoles in 1810 ousted local officials and took charge, all the while proclaiming their loyalty to the absent Ferdinand. This "legal" phase of the revolution took place in Venezuela, the Argentine, New Granada (modern Colombia), and Chile.

The legal phase of the revolutionary movement was of short duration. Radical leaders demanded independence and an end to the fiction of loyalty to Ferdinand. Simón Bolívar (1783-1830), leader of the rebels in Caracas, went to England to obtain British aid and convinced Miranda that the time had come to strike for complete freedom. Miranda re-

turned to Latin America in December 1810 and the following year proclaimed the independence of Venezuela.

Tragic reverses followed, and in 1812 Miranda felt compelled to make a humiliating surrender. Some of his fellow patriots, including Bolívar, were so furious with Miranda that they allowed him to be captured by the Spaniards. Thus repudiated, he was sent to a prison in Cádiz, where he died four years later. Successful royalist counterattacks in Venezuela ended the republican regime, and by 1815 Bolívar was in exile.

Other uprisings in Lima, La Paz, and Quito had been equally unsuccessful. The most tragic failure occurred in Mexico. In 1810 a premature effort for self-government led by a radical priest, Father Hidalgo (1753-1811), turned into a race war of Indian against white. Frightened by the specter of social revolution, wealthy Creoles and other conservatives supported the Spanish regime. Within a year Hidalgo was captured and executed, but his work for independence was carried on by another priest, Father José Morelos (1765-1815). In 1815 he suffered the same fate as Hidalgo.

The Liberators in action: Bolivar and San Martin. In 1814, following the defeat of Napoleon, Ferdinand VII was released by the French and was welcomed deliriously in Spain. Although the king might have rallied his subjects in the colonies by generous concessions, he ignored this opportunity and reimposed the Old Regime with all its hateful aspects. Soon embittered, the colonial independence forces rose from defeat to gain a complete triumph. This was the achievement of the Liberators, Simón Bolívar and José de San Martín (1778-1850), aided by a group of devoted and efficient lieutenants.

Bolívar, former leader of the abortive revolts in Caracas, was a wealthy Creole who gave his entire fortune to the revolutionary cause. A man of great personal charm, he was a born actor who liked to play the role of heroic leader and who sought the limelight and the plaudits of the crowd. Cultured, well traveled in Europe, and imbued with the liberal philosophy of the Enlightenment, he made the cause of independence both a crusade and an obsession.

LATIN AMERICA 1826

▨ European Colony

naval supremacy in the waters off Peru, San Martín transported his troops to this viceroyalty in 1820. In 1821 he entered Lima, where he formally announced the independence of Peru.

The two Liberators met in 1822. At this meeting basic differences in policy and strategy developed. It is said also that Bolívar did not relish being outshone by any rival. Thereupon, without any recriminations, San Martín withdrew from the scene and spent the remainder of his life abroad. His greatness was only tardily realized; not until 1880 were his remains brought back to Buenos Aires and buried in the cathedral there. Today his life is studied in the Argentine schools just as Washington's is in the United States.

After San Martín's withdrawal, Bolívar was left to dominate the scene. In 1824 his army delivered the knockout blow to Spanish power by winning a decisive victory at Ayacucho, situated on a high Peruvian plateau nearly twelve thousand feet above the sea. Here the last Spanish viceroy in the New World surrendered. By 1825 the revolution had run its successful course.

Independence won in Mexico and Brazil. Royalist elements in Mexico were deeply offended by the revolution of 1820 in Spain and the brief triumph of the liberal party (see p. 504). Therefore, in 1821, the conservatives supported Agustín de Iturbide (1783-1824), a military man of dubious reputation. Joining the rebel forces holding out in the mountains, he proclaimed the independence of Mexico. After plans to establish a monarchy in Mexico under a Spanish prince fell through, Iturbide proclaimed himself emperor. Guatemala also announced its independence, though for a time it seemed that it would fall under Iturbide's rule.

Independence also came to Brazil, where the members of the royal house of Braganza had arrived in 1808, in flight from Napoleon's armies. Fond of their new abode, the Braganzas remained in Rio de Janeiro after Portugal was freed of the French armies of occupation. Under the paternalistic hand of King John, industries grew, commerce flourished, and European traders and bankers helped the cause of colonial development.

San Martín was the complete opposite; he had none of Bolívar's glowing enthusiasm. Reserved and uncommunicative, he was not moved by praise or blame if he believed his cause just. Doing his duty without any regard for his own interests, San Martín rightly called himself a stoic.

Bolívar began his comeback early in 1817. With a small force he defeated the Spanish armies in northern South America. The most dramatic incident of his victorious campaign was the successful crossing of the formidable Andes. The Republic of Gran Colombia (made up of modern Colombia, Venezuela, and Ecuador) was established, and Bolívar was named the first president of this huge new state.

Further south, in the Argentine, San Martín prepared for a spectacular offensive against the royalist forces. In 1817 he led his army over the Andes in a desperate three weeks' march, surprising and defeating the Spanish forces in Chile. Aided by a former British officer, Lord Cochrane, who won

In 1820 a revolution in Portugal put the liberal party in power. Unfortunately, the colonial policy of the new government was reactionary, and King John decided that his presence was needed in Lisbon. Before he left, he told his young son Pedro, who was acting as regent: "If Brazil demands independence, grant it, but put the crown upon your own head." Shortly after his father's departure, Pedro ripped the Portuguese colors off his uniform and shouted, "Independence or death!" The Brazilians defeated the Portuguese garrison troops with the help of a British naval force. In December 1822 Pedro was crowned emperor of Brazil, under a parliamentary system of government.

Both the North American and the Latin American revolutions enjoyed the leadership of remarkable men, and both were civil wars in which a part of the colonial population remained loyal to the mother country. But there were important differences. In Spain and Portugal only a small percentage of the people favored the colonies; in England a substantial portion of the population did.

And in Spanish America fighting ranged over larger areas and was more bloodthirsty and cruel. We shall also see in a later chapter (Chapter 26) that while freedom brought political unity to the United States, in Spanish America it was the harbinger of internal turbulence and political fragmentation.

SUMMARY

The *philosophes* created an enlightened climate of opinion and a widespread tendency toward reform which influenced a number of European monarchs. But these enlightened despots failed to ward off the ultimate downfall of the Old Regime because their reforms were not sufficiently comprehensive and thorough.

The ideas of the *philosophes* and John Locke found ready acceptance among the colonists in British America—particularly the middle class. The advanced political and economic state of the colonies was a more important

Although the Spanish were better trained and equipped, Simón Bolívar led his ragtag army with such personal valor that he managed to liberate four countries. Below Bolívar leads his men against the Spanish in the battle of Araure in Venezuela.

cause of the American Revolution than any specific act that precipitated the struggle.

Some historians have asserted that the upheaval in France could not have taken place without the successful revolution in the thirteen colonies. The American Revolution gave France the example of a functioning and stable system of free government. But the excesses of the Jacobin dictatorship led to a revulsion in public opinion and to the meteoric career of Napoleon Bonaparte. Motivated primarily by personal ambition, this dominating figure spread French revolutionary ideals throughout Europe. And, in a way, he was also responsible for the independence of Latin America. Revolution broke out in the Spanish colonies because the French emperor had invaded Spain and dethroned the royal family.

The French Revolution was more radical and influential than the English and American revolutions that preceded it. For the first time, the goal of universal manhood suffrage was envisaged, although the net result of the Revolution was the triumph of the bourgeois class and its enshrinement in the government. The French Revolution also constituted the first great stimulus to a new, fervid nationalism in Europe. Furthermore, the Revolution was social as well as political; intellectual, economic, and religious freedoms were all given strong emphasis. Much of the history of the nineteenth century is concerned with the struggle to extend the Revolution's heritage of patriotic nationalism, representative government, and intellectual, religious, and economic freedom. The use of violence to achieve these goals was an ominous part of the Revolution's legacy for the future.

SUGGESTIONS FOR READING

Peter Gay, **The Enlightenment: The Rise of Modern Paganism,*** Vintage. An eloquent treatment of the thinkers who greatly influenced the shape of modern society. R. Anchor, **The Enlightenment Tradition,*** Harper & Row, is a very brief overview. See also K. Martin, **The Rise of French Liberal Thought,*** Torchbooks; W. H. Coates and H. V. White, **The Emergence of Liberal Humanism,** Vol. I of **An Intellectual History of Western Europe,** McGraw-Hill, 1966. J. Talmon, **The Origins of Totalitarian Democracy,*** Norton, stresses the influence of Rousseau.

G. Bruun, **The Enlightened Despots,*** 2nd ed., Holt, Rinehart & Winston. Good reading; brief. See also J. Gagliardo, **Enlightened Despotism,*** Crowell; Paul Bernard, **Joseph II,** Twayne, 1968; and the biographies of Frederick the Great and Catherine the Great cited in Chapter 19.

C. Brinton, **The Anatomy of Revolution,*** rev. ed., Vintage. A comparative study of the English, American, French, and Russian revolutions. See also the detailed study by R. R. Palmer, **The Age of the Democratic Revolution: A Political History of Europe and America, 1760-1800,** 2 vols., Princeton, 1959-1964.

Edmund S. Morgan, **The Birth of the Republic, 1763-1789,*** Univ. of Chicago. An excellent brief history of the American Revolution. Also recommended are L. H. Gipson, **The Coming of the Revolution, 1763-1775,*** Torchbooks; Gordon S. Wood, **The Creation of the American Republic, 1776-1787,** North Carolina, 1969; Merrill Jensen, **The Founding of a Nation,** Oxford, 1968.

R. R. Palmer, **The World of the French Revolution,** Harper & Row, 1970. Examines Europe before 1789, the Revolution, and its impact on European society. Other excellent syntheses are G. Rudé, **Revolutionary Europe, 1783-1815,*** Torchbooks; E. Hobsbawm, **The Age of Revolution: Europe 1789-1848,*** Mentor; and N. Hampson, **The First European Revolution: 1776-1815,*** Harcourt, Brace & World, 1969, which is profusely illustrated.

G. Lefebvre, **The Coming of the French Revolution,*** Vintage. Stresses the role of the reactionary nobility in precipitating the Revolution. C. Behrens, **The Ancien Régime,*** Harcourt, Brace & World, 1969, is brief and richly illustrated.

L. Gershoy, **The French Revolution, 1789-1799,*** Holt, Rinehart & Winston. A brief survey. Longer perceptive surveys are C. Brinton, **A Decade of Revolution, 1789-1799,*** Torchbooks; M. Sydenham, **The French Revolution,*** Capricorn; James M. Thompson, **The French Revolution,*** Galaxy. F. Kafker and L. Laux, eds., **The French Revolution: Conflicting Interpretations,*** Random House, 1968, samples the opinions of leading historians.

R. R. Palmer, **Twelve Who Ruled,*** Atheneum. Good reading on the Reign of Terror. James M. Thompson, **Robespierre and the French Revolution,*** Collier, is a sympathetic brief biography. G. Bruun, **Saint-Just: Apostle of the Terror,** Shoe String, 1966, describes a precursor of today's revolutionary student leaders. The importance of the class struggle is stressed in G. Rudé, **The Crowd in the French Revolution,*** Galaxy.

F. Markham, **Napoleon and the Awakening of Europe,*** Collier. A good popular introduction to the Napoleonic period. G. Bruun, **Europe and the French Imperium, 1799-1814,*** Torchbooks, is a notable survey. See also J. Godechot, B. Hyslop, and D. Dowd, **The Napoleonic Era in Europe,*** Holt, Rinehart & Winston, 1970; R. B. Holtman, **The Napoleonic Revolution,*** Lippincott, 1967.

F. Markham, **Napoleon,*** Mentor. The best brief biography. G. Lefebvre, **Napoleon,** 2 vols., Columbia, 1969, is a renowned study. P. Geyl, **Napoleon: For and Against,*** Yale, presents divergent evaluations by historians since 1815.

Irene Nicholson, **The Liberators: A Study of Independence Movements in Spanish America,** Praeger, 1969. Readable.

*Indicates an inexpensive paperbound edition.

Part Five

Europe's Century

■ The century from the battle of Waterloo to the outbreak of the First World War was one of sweeping change in the internal affairs of Europe. The impact of the powerful forces set in motion during this period made the nineteenth century one of the most complex, diverse, and significant eras in the history of modern civilization.

With Napoleon defeated, the Congress of Vienna met to remake the map of Europe. Dominated by the spirit of reaction, the statesmen at the Congress shelved the ideals of the French Revolution, ignored the burgeoning of nationalist and liberal sentiments, and attempted to restore autocracy and privilege intact. In the years which followed, this ultraconservative ideology was challenged again and again by those who espoused nationalism and economic and political liberalism—the creed of the growing middle class. This drive for liberty gained inspiration and emotional fervor from the romantic movement of the early decades of the nineteenth century. In the economic realm the bourgeoisie believed in the philosophy of laissez faire, the opposite to governmental regulation of business; in politics the middle class supported movements which best represented their own interests. Repeatedly—and with varying but on the whole increasing success—the bourgeoisie established parliaments and constitutions and brought about moderate reforms. But although these reforms benefited the middle class, the workers stood at one side, still without political power or social advantage.

A rapidly mounting antagonism between the business classes and the new urban proletariat produced still another ideological pattern, socialism, and contributed to the failure of the 1848 revolutions. In France, Italy, Prussia, and the Austrian empire, ardent hopes for political advancement were dashed. The price paid for such failures was high: ruthless realism rather than romantic idealism became the keynote for those in opposition to the status quo. Only in the more progressive European states—Britain, France, Denmark, Switzerland—was there a shift from middle-class liberalism toward mass democracy in the latter decades of the century. Elsewhere on the Continent, conservative governments continued in power, though often their control was hidden behind parliamentary trappings.

Economically, Europe was advancing by giant strides. Nineteenth-century industrialism introduced mass production, promoted the growth of large industrial complexes, and brought wealth to thousands of middle-class employers and investors. Not until latter decades of the nineteenth century, however, did the workers' plight receive much attention. Then, the enactment of social legislation raised the workers' living standards; the advance of unions gave them more effective bargaining power; and the spread of free education broadened their children's prospects. It was at this time that many socialists allied themselves with programs of gradual, rather than revolutionary, change, pointing to the welfare state. The class revolution of the proletariat, earlier predicted by Marx, was postponed indefinitely.

Perhaps as significant as the social and economic changes wrought by the end of the nineteenth century was the rise to preeminence of science and, with it, technology. There seemed no limit to the benefits which scientific and technological knowledge could bring to mankind. The work of such men as Pasteur and Lister promised an end to disease; and technological innovations resulted in an increasing number of new industries, new products, and new wealth. The development of man from lower beings was explained by Darwin, and Freud initiated the study and analysis of man's emotions. Indeed, in retrospect, the nineteenth century seems to have been one of the most promising in all history. And in power, wealth, and intellectual activity, Europe was the center of the world.

Yet in 1914 the Continent was plunged into catastrophic war. How did this disaster come about? The explanation lies both in the forces which made the century one of such bitter struggle and in those which made it a period of great promise. Nationalism eventually became more narrow and bellicose, and laissez-faire economics led to imperialistic rivalries. The rise to preeminence of science encouraged the translation of scientific Darwinism into social Darwinism, and this fallacious emphasis on the "survival of the fittest" led to racism, unbridled competition, and militant nationalism. Thus, despite a century of unprecedented scientific, technological, and social advances, the promise which they had offered was placed in mortal jeopardy by a military conflagration which spread beyond the confines of Europe itself to embroil peoples all over the world. And when the holocaust died down four years later, Europe had ceased to be the arbiter of mankind's destiny.

18. **Houses of Parliament, London** (1840-1860). Much nineteenth-century architecture combined a revival of stylistic elements from past cultures with a spirit of nationalism. Countries resurrected styles which they associated with their national glory. The new houses of Parliament, which replaced those destroyed by fire in 1834, were designed by Sir Charles Barry and hark back to the medieval English perpendicular mode.

19. (right) **New Guinea mask** (nineteenth century).
20. (below left) **Kwakiutl mask** (1850-1900). 21. (below right) **Benin mask** (c. seventeenth century). Europe held dominion over much of the non-European world in the nineteenth century. Yet artistically speaking, the conquerors learned from the conquered, who themselves gained little or nothing from the encounter. The indigenous styles of the people of Africa, Asia, the Americas, and Oceania began to wither away as the new European presence shattered the continuity of native traditions. Nor were these styles replaced by anything of comparable vitality. Meanwhile, the West began to understand the expressive power of these native arts and proceeded to enshrine examples of them in European and American museums. During the nineteenth and twentieth centuries native art has exerted a major influence on occidental art. In tribal societies the world over, the mask usually has played an important role in religion and ritual and thus in the art which served as a handmaiden to such ritual. Styles vary greatly, as illustrated here, from the cooly tempered and finely chiseled lines of the Benin mask, through the geometrically decorated surfaces of the New Guinea style, to the bold and elegant patterns of the Kwakiutl.

22. Edouard Manet: "Luncheon on the Grass" (1863). Manet is a central figure in a nineteenth-century dispute which developed between artist and public. The industrial and political revolutions of the late eighteenth century had effectively brought to an end the long-standing patronage of the church and the aristocracy. In consequence, progressive nineteenth-century artists turned their creative concerns inward, toward problems intrinsic to the painting medium, and away from literary subject matter, narrative, and editorializing sentiment. The public meanwhile continued to look for "message." What Manet here intended as a formal study of figures seated in a landscape, the public interpreted as a story-picture with dubious moral overtones. The ensuing clash helped widen a schism between modern artist and modern audience which has persisted down to the present day.

23. (below left) **Unknown limner: "Jonathan Benham"** (c. 1710) and **24.** (below right) **John Singleton Copley: "Mr. and Mrs. Thomas Mifflin"** (1773). Transplanted by Europeans into the New World, the fledgling culture of America was slow to beget an expressive manner of its own, even slower to develop an art of refinement and quality. The urgent need to tame a vast wilderness consumed nearly all the energies of the early colonists, few of whom, moreover, were well practiced in the art forms of the old country. By the early eighteenth century portraiture had become popular and, in the frequently untrained hands of the limner, took on a winsome, if naive, charm. The first native American genius in painting, J. S. Copley, came to maturity in the latter part of the century. With little help from teachers or other sources, he produced portraits whose diamond-like surfaces and sober realism won him international acclaim during his lifetime.

Chapter 21

Revolution: in Art, Thought, and Industry

Thought and Art (1800-1870);
The Industrial Revolution (1750-1870)

INTRODUCTION. Between 1750 and 1850 society was reshaped by several major historical forces. Among them was the romantic movement, which reached its height in the nineteenth century. An intellectual and esthetic reaction against eighteenth-century rationalism and classicism, romanticism permeated other fields in addition to literature and the arts. In particular, as we shall see, it interacted closely with the political movement of nationalism. These two forces shared a strong faith in the idea of progress, the perfectibility of man and his society. Even as the martial strains of the "Marseillaise" had carried the revolutionaries of France to triumph, so new "marching songs" in the form of poems, symphonies, and paintings accompanied the new era. European poets, composers, and painters of the romantic school sought new techniques of expression along with new subject matter, new harmonies, and new color patterns. Spurred on by their enthusiastic faith in man, the romanticists rebelled against both the intellectual standards of the previous century and all forms of political oppression and social injustice.

Meanwhile the landscape was being transformed by yet another major force—industrialism. Factory towns with their smoke-belching chimneys were springing up in western Europe, linked in turn by new railway networks and steam-driven engines. The owners of these factories and railroads—the bourgeoisie, or middle class—were rapidly propelled to the top of the social heap. In the political sphere, the bourgeoisie attained a dominant voice in government; in the economic sphere, they often profited from the doctrine of laissez faire, or economic liberalism, and piled up increasing wealth. But in time angry voices cried out against the poverty and social injustice resulting from bourgeois acquisitiveness and laissez-faire liberalism. Most trenchant and influential was that of the German socialist Karl Marx. As a result, much of the history of the western world after 1848, the year in which the *Communist Manifesto* was proclaimed, concerns the duel between the forces of capitalism and communism.

THE TRIUMPH OF ROMANTICISM

New forces at work. The clarion call of the French Revolution was summed up in three words: Liberty, Equality, Fraternity. Each of these concepts was to epitomize a major societal theme in the nineteenth century. Thus *liberty*, with its emphasis upon individual freedom and rights in the political and economic spheres alike, was championed by the middle class, whose triumph would be marked by the capturing of the ballot and control of representative government, as well as by the construction of new factories and the direction of an economic system based on the doctrine of laissez faire. The ideological expression of liberty is found in the term *liberalism.*

Meanwhile the rallying cry to overthrow monarchical absolutism had also emphasized the *equality* of all men, irrespective of their social antecedents or economic status. During the nineteenth century the peasants and urban workers would attempt to attain political equality with the middle class and support social philosophies that advocated egalitarianism. But whereas the middle class championed the doctrine of laissez faire, which legalized its ownership of the means of production, the working masses sought equality by means of a rival socioeconomic ideology, *socialism*—either within an evolutionary and democratic framework (as advocated in Britain) or, alternatively, by revolution and within a Marxist framework (as found in different countries on the Continent).

For its part, *fraternity* embodied what was to become perhaps the most powerful single force unleashed in the nineteenth century. The rebels who had stormed the Bastille, or those who had wintered at Valley Forge, were united by a shared community of interests, especially the ambition to be masters of their own territory and national destiny. In short, they were united by fraternal ties, and this sense of community and independence was embodied ideologically in the term *nationalism*—which was not only to sweep across nineteenth-century Europe but, in our lifetime, would engulf Asia and Africa as well.

Two other themes require mention because they in turn unleashed powerful new societal forces. One was industrialism, resulting from massive technological advances and the invention of new techniques in the production and distribution of goods on a world-wide scale. As we shall see in this chapter, it was within the interplay of bourgeois liberalism, socialism, and nationalism that the Industrial Revolution emerged. Its machines and factories were to produce complex urban life, an all-powerful business class, and a constantly growing mass of discontented industrial workers. Consequently, the clash of interests between business and labor—a product of the machine—becomes one of the major themes of modern history.

Meanwhile, as we saw in Chapter 18, new intellectual and political forces released during the second half of the eighteenth century brought to an end not only the primacy of the aristocracy in European society but also the dominance of rationalism. The Age of Reason was supplanted in the nineteenth century by an intellectual and cultural environment dominated by certain new trends. Among them was a widespread faith in the idea of progress—the perfectibility of man and his society—and the artistic and intellectual movement known as romanticism.

Romanticism and classicism compared. In contrast to the rationalism of the eighteenth century, with its exaltation of self-restraint and artistic self-discipline, the romanticism of the early nineteenth century was characterized by strong elements of individualism, idealism, and revolt against all rules and accepted authority.

To the classicist, man is a rational, finite being—an integral member of a society which is governed in accordance with law and well-defined rules of conduct. Within this well-ordered social structure, man finds fulfillment, even as, in his intellectual and artistic expression, he emphasizes form and order and harmony. To the romanticist, on the other hand, man is a creature of feeling no less than of thought. He seeks ever after the infinite because he is not simply a cog in a finite human society but instead an irreplaceable part of nature and the whole creative process. The romanticist argues that society's laws and rules of conduct serve only to confine the natural soaring instincts of man. While the classicist insists upon the overruling claims of society, the romanticist supports the right of self-determination, whether of the individual or of any group of like-minded individuals— for example, a nation. Where the classicist's esthetic ideal is manifested in elegance, symmetry, and order, the romanticist is charmed by the "natural," the wild, and the unruly. The classicist finds beauty in logic and in acceptance of what exists; the romanticist makes it synonymous with feeling and with longing after the ultimate. "Classicism is symbolized in the static perfection of the Greek temple, with its joy in the finite work of man. Romanticism soars restlessly into the unknown with the Gothic cathedral."[1] As we shall see in this chapter, the romanticists' concern with the Gothic was not accidental.

The preromantics: Rousseau, Schiller, Goethe. Jean Jacques Rousseau, whose *Social Contract* (1762) has been termed the Bible of the French Revolution, was a romanticist who believed that the human heart is the infallible source of wisdom, that we should trust in our instincts, that man is capable of constant improvement, and that men find their truest happiness in nature. Rousseau helped popularize the cult of the "noble savage" and urged mankind to return to a more "natural" form of society by abandoning artificial conventions and institutions. He proved a most potent influence both on the political rebels of his own century and on the romanticists of the next.

In the latter part of the eighteenth century Germany witnessed a dynamic cultural revival. Among the greatest of German writers was Johann Christoph Friedrich von Schiller, whose most famous drama, *Wilhelm Tell* (1804), deals with the struggle of the Swiss for their national independence and makes an impassioned attack on tyranny.

The works of Schiller's friend Johann Wolfgang von Goethe (1749-1832) constitute the finest example of the transition from eighteenth-century classicism to nineteenth-century romanticism. In 1774 Goethe published *The Sorrows of Young Werther*—an extravagantly sentimental tale of a youth, disappointed in love, who kills himself with the pistol of his successful rival. The novel had an enormous success all over Europe, delighting a public weary of classicism's repression of human emotions.

At Weimar, which he made the intellectual center of Germany, Goethe turned out lyric poems, novels, and plays. By far the greatest of his works is *Faust* (Part I published in 1808, Part II in 1832). Based on an old German legend, this verse drama relates the story of an aging scholar, Faust, who makes a pact with the devil, Mephistopheles. In return for twenty-four years of youth and pleasure, Faust gives his soul to the archfiend. In Goethe's adaption the legend becomes the vehicle for a magnificent philo-

For the prologue of Goethe's *Faust*, Eugène Delacroix envisioned the archfiend, Mephistopheles, as a fantastic winged devil.

sophical discussion of the trials and triumphs of the human soul. Faust is saved—but only because he ultimately rejects self-gratification and accepts service to his fellow man. This theme is in harmony with the tenets of romanticism. Goethe demands, on the one hand, a full realization of the individual personality through a multitude of experiences—intellectual, sensual, and spiritual alike—even at the risk of salvation. On the other hand, he seeks an integration of the now-developed personality with the collective good of the nation or society to which the individual must dedicate his gifts.

Romanticism in literature. In the early nineteenth century romanticism assumed many different aspects—all of them products of a state of mind in rebellion against accepted values. One was a strong interest in the folkways, ballads, and other romances of the Middle Ages. Several of Goethe's contemporaries in Germany reflected this

concern, while in France, Victor Hugo (1802-1885) recreated the medieval past in romances such as *Notre Dame de Paris*. In Britain, meanwhile, Sir Walter Scott (1771-1832) had stirred the imagination of contemporaries by his collection of Scottish border ballads, his antiquarian studies and narrative poems about the formative years of the Scottish national state, and his famous adventure story of medieval chivalry, *Ivanhoe* (1819).

Romantic poetry was marked by a strongly felt love of nature. Such emotional intensity is found in the work of Alphonse de Lamartine (1790-1869), in which French lyric poetry changed from classicism to the romantic style. The rhythm and music of his poetry displayed a profound feeling for the essence of things and for their symbols. In 1798 two young English poets, William Wordsworth (1770-1850) and Samuel Taylor Coleridge (1772-1834), published a volume of verse called *Lyrical Ballads*. In its preface Wordsworth defined poetry as "the spontaneous overflow of powerful feelings recollected in tranquillity"—a concept at once romantic and very much at odds with the views of the previous century. In expressing "universal passions" and "the entire world of nature," he rejected the high-flown and mythology-laden diction in which the classicists had delighted in favor of a simple vocabulary. Wordsworth believed that by contemplating nature in all its aspects, reality could be grasped intuitively—a view associated with the philosophy of transcendentalism, which was in turn taken up by Emerson and other New England intellectuals.

For his part, Coleridge stressed another facet of romanticism—delight in the supernatural and exotic. Especially vivid are the descriptions found in his *Rime of the Ancient Mariner* and *Kubla Khan*. Coleridge's interest in the nonrational and irrational elements in human experience would be shared later by Freud and other psychologists (see Chapter 25); these elements are often described in literature in terms of fantasy, symbolism, dream states, and the supernatural.

The romantic poet rebelled against the

constraints of his society. Thus the handsome, impulsive George Gordon, Lord Byron (1788-1824), gloried in the cult of freedom, and when the Greeks rose against the Turks in 1821 (see p. 506), he joined the cause of independence and died of fever in Greece. His friend Percy Bysshe Shelley (1792-1822) believed passionately that human perfectibility was possible only through complete freedom of thought and action. These romantic yearnings and dreams were shared by the German poet Heinrich Heine (1797-1856) who was, like Byron, a trenchant satirist of contemporary society and, like Shelley, a splendid lyricist. Today Heine is best remembered for his *lieder,* or songs, many of which were set to music by Schubert and Mendelssohn.

Unlike Shelley and Byron, John Keats (1795-1821) was not a social critic or rebel. Of prime importance to him was the worship of beauty—it was the motive and message of his poetry. Thus, in the concluding lines of *Ode on a Grecian Urn* (1820), he tells us that:

"Beauty is truth, truth beauty—that is all
Ye know on earth, and all ye need to know."

Thus Keats exemplifies an important aspect of the romantic movement—estheticism, or the acceptance of artistic beauty and taste as a fundamental standard, superior to ethical and other standards.

Revolt against classical painting. The romanticist painters rebelled against classical models and the emphasis upon precise draftsmanship because they felt that color was more important than drawing and that subject matter should give unhampered scope to the imagination and emotions. Old legends and exotic and picturesque scenes, such as were to be found in North Africa and the Near East, became popular. One of the first major rebels was Eugène Delacroix, a French artist whose flamboyant canvases convey the heightened emotional approach of the romanticists (see "Liberty Leading the People," p. 508). His "Massacre of Chios" (1824), painted under the direct impact of the news of the slaying of Christians on the island of Chios by the Turks, was unjustly dubbed the "Massacre of Painting" by conservative critics.

The effects of the cult of nature were no less marked upon romantic painting than upon poetry. Artists were inspired to look at nature with a fresh appreciation. The English painter John Constable (1776-1837) was in some respects the creator of the modern school of landscape painting. His choice of colors was revolutionary, for he used greens freely in his landscapes, an innovation considered audacious by men who had stressed the necessity of painting nature in browns. Another English painter whose originality created a profound stir was J. M. W. Turner (1775-1851). Gifted with a vivid sense of color and a powerful imagination, Turner was particularly adept in creating atmospheric effects. He used a color technique similar to that employed later in the century with dazzling success by the French Impressionists.

Romanticism in architecture: the Gothic revival. Until about 1830 architecture in Europe and America was based largely on classical models (see p. 415). But after 1830 occurred the great period of the Gothic

Lord Byron loved to have his portrait painted, particularly in the dark character of a corsair. He once asserted, "I am a poet by avocation and a pirate by vocation."

Landscape painting acted as a pivotal point of inspiration in nineteenth-century art. Romantic painters, such as J. M. W. Turner, used the form not only as a point of departure from the somber classicism of the eighteenth century but as a means of expressing the vitality of nature. In "Dutch Fishing Boats," by means of bold brushwork and a brilliant treatment of light (later adopted by the Impressionists), Turner couples man and nature in a swirling canvas, a reflection of the heightened emotionalism and idealism of his day.

revival, in which towers and pointed arches became the chief characteristics of architectural design (see Color Plate 18). The revival was stimulated in England by the romances of Sir Walter Scott, whose own residence at Abbotsford was designed along Scottish baronial lines; while in France the movement gained impetus from the publication of Victor Hugo's melodramatic novel of fifteenth-century life, *Notre Dame de Paris* (1831).

Romanticism in music. The nineteenth century brought radical changes in music; the regularity of the minuet, the precision of the sonata, and the limitations of the small chamber orchestra were not adequate to express the powerful forces of romanticism.

The genius who broke the classical mold and revitalized music was the German composer Ludwig van Beethoven (1770-1827), a titan who acted as a bridge between classicism and romanticism. A lover of nature and a passionate champion of freedom and the rights of man, Beethoven unleashed emotional forces never before heard in music. While retaining the classicist's sense of proportion in the structure of his works, he added flexibility to music forms by developing new harmonies and enlarged the scope of the orchestra to handle them. In short, Beethoven succeeded in freeing music from arid formalism.

The momentum of the forces which Beethoven set in motion carried through the entire century. Johannes Brahms (1833-1897) is generally regarded as the greatest symphonic composer of the second half of the century, but the age is studded with names of great composers—Chopin, Schubert, Liszt, Franck, and Tschaikovsky, to name only a few. This was an age marked by an outpouring of romantic symphonies, symphonic overtures, and concertos, all of which exploited the new and varied effects made possible by an orchestra which had been greatly expanded. Compositions made use of romantic subject matter infused with sentiment—and, not infrequently, sentimentalism. In addition, many composers turned for inspiration to their native folk music and dances.

Developments in opera were markedly influenced by nationalism and romanticism. In the fervid Germanic works of Richard Wagner (1813-1883), old Teutonic myths and German folklore were infused with typically romantic characteristics such as emphasis on the supernatural and the mystic. The romantic tragedy *Aïda* (1872) capped the career of Giuseppe Verdi (1813-1901), considered the greatest Italian composer of the nineteenth century.

As a result of significant changes in political and economic conditions, music was now supported chiefly by the middle classes and maintained by their thriving commercial prosperity. Public concerts, symphony orchestras, quartet societies, piano and song recitals, music festivals, public opera houses —all were attainments of the nineteenth century which had had only faint beginnings up to 1800.

ROMANTIC NATIONALISM

Nationalism, ally of romanticism. In glorifying the uniqueness of the individual and his rights, romanticism exhibited a close affinity with another powerful emotional force of this period—nationalism. With its emphasis upon the uniqueness of particular groups, nationalism was a potent historical catalyst among the peoples of nineteenth-century Europe. During this period feelings of nationalism came more and more to imply the willingness of an individual to live and die for his country. His loyalty to the state transcended all other loyalties. Unhappily, too, extreme nationalism implied that a state could do no wrong and that self-interest was the only test for its behavior. Here again we see the close affinity between romanticism and nationalism—the former advocating unrestricted self-expression for an individual, and the latter demanding unrestricted self-determination for a group.

Romantic nationalism in literature. This strongly felt emotion is well exemplified in a sonnet Wordsworth composed upon his return in 1802 from the Continent to England:

. . . Oft have I looked round
With joy in Kent's green vales; but never found
Myself so satisfied in heart before.
Europe is yet in bonds; but let that pass
Thought for another moment. Thou art free,
My Country! and 'tis joy enough and pride
For one hour's perfect bliss, to tread the grass
Of England once again. . . .[2]

The excesses of the French Revolution and Napoleon's perversion of its principles alienated many of the romanticists. But the pendulum swung back again as a result of the system of political reaction set up in 1815 by the Congress of Vienna (see Chapter 22). Some of the notable romanticists again became the champions of nationalism and revolution. In France, the leading figure was Victor Hugo, who expressed hostility toward tyranny at home and abroad, espoused the aspirations of the common man, and was a staunch supporter of the struggle for Greek independence. In Russia, where nationalism had been greatly stimulated by the people's heroic resistance to the Napoleonic invasion in 1812, still other romantic rebels were attracting the sympathetic response of the reading public (and also the hostile attention of the tsar's secret police). The greatest of the Russian romanticist poets was Alexander Pushkin, whose unrestrained personal life and literary lyricism justify his being called the "Byron of Russia." His subject matter was largely derived from Russian tales and folklore, and his dramas and his verse novel *Eugene Onegin* (1831) had a strong nationalistic appeal. Like Byron, Pushkin denounced tyranny and the reactionary movement which had set in after the Napoleonic Wars.

Romantic nationalism in philosophy and history. The glorification of the state became characteristic of various German thinkers, especially Georg Wilhelm Friedrich Hegel (1770-1831), perhaps the most influential philosopher of the time. To Hegel, history was a process of evolution in which the supremacy of primitive instincts gave way to the reign of clear reason and freedom— the "World Spirit"—as manifested in the state. Hegel believed that the Prussia of his day offered the best example of the state as a spiritual organism, because in Prussia the individual was given the greatest "freedom" —which to Hegel meant only the right to obey the laws of the governing group.

The nineteenth century produced a number of outstanding national historians. In France, Jules Michelet wrote a nineteen-volume *History of France* that was marked by liberalism and romantic nationalism and stressed the role of the common people. Across the Atlantic, George Bancroft produced a United States history described as "explaining the wonder-working providence of God in the United States."[3] In England, too, it was a splendid era for historians, of whom the most brilliant was Thomas Babington Macaulay. His famous *History of England,* a notable example of literary as well as historical craftsmanship which is still widely read, reflected the author's conviction that his age represented the best of all possible worlds.

THE TRIUMPH OF THE MACHINE

Interpretations of the Industrial Revolution. With the advent of industrialism, the economic life of Europe was modified drastically—a transformation called the Industrial Revolution. The first historian to give wide currency to the term was Arnold Toynbee of Oxford, the uncle of the famous British historian Arnold J. Toynbee. In *Lectures on the Industrial Revolution of the 18th Century in England* (1844) Toynbee pointed out that: (1) the beginning of the Industrial Revolution was sudden, starting in the year 1760; (2) the effects of the revolution were both sudden and cataclysmic, rudely overturning the whole edifice of society; (3) the Industrial

Revolution quickly pervaded all quarters of English manufacturing and for a substantial period was wholly an English phenomenon; and (4) for many decades the effects of the revolution upon the common people were completely evil.

This traditional interpretation has been criticized in recent years by various economic historians who assert that the change was less a revolution than a speeding up of technological evolution (see the Historical Critique, p. 837). Nevertheless, this accelerative process, and the economic and social changes which resulted, can still justify the use of the term *Industrial Revolution* as long as we set it within a larger chronological framework. During the Middle Ages there emerged a new machine technology which involved the exploitation of water and wind as important sources of energy (see Chapter 9). In the eighteenth century men came to rely on steam derived from coal and increasingly replaced wood with iron. This new technical phase—which was unique in its exploitation of new forms of energy and new raw materials and which called for new forms of economic and social organization—is identified with the Industrial Revolution, the term used in this chapter. (As we shall see in Chapter 25, the last decades of the nineteenth century witnessed the introduction of still other sources of energy, such as electricity; this succeeding technical stage has sometimes been called the Second Industrial Revolution.)

With the advent of the Industrial Revolution mechanization took over many tasks once performed by hand. An illustration from Diderot's famous *Encyclopedia* shows textile workers operating the spinning mule, which was powered by water.

Despite the advances of industry and technology, there remained the dark narrow tunnel through which young boys pulled and shoved heavy carts loaded with coal.

Mechanization of the textile industry. The Industrial Revolution began in England rather than on the Continent because England provided a more favorable climate for entrepreneurial activity. As the leading commercial and financial power England possessed a vast market and a surplus of liquid capital, its domestic system of industrial production (see p. 387) was more advanced than the guild system still predominant on the Continent, its labor supply was more mobile, and its government of wealthy landlords and merchants was more attuned to the needs of business.

During the eighteenth century in England the growing demand for cotton cloth, recently introduced from India, led to a series of inventions designed to increase and cheapen the methods of production. In 1733 John Kay, a spinner and mechanic, patented the first of the great textile inventions, the flying shuttle—a spring device that propelled the shuttle across the loom and permitted one person instead of two to weave wide bolts of cloth. Kay's invention upset the balance between weavers and spinners; one weaver now required ten spinners to produce sufficient yarn for him. With the invention of the spinning jenny in 1764 by James Hargreaves, a weaver and carpenter by trade, the production of spinners equaled that of

weavers. In 1769 a barber named Richard Arkwright patented the water frame. Powered by water, this machine was so heavy and expensive that it had to be housed in a factory, and Arkwright has been called the "father of the factory system." Ten years later Samuel Crompton, a spinner, combined the spinning jenny and water frame into the spinning mule, which is essentially the spinning machine still used today. The hand loom could no longer weave cloth as fast as the machine could spin yarn for it, and a country vicar named Edmund Cartwright set about to break this bottleneck. His power loom, patented in 1785, mechanized the weaving process.

The suppliers of raw cotton had great difficulty in meeting the increasing demands for their crop because cotton seeds were separated from the fiber by hand and the most skillful worker could prepare not more than five or six pounds a day. In 1793 a young American, Eli Whitney, invented a cotton gin which enabled one worker to clean as much as a thousand pounds of cotton a day.

Sources of power. With improvements in machinery came corresponding improvements in power. About 1705 an English mechanic, Thomas Newcomen, had devised an "atmospheric engine" in which a piston was raised by injected steam, the steam condensed, and the piston returned to its original position as it cooled off. Used to pump water from coal mines, Newcomen's invention doubled the depth in the ground at which coal could be worked but consumed large quantities of coal, which the mines could supply cheaply but which factories could not.

The transformation of the atmospheric engine into the true steam engine was the achievement of James Watt (1736-1819). This Scottish genius was employed at the University of Glasgow as a builder of scientific instruments. One day when repairing the university's Newcomen engine, Watt was struck by the waste of steam resulting from the alternate heating and chilling of the cylinder. Four fifths of the steam used was lost in heating the cold cylinder; only one fifth served a useful purpose by acting on the piston. Using steam to force the piston back and forth inside a closed cylinder, Watt devised a separate condenser to control the supply of steam. The first steam engines were used for pumping; after 1785 they were employed in cotton manufacturing; and still later they were adapted to the needs of the steam locomotive and the steamship.

Before 1870 the steam engine and the water wheel were the chief power sources, but the potentialities of oil were also explored. In 1859 the first oil well was drilled in Pennsylvania. The use of oil was destined to expand substantially the sources of power available to industry, for three and a half barrels of oil yield as much heat as a ton of coal. A further development came in 1860, when an electric spark was used to ignite gasoline in an internal-combustion engine, thus providing a momentous change in motive power.

Improved methods for refining iron and mining coal. Until 1784 iron was available only in an impure state—cast iron which would break rather than bend and which was too brittle to withstand hard strains and heavy blows. In that year a method was invented for making iron malleable by burning the impurities out and leaving the iron clean and tough. The molten iron was then stirred with a long rod, a technique known

as "puddling." Widespread adoption of this process enabled Great Britain to produce cheap wrought iron.

In the 1850's the smelting and refining of iron ore were substantially improved by Sir Henry Bessemer. With his new process, steel could be manufactured quickly and cheaply; in fact, between 1856 and 1870 the price of British steel fell to one half the sum formerly charged for the best grades of iron. At the same time production increased sixfold.

Improvements in the coal-mining industry included better means of ventilation in the mines by using large fans and by sinking a second shaft containing a fire, which made an upward draft and drew fresh air down the first shaft. But explosions were still a great hazard, for miners needed light to work by and the heat of the flame in their lamps ignited the gases present in the mine shafts and tunnels. By enclosing the flame of the miner's lamp with a wire gauze screen that was heat absorptive, this problem was solved.

Improvements in transportation: roads and canals. In 1815 the Scotsman John McAdam used a simple but revolutionary method in the construction of roads: small stones in compact layers were placed directly on the earth roadbed. The passage of traffic packed the stones down so tightly that a strong and fairly smooth surface resulted. *Macadam,* the term given today to roads of this type, is derived from the name of the inventor. Stagecoaches reached new top speeds as their horses galloped over the improved roads. It had taken four and a half days to travel the 160 miles from London to Manchester in 1754; thirty-four years later the journey had been shortened to twenty-eight hours.

Modern canal building in England began in the coal fields. In 1759 the construction of a waterway from the duke of Bridgewater's colliery to Manchester, a distance of seven miles, halved the price of coal in Manchester, and all England became "canal conscious." Seventy years later England had nearly four thousand miles of improved rivers and canals. Better roads and new canals made hauling of goods cheaper and easier. Many acres of new iron docks were constructed in London, making this port the largest in the world.

Canals were used so successfully in England that other countries were encouraged to plan elaborate systems of inland waterways. In 1825, for example, the Erie Canal, linking the Hudson River and New York City with the Great Lakes, was completed.

In 1869 the first great interoceanic canal joined the Mediterranean and the Indian Ocean by way of the Red Sea. Dug in the sands of the Egyptian desert, this new water artery, the Suez Canal, was nicknamed the "Big Ditch." Impressed by its strategic and commercial value, the British government purchased the shares of canal stock owned by the ruler of Egypt in 1875 and established control of the canal a few years later when English troops occupied Egypt (see p. 647). The Suez, which shortened the sailing time between London and Bombay by nearly half, became the lifeline of the empire.

The advent of railroads. In England the era of canal building was cut short by the advent of railroads. Before the locomotive was perfected, iron rails had been installed on public streetcar lines and in mines to reduce the friction on the wheels of horse-drawn vehicles. The forty miles of track between Stockton and Darlington in England served as a testing ground for the improved locomotive built in 1825 by George Stephenson, the brilliant son of a poor miner. Five years later, when his *Rocket* attained the terrifying speed of thirty-six miles an hour, the railroad era was on its way. Soon other countries began to lay the shining rails for locomotive transportation. In the United States the federal government subsidized the construction of the Union Pacific and Central Pacific railroads to connect Omaha and San Francisco. With their completion in 1869, it became possible to cross the entire North American continent by rail.

Clippers give way to steamships. The opening decades of the nineteenth century witnessed important advances in transportation at sea as well as on land. From the shipyards of New England came the beautiful clippers. These long, slender, sharp-bowed sailing vessels were the swiftest ships on the seven seas, often attaining a speed of eighteen knots. The finest clipper afloat, the *Flying Cloud,* made the voyage from New York to San Francisco via Cape Horn in eighty-nine days and eight hours, a record that still stands for sailing vessels.

Although others had used steam to propel boats earlier, the man who reaped the lion's share of glory for this feat was Robert Fulton, who used a Watt engine to drive his *Clermont* 150 miles up the Hudson River in 1807. About thirty years later Samuel Cunard initiated regular transatlantic passenger steamship service. This line still proudly bears the name of its Canadian founder. The clippers became obsolete; after 1870, smoking funnels progressively replaced the glistening sails.

Improvements in communication. Parallel with improvements in transportation went great advances in communication. The introduction of the penny post in 1840 in England made correspondence by mail substantially cheaper. Another revolutionary method of transmitting information appeared when Samuel Morse, an American artist and inventor, perfected the electric telegraph in 1844. Twenty-two years later Cyrus Field, another American inventor, laid the first successful Atlantic cable.

England, "workshop of the world." It was England's undisputed leadership in the Industrial Revolution that explained the tremendous volume of the nation's exports, its accumulation of vast amounts of capital, and its long-held position as the world's commercial center. Britain enjoyed a virtual monopoly in some manufacturing techniques until after 1870.

There were reasons for England's technological leadership. On this small island were rich deposits of coal and iron to supply the needs of industry. The wool of English sheep, unsurpassed in quality, provided essential raw material for some of the nation's textile mills. In the nineteenth century Britain's stable government catered increasingly to the interests of the trading and industrial classes, and its unrivaled navy not only protected the country from invasion but also kept open the routes for the mer-

With the spread of industrialization to the Continent, the iron and coal of the Saar region in Germany became increasingly important. Above is a metal foundry in the factory district of the Saar as it appeared about one hundred years ago.

chant fleet. There was also surplus capital, accumulated from trade with America and the Orient. Finally, England concentrated on staple goods, adaptable to mass production and mass consumption, whereas France, for example, specialized in luxury commodities demanding individual craftsmanship.

Industrialization outside England. During the nineteenth century industrial progress was much slower in France than in England. The development of heavy industry lagged. There was a shortage of coal, and although the output of iron ore increased about 65 percent between 1830 and 1865, the deposits of ore were not conveniently located. With the invention of the Jacquard loom (1801), on the other hand, French silk production came to exceed that of all the rest of Europe.

Early in the nineteenth century the prog-

ress of industrialism in Germany was retarded by political disunity, the conflict of interests between nobles and merchants, and, as in France, the existence of the guild system, which discouraged competition and innovation. But after the formation of a tariff union, the Zollverein, which by 1842 included most of the German states, industry was stimulated by the wider trade advantages now available. After 1850 improved methods in metallurgy were introduced, and in the next twenty years the output from German furnaces increased fourfold. Coal production likewise mounted rapidly.

The development of the Krupp works best exemplifies the remarkable growth of German industry. Inheriting a broken-down steel mill employing four men, Alfred Krupp introduced a steam engine into his factory and expanded his work force. From the invention and exploitation of a steel gun, cast-steel axles, and a breech-loading rifle, Krupp created a large-scale enterprise which by 1873 was employing sixteen thousand workers. The Krupp works was to become the symbol of German industrial efficiency and of Germany's successful application of technology to the weapons of war.

Belgium also achieved rapid industrial growth, helped initially by the adoption of British manufacturing techniques. During the nineteenth century, in fact, Belgium produced more coal and iron than its much larger neighbor, France, and Belgian railroad construction boomed until this small nation boasted a greater railroad mileage per capita than any other country. Meanwhile the Belgian factories and mills turned out quantities of lace, carpets, cutlery, and iron products.

By the 1840's factories and railroads had become important in the United States; by 1860 American textile, iron, steel, and shoe industries were developing rapidly. At mid-century, large-scale corporate enterprises had begun to replace small-scale businesses, and after 1861 the government was usually in the hands of legislators friendly to corporate enterprise, instead of under agrarian control as it had been in earlier decades. Protective tariffs were passed with the hope of assuring American manufacturers a ready home market, and the power of the states to regulate business was restricted; thus the basis was laid for large-scale industrial development, already stimulated by military needs during the Civil War. By 1870 the nation was crisscrossed with railroads, the northeastern part of the country was heavily industrialized, and new factories and mills were springing up everywhere.

Outside the industrial pale were Italy, Spain, Portugal, the nations of eastern Europe and the Balkans, and Russia, where industry either barely existed or grew very slowly. And before 1870 industrialism made little progress in South America, Africa, the Middle East, and Asia.

Progress in agriculture. The agricultural revolution which had begun in the eigh-teenth century was accelerated by the amazing progress of nineteenth-century technology. In 1831 Cyrus McCormick, a native of Vermont, demonstrated the first modern reaper. Later on came the harvester, which also bound the grain, and finally the combine, which threshed the grain as it reaped it. Further improvements in farm machinery came with the manufacture of the steel plow and other implements by John Deere of Illinois.

The marketing of foods was revolutionized by the widespread adoption of canning and refrigeration, permitting the storage of perishable crops. Railroads and steamships sped farm produce to market. During the second half of the nineteenth century international trade in farm products increased rapidly. For example, the annual export of wheat from the United States and Canada rose from 22 million bushels in the 1850's to 150 million in 1880.

CONSEQUENCES OF INDUSTRIALISM

New markets for new goods. An important result of industrialism was the increase in productivity. In some industries productivity increased a hundredfold; in others, as much as a thousandfold. It soon became apparent that home markets alone were not able to absorb all the goods the factories could produce, and western European powers therefore began searching for trade outlets all over the world. International trade required a network of world transportation, a need which was met by the development of the railroad and steamship. The world was becoming an integrated economic unit.

Accompanying the mounting demand for overseas markets was the need for raw materials. These aims led to the European penetration of African and Asian lands. Isolated and primitive peoples were brought into touch with western culture by traders seeking markets and raw materials. And with these traders usually came officials and troops to take over territories as protectorates

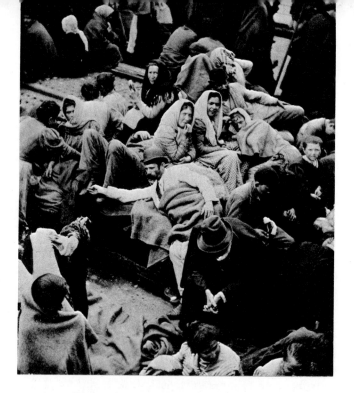

During the nineteenth century hundreds of thousands of European emigrants voyaged to the United States, hoping to make their fortunes in a relatively free and fast-developing country.

or colonies. Thus in the nineteenth century, and increasingly after 1871, the great industrial powers of Europe pursued a program of imperialism by which vast chunks of Asia and practically all of Africa came under European political and economic control.

Changing population trends. The best markets for the new products were still in Europe, where the industrial era was accompanied by a substantial and continuous increase in population. It has been estimated that Europe in 1800 had about 175 million people, whereas by 1900 it had 400 million.

Up to early modern times populations were checked by food scarcity, pestilence, and high infant mortality. Now the growing agricultural productiveness of European countries, achieved through intensive farming and the adoption of the techniques of scientific agriculture, supported larger populations. Because of the spread of transportation facilities, Europe was also able to import more food from other continents. In addition, achievements in medicine resulted in a lowered death rate. Infant mortality was re-

duced; in the eighteenth century it had been not uncommon for a mother who bore ten children to lose seven of them. By the latter part of the nineteenth century medicine and public health were slowly but surely conquering the dreaded plagues—cholera, typhus, and smallpox.

An increasing majority of the population were city dwellers. First in England, then in Belgium, France, and Germany, and later in other parts of the world, old cities outgrew their boundaries, and many new ones were founded. In general, from 1750 down to the present people have more and more tended to concentrate in cities, while population in the country has declined.

Aside from the country-to-city migrations, there were often regional shifts in population. For example, when coal and iron began to be exploited in northern England, industrial centers such as Birmingham and Manchester were founded in the vicinity of these raw materials. On a wider scale, the opportunities in America attracted thousands of immigrants, who joined the country-by-country migration.

The factory, symbol of the new order. The most important symbol of the new industrial order was the factory, for here was the site of the machinery and power that made industrialism possible. The factory system did not replace the cottage or domestic system of home manufactures overnight; the two existed side by side for decades. Until 1815 the hand-loom weaver in England did not suffer substantially, but after that he was forced to compete with machines that could produce more goods at lower cost. As a result, weavers had to accept lower and lower wages to compete with the cheaper goods made by the power looms. Ultimately, they lost their hopeless battle and were forced to move to the communities where the new factories offered employment.

This displacement of human skills by machinery, known as technological unemployment, remained a constant source of fear as the Industrial Revolution spread. Even today the twentieth-century advance in labor-saving machinery—automation—is causing serious concern to factory workers and their union leaders.

Wretched working conditions. The first factories thrown together during the extraordinary rise of such industrial centers as Manchester and Birmingham were lacking in the most elementary sanitary and safety facilities; horrible cases of mangling were a common occurrence among the factory workers. Furthermore, under English common law, any accident a worker might suffer was considered a result of his own negligence, for which the employer could not be held responsible. There was no system of workmen's compensation or health insurance; an injured worker was likely to be thrown out in the street destitute and his job given to one of the thousands who had flocked to the new cities in search of employment.

Despite the innovation of "labor-saving" machinery, the worker was certainly not saved any labor. Each day the factory bell summoned him to long hours of monotonous drudgery. Women were forced by poverty to work until a day or two before delivery of their children and then to report back to work shortly after the child was born.

Children were the most unfortunate victims of the factory system. The mills employed some youngsters only four or five years of age, and in the coal mines children were used to carry baskets of coal up ladders. Children working in the mills received almost no education, for schooling was neither compulsory nor free. The facilities for obtaining even the most rudimentary training were insufficient, and evening schools were of little benefit to children who had to toil twelve hours during the day.

Ugly, disease-ridden slums. Contemporary accounts of the workers' quarters in the new industrial cities fill us with loathing and pity. In his novel *Hard Times,* Charles Dickens described a typical English factory town of more than a century ago:

It was a town of red brick, or of brick that would have been red if the smoke and ashes had allowed it; but as matters stood it was a town of unnatural red and black, like the painted face of a savage. It was a town of machinery and tall chimneys, out of which interminable serpents of smoke trailed themselves for ever and ever, and never got uncoiled. It had a black canal in it, and a river that ran purple with ill-smelling dye, and vast piles of buildings full of windows where

Gustave Doré's nineteenth-century engraving depicts the filthy, overcrowded slums where the industrial workers of London lived.

there was a rattling and a trembling all day long, and where the piston of the steam-engine worked monotonously up and down, like the head of an elephant in a state of melancholy madness. It contained several large streets all very like one another, and many small streets still more like one another, inhabited by people equally like one another, who all went in and out at the same hours, with the same sound upon the same pavements, to do the same work, and to whom every day was the same as yesterday and tomorrow, and every year the counterpart of the last and the next.[4]

If we had visited a working-class district in Manchester early in the nineteenth century, we should have seen whole blocks of jerry-built homes, thrown together back to back by speculators so that the rear rooms had no windows. The houses faced on narrow, unpaved alleys or courts in which garbage and sewage were dumped. The living quarters for factory workers were chronically overcrowded and lacked adequate sanitary facilities. No wonder epidemics such as cholera were frequent. In 1842 a commission reported that the deaths caused by filth and lack of public sanitation outnumbered the loss in any wars that England had fought in modern times.

THE MIDDLE CLASS TRIUMPHANT

Liberalism: its meaning and impact. To this point we have been dealing with three major trends in the nineteenth century—romanticism, nationalism, and industrialism. We now meet a fourth—liberalism—which came to the forefront in the 1830's. Unlike romanticism and nationalism, liberalism was associated almost exclusively with the middle class. Let us see why.

Like romanticism, liberalism vigorously affirmed the dignity of man and the "pursuit of happiness" as his inherent right. Like the philosophy behind the American and French revolutions, the liberal philosophy was an outgrowth of the philosophy of the Enlightenment. But where romanticism accepted revolution as a justifiable means to give expression to the "rights of man," liberalism stood for gradual reform through parliamentary institutions. And where both the rationalists and the romanticists tended to speak of man in the abstract—that is, "Man"—and to conceive of him as a philosophical ideal in opposition to, say, the "state" or the "king," nineteenth-century liberals thought in terms of individual men who shared certain basic rights in common, who worked together to obtain parliamentary majorities and political power, and who made use of that power to ensure that each of them would be given a maximum of freedom from state or external authority.

In the economic sphere liberalism was expressed in the doctrine of laissez faire—competition among individuals with a minimum of governmental interference or regulation. The textbook of this school of thought, Adam Smith's *Wealth of Nations*, postulated that society benefited most from competition, which brought the more intelligent and more efficient individuals the greater rewards. Although governments were responsible for the protection of life and property, the hands of government should be kept off business; the best interests of society would be served by permitting the natural "laws" of supply and demand to operate unimpeded (see also p. 445).

In the new industrial societies the bourgeois entrepreneurs had everything to lose from revolution and everything to gain from governmental protection of property rights. To win such protection, however, they had to obtain a dominant voice in government. As government immediately after the Napoleonic Wars was largely controlled by the nobility and landed classes, this meant in turn that the middle class had to secure a limited extension of the suffrage—an extension that would give them the vote without granting voting privileges to the working classes. Thus the members of the middle class demanded political power commensurate with their steadily increasing economic strength. In England this goal was attained in 1832 with the passage of the Reform Bill (see p. 511).

We might pause here to note the change that has taken place regarding the meaning of *liberalism*. The term still stands for reform, in contrast to conservatism with its defense of the status quo or to radicalism with its demands for immediate, drastic change. But in the economic sphere especially, liberalism has undergone a profound modification. Unlike his nineteenth-century predecessor, the twentieth-century liberal believes that the state should take an active role in minimizing the extremes of wealth, in balancing the great power enjoyed by big business and big organized labor, in conserving natural resources, in providing social security, and in actively opposing racial discrimination.

The triumph of laissez faire. The bourgeoisie achieved their success in the era of industrial capitalism, which superseded the predominantly commercial, or trading, phase of business (see Chapter 17). In industrial capitalism profits were made primarily from investment in machinery and raw materials and from utilization of other people's labor. At first controlled and administered by factory owners, the new industrial capitalism soon resulted in important changes in business organization. The corporation, which could raise and utilize large sums of capital, became the characteristic form of business organization, largely replacing individual proprietorship and partnership, both of which proved inadequate to meet the needs of the factory system.

With the triumph of the middle class in the nineteenth century, we find also the triumph of their economic philosophy—laissez faire. This theory, known as "economic liberalism," held that it was impossible to correct the social evils of industrialism. Each man, enjoying free choice, could only improve his own circumstances by hard work, economy, and limiting the size of his family. Economists offered so little hope for improvement of the economic status of the common people that economics came to be known as the "dismal science."

Malthus' theory of population. Among the gloomier prophets was Thomas Robert Malthus (1766-1834), an English clergyman whose fame rests on his *Essay on Population* (1798). This study asserts that "the power of population is indefinitely greater than the power in the earth to produce subsistence for man."[5] In his own day Malthus could accurately point to a comparatively limited food supply and a population that was increasing by leaps and bounds. From this evidence, he deduced that the inevitable lot of the mass of mankind was misery, as the birth rate would always outrun the food supply. Malthus' only solution to what he believed to be a permanent problem was the practice of self-restraint in reproduction.

Ricardo's theory of wages. Using Malthus' line of reasoning in developing his own thesis, the English economist David Ricardo (1772-1823) advanced his subsistence theory of wages. Ricardo maintained that labor has a natural price and also a market price. The natural price is that "which is necessary to enable the laborers . . . to subsist and to perpetuate their race without either increase or diminution."[6] The market price depends on the law of supply and demand. When labor is scarce and in demand, it is well paid; when it is plentiful, it is poorly paid. In the first instance, the market price of labor exceeds the natural price; the result is prosperity for the laborer. In the second instance, the reverse is true.

Unfortunately, said Ricardo, labor tends to increase faster than available capital, so that wages fall to the natural price. Although varying circumstances might qualify the situation, Ricardo felt that he had stated an ironclad law which nothing could or should change.

Like all other contracts, wages should be left to the fair and free competition of the market, and should never be controlled by the interference of the legislature.[7]

Laissez-faire theory popularized and modified. Jeremy Bentham (1748-1832), a wealthy British jurist, devised the doctrine of utilitarianism, or philosophical radicalism, based on the two concepts of utility and happiness. He correlated these two terms by saying that each individual knows what is best for himself and that all human institutions should be measured according to the amount of happiness they give—Bentham's celebrated "pain and pleasure" principle. Bentham believed strongly that the function of government should be the securing of as great a degree of individual freedom as possible, for freedom made for happiness. Utilitarianism has been defined as "the greatest happiness for the greatest number."

John Stuart Mill (1806-1873) did not believe that the interests of the manufacturers would necessarily coincide with the interests of the workers; he advanced the theory that government should, if necessary, pass legislation to remedy injustices. Mill felt that when the actions of businessmen harmed people, the state should intervene for their protection. While admitting that the maximum freedom should be permitted in the processes of production according to natural law, he insisted that the distribution of wealth depends on the laws and customs of society, and these can be changed by the will of men. He upheld the rights of property and of free competition but only within reasonable limits. The liberty of the individual should be subordinated to the wider interest of the group. In this thought there are the germs of what came later to be known as the welfare state. John Stuart Mill's ideas gained influence slowly; and, until well past the middle of the nineteenth century, laissez-faire liberalism held its ground with little change.

In England "the Manchester School" was the name given to a group of politicians who strove in Parliament to defend and spread the tenets of economic liberalism. They advocated the repeal of various import duties on grain known as the Corn Laws, the adoption of free trade, and a foreign policy based on economic cooperation rather than international rivalry. During the middle years of the nineteenth century the policies of these men won wide acceptance and made supreme the economic and political prestige of a middle class devoted to laissez faire. Technologically more advanced than other countries, England adopted free trade for a time, thus indicating that it did not fear the competition of foreign products in its home market. In other countries, however, the middle class wanted business freedom at home but government protection against foreign imports which might undersell the local goods.

Theory and practice diverge. The philosophy of laissez faire seemed logical and was, in fact, a positive aid to social and economic progress. However, a wide gulf soon appeared between theory and practice. Because of monopolistic practices and secret collusion between competitors, the operation of competition did not always ensure fair prices. Nor did competition ensure the survival of honest and efficient businesses. Underhanded and unfair competition often wrecked the more ethical and scrupulous firms.

It also became increasingly difficult to reconcile the great wealth enjoyed by a few with the poverty borne by the many. Furthermore, legislation prevented them from achieving anything like an equal bargaining position with their economic masters. Drastic laws, such as the Combination Acts of 1799-1800 in England, forbade unions on the grounds that they would restrain trade. Strikes were classed as conspiracies, and strikers were harshly punished. While emphasizing the necessity for "freedom," the proponents of laissez faire completely disregarded the individual worker's lack of bargaining power.

Middle-class attitudes in Victorian England. By the 1840's England had entered a new era which coincided with the long reign (1837-1901) of the staunchly respectable Queen Victoria. This age was best symbolized by the opening of the Great Exhibition in London in 1851—a monument to the cult of material progress where one might see the latest wonders of an ever accelerating industrialism. "Material progress seemed, as by some new law of nature, to have been showered without stint on a people who rated industriousness, business efficiency, and private enterprise among the major virtues. This situation induced in large sections of the upper and middle classes a mood of comfortable complacency which later generations have found the most unattractive of Victorian characteristics. . . . Samuel Smile's *Self-Help* (which appeared in 1859, sold 20,000 copies that year and another 130,000 during the next thirty years) was rapidly succeeded by works with similar pious titles—*Thrift, Character, Duty*—which form a veritable catalogue of the Victorian 'virtues.' This long series of smug lay sermons on the virtues of industry and honesty, connecting always the practice of such virtue with the reward of material prosperity . . . was the instinctive creed of the prosperous industrialists and business men whose ethics now dominated English manners as they dominated English economic life."[8]

For its part, the fair sex had acquired a somewhat improved status. Women's colleges began to appear, and nursing by women was raised to professional status as a result of the initiative displayed by Florence Nightingale during the Crimean War. Sent to the military hospitals in the Crimea,

the "Lady with the Lamp" brought about a complete change in the treatment of the wounded. Under her efficient charge, medical facilities were improved so that the terrible mortality due to cholera, dysentery, and gangrene was materially reduced.

Victorian poetry: Tennyson and Browning. The spokesman of Victorian England, Alfred, Lord Tennyson (1809-1892), was poet laureate from 1850 to the year of his death. His popularity derived from his sympathetic understanding of the ideas and ideals of his countrymen; he had their "high seriousness" and self-consciousness along with their sentimentality and their admiration for the ornate. Yet the very qualities in his poetry that won him great acclaim in his own day have since worked against his reputation. Today the beauty of much of his

A sketch from an early edition of *Bleak House* illustrates the way in which Charles Dickens satirized the aggressive, middle-class "do-gooders" whose willful and stern philanthropy was often worse than no philanthropy at all. When the particularly aggressive Mrs. Pardiggle visited, the poor bricklayer, lying on the floor, answered the prying questions he knew were forthcoming: "An't my place dirty? Yes, it is dirty—it's nat'rally dirty, and it's nat'rally onwholesome; and we've five dirty and onwholesome children, as is all dead infants, and so much the better for them, and for us besides. . . . How have I been conducting myself: Why, I've been drunk for three days; and I'd been drunk four, if I'd a had the money."

verse seems somewhat artificial, his thought, shallow and conformist.

The other major English poet of the period was Robert Browning (1812-1889), whose sturdy optimism and faith in humanity won him many followers. Unlike Tennyson, however, Browning was not primarily a melodist; his talent lay in the skillful delineation of character. He created a new poetic form—the dramatic monologue—in which the thoughts and feelings of a character were depicted with a psychological insight which appealed to his readers, even though they could not always understand the poet's erudite allusions or his often cryptic mode of expression.

Victorian poets suffered from the tendency to express the moralistic and strongly conventional ideas of the members of the middle class for whom they wrote. Whereas the romanticists, as rebels, adopted an uncompromising attitude toward the world, the Victorians preferred to come to terms with it. Theirs was a more sober, perhaps a more responsible attitude, but it was not the exalted approach that makes for soaring flights of poetry. All too often such compromise was indistinguishable from a deep-rooted middle-class complacency.

Victorian novelists: Thackeray and Dickens. The snobbery and social climbing that went on in a society made highly fluid by the rise of the newly rich middle class provided ideal subjects for the genial satirist and moralist William Makepeace Thackeray (1811-1863). He is probably best known for his unscrupulous but engaging character Becky Sharp, the heroine of *Vanity Fair* (1848).

A note of social protest appears in the works of Charles Dickens (1812-1870). He painted in vivid colors the everyday life of the middle classes and the poor—and especially the struggle of the individual against the worst excesses of industrial expansion and social injustice. In *Oliver Twist, Dombey and Son, Hard Times, Bleak House,* and *David Copperfield,* to name but a few of his major works, Dickens blended romantic and realistic elements by combining a fundamental optimism and belief in progress with trenchant attacks upon existing slum conditions, the miseries of the poor, and the inhuman

debtors' prisons. This note of reaction against mid-Victorian self-satisfaction was soon to swell into a chorus of attacks, both moderate and radical, upon the existing social order.

CHALLENGES TO THE EXISTING ORDER

Social criticism: Arnold, Carlyle, and Ruskin. The state of culture in his day profoundly disturbed the English poet and essayist Matthew Arnold (1822-1888). Arnold believed that the materialistic standards of an industrialized society were completely incompatible with the great humanistic values inherited from Greece and the Renaissance. In his view, mid-Victorian culture was beset by personal self-seeking and lack of social purpose and moral strength. At one end of the social structure were the aristocrats, whom Arnold dubbed "Barbarians" because they were ignorant of the great western cultural inheritance and spent their lives in idleness and wordly pleasures. At the other end was the "Populace," the working class, which was now emerging from its traditional state of poverty and ignorance but which could, unless properly educated and directed, smash much that was irreplaceable in our civilization.

Then there was the middle class, about which Arnold was perhaps most concerned, since its members were now dominant in society. Arnold called them "Philistines" because they neither understood nor cared about culture in its humanistic terms. This new industrial bourgeoisie, he argued, thought only of power and riches and saw in the external signs of change proof of spiritual advancement. Philistinism led a man "to value himself not on what he is . . . but on the number of the railroads he has constructed."[9] In Arnold's judgment, state education was necessary in order to restore humanistic values and to make available to all classes in society the best of man's cultural heritage.

Another prominent figure, outspoken in

his criticism of the shortcomings of a society dominated by the middle class, was the Scottish essayist and historian Thomas Carlyle (1795-1881). He stormed against the worship of Mammon by the industrial capitalists, dubbing them the "Working Aristocracy." Railing against contemporary industrialism and the mass vulgarity which it produced, Carlyle argued that democracy's problems could not be settled by merely extending the ballot. Indeed, the grim-humored Scot feared what would happen when political power was placed in the hands of the multitude through the extension of the suffrage. Because Carlyle believed that "one wise man is stronger than all men unwise," he declared that "the few Wise will have, by one method or another, to take command of the innumerable Foolish."[10] This rejection of the democratic philosophy brings us to a central thesis of Carlyle—namely, that salvation could only be attained by the heroic deeds and leadership of history's "Great Men."

Another influential critic—but one whose formula for curing society's ills differed radically from Carlyle's—was John Ruskin (1819-1900). A leader of the protest movement often called the Esthetic Revolt, Ruskin believed wholeheartedly in the basic integrity and common sense of the people, for whom he advocated socialistic reforms and widespread education. Ruskin wrote eloquently to free his age from the ugly consequences of a soulless industrialism and to reform the arts and handicrafts, many of which were being destroyed by cheap mass production. Although Ruskin and his associates were not able to stem the tide of tasteless goods pouring from the machines, they helped stimulate a new appreciation of craftsmanship.

Stirrings of reform: Factory Acts. As critics of the existing order continued their protests, a movement to reform the worst evils of the Industrial Revolution gathered momentum. In England the landowning aristocracy constituted a powerful force in this camp. Resenting the rise of the *nouveaux riches* mill owners in the cities, the nobles were willing to curb middle-class power by passing Factory Acts setting various restrictions on woman and child labor and excessively long working hours. Although the Tory squires had little use for democracy, they possessed a humanitarian spirit and resented the callous indifference of the urban bourgeoisie toward human rights. Even among the factory owners themselves, a few men such as Robert Owen (see p. 495) realized that altruism and profits made a good team. If the conditions of the workers were improved, their efficiency and productivity would likewise rise.

The first effective Factory Act in Great Britain was passed in the year 1833. This law forbade the employment in textile factories of children under nine, restricted the hours of labor for children between nine and thirteen to forty-eight a week and the hours of children between thirteen and eighteen to sixty-eight, and made it illegal for anyone under eighteen to work at night. Government inspectors were to help administer the act. This piece of legislation prompted such manufacturers as John Bright to exclaim that it was "most injurious and destructive to the best interests of the country" and violated "the liberty of the subject" and "freedom of contract"—as though children of nine had freedom of contract in bargaining with mill owners.

Other reforms in England gradually whittled away at the old doctrine of laissez faire by broadening state regulation of economic enterprise. While conditions in the textile factories were improved by the 1833 Factory Act, those in the mines remained ghastly. Children of six and seven were employed underground twelve hours a day to open and shut ventilation doors and to be harnessed "like dogs to a go-cart" to haul coal wagons. In 1842 a law was passed forbidding the employment in the mines of women and of girls and boys under ten. In 1846 a law was enacted to limit the work of women and children in textile factories to ten hours a day, and in succeeding years other improvements were made in factory conditions. Inspection and enforcement of health and safety in factories and railways were required by law. As industrialization spread, other countries tended to pass regulatory legislation similar to that in England.

In 1836 Massachusetts passed the first act regulating child labor in the United States.

Labor unions legalized. In the field of labor relations, measures were enacted giving workers freedom to organize trade unions. In 1824 the harsh Combination Acts were repealed in Britain, and from this time on workingmen had the legal right to organize and to bargain peacefully with employers, though legal restrictions continued to limit trade union activity. For a long time the authorities vigorously opposed strikes, thereby restricting the strength and effectiveness of the unions.

In the meantime workers on the Continent turned more and more to unions as a means of obtaining their demands for higher wages, shorter hours, and more healthful working conditions. In France in 1864, workers were allowed by law to combine for strikes. During the 1860's trade unionism made progress in Germany, as it did in the United States, where the number of local unions multiplied almost fourfold between 1861 and 1865. In

1869 a temporarily powerful industrial union made its debut in America under the florid name "The Noble Order of the Knights of Labor."

Philanthropic movements. In the efforts to improve social and economic conditions, a significant role was played by private individuals with large fortunes—and with equally large hearts. Hospitals, orphan homes, schools, and other charitable agencies were established. In the United States, for example, mechanics' and apprentices' institutes, such as the Cooper Union in New York, sponsored free educational courses for workers and provided free access to books. Apprentices' and mercantile libraries in the United States laid the basis for the free public library movement, which began around 1850. Thus middle-class humanitarian sympathies and the emphasis upon the rights and dignity of individual men (both stimulated by the romantic movement) combined with the persistent influence of Christian doctrine to favor a humanistic rather than a mechanistic solution to social problems.

By the 1840's there had been substantial modification of the middle-class theory of laissez faire. The state was increasingly expanding its jurisdiction over industry, protecting workers in mines, factories, and on the railways. In addition, philanthropy by private individuals was doing much to make life easier and fuller for the masses. Yet despite these reformist efforts, there was evidence of a growing rift between the bourgeoisie and the workers. In Disraeli's novel *Sybil* (1845), the author points out that Queen Victoria really rules over two nations

A lithograph by Daumier, made in 1848, contrasts the gluttonous bourgeois in his frock coat and top hat with the earnest working man in his shabby clothes. A merciless critic of the bourgeois society of his native France, Daumier was once sentenced to prison for a particularly vitriolic cartoon.

between whom there is no intercourse and no sympathy; who are as ignorant of each other's habits, thoughts, and feelings, as if they were dwellers in different zones, or inhabitants of different planets; who are formed by a different breeding, are fed by a different food, are ordered by different manners, and are not governed by the same laws . . . THE RICH AND THE POOR.[11]

This rift intensified the rising class consciousness among the mass of the working people. In doing so, it contributed to the emergence of yet another major theory in the intellectual history of the nineteenth century, namely, socialism, which proposed complete social reconstruction.

The emergence of socialism. Attacking the nineteenth-century capitalistic system with its laissez-faire philosophy as both unplanned and unjust, socialists or communists (the two terms were once used synonymously) condemned the concentration of wealth and called for public or worker ownership of business. Above all, they insisted that harmony and cooperation—not ruthless competition—should control economic affairs. Generally convinced of the goodness of human nature, they dreamed of a happy future when

there will be no war, no crimes, no administration of justice, as it is called, no government. Besides there will be neither disease, anguish, melancholy, nor resentment. Every man will seek, with ineffable ardor, the good of all.[12]

This humanitarian idealism, a legacy of the Enlightenment, was typical of the theorists who created the early socialist movement.

Utopian socialism: Saint-Simon, Fourier, Owen. The early socialists of the nineteenth century are known as the Utopians. (They were so called by Karl Marx later in the century, and the name has persisted.) The first prominent Utopian was a French nobleman, Claude Henri de Rouvroy, Count de Saint-Simon (1760-1825). Defining a nation as "nothing but a great industrial society" and politics as "the science of production," he argued that men should voluntarily accept the rule of a paternalistic despotism of scientists, technicians, and captains of industry who would "undertake the most rapid amelioration possible of the lot of the poorest and most numerous class."[13]

François Fourier (1772-1837), another French reformer, also believed that future society must be cooperative. He spent much time in working out an ideal plan for a communal living unit, which he termed the "phalanstery." While his plan was endorsed by many prominent men of the day, attempts to found cooperative Fourierist communities were unsuccessful. The famous Brook Farm colony in Massachusetts was one such short-lived experiment.

A more practical reformer and Utopian socialist was Robert Owen (1771-1858), a successful mill owner in Scotland, who made New Lanark, the site of his textile mills, into a model community. Here, between 1815 and 1825, thousands of visitors saw neat rows of workers' homes, a garbage collection system, schools for workers' children, and clean factories where the laborers were treated kindly and where no children under eleven were employed. In 1825 Owen migrated to the vicinity of Evansville, Indiana, where he founded a short-lived Utopian colony called New Harmony.

Partly because of the impracticality of such colonies as New Harmony, which were usually based upon the somewhat naive notion that men naturally loved one another (or could be educated to love one another) and that men could live happily together in a communal society were it not that capitalist competition set man against man; partly because the Utopians made no practical, large-scale attempts to meet the problems of the depressed nineteenth-century industrial classes as a whole; and partly because ultimately Marxist socialism supplanted it—Utopian socialism failed.

Christian socialism. In addition to the Utopians, another nineteenth-century school of socialism arose that drew its inspiration directly from the teachings of Christianity. This group, the Christian socialists, aimed at showing that the doctrines of the Sermon on the Mount were socialistic in character. In England the Christian socialist leaders were drawn largely from the Broad Church party of the Church of England.

Abhorring violence and drawing upon traditional ideas of a universal Christian community, the Christian socialists preached good will between all classes and favored experiments with socialist colonies. They stimulated interest in working-class reforms and attempted to instill into organized Christianity a realization of the social aspects of the teachings of Christ.

Anarchism. Another socialist school of thought that became known as anarchism grew partly out of the ideas of the French theorist Pierre Proudhon (1809-1865), who wrote pamphlets urging the organization of society on a purely voluntary basis. The anarchists insisted that human nature is inherently good but is warped and depraved by authority. They repudiated all governmental compulsion, proposing instead free cooperation among the members of society. Proudhon's dictum, "Property is theft," was widely repeated by radicals everywhere.

In discussions on how to achieve their ends, the anarchists heard advocates of divergent tendencies—on the one hand, pacifists and humanitarian philosophers who were content to dream about a perfect society; on the other, devotees of violence. A member of the latter group was Michael Bakunin, an expatriate Russian revolutionary who insisted that God, the family, and the state must all be repudiated and that only when the world was without law would it be free (see p. 537).

Karl Marx and "scientific" socialism. Up to the middle of the century socialism remained a minor factor in European thinking, as the principal goal of groups of ordinary people was the winning of political equality and universal suffrage. Economic questions remained secondary. Furthermore, the theoretical tendencies of early socialism were not very alarming to the wealthy and aristocratic classes.

This calm was shattered in 1848 when workers on the Continent began demanding the "right to work" during the revolutions of that year. Simultaneously, and almost unnoticed, there appeared early in 1848 a new form of socialism that advocated violence, preached warfare between the classes, and repudiated traditional religion and morality. The instigator of this form of socialism was Karl Marx.

Born in the Rhineland, at Trier (Treves), of German-Jewish parents who had been converted to Christianity, Karl Marx (1818-1883) obtained his doctor's degree after studying the philosophical ideas of Hegel. Failing to find a career in university teaching, he was forced to make a precarious living as a journalist. He went to Paris, where he became interested in socialistic ideas and, while there, he began his lifelong friendship with Friedrich Engels (1820-1895), the son of a wealthy German factory owner. In 1845

Marx was expelled from France by the authorities, and with Engels he went to live in Brussels.

In January 1848 Marx and Engels published the famous *Communist Manifesto*. This stirring document contained practically all the elements of what they came to call "scientific" socialism. It opened with an ominous declaration: "A spectre is haunting Europe—the spectre of Communism." The *Manifesto* called for an implacable struggle against the bourgeoisie, proclaimed the inevitable revolution and the triumph of the masses, and closed with a stern warning:

The Communists disdain to conceal their views and aims. They openly declare that their ends can be attained only by the forcible overthrow of all existing social conditions. Let the ruling classes tremble at a Communistic revolution. The proletarians have nothing to lose but their chains. They have a world to win. Working men of all countries, unite![14]

The revolutions of 1848 (not in the least influenced by Marx, an obscure figure at the time) were welcomed by Marx as the dawn of a new era, the birth of a new society. Going to Germany to assist in its arrival, he was forced to flee when the revolutionary movement collapsed. From that time until his death in 1883, he lived a life of penury in London, supported largely by contributions from friends, especially Engels. Nearly every day Marx would make his way to the British Museum, where he collected material for his various books, especially *Das Kapital (Capital)*.

Basic theories of Marx. No matter what one may think of Marxian socialism, no one can doubt that *Das Kapital* (1867-1894) constitutes one of the most influential books of modern times. In the mid-twentieth century nearly half of the world has been organized on the basis of its teachings.

The following are the basic theories of Marx's socialist system:

(1) The materialistic conception of history: "economic determinism." Marx believed that economic forces basically determine the course of history; all other supposed factors —patriotism, religion, art—are only "ideological veils." For Marx, all history could be

explained in terms primarily of the social organization best adapted to the current means of economic production. When the economic organization of any era changed, it took the whole social and ideological structure with it to a new phase of history.

(2) "Dialectical materialism." Hegel, whose philosophy Marx had studied, felt that history is not just a matter of chance. It is dynamic and unfolds as the result of a definite plan or process of change. History is made up of a number of culture periods, each the expression of a dominant spirit or idea. After fulfilling its purpose, the period is confronted by another contradictory idea or set of values. In Hegelian phraseology the traditional "thesis" is challenged by the new "antithesis." Out of this struggle there emerges a "synthesis" of old and new. Then the cycle starts all over again. Thus, to Hegel, history is a process of unfolding, determined by an absolute purpose or idea, which orthodox Hegelians called God; the machinery of change was called "historical dialectic."

Marx adopted this concept of change—the dialectic—but modified Hegel's approach in an important respect. To Marx the combatants were material forces, not ideas. History became a series of clashes between the exploited and the exploiting group: slave against master in ancient Greece, plebeian against patrician in Rome, serf against lord in the Middle Ages. The bourgeoisie, who by means of the organization of trade and the Industrial Revolution had created a new urban and industrial society, were now opposed by the modern industrial proletariat. The bourgeoisie themselves had helped create the factory system of production—and with it their own nemesis, the proletariat. It was inevitable that when the proletariat realized its true power, it would overthrow its natural enemy, the bourgeoisie. Out of this conflict would appear the new synthesis, the classless society, the ultimate social organization of the modern industrialized era.

(3) The concept of "surplus value." Here Marx borrowed from the laissez-faire economists who held that economic value represented "congealed labor." Only human labor, Marx argued, can create new economic values. But under the capitalist system, the worker is not fully paid for all the values he creates. Suppose, for example, that a worker could produce in six hours the necessary economic values to supply his needs. However, the employer, as employers often did in the nineteenth century, keeps the worker producing goods for, say, twelve hours. The employer is in possession of a "surplus value" of six working hours, which he has "expropriated" from the worker. From this "stolen" surplus value the employer draws profits and capital. The workers are thus robbed of the fruits of their toil and become progressively poorer. Meanwhile, there is a concentration of capital in fewer hands as the most ruthless of the bourgeoisie destroy more and more of their competitors, forcing them into the ranks of the proletariat.

(4) The inevitability of socialism. Because the masses cannot buy all the goods they produce, economic crises, with overproduction and unemployment, will become the rule. Finally comes the day when the proletariat rises up and takes over the means of production. Then, says the *Manifesto:* "The knell of capitalism is sounded. The expropriators are expropriated."[15] In the apocalyptic new society private property will be abolished, exploitation of one class by another will cease, class warfare will end, and the millennium, a virtual heaven on earth, will arrive.

Devoting most of his ammunition to attacking the obvious injustices of unreformed nineteenth-century industrial society, Marx paid comparatively little attention to the kind of society that would supersede the bourgeois state. He once remarked that he had no interest in "writing the kitchen recipes of the future."

The First International. Marx helped to found an international organization of workers, the International Workingmen's Association. Organized in London in 1864, the First International failed to make much headway. There were savage quarrels between the anarchist group led by Bakunin and the majority commanded by Marx. While Marx and his followers would utilize the state as the agency for initiating their classless society, the anarchists bitterly opposed this extension of state activity. Finally, in 1873, the First International closed up shop.

Weaknesses in Marxist doctrine. Certain weaknesses and inconsistencies in Marx's arguments were soon perceived. In interpreting history, Marx sees at work in all ages his "dialectical materialism," the class struggle. Yet in some miraculous fashion this "dominant" feature of history is to disappear when the communist society is established.

Furthermore, there is something ironic in Marx's term *scientific socialism* (i.e., based upon supposed inevitable laws of social development "scientifically" observed and explained by Marx) "in contrast to the Utopian variety." With his talk of a final social stage in which there would be no coercion and no exploitation and with his vague notions about the organization of his ideal society, he really was akin to utopian dreamers of all ages.

By explaining all social and intellectual phenomena in terms of economics and class struggle, Marx's theory denied the importance of intellectual and idealistic influences. And yet Marxism itself as a body of ideas about history and social change became in time a great intellectual influence and historical force.

Another basic weakness in Marxian socialism was that Marx's materialism and atheism were unacceptable to most supporters of all the world's major religions. For the traditional religious belief in a happy afterlife where all earthly injustices and evils would be corrected, Marx substituted the promise of a heaven here on earth, the hope of a worldly utopia. Supporters of Marxist dogmas were assured that it was in the "nature of the historical process" (an ideological substitute for Divine Providence) that this should be so. One had but a single choice: to get into step with the "inevitable" or be destroyed. True believers were convinced that they alone possessed the truth. For this reason Marxism itself has been termed a "surrogate religion"—a secular substitute for religion.

Another difficulty Marxists encountered

was the patriotism of most European workers. Faced by a choice between supporting national interests, as in World War I, and supporting Marxist dogmas about the class nature of war under capitalism, most European workers chose to support their nations. Nationalism was a stronger influence than socialism.

Finally, as we shall see in Chapter 25, Marx's prediction that the mass of men under capitalism would become increasingly reduced to economic misery and near starvation did not come about.

SUMMARY

In this chapter we have presented a cross section of forces dominant in the western world from about 1750 to 1850. The romanticists were in revolt against what they felt was the one-sided rationalistic bias of eighteenth-century thought. In place of reason, they stressed intuition and the emotions. The result was one of the modern world's most fruitful epochs in literature and the arts. Closely allied to romanticism was another powerful emotional force of the period, nationalism, which caught up idealists in all nations and was in turn given eloquent expression by numerous poets.

For the economic historian, the most significant trend in this period resulted from the acquisition of steam as a new and dominant form of energy, accompanied by other inventions and new industrial processes—all summed up in the term Industrial Revolution. The consequent growth of populations and factory towns, the rise to dominance of the middle class, and the genesis of the class war in Marxian socialism added up to a radical transformation in the lives of men throughout the western world. Previously untapped sources of power were harnessed to operate railways and steamships. Efficient new machines gradually replaced hand methods of production, and factories replaced the domestic system of manufacturing.

Nineteenth-century liberalism, with its emphasis upon basic rights for the individual in both the political and economic spheres, became the social philosophy of the triumphant middle class. In effect, political liberalism stood for the rule of law, and evolutionary development rather than revolutionary change, while laissez faire, its counterpart in the economic realm, called for competition among individuals with the government maintaining a hands-off attitude.

Voices were soon raised against uncurbed competition, the exploitation of the many by the few, and the evils of rapid industrialization such as the employment of young children and the proliferation of squalid slums. Some of the worst abuses were corrected by reform legislation, while, in another vein, Utopian and Christian socialists proposed the complete reconstruction of society. In the *Communist Manifesto* (1848), Karl Marx thundered forth a hard and ruthless dogma. He contended that an unbridgeable chasm divided two warring classes—the bourgeoisie and the proletariat. The danger of a class war, however, was to be averted in most of the advanced industrial countries by social reforms and by improvements in the economic status of the masses.

In effect, despite its tempestuous and anguished moments, this was a forward-looking dynamic period, still sustained by a deep belief in the perfectibility of society. Thus the bourgeoisie of the mid-century could agree with Robert Browning when he had one of his poetic characters declare:

God's in his heaven—
All's right with the world![16]

SUGGESTIONS FOR READING

On economic and industrial developments during the nineteenth century, see H. Heaton, **Economic History of Europe**, rev. ed., Harper, 1948. Also recommended are T. Ashton, **The Industrial Revolution: 1760–1830**,* Galaxy; W. O. Henderson, **The Industrialization of Europe: 1780–1914**,* Harcourt Brace & World; and J. C. Chambers and G. E. Mingay, **The Agricultural Revolution**, Schocken, 1966.

H. D. Aiken, ed., **The Age of Ideology: the Nineteenth Century Philosophers**,* Mentor. Selections from the works of Hegel, Mill, and others. For a brief study of Marx and his ideas, see I. Berlin, **Karl Marx; His Life and Environment**,* Galaxy. R. Payne provides a portrait of his personal life in **Marx**, Simon & Schuster, 1968.

K. Marx and F. Engels, **Basic Writings on Politics and Philosophy**,* Anchor. A sizable selection from the writings of Marx and his chief associate, including the **Manifesto** in full, chosen to point up aspects of their thought that are having an impact on the world today, particularly in the underdeveloped countries. See also G. Hegel, **Selections**,* J. Loewenberg, ed., Scribner; and K. Marx, **Das Kapital**,* S. Levitsky, ed., Gateway.

For English literature see G. B. Woods, ed., **English Poetry and Prose of the Romantic Movement**, Scott, Foresman, 1950; and J. H. Buckley and G. B. Woods, eds., **Poetry of the Victorian Period**, 3rd. ed., Scott, Foresman, 1965. Other relevant works are G. L. Mosse, **The Culture of Western Europe, The Nineteenth and Twentieth Centuries: An Introduction**, Rand McNally, 1961; L. A. Willoughby, **The Romantic Movement in Germany**, Oxford, 1930; and B. Willey, **Nineteenth Century Studies**,* Torchbooks.

Vivid insights into the life and prevailing attitudes of the period are provided by contemporary fiction and by biographical studies of leading personalities. Recommended, for example, are the novels of Stendhal, such as **The Charterhouse of Parma**,* Penguin, which portrays post-Napoleonic Italy and life at a reactionary court. The novels of Charles Dickens depict not only the more attractive—albeit often sentimentalized—aspects of traditional English country society but also the social injustices and urban degradation which all too often accompanied the advent of the Industrial Revolution. G. L. Strachey, **Queen Victoria**, Harbrace Modern Classics, 1949, is an example of modern biographical analysis.

M. Raynal, **The Nineteenth Century: New Sources of Emotion from Goya to Gaugin**, Skira, 1952. A first-rate introduction to nineteenth-century painting. See also M. Brion, **The Art of the Romantic Era**,* Praeger, as well as relevant chapters in E. H. Gombrich, **The Story of Art**,* Phaidon; H. W. and D. J. Janson, **Picture History of Painting**,* Washington Square; and F. B. Artz, **From the Renaissance to Romanticism: Trends in Style in Art, Literature, and Music, 1330–1830**,* Phoenix.

For a better understanding of major developments in what has been described as music's "golden century," see M. Brion, **Schumann and the Romantic Age**, Macmillan, 1956; A. Einstein, **Music in the Romantic Era**, Norton, 1947; P. A. Scholes, **Romantic and Nationist Schools of the Nineteenth Century**, Vol. II of **The Listener's History of Music**, 3rd., Oxford, 1942; and H. C. Colles, **Ideals of the Nineteenth Century, the Twentieth Century**, Pt. III of **The Growth of Music**, Oxford, 1956. Well-written biographies of two titans in the world of music are M. M. Scott, **Beethoven**, Farrar, Straus, 1949; E. Valentin, **Beethoven: A Pictorial Biography**, Viking, 1958; and P. Latham, **Brahms**, Farrar, Straus, 1949.

*Indicates an inexpensive paperbound edition.

Chapter 22

To the Barricades

Reaction and Revolution: 1815-1850

INTRODUCTION. After the final defeat of Napoleon, the statesmen of the great powers assembled at the Congress of Vienna to resume the interrupted task of building a new Europe. Their solutions were conservative. Sincerely believing that the explosive forces of nationalism and democracy liberated by the French Revolution had been primarily responsible for more than two decades of destruction and suffering, they were determined to return as much as possible to the "good old days" before the Revolution. With this end in mind, they deliberately sought to extirpate the revolutionary ideas and attitudes that had been released by French republicanism; they restored the old order and endeavored to create among the nations of Europe a harmony and stability which would make a recurrence of revolutionary violence impossible. After this conservative peace had been established, international machinery known as the Congress System—or the Concert of Europe—was devised to defend the political arrangements of 1815 and to crush any attempts to upset them.

But the edifice of reaction built at Vienna could not withstand the forces directed against it. In the great revolutionary upheaval that had originated in France and spread through much of Europe, such ideas as popular suffrage, intellectual and religious freedom, pride in nation, and equality for all under the law had been given wide currency, and though the upheaval was ended, both the intellectuals and the underprivileged in many lands clung to these liberal concepts. In addition, during the revolutionary and Napoleonic eras the spirit of nationalism had risen in Russia, Spain, Italy, the Germanies, and other lands violated by French imperialism. After 1815 those peoples who enjoyed national liberty were resolved to defend it, while those who were denied this privilege and lived under alien governments were increasingly determined to throw off the foreign yoke. A flurry of revolts broke out in 1820 and 1821; another epidemic of revolutions challenged conservatism in 1830; and a climactic outbreak of rebellion and overthrow came in the historic year of 1848.

Another significant trend in the period under review was the growing antagonism between the workers and their employers, the new moneyed interests. As we saw in Chapter 21, the workers demanded democracy, universal suffrage, and equal political rights for all. The middle class, representing the philosophy of liberalism, championed the rights only of the well-to-do. The violent contradiction between these two attitudes was ignored for a time, while working class and middle class united to seize political power. But as the era of reaction following the Congress of Vienna faded, the course of several revolutions exposed the coalition as unnatural and unworkable. Much of the history of western Europe after the year 1850 will be concerned with the new power struggle between the forces of capital and labor.

REACTION AT VIENNA

The Congress of Vienna. In September 1814, during Napoleon's exile on Elba, a brilliant gathering of diplomats and rulers assembled at Vienna to remake the map of Europe. Representatives from every European state except Turkey were in attendance. The Austrian government acted as a lavish host to the treaty makers, sponsoring a round of festivals, hunts, balls, and musicales. Beethoven conducted the premiere of his *Seventh Symphony*. For ten months kings, princes, and diplomats, with their ladies, dined, danced, and worked—not too industriously—at remaking the Continent.

In this atmosphere of high society and what frequently turned out to be low diplomacy, the Congress as such never met. Instead, the new map of Europe was made in small, secret conferences. The leading delegates were Tsar Alexander I of Russia, Lord Castlereagh of Great Britain, Talleyrand of France, and Prince von Metternich, the spokesman for Austria.

The most important figure at the Congress was Metternich (1773-1859), the "prince of diplomats." During the Napoleonic period Metternich had become an inflexible opponent of the French emperor. After Waterloo, he resolved that there should be no return of the revolutionary ideas circulated by France between 1792 and 1815. At the conference Metternich exercised a kind of moral dictatorship. Witty, egotistical, and astute, he flirted elegantly with the ladies and influenced his fellow diplomats with his eloquent speech and his iron opposition to all revolutionary principles. His leadership initiated the reactionary era now termed the Age of Metternich, which was to last until 1848.

The task confronting the Congress. The task confronting the diplomats at the Congress of Vienna was threefold: What was to be done with France? How should the old governments and political boundaries so ruthlessly abolished by Napoleon be reconstituted? And, finally, how should the Congress deal with the radical ideas developed and spread abroad by revolutionary France?

Many Europeans, especially those of the middle class, hoped that the peace settlement would be guided by two principles that had grown rapidly during the stormy days from 1789 to 1815. These were nationalism on the one hand, and democracy and political liberalism on the other. The first principle promised all peoples the right to rule themselves, free of the control of foreigners. Both democrats and liberals opposed despotic government; but while democrats believed in the right of all citizens to participate in government, bourgeois liberals believed in control by the well-to-do.

Unfortunately, the Congress of Vienna was in no mood to respect the aspirations of the people. Much of the subsequent discontent and turmoil in nineteenth-century Europe resulted from the reactionary efforts of the Congress to restore as much of the Old Regime as could conveniently be retrieved.

Treatment of France. Regarding the future of France, the Congress proved to be sensible and moderate. The Treaty of Paris had given France about the same boundaries it possessed in 1792. But after Napoleon's escape from Elba, his so-called "Hundred Days" of freedom, and his ultimate defeat at Waterloo, a second and more severe treaty in November 1815 imposed a war indemnity and somewhat diminished French territory. Nevertheless, France's frontiers were more extensive than they had been in 1789.

Geographic and political realignment. In the reestablishment of the European political order, four principles were followed: (1) legitimacy, (2) encirclement of France, (3) compensations, and (4) balance of power. It was agreed that, wherever possible, the legitimate rulers who were in power before their deposition by Napoleon should have their thrones restored to them. Following this principle, all the rulers who had been established by Napoleon were removed. (The one exception was Bernadotte, one of Napoleon's marshals and founder of the present dynasty in Sweden.) In the person of Louis XVIII, the Bourbon House was restored in France, and other Bourbon rulers were re-

turned to their thrones in Spain and in the kingdom of Naples. The House of Savoy reigned again in Sardinia-Piedmont,* and the House of Orange in Holland.

In the reconstruction of the political boundaries of Europe, the keynote again was the restoration of the past. France, as we have seen, was reduced to substantially its former size; Spain, Holland, and other former Napoleonic possessions regained their independence. The map of Europe looked much as it had before the French Revolution (see Reference Map 7).

However, the pre-Napoleonic boundaries were not everywhere restored. The Holy Roman Empire remained dissolved; in place of the hundreds of states existing in pre-revolutionary times, the thirty-nine remaining German states were retained and organized into the German Confederation, dominated by Austria.

Certain features of the map of Europe were modified in accordance with the principle of encirclement. The allied statesmen were resolved that a protective belt should be fashioned to surround France, hem it in, and prevent any future French aggression. The Austrian Netherlands (Belgium) was turned over to Holland, making this country a stronger barrier on France's north; Savoy, belonging to the kingdom of Sardinia, was enlarged in order to block any French invasion of Italy; and Prussia was given extensive territory along the Rhine.

Another principle modifying the map of Europe was the granting of compensations to states surrendering territory. For example, Austria was compensated for the loss of the Austrian Netherlands by being given Lombardy and Venetia (Venice and the surrounding area) in northern Italy and part of the Adriatic coast as well. In such fashion the diplomats at Vienna portioned out the spoils so that no important power was slighted. When Sweden agreed to allow Russia to retain Finland, Sweden's compensation was the acquisition of Norway. England's share was the retention of colonies and naval bases

---

*Sardinia-Piedmont is often referred to as either Sardinia or Piedmont (the Continental portion of the kingdom). In the text hereafter, unless otherwise noted, *Sardinia* will be used to indicate Sardinia-Piedmont.

This engraving of a painting by J. B. Isabey depicts Europe's statesmen gathered at the Congress of Vienna being introduced to the Duke of Wellington, seen in profile at the far left. Metternich is standing before an empty chair, and Talleyrand appears at the right with his arm resting on the table. Although there was a great deal of work to do at the Congress of Vienna, there was also opportunity for entertainment and relaxation. The illustration at right shows a horse show staged to amuse the distinguished guests.

it had captured in the wars, notably the Dutch colonies of Ceylon and South Africa.

The diplomats also had to create a new balance of power among the nations. Among the Big Four there existed deep jealousies. Prussia coveted all of Saxony, while Austria feared growing Prussia. Russia wanted to expand by securing all of Poland. And Britain believed that an enlarged Russian state would menace the balance of power and—indirectly—British security. While the victors haggled, Talleyrand wormed his way into the good graces of Britain and Austria. A secret treaty was arranged, pledging the three countries to use force if necessary to restrain Prussia and Russia. Confronted by this threat, Russia and Prussia reduced their claims for more Polish and Saxon territory. The power struggle at Vienna demonstrated that making peace is often as dangerous as making war.

Nationalist sentiment disregarded. The most serious mistake in the territorial settlements made at Vienna was the disregard of the principle of nationalism. Italy was, in Metternich's disdainful phrase, only a "geographical expression," not a nation, and was

so treated. In Germany the weak and loosely organized German Confederation of thirty-nine states was established, with Austria at its head. This was largely Austria's doing again, for Austria saw in a united Germany a threat to its dominance in central Europe. The principle of nationalism was again violated when Norway was arbitrarily given to Sweden and the Belgians were turned over to the Dutch. Poles and Finns also simply exchanged masters. During the nineteenth century these peoples continued their struggle to secure national sovereignty.

Quadruple and Holy Alliances. The most vital problem facing the Congress was how to check the growth of revolutionary ideas. In November 1815, as a result of Metternich's influence, Austria, Prussia, Russia, and England signed the Quadruple Alliance. The object of this document was stated to be the maintenance of "tranquillity" in Europe, and for this purpose the members were to meet from time to time to agree on the proper measures to be taken. In 1818 France was admitted to the compact, making it a Quintuple Alliance.

Such an alliance system, providing for

collective security against any renewal of French aggression and for consultation on common problems, was both logical and desirable. Unfortunately, it became apparent soon after 1815 that the real purpose of the alliance was to crush any growth of liberalism and nationalism. After 1820 the Congress System became in effect a trade union of kings for suppressing the liberties of peoples.

The Holy Alliance, also formed at Vienna, was proposed by the visionary Alexander I of Russia and was joined by all the European rulers except the king of England, the sultan, and the pope. They agreed that they would base their policies on those of that "holy religion, namely, the precepts of justice, Christian charity, and peace." No one was quite sure just what Alexander meant by this pact, which Castlereagh described as "a piece of sublime mysticism and nonsense." Liberals and nationalists regarded the Holy Alliance as a sanctimonious device to conceal the reactionary designs of the Quadruple Alliance.

THE CONGRESS SYSTEM

Conservatism triumphant. The Congress of Vienna signaled the return of peace, though not of tranquillity. The spirit of Liberty, Equality, and Fraternity continued to stir the peoples of Europe; and almost immediately after the Congress disbanded, various groups began to work against the political arrangements made at Vienna. In most of Europe the forces of conservatism—based on the restored monarchies, the Church, and the aristocracy—were strong enough to stifle the forces of nationalism, liberalism, and democracy for some time after 1815. Despite the most careful precautions, however, violent revolutions soon broke out against the reactionary regimes in Italy and Spain. It was to safeguard against such uprisings that the Congress System, a significant experiment in collective security, was devised.

Reaction and revolution in Spain and Italy. In 1812, during the struggle against Napoleon, Spanish liberals had convened a parliament that had adopted a liberal constitution, but it was ignored by the Bourbon monarch Ferdinand VII after his restoration to the throne in 1814. The former privileges of the nobility and the Church were restored, the Inquisition was reinstated, and the Jesuits were given control of education. There was no parliamentary government, the press was gagged, and political offenders were imprisoned by the thousands. The more intelligent and liberal Spaniards were aroused by the pitiable conditions of their country, and in all the important towns revolutionary bodies called *juntas* were set up. Most dangerous to the reactionary monarchy was the rising discontent in the army, where bad food and lack of pay brought many troops to the brink of mutiny.

In Italy conditions were, if anything, worse. The consequences of the French Revolution had been felt here more than in any other land outside of France, because Napoleon had destroyed so many of the institutions of the Old Regime. The Napoleonic conquest had given the mass of the Italian people more liberty than they had ever known before and brought a considerable measure of political unity to their land. After the Congress of Vienna, however, the country was again fragmented. Lombardy and Venetia, as we have seen, were turned over to Austria; the rest of the country was divided into minor states, most of which were under the thumb of the Austrian government. The state governments returned to their old inefficient ways. Taxes were high, favoritism and corruption flourished, and desperate men took the easy road of brigandage as a way out. Many patriotic Italians joined a secret revolutionary society, the *Carbonari* or "charcoal burners," which had first organized in the mountain forests and soon spread throughout Italy.

In 1820 a mutiny in the Spanish army was followed by a general uprising. In answer to the rebels' demand that the liberal constitution of 1812 be restored, Ferdinand glibly agreed. When the news of this revolt reached the kingdom of Naples and Sicily, where the people were suffering under the oppressive regime of their Bourbon king, revolution broke out there also, and the king

was forced to grant his people a constitution patterned after the Spanish model.

Intervention in Italy and Spain. News of the revolts in Spain and Italy upset the conservative statesmen of Europe. Determined to stamp out rebellion and to support the 1815 settlement, Metternich set about organizing collective action for the suppression of the revolutions—the Congress System.

In 1820 the members of the Quintuple Alliance met in the Congress of Troppau to decide what should be done about the uprising in Naples. Despite England's opposition and France's lukewarm attitude, the three other powers (Prussia, Russia, and Austria) decided to intervene. In 1821 the conservative powers met again, this time at Laibach in Austria, and invited the king of Naples to appear before them. Once among his reactionary friends, the king repudiated his promises, supported intervention, and welcomed the use of an Austrian army that placed him back on his throne.

Meanwhile liberal sentiment in England was growing stronger, and the government was drifting further away from its ultra-conservative allies on the Continent. When another congress was convened in 1822 at Verona to consider intervention in Spain, the British soon withdrew their delegation and began their "splendid isolation" from permanent international commitments on the Continent that was to last until the end of the century. Because reactionaries in France had by now gained the upper hand, the French government volunteered to send an army into Spain to crush the reform movement. A brutal reaction followed. Terrible punishments were meted out to the patriots who had forced the king to restore the constitution of 1812; all acts of the liberal Spanish parliament since the rebellion of 1820 were annulled; and liberals were sought out and punished.

Weakening of the Congress System. Elated by its success in Italy and Spain, the conservative alliance sought to restore the authority

RUSSIA

AUSTRIAN EMPIRE

MOLDAVIA
Autonomous

Vienna

Buda Pest

Trieste

Belgrade

WALACHIA
Autonomous

Bucharest

SERBIA
Autonomous

ADRIATIC
SEA

MONTENEGRO

Danube R.

Sofia

BLACK SEA

Adrianople
Constantinople

ITALIAN
PENINSULA

Salonika

OTTOMAN EMPIRE

IONIAN
SEA

AEGEAN
SEA

Smyrna

GREECE

CHIOS

Athens

Navarino

**THE TREATY OF
ADRIANOPLE 1829**

CRETE

of the Spanish king over his rebellious subjects in Latin America. First revolting against Napoleon's intervention, then against the reactionary Ferdinand, most of the American colonies had secured their independence by the early 1820's. In trying to intervene in this struggle on behalf of the Spanish king, the European concert met its first defeat. Great Britain, which enjoyed a flourishing trade with the new Latin American states, displayed no enthusiasm for renewed Spanish control. As if the shadow of the British navy was not sufficiently daunting, President Monroe in 1823 warned the European powers that the United States would regard the proposed intervention as an unfriendly act. The Congress System was to receive a final shattering blow later in the decade when strategic and sentimental interests led some of the great powers to align themselves with the cause of revolution in Greece.

First nationalist successes in the Balkans. Outside the family of European nations and not represented at the Congress of Vienna, the Ottoman empire of the Turks ruled over a medley of restless and miserable subject peoples. In 1815 the sultan in Constantinople was still the head of an empire which included most of the Balkan peninsula as well as much of North Africa and Asia Minor (see Reference Map 7). The Christian subjects of the Turks were concentrated mainly in the Balkans, where they were known as *rayahs* (cattle). Formally, however, the Turks practiced religious toleration and in some cases supported the Church as a means of governing the *rayahs*.

The first people to obtain independence from Turkish rule were the Montenegrins, Serbians who lived in a particularly mountainous area near the Adriatic. In 1799, after a long, heroic struggle, these brave mountaineers had won a formal recognition of independence from the sultan.

In Serbia itself another independence movement had begun in 1804 with a general uprising led by a patriot named George Petrovich, popularly known as "Black George," who secured Russian support. In 1826 Turkey was forced to place Serbia under Russian protection.

Greece wins independence. It was the uprising of the Greeks in 1821 that attracted the serious attention of Europe. Stirred by the ideals of the French Revolution, Greek patriots rose in arms. Turkish officials in southern Greece were murdered, and in retaliation the sultan ordered the massacre of all Greeks in Constantinople. In 1822 the world was again horrified by news of the Turkish massacre of the entire Greek population of the island of Chios.

Metternich wanted the revolt to burn itself out, but the Greek cause had many friends. Hellas had been the cradle of European freedom and civilization, and liberals and intellectuals everywhere demanded that Greece be liberated. Lord Byron wrote:

The isles of Greece! the isles of Greece!
  Where burning Sappho loved and sung,
Where grew the arts of war and peace,
  Where Delos rose and Phoebus sprung!
Eternal summer gilds them yet,
But all, except their sun, is set.[1]

Philhellenic societies were formed, and both supplies and volunteers were sent to aid the Greeks.

It was the direct intervention of the great powers, however, that determined the outcome of the Greek independence movement. Although he detested revolutions, Tsar Nicholas I, who had come to the throne in 1825, was strongly interested in weakening Turkey in order to pave the way for Russian annexation of the Dardanelles. This policy alarmed Great Britain, and the upshot was an agreement in 1827 among Britain, Russia, and France, whereby these powers pledged themselves to secure the independence of Greece. This move proved a serious blow to Metternich's Congress System.

The three powers defeated the Turks on land and sea, and in 1829 peace terms were arranged by the Treaty of Adrianople. Greek independence was recognized, together with the autonomy of Serbia and Rumania (Wallachia and Moldavia), the latter becoming a protectorate of Russia (see map, p. 506).

Nationalism in the Balkans had registered important advances, but the victory was far from complete. Many Greeks still lived under Turkish rule, as in Crete; complete independence had still to be secured by Serbia and Rumania; and the restless Bulgarians still remained under the harsh Ottoman yoke.

FRANCE, ENGLAND, AND THE REVOLUTIONS OF 1830

France under Louis XVIII. The defection of Great Britain had heralded the demise of the Congress System, and by 1829, the year in which Greek independence was recognized, it was no longer an effective weapon of international conservatism. In 1830 additional sledge-hammer blows fell upon the machinery of coercion devised by Metternich and his backward-looking colleagues. The eruption began in France, the only great power which at all approached England in liberal political institutions.

The restored Louis XVIII, brother of the unfortunate Louis XVI, who had fallen victim to the guillotine in 1793, had been willing to accept many of the reforms of the French Revolution. In 1814 Louis "granted" his subjects a charter which established a form of constitutional monarchy. The king retained all executive power, which he exercised through ministers responsible to him, and he alone could initiate legislation. In the bicameral legislature, patterned after the British Parliament, members of the upper house were appointed for life by the king, and those of the lower chamber were chosen by a severely restricted franchise (only about one man in a hundred could vote) designed to vest power in the nobility and upper bourgeoisie. France in 1815 had a long way to go before it could claim to have democratic institutions.

The charter did grant the French people substantial social, religious, and legal rights. All citizens were now equal before the law. Freedom of speech and of religion were guaranteed, and arbitrary arrest was forbidden. The restored government of Louis XVIII accepted the abolition of feudalism and made no attempt to restore the properties confiscated from the Church and nobles during the Revolution. It was agreed, instead, to pay indemnities. Napoleon's most significant measures, such as the Civil Code, the Concordat with the pope, the centralization of local government, and the administrative system, were also retained. So, too, was the state's tight control over education.

Moderate though the restoration seemed, it had the backing of only a minority. Neither of the two politically important groups in France supported the restoration settlement. The Ultras, opponents of the Revolution and supporters of strong monarchy and privilege, thought the constitution too liberal and wanted to turn the clock back to the days of the Old Regime. At the core of the Ultra faction were some of the nobles, many just returned from exile, and the leaders of the Church, whose position in France had been seriously reduced by the Revolution.

At the other end of the political spectrum were the republican liberals and radicals—the disenfranchised lower bourgeoisie, students and intellectuals, and laborers in the larger cities—who wanted the constitution made more democratic and the electorate broadened to include themselves. The truth was that the Revolution, though over, was still an issue.

In his nine years on the French throne Louis XVIII managed with fair success to steer a middle course between the Ultras on the one hand and the liberal and radical reformers on the other. His aim was to "heal the wounds of the Revolution." During his reign a characteristic feature of modern French politics emerged—the multi-party system. Whereas in England there were but two political parties, both recruited in the main from similar strata of society and sharing a common political tradition, in France numerous loosely organized factions appeared, and it became necessary for ministries to be formed of men from a coalition of parties in the legislature instead of from one majority party as in England. Thus the basis

was laid for a pattern of government by frequently unstable parliamentary coalitions.

Charles X and the July Revolution. Louis XVIII was succeeded on his death in 1824 by Charles X, and the political balance maintained precariously by Louis at once swung heavily to the Right. Like the late monarch, Charles was a brother of the beheaded Louis XVI and had been an émigré during the Revolutionary era, but, unlike the late king, Charles X accepted none of the facts of his age and had long been leader of the Ultras. As a staunch exponent of divine right, Charles announced in 1829 that he "would rather saw wood than be a king of the English type."

When, in July 1830, the legislature refused to support his ultraroyalist program, Charles dissolved it and issued a series of ordinances

The barricades, symbol of revolution in France, are immortalized in Eugène Delacroix' painting of the July Revolution of 1830, "Liberty Leading the People" (1831).

gagging the press and limiting the franchise. Galled by this violation of the constitution, Parisians rose in rebellion. The then narrow streets of Paris were quickly choked with overturned carts, boxes, tables, and paving stones. Behind these barricades crouched the armed revolutionaries, who returned the fire of the soldiers with good effect. Again and again in nineteenth-century revolutions, insurrectionists fought from behind such barricades.

After three days a new liberal faction took over the government, and Charles fled to England. The new government was constituted by an agreement between the French republicans, led by the aging Marquis de Lafayette, and the liberal monarchist supporters of the Orleans branch of the Bourbon family.

The bourgeois monarchy (1830-1848) of Louis Philippe. The July Revolution gave France a new king, Louis Philippe, the duke of Orleans, and a new, definitely bourgeois outlook. Like William III of England in 1688, the new king had ostensibly accepted his crown from the people; he was "king of the barricades" and the "citizen king," in contrast to Louis XVIII and Charles X, who had claimed to rule by divine sanction. Thus the principle of the sovereignty of the people supplanted the principle of divine right. In token of this, the revolutionary tricolor once more replaced the white flag of the Bourbons as the emblem of France. The suffrage was extended to include the moderately wealthy bourgeoisie, but it did not yet include the lower middle class or the common people. The new regime was the first wholly middle-class-dominated government to be set up on the Continent.

Revival of Polish nationalism. Word of the July Revolution spread like the wind throughout western Europe, and nationalists and liberals elsewhere determined to strike for freedom against the Metternich system. Some of the most heroic and exciting events took place in Russian Poland, which, since the Congress of Vienna, had been ruled by the tsar as a semi-independent kingdom. Unrest among the Poles mounted under the rule of the ultrareactionary Tsar Nicholas I.

A few months after the July Revolution in France, the Polish Diet proclaimed Poland independent of Russia and asserted its right to select its own ruler. Despite some brilliant victories, Polish resistance was effectively broken by Russian arms in the summer of 1831. The national Diet was abolished, and Poland sank to the status of an ordinary Russian province, governed directly by Russian officials in St. Petersburg. Notwithstanding its tragic defeat, Polish nationalism continued to live on.

The Belgian revolution. In contrast to the disappointing outcome of the Polish revolution, nationalism and liberalism triumphed in Belgium. We recall that at the Congress of Vienna the Belgians had been united with Holland under the Dutch crown—a union which proved most unhappy. Wide differences in culture separated the two peoples. The Dutch were mainly Protestant, the Belgians Catholic; the Dutch were seafarers and traders, the Belgians farmers and industrial workers. The Belgians deeply resented the royal policies by which Dutch laws, officials, and language were imposed on them.

When news of the July Revolution in Paris reached the Belgians, nationalistic feeling rose high in Brussels. Rioting broke out in the city, and a Dutch army sent to quell the disturbances was repulsed with heavy losses. The Belgians then announced their independence and drew up a liberal constitution. The Dutch king immediately appealed to the conservative alliance for aid. But the Russian tsar was busy "tranquilizing" the Poles, and Austria was occupied with revolutions in Italy. No help was forthcoming from France, for Louis Philippe's government, created by revolution in 1830, was itself a repudiation of the principle of legitimacy laid down in 1815. England, whose political and commercial interests would generally be served by the independence of small states, saw no reason to oppose Belgian aspirations as long as the new state did not become a puppet of France.

Thus favored by fortune, a national assembly met in Brussels in 1831 and chose Prince Leopold of Saxe-Coburg-Gotha as king. The king of Holland had no choice but to recognize the independence of the kingdom of Belgium. In 1839 the international

With the end of the Napoleonic Wars, England ceased its war spendings, which resulted in an industrial depression. Unable to make a living, hand-skilled workers responded with acts of protest and sabotage. Finally, in 1819, a large demonstration was staged in Manchester, where the discontented, waving "love" signs, demanded universal suffrage. What they got instead was a cavalry charge that took at least eleven lives and political repression in the name of "law and order."

status of the new state was settled. A treaty declaring Belgium to be a "perpetually neutral state" was drawn up in that year and signed by England, Austria, Prussia, Russia, France, and Belgium. (This was the treaty which Germany dismissed as a "scrap of paper" when its troops invaded Belgium in World War I.) After centuries of foreign rule —under Burgundy, Spain, Austria, and Holland—the Belgians had finally secured their own government.

Depression and political reaction in England. The first decade after 1815 was a period of reaction in England as well as on the Continent. With the end of the Napoleonic Wars the government ceased its war

purchases, the country became overstocked with goods, and factories shut down. Unemployment, further augmented by demobilization, rose rapidly and resulted in widespread suffering. In a particularly sad state of distress and despair were the handloom weavers and other hand-skilled workers, who now began to feel the relentless squeeze of the machine; the severe drop in prices after 1815 made it impossible for them to make a living. In consequence, they turned to wrecking factories and smashing machines. The gangs of masked workers who took part in this violence were called "Luddites" after a legendary leader known as "Ned Ludd."

Instead of sympathizing with the plight of the poor, unemployed, and even starving lower classes, England's aristocrats saw in their discontent only the evil Jacobin influence of the French Revolution. The Tory party, controlling the government, followed the doctrine of "peace, law, order, and discipline." In 1819 a large meeting held in the city of Manchester to demand universal suffrage was dispersed by a cavalry charge with the loss of several lives. Terrified by what they believed to be the imminence of revolution, the ruling class enacted repressive legislation. Public meetings were restricted, liberal newspapers were repressed, heavy fines were imposed on "seditious literature," and in 1817 the Habeas Corpus Act was suspended.

Reform movement in England. The period of postwar reaction ended in the late 1820's with a series of reforms sponsored by the liberal branch of the Tory party under the leadership of Robert Peel and George Canning. These bills abolished capital punishment for over one hundred offenses, created a modern police force for London, began the recognition of labor unions, repealed old laws which forbade non-Anglican Protestants to sit in Parliament, and by the Catholic Emancipation Bill gave equal rights to members of the Catholic faith. Then in 1832 came the great crisis in political reform and its successful resolution.

The July Revolution of 1830 in France contributed the impetus for political reform in Great Britain. By this time not only was the

British working class incensed against the system of privilege which ruled it, but British businessmen were determined to break the monopoly of the aristocracy in government. In 1830 the Duke of Wellington, now prime minister, made a fateful speech in which he declared that the constitution of the country was quite satisfactory for all its needs. This so aroused public opposition that the "Iron Duke" was forced to resign, and Lord Grey, the leader of the Whig party, became head of the government, thereby ending sixty years of almost continuous Tory rule.

The new government under Grey immediately set about reforming Parliament. There had long been a need for such action. Representation in the House of Commons had virtually no relation to the population; it has been estimated that 3 percent of the population dictated the election of the members. Of 571 members of the Commons, 82 were elected by counties controlled by the landed aristocracy, and the remaining 489 members came from incorporated towns, called boroughs. Many "pocket" boroughs were under the control of political bosses who dictated the choice of the voters. In various depopulated "rotten" boroughs, members of Parliament were elected to represent areas which boasted only a handful of people or no longer contained any inhabitants. On the other hand, new and rapidly growing industrial towns, such as Manchester with 140,000 inhabitants and Birmingham with 100,000, had no representatives.

Reform Bill of 1832. Supported by the rising middle class and the workers, Grey's government introduced a bill to abolish the rotten boroughs, widen the franchise, and give representation to the new industrial towns. Defeated in the Commons at the outset, the bill was again introduced and passed, only to be defeated in the House of Lords. After the bill had been introduced a third time, the king, William IV, finally threatened to create enough new peers who would vote for the bill in order to pass the measure in the House of Lords. This threat forced the Lords to pass the bill.

The Reform Bill of 1832 transferred the balance of power from the landed gentry to the middle class and emphasized the growing supremacy of the Commons over the Lords. The important fact is that, while the great Reform Bill did not represent an immediate substantial widening of the franchise (the working class was still disenfranchised), the bill indicated a new sensitivity to popular forces and thus constituted an initial step in breaching the wall of political privilege.

Additional English reforms. Immediately following the first Reform Bill, several other notable reforms were enacted. Slavery was abolished in the British empire in 1833. The first important Factory Act (see Chapter 21) was passed in the same year, and in 1835 the Municipal Corporations Bill instituted a uniform system of town government with popular election. The historian Macaulay expressed the prevailing moderate view of preferring peaceful change to bloody revolution when he declared in the House of Commons:

Turn where we may, within, around, the voice of great events is proclaiming to us, "Reform, that you may preserve" . . . everything at home and abroad forbodes ruin to those who persist in a hopeless struggle against the spirit of the age. . . . Save the greatest, and fairest, and most highly civilized community that ever existed, from calamities which may in a few days sweep away all the rich heritage of so many ages of wisdom and glory. The danger is terrible. The time is short.[2]

The accession of the popular young Queen Victoria in 1837 was in itself a kind of reform. Victoria did much to save the monarchy by making it an accurate mirror of middle-class convention and creed. Under the young queen Great Britain rode out the storm of unrest that beset all the great powers in western Europe during the 1840's.

The Chartist movement. In the early 1830's a strong popular movement known as Chartism had developed in England. Its leaders published the People's Charter, containing six demands: universal suffrage, secret voting, no property qualifications for members of Parliament, payment of members so that poor men could seek election if they wished, annual elections to Parliament, and equal electoral districts. Twice, in 1839 and in 1842, the Chartists presented their petition, with over a million signatures, to the House of Commons. In each case the government ignored the petition.

In 1848, following the news of the February Revolution in France (see p. 514), a third petition was presented to Parliament, which again rejected the demands. A militant minority among the Chartists planned an armed insurrection in protest, but their plans were divulged by an informer and the ringleaders seized. The bulk of the English people, Chartists or otherwise, apparently preferred to avoid violence as an instrument of political and social reform. Although the Chartist movement subsequently declined, within the next century all but one of its demands—annual elections to Parliament—were enacted into law, forming the very foundations of modern British democracy.

A contemporary cartoon shows a demonstration of the kind that helped bring about repeal of the Corn Laws in 1846.

Repeal of the Corn Laws. Another reason why the Chartist movement declined so quickly was a basic change in the government's economic policy, which now leaned more toward economic liberalism and helped stimulate the rapid growth of employment, wealth, and industry after 1850. The Corn Laws, protective duties on imported corn (i.e., grain) which had favored the hitherto dominant farming gentry, were dropped in favor of a policy of free trade. These laws had been designed to encourage exports and to protect the English landowners from foreign competition. By the middle of the nineteenth century the population had increased to such an extent that English agriculture could no longer feed the country, and the price of bread rose alarmingly. The famine of 1845 in Ireland (see p. 551) dramatically spotlighted the seriousness of the situation. Repeal of the Corn Laws in 1846 made possible the import of low-priced wheat from abroad, cheaper food for the masses, and a more contented labor supply for the factory owners. At the same time, this victory of the free-traders reflected the growing political dominance of those members of the middle class who believed in laissez faire in England, feeling that tariffs restricted the free flow of goods. After 1846 the British economy was increasingly geared to industry, and England became dependent on imports to feed its population.

The repeal of the Corn Laws was shortly followed by the abandonment of customs duties of every kind. The free trade advocated by the followers of Adam Smith was at last a reality; another victory for liberalism had been achieved. For half a century the policy was eminently successful; the flourishing English industries needed no protection against outside competitors and the English economy throve on the stimulus of cheap imports of raw materials and food.

By mid-century Britain was a wealthy nation taking pride in the stability of its political institutions. The pattern of restraint and of gradual social and political reforms, so characteristic of England's history for the next hundred years, had been firmly established. Britain would move forward by evolutionary rather than revolutionary reform.

REVOLUTION RENEWED IN WESTERN EUROPE

Growing spirit of discontent. Throughout western Europe by the year 1848 discontent was rife. Idealistic romantics dreamed of liberty, practical businessmen sought the control of government, and city workers desired democracy and a more equal distribution of the profits of industry. A prophetic note for all Europe was sounded in the French legislature early in 1848, when Alexis de Tocqueville, who had written a famous book about democracy in America, warned his listeners:

We are sleeping in a volcano. . . . Do you not see that the earth trembles anew? A wind of revolution blows, the storm is on the horizon.[3]

France under Louis Philippe. The new forces of discontent were particularly strong in France. Since 1830 France had been ruled by the bourgeois monarch, Louis Philippe, who prided himself on being the representative of the business interests of his country. France was fairly prosperous, and the government, while not democratic, was moderate and sensible.

On the debit side, it soon became apparent that the July Monarchy had little concern with the lower classes. "Work, get rich, and then you can vote," was the government's advice. To Louis Philippe and his ministers, prosperity, order, and, above all, international peace required the maintenance of the status quo. The king believed that peace was threatened by the demands of many liberals and republicans that France aid the nationalists of Poland and Italy. "No reform!" became the platform of his reign.

What Louis Philippe failed to perceive was that new economic and social forces were at work which were bound to affect the political structure as well. The Industrial Revolution, entering France from England at an increasing tempo during his reign, was fattening the bourgeoisie whom he so sedulously represented, but it was also swelling the ranks of the politically conscious proletariat and creating those wretched conditions which gave rise to socialism, with its aim of

In his early years on the throne the "king of the bourgeoisie," Louis Philippe, made a point of walking about the streets of Paris in a frock coat and top hat and carrying a walking stick like any solid middle-class citizen. For a time he allowed ordinary citizens to flock through his palace, much as their American contemporaries poured through the White House during the presidency of Andrew Jackson.

redesigning the whole economic and political system.

Louis Blanc (1811-1882), a socialist theorist and journalist who had a large following among French workers, demanded that the state guarantee the "right to work" by establishing "national workshops" owned and operated by the workers. The discontented industrial workers concentrated in Paris and other growing factory towns added their demands for reform to the moderate requests of the lower bourgeoisie, who simply wanted the vote for themselves, and those of the intellectuals, who were devoted to republican principles.

Another cause of the government's general unpopularity was the corruption that pervaded the administration. Officials speculated with public funds, army commissions were sold, and a series of scandals in high society rocked the country. In addition, the reign of Louis Philippe was colorless and dull. "Business before national honor" seemed to be the king's policy in foreign affairs. Frenchmen began to think back fondly to the immortal deeds of the great Napoleon and yearn for national glory once again.

The Revolution of 1848. In February 1848 a Paris insurrection once more turned into a political revolution. Again, as in 1830, mobs of excited citizens began to congregate and the barricade—the inevitable symbol of revolution—appeared. More than 1500 barricades were thrown up in Paris. Republican leaders proclaimed a provisional revolutionary government, and Louis Philippe fled to England. Universal suffrage was immediately established, giving France a full political democracy.

The new regime, known as the Second Republic, had a brief and inglorious existence. Created without real preparation, it was hamstrung by the complete inexperience in democracy of both its officials and the newly enfranchised common people. In addition, the reformers who had been united in their opposition to Louis Philippe broke into diverse factions after his removal. The republicans at once split into two groups— the moderates, of bourgeois stamp, who favored political democracy within the existing social order; and the socialists, supported by mobs of unemployed Paris workers, who wanted the revolution to be economic and social as well as political. A provisional government representing both groups was set up, with the moderates well in the majority.

Within a few months the new regime came to grief over the issue of Louis Blanc's national workshops. The government approved the scheme but entrusted its organization and operation to men determined to discredit it. As a result, such projects as carrying dirt from one end of a park to the other soon made the workshops a laughingstock.

In June the workshops were disbanded, whereupon another violent insurrection, known as the "June Days," broke out in the streets of the capital. The unemployed workers hoisted a red flag as the sign of revolution—the first time that the red flag appeared as the symbol of the proletariat. With the cry of "Bread or Lead," these Paris workers

Stupidity and indifference characterize the paunchy, middle-class members of the French legislature in Daumier's scathing portrayal of the lawmakers in session under the July Monarchy.

erected barricades and sought to overthrow the government. Not since the Reign of Terror had the capital witnessed such savage street fighting. The insurrection was crushed after much loss of life. It left the working class with a bitter hatred of the bourgeoisie and the bourgeois element with a deep and lasting fear of left-wing violence.

Louis Napoleon and the Second Empire. The bloody upheavals in Paris produced a wave of reaction throughout the country. When the election for the presidency of the new republic was held, the victor was not one of the revolutionaries who had founded the new government but a hitherto obscure bearer of the magic name *Napoleon*—Louis Napoleon, nephew of Napoleon I.

Louis had assumed the headship of the Napoleon clan after the death of the emperor's only son in 1832. Early in life Louis became convinced of the magic of his name and the great destiny it was yet to play in the history of France. His efforts in 1836 and again in 1840 to overthrow the bourgeois

monarchy of Louis Philippe fizzled miserably, but at his trial he had an opportunity to address the nation:

I represent . . . a principle, a cause, a defeat. The principle is the sovereignty of the people: the cause is that of the Empire: the defeat is Waterloo.[4]

Sentenced to life imprisonment, Louis Napoleon occupied his time writing tracts and articles, which displayed an apparent concern for the depressed industrial workers and unemployed. He escaped from prison in 1846 and fled to England; two years later, with the overthrow of Louis Philippe, he returned to Paris. Free from any involvement in the June Days, he was able to obtain broad national support in his campaign for the presidency.

Louis Napoleon was elected president of the Second Republic by an overwhelming majority. He considered himself, not the legislature, as representing the national will. In December 1851, while serving as president under a constitution that did not permit him to succeed himself, Louis Napoleon forcibly dissolved the government, which had played into his hands by attempting to abolish universal male suffrage. Imitating the methods of his illustrious uncle and anticipating the techniques of modern dictators, he then carried out a plebiscite which gave almost unanimous support to his action. In 1852 Napoleon proclaimed himself emperor. The Second Republic was no more. France still did not seem to be ready for republican institutions.

CENTRAL EUROPE: THE RISE OF THE NATIONALISTIC SPIRIT

The Old Regime maintained in Austria. During the revolutions of 1820 and again in 1830, there had been sympathetic vibrations of unrest and minor insurrections in the German states and the Austrian empire. In the main, however, the political arrangements made at Vienna in 1815 were not seriously challenged. Under the strong hand of its chief minister, Metternich, Austria continued to be a bulwark of reaction throughout its sphere of influence among the multitude of states in Germany and Italy.

Nationalism menaced not only the Hapsburg domination of Germany and Italy but also the Austrian state itself, for the Austrian empire did not constitute a nation but rather a bewildering jumble of diverse nationalities. Austria proper, the seat of the governing house of the Hapsburgs, was German. To the east of Austria was the great plain of Hungary, the home of the Magyars, who were originally of Asiatic origin and spoke a language not related to most European tongues. All around the fringes of the Austrian and Hungarian center were primarily Slavic peoples: Czechs, Slovaks, and Poles to the north, Rumanians to the east, and Serbs, Croats, and Slovenes to the south. In addition, south of Austria were the large provinces of Lombardy and Venetia, purely Italian in population. In this polyglot Austrian empire the Germans were the ruling

nationality. Although they comprised only about 20 percent of the total population, they constituted the bulk of the upper and middle classes, controlling the government, the Church, the bureaucracy, and the army. In appearance, then, Austria was German, but it was actually "a Slav edifice with a German facade." Only by excluding the ideas of nationalism and popular government could this ramshackle empire be kept intact.

The middle class in the empire was very small; the great bulk of the inhabitants were peasants, either serfs, as in Hungary, or virtual serfs who owed half their time and two thirds of the crops to their lords. Government was autocratic, and the regional assemblies or Diets possessed little power and represented only the nobility.

The German nationalist youth movement. In the several dozen states of the German Confederation, Austrian influence was paramount. Here again Metternich perceived that his most menacing danger was nationalism, for a new German nation might repudiate Austrian leadership and stimulate nationalist aspirations within the Austrian empire.

Notwithstanding the stern opposition of Metternich, supported by most of the German rulers, nationalism and political liberalism advanced in the German states after 1815. Much of the inspiration for this movement was derived from the romantic nationalism so strongly expressed by German professors, poets, and philosophers (see Chapter 21).

In 1817 a great patriotic student festival was held at Wartburg Castle, where Luther had taken refuge and where now the students, emulating Luther's burning of the papal bull, threw reactionary books and pamphlets onto a great bonfire. The festival was followed by some disturbances, including the murder of a spy in the secret service of the Russian tsar. The response of Metternich was immediate and harsh. He persuaded the Diet of the German Confederation to issue the Carlsbad Decrees (1819), which dissolved student associations, muzzled the press, and throttled academic freedom.

Berlin follows the example of Paris. The echo of the 1848 revolution in France did not take long to reach discontented liberals and workingmen throughout Europe, leaving only Russia and Turkey untouched. At public assemblies convened in various German cities, patriotic liberals declared the unity of Germany and began to plan for a national assembly at Frankfurt which would draft a German constitution.

On March 15, 1848, the subjects of the Prussian monarch, King Frederick William IV, finally gave vent to their long-repressed political aspirations in serious rioting in Berlin. As in Paris, barricades sprang up all over the city, and for several days fighting went on between the people and the army. In this crisis the king lost his nerve, ordered his soldiers to leave Berlin, and proceeded to make peace with "his dear Berliners." Humiliated and coerced, the sovereign promised a constitution, a parliament, and support for a united Germany. Following this remarkable popular victory, the rulers of other German states agreed to establish constitutional governments and granted various privileges such as freedom of the press.

The Frankfurt Assembly. As the crowning symbol of the revolutionary fervor that was sweeping Europe in 1848, the Frankfurt Assembly opened its first session on May 18. Over five hundred members attended, coming from the various German states, from Austria proper, and even from Bohemia, which had a large German minority in its population. The guns boomed, the church bells pealed, and a vast crowd applauded as the newly inducted president of the Assembly announced: "We are to create a constitution for Germany, for the whole Empire."

This objective posed two fundamental problems: Just what was meant by *Germany*, and what manner of government should be devised for the new empire? In regard to the first problem, some believed that a united Germany should include all Germans in central Europe; such a state would include Austria proper (but not Hungary) and probably, because of its large and prosperous German minority, Bohemia. On the other hand, some representatives believed that Austria should not be included in the new Germany. The first faction wanted to offer

the new imperial crown to the Hapsburg sovereign in Vienna, the second to the Hohenzollern king of Prussia.

Failure of the Frankfurt Assembly and the "Humiliation of Olmütz." Perhaps the most tragic disappointment of 1848 was the failure of the Frankfurt Assembly and, with it, of the liberal cause in Germany. From May to December 1848, a period in which the need for action was imperative, the Frankfurt Assembly spent its time eloquently debating academic topics. Gradually the conservatives in the German states began to rally around their rulers to undo the work of the reformers. In Prussia King Frederick William regained his confidence; the army proved loyal; and the peasants apparently had little interest in political reform. By November 1848 the king and his army were again in full control of Berlin.

Even though the forces of reaction had definitely gained the ascendancy, the Frankfurt Assembly continued its work. It approved the Declaration of the Rights of the German People, an inspiring document which set forth the liberal political and social ideals of the reformers. In April 1849 a constitution was approved for a united Germany, with an emperor advised by a ministry and a legislature elected by secret manhood suf-

In 1848, following the example of the French, Germans rioted in Berlin, thus forcing Frederick William to promise governmental reforms, which he then failed to carry out.

In 1848, following the fall of Metternich, politically minded University of Vienna students sought to politicize the workers and turn them against the administration. The students are shown here collecting contributions "For the Workers."

frage. In this blueprint Austria was excluded for the simple reason that it had refused to join the new union. When the leadership of the new German Reich was offered to King Frederick William IV of Prussia, he refused to accept it, later declaring that he could not "pick up a crown from the gutter." After this contemptuous refusal, most of the members of the Assembly sadly returned to their homes. The Prussian army was called in to quell riots in various parts of the Germanies, and thousands of prominent middle-class liberals fled, many migrating to the United States.

In 1850 the Prussian king issued his own constitution, a document that paid lip service to parliamentary government but kept all real power in the hands of the sovereign and the upper classes. Prussia meanwhile sponsored a confederation of north German states, without Austria and with Frederick

William himself as head. This plan was not to the liking of either Austria or Russia, which feared the idea of a strong, Prussian-dominated Germany. A conference of the three interested powers followed at Olmütz in 1850. The Prussian king was persuaded to drop his plan, and it was agreed to restore the German Confederation as set up at the Congress of Vienna in 1815. Austria was still the mistress of central Europe, and Prussian ambitions to secure the leadership of the German states had been checkmated. Anti-Austrian Germans never forgot the "Humiliation of Olmütz."

Revolts in Austria, Hungary, and Bohemia. In the meantime the nationalist spirit was increasing among the Magyars of Hungary. Czechs, Poles, Croats, Serbs, and Bulgars also began to take pride in their distinctive national cultures, to agitate for national independence where it was lacking, and to feel a sense of kinship and common destiny with all Slavic groups. In Bohemia nationalist scholars studied the literature and customs of the Bohemian people, and newspapers in the Czech language were established.

In March 1848 the leading Hungarian nationalist, Louis Kossuth (1802-1894), gave a momentous speech before the Hungarian Diet. He electrified his listeners as he castigated the "stagnant bureaucratic system" and spoke of "the pestilential air blowing from the Vienna charnel house and its deadening effect upon all phases of Hungarian life." He demanded parliamentary government for the entire empire. Avidly read in Vienna, this speech inspired Austrian students and workers to rise in revolt. The frightened emperor forced Metternich to resign and flee to England. Meanwhile the Hungarian Diet declared the nation independent, tied to Austria only through a common sovereign. Constitutional rights were guaranteed, and serfdom and special privilege were ended.

The emperor accepted these reforms and promised a constitution for Austria and the end of serfdom in the empire. The once radical peasants now became conservative supporters of the regime. The emperor was forced to promise the Czechs in Bohemia the same concessions granted the Hungarians.

But in June 1848 German and Czech nationalists began to quarrel, and the upshot was that the Czechs revolted. Austrian forces bombarded and subdued Prague; thus ended all aspirations for an autonomous new kingdom of Bohemia.

Austria's success in Bohemia gave the emperor's advisers a pattern to follow. The quarrel between Germans and Czechs in Bohemia was being paralleled in Hungary. As head of the government, Kossuth was a proponent of rigorous Magyarization; he announced that he would not recognize the claims of any of the other national groups in Hungary. In protest, South Slavs under a capable Croatian named Jellachich attacked the Magyars, and civil war ensued. Taking advantage of the situation, the Austrian emperor made Jellachich an imperial general. Following his victory over the Magyars, Jellachich was ordered to Vienna, where, in October 1848, he forced the surrender of the liberals in control of the Austrian capital.

The next step taken to counter the revolution was to induce the weak and incapable Emperor Ferdinand I to abdicate in favor of his young nephew, Francis Joseph. The Austrian government then proceeded to repeal its concessions to Hungary, arguing that the new emperor was not bound by the acts of his predecessor. Infuriated at this treachery, the Hungarians declared complete independence and proceeded to put up a desperate defense against the invading Austrian armies. The intervention in Hungary of Tsar Nicholas I of Russia with 100,000 troops in the summer of 1849 ended any hope of victory, and in August all resistance ceased. Kossuth escaped and found refuge in the United States.

NATIONAL RESURGENCE IN ITALY

Mazzini and the Risorgimento. In Italy after 1815, the Hapsburgs ruled over some unhappy provinces in the north and northeast and dominated the little independent states throughout the peninsula. It was perhaps natural that this frustrated land should produce the most famous exemplar of romantic nationalism, Giuseppe Mazzini (1805-1872), the son of a professor at the University of Genoa. Fired by the revolutionary zeal of romantic poets such as Byron, Mazzini in the 1820's joined the *Carbonari* (see p. 504).

In 1830 Mazzini was implicated in an unsuccessful revolution against the royal government of Sardinia and was imprisoned for six months. Following his release, he established a new patriotic society known as Young Italy. Appealing mainly to students and intellectuals, he initiated a new phase of the Italian nationalist movement known as the *Risorgimento* (Resurgence).

Mazzini was intensely religious, and to him loyalty to the nation came midway between a man's loyalty to his family and that to his God. But unlike leaders of nationalism later in the century, who arrogantly preached the superiority of their own people, Mazzini

Giuseppe Mazzini's lifework was revolution. Catalyst of the *Risorgimento*, Mazzini decried the doctrine of individual rights as a breeding ground for selfishness and competition and espoused a "universal" nationalism whereby all men would be brothers.

believed that the people of every nation should work for the benefit of their brothers throughout the world.

Revolution, reform, and reaction in Italy. The year 1848 saw a rash of revolutions on the Italian peninsula. The Sicilians revolted against the corrupt rule of the king of Naples, forcing him to promise a liberal constitution; the Venetian populace rose against their Austrian rulers and proclaimed a republic; and in Milan, the center of discontent against Austria in Lombardy, a few homemade cannon and an assortment of firearms wielded by an indomitable citizenry forced the Austrian army to retreat northward. The king of Sardinia, Charles Albert of the House of Savoy, voluntarily promulgated a new liberal constitution, destined to become the constitution of a united Italy until the rise of Mussolini's Fascist dictatorship after World War I. Charles Albert also assumed the leadership in driving the Austrians out of Lombardy and Venetia.

Other states such as Tuscany granted their people liberal constitutions, and absolute government in Italy almost disappeared. In the Papal States a program of reform had begun as early as 1846, when Pius IX had been elected pope. Known as the "Reforming Pope," he released many political prisoners and initiated moderate political reforms.

The liberal triumphs achieved by revolution and reform were soon swept away. While regaining their mastery of Hungary, the Hapsburgs began throttling the liberal national movement in Italy. For their part, the Italians suffered not only from incompetent generalship but also from disunity; many wanted a republican Italy, not a united Italian monarchy. In July 1848 the Austrians defeated Charles Albert at the decisive battle of Custozza. After another defeat in May 1849, he abdicated in favor of his oldest son, who became Victor Emmanuel II. Victorious over the House of Savoy, Austria quickly helped restore old rulers and systems of government throughout Italy as they had been before 1848. And in the south, the Sicilian liberal movement was brutally crushed by the king of Naples, who abolished the new constitution.

The final episode of the Italian revolutions was the rise and fall of the republic of Rome. In November 1848, when Pope Pius IX refused to join actively against Catholic Austria in the struggle for a united Italy, his subjects forced him to flee from Rome. Early in the following year the papal domain was declared a republic, and Mazzini was called in to head it. The flight of the pope brought a wave of indignation in conservative circles throughout Europe, and Louis Napoleon, president of the Second French Republic, gained the support of French Catholics and conservatives by sending an expeditionary force which crushed the Roman republic in July 1849. The restored Pius IX was now bitterly hostile to all liberal and national ideas.

THE REVOLUTIONARY ERA IN RETROSPECT

Why democratic movements failed. The account of the rise and fall of the short-lived Roman republic ends the story of the widespread struggles for reform from 1848 to 1852. Looking back from the perspective of more than a hundred years, we can now see that the failure of the democratic movement in Europe in 1848 was one of the most decisive happenings in modern history; it helped shape the course not only of the nineteenth century but also that of the twentieth. What accounted for the failure?

One factor was excessive nationalism. It had been Mazzini's hope that men could be good Europeans as well as solid nationalists; but the events of 1848 showed that Europeans, whether democrats or reactionaries, were first and last Italians or Czechs or Germans, as the case might be. Kossuth, for example, refused to recognize the same national rights for the Croats and Serbs that he demanded for his own Magyar people. The problem posed to the men of 1848 was how to devise arrangements that would allow the various national groups to exercise political rights and enjoy cultural autonomy within some larger unit of cooperation. No progress was made in this direction.

Another element was the fact that romantic idealism was shown to be ineffectual in the realm of practical affairs. The idealist, the pacifist, and the internationalist were completely discredited. After 1848 romanticism in politics was superseded by the doctrine of realism, which placed its faith in power and resorted to any means to gain its ends.

Perhaps the most significant factor explaining the failure of the revolutions of 1848 was the emergence of class struggle as a factor in European politics. Since the peasants had little interest in revolution once the old feudal obligations had been removed, the movement became primarily the product of the middle class and the large-city workers. The leaders of the former wanted to transfer power from the aristocrats and upper bourgeoisie into their own hands; spokesmen for the latter wanted a social and economic change that would guarantee them a fair share in profits and in political control. In numerous instances a revolution was effected by a coalition between workers and bourgeoisie, but this cooperation soon broke down. The importance of the bloody June Days in Paris cannot be overestimated. The excesses of the Paris mob horrified both the intellectual and the bourgeois. By the end of 1848 it seemed that the observations of Marx and Engels in the Communist Manifesto issued on the eve of the revolutions of 1848 (see p. 496) might be justified—that perhaps there was an irreconcilable gulf between proletariat and bourgeoisie that could be resolved only by force.

Achievements of the 1848 revolutions. In spite of the overall failure of the revolutions of 1848, there were important immediate gains. Serfdom was not restored in the Austrian empire; Sardinia maintained its liberal constitution; and all the German states—even Prussia—had parliaments, even if most of them were not of the democratic variety. Even these limited successes offered fair indication that the nationalistic and democratic movements would continue to press forward in important areas, that the victory of absolutism and reaction would not be permanent. The movements of 1848 at least clarified what some of the unsolved problems were. Within the next twenty years the political structure of Europe was to be turned topsy-turvy, as constitutional government and nationalism made significant gains.

Metternich's place in history. As one looks back on this turbulent revolutionary era with its clash of opposing ideas, two symbols stand out in bold relief—the barricades and Metternich. In recent years some historians have been more kind in evaluating the Austrian statesman than were his contemporaries. Appalled by the chaos and conflict of the twentieth century, which they attribute to breakneck change, the fanaticism of nationalism, and the frequently emotional basis of politics in twentieth-century mass democracy, these scholars see a praiseworthy stability in the conservative system championed by Metternich from 1815 to 1848. Yet a complete absence of change is no better than too much change. Metternich failed to understand that the art of real statesmanship must provide for the attempt to bring together, in reasonable equilibrium, the best of the old forces and the most promising of the new. As a British historian has observed: "He saw no mean between revolution and autocracy, and since revolution was odious, he set himself to repress that which is the soul of human life in society, the very spirit of liberty."[5]

SUMMARY

The period from 1815 to 1850 witnessed such important events as the realization of Greek and Belgian independence, the passing of the Reform Bill of 1832 in England, the brief experiment with the Second Republic in France, and a rash of revolutions in Italy, the Austrian empire, and the Germanies in 1848. Behind all these events were four movements—nationalism, political liberalism, democracy, and romanticism. Nationalism moved all national groups to struggle for independence and the freedom to direct their own affairs without interference. Political liberalism—constitutional government dominated by the well-to-do—experienced significant victories and equally significant failures; and the ideals of democracy—full political equality—while remaining largely beneath the surface, were spreading. The intellectual and artistic movement known as romanticism glorified the rights of the individual and believed somewhat naively in the essential goodness of human nature.

An epidemic of revolutions in 1820-1821 and again in 1830 definitely showed that the European pattern laid out in 1815 by ultraconservative statesmen at the Congress of Vienna could not be maintained. In 1848 the great explosion came, leaving only Turkey and Russia untouched. A larger and more prosperous middle class had arisen, together with a numerous body of intellectuals who had been strongly moved by the gospels of freedom and nationality. And in the cities the Industrial Revolution was creating a growing mass of workers who resented their poverty and who also had dreams of their own.

The revolutionary fervor of 1848 did not, however, fulfill its expectations. Perhaps never has such a widespread, popular, and seemingly successful movement collapsed so quickly. The explanation for this failure is complex, but three factors of special importance should be singled out. The first was the inexperience and lack of realism of popular leaders. There was too much discussion and too little practical planning. Second, the force of nationalism, so powerful an enemy of autocracy at the outset, soon showed itself to be a selfish and exclusive movement that set the various liberated nationalities to quarreling among themselves. Third, the development of class consciousness put the middle class and the proletariat at odds.

Turning to the international scene, a significant phenomenon in European history during this period was the experiment in intergovernmental consultation and cooperation called the Congress System, or the Concert of Europe. Although the ends it sought were the prevention of change and although its effectiveness was short-lived, the Congress System—the first serious attempt to preserve peace by means of collective security—represented a positive step forward.

SUGGESTIONS FOR READING

The following are excellent on the general background of the period 1815-1850: J. McManners, **European History, 1789-1914,*** Torchbooks; A. J. May, **The Age of Metternich, 1814-1848,*** rev. ed., Holt, Rinehart & Winston (very brief); E. Hobsbawm, **The Age of Revolution: Europe, 1789-1848,*** Mentor; J. Droz, **Europe Between Revolutions, 1815-1848,*** Torchbooks; F. Artz, **Reaction and Revolution, 1814-1832,*** Torchbooks; W. L. Langer, **Political and Social Upheaval, 1832-1852,*** Torchbooks; J. Talmon, **Romanticism and Revolt: Europe, 1815-1848,*** Harcourt, Brace & World, 1967; Peter Stearns, **European Society in Upheaval: Social History Since 1800,*** Macmillan, 1967.

H. Nicolson, **The Congress of Vienna: A Study in Allied Unity, 1812-1822,*** Compass. Good reading. L. Seaman, **From Vienna to Versailles,*** Colophon, is a short diplomatic history especially good on the Congress System. See also Henry A. Kissinger, **A World Restored: Metternich, Castlereagh and the Problems of Peace, 1812-1822,*** Sentry; and Henry F. Schwartz, ed., **Metternich, the "Coachman of Europe": Statesman or Evil Genius?*** Heath.

G. Fasel, **Europe in Upheaval: The Revolutions of 1848,*** Rand McNally, 1970. A valuable short synthesis of recent scholarship. Priscilla Robertson, **The Revolutions of 1848: A Social History,*** Princeton, is colorful and entertaining. A scholarly reassessment is F. Fejto, ed., **The Opening of an Era, 1848: An Historical Symposium,** Fertig, 1966. G. Rudé, **The Crowd in History, 1730-1848,*** Wiley, describes how crowds were turned into bellicose mobs.

John B. Wolf, **France, 1814-1919: The Rise of a Liberal-Democratic Society,*** Torchbooks; A. Cobban, **A History of Modern France,*** Vol. II, Penguin. Notable surveys. For greater detail see F. Artz, **France Under the Bourbon Restoration, 1814-1830,** Russell, 1963; T. Howarth, **Citizen King: The Life of Louis-Philippe, King of the French,** Verry, 1961; G. Duveau, **1848: The Making of a Revolution,*** Vintage, 1968; F. A. Simpson, **The Rise of Louis Napoleon,** Longmans, 1950.

Asa Briggs, **The Making of Modern England, 1783-1867: The Age of Improvement,*** Torchbooks; E. L. Woodward, **The Age of Reform, 1815-1870,** 2nd ed., Oxford, 1962. Valuable surveys. On social and economic change from 1815 to 1885 see S. Checkland, **The Rise of Industrial Society in England,** St. Martin's, 1964.

A. J. P. Taylor, **The Course of German History,*** Capricorn. A short, pithy essay on German national history since the French Revolution. T. Hamerow, **Restoration, Revolution, Reaction: Economics and Politics in Germany, 1815-1871,*** Princeton, is highly praised. L. Namier, **1848: The Revolution of the Intellectuals,*** Anchor, is critical of the German liberals in the Frankfurt Assembly.

Barbara Jelavich, **The Habsburg Empire in European Affairs, 1814-1918,*** Rand McNally, 1969. An excellent brief history of the empire. A. J. P. Taylor, **The Habsburg Monarchy, 1809-1918,*** Torchbooks, is chatty and spirited.

A. J. Whyte, **The Evolution of Modern Italy, 1715-1920,*** Norton. A sound survey. G. Salvemini, **Mazzini,*** Collier, is an authoritative biography.

*Indicates an inexpensive paperbound edition.

Chapter 23

Nationalism and Authoritarian Regimes

The Politics of Power: 1850-1914

INTRODUCTION. After 1850 the tempo of political change in Europe increased rapidly as the forces of nationalism and democracy more and more predominated over the forces of conservatism and reaction. While these two progressive forces were usually present in varying degrees in every European state during this period, the present chapter will concentrate on the movement of nationalism —the major victories, partial successes, and failures of attempts to achieve national self-determination, together with the significant changes in the European power structure resulting from the pursuit of national interests. While some democratic institutions appeared in Germany, Austria-Hungary, and Russia, these essentially were window dressing covering the realities of authoritarianism. The major triumphs of democracy in Europe from 1850 to 1914 will be surveyed in Chapter 24. (For national and democratic movements in the non-European world during this period, see Chapters 26 and 27.)

Divided Italy, so long merely a "geographical expression," at last achieved national unification. Under Prussian rule the

German states were welded into a unified German empire. Austria achieved an uneasy accord as the Germans of Vienna and the Magyars of Budapest joined forces to check the aspirations of other nationalities in the creaky Hapsburg empire.

This era of nation-making is important not only for what happened but also for the attitudes of those involved. Political objectives were neither confused with the romantic dreams of poets nor modeled on the utopias imagined by idealistic intellectuals. Instead, they were practical goals, ruthlessly pursued by such pragmatic statesmen as Bismarck and Cavour.

Generally speaking, nationalism and nation-making in Europe was a bloody business. From 1815 to 1848 no single major conflict occurred, but from the midpoint of the century to the 1870's, six wars were fought—some of major proportions. Within this period every major European power went to war at least once. These conflicts swept away the settlements created at Vienna in 1815. The smashing defeat of France in the Franco-Prussian War (1870-1871) marked the demise of the Second French Empire and heralded the rise of the new German empire to a position of supremacy among the countries on the Continent.

The creation of major nations by extraordinary unification movements as in Italy and Germany was paralleled by the formation of several smaller nations from the European part of Turkey. The Balkan subjects of the Ottoman empire were infected with the nineteenth-century fever of European nationalism, and their efforts to attain national self-determination were repeatedly encouraged or frustrated by the major European powers, following their own national interests.

A prime objective of Russia's tsars during the nineteenth century was to partition the dominions of the Turks, seize Constantinople, and gain access to the eastern Mediterranean. This ambition was persistently blocked by British diplomacy and British arms. The conflict between the great powers—especially the rivalry between Russia and England—over the holdings of the decaying Ottoman empire came to be known as the Near Eastern Question. This international issue was complicated by continuing Balkan unrest and by emerging nationalist sentiment in Arab lands, also under Ottoman rule. The Near Eastern Question has continued into the twentieth century, becoming critical once again in the years following World War II. The Russians, whether tsarists or Communists, have never abandoned their plans to one day gain control of the Turkish Straits and extend their rule to the shores of the Mediterranean Sea.

NATION-MAKING IN ITALY

Common denominators in Italian and German unification. The two most important achievements of nineteenth-century European nationalism were the unifications of Italy and Germany. This addition of two new, powerful nation-states radically altered the European state system.

Both Italy and Germany were built around a dynamic nucleus—the kingdom of Sardinia, whose center was the mainland territory of Piedmont, and the kingdom of Prussia. Both Italy and Germany had a common obstacle to national unity—Austria, since 1815 master of central Europe. In the case of Italian unification, however, a special complication was the existence of the Papal States, ruled from Rome by the pope. The Italian nationalists were faced with the problem of stripping this great religious leader of his secular powers and absorbing his territories into a united Italy without incurring the wrath of the Catholic powers in Europe.

Both the German and the Italian unifications were ultimately achieved not by romantic poets or intellectuals but by the dispassionate calculations of practical statesmen who exercised the art of diplomacy divorced from ethical considerations. This kind of statecraft is known as *Realpolitik*; in Germany it became identified with the policy that Bismarck called "blood and iron."

Count Cavour. In the early part of the 1850's Italy still remained what Metternich had contemptuously called it—"a geographical expression." The Young Italy movement of Mazzini and the first phase of the *Risorgimento* had failed. Except in Sardinia, where young King Victor Emmanuel II refused to abrogate the liberal constitution granted by his late father, Charles Albert, there was reaction and repression. This victory of autocracy, however, was more apparent than real. Mazzini's appeal for a free Italy had taken root and proceeded to grow quietly but rapidly in the decade following 1848.

A new and vigorous phase of the Italian *Risorgimento* began with the career of Count Camillo Benso di Cavour (1810-1861), one of the most important statesmen of the nineteenth century. Born of a noble family in Sardinia, Cavour was educated for a military career, but after traveling in Switzerland, France, and England, he became a thoroughgoing liberal and began to ponder on how best to free Italy from Austrian domination. In 1852 Cavour became prime minister of Sardinia. Well aware that Sardinia alone could not oust the Austrians from the Italian peninsula, Cavour determined to "put Sardinia on the map," hoping to find an ally for his cause. His first move astonished Europe; in 1855 Sardinia joined Britain and France in their fight against Russia in the Crimean War (see p. 543). Although this step at first appeared ridiculous, it enabled Cavour to speak at the peace conference one year later, where he called attention to Italy's grievances.

The Austro-Italian War. Cavour's speech impressed Napoleon III, who became the ally Cavour was seeking. In 1858 the French emperor and Cavour held a secret meeting in France. It was agreed that if Cavour could trick Austria into war, France would come to Sardinia's assistance and help eject Austria from the Italian provinces of Lombardy and Venetia. Sardinia was then to rule over all of northern Italy. In return, France would receive from Sardinia two provinces—Nice and Savoy—which had been part of France during the Napoleonic period.

Within a year Cavour had tricked Austria into war by blowing up into major proportions a minor crisis over Austria's conscription of soldiers from Lombardy and Venetia. He offered sanctuary to Italian deserters and began to mobilize the Sardinian army— moves which prompted Austria to attack. Two bloody battles were fought at Magenta and Solferino, and the Austrian troops were driven out of Lombardy by Sardinian and French soldiers. Again the call for Italian unity was heard across the land. Revolutions broke out in Tuscany, Modena, Parma, and Romagna.

During the progress of the fighting, the Italians acclaimed Napoleon III as their savior and liberator. But before the allied armies could invade Austrian-held Venetia, the French emperor—without consulting Cavour—made a separate peace with Austria. Too late, Napoleon III realized that he had started a movement destined to unite not only northern Italy but the whole peninsula, creating a strong rival on the borders of France. He also suspected that Cavour had designs against the Papal States, a policy which would alienate French Catholics.

Although Cavour was furious, in 1859 he agreed to a peace settlement with Austria by which Lombardy was added to Sardinia, the exiled rulers of Parma, Modena, Tuscany, and Romagna were restored, and an Italian confederation was created in which Austria, as ruler of Venetia, was included. One year later, largely through the auspices of Great Britain, plebiscites were conducted in Italy. Tuscany, Modena, and Parma voted to join Sardinia. French expectations were satisfied when Nice and Savoy were ceded to France.

Garibaldi and his Red Shirts. The center of interest now shifted to southern Italy and to a new Italian leader. Giuseppe Garibaldi (1807-1882), a follower of Mazzini who had been forced into exile after the unsuccessful revolutionary movement of 1848, returned to Italy in 1854. Secretly subsidized by Cavour, Garibaldi recruited one thousand tough adventurers, his immortal Red Shirts, and in 1860 successfully invaded and conquered the island of Sicily, part of the reactionary, pro-Austrian kingdom of Naples and Sicily.

Next he turned to the mainland and attacked the remaining forces of the king of Naples and Sicily. The Neapolitan troops were not loyal, and Garibaldi took the city of Naples without a battle.

Garibaldi planned to set up a separate democratic government, which would have been a serious obstacle to the creation of a united Italy. Cavour therefore rushed troops to Naples, and Garibaldi surrendered his power to the king of Sardinia, Victor Emmanuel II. By November 1860 Sardinia had annexed the former kingdom of Naples and Sicily and all the papal lands except Rome and its surrounding territory, known as the Patrimony of St. Peter.

Garibaldi was a romantic nationalist and a daredevil adventurer, but he had little of the diplomat in him. Without realizing the political danger of his action, the conqueror of Naples resolved to attack the territories still under papal rule and force them to come into a united Italian kingdom. Such a move would alienate Catholics all over the world and probably precipitate war with France, since Napoleon III had stationed troops at Rome to protect the pope. To avoid the danger, Sardinian troops in 1862 forcibly restrained the Garibaldian volunteers from attacking Rome. This action disgusted Garibaldi, who had little use for high diplomacy. Refusing all the financial rewards and honors proffered him by Victor Emmanuel, he sailed once more into exile.

Unity achieved. Italy's first parliament met at Turin in February 1861. A new nation of 22 million citizens had been created, but the task had not yet been completed. Austria still controlled Venetia, while Rome and the Patrimony of St. Peter were still under papal control. Cavour, who died in 1861, did not live to see the full fruits of his works, but he realized that a united Italy was not far off. Although many have criticized his duplicity, he himself made no attempt to hide the true nature of his methods. He once said: "If we did for ourselves what we do for our country, what rascals we should be."[1]

In the decade following Cavour's death, Italian policy followed his principles. By acting as an ally of Prussia during the war between Prussia and Austria in 1866 (see p. 528), Italy obtained Venetia. And when the Franco-Prussian War broke out in 1870 and French troops were withdrawn from Rome, Italian troops took possession of the Eternal City. In 1871 Rome became the capital of a unified Italy.

Italy after unification. Italy still faced serious problems. The country had few natural resources, and the interests of the industrial north often clashed with those of the agricultural south. Furthermore, a religious issue seriously weakened the state: the seizure of Rome, the last remnant of the Papal States, had alienated the pope. Terming himself "the prisoner of the Vatican," the pope called on Italian Catholics to refrain from voting. In an attempt at conciliation, the Italian government passed the Law of Papal Guarantees, by which the pope was to have the Vatican as a sovereign state and was to be given an annual sum of $600,000. Although this offer was rejected, the law was not repealed.

THE UNIFICATION OF ITALY 1859–1870

- Kingdom of Sardinia to 1859
- To Kingdom of Sardinia 1860
- Annexed to Kingdom of Sardinia 1861; establishes Kingdom of Italy
- To Kingdom of Italy 1866
- To Kingdom of Italy 1870

In the field of politics, the people lacked experience in or aptitude for constitutional government. Seventy-five percent of the population was illiterate in 1861, and the franchise was very restricted. As late as 1904 only 29 percent of the adult male population could vote, and of this group only 38 percent actually went to the polls. Political life also suffered from unstable coalitions.

Another grievous burden for the country was its leaders' ambition to have Italy play a grand role in the world and thus fulfill the dreams of greatness built up during the *Risorgimento*. Too much money was spent on the army, and national resources were squandered in the unrewarding pursuit of empire in Africa.

Early in the twentieth century liberals joined socialists in demanding such reforms as compulsory education, freedom of the press, and better working conditions for the masses. As a result, in 1912 laws were passed providing for universal suffrage and for payment of deputies in parliament.

Although his dream of an Italian republic was not realized, Giuseppe Garibaldi remained a national hero because of his fight for the unification of Italy.

THE TRIUMPH OF BLOOD AND IRON IN GERMANY

Prussia and the German nationalistic movement. Although the German revolution of 1848 and the Frankfurt Assembly failed to achieve their liberal-national purposes, the nationalist movement in Germany was far from dead. German nationalism was accelerated by the activities of a group of remarkable German historians. Such scholars as Heinrich von Treitschke saw in the Italian struggle a clear example to follow; Treitschke eloquently advocated the union of all Germans under the leadership of Prussia: "There is only one salvation! One state, one monarchic Germany under the Hohenzollern dynasty."[2]

Economic factors also proved to be significant in the German unification movement. Of special importance was the Zollverein, or customs union, initiated by Prussia in 1834, which instituted free trade throughout Prussia and the territories of other member states (but excluded Austria). By 1842 most of the German states belonged to the Zollverein. This tariff union not only demonstrated that closer economic cooperation was good business for the various states but also strengthened the interest of the German middle class in the nationalist movement. Most important, by increasing the economic ties between the German states, the Zollverein made easier their political unity under Prussia. (All members of the Zollverein except Luxemburg eventually became part of the German empire.)

Prussian government and public administration were modern and efficient. Civil servants were well trained, honest, and highly devoted to the service of the state. The hierarchy of government bureaus and departments was logical and functional. By the middle of the century the general citizenry of Prussia attended public schools far in advance of those found in any of the other great powers, or in the United States; and Prussian higher education enjoyed an enviable reputation throughout Europe. By 1850 Prussia was rapidly building up the strength to compel central Europe to do its bidding, but it was twelve years before there appeared the man who was to formulate the necessary orders.

Bismarck and his policy of blood and iron. The unification of Germany was achieved through the genius of a consummate statesman, Otto von Bismarck (1815-1898). The future German chancellor grew up a typical Prussian aristocrat, or Junker, an enemy to all liberal ideas and an uncompromising supporter of the Prussian state and its king. As a university student, Bismarck made little impression on his professors but astonished his comrades by his beer-drinking capacity and gained renown as a duelist. In 1847 he entered politics and found this career to his liking. Soon he joined the diplomatic corps and served as Prussian ambassador in St. Petersburg and in Paris.

In 1862 Bismarck was called to be Prussian prime minister. His appointment coincided with a serious constitutional crisis: the king wished to strengthen the army, but the Chamber of Deputies would not approve the necessary appropriations. Following Bismarck's advice, the king successfully defied the legislature and levied the necessary taxes without its consent.

With meticulous care Bismarck prepared for the task of building a powerful new German empire. He was a superb master of diplomatic intrigue and a practitioner of *Realpolitik*—the "politics of reality." Boldly, he declared:

Germany does not look to Prussia's liberalism, but to her power. . . . The great questions of the day are not to be decided by speeches and majority resolutions—therein lay the weakness of 1848 and 1849—but by blood and iron![3]

Wars against Denmark and Austria. In 1864 Bismarck invited Austria to join Prussia in waging war on Denmark, the issue being the status of two duchies bordering on Prussia and Denmark—Schleswig and Holstein—which were claimed by both Denmark and the German Confederation. The Prussian army, aided by Austrian forces, easily smashed the Danish defenses; the administration of Holstein was awarded to Austria, while Schleswig came under Prussian rule.

Once Denmark had been defeated, Bismarck proceeded to isolate Austria and force it to withdraw from German affairs. The new kingdom of Italy was promised Venetia if it would assist Prussia should war come, and the French emperor was induced to be neutral by intimations of Prussian support should France seek to widen its frontiers. Bismarck then provoked war with Austria by expressing alarm over the way the Austrians were ruling Holstein and sending Prussian troops into the province. Hostilities broke out in 1866 and lasted only seven weeks. At the battle of Sadowa the Austrian army was defeated by superior Prussian forces, which had been made into the most efficient fighting machine in the world.

To avoid humiliating Austria, Prussia offered a moderate peace settlement, ending the old German Confederation. In its place the North German Confederation was formed under Prussian domination. Austria and the south German states (Bavaria, Württemberg, Baden, and Hesse-Darmstadt) were excluded —the former at the insistence of Bismarck, who wanted Austria removed from German affairs, and the latter at the insistence of the French emperor, who feared the power of a united Germany. Prussia annexed Holstein, Hanover, and a number of small states extending southward to the Main River, thus at long last bridging the gap between its major territories (see map, p. 530).

The Franco-Prussian War. Two barriers remained to Bismarck's plans for a united Germany under Prussian leadership—France with its centuries-old policy of keeping Germany disunited and weak, and the south German states with their distrust of Prussia. Both obstacles were removed when Bismarck succeeded in maneuvering Napoleon III into declaring war on Prussia.

As early as 1865 Napoleon III in a fateful conference with Bismarck had allowed himself to be completely hoodwinked. In return for vague promises—the German statesman mentioned securing for France "perhaps the Palatinate and the Rhine frontier, perhaps Luxemburg, perhaps part of Belgium or Switzerland"[4]—the French emperor pledged himself not to interfere in any Austro-Prussian war. After the conflict had been decided by the Prussian victory at Sadowa, Bismarck announced that he had no recollection of promises made to France. Napoleon III thereupon specifically raised the possibility of French compensation at the expense of Belgium, and an agreement was drawn up in which Bismarck backed this claim in return for French recognition of the federal union of all German states. Bismarck next saw to it that the document was made public in England, the nation where it would do the most harm to France. The British became openly hostile to Napoleon III, and Bismarck thus made certain that there would be no British support of France in case of war. At the same time, by supporting Russia during the Polish revolt in 1863 (see p. 539) and by offering Austria a moderate peace in 1866, Bismarck successfully isolated France from these two states.

Too late, Napoleon III realized that a great rival power was in the making and that France could no longer claim to be the "mistress of Europe." The cry, "Revenge for Sadowa," radiated from Paris. Bismarck also welcomed war. He was convinced that Napoleon's need to recoup his prestige would lead finally to his undoing. It was also Bismarck's belief that a war with France would stimulate patriotic feeling in the south German states and lead to the unification of all Germany.

The immediate cause of the war centered on the succession to the Spanish throne, left vacant after a revolution exiled the reactionary Spanish queen. Leopold, a Hohenzollern prince, was invited to become constitutional king of Spain. In the eyes of the French government, a Hohenzollern on the throne of Spain would be an unwelcome extension of Prussian influence. Because of French protests, Leopold withdrew his candidacy, but the French government then made a fatal mistake. The French ambassador was sent to Ems, where the Prussian king was visiting, to demand that William I promise that no Hohenzollern would ever sit on the Spanish throne. The king politely refused this unreasonable request and directed that a dispatch (the "Ems dispatch") be sent to Bismarck acquainting him with the results of the interview. Bismarck altered the dis-

A French cartoon published before the Franco-Prussian War shows France about to sweep away Bismarck's victim-laden web.

patch slightly in order to give the impression that the French ambassador had insulted the Prussian king and that the ruler had thereupon retaliated and insulted the ambassador. When this version of the dispatch was published, both the French and the Prussian people were infuriated.

France declared war in July 1870, and amid wild enthusiasm and shouts of "On to Berlin" the French regiments marched to the front. But there was no comparison between the superbly trained Prussian hosts and the badly disorganized French army. The French suffered reverse after reverse. In September came the crowning disaster—the surrender at Sedan, where an entire French army and the emperor himself were forced to capitulate. New leaders emerged to carry on resistance against the German forces, and Paris withstood a siege of four months before surrendering. By the Treaty of Frankfurt, France lost Alsace and part of Lorraine to Prussia and was required to pay a huge indemnity. Many Frenchmen never forgot this humiliation. History was to give France a chance to retaliate after World War I.

The Second (Hohenzollern) Reich. During the Franco-Prussian War the south German states, moved by patriotic enthusiasm, had joined the North German Confederation. Thus the common struggle against France removed the last obstacle to national unification. In January 1871, in the Hall of Mirrors at the palace of Versailles, King William of Prussia was proclaimed German emperor. The new German empire (Reich)—a federal union of twenty-six states with a population of about 41 million—included the kingdoms of Prussia, Bavaria, Saxony, and Württemberg, various grand duchies and duchies, three city republics, and the imperial territory of Alsace-Lorraine.

Headed by the German emperor, the imperial government consisted of a legislative upper house, the Bundesrat, representing the ruling houses of the various states; and a lower house, the Reichstag, representing the people. The 61 members of the Bundesrat voted as instructed by their royal masters.

The 397 members of the Reichstag were elected by manhood suffrage, but they had little power. Thus the Hohenzollern empire had a few parliamentary trappings, but behind this facade of democracy was the dominant power of reactionary Prussia.

The office of German emperor was vested in the Hohenzollern dynasty so that the king of Prussia was at the same time kaiser of the empire. The kaiser wielded considerable power in military and foreign affairs. As king of Prussia, he also controlled seventeen votes in the Bundesrat. No amendment to the constitution could pass this body if opposed by fourteen votes. Prussia also controlled the chairmanships of practically all the standing committees in the Bundesrat.

Appointed by the emperor and responsible to him alone, the chancellor was the actual head of the government. Unlike the situation in the English House of Commons or the French Chamber of Deputies, the German chancellor could defy or ignore any action

**THE UNIFICATION OF GERMANY
1815–1871**

- Prussia 1815–1866
- Annexed by Prussia 1866
- Joined Prussia in forming the North German Confederation 1867
- Joined with Prussia to form the German Empire 1871
- Alsace-Lorraine ceded to German Empire by France 1871
- German Confederation 1815–1866

With Paris about to fall to the Prussian armies, King William of Prussia is proclaimed German emperor by his princes in the Hall of Mirrors of the Palace of Versailles. Smiling with satisfaction, Bismarck stands foremost at the foot of the dais.

taken by the legislature, especially the Reichstag. In 1871 Bismarck was appointed the first imperial chancellor.

As the architect of German nationalism, Bismarck completed his most important work by 1871, although he remained chancellor of the German empire until 1890. To achieve his ends, he had used ruthless means. But perhaps, as in the case of Cavour, he felt that circumstances left him no alternative. It was a tragedy for the world that to Bismarck blood and iron seemed essential in forging a united Germany, for his successes strengthened the notion that war is a national business that can be made to pay big dividends.

The Kulturkampf. Bismarck's strong nationalism, together with his hatred of those who refused to subordinate themselves to the state, brought about his crusades against what he called "the black and the red menaces." The first so-called crusade was directed against "the black menace," the Catholic Church in Germany.

In the elections of 1871 the German Catholics had elected a large bloc of representatives to the Reichstag. These members supported the complete independence of the Church from state control and denounced divorce, secular education, and liberty of conscience. They also supported the new dogma of papal infallibility (see p. 588).

The conflict which began in 1872 was known as the *Kulturkampf* (the Civilization Struggle). The imperial government made it a penal offense for the clergy to criticize the government and prohibited religious orders from taking part in educational work in Germany. Next, all members of the Jesuit order were expelled from the country. Between 1873 and 1875 the Prussian government also passed severe measures. These Prussian May Laws required civil marriages, stopped appropriations to the Catholic Church, and required all priests to study theology at the state universities. Numerous religious orders were suppressed.

Pope Pius IX declared these repressive acts null and void and called on loyal Catholics to refuse to obey them. Bismarck was infuriated, and, remembering the time in the Middle Ages when the German emperor

Henry IV humbled himself before Pope Gregory VII, he grandiloquently declared, "We shall not go to Canossa, either in the flesh or in the spirit." Priests were imprisoned, Church property was confiscated, and pulpits were closed.

Bismarck's oppression of the Catholic clergy did not attain its end. The Center party—that is, the Catholic bloc—in the Reichstag gained greatly in membership. The wily chancellor, therefore, decided to beat a strategic retreat, and the majority of the anti-Catholic laws were repealed. Bismarck needed the support of all Catholics against what he regarded as a new foe of the state—socialism, which he dubbed the "red international."

Although Europe witnessed an ever increasing spirit of reform, democratic aspirations were often suppressed in the late 1800's. Germany, for example, saw the continuous struggle of the Social Democrats within the framework of an autocratic regime. "Conspiracy," an etching by Kaethe Kollwitz, shows workers secretly plotting their next move.

Drive against the socialists.

In 1875 the socialists in Germany had established the Social Democratic party. Traditionally, German socialists had opposed autocratic rule and Prussian militarism. Now they demanded not only a true parliamentary democracy but also comprehensive social legislation.

Bismarck watched the socialists' mounting strength in the Reichstag with grave concern. In 1878 two attempts were made on the emperor's life. Although the Social Democratic party had in no way sponsored or participated in these plots, Bismarck immediately launched an all-out campaign against all socialists. In 1878 socialist organizations were dissolved and their publications suppressed. Some five hundred persons were imprisoned, and restrictions were made on free speech and public assembly.

Despite these severe measures, the adherents of socialism increased rather than declined. Therefore, Bismarck shifted his tactics and sponsored important measures for ensuring the economic well-being of the masses. He declared:

Give the workingman the right to work as long as he is healthy, assure him care when he is sick, and maintenance when he is old . . . then the socialists will sing their siren songs in vain, and the workingmen will cease to throng to their banner.[5]

A sickness insurance bill was passed in 1883, an accident insurance bill in the following year, and in 1889 old-age insurance was introduced. Regardless of Bismarck's motives, these attempts to safeguard the economic interests of the German masses were pioneer efforts in modern social reform and were copied in many European countries. But despite Bismarck's efforts to lure the workers from socialism, the Social Democratic party continued to increase in size and influence.

Kaiser William II.

In 1888 William II, the grandson of William I, became German emperor. Just as Bismarck had stamped his policies and personality on the German nation for the more than twenty years that he was chancellor, so this young man was the focus of German history from 1890 to 1918.

In addition to having a strong militaristic bent, William was an ardent champion of the divine right of kings. He constantly reminded those around him that "he and God" worked together for the good of the state. Berliners, astounded at his wide if superficial interests, humorously said: "God knows everything, but the kaiser knows better." The loud dress, flashy uniforms, and oratorical outbursts of the emperor sprang from an inferiority complex, which probably had its origin in the withered left arm that he had had from birth. Restless and emotionally unstable, he was continually making undiplomatic speeches and casting off insulting phrases that alarmed and sometimes infuriated governmental circles in Europe.

William II came to the throne determined to dominate the German government personally. To the kaiser's mind it was "a question whether the Bismarck dynasty or the Hohenzollern dynasty should rule."[6] For two years the tension between emperor and chancellor mounted. Finally, in 1890, William rudely dismissed Bismarck.

Reasons for despotism. Despite advances in industry and science, Germany remained a "political kindergarten." There were several reasons why despotism existed in such a prosperous and advanced country. First, the nation had militaristic leanings. It had achieved its unity by blood and iron. Any liberal movement would, if necessary, be crushed by the armed forces, which were passionately loyal to the Hohenzollern dynasty. At the heart of this militarism were the aristocratic Prussian Junkers, who disdained business, gloried in war, and had an austere sense of their duty to the state.

What we may term the German tradition also played its part. The people had long been taught to serve the Prussian state unquestioningly and to look to their leaders for guidance. As the Germans expressed it, "Alles kommt von oben" ("Everything comes down from above"). The people also gave the government unquestioning loyalty because it was efficient and solicitous of their material welfare. Bismarck's social insurance program succeeded in keeping the German masses contented.

Another factor which kept most of the Germans in line was the school system. The masses went to the *Volksschule*, where they

This well-known cartoon, "Dropping the Pilot," appeared in the English magazine *Punch* in 1890, following the dismissal of Bismarck as chancellor of Germany. Kaiser William II, determined to dominate German government personally, watches from the ship of state as the former helmsman leaves the vessel. Despite the change in leadership, however, the tradition that Bismarck represented continued into the twentieth century, as Germany followed a course of ardent nationalism and military aggressiveness.

were given excellent training in the three R's and were taught obedience to the state. The businessmen and landed aristocracy, on the other hand, sent their sons and daughters to an altogether different school system that led to the university and produced the elite that ruled the nation. German education trained many followers and a few leaders.

The democratic movement. Notwithstanding the strength of autocracy, a remarkable democratic movement, whose spearhead was the Social Democratic party, manifested itself in Germany as the twentieth century dawned. Despite the opposition of the emperor and his conservative supporters (William II called the socialists a "treasonable horde"), the vote cast by the Social Democrats continued to increase during William's reign as it had under Bismarck. In 1914 this party could claim the support of one third of the German voters.

The outbreak of war in 1914 was to nip in the bud the promising democratic movement. As a result, revolution was later substituted for evolution, and the German people achieved a republic before they had been sufficiently trained to govern themselves.

THE DUAL MONARCHY: AUSTRIA-HUNGARY

Establishment of the Dual Monarchy. As we have seen in Chapter 22, the collapse of the liberal and nationalist movement in the Austrian empire in 1848 was followed by stern repression. An undisguised system of absolutism was imposed upon all peoples in the empire. Included in this system was the centralization of all governmental administration in Vienna and an active policy of Germanizing the non-Teutonic subject peoples.

These reactionary measures were doomed, however, by the defeat of Austria in 1859 by France and Sardinia. The old ways were thoroughly discredited, and Vienna realized that if the empire was to survive, the demands of the subject nationalities would have to be appeased. As a result, in 1861 a new imperial constitution was framed in which representatives were to be elected from the various provincial parliaments to a central, imperial Diet. The Hungarians, however, who were by far the strongest of the subject nationalities, demanded concessions which would virtually make Hungary an independent state. The resulting impasse ended following Austria's disastrous defeat by Prussia in 1866 when the emperor offered to establish the Magyars as equal partners in ruling the empire. The offer was accepted,

and in 1867 the constitution known as the *Ausgleich* (Compromise) was promulgated.

Setting up a unique form of government, a Dual Monarchy known as Austria-Hungary, the *Ausgleich* made the Hapsburg ruler king in Hungary and emperor in Austria. Each country had its own constitution, official language, flag, and parliament, but finance, defense, and foreign affairs were under ministers common to both countries. These common ministers were supervised by the "Delegations," which consisted of sixty members from the Austrian parliament and an equal number of representatives from the Hungarian legislature.

Problems in the Dual Monarchy. While the Germans of Austria recognized the equality of the Magyars of Hungary, these two dominant nationalities made few concessions to the aspirations of their subject nationalities (see map, p. 535). Increasingly restive under alien rule, these peoples wanted the right to govern themselves. In some cases, as in Bohemia, the people wanted to set up a new independent nation; or, in the case of the Italians and the Serbs, the goal was to join their countrymen living in adjacent national states.

The Dual Monarch, Francis Joseph I (1848-1916) of the House of Hapsburg, ruled a multilingual state in which there were 12 million Germans, 10 million Magyars, over 24 million Slavs, and some 4 million Latins—the latter Italians and Rumanians. There were North Slavs (Bohemians or Czechs, Poles, and Slovaks) and South Slavs (Serbs, Croats, and Slovenes). In addition, there were numerous small isolated islands of people in various parts of Austria-Hungary surrounded by masses of neighbors quite different in nationality and culture. The value of the official bank note of the Dual Monarchy was printed in eight languages on one side and in Magyar on the other.

Although the bicameral legislature in Austria was elected by general manhood suffrage after 1907, political life continued to be dominated by wealthy German businessmen and the landed aristocracy. The latter monopolized the leading positions in government, the army, and parliament. Strong racial and national antipathies also impeded the functioning of what, on paper, seemed a liberal constitution. Political parties were not based primarily on political principle but on nationality. Each major group—Czechs, Poles, Slovenes, and Italians —feared and detested the German ruling elite, and too often each disliked the other national groups. Although Austria gave its subject nationalities substantial local self-government, this concession had little mollifying effect.

If democracy was weak in Austria, it was practically nonexistent in Hungary. Here the aristocracy firmly held the reins of power, and the Magyars refused to share political control with the other nationalities—Croats, Serbs, Slovaks, and Rumanians—who were under their rule. Hungary was agricultural, with a small landowning class dominating a great mass of backward, landless peasants.

Despite the difficulties to which the existence of the Dual Monarchy gave rise, the defenders of the empire could point to the military strength and international influence it gave to a large part of eastern and southern Europe. Above all, the empire exhibited a certain economic unity, for its various parts complemented each other well. Hungary, for example, produced wheat; Croatia and Slavonia exported cattle and swine; Bohemia and Austria were important industrial centers; and the great capital city of Vienna was the heart of the empire's banking and commerce.

Another unifying force was the Hapsburg crown. Francis Joseph I was a sincere and kindly sovereign, well liked by most of his subjects. It was his firm belief that the function of his dynasty was to hold the various national groups in the empire together. He once said:

My people are strangers to one another, and yet it is for the best. They never have the same ills at the same time. . . . Each suspects his neighbor; they never understand one another. . . . Their mutual antipathies, however, conduce to order and to general peace.[7]

THE NATIONALITIES OF AUSTRIA-HUNGARY

- Germans
- Italians
- Magyars
- Poles

In Chapter 24 we shall see how the restlessness of the subject peoples in Austria-Hungary became enmeshed with a Pan-Slav movement exploited by Serbia and Russia. Nationalism was ultimately to prove the undoing of Austria-Hungary and to involve Europe in the First World War.

RUSSIA: AUTOCRACY, ORTHODOXY, AND NATIONALISM

Autocracy challenged: the Decembrist Revolt. In 1850 Russia comprised the largest continuous land empire in the world. Containing a sixth of the earth's land surface, with as many people as the rest of Europe combined, it stretched from the Baltic and Black seas to the Pacific. At this time, however, the great potential power that this immense land giant could exercise in world affairs was hidden under the inefficiency of its government, the isolation of its people, and its economic backwardness.

Following the defeat of Napoleon, Tsar Alexander I (1801-1825) had been ready to discuss constitutional reforms, but though a few were introduced, no thoroughgoing changes were attempted. The pseudo-liberal tsar was followed by his younger brother Nicholas I (1825-1855), who at the outset of his reign was confronted by an uprising. This revolt had an interesting background. During the Napoleonic Wars a number of well-educated Russian officers traveled in Europe in the course of the military campaigns, some of them ending their peregrinations in Paris with the army of allied occupation. On their return to autocratic Russia, their exposure to the liberalism of western Europe led them to ask, "Is it for this we liberated Europe?"

The result was the so-called Decembrist Revolt (December 1825)—the work of a small circle of liberal nobles and army officers who wanted to install Nicholas' brother as a constitutional monarch. The revolt was easily quashed and those involved were cruelly punished. Five were executed and over five hundred exiled to Siberia. This harsh retaliation made "December Fourteenth" a day long remembered and the inspiration for later revolutionary movements. It also made Tsar Nicholas ultrasensitive to revolution and liberalism. He turned away from the Europeanization program begun by Peter the Great and Catherine the Great and championed the maxim "Autocracy, Orthodoxy, and Nationalism."

Repression under Nicholas I. Under the reactionary Nicholas System, Russia became "frozen." Foreign visitors were carefully screened, and those with "dangerous ideas" were halted at the border. Foreign books were not permitted if they contained any tincture of liberalism. Even musical compositions were checked to see if the notes were a secret code. Schools and universities were placed under constant surveillance, and the students were provided with official textbooks. Police spies were everywhere. Would-be revolutionaries and often quite harmless liberals were packed off to Siberia; from 1832 to 1852 an estimated 150,000 persons were exiled there. A measure of the effect of this repressive system on Russian intellectual life can be gained by noting that in 1843 all Russian journals had a combined subscription of only 12,000 and the colleges contained less than 5000 students. The tsar had a special fear of intellectuals, who might be "perverted by foreign ideas."

As we saw in Chapter 22, it was during Nicholas' reign that the Polish nationalist revolution of 1830 occurred. The treatment of Poland after the unsuccessful revolution was quite in keeping with the Nicholas System in Russia proper. Poland was reduced to a Russian province, and every attempt was made to stamp out Polish nationalism. Russian was made the language of administration and the courts, Polish universities were closed, Polish soldiers were placed in Russian regiments, and a hostile policy was inaugurated against Roman Catholicism, the leading faith in Poland.

The Russian radical movement: Herzen and Bakunin. Although Russian liberalism had received a setback from the collapse of the Decembrist conspiracy, the reform movement continued. In the 1830's and 1840's the younger generation of the nobility began to study the ideas of French and English reformers. They also found inspiration in the work of two Russian authors, Alexander Herzen (1812-1870) and Michael Bakunin (1814-1876).

Herzen was a moderate socialist. He advocated the freeing of the serfs, the liberalization of the government, and freedom of the press. In 1847 he fled from Russia and settled in London, where he founded the famous paper *Kolokol (The Bell)* ten years later. It was widely read in Russia, even, it is said, appearing mysteriously on the table of the tsar.

Bakunin was much more radical and is regarded as the father of Russian anarchism. He advocated terrorism as an agent of social change, calling it "the propaganda of the deed." He preached that anarchy—complete freedom—can be the only cure for society's ills. To his mind, laws passed even by a majority of the people must be abolished:

In a word, we object to all legislation, all authority, and all influence, privileged, patented, official and legal, even when it has proceeded from universal suffrage, convinced that it must always turn to the profit of a dominating and exploiting minority, against the interests of the immense majority enslaved.[8]

Bakunin was shipped to Siberia, but he escaped and made his way back to western Europe where he joined forces with Karl Marx (see Chapter 21).

The ideological schism. Heavy-handed repression by Nicholas did not stifle the desire of Russian intellectuals for knowledge. One of them called this period "an amazing time of outward slavery and inner liberation." Liberals and reformers met in secret and argued during the long winter nights about freedom, the merits of parliamentary government, and the part Russia should play in world history.

The question of Russia's destiny had been brewing ever since Peter the Great's program of westernization had been put into operation early in the eighteenth century (see Chapter 19). Which path should Russia follow? Should it imitate Europe or renounce the West and return to the traditions of its

past? The first road was championed by the so-called Westerners; the second by the nationalistic Slavophiles, who heaped scorn on the "decadent" West. One Slavophile wrote:

In Europe the principle of personality is supreme; with us it is the communal principle. Europe is pagan, Russia—holy Christian. In the West reigns apparent liberty, a liberty like that of a wild animal in the desert. The true liberty is found among us, in the East.[9]

The Slavophiles preferred the collectivism of the medieval Russian *mir*, or village community, to what they regarded as the dog-eat-dog individualism of the West. Present-day communism in Soviet Russia owes a debt to the age-old social pattern of the *mir* as well as to the doctrines of Karl Marx.

Alexander II abolishes serfdom. Tsar Nicholas died with his philosophy in disrepute. One year earlier, in 1854, Russia had become involved in the Crimean War, a conflict fought primarily in the Crimean peninsula (see p. 543). Since playing a major role

The Emancipation Proclamation was an admirable legal document, but it brought the serfs neither widespread nor immediate economic benefits. Because of strong opposition from the nobles and a complicated bondage system, the life of the Russian peasant remained rather primitive for several decades.

in the defeat of Napoleon, Russia had been regarded as militarily invincible, but the reverses it suffered on land and sea in the Crimean War, the blunders committed by its generals, and the huge loss of its manpower exposed the rottenness and weakness of the Nicholas regime. Russia, it was said, was like a giant with feet of clay.

When Alexander II came to the throne in 1855, desire for reform was widespread. Many of his subjects, even the conservatives, believed that social and political conditions needed changing if Russia was to keep up with other European states. Although no liberal, the new tsar realized the necessity for moderate reform; his first move was against serfdom.

A growing humanitarian movement, which has been likened to that of the abolitionists in the United States before the Civil War, attacked serfdom, labeling it a national disgrace. In 1859 there were more than 23 million serfs living under nearly the same conditions as had the peasants of western Europe on twelfth-century manors. Russian serfs had no civil rights, could not own property, and owed heavy dues and services to their lords, who could even sell them or raise money by mortgaging them.

Alexander II made up his mind to end serfdom; in his own words, "[It is] better to abolish serfdom from above than to wait until it will be abolished by a movement from below." A committee appointed to study the matter drew up the Emancipation Proclamation, which was duly issued as a *ukase* (edict of the tsar) in March 1861. The freed serfs were promised land and granted ownership of their cottages, farm buildings, garden plots, domestic animals, and farm implements.

The serfs had expected a portion of the lord's land to be turned over to them without charge. Instead of receiving their lands as a gift, however, the freed peasants had to pay a special tax for a period of forty-nine years to the government, which had paid the landlords a handsome price for the land they had lost. In numerous instances the peasants complained that they had been given the poorest land. All the land turned over to the peasants was owned collectively by the *mir*, the village community, which divided the land among the peasants and supervised the various holdings.

The emancipation of the serfs was the single most important event in nineteenth-century Russian history. It was the beginning of the end for the landed aristocracy's monopoly of power. Emancipation brought a supply of free labor to the cities; industry was stimulated, and the middle class grew in numbers and influence. Above all, emancipation gave strong impetus to the liberal movement.

Nihilism. In the 1860's a remarkable movement known as Nihilism developed in Russia. For some time many Russian liberals had been dissatisfied by the empty discussions of the intelligentsia; they now launched a movement which aimed to put all things in Russia to the test of reason. Ivan Turgenev, in his novel *Fathers and Sons* (1861), described a Nihilist as "a man who does not bow down before any authority, who does not take any principle on faith, whatever reverence that principle may be enshrined in."[10] As might have been expected, this attitude of "nothing sacred" resulted in a radical reconsideration of the very basis of society. The Nihilists questioned all old values, championed the independence of the individual, and delighted in shocking the older generation:

Here is the ultimatum of our camp, what can be smashed must be smashed; whatever will stand the blow is sound, what flies into smithereens is rubbish; at any rate, hit out right and left, no harm will or can come of it.[11]

The Nihilists first attempted to convert the aristocracy to the cause of reform. Failing there, they turned to the peasants, and a veritable missionary movement ensued. Young college students became laborers and worked in the fields with the peasants. Others went to the villages as doctors and teachers to preach reform to the people. This "go to the people" campaign was known as the Narodnik movement (*narod*, "people").

Further reforms of Alexander II. While Nihilism and the Narodnik movement were gaining momentum, the Tsar Liberator, as Alexander II was called, proceeded to carry out additional reforms. In 1864 local government was transformed by the Zemstvo Law. In the country elective local boards (*zemstvos*) were established on which the gentry, the middle class, and the peasants were represented. These boards were given power to collect taxes for roads, asylums, hospitals, and schools. In the same year important reforms in the judicial system were carried out. Trial by jury in criminal cases was introduced, and justices of the peace were created to take care of minor cases. In 1870 city government was improved by the creation of municipal councils controlled by the propertied classes. Four years later conscription for the army affecting all classes was introduced. Before this most army conscripts had been peasants.

Alexander abandons reform. The reforming hand of Alexander was also felt in Poland, where the Nicholas System of repression was relaxed. But instead of propitiating the Poles, Alexander's concessions encouraged them to revive their nationalistic ambitions. In 1863 a Polish insurrection succeeded in establishing a provisional government, but the movement was soon crushed and a harsh policy of repression was reimposed, aimed particularly at the educated classes. And not only was repression felt in Poland: in 1866, after a university student tried to assassinate him, the Tsar Liberator turned to the use of repressive measures.

In the meantime the "go to the people" (Narodnik) movement had collapsed. The government had tried to extirpate it; and the peasants, who could not understand it, rejected it. In response to the growing reaction of the government, a radical branch of Nihilists advocated and systematically practiced terrorism. One after another, prominent officials were shot down or killed by bombs. Finally, after several attempts, Alexander II was assassinated in 1881, on the very day he had approved a proposal to call a representative assembly to consider new reforms.

Autocracy and reaction under Alexander III. Unlike his father, the new tsar, Alexander III (1881-1894), was throughout his reign a staunch reactionary who revived the repressive system of Nicholas I and rigidly adhered to its maxim of "Autocracy, Orthodoxy, and Nationalism." A confirmed Slavophile, Alexander III believed that Russia could be saved from chaos only by shutting itself off from the subversive influences of western Europe. Publications were censored, and schools and universities were regulated to prevent students from learning "dangerous" ideas.

The tsar's most influential adviser was Konstantin Petrovich Pobyedonostzev, tutor to Alexander III and his son Nicholas, and procurator of the Holy Synod from 1880 to 1895. He taught his royal pupils to fear freedom of speech and press and to hate democracy, constitutions, and the parliamentary system. Under Pobyedonostzev, terrorists were hunted down and a rigorous policy of Russification was carried out, particularly among the Poles and the Finns. One nation, one language, one church, and one government—an autocratic government—was the formula of administration. The Jews were bullied and sometimes massacred in terrible drives called pogroms, and thousands sought asylum in the United States.

Nicholas II and a new revolutionary movement. Alexander was succeeded by his son, Nicholas II (1894-1917), a weak man with little intellect and hardly any force of character. The Industrial Revolution, which had begun to exert a significant influence in Russia in the late nineteenth century, was quietly helping create forces that would finally overthrow this last "Tsar of all the Russias." Several distinct reform parties, either liberal or radical, emerged. The progressive elements among the businessmen and nobility formed the Liberals (Constitutional Democrats, or Kadets). They wanted a constitutional monarchy and believed in peaceful reform. The Social Revolutionaries combined socialism with the Narodnik tradition and advocated "the whole land to the whole people." Their specific goal was the distribution of the land among those who actually worked it—the peasants.

Another radical group was the Social Democrats, exponents of Marxist principles. Gathering their strength chiefly from the radical intellectuals and the workingmen in the cities, they believed in a complete social and economic as well as political revolution.

In 1903 the party split into two wings—the Mensheviks, or moderates, and the Bolsheviks, or extremists. The Mensheviks believed that Russian socialism should grow gradually and peacefully and that the tsar's government should be overthrown and succeeded by a democratic republic in which the socialists would cooperate with bourgeois political parties. Working under a democratic system, the socialists would gradually become the dominant political force and would secure their socialistic society by parliamentary means. On the other hand, the Bolsheviks, under Nikolai Lenin (see p. 581), advocated the formation of a small elite of professional revolutionists, subject to strong party discipline, to act as the self-appointed vanguard of the proletariat. Although the Bolsheviks posed as democrats, they advocated seizure of power by force.

The government struck back energetically. Nicholas' minister of the interior organized diversionary outbursts of anti-Semitism among the people. Bands of thugs, called Black Hundreds, were organized to carry out pogroms and to attack liberals; and the fierce Cossacks were frequently used to carry fire and sword into rebellious regions. In the ranks of the revolutionists the government planted *agents provocateurs*, who incited the insurgents to murder officials and then exposed them to the police.

The revolution of 1905: Bloody Sunday. In 1904 the clash of rival imperialism in Manchuria and Korea (see p. 640) led to war with Japan. The Russian fleet was destroyed, and on land the Japanese gained victory after victory. With the ignominious defeat of its armed forces, the tsar's corrupt regime became the target for almost universal criticism.

Disorders spread throughout the land in the last months of 1904. On January 22, 1905, occurred the tragic incident known as Bloody Sunday. On this day a priest led an enormous crowd to the Winter Palace in St. Petersburg to present a petition to the tsar. The document declared:

We, the workers of the town of St. Petersburg, with our wives, our children and our aged and feeble parents, have come to you, Sire, in search of justice and protection. We have fallen into poverty, we are oppressed, we are loaded with a crushing burden of toil, we are insulted, we are not recognized as men, we are treated as slaves who should bear their sad and bitter lot in patience and silence. . . . Do not refuse to protect your people; raise it from the grave of arbitrary power, poverty and ignorance; permit it to dispose of its own fate; free it from the intolerable oppression of officials; destroy the wall between yourself and your people—and let it govern the country with you.[12]

When the procession reached the Winter Palace, Cossacks opened fire on the defenseless crowd, killing hundreds and wounding many more. This massacre shocked the world. Subsequently it was discovered that the priest had once been an agent of the secret police.

The Russian masses were so aroused over the Bloody Sunday massacre that a general strike was declared. The strikers demanded a democratic republic, freedom for political prisoners, and the disarming of the police. Soviets (councils of workers) appeared in the cities to direct revolutionary activity. Most business and government offices closed, and there was no gas, electricity, or (in some areas) water. The whole machinery of Russian economic life creaked to a defiant halt. Russia was paralyzed, and the government was helpless.

Results of the revolutionary movement. In October 1905 Tsar Nicholas reluctantly issued the famous October Manifesto, which promised "freedom of person, conscience, speech, assembly, and union." A national Duma (legislature) was to be called without delay, the right to vote was to be extended, and no law was to go into force without confirmation by the Duma. The more moderate liberal groups were satisfied, but the socialists rejected the concessions as insufficient and tried to organize new strikes. Thus by the end of 1905 there was disunity among the reformers, and the tsar's position was strengthened considerably.

When the first Duma was convened in the spring of 1906, it proceeded to censure the government, demanding an investigation into the conduct of the Russo-Japanese War, autonomy for Poland and Finland, and the

Attempting to restore order after the revolution of 1905, Nicholas II instituted a national Duma with legislative power. Although the tsar's true colors were cloaked in this respectable institution, Nicholas never intended to be overruled. When the first Duma tried to assume its rightful duties, he disbanded it, but the members met in a wood.

freeing of political prisoners. The tsar dissolved the Duma in midsummer because, he said, its members "would not cooperate." An appeal by the liberal leaders of the Duma was met by apathy on the part of the people. Sensing the decline of revolutionary fervor, the tsar appointed a conservative prime minister, Piotr Arkadevich Stolypin, who mercilessly repressed all radical elements.

Yet Stolypin was no blind reactionary. Even without the tsar's full support, he managed to push through some significant agricultural reforms. All payments still owed by peasants under the Emancipation Law were abolished, and, with financial aid from the state, two and a half million peasants were enabled to withdraw from the village community (*mir*) and become private owners of their lands. By 1911, when Stolypin was assassinated by a Social Revolutionary— who was also, in the strange Russian manner, an agent of the secret police—Russia had taken a long stride toward becoming a land of peasant proprietors who, as in France,

would be conservative in politics because of their property interests.

Although Nicholas II had been forced to make some concessions, the loyalty of the army, the staunch support of the Orthodox Church, and division among the opponents of tsarism enabled him to continue his autocratic and inefficient regime for the time being.

STORM OVER THE BALKANS

The Near Eastern Question. The European subject peoples in the Ottoman empire, having become nationally conscious early in the nineteenth century (see p. 506), were to gain their independence during the course of the century. By the 1830's the Greeks, Serbs, and Montenegrins were free to develop their nationhood, but the heavy hand of Turkish misrule still lay upon the Bulgarians. The

Rumanians—the peoples of Wallachia and Moldavia, claiming descent from Roman colonists and proudly calling themselves Rumans (Romans)—languished under the "protection" of Russia. As nationalism sought fulfillment in the Balkans, the political scene was complicated by the rivalries of the great powers, especially the rivalry between Britain and Russia. These rivalries as they affected the Ottoman empire formed what was known as the Near Eastern Question.

The Near Eastern Question has also been defined as "the problem of filling up the vacuum created by the gradual disappearance of the Turkish Empire from Europe."[13] Britain, which consistently opposed Russian designs on the Near East, feared that if any great power should gain control in that area, the balance of power in Europe would be altered decisively. And, if Russia were to obtain the Straits, Russian naval power in the eastern Mediterranean would challenge Britain's communications with India. Although most Englishmen detested the corrupt rule of the sultans, during most of the nineteenth century the British government, following national rather then moral interests, supported the Ottoman empire.

In the nineteenth century this Near Eastern power struggle brought on three Russo-Turkish wars and two wars in which France, England, and Russia fought either with or against Turkey, in addition to numerous revolts by subject nationalities against the sultan's government. In the twentieth century the same Near Eastern Question led to three wars before 1914 and helped precipitate the catastrophe of the First World War. Today the Near Eastern Question in a new form—Arab-Israeli tensions, heightened by Russian-American rivalry—still endangers world peace.

Anglo-Russian rivalry in the Near East. Russian expansion at the expense of the Turks had begun during the reign of Catherine the Great. After six years of war the sultan had been compelled to sign the Treaty of Kuchuk Kainarji (1774), which awarded Azov and the north coast of the Black Sea to Russia, granted the Russians free navigation for their merchant ships in Ottoman waters (including the Straits), and recognized the tsar as the protector of all eastern Orthodox Christians in the Ottoman empire. On several occasions Russia was to use this final concession as an excuse to intervene in Turkish affairs.

In 1791 the famous British statesman William Pitt the Younger denounced Russia's ambition to dismember Turkey. Austria also was beginning to fear Russian expansion. Britain and Austria realized that Turkey was a danger to their national interests, not because Turkey was strong but because it was weak. Russia in the meantime continued to take over former territories of the Ottoman empire, thereby expanding westward along the north shore of the Black Sea and southeastward along its east shore into the Caucasus region. During the Greek revolt of 1821 the British feared that Russia would attack Turkey and thus expand further in the name of Greek independence. The jealousies of the big powers finally led France, England, and Russia to act cooperatively in putting an end to the fighting. The result was Greek independence without an undue expansion of Russian influence in the Balkans.

The Ottoman empire seemed on the very point of extinction in 1831, when the able Mehemet Ali, the virtually independent governor of Egypt, attacked his overlord, the sultan. To prevent the establishment of a new and probably stronger government at the Straits, Nicholas I sent an army to protect the Ottoman capital, extracting in return the Treaty of Unkiar Skelessi (1833), which, in essence, made Turkey a protectorate of Russia. The Straits were closed to all war vessels except those of the signatories, making the Black Sea a Russian lake. Chagrined by this Russian coup, British statesmen determined to stop Russia. The British view was that "If you do not stop the Russians on the Danube, you will have to stop them on the Indus." Diplomatic pressure was exerted by Great Britain, joined by Austria and France, and in 1841 the tsar agreed to renounce Unkiar Skelessi and sign a general guarantee of Turkish independence.

Turkey, the "Sick Man of Europe." Although Nicholas I was still determined to carry on his predecessors' policy of expansion at the expense of decrepit Turkey, he now decided to proceed by mutual agreement with other powers, particularly Great Britain. While visiting England in 1844, the tsar referred to Turkey as "a dying man" and proposed that England join in a dissection of the Ottoman carcass. British statesmen refused to be party to an agreement that would result in Russia's taking over Constantinople.

A quarrel over the management and protection of the holy places in Palestine gave Nicholas a new excuse to intervene in the affairs of the Ottoman empire. Ostensibly motivated by religious sentiments, the tsar reconfirmed Russia's protectorate over all Greek Christians in the Ottoman empire. His primary interest, of course, was the traditional Russian goal—to secure control of Constantinople and to ensure an entrance from the Black Sea to the Mediterranean.

The Crimean War. Russia invaded Turkish territory in 1853 but was soon confronted with a declaration of war from France and Britain. For his part, Napoleon III saw a war with Russia as an opportunity to enhance the reputation of his dynasty. In 1854 French, British, and Sardinian troops invaded the Russian Crimea and besieged the great fortress of Sevastopol.

Contrary to Russian expectations (Russia had aided Austria in crushing the Hungarian revolution of 1848), Austria refused to ally itself with Russia and maintained an unfriendly "neutrality" which forced Russia to evacuate Turkish territory (Rumania) near the Austrian borders. In September 1855 the fortress of Sevastopol finally fell. Thwarted in the attempt to carve up the "Sick Man of Europe," Russia sued for peace.

The Treaty of Paris (1856) affirmed the integrity of the Ottoman empire. Specifically, it provided for the neutralization of the Black Sea (neither Russia nor Turkey was to maintain forts or naval depots on its shores), closed the Straits to foreign warships, and declared that no power had the right to interfere on behalf of the sultan's Christian subjects. To reduce Russian influence in the Balkans, the Congress of Paris ended the Russian protectorate over Rumania that had been established in 1829 (see p. 507), placed

The Russian fortress of Sevastopol was the major scene of battle for most of the Crimean War. Fortified by the famed military engineer E. I. Todleben, the town withstood the attack of the allied army for eleven months.

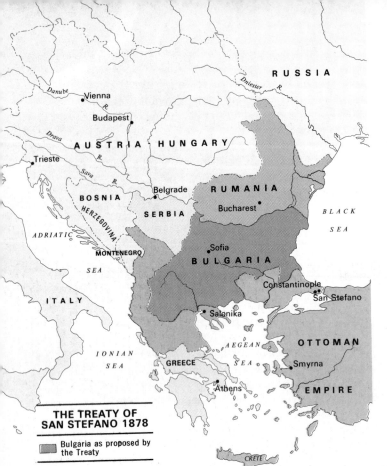

**THE TREATY OF
SAN STEFANO 1878**

▨ Bulgaria as proposed by
the Treaty

message of Slavic solidarity to the Balkans,
encouraging revolt.

Nationalist aspirations in the Balkans.
Meanwhile the Balkan peoples were slowly
moving toward nationhood. The Rumanian
provinces of Moldavia and Wallachia, though
self-governing, were still nominally under
Turkish control. Despite the opposition of
the Austrians and the British, who sought to
preserve the Ottoman empire from further
dismemberment, Rumanian nationalism
triumphed in 1862 when the great powers
recognized the two principalities as the
single nation of Rumania, although still
under the nominal rule of the sultan.

The story of Bulgarian nationalism became entwined with events in the whole
Balkan area and with the growing interests
of the great powers in this troubled region.
In 1875 peasants revolted in the district of
Bosnia, a Turkish-governed Serbian province not included in the autonomous Serbian
state. Following this insurrection Serbia and
Montenegro declared war on Turkey.

At the same time, the Bulgarians broke
into revolt, but the Turks crushed the rebels
with terrible cruelty. The "Bulgarian massacres" caused a gasp of horror among enlightened people all over the world. In one
incident over one thousand people, including children, were burned alive in a church
where they had sought sanctuary.

**The Treaty of San Stefano and the Con-
gress of Berlin.** While public opinion in
Europe was being aroused against the "unspeakable Turk," the Serbs and Montenegrins had been forced to sue for peace with
Turkey. Tsar Alexander II thereupon announced that the situation of the "oppressed
nationalities" in the Balkans was intolerable
and declared war on the sultan.

The Russo-Turkish War (1877-1878) was
hard fought. In one case a beleaguered Turkish army held off the Russians for five
months before surrendering. Faced with an
imminent Russian attack on Constantinople,
however, the sultan finally sued for peace.
The resulting Treaty of San Stefano (1878)
recognized the complete independence of
Serbia and Rumania, while reaffirming the
independence of Montenegro. A large Bulgarian state was set up, nominally still tribu-

the country under the protection of the great
powers, and permitted Turkey to maintain
its sovereignty.

The Crimean War momentarily halted
Russian advance into the Balkans. But it did
little to assuage the bitter international
rivalries in that area. Resentful of what was
regarded as gross Austrian "ingratitude,"
Moscow gave up the idea of having Austria
as an ally in the carving up of the Ottoman
empire and decided instead that this objective now required the weakening of Austria.

Pan-Slavism, agent of Russian expansion.
The nationalistic, antiwestern Slavophile
movement, which lauded Russian institutions, took on a political complexion after
the Crimean War. Known as Pan-Slavism,
this movement championed Russia as the
protector of its "little brother Slavs," with
the duty of freeing them from the rule of the
Turks. Moreover, exponents of Pan-Slavism
preached that it was Russia's destiny to create and rule a great Slavic empire. In the
1860's and 1870's Pan-Slavism carried the

tary to Turkey but actually under the dominance of Russia.

Britain was alarmed over the prospect of much of the Balkans coming under the domination of Moscow. And Austria was determined that Turkey as a political entity must be preserved or, at the very least, that its territory be prevented from falling under Russian influence. An Austrian statesman explained the Austro-Hungarian position in this way:

Turkey possesses a utility almost providential for Austria-Hungary. For Turkey maintains the status quo of the small Balkan states and impedes their [nationalistic] aspirations. If it were not for Turkey, all these aspirations would fall down on our heads . . . if Bosnia-Herzegovina should go to Serbia or Montenegro, or if a new state should be formed there which we cannot prevent, then we should be ruined and should ourselves assume the role of the "Sick Man."[14]

Accordingly, Britain and Austria later in 1878 forced a reconsideration of the Treaty of San Stefano at the Congress of Berlin, the last great nineteenth-century gathering of European statesmen in the pattern inaugurated at the Congress of Vienna. Russia was compelled to agree to a revision of Bulgaria's status, and the large Bulgarian state set up by the Treaty of San Stefano was divided into three parts. The northernmost part remained an independent principality paying tribute to Turkey; south of this region was an autonomous province to be occupied by Turkish troops; the southernmost region was given back to Turkey to administer. Among other provisions of the Berlin settlement, Austria was allowed "to occupy and administer" the provinces of Herzegovina and Bosnia (the latter was to be the scene of the incident that set off World War I), Britain was granted Cyprus, and France was promised Tunis.

Russian expansion had been checkmated and the so-called "Concert of Europe" shored up—but at a high price. The Turks continued to oppress and even massacre the Christians left under the rule of the sultan. The Russians proceeded to make a mockery of Pan-Slavism by trying to control the policies of their "brother Slavs" just freed from the Turks,

THE CONGRESS OF BERLIN 1878

Bulgaria as amended by the Congress of Berlin

particularly in Bulgaria. Russian satellites in eastern Europe and the Balkans, so much in evidence after World War II, are nothing new in history.

Despotism and misrule in the Ottoman empire: Abdul-Hamid II. In the closing decades of the nineteenth century the decaying Ottoman empire was a disreputable, vicious Oriental despotism. In 1876 a liberal constitution had been issued and a new sultan, Abdul-Hamid II, had come to the throne with the support of a liberal faction. But two years later the sultan abrogated the constitution and began to rule without parliament, aided by forty thousand spies. The strictest censorship was applied, and opponents of this tyranny mysteriously disappeared or were forced into exile.

At the same time Abdul-Hamid was fighting a losing battle to hold together the remainder of his empire. In North Africa, France, which had seized Algeria in 1830, annexed Tunis in 1881; Britain occupied Egypt in 1882; and by 1900 Italy had a covetous eye on Tripoli. But there remained under Turkish rule the Arab world of the Near East, inhabited by peoples who were proud of their traditions and who were Muslim in religion but not Turkish in nationality. The same nationalist spirit which had bestirred nineteenth-century Europe now began to arouse Arab leaders against Turkish rule.

Young Turks and Young Arabs. By the beginning of the twentieth century opposition to the sultan's tyranny was widespread among his Turkish subjects. The nucleus for this opposition was the organization known as the Young Turks, composed of reformers who had been educated in western European universities. Many converts to this reform group were made in the Turkish army, which provided the necessary military power for successful rebellion. When the Young Turks rebelled in 1908, Abdul-Hamid restored the liberal 1876 constitution. But after gaining what they desired for themselves, the Young Turks refused to share their victory with the non-Turkish peoples. The result was a counterrevolution, encouraged by the sultan, who sought to regain power. When Abdul-Hamid turned against the

In 1909 the rebellious Young Turks forced Abdul-Hamid II from his throne. This photograph shows the victorious insurgent forces on the march.

Young Turks, however, he was overthrown and replaced by his weak and innocuous brother.

Arabs in Syria, Lebanon, and the vast peninsula of Arabia were not happy with the new sultan. They writhed under the Young Turks program of Turkish supremacy and their policy of centralization, which left no opportunity for Arab home rule. When fighting against Turkey during World War I, Britain found it relatively easy to turn the Arab tribes against their overlord, the sultan.

Meanwhile the disintegration of the Ottoman empire proceeded apace. In the years between 1908 and 1913 Austria-Hungary annexed Bosnia and Herzegovina, two Turkish provinces on the Adriatic that had been occupied and administered by the Dual Monarchy since 1878; Greece annexed Crete; and Italy, in the course of a short war, seized Tripoli and Cyrenaica. Finally, the Balkan nations fought two wars with the Ottoman empire in 1912 and 1913 and partitioned Turkish Macedonia. How these annexations and wars brought about disputes among the great powers, and in particular how they created an explosive situation in the Balkans that touched off World War I, will be discussed in Chapter 24.

SUMMARY

From 1848 to the mid-1870's nationalism was the arbiter of history; democracy, for the moment, was overshadowed by the momentous events of nation-making. Nationalism's most important successes were registered by the unification movements in Italy and Germany, which produced two additions to the powers of Europe.

In central Europe, Magyar nationalism proved a significant force, leading in 1867 to the establishment of the Dual Monarchy of Austria-Hungary. But other less fortunate minority groups in this polyglot land were still denied political liberties and independence.

After the Napoleonic Wars, as after World War II, an iron curtain divided Europe. Russia remained isolated, remote from the modernizing forces of western Europe. Seemingly, defeat in war was necessary to bring about sweeping changes in the land whose maxim was "Autocracy, Orthodoxy, and Nationalism." Thus defeat in the Crimean War preceded the emancipation of the serfs, defeat by Japan led to the establishment of parliamentary government of a sort, and in a later chapter we shall see how Russia's defeat in World War I spelled the end of the tsarist regime.

But the fortunes of war had no permanent effect on Russia's determination to extend its political control to the shores of the Mediterranean. Russia's expansionist nationalism was disguised under the banner of Pan-Slavism; but the disguise failed to impress either the Ottoman empire, which even under the reforming Young Turks continued to perpetuate its hold on its subject peoples, or Britain and Austria-Hungary, which were strenuously opposed to any extension of Russia's boundaries. Complicating this international problem was the fervent nationalism of the Balkan peoples, the "little brother Slavs" whom Russia proposed to "liberate" from Turkish domination.

To most of us—even though we have often seen the term abused in our own lifetime—*liberation* suggests idealism and high purpose. But European diplomats and military leaders of this period had little interest in either high purpose or ideals. In his work *On War* (1832), the Prussian general Karl von Clausewitz gave classic expression to the hard-boiled *Realpolitik* that motivated these men:

War is only a continuation of State policy by other means. . . . War is not merely a political act, but also a real political instrument, a continuation of political commerce. . . . Is not war merely another kind of writing and language for political thought? . . . War is nothing but a duel on an extensive scale. . . . Let us not hear of Generals who conquer without bloodshed. . . . The best strategy is always to be strong.[15]

SUGGESTIONS FOR READING

R. C. Binkley, **Realism and Nationalism: 1852-1871**,* Torchbooks; C. J. H. Hayes, **A Generation of Materialism: 1871-1900**,* Torchbooks; J. Munholland, **Origins of Contemporary Europe, 1890-1914**,* Harcourt, Brace & World, 1970. Outstanding syntheses. A. J. P. Taylor, **The Struggle for Mastery in Europe, 1848-1918**, Oxford, 1954, and L. Seaman, **From Vienna to Versailles**,* Colophon, are well-written surveys of international relations.

K. Minogue, **Nationalism**, Basic, 1967; E. H. Carr, **Nationalism and After**, St. Martin's, 1945. Brief and stimulating historical surveys. B. C. Shafer, **Nationalism: Myth and Reality**,* Harcourt, Brace & World, is an outstanding fuller account. See also H. Kohn, **The Idea of Nationalism**,* Collier, and **Prophets and Peoples: Studies in Nineteenth Century Nationalism**,* Collier.

C. Delzell, ed., **The Unification of Italy, 1859-1861: Cavour, Mazzini, or Garibaldi?*** (European Problem Studies), Holt, Rinehart & Winston. See also Denis Mack Smith, **Italy: A Modern History**, Michigan, 1959, which deals with the period after 1861; and the same author's **Garibaldi**, Knopf, 1956.

W. Medlicott, **Bismarck and Modern Germany**,* Torchbooks. An excellent introduction to the era. Also recommended are E. Eyck, **Bismarck and the German Empire**,* Norton, and A. J. P. Taylor, **Bismarck: The Man and the Statesman**,* Vintage, which is generally hostile. Notable scholarly surveys are O. Pflanze, **Bismarck and the Development of Germany: The Period of Unification, 1815-1871**, Princeton, 1963; and H. Holborn, **A History of Modern Germany, 1840-1945**, Knopf, 1969. Michael Balfour, **The Kaiser and His Times**, Houghton Mifflin, 1964, describes the impact of William II on Germany and Europe. See also A. Rosenberg, **Imperial Germany: The Birth of the German Republic, 1871-1918**,* Oxford, 1970. The rebellious spirit of German youth is described in W. Laqueur, **Young Germany: A History of the German Youth Movement**, Basic Books, 1962.

C. Macartney, **The Habsburg Empire, 1790-1918**, Macmillan, 1969. A scholarly survey. See also works cited in Chapter 22.

M. Karpovich, **Imperial Russia, 1801-1917**,* Holt, Rinehart & Winston. Brief and valuable. H. Seton-Watson, **The Russian Empire, 1801-1917**, Oxford, 1967, and **The Decline of Imperial Russia, 1855-1914**,* Praeger, are excellent longer surveys. W. E. Mosse, **Alexander II and the Modernization of Russia**,* 2nd ed., Collier, is a brief biography. R. Charques, **The Twilight of Imperial Russia**,* Oxford, 1965, surveys the reign of the last tsar, Nicholas II. See also R. Massie, **Nicholas and Alexandra**,* Dell; Geroid Robinson, **Rural Russia Under the Old Regime**,* California; A. Yarmolinsky, **The Road to Revolution: A Century of Russian Radicalism**,* Collier, 1968; J. Joll, **The Anarchists**,* Universal.

William Miller, **The Ottoman Empire and Its Successors, 1801-1927**, Octagon, 1966. The standard work. L. Stavrianos, **The Balkans, 1815-1914**,* Holt, Rinehart & Winston, is a brief examination. R. H. Davison, **Turkey**,* Prentice-Hall, 1968, is a brief, well-written general history. See also Bernard Lewis, **The Emergence of Modern Turkey**,* 2nd ed., Oxford; and F. Ahmad, **The Young Turks**, Oxford, 1970.

Matthew S. Anderson, **The Eastern Question, 1774-1923**, St. Martin's, 1966. A new clarification. See also H. Kohn, **Pan-Slavism: Its History and Ideology**,* Vintage.

*Indicates an inexpensive paperbound edition.

Chapter 24

Hope and Holocaust

**Parliaments and Political Reforms: 1850–1914;
Forces for Peace and War: 1871–1918**

INTRODUCTION. Because of its steady and peaceful progress toward democracy, Britain was regarded by many nineteenth-century liberals as the model nation. Fearful of the rising influence of the business class, the English nobility allied itself with the growing labor class, which became politically ambitious and demanded an effective voice in government. In addition, many among the well-to-do had real fear of revolution; to them it seemed better to grant concessions to the masses than to risk bloodshed such as Paris witnessed in 1848 and 1871. Under Disraeli, city workers got the vote; under Gladstone, suffrage was extended to agricultural workers. Finally, the Parliament Bill of 1911 made Britain an almost completely democratic state.

The second great democratic power of the late nineteenth century was France, which, for the third time, attempted to adopt a republican form of government after its Second Empire went down in humiliating defeat at the hands of Prussia in 1870. The first important act of the Third French Republic was the defeat of the Commune, a revolutionary body which brought about a violent and bloody civil uprising in Paris. As the nineteenth century came to a close, France was further convulsed by a series of crises that threatened to discredit, and even to overthrow, the Republic. Although by 1914 democratic France seemed to have ridden out the storm, the feuds and scandals of the past had left scars.

The farther one traveled eastward from London and Paris, the more shallow-rooted democracy became. In the preceding chapter we have noted how Bismarck failed to give Germans an opportunity to exercise real political responsibility and how the discontent of submerged nationalities in Austria-Hungary stultified real parliamentary government. Yet we have also seen that even in the most backward parts of Europe the first steps toward modern parliamentary government had been taken—in Russia (1905) and in Turkey (1908).

Meanwhile, with progress in science and technology came progress in destructive armaments; and while the power of military weapons increased, little was done to remove the causes that led nations to rely upon these weapons. If men could be said to have ascended to a new level of civilization in their scientific and intellectual attainments, their tactics and outlook in international affairs were often reminiscent of the jungle. Europe, with its progressive and brilliant yet menacing and unstable civilization, was now the center of the world. It was the central position this little continent enjoyed that gave its promise and peril world-wide implications. Fanned by old rivalries and callous ambitions, a spark in that center was to grow and spread and finally engulf the world in flames, creating the holocaust known as World War I.

TOWARD DEMOCRATIZATION OF BRITISH LIFE

End of the Victorian Compromise. From 1850 to 1914 Great Britain manifested a slow but orderly progression to broadened horizons of political democracy and social justice. The period from 1832—the year in which the first Reform Bill was passed—to 1865 is often described as the era of the Victorian Compromise. During this period an alliance of the landed gentry and the middle class worked together to dominate the government and keep the lower classes "in their stations." The members of the middle class believed that the political reforms—which had been in large measure of benefit to them alone—had gone far enough. Although some social reforms were granted, they were exceptions in the general atmosphere of middle-class complacency.

The symbol of this conservatism was Lord Palmerston, who dominated the direction of foreign affairs from the 1830's until his death and ended his career by acting as prime minister during much of the period from 1855 to 1865. A viscount himself, he was quite satisfied with the rule of the aristocracy and the middle class.

Gladstone and Disraeli. The death of Palmerston in 1865 and the entry of two new political leaders into the limelight heralded the beginning of a new era in British affairs. For a generation English politics was little more than the biographies of William Ewart Gladstone (1809-1898), a Liberal, and Benjamin Disraeli (1804-1881), a Conservative, who alternated with one another as prime minister from 1867 to 1880. Following the death of Disraeli, Gladstone continued to dominate politics until his retirement in 1894.

The son of a rich Liverpool merchant, Gladstone had every advantage that wealth and good social position could bestow. Entering Parliament in 1833 at the age of twenty-four, the young politician quickly made a name for himself as one of the greatest orators of his day, on one occasion

The English satirical magazine *Punch* portrayed Benjamin Disraeli and William Gladstone as rival stars in the theater. Much to the displeasure of Gladstone, Disraeli had just become prime minister.

holding the attention of the House of Commons for five hours while he expounded the intricacies of the national budget. At first Gladstone was a Conservative in politics, a follower of the Tory leader Robert Peel. But gradually he shifted his allegiance to the Liberal (Whig) party, which he headed as prime minister for the first time in 1868. Gladstone was a staunch supporter of laissez faire, the belief that government should not interfere in business. His record as a social and economic reformer, therefore, was not imposing. But in political reforms his accomplishments were noteworthy.

The great rival of Gladstone, Benjamin Disraeli, had few advantages of birth and social position. The son of a cultured Jew who had become a naturalized British subject in 1801, Disraeli was baptized an Anglican. He first made a name for himself as a novelist with *Vivian Grey* (1826). Un-

like Gladstone, Disraeli swung from liberalism to conservatism in his political philosophy; he stood for office as a Conservative throughout his career and eventually became the leader of the Conservative (Tory) party.

The Reform Bill of 1867. By 1865 it was obvious that the Victorian Compromise could not be maintained any longer. With only one adult male out of six having the right to vote, English workmen had formed large organizations to agitate for the franchise. Both the Conservative party, drawing its strength mainly from the landowning gentry, and the Liberals, supported by the middle class, realized that reform must come, and each hoped to gain new political strength from the passage of a reform bill.

It was Gladstone's turn first. In 1866, Gladstone introduced a moderate reform bill giving the vote to city laborers. His proposal failed to pass, however, and the country was rocked by agitation and riots. The Conservatives then came into power, and Disraeli in 1867 successfully sponsored a reform bill that added a little more than a million city workers to the voting rolls. In 1832 the electorate had been increased 50 percent; in 1867 it was increased by 88 percent. Although women and farm laborers still could not vote, Britain was well on the road to political democracy. These reforms were not effected without arousing considerable conservative opposition, however. The famous Victorian writer Thomas Carlyle called the reform movement "Shooting Niagara," and another critic dolefully predicted:

The bag which holds the winds will be untied, and we shall be surrounded by a perpetual whirl of change, alteration, innovation, and revolution.[1]

Gladstone's "Glorious Ministry." To the dismay of Disraeli, the newly enfranchised voters brought the Liberals back to power in 1868 with Gladstone as prime minister. Gladstone's so-called "Glorious Ministry," which was to last until 1874, was one of great achievements.

With the enfranchisement of the city masses, it became imperative that their children be given an education. The Education Act of 1870 made possible the setting up of local school boards authorized to build and maintain government schools. Fees could be charged (they were not abolished until 1891), and attendance could be made compulsory from the age of five to thirteen. Government subsidies were given to the private schools, which were required to meet certain minimum standards. In ten years attendance in elementary schools jumped from one million to four million.

In the governmental and military administrations, most appointments and promotions had traditionally depended upon patronage and favoritism. In 1870 employment in the British civil service was finally based upon open examinations of a highly intellectual character. The war office also introduced changes. The terms of enlistment were improved, flogging was abolished, and the purchase of commissions was eliminated. An officer's rank had formerly been his own personal property that could be sold to the highest bidder.

Other long-needed reforms included a surer and speedier system of justice, introduction of secret balloting (1872), and removal of some of the restrictions on labor union activity. Gladstone's energetic efforts to solve the Irish problem, described later, extended through his second and third ministries. By the early 1870's, however, the reforming zeal of the Glorious Ministry had run down, and Disraeli wittily referred to Gladstone and his colleagues in the House of Commons as a "range of exhausted volcanoes."

Disraeli and Tory democracy. The story of the continued growth of democracy in Great Britain resumes with the election of Disraeli as prime minister in 1874. Attacking standpat conservatism, he advocated what became known as Tory democracy—a political alliance formed between the landed gentry and the workers against the businessmen. In the landed gentry Disraeli saw England's natural leaders—champions of the common people, who were being exploited by the middle class, the modern counterpart of the medieval nobility.

The social legislation enacted under Disraeli's ministry (1874-1880) substantially advanced Britain toward what we know now as the welfare state. Public health facilities were improved, peaceful picketing and the right to strike were fully legalized, a food and drug act was passed, and housing programs were inaugurated.

Reform measures of Gladstone. Returning to power in 1880, Gladstone in 1884 sponsored the third Reform Bill, a measure extending the vote to agricultural workers. This statute brought Britain to the verge of universal manhood suffrage. Gladstone also obtained passage of the important Employers' Liability Act, which gave the workers rights of compensation in five classes of accidents. Apart from these measures, Gladstone concerned himself primarily with attempts to solve the Irish problem, the principal question in British politics in the late nineteenth century.

The Irish problem. Although England is often credited with ability in government, a skillful hand seems to have been absent in its rule of Ireland—a case of chronic misgovernment. In the seventeenth century the British had planted large numbers of Scottish emigrants in the north of Ireland in Ulster, where a strong colony of Protestants (the so-called Scotch-Irish or Orangemen) developed. A number of oppressive laws were passed against the Irish Catholics, restricting their political, economic, and religious freedom and dispossessing them of their lands. Then by the Act of Union of 1801 the Irish legislature was abolished, and the Irish were required to send their representatives to the Parliament in London.

During the early nineteenth century the land problem in Ireland became very acute. A large part of the cultivable land was in the hands of parasitic landlords. As the population grew, the leased farms were subdivided into small portions scarcely capable of supporting tenants, and many peasants were evicted because of failure to pay rent. In 1845 the potato crop, the main staple of diet, failed, and a terrible famine ensued. Perhaps as many as 500,000 people died, and a huge exodus to America began—the beginning of the principal

Irish Catholic settlements in the United States. In 1841 the population of Ireland was 8,770,000; in 1891 it was less than 5,000,000.

The Irish, for their part, had managed to gain some victories in the course of the nineteenth century. In 1829 the British Parliament had passed the Catholic Emancipation Act, permitting Catholics to sit in Parliament. Earlier, the Irish members in Parliament had come from the Protestant minority and represented only the landlord class. During Gladstone's Glorious Ministry a land act was passed which protected tenants against arbitrary eviction, and the Irish Anglican Church was disestablished. The latter measure ended the use of Irish tax money to support a church to which 75 percent of the population did not belong. In 1881 Gladstone placed on the statute book his second land act, intended to give the country folk of Ireland what was called the "three F's": fair rent, fixed tenure, and free sale. The result was that by the close of the century the Irish peasants were gradually becoming landowners with at least a chance of earning a decent livelihood.

While the land problem was being ameliorated, the issue of Irish home rule came to the fore. The Home Rulers, led by Charles

Stewart Parnell (1846-1891), demanded that Ireland have its own legislature. Entering the House of Commons in 1874, Parnell did everything possible to obstruct business in that august body, hoping in this way to force the issue of home rule. Faced with such tactics, as well as with the fact that Parnell controlled eighty-five votes in the Commons, Gladstone in 1886 and 1893 introduced home rule bills. But both bills were defeated.

Finally, a third home rule bill was introduced and passed by Parliament in 1914. The Ulsterites, however, strongly opposed the measure and prepared to resist by force incorporation into a Catholic Ireland divorced from the government of Great Britain. Only the outbreak of war with Germany in 1914 prevented civil strife in Ireland. The 1914 act was never put into effect, and the question was not settled until 1921, when southern Ireland attained the status of a British dominion.

Rule of the new Liberals, 1905-1914. Gladstone's fight for Irish home rule split his party and paved the way for a decade of Conservative rule in Britain (1895-1905). Partly because Britain was enmeshed in foreign and imperial affairs, the Conservative party no longer adhered to Disraeli's Tory democracy and its program of social legislation. But by 1905 the need for social and political reform again claimed major attention. Over 30 percent of the adult male workers received a starvation wage of less than seven dollars per week. The pitifully small wages made it impossible for the workers to lay aside savings for increasingly frequent periods of unemployment. Numerous strikes gave evidence of discontent among the workers, and the newly founded Labour party (see p. 580) gained adherents. The Liberals, traditional champions of laissez-faire economics, decided to jettison their old ideas and embark on a bold program of social legislation. David Lloyd George (1863-1945), a leading member of the Liberal government, declared: "Four spectres haunt the Poor; Old Age, Accident, Sickness and Unemployment. We are going to exorcise them."[2]

Led by Prime Minister Herbert Asquith,

Having created the richest, most extensive, and most powerful empire in history, Britain was a natural target for criticism from other nations. Here the German caricaturist T. T. Heine pictures England dominating three continents—one foot in Great Britain, the other in Africa; one hand on Egypt, the other on India.

Lloyd George, and Winston Churchill—the last-named just beginning his fabulous career—the Liberal party, with the aid of the Labour party, carried through Parliament a revolutionary reform program that provided for old-age pensions, national employment bureaus, and sickness, accident, and unemployment insurance. In addition, labor unions were not to be held financially responsible for losses caused an employer by a strike, and members of the House of Commons, heretofore unpaid, were granted a moderate salary. This last measure enabled men without private means, chiefly in the new Labour party, to follow a political career.

For some time there had been ill-feeling against the House of Lords because it had tried to block the reform program of the Liberals. When the Lords refused to pass the 1909-1910 budget, which laid new tax burdens—including an income tax—on the richer classes in order to pay for the new social legislation, the Liberals and their Labour allies argued that a hereditary, irresponsible upper house was an anachronism in a democracy. The result was the Parliament Bill of 1911. Before this bill was passed, it was necessary for Asquith to announce (as had been done with the Reform Bill in 1832) that the monarch had promised, if necessary, to create enough new peers to pass the bill in the House of Lords. The bill took away from the Lords all power of absolute veto. No longer could the will of the people as expressed in the Commons be blocked; the Lords were left with power only to slow up and force reconsideration of legislation of which they did not approve.

The Pax Britannica. In nineteenth-century world affairs England's industrial might, its financial strength, and its smoothly functioning and stable government made it possible for this nation to play a unique role in world affairs. The very size of the British empire meant that Englishmen were involved in developments all over the globe. Enlarged and consolidated in the nineteenth century (see Chapter 27), the British empire consisted of 13 million square miles of land—the largest empire known to history. Although the *Pax Britannica* was not free of flaws or evils, in the absence of any world government there was a great deal to be said for a global system of law and defense which maintained stability in one quarter of the world's area.

FRANCE: PAINFUL PATH TO DEMOCRACY

Prosperity without liberty under Napoleon III. Since its establishment in 1852 (see p. 516), the Second French Empire of Napoleon III had prospered in both domestic and foreign affairs. Over a period of eighteen years, Napoleon III, the "emperor boss," gave his realm glory, prosperity, and, above all, order and discipline—nearly everything a great nation could desire, in fact, except liberty. Although the governmental structure retained the outward forms of a parliamentary regime, the suffrage was juggled to give the supporters of the emperor a safe majority in the legislature—which had little power anyway. An efficient secret police was established to hunt down "dangerous elements," the press was censored, and parliamentary debates were given no publicity.

But if the France of Napoleon III lacked liberty, it did enjoy prosperity. Large-scale industries and corporations developed, and in two decades production doubled. France sponsored the building of the famous Suez Canal (1859-1869), railway mileage increased fivefold, and steamship lines prospered. The condition of the masses was bettered in a number of ways, including the partial legalization of labor unions and the right to strike. An ambitious program of public works transformed Paris into a city of broad boulevards and harmonious architecture.

Successes and failures in foreign affairs. Napoleon III thought of himself as the first servant of the empire, devoted to the task of making the state prosperous and progressive. But though he claimed to be a man of peace, he was heir to the Napoleonic legend. He had no choice but to pursue a spirited role in international affairs.

For ten years Napoleon III's foreign policy was remarkably successful. Allying France with England in the Crimean War, the emperor gained the desired victory against Russia and appeared at the peace conference as the arbiter of Europe. In 1859 his support of Cavour in Italy against Austria earned him military glory and gained Nice and Savoy for France. Furthermore, during this period France secured a foothold in Indochina—the assassination of a French missionary providing the pretext to occupy the region around Saigon—raised the tricolor over Tahiti and other Pacific islands, completed the conquest of Algeria, and began to penetrate the Senegal River in West Africa.

Until 1861 Napoleon III could boast that France was mistress of Europe, but after this date the emperor seemed to lose his touch in foreign affairs, and the morale and efficiency of the Second Empire declined rapidly. In 1863, while the United States was distracted by civil war, Napoleon III embroiled France in the madcap scheme of placing Maximilian, a Hapsburg prince, on the Mexican throne. Some forty thousand troops were involved in this expensive adventure, which ended in the withdrawal of the French forces and the capture and execution of Maximilian by Mexican patriots (see Chapter 26). France suffered further humiliation in 1863 when the emperor talked boldly of aiding a Polish revolt against Russian rule and then failed to act.

Napoleon III's prestige at home and abroad reached a new low in 1866 when, as we saw in Chapter 23, his blunders contributed to the quick Prussian victory over Austria and the apparent certainty of a powerful united Germany rising on France's borders. To regain public support at home, Napoleon had gambled on a successful war with Prussia in which he unrealistically counted on Austrian and Italian aid. The result, as will be recalled, was complete disaster. Thus the glory of the Second French Empire and the power of its creator, Napoleon III, perished on the battlefield just as the empire of his uncle, Napoleon, had disintegrated before the unbending squares of British infantry at Waterloo.

News of this debacle swept the discredited Second Empire from power, and a republic was proclaimed in Paris.

The Third Republic. Born in 1871 amidst the humiliation of military defeat, France's Third Republic went through many years of precarious existence before it achieved a firm and popular foundation. A new national assembly, elected by manhood suffrage to fulfill the bitter task of making peace with Germany as well as to draft a new constitution, was overwhelmingly royalist. This led to a new revolutionary movement in Paris, where republicans and radicals of every description formed a Commune, in the tradition of the Paris Commune of 1792, to save the Republic. The Communards also favored governmental control of prices, wages, and working conditions. Karl Marx jubilantly welcomed the uprising, seeing in it a pattern for the future revolt of the proletariat against the capitalistic system. After several weeks of civil war the Commune was savagely suppressed, leaving France with a deep-seated heritage of class hatred. That the assembly finally voted a republican constitution for France in 1875 was due largely to the inability of various royalist factions to agree among themselves. A republic seemed the form of government on which there was least disagreement.

The improvised constitutional laws of 1875, passed by a margin of one vote, provided for the election by direct manhood suffrage of representatives to the Chamber of Deputies, the influential lower house. There was also a Senate, elected indirectly by electoral colleges in the major administrative districts, the departments. The president was elected by the legislature, and his powers were so limited as to make him merely a figurehead. The real executive was the ministry, or cabinet, appointed from whatever coalition of parties or factions held a majority in the legislature. As in England, the ministry was responsible to the legislature.

The Boulanger and Dreyfus affairs. In the mid-1880's there began a series of crises which, lasting more than a decade, threatened the very existence of the Republic. In 1886 General Boulanger, the minister of war,

During the civil war of 1871 between the government and the Paris Commune, many atrocities were committed. Illustrating the violence which occurred on both sides, this photograph shows the Communards assassinating sixty-two hostages.

became the toast of Paris and a national hero for seemingly advocating a war of revenge against Germany: "Remember, they are waiting for us in Alsace!" All antirepublican elements, from reactionary monarchists to radical workers, saw the "Brave General" as a "man on horseback" who would sweep away the Republic by a coup d'état as Louis Napoleon had done in 1851. But when the government ordered his arrest on the charge of conspiracy, Boulanger fled the country and later committed suicide.

In 1894 occurred an affair that eclipsed the Boulanger incident in the way in which it divided and embittered French opinion and challenged the fundamental ideals of French democracy. Captain Alfred Dreyfus (1859-1935), the first Jewish officer to secure a post in the general staff of the French army, was accused of selling military secrets to Germany. Disliked by many of his aristocratic fellow officers as a Jew, the unfortunate Dreyfus was found guilty, publicly stripped of his commission, and condemned to solitary confinement on Devil's Island, a notorious convict settlement near French Guiana.

The Dreyfus affair was not closed, however. French military secrets continued to leak, and a spendthrift officer named Major Esterhazy was brought to trial and then acquitted. When Émile Zola entered the fray, the first step in the ultimate exoneration of Dreyfus was taken. In "J'accuse" (1898), his famous open letter to the president of France, Zola attacked the military court-martial, accusing the judges of knowingly acquitting the guilty man, Esterhazy, who was a royalist.

The Dreyfus case developed into a bloodless civil war between friends and foes of the Republic—a war of which Dreyfus was the unwilling symbol and victim. The army, the Church, and the royalists were, generally speaking, anti-Dreyfusards; intellectuals, republicans, and socialists supported Dreyfus.

In 1899 the Dreyfus case was authorized for review, but even though Esterhazy had admitted his guilt, political passions were so strong that Dreyfus was again found guilty. The president of France, however, pardoned Dreyfus. In 1906 the highest civil court in France found Dreyfus completely innocent, thus asserting the power of the civil authority over the military that had condemned him. The victorious Republic then purged the army of its reactionary officers.

The anticlerical movement. The Church also had to pay for its alliance with the army during the Dreyfus affair. Convinced that the clergy was the Republic's main enemy—"at the bottom of every agitation and every intrigue from which Republican France has suffered"—leading republicans demanded an end to Church interference in the affairs of state. As one republican stated, "I want the priest outside of politics. In the Church, yes; on the public square, on the platform, never."[3]

In 1901 all Church schools were closed, and in 1905 Church and state were formally separated with the abrogation of Napoleon's century-old Concordat with the papacy (see p. 463). Henceforth, the state ceased to pay the salaries of the clergy—Protestant and Jewish as well as Catholic. Furthermore, all Church property was taken over by the state, annual arrangements being made for the use of Church buildings.

The Third Republic in 1914. By 1914 France was a prosperous land of more than 39 million people, although a falling birth rate put it far behind the prolific Germans, who numbered 70 million. And after a century of wars, revolutions, and crises, French republicanism had finally attained stability and wide public support.

Most Frenchmen enjoyed basic democratic rights, such as manhood suffrage, freedom of the press, and equality before the law. They tended, however, to regard government not as a servant but as a meddling, would-be tyrant. In consequence, officials found it difficult to impose direct taxation, and the machinery of the state was severely handicapped by a lack of funds.

Reflecting the extreme individualism of the French was the multi-party political system. There were so many different political groups represented in the Chamber of Deputies that prime ministers had to form cabinets made up of diverse elements. Like unstable chemical compounds, these cabinets blew up under the slightest pressure. French prime ministers came and went with bewildering rapidity, at the whim of the legislature. In spite of these weaknesses, however, France in 1914 was regarded as the most important democracy on the Continent and one of the great powers of the world.

Progress of democracy in the European small states. While achieving its greatest success in Great Britain and France, the trend toward democracy was evident throughout Europe during the late nine-teenth and early twentieth centuries. We have seen in Chapter 23 that political life in central and eastern Europe, where nationalism was the dominant force, was also marked by movements toward con-stitutional government and, in most states, universal manhood suffrage. The remaining, generally smaller, states of Europe also made democratic advances, often of a unique character.

In the latter part of the nineteenth century the Scandinavian nations in particular were developing into virtual sociological labora-tories, where "few should have more than they need, and fewer still should have less than they need." The enfranchisement of women was first introduced in Norway, proportional representation had its first trial in Belgium, and Switzerland invented the referendum and the initiative.

While political stability and protection of basic human rights were generally out-standing in the small states of northwestern Europe, Spain and Portugal were case studies of the failure of democracy. Popular dis-content, generated by political ineptitude and corruption on the part of too many politicians and general failure to provide education and better living conditions for the masses, was rife in these countries.

FORCES FOR PEACE AND WAR

Growing spirit of internationalism. As the nineteenth century came to a close, there was evidence of a growing spirit of inter-nationalism and a deep yearning for peace among the peoples of the world. The growth of world trade, augmented by new marvels in transportation and communication, served to knit men together into a world com-munity; and further evidences of such inter-nationalism were numerous. In 1865 a con-ference which met in Paris to discuss the coordination of telegraph lines and the problem of rates established the Interna-tional Telegraph Union, made up of twenty nations. To facilitate the handling of mail the world over, the Universal Postal Union was set up in 1875. As a protection for authors' rights, an agreement was drawn up in 1886 by an international copyright union. In 1896, as part of the growing internationalism, the ancient Greek Olympic games were revived. Held every four years, the games attracted participants from nearly every nation.

The peace movement. The modern, organized world peace movement began early in the nineteenth century. Motivated by Christian principles, the British Society for the Promotion of Permanent and Universal Peace was organized in 1816, and thirty years later the League of Universal Brotherhood was founded in the United States. While the first phase of the pacifist movement was for the most part religiously motivated, the second, beginning in the late 1860's, emphasized such practical problems as improvements in international law and the rules of warfare and creation of machinery for arbitrating disputes.

The first Pan-American Conference, consisting of eighteen countries, assembled in 1889 at Washington, D.C., to discuss matters of common economic interest as well as problems pertaining to the maintenance of peace in the Western Hemisphere. In 1899, also, the Russian foreign minister invited the great powers to attend a conference at The Hague on the reduction of armaments. Although no progress was made on disarmament, the conference did adopt a number of points in international law on rules of war relating to treatment of prisoners, outlawed the use of poisonous gas, and defined the conditions of a state of belligerency. A court of arbitration, the Hague Tribunal, was established; and a list of jurists from which nations could select judges was drawn up. Recourse to the court was voluntary and so was acceptance of its decisions. Yet arbitration between nations appeared to be on the increase. In the ten years following 1903, various powers signed 162 arbitration treaties, pledging the signatories to arbitrate certain matters.

The contributions of famous individuals were also important to the movement for world peace. Alfred Nobel, the famous Swedish manufacturer of dynamite, established the Nobel Peace Prize; and Andrew Carnegie founded the Carnegie Endowment for International Peace and built a Peace Palace at The Hague to be used for international conferences. (Ironically, the building was finished just before the outbreak of the First World War.)

Forces of antagonism. While some forces were working to bring about closer cooperation between nations and peoples, others were promoting distrust and rivalries. These antagonistic forces finally triumphed, and, as a result, Europe and most of the world with it were plunged into war in 1914. The underlying causes of this great conflict were the actions of national states in power politics, militarism, rival alliances, secret diplomacy, economic imperialism, and nationalism.

Europe in 1914 consisted of some twenty independent political units. Recognizing no higher authority, each of these states went its own way; international law was obeyed only if its dicta did not clash with a nation's interests. The great powers were ready to take advantage of any neighbor's weakness and to resort to war if the prize to be seized or the danger to be averted was substantial enough. War was an instrument of national policy, to be used whenever peaceful methods failed.

When force is the ultimate arbiter in international affairs, military strength becomes extremely important. By the end of the 1870's all six of the major European powers except Britain had introduced compulsory military training. By the first decade of the twentieth century, the great powers had nearly 4.5 million men under arms and were spending annually more than $2 billion on armaments. Thus the armament race began, and the faster it went, the higher tension mounted.

Living in this international anarchy, where a nation could not trust its neighbors, most states did not feel strong enough to rely upon their own military resources for protection. Therefore, nations whose interests ran along parallel lines joined together to muster more fighting power. But this, in turn, provoked nations outside the alliance to form a union capable of matching strength with strength. While the

«Amaos los unos á los otros.» (JESUCRISTO)

Symbolic of power politics and militaristic attitudes, European nations play billiards with cannon balls in this pre-World War I Spanish cartoon. The original caption was a Biblical quote: "You should love one another."

creation of two rival alliances was a feature of European diplomacy in the last part of the nineteenth century (see pp. 559-560), it brought no security to the states involved. In fact, the prospects of a major war were multiplied because the alliances made it unlikely that any conflict could be localized. This is what happened in the summer of 1914.

Closely connected with the system of alliances was the practice of secret diplomacy. Diplomats threatened, intimidated, jockeyed for power, and offered bribes. The activities of spies, the secret reports, and the unscrupulous methods of the foreign offices of Europe poisoned the atmosphere of international politics and heightened the tension still further.

After 1870 the world's markets were viewed as a battleground. Laissez faire increasingly gave way to a new kind of mercantilism in which governments acted as aggressive champions for their own business interests. One of the most significant features of this neo-mercantilism was economic imperialism, a struggle for the control of the colonial areas of the world. As we shall see in Chapter 27, governments began to use their diplomatic power and even their armies to secure control of areas rich in essential raw materials or valuable as markets for manufactured goods. In some cases economic competition led to war. Japanese designs upon the Asian mainland brought about war with China in 1894, and Great Britain fought the Boer War in South Africa in 1899-1902. Japan and Russia fought over Manchuria in 1904-1905, and Italy wrested Tripoli from Turkey in 1912.

The emotion of nationalism. Nationalism —particularly the narrow, blatant, and bellicose variety of the late nineteenth century— has been rightly regarded as one of the most potent causes of modern war. Among both subordinated and ruling groups, national loyalty was an intense, explosive emotion. Inflated patriotism became a new religion, the emotional adjunct to power politics. In the opinion of many observers, the most important fundamental cause of the First World War was rampant nationalism.

In Germany, for example, the Pan-Germanic League was organized to spread the doctrine of the superiority of the German race and culture. The League was a leader in anti-English agitation; it supported German colonial ambitions; it sought to retain the loyalty of all Germans to the fatherland no matter where they were living in the world; and it worked to promote a policy of German power both in Europe and overseas.

As it turned out, the greatest danger to peace was the flame of nationalism that burned fiercely in the new Balkan nations. Proud of their new freedom, they were determined to extend it to their brothers still under the Turks. Serbia in particular was ready to liberate the other Slavic groups and unite with itself the Slavs in Bosnia and Herzegovina and in Albania. This ambition, known as the Greater Serbia movement, was aimed not only against the Turks but also against the Hapsburgs, who ruled many South Slavs.

The Greater Serbia movement was a local manifestation of Russian-encouraged Pan-Slavism (see p. 544). Representatives of the various Slavic nations looked to Russia as the protector of all oppressed Slavs, especially those in the Dual Monarchy.

Anti-Semitism and Zionism. Speaking of Pan-Germanism and Pan-Slavism, a famous historian refers to their development as the "seed time of totalitarian nationalism." These pernicious ideas of racial superiority were later to develop into the hideous campaign of extermination which Adolf Hitler and his Nazi henchmen carried out against certain supposedly inferior peoples, concentrating primarily on the Jews.

A foretaste of what racial nationalism would bring in the twentieth century was provided by the treatment of the Jews in the later nineteenth century. After suffering from many injustices and restrictions during the Middle Ages, the Jews in western Europe and in the Americas secured practically all the rights of full citizens after 1800. With this advance came new opportunities; and Jews in many countries made significant contributions to art, music, literature, and science. About 1850, however, a strong anti-Semitic movement began to appear in Europe. German nationalists like Heinrich von Treitschke coined the phrase "The Jews are our calamity." In France anti-Semitism reached a climax in the Dreyfus affair. In eastern Europe the Jewish minorities suffered many injustices, but their hardest lot was in Russia. In the tsar's realm the Jews had to live in specified western provinces, the so-called Jewish Pale. They were forbidden to buy certain kinds of property; their admittance to schools was restricted; and they had to pay twice the taxes of corresponding non-Jewish communities. Used at times as scapegoats, many Jews were murdered in pogroms carried out with the encouragement of the government.

From the injustices of anti-Semitism in the last century grew the desire for a Jewish homeland. Thus the exaggerated nationalism of other peoples bred a nationalistic spirit among the Jews themselves. In 1896 a Hungarian Jew, Theodor Herzl, came forward with the program of Zionism, which had as its purpose the creation of Palestine as an independent state. Herzl claimed that the Jews were a distinct nationality and thus were entitled to have a country of their own. The first general congress of Zionists was held in Switzerland in 1897, and small-scale immigration to Palestine began.

THE LAMPS ARE GOING OUT

Bismarck's diplomatic footwork. After the conclusion of the Franco-Prussian War in 1871, the German chancellor was well aware that France would try to inflict revenge on Germany and take back Alsace-Lorraine. Therefore, Bismarck deliberately set out to isolate France diplomatically by depriving it of potential allies. In 1873 he made an alliance with Russia and Austria-Hungary, known as the Three Emperors' League; but at the Congress of Berlin (1878) he was forced to choose between the claims of Austria and those of Russia in the Balkans. Bismarck chose to support Austria because he trusted that empire more than he did Russia. He was afraid also that supporting Russia would alienate Great Britain.

A year later Bismarck negotiated the Dual Alliance with the Austrian government, and in 1882 a new partner, Italy, was secured, thus bringing into operation the Triple Alliance. The choice of Austria as a close ally in preference to Russia did not mean that Bismarck was reconciled to the loss of the latter's friendship. In 1881 the Three Emperors' League was renewed, but when rivalries between Austria and Russia in the Balkans made it impossible for these two powers to be in the same group, the alliance collapsed in 1887. To fill the gap, Bismarck negotiated a separate alliance with Russia called the Reinsurance Treaty.

Under the masterful hand of Bismarck, Germany retained hegemony over the European continent from 1871 to 1890. The chancellor had succeeded admirably in his diplomacy. Every effort was made to avoid challenging the interests of Britain, which continued its policy of "splendid isolation" (see p. 505). France had been kept in diplomatic quarantine without allies. Through amazing diplomatic acrobatics, Bismarck had managed to avoid alienating Russia while retaining an alliance with Austria.

In a single move, however, the preponderance of power built up by Bismarck was heedlessly cast away. In 1890 the new German kaiser, young William II, dismissed the old chancellor and took German foreign policy into his own hands. Foolishly allowing the Reinsurance Treaty to lapse, he permitted Russia to seek new allies. France immediately began to woo Russia; millions of French francs went to buy Russian bonds, and in 1894 France received what it had wanted for twenty years—a strong military ally. The Triple Alliance was now confronted by the Dual Alliance.

England ends its isolation. At the end of the nineteenth century Britain was involved in bitter rivalries with Russia in the Balkans and Afghanistan and with France in Africa. During the Boer War (see p. 618) all the great powers in Europe were anti-British. Only the supremacy of England's fleet effectively discouraged the development of an interventionist movement. More and more, Great Britain became disquieted by its policy of diplomatic isolation. It was

these circumstances which explained British overtures to Germany in 1898 and again in 1901.

Kaiser William II refused Britain's suggestions for an alliance, which he interpreted as a sign of British weakness, and embarked on an aggressive policy known as *Weltpolitik* (world politics). He was determined not only to make Germany the first military power in Europe but to expand its influence in the Middle East and the Balkans, secure more colonies overseas, and build a battle fleet second to none. A huge naval program was initiated in 1900, providing for the construction of a fleet strong enough to jeopardize Britain's naval supremacy within twenty years. For England the supremacy of the royal navy was a life-or-death matter. Since food and raw materials had to come by sea, it was crucial that the royal navy be able to protect British shipping. The British were disturbed also at the tremendous strides made by German industry, as well as the Kaiser's threatening and irresponsible speeches and unpredictable behavior. Rebuffed and challenged by Germany, Britain turned elsewhere to establish friendly relations.

In 1904 Britain and France settled their outstanding differences and proclaimed the *Entente Cordiale*, a French term meaning "friendly understanding." The Entente Cordiale, together with England's alliance with Japan in 1902, ended Britain's policy of isolation and brought it into the diplomatic combination pitted against Germany's Triple Alliance. In 1907 Britain settled its problems with Russia, thereby establishing the Triple Entente. Great Britain made no definite military commitments in the agreements with France and Russia. Theoretically it retained freedom of action but, for all this, it was now part of the alliance system.

Diplomatic crises: 1905-1914. For a decade before the First World War, Europe experienced a series of crises brought about as the two alliance systems flexed their muscles and probed each other's strength. As each new diplomatic crisis arose, Europe teetered on the abyss of war.

The first serious diplomatic crisis occurred in 1905 over Morocco. France sought control of this territory in order to establish a stretch of contiguous dependencies from the Atlantic across the North African coast to Tunisia. Carefully timing his moves, the German chancellor arranged for the kaiser to visit the Moroccan port of Tangier, where he declared that all powers must respect the independence of the country. The French were forced to give up their immediate plans for taking over Morocco and agree to Germany's suggestion that an international conference be called at Algeciras (1906) to discuss the matter.

At this meeting the German hope that a rift might appear between the British and French did not materialize. On the contrary, all but one of the nations in attendance—even Italy—supported France rather than Germany. Only Austria remained at the side of Germany. It was agreed that Morocco should still enjoy its sovereignty but that France and Spain should be given certain rights to police the area. The events at

Algeciras and the British agreement with Russia the following year (1907) filled the Germans with dread.

In 1911 a second Moroccan crisis heightened the tension. When France sent an army into the disputed territory "to maintain order," Germany countered by dispatching the gunboat *Panther* to the Moroccan port of Agadir. Great Britain came out with a plain warning that all its power was at the disposal of France. A diplomatic bargain was struck whereby France got a free hand in Morocco, and Germany was granted French holdings in equatorial Africa.

The Balkan nemesis. Although the two rival alliance systems had managed to avert an armed showdown over Morocco, these happy auguries were of no avail against the forces of rival imperialism and nationalism in the Balkans, where both Germany and Austria were opposed to Russia's Pan-Slavic ambitions. German motives were largely economic; the Germans en-

DIPLOMATIC CRISES
1905-1914

visaged a great continuous economy stretching from the Baltic to the Persian Gulf. The Austrian concern in the Balkans was primarily defensive. A polyglot empire containing millions of Slavs, Austria-Hungary feared an expanding Serbia, egged on by Russia. To counter the advance of the Greater Serbia movement, Austria in 1908 annexed the provinces of Bosnia and Herzegovina, which it had administered since 1878. This high-handed move produced a dangerous crisis. Russia was furious and Serbia was equally exercised over the incorporation of more South Slavs into the Hapsburg domain. But because Russia had come out of its war with Japan (1904-1905) badly battered, it could not support Serbia against the combined might of Germany and Austria. In this crisis the Triple Alliance had humbled Russia and thwarted the plans of Russia's protégé Serbia.

In 1912 Serbia and its neighbors, especially Greece and Bulgaria, formed an alliance with the objective of expelling Turkey from Europe. The First Balkan War began later in that year and was quickly terminated as Turkish resistance crumpled. The victorious Balkan nations were not permitted to divide their spoils, however, and this led to the Second Balkan War. Denied Albania by Austria, the Serbs, supported by the Greeks, demanded territory originally promised to Bulgaria. Bulgaria attacked its former allies, and Turkey and Rumania in turn entered the war against Bulgaria, which was no match for its numerous opponents. A peace was signed by which Bulgaria gave its former allies most of the territory it had originally taken from Turkey. The Turks retained only a precarious toehold in Europe, the small pocket around Constantinople.

By the end of 1913 no permanent solution had been found to the Balkan problem. Austria was more fearful than ever of the Greater Serbia movement, and Serbian ambitions had grown larger, since its territory had doubled as a result of the recent wars. The Serbian prime minister is quoted as saying: "The first round is won; now we must prepare the second against Austria." As for Russia, its Pan-Slavic dreams had not

been completely blocked but only interrupted. The dynamite in the Balkan bomb was the involvement of the major powers.

The archduke assassinated. The fateful spark came on June 28, 1914, when Archduke Francis Ferdinand, heir to the Austrian throne, and his wife were assassinated in the town of Sarajevo in Bosnia. This deed was the work of a young Bosnian student inspired by Greater Serbia propaganda. He and two associates received assistance from high Serbian officers, although the direct complicity of the Serbian government has not been proved. Even so, it seems unlikely that the government could have been ignorant of the plot.

Count Leopold von Berchtold, the Austrian foreign minister, believed that the assassination justified crushing, once and for all, the anti-Austrian propaganda and terrorism emanating from Serbia. Austria hesitated to act, however, without securing the support of its German ally. The kaiser felt that everything possible must be done to prevent Germany's only reliable ally from being weakened by such forces as Serbian terrorism, and so he assured the Austrian government of his full support. Thus Berchtold obtained a blank check from Germany. Vienna wanted only a local Austro-Serbian war, and Germany favored quick action to forestall Russian intervention.

The Austrian ultimatum and Russian mobilization. On July 23 a harsh Austro-Hungarian ultimatum was presented to the Serbs. Intending that the ultimatum be turned down, Berchtold demanded unconditional acceptance within forty-eight hours. On July 25 the Austrian government announced that Serbia's reply was unsatisfactory and mobilized its armed forces. Meanwhile the German chancellor urged Austria to negotiate with Russia, which was following developments closely. Russia realized that if the Austrians succeeded in humbling Serbia, Russian prestige in this area would suffer tremendously. The French in the meantime assured the Russians of their full cooperation and urged strong support for Serbia, while the British advised negotiations, but without success.

Fearful that Serbia would escape from his

clutches, Berchtold succeeded on July 27, thanks in part to falsehood, in convincing the Hapsburg emperor that war was the only way out. On the following day, war was declared against Serbia. As the possibility of a general European war loomed, Berlin sent several frantic telegrams to Vienna. The German ambassador was instructed to tell Berchtold: "As an ally we must refuse to be drawn into a world conflagration because Austria does not respect our advice."[4] At this critical stage, when German pressure on Austria might have opened a path to peace, an event took place which wrecked any further attempts at negotiation. This was the Russian mobilization on July 30.

To Germany, the question of Russian mobilization was especially vital, because, in the event of war with Russia and its ally, France, Germany would be confronted with enemies on two fronts. The best plan seemed to be to launch a lightning attack against France, crush France, and then turn to meet Russia, which could ordinarily be expected to mobilize rather slowly. To allow Russian mobilization to proceed would jeopardize this strategy.

War declared. On July 31 the government in Berlin dispatched ultimatums to Russia and France demanding from the former cessation of mobilization and from the latter a pledge of neutrality. Failing to receive satisfactory replies, Germany declared war on Russia August 1 and on France August 3. On August 2 an ultimatum was delivered by the German ambassador in Brussels, announcing his country's intention of sending troops through Belgium. The Belgian cabinet refused to grant permission and appealed to Russia, France, and Great Britain for aid in protecting its neutrality. A majority in the British cabinet did not favor war, but with the news of the German ultimatum to Belgium, the tide turned. Sir Edward Grey, the British foreign secretary, sent

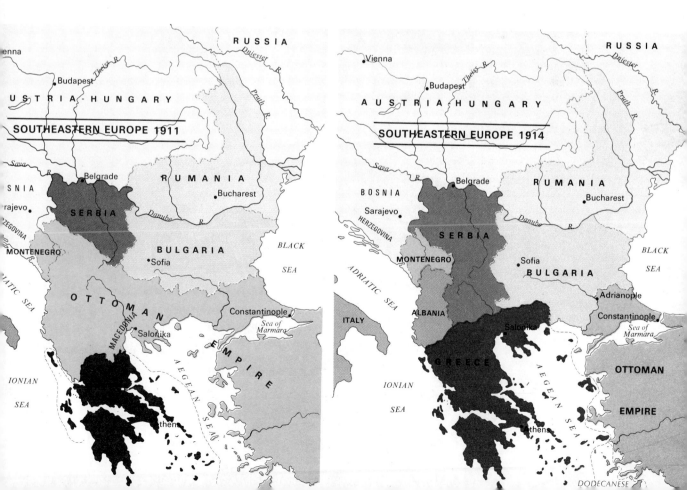

an ultimatum to Germany demanding that Belgian neutrality be respected. This Germany refused to do, and on August 4 Great Britain declared war.

On the basis that Germany and Austria were not waging a defensive war, Italy refused to carry out its obligations under the Triple Alliance and for the time being remained neutral. In the latter part of August, Japan joined the Allies; and in October, Turkey, fearing the designs of Russia, threw in its lot with the Central Powers, Germany and Austria.

The question of war guilt. Germany made a serious blunder when its chancellor referred to the treaty of 1839 guaranteeing the neutrality of Belgium—signed by the European powers, including Prussia—as "a scrap of paper." Germany thus put itself morally in the wrong as a breaker of treaties, a position that lost it support and sympathy the world over. Equally important, Germany's declaration of war on Russia and France had brought on a general war.

The structure of the Treaty of Versailles, as we shall see later, rested in large part on the assumed "war guilt" of Germany. When the treaty was first written, scholars and laymen alike in the Allied nations sincerely believed that Germany was completely responsible for the war. In time it became increasingly clear that the problem was more complex than had been originally thought. Today most historians agree it is next to impossible to try to explain the war in terms of the actions of any one of the great powers. Rather, all the major participating nations must accept, in some measure, responsibility for the outbreak of the First World War. In the final analysis, it is needless to try to apportion the blame, for the tragedy was inherent in the prevailing order —or disorder—of international anarchy.

In the last few days of peace, diplomats strove desperately to avert general war. Through confusion, fear, and loss of sleep, the nervous strain among them was almost unbearable. Many broke down and wept when it was apparent they had failed. This atmosphere of anguish and gloom is reflected in a passage from Sir Edward Grey's autobiography:

A friend came to see me on one of the evenings of the last week [before the war]—he thinks it was on Monday, August 3. We were standing at the window of my room in the Foreign Office. It was getting dusk, and the lamps were being lit in the space below on which we were looking.

"The lamps are going out all over Europe . . ."—these words of Sir Edward Grey, the British foreign secretary, are illustrated in a *Chicago Daily News* cartoon of July 30, 1914, a few short days before World War I became a reality.

My friend recalls that I remarked on this with the words: "The lamps are going out all over Europe; we shall not see them lit again in our life-time."[5]

THE FIRST WORLD WAR

Scope of the conflict. Although the terrible struggle that racked mankind from 1914 to 1918 was fought chiefly on the European continent, it can justly be called the First World War. Altogether, twenty-seven powers became belligerents, ranging the globe from Tokyo to Ottawa and from Rio de Janeiro to Capetown. Tremendous fighting strength was mustered. The Central Powers—Germany, Austria, Bulgaria, and Turkey—mobilized 21 million men; their opponents, the Allies, mustered 40 million of whom 12 million were Russian. Since the Russian divisions were poorly equipped and often ineffectively used, these total figures are somewhat misleading in that they indicate a more decisive advantage than the Allies actually enjoyed. Furthermore, in the German army, the Central Powers boasted superb generalship and discipline, and they fought from an inner or central position and were therefore able to transfer troops quickly and efficiently to various fronts. In their favor, the Allies had greater resources of finance and raw materials; and Britain, helped by its empire, had the advantage of a splendid, powerful fleet with which to maintain control of the seas.

The initial shock of war. The belligerent nations went into battle in a champagne mood. Each side believed the conflict would soon be over, concluded by a few decisive battles, and each side believed its victory was inevitable. Allied naval supremacy cut off the Central Powers from vitally needed sources of raw material from overseas. Germany was therefore determined to strike a quick knockout blow to end the war. Pushing heroic Belgian resistance aside, German armies drove rapidly south into France. The strategy was to wheel west of Paris, outflanking the French forces, and then to drive them toward Alsace-Lorraine, where they would be met by another German army and destroyed by this hammer-anvil maneuver. Meanwhile, a small German force would be holding the Russians at bay in East Prussia.

But this strategy failed. After reaching to within twenty-five miles of Paris, the Germans were hurled back by a bold counteroffensive launched by the French and a small British expeditionary force. Following this all-important battle of the Marne, a race to the sea began with each army trying to reach the vital ports along the English Channel first. After much desperate fighting, battle positions were stabilized, and the "western front" was created in a solid line of opposing trenches stretching from the Channel to Switzerland. On the "eastern front" rapidly moving Russian armies had penetrated East Prussia and had quickly overrun the Austrian province of Galicia. The Russians, however, suffered two catastrophic defeats in East Prussia, and the eastern frontiers of Germany were never again seriously menaced. Toward the end of 1914 all combatants began to realize the terrible consequences of modern war. Single battles devoured hundreds of thousands of lives, and the toll during the first few months of conflict ran as high as a million and a half dead and wounded.

Allied setbacks in 1915. In 1915 Britain undertook a major campaign in an attempt to force open the Dardanelles, closed by Turkey when it had joined the Central Powers. This plan, attributed mainly to Winston Churchill, then first lord of the admiralty, was designed to open up a sea route to Russia, which was badly in need of war supplies. After heroic and costly attacks, Australian and New Zealand troops, known as Anzacs, were compelled to withdraw from their landing positions on the Gallipoli peninsula in European Turkey.

Another major Allied setback in 1915 was the defeat of Russian forces in Poland. More than 1,200,000 Russians were killed or wounded, and the Germans captured nearly 900,000 prisoners. While Russia somehow remained in the war, it now ceased to be a major threat to the Central

WORLD WAR I

- Triple Entente
- Central Powers
- Allies of Triple Entente
- Neutral nations
- → Allied thrust
- ➤ Central Powers' thrust

Battles:
- × Allied victory
- ⊗ Central Powers' victory

Powers. These defeats generated rising criticism against the tsar's government, and the Russians' morale began to break down.

Serbia was the next victim. Its conquest was made all the easier because in September Bulgaria entered the war on the side of the Central Powers. Surrounded by enemies, Serbia was helpless and resistance was quickly crushed.

The only bright spot for the Allies in 1915 was the entry of Italy into their ranks. This nation had remained neutral in August 1914, and its defection from the Triple Alliance was secured in 1915 by promises

the Allies made in the secret treaty of London. This agreement promised Italy lavish concessions of territory following a victory by the Allies.

Stalemate, 1916. The Allied strategy was to restrict attacks in France to intermittent nibbling, thus conserving manpower and at the same time concentrating on their naval blockade. Denied badly needed imports, the German war effort would be seriously weakened. Countering this tactic, the German high command launched a tremendous offensive against the important fortress of Verdun in the spring of 1916, compelling the French to commit hundreds of thousands of men to its defense. Attrition on both sides resulted from this incredible bloodbath—the total loss in wounded and dead of some 700,000 men.

To ease the grinding pressure against Verdun, the British army began an offensive along the Somme on the western front. The attackers' losses were tragic: 60 percent of the officers and 40 percent of the men became casualties on the first day of the battle. Despite these awesome figures, the attacks continued for several months without any substantial gains. The total German casualties at Verdun and on the Somme were slightly less than those of the Allies.

The battle of Jutland (May 31–June 1, 1916), in the North Sea west of Denmark, was another crucial engagement, since control of the seas was vital to Britain. At Jutland, the only major naval engagement of the war, the Germans maneuvered brilliantly and took risks. They could afford to gamble, for defeat could in no way worsen their existing strategic position. The British fleet, on the other hand, acted with extreme caution, since the British admiral "was the one man who could have lost the war in an afternoon."[6] British losses were heavier, but the German battleships retreated to their bases to remain there for the duration of the war. British naval supremacy continued intact.

On the eastern front in 1916 the Russians staged an unexpected comeback by inflicting a major defeat upon Austrian forces. German armies saved their ally from destruction, but, impressed by the Russian victory, Rumania threw in its lot with the Allies and launched an attack against Hungary. Despite initial success, Rumania was later invaded by German and Bulgarian forces and compelled to capitulate.

At the close of 1916, after more than two years of fighting, neither the Central Powers nor the Allies could envisage victory. The war had turned into a dreary contest of stamina.

Total war, a new reality. War had also branched out into a whole new dimension—the nonmilitary struggle to sustain the will of the civilian population. In fact, the war on the home front rivaled that fought on the battlefield. As an English observer put it:

> The War has passed out of the phase of a mere battle. It is now a contest between the will and determination of whole nations to continue a life-and-death struggle in which "battle" takes a very small part.[7]

The citizens of the belligerent nations were urged to eat less food, buy more bonds, and manufacture more shells. Women were urged to take men's jobs in order to release more manpower for military purposes. People were deluged by a barrage of propaganda inciting them to hate the enemy, to believe in the righteousness of their cause, and to support the war effort without complaint or criticism. Civil liberties suffered, and in some instances, distinguished citizens were clapped into prison for opposing the war effort. In England, for example, the philosopher and mathematician Bertrand Russell was imprisoned for a short time. Governments took over the control of their national economies. Strikes were outlawed, and currencies and foreign trade were rigidly controlled.

Changes in public opinion. On the home front all was flag waving and enthusiasm in 1914. There was much idealism, sense of sacrifice, and patriotism, with little comprehension of the horror, death, and degradation accompanying modern mechanized war. The spirit was expressed by the English poet Rupert Brooke when he wrote:

> If I should die, think only this of me:
> That there's some corner of a foreign field
> That is forever England. There shall be
> In that rich earth a richer dust concealed;
> A dust whom England bore, shaped, made aware,
> Gave, once, her flowers to love, her ways to roam,
> A body of England's, breathing English air,
> Washed by the rivers, blest by suns of home.[8]

But this early euphoria gradually changed to one of war weariness and utter futility. This growing awareness is illustrated by the poetry of the young British officer and poet Wilfred Owen, himself a victim on the western front, who poignantly observed:

What passing-bells for those who die as cattle?
Only the monstrous anger of the guns . . . .

No mockeries for them; no prayers nor bells,
Nor any voice of mourning save the choirs,—
The shrill, demented choirs of wailing shells;
And bugles calling for them from sad shires.[9]

By the end of 1916 there was a deep yearning for peace. Sensing this mood, leaders on both sides tendered rather half-hearted peace feelers. But these achieved nothing. Continuance of the war was made possible largely by use of propaganda. All the people in the warring nations were made to believe that they were part of a crusade for a better world. The Germans were labeled "Huns" by the Allies; the Russians "savages" by the Germans. The followers of the kaiser sang their "Hymn of Hate" with patriotic gusto:

Hate by water and hate by land;
Hate of the heart and hate of the hand;
We love as one; we hate as one;
We have but one foe alone—England.[10]

Allies near the breaking point in 1917. In 1917 British and French military strength reached its highest point, only to fall to unprecedented depths. Allied commanders were hopeful that the long-planned breakthrough might be accomplished, but a large-scale attack by the French was beaten back with horrible losses. French regiments mutinied rather than return to the inferno of no man's land. The British army meanwhile launched several massive offensives, only to lose hundreds of thousands of men without any decisive results. The Allies also launched unsuccessful offensives in Italy, where catastrophe threatened. Aided by the Germans, the Austrian army smashed the Italian front at the battle of Caporetto (1917), so vividly described by Ernest Hemingway in *A Farewell to Arms*. Italian resistance finally hardened, but collapse was barely averted.

This frustration of Allied hopes was deepened by the growing menace of the German submarine campaign. By 1917 shipping losses had assumed catastrophic proportions. In three months 470 British ships alone fell victims to torpedoes. Britain had no more than six weeks' supply of food, and the

The participants of World War I experienced a tragic consequence of industrialization as the tools of peacetime prosperity became the weapons of wartime destruction. Due to their effectiveness in surprise attack, submarines achieved widespread use as military weapons. Below a submarine takes on supplies while moored in a German harbor. The British secretly developed the military tank under the pretext of building water tanks. German soldiers were terrified when these strange steel monsters first appeared in September 1916. The "dogfight" between German and Allied planes was a typical scene during the Great War. Although the aircraft of those days are now obsolete, their maneuverability has never been matched.

situation became critical for the Allies. But the very weapon that seemed to doom their cause was to prove their salvation, for the submarine brought the United States into the war on the Allies' side.

American sentiment lies with the Allies. After Italy joined the Allies in 1915, the United States was the only great power remaining neutral. In 1914 President Wilson had announced the neutrality of the United States and declared that the people "must be impartial in thought as well as in action." The events of the following two years showed that this was no easy task.

From the beginning of the conflict, American sentiment was predominantly with the Allies. There was the strong tradition of friendship with France because of that country's help to the American colonies during the revolutionary war, and between Britain and America there were strong cultural ties of language, literature, and democratic institutions. British propaganda, moreover, had the United States as its special target and was much more effective than that of the Central Powers.

Another factor favoring the Allied cause was the American belief that Germany had grossly violated international law by invading Belgium. Partly because of the kaiser's saber-rattling speeches, the German government was regarded as undemocratic, unpredictable, and unstable. In some circles it was believed that a German victory would upset the world balance of power and that a victorious and expansionist Germany might imperil American security.

As the war progressed, it became apparent that the British blockade would permit United States trade to be carried on with only the Allies, and before long American factories and farmers were producing munitions and food exclusively for Great Britain and France. Industry expanded and began to enjoy a prosperity dependent upon the continuance of Allied purchases. Between 1914 and 1916 American exports to the Allies quadrupled. During 1915 and 1916 Allied bonds totaling about $1.5 billion were sold in the United States.

German U-boat campaign precipitates war. The immediate cause of the United

States entry into the war on the side of the Allies was undoubtedly the German submarine campaign. Blockaded by the British navy, Germany decided to retaliate by halting all shipping to the Allies. Its submarine campaign began in February 1915, and one of the first victims was the luxury liner *Lusitania*, torpedoed with the loss of more than a thousand lives, including more than one hundred Americans. This tragedy aroused public opinion in America.

In the fall of 1916 Wilson was reelected to the presidency. One of his election slogans was "He kept us out of war." But this boast was soon invalidated by the force of events. The discovery of German plots to embroil Mexico in the war against the United States and more submarine sinkings aroused violent American resentment. Finally the President asked Congress to declare war against Germany. This action was taken on April 6, 1917.

The motives back of this decision, as in any great historical happening, were incredibly complex and have caused considerable debate among historians. After the First World War much attention was paid to the important role played by British propaganda and to the American financial interest in the Allied powers. Careful students point out that though the economic situation did influence the final decision to go to war, "the financial community as a whole . . . favored American neutrality rather than American participation; for neutrality afforded Wall Street all the profits of war without the compensating sacrifices and taxation. And there is not a shred of evidence to support the allegation that Wilson was at any time influenced by the financial 'stake' in his relations with Germany."[11]

No matter what causes had operated to bring America into the war, the United States was now fighting, in the words of President Wilson, "to make the world safe for democracy." The spell of Wilson's lofty principles caused a great welling of idealism among Americans.

Germany's last effort. While the United States mobilized its tremendous resources of manpower and materials, the German government decided to win the war before American aid became effective. The British army had been bled white from the fruitless offensives of 1917, and the French divisions had barely recovered from the mutinies. Furthermore, the Russian war effort had collapsed. In the revolution of November 1917 the Bolsheviks seized power in Russia; and by the Treaty of Brest Litovsk early in 1918, they made peace with Germany. The terms were harsh. Russia lost 500,000 square miles of territory and 66 million people.

Freed from the necessity of fighting on the Russian front, Germany launched a series of great offensives against British and French positions in the spring of 1918. During one of these attacks a brigade of American marines covered itself with glory by halting a German onrush at Chateau-Thierry. A final effort was made against the French in July 1918. It was described as the *Friedensturm*, the peace offensive. Thus far German forces had made substantial gains but had not scored the essential breakthrough. By this time the momentum of attack was slowing down, and more than one million American "doughboys" had landed in France. The last German offensive was hurled back after a slight advance.

German collapse and armistice. The German drive had hardly been halted when the supreme Allied commander, Marshal Foch, counterattacked. Badly beaten and continually harassed, the German troops fell back in rapid retreat. By the end of October the German forces had been pushed out of most of France, and Allied armies were advancing through Belgium. The war of fixed positions separated by no man's land was over. With a preponderance of tanks, the Allies had smashed trench defenses and were now in open country.

On October 1 the German High Command urged the kaiser to sue for peace, and three days later the German chancellor sent a note to President Wilson requesting an end to hostilities. The president's reply notified the German government that peace was impossible so long as the autocratic regime in Germany existed. Although the German chancellor tried to retain the monarchy by introducing certain liberal reforms,

it was too late. Revolution broke out in many parts of the country, the kaiser abdicated, and a republic was proclaimed.

While Germany was staggering under the relentless pounding of Foch's armies, the German allies were suffering even greater misfortunes. Bulgaria surrendered on September 30, and Turkey capitulated a month later. Austria gave up the struggle against Italy on November 3; nine days later the Hapsburg empire collapsed when Emperor Charles I fled Vienna for sanctuary in Switzerland.

At five o'clock on the morning of November 11, 1918, in a dining car in the Compiègne Forest, the German delegates signed the terms of the armistice presented to them by Marshal Foch. At eleven o'clock the same day hostilities were halted. Everywhere the news was received with an outburst of unrestrained joy. The world was once more at peace, confronted with the task of binding up its wounds and removing the scars of conflict. Delegates from the Allied nations were soon to converge on Paris, where the peace conference was to be held.

For the troops of the victorious Allies, November 11 meant returning home to a joyful conqueror's welcome; to those of the Central Powers, it meant a return saddened by the realization of failure. The exodus of German forces has been vividly described by the German novelist Erich Maria Remarque.

Along the road, step upon step, in their faded, dirty uniforms tramp the grey columns. The unshaved faces beneath the steel helmets are haggard, wasted with hunger and long peril, pinched and dwindled to the lines drawn by terror and courage and death. They trudge along in silence . . . into peace.[12]

SUMMARY

By the end of the nineteenth century western Europe had experienced a veritable revolution in many basic aspects of its pattern of life. The political predominance of the aristocracy and the business classes was coming to an end; the bourgeois creed of political liberalism with its restricted suffrage had been undermined by the creed of mass democracy; and, in the economic field, state intervention to assure a measure of economic security had begun to replace laissez faire. This democratically oriented type of welfare state advanced much more rapidly in western than in eastern Europe. Great Britain, France, Norway, and Switzerland best represented the western democratic tradition. In contrast to these nations, a number of other states in Europe lacked democratic traditions and experience in self-government. The Nazi dictatorship, the despotism of Soviet Russia, and the tyranny in Russia's satellites—all have their roots in the failure of parliamentary government to become established in parts of central and eastern Europe before 1914.

Europe's golden age—the nineteenth century—was brought to an end by a combination of tragic forces: militarism, rival alliances, economic imperialism, secret diplomacy, and, most important of all, narrow and bellicose nationalism. All these forces operated in their most virulent form in the Balkans, where they finally exploded. And so powerful and pervasive were they that they not only involved Europe in general war but most of the rest of the world as well.

For more than four years the science, industry, wealth, and power of Europe were concentrated upon destruction. The Great War of 1914-1918 was a total war—a war fought not only on land, at sea, and in the air but also on home fronts far from military conflict. The campaigns fought at the beginning of the war—the Marne and Tannenberg and, a little later, the Dardanelles and Jutland—ended any hope of a quick victory on either side. The belligerents were condemned to the grinding horror of a war of attrition and stalemate. With the entrance of the United States into the war in the spring of 1917, however, this standoff finally ended. In the autumn of 1918 Germany collapsed and sued for peace.

SUGGESTIONS FOR READING

C. Morazé, **The Triumph of the Middle Classes,*** Anchor. A study of the rise and influence of the middle class in the nineteenth century. J. Munholland, **Origins of Contemporary Europe: 1890-1914,*** Harcourt, Brace & World, 1970, is a brief, highly recommended synthesis. Barbara Tuchman, **The Proud Tower: A Portrait of the World Before the War, 1890-1914,** Macmillan, 1966, is very readable.

D. Thomson, **England in the Nineteenth Century (1815-1914),*** Penguin; J. Conacher, ed., **The Emergence of Parliamentary Democracy in Britain in the Nineteenth Century,*** Wiley, 1970. Valuable brief accounts. See also the surveys cited in Chapter 22 and R. Ensor, **England, 1870-1914,** Oxford, 1936; G. Kitson Clark, **The Making of Victorian England,*** Atheneum; George M. Young, **Victorian England: Portrait of an Age,*** Galaxy; P. Magnus, **Gladstone,*** Dutton; Robert Blake, **Disraeli,*** Anchor. G. Dangerfield, **The Strange Death of Liberal England, 1910-1914,*** Capricorn, describes the inability of the Liberals to deal with major problems.

Donald J. Harvey, **France Since the Revolution,*** Free Press, 1968; D. W. Brogan, **The French Nation: From Napoleon to Pétain,*** Colophon. Short perceptive surveys. See also B. Gooch, **The Reign of Napoleon III,*** Rand McNally, 1970; D. Thomson, **Democracy in France Since 1870,*** 5th ed., Oxford; Roger L. Williams, ed., **The Commune of Paris, 1871,*** Wiley, 1970; N. Halasz, **Captain Dreyfus: The Story of a Mass Hysteria,*** Simon & Schuster, 1968.

W. L. Langer, **European Alliances and Alignments, 1871-1890,*** Vintage, and **The Diplomacy of Imperialism, 1890-1902,** Knopf, 1951. Standard accounts. Bernadotte Schmitt, **Triple Alliance and Triple Entente,** Fertig, 1934, is a compact introduction. See also R. Albrecht-Carrié, **A Diplomatic History of Europe since the Congress of Vienna,** Harper & Row, 1958, and the surveys by Taylor and Seaman cited in Chapter 23.

S. B. Fay, **The Origins of the World War,*** 2 vols., 2nd ed., Free Press. Sympathetic to Germany and Austria and long considered the standard guide, but see now F. Fischer, **Germany's Aims in the First World War,*** Norton, and W. Laqueur and G. Mosse, eds., **1914: The Coming of the First World War,*** Torchbooks. See also L. Lafore, **The Long Fuse: An Interpretation of the Origins of World War I,*** Lippincott, 1965; and J. Remak, **Sarajevo: The Story of a Political Murder,** Phillips, 1959.

A. J. P. Taylor, **History of the First World War,*** Berkley; H. Baldwin, **World War I,*** Grove; C. Falls, **The Great War,*** Capricorn. Good short accounts. Excellent special works include Barbara Tuchman, **The Guns of August,*** Dell; A. Moorehead, **Gallipoli,*** Harper & Row; A. Horne, **The Price of Glory: Verdun, 1916,*** Colophon; E. Coffman, **The War to End All Wars: The American Military Experience in World War I,** Oxford, 1968; Frank Chambers, **The War Behind the War, 1914-1918,** Harcourt, Brace, 1939 (the home fronts).

*Indicates an inexpensive paperbound edition.

Chapter 25

Survival of the Fittest

Science, Thought, and Art: 1870-1914

INTRODUCTION. For Europe the nineteenth century was a golden age of advancement and prosperity. Electricity and other new forms of energy accelerated man's technological capabilities to produce more goods and raise living standards; transportation and communication networks expanded across continents and oceans and telescoped time-distance relationships; and Europe became the workshop of much of the world. At the same time the earlier fear of class warfare waned as governments showed increasing solicitude for their peoples' economic and social needs. Illiteracy was being reduced by the spread of public school systems. The franchise was being broadened; parliamentary government and mass suffrage were crowding out aristocratic plutocracy; political liberty was on the march.

Buoyed by their firm conviction that "God's in his heaven—All's right with the world,"[1] the Victorians faced the second half of their century with optimism. After 1850, however, marked changes took place in the intellectual and social environment. The members of the prospering middle class still had little reason to doubt that theirs was the best of all possible worlds—but was God in His heaven? Between the latest findings of science and the traditional religious faith on which their beliefs and moral values rested, a great conflict had arisen. The mid-Victorians had been brought up to believe that the creation of the world and the forms of life thereon had been an act of God and that nature revealed the workings of His moral law. But when Darwin in 1859 put forward his famous thesis that species were continually evolving through a ceaseless struggle for existence among living things and that the survival or extinction of all species depended on their adaptability, nature was seen as simply a blind life-and-death struggle, stripped of all morality. This harsh and uncompromising doctrine set off a bitter debate between many advocates of science and those of religion.

However abhorrent to traditional religious beliefs, the doctrine of the survival of the fittest was in fact thoroughly compatible with political, economic, and even intellectual activities after the revolutions of 1848. European powers amassed armies and fleets and entered into alliances that made right subservient to might; in Asia and Africa they annexed vast tracts of land at the expense of "lesser breeds without the law." This chapter examines the manifold ways in which industrialism, science, philosophy, and the arts contributed to or reflected the increasingly realistic—and materialistic—attitudes to be found throughout western Europe and the United States.

This period was distinguished by unprecedented scientific advancement. In addition to the work of Darwin and his associates in biology, fundamental discoveries were made in physics, such as in thermodynamics and electrodynamics, in chemistry with the arrangement of the periodic table, and in medicine with the development of the germ theory of disease. A new model of celestial mechanics was provided by Einstein, while Freud delved into hitherto little-understood levels of human consciousness. On the other hand, there also developed a cult of science whose practitioners were too often guilty of intellectual arrogance and of a dangerous oversimplification of human affairs. With such people it became all too easy to think of social needs and human values solely in materialistic terms.

In literature, painting, and sculpture, the impact of scientific and technological achievements took the form of realism, later extended into a facts-of-life school known as naturalism. At the same time, an increasing number of writers protested against injustices perpetrated in a society where cutthroat competition was defended and human exploitation excused as immutable elements in the struggle to survive. Still other artists, reacting against the baldly mechanistic view of man, devised new movements in the arts—expressionism and symbolism—each with special techniques for representing the subjective feelings of the individual.

THE NEW INDUSTRIALISM

Chief characteristics. As we saw in Chapter 21, the advent of the Industrial Revolution brought about remarkable advances in industrial production and transportation. This steam-and-iron age was accompanied by a concentration of labor and produce in congested factory towns. The second half of the nineteenth century saw a new surge of technological and industrial development of such magnitude that it has sometimes been called the Second Industrial Revolution. (We are still in this technical stage, though of course the term is relative inasmuch as the decades

ahead promise to revolutionize our technology and way of life at an increasing tempo.)

Between 1870 and 1914 the new industrialism displayed the following characteristics: (1) New sources of energy, particularly electricity and the power produced by the internal combustion engine, were introduced. (2) New materials including steel and a variety of lighter metals and alloys were employed, along with a host of synthetic products and new types of explosives. (3) Mass production methods involved the use of interchangeable parts and the assembly line, which came into its own in the automobile age when Henry Ford began turning out Model T's. (4) Industry increasingly allied itself with the laboratory; invention became systematic rather than accidental, involving research teams. (5) New and faster means of mass transportation provided a new capacity to disperse industry and decongest factory towns and to plan for the social improvement of the human landscape (though large-scale social planning had to await later decades in the present century).

New inventions. This new stage of industrialism was marked by a veritable avalanche of inventions. In 1876 a working dynamo was invented that could produce electricity in any required amount. With the harnessing of this new form of power, the western world entered the age of electricity, which now ran its factories, lighted its homes and city streets, and moved its tramcars. The self-taught American genius, Thomas Edison, supervised the construction in New York City of the world's first central electric power plant, and many of his more than 1200 patents involved machines powered by electricity.

The field of communications was revolutionized by the introduction of electrical devices. The first telephone was invented by Alexander Graham Bell in 1876, and in 1895 Guglielmo Marconi revealed his brainchild —wireless telegraphy. Three years later wireless messages were being transmitted across the English Channel, and within six years, across the Atlantic.

No less a revolution was taking place in transportation. In the 1880's a successful internal-combustion engine using gasoline as fuel was constructed and then applied to a bicycle and a carriage. From these crude beginnings came the motorcycle and the automobile. In the field of automobile manufacturing the United States took an early lead. Henry Ford began large-scale production of his Model T in 1909, and by 1914 some two million motor cars were registered in the United States. Another form of the internal-combustion engine—designed to burn crude oil, a much cheaper fuel than gasoline— was designed by a German engineer, Rudolf

Diesel, who took out his patent in 1892. A successful competitor to the steam engine and the electric motor, the Diesel engine was used especially for driving locomotives, electric generators, and marine pumps.

During this period man acquired wings. In the 1890's attempts were made to construct a heavier-than-air craft with propellers run by internal-combustion engines. The climax came at Kitty Hawk, North Carolina, on December 17, 1903, when Orville and Wilbur Wright succeeded in keeping their fragile biplane aloft for twelve seconds.

Other important inventions were also making their appearance. The invention in 1886 of the linotype machine (which made typesetting by hand obsolete) and the manufacture of cheap wood-pulp paper made possible the production of urban newspapers on a mass scale. In 1888 the Kodak camera was developed. Entertainment was enlivened by Edison's invention of the phonograph in 1877 and of the motion picture, first exhibited publicly in 1896.

The spread of industrialism. Between 1870 and 1914 the world could be divided into three economic areas. The highly industrialized area was concentrated in western Europe, in the northern United States, and in Japan. In the area just beginning to be touched by industry were such countries as Italy, Spain, the Balkan states, Russia, and Canada. The third area, consisting of all of Africa, the Middle East, and all of Asia except Japan, was outside the industrial realm. This third zone can be called "the world of empire," for most of its vast territories were colonies of the industrial powers or objects of foreign exploitation.

As we saw in Chapter 21, Great Britain was the pioneer in industrialization. But after 1870 new and vigorous competitors, primarily the United States, Germany, and Japan, became important industrial nations. In 1870 Britain had more textile spindles and looms and produced more coal and iron than all the rest of the world. By 1910 it had only 40 percent of the spindles and 30 percent of the looms of the world and produced only 26 percent of the world's coal and 14 percent of the world's iron. In banking and shipping, however, Britain still led the pack. Its

By the end of the nineteenth century the term *industrialization* had acquired world-wide significance. The technological revolution which originated in western Europe was now reaching every continent and affecting almost every aspect of life. In Germany Alfred Krupp discovered a new method for producing large quantities of steel and turned a small family company into the famous and self-sufficient Krupp munitions plant (right). The Japanese government decided to take advantage of a profitable export item—raw silk. It set up a factory at Tomioka (bottom right) and employed a new silk-reeling technique introduced from Europe. Even France, which tended to lag behind other industrial nations, was showing signs of technological progress. A steam-driven tractor exhibited at the Philadelphia exposition in 1876 attracted the attention of the French magazine *L'Illustration* (bottom left).

ships carried 40 percent of all the world's commerce, and London was the world's main source of capital. Although Britain had an "unfavorable" balance of trade (imported more goods than it exported), it received nearly a billion dollars annually from overseas investments, shipping fees, insurance, and banking services. These "invisible exports" kept Great Britain out of the red.

After the conclusion of the Civil War, industrialization in the United States proceeded at an amazing rate (see p. 605). In 1860 the total value of American manufactures was less than $2 billion; by 1900 the figure was nearly seven times as large.

The unification of the German empire was in part responsible for the astounding growth of German industrialization. Other factors included the acquisition from France in 1871 of the extremely rich iron-mining and manufacturing districts of Alsace and Lorraine; the payment by France of a war indemnity of 5 billion francs, which gave Germany a sharp increase of capital for industrial purposes; and the rapid growth of population (from 41 million in 1871 to almost 65 million in 1910). The Germans concentrated primarily on the development of such new enterprises as the chemical and electrical industries. The government played a decisive role in this expansion by designing tariffs to aid the new industries and by setting up technical schools to train personnel. In the chemical industry the Germans seized undisputed first place—by 1900 they produced four fifths of the world's dyestuffs—and in the electrical industry Germany's skilled technicians were soon producing intricate equipment destined for all countries of the world.

After isolated Japan had been opened to the West in the mid-nineteenth century, industrialization was introduced. Economic changes came with pell-mell rapidity: the labor market was large, and workmen could always be found to work at a low wage, enabling the Japanese manufacturer to undersell his rivals in other nations. The government aided industrialization by subsidizing railroads and steamship lines, and large supplies of coal were available. Specializing in textiles, Japan created serious competition for the mills of Manchester. The pace of industrialization in Japan is best indicated by the following facts: in 1870 no manufactured goods were exported; in 1906 the value of manufactures exported had reached $100 million.

Growth of world trade. The new industrialism set in motion strong forces binding the world into one interdependent economic unit. The tremendous increase in manufacturing productivity caused the most highly industrialized regions of the world to seek new markets in the backward zones. There was also a demand for huge quantities of raw materials—cotton, tin, oil, tea, coffee, wheat, sugar, and timber. In 1860 world trade amounted to slightly more than $7 billion; in 1913 the figure was nearly $42 billion.

A world-wide market existed in which commodities, capital, currency, and economic services were freely exchanged. In 1879 an era of free trade ended as tariffs began to go up, but the rates remained moderate, and the effect on world commerce was slight. All the important currencies—the dollar, franc, mark, and pound—were redeemable in gold, and their exchange rates were stable. One nation might have an unfavorable balance of trade with several nations but at the same time a favorable balance with others, so that in the long run the debit and credit transactions balanced out.

The great industrialized area of western Europe accumulated vast sums of wealth between 1870 and 1914. Capital investments at home and abroad doubled in Britain and France and tripled in Germany. This outflow of capital helped the backward regions to develop; and in turn the borrowing countries could sell their commodities, mainly raw materials, to the industrialized nations.

Materially aiding this world economic interdependence was what might be termed the export of people. The higher standard of living and lower death rate in western Europe let to an unparalleled increase in population. From 1870 to 1914 the European continent registered an increase of 100 million people. At the same time a quarter of that number migrated to the great unsettled regions of North and South America, to Australia, and, to a lesser extent, to South Africa. This vast movement of people helped to develop backward and underpopulated lands and also created expanding markets for European goods.

Business consolidates. In the rush of new products and factories, businessmen became aware of the advantages of consolidation. By being big, a business could enjoy the economies of mass production, could buy raw materials in huge amounts and at low prices, and could use its power to crush competition and, if necessary, to lobby for favorable government legislation. In addition, big business could effectively discourage unionism, could place labor agitators on a black list, and, in the event of a strike, could employ strikebreakers. In the United States there arose such business giants as the United States Steel Corporation, the American Tobacco Company, International Harvester, the Standard Oil Company, and the United States Rubber Company.

Business consolidation took the form not only of larger corporations but also of mergers and alliances of separate units. One form was the trust, in which a body of trustees held a majority of the stock and thus controlled the wage, price, and merchandising policies of the several companies involved. Another form was the holding company, in which a corporation was organized to perform the same functions as the more informal trust. In Europe business integration took the form of huge industrial combines known as cartels. These great industrial units were hooked together from country to country in international affiliates controlling such products as steel or rubber.

To create and operate such huge industrial organizations required larger sums than the manufacturer could ordinarily provide; as a result, capitalism passed into a new stage of development. Just as commercial capitalism had been replaced by industrial capitalism in the eighteenth century, industrial capitalism in the last two decades of the nineteenth century was superseded by finance capitalism. As the financial houses arranged for the vast amounts of capital investment demanded by industry, more and more control of business fell into their hands. In this era the financier rather than

the manufacturer became the dominant figure in the business arena.

With the growth of the size of the business unit, gains in economy and efficiency were registered. But there were also danger signals. In too many instances key industries providing services or commodities vital to the health and well-being of society were dominated by a few huge enterprises controlled by a relative handful of men. And in the hectic pursuit of profits, businessmen too often neglected the legitimate responsibilities of industrial management and dabbled in stock "deals" or in other speculative schemes.

Workers unite. Consolidation in business was paralleled by consolidation in the ranks of labor. In response to the seemingly all-powerful position of big business in wage bargaining and in reaction against management's tendency to regard workers merely as commodities, the workers (as we have seen in Chapter 21) began to organize into trade unions.

The first unions were craft unions made up of skilled workers. Then unskilled wage earners were organized. Some of the unions formed were industrial unions, taking in all the workers employed in one industry. In this case, when any given group of workers felt compelled to strike, all union men in the industry would join them. As another means of gaining strength, associations of unions, such as the English Trade Union Congress, were formed on a national basis. In 1881 a federation of autonomous craft and industrial unions was founded in the United States with a membership that soon numbered in the millions. This was the American Federation of Labor, headed by Samuel Gompers; it became the most powerful voice of American workers.

The immediate result of the growth of unionism was better protection for the working masses, a stronger voice when it came to collective bargaining with the bosses, and consequently higher wages. Big unionism, like big business, made for more efficient methods, but in both cases bigness created power and with it the need for responsibility in its exercise. This problem was to become paramount in industrial relations by the mid-twentieth century. While in some instances, as in syndicalist-controlled unions (see p. 581), labor organizations sought to overthrow the capitalist system, the vast majority of unions both in Europe and in the United States were moderate and gradualistic in both their aims and methods.

NEW ECONOMIC AND SOCIAL FORCES

The new trends. From the standpoint of conditions in 1848, it looked as though Marx's predictions in the *Communist Manifesto*—the inevitability of revolution and the destruction of capitalism and the bourgeoisie—would come true. Fortunately, they did not. The latter part of the nineteenth century and the decade preceding the First World War saw improvement in three basic areas: (1) the granting of such basic political rights as universal suffrage, civil liberties, and free expression of opinion (discussed in Chapter 24); (2) an increase in the democratic distribution of wealth, also known as economic democracy; and (3) the spread of education.

Democratic distribution means, simply speaking, more equal sharing in the wealth of a nation. The growth of labor unions gave workers more bargaining power with their employers, and they used this power to gain better wages. It has been estimated that the "real" wages of workers (the amount of goods that their wages could actually buy) increased 50 percent in industrial nations between 1870 and 1900.

Not only did real wages improve, but the state increasingly guaranteed the popular standard of living. More and more governments made it their business to provide such benefits as unemployment insurance, old-age pensions, and accident compensation. Because this social legislation was paid for out of tax revenues, England introduced a graduated income tax, by which every individual paid a sum relative to his earnings.

Business management became less exclusively a monopoly of the capitalists. Labor unions began to assert their right to have some say in the operation of industry, and government itself assumed the right to regulate and control great industries when the public interest was involved. Governments, moreover, sought to prevent the unjust exercise of economic power by the enactment of legislation such as the Sherman Anti-Trust Act and the Clayton Act in the United States. However, the effective subordination of big business in the highly industrialized western nations was not fully taken in hand until the advent of world depression in the 1930's.

Workers also attempted to make business production more democratic by establishing cooperatives. Capital was secured by the sale of stock, goods were sold at prevailing prices, and profits were distributed annually to stockholders in proportion to the amount of goods each had purchased. By 1913 at least half the population of the British Isles were buying some of their goods from cooperatives.

The final aspect of the democratic movement in the second half of the nineteenth century was education. When the common people won the franchise, it was painfully apparent that they needed at least the rudiments of education to vote intelligently. As the result of an education bill passed in 1870 under Gladstone, school attendance in England jumped from one to four million in ten years. Similar acts were passed in France, Germany, the Low Countries, and Scandinavia. Although educational progress lagged in southern and eastern Europe, with 80 percent of the people of Russia and the Balkans remaining illiterate, by 1900 free and compulsory elementary education became almost universal in western Europe.

Liberalism fades; the welfare state appears. Only through the drastic modification and weakening of the middle-class doctrine of laissez-faire liberalism could the government's increased solicitude for the masses have come about. The expansion of a government's responsibilities for the economic security of all its people pointed toward the welfare state. That government moved away from laissez-faire liberalism and in the direction of the welfare state must be regarded as one of the fundamental trends of the late nineteenth century.

By the end of the century this trend had also received the official stamp of approval of the Catholic Church. Reversing the position of Pope Pius IX, whose *Syllabus of Errors* (see p. 588) had stated bluntly that it was an error to believe that "the Roman Pontiff can and should reconcile and align himself with progress, liberalism, and modern civilization," Pius' successor, Leo XIII (1878-1903), revived the progressive outlook of St. Thomas Aquinas and reconciled the Church with the modern age. His most important pronouncement, *Rerum novarum* ("concerning new things," 1891), inaugurated what became known as "Christian democracy." The pope condemned Marxism and upheld capitalism, but he severely criticized the evils afflicting the working class. To ameliorate the lot of the workers, Leo advocated social legislation and the formation of Catholic labor unions and political parties. Soon Catholic parties, using the slogan and often the name of Christian democracy, began to play a major role in European politics—as they continue to do today.

Factory legislation, social legislation, the recognition of trade unions, and middle-class philanthropy all helped to achieve some degree of reconciliation between the proletariat and the bourgeoisie. A compromise had been reached. The workers were not completely satisfied but were willing in most instances to cooperate with management in the hope that the future would see more substantial gains. Speaking of the situation before 1914, a famous historian has written: ". . . most men are so constituted that they will abate something of their extreme demands in the interest of social peace. They will seek a compromise; and compromise has, on the whole, been the most characteristic feature in the relation of the two classes, employers and employees."[2] That the same spirit of compromise prevailed among most socialists also became clear.

Socialism compromises. In the early 1870's the growth of socialism was slow; but as the decade progressed, the movement gained momentum. The Social Democratic party, organized in Germany in 1875, became the strongest of its kind in Europe and a model for similar parties in other nations. In the 1880's Marxist parties also arose in Italy, Austria, Scandinavia, and the Low Countries. In France the socialist movement—discredited by the Paris Commune of 1871—broke into a number of acrimonious factions.

Influenced to a greater degree by the maxims of Christian socialism than by the dogmas of Marxism, British socialists placed their faith in parliamentary reform rather than in any uprising of the proletariat. The most important socialist group was the Fabian Society, organized in 1883 and including such brilliant intellectuals as George Bernard Shaw, Sidney and Beatrice Webb, and H. G. Wells. (The Fabian group derived its name from the cautious Roman general Quintus Fabius Maximus, who wore down his enemy Hannibal by being content with small gains.) Chiefly through the efforts of the Fabian Society, the Labour party was formed in 1900 with the support of trade unions and various socialist groups. Much of the credit for British social legislation goes to the Labour party, which supported the Liberal party's program before World War I.

Moderate socialists were not limited solely to England, for the Fabian gospel of moderation—or revisionism, as it came to be called—spread to the Continent. Encouraged by a general improvement in the lot of the common man, the socialists became less revolutionary and more willing to cooperate with governments which were genuinely interested in raising the standards of living of the working people. In the 1890's the movement grew rapidly.

For revisionist socialism to be effective, it had to wield power within the government; and by the early 1900's socialistic parties had achieved this goal in numerous European capitals. The German workers' representatives in the Reichstag had numbered only two in 1871, but in the 1912 election the socialists won 110 seats in the lower house. Through a coalition of the various parties, the socialists in France had cornered 102 seats in the Chamber of Deputies by

1914. Socialists from many countries joined the Second International after its founding in 1889; by 1914 it boasted a membership of twelve million.

Syndicalism. The progress of revisionist socialism seemed to confound the dire prophecies of Marx. But there were radicals who refused to discard the doctrines of revolution, who viewed the growing moderation of the socialists with dismay, and who suspected that their old leaders were becoming the tools of the capitalists. A new radical movement known as syndicalism (from the French word *syndicat*, meaning "trade union") emerged in the 1890's with its center in France. The ultimate goal of syndicalism was imprecise. Apparently the bourgeois state would be overthrown by a general strike, and society henceforth would consist of "cells," each representing an industrial union.

Orthodox Marxism in Russia. By 1900 the picture of workers "having nothing to lose but their chains" had been substantially altered in western Europe by the advance of social legislation and the rise of "real" wages. But if Marx could have risen from his grave in that year, he would have found in Russia the "1848" he once described in the *Communist Manifesto*. Here industrialization was just gaining momentum, and bewildered peasants seeking work in city factories were shamefully exploited. There were no traditions of peaceful reform, gradualism, or compromise in Russia—only the memory of ruthless government suppression and of equally violent attempts at retaliation. It was natural, therefore, that when socialism appeared in Russia, its adherents passionately embraced Marx's original doctrines of class war and revolution. While the tsars still reigned, the socialist leaders were preparing for the day when the people would overthrow the regime and win control of the government. One such leader was Lenin.

Born Vladimir Ilich Ulyanov in a small city in the Volga River valley, Lenin (1870-1924) grew up in moderate and respectable circumstances provided by his father, a teacher of physics. In 1887 his elder brother was arrested for plotting against the life of the tsar and was executed. Shortly thereafter, Lenin began to read his dead brother's copy of *Das Kapital* and joined a secret Marxian discussion club. He was arrested in 1895 and sentenced to exile in Siberia. After he was released in 1900, he and his wife made their way to Switzerland. There, Lenin helped to found the socialist paper *Iskra* (*Spark*), whose motto was "From the spark—the conflagration."

Lenin stood for a socialism whose weapon was violence and whose creed allowed no compromise with the bourgeoisie. While Marx believed that capitalism would break down of its own accord, Lenin wanted to smash it. He took nothing for granted. To destroy capitalism, he devised a technique of revolution whereby an elite leadership would enforce its dictates on the populace with iron discipline. The organization of communist activity would be of two kinds. On the surface would be the legal and peaceful workers' movement. But below was to be a revolutionary network, infiltrating the government, the police, and the army.

Lenin also disagreed with Marx on the dictatorship of the proletariat. Engels and Marx did not envisage a police state but rather a republic of workers. Engels in 1891 wrote:

If anything stands, it is that our party and the working-class can only come to power under the form of a democratic republic. This is the specific form of the dictatorship of the proletariat.[3]

Lenin had other notions. His dictatorship of the proletariat would be a highly centralized despotism whose word was law. The shattering impact of World War I would give Lenin and his followers the opportunity to seize power.

THE RISING TIDE OF SCIENCE

Science comes of age. As previously pointed out, the nineteenth century saw a new and intimate application of science to industry and everyday life, with increasingly spectacular results. Indeed, the extraordinary achievements of science in this era seemed to fulfill the dream of the pioneer scientists of the seventeenth century—a full understanding of nature's order and man's part in it. Science was now seen to be an indispensable component of basic human activity, and scientists were welcomed into the hitherto classics-centered universities. In short, science had become "respectable" and was increasingly capturing popular imagination and applause.

The theory of evolution. The nineteenth century witnessed the spread of a doctrine which was to have powerful repercussions on science, philosophy, and religion. This was the theory of evolution—namely, that all complex organisms have developed from simple forms through the operation of natural causes and that no species is fixed and changeless. Some classical philosophers had envisaged such a hypothesis, while in 1785 James Hutton had ascribed the earth's development to natural rather than supernatural causes (see p. 407). In the nineteenth century Sir Charles Lyell's epoch-making *Principles of Geology* (1830) confirmed Hutton's views that the earth's surface had been formed by still continuing natural causes operating over a vast period of time. This conception of geologic time was essential for any theory of biological evolution based on changes in species over many thousands of generations.

In the first decade of the century a French scientist, Jean Baptiste Lamarck (1744-1829), argued that every organism tends to develop new organs in order to adapt itself to the changing conditions of its environment. The changes that take place in an organism are transmitted by heredity to the descendants, which are thereby changed in structural form. In supporting his doctrine of the inheritance of acquired characteristics, Lamarck claimed that the giraffe had to develop a long neck to reach the high leaves and branches of the trees on which it fed. The slight gain in length of the neck made by each generation was handed on to the next.

Darwin's contribution. The scientist chiefly responsible for furthering the evolutionary hypothesis was Charles Darwin (1809-1882). After studying medicine and preparing at Cambridge University for the ministry, Darwin became a naturalist. From 1831 to 1836 he studied the specimens he had collected while on a surveying expedition with the ship *Beagle*, which had sailed along the coast of South America and among the Galápagos Islands.

Two works that had a marked influence upon the development of Darwin's theories were Lyell's *Principles of Geology* and Malthus' *Essay on Population.* The latter suggested to Darwin that the struggle of men for existence in a world in which the population increases faster than the food supply was a problem that could be extended to all nature. In 1859 Darwin's views appeared under the title *The Origin of Species by Means of Natural Selection, or the Preservation of Favored Races in the Struggle for Life.* In this work he contended:

. . . that species have been modified, during a long course of descent . . . chiefly through the natural selection of numerous successive, slight, favourable variations; aided in an important manner . . . by the direct action of external conditions, and by variations which seem to us in our ignorance to arise spontaneously.[4]

The Origin of Species was to prove one of the most significant books in scientific literature, revolutionizing concepts about the origin and evolution of life on the planet. Furthermore, this pioneer work brought into the open the mounting differences between science and theology over the Biblical account of creation—differences to which Lyell's *Principles of Geology* had already markedly contributed. The mid-Victorians might employ the Darwinian theory to bolster their belief in the inevitable improvement of mankind, but while they shared this conviction with the earlier romanticists, they had lost much of the latter's idealism and optimism. There were too many new tensions to contend with, thanks alike to science and to a highly industrialized society. Romanticism was giving way to realism.

Darwin's next bombshell was *Descent of Man and Selection in Relation to Sex,* published in 1871. In this work Darwin applied the principle of natural selection to human beings and reached the explosively controversial conclusion that man's ancestors were probably monkey-like animals related to the progenitors of the orangutan, chimpanzee, and gorilla.

There are five main points in the Darwinian hypothesis. First, all existing vegetable and animal species are descended from earlier and, generally speaking, more rudimentary forms. Second, species evolve through the inheritance of minute differences in individual structures due to the direct effect of the environment. Third, in the struggle for survival, the fittest win out at the expense of their rivals. Fourth, a species may also be altered by the cumulative workings of sexual selection, which Darwin declared is "the most powerful means of changing the races of man." Finally, some variations seem to arise spontaneously, a view of Darwin's which pointed toward the doctrine of mutation.

Biology after Darwin. By the close of the nineteenth century scientists were in virtual agreement regarding the general validity of Darwin's hypothesis, though, as we shall see, it was later modified in certain important respects. Meanwhile, largely as a result of Darwin's unifying principle of evolution, biology was progressively transformed from a descriptive science into a search for genetic relationships between living organisms.

One of the most significant developments in biology concerned the question of heredity. In the 1870's the German biologist August Weismann, basing his investigation on an earlier theory that all living things originate and develop in very small structural units, or cells, distinguished two types of cells. One type—the somatic cell—dies with the individual, while the other—the germ cell—transmits through reproduction a continuous stream of protoplasm from one generation to the next. Later, Weismann produced experimental evidence that germ cells, which transmit hereditary characteristics, are not affected by changes in the somatic cells—in other words, that acquired characteristics cannot be inherited.

An Austrian monk, Gregor Mendel (1822-1884), formulated definite laws of heredity on the basis of experiments with the crossing of garden peas. Because he published his important findings in an obscure scientific journal, his work was overlooked until about 1900. Mendel's laws not only proved a valuable help in the scientific breeding of plants and animals but also demonstrated that the evolution of different species was more complex than had been deduced by Darwin.

From the work of Mendel and Weismann, biologists began to conclude that the nuclei of the germ cells possess chromosomes which carry the characteristics of an organism. Further research substantiated the mutation theory, which states that sudden and unpredictable changes within the chromosomes can be transmitted by heredity to produce new species.

Meanwhile, a cousin of Darwin, Sir Francis Galton, carried the study of heredity into still more new areas. Struck by the similarity of characteristics among members of one family, Galton concluded that mental as well as physical characteristics must be inherited. He invented mental testing and pioneered in the new science of eugenics.

Modern medicine emerges. In the 1840's the value of ether and chloroform in alleviating pain during operations had been discovered. Another step of the greatest value was the introduction into surgery of asepsis —that is, methods for preventing the entry of infection into a wound. In the 1860's an Edinburgh University surgeon, Joseph Lister, made use of revolutionary techniques in conducting operations. These included both asepsis and antisepsis, the latter being the method of disinfecting wounds so as to destroy dangerous bacteria. Both techniques sprang from a knowledge of the germ theory of putrefaction developed by Lister's brilliant friend, the French scientist Louis Pasteur (1822-1895).

Probably the most important single advance in medicine during the latter part of the nineteenth century was the substantiation of the germ theory of disease. The validation of this theory by Louis Pasteur and his younger disciple, the German bacteriologist Robert Koch, came as the result of a search for a cure for anthrax, a fatal disease which in the late 1870's was destroying over 20 percent of the sheep in France. Pasteur and Koch discovered that anthrax bacteria could be grown in a culture of meat-broth

A nineteenth-century issue of the French magazine *L'Illustration* pictures Louis Pasteur in his laboratory.

jelly and that the injection of the bacteria into a healthy animal produced anthrax. In 1881 Pasteur inoculated twenty-five sheep with weakened anthrax bacteria and left the same number unvaccinated. Later, all fifty were given a virulent form of the disease; the unvaccinated animals died while the treated sheep remained sound. With the establishment of the principle that the injection of a mild form of disease bacteria will cause the formation of antibodies which will prevent the inoculated person from getting the virulent form of the disease, the end of such scourges as typhoid and smallpox was in sight.

In 1885 Pasteur showed that by the injection of a vaccine an animal could be made resistant to rabies *after* having been bitten by a mad dog. For his part, the brilliant Koch discovered the organisms that caused eleven diseases, including tuberculosis and cholera. As a result of the work of Pasteur and Koch, the twin sciences of bacteriology and immunology were established on a firm footing.

Chemistry and related fields. Meanwhile modern chemistry had been securely founded upon the atomic theory advanced by an English Quaker schoolmaster, John Dalton (1766-1844). This pioneer believed that all matter is made up of invisible particles, or atoms, which remain unchanged upon en-

tering or leaving any chemical combination. Moreover, the basic substances or elements which are to be found in the world of matter differed by virtue of the size and weight of the atoms composing them.

It now became possible to arrange chemical elements according to their atomic weights, beginning with the lightest, hydrogen. It was seen that the elements fell into groups of eight which possess similar properties. In 1869 the Russian chemist Dmitri Mendelyeev (1834-1907) drew up his periodic table, in which all the known elements were classified according to their weights and properties. From gaps in this table, chemists were able to deduce the existence of still other undiscovered elements.

In the latter part of the century considerable research was conducted on proteins and on nutritional problems. For a long time the value of fresh fruits and vegetables in treating scurvy had been demonstrated, but the reason was unknown. Now investigations showed that this and other diseases were caused by nutritional deficiencies. The true significance of vitamins was first disclosed in 1912, and the way was paved for isolating and synthesizing nearly all known vitamins in the laboratory.

Biochemical research in this period also threw light on the presence and purpose of the ductless glands. Research showed that the glands poured their secretions, called hormones, directly into the blood stream and that some of these hormones were essential for survival. This discovery led to the search for various kinds of hormones, such as the secretion from the pancreas (insulin), which prevents diabetes.

Meanwhile a German biochemist, Paul Ehrlich (1854-1915), had been experimenting with drugs that could destroy bacteria and other organisms without harming the individual who harbored them. After more than six hundred unsuccessful attempts, Ehrlich in 1909 produced an organic arsenic compound, "606," later named "salvarsan" which, without being too toxic to the individual, destroyed syphilis bacteria in the body. Following this major triumph for chemotherapy, practitioners later in the century were to score a spectacular breakthrough in the never ending struggle against disease by their development of sulfa drugs, penicillin, and other antibiotics.

One of the most impressive advances in the field of chemistry was the making of chemical synthetics. A French scientist demonstrated how artificial silk could be made from cellulose, while chemists in Germany and elsewhere turned out synthetic dyes from coal-tar residues. In 1913 a process by which nitrogen could be obtained from the atmosphere was perfected. This process proved vital to the Germans during World War I; it enabled their munitions program to survive despite an Allied blockade that cut off the importation of nitrates from Chile.

Revolution in physics. Remarkable progress in physics led to questioning the very nature of the universe which, since Newton's time, had seemed the perfect model of rational stability. Moreover, many of the outstanding new inventions discussed earlier were the outcome of spectacular discoveries in the sphere of pure scientific research. Especially important was the work done in thermodynamics and electrical phenomena. Thermodynamics, that branch of research which deals with the relations between heat and motive power, was of particular importance because of industry's dependence upon the steam engine.

Scientists had believed previously that heat was a mysterious fluid called "calorie," but research showed that friction generated heat in proportion to the amount of energy expended. After physicists had found out how much mechanical energy was required to raise the heat of any given body, it became possible, in 1847, to formulate the first law of thermodynamics. This law states that the sum total of energy in the universe is constant—it cannot be either created or destroyed but can only be transformed from one form into another. Meanwhile scientists engaging in the converse problem of transforming heat into energy found that heat can in fact never be completely converted into energy. From their experiments emerged the second law of thermodynamics: although the total amount of energy in the universe remains constant, the amount actually available is always diminishing through its transformation into nonavailable, or dissipated, heat.

Nineteenth-century scientists prepared the way for the use of electricity as a source of power. The most prominent figure in the field of electrodynamics during the earlier part of the century was Michael Faraday (1791-1867). In 1831 Faraday produced an electric current by rotating a copper disk between the two poles of a horseshoe magnet, thereby inventing the first electric dynamo. This simple dynamo made possible the development of the electric motor, the transmission of large currents over long distances, and (later in the century) the invention of the electric telegraph, the telephone, and electric lights.

Electromagnetism and radiation. Some of the most significant discoveries in science made after 1870 resulted from research in the field of physics. In his famous work *A Treatise on Electricity and Magnetism* (1873), the Scottish scientist James Clerk-Maxwell advanced the theory that "electricity is matter moving in waves like those of light and radiant heat," thereby linking optics and electricity; and he maintained that light, radiant heat, and invisible ultraviolet radiation are all electromagnetic phenomena.

Working with the electromagnetic theory of light, a German physicist named Heinrich Hertz was able to demonstrate in 1886 the existence of electromagnetic waves—as predicted by Clerk-Maxwell—and to measure their velocity. It was these "hertzian waves" (later known as radio waves) which provided the theoretical basis for Marconi's subsequent invention of wireless telegraphy. In addition, Hertz' studies of the optical properties of these waves led to his discovery of photoelectricity, which was fundamental for the development of television.

Toward the end of the century two new events occurred in the field of electrical research that were to have equally far-reaching repercussions. In 1895 a ray which could penetrate a nontranslucent mass was discovered, and, because the nature of this strange phenomenon was not at first understood, the term *x-ray* came into use. Shortly thereafter, it was learned that uranium gives off similar rays. Then in 1898 the French scientist Pierre Curie and his Polish wife Marie extracted radium from pitchblende, an ore of uranium, and the world began to become conscious of the potency of radioactivity. Radiation was soon utilized in medicine.

Studies of the scattering of x-rays led to the conclusion that electricity is composed of particles which are constituent parts of atoms. This deduction led to the electron theory—namely, that the atom contains negatively charged particles known as electrons. The next major step in understanding the structure of the atom was made in 1911 by the British physicist Ernest Rutherford, who advanced the theory that each atom has a central particle, or nucleus, which is positively charged. Later, scientists determined that the atom is like a miniature solar system; most of the weight is concentrated in the central, positively charged nucleus, around which the negatively charged electrons revolve. These discoveries smashed one of the foundation stones of traditional physics—the belief that the atom was indivisible and solid. The way was now clear to demonstrate conclusively that the universe is composed not of matter in the traditional sense but of atomic energy.

Quantum and relativity theories. Traditional physics received another jolt from the research of the German physicist Max Planck (1858-1947). Planck had been studying radiant heat, which comes from the sun and is identical in its nature with light. He found that the energy emitted from a vibrating electron proceeds not in a steady wave—as traditionally believed—but discontinuously in the form of calculable "energy packages." To such a package Planck gave the name *quantum* — hence the term *quantum theory*.

Planck's quantum theory, which was to prove invaluable in the rapidly growing study of atomic physics, found support in the studies of Albert Einstein (1879-1955). In 1905 Einstein contended that light is propagated through space in the form of particles which he termed *photons*. Moreover, the energy contained in any particle of matter, such as the photon, is equal to the mass of that body multiplied by the square of the velocity of light, which is a constant

figure. The resulting equation—$E=mc^2$—provided the answer to many long-standing mysteries of physics—for example, how radioactive substances like radium and uranium are able to eject particles at enormous velocities and to go on doing so for millions of years. The magnitude of the energy that slumbers in the nuclei of atoms could be revealed. Above all, $E=mc^2$ shows that mass and energy are convertible.

In 1905 Einstein also revealed his epoch-making Special Theory of Relativity, which called for a radically new approach to explain the concepts of time, space, and velocity. For example, he maintained that time and distance are interrelated, that the mass of a body increases with its velocity, and that, as mentioned previously, mass and energy are convertible, i.e., $E=mc^2$.

In 1915 Einstein produced his second installment, or the General Theory, in which he incorporated gravitation into relativity. He showed that gravitation was identical to acceleration and that light rays would be deflected in passing through a gravitational field—a prediction confirmed by observation of an eclipse in 1919. The theory of relativity has been subsequently confirmed in other ways as well; thus the interconversion of mass and energy was dramatically demonstrated in the atomic bomb, which obtains its energy by the annihilation of part of the matter of which it is composed.

The universe as conceived by Einstein is not Newton's three-dimensional figure of length, breadth, and thickness but a four-dimensional space-time continuum in which time itself varies with velocity. Such a cosmic model calls for the use of non-Euclidean geometry. Einstein's theory has reoriented our attitude toward the structure and mechanics of the universe, and its relativistic implications have permeated not only this century's scientific theories but our philosophical, moral, and even esthetic concepts as well. Moreover, Einstein's contribution aptly illustrates one of the yardsticks sometimes employed to measure "progress." According to this yardstick, progress occurs when our knowledge and understanding of the phenomenal world are enlarged. Thus Einstein's theory of gravitation covers all the explanations provided by Newton's theory of gravitation and also "fits the facts" in a still wider field where the other fails.

Advances in psychology. The study of psychology was given a marked impetus by numerous investigators, one of the most famous of whom was a Russian, Ivan Pavlov (1849-1936). In 1900 Pavlov conducted a series of experiments in which food was given to a dog at the same time that a bell was rung. After a time, the food and bell became inseparably identified by the dog. Henceforth when the bell was rung alone, the dog produced saliva just as if food had been brought. Thus Pavlov demonstrated the influence of physical stimuli on an involuntary process.

This psychology of "conditioned reflexes" achieved a wide vogue, especially in the United States, where it was used to help substantiate the tenets of a school of behaviorism which considered man more or less as a machine responding mechanically to stimuli. Behaviorism stressed experimentation and observational techniques and did much to create relatively valid intelligence and aptitude tests. It also strengthened the materialistic philosophies of the period.

Freud and psychoanalysis. Probably the most famous name associated with psychology is that of the Austrian Sigmund Freud (1856-1939). Placing far greater stress than any predecessor on the element of the unconscious, Freud pioneered in psychoanalysis. This form of psychotherapy is based on the theory that mental symptoms express forbidden desires which are not consciously acknowledged. Freud treated emotional disturbances by bringing deeply repressed, "pathogenic" motives and memories to the surface with the help of dream interpretation and free association. He believed that the source of all adult adjustments and maladjustments is the Oedipus complex, whereby a child is sexually drawn to the parent of the opposite sex and jealous of the other parent. All in all, in revealing the heretofore unappreciated intricacies of the human mind, Freud had a far-reaching influence upon the understanding of human behavior. He made current a whole new vocabulary, employing such terms as *libido, id, ego, inhibition, fixation, defense mechanism,* and *repressed desire.* The twentieth-century outlook on man, expressed in such fields as literature and art, owes much to the influence of Freud.

THE CULT OF SCIENCE

Science versus faith. With its spectacular successes in both pure research and technological application, science gripped the popular imagination of the pre-1914 generation to an extent never before equaled. Science was elevated to a cult by means of which all human problems were to be solved. Many men and women became skeptical and uneasy about whatever could not be proved in the laboratory.

It can be readily seen that a conflict was certain to ensue between the traditional doctrines of religion and the new scientific

Skepticism was a typical reaction to Darwin's *The Origin of Species.* This *Punch* cartoon about the evolutionary process portrays man evolving from a worm through all of the intermediate stages, including a grotesque "missing link."

PUNCH'S ALMANACK FOR 1882.

MAN·IS·BVT·A·WORM

tenets, especially those of Darwinism. Thomas Huxley, a strong popularizer of Darwin's theories, contended that for the advocate of science "skepticism is the highest of duties; blind faith the unpardonable sin."[4] Certainly, established religion was thrown on the defensive, and many of the most sensitive minds of the period suffered anguish and even despair in their attempts to reconcile their religious beliefs with the new scientific tenets.

As time went on, however, more than one thinker came to believe that the evolutionary theory supplemented rather than contradicted the basic tenets of faith. As they saw the bounds of the universe pushed back by science, they perceived growth and development in the constant changes and felt that God was revealing Himself to man through the evolutionary process. Interestingly enough, Darwin himself had expressed a similar view in the conclusion of his *The Origin of Species*:

When I view all beings not as special creations, but as the lineal descendants of some few beings which lived long before the first bed of the Cambrian system was deposited, they seem to me to become ennobled. . . . There is grandeur in this view of life, with its several powers, having been originally breathed by the Creator into a few forms or into one; and that, whilst this planet has gone cycling on according to the fixed law of gravity, from so simple a beginning endless forms most beautiful and most wonderful have been, and are being evolved.[5]

The Roman Catholic position. In 1864 Pope Pius IX had issued the *Syllabus of Errors*, which warned the faithful against "the principal errors of our time"—in particular, that God did not exist, that His action upon man was to be denied, that human reason was alone the sole arbiter of truth, and that the miracles found in the Scriptures were fictional. Next, in 1870 the Vatican Council—the first general council of the Church to gather in centuries—defined the doctrine of papal infallibility. This declared that when the pope spoke *ex cathedra* (from the seat of authority), he possessed "that infallibility with which the divine Redeemer willed that his Church should be endowed for defining doctrine regarding faith or

morals."[6] Thus the Roman Catholic Church categorically reaffirmed its historical position.

Biblical criticism. Just as certain historians were developing scientific methods to determine the validity of secular evidence about the past and thereby put history on a more scientific basis (see below), so other scholars—mainly Protestants—sought to subject Biblical texts and problems of authorship to the same type of rigid examination. This type of study was known as the "higher criticism."

When the Old Testament was thus critically analyzed, Genesis and other books were questioned in the light of the latest historical and scientific evidence. Advocates of the higher criticism contended that the New Testament, no less than the Old, recounted human rather than divine events and reflected the moral and ethical attitudes of the society which produced it. In addition, some scholars argued that many of the narratives found in the Gospels must be considered only myths and not historical facts.

The science of man. The apostles of science were also anxious to place human institutions on a scientific foundation. Such was the intention of the noted French student of society, Auguste Comte (1798-1857). Comte held that the history of mankind had passed through three stages of evolution. The first two of these, the theological and the metaphysical, had outlived their usefulness. Now the time had arrived to embark upon what he called the positive stage, in which scientific standards of observation and judgment would dominate. At the apex of all the social sciences, Comte placed the study of man in society, a new science to which he gave the term *sociology*.

Scientific history. The scientific approach was also brought to bear upon the writing of history. The founder of "scientific history" is the German Leopold von Ranke (1795-1886). His system called for a thorough search for all relevant evidence on a given subject, rigorous examination of this evidence to ensure its authenticity, and the restriction of conclusions to what could logically be drawn from the evidence. Ranke's methods initiated a more rigorous methodology among historians and demanded that they subordinate their personal views and preferences to a concern for the truth.

Darwin's work *The Origin of Species* caused further repercussions in the study of history. More than one historian began to analyze his subject matter strictly in terms of environment and heredity, stressing such factors as soil, topography, climate, food, race, and the inheritance of various traits. Sometimes this approach led to the treatment of societies and institutions as though they were simply biological organisms—a fallacy which could have pernicious results. On the more constructive side, the Darwinian hypothesis encouraged students to view history in terms of growth and adaptation.

Social Darwinism. One American thinker at the close of the nineteenth century wrote:

The life of man in society, just like the life of other species, is a struggle for existence. . . . The progress which has been and is being made in human institutions and in human character may be set down, broadly, to a natural selection of the fittest habits of thought and to a process of enforced adaptation of individuals to an environment which has progressively changed with the growth of the community and with the changing institutions under which men have lived.[7]

Here we see clearly how the concept of the survival of the fittest was used to explain not only the development but the progress of both human institutions and human character. Although Darwin himself had confined the principle of natural selection to the sphere of biology, others eagerly applied it to the field of human affairs. This application of Darwin's principles to man and his efforts was called "social Darwinism"; it became a vogue that swept western thought in the late nineteenth century. It also became a convenient doctrine for justifying various economic and political theories (see the Historical Critique, p. 840).

Herbert Spencer (1820-1903), an English philosopher from whom Darwin borrowed the phrase "survival of the fittest," was one of those who regarded society as a living organism. Spencer opposed any interference by the state with the natural development of

society. The sole function of the state, in his view, was negative—namely, to ensure freedom of the individual, who if left alone through enough generations would become perfect. Spencer used this doctrine to advocate unfettered business competition and to oppose all state aid to the poor, whom he regarded as unable to compete successfully in the struggle for survival and consequently better eliminated. At the same time, he favored private charity to develop altruistic traits in the donors.

The "justification" of racism and war. The pseudoscientific application of a biological theory to politics, whereby a nation is regarded as an organism, constituted possibly the most perverted form of social Darwinism in the period under review. It led to racism and anti-Semitism (see p. 559) and was used to show that only "superior" nationalities and races were fit to survive. One of the most influential advocates of racism was Comte Joseph Arthur de Gobineau (1816-1882), who argued that the different races are innately unequal in ability and worth and that the genius of a race depends upon hereditary and not environmental factors. The white peoples were alone capable of cultural creativity, which in turn could be destroyed by racial intermixture.

Social Darwinism was also employed to justify the use of military power to ensure that the "fittest" state would survive. Most influential as an advocate of war was the German philosopher Friedrich Nietzsche (1844-1900). His ideal, the superman, was characterized by bravery, strength, egoism, arrogance, and ruthlessness. Nietzsche challenged the world with: "You say, 'A good cause sanctifies even war,' but I say, 'A good war sanctifies every cause'!" Nietzsche viewed Christianity with contempt because he regarded gentleness as weakness and humanitarianism as protection of the unfit and spineless. Likewise, he ridiculed democracy and socialism for protecting the worthless and weak and hindering the strong.

Developments in philosophy: pragmatism and vitalism. Philosophy had been profoundly influenced by the implications of Darwin's work. Stressing the roles of change and chance in nature, the Darwinian theory strengthened the trend away from absolute standards.

Among American philosophers arose a school known as pragmatism. Led by the noted psychologist William James (1842-1910), the pragmatists argued that men think for the practical purpose of getting on with the job of living; and since the validity of any idea lies not in its approximation to some ultimate truth but in its ability to effect desired action, it must be tested by its logical or empirical results. As James put it, "An idea is 'true' so long as to believe it is profitable to our lives." Pragmatism, in effect, rejected any concept of truth or reality as absolute. Although it has been credited with bringing formal philosophy out of the clouds and relating it more concretely to the major scientific and intellectual trends of the day, the pragmatic approach resulted in a strongly utilitarian bent on the part of some of its adherents, with whom truth became indistinguishable from success.

Influenced by contemporary scientific currents in both biology and physics but differing widely from pragmatism was the philosophy of Henri Bergson (1859-1941). Bergson attributed evolution to a spontaneous creative force which he called the vital impulse (*élan vital*). Nothing is fixed; everything in life changes ceaselessly. The intellect is incapable of grasping the true nature of reality, which flows like an uninterrupted stream, and instead cuts reality up into discontinuous parts in much the same way that a movie film divides a single action into separate pictures. Bergson believed, however, that man has another faculty, intuition, which is capable of grasping life in terms of wholes. This, he maintained, is the ability employed by artists.

Bergson's philosophy of vitalism, which made its greatest impact in the years preceding World War I, represented a revolt against scientific determinism. While making use of the Darwinian thesis of change, it conceived evolution to be creative and not a blind struggle for survival. With its insistence that mental processes could not be reduced to simple mechanistic terms, this vitalistic philosophy was to influence many intellectuals of the time.

FROM REALISM TO EXPRESSIONISM

The realistic novelists. By 1870 writers were not only responding in various ways to the growing cult of science and to the impact of philosophical rationalism; they were also in revolt against the now-spent romanticism that survived in the form of sentimentalism. A down-to-earth attitude had become the order of the day. The nineteenth-century realists did not hesitate to describe in graphic detail social and personal problems which had hitherto gone unmentioned because they were not "nice." Their creed was to chronicle without comment, to photograph without touching up.

This new trend in literature had already been foreshadowed in the work of the French novelist Honoré de Balzac (1799-1850), the author of *La Comédie Humaine* or "The Human Comedy," a panorama of ninety volumes concerning French city and country life in the first half of the nineteenth century. In his novels the crudities and avarice of the French petty bourgeoisie were depicted in detail. The first thoroughgoing French realist was Gustave Flaubert (1821-1880). His masterpiece, *Madame Bovary* (1856), describes how the boredom of a romantic-minded young provincial wife led her into adultery, extravagance, and ultimately suicide. By implication Flaubert was pointing to the pitfalls of romanticism as a way of life.

Realism served as the keynote for the most important novelists of the late nineteenth century. Count Leo Tolstoy's epic novel *War and Peace* (1869), a magnificent tapestry of life in Russia during the Napoleonic invasion of 1812, stripped every shred of glory or glamour from that conflict. His *Anna Karenina* (1877) relentlessly detailed the story of two lovers who openly defy social conventions. Another great Russian novelist, Feodor Dostoevski, traced the causes and effects of murder in two masterpieces of suspense and psychological analysis, *Crime and Punishment* (1866) and *The Brothers Karamazov* (1880).

A notable English realist was Thomas Hardy, who dealt with the struggle of the individual—almost invariably a losing struggle —against the impersonal, pitiless forces of his natural and social environment. In America Henry James, the brother of the American pragmatist William James, attempted, as he put it, to catch "the atmosphere of the mind" in his works. His stories and novels serve as a framework for the lengthy, subtle analyses of human motives. Another well-known American writer of the period was Samuel Clemens, whose fame as the humorist Mark Twain should not blind us to the realistic character of his work. His writings abound not only with robust humor but also with accurate descriptions of the Middle and Far West. Like Dickens, he could employ humorous satire to underscore social injustice.

In the hands of some writers realism developed into an extreme form of presentation known as naturalism The naturalists wished to apply scientific objectivity to their subject matter and to deal with their characters as with animals in a laboratory, whose every move was determined by environment or heredity. The most outstanding practitioner of this literary doctrine was Émile Zola, who made a case study twenty volumes long of a middle-class family. In this series of works, which included *Nana* (1880) and *Germinal* (1885), Zola employed a clinical approach, amassing huge notebooks of information on such subjects as the stock market and the mining districts before describing these settings.

The problem play: Ibsen and Shaw. The exposure of social problems was an important aspect of the new literary realism. The problems facing *fin de siècle* (end of the century) society were more subtle in character than the obvious injustices of child labor and cholera-infested slums, which had monopolized the attention of social critics earlier in the century. Thus, perhaps, was provided the impetus for the development of a new, sophisticated form of drama called the "problem play."

The dramas of the Norwegian Henrik Ibsen were the first of the problem plays. One of his best known works is *A Doll's House* (1879), in which he assailed marriage without love as being immoral. In other plays he attacked social greed masked by conventional respectability and delineated with great sensitivity the human dramas latent in the strains and stresses of ordinary life. A disciple of Ibsen and, like the Norwegian, an ardent assailant of bourgeois complacency, was the brilliant Irish playwright George Bernard Shaw. In a series of shrewdly satirical and highly diverting stage successes, he cajoled, bullied, and shocked the English-speaking public into reassessing their conventional attitudes on a variety of social subjects, ranging from private and public morality to militarism and religious beliefs.

The search for new standards. All the writers of this period were not proponents of the realistic school. Some, like Oscar Wilde in England, made a cult of their revulsion

The life and works of Tolstoy are evidence of his strong identification with the common man. Although wealthy, this famous novelist did manual labor as he tried to simplify his own life.

1893, *[signature]*

against the crudities and vulgarity of a realism-ridden age. To them, the only valid standard was "art for art's sake." Moral, social, or ethical criteria were unimportant in themselves; the artist might do as he pleased so long as his work possessed artistic integrity. In the name of such integrity, the devotees of this school—both as writers and as individuals—often lapsed into decadence.

Still other writers sought new standards and modes of expression. A group of poets known as the symbolists, found for the most part in France during the last two decades of the nineteenth century, made use of images, archaic and mystical terms, and other devices in order to convey the inner feelings of an individual or group. Their experimentation also led them to employ free verse and the prose poem, while their efforts to express the subjective and introspective often made their works obscure to all but themselves.

Realism in painting. The major trends in literature between 1870 and 1914 were paralleled by developments in painting in the same era. Already, by the 1850's various artists in France had been rebelling against traditional subject matter and techniques. Feeling that the canvases exhibited on academy walls were for the most part too "respectable" and hence artificial, they chose instead to paint life as they saw it.

Gustave Courbet, probably the outstanding French realist, expressed his contempt for religious and Neoclassical themes when he mocked: "Show me an angel and I will paint one." When he looked at nature, he consciously dropped the affectations of both the romanticists and Neoclassicists and painted uncompromising, often brutal canvases. Courbet's view that "realism is an essentially democratic art" was shared by his compatriot Honoré Daumier, who knew Parisian life intimately. His lithographs were biting satires of life among the bourgeoisie, in the courts of law, and in political circles (see illustrations, pp. 494, 514).

Impressionism in France. As we have seen, realism in literature was developed by Zola and others into naturalism, whereby the writer sought to observe phenomena in their natural state and to record them with scientific precision. In painting we find a similar development in Impressionism. Preoccupied with problems of color, light, and atmosphere, the Impressionists sought to catch the first impression made by a scene or object upon the eye, undistorted by the intellect or any subjective attitude. The result was that the Impressionists worked in terms of light and color rather than solidity of form. In doing so, they found that a more striking effect of light could be obtained by placing one bright area of color next to another without any transitional tones. They also discovered that shadows could be shown not as gray but as colors complementary to those of the objects casting the shadows. At close range an Impressionist picture may seem little more than a splotch of unmixed colors, but at the proper distance the eye mixes the colors, and a vibrating effect of light and motion emerges. Through their technique the Impressionists helped revolutionize modern painting.

An outstanding Impressionist was Pierre Auguste Renoir, who skillfully employed color to capture flesh tones and texture. Renoir painted all sorts of subjects, among them the opera, landscapes, and houseboats on the Seine. His canvases all reveal his rich sense of color; the sunlight plays across his paintings, giving the sense of a passing moment held in paint (see p. 594).

To France must go credit for the development not only of this new style of painting but of related techniques in other arts as well. The outstanding sculptor of the late nineteenth century, Auguste Rodin, has been described as the father of modern sculpture. He infused his work with a realistic honesty and vitality that made him the object of stormy controversy during much of his lifetime. Sharing with the Impressionist painters a dislike for studied finality in art, Rodin preferred to let the imagination of the beholder play on his sculpture. Rodin's technique of rough finish shows to advantage in his bronze works. By this technique the sculptor achieved two effects: a glittering surface of light and shadow and a feeling of immediacy and incompleteness that emphasized the spontaneous character of the work.

Post-Impressionism. By conveying a sense of motion and of the moment, Impressionism had given painting—and, through Rodin, sculpture—a fresh vitality. But it had done so at a price. For one thing, its effects with color and atmosphere had been achieved by sacrificing much of the clarity which continued to be a hallmark of the classical tradition. Again, while bringing the surface of things alive in an exciting fashion, the Impressionist seemed unable to give his objects the solidity and structure which were theirs by nature. How could artists get the best of both worlds?

This was the difficult intellectual and artistic problem to which Paul Cézanne (1839-1906) addressed himself. For years this painter—a one-time realist and friend of Zola—experimented with new techniques. He sought to simplify all natural objects by emphasizing their essential geometric structure. As Cézanne said, everything in nature corresponds to the shape of the cone, the cylinder, or the sphere. Proceeding on the basis of this theory, he was able to get below the surface and give his objects the solidity which had eluded the Impressionists. Yet, like the latter, he made striking use of color—in his case, to establish the relationships of his objects in space (see Color Plate 29). The successful pioneering work of Cézanne was to have important consequences.

One or two other late nineteenth-century painters were also successful, by reason of their individualism, in contributing to the rise of Post-Impressionism. One was Vincent van Gogh (1853-1890), a Dutch painter whose short life of poverty and loneliness was climaxed by insanity and suicide. In many of his paintings he employed short strokes of heavy pigment which accentuated forms and rhythms. Van Gogh was concerned not with presenting simply a photographic representation of what lay before him but wanted to convey also the intense feelings evoked in himself by his subject. As a consequence, he was ready to distort what he saw in order to depict these sensations, even as Cézanne had abandoned perspective where necessary so as to concentrate on form and spatial relationships.

Following the example of the Impressionist painters, Auguste Rodin brought the "unfinished" look into the realm of sculpture. His best known work, "The Thinker," was originally designed as part of a massive entrance inspired by Dante's *Inferno;* the figure was to ponder a wretched view below.

Expressionism and Cubism. Continuing to experiment, artists became increasingly concerned with painting what they felt about an object rather than the object itself. This method of using an object as a means of expressing subjective feelings is known as Expressionism, an approach similar to that of the symbolist school in literature. Among the early Expressionists—or *les fauves* (the wild beasts), as they were derided by their critics—was Henri Matisse, who had learned to simplify form partly from African primitive art and had studied the color schemes of oriental carpets. His decorative style was to influence design strongly in our own day.

Experimentation took still other subjective forms. We have already noted that in order to achieve a sense of depth and solidity, Cézanne used geometric shapes and

Auguste Renoir, the French Impressionist, used vibrant color and scintillating light to achieve delightful visual effects. Many of his paintings, such as "Canoeists' Luncheon" (top), portray the pastimes of the lower and middle classes in informal outdoor scenes. Influenced both by Impressionist works and by Persian art, Henri Matisse emphasized the arrangement of simple rhythmic forms, rich textures, and vivid areas of color in paintings like "Goldfish and Sculpture" (right).

depth relationships on the two-dimensional painting surface. Further developments along these lines resulted in the emergence of a new school—Cubism. Cubists would choose an object, then construct an abstract pattern from it. In doing so, they went far beyond the traditional manner of reproducing the object from one vantage point; instead, they viewed it from several points of view simultaneously. In a Cubist canvas one might see a given object—say a violin—from above, below, outside, and inside, with all the dissected elements interpenetrating (see illustration, p. 798). Such a pattern is also evident in "Three Musicians" by the Spanish artist Pablo Picasso, probably the most influential single figure in twentieth-century painting.

Architecture reflects the machine age. For a great part of the nineteenth century, architectural styles were largely derivative. Structures were designed in the Gothic and Rococo and other styles as well. This eclectic approach was due in no small measure to the fact that large houses and factories alike were often erected for middle-class entrepreneurs who believed that the best way to prove that they had arrived socially was to build in styles traditionally associated with the aristocracy. Meanwhile, public buildings in the rapidly growing towns were designed in a massive and ornamental style calculated to reflect civic grandeur and opulence. From the standpoint of today's architects, there was a total lack of sensitivity in the way that buildings were related—or, rather, unrelated—to their sites.

Nevertheless some exciting new thinking had been concentrated on commercial architecture. Aided by advances in industry and technology, architects were now able to design structures that could span greater distances and enclose greater areas than had hitherto been possible. However much of a tragedy, the great fire that leveled much of Chicago in 1871 had the benefit of putting that city in the forefront with a new form of architecture, the steel-skeleton skyscraper. Whereas high buildings had formerly required immensely thick masonry walls, a metal frame now allowed the weight of the structure to be distributed on an entirely

different principle and permitted a far more extensive use of glass than ever before. Outstanding among the pioneers in this new architecture was Chicago's Louis Sullivan (1856-1924). Like others, Sullivan perceived the value of the skyscraper in providing a large amount of useful space on a small plot of expensive land, such as that in Chicago's Loop or in Manhattan. Unlike others, he rejected all attempts to disguise the skeleton of the skyscraper behind some false facade and boldly proclaimed it by a clean sweep of line. Sullivan's emphasis upon the functional was to have far-reaching influence.

One of Sullivan's pupils, the brilliant Frank Lloyd Wright (1869-1959), was meanwhile originating revolutionary designs for houses. One feature of Wright's houses was the interweaving of interiors and exteriors by the use of terraces and cantilevered roofs. He felt that a building should look appropriate on its site; it should "grow out of the land." His "prairie houses," with their long, low lines, were designed to blend in with the flat land of the Midwest. Much that is taken for granted in today's houses derives directly from Wright's experiments at the turn of the century.

In the decade prior to World War I, there developed in Germany a fairly widely accepted style of architecture that broke with tradition and stressed the use of new forms reflecting the machine age. In 1914 one of the outstanding leaders of this movement, Walter Gropius, designed an exhibition hall in Cologne which, with its emphasis on horizontals, its use of glass, its exposure of staircases, and its undisguised functionalism, we would accept today as contemporary. The new movement in architecture resulted in the establishment of a school of functional art and architecture, the Bauhaus, in 1918.

Impressionism and experimentation in music. In the early years of the period 1870 to 1914, romanticism was still the main style in the musical world. As we will recall from Chapter 21, Brahms and Tschaikovsky were offering the public new orchestral works, and Verdi and Wagner were writing operas. A post-Wagnerian school persisted well into the twentieth century. One of its

Louis Sullivan and Walter Gropius produced revolutionary architectural designs born of the concept that external form should express the purpose of a building, its internal structure, and the materials used. Adhering to his maxim "form follows function," Sullivan expressed tremendous strength in the Carson, Pirie, Scott Store (left) with sharply cut horizontal windows which fulfilled their indispensable purpose—the admission of light. Similarly, Gropius achieved a very transparent effect in the Bauhaus (below) by means of a continuous glass curtain wall between two ribbons of white concrete.

outstanding members, Richard Strauss, enlivened the musical scene with his brilliant orchestrations and his dramatic music.

A striking departure from musical tradition occurred with the rise of the French school of impressionism, whose foremost exponent was Claude Debussy (1862-1918). Just as the painters of the period had achieved new atmospheric effects by their technical innovations, so composers now engaged in "tone painting" to achieve a special mood or atmosphere. Such an effect is immediately recognizable in Debussy's prelude "L'Après-midi d'un faune" ("The Afternoon of a Faun"), which astounded the musical world when it was first performed in 1892. The Impressionist painters had obtained their effects by juxtaposing different colors. The composers in turn juxtaposed widely separated chords to create similarly brilliant, shimmering effects with sound.

A number of other composers rebelled strongly against romanticism and engaged in striking experimentation. Breaking with the major-minor system of tonality, which had been the western musical tradition since the Renaissance, some of them began to make use of several different keys simultaneously, a device known as polytonality. Outstanding among such composers, Igor Stravinski (1882-1971) has done for modern music what innovators like Picasso have done for modern painting. Unlike the romanticists, Stravinski was less concerned with melody than with achieving his effects by means of polytonality, dissonant harmonies, and percussive rhythms. Meanwhile other composers were experimenting with atonality (the absence of any fixed key). In this regard, we should mention Arnold Schönberg (1874-1952), who developed a twelve-tone system. Compositions of this structure depart from all tonality and harmonic progressions, while at the same time stressing extreme dissonances.

With the work of composers like Schönberg, we arrive at expressionism in music. Just as the Expressionist painters were attempting to create a new inner reality, so composers sought to give shape to their innermost feelings by getting below the surface. Although harsh and unpleasant to many ears, these experiments with polytonality and atonality had validity for a century in which the old absolute values were being broken down—a century, as two world wars were to prove, of clashing dissonance.

SUMMARY

Between 1870 and 1914 new industries and inventions revolutionized manufacturing. This technical stage was characterized by new sources of energy, new materials, an ever-increasing alliance between science and industry, mass-production methods, and a new capacity to disperse industry and the urban population. The outpouring of goods during this period enormously increased the wealth and power of Europe, making it the financial, cultural, and military center of the world. The masses' living standards were raised, and the philosophy of laissez faire shrank before that of the welfare state. Old-age pensions, unemployment insurance, and accident compensation gave the masses more security. The Fabians and other revisionist socialists were content to call for continued social and economic reform. Yet revolutionary socialists persisted; the syndicalists advocated the use of the general strike to paralyze capitalism, and the Leninist Bolsheviks fostered revolution in order to implement the doctrine of Marx.

The period from 1870 to 1914 also constituted the zenith of western intellectual and social dominance. Traditional concepts in physics were challenged by a number of remarkable developments: Clerk-Maxwell's experiments with optics and electricity, the discovery of x-rays, Planck's quantum theory, and Einstein's theory of relativity. No less spectacular was the progress made in other sciences. Scientists learned about proteins and vitamins, about the purpose of ductless glands, and about the uses of chemotherapy in the treatment of disease; the twin sciences of bacteriology and immunology were established firmly; and the study of biology was advanced by the research of Mendel and

Galton. In psychology the behavioristic school flourished, while Freud pioneered in psychoanalysis.

These spectacular advances in science were responsible for the rise of a cult of science and the development of a vigorous struggle between the claims of science and those of organized religion. Although Darwin had already shaken a previous era with his evolutionary hypothesis, it was this period that experienced its full impact in both the scientific and social spheres. Perhaps the most pernicious aspect of the cult of science was that of social Darwinism, which applied the doctrine of the survival of the fittest to the economic, political, and military spheres with disastrous results.

The writers and artists of these decades had been turning away from the romanticism of the first half of the nineteenth century to embrace a down-to-earth, photographic approach known as realism. Carried to its extreme form of presentation, realism was known in literature as naturalism. In the theater the problem play heralded the rise of social criticism. In painting, following the brilliant results achieved by the Impressionists in obtaining new surface and atmospheric effects, other painters continued to experiment in various ways, and the schools of Expressionism and Cubism were the result. Architects broke with the largely derivative styles of the preceding period and experimented with new materials and designs to satisfy the requirements of a highly industrialized society.

Our survey closes in 1914, the year of the outbreak of the First World War—itself the logical culmination of the doctrine of the survival of the fittest. The physical waste and moral bankruptcy of this conflict are bitter indexes of the hideous perversion of such a theory when misapplied to human society.

SUGGESTIONS FOR READING

For an introduction to European scientific, intellectual, and esthetic developments during this period, see C. J. H. Hayes, **A Generation of Materialism: 1871–1900,*** Torchbooks; W. W. Wagar, ed., **European Intellectual History Since Darwin and Marx,*** Harper & Row; and R. N. Stromberg, **An Intellectual History of Modern Europe,*** Appleton.

In **The Voyage of the Beagle,*** Anchor, Darwin has left a journal of his experiences and observations about natural history and geology that led to the revolutionary **The Origin of Species,*** Collier. See also J. Huxley, ed., **The Living Thoughts of Darwin,*** Premier. Making use of unpublished documents, G. Himmelfarb in **Darwin and the Darwinian Revolution,** Norton, 1968, sheds valuable light on both the scientist's character and the age in which he lived. See also G. De Beer, **Charles Darwin,*** Anchor.

C. C. Gillispie, **Genesis and Geology,*** Torchbooks. A review of the controversy between religion and science which preceded the publication of *The Origin of Species.* The involvement of Darwin and Thomas Huxley in the intellectual furor is dealt with in W. Irvine, **Apes, Angels, and Victorians,*** World.

S. Tax, ed., **Issues in Evolution,** Vol. III of **Evolution After Darwin,** Univ. of Chicago, 1960. An assessment of the effects of Darwin's theories on modern-day science, philosophy, and religion. Excellent accounts of modern evolution are found in J. Huxley, **Evolution: the Modern Synthesis,** Allen and Unwin, 1958; T. Dobzhansky, **Genetics and the Origin of Species,** Oxford, 1951; and G. G. Simpson, **The Meaning of Evolution,*** Mentor. In his admirable **Social Darwinism in American Thought,*** Beacon, R. Hofstadter details the cult of force, struggle, and militarism in the United States during this period.

Excellent biographies of important scientists include W. W. Cheyne, **Lister and His Achievements,** Longmans, 1925; E. Curie, **Madame Curie,*** Pocket Books; H. Iltis, **The Life of Mendel,** Hafner, 1932; and R. Dubos, **Louis Pasteur, Free Lance of Science,** Little, Brown, 1950.

C. Singer *et al.,* eds., **The Late Nineteenth Century, 1850–1900,** Vol. V of **A History of Technology,** Oxford, 1958. Lavishly illustrated and clearly written, perhaps the best single work on technological accomplishments during this period. For a survey covering a longer time space, see D. W. Landes, **The Unbound Prometheus: Technological Change and Industrial Development in Western Europe from 1750 to the Present,*** Cambridge.

A. Maurois, **The Life of Balzac,** Harper & Row, 1966; and H. Troyat, **Tolstoy,** Doubleday, 1967. Outstanding studies of notable literary figures.

For significant developments in esthetic theory and painting in the decades preceding World War One, see C. Edward Gauss, **The Aesthetic Theories of French Artists: From Realism to Surrealism,*** Johns Hopkins; and E. F. Fry, **Cubism (World of Art Series),*** Thames and Hudson. For an overall survey of developments during the past two centuries see H. L. C. Jaffe, **The Nineteenth and Twentieth Centuries,** Vol. 5 of the **Dolphin History of Painting,*** Thames and Hudson. A number of outstanding painters and their works are treated in individual publications; Fontana has issued a series of **Paintings,*** in its **Art Books,** separately for Manet, Matisse, and Picasso. M. De Micheli has written **Cezanne*** and **Picasso*** for Thames and Hudson.

*Indicates an inexpensive paperbound edition.

Part Six

The West
Dominant

■ In the eighteenth and nineteenth centuries European influence spread to virtually all parts of the non-European world. Two sorts of communities were created by this expansion: the centers of settlement for the millions of people from Ireland, England, Germany, France, and Italy who migrated to the Americas, South Africa, and Australasia; and the colonies of exploitation, those African and Asian territories and islands which were developed largely for economic gain. The settlement of new and largely uninhabited lands by Europeans gave birth to new nations, and the conquest of areas unsuited for European settlement resulted in a system of imperialism by which a minority of foreign officials and soldiers controlled a majority of native peoples. The colonies in imperial systems brought wealth to the controlling western powers, but at the same time European rule helped introduce new forces that ultimately were to challenge and sweep away imperialism.

Although there was variance in the centers of settlement—which can be called new Europes—because of differences in the national origins of the colonists and in the indigenous societies they encountered, all can be said to have derived their culture mainly from Europe. Thus though the United States grew and broke away from its mother country while Canada flourished and remained in the English fold, the outstanding traits of both—their governmental structure and principles, their social make-up, and their language—reflect their common European origins. And all these new Europes had certain common problems—the challenge of exploring and occupying hitherto unsettled lands, the problem of native peoples, the necessity of taming nature and using natural resources, and the task of building nations. Furthermore, all of them experienced the same urge to broaden democratic rights. A number of the new Europes in the Americas had one unique characteristic, a large black population resulting from the importation of slaves from West Africa. This ethnic element influenced the course of history especially in Brazil and the United States.

The stage on which history was being made in the nations of the New World was different in many ways from that of the mother countries in Europe. On both, however, the plot and the action had much in common. The leading actors—statesmen and administrators—had to direct and cope with the same basic forces, such as nationalism, industrialism, and democracy. For example, the American Civil War, the federation movement in Canada, and the efforts of Bismarck and Cavour in Germany and Italy all concerned the same basic principle of national unity; and the quest for expanding democratic freedoms in the Jacksonian era in the United States had its counterpart in the widespread revolutions of 1830 and 1848 in Europe.

While European immigrants were settling the new Europes, their home governments were extending their control over African and Asian peoples. By the end of the nineteenth century practically all of Africa had been partitioned and placed under European rule, along with most of southern Asia and the islands of the Pacific. Although China remained technically independent, this vast, tradition-bound land also was controlled in many ways by the western imperial powers. Japan alone succeeded in modernizing itself and thus avoided being caught in the imperialist net. In the half-century before World War I, western supremacy, symbolized by imperialism and the colonial system, was one of the major facts of international life.

The morality of imperialism has been a hotly debated subject. Critics have emphasized such negative aspects as arbitrary rule, economic exploitation, and hypocrisy and greed on the part of the imperialists. On the other hand, imperialism has been justified on economic, religious, nationalistic, and even humanitarian grounds. Such well-known champions of imperialism as Livingstone, Rhodes, and Kipling believed that, in promoting their country's seizure of foreign lands and riches, they were doing the best thing for all concerned. The theory that only the selfish have followed the course of imperialism is not borne out by the facts of history.

What is perhaps the most significant and enduring influence of imperialism has not been appreciated. Western colonialism was the instrument for culture diffusion on a huge scale. The colonial officials, missionaries, planters, and educators spread new ideas about science and technology, developed natural resources, cured the physical ills of the native peoples, and taught concepts of democracy and Christian morality.

This impact of western culture subtly modified the outlook and habits of the peoples under the colonial system. Ideals of freedom and nationalism began to stir. National movements gained strength in the early years of the twentieth century and after World War II gathered sufficient momentum to challenge and largely demolish colonialism. Thus the western world provided the knowledge and inspiration which was to uplift and release the very people it had exploited. The golden age of imperialism ended more than half a century ago, but it had changed the course of history for all time.

Chapter 26

New Europes Overseas

**The United States, the British Dominions,
and Latin America: 1650-1914**

INTRODUCTION. In the four centuries before the twentieth, the greatest transplantation of peoples in human history took place as millions of Europeans left their homelands, crossed oceans, and made for themselves new homes in overseas lands. These immigrants brought with them what has been aptly called their "cultural baggage"—their language, religion, folk habits, and political institutions. At the same time, the slave trade brought vast numbers of Africans to the Americas.

In the new areas of settlement—the Americas, South Africa, Australia, and New Zealand—new Europes were founded and developed. In many ways these settlers perpetuated the culture of their homelands. Moreover, the most important developments in Europe after Waterloo—the ambitions of the middle class, the search of the masses for full political rights, the increased interest in a better standard of living, and the pervasive force of nationalism—all these became important factors in the overseas communities. Yet if the history of the new Europes is to be studied profitably in comparison with that of Europe itself, it should be remembered that certain common conditions and problems distinguished the history of these new nations: the challenge of geographical exploration, the problem of what to do with the indigenous peoples, and the search for a new national way of life. In the Americas there was also the problem of how best to treat the Negro, as a slave and then as a free man. Furthermore, some historians have stressed the deep influence in all the new Europes of frontier life with its fostering of democracy, individualism, resourcefulness, and optimism. As a complete explanation of the course of history in the new Europes, this thesis has been overdone. But some of its relevance remains.

In this chapter we shall see how the founding of colonies in Canada, Australia, New Zealand, and the Union of South Africa illustrates the transplanting of British culture to remote parts of the world. One interesting aspect of the story of the new Britains overseas during the nineteenth century is that they finally arrived at a status of full national independence or sovereignty without recourse to arms. At the same time they remained closely associated with the mother country as members of the British Commonwealth of Nations. Since the political development of Canada was a model for other English colonies, we shall emphasize Canadian history in our survey of the British dominions.

The United States stood apart from the other republics in the New World by reason of its spectacular economic advances, political stability, and successful democratic system. Its greatest failure was its inability to avoid the costly Civil War and delay in recognizing the legitimate aspirations of its black citizens.

Latin America faced certain unique problems in its struggle to win greatness. Here the Indian problem was far greater than it was in the United States, and relations between the two races were very different. From the time of the successful revolt against Spain and Portugal in the first quarter of the nineteenth century, the history of Latin America has been marked by civil wars and local struggles for political power. As this chapter discloses, threats from the outside and attempts by other powers to gain economic if not political control of Latin America did much to retard the growth of Latin America as a whole. Nevertheless, by the first quarter of the twentieth century a degree of stability and prosperity had been achieved in parts of Latin America, and the cultural patterns that developed there constitute a valuable component of world civilization.

THE MAKING OF A NEW NATION: THE UNITED STATES

Brave new world. The revolutionary movements in Europe during the nineteenth century had a two-pronged problem: they faced the vestiges of a feudal order of lord and peasant in which political, economic, and social privilege was concentrated in an aristocratic class; or they faced restless nationality groups that sought to unite under their own government by throwing off alien rule —or both. The nineteenth-century movements in the United States were not quite the same, since there was no significant heritage of feudal lord and peasant relationship in *English* North America and no counterpart to the conflicts with outside powers over national unification that troubled the Germans, Italians, Serbs, and other peoples of central and southeastern Europe. In place of these problems the United States had two major and interrelated problems of its own— the annexation, settlement, and development of a sparsely populated continent, and slavery. Free land and unfree men: these were the sources of the many political confrontations that culminated in the Civil War, the greatest revolutionary struggle in nineteenth-century America.

Democratic influences of the frontier. In 1783, the year the United States became a sovereign state, the young nation could not be called a democracy. Six years later only one male in seven possessed the franchise.

Religious requirements and property qualifications kept many of the common people from participating in governmental affairs. For the first forty years of its existence the government of the United States was largely in the hands of established families from the South, such as those of Washington and Jefferson, or of men of wealth and substance from the middle class of the North, such as Adams. It has been said that it took fifty years after the Declaration of Independence "to reach a vital belief that the people and not gentlemen are to govern this country."[1]

The influence of the western frontier helped move America closer to full democracy. Even before the Constitution was ratified by the thirteen states, thousands of pioneers crossed the Appalachian Mountains into the new "western country." Here on the frontier, land was to be had for the asking. Here social caste did not exist; one man was as good as another. Vigor, courage, and self-reliance counted, not birth or wealth. Throughout most of the nineteenth century, as pioneers moved westward, the West was to be a source for new and liberal movements which challenged the ideas prevalent in the more conservative and settled areas of the country.

Until the War of 1812 the growth of democracy was slow. In 1791 Vermont had been admitted as a manhood-suffrage state, and the following year Kentucky followed suit; but Tennessee, Ohio, and Louisiana entered the Union with property and tax qualifications for the suffrage. After 1817 no new state entered the Union with restrictions on male suffrage except for slaves. Most appointive offices became elective, and requirements for holding office were liberalized.

Jacksonian democracy. In 1828 Andrew Jackson was elected to the presidency, following a campaign which featured the slogan "Down with the aristocrats." Jackson was the first president produced by the new West; the first, excepting Washington, not to have a college education; and the first to have been born in poverty. He owed his successful election to no congressional clique but to the will of the people. The common people idolized "Old Hickory" as their spokesman and a fearless leader of men.

The triumph of the democratic principle in the 1830's set the direction for political development down to this day. With the new president came the idea that any man, by virtue of being an American citizen, was worthy of holding any office in the land. Educational opportunities were widened with the growth of the public school system, class barriers became less important, and government became more responsive and responsible to the average or common man. Indeed, it has been thoughtfully said that "the 1830's saw the triumph in American politics of that democracy which has remained pre-eminently the distinguishing feature of our society."[2]

Acquisition of new lands. From 1800 to 1860 the westward movement proceeded at an amazingly rapid pace. The Louisiana territory, purchased from France for about $15 million in 1803, doubled the size of the United States. The annexation of Texas in 1845 was followed by war with Mexico in 1846. Two years later Mexico signed a peace treaty whereby California, all title to Texas, and the country between California and Texas were ceded to the United States. The same year that war broke out with Mexico, the Oregon territory was occupied after the settlement of a boundary dispute with Great Britain (see p. 621). As a result of these acquisitions, by 1860 the area of the United States had increased nearly two thirds over what it had been in 1840.

The slavery issue. The acquisition of new territory forced the issue of whether slavery should be allowed in these areas. At the same time, the whole issue of slavery was being vigorously condemned by abolitionists in the North, particularly in New England. Henry Clay's Missouri Compromise of 1820, by which slavery was permitted in Missouri but forbidden in the remainder of the Louisiana Purchase, had satisfied both sides temporarily, but the antislavery forces grew more insistent. In the senatorial campaigns of 1858, Abraham Lincoln declared:

"A house divided against itself cannot stand." I believe this government cannot endure permanently half slave and half free. I do not expect the Union to be dissolved—I do not expect the house to fall—but I do expect it will cease to be divided. It will become all one thing, or all the other.[3]

Slavery was a fundamental issue; from its existence stemmed many differences and tensions which separated the North from the South. In a sense the North and the South had become two different civilizations. The former was industrial, urban, and democratic; the latter was mainly agricultural, rural, and dominated by a planter aristocracy. The South strongly opposed the North's desire for higher tariffs, government aid for new railroads, and generous terms for land settlement in the West.

The Civil War. Soon after the inauguration of Lincoln as president, the southern states seceded from the Union and formed the Confederacy. The first shot of the Civil War was fired at Fort Sumter in 1861. Four agonizing years of conflict and the bloodiest war experienced by any western nation to that time followed. The Civil War ended

when General Lee surrendered to General Grant at Appomattox in April 1865; a few days later the joyful North was stunned by the assassination of President Lincoln. With the final collapse of the Confederacy before the overwhelming superiority of the Union in manpower, industrial resources, and wealth, the Civil War became the grand epic of American history in its heroism, romance, tragedy, and incalculable results.

In the largest sense the American Civil War can be explained in its relation to the great historical movements of the nineteenth century—liberalism, democracy, and nationalism—which were transforming Europe. It was the desire for freedom that sparked the revolutions in Europe in 1830 and 1848; and likewise in the United States many people had come to believe that slavery was an inhuman and immoral institution. The sentiment of nationalism was equally strong in Europe and in the United States. Just as wars were fought to attain German and Italian unity, a great struggle took place in

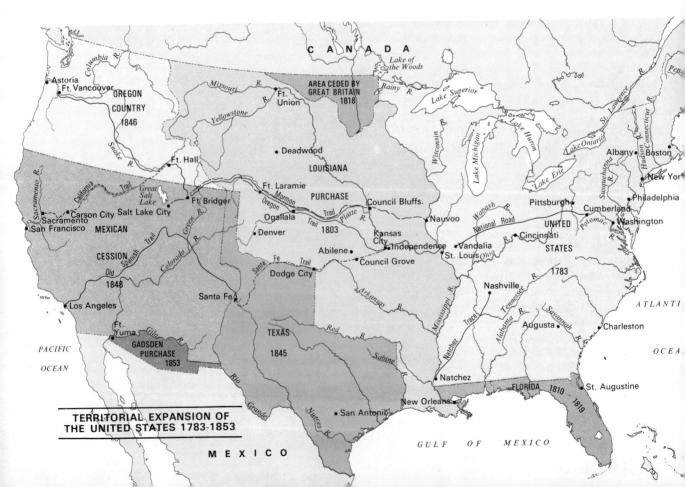

TERRITORIAL EXPANSION OF THE UNITED STATES 1783-1853

America to maintain national unity. If the causes of the American Civil War are complex, the all-important result was simple. It settled the issue of whether the United States was an indivisible sovereign nation or a collection of sovereign states. The Federal Union was preserved, and nationalism triumphed over the sectionalism of the South.

Aftermath of the Civil War. Following the conflict, federal military occupation and force were used to try to convert the South to democratic voting and property rights for the Negro. Eventually this so-called Reconstruction period (1865-1877) was ended by a tacit political agreement between the industrial North and white southern leaders. The latter now proceeded to deprive Negroes of their voting rights. As second-class citizens, freed but landless, the ex-slaves became essentially a sharecropping class. More than one hundred years after the Civil War, black Americans had still not achieved the place in a politically and economically free society which radical reformers attempted to ensure at the beginning of the Reconstruction. In a sense, the civil rights movement of the twentieth century is the belated aftermath of uncompleted Reconstruction.

Industrial expansion. The victory of the North also foreshadowed an irresistible trend toward industrialism. In its lasting effects the economic revolution in the United States that followed the Civil War was more significant than the conflict itself. Railroads were built across broad prairies, and the first transcontinental railroad, the Union Pacific, was completed in 1869. Thousands of settlers swarmed westward.

Between 1850 and 1880 the number of cities with a population of 50,000 or more doubled. The number of men employed in industry increased 50 percent. In 1865 there were 35,000 miles of railroads in the country; eight years later this figure had been doubled. By 1900 the trackage was estimated to be about 200,000 miles, more than in all of Europe. In 1860 a little more than a billion dollars was invested in manufacturing; by 1900 this figure had risen to twelve billion. The value of manufactured products increased proportionately. In 1870 the total production of iron and steel in the United

THE DIS-UNITED STATES—A BLACK BUSINESS.

The growing tensions between the North and South gained world-wide attention. *Punch*, the English humor magazine, viewed the situation like this in 1856.

States was far below that of France and England. Twenty years later the United States had outstripped them and was producing about one third of the world's iron and steel.

In the age of rapid industrialism and materialistic expansion, many who pursued profits lost sight of ethical principles both in business and in government. In five years, between 1865 and 1870, the notorious Tweed Ring cost the city of New York at least $100 million. Ruthless financiers, such as Jay Gould and Jim Fisk, tampered with the financial stability of the nation. During General Grant's administration as president, the country was shocked by scandals and frauds. A new rich class, elevated to power and wealth overnight, failed to appreciate its responsibilities to society. Corruption in business was a blatant feature of the new economic order.

End of the era of expansion. For roughly a century the gospel of the new nation of America had been rugged individualism. As in Europe, government interference in business was unwelcome because it was felt that the individual should be free to follow his own inclinations, run his own business, and enjoy the profits of his labors. In an expanding nation where land, jobs, and opportunity beckoned, there was little to indicate that the system would not work indefinitely. By

1880, however, the end of the frontier was in sight. Free land of good quality was scarce, and the frontier could no longer act as a safety valve to release the economic and social pressures of an expanding population.

Between 1850 and 1900 the United States became the most powerful state in the Western Hemisphere, increased its national wealth from $7 billion to $88 billion, established an excellent system of public education, and fostered the enjoyment of civil liberties. But there were many disturbing factors in the picture. Unemployment, child labor, and industrial accidents became common in the rapidly growing industrial areas. In large cities, slums grew and served as breeding places for disease and crime. Strikes, often accompanied by violence, demonstrated the tension developing between labor and capital.

The progressive movement. The United States obtained its independence in 1783, became a political democracy early in the nineteenth century, and prevented the collapse of the Federal Union between 1861 and 1865. By 1890 a new challenge had arisen—the need for economic reform. At this point, as had happened in England and elsewhere at about the same time, a powerful movement whose object was the removal of economic inequalities began. The so-called progressive movement agitated for the elimination of sweatshops, of exploitation of foreign labor, and of waste of the nation's natural wealth. This era of the muckrakers lasted roughly from 1890 to 1914.

The success of the progressive movement was reflected in the constitutions of new states admitted to the Union and in their introduction of the direct primary, the initiative and referendum, and the direct election of senators. All these measures tended to give the common man more effective control of his government. After the enactment in 1887 of the Interstate Commerce Act, which had introduced federal regulation of the railroads, a steady expansion of governmental regulation of industry began. As president of the United States from 1901 to 1909, Theodore Roosevelt launched an aggressive campaign to break up the trusts, to conserve national resources, and to extend the regulation of the national government over the railroads, food, and drugs. In 1913 President Woodrow Wilson inaugurated a militant campaign of reform called the "New Freedom." The tariff was reduced because it was too much the instrument of special economic privilege; banking reform was effected by the Federal Reserve Act in 1913; and governmental regulation of business for the protection of public interests was further extended both by the passage of the Clayton Anti-Trust Act in 1914 and the establishment of the Federal Trade Commission in the same year.

The United States in 1914. In 1914 the United States was the most populous, rich, and influential of the new countries which had sprung from motherlands in Europe. In 1790 the population of the United States had been just under 4 million; the census of 1910 showed an increase to nearly 99 million. During the nineteenth century and the first decade of the twentieth century, more than 25 million immigrants had made America their new home. Since the days of George Washington, the national wealth had increased at least a hundredfold. Once the producer of raw materials only, the United States in 1914 was the greatest industrial power in the world. In 1900 it was producing more steel than Great Britain and Germany combined; and one of its concerns—United States Steel—was capitalized for $1,460 million, a sum greater than the total estimated wealth of the country in 1790. In 1914 many people in the United States and in the rest of the world failed to appreciate the significance of the amazing growth of the United States. Only World War I could give tangible proof that the New World nation had surpassed the power and economic importance of its mother country.

THE UNITED STATES AND WORLD AFFAIRS

Beginnings of isolationism. The tremendous development of the United States in wealth, population, and industrial power during the nineteenth century was reflected in its growing importance in world affairs. After the achievement of independence in 1783, three purposes may be identified as controlling American foreign policy: a basic concern for national security, the desire to protect and foster foreign trade, and, last, the feeling of a national mission in sympathizing with and encouraging the growth of freedom throughout the world.

During the first quarter century after gaining its independence, the new republic fought a brief naval war with France, became embroiled with Britain in the War of 1812, and sent two expeditions to the Mediterranean to teach the Barbary pirates a lesson. These complications notwithstanding, isolationism became the cardinal principle of American foreign policy. Thomas Jefferson's words on the subject have been quoted often:

Peace, commerce and honest friendship with all nations—entangling alliances with none.[4]

The Monroe Doctrine. Early in the 1820's the policy of noninvolvement was seriously challenged when the conservative Quadruple Alliance gave notice of helping the Spanish monarchy regain control over its rebellious colonies in Latin America. Both Britain and the United States regarded this possibility with alarm. George Canning, the British foreign secretary, suggested that his government and that of the United States make a joint declaration warning against European intervention in South America. This invitation was considered seriously by President James Monroe, but joint action was not deemed necessary. In his message to Congress in December 1823, Monroe warned the European powers against any attempt to extend their system to the Western Hemisphere and also made it clear that the United States had no intention of interfering in European affairs. In 1823 we could have our cake in foreign affairs and eat it too. The complications and dangers inherent in European intervention had been avoided—and without the necessity for any formal alliance. The shield of the British fleet stood behind the Monroe Doctrine with or without an alliance between Washington and London.

Challenges to American isolationism. On occasion, difficulties arose in reconciling isolationism with American interest in the cause of freedom throughout the world. Although much sympathy was expressed for the cause of the Greeks as they fought against Turkish tyranny in the 1820's, this sympathy did not lead to active support. In an Independence Day address, an elder statesman made it quite plain that while the United States was sympathetic to the cause of freedom

she goes not abroad in search of monsters to destroy. She is the well-wisher to the freedom and independence of all. She is the champion and vindicator only of her own.[5]

Some modifications of the American policy of isolationism became apparent in the two decades before 1860, however. The United States began to evince a growing interest in the Pacific and Asia (see Chapter 27). In 1844 the United States made its first treaty with China, opening certain Chinese ports to American trade and securing the right of our merchants and sailors to be tried in American tribunals in China. In 1853 Commodore Perry visited Japan, and by his show of force he persuaded the Japanese to open some of their harbors to American vessels. By 1854 the government of the United States was considering the annexation of the Hawaiian Islands. In 1867 the United States purchased Alaska from Russia for the amazingly small price of $7,200,000.

After the Civil War came to an end, the United States also moved to strengthen the Monroe Doctrine, which had been challenged by France's emperor, Napoleon III, while the United States was preoccupied with civil conflict. With French bayonets, Napoleon III had established a Mexican empire under Maximilian. Warnings by the United States secretary of state went unheeded until after the Civil War, when the protests to Napoleon were backed up by the force of 900,000 veterans. The French position in Mexico was now untenable, and Napoleon was forced to withdraw his military and financial support from Maximilian. In 1867 the emperor died before a Mexican firing squad.

After this post-Civil War flurry of activity in foreign affairs, isolationism again came to the fore as the United States set about domestic development. The building of railroads, the opening of western lands, the assimilation of millions of immigrants, the expansion of industry—all these activities monopolized attention. Foreign affairs were almost forgotten. A New York newspaper reflecting the prevailing mood went so far as to suggest the abolition of the diplomatic service!

By 1885, however, new forces began to emerge that were to carry the United States increasingly away from isolationism in the closing years of the nineteenth century. The United States began to seek an outlet for its vast national energy now that the frontier had disappeared and most of the fertile land was occupied. Foreign trade increased from a value of $393 million in 1870 to more than $1,333 million in 1900. Investments abroad in the same period increased from practically nothing to $500 million. At the same time, American missionary activity in Africa, in the Middle East, and in Asia greatly expanded. In common with the same intellectual trend in Europe, many American leaders were influenced by Darwinism, especially by its application to political affairs. The slogan "survival of the fittest" had its followers in Congress as well as in the British Parliament, the French Chamber of Deputies, and the German Reichstag. In order to be great, many argued, the United States must expand and must assume a vital role in world politics.

In Chapter 27 the growth of an American colonial empire will be described as the Stars and Stripes came to wave over Guam, the Philippines, Hawaii, and Puerto Rico. This urge to acquire dependencies did not long endure, however; by 1905 it was definitely waning. Nevertheless, the imperialistic urge was a manifestation, however fleeting, of deeper currents of history that were carrying the United States into the full stream of world affairs. The ambitions of expansionist powers such as Germany and Japan and the advance of technology that would soon destroy American geographical remoteness were rapidly eroding the time-honored belief that isolationism was the best buttress of national security.

New dynamism in foreign affairs. In 1883 the building of a modern navy was begun, and by 1890 the buildup had accelerated greatly. Care was taken not to alarm isolationist circles, however, for the new ships were officially known as "seagoing coastline battleships," a nice nautical contradiction. When this naval program was initiated, the United States Navy ranked twelfth among the powers; by 1900 it had advanced to third place.

The growing international stature of the United States was given startling confirmation in the border dispute between Britain and Venezuela in 1895. While Britain dallied before agreeing to submit the issue to arbitration, the State Department of the United States drafted a blunt note to the British Foreign Office. According to the United States, grave consequences would follow a refusal to accept arbitration, and it was added:

To-day the United States is practically sovereign on this continent, and its fiat is law upon the subjects to which it confines its interposition . . . its infinite resources combined with its isolated position render it master of the situation and practically invulnerable against any or all other powers.[6]

Fortunately for the cause of peace, Britain was too occupied with the Boers in South Africa, with tensions with Germany, and with rivalry with France in the Sudan to offer strenuous objections. Arbitration was accepted, and the greater part of the disputed area was awarded to British Guiana.

In Asia there was also evidence of the new dynamism in American foreign affairs. In 1899 the American secretary of state, John Hay, took the initiative in maintaining equal commercial rights in China for the traders of all nations, and the Open Door Policy in China became a reality. And in the melodrama of the Boxer Rebellion, the United States again was a leader rather than a follower (see Chapter 27).

Theodore Roosevelt. The quickened activity of the United States in international affairs is best symbolized by the ideas and actions of Theodore Roosevelt (1858-1919). In his terms as president he was one of the leading figures on the world stage. At the request of the Japanese, he assumed the role of peacemaker in the Russo-Japanese War. The peace conference, which met at Portsmouth, New Hampshire, in 1905, successfully concluded a treaty (see p. 640). In 1910 Roosevelt received the Nobel Peace Prize.

Roosevelt was not always a man of peace, however. Whenever he believed the legitimate interests of the United States to be threatened, he had no compunctions about threatening to use force or actually using it. The most significant illustration of Roosevelt's determination to protect vital national interests took place in the Panama incident. In 1901 the British conceded the exclusive right of the United States to control any Isthmian canal that might be dug. For $40 million the United States bought the rights of a private French company which had already begun work on a canal; and a lease was negotiated with Colombia, through whose territory the canal would be built. But the Colombian senate refused to ratify the treaty, claiming that the compensation was too small. Roosevelt is reputed to have explained, "I did not intend that any set of bandits should hold up Uncle Sam."[7] The upshot was a revolution, financed with money borrowed from J. P. Morgan; and Panama—the new republic which seceded from Colombia in 1903—concluded a satisfactory canal treaty with the United States. In 1914 the canal was opened.

By the first decade of the twentieth century, the United States had moved far from its traditional isolationism. But while active in international affairs, it was not yet willing to commit itself to definite foreign entanglements. A few observers warned of dangers soon to come. They stressed the importance of supporting nations whose interests coincided with those of the United States. Some publicists in America identified Russian imperialism as the great potential danger; others were more concerned over German ambitions. The history of the first half of the twentieth century was to prove both schools of observers correct.

LATIN AMERICA STRUGGLES TO WIN GREATNESS

Early disappointments in freed Latin America. Influenced by the liberal intellectual currents of the Age of Reason in Europe and irked by oppressive and corrupt controls from Madrid and Lisbon, the first decades of the nineteenth century witnessed an irresistible movement for independence in the Latin American colonies (see Chapter 20). By 1825 Spanish and Portuguese power was broken in the Western Hemisphere, and nine new political units emerged in Latin America. Mexico, Guatemala, Great Colombia, Peru, Bolivia, Paraguay, Argentina, and Chile were free of Spain, while Brazil, retaining a liberal monarchy, had gained its independence from Portugal. While the stirring military achievements of the rebel armies under Bolívar, San Martín, and others should not be underemphasized, it was British and American sympathy, as we have already seen (p. 607), that helped the Latin American republics attain independence.

For most of the new nations, unfortunately, the first half century of independence was a period of retrogression and disillusionment. The great Liberators were unable to maintain control of the nations they had freed, nor were the liberal, urban Creoles who had begun the independence movement able to agree with one another on elementary political matters. Impractical and inexperienced, they soon lost power to crude military leaders, or *caudillos*, whose armed gangs seized and lost the seats of power in a confusing series of tumults. A growing sectionalism appeared, and the mammoth states broke up into puny republics which in turn were threatened with localism.

The unpromising heritage. The Spanish colonial system had offered American-born whites little responsibility or opportunity in government, and the tradition of autocracy and paternalism was a poor precedent for would-be democratic republics. The emphasis on executive power inspired later presidents, generals, landowners, tribal leaders, and even clerical officials to wield authority with extreme arrogance. Independent legislative organs never flourished. Spain's economic system encouraged concentration of land and other forms of wealth in a few hands and an extractive economy. Finally, the Church, with its great properties and its hold on education and welfare agencies, was to complicate the politics of every new nation.

The effects of the wars of independence were also ruinous. Some of the most productive areas were devastated. Hatreds and divisions long persisted. Also, many men who had fought the royalists remained armed, fond of a life of violence and pillage, and likely to group themselves about the *caudillos* who promised them adventure or gain in revolutions.

Racial disunity. When independence was achieved in the first quarter of the nineteenth century, there were from fifteen to eighteen million people in the former Spanish empire. About three million of these were whites, among whom were included almost all the property-owning and educated groups. (Immigration from Europe did little to increase their numbers until the last third of the century, when a deluge began.) About the same number of people were *mestizos*, who scorned the Indians but were usually not accepted by the whites, though they were steadily increasing in number and ambition during the period when new nations were being formed. During the nineteenth century at least half of the population in some states was Indian. Deprived of the small protection once offered by the Spanish crown, they either sank into peonage or lived in semi-independence under their tribal rulers. Finally, in Brazil and most of the Caribbean islands, Negroes, most of them slaves, were in a large majority. Conflicts of interest quickly developed between these broad racial groups, particularly between the Creoles and the *mestizos*.

Mexico. The pernicious effects of these divisive factors in the newly independent Latin American world can be seen in the experiences of each nation. Mexico, which

had seemed such a promising new country in 1821, had half a century of turmoil. The empire of Iturbide (see p. 468) lasted only a few months, and a federal republic was then established. In less than ten years, however, a preposterous military leader named Antonio López de Santa Anna (1795-1876) had become dictator. (It was Santa Anna who massacred the defenders of the Alamo in 1836). The debasement of Mexican public life and the humiliation of Mexico by the United States in the war of 1846-1848 must be charged to this strutting, corrupt *caudillo*. Upon his final overthrow in 1855, the injuries inflicted on Mexican pride during his regime brought more thoughtful and circumspect men into politics; and the liberals, whose eventual leader was the Indian Benito Juárez (1806-1872), set out to implement their program, the *Reforma*. They planned to establish a more democratic republic, to destroy the political and economic force of the Church, to hasten the inclusion of *mestizos* and Indians in political life. A terrible civil war followed their anticlerical measures; it ended in 1861 with the apparent victory of Juárez, but inability to meet payments on debts owed to foreigners brought an invasion of Mexico by European powers and the establishment of a French puppet regime (see p. 554).

When pressure from the United States had driven French troops from Mexican soil, Juárez again set about instituting the *Reforma*, but the poverty of the country hampered progress. Soon after Juárez died, power went to one of his adherents, Porfirio Diaz (1830-1915), who served as president from 1877 to 1880 and from 1884 to 1911. Under his administration Mexico became an orderly country. Foreign capital entered in large amounts. Factories, railroads, mines, trading houses, plantations, and enormous ranches flourished, and Mexico City became one of the most impressive capitals in Latin America. Yet Diaz' rule, though outwardly conforming to the constitution, was a dictatorship. If there was much encouragement of art and letters, there was no liberty. The Indians sank lower into peonage or even outright slavery, and the Indian heritage was disdained. In spite of the anticlerical laws of the Juárez period, the Church was quietly permitted to acquire great wealth; and foreign investors exploited Mexico, creating a long-lasting hatred of foreigners.

In 1910 the critics of Diaz found a spokesman in a frail, eccentric man named Francisco Madero (1873-1913), who undertook to lead a revolutionary movement and surprised the world by succeeding. The Diaz machine crumpled abruptly in 1911. Although Madero was murdered two years later and Mexico underwent another period of turmoil in which the country was controlled mainly by self-styled local rulers, a determined group was able to organize a revolutionary party and to bring about the only genuine social revolution that Latin America has experienced since the Spanish conquest. As we shall see in a later chapter, the Mexican constitution of 1917 has served as an inspiration to much of Latin America.

Argentina. Probably the most advanced Spanish-speaking country in the world, Argentina attained this position in a period of sudden growth that followed half a century of torpor. Its beginning as a free nation was promising. Soon, however, the bustling port city of Buenos Aires, whose energetic population sought to encourage European capital and commerce, found itself overawed by the great ranchers of the interior, *caudillos*, and their retainers, the primitive *gauchos*—colorful, nomadic cowboys and bandits, whose way of life is now regarded as romantic. The *caudillos* intimidated the adherents of constitutional government in

This mural by Diego Rivera depicts the historical and cultural forces behind the Mexican Revolution. Ostensibly only a group picture, it really shows a hierarchy of power. The foreign companies, wielding the most pervasive influence, are pictured at top. The degree of power then moves downward to the two opposing political leaders Madero and Diaz pictured with swords, the journalists and intellectuals, and, at bottom, the Indian, sunk pitifully into peonage. The Catholic Church, regarded as an enemy of the Revolution, is portrayed by the grim-faced padre near the top left.

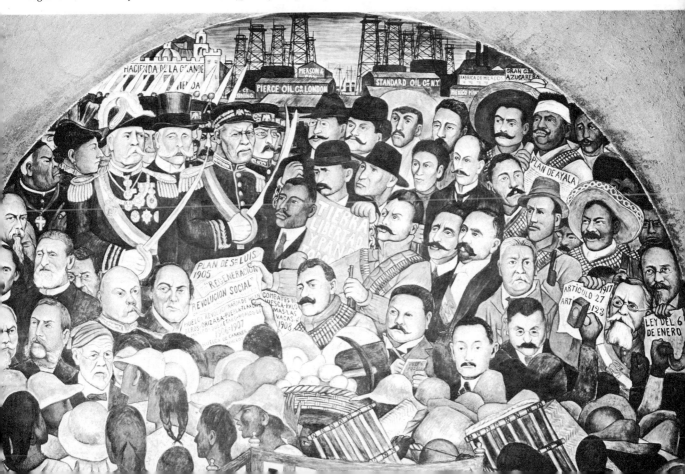

Buenos Aires, and until midcentury Argentina was not a republic but rather a *gaucho* paradise, isolated and ruled by men who wanted to keep European influences out.

In 1852 a combination of progressive elements overthrew the *gaucho* leader; commerce with Europe was revived, and by 1862 Argentina at last became a united republic and began a period of admirable stability. The constitution was usually observed, and individual rights were respected to a high degree. Immigrants poured in, and soon the population of Argentina became the most European of any major land of the New World, for it had few Indians or Negroes. Foreign capital, especially British, brought about amazing developments; port facilities, railroads, light industries, and urban conveniences were among the most advanced in the world. Buenos Aires became by far the largest and most beautiful city in Latin America, despite its location on a monotonous flat plain beside a muddy estuary.

This flat plain, or pampas, is perhaps the richest land in the world for grass and wheat; and livestock have been multiplying there for centuries. About 1880, refrigerated ships made it feasible to transport enormous quantities of fresh beef to Britain in exchange for capital and finished goods. About 1900 wheat joined beef as a major Argentine export. This intimate commercial relationship with Britain, which lasted until after World War II, affected nearly every aspect of Argentine life. Nevertheless, though top-drawer society was dominated by leaders who were pro-British in business and pro-French in culture, a true Argentine nationalism was developing. Along with the growth of this powerful sentiment came urgent demands for more democracy and wider distribution of wealth.

Brazil. For many years the former Portuguese colony of Brazil escaped the turbulence and disorders that befell its Spanish-speaking neighbors, probably because it had achieved independence without years of warfare and military dominance and because it enjoyed the continuity and legitimacy afforded by a respected monarchy. A constitution was granted by the first emperor, Pedro I, in 1824, and the secession to the throne of Pedro II in 1840 inaugurated a period of political liberty and economic and cultural progress that was to endure throughout his fifty-year reign.

Immigrants were attracted to this peaceful land in the New World, and foreign investments were heavy, though not with the arrant exploitation that Mexico experienced under Diaz. But economic growth tended to favor the southeastern part of the country at the expense of the great sugar plantations in the tropical north; and when the sugar lords were further injured in 1888 by the abolition of slavery, they ranged themselves in opposition to the emperor. Joining them were army officers, who resented the civilian nature of Pedro's regime, and a small number of ideological republicans. In 1889 the aging emperor was forced to abdicate.

For nearly ten years the new federal republic of Brazil underwent civil wars and military upheavals not unlike those in other Latin American countries. Finally, the republic was stabilized with the army in control, and Brazil resumed its progressive course. Foreign capital continued to enter, and immigration from Europe remained heavy. By World War I Brazil was generally stable and prosperous, with a growing tradition of responsible government.

Other Latin American nations. Political turmoil, geographical handicaps, and racial disunity all played a part in the development of the other new nations in Latin America. Bolivia, named so hopefully after the Liberator, underwent countless revolutions which to an outsider seem almost pointless. Peru's course was almost as futile. The state of Great Colombia dissolved by 1830, and its successors—Colombia, Venezuela, and Ecuador—were plagued by instability and civil wars. Paraguay endured a series of dictatorships; and Uruguay, created in 1828 as a buffer between Argentina and Brazil, long suffered from interventions by these two countries. An exception to the prevailing pattern of political chaos was the steady growth of the republic of Chile. In 1830 Chile came under the control of a conservative oligarchy. Although this regime proved to be generally enlightened, the country was kept under tight control for a century and was ruled for the benefit of the large landlords and the big businessmen.

Central America narrowly escaped becoming part of Mexico in 1822. After a fifteen-year effort to create a Central American confederation, Guatemala, San Salvador, Honduras, Nicaragua, and Costa Rica asserted their independence. Except for Costa Rica, where the whites comprised the bulk of the population, racial disunity delayed the creation of national feeling. In the Caribbean the Dominican Republic, after decades of submission to more populous but equally underdeveloped Haiti, maintained a precarious independence.

Foreign investments. The Industrial Revolution came into full stride just after the Latin American republics were born. The great industries of western Europe, and later those of the United States, demanded more and more raw materials and new markets in which to sell the finished products. Capital accumulated, and investors eagerly sought opportunities to place their money where high rates of interest could be obtained. This drive for markets, raw materials, and outlets for surplus capital led to the movement known as economic imperialism. As the following chapter shows, imperialism was particularly active in Asia and Africa, but Latin America did not escape unscathed.

The continual disorder and the lack of strong governments in Latin America gave businessmen ample opportunity to obtain rich concessions and float huge loans. Many of the Latin American governments, created by revolution and interested only in filling their own pockets, often resorted to the vicious practice of selling concessions to foreign corporations for ready cash. Political bosses bartered away the economic heritage of their lands, for Latin America was rich in minerals, oil, and other important resources. Sometimes the foreign investor acted in good faith, providing capital at a reasonable rate of interest to Latin American regimes which, it developed, had no intention of fulfilling the contract. On other occasions unscrupulous capitalists took full advantage of officials in ignorant or helpless governments. In many cases defaults occurred and controversy ensued.

The injured foreign investor usually appealed to his government to intercede in his behalf, and an unending stream of diplomatic correspondence over debt claims was begun, for neither the United States, Great Britain, Germany, France, Italy, nor Spain—the chief investor states—would see its nationals mistreated in their ventures into foreign investments.

Roosevelt and the Monroe Doctrine. Another threat to Latin America developed in 1902 and 1903. A dispute between Venezuela and a coalition formed by Germany, Great Britain, and Italy provoked the three European powers into blockading Venezuela and even firing upon coastal fortifications to remind the Venezuelan dictator of his obligations to some of their nationals. At first inclined to stand by and let Venezuela take its punishment, the United States soon became suspicious of German intentions. President Theodore Roosevelt matched threat with threat; and the European nations retreated quickly into the safer field of international arbitration. The Venezuelan imbroglio was resolved, but it left the United States and President Roosevelt with an increasing determination never again to allow Europe so much rope in the Western Hemisphere, no matter how just the cause.

If the Monroe Doctrine was to prevent Europe from pursuing the legitimate task of protecting its nationals—even to the employment of force—then it was natural for Europe to charge the United States with the responsibility of protecting European creditors as well as its own. In 1904 the American president proclaimed the Roosevelt Corollary to the Monroe Doctrine. This doctrine was a frank statement that chronic wrong-doing on the part of Latin American governments might force the United States to exercise an international police power. Picturesquely described as the policy of speaking softly but carrying a big stick, the Roosevelt pronunciamento thus launched the era of the Big Stick. The United States not only established a customs receivership in the Dominican Republic but exercised similar control in Nicaragua and Haiti. In addition, the Monroe Doctrine was now used not only for its original purpose of keeping out European political interference in Latin America but also as an agency for expanding the commercial interests of the United States.

Cuba becomes a protectorate. In 1898 the United States went to war with Spain over the way the Spaniards were ruling Cuba. For decades the mistreatment of the Cubans had offended humanitarian sentiments of the Americans—an altruism strongly colored by the fact that the evils of Spanish rule also injured American commercial interests in the island. Victory in the brief, dramatic Spanish-American War brought the United States recognition as a world power and a conglomeration of islands in the Pacific Ocean as well as in the Caribbean. Puerto Rico was annexed; the Philippines were brought under American rule. Sensitive of accusations of outright imperialism in Cuba, the government offered Cuba an imperfect, closely tutored independence, and the Cubans were obliged to acknowledge by law the right of the United States to intervene for the "preservation of Cuban independence" and the "maintenance of a government adequate for the protection of life, property, and individual liberty." These and other restrictions on Cuban independence were embodied in the so-called Platt Amendment (1901) to the new Cuban constitution. Thus the United States established its first American protectorate. Panama soon became another protectorate of the United States. In all these areas American business interests throve, but so did the material welfare of the inhabitants.

Dollar diplomacy. The next manifestation of the imperialistic mood of the United States has been appropriately called dollar diplomacy, an American policy which prevailed from the Theodore Roosevelt through the Coolidge administrations. Dollar diplomacy referred to the coordinated activities of American foreign investors and their State Department, who worked in close cooperation to obtain and protect concessions for investors, especially in those sections of the Caribbean countries which produced sugar, bananas, and oil. From 1890 to 1914 this policy acutely affected nearly a dozen of the Latin American republics. The United States government could in the last analysis—and at times did—control the policies of these states.

The "Colossus of the North." Although the growing assertiveness of the United States in the Western Hemisphere was accompanied by increasing alarm among the Latin American peoples, a movement which held hope for greater harmony between the United States and the Latin American states was developing. Some liberal thinkers in the United States had long envisioned a fraternity of the Americas indissolubly linked by common bonds of geography and democratic political ideals. Expressed by periodic conferences, the first of which was held in 1889, and the establishment of a permanent secretariat in Washington known as the Pan American Union, Pan-Americanism was carefully nursed by Washington officialdom.

Yet barely a decade after the first Pan-American Conference, United States imperialism shook the foundations of the new movement. If Latin American nations had ever felt a grateful appreciation for the protection afforded by the Monroe Doctrine, its benign aspect was forgotten in their concern over what they now chose to call the "Colossus of the North." Recognizing the familiar stamp of "made in the U.S.A.," the more suspicious of the Latin Americans began to see Pan-Americanism as a "skillful move in the expansionist policy of the North, and a suicidal tendency of the simple-minded South."[8] By 1913 the general resentment evoked such charges of hypocrisy that an important South American diplomat undiplomatically felt prompted to state in all sincerity: "There is no Pan-Americanism in South America; it exists only in Washington."[9] More sarcastic colleagues referred to the Pan American Union as the Colonial Division of the Department of State.

Latin America in 1914. Thus by 1914 Latin America's relations with the outside world were neither healthy nor comforting. Although a century of independence had elapsed, Latin America still lingered on the margin of international life. Left to shift for itself in the face of a future shaded by Yankee imperialism, Latin America saw only a hard road ahead in its relations with the outside world.

BLACK AFRICANS
IN THE NEW EUROPES

Migration in history. Mankind has been a wanderer as much, or perhaps more so, than a home stayer. It has well been said that "Man's history is a story of movement, of the conquest of land from nature and from fellowman, of adaptation to new environment, of the blending of blood and the intermixture of cultures."[10] Intercontinental migration constituted one of the significant dynamics of modern world history from 1500 to 1900. During this period various major types of migration can be singled out, such as (1) from all of Europe to North America, (2) from Latin Europe to Central and South America, and (3) from Great Britain to South Africa, Australia, and New Zealand.

There was, however, another form of migration. Millions of Africans were seized and forcibly transplanted to the Americas. The slave trade in Latin America began shortly after 1502. As many native Indians died off and could not supply the mounting demand for the labor required by the plantations, the influx of black slaves increased rapidly. The first to be imported into Brazil came in 1538. By 1600 blacks formed the basis of the economy in Brazil, along the Peruvian coast, in the hot lands of Mexico, in Santo Domingo and Cuba, and in the mines of Colombia. By 1800 the population of Haiti was predominantly black or mulatto, and the African element was substantial in Brazil and Cuba and much less in the Dominican Republic, Panama, Venezuela, and Colombia.

Slavery in the English colonies. A century after the African was brought to Latin America, he appeared in the English colonies to the north. The first Negroes were landed in Jamestown in 1619, but their status was uncertain for some fifty years. Between 1640 and 1660 there is evidence of enslavement, and after the latter date the slave system was defined by law in several of the colonies. The labor of white immigrant indentured servants—initially an important factor in these colonies—provided unfree, cheap labor for only brief terms and declined as the use of black, lifetime slaves proved to be a less costly labor supply in the plantation system. In 1790 when the white population was just over three million, there were some 750,000 Negroes in the United States.

During the American Revolution there was a quickening of conscience about the rightness of slavery. For some people there was an embarrassing contradiction between the ideals of the Declaration of Independence and human bondage. The incipient antislavery sentiment waned, however, as concern mounted over a bloody slave insurrection in Santo Domingo, unrest among American slaves, and the unsettling economic and social consequences of liberal opinion. Slave rebellions in the early 1800's shocked many quarters. It was the Industrial Revolution in England, however, that did the most to fasten slavery on the economy of the southern states. An increased supply of cotton was needed for the new textile mills early in the nineteenth century. New technology and new lands made the plantation system more profitable, creating a rising demand for slaves even as the importation of slaves was ended in 1808. Eventually the belief in Negro inferiority was elevated into a pseudoscientific racist doctrine defending slavery.

Emancipation without equality. While human servitude was legally outlawed after the defeat of the Confederacy in the Civil War, the full "blessings of freedom" were denied to the "free" Negro during the remainder of the nineteenth century. In fact, while social Darwinists (see p. 589) upheld the rectitude of European imperialism's rule over the "lesser breeds" in Africa and Asia, an analogous American school of thought, based upon the spurious logic of biology, championed beliefs apportioning blacks a lowly and subordinate role in society. Following emancipation Negroes in the South were progressively disfranchised by state laws or by various devices such as poll tax requirements, literacy tests, property qualifications, and naked intimidation. A pattern of segregation in schools, restaurants, parks, and hotels was more thoroughly applied. Laws were passed prohibiting interracial marriage, and blacks were generally excluded from unions. Between 1885 and 1918 more

Editor of the *Crisis*, official publication of the NAACP and an important organ of Negro expression in the United States, W. E. B. DuBois directs the operations of the newspaper's editorial offices.

than 2500 Negroes were lynched in the United States. Blacks were generally poorly educated, socially denied, and economically depressed; it has been said that "the years from 1890 to 1920 were the darkest for the dark people of America."[11]

Notwithstanding numerous and often painful obstacles, however, black Americans in 1913, fifty years after the Emancipation Proclamation, could point to some solid advances: a professional class estimated at 47,000, at least 70 percent literacy, ownership of 550,000 homes, 40,000 businesses, and savings of some 700 million dollars. Their churches, banks, and insurance companies had become substantial institutions.

In addition to improving their own lot, blacks made rich and distinctive contributions to American culture. In music, folk spirituals are known all over the world, and modern rhythmic forms so dominant after World War I had their origin in black rhythm and blues. At the turn of the century Henry Ossawa Tanner was recognized as a distinguished painter specializing in biblical scenes. Receiving over fifty-seven patents for his various inventions, Elijah McCoy was a pioneer in perfecting automatic lubricating devices; appliances for lubricating railroad cars were not considered adequate without the "McCoy" trademark. The achievements of George Washington Carver in the field of

agricultural chemistry illustrate the contributions of black Americans in science. W. E. B. DuBois, a social scientist of national stature, began the first effective black protest early in the century. In the 1920's New York experienced its Harlem Renaissance, as such notable black writers as Alain Locke, Claude McKay, and Langston Hughes produced outstanding literature. The first phase of this Renaissance ended in 1930, but its dynamism and strength carried on and still continues.

Africans in Latin America. The history of African peoples in the new Europes of Latin America has generally been different from that north of the Rio Grande. Long contact of the Spanish and Portuguese with the dark-skinned Moorish people in the Iberian peninsula and their early African explorations had helped prevent the development of the form racism took in North America. There was also an important difference in the status of the slave in North and South America. In the former, the slave was regarded as a mere chattel with no legal or moral rights. In the latter, partly explained by the tradition of the Roman law and some influence of the monarchs and the Catholic Church, slaves had a legal personality and moral status. Thus while the slave status was generally considered to be perpetual, manumission was not difficult in Latin America. By 1860 free blacks outnumbered slaves 2 to 1 in Brazil, while slaves outnumbered free blacks 8 to 1 in the United States. In 1888 slavery ended in Brazil without armed conflict.

There has been greater racial mixing in Latin America. The greatest meld of races—white, red, and black—in the history of the world has taken place. Perhaps more than half of the population has mixed blood. This intermingling may have eased racial tensions and made impossible North American practices such as segregation.

What did the African contribute to the new Europes of Latin America? Demographically, he helped fill the vast empty tropical spaces. Economically, he played a vital role in the production of colonial wealth as a herdsman, an artisan, and a farm worker. "During this era, the frontiers of European influence in the New World tropics were established on the base of African manpower."[12] Culturally, he contributed to the life style of the society in which he lived. Reflecting on this contribution and the racial blending that has taken place, a historian of South America has written: "The African peoples . . . have a rich cultural heritage and have transferred this heritage to the New World; the talents, the temperament, the beliefs, the physical traits of the Negro are ingredients in that new race of man—the American."[13]

SOUTH AFRICA, AUSTRALIA, AND NEW ZEALAND

Dutch settlement of South Africa. The area later known as the Union of South Africa, located at the tip of Africa, first came within the ken of Europe when Bartholomew Diaz reached the Cape of Good Hope in the year 1487. Ten years later Vasco da Gama rounded the Cape on his way to the Indies. In the seventeenth century, when large fleets of merchantmen from Holland made their way around Africa to the Indies to trade for spices and oriental wares, the Cape became of great importance as a place to obtain fresh water and to replenish supplies.

In 1651 the Dutch established a settlement at the Cape of Good Hope named Cape Town, which grew slowly. As the Dutch settlers pushed into the interior, they came into conflict with the Kaffirs, or Bantu native people, who put up stout resistance against the expansion of the whites.

British rule. The Dutch period of South African history came to an end when Great Britain acquired the colony in 1806 during the Napoleonic Wars. From the beginning of English rule, there was bad blood between the two nationalities. The English did not cater to the sensitivities of the Boers, the Dutch burghers, who were a proud and independent people. The Dutch had many slaves, and the British emancipation of all slaves in the empire in 1833 caused much ill feeling. Moreover, the Boers disliked the attitude of the missionaries, who were continually accusing the Dutch of abusing the natives.

In 1836 the Boers began an epic journey in their great ox-drawn wagons to a new country where they could pursue their way of life without interference. This Great Trek was a folk movement similar in its importance to the covered-wagon epic of our own West. For several years the Boers were on the march. Finally, on the high veld, they established two little republics far away from the British—the Orange Free State and the Transvaal. The British, in the meantime, extended their settlement along the eastern coast north of the Cape and founded the colony of Natal.

The Great Trek did little to solve the difficulties of the Boers. In the mid-nineteenth century there was much fighting with the natives. The British government was forced to intervene because the native warriors, out to "blood their spears," made no distinction between Boer and Briton. In 1852 and 1854 the British government made treaties with the Boers, acknowledging their indepen-

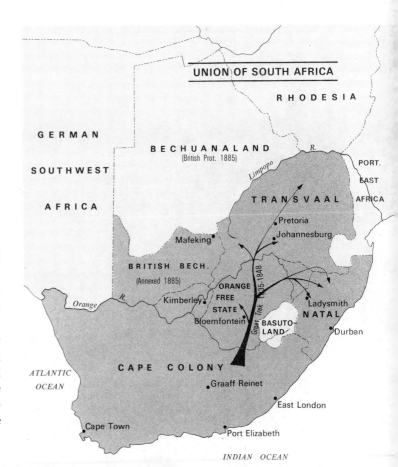

dence but retaining a shadowy right to have a voice in the foreign affairs of the two little republics.

The Boer War. The discovery of gold in the Transvaal in 1885 indirectly brought on the Boer War. Thousands of Englishmen and people of other nationalities thronged to the mines, and in a few years the boom town of Johannesburg numbered more than 100,000 inhabitants. Paul Kruger, president of Transvaal from 1883 to 1900, distrusted the British and was determined that the alien element should not gain control. Heavy taxes were imposed on the miners, or *Uitlanders* (foreigners), who complained that they paid taxes but that their children were denied adequate educational facilities and that it was almost impossible to become a naturalized Boer citizen. In their anger the *Uitlanders* appealed to the British authorities for assistance. Relations between Boer and Briton went from bad to worse, and in 1899 hostilities broke out between Great Britain and the two Dutch republics.

The world was amazed at the developments in the war which followed. The Boers were

During the Boer War farmers left their fields to take up arms against the British.

crack shots and splendid horsemen. Knowing every inch of the ground on which they fought, they frequently outmaneuvered the British troops. But the tide turned in 1900 when Lord Roberts and General Kitchener inflicted several disastrous defeats upon the Boers.

Formation of the Union. After the Boers surrendered in 1902, the British government treated them magnanimously. Loans were furnished to rebuild burned farmhouses and buy cattle. In 1906 the right of self-government was given to the Transvaal and, two years later, to the Orange Free State. The Liberal government in Great Britain then permitted the Boer and English states to unite and form the Union of South Africa in 1909. Only seven years after the war Boer and Briton joined hands in creating a new self-governing dominion in the tradition of Canada and Australia. The first prime minister of the Union was Louis Botha (1863-1919), who had been a Boer general in the late war. Botha's primary purpose was to create not an English or a Boer nationality but a blend of the two in a new South African patriotism.

Discovery and development of Australia. The discovery of Australia dates back to the seventeenth century, when Dutch explorers sighted its shores. It was the South Seas voyage in 1769 of the famous English explorer Captain Cook, however, that paved the way for English settlement. In 1788 a group of English convicts were transported to Australia and settled at Sydney. From the parent colony of Sydney, later called New South Wales, five other settlements were founded.

Although most of the first Europeans in Australia were convicts, in general they were not habitual criminals but political prisoners and debtors. After seven years of servitude many were liberated and as "emancipists" entered civil life and became valuable citizens. Quite early in the nineteenth century many free settlers also came to Australia. Soon they began to agitate against the transporting of convicts, and the first step in this direction was taken by Britain in 1840. By 1850 the Australian colonies were enjoying a liberal form of self-government.

During the first half of the nineteenth century the Australian colonies grew slowly. Sheep raising became the principal basis of economic prosperity. In 1850 the population of the country was about 400,000; a decade later it had nearly doubled. Although the discovery of gold in 1851 quickened the tempo of development, agriculture continued to be the mainstay of Australia's economy. Railway mileage was expanded, and large amounts of foreign capital flowed in to assist the young nation in developing its resources. In the decade preceding 1914 the population increased from just under four million to five million people.

The Commonwealth formed. In 1901 the six Australian colonies formed a federal union known as the Commonwealth of Australia, which bore many resemblances to the American system of government. The Commonwealth has a legislature composed of a House of Representatives and a Senate. The members of the latter house, six for each state, are elected without regard to changes in population, while the lower house is made up of members elected by each state in accordance with its population. As in Canada, however, the Commonwealth government makes the chief executive, the prime minister, responsible to the legislature and thus does not provide him with the fixed tenure guaranteed the American president.

New Zealand's development. About a thousand miles from the Australian mainland is a group of islands, two of which are of particular importance. These lonely projections of British influence in the South Pacific constitute the self-governing Dominion of New Zealand. The total population of this country, which has an area five sixths the size of Great Britain, is just over 1,500,000. The earliest settlers were desperate convicts who had escaped from the penal settlements in Australia. The activity of other colonizers forced the British government to assume protection of the islands in 1840, and a treaty was signed by British agents guaranteeing certain rights, especially land rights, to the indigenous Maoris.

New Zealand gradually became a rich pastoral, farming, and fruit-raising country. The chief export, then as now, was wool. Later the development of refrigeration enabled large quantities of meat and dairy products to be shipped to foreign markets, especially to Great Britain.

Social advances in the dominions. New Zealand and Australia have been termed sociological laboratories because of their pioneer activities in democratic government and social welfare legislation. As early as 1855 the state of Victoria in Australia introduced the secret ballot in its elections. The Australian ballot was later adopted in Great Britain, the United States, and the world over. Woman suffrage was introduced in New Zealand in 1893 and in Australia nine years later. In New Zealand a program of "land for the people" was carried out by imposing heavy taxes on large tracts of land held by absentee landlords. This dominion led the world in the adoption of noncontributory old-age pensions in 1878 and the establishment of a national infant welfare system in 1907. Before 1914 Australia had passed similar measures.

BICULTURISM IN CANADA

French Canada. From 1534—the year Jacques Cartier sailed up the St. Lawrence River and claimed the area for France—until 1763, Canada was part of the French empire. Unlike the English colonies in the New World, the French colony of Canada was rigidly supervised by the home government. All trade activities were carefully regulated; the Catholic Church monopolized education; and few Protestants were allowed to settle in New France. The French king granted huge tracts of land to nobles, who in turn parceled their estates out to peasant farmers. On the whole this introduction of an adaptation of European feudalism seriously restricted the development of the colony; it retarded expansion by denying free land to pioneers, and it subjected the "habitant" to unduly rigid control by priest, seigneur, and royal official.

The French-British quarrels. Early in the history of New France, English activities in North America plainly endangered the future of French Canada. In addition to England's interest in its Atlantic seaboard colonies, English fishermen frequently landed at Newfoundland, and in 1670 the Hudson's Bay Company was founded to carry on trading activities, especially in furs, with the Indians in the territory around Hudson Bay. When war broke out in Europe between England and France, their colonies in the New World went to war also (see Chapter 19). The ultimate English victory in the struggle for the New World was foreshadowed by the Treaty of Utrecht (1713) in which France ceded Acadia (later known as Nova Scotia), surrendered claims to Newfoundland, and recognized the Hudson Bay territory as British.

The British acquire Canada. Peace in New France was interrupted by renewals of the duel for world empire between Great Britain and France. The last of four colonial wars ended in a complete victory for Britain. In 1763, by the Treaty of Paris, Canada passed entirely into British hands. The victors took care to assure the loyalty of the French Canadians by means of a royal proclamation guaranteeing the political rights of the inhabitants and their freedom to worship as Roman Catholics. In 1774 the British government passed the famous Quebec Act, termed the "Magna Carta of the French Canadian race." This act reconfirmed the position of the Catholic Church and perpetuated French law and custom. No representative assembly, such as existed in the English-speaking colonies, was provided for, however, because the French lacked both interest and experience in self-government.

Canada's formative period. Great Britain's conquest of Canada ushered in Canada's formative period, which lasted from 1763 to 1867 and was characterized by the following important developments: the addition of an English-speaking population, the repulse of an attempt at conquest by the United States, the grant of local self-government, and, finally, the confederation of Canada into a dominion in 1867.

The addition of an English population to French Canada came as a result of the American Revolution. Although the rebellious colonists tried to conquer Canada, the French remained loyal to Britain, largely because

of the liberal concessions of the Quebec Act, and the invasion failed. Those inhabitants of the thirteen colonies not in favor of separation from Great Britain (Tories) suffered at the hands of the patriots, and a large number of them emigrated to Canada. The immigrants, known as United Empire Loyalists, settled in Nova Scotia, along the St. Lawrence River, and north of the Great Lakes.

The newcomers resented the absence of representative government in their new home and agitated for a measure of self-government. Numerous controversies also arose between the French Canadians and the newly arrived Loyalists. To meet this situation the British government in 1791 divided British North America into two separate provinces called Upper and Lower Canada and granted each a representative assembly. The quarrel between the French and English continued, causing discontent with the government in both provinces of Canada.

Open rebellion in 1837 was quelled only after serious fighting. From London, a special commissioner, Lord Durham (1792-1840), was sent to Canada to study the problem and make recommendations. A statesman with vision, Durham realized that a much larger degree of self-government must be granted if the home country was to hold the loyalty of its colonies. He recommended that certain matters of imperial concern, such as the control of foreign relations, should be left to the discretion of the mother country, but that Canada alone should control its own domestic affairs. By the mid-nineteenth century local self-government was granted to Canada. Unlike the thirteen colonies, who severed their connection with the mother country by revolution, Canada achieved virtual independence peacefully and remained loyal to Britain.

Confederation. Fear of the United States, the need for a common tariff policy, and a concerted effort to develop natural resources led Canadians into confederation. A plan of union—the British North America Act—was drawn up, approved by the British government, and in 1867 passed by the Parliament in London. This act united Canada (then divided into the provinces of Quebec and

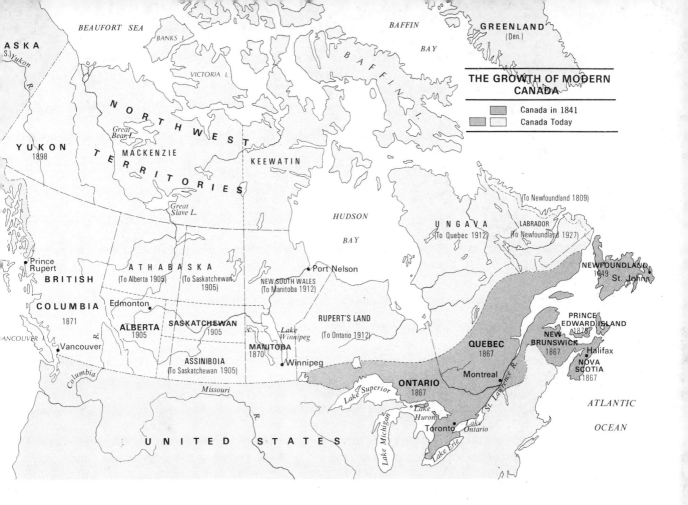

THE GROWTH OF MODERN CANADA

Canada in 1841
Canada Today

Ontario), Nova Scotia, and New Brunswick. Canada was now a federal union of four provinces, somewhat similar in political organization to the United States. The government of Canada, however, adopted the English cabinet system with its principle of ministerial responsibility. As a symbol of Canada's connection with the mother country, provision was also made for a governor-general who was to act as the personal representative of the British king.

Obstacles to Canadian development. With the passage of the British North America Act in 1867, Canada's national existence began. But the new nation encountered many problems. Communications were poor. In 1869 the Dominion purchased the vast territories of the Hudson's Bay Company;* in 1871 a new colony, British Columbia, far off on the Pacific coast, joined the Dominion on the promise of early construction of a transcontinental railroad to link British Columbia with eastern Canada.

Another disturbing factor was the lack of cordial relations with the United States. After the Civil War anti-British sentiment was fanned by Irish patriots in the United States who, in the cause of freedom for Ireland, conducted armed forays over the Canadian border. But in 1871 the major differences between Canada and the United States were ironed out in the Treaty of Washington, a landmark in the use of arbitration.

*The Hudson's Bay Company had been incorporated in 1670 as the company of Gentlemen Adventurers of England Trading into Hudson's Bay. Early in the nineteenth century the company established posts throughout the Canadian west, and the vast territory extending from what is now the province of Ontario to British Columbia was administered by this great trading organization. In 1824 the company built Fort Vancouver on the Columbia River (in the present state of Washington), which was the trading center for the Oregon territory. Here the serious boundary dispute that developed between the company and American settlers caused Americans in 1844 to raise the cry "54-40 or fight" and "All of Oregon or none." Two years later the controversy was settled amicably when Great Britain and the United States accepted a boundary at the 49th parallel. The history of the Canadian west and even that of the United States was greatly influenced by this company. While the company no longer possesses its former administrative powers, it still continues to play an important part in the economic life of Canada.

The United Empire Loyalists, former colonists still loyal to England, fled north from the United States to escape persecution by those favoring independence and helped settle Canada above the Great Lakes. This addition of an English-speaking population marked the beginning of Canada's cultural pluralism. Above is a new Loyalist settlement at Johnston, Ontario.

One state: two nations. Canada has aptly been called "a classic instance of a two-fragment society,"[14] a pluralism that has seriously hindered its development. As we have seen, this dualism was not born with the British conquest in 1761. At this time the entire population was French, but an historic change began with the American Revolution, when English-speaking American Loyalists wishing to retain their British allegiance fled to Canada. In 1761 there were only 65,000 people in New France; by 1815 the population of all the British North American colonies had increased to 600,000, of whom only 250,000 were French. Between 1815 and 1850 a second wave of immigrants from Britain brought the entire population to 2,400,000, of whom less than one third were French. During the nineteenth century, and indeed down to the present, the population of French origin has remained between 28 and 31 percent of the total.

From the first arrival of significant numbers of British, the relations between the French and English have been strained. In his investigation of Canadian unrest in 1837, Lord Durham eloquently observed, "I found two nations warring in the bosom of a single state; I found a struggle not of principles but of races." In this reference to the ill will and on occasion downright hostility between English and French Canadians, Durham singled out the most persistent and disturbing problem in Canadian national life.

The reasons are complex and numerous. The memory of the British conquest has often rankled the French; the English, on the other hand, have felt pride in this victory and with their tie to "mother country." There was also a clash in the religious field. New France was highly conservative, ruled by an authoritarian regime. When this political authority was removed, the Catholic Church in Quebec became the main defender and citadel of French Catholic culture. The English-speaking Canadians, however, tended to be antagonistic to this Catholic role.

Complicating the situation was the fact that the French minority was largely agricultural with a high rate of illiteracy. The French lived an unhurried existence, dominantly rural, suspicious of the outside world. Their education, often centered in convents and seminaries, was classical and theological in emphasis. The more secular-minded English, on the other hand, eagerly sought training in economics and science. It was natural, therefore, that the English dominated business. And while the federal constitution sought to create a bilingual society and a dual school system, the French were bitter over the progressive erosion of this guaranteed equality in the western provinces, where no appreciable French population developed. Tension was also generated by the inclination of some English Canadians to assume a pose of superiority; they denigrated French-Canadian culture and made little effort to learn French.

At the end of the nineteenth century, while Canada was a united federation in political structure, a common Canadianism had not been achieved. The French had no intention of being absorbed by the culture of the majority. How to create a single nationality comprised of two separate but officially equal cultures was to emerge in the mid-twentieth century as Canada's cardinal problem.

Canada's national development. Under the leadership of the Dominion's first prime minister, Sir John A. Macdonald (1815-1891), Canadians resolutely set about the task of national development. Bounties were offered to new industries; a railroad was completed from the east to British Columbia in 1885; and an active program for attracting immigrants was pursued.

Macdonald's work was carried on by Sir Wilfrid Laurier (1841-1919), who as prime minister dominated Canadian politics from 1896 until 1911. Between 1897 and 1912 Canada received 2,250,000 new citizens, bringing the country's total population to over 7,000,000. New provinces were also carved out of land formerly controlled by the Hudson's Bay Company so that in 1914 the Dominion consisted of nine provinces.

After the turn of the century certain problems began to appear as the result of the country's rapid growth. The advance of industrialism produced labor problems and discontent among the common people. The influence of big business began to permeate the halls of the Canadian parliament. The competition of wheat from Russia, South America, and the United States and the vagaries of the climate had serious economic effects on the Canadian farmer. This period saw the rise of agrarian unrest resembling the Populist movement in the western United States about 1890. In 1904 the Canadian government created a body for regulating the railroads similar to the Interstate Commerce Commission of the United States. Canada was becoming a mature nation, with all the accompanying problems of depressions, the maldistribution of wealth, and the need of governmental restraint of business.

COMMON DENOMINATORS

Immigration. The vast, fertile lands of the new Europes provided an almost magnetic attraction for the poor and landless peoples of Europe. A tremendous tide of immigration entered the new lands; it is estimated that 40 million emigrants sailed from their European homes from 1815 to 1914. By the latter date the number of people of European stock living in the new Europes totaled 200 million—a figure which is almost equivalent to the total population of Europe at the time of Napoleon's defeat.

For some 350 years this mass movement from Europe was accompanied by an equally significant forced migration from West Africa to the Americas. The number transported in the slave trade ran into the millions, and since many died from ill treatment at the time of capture and at sea during the nefarious Middle Passage—the forty-day voyage across the Atlantic—this trade perhaps cost Africa 50 million of its people; this estimate does not include the Arab slave trade from the East African coast.

In various and different ways the new Europes reflected the nineteenth-century movements that had originated in western Europe—nationalism, democracy, industrialism, and even imperialism. In addition, they had problems and opportunities which sprang specifically from factors and conditions shared in their new environments. These common denominators, with some variants, will be considered here.

Exploration. In all the new Europes vast spaces had to be explored, paths to the interior mapped, and natural resources evaluated. In what is now Canada, Alexander Mackenzie in 1789 traveled to the Great Slave Lake, then down the river that now bears his name to the shores of the Arctic. Four years later he crossed the Rocky Mountains to the Pacific and thus became the first European to traverse North America at its greatest width. In the United States the famous expedition of Meriwether Lewis and William Clark started from St. Louis in the winter of 1803-1804, blazed a trail through the unknown Northwest, and reached the Pacific two years later. For half a century the process of exploration and mapping continued, reaching its climax in John Frémont's expeditions to Oregon and California during the 1840's.

The most famous figure in the exploration of South America was the German naturalist Alexander von Humboldt, who from 1799 to 1804 carried on explorations in Mexico, Cuba, and South America; he investigated the valley of the Orinoco, crossed the Andes, and studied the sources of the Amazon. Although others have carried on the work he began, the huge Amazon basin—a tropical wilderness covering an area as large as the United States—has not been completely explored to this day.

Not until after the midpoint of the nineteenth century was the continent of Australia crossed from north to south. Between 1860 and 1862 John McDouall Stuart made three attempts before he successfully completed the journey from Adelaide to Van Diemen's Gulf. The penetration of the interior of South Africa differed from explorations in the other new Europes. It was achieved by the gradual expansion of white settlement in such valiant movements as the Great Trek rather than by expeditions of exploration, although discovery further north was accomplished by such men as Livingstone and Stanley (see Chapter 27).

Race problems in the new Europes. Race relations have been an important component in the history of most of the new Europes and have remained so in some. Estimates of the number of Indians in North America at the time of the coming of the white man are conjectural. In Canada the estimate is about 200,000; in the United States, about 850,000. Since the coming of the white man, the number of Indians in North America has been reduced by approximately half. In Canada, where the Indian population was not so great as in the United States, the Canadians encountered less difficulty with the natives as they moved westward to the Pacific. In the United States, however, there were frequent Indian wars and, generally speaking, a much more severe impact of an advanced civilization upon the culture patterns of the Indians. While in modern times some attempts have been made to help the Indian make a place for himself in contemporary urban society, these efforts have generally been inadequate. The Indian remains the most neglected and isolated minority in the United States.

The aborigines of Australia and Tasmania —numbering possibly 300,000 at the time of the arrival of the Europeans—could not withstand the ravages of new diseases and of the intoxicating liquors brought by the white men. Nor could they adapt themselves to new ways of life made necessary by the disappearance of their hunting lands. At times they were treated brutally: in some localities they were shot in batches; sometimes the whites got the natives drunk and then gave them clubs to fight each other for the amusement of the "civilized" spectators. The natives of Tasmania are now extinct, and the aborigines in Australia are a declining race.

In New Zealand the native Maoris had a more advanced culture than the Australian aborigines and were better able to stand up to the whites. After serious wars in the 1860's peace was finally secured, and slowly the Maoris accommodated themselves to the new world created by the whites. Since 1900 the Maoris have shared the same political rights and privileges as the European settlers and have obtained the benefits of advanced education. In the 1920's the pure Maori community was estimated to be fifty thousand. They now constitute 5 percent of the population, and their numbers are increasing.

In two of the areas colonized by European stocks, Latin America and South Africa, the indigenous peoples greatly outnumbered the white pioneers. Some authorities, for example, estimate that the population of Latin America in pre-Columbian days was at least 25 million. While a large percentage of these people died out following the initial European impact, because of disease, war, and famine, in the long run native stocks did not dwindle away but substantially increased. There was much racial mixing between the Indians and Europeans, giving rise to the *mestizo*, and this mixed strain together with the Indian soon outnumbered the white population. In the early twentieth century population statistics were estimated to be: 20 million pure Indian, 30 million *mestizos*, 26 million black and mulatto, and 34 million white. Only in Argentina, Chile, and a few smaller states such as Costa Rica, Cuba, and Uruguay have European stocks overwhelmed the Indian.

Although the indigenous peoples in South Africa were not exterminated, neither were they given the opportunity to share in European civilization. The fierce fighting between the European frontiersmen (mainly the Dutch) and the Bantu caused constant misunderstanding and fear. Despite many political and economic disabilities, in the nineteenth century the South African natives showed a substantial increase in numbers. By 1904 the Europeans numbered about 1,150,000, as compared with about 7,000,000 others, mainly Bantu, "coloured,"* and a small community of Indians originally brought to the country as indentured workers from India. Unlike the situation in Latin America, the European minority—both English and Boer—have resolutely opposed any miscegenation with the indigenous Bantu peoples. Socially, politically, and economically there has been implacable segregation. This horizontally stratified society of endogamous classes, set apart by color, has been defined as "pigmentocracy."[14]

Isolation. Another common denominator in the new Europes was that generally the new nations remained outside the main current of world affairs in the nineteenth century. The British overseas nations accepted British leadership in international affairs. They were also effectively sheltered by the British fleet, a dependence that largely explains their reluctance to assert their complete independence.

During most of the nineteenth century the United States lavished its main efforts upon the exploitation of its vast natural resources and on the Americanization of the millions of immigrants who flocked to its shores. Evidence of its future role in world affairs became increasingly apparent, however, as the century drew to a close. In fact, the en-

The indigenous Maoris and the white colonialists in New Zealand fought two series of bloody wars over land rights. The courage the Maoris displayed during these wars won them the colonists' respect, and they were given representation in the New Zealand parliament. Eventually they adapted to the dominant white culture.

trance of the United States onto the world stage was to be one of the cardinal factors in the drama of twentieth-century international affairs.

It would not be wholly correct to say that the nations of Latin America remained aloof from the flow of world politics. Politically unstable but rich in natural resources, these countries were tempting bait for great powers in Europe and also for the "Colossus of the North"—the United States. But the cruder imperialistic partitions and outright annexations so evident in Africa, China, and Southeast Asia were avoided. This lack of complete exploitation was due to luck rather than to the virtue of the outside powers. The national interests of the United States and to some extent of Britain coincided with the maintenance of the independence of various Latin American nations.

Progress of democracy. In general the liberal and equalitarian trends originating in western Europe found a fertile soil in the new Europes. Opposition to authority and

Coloured is a special South African term used to refer to the Cape Colored, a people of mixed racial ancestry.

to long-established traditions were at the heart of the revolutions that expelled the influence of Britain, Spain, and Portugal from the New World. Some historians have emphasized another factor in the progress of democracy—the influence of the frontier. Among the frontiersmen existed an absence of class distinctions, a refusal to truckle to authority, and a strong belief in the rights and capacities of the individual.

It is interesting that this frontier thesis worked in reverse in Australia. In this new Europe, land was not free or as productive as in the United States. As a result, in the remote "outback" vast sheep and cattle stations were established as rural capitalistic enterprises. On what has been called the "big man's frontier"[15] there was little opportunity for the squatter and little man. This rural proletariat, therefore, escaped to the city. In this urban environment it supported radical and reformist causes that help explain the strong democratic trend in late nineteenth-century Australian politics. To a striking degree the same reverse frontier development occurred in Argentina.

In the United States the impediments to social democracy remaining after independence were largely removed by the 1820's; and during the remainder of the nineteenth century the country progressively perfected its democratic structure. In Canada the greatest stimulus to the growth of democracy was the achievement of responsible government. The trend toward social democracy evident in the United States was outstripped in Australia and New Zealand. In fact, New Zealand led the world in the direction of what is known as the welfare state.

With few exceptions, such as Mexico under the first Juárez administration, the Latin American republics in the nineteenth century paid mere lip service to the concept of social and political democracy. Society did not have the mobility existing in the United States and Canada. The new Latin American nations suffered from chronic political instability; changes in government came too frequently from bullets, not ballots.

Search for a nationality. Among all the new Europes, the United States has found the quest for nationality easiest. Its power,

size, available resources, and heritage of freedom and the rule of law from its mother country have all contributed to a distinctive and recognizable national ideal. The greatest threat to national sovereignty—the Civil War—ended with the triumph of the forces of national union. In the nineteenth century the United States was the melting pot for thousands and thousands of immigrants; it stood for nonmilitarism and for the hope of the common man. And this democratic ideology consisted not only of faith but also of works.

The search for a national identity has not been easy in Canada. The establishment of the Confederation in 1867 increased nationalistic sentiment. But the Canadian, then as now, continued to be drawn like a magnet to the colossus of the south. He prefers baseball to cricket; he even joins affiliates of American labor organizations. Another problem complicating the search for a national identity is the existence of a closely knit French Canadian minority that tenaciously clings to its own language and culture. To some, Canada is a country with two nationalities: Toronto the symbol of one and old Quebec that of the other.

Nationalism has burned as brightly in each of the Latin American nations as in the other new Europes. In fact, the sentiment of nationalism has seemed the stronger as if in compensation for the obvious failures in political stability. The eight major administrative divisions in the late colonial era have fragmented into nineteen states—a process accompanied by costly and bloody wars. The whole of Latin America, however, exhibits a cultural homogeneity which has perhaps been some compensation for political turmoil.

Australia and New Zealand have found the search for nationality difficult. Remote from Europe, these islanders have clung to the traditions and ways of life of their forebears. New Zealanders brag about being more English than the English. This sentiment notwithstanding, a recognizable national character has developed in both countries—strongly equalitarian and fiercely nationalistic in its pride of the immensity and beauty of its lands.

Unlike Canada, where the original European community became a national minority in a new country created by the victorious British, the Union of South Africa has a majority of Boers instead of British in its European community. Of all the people of the new Europes, the South African Boers, who now call themselves Afrikaners, have developed the strongest sense of national identity. Continuously challenged by the alien culture of their English neighbors and potentially endangered by the Bantu majority, these beleaguered people have developed a distinctive, unbending culture. Two of its main pillars are a rigid Calvinism brought from Europe in the seventeenth century and a new language, Afrikaans, developed from the Dutch tongue. As in the case of Canada, a unicultural and national South Africa (at least as far as Europeans are concerned) has been weakened by the antipathy between its English and Afrikaner segments. In recent years, however, this division has been lessened by a common fear of Bantu domination and also by resentment directed against the outside world for its criticisms of South African racial policies.

SUMMARY

In little more than two and one half centuries (1650-1914) the greatest human migration from the smallest of continents, Europe, had taken place. It surpassed in scope such momentous human wanderings of the past as those of the Indo-Europeans into India and southern Europe and the historical incursions of the Germanic tribes into the Roman Empire. Transoceanic in character, this mass movement originated in Europe which, during this period, forged ahead of the rest of the world in industry, technology and science, wealth, and military power.

These advances were reflected in the tremendous increase in Europe's population that reached full tide in the nineteenth century. From 1815 to 1914 that continent's numbers increased from 200 million to 460 million; yet, during this time span, more than 40 million immigrants sought homes in the new Europes overseas. In 1815 there were less than 20 million abroad. By 1914 the figure had grown to 200 million. As many people of European stock lived outside Europe by this latter date as had been in it when Napoleon was defeated at Waterloo in 1815. Concurrent with the European immigration to the Americas was the transfer of millions of Africans to the New World by the slave trade.

The transoceanic dispersal of Europeans has been treated mainly in the history of the United States, the British Dominions, and Latin America. The story of the United States, albeit familiar to most students, has been treated at some length because it is by far the most important of the new Europes in the nineteenth century and because of the profound differences in its development, despite a common European heritage. The frontier and slavery both influenced the formation of a distinctive society, and the latter bequeathed to the country the most intractable of its twentieth-century domestic problems. The Civil War had more "revolutionary" consequences, socially, economically, and politically, than any other event occurring in the new Europes.

African peoples were a potent economic factor in developing the vast natural resources of their new homes; and where they constituted a substantial ethnic element, they made significant contributions to the culture of their society. In Latin America there was considerable racial intermingling, abolition of slavery was progressive and peaceful, and discrimination by whites over blacks relatively mild. In the United States, a new Europe and to some extent a new Africa, the concept of Negro inferiority was more potent, and even after emancipation blacks continued to be treated as second-class citizens. Only in the last two decades, following the migration of hundreds of thousands of blacks to northern cities and the general ascendancy of the concept of human rights in the world, has the demand of black Americans for the full rights of citizenship initiated a critical phase in race relations in the United States.

The British dominions became self-governing without breaking the political tie binding them to Britain. With the exception of South Africa, these communities were dominantly British in stock. Their language and culture were English; their governmental habits Anglo-Saxon. In the case of Canada, however, there was a strong French Canadian minority in Quebec inherited from the original French regime. In South Africa, following a confused history of rivalry and finally a war between the British and Dutch colonies, a rather shaky union was achieved in which the Dutch were the dominant element. There were no complications of rival nationalities in Australia and New Zealand. These colonies were settled by the British in the beginning and did not have to adjust themselves to an influx of other European peoples.

Both Australia and Canada, continental areas in their dimensions, took a leaf out of United States history. They attained their political unity by the merging of a number of colonies into a single government. Canada as a dominion became a confederation in 1867, and Australia attained the same status as a commonwealth in 1901.

Much the same problems of exploration, pushing back the frontier, and development of natural resources that were found in the American and British new Europes were also factors in the development and growth of Latin America. But instead of political unity, the sequel to the Spanish empire was fragmentation and a multiplicity of nationalities. There were also intermittent civil wars; revolutions and new regimes came and went with alarming and costly regularity. Dictators rather than democrats called the tune. In such an atmosphere economic development could not thrive; the bulk of the people lived in poverty. This internal disorder and weakness invited foreign intervention. The United States, in particular, extended its influence, political and economic, into Central America and the Caribbean region.

SUGGESTIONS FOR READING

O. Handlin *et al.*, eds., **The Harvard Guide to American History,** Harvard, 1954. The indispensable bibliography. R. B. Morris, ed., **Encyclopedia of American History,** Harper, 1953, is the most convenient reference work. Recommended general surveys are S. E. Morison, **The Oxford History of the American People,** Harper & Row, 1965, a graphic survey by a distinguished historian; and R. Hofstadter, **The American Political Tradition,*** Vintage, a brilliant and unorthodox interpretation of men and ideas from the Founding Fathers to F. D. R.

M. Cunliffe, **The Nation Takes Shape: 1789-1837,*** Univ. of Chicago. A brief and stimulating survey of the first half of American history. Also recommended is A. M. Schlesinger, Jr., **The Age of Jackson,*** Mentor, a Pulitzer Prize-winning study. A. Craven, **The Coming of the Civil War,*** Phoenix, 1957, is a challenging discussion of the various forces responsible for the conflict. One of the best treatments of the war is B. Catton, **This Hallowed Ground,*** Pocket Books. Also recommended is Carl Sandburg, **Abraham Lincoln: The Prairie Years** and **The War Years,*** 3 vols., Dell.

Edward C. Kirkland, **Industry Comes of Age,** Quadrangle, 1961. A new interpretation of a crucial era. The best introduction to the progressive movement is R. Hofstadter, **The Age of Reform,*** Vintage. T. C. Smith, **The United States As a Factor in World History,*** Holt (Berkshire Studies), is a useful account of how the nation became a world power.

R. W. Logan, **The Negro in the United States,*** Anvil. Traces the progress of the American Negro. See also C. Vann Woodward, **The Strange Career of Jim Crow,*** Oxford; Lerone Bennett, Jr., **Before the Mayflower,*** Penguin; Winthrop D. Jordan, **White Over Black,*** Penguin; and L. H. Fishel and B. Quarles, **The Negro American,*** Scott, Foresman, a comprehensive anthology.

A critique of the American scene which has become a classic in the field of political analysis is Alexis de Tocqueville, **Democracy in America,*** R. D. Heffner, ed., Mentor. For an analysis of politics and military policy by a renowned military historian see W. Millis, **Arms and Men,*** Mentor. Brevity and scholarship mark the following two biographies: H. F. Pringle, **Theodore Roosevelt,*** Harvest; and E. M. Hugh-Jones, **Woodrow Wilson and American Liberalism,*** Collier. An excellent introduction to intellectual history since the 1880's is H. S. Commager, **The American Mind,*** Yale.

T. H. Raddall, **The Path of Destiny,** Doubleday, 1957. A history of Canada from the British conquest to self-government in 1850. For two important aspects of Canadian history see Bruce Hutchison, **The Struggle for the Border,** Longmans, 1955, a lively account of Canadian-American relations; and J. B. Brebner, **Canada,** Univ. of Michigan, 1960.

John Harre and Keith Jackson, **New Zealand,** Walker, 1969. Study of a multiracial society: Europeans and Maori. For provocative studies of history and society see O. H. K. Spate, **Australia,** Praeger, 1968, and Douglas Pike, **Australia,** Cambridge, 1969. On the rise of the gold and diamond industries and the background of the Boer War see C. W. De Kiewiet, **A History of South Africa, Social and Economic,** Oxford, 1941. Also recommended is L. M. Thompson, **The Unification of South Africa, 1902-1910,** Oxford, 1960. For a comparative cultural study of the new Europes see Louis Hartz, **The Founding of New Societies,** Harcourt, Brace, & World, 1964; and C. Hartley Grattan, **The Southwest Pacific Since 1900,** Univ. of Michigan, 1963.

*Indicates an inexpensive paperbound edition.

Chapter 27

The Apogee of Imperialism

Global Imperialism: 1650-1914

INTRODUCTION. Europe, as we have seen, not only sent millions of her sons and daughters to found colonies of settlement that eventually became independent states but also acquired and controlled vast tropical territories around the globe in a significant movement known as *imperialism*. This latter movement, mainly in the form of protectorates or colonies, involved few or no European settlers as was the case of Australia or the United States. The majority of indigenous peoples were ruled by a small group of colonial officials, while the natural resources were exploited by western businessmen.

But no matter what form modern colonialism assumed, imperialism is as old as the history of man. In all ages certain groups of people have possessed more power and dynamism than others, and in their search for more food, precious metals, or other valuable materials, they have attempted to conquer weaker groups more fortunately endowed by nature. But man does not live by bread alone; from the dawn of history, psychological and spiritual motives have played roles in the extension of one people's power over another. Leaders have made their conquests as agents of the gods or have created great empires to exalt the prestige of their dynasties.

In Europe's golden age of imperialism (1870-1914) its most eloquent spokesman, the English poet Rudyard Kipling, urged his countrymen:

"Take up the White Man's burden—
  Send forth the best ye breed—
Go bind your sons to exile
  To serve your captives' need . . ."[1]

At the outset, this imperial mission had few critics, but after 1900 there progressively developed a crescendo of denunciation against colonial rule. No matter what the ultimate verdict may be on the significance of Europe's intrusion into many parts of the world, this imperialistic thrust is an intriguing and arresting saga in which one can follow intrepid explorers, dedicated missionaries, businessmen—avaricious or honest—and colonial officials, both good and bad. And most important, one can observe the impact of imperial rule upon the indigenous peoples as they seized upon such western dynamic traits as nationalism, democracy, science, and technology and began first to question and then to challenge the overlordship of their colonial masters.

In this chapter we shall first examine the forces of imperialism, analyzing the whys and hows of the movement; then we shall see what the relations of Europe to the nonwestern world were from about 1650 through the advent of modern imperialism in the 1870's to 1914; and finally we shall weigh in the balance sheet the pros and cons of this explosive development.

THE DYNAMICS OF IMPERIALISM

Imperialism defined. The word *imperialism* has come to mean many things to many people. Broadly speaking, the term refers to the extension of authority or control, whether direct or indirect, of one people over another. But we use the term *imperialism* in a more restricted sense to refer to the period from 1870 to 1914, when western Europe—which controlled much of the world's finance, commerce, military power, and intellectual life—extended its power over the peoples of the Orient and Africa.

The traditional periodization of nineteenth-century imperialism, which describes European expansion as lukewarm from 1815 to 1870 and thereafter as tumultuous and energetic, has recently been attacked by some British historians.[2] Dealing exclusively with British imperial history, they have sought to obliterate the differentiation between political and nonpolitical categories of British expansion, between "informal and formal" empires, putting both into "the vital framework" of nineteenth-century imperialism. It is pointed out that before 1870 Britain advanced its commercial interests by such informal means as political influence exerted upon weaker states, by the lever of loans and trade treaties, and by the acquisition of strategic bases and entrepôt sites that guarded British interests along the main routes of trade. "Until the 1870's much of the empire was held, with the grand exception of India, by indirect interest rather than formal control." It was an empire of "trade not dominion."[3] Notwithstanding this form of British "indirect imperialism," the formal annexation of vast territories by Great Britain and other powers and the climax of imperial rivalries came after 1870. The term *imperialism*, therefore, is especially appropriate for this period in which the great colonial empires of modern times were acquired.

Waning European interest in colonization. From the end of the Middle Ages to the close of the eighteenth century, a large part of Europe was expansive. Aggressive national states strove to stake out colonies and to monopolize overseas trade with their colonial possessions; the subsequent rivalries between nations helped bring on the great colonial wars of the eighteenth century. But by the end of that century interest in colonization declined. The loss of the thirteen colonies in 1783 dampened British ardor. By 1815 France had lost nearly all of its colonial possessions, and a few years later Spain and Portugal were forced to grant independence to most of their colonies. At the same time, the school of laissez faire argued that there were no advantages in possessing colonies and that the cost of defending them was an expensive burden. It was also believed that the whole world would soon be opened to free trade. Thus, between 1815 and 1870, as the gospel of free trade and laissez faire became dominant, colonial expansion was comparatively small.

Revival of imperialism. When the tide turned, however, it came with a rush. In his six years as English prime minister, Disraeli annexed Fiji and Cyprus, fought a war against the Zulus in southeastern Africa, purchased a controlling interest in Suez Canal shares, and proclaimed Queen Victoria empress of India. Other European powers avidly followed Britain's lead, and early in the 1880's the colonial scramble began in earnest. The United States also felt the imperialistic urge.

This expansion of the western peoples had come about with amazing rapidity. It has been estimated that in 1800 fully one half of the world's surface was unknown to Europeans. A century later more land had been explored and acquired than in the entire period from the middle of the fifteenth century to the midpoint of the eighteenth. By 1914 the European nations could claim control of about 60 percent of the world's surface.

Economic motives for imperialism. What were the motives behind this amazing expansion of western power? The most obvious and powerful were economic. Britain had been the home of the Industrial Revolution; by the middle of the nineteenth century other nations began to industrialize. To compete with British industry, these nations placed protective tariffs on imports. The free commerce of the early nineteenth century waned as tariff walls rose in the United States, Russia, France, and Germany. Great Britain and its new competitors— now producing a surplus of manufactured goods—began to search for trade outlets; building colonial empires appeared to be the solution to the problem.

Besides increased markets for European goods, colonies and trading posts could supply burgeoning industries with raw materials such as cotton, silks, rubber, exotic woods, tin, manganese, copper, and oil. And growing populations continued to increase the demands for foods raised in exotic lands.

Banks provided capital for trading enterprises and for the development of resources in distant lands. Money invested overseas could earn 10 to 20 percent. This impetus to wealth led one wag to remark that the French colonist was the franc. To safeguard these important investments and recover defaulted loans, European governments sometimes established spheres of influence or protectorates over the territories of weak native rulers and in certain cases subjected these lands to military occupation or to annexation.

Marxian socialists have stressed only the economic motives underlying imperialism. In his famous work *Imperialism, the Highest Stage of Capitalism* (1916), Lenin argued that the wages of the workers did not represent enough purchasing power to absorb the output of the capitalistic factories, and, moreover, that vast amounts of capital accumulated which could not be profitably invested in the home country. Therefore, to the Marxists, imperialism was an inevitable phase in the development of capitalism. That the profit motive in imperialism is strong is undeniable, but that it is the sole motive is false. It is also false that imperialism is a policy exclusive to capitalist powers, as can be proved by examples of Communist imperialism in the twentieth century.

Population pressure as a motive for imperialistic expansion. In the middle of the eighteenth century the population of Europe numbered about 140 million; by 1914 this figure had increased to 463 million. Hearing that land was more plentiful and jobs easier to secure overseas, no less than 9 million British subjects and 6 million Germans, to say nothing of millions of Italians, left their homelands. These migrations provided one of the greatest population movements in history.

But while some European statesmen, particularly in Germany and Italy, thought of the acquisition of new colonies as a means whereby their surplus population could be settled in sparsely settled lands without escaping the political control of the motherland, this belief proved to be a delusion. Few Europeans migrated to the tropical colonies; the great majority made their new homes in the United States and the temperate regions of Latin America. In such areas the loyalty and support of these sons and daughters of Germany, Italy, and other nations were lost to the homeland.

Nationalism as a force for imperialism. While the economic forces behind nineteenth-century European expansion were strong, the psychological factors were equally important. A dominant factor was the new nationalism. Fresh from the achievement of national unification, Germany and Italy were eager to show off their new national strength; both demanded a place in the sun. In Great Britain also, a strong nationalist spirit existed. Britain was ready to take on any antagonist who stood in the way of its imperialistic ambitions.

Closely enmeshed with the nationalistic justification of imperialism was the philosophy of social Darwinism (see Chapter 25). Just as Darwin believed that progress in the biological sphere was measured by the survival of the fittest, so political and social theorists saw this concept of the "fittest" as an immutable factor in the onward march of civilization.

The military factor. If the use of force and the survival of the fittest were essential features of progress, then the military factor was important. A nation had to be strong enough to defend its interests. Colonies could be used as naval bases to protect a nation's commercial lifelines or to destroy those of a rival. Or a colony could be obtained as a buffer state to protect another colony against the designs of a rival.

Humanitarian and religious motives. The acquisition of colonies cannot be explained on economic, political, or strategic grounds alone, however. Many colonial administrators honestly felt that they were carrying the "white man's burden"—that it was a sacred task to bring the best aspects of western civilization to their undeveloped wards. The religious motive was likewise especially strong. In the nineteenth century British missionaries were particularly active, and there were large numbers of missionaries from France, Germany, and the Scandinavian countries.

Toward a new understanding of imperialism. In recent years there has been significant scholarly reexamination of the dynamics of nineteenth-century imperialism. In general the original overemphasis upon economic factors has been rectified. The scramble for territory in Africa, for example, has been shown to spring not so much from the economic competition between European states as from their international rivalries, stemming from problems of the balance of power in Europe that were extended to Africa.[4] Reflecting the mounting recognition of the role psychological factors play in human affairs, some scholars have turned to this area for an explanation of imperialism. One theory is that the nineteenth-century ruling classes purposely diverted the attention of the masses from their wretched living conditions by offering them the exciting diversion of adventure and glory in imperial enterprises.[5] Another ingenious explanation, influenced by the effect of "the dark powers of the subconscious," sees imperialism as the result of primitive aggressive instincts that still inhere in mankind. "Imperialism thus is atavistic in character. It falls into that large group of surviving features from earlier ages that play such an important part in every concrete social situation."[6] Thus nations sought colonies not so much as ends in themselves but rather for the satisfaction derived in fighting for them and in dominating them.

The final word on imperialistic motivation is a long way off, but it may be said at this time that no single simplistic cause is adequate. Stressing the importance of multiple causation and the fact that numerous motives recur but in different combinations, a student of African history has said that:

The missionary movement will be important in one case, strategic considerations in another, economic motives in a third, and so on. We have now reached the paradoxical situation of knowing so much about European imperialism that generalization about its causes is almost impossible.[7]

BRITISH RULE IN INDIA

Twilight for the Mughul dynasty. During the Mughul era in the seventeenth century, Europeans came to India to establish trading posts. As European infiltration continued, Mughul authority rapidly declined.

The reign of Shah Jahan (1628-1658) had marked the height of Mughul power, and conditions appeared auspicious for his successor. But his son Aurangzeb (1658-1707) was a ruthless and fanatical man who intended to rid India not only of all vice but also of all art and all views alien to the Muslim faith. He terrorized millions of his Hindu subjects by his fanaticism. By 1690, when Mughul territorial expansion reached its greatest point, Aurangzeb's empire encompassed the whole of the Indian peninsula. But this period of power was followed by one of decline. Aurangzeb's realm seethed with corruption, oppression, and revolt; fifty years after his death the great Mughul empire crumbled and perished.

The condition of India during this time may be summed up in one word—misery. Marauding armies, nobles bent on gaining power, and officials who oppressed the people brought anarchy to India. Delhi was sacked in 1739 by invaders from Persia and again in 1757 by marauders from Afghanistan. The Mughuls kept the imperial title until 1858, but their dynasty was a mere shadow of its former grandeur and strength.

The British East India Company. The collapse of the central government in India left the field open to a new authority. For more than one hundred years English and French trading companies had fought one another for supremacy, and by the middle of the

eighteenth century a great duel for empire was taking place. During the Seven Years' War (1756-1763) Robert Clive, the British leader in India, defeated the Indian ruler of Bengal at the decisive battle of Plassey (1757), a victory which ushered in the beginning of a new period in Indian history, that of British rule.

The French in turn were defeated in 1760, and after their elimination, the most important problem facing the East India Company was its relationship with the Indian people. As the Mughul emperor became more and more a puppet ruler, anarchy spread until the company accepted the role of policeman in India. By 1818 the East India Company was master of India. Some local rulers were forced to accept its overlordship; others were deprived of their territories. Thus the Indian subcontinent (until its independence in 1947) became divided into British India, which the British administered directly, and Indian India, where native dynasties were

retained under British supervision (see map, p. 633).

The British Parliament, disturbed by the idea that a great business concern interested primarily in profits was controlling the destinies of millions of people, passed acts in 1773 and 1784 which gave it the power to control company policies and to appoint the highest company official in India, the governor-general. This system of dual control lasted until 1858.

Earlier in the century the British introduced many significant reforms in India. The practice of *suttee*, in which widows burned themselves on the funeral pyres of their deceased husbands, was prohibited; the custom in some areas of killing girl babies was combated; and a notorious system of banditry and murder called *thuggee* (hence our word *thug*) was broken up by the British secret police. In addition, a comprehensive educational system including secondary schools and universities was introduced.

The Indian Mutiny. In the spring of 1857 the progress of reform was suddenly inter-

After Robert Clive, as the servant of the British East India Company, had defeated the ruler of Bengal, thus becoming the real power in this province, he decided to continue the fiction of Indian authority. In this contemporary print Clive receives "Dewanee," the right to collect taxes, from the Mughul emperor.

rupted by a serious rebellion. This uprising was initiated by Indian troops, called sepoys, who formed the bulk of the company's armed forces. The sepoys complained that a new cartridge issued to them was smeared with the fat of cows and pigs. This infuriated the Hindus, who regarded the cow as sacred, and horrified the Muslims, who considered the pig unclean. Fortunately for the British, many areas in India remained loyal or at least quiescent, but the revolt was crushed only after fierce fighting and the loss of many lives.

One important consequence of the Indian Mutiny was the final collapse of the Mughul dynasty. The last of the Mughul emperors permitted to maintain a court at Delhi had in 1857 been proclaimed by the mutineers as their leader. After order had been restored, the British exiled him to Burma. The mutiny also ended the system of dual control under which the British government and the East India Company shared authority. The government relieved the company of its political responsibilities, and in 1858, after 258 years of existence, the company terminated its rule. A trained civil service was recruited from honor graduates of British universities, and these men set out to rule India benevolently and efficiently.

Growth of Indian nationalism. By 1880 it was apparent that Indian nationalism was growing rapidly, the fruit of the influx of western ideas and technology. In 1885, with the aid of several Englishmen who had interested themselves in Indian political ambitions, the Indian National Congress was formed.

The British educational system served as one of the most potent forces back of the new movement. As Indians became acquainted with the story of the rise of self-government in England, the desire for the political freedom of their own land grew. Unable to obtain white-collar employment in governmental service and disdainful of manual labor, thousands of newly educated but unemployed Indian youths turned in wrath against the government. Confronted by the spread of violence, the British carried through a major shift in policy between the years 1907 and 1909. The various provincial legislatures in India were granted elected Indian majorities, and an Indian was seated in the executive council of the governor-general. The legislature of the central government, however, remained under British control. Moderate nationalists were satisfied for the time being, but their more radical comrades were not appeased. The twentieth century in India would see the spirit of nationalism become ever more insistent.

MANCHU CHINA AND THE WEST

The last dynasty. In the middle of the eighteenth century China had a population of 300 million and comprised an area of more than 4 million square miles. The ruling dynasty was the Ch'ing established by the Manchu, who in 1644 had superseded the Ming. Descendants of Tatars who for centuries had lived in Manchuria, the Manchu appreciated Chinese civilization and adopted a conciliatory attitude toward their subjects. They refused, however, to allow intermarriage with the Chinese, for they realized that only their blood difference kept them from being assimilated and conquered. By and large, however, the Manchu gradually became Chinese in their habits and attitudes.

The Manchu emperors were remarkable conquerors. The reign of Ch'ien-lung (1736-1795) was a period of great expansion, when the Manchu government attained suzerainty over eastern Turkestan, Burma, and Tibet. By the end of the eighteenth century Manchu power extended even into Nepal, and the territory under Ch'ing control was as extensive as under any previous dynasty.

Jesuit missionaries were active in China during the seventeenth century, occupying high positions at the Ming and Ch'ing courts. They made important contributions to Chinese scientific information and technology and helped the government survey its territories. While this diffusion of western knowledge was a factor in Ch'ing dynamism, the introduction of elements of Chinese culture into Europe by the Jesuits was more significant. The political and philosophical concepts they introduced played an important role in the intellectual climate of the European Enlightenment, and in the arts the stately homes of both England and France became graced by the decorative cult of *chinoiserie.*

In spite of these evidences of dynamism, however, uncritical acceptance and reverence for traditional thought (particularly Confucianism), augmented by the scholar rule of a civil service trained almost exclusively in the classics, had tended to make Chinese culture excessively backward-looking and conservative. Thus the amazing continuity which Chinese civilization had exhibited for thousands of years was gained at a heavy price. In addition, the prevailing attitude of superiority to the cultures of all other peoples was an unwholesome one for China, leading to what has been called "progressive sterility."[8]

Trade relations with the West. Meanwhile a new factor, destined to have momentous consequences for China, had entered the scene: European trade. During the eighteenth century merchants from western Europe came to China in increasing numbers. Only with great difficulty was trade carried on, however. Foreign merchants were confined to Canton and the Portuguese colony of Macao. Nor would the Manchu government recognize or receive representatives of foreign powers.

European traders were irritated by the high customs duties the Chinese forced them to pay and by the attempts of Chinese authorities to curb the growing import trade in opium. In 1800 its importation was forbidden by the imperial government. Still, the opium trade continued to flourish. Privately owned vessels of many countries, including the United States, made huge profits from the growing number of Chinese addicts.

War and western exploitation. Early in the nineteenth century serious internal weaknesses developed in the Manchu empire. The standing army became corrupt, and rapacious governors fleeced the people. Weak emperors proved inadequate to meet the challenges of the time.

IMPERIALISM IN CHINA
ABOUT 1900

Canton - Major Treaty Ports

In 1839 war broke out with England—ostensibly over the opium traffic. But this was basically a secondary issue. As a Chinese historian has observed: "The war between China and England, caused superficially by the problem of opium prohibition, may actually be viewed as a conflict of Western and Eastern cultures."[9] Traditional China was no match for English military power, and in 1842 China agreed to the provisions of the Treaty of Nanking. Hong Kong was ceded to Great Britain, and certain ports, including Shanghai and Canton, were opened to British residence and trade.

In 1856 a second "Opium War" with England, aided by France, took place, and China was again defeated. By the terms of the Treaty of Tientsin (1858), new ports were opened to trading, and foreigners with passports were permitted to travel in the interior. Christians gained the right to propagate their faith and to hold property, thus attaining another means of western penetration. The

United States and Russia obtained the same privileges in separate treaties, and China appeared well on the way to ultimate physical dismemberment and economic vassalage. Three provisions of these treaties, in particular, caused long-lasting bitterness among the Chinese: (1) extraterritoriality, (2) customs regulation, and (3) the right to station foreign warships in Chinese waters. Extraterritoriality meant that, in a dispute with a Chinese, a westerner had the right to be tried in his own country's consular court. Europeans argued that Chinese concepts of justice were more rigid and harsh than those in the West. But the Chinese felt that extraterritoriality was not only humiliating to China's sovereignty but also discriminative in favor of the western nations.

Difficulties of the Manchu. The concessions to the "foreign devils" resulted in a great loss of prestige for the Manchu rulers. Serious internal difficulties further diminished their power, and the Taiping Rebellion of 1850 to 1864 almost overthrew the dynasty. That the Manchu dynasty managed to survive another half century was largely due to the statecraft of a remarkable woman, Tzu Hsi, the dowager empress, popularly known as "Old Buddha." From 1861 to her death in 1908, she was the real power behind the throne. Shrewdly and unscrupulously, Tzu Hsi crushed internal revolts and restored a measure of prestige to her homeland. Convinced that security for China lay in adhering to ancient traditions and customs, she encouraged antiforeign sentiment—an attitude her subjects shared. A relatively weak central government and general lack of national unity, however, made it impossible for China to resist foreign encroachments.

Sino-Japanese War. By 1860 Russia had annexed the entire area north of the Amur River; by 1885 France had taken Indochina and Britain had seized Burma; and in 1887 Macao was ceded to Portugal. China was too weak to resist these encroachments on its borders. But the crowning blow came not from the western nations but from Japan, a land which the Chinese had long regarded with amused contempt.

Trouble had brewed for some time between China and Japan, especially over the control of Formosa and Korea. In a dispute over China's claim to suzerainty in Korea, war broke out in 1894, and the brief Sino-Japanese struggle resulted in a humiliating defeat for China. By the Treaty of Shimonoseki (1895), China was forced to recognize the independence of Korea and hand over the rich Liaotung peninsula and Formosa.

Spheres of influence in China. The Chinese defeat was the signal for the renewal of aggressive actions by western powers, who forced Japan to return the strategic Liaotung peninsula to China. Shortly thereafter, the European powers made their demands of the Manchu. In 1897 Germany demanded a ninety-nine-year lease to Kiaochow Bay and was also given exclusive mining and railroad rights throughout Shantung province. Russia obtained a twenty-five-year lease to Dairen and Port Arthur and gained the right to build a railroad across Manchuria, thereby achieving complete domination of that vast territory. In 1898 Britain obtained the lease of Weihaiwei, a naval base, and France leased Kwangchowan in southern China (see map, p. 636).

A halt, or at least a hesitation, in the process of disintegration was brought about by the United States, not from high-minded desires but largely because Washington was alarmed at the prospect of American businessmen being excluded from China because the United States had no sphere of influence. In 1899 Secretary of State John Hay asked the major powers to agree to a policy of equal trading privileges. In 1900 several powers did so, and the famous Open Door Policy was born.

The Boxer Rebellion. The humiliation of the defeat by Japan had incensed the younger Chinese intellectuals, who agitated for reform. Sympathetic to their cause, the young emperor in 1898 instituted what came to be known as the "hundred days of reform." Unhappily for China, however, the reactionaries at court viewed all innovation with disfavor and formed a powerful faction about the dowager empress, Tzu Hsi.

In 1689 China and Russia concluded a treaty—the first treaty between China and any western power—providing for frontier control and triennial visits of Russian trade caravans to Peking. In this contemporary print the Russian caravan passes through a gate in China's Great Wall. In the valley beyond the gate the caravan of horses and camels laden with trade items passes the walled city of Xogon Koton.

In September 1898 she imprisoned the emperor and took over the government.

After the suppression of the reform movement, a group of secret societies united in an organization known as the "Righteous Harmony Fists"; the members were called "Boxers" by westerners. At first the Boxers were strongly anti-Manchu because of the reactionary measures of "Old Buddha," but by 1899 the chief object of their hatred had become the foreign nations who were stripping China of land and power.

The Boxers started a campaign to rid China of all "foreign devils." Many Europeans were killed, and the legations at Peking were besieged. In August 1900 an international army forced its way to Peking and released the prisoners. China was then forced to apologize for the murder of foreign officials and to pay a large indemnity. The United States returned most of its share of the indemnity, which the Chinese government set aside to send students to American universities.

Only a decade after the conclusion of the rebellion, a revolution was to break out all over China, and in 1912 the Republic of China was proclaimed with Sun Yat-sen as president. This story of China's giant step into modern times will be discussed in Chapter 29.

JAPAN MODERNIZES

Two centuries of isolation, 1639-1854. At the beginning of the seventeenth century Japan was being ruled from Edo (now Tokyo) by the head of the Tokugawa clan, who in 1603 had made himself shogun. As a military dictator with a retinue of feudal lords and warriors, the shogun kept the country united and at peace. Meanwhile, the emperor—nominal head of the government—lived a meaningless existence at Kyoto.

As in the case of China, European merchants and missionaries posed a problem to the Japanese authorities. We have noted earlier (see p. 375) that the shoguns insulated Japan effectively from the outside world by expelling the European traders and crushing Christianity. Nevertheless, despite the attempts of the shoguns, change could not be averted. There was remarkable economic growth, accompanied by rapid urbanization, the spread of education, and the rise of new social classes, especially young aggressive *samurai*, merchants, and intellectuals, many interested in western culture. Thus, in spite of Tokugawa isolationist policies, a new ferment was preparing the way internally for the "opening of Japan."

Commodore Perry and the Treaty of Kanagawa. On July 7, 1853, two steam frigates and two sloops of war sailed into the bay of Edo. The commander of the fleet, Commodore Matthew Perry, had been dispatched by the United States government to convince the Japanese ruler that a treaty opening trade relations between the two countries would be of mutual interest. Perry had been instructed to be tactful and to use force only if necessary.

When Perry returned the following year with a greater force, the shogun prudently agreed to sign the Treaty of Kanagawa, the first formal treaty between Japan and a western nation. Shipwrecked sailors were to be well-treated, and two ports were opened for the provisioning of ships and a limited amount of trade. Europeans soon obtained similar privileges plus, as in China, the right of extraterritoriality.

The westernization of Japan. With his prestige lost, the shogun in 1867 was forced to restore supreme authority to the emperor —the *Tenno*, or "Heavenly King" (called "Mikado" in the West). The new leaders responsible for the restoration movement were remarkably young and largely of *samurai* origin. Clearly recognizing that the West was the greatest threat to Japan's integrity and existence, they proposed as the best defense to build "a rich country and strong military," based on western technology and institutions adapted to their country's needs.

The young emperor, whose reign was known as the *Meji* (enlightened government), ruled from 1868 to 1912. With his reign are associated those epoch-making events that transformed Japan from a sleepy oriental island kingdom into a dynamic, semimodernized power which the European nations had to recognize as an equal.

The restoration of the throne's supreme authority was aided by the voluntary abolition of feudal rights; in 1871 the abolition of the feudal system became official, although it was far from an actual fact.

In 1882 a commission was established to study the world's various governmental systems and to frame a new constitution for Japan. The committee members were particularly impressed by the German system developed by Bismarck. Thus the new constitution, promulgated in 1889, gave the premier a position analogous to that held by the chancellor in Germany, and the cabinet was made responsible to the emperor alone. Only the army and navy could appoint their respective ministers. Since no statesman could form a cabinet without a war minister and the army could overthrow any cabinet by simply withdrawing its minister, final control of policies rested in the hands of the military clique. The constitution provided for a Diet, but the property qualifications at first limited the electorate to a small number. While the cabinet was independent of the Diet, the latter body wielded a modicum of power in financial matters because in peacetime it could hold up an unpopular budget by refusing to vote supplies. Promulgated in 1889, the constitution stressed the position and powers of the emperor, who was considered "sacred and inviolable." Only the emperor could initiate constitutional amendments.

In other ways the Japanese showed skill in exploiting their knowledge of western institutions. In 1876 national conscription went into effect, and a modern military machine was created whose officers were trained by European experts—the army by the French and Germans, the navy by the British. The government initiated the founding of banks, factories, and business concerns and later, when they became successful, turned them over to private ownership and management while continuing to supervise them closely. Thus Japan avoided the dangers to sovereignty which imperialism offered to other undeveloped countries such as China.

Many other changes began to transform the "land of the rising sun." Railways, telegraphs, lighthouses, and dockyards were constructed, and orders were placed in England for the construction of warships. American advisers were consulted regarding national education, and imperial universities as well as a number of technical schools were founded. More foreign experts were brought in to teach the Japanese about medicine, engineering, and agriculture, and many Japanese went abroad to study.

Japanese westernization: a facade? The modernization of Japan was one of the amazing phenomena of modern world history. But there were some disturbing features in the way western technology and institutions were adapted by the Japanese for their own purposes. On the surface, Japanese government was liberal and parliamentary. In reality, however, the constitution was ultra-conservative, giving the emperor and his cabinet dominant power. Though Japan was the first Asian nation to achieve a high degree of literacy, education was the tool of the government, and its primary function was to produce docile servants of the state. The press was subject to wide control and censorship. The army was used as a means of instilling conscripts with unquestioning loyalty and obedience to the emperor. In army

The influence of western technology and culture is evident in a Japanese woodcut of Yokohama harbor in the late nineteenth century. A steam locomotive carries passengers along the dock as Yokohama citizens dressed in western attire watch a ship set sail.

barracks young soldiers learned that the noblest fate was death on the battlefield.

Unlike the Chinese, who revered the scholar, the Japanese admired the soldier; warfare was the supreme vocation, and a tradition of Japanese invincibility had grown up. Since prehistoric times the Japanese islands had not been invaded successfully, and on several occasions the Japanese themselves had invaded the Asian continent. Thus the Japanese were ready to seize new methods and new ideas to serve their own militant ends.

Another prominent characteristic of Japanese culture was the meticulous attention paid to formal manners and "face." Like the Chinese, the Japanese took great pride in their dignity and status; to be shamed, degraded, or dishonored was a mortal offense. Awareness of these culture traits is basic to an understanding of Japanese reactions to the modern world and the policies that the rulers of Japan adopted to meet the challenges of the twentieth century.

The Russo-Japanese War. In the eyes of European diplomats, Japan's prestige began to increase soon after the conclusion of the Sino-Japanese War of 1894-1895. In 1902 Japan scored a diplomatic triumph by allying itself with Great Britain. Both nations viewed the alliance primarily as a deterrent to Russian expansion.

Fearful of Russia's designs on both Manchuria and Korea, Japan attempted to negotiate a division of the area into spheres of influence. Believing that Japan could be defeated easily, the Russians were inflexible. In February 1904 Japan broke off negotiations and, without declaring war, attacked Port Arthur and bottled up Russia's fleet. The world was astounded by the quick series of Japanese victories which followed.

By the Treaty of Portsmouth, signed in September 1905, Japan acquired half of the island of Sakhalin, the leaseholds to the Liaotung peninsula and Port Arthur, and various Russian railway and mining rights in southern Manchuria. Japan's paramount position in Korea was also conceded, paving the way for Japanese annexation of that nation in 1910. Japan was now accepted as a first-class power.

IMPERIALISM IN SOUTHEAST ASIA AND THE PACIFIC

Establishment of western rule. At the southern tip of the Asian mainland, wedged between India and China and including a multitude of islands in the Indian and Pacific oceans, is the complex area of Southeast Asia. Its diverse peoples and countries began to come under European colonial rule with the arrival of the Portuguese and Spanish in the sixteenth century and the Dutch in the early years of the seventeenth. In the nineteenth century imperial control was completed when the British gained power over Ceylon, Burma, and Malaya and the French over Tahiti and Indochina. While European imperialism pushed eastward by way of the Indian Ocean into Southeast Asia, the United States, expanding westward, had reached the shores of the Pacific. By mid-nineteenth century it began to extend its influence and control into the Pacific area, ultimately securing control of Hawaii and the Philippines with naval bases at Pearl Harbor and Manila as well as Guam and Pago Pago in Samoa.

Throughout Southeast Asia, western rule made a substantial imprint. A plantation economy was established with foreign capital to develop the rich natural resources; vast quantities of petroleum, tin, coffee, tea, pepper, and other tropical products were produced for the world market. Chronic civil war and banditry were ended. Law and order, together with public health facilities, came in with colonial rule and brought about a rapid increase in population.

Throughout the colonial lands of Southeast Asia, the impact of European ways of life, and especially western education, created a new generation of nationalists. More and more irked with alien rule, this minority of young intellectuals finally aspired to complete independence. Little was done to satisfy these aspirations in the Dutch East Indies or in French Indochina. Britain provided some training in self-government in Burma and Ceylon, but it was in the Philippines that benevolent imperialism most consciously moved in the direction of ultimate freedom.

British rule in Ceylon, Malaya, and Burma. In the sixteenth century the chief ports on the island of Ceylon were occupied by Portuguese and Dutch adventurers. In 1796 the British forced the Dutch to give up their holdings in Ceylon, which became one of the most valuable British colonies as the nineteenth century unfolded; such prized commodities as tea, rubber, lead, cocoa, and sapphires were produced in this area.

British influence in the Malay peninsula began in 1796 when a coastal strip was obtained. In 1819 Sir Thomas Stamford Raffles, an energetic English colonial official, secured the uninhabited island of Singapore from a Malay sultan; later acquisitions brought British Malaya in contact with the frontiers of Siam. Singapore's commercial and strategic value was apparent in the nineteenth century; it became one of the world's greatest ports and it provided a vantage point from which Britain could dominate the seas surrounding southern Asia. British Malaya itself became one of the richest colonial areas in the world, particularly in tin and rubber.

The economic development of the Malay peninsula has been mainly the work of Chinese and Indian emigrants. The Malayan natives, living contentedly in their great jungle forests where luxuriant tropical growth easily supplied most of their wants, had little interest in hard work. Today, in the southern Malay peninsula, the Chinese not only outnumber the Malayan natives but also monopolize higher education and dominate such professions as medicine and law.

Adjoining India on its eastern land frontier is Burma. In three separate wars between 1823 and 1885, this kingdom was progressively conquered by Britain and annexed to India.

The French. In contrast to Britain, France, which had lost its empire to the British by the end of the eighteenth century, had no geographical or commercial basis for expan-

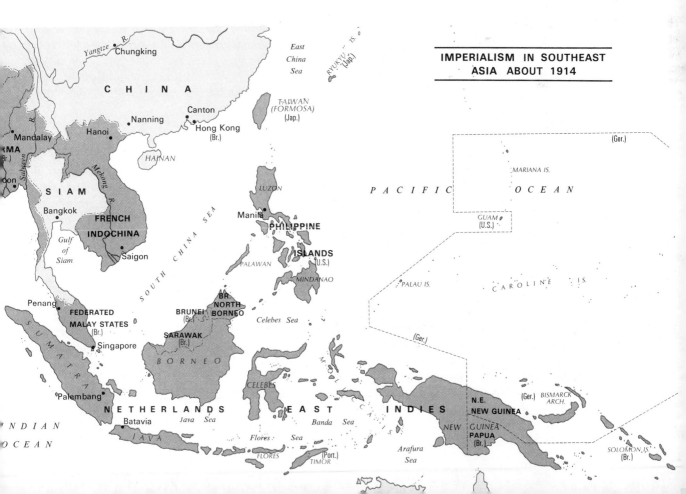

IMPERIALISM IN SOUTHEAST ASIA ABOUT 1914

sion in Southeast Asia. French imperialism was initially impelled by a nationalistic need to rival Britain and was supported intellectually by the concept of the superiority of French culture and of France's special *mission civilisatrice*—the civilizing of the native through his assimilation to French culture. The immediate pretext for French imperialist expansionism in Indochina was the protection of French religious missions in the area, coupled with a desire to find a southern route to China through Tonkin, the northern region of North Vietnam.

French religious and commercial interests were established in Indochina as early as the seventeenth century, but no concerted effort at stabilizing the French position was possible in the face of British strength in the Indian Ocean and the French defeat in Europe at the end of the eighteenth and beginning of the nineteenth centuries. A mid-nineteenth-century religious revival in France provided the atmosphere within which interest in Indochina grew. Anti-Christian persecutions in the Far East provided the immediate cause. In 1856 the Chinese executed a French missionary in southeastern China, and in 1857 the Vietnamese emperor, faced with a domestic crisis, tried to destroy foreign influences in his country by executing the Spanish bishop of Tonkin. Paris decided that Catholicism would be eliminated in the Far East if France did not go to its aid, and accordingly the French joined the British against China from 1857 to 1860 and took action against Vietnam as well. By 1860 the French occupied Saigon.

By a Franco-Vietnamese treaty in 1862, the Vietnamese emperor ceded France outright the three provinces of Cochin China in the south; France also secured trade and religious privileges in the rest of Vietnam and a protectorate over Vietnam's foreign relations. Gradually French power spread through exploration, the establishment of protectorates, and outright annexations. Their seizure of Hanoi in 1882 led directly to war with China (1883-1885), and the French victory confirmed Paris' supremacy in the region. France governed Cochin China as a direct colony, and Annam (central Vietnam), Tonkin, and Cambodia as protectorates in

one degree or another. Laos too was soon brought under French "protection."

By the beginning of the twentieth century France had created an empire in Indochina nearly 50 percent larger than the mother country. A governor-general in Hanoi ruled Cochin China directly and the other regions through a system of residents. Theoretically, the French maintained the precolonial rulers and administrative structures in Annam, Tonkin, Cambodia, and Laos, but in fact the governor-generalship was a centralized fiscal and administrative regime ruling the entire region. Although the surviving native institutions were preserved in order to make French rule more acceptable, they were almost completely deprived of any independence of action. The ethnocentric French colonial administrators sought to assimilate the upper classes into France's "superior culture." While the French improved public services and provided commercial stability, the native standard of living apparently declined and precolonial social structures were to all intents and purposes in the process of erosion. Indochina, which had a population of over eighteen million in 1914, was important to France for its tin, pepper, coal, cotton, and rice. It is still a matter of debate, however, whether the colony was commercially profitable.

Siam, an independent buffer state. Although its territory was pared down by both Britain and France, Siam maintained its existence—partly because both western nations welcomed the retention of an independent Siam as a buffer between their holdings and partly because the royal house of Siam showed shrewdness and sagacity.

The Dutch East Indies. Late in the sixteenth century the Dutch had wrested most of the East Indies from the Portuguese, and in 1602 the Dutch East India Company was organized to exploit the resources of the Spice Islands. By the middle of the next century it had eliminated all rivals in the area. In time, however, the company became corrupt, and it was abolished in 1798, with all holdings transferred to the Dutch crown.

For some time the spice trade had been declining, and early in the nineteenth century the Dutch set about raising new products. In the 1830's the so-called "culture system" was introduced, under which one fifth of all native land was set aside to raise crops for the government and one fifth of all the natives' time was required to till these lands. The production of tobacco, sugar, coffee, tea, indigo, pepper, and cinnamon increased enormously. In the long run, the culture system gave the islands a prosperous system of raising crops, but because it was based on forced labor, it often prevented the natives from having enough land for their own use. By 1900 the Dutch had abandoned the culture system, and the natives enjoyed a better life. Less commendable was Dutch neglect of higher education and the failure to prepare their wards for eventual self-government.

Spanish rule in the Philippines. Little more than 250 miles north of the Dutch East Indies is the Philippine archipelago, known to Europe only after the Portuguese explorer Magellan discovered it for Spain in 1521. In contrast to the harsh regimes imposed on the Indians of Latin America, Spanish rule in the Philippines was humane. But the Filipi-

nos were given no opportunities to participate in government. Discontent arose, especially among educated liberals, and a widespread revolt broke out in 1896.

United States imperialism. While Spain wrestled with Filipino discontent, a new imperialist power was emerging in the Pacific—the United States. In 1867 the Midway Islands were occupied and Alaska was purchased from Russia. The next advance of the United States was in the Hawaiian Islands, where, during the nineteenth century, Europeans and Americans had developed large sugar plantations. American capital continued to pour in, and by 1881 the islands had been spoken of by an American secretary of state as part of the "American system." A revolt in 1893, engineered with the assistance of United States Marines, deposed the Hawaiian queen and set up a republic. Five years later Hawaii was annexed by joint declaration of both houses of Congress.

As we saw in Chapter 26, the United States went to war against Spain in 1898. After Admiral Dewey destroyed the Spanish fleet at Manila in May of that year, American sol-

After "liberating" the Philippines from Spanish rule in 1898, a direct result of the Spanish-American War, the United States failed to grant the independence expected by the islanders. Hostilities broke out in 1899 between Filipino patriots and American occupation forces (captured insurrectionists below), an ironic replay of the fighting between native resisters and Spain three years earlier. Many Americans, disillusioned by imperialism, were ready to lay down the "white man's burden."

diers landed in the Philippines. Here, as in Cuba, Spanish resistance crumbled quickly, and in the treaty of December 1898 Spain ceded the Philippines, Guam, and Puerto Rico to the United States. One year later the United States occupied the small Pacific outpost of Wake Island.

Some of the Filipino patriots who had assisted the American troops against the Spanish had no wish merely to exchange masters and to see the United States acquire the Philippines. In 1899 fighting broke out and hostilities lasted for three years. The ironic spectacle of American forces being used in a second conquest of the Philippines brought about a strong revulsion against imperialism in many quarters in the United States. A New York newspaper plaintively addressed Kipling, the archspokesman of imperialism, thus:

We've taken up the white man's burden
  Of ebony and brown;
Now will you kindly tell us, Rudyard,
  How we may put it down?[10]

Yet American colonial administration in the Philippines proved to be liberal and well-intentioned for the most part. In 1913 the legislature became dominantly native, although final authority in the most important matters was still reserved for the United States Congress. The Philippine tariff was shaped to favor American trade; and large amounts of capital from the United States were invested in the islands. Increased educational facilities produced educated Filipinos, among whom the desire for independence grew increasingly strong. In their eyes, American government in the Philippines, no matter how efficient or humanitarian, was no substitute for self-government.

Notwithstanding substantial reservations in the minds of many Americans, there could be no doubt that by 1900 the United States sat astride the Pacific basin as did no other power. The consequences of this Pacific imperial posture were to become a major and costly constituent of American life in the twentieth century. A massive conflict with Japan, another in Korea, and a tragic war in Vietnam lay in the future. Whether such involvement was essential for American basic interests was to become a crucial and painful dialogue after the late 1960's.

BRITAIN AND RUSSIA IN CENTRAL ASIA

Character of Russian imperialism. Ordinarily one does not think of tsarist Russia as a colonial power such as Britain or France. The reason is the manner of Russian expansion: unlike Britain, which had to expand overseas, the Russian empire grew from the center outward by a process of accretion. From the grand duchy of Moscow, the Russians pushed out into the great plain that surrounded them.

Four specific types of Russian expansion may be identified. First, there was the occupation of uninhabited territory by a vigorous, land-hungry people. Then, during the Middle Ages, substantial portions of the Russian homeland which had been occupied by Poles and Lithuanians were reconquered and joined to the grand duchy of Moscow. This assimilation of various adjoining areas closely resembled the growth of France around the Ile de France, of Spain around Castile and Aragon, of Italy around Piedmont, and of Germany around Brandenburg-Prussia. A third aspect of Russia's expansive movement—the absorption of backward, non-Russian tribes and peoples— was similar to Britain's conquest of primitive tribes in Africa.

The fourth feature of Russian expansion was unique: the struggle of a landlocked country for access to the warm water of the sea. We have already followed the imperialistic efforts of the eighteenth-century rulers Peter the Great and Catherine the Great for Russian expansion toward the Baltic and the Mediterranean seas (see Chapter 19). At the same time the Russians had crossed the Ural Mountains and penetrated the huge expanses of Siberia, occupying the territory as far east as the Sea of Okhotsk and the Kamchatka peninsula.

Britain and the defense of India. The defense of India's land frontiers and the control of all sea approaches to the subcontinent via the Suez Canal, the Red Sea, and the Persian Gulf became twin elements in British foreign policy during the nineteenth century. While the East India Company was consolidating its hold on India, Russian expansion had moved steadily eastward to the Pacific, then toward the Middle East, and finally to the frontiers of Persia and Afghanistan, both latter territories adjacent to India. Russia had annexed the kingdom of Georgia between the Black and Caspian seas in 1801 and had fought several wars with Turkey and Persia. As the Russians drove southward into the mountainous lands of the Caucasus, the indigenous people fought desperately but were finally overcome in the 1860's.

Russian conquest of Turkestan. In Turkestan, north of Afghanistan, lived various backward nomadic tribes—a mixed lot of Mongols, Afghans, Turkomans, and Tatars, predominantly Islamic in culture. Long traversed by caravan routes, the territory had a few important trading cities, notably Samarkand, Tashkent, Merv, and Bokhara. Here Russian merchandise was traded for raw cotton. When the wild Turkestan tribes began to stop and rob the caravans, the Russians countered by sending troops, which fought against resolute resistance. Finally, early in the nineteenth century, Russian armies and colonists pushed across the steppes north of the Aral Sea into Turkestan. By the 1870's the little states, or khanates, had been conquered. Russia had now pushed south to the frontiers of Afghanistan and India. By 1914, if Siberia is excluded, the Russian empire was more than three million square miles in area.

Russia's advance had been won not only by the bravery and resolution of Russian troops but also by the construction of the Trans-Caspian Railway, which at its completion in 1888 reached 1064 miles into the heart of Asia. The Orenburg-Tashkent Railway, completed in 1905, stretched 1185 miles farther, led to a great increase in Russian commerce, and revived the ancient cities of eastern Turkestan. Accomplished with great difficulty, the feats of Russian arms and engineers inspired some Russian imperialists to dream of conquering Afghanistan and

even penetrating India itself. While Britain did not rule out the latter eventuality, it was thought more probable that Russian pressure against India was designed primarily as a counter against Britain in other areas of big-power rivalry. As a Russian general admitted: "The stronger Russia is in Central Asia, the weaker England is in India and the more conciliatory she will be in Europe."[11]

Afghanistan and, to a lesser extent, Tibet continued to be serious areas of tension during much of the nineteenth century. Russian designs against the former were finally effectively blocked by Britain, and the intrusion of Muscovite influence into Tibet was countered by a British military expedition to Lhasa in 1904.

Anglo-Russian rivalry in the Middle East. The royal navy was in command of Britain's sea communications with India. A naval station at Aden guarded the entry into the Red Sea; and along the Arabian coast Britain, by treaty relations, controlled and protected a number of friendly minuscule sheikdoms, such as Muscat, Oman, Bahrein, and Kuwait.

A contemporary Russian drawing shows a construction train on the Trans-Caspian Railway. The completion of this railroad allowed Russia to convey and supply troops in Central Asia and to greatly extend its economic influence there.

The maintenance of this sphere of influence blocked efforts of both Germany and France to secure footholds on the Persian Gulf. The former unsuccessfully sought to build a terminus on the gulf for its projected Berlin to Baghdad railroad. In 1903 the British foreign secretary issued what has been termed a British Monroe Doctrine over this area:

I say without hesitation, we should regard the establishment of a naval base or a fortified port in the Persian Gulf by any other power as a very grave menace to British interests, and we should certainly resist it by all the means at our disposal.[12]

While Britain had forestalled Russian influence in Afghanistan, the decline of Persian power and the mounting interference of Moscow into the shah's land caused grave concern in London. There was the possibility that the Russian Trans-Caucasian Railway might be extended south through Persia to the warm waters of the Persian Gulf; in this event, the government of the tsar might not only profit commercially but also construct a naval base that would be a potential threat to the British sea route to India.

Persia was in no position to resist Russian pressure. Its government was corrupt, inefficient, the tool of a medieval parasitic aristocracy. Russia moved into this vacuum and by the twentieth century was in complete control of the northern part of the country. Russians trained the Persian army, erected telegraph lines, established a postal system, and pursued profitable trade. The Russian ministry of finance founded the Discount and Loan Bank of Persia with branches in many parts of the nation. This bank loaned the Persian government 60 million rubles and provided 120 million rubles to Persian merchants to enable them to purchase Russian goods.

No. 10 Downing Street had no desire to see Russian power athwart the Persian Gulf and the British lifeline to India. To counter Russian moves, the British advanced into Persia from the southeast, established the Imperial Bank of Persia with a capital of £1,000,000, and set up a profitable tobacco monopoly.

To make matters more complicated, the exponents of a reformist and patriotic movement in Persia began to initiate a revolution. In 1906 a parliament was established and the work of reform carried forward. An American financial expert, Morgan Shuster, was brought in to overhaul the treasury.

The Anglo-Russian entente. In 1907 Britain and Russia signed an agreement which—on the surface—ended their rivalry in Central Asia. Russia agreed to deal with the sovereign of Afghanistan only through the British government. For its part, Great Britain consented neither to occupy nor to annex Afghanistan so long as it fulfilled its treaty obligations.

Persia was divided into three zones: the northern was a sphere of interest for Moscow, the middle was a neutral zone, and the south gave Britain a free hand. In effect, Persia was under Anglo-Russian dual control. This partnership, however, was only a marriage of convenience. Russia increasingly intervened in Persian domestic politics. Shuster, the American financial expert, was forced to give up his post, and the Russians threw their support to a willing dupe, the shah, who was ready to do their bidding. Shuster described this puppet as "perhaps the most perverted, cowardly, and vice-sodden monster that had disgraced the throne of Persia in many generations."[13]

Though sorely disturbed over the Shuster incident, Britain chose not to alienate the Russians because of vital national interests. Britain now had a growing fear of German ambition in strategic areas such as Africa and China—fears which Russia shared. Thus Britain and Russia chose to reach an uneasy compromise in Persia. Both ethics and Persia were the victims of power politics.

THE GREAT AFRICAN COLONY HUNT

Exploration of Africa. The best area in which to follow the course of nineteenth-century imperialism is Africa, for nowhere else on the globe were colonial empires achieved so quickly. A great continent many times the size of Europe with nearly 150 million people came almost completely under the control of European powers (see Reference Map 9).

Late in the eighteenth century the opening of Africa began in earnest, and by 1835 most of northwestern Africa had been mapped by Europeans. The greatest of the European explorers was David Livingstone, a Scottish missionary who traversed vast barren wastes and jungles from the Cape of Good Hope as far north as Lake Tanganyika and from the Atlantic to the Indian Ocean. It was Livingstone who discovered Victoria Falls and the Zambezi River. "The very great doctor," as the natives called him, began his series of explorations in 1853. After his death in 1873, explorations of the interior were carried on by Henry Morton Stanley, a British explorer and journalist who had located Livingstone in 1871 and had casually greeted him, "Dr. Livingstone, I presume." By the end of the century Africa was no longer the "Dark Continent." The source of the Nile had been discovered, the courses of the Niger and Congo had been traced, and the world now realized the rich resources of Africa.

On the eve of the European scramble for Africa, only 10 percent of the continent was under the control of western nations. In 1875 the two most important European holdings were Algeria, administered by France, and Cape Colony, held by Great Britain. In South Africa there were Dutch farmers in two small republics, the Orange Free State and the Transvaal. Most of the other European holdings were mere coastal ports. The interior still remained a mysterious land.

Belgian interest in Africa. Stanley's explorations galvanized the European nations into action, although at first his ideas found little support except from the Belgian king. Leopold II, who in 1876 had organized the International African Association, enlisted Stanley in his service. The association, composed of scientists and explorers from all nations, was ostensibly to serve humanitarian purposes, but the crafty king had other motives. As an agent of the association, Stanley was sent to the Congo region, where he made treaties with several African chiefs and by 1882 obtained over 900,000 square miles of territory.

The British in Egypt. Meanwhile, important developments were taking place in the Nile valley. Shortly before the completion of the Suez Canal in 1869, Ismail, the ruler of Egypt, borrowed enormous sums from French and English bankers at high rates of interest. By 1875 he was involved in financial difficulties and was forced to sell his block of 175,000 shares in the Suez Canal. The shares were snapped up by the astute prime minister of Great Britain, Disraeli, in order to give his country practical control in the management of this strategic waterway between Europe and the East. When Ismail repudiated his debts in 1879, Great Britain and France assumed joint financial control over Egypt, forcing the Egyptian ruler to abdicate in favor of his son, Tewfik.

The Egyptian ruling classes did not relish foreign intervention, and when a serious revolt broke out in 1882, many Europeans lost their lives in riots in Alexandria. The French fleet withdrew at this point, but Great Britain decided to quell the revolt and assume responsibility for the administration of Egypt. To reorganize Egyptian finances, eliminate corruption from the administration, and improve the cotton industry, Sir Evelyn Baring, later Lord Cromer, was sent to Egypt and actually ruled the country from 1883 to 1907. In reducing corruption, he overhauled the system of government. The use of forced labor was curbed, and huge dams were constructed to improve the fertility of the soil. Indeed, it has been said that the best record of imperialism is to be found in Egypt. Nevertheless, the twentieth century was barely under way before the Egyptians voiced a growing demand for self-government.

Organization of imperial policy. The occupation of Egypt and the acquisition of the Congo were the first moves in what came to be a precipitous scramble for African territory. In 1884 Bismarck convened a conference in Berlin to discuss the Africa problem. This assembly of diplomats paid lip service to humanitarianism by condemning the slave trade, prohibiting the sale of liquor and firearms in certain areas, and expressing concern for proper religious instruction for the natives. Then the diplomats turned to matters they considered much more important. They laid down the rules of competition by which the great powers were to be guided in seeking colonies, and they agreed that the area along the Congo was to be administered by Leopold of Belgium, that it was to be neutral territory, and that in this area trade and navigation were to be free. No nation was to peg out claims in Africa without first notifying other powers of its intention. No territory could be claimed unless it was effectively occupied, and all disputes were to be settled by arbitration. In spite of these encouraging declarations, the competitors ignored the rules when it was convenient to do so, and on several occasions war was barely avoided.

The methods Europeans used to acquire land continued, in many cases, to involve the deception of the native peoples. Europeans obtained huge grants of lands by presenting ignorant chiefs with treaties which they could not read and whose contents they were not permitted to comprehend. In return, the natives were rewarded by bottles of gin, red handkerchiefs, and fancy-dress costumes. Since in many cases native custom reserved ownership of land to tribes, allowing individuals only the use of it, the chief granted land to European settlers with no idea that he was disposing of more than its temporary use. When later the settler claimed ownership, the natives were indignant, feeling that the tribe had been robbed of land contrary to tribal law.

The Belgian Congo. Shortly after the Berlin conference Leopold organized his African territories as the Congo Free State, subject to no control, not even that of the Belgian parliament. He began to exploit the colony's economic resources by granting concessions to private companies, reserving for his own administration an extensive rubber area ten times as large as Belgium. A system of forced labor was introduced, and soon stories of filthy work camps, horrible whippings, and other atrocities leaked out of the Free State, now undergoing the process of "civilization."

In the face of a rising tide of international indignation, Leopold in 1908 was forced to turn over the Free State to the Belgian government, which renamed the area the Belgian Congo. Under the direct administration of the government, conditions in the colony improved.

German interest in Africa. In the 1880's Germany acquired three colonies on the west coast of Africa: German Southwest Africa, Togoland, and Cameroons. It was on the east coast of the African continent, however, that the most important German acquisitions were made. German penetration there was largely the work of one man, Carl Peters, who had studied British methods of colonization. In 1884 he and three other colonial enthusiasts, disguised as English workingmen, set out on a secret mission to eastern Africa. Peters succeeded in obtaining treaties from chiefs giving him control of sixty thousand square miles. In 1885 Bismarck proclaimed the region German East Africa.

British penetration in Africa. The British had been pegging out claims to the region directly north of Peters' concessions, and in 1886 and 1890 rival German and British claims were settled amicably. Germany received several concessions from Britain, notably the strategic island of Helgoland in the North Sea, which was to become an important pivot of German naval power. Britain also recognized the Germans' claim to their protectorate in East Africa (later called Tanganyika). After the agreement in East Africa, the British held Uganda, along the shores of Lake Victoria; British East Africa (later known as Kenya), fronting along the coast of the Indian Ocean; the rich spice (cloves) island of Zanzibar; and the area of Nyasaland.

Meanwhile, by 1884 Great Britain had obtained control over a stretch of African coast fronting on the Gulf of Aden. This protectorate (British Somaliland) was of great strategic value since it guarded the lower approach to the Suez Canal. Even more important were the headwaters of the Nile, situated in the area known later as the Anglo-Egyptian Sudan. In 1898 the British conquered this area also. Among the British acquisitions on the west coast of Africa, the most important were the territories around the mouth of the Niger, stretching back toward the Sudan. These British possessions included Gambia, Sierra Leone, the Gold Coast, and Nigeria.

Cecil Rhodes, empire builder. During this same period Great Britain's influence in southern Africa had expanded northward from Cape Colony to German East Africa. The main impetus in this drive north came from the British capitalist Cecil Rhodes, who dreamed of an uninterrupted corridor of British territory from the Cape of Good Hope to Cairo.

Shortly after Rhodes' arrival in southern Africa as a young man, diamonds were discovered north of Cape Colony. In time Rhodes became the leading figure in the fabulously wealthy De Beers diamond syndicate and the owner of many valuable gold-mining properties in the Transvaal. By 1890 his annual income was estimated to be at least five million dollars.

In 1885 Rhodes was instrumental in getting Britain to declare a protectorate over Bechuanaland, a territory wedged between the Dutch Transvaal and German Southwest Africa. Without Britain's domination over this region, Rhodes' dream of a Cape-to-Cairo railroad under British control could not be realized. By unscrupulous methods the empire builder secured extensive set-

tlement and mining rights to the high and fertile plateau through which flowed the great Zambezi River. In 1890 the capital, Salisbury, was founded and the region was named Rhodesia.

By 1890, as prime minister of Cape Colony, Rhodes had one remaining task: uniting Boer and Briton in South Africa into a single nation. But Rhodes made the fatal mistake of conspiring to use force to achieve his ends. This only widened the breach between the two peoples and did much to bring on the Boer War in 1899 (see p. 618).

In 1902 Cecil Rhodes died, leaving a huge legacy to endow 175 scholarships at Oxford for students from the British Dominions, the United States, and Germany. He believed that if harmony and understanding could be achieved among these countries, the peace of the world would be assured. Rhodes was a complex combination of astute financier, fanatical nationalist and empire builder, and confused seeker after world peace.

French colonies in Africa. The first important French colonial acquisition in Africa had been made decades before the renewed European interest in colonization in the 1870's and 1880's. In the 1820's, during the reign of Charles x, French statesmen had seen in North Africa a chance to counterbal-

Before the European scramble for Africa began, western nations controlled only 10 percent of the continent. By the early 1900's, however, Great Britain alone commanded over three million square miles of African territory, wielding power over such strategic areas as the Suez and the headwaters of the Nile. Made commander-in-chief of the Egyptian army in 1892, Lord Kitchener here reviews the troops.

ance political unrest at home. For some time France had been complaining of the piratical activities of the Algerians, and when in 1827 the Algerian ruler insulted the French consul in public by hitting him on the head with a flyswatter, France was furnished with a good pretext for intervention. In 1830 a large army was dispatched to occupy the country, but seventeen years elapsed before the French succeeded in subduing the fierce Berber tribes. Algeria was then made an integral part of the French state.

With the acquisition of Tunisia in 1881 and a huge section of equatorial Africa along the right bank of the Congo River in 1884, France began to develop an ambitious colonial program. From trading posts along the west coast of Africa, France pushed into the interior and thus obtained most of the basins of the Senegal and Niger rivers, while expeditions from Algeria and Tunisia penetrated the Sahara. Although the French did not succeed in getting to the Nile, by 1900 they controlled the largest empire in Africa, one which stretched eastward from the Atlantic to the western Sudan and southward to the Congo River. In addition, the French annexed the large island of Madagascar in the south Indian Ocean and in 1911, despite the opposition of Germany, made Morocco a French protectorate.

Italy's African ventures. If overpopulation, lack of trade, and widespread poverty constitute the most compelling reasons for obtaining colonies, Italy should have gained the most extensive areas in Africa. But Italy came out of the scramble with very little territory. When Tunisia became a French protectorate in 1881, Italian ambitions there were blocked. Italy turned to East Africa, obtaining a piece of Red Sea coast and a slice of barren and desolate land on the Indian Ocean, but these areas were of little value without the rich plateau of Abyssinia (Ethiopia) in the hinterland. An attempt to annex this ancient empire in 1896 ended in the destruction of an Italian army.

Italy then shifted its attention to the Turkish territory of Tripoli, which was acquired with the secret consent of Spain, France, Great Britain, and Russia. Italy declared war on Turkey in 1911 and forced the

European Territorial Expansion in Africa

	SQUARE MILES	POPULATION
France	4,200,000	25,000,000
Great Britain	3,300,000	35,000,000
Germany	1,100,000	12,000,000
Belgium	900,000	7,000,000
Portugal	800,000	8,000,000
Italy	600,000	1,000,000
Spain	75,000	200,000

Turks to cede the area in 1912. This event temporarily marked the end not only of Italian expansion but also of the race for colonial empires by European powers.

The economic wealth of Africa surpassed the expectations of the most avid imperialist. By the first decade in the twentieth century it was the world's greatest producer of gold and diamonds. In addition, rich resources of tin, phosphates, and especially copper were uncovered. From the once "Dark Continent" poured rubber, coffee, sisal, palm oil, and cotton—products which became more and more essential for the great industrial nations of the world. The table above shows the shares of African territory taken by European nations during the nineteenth century and the first decade of the twentieth.

Africa and the European impact. If the first period of Europe's encounter with Africa, ending about 1800, was primarily of trade and slaving, the second was the onset of exploration ending after three quarters of a century with the hectic scramble for colonies. Last, there was the era of imperial consolidation, beginning in the 1890's, when the various European powers established their techniques and policies of colonial rule and undertook various forms of economic development.

It was inevitable that the process of acculturation—that is, the social change caused by the interaction of significantly diverse cultures—should have been more profound and widespread in Africa than that occasioned by British rule in India. In India the resulting acculturation involved some disintegration and modification of the traditional pattern of culture, but the main core of the ancient Hindu way of life remained intact. This was not so in Africa, where for the first time the villagers were compelled to pay money taxes to a distant central authority. In most cases Africans had lived within a small tribal area of law and political affiliation. With the advent of imperial rule, dozens of formerly distinct—and often antagonistic—tribes were gathered together, as in the case of Nigeria, into one colony. In some cases boundaries divided large tribes into two or three European colonial segments. Colonies, therefore, were usually not homogeneous nations in the modern sense, a fact later to prove a serious complication when these colonies became independent "nations" following World War II.

The process of colonization in Africa added up to the massive impact of a dynamic, self-confident, and technologically advanced civilization upon cultures that had been isolated from the mainstream of world affairs, politically and technologically arrested, and psychologically overawed. Kinship and family ties were weakened when villagers sought wage employment in distant towns or mines. In some areas, as many as 50 percent of the young males sought jobs in European mines hundreds of miles distant. Migrant workers sought money to pay the new hut taxes or to buy cheap, enticing European wares. Undoubtedly wage remittances from absent husbands did help raise standards of living, but the effect upon family ties and tribal loyalty was destructive. Old handicrafts declined as trade came to be dominated by Europeans and by Indian and Syrian merchants. The old ways of life were most disrupted in colonies that attracted European settlement, as in Kenya and Southern Rhodesia. In such areas Africans were limited to "native reserves" or to segregated areas in the towns. On occasion large tracts of land were allocated exclusively for European use. It was in these plural societies that racial tensions most rapidly developed.

For some fifty years after the African scramble began, the incidence of social change was uneven. In some remote areas Africans may never have seen a white man, let alone worked for him. But tribal life was gradually transformed by the introduction of new forms of land tenure, enforcement of alien systems of law, and the growth of a money economy. The obvious material superiority and military power of Europeans deeply impressed Africans. They sought consciously to imitate their rulers, to accept the white man's gods, and if possible to obtain a modicum of western education. The African in consequence became "detribalized" and often bewildered, alienated from much of his traditional culture but yet unable to understand and be part of the new.

Although the transformation of Africa was desirable and indeed inevitable, it was unfortunate that this revolutionary change occurred so quickly and at the hands of intruders whose motives were so mixed and who too frequently denigrated all African culture, dismissing the African as barbarous and uncivilized. Perhaps colonialism was a necessary, if abrupt and rude, awakening. It *did* introduce peace between tribes, administrative techniques, communications, harbors, western education, and a money economy—all essential before any African area could develop into a modern state. Some scholars disagree; Basil Davidson contends:

There is indeed nothing in that episode to show that these people could not or would not have worked this transformation for themselves, far less expensively in life and suffering and self-respect, without the coercion of outside interference.[14]

IMPERIALISM: THE BALANCE SHEET

Spread of imperialism. By 1914 some 283 million whites in Europe and the United States, together with about 54 million Japanese in Asia, directly controlled over 900 million non-Europeans, mainly in Africa and Asia, and dominated millions more in vast areas like China and Latin America. Britain, the greatest of the empire builders, boasted that "the sun never set" on its empire. Russia's colonial domain, mainly in central and eastern Asia, was at least half the size of Britain's empire. France was the third largest imperial power, with Germany a poor fourth. Belgium, Portugal, and Holland had substantial colonial holdings, though Italy made a poor showing. In 1914 the United States, as an imperial power, controlled over 700,000 square miles of territory outside the confines of continental United States. Its three most important possessions were Hawaii, Alaska, and the Philippines, but its shadow loomed gigantically over Latin America as well.

Imperialism: positive aspects. Today classical imperialism would find few, if any, really enthusiastic supporters. However, the significance of western colonial rule in the scheme of world history is becoming clearer following the achievement of independence by a large number of colonies after World War II. It is now evident that many of the native peoples living under imperial rule took the ensuing law and order for granted. It should not be forgotten that the slave trade in tropical Africa was smashed in the mid-nineteenth century largely by British efforts; that the French ended piracy in North Africa; and that in India *thugee* was extirpated by British rule. Even as late as 1900 much of Nigeria was in a state of chaos, with powerful Muslim chieftains carrying out ruthless slave trading.

In many of the areas that came under imperial control, tribes or nations had been constantly at war with each other. This was especially true in Africa, Malaya, and the Dutch East Indies. One law was imposed over an entire area, providing advantages of political and economic unity heretofore unknown. As we shall see in a later chapter, the granting of independence revived the old tribal and sectional loyalties. Regions such as India broke apart; unity has been maintained with extreme difficulty in Indonesia. The recent breakaway effort of the Ibos in Nigeria to create a new state of Biafra exemplifies the tendency toward a continued fracturing of the African political map.

On the economic front, western nations constructed roads, public buildings, postal, telegraph, and railway systems, and dams, while their businessmen dug mines, tapped oil fields, and established plantations. With the end of imperial control, many of these improvements remain, performing invaluable functions. Moreover, these underdeveloped areas still require the capital and technical skills of more developed nations.

Nor should the positive side of the ideological impact of imperialism be minimized. To civilizations, such as the Chinese, that were no longer dynamic, and to certain areas, such as tropical Africa, where modern technology had never existed, the West brought dynamic ideas of progress, nationalism, effective public administration, democracy, and faith in science. This ideological impact of nationalism and democracy, made possible by imperial rule, ultimately led to a demand for independence.

Among the most important agencies diffusing western ideas were the Christian missionaries. Their missions, hospitals, churches, schools, and colleges made a unique contribution. True, missionaries sometimes failed to respect or understand the intrinsic worth of aspects of indigenous culture. They believed such customs or beliefs undesirable because they were non-western (or non-Christian). But much selfless labor also was devoted to humanitarian objectives in the world's colonial regions.

Imperialism: negative aspects. A strong anticolonial school in the West has produced a massive literature against imperialism. Thus its critics charge that it was imposed "by self-seeking interests which appeal to the lusts of quantitative acquisitiveness and of forceful domination surviving in a nation from early centuries of animal struggle for existence."[15] Unquestionably imperialism had its ruthless and exploitative side. Large territories were taken by force or fraud, and on occasion lands were seized from native populations without compensation.

In the political and economic sectors, while imperial rule did create law and order, it was often achieved by perpetuating an indigenous hierarchical structure and endowing this elite with wealth and authority in return for maintaining a status quo that was advantageous for the imperial power. One result was to retard the development of national forms of representative government, of needed educational opportunities, or of the ability of the indigenous peoples to profit from the exploitation of their own natural resources. Often the construction of roads, transportation systems, hospitals, and schools was designed to serve the economic and societal interests of the colonial administrators and western business community so that the great masses remained both illiterate and at the bottom of the economic ladder, often at the bare subsistence level. Moreover, so well did western economic interests become entrenched that the eventual transfer of independence in the political sphere was seldom accompanied by a concomitant transfer of economic control and resources to the indigenous community, thereby creating a condition known as "neocolonialism."

On the sociological side, the large-scale destruction of culture patterns in Asia and Africa had massive repercussions. This is not to suggest that imperialism deliberately set out to practice either physical or cultural genocide. Rather, when drawing up an overall historical balance sheet, we must recognize that the penetration of western culture armed with a dynamic technology had a devastating impact which imperialism *per se* did little or nothing to alleviate. Whether the charge is valid or not, it is widely believed in the new Asian and African nations that imperialism accentuated the destructive forces inherent in western political, economic, and cultural penetration.

Finally, on the psychological side, the positive contributions of western imperialism were not sufficient in themselves to counter the charge of cultural arrogance implicit in the concept of "the white man's burden"—namely, that the conquest of nonwestern lands and the exploitation of their wealth could be justified on the basis of a civilizing mission. Nor were they sufficient to counter a slogan raised in more than one colonial region that "Good government is no substitute for self-government." The forces of nationalism were to prove irresistible and only after they had become masters in their own house would the newly independent peoples come to realize that the converse of that slogan is also true. But in any event, there would be no going back to the old order.

SUMMARY

Before 1870 Europe had little interest in colonial expansion. But with the completion of the unification of Germany and Italy, the mounting of tariffs, and the need for markets, raw materials, and areas for investing surplus capital, the western nations avidly turned their attention to imperialism. The economic forces back of this expansion have usually been overemphasized, the psychological underestimated. By 1870 Europe had unbounded faith in its destiny and in its powers. What has been called "a certain indefinable national energy"[16] impelled nations such as France, Britain, and Germany to spread their rule, power, and culture. Love of adventure and scientific curiosity also impelled explorers and administrators to peg out colonial claims.

In the Far East, China was opened in the 1840's and 1850's—somewhat before the real onset of western imperialism. This huge and inert empire was callously treated and exploited by the western nations. But China, with its unbending ethnocentrism and sense of cultural superiority, refused to adapt to the needs or realities of a rapidly changing world. On the other hand, Japan had a long tradition of borrowing from the outside. Once convinced of the necessity of modernization, this feudal island kingdom engaged in a pell-mell adoption of western culture. But while foreign customs and techniques were borrowed, they were shaped to fit Japanese needs as seen by Japan's leaders. Education, the press, the armed services, and the government so functioned as to produce a docile, obedient citizen and a fanatical, dedicated soldier.

Following the Indian Mutiny in 1857, Britain consolidated its rule in India and built up flourishing colonies in Ceylon, Malaya, and Burma. The French acquired Indochina, and the Dutch exploited the riches of the East Indies. In the Pacific a feature of the late nineteenth century was the growing imperialism of the United States.

Russian imperialism in the nineteenth century is often overlooked. Its empire was not a scattered series of territories located in various continents and separated by the seven seas but a continuous land area, a group of territories that had originated from a nucleus—Moscow. By 1900 Russia had expanded to the Pacific and marched southward to the passes of India and Afghanistan and was pushing into the Middle East toward the warm waters of the Indian Ocean. Because of Anglo-Russian rivalry in this latter area, Persia was in effect partitioned.

Africa was the largest area to be partitioned. By the end of the colonial scramble only two independent countries remained: Ethiopia and tiny Liberia. In addition to its control of South Africa, Britain had gained Egypt, British Somaliland, Anglo-Egyptian Sudan, Kenya, Uganda, Rhodesia, Nigeria, Gambia, Sierra Leone, and the Gold Coast. In addition to its extensive holdings in North Africa, France ruled Madagascar, French Equatorial Africa, and the huge stretch of French West Africa reaching from Dakar on the Atlantic coast to the valley of the Nile. Little Belgium controlled the vast Belgian Congo, and Germany had fairly extensive holdings. Only ambitious Italy had failed in the great African colony hunt.

By the end of the nineteenth century European imperialism had reached its apogee. Colonial officials ordered the lives of millions of seemingly complacent Afro-Asian subjects. Even the United States, once a colony herself, joined the imperial act, acquiring such territories as the Philippines, Hawaii, and Puerto Rico.

SUGGESTIONS FOR READING

P. T. Moon, **Imperialism and World Politics**, Macmillan, 1953. A keen analysis of why Europe shouldered the "white man's burden." Other provocative studies on nineteenth-century imperialism are G. H. Nadel and P. Curtis, eds., **Imperialism and Colonialism**,* Macmillan; H. M. Wright, ed., **The "New Imperialism,"*** Heath Problems; A. P. Thornton, **Doctrines of Imperialism**,* Wiley. See also R. Koebner and H. Schmidt, **Imperialism**, Cambridge Univ., 1964, which deals mainly with British imperialism; James Morris, **Pax Britannica**, Harcourt, Brace & World, 1968; and Donald C. Gordon, **The Moment of Power**,* Prentice-Hall, the historical significance of the British empire in the nineteenth and twentieth centuries.

Alan Burns, **In Defence of Colonies**, Verry, 1957. A vigorous defense of the motives and positive results of British imperialism. Two famous attacks on imperialism are J. A. Hobson, **Imperialism**,* rev. ed., Univ. of Mich.; and V. I. Lenin, **Imperialism, the Highest Stage of Capitalism**,* China Books. See also Ernest Barker, **The Ideas and Ideals of the British Empire**, Cambridge Univ., 1941.

Z. Marsh and G. W. Kingsnorth, **An Introduction to the History of East Africa**,* Cambridge Univ.; and J. D. Fage, **An Introduction to the History of West Africa**,* Cambridge Univ. Two brief, useful studies. See also R. Hallett, **The Penetration of Africa**, Praeger, 1965; R. Slade, **Belgian Congo**,* Oxford, a detailed history from 1885 to 1908; Ronald Robinson and J. Gallagher, **Africa and the Victorians**, St. Martin's, 1961; and Peter Duignan and L. H. Gann, eds., **Colonialism in Africa**, Cambridge Univ., 1969, perceptive essays on the motivation of imperialism. English historian Reginald Coupland gives a vivid picture of the horrors of the slave trade and of the long campaign against it in **The British Anti-Slavery Movement**, 2nd ed., Barnes and Noble, 1964. The challenge of Britain's imperial mission in Africa is mirrored in the lives of three men: F. Gross, **Rhodes of Africa**, Praeger, 1957; Lord Elton, **Gordon of Khartoum**, Knopf, 1955; M. Perham, **Lugard, The Years of Adventure**, Archon, 1968. See also A. Moorehead, **The White Nile**,* Dell, and **The Blue Nile**,* Dell, fascinating accounts of exploration in central Africa; and R. and C. Oliver, eds., **Africa in the Days of Exploration**,* Spectrum.

For valuable insight into British rule and its consequences see M. Edwardes, **British India**, Taplinger, 1968; and S. Gopal, **British Policy in India**, Cambridge Univ., 1966. See also P. Speare, **Twilight of the Mughuls**, Cambridge Univ., 1951, a description of the once mighty Indian dynasty on the eve of its oblivion; S. N. Sen, **Eighteen Fifty-Seven**, India Ministry of Information, Delhi, 1957, the official history of the Indian Mutiny of 1857; P. Woodruff, **The Men Who Ruled India**,* 2 vols., Schocken; and Francis G. Hutchins, **The Illusion of Permanence**, Princeton, 1967, which deals with the problems of British imperial rule in India.

Li Chien-nung, **The Political History of China**, Van Nostrand, 1956. The best history of Chinese domestic affairs in the nineteenth century. J. Meskill, ed., **The Pattern of Chinese History**, Heath, 1965, is a useful collection of articles from various interpretive schools. See also A. Feuerwerker, ed., **Modern China**, Prentice-Hall, 1964; and F. Wolfgang, **China and the West**, R. A. Wilson, trans., Harper & Row, 1967. P. S. Buck, **Imperial Woman**,* Pocket Books, is a lengthy, colorful biographical novel of the last empress of China, who rose from concubinage to the throne of the Manchu.

For an investigation into the early contacts between Europe and Asia see George B. Sansom, **The Western World and Japan**, Knopf, 1950. See also W. G. Beasley, **The Modern History of Japan**,* Praeger; and O. Statler, **Japanese Inn**, Random House, 1961, a colorful and dependable overview of Japanese history in the last three centuries.

Recommended for the coverage of events in Southeast Asia are D. G. E. Hall, **A History of South-East Asia**, St. Martin's, 1968; H. J. Benda and J. A. Larkin, **The World of Southeast Asia**, Harper & Row, 1967.

*Indicates an inexpensive paperbound edition.

Part Seven

The World Adrift

■World War I had been described as a major watershed in modern history. It brought to a dramatic close a century of relative peace and ushered in what has been referred to as the Age of Violence. As we have seen, before 1914 Europe was the center of the world in political influence, cultural creativity, and military and financial power. This small continent ruled a vast colonial structure and with it hundreds of millions of dependent peoples. Ideologically, political liberalism and parliamentary institutions had flourished and multiplied. Democracy, it seemed, was destined to spread all over the globe. And capitalism was the prevailing economic creed, with the middle class its master and chief beneficiary.

First of the total technological conflicts, the 1914-1918 conflagration had far-reaching consequences, which include World War II in turn. Because of the fearful price paid by the men who endured World War I, they had to believe that a better world would emerge. They were soon disillusioned. Although the statesmen of the victorious Allies had championed the democratic and humanistic traditions of western civilization, their motives in making the peace were often as vindictive and nationalistic as any preparations for war. And though internationalism was activated in the form of the League of Nations, it was given neither the strength nor the support required to bring peace and security during the troubled 1920's and 1930's.

In these years democracy began its struggle with new totalitarianisms. In war-exhausted Russia, Marxist tenets were embraced by revolutionaries, and a Communist society took shape under Lenin. Another authoritarian system, Fascism, gripped Italy. And the most frightening ideology of all, Nazism, grew to terrifying fruition in Germany, where a people embittered by the humiliation of World War I and the Treaty of Versailles staked their future on a madman named Hitler.

By the 1920's and 1930's the non-European world had discovered the concept of nationalism. In the Middle East, Arab national ambitions had flared in 1916 into a revolt against Ottoman rule. The immigration of European Jews to Palestine led to conflict between Arabs and Jews, which was to increase as time passed. In North Africa, the Middle East, India, southeastern Asia, and Oceania, the indigenous peoples were gathering strength in their battle to oust the Europeans completely and govern themselves; and in the huge colonial area south of the Sahara, Africans were beginning to stir restlessly against European rule. Even China, tradition-bound for centuries, turned to revolution to regain the power and prestige it had lost during the era of imperialism. But though Chiang Kai-shek won an internal power struggle and organized the government, the country remained poor and weak. Meanwhile Japan continued its amazing technological, industrial, and military growth and became as a world power.

The world depression in the 1930's gave the totalitarian movements an opportunity to expand their despotism at home and to launch aggression abroad. From 1931 to 1939, starting with the Japanese invasion of Manchuria, their belligerence mounted. The new dictatorial regimes went from one success to another, glorifying militarism and the potency of the state, regimenting their citizens, and intimidating their neighbors. The older democratic nations, such as Britain and France, were paralyzed with indecision and fear and did little to halt the dictators. Appeasement was tried, but the aggression continued. Finally, in 1939, the British and French realized that their own nations were next in Hitler's march of conquest and took up arms. The Second World War began. In 1941 the Soviet Union, which had been allied earlier with the Nazis, and the United States, which for two decades had been attempting to ignore the mounting tensions abroad, were forced into the struggle. The horrors which this global conflict brought were the familiar ones of ruthless enemy occupation, the rigors of battle, and the loss of life and property, and the new ones created by dread new weapons and methods of warfare, the organized slaughter of certain nationality groups, and the repeated bombing of civilian centers.

Victory came to the Grand Alliance in 1945 and with it total defeat of Hilter's Third Reich and the fascist states established in Italy by Mussolini and in Japan by Tojo. As in 1919 the victors were confronted with the immense task of rebuilding and reestablishing a great part of the world. This task was made more difficult by the knowledge of the failures of the peace of 1919 and the dismaying realization that as the Second World War was more encompassing and vastly more destructive than the First, so a Third World War would be more shattering than the Second and, with the advent of nuclear weapons, might bring about the annihilation of man.

25. Claude Monet: "La Grenouillère" (1869). The subject matter of progressive painting in the later nineteenth century turned from Neoclassic and romantic idealization toward realism, toward an immediacy and objectivity which reflected the environment of a technologically oriented middle-class society. The form and method of painting likewise changed radically. In an attempt to depict outdoor light, the Impressionist Monet employed pigment loosely, in short, choppy strokes and staccato patches. He thus achieved a quality of light that shimmers and dazzles as it does in the out-of-doors and a texture that avows the presence of air between foreground and background. While the finished painting is thus truer to the eye, it is, paradoxically, rendered almost abstractly, as if by a kind of visual shorthand. And while it conveys a convincing sense of distance, it retains at the same time a curiously flat playing-card effect. Thus a tension arose in nineteenth-century painting between naturalism and abstraction. In its later resolution by the Post-Impressionists—toward abstraction—a fundamental direction in modern art was set.

26. (opposite page) **Victor Horta: Hotel van Eetvelde, Brussels** (1899); **27.** (above) **Edvard Munch: "The Cry"** (1893); and **28.** (below) **Thomas Eakins: "The Gross Clinic"** (1875). The art of the last years of the 1800's looked back upon the century's achievement at the same time it looked forward to the future, and both glances were accompanied as often by anxiety as by assurance. The modern revolution in technology, economics, politics, and mores proceeded apace. In 1881 it was possible for Thomas Eakins, painting in the pragmatically optimistic atmosphere of America, to look on the world with a naturalist's eye, confident that both science and art could cope with reality at the material level. By 1896, however, the paintings of the Norwegian Munch strongly suggested that the brave new society was fraught with frightening new perils, among them a personal psychological dislocation born of the fragmentation of those values in which security had traditionally been found. Even Munch's painterly means are here more abstract—less trusting of superficial material facts—than Eakins'. Meanwhile, architects sought to cast off the hidebound old "revival modes" which had weighed so heavily on nineteenth-century building. The art nouveau manner, shown here at the crest of its popularity, was intended to freshen the mainstream of western style, as well as to revivify a sense of craftsmanship which machine technology had greatly undermined. Oddly, Horta's imaginative use of iron did much to demonstrate the esthetic as well as practical possibilities of this most industrial of materials.

29. Paul Cezanne: "Still Life with Peppermint Bottle" (1890-1894). The still lifes of Cezanne are not so much pictures of apples, bottles, and other memorabilia of the visible world as essays in pictorial architecture. Though he employed many Impressionist devices, such as direct color and bold brushwork, Cezanne replaced the breezy and casual composition of the Impressionists with a firmer, more calculated order. To create this soundness of structure, he positioned and modeled his forms with scrupulous care. Occasional distortions (note the asymmetry of the bottle) were allowed in order to achieve a tighter, more dynamic organization.

Chapter 28

New Vistas and Ominous Fears

The Course of Politics in the West: 1918-1930

INTRODUCTION. When World War I ended in 1918, a weary world began the herculean task of transforming its efforts from those of war to peace. Underlying this transition was the prevalent belief that somehow the sacrifices made during the war would lead to a better life for all mankind. Accordingly, there were roseate predictions of the ultimate triumph of democratic institutions everywhere. Had not four antidemocratic imperial governments—in Germany, Turkey, Austria-Hungary, and Russia—been overthrown? And millions of people, invoking nationalism's creed of self-determination, were escaping alien rule and establishing their own democratic governments. In addition to this faith in democracy and nationalism, there was an ambivalent adherence to the cause of internationalism so eloquently espoused by President Wilson. A new international order was to be achieved by the creation of a world organization designed to outlaw war and encourage amity between nations.

Europeans generally viewed their continent's prospects optimistically. They were prone to believe that Europe could regain its preeminence in the world—in finance, industry, and military power. It soon became evident, however, that such hopes were not justified. The war's economic consequences were both underestimated and only dimly understood. Nations such as Great Britain had lost export markets; disagreements over war debts and reparation claims against former enemies, as well as runaway inflation, plagued various nations after 1918. Economic recovery was also hindered, and the general morale tarnished, by the destruction of millions of Europe's young men on the battlefields of the Marne, Tannenberg, and Verdun.

The postwar decade soon exposed the lack of realism concerning nationalism and democracy. Newly created democracies in central and eastern Europe, whose people had little experience in representative government, were soon superseded by dictatorial regimes. Most challenging to the future of democracy was the establishment of two dictatorships—the Communist in Russia and the Fascist in Italy. Another menacing portent was the emergence of a racist and antidemocratic Nazi movement in republican Germany. Democratic institutions were destroyed in Russia and Italy, and even in the traditional bastions of democracy, in Great Britain, France, and the United States, there seemed to be a lack of purpose, of vitality, and of confidence. While France and Britain failed to come to grips with their basic problems, the United States, mainly aloof from world affairs, concentrated on what appeared to be dazzling prosperity. During the postwar decade all three nations exhibited various symptoms of moral fatigue and disillusionment.

Against this background, and confronted by the defeated nations' belief that the peace treaties were unjust, the newly created League of Nations began its task of safeguarding world peace and encouraging international conciliation. In retrospect, it is hardly surprising that its record was not impressive. Its usefulness was also compromised by the refusal of the United States to become a member of the League.

As the 1920's neared an end, the general course of international affairs seemed reasonably calm; former enemies such as France and Germany were apparently burying the hatchet, and economic recovery and prosperity was fairly widespread. Yet below the surface remained serious tensions and problems, both political and economic, bequeathed by the First World War. These, then, were the historical ingredients of the complex 1920's, which were ushered in following the end of hostilities by the immediate and crucial task of trying to fashion a "just peace" between the victors and vanquished.

THE PEACE SETTLEMENT

Wilson's blueprint for peace. Woodrow Wilson had declared that World War I was

a war for freedom and justice and self-government amongst all the nations of the world, a war to make the world safe for the peoples who live upon it and have made it their own, the German people themselves included.[1]

In January 1918, in an address before both houses of Congress, the president had enunciated his famous Fourteen Points as the basis for a lasting peace. With this speech, Wilson made himself a new kind of world leader, representing not wealth and power but morality and justice. Millions of men and women, at home and abroad, in the Allied nations, in the enemy countries, and in neutral states, flocked to his standard. The Fourteen Points seemed to open the way not only for a speedy cessation of hostilities but for a peace that could endure.

The first five points were general in nature and may be summarized as follows: "Open covenants openly arrived at"; freedom of the seas in peace and in war alike; the removal of all economic barriers and the establishment of an equality of trade conditions among all nations; reduction of national armaments; a readjustment of all colonial claims, giving

Thirty-two Allied nations sent representatives to Paris to put the stamp of finality and justice on the "war to end all wars." But the settlements which came out of the Peace Conference were marked by national rather than global interests, and by hostility rather than assistance for the defeated nations. Four influential men who clashed over their individual plans for a lasting peace were David Lloyd George, prime minister of Great Britain; Vittorio Orlando, prime minister of Italy; Georges Clemenceau, premier of France; and Woodrow Wilson, president of the United States.

the interests of the population concerned equal weight with the claims of the government whose title was to be determined. The next eight points dealt with specific issues involving the evacuation and restoration of Allied territory, self-determination for submerged nationalities, and the redrawing of European boundaries along national lines. The fourteenth point in Wilson's speech contained the germ of the League of Nations: the formation of a general association of nations under specific covenants for the purpose of affording mutual guarantees of political independence and territorial integrity to great and small states alike.

Cross-currents at the peace conference. All the Allied powers sent delegations to the peace conference at Paris, but the vanquished nations were not accorded representation. This exclusion was not in the spirit of Wilson's idealistic pronouncements before the armistice.

Three personalities dominated the Paris Conference: Wilson, Lloyd George, and Clemenceau. In the eyes of the war-weary and disillusioned peoples of Europe, Wilson was a veritable Messiah. But it soon became

apparent that he would be unable to prevent his ideals and promises from being sabotaged by the other Allied statesmen. Against the wily Lloyd George and the cynical Clemenceau, the idealistic American scholar had little chance of holding his own. In addition, certain factions in Congress were preparing to repudiate Wilson's program. Handicapped by a cold and imperious personality, Wilson (1856-1924) was so thoroughly convinced of the validity of his own ideas that he seldom recognized a need to "sell" them to others and often refused to consider the possibility of merit in the ideas of his opponents.

Lloyd George (1863-1945), the prime minister of Great Britain, was a consummately clever politician who could use the arts of diplomatic bargaining with a rare skill. He came to the conference just after a triumphant victory at the polls in which his party had promised the electorate the "hanging of the kaiser" and the "squeezing of the German lemon until the pips squeaked." He was determined to destroy the commercial and naval power of Germany, to acquire the German colonies, and to compel Germany to pay a large share of the cost of the war.

The strongest personality of the conference was the French premier—the seventy-seven-year-old Clemenceau (1841-1929), who for more than half a century had been a colorful part of French life and politics. A fierce individualist, Clemenceau had continuously opposed corruption, racism, and antidemocratic forces. His burning ambition was to ensure the security of France in the future; his formula was restitution, reparations, and guarantees. Clemenceau had little confidence in what, to him, were the unrealistic and utopian principles of Wilson, observing, "Even God was satisfied with Ten Commandments, but Wilson insists on fourteen."

Prearmistice peace principles and secret treaties. The Germans had surrendered with the understanding that the peace would in general follow the Fourteen Points and coincide with Wilson's speeches. In February 1918 the president had announced, "There shall be no annexations, no contributions, no punitive damages"; on July 4 he had said that every question must be settled "upon the basis of the free acceptance of that settlement by the people immediately concerned."

Complicating the promises of Wilson, especially the Fourteen Points, were the secret treaties the Allies had made during the war. In 1915 Italy had been induced to enter the conflict by promises of Austrian territory which would make the Adriatic an Italian sea. Italy was also promised an extension of its African colonies and a sphere of influence in Asiatic Turkey. Nearly all these proposed transfers violated the Wilsonian concept of national self-determination.

Other secret treaties gave Russia the right to take over the Dardanelles and Constantinople, Rumania the right to secure substantial territory at the expense of Austria-Hungary, and Japan the right to retain the German territory of Kiaochow in China. In return for Arab aid against the Turks, Britain had made vague promises of independence for the Arabs. In 1916, however, Britain and France had divided Turkish Iraq and Syria into their respective spheres of interest. Palestine, with its holy places, was to be placed under international administration; and in 1917 Great Britain pledged its support

of the "establishment in Palestine of a national home for the Jewish people."

President Wilson professed ignorance of the existence of the treaties, but their contents were common knowledge before the end of the war. In fact, in 1917 the Bolshevik government had released their texts, which were then published in American and English newspapers. Wilson may have believed that the secret agreements could be ignored, for he hoped to sway European statesmen to the necessity of founding the peace on his principles.

The League Covenant. When the statesmen assembled in their first plenary meeting on January 18, 1919, the first difficulty arose over the question of a league of nations. Wilson was insistent that the initial work of the conference must be to agree upon a covenant of a league of nations which was to be made part of the peace treaty. After much wrangling, the Covenant was approved by the full conference in April 1919. In order to gain support for the League, however, Wilson had to compromise on other matters. His Fourteen Points were thus partially repudiated, but he believed firmly that an imperfect treaty incorporating the League was better than a perfect one without it.

The Covenant of the League of Nations specified its aims: "to guarantee international cooperation and to achieve international peace and security." To implement this goal, Article x, the key article of the Covenant, stipulated that:

The Members of the League undertake to respect and preserve as against external aggression the territorial integrity and existing political independence of all Members of the League. In case of any such aggression or in case of any threat or danger of such aggression the Council shall advise upon the means by which this obligation shall be fulfilled.[2]

Redrawing German boundaries. The conference also faced the task of redrawing German boundaries. Alsace-Lorraine was turned over to France without question, in accordance with one of the Fourteen Points. Three districts formerly belonging to Germany were given to Belgium, after a dubious plebiscite conducted by Belgian officials. Another plebiscite gave half of Schleswig back to Denmark.

Clemenceau was determined that a buffer state consisting of the German territory west of the Rhine should be established under the domination of France. In the eyes of the American and British representatives, such a crass violation of the principle of self-determination would only breed future wars; and a compromise was therefore offered Clemenceau, which he accepted. The territory in question was to be occupied by Allied troops for a period of from five to fifteen years; and a zone extending fifty kilometers east of the Rhine was to be demilitarized. In addition, Wilson and Lloyd George agreed that the United States and Great Britain, by treaty, would guarantee France against aggression. The importance of this pledge cannot be overemphasized.

Along Germany's eastern frontier the creation of the Polish Corridor, which separated East Prussia from the rest of Germany, raised grave problems. Large sections of German territory in which there were Polish majorities but also a goodly number of Germans were turned over to Poland. (The land in question had been taken from Poland by Prussia in the eighteenth century.) A section of Silesia was likewise given to Poland, but only after a plebiscite. Danzig, a German city, was handed over to the League for administration. All in all, Germany lost 25,000 square miles inhabited by some six million people.

Although Clemenceau also claimed the Saar Basin, a rich coal area, this was not given outright to France but instead was placed under the administration of the League. The French were given ownership of the mines to compensate for the destruction of their own in northern France. It was agreed, however, that after fifteen years a plebiscite would be conducted to determine the future status of the Saar region.

The mandate system. A curious mixture of idealism and revenge determined the allocation of the German colonies and certain territories belonging to Turkey. Because outright annexation would look too much like unvarnished imperialism, it was suggested that the colonies be turned over to the League, which in turn would give them to certain of its members to administer. The colonies were to be known as mandates, and praiseworthy precautions were taken to ensure that the mandates would be administered for the well-being and development of the inhabitants. Once a year the mandatory powers were to present a detailed account of their administration of the territories to the League. The mandate system as such was a step forward in colonial administration, but Germany nevertheless was deprived of all colonies, with the excuse that it could not rule them justly or efficiently.

Reparations. Germany had accepted the armistice terms with the understanding that it was to pay for damage done to the Allied civilian population. At the conference the British and French delegates went much further by demanding that Germany pay the total cost of the war, including pensions. The American representatives maintained that such a claim was contrary to the prearmistice Allied terms and succeeded in achieving a compromise. It was agreed that, except in the case of Belgium, Germany was not to pay the entire cost of the war, but only war damages, which included those suffered by civilians and the cost of pensions. These payments, called reparations, were exacted on the ground that Germany was responsible for the war.

Although the Allies agreed that Germany should be made to pay, they were unable to decide on the sum. Some demands ran as high as $200 billion. Finally it was decided that a committee should fix the amount and report no later than May 1921. In the meantime Germany was to begin making payments which, by the time the reparations committee's report was ready, would total nearly $5 billion.

Other Allied demands. Germany was required to hand over most of its merchant fleet, construct one million tons of new shipping for the Allies, and deliver them vast amounts of coal, equipment, tools, and machinery. In military matters the demands were even more drastic. Germany was permitted a standing army of only 100,000 men, the size of the fleet was drastically reduced, possession of military airplanes was forbidden, and munitions plants were to be placed under close supervision. The treaty also provided that the kaiser be tried by a tribunal "for a supreme offense against international morality and the sanctity of treaties" and cited some eight hundred German officials for trial on charges of war atrocities. But the kaiser had fled to Holland after the German revolution; and when that country refused to surrender him, no further steps were taken by the Allied governments, which had inserted the clause providing for the punishment of the kaiser largely for home consumption.

The Treaty of Versailles signed. The Treaty of Versailles was built around the concept that Germany was responsible for the war. It stated explicitly that:

The Allied and Associated Governments affirm and Germany accepts the responsibility of Germany and her allies for causing all the loss and damage to which the Allied and Associated Governments and their nationals have been subjected as a consequence of the war imposed upon them by the aggression of Germany and her allies.[3]

Before coming to Paris in April 1919 to receive the Treaty of Versailles, the German delegation had been given no official information as to its terms. Upon obtaining the treaty on May 7, the German foreign minister stated:

It is demanded of us that we shall confess ourselves to be the only ones guilty of the war . . . . We are far from declining any responsiblilty . . . but we energetically deny that Germany and its people . . . were alone guilty. . . . In the last fifty years the Imperialism of all the European States has chronically poisoned the international situation . . . .[4]

The menace of Allied invasion gave the Germans no alternative but to sign, and the government therefore instructed its delegates to accept the treaty for Germany "without abandoning her view in regard to the unheard-of injustice of the conditions of the peace." On June 28, on the anniversary of the assassination of Archduke Francis Ferdinand and in the Hall of Mirrors at Versailles where the German empire had been proclaimed in 1871, the treaty was signed.

After witnessing this ceremony, an American delegate wrote in his diary:

I had a feeling of sympathy for the Germans who sat there quite stoically. It was not unlike what was done in ancient times, when the conqueror dragged the conquered at his chariot wheels. To my mind, it is out of keeping with the new era which we profess an ardent desire to promote. I wish it could have been more simple and that there might have been an element of chivalry, which was wholly lacking. The affair was elaborately staged and made as humiliating to the enemy as it well could be.[5]

Other World War treaties. The Allies also concluded treaties with the rest of the Central Powers. The treaty with Austria, the Treaty of St. Germain (1919), legalized the nationalist movements of Czechs, Poles, and South Slavs and converted the rest of the empire into the separate states of Austria and Hungary. By the treaty terms, the Austrian empire was reduced in area from 116,000 to 32,000 square miles and in population from 28,500,000 to 6,000,000. *Anschluss*—union of the Germans in Austria with their kinsmen in the new German republic—was forbidden. The treaty also awarded Italy sections of Austria—the territory south of the Brenner Pass, South Tyrol, Trentino with its 250,000 Austrian Germans, and the northeastern coast of the Adriatic with its large number of Slavs. To complete its acquisition of the Adriatic, Italy needed to obtain a slice of the Dalmation coast and the port of Fiume. The latter, however, was the natural port for the newly created state of Yugoslavia and had not been promised to Italy in 1915. Wilson declared that the Italian claim was in flat contradiction to the principle of self-determination; the ensuing controversy nearly wrecked the peace conference. The explosive issue of Italian claims in the Adriatic was not settled until 1920, when Italy renounced its claims to Dalmatia and when Fiume became an independent state. Four years later, however, Fiume was ceded to Italy.

By the Treaty of Sevres (1920) the Ottoman empire was placed on the operating table of power politics, dissected, and divided among Greece, Britain, and France. Greece was given nearly all of European Turkey and some islands of the Aegean Sea. The city of

THE PEACE SETTLEMENT IN EUROPE

Newly Created States
Ceded Territories

Smyrna was put under Greek administration, but Armenia achieved full independence. Syria was mandated to France, and Palestine and Iraq to England. To the Arabs, these transfers to Britain and France were a violation of wartime pledges. As for the Straits, this strategic waterway was to be under international control.

Two other treaties affected the Balkans. By the Treaty of Trianon (1920) Hungary lost territory to Czechoslovakia, Yugoslavia, and Rumania. The Treaty of Neuilly (1919) cut off Bulgaria from the Aegean Sea, imposed an indemnity, and provided for compulsory demilitarization. Bulgaria lost nearly one million subjects.

Evaluation of the peace settlement. During the first postwar decade tons of paper and barrels of ink were used in hot justification or acrid denunciation of the peace settlement. On the whole, the peace settlement was inadequate and unrealistic. In his indictment of the economic provisions of the peace, the world-famous economist John Maynard Keynes wrote in 1919:

The treaty includes no provisions for the economic rehabilitation of Europe,—nothing to make the defeated Central Empires into good neighbours, nothing to stabilise the new States of Europe, nothing to reclaim Russia; nor does it promote in any way a compact of economic solidarity amongst the Allies themselves; no arrangement was reached at Paris for restoring the disordered finances of France and Italy, or to adjust the systems of the Old World and the New.[6]

One of the weakest aspects of the peace settlement was the complete disregard of Russia. While the peace conference was in session, Russia was convulsed by civil war, complicated by the intervention of Japanese, American, French, and British troops. The Allied representatives at Paris disagreed on the policy to adopt toward the Communist government in Russia. The Soviets proposed to accept the huge prewar debts contracted by the tsar's government if the Allies would stop aiding the anti-Communist forces and restore normal commercial and diplomatic relations. The statesmen at Paris did not take this offer seriously, for they believed that the Communist government would soon collapse. Whether the new regime in Russia and the Allies could have reached some kind of an agreement leading to Russian participation in the peace settlement is uncertain, but the possibility was not seriously explored. George F. Kennan, an American authority on Soviet affairs, maintains that the sacrifice of this possiblilty had tremendous consequences for "the long-term future of both the Russian and American peoples and indeed of mankind generally."[7]

Some historians blame the errors of the treaties upon the defects of the personalities who made them. This view oversimplifies the problem and furthermore assumes that the statesmen at Paris were free agents. In truth, the delegates were the prisoners of their own people, who had been so influenced by propaganda, whose enmity was so bitter, and whose knowledge was so meager that any indication of reasonableness shown to the ex-enemies would have meant the repudiation of the harassed peacemakers. Perhaps no one possessed enough wisdom to cope with the many problems created and accentuated by four years of global war. Perhaps no other group of leaders could have made a better peace.

PROBLEMS OF STABILITY AND SECURITY

The "new world" and the powers. The prophecy that peace would usher in "a world fit for heroes" was quickly repudiated in the early troubled years of the postwar decade. The unity among the Allies wrought by the necessities of war did not long survive victory. During the Paris Conference and in the years following, serious differences emerged over such basic issues as reparations, war debts, disarmament, and the structure and functions of the League of Nations.

Italy was angry with its former allies for being so niggardly with the spoils of war. Great Britain was ready to let bygones be bygones; the "nation of shopkeepers" was anxious to see prosperity return to central Europe. On the other hand, France feared a resurgent Germany and was determined to enforce all the peace treaties.

And what of the vanquished? Germany was resentful of the peace settlement and determined to repudiate it. Hungary, Austria, and Bulgaria held similar views. Alone of the defeated powers, Turkey was fairly content, as it had been able to secure better treatment in a new treaty—the Treaty of Lausanne (see p. 697).

The United States refuses to join the League. In 1919, the year of its establishment, the League of Nations constituted a promising agency for improving the status of mankind everywhere. At the outset, however, it suffered a great blow to its prestige: the United States refused to become a member of the League. During the war Americans had been proud of Wilson's proposals for a new world order. After the war, however, their sense of a world mission and crusade for internationalism quickly ebbed away.

Disillusionment with the consequences of the peace settlements rekindled isolationism, and idealism born during the conflict was superseded by apathy and cynicism over world affairs. Unfortunately, President Wilson was both physically unable and politically maladroit in campaigning for Senate ratification of the League Covenant. In 1920 his program was repudiated at the polls, for the victory of Warren G. Harding, the Republican candidate for president, meant that the Covenant would never be ratified by the Senate.

The United States refusal to support the League was a fateful decision and, in retrospect, probably a serious blow to the cause of world peace. When the United States did join an international organization, the United Nations, in 1945, obstacles to world peace were much more complicated and obdurate than in 1919. But at the outset of the 1920's the chaos of the future and the coming of World War II were hidden in the yet unturned pages of history. The mass of Americans lapsed into complacent isolationism and normalcy with Harding.

France and the Little Entente. When both Britain and the United States repudiated the treaty guaranteeing France from aggression, the French, having little faith in the League as an instrument for their security, set about establishing their own military system. Allies were obtained through defensive treaties made, between 1920 and 1927, with Belgium, Poland, Czechoslovakia, Rumania, and Yugoslavia. The last three states constituted a diplomatic bloc, the Little Entente, whose power rested upon huge French loans and military assistance. For a brief ten years France with these allies dominated Europe; Germany was economically weak and militarily impotent.

The shift to a peace economy. One of the chief obstacles to postwar peace was the confused and desperate situation into which the European economy had been plunged. It has been estimated that the cost of the war was about $350 billion. It was the financial consequences of war that did the most to continue the enmity between victors and vanquished and also to alienate the nations, formerly allies, which had defeated Germany.

Following the armistice, there was an urgent need for getting back to a peacetime economy, which meant the production of peacetime goods instead of munitions, the demobilization of millions of soldiers, and the absorption of these veterans into the business structure. But it was not easy to return to the prosperous world economy that had existed before 1914.

The conflict had brought about many changes in world trade. Europe in particular had suffered a serious decline in its share of the world's commerce because of war blockades, the reduction of consumer purchasing power, the loss of shipping, and the capture of overseas markets by the United States, Latin America, and Japan. These economic setbacks were felt keenly by Germany and Great Britain. Furthermore, the peace treaties had multiplied national boundaries, which soon became obstacles to the flow of goods.

Serious problems also existed in the domestic economies of the European nations. As a result of the war, the public debts of the participant nations zoomed, often accompanied by the circulation of paper money not backed by adequate reserves. Furthermore, the war left a legacy of tension between economic groups. Labor unions were determined not to give up wage gains acquired during the war.

For a brief period many of these economic problems were obscured by an artificial postwar boom. The peak of prosperity was reached in 1920, after which world trade and industrial activity diminished. Strikes, unemployment, and other industrial problems multiplied; and for the next five years the nations, particularly in Europe, tried to extricate themselves from this economic morass.

The inter-Allied debt problem. The most serious problem facing Europe as it strove to achieve a prosperous peace economy was the revolution in its financial position in relation to the rest of the world. In 1914 the United States had been a debtor nation, mostly to Europe, for the amount of $3.75 billion. The war reversed the situation, and in 1919 the United States was owed more than $10 billion by its fellow victors. This tremendous debt posed what economists call the transfer problem. Such international obligations could only be paid by the actual transfer of gold or by the sale of goods to the creditor country.

The various Allied powers in Europe had lent each other funds, with Britain acting as the chief banker. When their credits had been used up, they had turned to the United

States for financial help. Britain owed huge sums to the United States but was still a net creditor of $4 billion because of its European debtors. France, on the other hand, was a net debtor of $3.5 billion. Some of the former Allies argued that the inter-Allied debts were political, that all of them had in effect been poured into a common pool for victory, and that, with victory, all should be canceled.

In the summer of 1922 Great Britain proposed that it collect no more from its debtors —Allies and Germany alike—than the United States collected from Britain itself. It was becoming manifest to British statesmen that Germany would not be able to meet its reparation payments, and without them the payment of the inter-Allied debts—especially the debts owed to the United States—would be extremely difficult, if not impossible, to make.

Although the American government insisted that there was no connection between the inter-Allied debts and German reparations, negotiations were carried on, and debt payment plans were set up with thirteen nations. No reductions were made in principal, but in numerous instances the rate of interest was decreased. The total amount to be paid came to more than $22 billion.

France invades the Ruhr. It became apparent that the Allies had placed an impossibly heavy burden on Germany. In 1921 its total indemnities had been fixed at $32 billion. During the same year Germany made a payment of $250 million, which reacted disastrously upon its currency system. Upon the default of some of Germany's payments, French troops, supported by Belgian and Italian contingents, marched into the rich industrial German district of the Ruhr, undeterred by British and American opposition. Defying the French army, German workers went on strike. Many were imprisoned, and the French toyed with the idea of establishing a separate state in the Rhineland which would act as a buffer between Germany and France. While chaotic conditions in the Ruhr led to catastrophic inflation of German currency, the French gained little economic benefit from their occupation. Meanwhile, public opinion all over the world had been shocked by France's strong-arm tactics in the Ruhr.

Change for the better. Midway in 1923 the prospect of a tranquil and cooperative world seemed far off indeed. But while not apparent to the harassed statesmen of the period, the worst of the war's aftermath had run its course. The Franco-British quarrel, mainly over the Ruhr, was patched up, and French troops were evacuated from the Ruhr in 1924. In the same year a commission under the chairmanship of an American banker, Charles Dawes, formulated a more liberal reparations policy. Installments were reduced and extended over a longer period, and a large loan was floated to aid Germany's recovery. Reparations payments were now renewed, and the former Allies paid their debt installments to the United States on schedule.

There was also a spectacular development in international relations. At the Locarno Conference in 1925 Germany, Great Britain, Belgium, France, and Italy signed a treaty guaranteeing the existing frontiers along the Rhine, providing for a demilitarized German zone extending fifty kilometers east of the Rhine, and, in effect, pledging the signatories not to resort to aggression against each other. The Locarno Pact heralded a new era in European affairs. Germany accepted an invitation to join the League of Nations, and there were good grounds for believing that

"It is for peace that this hammer works." Hope for international disarmament and cooperation is reflected in this French cartoon, showing Aristide Briand, the French minister of foreign affairs, smashing his guns while the British and German ministers wait their turn.

the hatreds of the past war were now on the wane.

Organization of the League of Nations. The League of Nations was the first ambitious attempt in world history to create an organization designed to prevent war and to promote international conciliation. Its main organs were a Council, an Assembly, and a Secretariat. The Council was the most important body, dominated by the great powers. It dealt with most of the emergencies arising in international affairs. The Assembly served as a platform from which all League members could express their views. It could make specific recommendations to the Council on specific issues; but all important decisions required the unanimous consent of its members, and every nation represented in the Assembly had one vote.

The Secretariat represented the civil service of the League. Numbering about seven hundred, the personnel of the Secretariat constituted the first example in history of an international civil service whose loyalty was pledged to no single nation but to the interests of all nations in common. All treaties made by members of the League had to be registered with the Secretariat; its fifteen departments had charge of the matters of administrative routine arising from the mandates and dealt with questions relating to disarmament, health problems, the protection of racial minorities, and any other problems which the League was considering.

In addition to the Council, the Assembly, and the Secretariat, two other important bodies were derived from the Covenant of the League. The first was the Permanent Court of International Justice, commonly referred to as the World Court. Its main purpose was to "interpret any disputed point in international law and determine when treaty obligations had been violated." It was also competent to give advisory opinions to the Council or Assembly when asked for them. (By 1937 forty-one nations had agreed to place before the World Court most basic international disputes to which they were a party.) The second international body affiliated with the League was the International Labor Organization. Pledged "to secure and maintain fair and humane conditions of labor for men, women, and children," this organization consisted of three divisions: a general conference, a governing body, and the International Labor Office.

The League as a peace agency. The record of the League from 1919 to 1929 was one neither of dismal failure nor of complete triumph. Restrained optimism was the mood of its supporters. Its greatest handicap was the refusal of the United States to become a member. Such threats to peace as disputes between Sweden and Finland, Poland and Germany, and Britain and Turkey were resolved. When a great power defied the League, as in the case of Fascist Italy's quarrel with Greece, the organization proved impotent. Little progress was made in the field of world disarmament. On one occasion, perhaps because of its relative military weakness, Russia proposed complete disarmament to League members. This proposal did not get very far because the British delegates were suspicious of the Russian government's sincerity. When this Russian proposal was made, one of the delegates replied:

If Mr. Litvinov [the Russian member] promises not to be angry I'll narrate a fable. . . . A conference of the beasts once discussed the question of disarmament. The lion spoke first and looking at the eagle suggested the abolition of wings. The eagle turning to the bull asked for the suppression of horns. The bull in his turn regarded the tiger and demanded the elimination of claws. It remained for the bear to speak and he proposed total abolition of every means of attack and defense so that he might take them all into his loving embrace.[8]

Other League activities. While the effectiveness of the League as a peace agency is debatable, certain of its activities deserve high praise. The League supervised the exchange and repatriation of thousands of prisoners of war and saved thousands of refugees from starvation. With its assistance, Austria, Bulgaria, and Hungary obtained badly needed loans, and the League rendered valuable service in administering the region of the Saar Basin and the Free City of Danzig. The League's efforts in the fields of health, humanitarianism, and intellectual activity were especially noteworthy. The League investigated the existence of slavery in certain sections of the world, sought to control the traffic in dangerous drugs, and stood ready to offer assistance when great disasters brought suffering and destruction to any portion of the world's population. It published books and periodicals dealing with national and international problems of all kinds and broadcast important information, particularly in the field of health, from its own radio station.

Naval disarmament. While little progress in the reduction of land armaments was made in the League, more encouraging success was registered outside its jurisdiction in naval reduction. The Washington Conference (1921-1922), called by the United States, reached agreement on the relative naval strength of the major naval powers. The United States, Britain, Japan, France, and Italy not only scrapped a large number of fighting craft but also agreed to a ten-year holiday in the construction of capital ships. Subsequent conferences at Geneva (1927) and London (1930), however, made little progress in limiting smaller naval craft, such as submarines and light cruisers.

Hopeful trends on the diplomatic front. Despite some serious initial crises and problems following World War i, the years from 1925 and 1929 seemed to indicate that a new era of international cooperation had commenced. Especially promising was a treaty to outlaw war, the Kellogg-Briand Pact (1928), pioneered by France and the United States. Within four years it had been signed by sixty-two nations. But while this pact renounced war as an instrument of national policy, it contained no provisions for enforcing the agreement.

Other attempts to improve international relations included further corrections of some of the worst abuses in the World War i treaties. In the field of reparations, a new schedule of payments, known as the Young Plan, was agreed upon in 1930. The total amount to be paid was greatly scaled down. It was also agreed that Allied occupation troops would be evacuated from the Rhineland five years in advance of the time stipulated by the Treaty of Versailles. In addition to these encouraging signs, there was a strong movement for European union at the end of the 1920's. Various congresses were held, and Aristide Briand, French minister of foreign affairs, prepared a comprehensive memorandum for a European Federal Union.

With these promising events in the background the League of Nations celebrated its tenth birthday in 1929. Speaking at Oxford about the first decade of the League, General Jan Smuts of South Africa, a founder of the international organization, declared:

Looked at in its true light, in the light of the age and of the time-honoured ideas and practice of mankind, we are beholding an amazing thing— we are witnessing one of the great miracles of history. . . . The League may be a difficult scheme to work, but the significant thing is that the Great Powers have pledged themselves to work it . . . [they have] bound themselves to what amounts in effect to a consultative parliament of the world. . . . The great choice is made, the great renunciation is over, and mankind has, as it were at one bound and in the short space of ten years, jumped from the old order to the new. . . .[9]

These noble and reassuring sentiments reflected what appeared to be an encouraging trend in international affairs after 1925. But what of the course of events within the major western nations? In particular, had democratic institutions in the 1920's held their own and lived up to the great promise envisaged by leading Allied statesmen during World War i? Lamentably, in the postwar era, the forces of democracy were confronted by dynamic new rivals, ideologies born of the extreme Left (Communism) and extreme Right (Fascism and Nazism) but united in their common denial of democratic values.

DICTATORSHIP OF THE PROLETARIAT IN RUSSIA

Prelude to revolution in Russia. Tsar Nicholas ii and his subjects entered World War i in a buoyant mood of enthusiasm and patriotism. The weaknesses of the Russian economy, and the inefficiency and corruption in government, were hidden for a brief period under a cloak of fervent nationalism. By the middle of 1915, however, the impact of war was demoralizing the nation. Food and fuel were in short supply, war casualties were staggering, and inflation was mounting ominously. Strikes increased among the low-paid factory workers, and the peasants, who wanted land reforms, were restive. Confronted with these danger signals, the tsar showed little leadership.

Perhaps most serious was the fact that Nicholas and his empress were strongly influenced by a small clique of corrupt adventurers, notably the scandalous Rasputin. Sojourning briefly with a monastic sect notorious for its alternation of sexual orgies with spiritual raptures, Rasputin became a sham holy man who believed that "great sins made possible great repentances."[10] Despite his moral lapses, Rasputin gained wide recognition for supposed magical powers. This charlatan obtained tragic influence over the royal family, especially the empress, by claiming that his treatment of her only son protected him from his dread affliction of hemophilia.

In 1915 the tsar left his capital to assume command of the army at the battlefront, leaving the empress to administer the affairs of state. In effect, this allowed Rasputin a free hand in manipulating the empress to his own ends. Generals and ministers were cavalierly dismissed, the work of government departments seriously impaired, and military operations endangered. In December 1916 a group of patriotic Russian nobles, dismayed by Rasputin's malevolent power, assassinated him. The "mad monk" thus passed from the scene, but by this time the Romanov regime was beyond repair.

The revolution begins. On March 3, 1917, a strike occurred in a factory in Petrograd. Within a week nearly all the workers in the city were idle, and street fighting broke out. On March 11 the tsar dismissed the Duma and ordered the strikers to return to work. These orders precipitated the revolution. The Duma refused to disband, the strikers held mass meetings in defiance of the government, and the army openly sided with the workers. A few days later a provisional government headed by the moderate liberal, Prince Lvov, was named by the Duma, and the following day the tsar abdicated. There is little evidence to indicate that there was a

calculated conspiracy behind the overthrow, which has been termed "one of the most leaderless, spontaneous, anonymous revolutions of all times."[11] Thus far the revolution had been, on the whole, peaceful.

Many historians have analyzed the complex background and causes of the revolution. Undoubtedly Rasputin was an important factor, but his role has generally been overemphasized; he was a symptom, not a cause. For a century or more the whole tsarist regime had become an anachronism, completely unable and unwilling to reform itself to meet the needs of its people. As an English historian has noted: "The complex revolutionary situation of 1917 was the accumulated deposit of Russian history, detonated by the explosion of war."[12]

Dominated by liberal middle-class representatives, the Duma hoped to achieve a political but not an economic revolution. Meanwhile the Marxian socialists in Petrograd had formed a soviet (council) of workers and soldiers' deputies to provide them the representation they lacked in the Duma. Determined that a thoroughgoing change should take place in accordance with Marxist teachings, the radical soviet cooperated with the provisional government for a few months.

In July, Lvov resigned and was succeeded by Aleksandr Kerenski, who was more progressive than his predecessor but not radical enough for the Bolsheviks. While Kerenski's government marked time, the Marxist soviet in Petrograd extended its organization all over the country by setting up local soviets. The new provisional government made a serious mistake when it decided to prosecute the war and honor its commitments to the Allies. Such a policy was increasingly unpopular with the masses, who were completely disillusioned by the heavy sacrifices demanded by the war effort.

Meanwhile Lenin, the exiled Marxist, who had been living in Switzerland, was anxious to return to Russia and transform the revolution according to his Bolshevik ideas. Hoping that widespread strife and chaos would cause Russia to withdraw from the war, Berlin helped Lenin return to Petrograd. A tumultuous reception by thousands of peasants, workers, and soldiers took place as Lenin's train rolled into the station. Lenin addressed the crowd with this message:

The people need peace; the people need bread; the people need land. And they give you—war, hunger, no bread; they leave the landlords on the land. . . . We must fight for social revolution, fight to the end, till the complete victory of the proletariat. Long live the worldwide Socialist revolution.[13]

Lenin's coup d'état. After many behind-the-scenes maneuvers, the soviets seized control of the government in November 1917, and drove Kerenski and his moderate provisional government into exile. This liberal and largely middle-class regime had lacked dynamism and forcefulness and could not cope with the complete ruthlessness of Bolshevik tactics. Lenin's coup d'état was an amazing feat. With audacity, careful organization, and astute propaganda, he had placed a party with a membership estimated at 30,000 in control of a nation of more than 170,000,000 people.

Lenin did not become a national hero overnight, however. In the free elections held to form a constituent assembly to frame a constitution, he and his followers were

A leader who always stressed unity with the masses, Lenin addresses a group of Bolsheviks in this Russian painting by Serov.

chagrined to receive just under 25 percent of the votes. When the assembly, which met in January 1918, refused to become a rubber stamp of the Bolsheviks, it was dissolved by the bayonets of Lenin's troops. It was Russia's last free parliament. With the dissolution of the constituent assembly, all vestiges of bourgeois democracy in Russia were removed. Moreover, this decisive step sealed the fate of the Mensheviks. Having ended the handicap of a democratic opposition, Lenin next freed his regime from the war problem by the harsh Treaty of Brest Litovsk (1918) with Germany, although with great sacrifice of Russian territory.

The Bolshevik fight for survival. The worst was yet to come. A powerful group of counterrevolutionaries termed White Russians began to make war on the Bolsheviks. At the same time the Allied powers sent several expeditionary armies to Russia to support the anti-Leninist forces. The Allies were fearful that the Bolsheviks were in a conspiracy with the Germans because of the Treaty of Brest Litovsk; they also hoped the White Russians might renew hostilities against Germany. In the fall of 1918 the Bolshevik regime was in a perilous condition, opposed by Russia's former allies and challenged by internal foes.

To counteract this ominous emergency, a ghastly reign of terror was begun within Russia as the Red Army and the Cheka (the secret police) destroyed all enemies of the revolution as well as those who were only lukewarm in their support of the revolution. The royal family, under arrest since the outbreak of the revolution, was made to pay for all the years of cruel and inept Romanov rule. In July 1918 they were herded into a cellar and shot. By 1920 all White Russian resistance had been crushed, the foreign armies had been evacuated, and about one million White Russian anti-Communist refugees were scattered over the earth.

After the surrender of the Central Powers in November 1918, Allied intervention in Russia ceased, and the Bolsheviks were able to concentrate their energies against the White Russians. Other factors contributing to the Bolshevik victory were the fanatical, do-or-die spirit of Lenin and his followers, the resentment against foreign intervention, and the lack of appeal of the White Russian movement, which sponsored no program of land and social reform.

Lenin's contribution to Marxist thought. As we have previously noted (see p. 581) Nikolai Lenin had made an important contribution to Marxist theory that set the pattern by which socialism in Russia would be guided. Opposing all democratic parliamentary procedures, such as an officially recognized opposition party, he believed that the new order should be established by a revolutionary "dictatorship of the proletariat" under Bolshevik leadership. The opposition group, the Mensheviks, charged that Lenin was confusing the dictatorship *of* the proletariat with the dictatorship *over* the proletariat, while they in turn were accused of having capitulated to gradualism by adopting a revisionist program. Both groups agreed, though, that the socialist revolution could be consummated in Russia only as part of a general uprising of the proletariat throughout Europe. As we have seen, the Bolshevik-Menshevik feud continued until the Revolution of 1917.

As a Marxist, Lenin accepted the two-revolutions sequence—that is, that the proletarian-socialist revolution must be preceded by a bourgeois-democratic revolution. He interpreted the toppling of the tsarist regime in March 1917 and its replacement by a provisional government of moderates and liberals as the first democratic revolution. His coup d'état in November 1917 engineered the second or proletarian-socialist revolution. Lenin justified the dissolving of the constituent assembly on the grounds that a higher form of the democratic principle had now been achieved which rendered a constituent assembly superfluous: the proletarian-socialist revolution had vested all power in the Russian republic in the people themselves, as expressed in their revolutionary committees or soviets.

The state: theory and practice. Many orthodox Marxists believed that once the dictatorship of the proletariat had liquidated the bourgeoisie, the way would be open for the progressive disappearance of the state and the abolition of the standing army and the bureaucracy, the two most characteristic institutions of the centralized bourgeois state. While Lenin thought that the state would eventually wither away, at the same time he believed that during the dictatorship of the proletariat the latter's power must be wielded by an "iron party" (the Bolsheviks). Ironically enough, the events which transpired between his coup d'état in 1917 and his death seven years later served not to weaken but to strengthen the role of the state in Russia.

In this period occurred three major developments relating to the Communist party. (The Bolsheviks were renamed Communists in 1918.) First, all other parties were eliminated. Second, the function of the Communist party was modified. No longer charged with the overthrow of existing institutions, the party now became the controlling element within the new governmental machinery of the state; the concentration of authority and power in the party was justified as "democratic centralism." Third, within the party itself authority was consolidated in the hands of a small elite group, the Politburo, which was composed of five members with Lenin as the chairman. The second major organ of the party was the Secretariat for the Central Committee.

The state was known as the Russian Socialist Federated Soviet Republic (R.S.F.S.R.). As the power of this government grew and the anti-Bolshevik forces were repelled, the jurisdiction of the R.S.F.S.R. expanded. In 1922 the Union of Soviet Socialist Republics (U.S.S.R.) was established, consisting of four constituent socialist republics: the original R.S.F.S.R., the Ukraine, White Russia, and Transcaucasia.

The constitution, adopted in 1924, established a federal system of government based on a succession of soviets which were set up in the villages, factories, and cities and in larger regions. This pyramid of soviets in each constituent republic culminated in the All-Union Congress of Soviets, which was at the apex of the federal government. But while it appeared that the congress exercised sovereign power, this body was actually governed by the Communist party, which in turn was controlled by the Politburo. So great did the authority of the Communist party become over the formation and administration of policy that before Lenin's death in 1924 it could be said without exaggeration that party and state were one. Consequently, whoever controlled the former must be master of the latter as well.

The period of war communism. One of Lenin's central beliefs was equalitarianism. He championed the program of "from each according to his ability; to each according to his needs" and believed in the principle of "maximum income," by which no state employee would receive a salary higher than a qualified worker. Following both Marx and Engels, Lenin subscribed to the ultimate goal of large-scale collective farming and the elimination of private ownership of land.

The period from the consolidation of the Bolshevik Revolution in 1918 until 1921 is known as the period of war communism, when the Bolsheviks sought to apply undiluted Marxist principles to the Soviet economy. Banks, railroads, and shipping were nationalized; the money economy was restricted; and private property was abolished.

Strong opposition to this program soon developed. The peasants wanted cash payments for their products and resented having to surrender their surplus grain to the government. Many laborers grumbled at being conscripted to work in the factories, and former business managers showed little enthusiasm for administering enterprises for the benefit of the state. This period was also a time of civil war, when the White Russians, aided by the Allies, were attempting the overthrow of the Communist regime.

,The early months of 1920 brought the most dangerous crisis yet faced by the government. The years of civil strife had left Russia in a state of confusion and disruption. Total industrial production had been reduced to 13 percent of what it had been in 1913. Added to the misery caused by wartime dislocations and the shortages caused by inept or wasteful management in the recently nationalized industries was the suffering that followed the crop failures of 1920. Famine marched over the land, bringing more than twenty million people face to face with starvation.

In the meantime serious controversy developed between Poland and Russia over their boundaries. War followed in 1920, and after defeating Russia, Poland annexed a large slice of its territory, thereby sowing the seeds of later conflict. During these turbulent years other areas of Russia were chopped off to form Finland, Estonia, Latvia, and Lithuania. While the collapse of the first Marxist state seemed imminent, Lenin remained indomitable.

The NEP. Confronted with the collapse of the nation, Lenin beat a strategic retreat in spite of strenuous opposition from his colleagues. He felt that the new regime had run into difficulties because it had been too eager to change everything at once. A return to certain practices of the capitalistic system was recommended, and the New Economic Policy, or NEP, was inaugurated.

The retreat from war communism operated from 1921 to 1928. The peasants were freed from the onerous wholesale levies of grain; after paying a fixed tax, they were allowed to sell their surplus produce in open market. Factories employing less than twenty men were returned to private management, and a graduated wage scale was granted to the workers in the state industries. Commerce was stimulated by permitting private retail trading. Although simon-pure Communists criticized the wealthy peasants or *kulaks* who benefited from the new order of things and dubbed the private businessmen "Nepmen," such compromise proved highly beneficial and the economy revived. The NEP was designed as only a temporary strategic retreat from the former outright socialist system; the state continued to be responsible for banking, transportation, heavy industry, and public utilities.

The NEP was Lenin's last outstanding achievement. In spite of broken health, Lenin worked unceasingly until his death in January 1924. His tomb in Moscow's Red Square is a Mecca for thousands of followers who come to pay homage to the creator of the first Marxist state in history.

Stalin vs. Trotsky: the politician and the intellectual. Upon the death of the one man in the party who had possessed unchallenged authority and whose decrees were binding, a struggle for power broke out, and conflicts of policy and personality appeared. Two rivals who took different sides on most issues were Trotsky and Stalin.

Leon Trotsky (1879-1940), whose real name was Bronstein, had turned to Marxism in his early youth and, like Lenin, had known exile. During the revolution Trotsky had come to the forefront. He was a magnificent orator; and by his personal magnetism and his demonic energy, he had led the Red Army to victory. During his hectic career Trotsky wrote an amazing number of brilliant and provocative articles and books. A theorist and scholar, this intellectual, professor-like leader had personal defects of arrogance and egotism which contrasted with the peasant shrewdness and cunning of his less colorful but more calculating rival.

Stalin, born Joseph Dzugashvili in 1879 in the Georgian region of Transcaucasia, was the son of a poor shoemaker. Admitted to a seminary to be trained for the priesthood, young Stalin was later expelled for radical opinions. Before the revolution he engaged in much activity in the underground and was sent into exile four times. In 1922 *Pravda* carried a brief announcement that the Central Committee had confirmed Stalin as general secretary of the Secretariat—a decision that was to have momentous consequences after Lenin's death.

Trotsky, like Lenin, believed that the U.S.S.R. could not maintain itself indefinitely as a socialist island in a capitalist ocean and that it was therefore the duty of the Russian Communists to foster revolution elsewhere. Stalin, less the theorist than the political realist, viewed Trotsky's ideas of world revolution as premature. He noted that Marxism had made little headway outside of Russia, despite the existence of what from the Marxist standpoint were the most advantageous circumstances for revolution. The impoverished and war-disillusioned workers of Germany had not turned against the bourgeoisie, while in Italy socialist opposition had been crushed by Mussolini. Stalin advocated a new policy, which was to become known as "building up socialism in a single state."

In the struggle that ensued, Trotsky had the initial advantage of being one of the chief architects of the revolution and (second to Lenin) the best known Bolshevik in the Soviet Union. With his outstanding record and his mastery of ideological analysis, Trotsky not unnaturally expected to assume Lenin's mantle of leadership. But he reckoned without the political astuteness of Stalin, who had obtained a key administrative post in the party apparatus. Quietly and systematically, Stalin proceeded to shunt his rival aside. He placed his supporters in important posts in the government, assumed the powerful chairmanship of the Politburo, and by 1927 had brought about the expulsion of Trotsky and his followers from the party. Trotsky was exiled and led a hare-and-hounds existence until 1940, when he was struck down by the ax of an assassin in Mexico, probably on Stalin's orders.

With a well-organized governmental structure and an obedient bureaucracy and with the Trotskyites either exiled or rendered powerless, Stalin was ready by 1928 to put a daring new program into operation. The NEP was to be scrapped and replaced by a Five-Year Plan, which called for a highly ambitious program of heavy industrialization and the collectivization of agriculture. In spite of breakdowns and failures, the first Five-Year Plan achieved amazing results (see Chapter 30), mainly because of the heroic sacrifices of the common people. Russia, an inert sleeping giant before 1914, now became industrialized at an unbelievable speed, far surpassing Germany's pace of industrialization in the nineteenth century and Japan's early in the twentieth.

Changes in Soviet society. While the Russian economy was being transformed, the social life of the people underwent equally drastic changes. From the beginning of the revolution, the government attempted to weaken the importance of the family. A divorce required no court procedure; and to make women completely free of the responsibilities of childbearing, abortion was made legal. The policy of "emancipating" women had the practical objective of increasing the labor market. Girls were encouraged to secure an education and pursue a career in the factory or the office. Communal nurseries were set up for the care of small children; and efforts were made to shift the center of the people's social life from the home to educational and recreational groups, the soviet clubs.

Most observers in the 1920's credited the regime with abandoning the tsarist policy of persecuting national minorities in favor of a policy of tolerance toward the more than two hundred minority groups in the Soviet Union. Another feature of the regime that received praise was the extension of medical services. Campaigns were carried out against typhus, cholera, and malaria; the number of doctors was increased as rapidly as facilities and training would permit; and death and infant mortality rates steadily decreased.

In addition to the political and economic measures which weakened Russian religious institutions, the Bolsheviks pursued a propaganda campaign to stifle religious fervor. This Soviet antireligious poster portrays a Russian Orthodox priest as a spider-like monster who draws the people into his web.

Coming under heavy fire in the West, however, were the Communist policies toward education and religion. Although education was made available to millions of children, the primary purpose of the school system was to indoctrinate the pupils with Communist precepts and values. There was also widespread religious persecution. Religious leaders were sentenced to concentration camps. Members of the party were forbidden to attend divine services. The Church was shorn of its powers over education, religious teaching was prohibited except in the home, and antireligious instruction was stressed in the schools.

Foreign relations in the 1920's. During the decade and a half following the Russian Revolution, the Soviet Union was not considered a member in good standing in the family of nations. From the beginning of the revolution, relations between the western democracies and the new Soviet regime had been cool. The Communists resented the intervention of Allied troops during the civil war, which they interpreted as a calculated capitalistic attempt to crush the Marxist revolution. For their part, the Allies were aroused over the separate peace Lenin made with Germany, the seizure of foreign property in Russia, and the repudiation of all foreign debts.

Probably the greatest barrier to friendship (or at least mutual tolerance) between the West and Soviet Russia was the Third Communist International, or Comintern, organized in 1919 and dedicated to the overthrow of capitalism the world over. Specific aims of the organization were to disseminate Communist propaganda, to establish Communist parties in all the important nations of the world, and to secure control of labor unions and other working-class groups wherever possible. In the 1920's the Comintern encouraged the organization of Communist parties by radicals who had broken off from moderate socialist groups all over the world. Communists of all countries became members of the Comintern, meeting in congresses held in Moscow and setting up committees to coordinate their activities. Thus the Communist party became basically different from all national political groups;

Under Stalin, the school became the mouthpiece of the new regime, as students were taught to conform, to love their country, and to believe in the infallibility of their leaders. These Russian school-children were photographed under a poster of Stalin hugging a Siberian girl.

all Communists owed their allegiance to an international organization rather than to the nations in which they resided.

Another basic aim of the Comintern was to undermine colonialism. As we have seen earlier (see p. 631), Lenin's anti-imperialist beliefs were given wide publicity. Not so well known, however, was his idea that communism could conquer Europe and America by gaining control of Asia. He is reported to have once stated that London and New York could be conquered on the Yangtze.

RISE OF FASCISM IN ITALY

Problems in postwar Italy. During World War I the Italian armies had been badly mauled by their enemies, and Italy emerged from the peace conference a victor with only modest gains. The First World War aggravated the weaknesses of the Italian economy.

The lira fell to a third of its prewar value, unemployment rose, and severe food shortages developed. People refused to pay their rent, strikes broke out in industrial centers, and workers seized factories. Italy's economic plight invited agitation by extremists from both Right and Left.

Mussolini and the birth of Fascism. Within four years following the armistice in Italy, five incompetent premiers came and went. The situation seemed propitious for the appearance of a strong leader on the political stage. When he appeared, he was the jutting-jawed son of a blacksmith named Mussolini, and he bore the Christian name of Benito in honor of the Mexican revolutionary hero Benito Juárez.

Born in northern Italy, Benito Mussolini (1883-1945) had grown up in left-wing circles. Although he became editor of the influential Italian socialist newspaper *Avanti (Forward)* in 1912, he was far from consistent as regards his belief in socialism and its doctrinal opposition to "capitalist" wars. When a majority in the Italian Socialist party called for neutrality in World War I, Mussolini urged intervention. The *Avanti* was taken from his control and Mussolini was expelled. Undaunted, he founded his own paper *Il Popolo d'Italia (The People of Italy)*, in which he continued to advocate Italian intervention in the war on the side of the Allies. As part of his campaign for Italian participation in the war, Mussolini organized formerly leftist youths into bands called *fasci*, a name derived from the Latin *fasces*, the bundle of rods bound about an ax which was the symbol of authority in ancient Rome. When Italy entered the war, Mussolini volunteered for the army, saw active service at the front, and was wounded. After his return to civilian life, he reorganized the *fasci* into the *fasci di combattimento* ("fighting groups") to attract war veterans. The ultimate purpose of these groups was to capture the control of the national government.

The march on Rome. In the elections of 1919 the socialists capitalized on mass unemployment and hardship to emerge as the strongest party. Although the Fascists failed to elect a single candidate to the Chamber of Deputies, they succeeded in obtaining both approval and financial aid from industrial and landowning groups fearful of the triumph of Marxist socialism in Italy. Mussolini's black-shirted toughs broke up strikes and workers' demonstrations and, by beatings and overdoses of castor oil, "persuaded" political opponents of the error of their views. The central government remained virtually impotent during these outbreaks of violence.

Elections held in May 1921 resulted in a plurality for the liberal and democratic parties. A few Communists were elected to the Chamber of Deputies, and only thirty-five Fascists, among them Mussolini. But their leader had no intention of allowing the country to achieve economic recovery and political stability by following a liberal-democratic course. In November Mussolini established the National Fascist party.

Events in 1922 conspired to favor Mussolini's bid for power. The liberal-democratic government of the day was ineffective, and the socialists were divided among themselves, while the ranks of the Fascists had been strengthened by the enrollment of thousands of disaffected bourgeoisie, cynical and opportunistic intellectuals, and depression-weary workers. The general strike called in August by the trade unions in order to arouse the country to the menace of Fascism was smashed. On October 24 a huge crowd attending a Fascist rally at Naples shouted "On to Rome!" When some fifty thousand Fascist militiamen swarmed into the capital, King Victor Emmanuel III invited Mussolini to form a new government.

Mussolini organizes the Fascist state. Mussolini's first act as prime minister was the passage in 1923 of an enabling law which gave him dictatorial powers. By this means Mussolini acquired a temporary "legal" right to govern without democratic procedure. He quickly used his newly acquired power to dissolve all other political parties and thus completely eliminate opposition to his regime. The Fascist party was now in a position to recast the entire governmental apparatus.

The Fascist state was ruled by an elite in the party, which ruthlessly crushed all free expression and banished critics of the regime to penal settlements on islands off the southern Italian coast. Censorship of the press was established, and a tribunal for defense of the state was set up to punish any individuals not conforming to Fascist practices. Thus Fascist ideology was a continuation of the antirational, elitist cult of the leader or "great men" school prominent before 1914 and exemplified by such thinkers as Nietzsche. Fascism glorified force, accepting the tenets of social Darwinism. It was above all antidemocratic.

Parliamentary institutions of the pre-Fascist era were not destroyed overnight, however. The Senate continued to exist, even though completely dominated by Fascists; the Chamber of Deputies withered on the vine until the 1930's, when it was replaced by the Chamber of Fasces and Corporations. Meanwhile, all real power in the new state had been vested in the Fascist Grand Council, headed by Mussolini. The members of the council occupied the government's ministerial posts; in fact, at one time Mussolini himself held no less than eight offices. During 1925 and 1926 the Italian cities

Peter Blume's "The Eternal City" represents a young American artist's impressions of Italy ten years after Mussolini's march on Rome. A terrifying but flimsy jack-in-the-box of a Mussolini dominates a city of apathetic people living among the ruins of the past. But out of this nightmare emerges hope for the future; in the background, people climb out of the darkness into the sunlit forum, where others are already attempting to drag their Fascist masters from their mounts.

were deprived of self-government. With all units of local and provincial government welded into a unified structure dominated from Rome, the Fascist administrative system constituted the ultracentralization of government.

In 1929 Mussolini negotiated the Lateran Treaty with representatives of the Roman Catholic Church. By the terms of this agreement, Roman Catholicism was recognized as the state religion in Italy; and Vatican City, a new state of 108 acres located in Rome itself, was declared fully sovereign and independent. In addition, the Vatican was promised sums amounting to $91 million. Thus the long-standing controversy concerning the relationship of Church and state in Italy was settled amicably.

The corporate Fascist state. There is a marked difference in economic theory between Communist and Fascist states. The Communists are determined to destroy private capital and to liquidate the managerial-capitalist class. The Fascist system, some-times defined as state capitalism, aims to abolish the class war through cooperation between capital and labor, by the compulsion of the state if need be. In Communist theory, labor is the state itself; in Fascism, labor and capital are both instruments of the state.

Mussolini based his ideas of economics on the views of the syndicalists (see p. 683), who believed that industrial unions should be the cells of society and that a confederation of these unions, or syndicates, should constitute the governing body of the state. Syndicalism was adapted to the objectives of Fascism, creating what is called the corporate state. Economically, Italy was divided into thirteen syndicates or corporations: six were formed from the ranks of labor, an equal number represented capital or management, and a thirteenth syndicate was established for the professions. Under the control of the government these bodies were to deal with labor disputes, guarantee adequate wage scales, control prices, and supervise working conditions. Strikes by workers and lockouts by employers were prohibited.

The corporate state also included the concept of economic functionalism—that is, the representation of all major national economic segments in the political process. In 1928, for example, a law set the membership of the Chamber of Deputies at four hundred. Eight hundred candidates were to be named by worker-employer groups and two hundred by various charitable and cultural organizations. From this master list the Grand Council then selected four hundred deputies. Mussolini liked to claim that the corporate state, embodying in theory a classless economic system together with economic functionalism, was one of Fascism's greatest contributions to political theory.

Economic goals of Fascist Italy. Some of the main economic goals of Fascism were to make Italy more self-sufficient, especially in the matter of food; to increase the power resources of the nation; and to expand foreign trade. A campaign called "the battle of the wheat" increased the home yield of this grain 70 percent. Extensive marshland was reclaimed and hydroelectric power resources increased. To some extent the intention to increase Italy's natural resources was commendable, but the drive was carried on to an extreme and uneconomic degree. Mussolini's desire to attain national self-sufficiency, a policy known in international economics as autarky, was primarily motivated not by the exigencies of economics but rather by those of war. In achieving this goal, much was accomplished, though often at a ruinous cost. Many projects were launched to provide for a home supply of materials which could be obtained much more cheaply from other nations.

Fascism's glorification of the state and war. The concept of the "inevitability" of war, added to the exaltation of the state and of its "destiny," created a supernationalism whose adherents tended to interpret the right of self-determination in terms of the expansion of the Fascist state at the expense of other nations. A foretaste of Mussolini's contempt for peace and his defiance of the League of Nations soon became apparent when he humiliated Greece in 1923 by the bombardment of Corfu. Mussolini warned the world that Italy intended to expand or explode, and his encouragement of a high birth rate in conjunction with meager territorial and natural resources pointed in only one direction—imperialism.

Fascism has been defined as "the cult of state worship." In the Italian totalitarian state the individual had no significance except as a member of the state. The Fascists were taught "to believe, to obey, and to fight" (*credere, obbedire, combattere*). Fascist ideology governed the educational system. The first sentence pronounced by children at school was "Let us salute the flag in the Roman fashion; hail to Italy; hail to Mussolini." Textbooks emphasized the glorious past of the ancient Romans, the limitations imposed upon the present inhabitants by geography and western "plutocratic" nations, and the imperial destiny that awaited Italy's future development.

Mussolini provided the trappings of greatness while he talked of acquiring the substance. The ruins of imperial Rome were revered at the same time that new, ostentatious monuments, buildings, and official sculptures were erected. All public functions and displays of the state were clothed in propaganda, from the dedication of farm land salvaged from ancient swamps to the regime's vulgar displays of military might and its gigantic sports rallies.

As in the case of other dictatorial regimes, the Fascist social program had some commendable features, such as its slum clearance, its offensive against illiteracy, its campaign against malaria, and its system of child welfare clinics. To the casual observer the country seemed rejuvenated. For example, the notoriously erratic Italian trains now ran on time. But any positive achievements were more than outweighed by such nefarious results as the deification of war, excessive armaments budgets, and the fraudulent claim of the corporate state to protect the workers while it actually benefited the large landowners and industrialists. By 1930 Italy had the lowest standard of real wages in western Europe. The basic weakness and sham of Fascism, however, would not be exposed for another decade.

WEIMAR DEMOCRACY:
THE REPUBLIC THAT FAILED

Revolution in Germany. Near the close of World War I, Woodrow Wilson had made it clear that the Allies would not enter into peace negotiations with the imperial government of Hohenzollerns. By November 1918, sick of the war and its privations, the German people were ready to do anything to bring the conflict to an end. The revolution that caused the kaiser to pack his bags and escape to Holland began in the navy. News of the revolt flashed like lightning through Germany, and the authority of the old government crumbled. On the same day that the chancellor turned over his authority to Friedrich Ebert—the leader of the majority socialist party, the Social Democrats—the republic was officially proclaimed.

The collapse of the imperial government provoked vigorous disagreement over the type of administration that was to replace it. The Communists wanted a complete social revolution as well as a political revolution, while Ebert's Social Democrats favored a democratic system in which the rights of private property would be safeguarded. In December 1918 and January 1919 the moderates and the radicals clashed violently; the Communists in Berlin were scattered and their leaders murdered. In a national election held to select a constitutional convention, the parties stressing moderation were triumphant, with the Social Democrats securing the most votes. The German revolution was democratic and bourgeois.

Problems of the Weimar Republic. The new constitution was adopted in midsummer of 1919 at Weimar, famous as the residence of Germany's greatest poet, Goethe. It provided for a president, a chancellor who was responsible to the Reichstag, and national referendums. The rights of labor were guaranteed, personal liberties were safeguarded, and compulsory education was planned for everyone up to the age of eighteen.

Parliamentary government in the Weimar Republic exhibited certain basic weaknesses, however. The principle of proportional rep-

During the years of the Weimar Republic inflation destroyed the financial foundations of the German middle class, and continued economic depression gave added impetus to Hitler's rise in popularity. If formerly prosperous people were forced to stand in line for bread, they were also prone to listen to Hitler's promise of a higher standard of living.

resentation was carried so far that innumerable separate parties arose, and only the formation of coalitions enabled the government to function. Frequently unable to muster sufficient votes among a multiplicity of parties, the government was tempted to employ a constitutional provision that enabled the president to enact measures by decree in the event of disorder. By weakening the legislative process, such actions were bound to help discredit the parliamentary government in Germany.

In spite of difficulties and the opposition of Communists and monarchists, the Weimar Republic restored political stability to Germany and surmounted serious financial problems. (The reparation problem was discussed on p. 661.) In 1923, when French and Belgian troops occupied the Ruhr, the wild inflation of the mark wiped out savings, especially of the middle class, and political moderates gradually lost their influence to ultranationalists and reactionaries. But after the French withdrew and the Dawes Plan enabled Germany to meet its schedule of reparation payments and to obtain large loans from abroad, the German economy took a turn for the better, and from 1925 to 1929 Germany enjoyed economic prosperity. Large public works projects were undertaken, industry was expanded, and Germany became the second largest industrial nation in the world. But disturbing forces were at work.

Factors favoring the growth of dictatorship. Germany in the late 1920's was a compound of numerous ingredients, many of which had been in existence for at least a century. With Prussia as their model, such men as Hegel and Treitschke had exalted the state at the expense of the individual; and the government of the kaisers had fostered despotism. Lack of experience in democratic government made the success of the Weimar Republic doubtful from the start. There were too many political parties; the army, which had never reconciled itself to the abolition of the empire, was not brought under effective civilian control; and the republic was too complacent and did not take the drastic measures essential to destroy the enemies of democracy. In short, "German democracy was utterly fair, legalistic, but not militant."[14]

Other difficulties threatening the new government stemmed from the resentments and frustrations engendered among the people by defeat in war. The powerful Prussian militaristic clique fanned the flames of discontent by fostering the legend that the German army had not been defeated on the field of battle but had been stabbed in the back by pacifist liberals and "decadent" democrats on the home front. The legend of the betrayal of the Fatherland was to be increasingly the refrain of those who came to favor Nazi militarism. The resurgence of strong feelings of nationalism was evidenced by the election to the presidency in 1925 of Field Marshal von Hindenburg, a stalwart Junker and hero of World War I.

The Treaty of Versailles embittered many Germans, and its use by the French to justify the invasion of the Ruhr sowed further seeds of hate. The so-called war guilt clause of the treaty, by which the Germans were forced to proclaim sole responsibilty for starting the war—which most impartial historians have been unable to assign to any single nation—was particularly rankling.

The ultranationalists made effective appeals to the industrialists and landowners, who were convinced that the republic could not effectively discourage the internal threat of communism. As a result of the war and the postwar inflation, professional people, white-collar workers, and skilled tradesmen feared the prospect of being dragged down to the level of the masses. Especially after the debacle of inflation, a deep sense of despair and futility fell upon the people. Blaming their elders for the catastrophe of 1918 and the humiliations that followed, German youth repudiated the past and sought a cause to redeem the Fatherland. They were vulnerable to the blandishments of any spellbinding would-be dictator.

Hitler's rise to prominence. The creator and high priest of German fascism was Adolf Hitler (1889-1945), the son of a minor customs official in Austria. An orphan at the age of seventeen, Hitler went to Vienna in 1908 hoping to become an architect or artist. While in the Austrian capital, he read pamphlets written by racists and proto-Fascists who championed such ideas as the leader concept and social Darwinism and became interested in Marxist socialism and Pan-Germanism. He experienced dire poverty in Vienna and a few years later moved to Munich, where he earned a scanty living by selling drawings.

When war broke out, Hitler joined a German regiment and was sent to France. The armistice of 1918 found him in a hospital. He said later that news of Germany's defeat caused him to turn his face to the wall and weep bitterly. Following his return from the war front, Hitler was hired by the authorities in Munich as a special agent to investigate Communist and other extremist movements. In the line of duty he was asked to check on a small organization called the German Worker's party. Hitler joined this group, whose fervently nationalistic doctrine was at once antidemocratic, anticapitalist, anti-Communist and anti-Semitic.

Before long the movement took the name

"National Socialist German Workers' party," and the words "National Socialist" *(Nationalsozialistische)* became abbreviated to "Nazi." In 1920 the party obtained a newspaper as a mouthpiece; soon thereafter the first of the paramilitary organizations, Storm Troops, or SA, was organized. Adopted as the emblem of the party was the swastika set against a red background signifying the community of German blood.

Hitler was now becoming better known. His remarkable oratorical gifts began to attract large crowds in Munich. With a kind of mystical exaltation, this charismatic leader had the uncanny ability to arouse and move mass audiences with his bombastic, passionate oratory. Likened to a "human phonograph," he has been termed the "greatest demagogue in history." Sometimes he would hire a dozen beer halls and dash from one to the other in an automobile, delivering fiery harangues at each. His initial political program called for land reform, the nationalization of trusts, abolition of all unearned incomes, and—in the field of foreign relations—a greater Germany to include all German-speaking peoples in Europe, the abrogation of the Versailles Treaty, and the restitution of Germany's prewar colonies. In 1923 Hitler staged his *Putsch*, or revolt, in Munich; coming prematurely, it failed, and he was sent to prison.

Mein Kampf. Before his release from prison in 1925, Hitler began to write *Mein Kampf (My Battle)*, at once an autobiography and a long-winded exposition of Nazi philosophy and objectives. In this work Hitler contends that history is fashioned by great races, of which the Aryan is the finest; that the noblest Aryans are the German people, who are destined to rule the world; that the Jews are the archcriminals of all time; that democracy is decadent and communism criminal; that foreign expansion into the Russian Ukraine and the destruction of Germany's prime enemy France are rightful courses for the German people; and that war and force are the proper instruments of the "strong." Again and again his sentences drip with acid as he fulminates against the Jews, Russia, and France. With his irrational creed and his ritualistic gestures, badges,

and uniforms, Hitler would one day surpass his predecessor Mussolini in Italy by becoming *Führer* (leader) of a new Germany based on despotism and terror.

DISILLUSIONMENT IN THE DEMOCRACIES

Democracy on the defensive. "In this autumn of 1919, in which I write, we are at the dead season of our fortunes. The reaction from the exertions, the fears, and the sufferings of the past five years is at its height. Our power of feeling or caring beyond the immediate questions of our own material well-being is temporarily eclipsed. The greatest events outside our own direct experience and the most dreadful anticipations cannot move us. . . . We have been moved already beyond endurance, and need rest."[15] Thus wrote the famed English economist John Maynard Keynes; his mood of apathy, disillusionment, and despair was shared by many people in the West.

The postwar period witnessed an inevitable reaction against wartime controls. In the English-speaking democracies, which were the chief bastions of laissez-faire economics, governmental controls were thrown off with all possible speed. The slogan "back to normalcy" in the United Stated indicated a desire to return to prewar economic habits and creeds. And halted throughout most of the democratic-capitalist world were the strong prewar movements to advance social welfare legislation and to regulate traditional laissez-faire economics. An unhealthy inertia resulted in the suspension of badly needed socioeconomic reforms.

The national mood and psychology prevailing in the democracies, whether long-established or newly created, differed basically from the mood and psychology in the rising dictatorships. The democracies drifted into listlessness and futility, while the totalitarian states exhibited resolution, dynamism, and purpose, even though of a ruthless variety. Hence the history of nations such as Britain and France was not so colorful and fascinating as that of the new dicator-

The coal mining regions of South Wales suffered severely during Britain's economic decline in the 1920's. Hampered by poor organization, old machinery, and inefficient methods, the coal industry was hard pressed to give either employment or compensation to the protesting miners.

ships. The attributes of democracy—tolerance, government by consensus, and protracted action—often seem rather unexciting. Furthermore, during the postwar period the democracies had no burning sense of national injustice as did Germany and, to some extent, Italy. After their herculean efforts for victory, they suffered a kind of national weariness. Because victory had not solved deep-seated problems, there was a feeling of disillusionment in western Europe. The inability of the democracies to measure up to the needs of the time gave the 1920's its characteristic mood and quality.

Unstable coalition governments in France. More than one million Frenchmen had been killed and some 13,000 square miles of French territory laid waste in the holocaust of World War I. Years later the nation would still feel the heavy loss of manpower and the economic devastation of a war that had been fought largely on French soil. While a commendable record was achieved in foreign affairs, especially the rapprochement with Germany, in internal affairs the country was plagued with inflation endangering the franc

and a spurious prosperity. In addition, parliamentary government was hindered by a multiparty system and by the brief tenure of unstable ministries. In sum, the story of the Third French Republic in the 1920's is a mixed plot of progress and setbacks, of successes and failures. Fundamentally, a national spirit and a sense of purpose were lacking. The war had sapped the vigor of the French nation, and the unhealthiness and lack of dynamism characteristic of the postwar mood were evident.

Evolutionary socialism comes to Britain. The 1920's were not a tranquil period for Britain. During these dismal years unemployment and bitter labor disputes disrupted the nation. In 1924 Ramsay MacDonald became Britain's first Labourite prime minister. The goal of the Labour party was to introduce socialism slowly and within a democratic framework. During four years of power the Labour government registered some successes in foreign affairs but at home generated little dynamism in solving Britain's critical economic problems. Following MacDonald's defeat at the polls in October 1924,

Britain was for the next five years led by a Conservative government under Stanley Baldwin, who was even less successful than his predecessor in providing vigorous leadership. Thus the decade following victory in 1918 saw an absence of forward-looking programs of economic development and reform and a seeming inability to measure up to the demands of a difficult new age. To many young English people, unemployed and maintained on a government pittance, the postwar period was aptly symbolized by a popular play of the time—*Love on the Dole*.

Change and ferment in the British empire. During this period serious tensions, mainly demands for home rule, were emerging in various parts of the British empire, mainly in India, Ceylon, Burma, and Egypt. An ominous trend was the growing antagonism between the Arab inhabitants of mandated Palestine and the Jewish Zionist immigrants (see Chapter 29). Happier developments were the attainment of home rule by the Irish Free State (the southern part of Ireland) in 1921 and Britain's recognition in 1931, in the Statute of Westminster, of a new national status for the dominions (Canada, Australia, New Zealand, and South Africa). Henceforth, the dominions and Great Britain were held together only by loyalty to the crown and by a common language, legal principles, tradition, and economic interests. Collectively these states were now known as the British Commonwealth of Nations.

Developments elsewhere in Europe. What had happened to the countries of southern Europe—Austria, Hungary, Bulgaria—which had been on the losing side in the war? For ten years after its creation, the new mini-state of Austria wrestled with widespread unemployment, substantial opposition to its republican government, and the specter of bankruptcy. Little need be said about the depressing history of Hungary and Bulgaria. It immediately became evident in both these states that democracy did not have the slightest chance of taking firm root. Reactionary cliques blocked urgent reforms, anti-Semitism flourished, and Fascism attracted numerous adherents. Authoritarian regimes were the general rule in Europe by the early 1930's.

What were the chances for democracy in the states of Europe which had been created from the debris of the Austro-Hungarian empire and had never known democratic traditions? Among the most important of the succession states was Czechoslovakia. Four hundred years of Austrian rule had not diminished the patriotic zeal of the Czechs, and in November 1918, after the collapse of Austria, they joined with the Slovaks in establishing a republic, with Thomas Masaryk as president and Eduard Beneš as foreign minister. In addition to Czechs and Slovaks, the new republic included such minority groups as Germans in the Sudeten area, Ukrainians (Ruthenians), and Hungarians, constituting one third of the total population of fifteen million. Despite some tensions among these minorities, Czechoslovakia prospered, a large foreign trade was built up, and the government assisted small farmers by breaking up large estates. The people demonstrated that they were industrious and conscientious citizens. The country gave every indication of growing into a healthy democracy. Unlike Czechoslovakia, the neighboring succession states—Poland, Rumania, Yugoslavia—were the scenes of political instability, exploitation of the masses, and violence culminating in dictatorship.

In Finland and the Scandinavian countries (Norway, Sweden, and Denmark) representative government operated smoothly and economic prosperity was the general rule. During the 1920's democratic institutions together with relatively high living standards were also enjoyed in Switzerland, the Netherlands, and Belgium.

Prospects for democracy and enlightened rule were not so promising in the Iberian peninsula, where military and aristocratic privilege were still strongly in vogue, and where the peasants continued to live a drab and often miserable existence. In the 1920's the republic of Portugal was plagued by political instability. In 1928 Dr. Oliveira Salazar, a professor of economics, became the minister of finance and, in 1932, the leading figure in an outright dictatorship. He exercised his power unobtrusively, perhaps as befitted a professorial dictator. Spain witnessed the creation of a dictatorship in 1923, growing mass discontent, and the end of the monarchy with the declaration of a republic in 1931. At a time when many other countries were turning to dictatorship, it was heartening to witness the triumph of democracy in Spain. This triumph, however, was to be short-lived (see Chapter 30).

Growth of democratic ideals in Latin America. Across the seas in the lands to which Iberian culture had been transplanted, various nations were beginning to tackle their economic problems and were trying to make their governments democracies in more than name.

The huge wartime demands for Latin American products resulted in an economic boom; and though the end of the war brought about a familiar situation—a crisis in the economy—business expansion began again in the 1920's. However, a crucial weakness remained—the dependence of the economies of Latin America's twenty republics upon only a few products or, in some cases, upon a single product. Thus Brazil's prosperity depended on the world coffee market, which absorbed half its exports. Cuba depended on sugar; Bolivia, tin; Mexico, oil and silver; Venezuela, oil; Argentina, meat and wheat. Various Central American "banana republics" were equally dependent on the sale of bananas. Another weak spot was the land problem. On many large estates conditions resembled medieval serfdom. Because the Church was a great landowner, certain churchmen combined with the landed interests to oppose land reforms.

During the 1920's the movement for social reform in Latin America was spearheaded by Mexico, which came under a series of administrations, all claiming to be heir to the revolutionary spirit of the revolt of 1910. The government sought to exercise increasing control over the vast oil properties run by foreign investors; and the agrarian problem was partially solved at the expense of large landowners. These changes were accompanied by a wave of anticlericalism. Much Church property was seized, many churches were destroyed, and the priesthood had to go underground for a time.

Conditions in Mexico exerted a strong influence on other Latin American countries,

and between 1919 and 1929 seven nations adopted new, liberal constitutions. In addition, there were growing demands for better economic and social opportunities, for a breakdown of the barriers that divided the few extremely rich from the many abysmally poor, and for improvements in health, education, and the status of women. Above all, there was an increasing desire for more stable political conditions.

Era of normalcy and big business in the United States. By 1919 wartime industrial expansion had won for the United States the supreme position in industrial equipment and wealth among the family of nations. Moreover, the nation had been transformed from a debtor nation to the world's greatest creditor. But while other nations increasingly looked to it for leadership, the United States turned away from the international scene. The wartime democratic idealism of President Wilson was shelved, the League of Nations was ignored, and isolationism triumphed over internationalism.

Internally, industrial strife and a wave of intolerance directed against immigrants, Catholics, Jews, and the League of Nations marked the postwar years. One important event was the ratification of the Eighteenth Amendment prohibiting the sale and possession of intoxicating liquors. However laudable its purpose, the law was broken by great numbers of citizens, and it strengthened the "bootleg" underworld and led to widespread violence and corruption.

In 1921 the inauguration of Warren G. Harding (1865-1923) as president on the platform of a "return to normalcy" ushered in a decade of Republican dominance. It soon became apparent that by "normalcy" the Harding administration meant resistance to pressure for such progressive measures as low tariffs and antitrust prosecutions. In foreign affairs the new president was bent upon isolationism and the repudiation of the League of Nations. In fact, the American ambassador in London was "instructed to inform the League's authorities that as the United States had not joined the League she was not in a position to answer letters from it."[16] Harding died suddenly in 1923, on the eve of the exposure of widespread corruption in his administration. The worst scandal concerned the leasing of government oil reserves at Teapot Dome, Wyoming, to private operators for $400,000.

Harding's vice president and successor, Calvin Coolidge (1872-1933), advocated high tariffs and reduction of taxes. His credo was summed up in these words: "The business of the United States is business." The Democrats tried in vain to raise the issue of corruption so rampant during Harding's regime, but under the glow of rising prosperity the voters in the 1924 presidential elections decided to "keep cool with Cal" and the Republicans won easily.

Little outstanding legislation was enacted during the second Coolidge administration. A difficult problem was agriculture. Although farm income continued to decline while the fixed payments for debts contracted during agriculture's wartime expansion had to be kept up, bills to ease the farmers' plight were repeatedly vetoed by Coolidge. Other segments of the national economy enjoyed what appeared to be dazzling prosperity in 1927 and 1928. Growing quantities of autos, radios, and refrigerators were purchased either with cash or, increasingly, on the installment plan. Stock speculation became a virtual mania. The stock market, mass production, high tariffs, large foreign loans, and installment buying—all seemed to be working together in harmony. These years marked the high tide of American big business and economic self-satisfaction.

In the 1928 presidential elections, Herbert Hoover (1874-1964), a successful mining engineer who had directed Belgian relief during the war, had as his Democratic opponent the governor of New York, Alfred E. Smith. A product of the "sidewalks of New York" and the first Catholic to obtain the presidential nomination, Smith as governor had sponsored progressive social legislation. In the election campaign he called for the repeal of prohibition because of the problems to which it had given rise, but Hoover won the the day on what one historian termed "prosperity, prohibition, and prejudice." When Hoover took office in 1929, he was supported by a Republican Congress and a nation enjoying unbounded industrial prosperity.

In retrospect the 1920's did little to enhance the national image and luster of the United States. After championing the first ambitious attempt to create an effective international organization, the League of Nations, the United States retreated into the comfortable cocoon of insular isolationism. Basic domestic issues were generally merely trifled with or ignored, and party dialogue in politics was seldom inspiring or informative. But most of the country enjoyed frenetic prosperity, whose unhealthy foundations were destined to crumble in the early 1930's.

SUMMARY

During the First World War various statesmen had uttered eloquent statements promising mankind a "world safe for democracy" and one progressively free of war. This anticipation was soon revealed as naively optimistic at the peace conference in Paris. Negotiations exposed the same old national rivalries and chauvinistic ambitions. The peace treaties, therefore, were neither fish nor fowl; they incorporated both the victor's traditional attitude of humiliating the vanquished and the concepts of a new international morality symbolized by the League of Nations.

Understandably the first five years after 1919 witnessed little but confusion and strife. The Germans balked at paying reparations, the French invaded the Ruhr, and numerous nations were agitated by civil strife and tensions with their neighbors. From 1925 to 1929, however, the feuds and discontent began to subside, giving way to peace and rising prosperity. The League of Nations registered encouraging, if not spectacular, progress.

While the western nations in the 1920's were striving to normalize and stabilize relations *between* themselves, significant developments were taking place *within* these various states. In the three great democracies —the United States, Great Britain, and France—this was in many ways a period of opportunities lost and important challenges ignored. The United States turned to isolationism, refusing to accept membership in the League of Nations, and at the same time engaged in a hectic economic boom compounded of stock market speculation, mass production, and the new installment buying. Britain "muddled" along prosaically with its traditional parliamentary institutions, even though they failed to cope adequately with the country's ills. France, under the Third Republic, presented a confusing spectacle of unstable and short-lived governments.

This chapter has emphasized the new totalitarian, antidemocratic systems because, unfortunately, in the postwar era they seemed the most vital and dynamic countries, destined to direct the course of history, no matter how tragic it was to be. A Communist, Marxist regime—both antidemocratic and anticapitalistic as well as implacably opposed to organized religion—was established in Russia over the debris of a discredited tsarist monarchy. The driving force behind this achievement was the audacity and leader-

ship of Lenin. This founder's mission was further advanced in the late 1920's by Stalin, who inaugurated a ruthless program of industrialization. Another antidemocratic system was initiated in Italy by its high priest and leader, Benito Mussolini. Defined as the "cult of state worship," Italian Fascism glorified war and called for the rule of one party, which manipulated all economic power by means of the corporate state. Defeated Germany had entered the 1920's with a new government, the democratic Weimar Republic. Political inexperience, however, augmented by heavy economic burdens and a festering feeling of injustice spawned by the Versailles peace treaty, combined to discredit the government. Dispirited and frustrated, Germans began to turn to Adolf Hitler and his ultranationalist and racist movement of Nazism. This fanatic and his followers were intent upon destroying the established order and rectifying the "injustices" of Versailles.

SUGGESTIONS FOR READING

R. Aron, **The Century of Total War,*** Beacon. A thoughtful analysis of the happenings in the world since 1914. See also H. S. Hughes, **Contemporary Europe,** Prentice-Hall, 1961; G. M. Gathorne-Hardy, **A Short History of International Affairs, 1920–1939,** Oxford, 1950; J. M. Keynes, **The Economic Consequences of the Peace,** Harcourt, 1920; U. Faulkner, **From Versailles to the New Deal,** Yale, 1951; and E. Leuchtenburg, **The Perils of Prosperity,** Univ. of Chicago, 1958.

E. Golob, **The Isms,** Harper, 1954. A useful introduction to modern political and economic ideologies. See also J. H. Hallowell, **Main Currents of Modern Political Thought,** Holt, 1950; C. J. Friedrich and Z. Brzezinski, **Totalitarian Dictatorship and Autocracy,*** Praeger; and H. Arendt, **The Origins of Totalitarianism,*** Meridian.

H. Seton-Watson, **From Lenin to Khrushchev,*** Praeger. A history of the Communist movement in the twentieth century. The most useful single volume on Russian history in this century is D. Treadgold, **Twentieth Century Russia,** Rand McNally, 1964. For the standard balanced history of the subject see W. H. Chamberlain, **The Russian Revolution, 1917–1921,** 2 vols., Macmillan, 1952. See also J. Reshetar, Jr., **A Concise History of the Communist Party of the Soviet Union,*** Praeger; G. F. Kennan, **Russia and the West,** Little, Brown, 1960.

S. W. Halperin, **Germany Tried Democracy,*** Norton. The best short history of the Weimar Republic. For an insightful look at Versailles and the birth pangs of the Weimar Republic see Richard M. Watt, **The Kings Depart: The Tragedy of Germany,*** Simon & Schuster. Should be supplemented by F. L. Schuman,

Germany Since 1918, Holt, 1937; W. L. Shirer, **The Rise and Fall of the Third Reich,*** Simon & Schuster; and G. Hilger and A. G. Meyer, **The Incompatible Allies: German-Soviet Relations,** Macmillan, 1953.

Three excellent critiques of Italian Fascism are A. Rossi, **The Rise of Italian Fascism,** Methuen, 1938; L. Fermi, **Mussolini,*** Phoenix; and E. Wiskemann, **Fascism and Italy,*** St. Martin's.

C. L. Mowat, **Britain Between the Wars,** Univ. of Chicago, 1955. An excellent treatment of the period. For a disquieting analysis of Britain's foreign policy up to the eve of Munich see R. W. Seton-Watson, **Britain and the Dictators,** Fertig, 1968.

H. Wish, **Contemporary America,** 4th ed., Harper & Row, 1966. A standard survey. Two sound economic surveys are B. Mitchell, **Depression Decade,** Holt, Rinehart & Winston, 1947; and J. K. Galbraith, **The Great Crash,*** Houghton Mifflin. See also A. M. Schlesinger, Jr., **The Crisis of the Old Order, 1919–1933,*** Sentry.

Important works on individual states in the international scene are M. MacDonald, **The Republic of Austria, 1918–1934,** Oxford, 1946; C. Macartney, **Hungary and Her Successors,** Oxford, 1937; M. Childs, **Sweden,*** Yale; S. H. Thomson, **Czechoslovakia in European History,** Princeton, 1953; O. Halecki, **History of Poland,** Roy, 1956; R. West, **Black Lamb and Grey Falcon: A Journey Through Jugoslavia,*** 2 vols., Compass; and L. Hanke, **Modern Latin America,*** 2 vols., Anvil.

*Indicates an inexpensive paperbound edition.

Chapter 29

Africa and Asia Astir

Africa, the Middle East, and India (1914-1939);
China and Japan (1914-1930);
Southeast Asia (1914-1939)

INTRODUCTION. By the first decade of the twentieth century, after fifty years of aggressive expansion, the dynamic, highly industrialized, militarily invincible western powers had Europeanized much of the world. Both the powers themselves and the territories over which they gained control derived numerous benefits from this march of imperialism. Evils as well as benefits resulted from imperialistic control, however; sometimes the western powers brought enlightened rule, but all too often native peoples had to pay a heavy price—ruthless economic exploitation, racial discrimination, and harsh administrative controls—for whatever advantages they received.

The most significant achievement of imperialism was its transmission of revolutionary western political and social ideas to undeveloped societies. The explosive ideas of democracy, parliamentary government, and nationalism, in association with western science and technology, reawakened and revitalized the societies of the nonwestern world with their hundreds of millions of people. After World War I colonialism was never quite the same. The colonial peoples had heard and seen too much for them ever again to give the white man unquestioning obedience. Yet while the influence of World War I was revealed in the growth of nationalism in India and China and among the Arabs of the Middle East, the activities of many nationalist programs and anti-imperialist movements remained tentative and secret, attracting little attention. But over the years the forces of liberation gathered their strength; and with the impact of World War II, they exploded into action.

After the First World War a chapter in modern world history—the dominance of the West—began to draw to a close. In an-cient and medieval times—before Europe's amazing advances in knowledge, wealth, and power—East and West were in rough balance. After the Renaissance, the scientific and industrial revolutions, and the spread of democracy and nationalism, the West took a commanding lead. Springing from this imbalance, western imperialism should perhaps be regarded as an inevitable development. But the colonial system and the West's power monopoly could not last; from its height in 1919, western superiority went into a rapid decline, and by the 1930's it was becoming apparent that fundamental changes were taking place in the nonwestern world. We shall see how the tempo of these changes increased until the ferment in Africa and Asia created a critical challenge for the statesmen of the contemporary world.

NEW FORCES IN AFRICA

Pan-Africanism and Negro nationalism. In Africa opposition to imperialism grew during the war years, as democracy and self-determination of nations were so widely publicized by President Wilson. American Negro leaders demanded greater recognition of Negro rights, particularly in Africa. Dr. W. E. B. Du Bois (1868-1963), editor of the influential newspaper *Crisis*, believed that the Paris Peace Conference should help form an internationalized, free Africa. He proposed the nucleus for a state of some twenty million people, guided by an international organization. At the war's end, Du Bois and other American Negro leaders journeyed to Paris in order to present their ideas in person to the delegates at the peace conference. While in Paris, Du Bois was instrumental in convening a Pan-African Congress with representatives from fifteen countries; the gathering urged that the former German colonies be placed under an international agency, not under the rule of one of the victorious colonial powers such as Britain.

Complementing the sentiments expressed at the Pan-African Congress were the ideals of Negro nationalism. In a convention held in New York in 1920, the members issued the Declaration of Rights of the Negro Peoples of the World, a document which went on record against race discrimination in the United States and the "inhuman, unchristian, and uncivilized treatment" of the African in colonial empires.

The mandate system in Africa. As a result of the Pan-African movement—coupled with a growing liberal sentiment in various nations, especially Britain—all territories conquered by the Allies in World War I were declared to be mandates. Article XXII of the League Covenant stated that the "well-being and development" of backward colonial lands was a "sacred trust of civilization." In essence, the mandate system was a compromise between annexation of the spoils of war by the victors and establishment of an international trusteeship. Parts of the Cameroons, Togoland, and German East Africa (Tanganyika) went to Great Britain. The remaining portions of the Cameroons and Togoland became French mandates. Belgium received the mandate of Ruanda-Urundi (also a part of German East Africa), while the former German colony of Southwest Africa was allotted to the Union of South Africa.

Annual reports from the governments administering the mandates were subject to the scrutiny and evaluation of the Permanent Mandates Commission. While the commission had no effective power to rectify unsatisfactory conditions in a mandate, it could place the matter before the eyes of the world. On numerous occasions the suggestions and criticisms of the commission were heeded by the mandatory powers.

Judgments of the mandate system, a radically new concept in colonial administration, have differed widely. To many critics, international supervision was a unique invasion of national sovereignty. To others, the Permanent Mandates Commission did not have enough power, especially the right to send its own observers into the mandated areas.

Growth of African studies. Closely connected with Pan-Africanism and Negro nationalism was the movement among black intellectuals to rediscover the African past, to prove that Africa had known days of glory. One American writer maintained that the stirring cultural forces which had brought about the Renaissance in Europe had originated in Africa. He also declared that prior to the fifteenth century the cultural level in West Africa was equivalent to that in Europe.[1]

While this propaganda stemming from enthusiastic Negro nationalistic feelings was appearing, a more promising development was also taking place—a rising interest in African life and culture among some anthropologists, missionaries, and learned societies. Up to this time relatively little information was available concerning the religious systems, tribal organization, and agriculture of sub-Saharan Africa. Students of social anthropology, a new branch of the social sciences, undertook field trips to Africa; their findings made it clear that the backwardness of the African native was attributable in large part to disease and isolation. In 1926 the International Institute of African Languages and Cultures was organized. It was claimed with some justification that the project opened up a new era of international cooperation in the service of Africa. As an indication of the rising interest in this area, new departments in the field of African studies were set up in various European universities, and a small number of Africanists began to be trained in the United States.

Impact of western colonial rule. The two decades following World War I witnessed the first massive and pervasive impact of European culture upon the African, which, to some degree, penetrated to all parts of the continent. While in some isolated bush areas tribesmen lived in Neolithic isolation, in the new cities many Africans led lives almost wholly European, at least in externals. Under colonial rule Africans now had to obey the laws and regulations of white administrators as well as those of their tribal councils and chiefs. To pay for better roads, public buildings, health and agricultural departments, taxes now had to be paid in cash, forcing many Africans to seek employment outside of their tribal areas in the towns, in the mines, in menial domestic or government service or on plantations run by Europeans. Habits of living changed, new modes of dress were adopted, new farming methods designed to produce cash crops were introduced, and a desire to buy enticing imported goods developed.

Contact with European modes of life rapidly undermined old faiths, customs, tribal loyalties, and social institutions—a process known as detribalization. But the African as yet belonged exclusively neither to his old tribal world nor to that of the white man. No longer bound by his tribe's laws, he was uneasy about the courts and the law of the Europeans; while accepting Christian doctrines, he secretly believed in the powers of his tribal deities. No matter what the benefits of imperial rule might be, it was paternal at its best and exploitive at its worst. Perhaps it was necessary and indeed desirable that Africa be brought into the mainstream of world forces; but it was a profoundly disrupting experience.

While colonial systems of administration varied, few Africans, outside of their tribal affairs, were allowed to participate in the important organs of colonial government. In British and French colonies a modicum of training in self-government was available to a small minority. Thus in 1922 in British

Nigeria, one of the most advanced colonies for African political participation, the Legislative Council of forty-six members included ten Africans, four of whom were elected. These were the first elected Africans in the legislatures of British tropical Africa.

New African leadership. The most significant consequence of colonial acculturation was the creation of a small nucleus of African intellectuals. Educational opportunities were generally meager. The great mass of Africans never attended school, and only an infinitesimal fraction was able to secure the equivalent of a high school education. But a few ambitious and competent young men did so manage and then continued advanced studies abroad, mainly in Britain, the United States, and France. It was largely from their ranks that the future leaders of independent Africa were recruited.

One of the first of these young students was Jomo Kenyatta, of the Kikuyu tribe, born in 1903 in what is now the independent state of Kenya and educated in a Scottish mission. Kenyatta became active in politics in the

In the rich gold mines of the Witwatersrand ("ridge of white waters") in Southern Transvaal, white laborers held relatively high-paying, skilled jobs, while native workers performed grueling tasks for miserable wages. Before the installation of modern air cooling, Africans endured temperatures of more than 100 degrees as they drilled the veins in cramped tunnels often more than a mile and a half below the surface of the earth.

early 1920's, and a pioneer nationalist, he published an African newspaper to disseminate his views. In 1929 he was a member of a delegation sent by the Kikuyu tribe to present a petition to the British Colonial Office regarding certain grievances. In 1931 he went to England again. After attending a small college and teaching Africans phonetics, Kenyatta studied anthropology at the London School of Economics. As a result he wrote a significant study, *Facing Mount Kenya*, which emphasized the disintegration of African tribal life following European colonial control. Kenyatta did not return to East Africa until 1946, and during his long sojourn abroad he traveled extensively in Europe and for a brief period attended Moscow University. After World War II Kenyatta became one of the most important and controversial African national leaders.

One of the earliest and most prominent young Africans to study abroad was Léopold Sédar Senghor. Born in 1916 in the French West African colony of Senegal, of a prosperous family, he attended a Catholic mission and then passed brilliantly from the *lycée* in Dakar. He pursued further studies in Paris, becoming the first African qualified to teach in a *lycée*. Senghor taught in several advanced institutions in France and carried on special studies in African cultures at the Sorbonne. In 1939, with the outbreak of war, he joined the French army. Taken prisoner, Senghor was approached by his German captors to desert the French cause, but he spurned these blandishments.

Senghor became one of the best educated African leaders. In the 1930's the young Senegalese's writings began to stress the beauty and complexity of African art, music, and psyche. Widely known as a gifted poet, Senghor exerted a strong influence upon the African intellectual revival after World War II. Interestingly he is a symbol of the psychological ambivalence often noted among African intellectuals. Married to a French lady, he probably is more at home in Paris than in Dakar. A master stylist in French, an ardent admirer of France and its contributions to world culture, Senghor yet belongs to the world of his ancestors. He became a vigorous champion of the traditions of his people and of the positive features of their indigenous culture.

Additional young Africans who studied abroad and became acquainted with western ideology could be mentioned, such as Kwame Nkrumah, from the Gold Coast (now Ghana), and Dr. Benjamin Azikiwe, from Nigeria. Both these students, who were later prominent in the new Africa, attended American universities. With these educational advantages they developed a renewed confidence in the destiny of Africa and a burning desire to have a part in ending colonial control. Thus, ironically, imperialism provided the essential dynamic for its eventual overthrow.

Segregation in the Union of South Africa. The most explosive area in the period between the First and Second World Wars was the Union of South Africa. Here the discontent of the African was the deepest, the confusing process of detribalization the most widespread.

South Africa is a plural society; that is, "a society comprising two or more elements or social orders which live side by side, yet without mingling, in one political unit."[2] The Dutch Europeans (the Boers) were rivals of the British settlers. Since 1902, when Britain defeated the two Boer republics, there had been bad blood between victors and vanquished. In 1909, through the union of the two former republics (the Transvaal and the Orange Free State) with the British colonies of Cape Colony and Natal, South Africa became a self-governing dominion in the British Commonwealth. But union did not bring cooperation. The Boers obtained official recognition for their language Afrikaans (developed mainly from seventeenth-century Dutch); they insisted upon their own flag and national anthem; and they talked about secession from the Commonwealth.

The rift between Briton and Boer was serious. More dangerous, however, was the increasing numerical gap between all Europeans on the one hand and the native population on the other. After World War I the Europeans began to eye the statistics nervously. The figures disclosed that there were 5,500,000 pure Africans in the Union and 1,800,000 whites, just under 50 percent of

them of British stock. In addition there were 200,000 Asiatics and 600,000 "coloured." Fearful of being overwhelmed by sheer numbers, many whites became convinced that the natives had to be kept separate from the European community socially and politically and that all political control must remain in the hands of the Europeans.

Segregation and the color bar spread rapidly in the 1930's. Africans were required to live on their tribal reserves. Only those who obtained special permission could work on farms owned by Europeans or in the cities; and in urban areas they were obliged to live in squalid, segregated "locations" and had to carry passes and identity cards under penalty of arrest and fine or imprisonment if found without them. Native labor unions were discouraged and strikes forbidden. In addition, governmental regulations or the white labor unions excluded Africans from certain skilled trades. Because of the enormous supply of unskilled native laborers, who would work for miserably low wages, uneducated Europeans—the "poor whites" —found it difficult to make a living. To favor this group, laws were passed earmarking certain jobs on the railroads and in city services for Europeans; wages for these jobs were raised, and the cost was paid by special subsidies. The practice was most discriminatory; the average wage for Europeans was just under four dollars a day, while that of the Africans was just over three dollars a week. In addition to the color bar in industry, the African was effectively barred from politics: he could not vote or hold office in any influential elective body or parliament outside his own tribal reserve.

African unrest was manifested in the increasing crime rate in the cities, in the formation of underground organizations, and in the determined efforts to secure political rights. Here and there in the back alleys and cellars of cities such as Johannesburg, young Africans ran their mimeograph machines, turning out handbills and papers advertising their grievances. One two-page sheet called the *African Liberator* declared:

Africa has come to the parting of the ways . . . Black South Africa has been bought and sold to some wolves in clothing of sheep who profess to be their friends. What does the African want? He wants liberty, equality, and opportunity. We demand our rights to have the same vote as Europeans, the same education, the same right to defend the country, the same right to sit in Parliament, Provincial Councils, and Town Councils. We do not want two nations in South Africa.[3]

Although the ferment of change and unrest began to be detected in other areas, only in the Union were African nationalist aspirations widespread. The unappeasable upsurge of nationalism was to wait until after World War II.

TENSIONS IN
THE ARAB WORLD

Cultural links between Asia and Africa. The heart of the Arab world is the Middle East, a difficult region to define. The term is used most often in reference to the lands connecting Asia with Africa, the chief boundary markers being Cairo, Istanbul, Teheran, and the south coast of the Arabian peninsula. Nearly all the peoples of the Middle East are united in a common faith (Islam) and share common elements of Islamic culture and a common tongue, Arabic. Because of the unifying force of this heritage, Muslim North Africa (Morocco, Algeria, Tunisia) will be treated here as part of the Arab world.

With the exception of Morocco, North Africa at the beginning of the nineteenth century was nominally under the sovereignty of the Ottoman Turks, whose capital city was Constantinople. In practice, however, the various states in this area were self-governing. After 1815 all of North Africa from Casablanca in Morocco to Cairo in Egypt came under European imperialistic rule, while the other Arab lands in the Middle East continued under the despotic control of the sultans.

The Arab revolt. Just before the outbreak of the First World War, the Arabs within the Ottoman empire had reached the breaking point in their relations with the Turkish government. In 1913 an Arab Congress meeting in Paris demanded home rule and equality with the Turks in the empire. Because the Middle East was strategically important to Britain, the British government followed the rise of Arab discontent with great interest. During 1915 extensive correspondence was carried on between the British high commissioner in Cairo and Sherif Husein of Mecca (Husein ibn-Ali, 1856-1931), guardian of the holy places in the Hejaz. In the event of an Arab revolt, Great Britain would recognize Arab independence except in those regions of coastal Syria which were not wholly Arab—presumably excluding Palestine—and in those which might be claimed by France. But British commitments were purposely vague, and the whole correspondence has been described as a "monument of ambiguity."

In addition to the British alliance with the Arab nationalist movement, the indomitable desert warrior Abdul-Aziz ibn-Saud (1880-1953), sultan of Nejd in south-central Arabia, was induced to adopt a policy of benevolent neutrality toward Britain. The wooing of the Arabs thwarted the Turkish attempt to rouse the whole Muslim Middle East by preaching a *jihad*, or holy war, against the British.

Late in 1916 the Arab revolt began. Husein raised the standard of rebellion in the Hejaz, proclaimed independence from the Turks, and captured Mecca for his cause. In the fighting that followed, the Arab forces were commanded by the third son of the Sherif Husein, Emir Faisal (1885-1933), who was assisted by a remarkable English officer, Colonel T. E. Lawrence (1888-1935), later known as Lawrence of Arabia.

Under Lawrence, the Arabs took a decisive part in the last battle against the main Turkish forces in September 1918. When the war ended, Syria was occupied by the victorious Allied forces; a small French force was located along the coast of Lebanon; Emir Faisal and his Arab forces were in the interior, grouped around Damascus; and the British controlled Palestine.

The peace settlement. With Turkey defeated, the Arab leaders sought the independence they thought Britain had promised in the correspondence with Husein. When the peace conference met in Paris, it became painfully clear that the problem of political settlement in the Middle East was a jumble of conflicting promises and rivalries.

During the war years a number of important commitments had been made, starting with the British pledge in 1915 to Sherif Husein. In 1916, in the Sykes-Picot Agreement, Syria and Iraq had been divided into four zones, with Britain and France each controlling two. Palestine was to be placed under an international administration. The most important pronouncement bearing upon the postwar history of the Middle East was Britain's declaration to the Jewish Zionist organization in 1917.

Jewish aspirations to create a national home in Palestine had been rapidly growing after 1900. In 1903 a sympathetic British government had offered Theodore Herzl, the creator of the Zionist idea of a Jewish state, land in East Africa for a Jewish settlement. This proposal, however, had not been accepted. Following Herzl's death in 1904, the leadership of the Zionist movement had been assumed by Dr. Chaim Weizmann. Of Russian birth, Weizmann became a British subject and developed an intimate intellectual friendship with the English statesman Arthur James Balfour, who became keenly interested in the Zionist program. Balfour's admiration for Jewish religious and cultural contributions was profound; and he believed strongly that "Christian religion and civilization owed to Judaism a great debt and [one] shamefully repaid."[4]

During the course of World War I, the British government—strongly influenced by Balfour, then foreign secretary—became convinced that its support of a Zionist program in Palestine would not only be a humanitarian gesture but would also serve British imperial interests in the Middle East. Thus in November 1917 Britain issued the Balfour Declaration which stated:

His Majesty's Government view with favour the establishment in Palestine of a national home for the Jewish people, and will use their best endeavors to facilitate the achievement of this object, it being clearly understood that nothing shall be done which may prejudice the civil and religious rights of existing non-Jewish communities in Palestine. . . .

Zionists were disappointed that the Declaration did not unequivocally state that Palestine should be *the* national home for the Jewish people. In 1918 Great Britain made several declarations recognizing Arab national aspirations, and an Anglo-French pronouncement pledged the establishment of national governments "deriving their authority from the initiative and free choice of the indigenous populations."

At the Paris Peace Conference Emir Faisal, aided by Lawrence, pleaded the cause of Arab independence, but in vain. Faisal was still ruler in Damascus, and in March 1920, while the statesmen in Paris argued, a congress of Syrian leaders met and resolved

Shy and physically slight, Lawrence had roamed the Arab lands, studying the language and habits of the Muslims. In 1914 the British government engaged Lawrence to take part in the Arab guerrilla campaign against the Turks. Idolized by the Bedouin tribesmen he knew so well, Lawrence disrupted Turkish communication lines and destroyed so many locomotives that the Turks called him *El-Orens* ("destroyer of engines").

that he should be king of a united Syria, including Palestine and Lebanon. But in April the San Remo Conference of the Allied powers turned over all Arab territories formerly in the Ottoman empire to be administered as mandates. Syria and Lebanon were mandated to France; Iraq and Palestine, to Great Britain. To the Arabs the mandates were a poor substitute for independence and a flimsy disguise for imperialism.

From the Arabs' point of view, the peace settlement in the Middle East was a shabby piece of statesmanship compounded of ignorance, deception, and conflicting aims. Apologists for Britain and France point out that Britain made promises to France during the war because the British could hardly deny the requests of their most important ally, which had close missionary and educational ties in Syria. In 1916 Britain made its ambiguous pledge to Husein because of its desperate need for Arab friendship. Again, in the Balfour Declaration, Britain acted according to short-range interests; in order to swing the support of the world's Jews to the Allied cause and to maintain communications in the Middle East, Britain promised to open the Arab region of Palestine to Jewish settlement. It should be kept in mind that British statesmen sincerely believed that a Jewish national home could be reconciled with Arab interests; they had no idea of the massive influx of Jewish immigration during the 1930's. The plain fact remains, however, that the Allied statesmen at Paris were profoundly ignorant of the intensity of Arab nationalism.

The French in Syria and Lebanon. In 1920, following the San Remo Conference, a French army moved against Damascus and ejected Faisal from the throne. After this incident, France took over the mandate of Lebanon and Syria. Following a policy of divide and rule, the French attempted especially to woo the large Christian Arab groups in Lebanon. But they were not successful; the Arabs remained hostile. Strikes, demonstrations, and revolts were not uncommon.

Politically, French rule was a failure in Syria and Lebanon. At the outset a popular Arab king had been ejected, and for the next twenty years the French administration often suppressed personal and political liberties. Under French mandatory rule, however, the modernization of Syria-Lebanon proceeded: roads and public buildings were constructed, and the use of electricity and irrigation works was extended.

British policy in Iraq. Great Britain's vital interest in the mandate of Iraq was prompted largely by Iraq's rich oil resources, its growing importance in East-West air transportation, and its proximity to the Persian Gulf. But this interest did not prevent the British from taking steps to satisfy Iraqi nationalism after the outbreak of rebellion in June 1920. In March 1921 the Iraqi throne was offered to Faisal, who had lost his throne in Syria. A plebiscite strongly supported Faisal as ruler of the Iraqi, and a few months later he was proclaimed king. In 1922 Britain and Faisal's government signed a treaty which stipulated that Britain was to supervise the finances and military affairs of the new state. Three years later a constitution was adopted making the country a constitutional monarchy with a bicameral legislature. An Anglo-Iraqi treaty signed in June 1930 granted Iraq full independence, and in 1932 Iraq was admitted to the League of Nations. By these concessions Britain avoided the conflict that France experienced in Syria-Lebanon.

Arab-Jewish conflict in Palestine. Between the two world wars, Palestine was the most tempestuous area in all the Middle East, as Britain sought to protect its imperial interests and at the same time reconcile them with Zionism and Arab nationalism. Almost as soon as the mandate was set up, Arab riots broke out in Palestine. In 1919 the population was given at 700,000, with 568,000 Arabs, 58,000 Jews, and 74,000 others, mainly Christians. Realizing the apprehensions of the Arabs, the British sought to define the Balfour Declaration more precisely. While not repudiating Palestine as a national home for the Jews, the British government declared it "would never impose upon them [the Arabs] a policy which that people had reason to think was contrary to their religious, their political, and their economic interests."[5]

Such pronouncements and the fact that Jewish immigration was not large made possible a period of peace and progress from 1922 to 1929. As the Zionists reclaimed land, set up collective farms, harnessed the Jordan for power, and established many new factories, a veritable economic revolution took place. Tel-Aviv grew into a thriving modern city, an excellent university was founded at Jerusalem, and Palestine became the center of a Hebrew renaissance.

The era of peace ended in 1929 when serious disorders broke out, mainly Arab attacks on Jews. Violence continued to erupt in the early 1930's as the Nazi persecution of the Jews brought about a steep rise in immigration to Palestine and threatened the Arabs' predominant position in the area. In 1937 a British commission of inquiry recommended a tripartite division: Palestine would be divided into two independent states, one controlled by the Arabs and one by the Jews, with Britain holding a third portion, a small mandated area containing Jerusalem and Bethlehem. This recommendation satisfied no one and was not accepted.

Throughout the 1930's the "Palestine Question" was violently discussed in many parts of the world. Zionists argued that they had a historic right to the Holy Land, their original home, that Palestine had been promised to them in the Balfour Declaration and legalized by the League of Nations; that Jewish colonization constituted a democratic and progressive influence in the Middle East; and that Arab antipathy was mainly the work of a few wealthy effendis, since the mass of Arabs were profiting from the wealth being brought into Palestine. On the other hand, the Arabs argued that Palestine had been their country for more than a thousand years and declared that the Balfour Declaration did not bind them because they were not consulted in its formulation. They further insisted that much of Zionist economic development was not healthy because it depended upon subsidization of huge amounts by outside capital. Finally, they asked how could any people be expected to stand idly by and watch an alien immigrant group be transformed from a minority into a majority.

As war with the Axis powers loomed in 1939, Britain sought desperately to strengthen its position in the Middle East by attempts to regain Arab good will. A "white paper" was issued declaring that it was Britain's aim to have as an ally an independent Palestine established at the end of ten years, with guarantees for both the Arab and Jewish populations. During this ten-year period land sales were to be restricted. After the admission of 50,000 Jews, with the possibility of another 25,000 refugees from Nazi Germany, no more immigration would take place without the consent of the Arabs. The outbreak of World War II shelved the Zionist-Arab quarrel in Palestine; but after the war the controversy was to break out again with fatal virulence.

Emergence of Saudi Arabia. In the cradle of Islamic civilization—the Arabian peninsula—the various local rulers were largely outside the sphere of western control. The collapse of Ottoman rule in 1918 left several rival independent states such as Yemen, Hejaz, and Nejd to adjust their relations, plus a few British protectorates on the Arabian Sea and the Persian Gulf. Following hostilities between various contenders for leadership in the Arabian peninsula, ibn-Saud welded all tribal groups into a strong political unit. The new kingdom, Saudi Arabia, became endowed with enormous economic resources obtained from vast oil reserves discovered in 1932.

Riza Shah Pahlavi rules Iran. Persia, (or Iran as it came to be known in the 1920's), a land Muslim in religion but not Arabic in culture, had been the scene of strenuous British and Russian imperial rivalry before World War I. Following this conflict, a brilliant millitary officer, Riza Shah Pahlavi (1877-1944), seized the throne and established his own dynasty. A strongly nationalist reformer, Riza Shah abolished some of the special privileges enjoyed by foreigners —especially those of the Anglo-Iranian Oil Company. The army was modernized, education improved, trade and industry fostered, and important new railway lines constructed. But notwithstanding this impressive record, the Shah progressively developed the mind of a tyrant. Organs of government were relegated to puppetdom, and corruption increased. The decaying rule of Riza Shah was destined to collapse during World War II.

The problem of Egyptian sovereignty.
While the Arabs in the mandates had been
struggling for the right of self-determination,
a parallel development was taking place in
Egypt. When the British refused a delegation
of Egyptian nationalists permission to attend
the Paris Peace Conference and deported
the spokesman of the group and his followers, the Nile valley rose in revolt.

After three years of disorder the government in London announced that Egypt was
no longer a British protectorate. It was to be
a sovereign state. Britain, however, was to
remain responsible for the defense of the
country, for the protection of foreign interests, and for communications vital to the
British empire, above all the Suez Canal.
Egypt grudgingly adapted itself to this
declaration, made its sultan a king, and proclaimed a constitution in 1923. Anglo-Egyptian relations remained unsatisfactory, how-

ever, and frequent negotiations between the
two governments were fruitless.

Respite in the long record of Anglo-Egyptian acrimony came about through the threat
of Italian Fascist aggression in Africa following Mussolini's conquest of Abyssinia
(see p. 723). In 1936 Britain and Egypt negotiated a treaty of alliance. In the case of war
there was to be mutual assistance on a wide
scale, and the status of the Sudan (theoretically under the dual sovereignty of Britain
and Egypt but actually under British control)
was to continue unaltered.

**Aggressive nationalism in North Af-
rica.** Long before the outbreak of World
War I, Algeria had become politically integrated with France; Tunisia had prospered
under French rule and had maintained its
native ruler, the bey; and the native sultan
had also been retained in the protectorate
France established in Morocco in 1911.
Nevertheless, the storm signals of bitter
nationalism had appeared, particularly in
Morocco.

Following a revolt in 1912, the Moroccans
in the 1920's vented their feeling against
French rule on several occasions by riots and
armed outbreaks. In the 1930's a modern
nationalist movement began to function, but
it was relatively weak. Tunisia, the most
westernized area in French North Africa,
also had a nationalist movement, but it was
driven underground. In Algeria, which was
part of metropolitan France, political agitation was slight. The growing desire of
Muslims for French citizenship, strongly
opposed by settlers from France, caused
much resentment.

France deserves much credit for its colonial rule. Administration on the whole was
just and efficient, the economy prospered,
and living standards advanced. Nevertheless, a fundamental split existed between the
privileged Christian minority and the overwhelming Muslim majority; the Arab populace admired examples of Arab assertiveness, as in Egypt and Morocco. Until 1939
the nationalist movement in North Africa
was largely a monopoly of the relatively
small intellectual groups and middle class.
The mass of peasants remained quite apathetic.

Just as the Arabian garb of Lawrence, an Englishman,
indicated his dedication to the Arab cause (see photo,
p. 693), so the western dress of Kemal represents his
attempt to westernize the Turkish nation. Under his
leadership Turkey made more progress in the two decades after World War I than had been registered during
the entire nineteenth century. In 1934 the people bestowed upon their leader the title of *Atatürk*, meaning
"father of the Turks."

Mustafa Kemal's rise to power in Turkey. We have seen in Chapter 24 how reform measures had been initiated by the Young Turks just before World War I. Defeat in the war, the revolt of the Arabs, and the impotence of the sultan's government convinced some patriots that only the most drastic measures could save the Turkish nation. In addition, they were embittered by the harsh terms of the Treaty of Sèvres (1920). It was bad enough to lose their empire, peopled by Arabs, but it was much worse to see their homeland, mainly Anatolia and the city of Smyrna, partitioned and invaded by the Greeks and Italians.

Imbued with a new spirit of nationalism, the patriots rallied around the military hero Mustafa Kemal Pasha (1880-1938), who had a brilliant record against the British at Gallipoli in World War I. An important figure in the Young Turks movement, Kemal was a born leader, thoroughly western in education and outlook. After the defeat of Turkey, he had been sent by the sultan to demobilize the Turkish troops in Asia Minor, but, disregarding his instructions, he had reorganized the troops and successfully defied the Allies. A new government was set up in Ankara, and Kemal was selected as president and commander in chief. Turkish patriotism was galvanized by the National Pact, a declaration of principles supported by Kemal. This document upheld the rule of self-determination for all people, including the Turks, and also proclaimed the abolition of the special rights heretofore enjoyed by foreigners in Turkey.

In 1921 Greek designs on Turkish territory were defeated by Kemal's armies. And in the following year the sultanate was abolished, followed by the establishment of a republic. The Allies agreed to a revision of Sèvres, and the Treaty of Lausanne, signed in 1923, returned to Turkey some Aegean islands and territory adjoining Constantinople. The heartland of Turkey—Anatolia—remained intact, and no reparations were demanded.

Kemal's reforms. The new constitution was democratic in form, but in reality Kemal was a dictator who brooked no interference with his plans. His dictatorship does not belong in the same category as those fashioned in Nazi Germany, or Fascist Italy, or Communist Russia, however. In the new Turkey there was little of the cult of the superior race; the brutal efficiency of the purge and the concentration camp was practically unknown. Dictatorship was regarded as the rough but essential highway to parliamentary government. Kemal envisioned a dictatorship as a necessary stage in raising his people to that level of education and social well-being which democratic government requires.

Under his rule the old institutions and customs of a backward oriental state were transformed or replaced within a few short years. In modern times such a wholesale adoption of new culture traits is duplicated nowhere except perhaps in Japan. The caliphate, the sultan's spiritual leadership of the Muslim world, was abolished. The courts of the Greek Orthodox Church were discontinued, and new law codes were promulgated. Education was taken out of the hands of the Orthodox Church, and school attendance was made compulsory to the age of sixteen. Use of the fez by men and the veil by women was forbidden. Polygamy was prohibited. In addition, the western Gregorian calendar and European numerals were introduced, and the Latin alphabet replaced the Arabic. Thus, Turkey was rejuvenated by its indefatigable leader, who created a new capital at Ankara.

INDIA SEEKS TO RULE ITSELF

Moves for self-government. Many observers had predicted that in the event of war Great Britain would find India a serious liability. But when hostilities began, nearly all unfriendly acts against Britain ceased. By 1917, however, it became apparent that the Indian people expected compensation in the way of more self-government. Parliament's reply indicated that the goal to be attained in India was the gradual development of self-government within the British empire.

The great leader of the Indian independence movement was Gandhi. He is shown here just after he arrived in England in 1931 to attend a round-table conference on the future of India.

In 1918 a British commission was sent to India to investigate the problem of Indian self-government. The result was a new constitution. The Government of India Act provided for a system of dyarchy, or double government, in the provinces, by which certain powers were reserved to the British while the provincial legislatures were accorded other, generally lesser powers. Thus the act represented only a step toward self-government.

Chances for India's acceptance of the act of 1919 were swept away by the outbreak of a struggle between the British and the Indian nationalists. In an ill-advised moment the British passed the Rowlatt Act (1919), which allowed the police and other officials extraordinary powers in ferreting out subversive activity. Although the act was never enforced, it was deeply resented as a token of repression. Disgruntled and disheartened, many nationalists demanded sweeping changes.

Gandhi and civil disobedience. The foremost nationalist leader in India was Mohandas K. Gandhi (1869-1948). Born of middle-class parents, Gandhi had been sent to London to study law; later he went to South Africa, where he built up a lucrative practice. During these years his standard of values changed completely. The new Gandhi repudiated wealth, practiced ascetic self-denial, condemned violence, and believed firmly that true happiness could be achieved only by service to one's fellow men.

Gandhi began his career as reformer and champion of his people in South Africa. The Indians there were subject to numerous restrictive laws which hampered their freedom of movement, prevented them from buying property, and imposed upon them special taxation. By the use of passive resistance, or noncooperation, Gandhi forced the government to remove some restrictions. Disdaining the use of violence, he believed that a just cause triumphs if its supporters attempt to convince those in power of injustices by practicing "civil disobedience." With Gandhi as their leader, the Indians in South Africa carried on various strikes, including hunger strikes; they refused work, held mass demonstrations, and marched into areas where their presence was forbidden by law.

When he returned to his native land shortly after the outbreak of World War I, Gandhi was welcomed as a hero. During the war he cooperated with the British government, but the Rowlatt Act and the disappointing concessions in the new constitution led him to announce his determination to force the British to give India self-rule.

In 1919 Gandhi introduced his campaign. A mass strike was declared in which all work was to cease and the population was to pray and fast. Contrary to Gandhi's plan, however, riots took place, Europeans were killed, and soldiers were sent to try to restore order. Although public gatherings were forbidden, a large body of unarmed Indians assembled at Amritsar. They were dispersed by gunfire, and several hundred were killed. All hope of cooperation between Indian and Briton was temporarily at an end. Arrested in 1922, Gandhi seemed to welcome being placed on trial; he assured the British magistrate that the only alternative to permitting him to continue his opposition was to imprison him. Sentenced to six years' imprisonment, Gandhi suffered a temporary eclipse.

There was little peace in India in the 1920's. During 1928 and 1929 a group of political experts from Great Britain, the Simon Commission, toured the country. The survey issued by the commission in 1930 suggested only a cautious advance in the direction of self-government. Meanwhile Gandhi initiated another campaign toward that goal.

British reform gestures. A promising road to conciliation opened in 1930, when a series of round-table conferences was arranged in London. A new scheme of government was hammered out, providing for a federal union which would bring the British provinces and the states of the princes into a central government. In the provinces the system of dyarchy was displaced by full autonomy, while in the federal government all powers were transferred to the Indians except defense and foreign affairs, which remained in the control of the British viceroy. From 1937, when this new Government of India Act came into operation, to 1939 the scheme of self-government worked smoothly. The possibility of federation, however, faded away as the native princes refused to enter the central government.

The Indian National Congress. The new system of government failed to satisfy the demands of the Indian nationalists, who continued to espouse the cause of complete independence for India. The chief element in the nationalist movement was the powerful Indian National Congress, which had become the organ of the militant nationalists. Membership, estimated at several million, was predominantly Hindu but also included many Muslims and members of other religious groups. Soon after the First World War, the Congress had come under the leadership of Gandhi, whose personal following among the people was the chief source of the party's tremendous influence. He transformed the Congress, which had been primarily a middle-class organization, into a mass movement including the peasants. Gandhi had other goals besides the independence of India; he sought to end all drinking, to raise the status of women, to remove the stigma attached to the untouchables, and to bring about cooperation between Hindus and Muslims. Permeating all of Gandhi's ideas and actions was his belief in nonviolence; he was convinced that injustices and wrongs could be destroyed only through the forces of love, unselfishness, and patience.

In the 1930's Gandhi came to share his leadership with Jawaharlal Nehru (1889-1964), who came from a Brahmin family of ancient lineage. In his early youth Jawaharlal had all the advantages of wealth: English tutors, enrollment in the English public school of Harrow and later in Trinity College, Cambridge, where he obtained his B.A. in 1910 and was admitted to the bar in 1912. Upon his return to India, Nehru showed little interest in the law and gradually became completely absorbed in his country's fight for freedom.

Although born a member of the Brahmin caste, Nehru rejected India's rigid class system and devoted himself to the welfare of the masses, eventually becoming second only to the beloved Mahatma in the independence movement.

A devoted friend and indeed a disciple of Gandhi, Nehru could not agree with the older leader's asceticism, mysticism, and his antagonism against western industrialism. At heart Nehru was a rationalist, an agnostic, an ardent believer in science, and a foe of all supernaturalism. Above all he was a blend of the cultures of both East and West, with perhaps the latter predominating. As he himself said: "I have become a queer mixture of the East and the West, out of place everywhere, at home nowhere. Perhaps my thoughts and approach to life are more akin to what is called Western than Eastern, but India calls to me."[6]

The Hindu-Muslim clash. India is a classic example of a plural society. The division in India was between the Hindus and Muslims and was known as the "communal problem." As Britain's imperial control over India began to show signs of ending, hostility between the two communities quickened. They were poles apart in culture and values. In a word, Islam and Hinduism represented a fundamental antithesis in nearly all facets of life. Many Muslims believed that in the event of independence they would be relegated to an ineffectual minority; in this sense the rivalry was a struggle for political power.

During the 1920's differences between Muslim and Hindu progressively developed. In the early 1930's the Muslim League, a political party, began to challenge the claim of the Indian National Congress to represent all of India. Its leader, Muhammad Ali Jinnah (1876-1948), originally a member of Congress and once dubbed by Indian nationalists as the "ambassador of Hindu-Muslim unity," had become alienated by what he considered the Hindu domination of Congress and its claim to be the sole agent of Indian nationalism. The Muslim League began to advance the "two-nation" theory, and in 1933 a group of Muslim students at Cambridge University circulated a pamphlet calling for the establishment of a new state to be known as Pakistan. This leaflet was a portent of momentous developments. In the fall of 1939 the Muslim League emphatically denounced any scheme of self-government that would mean majority Hindu rule.

NATIONALISM IN SOUTHEAST ASIA

Roots of decolonization. Southeast Asia underwent dramatic changes between World Wars I and II. Inspired by the Wilsonian ideal of "self-determination of peoples" or by the social revolutionary ideals of European socialism and the Russian Revolution, or by a combination of both, more and more Southeast Asian political, intellectual, and business leaders joined the anti-imperialist struggle, promoted national self-consciousness, and sought by one means or another the path to independence. The rise of Japan to the status of a world power indicated to Southeast Asian elites that the West was not alone in its ability to master technology and politics for purposes of national renewal. Furthermore, the spectacle of westerners barbarously slaughtering westerners in World War I gave birth to grave doubts concerning the validity of the West's claims of being a civilizing agent.

The imperialist powers continued to exploit their colonial possessions, apparently undaunted by the political ideals they had subscribed to during the First World War. But Southeast Asian populations grew dramatically. From 1930 to 1960 the populations of Siam, Malaya, and the Philippines increased by over 100 percent while the populations of Indonesia, Burma, and the states of Indochina all increased by well over 50 percent. Increased population pressures naturally contributed to unrest and the growth of nationalist movements.

Certain economic trends also characterized most of the region. The Chinese played a more and more important role as merchants and middlemen in the local economies. In Burma, Indians played the same role. European and Chinese capital investment brought about a rapid growth in the exploitation of natural resources, such as mines and forest products. In some countries, such as Siam and Indochina, rice production grew more rapidly than population, and they became rice-exporting economies. Imperialist exploitation coupled with an irregular world market, which crashed in 1929, led to the increasing impoverishment of large numbers of the population. This seemed to validate the Marxist-Leninist view of imperialism.

Throughout the area the elite became more assimilated to European culture as increasing numbers of young people went to the "mother countries" for education. The masses were hardly touched by this process, however, and the result was an increasing cultural and social dichotomy between the indigenous leadership and the people at large. With the exception of the United States in the Philippines and Great Britain in Burma and Ceylon, moreover, none of the imperialist powers undertook to prepare their colonies for self-government, as they had no intention of relinquishing them.

The Philippines. American civil government was established in the United States newly won Far Eastern possession on July 4, 1901, under William H. Taft. President McKinley declared that the primary American aim was to prepare the Filipinos for self-government. The first elections were held in 1907, and by 1913 Filipinos dominated both houses of the island legislature, while an American remained as governor-general or chief executive. By 1935, when the Philippine Commonwealth was inaugurated with a new constitution and the promise of independence in ten years, the islands had developed a complex political structure and a sophisticated political life.

Economic developments, however, decreased Philippine independence at the same time that the islands were being prepared for political independence. Before the outbreak of World War II, four fifths of Philippine exports went to the United States, and three fifths of its imports were American. Like most underdeveloped economies, the export trade was dominated by a very few products: hemp, sugar, coconuts, and tobacco. Independence, with its accompanying imposition of tariffs, would be economically difficult. Socially, the United States had prevented the development of a colonial-type plantation economy by forbidding non-Filipinos to own plantation lands. But native landlordism was rampant, and agrarian discontent manifested itself in brief uprising in the mid-thirties.

The Dutch East Indies. The growth of Indonesian self-consciousness and nationalism was paradoxically facilitated in the interwar period by the spread and increasing efficiency of Dutch rule. Stretched over 3100 miles of water, the numerous islands of Indonesia were integrated into political and communications systems by the Dutch. At the same time, the stringent limits put on the power and advancement of native elites led to bitterness and resentment. A Communist party was organized in 1920, and in late 1926 and early 1927 it attempted uprisings in Java and Sumatra, but they were unsuccessful. Police repression increased, and in 1930 the Dutch attempted to crush the Nationalist party by arresting one of its leaders, Sukarno, who became the first president of independent Indonesia after World War II. The colonial administration banned all discussions of any subject that might involve the concept of national independence. Even the name Indonesia was banned from official publications.

Burma and Malaya. India was the model for the development of Burmese nationalism and agitation for independence. The Indian Congress party stimulated Burmese political thought, but Buddhism provided the focus for organizational activity. In 1906 a Young Men's Buddhist Association was formed, and in 1921 it organized a General Council of Burmese Associations which gave organizational expression to nationalism on the village level. British promises to promote Indian self-government created a similar demand in Burma; in 1937 Burma was administratively split off from India, and a parliamentary system was inaugurated with a Burman prime minister under a British governor who was responsible for foreign relations, defense, and finance.

Malaya, in contrast to Burma, did not develop a strong nationalist movement. Perhaps the major reason for this was the existence of large ethnic groups that distrusted each other more than they felt the need to make common cause against the British. The Malays feared Chinese ethnic domination; eventually, the Chinese came to outnumber the Malays themselves. The Chinese were primarily interested in commerce and in developments in China, while the Indians, for the most part workers on plantations and in mines, looked toward India, rather than Malaya, as their homeland.

Indochina. The story of the Indochinese, and particularly the Vietnamese, struggle for independence is far too complex to be related here in anything but the most general terms. In fact, it has not yet ended. French rule in Indochina was in some ways the least enlightened of all the colonial regimes in Southeast Asia. In 1942, for instance, the colonial government had the highest proportion of Europeans in its service of any in the region, some 5100 French officials to 27,000 Indochinese.[7] Four fifths of the population was illiterate, and with over 21,000,000 people only about 500,000 children received any education at all, with only a few thousand receiving any higher education. French rule was characterized by political oppression, severe economic exploitation, and a rigid and stagnant traditional culture.

Revolution alone seemed the answer to Vietnam's problems. During World War I over 100,000 Vietnamese laborers and soldiers were sent to France, where many of them came into contact with liberal and radical thinking, which they then brought home. The Vietnam Nationalist party, patterned organizationally and intellectually on the Chinese Kuomintang, was denied any legal existence and, by the late 1920's, resorted to terrorism as the only form of political expression open to it. Communism rapidly became the major revolutionary ideology in the French colony. In 1920 a young Vietnamese calling himself Nguyen Ai Quoc ("Nguyen, the Patriot"), and later known to the world as Ho Chi Minh, participated actively in the formation of the Communist party in France. In 1930 he organized in Hong Kong what eventually became the Vietnamese (later Indochinese) Communist party. The 1930's in Vietnam were characterized by the spread of Communist ideas and organization, Vietnamese uprisings against French oppression, and strong repressive measures by the colonial government. As a result, the Communist party entered World War II as the major vehicle for the expression of Vietnamese nationalism.

Siam. In the interwar period Siam, which changed its name to Thailand in 1939, continued to modernize. Educational improvements, economic growth, and increasing political sophistication contrasted sharply, however, with the political and administrative domination of the country by the rather extensive royal family. In 1932 a French-trained law professor led a bloodless coup d'état, and a new constitution was promulgated with the agreement of the king, turning him into a reigning, but not ruling, monarch. Since then the country has been ruled by an alliance of army and oligarchy.

CHINA TRIES TO CHANGE

The end of the dynasty, the birth of the republic. During the course of the nineteenth century the once mighty Chinese empire increasingly felt the encroachments of the great imperialist powers. Loss of territory, the imposition of extraterritoriality, and foreign control of the tariff were symbols of China's impotence. But in the first decade of the twentieth century a strong nationalistic movement with liberal overtones emerged, determined to depose the Manchu dynasty, establish a republic, and modernize China. Only by these measures, it was felt, could China be saved.

Sun Yat-sen (1867-1925) emerged as the most important political leader of the new movement. Born near Canton, the son of a tenant farmer, he received a western education in Hawaii, was converted to Christianity, and in 1892 earned a diploma in medicine in Hong Kong. Shortly after, he became a leader in the Chinese nationalist movement, directing his energies toward the overthrow of the Manchus and the formation of a republic. Forced into exile in 1895, he traveled widely in Asia, Europe, and America, seeking political and financial aid from Chinese living abroad. During this period he organized the movement that eventually became the Kuomintang, or Nationalist party.

In 1911 a revolt broke out in China over a foreign loan to finance railways, and the outbreak spread like wildfire throughout the country. Yüan Shih-kai (1859-1916), an outstanding modernized military leader in North China and a confidant of the dowager empress Tzu Hsi (see p. 637), persuaded the imperial clan that the Manchu dynasty was doomed. In February 1912 the child emperor abdicated, and Yüan was asked to form a republican government. Although a few months earlier a revolutionary assembly in Nanking had elected Sun president of the new republic, he now stepped aside in the interest of national unity, and the Nanking assembly elected Yüan.

Dissension and warlordism. During the next decade and a half China went through a period quite similar to the dynastic interregnums that had punctuated all her previous history. It is impossible here to trace the confusion in Chinese politics in more than the barest outline.

In 1913 trouble broke out when Yüan negotiated a large loan with bankers from Britain, France, Germany, and Russia, thus giving these powers substantial influence in the government of the republic. The outcome was a new rebellion, endorsed by Sun. Yüan suppressed the revolt, and Sun fled to Japan. Now firmly entrenched, Yüan dismissed parliament and announced the imminent restoration of the monarchy with himself as emperor. Rebellion broke out again, Yüan's prestige evaporated, and in June 1916 the discredited dictator died.

China now entered a period of political anarchy. Warlords at the head of armies based on local power centers marched and countermarched across the country. The prize was the capital at Peking, possession of which apparently was thought to confirm the legitimacy of its occupier. The political picture was complicated by strained relations with Japan during World War I (see p. 706) and China's entry into the war. For a time the country was divided between two would-be governments, one in the north at Peking, the other in the south at Canton. Composed largely of those who had engineered the revolution of 1911-1912, the Canton government elected Sun as president in 1921.

The Three Principles of the People. Unable to obtain aid from the western powers to overcome the Peking government, Sun requested advisers from the Soviet Union. A military and political advisory group arrived, led by a brilliant Communist and international revolutionary, Michael Borodin. Under Borodin's guidance, the Kuomintang adopted many of the planks of the program subscribed to by the Communist party in the Soviet Union as well as its organizational structure.

Sun died in 1925. More skillful as a propagandist and revolutionist than as a political administrator, he had failed to reunite the Peking regime with his Kuomintang government. However, his social ideology had important results for the future. His most famous work, a series of lectures entitled *Three Principles of the People,* became the political manual of the Kuomintang. The three principles are: (1) nationalism—the liberation of China from foreign domination and the creation of a Chinese nation-state; (2) democracy—"government by the people and for the people"; (3) livelihood—economic security for all the people.

Chiang Kai-shek "unites" China. Sun's eventual successor as leader of the Kuomintang was the son of a petty landlord family, Chiang Kai-shek (1886-   ). Chiang studied at a military academy in Japan, was stirred by Sun's vision of a new China, and returned home to take an active part in the revolution. His obvious abilities attracted Sun's attention, and in 1923 he was sent to Russia for a brief period of indoctrination.

Under Chiang the armies of the Kuomintang began to drive northward in 1926. They encountered little opposition, and by early spring of the following year they reached the Yangtze valley and occupied Shanghai. But dissension broke out between radical and conservative elements in the Kuomintang, and a split became inevitable. The moderates under Chiang created a government at Nanking, and before the end of 1927, public opinion had crystallized behind this regime. Chiang used force against the leftist elements; the end of the Kuomintang alliance with the Communists was written in blood when a proletarian uprising in Canton was quelled with the loss of more than five thousand lives. Back to the Soviet Union went the Communist advisers; many radicals (including the widow of Sun Yat-sen) were driven into exile; and the Chinese Communists were scattered to the hills and mountains of south China, where they set up their own administrative units.

In retrospect, the split of 1927 stands out as a major event in modern Chinese history. Not only were Marxist radicals ousted, but moderate liberals also began to be eliminated. Nationalist strength lay with the city professional, banking, and merchant classes, and the Nanking government came to depend for financial support upon the foreign bankers at Shanghai. The regime began to take on a conservative character which hindered its leaders from understanding and dealing with the problems of the peasants.

With his government established at Nanking, Chiang's armies and his warlord allies again moved north and occupied Peking; China appeared once more to be united. Actually, however, China's unity was more appearance than fact. While large areas of the country had been conquered by Chiang's forces, other regions came under the Kuomintang by agreement between Chiang and local warlords. In theory the warlords were subordinate to Chiang, but they maintained power in their spheres of influence.

During the 1920's Chinese foreign relations improved. China's territorial integrity was guaranteed by the Nine-Power Treaty of 1922 (see p. 707), and China was a member of the League of Nations. The Chinese government obtained the power to fix its own tariffs in 1929, and ten foreign powers gave up or lost the right of extraterritoriality. In addition, during this period Japan appeared relatively conciliatory toward its neighbor. But the sympathizers of the young republic could not overlook certain problem areas. In many regions the people were still tyrannized by bandits, and famine in the northwest cost the lives of millions.

A fervent patriot, Chiang nevertheless had little appreciation for the social and economic problems of his people. He placed much more store in their moral regeneration by traditional means. Strongly versed in Confucian teachings and at the same time a Christian, Chiang in the mid-thirties established the New Life Movement, which was a combination of Christian and Confucian ethics. He would have done better to appreciate the intellectual changes taking place in China and the social and economic aspirations of the peasants.

The New Culture Movement and Chinese communism. During World War I a Chinese intellectual revolution began at Peking University and then spread to students all over the country. Its first influential voice was the magazine *New Youth*. Returning from universities in the United States and Europe, students brought ideas of western science, liberalism, and democracy. In essence they sought to establish a new order and a new set of values to replace much of the discredited Confucian tradition.

Disillusionment with western values rapidly set in, however, following the Versailles peace treaty which tendered Chinese Shantung to Japan. Antiwestern sentiment was expressed in a violent student demonstration on May 4, 1919. A new ideological orientation now began in the New Culture Movement. Study groups were formed, especially at Peking University, where professors and students began to read Marx and Lenin and to apply their thought to the Chinese scene. Lenin's analysis and attack on imperialism struck a responsive chord. With some guidance from Russian Comintern agents, the First Congress of the Chinese Communist party was held in July 1921. A young student at Peking university named Mao Tse-tung was a delegate. About the same time, Chinese worker-students in France established the Young China Communist party in Paris. One of its leaders was Chou En-lai, later premier of Communist China.

Mao Tse-tung was born in December 1893 in Hunan province, a traditional center of Chinese revolutionary activity. In 1918 he went to Peking University, where he worked as library assistant under Li Ta-chao, the founder of an important Marxist study group and one of the founders of the Chinese

Communist party. Mao began to emerge as a distinctive leader with a new program for revolution when he wrote a report for the Communist party in 1927 about the peasant movement in Hunan. His belief that the revolution must base itself on peasant uprisings was condemned by the Central Committee of the Chinese Communist party, which adhered closely to the Moscow policy of basing the revolution on the urban proletariat. Nevertheless, Mao led a Hunanese peasant uprising that became known as the "Autumn Harvest Uprising." It was crushed, and in May 1928 Mao and other Communist leaders joined forces in the border region of Hunan and Kiangsi provinces. Acutely conscious of peasant needs, Mao organized the peasants in his region into a Chinese "soviet." Other Communist leaders did the same in other regions, and in 1931 delegates from the various local soviets in China met and proclaimed the birth of the Chinese Soviet Republic. Meanwhile, Chiang Kai-shek's agents had destroyed the Shanghai apparatus of the Communist party. Within three years large Communist enclaves with a total population of about nine million existed in South China.

Mao Tse-tung's success as a Communist leader depended largely on his realization that it was the Chinese peasant, not the urban worker, who could be made the agent of revolution. Farmers' cooperatives were established and tax systems reformed. More drastic measures included the seizure and division of moderate-sized and large farms and the distribution of the goods taken from the landowners.

The Nationalists, who had neglected the countryside for the cities, were apprehensive of Mao's success. From 1931 to 1934 Chiang launched five military campaigns against the Communists, the last employing one million men and a German military staff. To escape annihilation, the Communists made their famous Long March two thousand miles to the northwest. Only a remnant of the original force reached Yenan, in Shensi province, where a new Communist stronghold was set up in 1935.

Changes in Chinese life. The changes that took place in Chinese life between the

Mao Tse-tung's belief that the revolution must be based on peasant uprisings was rejected by the early Chinese Communist party and was counter to the Marxian doctrine held by Moscow. Here a young Mao gives a speech at a meeting of Chinese Communists.

times of the Nationalist revolution and the beginning of World War II in the Far East were noteworthy. The number of Chinese receiving an education, though still small, increased remarkably. Chinese intellectuals championed the use of a new and simplified written language, while scholars labored for the adoption of Mandarin as a national speech so that men from all parts of China could speak together. Social customs were also considerably altered; in urban areas folkways and dress began to give way to occidental customs and fashions. Telephones, electric lights, modern water systems, and movie palaces appeared in the large cities.

Chinese commerce increased rapidly. Total foreign trade was seven times as great in 1929 as it had been in 1894. Nevertheless, civil warfare, currency insecurity, inefficient transportation systems, and national poverty all combined to keep China virtually an undeveloped nation. For the most part industry was controlled by foreign entrepreneurs, who raked in the profits. Because the impressive economic potentialities of China were not exploited for the advantage of the Chinese, the inhabitants of the republic continued to suffer.

JAPAN BECOMES A WORLD POWER

The Twenty-one Demands. As the twentieth century dawned, Japan had astonished the world by the tempo of its modernization. From a static, militarily weak, and dominantly agricultural nation, it was rapidly becoming a dynamic, militarily powerful, and highly industrialized state. There were serious problems ahead, however. The liberal statesmen of Japan sought means not only to support the rapidly increasing population but also to democratize the constitution. Unfortunately, Japan followed a path that led ultimately to aggression against its neighbors and to more, not less, dictatorial government at home.

When the First World War broke out in 1914, Japan ordered Germany to remove its warships from the Far East and to surrender the Kiaochow territory in China to Japan "with a view to the eventual restoration of the same to China." When Germany failed to reply to this request, the Japanese government declared war and seized the territory. Japan had not consulted China at all during this time, nor did the Japanese hesitate to violate Chinese neutrality.

In January 1915 Japan presented China with the notorious Twenty-one Demands, which startled the world by their frank disclosure of Japanese imperialistic designs on the Asian continent. Preoccupied as they were with the gigantic struggle in Europe, the European powers did little to hinder the Japanese, and indignant China had not the physical means to protest effectively. Under threats of coercion, the Chinese government acceded to the first sixteen demands in May; the remainder were reserved for later consideration. The intervention of the

United States helped nullify the most dictatorial of the demands, which would have brought China completely under Japan's domination. China was forced, however, to acknowledge Japan's authority in Shantung province and to extend Japanese railway and land concessions in southern Manchuria.

In 1917 the Allied powers secretly agreed to support Japanese claims in the peace conference that would follow the First World War. While not a party to the agreement, the United States in the Lansing-Ishii agreement (1917) declared somewhat reluctantly that Japan deserved "special interest in China" owing to "territorial propinquity." Japan, in turn, agreed to respect the Open Door Policy in China. The Allies' position toward China was most embarrassing; China had entered the war on their side, chiefly to secure a spot during peace negotiations so that Japanese ambitions might be checked. China's only hope for preserving its independence lay in the growing tension between the United States and Japan.

Japanese foreign relations in the 1920's. Japan profited from its role in the war; in one way or another it controlled Shantung, Manchuria, southern Mongolia, and the German islands north of the equator, besides the territories and concessions it had wrested from China and Russia prior to the war. The increased power of Japan was particularly alarming to the United States and the British dominions in the Pacific. In 1921 Great Britain allowed its treaty with Japan, which Britain had renewed in 1911, to terminate without further renewal.

The growth of Japan's hold on China is revealed in a comparison of the investments by foreign powers in that country. In 1902 Japanese investment in China was negligible, but in 1914 it rivaled the investments of both Russia and Germany, and by 1931 it was second only to Great Britain's. In 1931 Japanese capital represented about 35 percent of all foreign investment in China. At the Washington Conference in 1921, the agreement by the three leading naval powers —Great Britain, the United States, and Japan—to reduce the tonnage of their capital ships in order to achieve a respective ratio of 5-5-3 recognized the position of the Japanese navy as the third most powerful in the world.

In 1922 the Nine-Power Treaty was signed at Washington. All the signatories agreed to respect the independence, sovereignty, territoriality, and administrative integrity of China. Furthermore, they were to use their influence to preserve the Open Door Policy and "to refrain from taking advantage of conditions in China in order to seek special rights or privileges which would abridge the rights of subjects or citizens of friendly states, and from countenancing action inimical to the security of such states."[8] It is impossible to reconcile Japan's later acts in China after 1931 with the pact which it signed in 1922, just as it is difficult for the other signatories to excuse their apathy toward Japanese aggressions in China before they were themselves drawn into war against Japan.

The struggle for liberalism. From 1889, when Japan's new constitution was promulgated, to 1918, the government was mainly in the hands of an aristocratic oligarchy of elder statesmen called the *Genro*. By the end of World War I most of these political patriarchs had passed away, and the field of politics was now open for new blood, a fact signalized by the election to the post of prime minister of the first commoner ever to hold that office, Hara Takashi.

The period from 1918 to 1930 was of crucial importance. Japan seemed to be moving toward the establishment of a democratic, parliamentary government under its new liberal political leaders. There were serious obstacles to be overcome, however—not only the lack of a widespread popular liberal tradition and inexperience in parliamentary politics but also other factors. The concentration of wealth in the hands of a few fantastically rich families was not democratically healthy. Militarism, based on the revered *samurai* tradition which exalted war, was strong, and to this militaristic virus in the Japanese blood stream was added a strong authoritarian tradition, fostered by secret societies and the cult of Shintoism.

Many secret societies were connected with the army and were ultranationalistic and terroristic. Long a feature of Japanese life, they multiplied rapidly in membership after 1930. Originally a simple nature cult, Shinto by the end of the nineteenth century had been transformed into the cult of emperor worship and the deification of the state. Thus the Japanese were able to build a strong regime upon cults that already occupied an important position in the lives of the people, while the Nazis were forced to resurrect Teutonic cults that had been extinct for centuries in order to arouse national fervor.

It was with these serious handicaps that parliamentary government after 1918 sought to lead the nation away from excessive nationalism and militarism. Liberals in the Diet showed great promise and courage as they pressed reform and criticized the imperialistic intervention in Siberia of the Japanese army (along with other Allied forces) during the confused civil war following the Russian Revolution. Although liberalism suffered a serious setback in 1921 with the assassination of Prime Minister Hara, liberal strength returned in 1925 when the Universal Manhood Suffrage Bill was passed, granting the franchise to most males over twenty-five. However, liberal progress was often paid for with conservative legislation. Soon afterward a reactionary government came to power, advocating a stronger policy toward China; but this militaristic regime was in turn quickly succeeded by the most liberal government Japan had ever had. Led by Prime Minister Hamaguchi Yuko, this liberal regime assumed a policy of conciliation toward China, reduced army expenditures, and signed the London Naval Treaty.

Economic progress. In the economic sphere, Japan forged ahead rapidly. Thousands of factories were built, and Japanese manufacturers undersold foreign competitors in the world market, owing in part to the low Japanese wage standard and in part to the modern machine techniques which Japanese industrialists were swift to adopt. In textiles especially, Japan captured one market after another. Commerce and industry were controlled by a few giant concerns, in whose hands the greater part of the country's wealth was concentrated. By the 1930's Japan had become the first exporter in rayon, cotton textiles, matches, and raw silk.

Japanese economic prosperity was, however, more apparent than real. Serious economic weaknesses existed. The country lacked natural resources such as coal, iron, petroleum, timber, and cotton. The population was growing at an unbelievable rate. In 1920 the population was 56 million; in 1931 it had reached 65 million persons, crowded into a land area smaller than the state of California. In 1932 the annual increase reached 1,000,000. The Japanese economy needed to find 250,000 new jobs for young workers every year, to say nothing of feeding 1,000,000 additional mouths annually. Up to 1930 Japan had managed to pay its way by expanding its exports, which gave the nation foreign credits to buy raw materials and foodstuffs abroad. Should these exports suffer a substantial contraction, Japan would then be confronted with a serious national crisis. Just such a crisis occurred in the world depression which began in the 1930's.

Military fascism comes to Japan. Economic depression came to Japan with little warning and with shattering impact. Between 1929 and 1931, the Japanese export trade was cut almost in half. The sale of raw silk, which amounted to 40 percent of Japanese exports, rapidly plunged downward as the United States drastically reduced purchases. Unemployment, wage cuts, and strikes became common. As in Germany on the eve of Hitler's rise to power, frustration among the younger generation was widespread.

In 1929 and 1930 the liberal prime minister, Hamaguchi, sought with relatively little success to meet the depression. He also followed a conciliatory policy toward China and was willing to cooperate in disarmament proposals—aims bitterly opposed by the militaristic clique. Shot in November 1930, the prime minister died the following spring. This assassination was a tragedy from which Japanese liberalism never recovered in the decade before the Second World War.

A new group of ultranationalistic and militaristic leaders came into power. In contrast to the personal dictatorships in Nazi Germany and Fascist Italy, however, Japan was dominated by a military clique, which terrorized the civilian members of the government. Scoffing at democracy and peace, these leaders plotted to shelve parliamentary government in Tokyo and to use force on the mainland of China to secure essential raw materials and markets for goods, to spread the "superior" Japanese culture throughout Asia, and to find space for Japan's overcrowded population. This "beneficial mission" was known as the New Order in Asia.

SUMMARY

Between the two world wars imperialism went on the defensive before the rise of nationalism in the nonwestern world. The nationalistic stimulus in sub-Saharan Africa stemmed from the Pan-African movement of educated Negroes outside their homeland as well as from a very small educated class within the African states. This group sought to replace alien imperialistic control with self-government and to bring about the cultural resurgence of a people whose tribal way of life was slowly disintegrating as the black man came into contact with the numerous facets of western culture. The Pan-African movement did not affect the masses of the people in most areas, however; only in the troubled multiracial society of the Union of South Africa was there widespread unrest among Africans.

Nationalism was much stronger in the Arab world. In the lands formerly controlled by the Ottomans, Arab nationalists bitterly contested European control as set up in the mandate system; the British were ultimately forced to grant complete independence to Iraq, and outbreaks of violence occurred in the French mandate of Syria-Lebanon and especially in Palestine, where the Arabs resented the British attempt to set up a national home for the Jews. In Iran the nationalists threw off the influence of Britain and set up a government under the control of Riza Shah Pahlavi. Dissatisfaction with

French rule mounted in North Africa, and self-government was granted to Egypt by the British. In other areas of the Middle East Turkish nationalists under Mustafa Kemal built a new Turkey, while in the Arabian peninsula a new Arab power, Saudi Arabia, emerged under the dynamic leadership of ibn-Saud.

The strongest nationalism in all the colonial areas developed in India under the powerful leadership of Mahatma Gandhi. The effective use of nonviolence in his civil disobedience campaigns forced Britain to grant a substantial measure of self-government to the Indians.

In Southeast Asia nationalism began to rise steadily, although it did not as yet affect the majority of people. In Burma, Britain conceded some degree of self-government; unrest grew stronger in the French and Dutch colonies. In the Philippines nationalism was given ample opportunity to develop, and self-government was finally granted.

China was not, strictly speaking, a part of the colonial world, yet in many ways this vast and backward land was under the indirect influence of the great western powers. Faced with the prospect of virtual partition by these nations, Chinese nationalists, under the leadership of Sun Yat-sen, overthrew the Manchu dynasty and established a republic. After years of confusion and conflict between rival factions, power was consolidated under the Kuomintang and Chiang Kai-shek. The Chiang regime effected a gradual modernization of urban China, though agrarian reform was largely neglected.

Japanese history in the opening decades of the twentieth century was characterized by amazing progress in industrialization and by an attempt to introduce a democratic and responsible system of government. By 1919 the island kingdom had become one of the world's great powers. But its spectacular rise to greatness was also characterized by serious omens. There was disturbing evidence that military fascism was more potent than democracy and expansionist ambitions more powerful than love for peace.

SUGGESTIONS FOR READING

Barbara Ward, **The Interplay of East and West**, Norton, 1957. A stimulating study of the interacting influences between East and West from ancient times to the present. P. Welty, **The Asians**,* Preceptor; and H. G. Matthew, ed., **Asia in the Modern World**,* Mentor, are handy introductions. For valuable comparative studies see R. Emerson, **From Empire to Nation: The Rise of the Asian and African Peoples**,* Beacon; and J. Romein, **The Asian Century: A History of Modern Nationalism in Asia**, California, 1962.

H. Kohn and W. Sokolsky, **African Nationalism in the Twentieth Century**,* Anvil. A summary of twentieth-century developments. Significant articles from the magazine **Foreign Affairs** can be found in Philip W. Quigg, ed., **Africa**, Praeger, 1964. Two astute observers survey Africa as it was before the Second World War: J. Huxley, **Africa View**, Harper, 1931; and W. M. Macmillan, **Africa Emergent, A Survey of Social, Political, and Economic Trends in British Africa**,* Penguin.

G. Lenczowski, **The Middle East in World Affairs**, Cornell, 1956. A first-rate survey. See also S. N. Fisher, **The Middle East**, Knopf, 1959; Howard M. Sachar, **The Emergence of the Middle East**, Knopf, 1939; and W. C. Smith, **Islam in Modern History**,* Mentor. A good short history of the Jewish people is Abba Eban, **My People**, Random House, 1969. See also B. Halperin, **The Idea of the Jewish State**, Harvard, 1961. The Arab view of the political control of Palestine is presented eloquently in G. Antonius, **The Arab Awakening: The Story of the Arab National Movement**,* Capricorn. On the impact of westernization on Turkey see N. Berkes, **The Development of Secularism**

in Turkey, McGill Univ., 1964; and D. E. Webster, **The Turkey of Ataturk**, Amer. Academy of Pol. and Soc. Science, 1939. Other special studies are S. H. Longrigg, **Syria and Lebanon Under French Mandate**, Oxford, 1958, and **Iraq, 1900 to 1950**, Oxford, 1953.

T. W. Wallbank, **India: A Survey of the Heritage and Growth of Indian Nationalism,** Holt (Berkshire Studies), and **India in the New Era**, Scott, Foresman, 1951. Two useful, authoritative surveys. For invaluable studies of the architects of Indian nationalism see Stanley Wolpert, **Tilak and Gokhale**, California, 1962; and Krishna Kripalani, **Rabindranath Tagore**, Oxford, 1962. An absorbing autobiography is Jawaharlal Nehru, **Toward Freedom**,* Beacon.

J. Cady, **Southeast Asia**, McGraw-Hill, 1964. See also the perceptive appraisal by D. Dubois, **Social Forces in Southeast Asia**, Harvard, 1959. G. M. Beckmann, **The Modernization of China and Japan**, Harper & Row, 1962, interrelates the process of modernization in these two nations. K. S. Latourette, **A History of Modern China**,* Penguin, is an excellent resume. For the basic study of the Kuomintang regime see Ch'ien Tuan-Sheng, **The Government and Politics of China**,* Stanford. E. O. Reischauer, **Japan, Past and Present**, Knopf, 1964, emphasizes the modern period. For a detailed description of how the military extremists undermined parliamentary government in Japan see R. Storry, **The Double Patriots**, Houghton Mifflin, 1957.

*Indicates an inexpensive paperbound edition.

Chapter 30

The Tragic Decade and Global Conflict

Depression and World War II: 1930-1945

INTRODUCTION. On September 1, 1939, Hitler's legions marched into Poland, and the Second World War began. This outbreak of terrible violence marked the end of a tragic decade.

Ten years earlier the Wall Street stock market crash had ushered in a world-wide financial crisis—the Great Depression. Nation after nation fell victim to industrial decline, bank failures, deflated prices and profits, and commercial stagnation. People the world over suffered from lowered standards of living, unemployment, hunger, and fear of the future. In the western democracies the buoyant optimism of the 1920's was superseded by self-criticism and despair.

In desperation governments sought economic recovery by adopting restrictive autarkist policies—high tariffs, import quotas, and barter agreements—and by experimenting with new plans for their internal economies. The United States launched the New Deal, and Britain adopted far-reaching measures in the development of a planned national economy. In Nazi Germany economic recovery was pursued through rearmament, conscription, and public works programs, while in Italy Mussolini tightened the economic controls of his corporate state. Observers in many lands saw in the gigantic economic planning and state ownership of the Soviet Union what appeared to be a depression-proof economic system and a solution to the crisis in capitalism.

The economic malaise of the 1930's gave dictators their chance: Hitler took over control in Germany, and a militaristic clique grasped the reins of power in Japan. In 1931 the Japanese pounced upon Manchuria, and when the League of Nations proved powerless to interfere, war between Japan and China raged intermittently throughout the decade. While China was fighting for its national existence, Italy conquered Abyssinia, fascism emerged triumphant from the Spanish civil war, and by a series of "incidents" Hitler swelled the territory of the Third Reich and increased its power. Faced with blatant aggression by the Axis powers (Germany, Italy, Japan), England and France abandoned their faith in collective security and the League of Nations and adopted a policy of appeasement. Meanwhile, the Soviet Union played for time to build up its own defenses, and the United States detached itself from the increasing world tensions by maintaining its traditional policy of isolationism. Finally driven to the limit by the Axis, the European democracies and later the Soviet Union and United States took up arms to defend their independence and end the threat of world conquest.

Far more than World War I, World War II represented global conflict. Furthermore, the Second World War was a "total war" in that never before had civilian populations been so deeply involved. They were targets of the guns and falling bombs, and many were participants, often fighting beside the soldiers.

In many ways this was a new kind of war, not only in its enormous scope but also in its techniques and in its weapons. Technology made possible the mass bombing raids, the air-borne invasions, the amphibious assaults, the operations of carrier-based planes, the maneuvers of armored divisions, the coordinated efforts of the giant naval task force, and the mass murders of Nazi concentration camps; and science and technology combined to create the ultimate in efficiency and horror—the nuclear bomb. Yet World War II was also a war of men, fighting as men have fought throughout human history. After the weapons and techniques of modern technological warfare had done their worst, it was men who had to win or lose the battles. It was men who finally destroyed the Axis.

DEPRESSION THREATENS DEMOCRACY AND BREEDS TOTALITARIANISM

Phony prosperity of the "roaring twenties." In 1929 the world's most prosperous nation was the United States. President Hoover declared in his inaugural address:

Ours is a land rich in resources, stimulating in its glorious beauty, filled with millions of happy homes blessed with comfort and opportunity. . . . I have no fears for the future of our country. It is bright with hope.[1]

But despite the buoyant optimism in the United States and the apparent economic well-being in other countries, the world economy was in an unhealthy state. One by one, the cornerstones of the pre-1914 economic system—multilateral trade, the gold standard, and the interchangeability of currencies—were crumbling.

The desire for self-sufficiency, or autarky, led nations to manufacture goods or grow products at home, even though this policy was sometimes more expensive than importing what they needed. Then, to protect home products against competition from foreign imports, high tariff walls were raised. The United States led the movement toward higher tariffs. Other nations quickly retaliated with discriminatory tariffs against the United States and each other, American foreign trade seriously declined, and the volume of world trade steadily decreased.

The high tariffs had a crucial effect on the payment of war debts. As a result of America's high tariff, only a sort of economic ring-around-the-rosy kept the reparations and war-debt payments going. During the 1920's the former allies paid their war-debt installments to the United States chiefly with funds obtained from German reparations payments, and Germany was able to make these payments only because of large private loans from the United States and Britain. Similarly, American investments abroad provided the dollars which alone made it possible for foreign nations to buy American products. By 1931 the world was reeling from the worst depression of all time, and the entire structure of reparations and war debts collapsed.

Panic on Wall Street: the crash of 1929. In the postwar decade the activities of daring and often unscrupulous speculators made international finance a precarious and exciting world of its own. Operating on an international scale, the Swedish swindler Ivar Kreuger cornered the match market; in the United States, Samuel Insull's attempts to maintain a vast public-utilities empire helped push stock prices to dizzy heights; and an English speculator, Clarence Hatry, indirectly touched off the Wall Street crash. When Hatry's shaky companies failed, his English victims dumped their American securities to get ready cash. This in turn triggered a sickening slump in stock prices on Wall Street. The crash came in 1929, on October 24, "Black Thursday." "Prices fell farther and faster, and the ticker lagged more and more. By eleven o'clock the market had degenerated into a wild, mad scramble to sell. In the crowded boardrooms across the country the ticker told of a frightful collapse. . . . The uncertainty led more and more people to try to sell. . . . By eleven-thirty the market had surrendered to blind relentless fear. This, indeed, was panic."[2] Within a few weeks, stock prices had declined 40

percent. Fortunes were wiped out, business confidence was blasted, and the demand for goods plummeted. The growing paralysis in the American economy spread all over the world as the United States began to call in its foreign loans and decrease its imports.

In the face of impending world-wide disaster, President Hoover in 1931 succeeded in obtaining a moratorium of one year on all intergovernmental debts. At the Lausanne Conference (1932) German reparations payments were practically canceled in the hope that the American government also would make a substantial concession in reducing war debts, but the United States refused to concede that there was a logical connection between reparations and war debts. As the depression deepened, the debtors could not continue their payments. France refused outright in 1932; Great Britain and four other nations made token payments for a time, then stopped entirely in 1934; and only Finland continued to meet its schedule of payments. In the meantime, Germany had completely stopped paying reparations.

The depression begins. The effects of the depression were catastrophic the world over. Governments could not balance their budgets, factories shut down, and harvests rotted in the fields. The price of wheat fell to the lowest figure in more than three hundred years. The lives of the grower of cacao in the African Gold Coast, the coffee grower in Brazil, and the copra plantation worker in the Dutch East Indies were blighted, as were those of the factory worker in Pittsburgh, Sheffield, Lille, and Frankfurt. In the "land of plenty," one of the popular songs of the day was "Brother, Can You Spare a Dime?"

During the years following the crash most nations strengthened their resolve to employ autarky as their guiding economic principle. To increase exports and decrease imports, quota systems were put into operation, and tariffs were boosted to new highs. After almost a century of free trade, modified by a few protective duties levied during and after World War i, Great Britain enacted a high tariff in 1932 but allowed for the system of imperial preference, whereby lower tariffs were levied on members of the empire than on outside nations. The net effect was the increase of trade within the empire at the expense of trade with outside countries.

Another technique for increasing exports was to depreciate the currency, which meant reducing the value of a nation's money. When Japan depreciated the yen, an American dollar or a British pound could buy more Japanese goods. In effect, depreciating the yen lowered the price of Japanese exports. In most cases, however, devaluation brought only a temporary trade advantage; other countries could play the same game. In 1934 the United States reduced the amount of gold backing the dollar by about 40 percent.

The disturbances in the natural flow of world trade caused by the depression led nations to hoard their gold reserves—a trend strengthened by the fact that most nations had comparatively little gold, the United States, Great Britain, and France controlling three fourths of the world's supply. Many nations went off the gold standard, which meant that they would not pay foreign creditors in gold. Great Britain abandoned the gold standard in 1931; two years later the United States did likewise. Without gold as the medium of exchange between countries, barter became more and more prevalent in international trade.

The depression had profound implications for politics. The rash of democratic constitutions adopted after World War I had seemed to assure government by and for the common man, but in the tragic thirties democracy in many nations went into eclipse as unemployed and starving masses turned to dictators who promised jobs and bread. The hardships of the depression formed a dismal backdrop on a political stage where dictators seized the leading roles.

Considering the shattering impact of this world economic malaise, there has been relatively little research and comprehensive literature about its background and causes. Was it the inevitable consequence of unwise peace treaties; was it the result of the economic losses and disruption of trade suffered by the belligerents during World War I; or was it mainly caused by the United States tariff and reparations policies compounded by a fanatical fever of stock speculation? A

noted economist has called attention to a number of unhealthy conditions in the American economy: (1) the uneven distribution of income between the very rich and the extremely poor; (2) the lack of stability, honesty, and good management in the corporate structure; (3) an inherently unsound banking system; and (4) the lack of adequate economic intelligence available to businessmen.[3] Although all these factors existed to some degree in other national economies, the United States occupied such a central position in world finance that any substantial reverse or breakdown in its economy inevitably had world repercussions. As the dean of a noted American school of business administration has stated: "I can only repeat that I think it was primarily of American domestic origin, though with many complicating circumstances."[4]

The Five-Year Plans in the Soviet Union. The years from 1929 to 1939 comprised a dark decade in Russia—a period of massive industrialization and of convulsive inner struggles as Stalin established a personal dictatorship both total and terrible. While in the capitalist countries factories and mines were idle or running on reduced schedules and millions were unemployed, the Soviet people worked many hours a day, six days a week, in an all-out attempt to revolutionize Russia's economic structure. For the first time in history, a government controlled all economic activity.

In 1928 Stalin proposed a Five-Year Plan, the first of a number of such schemes aimed at the relatively swift accumulation of capital resources through the buildup of heavy industry, the collectivization of agriculture, and the restricted manufacture of consumers' goods. Although capitalism in the form of the NEP was abolished, citizens were permitted to own certain types of private property—houses, furniture, clothes, and personal effects. They could not, however, own property which could be utilized to make profits by hiring workers. The only employer was the state.

As part of the plan, the government took control of agriculture through the state farms. By the beginning of the Second World War 90 percent of the Russian land under cultivation was organized in one of two ways. The state farm (*sovkhoz*) was owned outright by the government and run by paid laborers. The collective farm (*kolkhoz*) was created from land given up by the peasants who accepted the government's decree to merge their holdings and from land taken from the *kulaks*—well-to-do farmers. The *kolkhoz* members worked the land under the management of a board of directors. At the end of the year the farm's net earnings were computed in cash and in kind, and the members were paid on the basis of the number of days they had worked.

A second Five-Year Plan, begun in 1933, sought to redress some of the mistakes of the first; greater emphasis was placed on improving the quality of industrial products and on manufacturing more consumers' goods. The year 1938 witnessed the initiation of the third Five-Year Plan, in which national defense became the major consideration. Industrial plants were shifted inland to the east, and efforts were made to develop new sources of oil and other important commodities. The world's largest tractor factory was erected in Chelyabinsk, the greatest electric power station in Dnepropetrovsk, and the largest automobile plant at Gorki.

The plans achieved remarkable results. Soviet authorities claimed in 1932 an increase of industrial output of 334 percent over 1914, and in 1937 a further increase of 180 percent over 1932. However, the high volume of production was often coupled with mediocre quality, and the achievements were secured only at an enormous cost in human life and suffering. At first a bare subsistence scale of living was imposed on the people by the burdensome expense of importing heavy machinery, tools, equipment, and finished steel from abroad. These purchases were paid for by the sale of food and raw materials in the world's markets at a time when the prices of such goods had drastically fallen. An even greater cost was the terrible loss of life brought about by the callous collectivization of agriculture. By a decree of February 1930, about one million *kulaks* were forced off their land and all their possessions confiscated. Many farmers consistently opposed regimentation by the state,

often slaughtering their herds when faced with the loss of their land. In some sections they revolted, and thousands were executed. A serious famine broke out and several million peasants died of starvation.

Another casualty of the Five-Year Plans was Lenin's basic concept of economic equalitarianism. In 1931 Stalin declared that equality in wages was "alien and detrimental to Soviet production" and a "petit-bourgeois deviation." So much propaganda was used to implant this ideological twist that the masses came to accept the new doctrine of the inequality of wages as a fundamental Communist principle. Piecework in industry became more prevalent, and bonuses and incentives were used to speed up production. It was indeed ironic that capitalistic practices were introduced to stimulate the growth of communism.

The great purges. While the Five-Year Plans were forging ahead, Stalin was establishing an all-powerful personal autocracy. From 1928 to 1931 and again from 1935 to 1938, Stalin settled his accounts with all his rivals through barbaric purges. The long arm of the secret police gathered in thousands of Soviet citizens to face the firing squad. Of the six original members of the 1920 Politburo who survived Lenin, all were purged by Stalin. Old Bolsheviks who had been loyal comrades of Lenin, high officers in the Red Army, and directors of industry were liquidated. It has been estimated that between 5 and 6 percent of the total population passed through the pretrial prisons of the secret police. The fitting climax to the purges came in 1940, when Stalin's archcritic Trotsky, living as an exile in Mexico, was murdered by a Soviet agent.

In 1936, notwithstanding the terror of his secret police, Stalin ostensibly turned to constitutionalism. A new constitution declared that: "All power in the U.S.S.R. belongs to the toilers of town and country as represented by the Soviets of Toilers' Deputies." On the surface many basic rights, such as free speech, secret ballot, and universal suffrage, were granted, together with a number of important economic and social rights. In practice, however, much of the new document was mere window dressing.

The people, however, were given some feeling of participation in their government by means of parades, rallies, and carefully supervised elections. The liberal features of the new constitution also improved Soviet Russia's image abroad. Nevertheless, the Communist party, with less than 1.5 percent of the population, still continued to dictate the government policy.

Crisis in Germany. World depression, accompanied by the cancellation of foreign loans to Germany and the withdrawal of foreign investments, was the culminating blow to the ill-fated Weimar Republic. In 1931 all banks were forced to close, and disorders broke out in many cities. A year later the number of unemployed had reached six million; and desperate, jobless workers roamed the streets shouting, "Give us bread." Night after night, police and military troops battled hungry mobs.

Up to this time the Nazi party had attracted only lukewarm support; there were but a handful of Nazi deputies in the Reichstag. By the summer of 1932, however, their number had swelled to 230, and the Nazis had become the largest political party. Hungry, frightened, and desperate, the impoverished masses turned to Hitler as a source of salvation. And, ironically enough, the rich also saw their salvation in Nazism. Alarmed at the growth of the German Communist movement, the great industrialists supported Hitler—a rabid anti-Communist—and his Nazi party as a shield against a proletarian revolution.

Once the Nazi movement began to gain popularity, Hitler and his master propagandist, Joseph Goebbels, utilized every type of persuasion to make the mass of the people permanent converts to Nazism. All over Germany huge meetings were organized. Then thousands of Storm Troopers marched into stadiums to form a great swastika, while martial music, the roll of drums, and the trumpeting of bugles filled the air. At first, no speaker was seen on the platform, starkly illuminated by a huge spotlight. Then, as the suspense became almost unbearable, into the beam of light stepped Goebbels or, on major occasions, Hitler himself. For hours the speaker poured forth a torrent of words.

Theoretically collective farms are voluntary cooperatives, but in reality communal organization was forced on the rural population of the Soviet Union by Communist officials. Here workers on a Ukrainian collective farm assemble to discuss their work.

"Germany is in ruins," "This is the result of reparations," "The Jews are behind all our woes," "It is only the Nazi party that can make Germany strong and prosperous, that will repudiate the reparations and make Germany's army and navy the fear of all Europe." Thrilled by these colossal displays and mesmerized by rituals and ranting speeches, the masses gave the Nazis increasing support.

Hitler becomes chancellor. For the Nazi party, 1932—when Hitler ran against the incumbent Paul von Hindenburg for the presidency of the German republic—was a crucial year. Although Hitler was defeated, Hindenburg asked the Nazi leader to join coalitions on two subsequent occasions. Hitler refused, demanding what was equivalent to dictatorial power.

It became increasingly difficult for the German ministries to carry on the government, and a second general election held in November was so costly to the Nazis that

With crusading zeal, Hitler used every type of propaganda to make the German people permanent converts to Nazism: huge meetings, parades, sporting events. Here, Hitler makes his entrance at the annual Nazi rally in Nuremberg, where he made some of his most virulent speeches.

the party treasury almost went bankrupt. Some observers believed that the Nazis had passed the crest of their power. At this point, however, a clique of aristocratic nationalists and powerful industrialists, fearful of a Communist revolution and the growing strength of the trade union movement, offered Hitler the chancellorship. In January 1933 a mixed cabinet of nationalists was created with Hitler at the head. Because he did not have a clear majority in the Reichstag, Hitler called a general election for March 5. During the campaign, radio broadcasts were monopolized by Nazi propaganda, and Storm Troopers bullied and coerced the voters. But many Germans became disgusted with the strong-arm methods, and the Nazis needed a dramatic incident to clear a majority in the election.

Just before the election, fire gutted the Reichstag building. The blaze was blamed on the Communists, though there was strong suspicion that the Nazis themselves had started it. When the votes were counted, Hitler controlled 44 percent of the deputies. The added support of the Nationalists (another 8 percent) gave the Nazis a bare majority. Quickly the Reichstag passed the Enabling Act, which granted Hitler the right to legislate by decree for the next four years. The Weimar constitution was never formally—only effectively—abolished; the Reichstag continued as a phantom legislature, but nearly all political power was exercised by one organization, the National Socialist party.

A dread intimation of things to come was Germany's withdrawal from the League of Nations in 1933. Two years later, in defiance of the Treaty of Versailles, Hitler introduced conscription. When President von Hindenburg died in 1934, Hitler became both chancellor and president; he was known as Führer (leader), and the new regime was described as the Third Reich.*

Persecution of the Jews. Hitler ruthlessly uprooted and smashed the democratic institutions by which he was brought to power. All rival political parties were disbanded by force, and individuals who had spoken out against Nazism mysteriously disappeared after midnight visits from the dreaded Gestapo—the Nazi secret police. Concentration camps were built to house thousands of prisoners. It has been estimated that in 1933 nineteen thousand Germans committed suicide and sixteen thousand more died from unexplained causes. Not until the end of World War II was the full horror of Nazi brutality revealed (see p. 733).

The doctrine of Aryan racial superiority was an integral part of Hitler's program, and the Jews bore the brunt of Nazi persecution. They were blamed for the Versailles Treaty, for all that was bad about capitalism, for revolutionary communism, for pacifism, and for internationalism—all represented as being facets of a Jewish plot to destroy Germany and seize control of the world. That such a fantastic tale was seriously believed by a considerable number of the citizens indicated the state of near psychosis into which Germany had fallen.

Once he was dictator, Hitler did everything to stifle and to destroy the Jews. They were prohibited from owning businesses, barred from public service, and deprived

*The First Reich was created by Otto the Great in 962; the Second by Bismarck in 1871.

of citizenship. Marriage between "Aryans" and "non-Aryans" was forbidden. Six million Jews were killed in extermination camps, where the Nazis used the most refined techniques of science to carry out loathsome mass murders. The German commandant of one of these camps has described its methods:

I used . . . a crystallized prussic acid dropped into the death chamber. It took from three to fifteen minutes to kill the people in the chamber, according to climatic conditions. We knew when the people were dead because their screaming stopped. We usually waited about half an hour before we opened the doors and removed the bodies. After the bodies were removed, our special commandos took off the rings and extracted the gold from the teeth of the corpses. . . . we built our gas chambers to accommodate two thousand people at one time. . . .⁵

Nazi propaganda and education. A Reich culture cabinet was set up to instill a single pattern of thought in literature, the press, broadcasting, drama, music, art, and movies. Forbidden books, including the works of some of Germany's most distinguished men of letters, were seized and destroyed in huge bonfires.

The school system was integrated with the German Youth Movement, which drilled and regimented boys and girls between the ages of ten and fourteen. The boys were taught above all else to be ready to fight and die for their Führer; the girls, to mother the many babies needed by the Third Reich. The German universities, once famous throughout the world for their academic freedom, became agencies for propagating such ideas as the racial myths of Nazism; and since Nazi doctrine elevated the state above all else, a movement was instigated to subordinate religion to the Hitler regime. Enrollment in the universities was limited to good Nazi material, and professors were dismissed by the score.

Public works and rearmament. In theory and in outward form, Nazism retained capitalism and private property. Business and labor, however, were rigidly controlled by the state. Labor unions were dissolved, and both workers and employers were enrolled in a new organization, the Labor Front. As in Mussolini's corporate state, the right of the workers to strike or of management to call a lockout was denied. Compulsory dues were taken from workers' wages to support Nazi organizations. As a sop, the government established the Strength Through Joy movement, which provided sports events, musical festivals, plays, movies, and vacations at low cost.

The government's attempts to solve Germany's economic problems included levying a huge tax load on the middle class and increasing the national debt by one third in order to provide work for the unemployed. To create jobs, the first Four-Year Plan, established in 1933, initiated an extensive program of public works and rearmament. The unemployed were put to work on public projects (especially noteworthy was a great network of highways, or *Autobahnen*), in munitions factories, and in the army. The program led to the production of vast arma-

In "White Crucifixion" Marc Chagall takes as his theme the persecution of Jews during modern times. Note the burning synagogue, upper right, and the Jewish refugees throughout the picture. To give universality to his message and to symbolize man's ravaged innocence, Chagall focuses on the crucified figure of Christ.

ments and to their eventual utilization in aggression against other states.

Overlapping the first program, the second Four-Year Plan was initiated in 1936. The objective of this plan was to set up an autarkist state. In order to achieve self-sufficiency, quantities of substitute (*ersatz*) commodities —frequently both inferior in quality and more costly than those purchasable on the world market—were produced by German laboratories, factories, and mills. The standard of living continued to decline.

Nazism—Why? The rise and victory of the brutal, atavistic Nazi movement in such a culturally advanced nation as Germany must be regarded as one of the most momentous events of the twentieth century. How to account for this phenomenon and its leader, Hitler, constitutes one of the most complicated and fascinating problems in historical causation.

One school of thought has found the answer in the logical outcome of German history. Over the centuries national traditions had progressively united such elements as authoritarianism, submissiveness on the part of the individual, strains of unstable and explosive mysticism, anti-Semitism, and a belief in the superiority of the "Germanic-Nordic race." Other historians deny that a German national character had anything to to do with Nazism; they assert that it was the understandable result of the catastrophic impact of the Treaty of Versailles and the depression. Marxist explanations see Fascism coming to power in Germany because of the Communist menace and its threat to a crumbling capitalistic system. Such arguments naturally emphasize the financial assistance Hitler received from German big business. The role of the army has also received attention. The army had always been an important, influential, and respected force in public life, and the military chiefs, unhappy with their lot under the Republic, gladly turned their support to Hitler in 1933.

Social psychologists maintain that the key is to be found in the psychological mood of the German people. Generally the populace was in a condition of stress, insecurity, and frustration. The immediate post-1918 trends had had a painful effect upon all Germans, no matter what their social position. The depression, with its massive unemployment, political instability, and ineptitude of the leaders of the republic, left millions in a state of traumatic shock. "Hitler succeeded not because of a conspiracy of the few but because his movement gave high hope to the many of solving the pressing psychological demands of a people living under conditions of acute stress. Defeated by war and broken by inflation, the uprooted, humiliated, and insecure Germans were attracted to Nazism because they felt that their personal problems would be solved by a movement that promised to supply everything they lacked as individuals: dramatic action, a sense of purpose, a feeling of power."[6] Other nations, however, experienced shocks to their national lives, perhaps as traumatic as Germany's, and yet did not accept the extreme solution of Nazism. There were, then, certain elements in the German situation that were unique and conducive to a Nazi victory. Not least of these was the charismatic leadership of Hitler. Some observers maintain that there could have been no Third Reich without this perverted genius.

Depression under Italian Fascism. In 1933 the number of unemployed in Italy totaled more than one million, and the public debt reached an alarming figure. Italian wages were the lowest in Europe, and living standards had sunk to a level below that of 1914. To strengthen the Fascist economy, the nation was reorganized in 1934 into twenty-two government-controlled corporations, each consisting of syndicates of workers and employers. But in spite of a grandiose program of public works and the adoption of measures to increase agricultural output, Mussolini's corporate state continued to suffer from the depression.

In racial matters, the Fascist regime made half-hearted attempts to copy the Nazis. Italians were urged to be "race conscious," but the decrees issued against Jews were not rigidly enforced.

Parliamentary demoralization in France. The lack of vigorous leadership in the democratic nations and the mounting crisis in their capitalistic systems were best exemplified in France. Although the prosperity of the twenties carried over after other nations were engulfed in depression, in the early thirties France was faced with rising unemployment, budget deficits, the drying up of the lucrative tourist trade, and heavy military expenditures for security against a rearming Germany. Ministry after ministry was organized, only to collapse a few months later; citizens became more and more impatient with the government.

Disgust with the administration increased with the exposure of corruption in high places. It became known that many prominent politicians were involved in the machinations of Alexander Stavisky, who had cheated French investors out of some 600 million francs. When the ministry in power ignored public furor and refused to authorize an investigation, thousands of angry citizens thronged the streets of Paris on the evening of February 6, 1934, and tried to storm the Chamber of Deputies.

The outcome was a new government, the National Union, which ignored pleas for constitutional reform and for a grant of increased power to the prime minister. The agent of the wealthy and privileged classes, the National Union grew ultraconservative but continued to rule under a variety of prime ministers.

In 1936 emerged the Popular Front, a coalition composed of liberal parties united in opposition to the conservative elements in the government. In June the Popular Front won a national election; and Léon Blum (1872-1950), a noted lawyer and writer, became premier. The Popular Front endeavored to stem the influence of fascist ideas, to improve the country's finances, and to bring about certain fundamental economic reforms. In particular, the Popular Front promised to "break the power of the two hundred families who control the economic life of the nation."[7] In foreign policy the Popular Front was friendly to Great Britain and supported the League of Nations. This coalition faced numerous dilemmas. The central problem was how to cooperate with the Communists without being captured by them. Many Frenchmen were reluctant to support the Popular Front for fear it might commit France to fight against Germany for the benefit of the Soviet Union.

An epidemic of sit-down strikes embarrassed the new government, but gradually labor was conciliated by the passage of laws introducing a forty-hour week, higher wages, collective bargaining, and vacations with pay. Furthermore, the government extended its control over the Bank of France and initiated a public works program. Although the Blum government stood resolutely for the laborer and against monopoly and big business, it was equally against communist collectivism or fascist centralization. After only a year in office, however, Blum was forced to resign. Unfavorable trade balances, an enormous public debt, and an unbalanced budget proved too much for the Popular Front government. France swung back to conservatism. The forty-hour week was ended, and strikes were energetically suppressed.

The National Union and the Popular Front mirrored the widening chasm between the upper and lower classes. The working classes believed that the reforms of the Popular Front had been sabotaged and that a France ruled by a wealthy clique deserved little or no allegiance. On the other hand, some businessmen and financiers were horrified at the prospect of communism and flirted with fascism. The cleavage between classes was secretly encouraged by subtle propaganda from the totalitarian countries. While Frenchmen quarreled and France's economic strength was being sapped, Hitler's Germany, regimented and feverishly productive, was rapidly outstripping France in the manufacture of armaments. The ingredients for the tragic fall of France in the spring of 1940 had now been supplied.

Democracy in crisis elsewhere in Europe. Except in Finland and Czechoslovakia, a progressive weakening of parliamentary systems occurred in the smaller European states of eastern and Balkan Europe. These states retained a meaningless appearance of parliamentary forms. Behind the false front, however, a small clique—aided by secret police, censorship, and armed political supporters—stifled all opposition to the government in power.

"Muddling through" in Britain. It was inevitable that the depression would have catastrophic effects in the highly industrialized and heavily populated island of Britain. In two years exports and imports declined 35 percent, and three million unemployed roamed the streets.

A Labour administration, with James Ramsay MacDonald as prime minister, took office in 1929. Little was accomplished, and unemployment became more widespread as the depression deepened. When the Labour government fell, MacDonald retained his office by becoming the leader of a National Coalition government, which was primarily conservative. The bulk of the Labour party constituted the opposition.

Nothing spectacular was undertaken, but the country in typical British fashion did "muddle through." Unlike Germany, which gave up democracy, and France, which kept it but did not know what to do with it, Britain adhered strongly to its traditional parliamentary system. By 1937 a substantial measure of prosperity had been regained, and production registered a 20 percent increase over that of 1929. To achieve this comeback, much of what remained of laissez-faire policy was discarded. The government now regulated the currency, erected high tariffs, gave farmers subsidies, and imposed a heavy burden of taxation. The rich had a large proportion of their income taxed away, and what might be left at death was decimated by inheritance taxes. It was ruefully declared that the rich could hardly afford to live, much less to die.

Despite improvements in the economic picture, an increasing demand for the extension of the welfare state existed. There were pleas for expanded educational and health facilities, better accident and unemployment insurance, and more adequate pensions. A survey of Britain's social services, made in 1941 by the noted economist Sir William Beveridge, recommended a comprehensive system of social insurance. This plan served as the blueprint for Britain's post-World War II legislation that tried to give security "from the cradle to the grave."

The British Commonwealth weathers the storm. In common with the rest of the world, Britain's self-governing dominions were hard hit by the depression. Like Latin America, they were painfully susceptible to the effects of the world slump because they were primarily producers of basic materials, such as wheat, meat, lumber, and minerals. When prices of such products dropped to rock bottom, the dominions (which had borrowed heavily on outside capital) were able to avoid defaults on their obligations only by the most stringent economies. But democracy did not succumb; there were no violent overthrows in Australia, New Zealand, Canada, or South Africa, for parliamentary traditions were strong and natural resources were abundant.

Political instability in Latin America. The Latin American countries, which depended on the export of a few all-important raw materials for their prosperity, suffered serious economic crises as world prices collapsed. Largely as a result of the depression, six South American nations experienced revolutions in 1930.

Out of the increased industrialization and land reform resulting from the revolutions came the gradual development of a middle class, where before there had been only a small group of the extremely rich and great masses of the poor. Rising political, economic, and social standards promised better health and education for more people. The Catholic Church, accused by many of being the ally of the wealthy and powerful, was subject to growing anticlerical attacks, although the continent continued to be almost totally Catholic.

In 1933 the United States inaugurated the Good Neighbor Policy, whose beginnings can be traced back to the Hoover administration. By stimulating trade and formally agreeing that "no state has the right to intervene in the internal or external affairs of another," the United States demonstrated the sincerity of its overtures to the southern continent. In 1934 an Export-Import Bank was established in Washington to help finance foreign trade, especially with Latin America. It has been estimated that between 1934 and 1941 this institution created $560 million worth of American trade.[8] Rivalries among industrialized nations for the Latin

American market became very intense during the thirties. Nazi Germany concluded many barter agreements with Latin American customers and at the same time penetrated the countries politically by organizing German immigrants into pro-Nazi groups, fostering fascist politicians, and developing a formidable propaganda system. When war came and the chips were down, however, Latin America eventually lined up with the democracies.

The New Deal fights depression. In shocking contrast to the golden days of prosperity, the frenzied boom on the stock market, and the smug complacency of American businessmen in the 1920's was the economic paralysis which gripped the United States in 1930. By 1932, business failures numbered at least thirty thousand, and the number of unemployed was somewhere between twelve and fifteen million.

In the first few years after the crash President Hoover tried to prop up shaky businesses with government money in the hope that the benefits would filter down to the workers. Because the President believed that the government should not compete with private concerns, only a few public works projects were started. Hoover avoided federal relief, leaving to private charities and local governments the heavy responsibility for caring for the hungry. Toward the end of his term the depression steadily worsened, and thousands of people went hungry because they had no money for food.

The general dissatisfaction with the government was evidenced by the sweeping victory of Franklin D. Roosevelt (1882-1945), the Democratic standard-bearer, who was inaugurated in 1933. Under his leadership the New Deal, a sweeping program to cope with the national emergency, was put into operation. The three objectives of the New Deal were relief, recovery, and reform. Millions of dollars were appropriated for the relief of the unemployed, and vast sums were expended for the construction of public works in the belief that such activity would stimulate economic recovery. A combination work and relief program, the Civilian Conservation Corps, offered employment and education to thousands of young men. To encourage building activity, the Federal Housing Administration offered liberal terms to finance new homes, especially for low-income families. Most significant was the Social Security Act, passed in 1935. For the first time in the history of the United States, a comprehensive scheme for unemployment insurance and a plan for old-age benefits were introduced.

To prevent a recurrence of the crash, measures were instituted to guarantee the savings deposits of small investors; and the sale of stocks and bonds was regulated by the Securities and Exchange Commission. The Tennessee Valley Authority was established to produce power at reasonable rates that would constitute a yardstick for public utilities. On the labor front, the National Labor Relations Board was designed to protect labor and give it the right to bargain collectively.

The measures and objectives of the New Deal aroused much controversy. Its opponents contended that it gave too much power to the labor unions, that it created a vast, irresponsible bureaucracy at Washington, D.C., that it spent public funds in a profligate fashion, and that it sought to destroy the capitalist system. Its supporters, on the other hand, maintained that the New Deal did not aim to destroy capitalism but rather to preserve it by adapting it to new circumstances, and that thus it represented a reasonable compromise between the discredited system of laissez faire with its unbridled opportunities for exploitation and, at the other extreme, the pervasive and all-powerful economic controls exercised by states under totalitarian regimes.

AGGRESSION AND APPEASEMENT

Japanese aggression in Manchuria. The first challenge to world peace occurred in September 1931, when Japan moved into Manchuria. Unable to cope with the invader, the Chinese appealed to the League of Nations, which appointed a committee of inquiry. The committee report condemned the aggression while trying not to affront Japan, which nevertheless resigned its League membership two years later. The significance of the Manchurian campaign was dreadfully clear. A demonstration that a great power could embark on aggression without any effective opposition from League members marked the beginning of the collapse of the League.

When the Chinese resorted to a nationwide boycott of Japanese goods, the Japanese attacked Shanghai and early in 1933 began to push deeper into northern China. To slow down the invasion and give themselves a chance to prepare for the inevitable struggle, the Chinese agreed to the Tang-ku Truce, which recognized Japanese conquests in Manchuria and northern China. The truce remained in effect for about four years, while the Japanese consolidated their position and the Chinese wrestled with internal threats.

The united front in China. In addition to the invaders, the Nationalist forces of Chiang Kai-shek had to contend with the Chinese Communists (see p. 705). The Chinese Communists demanded a united front against the Japanese, stating that the first objective of all China should be whole-hearted resistance against foreign imperialism and aggression. In 1936 the Communists kidnaped Chiang and held him for two weeks. There was a great outcry from the Chinese people, and, influenced by the obvious national solidarity behind Chiang, the rebels asked him to lead a united China against the common enemy. In order to allay suspicion and achieve a united front, Mao Tse-tung agreed to end land confiscation and armed opposition to the Nanking government, to abandon the system of soviets, and to permit the incorporation of the Communist forces into the fight against Japan. Neither of the parties to the truce trusted each other, but they both feared the Japanese. China was unified just in time to meet the next Japanese thrust.

Japanese conquests continue. In 1937 fighting broke out again, this time around Peking. Farther south, Japanese troops captured Shanghai and advanced rapidly up the Yangtze valley to Nanking. The Chinese retreated westward, establishing a new capital at Chungking. In North China the Chinese armies were also forced to retreat, and the Japanese set up a government at Peking.

In 1938 Japan proclaimed the New Order in eastern Asia. Its objectives were the destruction of Chiang Kai-shek's regime, the expulsion of western interests in eastern Asia, and the establishment of a self-sufficient economic bloc to include Japan, Manchuria (which was renamed Manchukuo by the Japanese), and China.

The outbreak of war in Europe gave Japan its golden opportunity to extend the New Order in China and into the Asian colonies of the western powers. The year 1939 saw several strong but inconclusive offensives in China and the seizure of the island of Hainan, of strategic importance in relation to French Indochina, British Malaya, and the Dutch East Indies. After the fall of France (see p. 727), the Vichy government allowed Japan to build naval and air bases in Indochina. Japanese pressure was also exerted on the Dutch East Indies and on British settlements in China. By the time Japan was ac-

On September 18, 1931, Japan blew up a bridge on the South Manchuria Railroad, ending a decade of treaty-making and relative peace. The League's failure to stop Japan's seizure of Manchuria led Hitler and Mussolini to believe that aggression in other parts of the world could be just as profitable.

tively engaged in the Second World War, the New Order was being rapidly expanded over much of Asia.

Of the three great powers which might have halted Japanese banditry in the 1930's, Britain was in the throes of an economic crisis, France suffered both political and economic paralysis, and the United States, feverishly occupied with its New Deal, was still isolationist, holding to the view "that foreign affairs are something not pleasant that happens to other people."[9]

Italy swallows up Abyssinia. Italian aggression in Abyssinia followed Japan's lead. As his first victim, Mussolini chose Abyssinia, the only important independent native state left in Africa and the nation which in 1896 had handed the Italians a humiliating defeat. Late in 1934 fighting broke out between the Abyssinians and the Italians, and in the following year the Italians made a wholesale invasion of Abyssinia. Emperor Haile Selassie appealed to the League, which tried to arrange for arbitration. Despite the Italian delegates' audacious argument that Abyssinia, not Italy, was the aggressor, the League voted to prohibit shipment of certain goods to Italy and denied it credit. But the effect of the sanctions was nullified because oil—without which no modern army or navy can fight—was not included in the list of prohibited articles. Apprehensive of alienating Italy, France and Britain were only lukewarm in their support of the sanctions; and since they were not League members, the United States and Germany largely ignored the prohibitions.

Using bombs, mustard gas, and tanks, the Italians advanced swiftly into Abyssinia and crushed the resistance of Haile Selassie's valiant soldiers. The whole sorry story ended in July 1936, when the sanctions were removed. Haile Selassie, an emperor without a country, went to live in England, the first of several royal exiles.

Germany marches into the Rhineland. The conflict over Abyssinia gave Hitler his first big opportunity to use the military force he had been building up. In March 1936, while the wrangle over the sanctions against Italy was taking place, German troops marched boldly into the Rhineland in defiance of the Treaty of Versailles and the Locarno agreements (see Reference Map 8). France immediately mobilized 150,000 troops, but Britain refused to support the use of force to compel Germany to withdraw. Many Englishmen thought it hardly worth while to risk war over Germany's demand to fortify its own territory. Others, however, recognized the danger in allowing Hitler to break an agreement with little or no protest.

Alliance of the Axis powers. Up until 1935 Germany had been diplomatically isolated in Europe, faced by the United Front of Great Britain, France, and Italy. But the Abyssinian incident and the imposition of sanctions broke up the United Front, and Italy became Germany's friend. In 1936 the friendship was formalized in the Rome-Berlin Axis, and one year later Mussolini followed Hitler's lead by withdrawing from the League.

Japan, the third major member of the Axis powers, joined forces with Germany in 1936 in the Anti-Comintern Pact. A year later Italy subscribed to the agreement. On the surface the agreement was directed against the international activities of communism; in reality the pact was aimed at Russia. The members of the Rome-Berlin-Tokyo Axis were preparing for expansion.

Dress rehearsal in Spain. In 1936 civil war broke out in Spain, shattering that country and threatening to involve all of Europe. The Spanish republic had been established five years earlier. Long overdue reforms were enacted: new schools were constructed, great estates were broken up, and the army was purged of its parasitic officers. But the republic brought neither prosperity nor stability to Spain. Reactionary groups tried to gain control of the government while left-wing groups resorted to terrorism. The middle-of-the-road reformist government became increasingly powerless to maintain order, and an uprising inspired by reactionary and military cliques began in July 1936.

The totalitarian powers—Italy and Germany—seized the opportunity to ensure a Fascist victory. Large numbers of Italian planes were made available to the Fascist insurgents, led by General Francisco Franco (1892-   ). Most of the regular army troops were faithful to Franco, and a quick victory was anticipated. But many groups stood by the Republic, and, as Communists gained increasing strength in the Republican government, the Soviet Union provided it with aid. Foreign Communists flocked to Spain, as did many idealistic anti-Fascists who were not Communists, including a number from Britain and the United States. The Republicans mustered stronger resistance than expected, and Franco's drive was checked at the outskirts of Madrid.

Instead of permitting arms to be sent to the recognized legal Loyalist government, which had the right under international law to purchase them in self-defense, Great Britain and France, fearful that the conflict would spread, set up a nonintervention system by which the nations of Europe agreed not to send arms to either side. France, Britain, the British Commonwealth, and the United States were the only nations that held to the agreement. Germany and Italy sent troops and equipment to the Fascists, while Russia sent matériel and personnel to the Loyalists at Madrid. Germany, Italy, and Russia tried out their new cannon and combat planes on Spanish battlefields. Internal dissensions weakened Russian assistance, which was not sufficient to offset German and Italian aid. In March 1939 Madrid fell, and the Spanish republic was no more. Franco, at the head of the new state, was endowed with absolute power. The Spanish civil war was not only a national catastrophe, which left permanent scars on a proud and gallant people, but also a dress rehearsal for the tragic global drama of World War II.

British appeasement and Allied weakness. Neville Chamberlain (1869-1940), whose name was to symbolize the policy of appeasement, had become the British prime minister in 1937. Determined to explore every possibility for reaching an equitable understanding with the dictators, Chamberlain persisted in trying to ease international tension despite snubs from those he wished to placate and also warnings from some of his colleagues and from experts in the British foreign office. Chamberlain's policies were strongly supported in England. Many Englishmen had a feeling of "peace guilt"—

namely, that Germany had been unfairly treated in the Treaty of Versailles. In other quarters, there was reluctant admiration for the Nazi regime and the belief that a strong Germany could serve as a buffer against Communist Russia. Most important, however, was the passionate and widespread desire for peace, arising from the war weariness and disillusionment suffered by the democratic peoples after World War I.

The world was uneasily aware of the growing weakness of the democracies and of the major shift in the European balance of power. The small states began to draw away from the impotent League of Nations. Some tried to make deals with Germany and Italy; others, such as the Scandinavian countries and Holland, ran for the dubious shelter of neutrality and "innocent isolation." Belgium gave up its alliance with France, and Poland signed a nonaggression pact with Germany. In the Little Entente of Czechoslovakia, Rumania, and Yugoslavia, only Czechoslovakia remained loyal to Paris. Hitler was fully aware of the pervading obsession for peace in Britain and of the decline of the French alliance system.

Hitler's Austrian coup. In announcing the military reoccupation of the Rhineland in the spring of 1936, Hitler had stated, "We have no territorial demands to make in Europe." The course of events was to belie this statement. By 1938 the German army had amazing strength, the *Luftwaffe* was at its peak, and Hitler was ready to embark on a daring program of expansion. His "territorial demands" were to prove limitless.

Hitler's first victim was his neighbor Austria. Previously, in 1934, Hitler had attempted to annex Austria; and the Austrian chancellor, Engelbert Dollfuss, had been murdered by Nazi agents. Partly because of Mussolini's opposition, this *Putsch* (coup) failed. Four years later, after Mussolini had become his ally, Hitler tried again.

The blow fell on Friday, March 11. American radio listeners were told at 2:15 P.M. that the Austrian chancellor had resigned, at 2:45 that German troops were crossing the frontier, and at 3:43 that the swastika had been hoisted over the Austrian chancellery. Meanwhile, Nazi agents in Austria took over the government; on Saturday German troops occupied most of the country.

Germany aspires to the Sudetenland. After the Austrian coup, Hitler moved on to his next objective, the annexation of the Sudetenland, an area in Czechoslovakia bordering on Germany and peopled mainly by Germans. In September 1938 the Führer bluntly informed Chamberlain that he was determined to secure self-determination for the Sudeten Germans. Chamberlain then persuaded Edouard Daladier, the French premier, that a sacrifice on the part of Czechoslovakia would save the peace. When France, previously counted as an ally by the Czechs, joined England in pressing for acceptance of the Nazi demands, Czechoslovakia had little choice but to agree. Chamberlain gave this news to Hitler, only to discover that the German demands had increased considerably. Hitler demanded that within one week the Czechs evacuate certain areas and that all military matériel, goods, and livestock in these areas be turned over to the Germans immediately. Astonished and embittered at the Führer's duplicity, the British prime minister refused to accept the new terms.

Munich seals the fate of Czechoslovakia. On September 28, 1938, the British House of Commons assembled to hear a report by the prime minister. As he neared the end of his address, a messenger delivered a note from Hitler inviting him to attend a conference at Munich. The following day Hitler, Mussolini, Daladier, and Chamberlain met at the Nazi headquarters in Munich and for thirteen hours worked out the details of the surrender of the Sudetenland. No Czech representative was present. Though an outspoken ally of Czechoslovakia, Russia was completely disregarded. (French and British statesmen distrusted Russia and presumably thought that Hitler's hatred of communism would not permit the attendance of a representative from Moscow.) Not only were all of Hitler's demands accepted, but Poland and Hungary also received slices of Czechoslovakia (see Reference Map 8).

Munich brought relief to millions of Europeans half-crazed with fear of war, but it was still a question whether this settlement would be followed by another crisis. Many hoped for the best but feared the worst. Immediately after Munich, Winston Churchill solemnly warned:

And do not suppose that this is the end. This is only the beginning of the reckoning. This is only the first sip, the first foretaste of a bitter cup which will be proffered to us year by year unless, by a supreme recovery of moral health and martial vigor, we arise again and take our stand for freedom as in the olden time.[10]

The mounting fears of French and British statesmen were confirmed in 1939. Early in March a bitter attack against the Czech government was inaugurated by the German press. Another coup was in the making. On March 14, Hitler summoned the Czech president, Hacha, to Berlin. Subjected to all kinds of threats during an all-night session, Hacha finally capitulated and signed a document placing his country under the "protection" of Germany. His signature was a mere formality, however, for German troops were already crossing the Czech frontier. Not to be outdone, Mussolini seized Albania the following month, and the two dictators celebrated by signing a military alliance, the so-called Pact of Steel.

The shock of the final conquest of Czechoslovakia and Hitler's callous violation of pledges made at Munich ended the appeasement policy of France and Great Britain. For the first time in Britain's long history, the government authorized a peacetime draft. A tremendous arms program was launched. In Paris, Daladier obtained special emergency powers to push forward national defense.

Isolationism in the United States. The United States had been disillusioned by the results of the "war to make the world safe for democracy." Influential spokesmen asserted that World War I had been caused by the greed of munitions makers and stressed the centuries-old hatreds and rivalries in Europe; America, therefore, should insulate itself from these potent causes of international conflict. Reflecting this mood, Congress passed neutrality legislation between 1935 and 1937 which made it unlawful for any nation at war to obtain munitions from the United States.

As the Nazi and Fascist menace became apparent in the late 1930's, President Roosevelt and the state department worked strenuously to arouse the American people to the dangers of the world situation. In 1937, in his famous "quarantine speech," Roosevelt declared:

The peace, the freedom and the security of 90 per cent of the population of the world is being jeopardized by the remaining 10 per cent who are threatening a breakdown of all international order and law.

Surely the 90 per cent who want to live in peace under law and in accordance with moral standards that have received almost universal acceptance through the centuries can and must find some way to make their will prevail. . . . There must be positive endeavors to preserve peace.[11]

In May 1939 the president told leaders in the House of Representatives "that in case of war there was at least an even chance that Germans and Italians might win."[12] So strong was isolationist sentiment, however, that the warning went unheeded.

The Polish question and the Nazi-Soviet pact. It was Germany's aggression against Poland that precipitated the Second World War. The Treaty of Versailles had turned over West Prussia to Poland as a Polish Corridor to the sea (see map, p. 663). While 90 percent of the Corridor's population was Polish, the Baltic port city of Danzig was nearly all German. Late in March 1939 Hitler proposed to Poland that Danzig be ceded to Germany and that the Nazis be allowed to occupy a narrow strip of land connecting Germany with East Prussia. Chamberlain, with France concurring, warned the Nazi government that "in the event of any action which clearly threatened Polish independence," the British would "at once lend the Polish government all support in their power." In the months that followed the Allied warning, France and Britain competed with Germany for an alliance with Russia.

The Soviet Union had long been seriously concerned about the twin menaces of Nazi Germany and expansionist Japan. The Kremlin had supported the collective security system of the League and had supposedly called off the subversive activity of the Com-

intern (see p. 674) in favor of popular-front governments to oppose the rising tide of Axis aggression. On the other hand, Soviet pledges to call off Comintern activity were openly violated; and the purge trials not only alienated public opinion in many parts of the world but seriously weakened the Red Army, whose leading officers had been removed.

As we have seen, Chamberlain and Daladier ignored the Soviet Union at Munich. Now, with the Polish question of paramount importance, Britain and France desperately needed Russia as an ally. But while British and French negotiators attempted to convince the Kremlin that their nations really desired an effective alliance against Nazi Germany, the Nazi and Soviet foreign secretaries were secretly working out the details of an agreement. On August 23, 1939, Russia and Germany signed a nonaggression pact, an utterly cynical arrangement between two inexorably antagonistic foes.

Through this agreement Stalin gave Hitler a free hand in Poland, thus precipitating war between Germany and Britain and France. Russian political strategy was that such a conflict would give the Soviet Union time to build up its armaments and would weaken the antagonists. With the pact in his pocket, Hitler could attack Poland without fear of intervention by his great rival to the east. Furthermore, he believed that Britain and France would not dare oppose his ambitions. But France and Britain at last understood that if they wished to stop Germany from dominating all of Europe, they must fight.

Basic causes of Hitler's war. Undoubtedly Germany nursed a sense of grievance over what were regarded as the injustices of Versailles. The most important cause of the war, however, was the ruthless ambition of an irrational dictator to gain control of Europe and as much of the rest of the world as he could master. Aiding and abetting his sinister ambition was the strong, even obsessive desire of the democracies for peace. Because Britain and France had long turned the other cheek, Hitler believed that they would not fight under any provocation. Hitler scoffed at the democracies: "Our enemies are little worms. I saw them at Munich."[13]

One of the great lessons of 1939 is that appeasement does not guarantee peace and that it does not take two equally belligerent sides to make a fight. Hitler was genuinely surprised to discover that he had pushed the democracies too far and that he had a real war on his hands. When he was handed the British ultimatum, he turned to Ribbentrop, his foreign minister, and asked: "Well, what now?" There was no reply, but Hermann Goering, the commander of the *Luftwaffe*, exclaimed: "Heaven help us, if we lose this war."[14] Unlike the controversy following World War I over the "war guilt" of the various nations, there has been virtually unanimous agreement that Nazi Germany was responsible for the war.

THE WORLD DIVIDED

Blitzkrieg in Poland. Without a declaration of war, Nazi troops crossed the Polish frontier early in the morning of September 1, 1939, and the *Luftwaffe* began to bomb Polish cities. On the morning of September 3, Chamberlain sent an ultimatum to Germany, demanding that the invasion be halted. The time limit was given as 11 A.M. of the same day. At 11:15 he announced on a radio broadcast that Britain was now at war. France also declared war, and after an interval of only twenty-one years since World War I Europe was again plunged into conflict.

For the first time the world had the opportunity to witness the awesome power of Nazi arms. Polish resistance crumbled, and at the same time Russian forces attacked from the east. In less than a month Poland had been partitioned by the Russo-German treaty. Britain and France did not try to breach the Siegfried line along the Rhine. With their blockade and mastery of the seas, they hoped to defeat Hitler by attrition.

Dunkirk. All seemed to be going according to this plan during the winter of 1939-1940. There was little fighting along the Franco-German frontier during this period of the "phony war," or *Sitzkrieg*. Russia,

however, took advantage of the opportunity to force Finland to cede substantial territory, but only after unexpected stubborn resistance. In the late spring there were signs that the Nazi High Command was not prepared to accept a long war of attrition. Neutral Norway and Denmark were invaded and occupied. A month later, in May 1940, German armies overran neutral Holland and Belgium. From the latter, armored columns knifed into France through an undefended gap north of the Maginot line. German forces swept to the English Channel trapping an Anglo-French army of nearly 400,000 on the beach at Dunkirk.

The reverses in Norway and a military crisis in France led to Chamberlain's resignation, and Winston Churchill (1874-1965) became prime minister of Great Britain. While he had intermittently occupied high office during his long career in Parliament, which dated back to 1900, Churchill had suffered numerous frustrations and in the 1930's enjoyed little popular support. At that time he was described as "a might-have-been; a potentially great man flawed by flashiness, irresponsibility, unreliability, and inconsistency."[15] Yet in 1940 Churchill's qualities of leadership rose to match his nation's peril. During the next five years he was the voice and symbol of a defiant and indomitable Britain.

Confronted with the prospect of destruction of the British army at Dunkirk, Churchill refused to be dismayed. Appearing before Parliament as the new prime minister he announced, "I have nothing to offer but blood, toil, tears, and sweat," preparing the people for a long and desperate conflict. By herculean efforts hundreds of small craft, protected by an umbrella of the Royal Air Force, successfully evacuated some 335,000 soldiers. An army had been brought home, but all its heavy equipment had been lost.

The fall of France. After Dunkirk, the fall of France was inevitable. Anxious to be in on the kill, Mussolini declared war against France and Britain. Designated an "open city" by the French, Paris fell on June 14. As the German advance continued, the members of the French government who wished to continue resistance were voted down;

and Marshal Pétain, the eighty-four-year-old hero of Verdun in the First World War, became premier. Pétain immediately asked Hitler for an armistice, and in the same dining car in which the French had imposed armistice terms on the Germans in 1918, the Nazis and the French on June 22 signed the armistice agreement. France was split into two zones, occupied and unoccupied. In unoccupied France, Pétain's government at Vichy was supposedly free from interference, but in reality it was a puppet of the Nazis. And so the Third Republic, created in 1871 from the debris of defeat suffered at German hands, now came to an end because of a new blow from the same quarter. However, a remarkable patriot, General Charles de Gaulle (1890-1970), fled to London and organized a Free French government, which adopted as its symbol the red cross of Lorraine (flown by Joan of Arc in her fight to liberate France centuries earlier) and continued to aid the Allied cause throughout the war.

The crucial battle of Britain. With millions of Europeans already his captives and with millions more living in constant dread of his screaming dive bombers and clanking panzer divisions, Hitler demanded that the British lay down their arms. But in the face of almost hopeless odds, they rallied to the support of their homeland. Churchill's eloquent defiance of Hitler stirred not only his own countrymen but all of the free world:

We shall go on to the end . . . . we shall defend our Island, whatever the cost may be, we shall fight on the beaches, we shall fight on the landing grounds, we shall fight in the fields and in the streets, we shall fight in the hills; we shall never surrender. . . .[16]

As a prelude to invasion, the Germans sought to gain control of the air over England. Their fighter and bomber squadrons crossed the Channel but were turned back with heavy losses by the R.A.F. All through the winter of 1940-1941, however, England continued to be racked by terrible raids. Night bombing destroyed block after block of England's cities; St. Paul's Cathedral in London stood as a solitary survivor in the midst of acres of desolation. Evacuating their children and old people and sleeping in air-raid shelters, Britain's people stood firm. Their air force retaliated in some

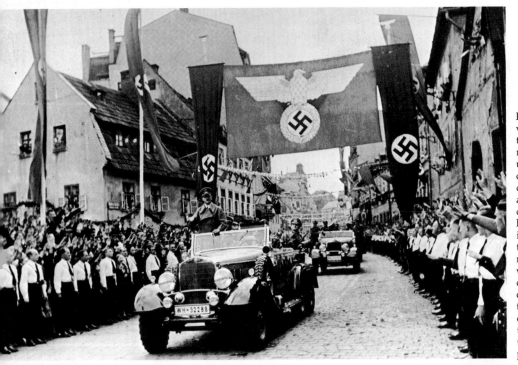

Hitler's victory in Czechoslovakia was only a prelude to the fear and aggression which many nations experienced under the force of Axis conquest. Once war was formally declared, the German, Italian, and Japanese armies proceeded to destroy the strongholds of the Allies, inflicting terrible losses. And like this Frenchman, people from many nations were forced to watch the Axis powers take over their country while their own forces either laid down their arms or escaped into exile. For a while, Axis victory indicated to the world that an Allied defeat was very possible.

measure by raiding the industrial cities of the Ruhr, and their naval forces remained on the offensive.

Italian failures and Nazi successes. Meanwhile, Mussolini was eager to share in the spoils. In October 1940 he invaded neutral Greece, but this thrust proved to be a costly failure. Other defeats were met in North Africa, and Abyssinia was recaptured by British forces. Hitler, on the other hand, continued to expand his domination over Europe. Rumania, Bulgaria, and Hungary became Nazi satellites. In the spring of 1941 Yugoslavia and Greece were overrun.

By the spring of 1941 nearly all of Europe had come under the iron heel of the Third Reich. Only Portugal, Switzerland, Sweden, and Turkey remained neutral. While ostensibly neutral, Spain under Franco was pro-Nazi. Britain, though still dangerous, was powerless to interfere on the Continent. The United States was profoundly disturbed over the Nazi successes but was still unprepared.

Hitler turns on the Soviet Union. Thwarted in his invasion plans of England, Hitler made the fatal decision to invade Russia. Stalin had no illusions about Nazi friendship. When he had signed the nonaggression pact with Hitler in 1939, Stalin had expected that in the event of war the antagonists would wear themselves out and suffer terrific losses. But now Hitler was master of western continental Europe. *Lebensraum* (living space) and badly needed raw materials could be had by expansion to the east.

In June 1941, without warning, a gigantic German attack was launched against Russia, even though many of Hitler's generals were apprehensive. Along a battlefront eighteen hundred miles long, nine million men became locked in struggle. At the outset, the Nazi armored panzer units were irresistible. Russian troops were killed or captured in enormous numbers. In October, Hitler's troops neared the suburbs of Moscow; Russia appeared to be on the verge of collapse. With the coming of winter, however, the Nazi offensive bogged down. Weapons froze, troops were inadequately clothed, and heavy snows blocked the roads. The German attack not only halted, but in the spring of 1942 the Russian army began to recover territory.

The "arsenal of democracy." Following the collapse of France and during the battle

THE CREST OF AXIS POWER

Allies and areas they controlled
Axis nations
Area occupied by the Axis
Vichy France
Neutral nations

Battles: Allied victory × Axis victory ⊗
Thrusts: → →

ARCTIC OCEAN

ATLANTIC OCEAN

Murmansk
WHITE SEA
Arkhangelsk
N. Dvina R.

FAEROE IS. (Den.)
SHETLAND IS. (Br.)
ORKNEY IS.
Scapa Flow

Narvik

NORWAY
SWEDEN
FINLAND
Lake Onega
Lake Ladoga
GULF OF BOTHNIA

Trondheim 1940
Bergen
Oslo
Goteborg

Helsinki
Stockholm
Tallinn
Leningrad

SOVIET

Kazan
Gorki
Moscow

Glasgow
GREAT
IRELAND
Dublin
Liverpool
BRITAIN
Birmingham
Air battle for Britain July-Oct. 1940
London
Southampton
Dunkirk May-June 1940 ⊗

NORTH SEA
BALTIC SEA

DENMARK Copenhagen (Apr. 1940)
Hamburg
Hanover
Berlin
Danzig
Warsaw

ESTONIA
Pskov
LATVIA
Riga
LITHUANIA
Kaunas
Minsk
Smolensk

UNION

Voronezh
Don R.
Volga R.
Sara

NETHERLANDS May 1940
BELGIUM 1940
Cologne
Dresden
GERMANY
POLAND
Krakow
Lvov
Kiev
Dnieper R.
Kharkov
Rostov

Nantes
Paris
LUX.
Frankfurt
Prague
CZECHOSLOVAKIA Mar. 1939
Loire R.
Rhine R.
La Havre

FRANCE
Munich
Vienna
AUSTRIA Mar. 1938
Dniester R.
Sea of Azov

Bordeaux
Vichy
Lyons
SWITZERLAND
HUNGARY Oct. 1940
Budapest
RUMANIA Nov. 1940
Odessa
Sevastopol

VICHY FRANCE
Milan
Venice
Trieste
YUGOSLAVIA Apr. 1941
Belgrade
Bucharest
Danube R.
BLACK SEA

Marseilles
Genoa
ADRIATIC SEA
BULGARIA Mar. 1941
Sofia
Trabz

SPAIN
Madrid
Barcelona
CORSICA
Rome
ITALY
ALBANIA Apr. 1939
GREECE Apr. 1941
Salonika
Istanbul
Ankara
Kizil R.
TURKEY

Valencia
BALEARIC IS.
SARDINIA
TYRRHENIAN SEA
Naples
IONIAN SEA
Athens
AEGEAN SEA
Smyrna
Adana
Aleppo
SYR

MEDITERRANEAN
Palermo
SICILY
MALTA (Br.)
CRETE
CYPRUS (Br.)
Beirut
Damasc

Oran
Algiers
Bône
Tunis

ALGERIA
TUNISIA
LIBYA
Tripoli
Bengasi
Alexandria
Cairo
EGYPT
Nile R.
Suez Canal
RED SEA

Jerusalem
PALESTINE
TRANSJORDAN
SAUDI ARABI

of Britain, the American public began to understand the full implications of an Axis victory. After Dunkirk, arms were sent to Britain, a great rearmament program was undertaken, and compulsory military service was introduced. The Lend-Lease Act of 1941 empowered the president to make arms available to any country whose defense was thought vital to the national interest. Despite ideological differences, munitions were sent to Russia, Nazi Germany's new foe.

To define the moral purpose and principles of the struggle, Roosevelt and Churchill drafted the Atlantic Charter in August 1941. Meeting "somewhere in the Atlantic," the signatories pledged that after "the final destruction of Nazi tyranny," they hoped to see a peace in which "men in all the lands may live out their lives in freedom from fear and want." If the United States was not yet a belligerent in the fall of 1941, it was certainly not neutral.

Pearl Harbor draws the United States into war. It was Japan's expansionist policy which brought the United States directly into the conflict. Confronted with Japanese ambitions for the New Order in Asia, the United States froze Japanese funds and refused to sell it war matériel. In spite of this pressure, Japan made the fateful decision to continue its expansion; in October 1941, General Tojo, an avid militarist, became premier.

On Sunday, December 7, while special "peace" envoys from Tokyo were negotiating in Washington, ostensibly to restore harmony to Japanese-American relations, Japanese planes attacked Pearl Harbor, the American bastion in the Pacific. Half the United States fleet was crippled, and planes were wiped out on the ground. On the following day Congress declared war on Japan. In a few days Italy and Germany declared war on the United States; and Britain, together with the dominions, the refugee governments of Europe, and the Central American republics, ranged themselves with the United States against Japan. On January 2, 1942, the twenty-six nations which now stood arrayed against Germany, Italy, and Japan solemnly pledged themselves to uphold the principles of the Atlantic Charter and declared themselves united for the duration of the conflict.

High tide of the Axis. After Pearl Harbor, Japanese power expanded over the Pacific and into Southeast Asia (see map, p. 732). Hong Kong, Singapore, the Dutch East Indies, Malaya, Burma, and Indochina were conquered. An American army was forced to cease its defense of the Philippines when it surrendered at Bataan. The Chinese, however, in their remote inland fortress-capital of Chungking, managed to hold off the Japanese. The summer of 1942 was an agonizing period for the foes of the Axis. A new German offensive pushed deeper into Russia, threatening the important city of Stalingrad. Egypt was placed in peril when the gifted German general, Rommel, inflicted a decisive defeat on the British army in Libya. All over the globe the Axis powers were in the ascendancy.

The road to victory for the Allies. Imminent defeat was suddenly and miraculously transformed to hope of victory in 1942. Further Japanese expansion in the Pacific was halted by two American naval victories —Coral Sea and Midway—and at Guadalcanal American marines began the conquest of Japanese-held islands. In November 1942 British and American troops landed in North Africa, and Axis forces were defeated by the British at Alamein. By May 1943 all Axis troops in North Africa had been destroyed or captured. Hitler fared no better in Russia, where in February 1943 an entire German army was surrounded and captured at Stalingrad. The next Allied thrust was against Italy; in July 1943 Sicily was captured. The whole edifice of Fascism now collapsed. Mussolini was stripped of his office and was later kidnapped by Nazi agents. A new Italian government signed an armistice as Allied forces landed in Italy. Rome was not captured until June 1944, and German resistance continued in northern Italy until the end of the war.

By the end of 1943 the initiative had definitely passed to the Allies. Russian divisions pushed into Poland and wheeled south into the Balkans. On D-Day, June 6, 1944, a vast armada of ships landed half a million men on the beaches of Normandy.

After violent fighting, British and American forces entered Germany in October. At the same time, Russian troops closed in from the east.

With victory in Europe in sight, Stalin, Roosevelt, and Churchill met at Yalta in the Crimea in February 1945 to discuss the peace arrangements. It was agreed that the Soviet Union could have a slice of Poland and territory and privileges in the Far East, a decision later severely criticized. It was also agreed that Russia would enter the war against Japan and that postwar Germany would be split into four zones. Yalta was the high point of the alliance. After this conference, relations between the Soviet Union and its allies quickly deteriorated.

As the Allied troops advanced through Germany, they uncovered the secret hell of Nazi inhumanity toward the people Hitler despised. In the concentration camps—Belsen, Buchenwald, Dachau, and others—they found the gas ovens which had de-

stroyed millions of lives, the wasted bodies of slave laborers who had starved to death, and the living dead who had somehow survived torture and the cruel medical experiments to which they had been subjected. Between 1939 and 1945 the Jewish population in Nazi-occupied Europe had decreased from 9,739,200 to 3,505,800; and another 6,000,000 people—Poles, Czechs, Russians, and others—had also fallen victim to Nazi cruelty.

The Axis leaders did not live to see defeat. Mussolini, a cringing fugitive, was seized by anti-Fascist partisan fighters and shot to death; his mutilated body, with that of his mistress, was trussed up in the public square at Milan, an object of derision and hatred. While street fighting raged in Berlin, Hitler committed suicide. His body and that of the mistress he had just made his wife were doused with gasoline and set afire. Nor did the great wartime leader of the United States live to see the end of the war, although

he realized the imminence of victory. Franklin Roosevelt died suddenly in April 1945, less than a month before the German armies surrendered. The final surrender ceremony took place in Berlin on May 8, designated by President Harry Truman as V-E Day, Victory Day in Europe.

End of the war. While the Allied armies were finishing off the Germans, the Americans had been "island-hopping" their way to Japan, capturing in turn Tarawa, Kwajalein, and Saipan, after bloody struggles on the sandy beaches. In October 1944, with their victory in the battle for Leyte Gulf—the greatest naval engagement in all history—the Allies ended the threat of the Japanese fleet; and in January 1945 General MacArthur returned to the Philippines. The final phase of the war against Japan was unfolding. Only a few hundred miles from Japan, Iwo Jima and Okinawa were conquered; and from such advance bases, waves of American bombers rained destruction on Japanese cities. In the China-Burma-India theater, the Chinese, with American aid, were making inroads on areas previously captured by Japan.

From the Potsdam meeting of the Allied leaders in July-August 1945 came a warning to the Japanese that the war against them would take a new and angry turn. When Japan refused to surrender, an American bomber dropped the most terrible weapon yet invented by mankind—the atomic bomb —on Hiroshima. As the mushroom-shaped cloud rose over the city, only charred ruins were left beneath; an expanse of approximately three miles square—and 60 percent of the city—was almost completely obliterated. The Japanese government estimated that 60,000 people died, 100,000 were wounded, and 200,000 were left homeless. Whether or not the use of the bomb was justified is still a question for debate, but the new weapon achieved its purpose. A few days after the dropping of a second atomic bomb on Nagasaki, the Japanese sued for peace. The surrender ceremony took place September 2 on board the battleship *Missouri*, almost six years to the day after Hitler had plunged the world into the Second World War.

The nightmare of Nazism is only suggested by these piles of bodies at the concentration camp at Belsen, Germany. These victims died of disease and starvation, but millions more—men, women, and children—were deliberately murdered.

SUMMARY

From 1929 to 1945 the world was in turmoil. People were caught up in a bewildering procession of economic problems, of toppling governments, and of aggressions and finally in a world conflagration. As the focal point of the world's economy, the Wall Street crash of 1929 set off an international depression. To survive this economic earthquake, governments were forced to modify the capitalistic structure by increasing their controls, particularly in the United States and England.

The depression brought Hitler to power in Germany, and a chain of events leading to global conflict was set off. In the 1930's the Axis powers—Germany, Japan, and Italy—carried out a series of aggressions with little opposition. Manchuria, China, Abyssinia, Austria, and Czechoslovakia all heard the tramp of invading troops. By 1939 Hitler had thrown off his mask and revealed his real intentions: the expansion of Germany until much of the world was under the Nazi heel.

The Allied policy of appeasement ended abruptly with the invasion of Poland, and the Second World War was on.

This gigantic struggle can be divided into a series of stages. During 1939 and 1940 Germany virtually mastered Europe. Only Britain remained a defiant and lonely opponent. Following the fall of France, the United States made every effort to aid Britain and then Russia to forestall domination of the world by the Axis.

The totalitarian powers came perilously close to winning in the summer of 1942. After a sneak attack against the United States base at Pearl Harbor, the Japanese invaded island after island in the Pacific. Hitler marched through Russia up to the outskirts of Stalingrad. In North Africa British troops were pushed back into Egypt by General Rommel. By the end of 1942, however, the tide began to turn with an Allied victory in North Africa and a Nazi

debacle in the icy streets of Stalingrad. Italy surrendered, the Germans were harassed out of Russia, the submarine menace so destructive to Allied shipping was brought under control in the Atlantic, and the Americans went on the offensive in the Pacific. Germany surrendered in May 1945; the Japanese in August.

In this titanic struggle there was no clear-cut ideological alignment. The exigencies of war helped conceal basic and even conflicting differences in ideology between Britain and the United States on the one hand and Russia on the other. At the same time, the explosion of two atomic bombs registered the awesome warning that world wars in the future would be suicidal for all concerned. Yet the world, numbed by its suffering and exhausted by its efforts, did not understand the danger inherent in the opposing aims of the two ideologies and the vital need to prevent their clash.

SUGGESTIONS FOR READING

J. K. Galbraith, **The Great Crash, 1929,*** Sentry. Dramatic account of the onset of the depression in the United States. F. L. Allen, **Since Yesterday,*** Bantam, is a lively social history of the 1930's. See also S. Adler, **The Isolationist Impulse,*** Collier; and D. Perkins, **The New Age of Franklin Roosevelt: 1932–1945,*** Univ. of Chicago.

W. L. Shirer, **The Rise and Fall of the Third Reich,*** Fawcett. A full account by a journalist. Also notable are T. L. Jarman, **The Rise and Fall of Nazi Germany,*** Signet; and H. R. Trevor-Roper, **The Last Days of Hitler,*** Collier.

On the crisis in the west European democracies on the eve of World War II, the following are recommended: A. Werth, **The Twilight of France, 1933–1940,** Harper, 1942; J. F. Kennedy, **Why England Slept,*** Dolphin; H. Thomas, **The Spanish Civil War,*** Colophon.

For various viewpoints on its origin see J. L. Snell, ed., **The Outbreak of the Second World War,*** Heath; A. J. P. Taylor, **The Origins of the Second World War,*** Premier; and L. Lafore, **The End of Glory,** Lippincott, 1970.

E. McInnis, **The War,** 6 vols., Oxford, 1940–1946. One of the best accounts of World War II. W. Churchill, **The Second World War,*** 6 vols., Bantam, is a brilliant panoramic survey. Good single-volume histories are P. Young, **A Short History of World War II,*** Apollo; and L. L. Snyder, **The War: A Concise History,*** Dell. See also A. Werth, **Russia at War, 1941–1945,*** Avon; C. Wilmot, **The Struggle for Europe,*** Colophon; D. D. Eisenhower, **Crusade in Europe,*** Dolphin; H. Feis, **Japan Subdued,** Princeton, 1961; G. Wright, **The Ordeal of**

Total War,* Torchbooks. Good discussions of wartime diplomacy are J. L. Snell, **Illusion and Necessity,*** Houghton Mifflin, 1963; and H. Feis, **Churchill, Roosevelt, Stalin,*** Princeton.

T. Taylor, **The March of Conquest,*** Simon & Schuster, 1958. The amazing story of the initial German military triumphs. P. Fleming, **Operation Sea Lion,*** Ace, is an absorbing account of Hitler's plans to invade Britain. Excellent works on other highlights of the war include H. E. Salisbury, **The Nine Hundred Days: The Siege of Leningrad,** Harper & Row, 1969; C. Ryan, **The Longest Day: June 6, 1944,*** Crest, and **The Last Battle,** Simon & Schuster, 1966; C. Fitzgibbon, **Officers' Plot to Kill Hitler,*** Avon; J. Toland, **Battle: The Story of the Bulge,*** Mentor; L. Collins and D. Lapierre, **Is Paris Burning?*** Pocket Books; R. W. Thompson, **The Battle for the Rhine,*** Ballantine; and J. Hersey, **Hiroshima,*** Bantam.

Four studies documenting the enormity of the crimes perpetrated by the Nazis are L. Poliakov, **Harvest of Hate,** Syracuse, 1954; P. Tillare and C. Levy, **Betrayal at the Vel d'Hiv,** Hill and Wang, 1969; Lord Russell, **The Scourge of the Swastika,** Philosophical Lib., 1954; W. R. Harris, **Tyranny on Trial,** Southern Methodist Univ., 1954.

Important World War II novels include the trilogy by T. Plievier: **Stalingrad,*** Berkley; **Moscow,*** Ace; and **Berlin, A Novel,*** Ace. Other excellent works are I. Shaw, **The Young Lions,*** Signet; N. Mailer, **The Naked and the Dead,*** Signet; N. Monsarrat, **The Cruel Sea,*** Pocket Books; and J. Hersey, **The War Lover,*** Bantam.

*Indicates an inexpensive paperbound edition.

Part Eight

Toward a
New World

■ At the end of World War II mankind set about to construct a peace worthy of the sacrifice of millions of lives. Statesmen of the victorious powers assumed that they could transform their wartime "Grand Alliance" into an enduring alliance for peace. Upon this assumption the United Nations was created in 1945, and the defeated Axis powers were occupied. Yet almost overnight a different transformation occurred: former allies became antagonists, former enemies became allies, and peace became the cold war.

In the fast-changing decades since 1945, three major worlds have emerged, each with its recognizable way of life. The western world comprises almost all of the Americas, western and southern Europe, Australia and New Zealand, as well as South Africa and Japan. Stretching across the vast Eurasian heartland, from Berlin to Peking, is the Communist world. The underdeveloped nations of Africa and parts of Asia make up the Third, or nonaligned, World. The conflicting interests of these three worlds form much of the story of our times.

For most of the last twenty-five years, however, the fate of the world has depended upon the rivalry and confrontation tactics of the western and Communist power blocs, as summed up in the term cold war. Each armed itself with thermonuclear weapons and an intercontinental delivery system capable of annihilating the other. With the United Nations powerless to keep the peace between these blocs, the world had to depend upon a "balance of terror," with the two superpowers leading a number of regional security alliances. Twice the western and Communist worlds lunged to the brink of war: over control of Berlin and Soviet attempts to install offensive missiles in Cuba. However, as of 1970, because of the dangers attending an increase in the number of countries possessing nuclear weapons and the massive financial burdens involved, Washington and Moscow were seeking to limit strategic arms by treaty, despite Communist China's opposition. Meanwhile, cold war bipolarity had been giving way to polycentrism. Not only were the former defeated Axis powers reemerging as dynamic—and democratized—societies, but both America's allies and the Soviet Union's sought to acquire more independence in world affairs.

The most dramatic changes occurred in the Third World, where scores of former colonies in Asia and Africa became independent and together constituted a majority in the enlarging membership of the United Nations. To the poverty- and disease-ridden peoples of the underdeveloped world, nationalism offered swift transition from second-class status to equality.

Given their past condition, it was understandable that the impatient Asian and African masses should view their problems in uncomplicated terms—an approach emphasized by many nationalist leaders who promised a veritable millennium. But the actual attainment of freedom has instead opened the floodgates to a torrent of new problems—psychological, economic, social, and, at worst, military. The easily given promises of the pre-independence period must now be redeemed by performance. Little wonder that the Third World has been marked by both political and economic instability—in many countries capsizing into outright chaos. Yet despite the massiveness of their problems, the peoples of Asia and Africa have determined that their road from dependence to independence is irreversible.

In all three worlds entire societies are engaged in a new—and often seemingly frantic—search for identity. In western countries, such as the United States, minorities have been seeking to enter the mainstream of social development and be accepted as equal in all respects. In the Communist world the ideological postulates which helped channel the energies of an earlier generation along revolutionary avenues are increasingly resented by the youth as outmoded and constricting. In the Third World the search takes the form of rediscovering the values and forms of precolonial Asian and African cultures and of adapting them to meet the social and psychological needs of nation-building in this century.

Change is inherent in human affairs, and man has always been discovering new knowledge and solving new problems. This planetary process has now been accelerated beyond anything known in the past. A veritable knowledge and cultural explosion is revolutionizing the second half of the twentieth century. Some of the sciences are doubling their information almost every decade, while a communications revolution has broken down the traditional political and social barriers around the globe. The major problems confronting mankind cut across national boundaries: the population explosion, urbanization, the dwindling of nonrenewable natural resources, and pollution. Science and technology are at once contributing to the existence of these problems and proving essential to their solution. But will the traditional political and social institutions be able to transform themselves either swiftly or fundamentally enough to enable mankind to continue to survive—and prosper—on a plundered and polluted planet? These questions challenge today's youth, who are attempting to develop a new life style appropriate to their approaching role of responsible decision-making.

30. R. Buckminster Fuller: American Pavilion, Montreal World Fair (1967). The magnitude of the revolution in modern architecture can be measured by the great diversity of forms it has engendered. Architects of the nineteenth century were often more interested in the outward style manifestations of the building than in its structure. The modern designer, contrarily, has more notably rooted his art in the materials and techniques of modern industrial technology, and let the style—if any—emerge from the most resourceful use of those materials and techniques. Buckminster Fuller's researches in the geodesic dome have led to an extraordinarily light prefabricated structure, as economic in its means as it is fundamental in design and flexible in use. Its simplicity has enabled builders to utilize it for functions as practical as manufacturing and—witness the American pavilion at Expo 67—as ceremonial as a national exposition hall.

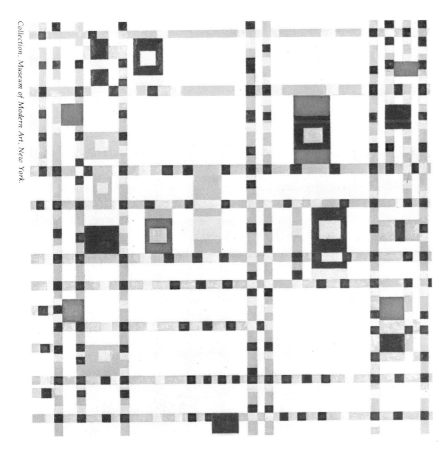

31. (opposite page) **Pablo Picasso: "Dancer"** (1906); **32.** (above) **Piet Mondrian: "Broadway Boogie-Woogie"** (1944); and **33.** (below) **Constantin Brancusi: "Mlle. Pogany"** (1919). The three works shown here only begin to illustrate the immense variety of expressive modes which have turned twentieth-century art into a kaleidoscope of styles and theories of art. Neglecting almost all references to past western painting, Picasso about 1906 borrowed the brusque forms of African tribal sculpture to initiate a radical abstraction which pushed painting ever further away from the descriptive and the mimetic. The objective here is a forceful new imagery and an inventive new system of pictorial structure. Mondrian, implacably following the logic of Picasso's faceted forms, eventually dismissed recognizable subject matter from his painting altogether and constructed severely proportioned compositions of pure geometric shapes. Between these two extremes—Picasso's vehement confrontation of the figure and Mondrian's cerebrally refined ordering of space—lies much of modern art. Brancusi's marble head, for example, is an image as evocative as Picasso's, but its mystery is kept cool by a restraint reminiscent of Mondrian's clean surfaces.

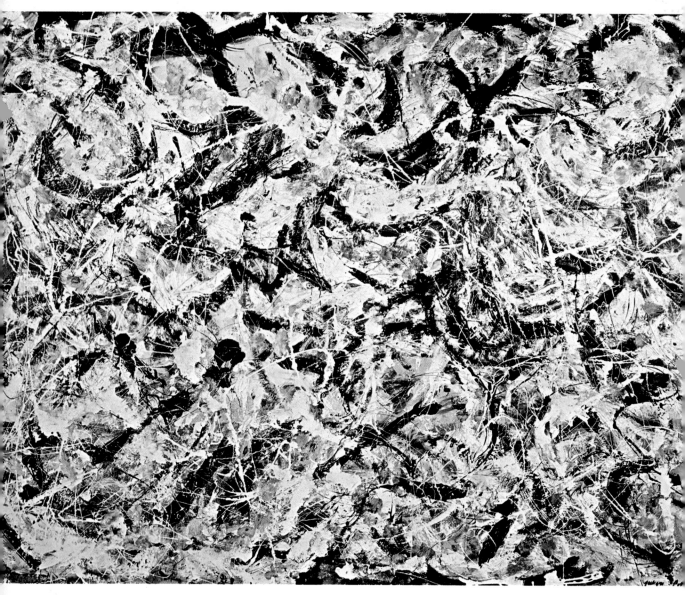

34. Jackson Pollock: "Grayed Rainbow" (1953). The Second World War left the western world a profoundly and unalterably different place, and this fact, as usual, was reflected in the arts. Vanguard painters in America, as if responding to the central role that country was now assuming in the international community, developed an extreme and urgent new abstract style in which traditional pictorial structure and organization were shredded by an explosion of sheer painterly energy. Fluid forms hurtled with uncontained violence through the space of a greatly enlarged picture format. Abstract expressionism, as this uniquely American manner came to be known, dominated the 1950's. Jackson Pollock was one of its most important and eloquent spokesmen.

Chapter 31

Two Worlds: Confrontation and Détente

The West and Communism Since 1945

INTRODUCTION. As the guns stopped firing on the battlefields of Europe and Asia, a great longing to return to the pursuits of peace motivated most of mankind. These pursuits called not only for repairing the most massive destruction in history but equally for implementing the wartime pledge to create a world free from fear and want. In the eloquent phraseology of the United Nations Charter, the peoples of the postwar era were determined "to reaffirm faith in fundamental human rights, in the dignity and worth of the human person, in the equal rights of men and women and of nations large and small, and . . . to promote social progress and better standards of life in larger freedom."

Amid hopes for the future, urgent problems called for immediate attention. While the tasks of reconstruction were undertaken with determination and energy, the statesmen of the victorious Allied powers met to draft peace treaties and to work out policies for occupying the defeated nations. And in San Francisco they organized a new international institution, the United Nations, "to save succeeding generations from the scourge of war, which twice in our lifetime has brought untold sorrow to mankind."

For a brief period these arrangements concealed the more profound consequences of the global conflict: the drastically reduced potential of western Europe in international affairs, marking the end of its four-hundred-year dominance of world affairs; the granting of sovereign status to scores of colonies in Asia and Africa (discussed in Chapter 32); and the upsurge—and later victory—of Communist power in China. The most immediately significant consequence, however, was the emergence of two superpowers, the United States and the Soviet Union, which superseded western Europe as centers of power. Championing antithetical social and economic systems, Washington and Moscow created rival political and military blocs, thereby restructuring the postwar world into a bipolar configuration. The resulting confrontation between the western and Communist worlds came to be known as the cold war, a struggle that was neither war nor peace in the conventional sense but a constant maneuvering for advantage combined with incessant glowerings and threats. For a quarter of a century the world had to live with this cold war, which spasmodically threatened to burst into sudden and uncontrollable nuclear holocaust.

Yet in nature and human affairs alike, nothing remains static or permanently fixed. Although the cold war persisted through the 1950's and into the succeeding decade, and the two superpowers continued to stockpile nuclear arms and to eye each other warily, each knew that it could not expect to destroy the other without risking almost certain thermonuclear annihilation itself. Each recognized the other's sphere of influence, so that an unspoken agreement not to interfere in the internal affairs of the other bloc appeared to have been reached. Thus Moscow could crush the Hungarian uprising of 1956 without real fear of American intervention leading to a Third World War, and Washington in turn was able to contain Communist ambitions in the Atlantic area fairly certain that the Soviet Union would not retaliate, as demonstrated by Moscow's backdown over the Cuban missile crisis. An equilibrium of tension based on two military alliances in Europe—NATO and the Warsaw Pact—provided the basic structure of the world's power division, which was symbolized concretely by the Berlin Wall.

Paradoxically, however, this equilibrium was to be disturbed less by superpowers themselves than by changes within their respective blocs. In short, the Sino-Soviet and the American-European alliances began to come apart. France in the West and China in the East pursued independent policies with increasing vociferousness. Moscow and Washington found they had diminishing control over their client states, and both were challenged by the rising power of Communist China with its quarter of the world's population. A bipolarized world was undergoing still another transformation as new loci of power emerged—thereby adding to existing tensions, notably in the Middle East and Southeast Asia. Yet what has been called the "stalemate of terror" seemed to guarantee that the United States and the Soviet Union would avoid challenging each other directly, lest the dreaded Third World War become a reality and civilization be reduced to radio-active rubble.

THE COLD WAR ABORTS THE GREAT HOPE

The United Nations—purposes and structure. The memory of the failure to build a lasting peace after World War I convinced Allied statesmen that the survival of civilization required an efficient international machinery to maintain peace and security.

With this goal in mind, the representatives of fifty governments met at San Francisco from April to June 1945 and drafted the Charter of a new organization, the United Nations. To achieve its purposes, the United Nations was equipped with six major organs:

The bombing of Hiroshima on August 6, 1945, followed three days later by the bombing of Nagasaki (right), brought with it a new awareness of man's ability to destroy himself. The fact that only two bombs had killed 114,000 people did not deter nations from developing and stockpiling more sophisticated nuclear weapons.

the Security Council, to maintain peace and order; the General Assembly, to function as a form of town meeting of the world; the Economic and Social Council, to improve living standards and promote fundamental human rights; the Trusteeship Council, to advance the interests of dependent peoples; the International Court of Justice, to resolve disputes between nations; and the Secretariat, headed by a secretary-general, to serve the needs of the other major organs. Though lacking the sovereign powers of its member states, the United Nations was a more wide-reaching instrument than its defunct predecessor, the League of Nations.

The most controversial issue at San Francisco was over the right of veto in the Security Council. The smaller countries held that it was undemocratic for certain governments to be privileged to block the wishes of the majority, but the Big Five—the United States, the Soviet Union, China, France, and Great Britain—maintained that singly and collectively they had special interests and responsibilities in maintaining global peace and security. Realists recognized that given

the actualities of power in 1945, peace could not be kept unless the five permanent members of the Council—in particular the Big Two—were willing to cooperate.

Advent of the Atomic Age. The United Nations Charter was signed on June 26, 1945; the first atomic bomb in history was dropped on Hiroshima some six weeks later, on August 6. This second event—and its timing—had two implications of far-reaching significance. First, the advent of nuclear weapons completely altered man's capacity to wage war and to destroy his physical and societal environment; second, because the Charter had been drafted in a prenuclear context, the newly established United Nations was not equipped with formal, far less specific, powers to internationalize the control of atomic energy for peaceful purposes only. Henceforth, those states with nuclear—and later thermonuclear—weapons would possess a life-and-death advantage over nonpossessors; at the same time, the very disparity in power relations would almost certainly propel the latter to bend every effort to acquire these weapons in the absence of any effective international control system. Consequently, the years following World War II were marked by the progressive acquisition of atomic weapons by the larger nations and by ineffectual attempts to limit the proliferation of nuclear weapons and to put brakes on what was to prove the most costly armaments race in history.

Problem of the ex-enemies. At the Potsdam Conference in 1945 the Council of Foreign Ministers of the Big Five was set up to draft the peace treaties. Only minor difficulties were encountered in adopting treaties in 1947 with Italy, Rumania, Bulgaria, Hungary, and Finland. The future of Austria remained uncertain until 1955, when a peace treaty was signed and occupation forces withdrawn. What proved to be roadblocks to international cooperation were treaties with the major ex-enemies, Japan and Germany. Postwar Japan was given a new and more democratic constitution, the national economy was liberalized, workers were encouraged to join trade unions, and the great trusts were broken up. A peace treaty between Japan and the West, signed in 1951 over Soviet objections, reestablished that country as a sovereign state, while a Japanese-American security pact made allies of ex-enemies less than ten years after Pearl Harbor.

It was in Germany that Allied and Soviet policies collided headlong. The defeated country had been divided into zones of temporary occupation; the eastern zone remained under Soviet control, while western Germany was partitioned into American, British, and French zones. Berlin, forming an enclave within the Soviet zone, was placed under four-power administration. This arrangement created serious tensions. Moscow closed its zone to western inspection, stripped the area of raw materials and industry, and in effect demonstrated its aim to keep Germany politically and economically impotent and to foster a Communist regime. With Germany physically and ideologically split, the two superpowers found themselves in serious confrontation in central Europe.

The iron curtain falls. Collaboration among the major Allies had won the war and was supposed to serve as the basis for post-war reconstruction and security, as the United Nations Charter attested. At the wartime Yalta Conference, pledges had been made to permit "free and unfettered elections" in Poland, but a Communist regime was imposed without reference to the will of the people. By 1947 similar governments had been forced on Rumania, Yugoslavia, Hungary, Bulgaria, and Albania, and the following year saw a Communist take-over in Czechoslovakia. Even before some of these events, Winston Churchill had warned at Fulton, Missouri, in 1946, "From Stettin in the Baltic to Trieste in the Adriatic, an Iron Curtain has descended across the Continent."

The bipolarization of Europe became progressively apparent. In 1946 Soviet support of Communist guerrilla activities in Greece and territorial demands upon Turkey revealed Russian designs in the eastern Mediterranean. Such expansionist aims did not go uncountered; President Harry S. Truman (1884-   ) announced in 1947 that the United States would support any country threatened by Communist aggression. This "Truman Doctrine" was followed by the dispatch of economic and military aid to Greece and Turkey—a move usually regarded as marking the start of the cold war.

This American initiative was followed by an offer, announced by Secretary of State George C. Marshall, to help Europe solve its dire economic problems. Western European nations eagerly accepted this American proposal, which was, however, rejected by the Soviet Union for itself and the countries of eastern Europe. Congress subsequently appropriated billions of dollars to implement the European Recovery Program—better known as the Marshall Plan—which proved so effective that within four years the industrial production of the recipient nations had climbed to 64 percent over 1947 levels and 41 percent over prewar figures.

To enable western Germany to participate in the Marshall Plan, the western Allies helped create the new Federal Republic of Germany, which comprised West Germany and West Berlin. Almost immediately the Soviet Union established the German Democratic Republic in East Germany and began to apply pressure to gain control over West Berlin as well. In 1948 all surface communication between Berlin and western Europe was suddenly cut off. American and British authorities met this blockade by organizing an air lift to supply food and fuel to the two million inhabitants of West Berlin. In 1949 the Soviet Union agreed to lift the blockade, a notable victory for the West in central Europe.

Collective security by regional alliances. Deadlocks in the United Nations and its inability to guarantee international security, coupled with Soviet expansionism, led to the establishment of the North Atlantic Treaty Organization (NATO) in 1949. Composed of nations of western Europe (Great Britain, France, Belgium, Luxemburg, the Netherlands, Norway, Denmark, Portugal, and Italy) together with Iceland, the United States, and Canada, NATO was a regional alliance for mutual assistance in the North Atlantic area; in 1952 its territorial limits were extended to include Greece and Turkey; in 1955 West Germany also joined. NATO represented a profound shift in the foreign policies of the United States and Canada, neither of which had previously made peacetime overseas military commitments. NATO employed forces from its members to set up a defensive shield against possible sudden attack from behind the iron curtain.

The Communists for their part had not been inactive. In September 1949, following the driving of Chiang Kai-shek's government from the Chinese mainland to the island of Formosa, Mao Tse-tung proclaimed the People's Republic of China, and early the following year Moscow and Peking signed a thirty-year treaty of "friendship, alliance, and mutual assistance." West Germany's entry into NATO in May 1955 was swiftly followed by the creation of the Warsaw Pact, which provided for a unified Communist military command in Soviet-dominated eastern Europe.

The Korean War and additional regional alliances. After Japan's surrender Korea had been divided into American and Soviet zones of occupation. The departure of occupation forces left behind two hostile regimes, each claiming jurisdiction over the entire

TERRITORIAL CHANGES
IN EUROPE AFTER
WORLD WAR II

Annexed by the Soviet Union
Annexed by Poland
Annexed by Bulgaria
Annexed by Yugoslavia

country. On June 25, 1950, North Korean troops crossed the 38th parallel into South Korea. Washington immediately called for a special meeting of the United Nations Security Council, whose members demanded a cease-fire and withdrawal of the invaders. (The Soviet delegate was boycotting the Council at the time and was not present to veto its action.) When the demand was ignored, the Council undertook to furnish assistance to the South Korean government in order "to repel the armed attacks and to restore international peace and security in the area." After three years of costly fighting —during which the United States carried the brunt of the burden in defending South Korea while Communist China dispatched "volunteers" to assist the North Koreans— an armistice was secured in July 1953. The status quo *ante bellum* was reestablished and South Korea's independence maintained. Although the peninsula had not been reunited, Communist expansion in the area had been contained.

Following the Korean outbreak, the concept of regional collective security was extended to the Pacific and the Middle East. The year 1951 saw the establishment not only of the previously mentioned American-Japanese defense treaty but also of the ANZUS Pacific Security Pact, entered into by the United States, Australia, and New Zealand. The year 1954 was marked by the creation of two more regional alliances spearheaded by the United States, one with the Chinese Nationalist government on Formosa, the second in Southeast Asia following the establishment of a Communist regime in North Vietnam. Known as the Southeast Asia Treaty Organization (SEATO), it was formed for mutual security by the United States, Australia, New Zealand, France, Great Britain, Pakistan, the Philippines, and Thailand and also brought Cambodia, Laos, and South Vietnam under its protection. The fear of Soviet penetration into the Middle East resulted in yet another mutual security arrangement. Negotiated in 1955, with Great Britain, Turkey, Iran, Iraq, and Pakistan as full members and the United States as an "observer," it was originally called the Baghdad Pact but was renamed the Central Treaty Organization (CENTO) after the withdrawal of Iraq in 1959. International affairs in the 1950's thus were characterized by a bipolar confrontation of two global power systems.

A new era in American-Soviet rivalry. With the death of Stalin in 1953, Soviet foreign policy shifted from crude brinkmanship to a more sophisticated approach. Nikita Khrushchev (1894-   ), the new leader, realized that nuclear war would be suicidal to all concerned. By enunciating the doctrine of "peaceful coexistence," he repudiated the Stalinist view that war between the socialist and capitalist worlds was inevitable. Rivalry between the two systems would continue, however, and Khrushchev boasted that in the near future the Soviet Union would overtake the United States economically, scientifically, and in the area of social justice. In his own words, "We shall bury you."

Thus coexistence did not mean the end of tensions, which were reflected in the formation of previously mentioned regional pacts during Khrushchev's period of control in the Kremlin (1953-1964). Again, the brutal suppression of the Hungarian revolt by Soviet arms in 1956 (see p. 750) caused widespread revulsion in the West. This action was especially disillusioning, because a summit conference of the Big Four at Geneva the previous year, during the first term of Dwight D. Eisenhower (1890-1969), had been the first such conclave since the Potsdam conference a decade earlier. Following the meeting many observers had felt that the danger of a hot war was receding and that a beginning had been made in removing tensions by negotiation rather than by force.

Meanwhile two Soviet technological triumphs appeared to affect the cold war. In 1957 Soviet scientists put the first artificial satellite in orbit and began producing intercontinental ballistic missiles (ICBM's). Following this scientific coup, Khrushchev took a tougher line in foreign policy, especially in regard to Berlin, which had long been a thorn in the Soviet side. West Berlin had become a showplace of freedom and affluence compared with East Berlin, and it was also a magnet for attracting manpower from East Germany. In 1958 Khrushchev demanded the withdrawal of all western forces and recognition of Berlin as a "free city," presumably seeking to bring the whole metropolis under Communist control. The United States refused to accede to this demand, its attitude strengthened by substantial advances in rocket power.

The early years of the 1960's were marked by dangerous tensions that threatened to engulf the superpowers in a nuclear conflict. A summit meeting convened in Paris in 1960 broke up angrily, the situation exacerbated by an American U-2 reconnaissance plane having been discovered and shot down over the Soviet Union. During the same year Khrushchev, speaking at the United Nations, demanded the resignation of the secretary-general, Dag Hammarskjöld, and denounced American foreign policy. The following year Moscow again demanded the withdrawal of Allied forces from West Berlin, and once more Washington refused to back down. President John F. Kennedy (1917-1963) declared that the Communists would not be permitted to gain control either gradually or by force, and the NATO alliance stood firm in the crisis. Backed by Moscow, the East German government erected a wall between East and West Berlin, thereby blocking the escape route formerly used by thousands.

The most serious crisis occurred in 1962 within ninety miles of the American mainland. Three years earlier Fidel Castro had wrested power from a right-wing dictatorship in Cuba and had set about to transform the island into a Communist state and to create an anti-American springboard for the diffusion of Communist subversion into Latin America (see p. 747). A setback to the Kennedy administration occurred when some Cuban exiles, trained under American auspices, invaded their homeland in April 1961 and were decisively defeated at the Bay of Pigs. A year later American intelligence discovered that the Soviet Union was building rocket sites in Cuba and sending missiles which, if installed, could constitute a decisive advantage in the cold war. Kennedy ordered a naval blockade set up around Cuba and demanded that Moscow withdraw these offensive weapons. After a few days of "eyeball to eyeball" crisis, Khrushchev ordered the rockets removed.

The Cuban imbroglio underscored the urgency of reducing the peril of atomic war. The result was a limited nuclear test ban treaty, signed in 1965 by Great Britain, the Soviet Union, and the United States, which outlawed the testing of nuclear devices in outer space, in the atmosphere, or under water. Although France (now a nuclear power) and Communist China (soon to become one) refused to sign, one hundred other states did. This test ban registered some lessening of tension, and relations between the superpowers improved in other ways. Scientific and agricultural exchanges were encouraged,

and a "hot line" between the White House and the Kremlin was set up to prevent a communications breakdown and to facilitate understanding of their respective positions.

FROM BIPOLARITY TO POLYCENTRISM

Developments in the western alliance. The United States had emerged from World War II with its landscape unscathed and its economy the most powerful in history; now technological change and postwar conditions were to hurtle American society to new plateaus of efficiency and prosperity. By 1967 the annual gross national product (GNP) approached $800 billion, or nearly half that of the whole world, with the eleven northeast states generating a GNP equal to that of the Soviet Union. The burgeoning of this industrial power made possible the vast number of global responsibilities undertaken by the American people after 1945: the expenditure of $128 billion (through 1967) for military and economic foreign aid; the maintenance of armed bases around the world; and the waging of two protracted wars in Asia. These developments abroad were accompanied by major domestic programs aimed at improving educational and economic opportunities and for extending benefits in such areas as unemployment insurance, public housing, urban renewal, social security, and medicare for the aged.

The administration of President Lyndon B. Johnson (1963-1968) was marked by notable reforms on a broad domestic front. However, various problems—including the reconstruction of urban "inner cores" and a vigorous attack against the accelerating pollution of the national environment—remained unsolved pending the termination of an unpopular Vietnamese war which was costing the economy upwards of $30 billion annually as of 1969. Meanwhile the problem of race relations became especially acute in the mid-1960's as the black minority sought to secure recognition of its civil rights, to improve its economic status and educational opportunities, and to be accepted fully into the mainstream of American life.

While Americans were reassessing their national commitments and goals on both the foreign and domestic fronts, their European allies had in turn been experiencing profound changes of status and outlook since the war-devastated days of 1945. Assisted initially by the Marshall Plan, western Europe had made a remarkable recovery, and by 1964 its economic power stood next to the United States. Non-Communist Europe's economic advance was largely attributable to the creation in 1957 of the European Economic Community, better known as the Common Market. Its members—France, West Germany, Italy, Belgium, Luxemburg, and the Netherlands—aimed to abolish gradually all custom duties among them, to reach agreement on a common tariff, to facilitate a common trading market, and, eventually, to attain some form of political integration. Parallel with the Common Market was a smaller free trade group known as the European Free Trade Association (EFTA), established in 1959 by Great Britian, the Scandinavian countries, Switzerland, Spain, and Portugal.

Britain's changing role. The remarkable postwar European economic advances were not shared by Great Britain, which had incurred huge losses of overseas investments and a marked decline in foreign trade. Moreover, its problems had been increased by inefficient industrial management and featherbedding among trade unions, while its welfare state programs, calling for expanded social services and higher wages, could only be maintained by a favorable balance of international payments. But imports kept exceeding exports, threatening the position of the pound sterling and creating balance-of-payment crises in the 1960's. By 1970, however, Britain's overall economic position had improved.

Perhaps Britain's most notable postwar achievement was the peaceful liquidation of its once vast empire (see Chapter 32). This imperial loss, coupled with domestic economic problems, caused British statesmen to develop a new posture in world affairs, such as seeking closer ties with countries across the English Channel. In 1962 London formally applied for membership in the Common Market, but President de Gaulle abruptly vetoed the application. Realizing that it could only exercise influence in world affairs by becoming part of an integrated Europe, Britain continued to explore this possibility, especially following de Gaulle's retirement from public office. Though London played down the implications of such an historic shift, this move would tend to weaken the traditional Anglo-American community of interests and to strengthen the growing European locus of power and prestige.

De Gaulle's France. Overwhelmed by defeat in 1940, France owed its resurgence primarily to General Charles de Gaulle (1890-1970). At the war's end he became provisional president, only to resign in 1946 when denied the strong executive powers he had demanded. However, a new constitution, adopted for the Fourth Republic, proved inadequate to cope with France's political ills at home or in Indochina and Algeria. Finally, by popular mandate, de Gaulle resumed control of the government in 1958 and obtained another constitution vesting decisive powers in the president. The center of political gravity in the Fifth Republic shifted to the masterful de Gaulle.

During the next decade de Gaulle spoke and acted for France. Thus he resolved the Algerian imbroglio, introduced welfare legislation at home, and stimulated French initiative in such fields as atomic energy and supersonic aircraft. In giving France a status in world affairs which it had not enjoyed for decades, de Gaulle challenged two fundamental postwar theses: (1) NATO was indispensable for western security; and (2) the United States must maintain leadership in the western alliance. De Gaulle saw the situation differently. Post-Stalinist Russia was no longer expansionist in Europe, while a Germany split into two segments entrenched in rival power blocs offered little chance of upsetting the postwar equilibrium—nor were many people seriously interested in seeing Germany reunited. In short, the threat of war on the European landscape had receded over the horizon.

De Gaulle's distinctive French foreign policy rested on three pillars. He opposed Anglo-American hegemony in the West. He believed that a united Europe, hopefully under French leadership, would become a major force in world politics, along with the Soviet Union (if it did not join the new European structure), the United States, and China. He was also concerned with the Afro-Asian world, whose newly emergent nations in his opinion should not be committed to either the East or the West. In pursuit of this foreign policy de Gaulle recognized mainland China, began to build an entente with the Soviet Union, sought greater French influence in Asia and Africa, and opposed Britain's entry into the Common Market lest the United States, through Anglo-American shared interests, would dominate it. Far from least, de Gaulle withdrew his military forces from NATO, broke five treaties with the United States, forced American bases off French soil (along with NATO headquarters), and proceeded to develop an independent French nuclear capability.

In mid-1968, however, the Czechoslovakian crisis raised serious doubts in Paris as to the future of France's anti-American and anti-NATO orientation, and the de Gaulle regime was profoundly shaken by a student uprising and nation-wide strikes. In 1969 the president resigned and was replaced by his former prime minister, Georges Pompidou, who for his part would have to make sensitive readjustments in France's domestic affairs and foreign policy postures, now that "le grand Charles" was no longer on the scene to impose his imperious will. These readjustments would not be easy; they would have to take care of student disaffection with an outmoded educational system, worker demands for higher wages to meet a continuing rise in living costs, and regional demands for less bureaucratic centralization of power in Paris. Having to give first priority to domestic and especially economic problems, the new president could hardly expect

ECONOMIC INTEGRATION OF WESTERN EUROPE

European Common Market (Inner Six)

European Free Trade Association (Outer Seven)

to retain the role for France in European affairs which his predecessor had so ably played. Foreign observers expected France to be replaced by West Germany as the dominant power in western Europe and an improvement of French relations with the United States.

Resurgence in West Germany. The dramatic story of West Germany's recovery from an occupied territory to membership in the western alliance began with the establishment of the Federal Republic in 1949 and the end of Allied occupation five years later. Under its aged but forceful chancellor, Konrad Adenauer (1876-1967), West Germany surged forward economically, while politically Adenauer wedded his country's fortunes to those of the western democracies.

Central to future peace is how firmly democratic institutions have taken hold in the former Nazi homeland. As elections succeed one another, the democratic process seems to be acquiring firm roots. Another factor impinging on the peace is the problem of the division of Germany. However desirable to the German masses, as of 1970 unification remained unattainable in the foreseeable future, given the might of the Soviet Union and its fear of German industrial and military strength as experienced in two world wars. The West Germans have come to realize that unification will be a long-term objective and that perhaps the first step should be the attainment of closer contacts with eastern Europe by expanding trade and diplomatic relations.

In October 1969, for the first time in some forty years, the Social Democratic Party was able to form the government—under its leader and new chancellor, Willy Brandt—on election promises that included improved relations with Germany's Communist neighbors and the Soviet Union. In March 1970 the leaders of West and East Germany held direct meetings, followed a few months later by Brandt's trip to Moscow where he concluded an important treaty. By its provisions, the German Federal Republic and the Soviet Union renounced the use of force in the settlement of disputes; the parties accepted the concept of eventual reunification of the two Germanies; and for its part

Arriving in Moscow to sign a treaty with the Soviet Union in August 1970, West German chancellor Willy Brandt, escorted by Soviet premier Aleksei Kosygin, reviews an honor guard at the airport. Not since 1955 had a West German head of government visited Moscow.

West Germany recognized the continued existence of the Oder-Neisse line as the western boundary of Poland.

Normalization of relations with West Germany's Communist neighbors could pave the way for increased trade and cultural exchanges. Meanwhile the remarkable strength of German industry and an economic prosperity unrivaled in Europe attested to West Germany's preeminence in the Common Market community. No less clearly, as demonstrated in the 1969 elections, the West German population has shown its determination to adhere to democratic institutions and policies by roundly repudiating the new-Nazi forces at the polls.

Latin America: reform or revolt. The term *Latin America* comprises enormously different regions: Spanish- and Portuguese-speaking areas; homogeneous societies of European stock (Argentina, Uruguay, and Chile); dualistic Indian-Spanish societies (Peru, Bolivia, Ecuador, and Mexico); what has been described as "melting-pot" societies in Brazil and Venezuela; industrially developed economies (Argentina, Mexico, and southern Brazil); and largely agricultural economies such as Ecuador and Paraguay. As a continent, Latin America shares many of the problems associated with the developing nations of the Third World. Nevertheless, for many observers, Latin America "has the greatest affinities, as regards both culture and institutions, with the Western world" and can be better described "as a peripheral area of the industrialized West than as a component of the Third World."[1]

The period following World War II witnessed much political instability and rising social unrest in the region. The only countries with continuous elected governments from 1950 to 1966 were Chile, Mexico, Costa Rica, and Uruguay. Between these dates fourteen governments were toppled by force, and dictatorial rule was imposed on more than half of the Latin American population. Political instability and the seeds of social upheaval spring from appalling socioeconomic disparities. Despite the region's great natural resources, the poverty of the average Latin American is cruel. Shanty towns on the edges of the large cities house thousands amid filth, disease, hunger, and vice. Life expectancy in Latin America is about forty; more than half of the adults are illiterate.

Four of the problems currently afflicting Latin American societies can be enumerated. First, agricultural productivity must be improved in order to lower food costs, increase supplies for both home consumption and export, and raise rural incomes. Second, the population explosion must be controlled; with a yearly increase around 3 percent, Latin America has the fastest-growing population in the world. In the mid-1960's the region's population was about 200 million; it is entirely possible that the figure will climb to 600 million by the year 2000. Third, national economies—especially those that are relatively developed—have suffered from inflation which has created far-reaching economic and social disturbances. Finally, Latin America must not only accelerate industrialization but also develop greater regional integration and better access to domestic and foreign markets.

These massive problems have made Latin America a battleground for opposing ideologies. Since 1948 the countries south of the Rio Grande have been aligned with the United States in the Organization of American States (OAS), a regional alliance to establish a security zone in the Western Hemisphere. Dominated by the "Colossus of the North," the OAS has sought to prevent Communist regimes from acquiring control in Latin American countries; conversely, Communist elements have sought to exploit social restlessness and economic misery in the region. In the 1950's this explosive situation was not appreciated by Washington, preoccupied with combating Communist expansion in western Europe. It demanded attention, however, in 1959 when Castro rapidly transformed Cuba into a Communist dictatorship. His attempts to export his brand of politics were countered by a boycott set up by the OAS. Under Castro, educational and health standards rose appreciably, as did living conditions among the peasantry; but the professional and middle classes suffered losses in both living standards and personal liberties,

and many thousands fled to the United States. The loss of these professional skills added to Castro's problems, which were already great because of Cuba's dependence upon a one-crop economy, sugar, and especially upon its export to other Communist countries.

Realizing that the United States should pay more attention to its southern neighbors in order to protect its own interests and to prevent the further spread of communism from Cuba, President Kennedy initiated, with Latin American cooperation, the Alliance for Progress. For the first decade, the United States pledged $20 billion, to which the recipients were to add $80 billion. It was thus hoped that democratic and economic reforms could eradicate those conditions against which communism's attack was chiefly directed.

Unfortunately, the Alliance has so far not made the progress originally expected. Its concept has failed to capture the public imagination, and although a number of agrarian and other reform laws have been enacted in different countries, implementation has proved tardy. Given the social traditions of paternalism and oligarchic rule, there has been little correlation between economic and political reform. Moreover, extreme inequalities exist in the distribution of income. According to a United Nations estimate for 1965, half of Latin America's population received only 14 percent of the region's total income, while 31.5 percent went to top income brackets comprising only 5 percent of the population. In effect, while a number of sound programs have been attempted, Latin America is far from reaching the point of economic takeoff. It is still in a race between reform and revolt.

Japan: economic and social transformation. In striking contrast to lethargically paced developments in Latin America stands the brilliant recovery and development of Japan since 1945. Allied occupation reforms in the educational, social, and political spheres, together with close economic political ties with the United States, made Japan a member of the western bloc—both America's chief ally in Asia

Rapidly recovering from the devastation of World War II, Japan has become one of the world's leading industrial nations, a major producer of steel, electricity, and automobiles.

phenomenal postwar economic growth was making its presence felt. The 1970's could be expected to see a growing involvement by Japanese businessmen and statesmen alike in the trade and politics of East and Southeast Asia, the latter region offering both raw materials and a potentially large market for Japanese exports.

Considering the fascist character of its pre-1945 politics, it is remarkable that Japan has maintained stable parliamentary government during the postwar years. The political situation, however, is subject to serious domestic pressures. Conservative parties, largely pro-American, have been in power continuously since 1948, the main opposition coming from the Socialists, who are frustrated by their being perennially in opposition. And while Japanese leadership has demonstrated extraordinary talent in economics, the same vision and dynamism have been lacking in politics. The various parties have not sufficiently assessed the importance of anticipating the needs of a rapidly changing society. Traditional prejudices and bitterness between the advocates of different political faiths constitute a serious weakness in the political arena. An American observer warns: "Japan's imported institutions may perhaps be taken for granted, but their capacity to endure and evolve is always open to question."[2]

The fracturing of monolithic communism. Just as the structure and behavior pattern of the western alliance underwent profound changes in the quarter of a century following World War II, so a once monolithic Communist world was to find itself irretrievably shattered by inner tensions and conflicts. Briefly stated, the fracturing process was due to the inability of an ideology which professes to be international to contain, far less direct, the upsurge of historically nurtured nationalisms within the geographical orbit which had been largely delimited by Soviet force.

The Soviet Union after victory. Ravaged by war—with millions killed and many millions more left homeless, with cities blasted into rubble and vast areas of the countryside laid waste—the Soviet Union

and its second trading partner. The American alliance, however, caused considerable division in Japanese public opinion. Leftist groups tended to be anti-American, an attitude accentuated by the unpopularity in Japan of the war in Vietnam. The students were especially critical of the renewal, in 1960, of their country's security pact with the United States, and its adoption set off a rash of riots. The retention of the American military base in Okinawa also affronted national sensibilities.

Relations with neighboring mainland China were of continuing concern to Japan. Since China offers an immense potential market, Tokyo made a limited trade pact with Peking in 1962. At the same time, however, Japan was apprehensive over China's growing military power and nuclear capability. As an ally of the United States, therefore, Japan followed a diplomatic policy of nonrecognition. With the highest standard of living in Asia, a GNP twice that of Latin America, and the status of the third largest industrial power, Japan enjoyed the longest sustained economic growth of any nation in the two decades following 1945. Throughout the world, in fact, Japan's nevertheless faced the postwar years in a determined, aggressive mood. Early in 1946 the Soviet government inaugurated its fourth Five-Year Plan, designed to restore the war-damaged economy, accelerate heavy industry and the mechanization of agriculture, and expand the country's military capability. In contrast to the speedy demobilization of American forces, the Soviet Union maintained a huge army and increased military expenditures from 66 billion rubles in 1948 to 96 billion three years later. Production of consumer goods was limited and in some areas lagged behind the prewar level. Soviet citizens were prevented from traveling abroad, from reading unauthorized publications, and from listening to foreign radio programs, which were in turn systematically jammed.

Stalin died in 1953, his last years marked by brutality and a paranoid fear of even his close associates. On the eve of his demise there were ominous portents of yet another blood purge. The Stalinist regime has been described as combining "all the horrors of early industrialism, Victorian imperialism, political tyranny, and ideological infallibility into a single totalitarian whole."[3]

Following Stalin's death, the Soviet government announced that henceforth it would be guided by the "collective leadership" of the top Communists. It was not long, however, before the shrewd, stockv Ukrainian Nikita Khrushchev succeeded in making himself undisputed master of the Soviet world. The new premier gave top priority to heavy industry, so that steel production doubled between 1950 and 1957 and made possible a complex of plants throughout the country. The Seven-Year Plan, announced early in 1959, aimed at further strengthening the country's economic and military might and at surpassing the leading capitalist countries in per capita output. The annual production of steel was to be increased to about 90 million tons, and agricultural output raised by 70 percent. Education was to be expanded until by 1965 the number of engineers and technocrats would total some four million, or half as many again as at the start of the plan.

Many discounted these ambitious plans, but Khrushchev's ebullience sprang from his awareness of Soviet industrial and technological capabilities. His confidence was rewarded with the launching of the first space satellite, Sputnik, in 1957 and the moon rockets, Lunik I, II, and III, two years later.

Soviet imperialism and eastern Europe. After 1945, while western powers were relinquishing control over their extensive colonial holdings, the Soviet Union staked out a colonial area of its own in eastern Europe. Russian expansionism followed a common pattern. With variations here and there, the process was first for Moscow to secure the establishment of a coalition government in which certain key ministries, especially that of interior and police, were given to the Communists. Full-scale elections were held only after these ministries had made certain that the opposition was either imprisoned or barred from voting. In short order, and despite western protests, Poland, East Germany, Rumania, Bulgaria, Hungary, and Czechoslovakia were transformed into Communist dependencies of the Soviet Union. Throughout eastern Europe, the Soviet Union effectively exercised political control, directed economic activities, and forbade any cultural or educational initiative that ran counter to Marxism-Leninism as interpreted by the Kremlin leadership.

Nevertheless, one Soviet satellite, Yugoslavia, broke Moscow's grip. Marshal Tito (1892-   ), a tough wartime resistance leader and top Communist in that country, at first went along with the Soviet "line." However, his national strength and geographical distance from Soviet forces enabled him to display a growing resentment of Russian interference. When Tito made a final political break with Soviet policy in 1948, he was encouraged by the western powers and held his ground despite Moscow's economic reprisals and threats of war.

While Tito remained a Communist and used western financial aid in such ideologically "correct" ventures as the build-up of heavy industry and the collectivization of agriculture, his successful defection proved a continuing source of embarrassment to the Kremlin. Moreover, Yugoslavia's example stirred thoughts of rebellion in other satellites that wanted to regain some semblance of national independence.

Following the organization of the eastern zone of Germany into the German Democratic Republic, the East German regime proceeded to break up the large farms and expand heavy industry. As living standards stagnated, or in some instances declined, discontent mounted. Thousands of East Germans fled each week to West Germany; and in June 1953 severe food shortages, coupled with new decrees for longer working hours, touched off a workers' revolt. The uprising was quickly put down, but the world was left in no doubt as to what most East Germans thought of their "workers' democracy."

In Poland, as in Yugoslavia, communism acquired a national coloration. Wladyslaw Gomulka, a formerly imprisoned national Communist, gained control of the Polish United Workers' (Communist) Party in 1956. Subsequently, he sent important Soviet officials back to Russia and permitted Polish workers considerable freedom of expression. He also extended greater autonomy to the Catholic Church (to which most Poles continued to belong). However, foreign observers ruled out any chance of Titoism in Warsaw for the foreseeable future.

Meanwhile national communism had been gaining ground in Hungary. The climax was reached in a widespread revolt in the fall of 1956, the creation of a popular government, and the withdrawal of Russian forces from Budapest. Reinforced Soviet troops, however, quickly returned to the capital where they stamped out the flames of national independence. Large numbers of freedom fighters died in the struggle, while more than 200,000 refugees fled to the West.

Communism triumphs in China. Another momentous transformation foreseen by few during the war was the swift victory of communism in China. During that conflict Chiang Kai-shek's Nationalist government and the Chinese Communist leaders had waged a common struggle against the Japanese invaders. The Communists emerged from the conflict with increased popular support and in control of an area containing some 90 million people as well as an army of 500,000 under the leadership of Mao Tse-tung.

Civil war broke out in October 1945. The Nationalists had failed to retain the loyalty of the masses and could be saved neither by American mediation nor by international relief supplies. Notwithstanding Chiang's attempts at limited reform, the long struggle with Japan had resulted in catastrophic inflation, a situation made more critical by widespread corruption among government officials. Above all, the Nationalist regime favored big business and had neglected the long-existing poverty and problems of the farmers. Chiang's strength collapsed in Manchuria in 1948, and the following year saw the complete rout of his armies. By the middle of 1950 Mao had become master of mainland China, and Chiang and a remnant of his forces fled to Formosa (Taiwan). The People's Republic of China, already established in Peking in 1949, was immediately recognized by the U.S.S.R., and subsequently the two countries formed a thirty-year alliance. Soviet attempts to gain for Peking the seat in the United Nations held by Nationalist China failed, however, largely because of United States opposition.

Communist consolidation and problems in China. Following their victory over Chiang's Nationalist government, Mao and his colleagues imposed a tightly centralized administration extending to Manchuria, Inner Mongolia, and Chinese Turkestan; and in 1950 Red Chinese armies moved into Tibet. In order to cast China into a solid Marxist mold, intensive efforts were employed to redirect the whole course of society away from traditional patterns, and all organized opposition to the regime was liquidated. Landlords were dispossessed, business firms either nationalized or brought under rigid control, and intellectuals subjected to "thought reform" in order to eliminate "incorrect thinking" which might offer a threat to the government.

As in the Soviet system, all power was concentrated in the Communist party, governed by the People's Central Committee, whose members occupied the chief civilian and military posts. The day-to-day work of the committee was entrusted to a smaller Politburo headed by Mao, who was also chairman of the republic—that is, head of the state. Elected representative bodies existed, but the political levers were manipulated by the Central Committee.

After checking two flagrant evils that had afflicted the Nationalist regime—namely, corruption and inflation—Mao's government began to grapple with China's basic problems: a desperately low standard of living, too many people on overworked land, and an urgent need for industrialization. Millions of acres, confiscated from their owners without compensation, were set up as state farms, and other land was organized into collectives. The first Five-Year Plan (1953-1957) showed significant economic growth, especially in heavy industry. Agriculture, on the other hand, tended to be neglected. A grandiose second Five-Year Plan was launched in 1958, and the "Great Leap Forward" began. The entire population was mobilized on the land and in the factories. In agriculture gigantic communes were set up, each served by public mess halls, dormitories, and nurseries. It soon became evident, however, that the Great Leap Forward had proved overly ambitious and ill planned. The communes, dehumanized by western standards at least, failed to produce more food, industry bogged down in a mire of mismanagement, and severe floods compounded the economic fiasco.

The Sino-Soviet split. During the 1950's most Americans had assumed that Communists everywhere were united in seeking to destroy the western world—an attitude reinforced by oft-reiterated pledges of "eternal friendship" and "comradely cooperation" between Moscow and Peking, bound in turn by their thirty-year alliance. In the 1960's, however, evidence began to mount that the two Communist giants were at odds. Many Americans were skeptical of this evidence because of "an exaggerated belief in the unifying power of Communist ideol-

ogy and an inadequate appreciation of the long-standing differences between the Russians and Chinese. Very few Americans, for example, had any idea of how bitter and frequent Russian-Chinese conflicts have been over the centuries. Actually, the remarkable thing is that Moscow and Peking were able to maintain the appearance of friendship as long as they did. It was implicit in their background that even though both claimed allegiance to Marxism-Leninism they should become rivals and finally enemies."[4] The Sino-Soviet split has been described as "the most important international political development of the first half of the nineteen-sixties."[5]

The previous decade had witnessed large-scale cooperation and forms of Soviet assistance to China. These included cash loans, credits for industrialization, the training of thousands of Chinese students at Soviet universities and factories, and the dispatch of thousands of Soviet technicians to help

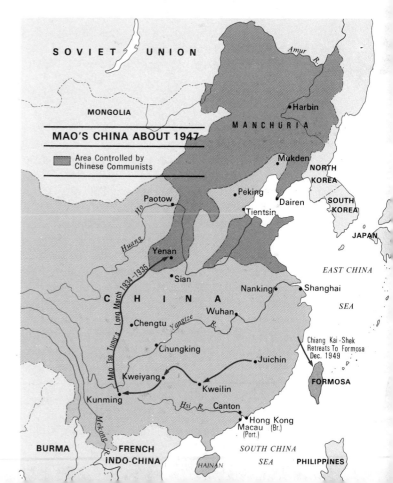

SOVIET UNION

MONGOLIA

MANCHURIA

MAO'S CHINA ABOUT 1947

▨ Area Controlled by Chinese Communists

Amur R.

Harbin

Mukden

NORTH KOREA

SOUTH KOREA

JAPAN

Peking

Dairen

Tientsin

Paotow

Ho R.

Huang R.

Yenan

Sian

EAST CHINA SEA

Nanking

Shanghai

C H I N A

Wuhan

Yangtze R.

Chengtu

Chungking

Juichin

Kweiyang

Kweilin

Kunming

Hsi R.

Canton

Hong Kong
Macau (Br.)
(Port.)

Mao Tse Tung's Long March 1934-1935

Chiang Kai-Shek Retreats To Formosa Dec. 1949

FORMOSA

BURMA

FRENCH INDO-CHINA

Mekong R.

HAINAN

SOUTH CHINA SEA

PHILIPPINES

After crossing the icebound Ussuri River, Chinese soldiers attacked Soviet border guards in an effort to penetrate Damansky Island. The border conflict was further evidence of the continuing power struggle between the Soviet Union and China as each tried to emerge as the leader of world communism.

build new factories, mines, and power plants in China. Throughout the 1950's the Soviet Union was China's principal source of machinery and other needed goods and its biggest customer.

On the other hand, during that same decade tensions were building up. Thus Mao made sure that the Russians abandoned their special position in Manchuria, including their half-ownership of the Chinese Eastern Railroad and the basing of Soviet troops in Port Arthur and Dairen. For their part, the Kremlin leaders made clear that the supplies they provided the Chinese forces during the Korean war were not a gift but a loan which Peking was expected to repay, and in 1958 Khrushchev did not disguise his basic disagreement with China's Great Leap Forward. Moreover, both giants were competing in a prestige race to determine which one would be first to reach Marx's goal of pure communism and in the process could claim to be leader of the Communist world.

As far back as the seventeenth century, with the drive of tsarist governments across Eurasia to the Pacific, Sino-Russian relations had experienced serious tensions. In their advance, the Russians encountered Chinese subjects living in the Amur River valley and elsewhere. In time the newcomers acquired at Chinese expense some half a million square miles of what now comprises the Soviet Far East and much of Soviet Central Asia. In addition, the Soviets succeeded in transforming Outer Mongolia into a protectorate.

Like other European powers, Russia had gained territory when China was weak; now that the latter has acquired new strength—along with a thermonuclear capability—it seeks to regain as much of its former territory as possible. Territorial issues were raised publicly in 1963 when the Sino-Soviet split broke into the open, and since then tensions and armed conflict have intensified along the disputed borders as well as over the highly strategic province of Sinkiang, which contains important sources of oil as well as China's nuclear installation sites. In 1969 much publicized fighting occurred over an uninhabited island in the Ussuri River which separates Manchuria from Soviet territory to the East. The island itself—called "Chenpao" by the Chinese and "Damansky" by the Russians—has no territorial or strategic value, but made world headlines simply because it served as a focal point of a continuing conflict, at once geopolitical and ideological.

The Sino-Soviet power struggle can be described in terms of two epithets: the charge of "adventurism" which Moscow hurls at Peking, and of "revisionism" with which the latter assails the Kremlin leadership. Each claims to represent Marxism-Leninism in its pure form and charges the other with betraying world communism. The Soviet leaders argue that in a thermonuclear age, when hydrogen bombs could destroy the whole world, communism must coexist with capitalism. In their view, the Chinese leadership either does not sufficiently understand the ecological risks of a nuclear conflict or expects that sufficient numbers of the huge Chinese population would survive to ensure Peking's primacy in any aftermath. In addition, Moscow charges Mao Tse-tung with substituting for Marx's teachings about labor-capital conflict his own revisionist doctrine that pits peoples of the "countryside" (the underdeveloped nonwhites of Asia, Africa, and Latin America) against those of the "city" (the developed white populations of Europe, the Soviet Union, and North America).

For their part, the Chinese Communists charge Moscow with maintaining the international status quo of which, as a superpower, it is a major beneficiary. Hence, the Kremlin's leaders have abandoned Marxist revolution in favor of reaching a détente with Washington in order to ensure continued American-Soviet hegemony over the world. Soviet warnings about the dangers of nuclear warfare need not discourage Communist revolutions which can be prosecuted without recourse to atomic weapons (as the Vietnam struggle attests). The present Kremlin leaders have revised Marxism to the point where they are reintroducing some elements of capitalism into the Soviet Union and its client states and are placing national interests before those of international communism. They must be replaced by leaders dedicated to a world Communist revolution.

After attending Ho Chi Minh's funeral in North Vietnam in September 1969, Soviet leaders paid a call on their counterparts in Peking, apparently in an attempt to reach agreement on the dangerous border situation and other contentious issues. As of early 1970, however, no appreciable lessening of tensions, or of verbal abuse, had occurred. Meanwhile the Sino-Soviet split has served to accentuate centrifugal forces within the once monolithic Communist world, as various national governments have felt obliged to support one or the other giant protagonist. Chinese attempts, sometimes successful, to bar the Russians from conferences of Asian and African nations on the grounds that the Soviet Union is really a European state underscore a major difference which an international ideology does not seem to be able to bridge successfully. This is that the Russian people have most in common, both culturally and historically, with those of Europe and the United States, whereas the Chinese are more closely related to the other peoples of Asia.

THE NEW SEARCH FOR IDENTITY

Domestic developments in the United States. The breakdowns within the western and the Sino-Soviet alliances were accompanied, throughout the 1960's, by important internal developments in the three great powers—the United States, the U.S.S.R., and Communist China—which inevitably affected their capacities on the international scene.

The 1960's found the United States involved in massive efforts to accord equal status, treatment, and opportunities to all its citizens. Since the 1954 decision of the Supreme Court calling for desegregation of public schools, the nation had sought to make the Constitution's provisions real and substantial for every American. Integration in schools and public facilities and equal voting rights for black Americans, who comprise one tenth of the nation's population, have been the dramatic objectives of the overall civil rights issue. By the middle of the decade those rights had been largely enacted into law, mainly because of pressures brought to bear by the civil rights movement, which in the fifties and early sixties was characterized by nonviolence. From 1965 to 1968, however, the nation was rocked by violence in the ghetto slums of cities as far apart as Los Angeles, New York, Detroit, and Washington. It had become apparent that the legal extension of guaranteed civil rights to the black population was not a sufficient answer to the social and racial problems of the nation.

The urban violence that characterized the middle of the decade was closely linked to the problem of continuing pockets of poverty in the world's wealthiest nation. The problem involves not only the black and the white sharecroppers of Alabama and Georgia and the Spanish Americans of the Southwest but the tenement dwellers of Harlem and Chicago; not only the unemployed of Appalachia but the school dropouts in Detroit who, as unskilled members of the labor force, are inevitably "the last hired, the

first fired." By the mid-1960's many observers felt that too little was being done too
late to help the cities solve their social and
economic problems. Congress was slow in
providing the massive funds required to
improve the living conditions of the ghetto
dwellers. One of the reasons was budgetary:
the rapidly escalating costs of the Vietnam
War made Congress reluctant to vote funds
for internal development if that meant an
an increase in taxes.

Consequently, the internal struggle for
economic rights, which had largely supplanted the struggle for civil rights, became
more and more linked with the war in Vietnam, or, more precisely, the civil rights
movement increasingly joined with the antiwar movement. Thus Dr. Martin Luther
King, Jr., the Nobel laureate who had led
the nonviolent civil rights movement, became a leader in the movement against the
Vietnam War as well—until he fell victim
to an assassin's bullet in 1968. Frustration
with the slow pace of reform resulted in a
more radical civil rights movement, and
many younger Negro spokesmen began to
demand political action and influence under
the banner "Black Power." The more militant leaders, who also opposed the Vietnam War, emphasized that they were prepared, as they put it, to meet violence with
violence in the attainment of their objectives
of equal social, educational, and economic
status for black Americans throughout the
country.

The antiwar movement itself increased in
importance as the war escalated. Beginning
in the early 1960's with only a handful of
urban and university intellectuals, by 1967
it included many of the most influential
members of both houses of Congress from
both political parties. On the nation's campuses and elsewhere, dissatisfaction with
the draft laws and frustration at the slow
progress being made in such fields as poverty legislation led to increasing disaffection
with the government. In March 1968 President Johnson announced that he would not
seek reelection but would spend the remainder of his term seeking to end, or at
least shorten, the conflict.

The presidential election of 1968 was
waged over a number of strongly felt
issues: the continuing war in Vietnam;
urban decay; racial inequalities in housing,
health, and job opportunities; an increasing
breakdown of law and order (especially in
the big cities); and the dangerously mounting pollution of the natural environment.
The election results disclosed that none of
the three presidential candidates had won a
majority of the votes, but the Republican,
Richard M. Nixon (1913-   ), amassed
more votes than either of his opponents
and also a majority of the electoral votes.
Following an inaugural address that called
for a calming of the national temper and a
lowering of contentious voices, President
Nixon employed his first eighteen months
in office to develop new priorities and
policies.

In foreign affairs he sought to improve
understanding between the United States
and its western allies (notably with President Pompidou's France) and to emphasize
that relations with the Soviet Union and
other Communist countries should move
from "confrontation" to a more businesslike and flexible policy of mutual understanding. At the same time, he called for
the development of a new Anti-Ballistic
Missile system (ABM). Despite strong opposition from congressional critics who
feared both its costs and the dangers of
further escalating the arms race, Nixon
maintained that it· was essential to the
country's defenses against Soviet military
threats in the 1970's and possible Chinese
threats as well.

Domestically the new administration
slowed the pace set by preceding administrations in the fields of civil rights and
educational integration, while new appointments to the Supreme Court and other key
offices showed a distinct shift toward a
more conservative political philosophy.
Economically, the country found itself in
an unusual situation. The gross national
product continued to rise—and could well
reach a trillion dollars by 1971—and it
was possible that the average American
family's annual income would rise to
$25,000 by the end of the century. Yet
this economic growth had been accompanied

With the escalation of the Vietnam War, massive anti-war demonstrations were staged throughout the United States, climaxed in November 1969 by the Moratorium Day protest in Washington D.C.

in the late 1960's by an overheating of the economy, resulting in inflationary pressures which threatened to get out of hand. To remedy matters, the administration introduced restrictive fiscal and monetary measures. As of May 1970, however, the economy was experiencing a recession, marked by a fall in stock market values and rising unemployment rates.

Two major concerns of the American people as they entered the 1970's were the war in Vietnam (see p. 787) and the deterioration of the natural environment at home. Enmeshed in Southeast Asia in what had become probably the most unpopular war in American history, the Nixon administration sought to find an acceptable and viable solution. Troop withdrawals from Southeast Asia were begun as part of a new policy of "Vietnamization"—that is, of transferring the prosecution of the war progressively to the South Vietnam government. Public opinion polls showed that this new policy

had the overwhelming endorsement of a war-weary electorate, but it represented an obvious calculated risk. Its success depended on certain variables: the ability of the South Vietnamese army to prevent a Communist take-over in the field once American fighting forces had been withdrawn; and the ability of the South Vietnamese government to function on the civilian front once the American presence—and money—had been drastically reduced. Moreover, March 1970 saw the fighting spread to Laos, while on April 30 President Nixon ordered American troops into Cambodia in an effort to destroy "sanctuaries" from which the enemy had been attacking South Vietnam.

Meanwhile millions of Americans became familiar with the significance of the word *ecology* and its implications for their environment. Pollution had been going on for decades, but now a critical point had been reached, not only in the smog covering every major city in North America but in the recuperative powers of the physical environment itself to regain its former balance, upon which all life on this planet depends. The ecologists were joined by increasing numbers of university students who began to demonstrate to draw attention to the urgency of taking drastic remedial steps.

The Soviet Union. On November 7, 1967, the Soviet Union celebrated the fiftieth anniversary of the Bolshevik Revolution. The half-century mark had been reached as the U.S.S.R. showed signs of political and social maturation and change. Symbolic of the maturity that the regime had achieved was the manner in which the leadership was changed in October 1964, when Nikita Khrushchev was ousted from power and replaced by a duumvirate composed of Aleksei Kosygin as premier and Leonid Brezhnev as chief of the Communist party.

Three factors in particular were striking about the new regime. First, it did not engage in a violent and widespread purge of its opponents or members of the old regime. The change of power was carried out by a vote in the Central Committee of the Communist party; while it had many of the earmarks of a coup, Khrushchev was permitted to retire quietly and was occasionally seen in public in the following years. Second, the regime approached the Soviet people carefully. Khrushchev's ouster had been a shock to Communist parties in eastern Europe and the West. But the caution with which the new leaders changed top governmental personnel and developed new policy mo es indicated that they sought the support of public opinion rather than its repression through terror. Finally, the new leadership consisted of men who were accomplished bureaucratic politicians and technocrats. For instance, many Khrushchev appointees were supplanted through the merging of party control organizations in the industrial and agricultural sectors throughout the Soviet Union.

The 1960's witnessed the rise of new spokesmen in Soviet economic planning who were interested in the use of the profit motive and material incentives to increase consumer production. While the Twenty-Third Congress of the Communist party of the Soviet Union, which met in 1966, retained centralized planning as the keystone of the country's socialist system, it also introduced more liberal regulations based on the principles of a free market. A price system reflecting supply and demand as well as distribution and production costs was widely considered. By the end of 1966 some four hundred economic enterprises were operating under the new system.

Socially the Soviet government was disturbed by a persistent problem of "hooliganism," or crime. Under Khrushchev's regime a system of "people's militia" patrols deputized citizens to deal with petty crimes, but it had next to no effect. Under the new regime a Ministry of Public Order was created in 1966 for the same purpose. No adequate explanation for the rise of "hooliganism" has emerged, but it is possibly one outlet for Russian youth who find traditional Marxist dogma irksome and progressively irrelevant in their changing outlook.

The 1960's also witnessed growing pressure for the liberalization of intellectual life and greater freedom of artistic expression and experimentation. While some progress was made, it was far from steady, and the strong voices of the young poets like Yevgeny Yevtushenko, or again of novelists who revealed inhuman conditions in Soviet labor camps, were all too often drowned out by official censure at the trials of writers who had made the mistake of criticizing the regime too openly or of publishing in the West. Evidence for any controlled liberalization in the intellectual realm to match that in the economic sphere was tenuous. The anniversary year of 1967 saw the escape to the West of Stalin's daughter, a development that created propaganda difficulties for the Kremlin and was followed in 1968 by a spate of new trials of writers and intellectuals.

Developments in Communist Europe. The restiveness of Russian youth is directed against artificial restraints imposed by their own government; the restiveness, and occasional violent flare-ups, of their counterparts in eastern Europe is directed against the control and subordination of their national societies by alien, Soviet power in both the military and the bureaucratic sectors. Several factors appear responsible for the contemporary ferment in eastern Europe. One is the resurgence of nationalist feelings among peoples possessing long and proud societies. Another is recognition of the fact that since successful revolution against a neighboring superpower equipped with the most advanced military technology is seemingly impossible, changes in the theory and practice of government imposed by that neighbor should be attempted by evolutionary, peaceful means. Hence the growing insistence among the Communist satellites that the Kremlin accept the theory of many paths to socialism. As we have seen, Tito's Yugoslavia was the first to employ and successfully apply this theory, so that his "deviation" served as the initial augury of polycentrism.

The emancipation of east European ruling elites from direct Moscow control has been attempted in several countries with varying degrees of success. In Poland, for example, the intellectuals and students have recognized that since theirs is a relatively small country within the Soviet sphere of influence, they must resign themselves to continued Communist government. At the same time, they have sought to reconcile this ideology with Polish interests, which include development of greater trade and cultural contacts with the West. In attempting to walk a razor's edge to satisfy both national aspirations and Soviet demands, Gomulka has permitted abstract art, miniskirts, and rock and roll, while suppressing revisionist comment of his regime. Following the brutal suppression of the Hungarian uprising in the 1950's, the Kremlin permitted the leader of their choice, Janos Kadar, to soften the more repressive aspects of control which led to the revolt.

In the 1960's Czechoslovakia provided the most dramatic example of the search of east Europeans to find a new, appropriate identity of their own by eroding the constraints of Russian-imposed Communist ideology and behavior. During the previous decade, while discontent in neighboring countries had risen to the boiling point, as in East Germany, Poland, and Hungary, the Czechs had remained relatively passive towards their own Communist regime. But the forces of dissension were in the ascendancy, due to economic stagnation which antagonized the trade union membership, to a failure to initiate educational reforms which alienated the students, to the denial of civil liberties which frustrated the intellectuals, and to an inefficient bureaucratic regime which caused the more progressive Communist politicians to work for reforms within the existing system.

At last, reformist political forces, led by Alexander Dubcek, acquired power and instituted programs aimed at liberalizing and revitalizing the economic sector for the benefit of the consumer and labor force; at restoring freedom of the press and encouraging greater intellectual and commercial contacts with Czechoslovakia's western neighbors; and at correcting Communist party errors of policy and behavior alike. Unhappily, this dramatic move to realize a

When Soviet troops invaded Czechoslovakia on August 20, 1968, students erected barricades around the Prague radio building so that for as long as possible the station could broadcast to the world what was happening to the country.

new vision of democratic socialism was aborted on August 20, 1968, when Soviet tanks and armed forces invaded the country and completely suppressed the national movement. Following this intervention, the Kremlin leaders began systematically to force the Czech Communist reformers to abrogate their programs and finally ousted Dubcek and his associates from all decision-making offices.

As of 1970 the forces of reaction had apparently triumphed in Czechoslovakia. Yet despite this setback, it is doubtful whether Moscow can continue to suppress pressures in eastern Europe demanding liberalization of existing dogmas and governmental behavior. The search for a viable, and acceptable, ideology goes on. The leader of Rumania, Nicolae Ceausescu, for example, insists on his country's sovereignty and freedom to develop an independent foreign policy that includes improving relations with the United States and other western nations, as well as with Moscow's most dangerous Communist competitor, China. Similarly, the Rumanian government is in turn experimenting with more liberal economic and social policies at home. In the eyes of some foreign observers, these activities risk a repetition of the same armed intervention of which the Kremlin had been guilty in August 1968; but others point out that this crude maneuver lost the Soviet Union so much credibility both abroad and among its own intellectuals that the Kremlin could not afford to repeat it. In short, in the Communist world as elsewhere, the appearance of the 1970's was witnessing continued polycentrism accompanied by the search for identity.

Communist China. While the Soviet Union took fitful but evident steps in the direction of liberalization, Communist China rushed headlong into social and political radicalization. By the end of the 1950's it was evident that the solidarity which had characterized Chinese Communist leadership since the Long March in the mid-1930's was beginning to fracture. In the aftermath of the failure of the Great Leap Forward it became apparent that there were at least two groups divided

over policy: the "liberals," who wanted to proceed slowly and carefully with economic development and social change, and the "radicals," who evidently were impatient to effect a drastic restructuring of Chinese society. It is probable that Mao Tse-tung was the leader of the radicals.

By the middle of the 1960's a perplexed world could perceive the development of a gigantic ideological and political conflict inside China. Mao Tse-tung and his supporters had organized a movement known as the "Red Guards," composed chiefly of bands of high school and college age youths whose primary responsibility was to attack the radicals' liberal opponents, to whip up ideological fervor, and to enforce a strict radical orthodoxy on the entire population. Temporarily placing political purification higher on the Chinese priority list than economic development, the Red Guards were, at first, permitted to interfere with production processes. Vast rallies and demonstrations were held in Peking; the Red Guards set out on cross-country marches in emulation of the Long March; the entire educational system from top to bottom was closed down for a year to permit the ideological correction of texts and teachers; and those considered the carriers of outmoded ways of life and thought were often physically attacked in their homes and on the streets.

Known as the "Great Proletarian Cultural Revolution," this radicalization movement was based ideologically on what came to be known as the "thought of Mao Tse-tung," conveniently summarized in "the little red book" entitled *Quotations from Chairman Mao Tse-tung.* This collection of excerpts from Mao's writings became the catechism of the Maoist movement, and memorization and repetition of quotations in speech and song were intended as an educational device to instill in everyone the essentials of Mao's thought. The study of Mao's thought was claimed to have efficacious results in all fields of human endeavor, from agricultural and industrial production to medicine and interpersonal relations.

Among the important issues the Cultural Revolution was meant to resolve was the question of "Red or expert?"; whether, in other words, basic technical and economic decisions should be made at all levels by the party, because of its adherence to the "general line" of Maoist thinking, or by technical personnel, thoroughly educated in their specialties but not always or necessarily ideologically pure. In other words, should politics or rational economic development occupy the prime position in the process of constructing a new China?

The Cultural Revolution appeared to be a device for deciding the issue on the basis of the doctrine that politics is always primary. Maoism considered the human element and "revolutionary correctness" more important than professional or technical training; dependence on the latter was considered "bourgeois thinking" and was the prime target of the Red Guards and their Cultural Revolution. As such, the Cultural Revolution must be seen as more than a power struggle between two factions within the Communist party. On another level, it was nothing less than an attempt to reorganize the pattern of thought of an entire nation, a gigantic campaign to remake the Chinese in the image of the "new socialist man." In contrast to traditional Marxists, who believed that a new, unalienated socialist man would emerge from the structures of socialist society, the Maoists apparently believed that a socialist society could only be built by the new socialist man.

The total purpose of the Cultural Revolution—the welding of a common mind in a new society—was summarized in the last quotation in the "little red book":

In order to have a real grasp of Marxism, one must learn it not only from books, but mainly through class struggle, through practical work and close contact with the masses of workers and peasants. When in addition to reading some Marxist books our intellectuals have gained some understanding through close contact with the masses of workers and peasants and through their own practical work, we will all be speaking the same language, not only the common language of patriotism and the common language of the socialist system, but probably even the common language of the communist world outlook. If that happens, all of us will certainly work much better.

Workers on a Chinese state farm read from a collection of Chairman Mao's ideological writings, one of many attempts to redirect the nation's pattern of thought.

Without our passing judgment on the aims and methods of the Cultural Revolution, future historians will doubtless view it as one of the most ambitious and remarkable social and psychological experiments in history.

By 1967 the Red Guards themselves had to be brought under control by their creators. In addition, opposition to the Red Guards appeared in many areas of China and segments of society, and open conflicts occurred in many cities and provinces between the Red Guards and army detachments. Nevertheless, unrestrained western predictions of civil war and a return to warlordism appeared to be the product more of wishful thinking than of reasoned analysis.

Despite the intense radicalization of its internal politics, in foreign affairs China continued the essentially conservative policy it had followed since the end of the Korean War. Verbally bellicose, it exercised a self-restraint appropriate to the realities of international power, although numerous situations and incidents, such as the Vietnam War and American flights over Chinese territory, might have served as occasions for foreign adventures. In 1962, it is true, China came into direct armed conflict with India. China's primary aim in the Sino-Indian conflict, in addition to securing the frontiers of its Tibetan territory, was probably to demonstrate its strength in contrast to India's. Until 1962 India had been held up by the West as an alternative model of Asian development, as against China's stringently regimented Communist system. China's advance into territory claimed by India was a strictly controlled affair, and having achieved its objectives, Peking withdrew its forces. Although undoubtedly tempted to enter actively the neighboring Vietnam situation, China gave Hanoi and the Viet Cong verbal rather than military aid, and its contributions of military matériel and economic support appear to have been less than the Soviet Union's. Nevertheless, the Vietnam War remained, throughout the 1960's, the primary issue in Chinese foreign policy, as it was in the foreign policies of the Soviet Union and the United States as well.

To American and Soviet decision-makers alike, the problem of assessing Chinese foreign policy and behavior in the 1970's had to be given major priority, since Peking would probably soon possess an intercontinental capability of delivering its thermonuclear weapons. As noted previously, Mao's Cultural Revolution has sought to create a new society and to uproot those traditional forces standing in the way. On the other hand, as in all other human societies, the old and the new, the continuous and the discontinuous, coexist as constant factors of change.

A prominent American Sinologist, John K. Fairbank, has drawn attention to three major traditions that have attended the creation and retention of the Chinese order.

One is the strategic primacy of Inner Asia, a sparsely populated arc running from Tibet and Sinkiang around to Mongolia and Manchuria. Traditional Chinese foreign policy has always sought to control Inner Asia outright; conversely, when non-Chinese regimes control segments of this arc, foreign policy is consciously concerned with restoring the traditional land frontier. This explains the planting of Chinese farming colonies in Sinkiang and Tibet, and Peking's current concern over disputed areas with the Soviet Union and Outer Mongolia.

A second major tradition has been China's disesteem of sea power; true, in the early decades of the fifteenth century, its warships sailed as far as Aden and the coast of Africa, but subsequently the country remained self-sufficient and land-based. In this century Peking's reported submarine fleet would appear to be a defensive force at most. The third tradition is the doctrine of cultural superiority—a posture difficult to sustain in times of military weakness. "The tradition of Chinese superiority has now been hyperactivated, both by a new consciousness of the past century's humiliations and by the peptic euphoria of revolutionary leadership. It will confront us for a long time to come."[7]

On the basis of these traditions, Fairbank concludes that continued Chinese concern with Inner Asia is much more likely than possible expansion into Southeast Asia. "History suggests that China has her own continental realm, a big one; that Chinese power is still inveterately land-based and bureaucratic, not maritime and commercial; and that we are likely to see emerging from China roughly the amount of expansion that we provoke."[8]

Three views of man. The great ideological divisions that characterized civilization after World War I not only survived World War II but have become more profound with the passing decades. As a result, today's citizen is assailed by grave doubts that go far deeper than the problem of choice among alternative policies to resolve specific political, social, or economic issues. The very nature of man and the structure of society are being called into question.

In the West, where philosophical liberalism has provided the basis for some of man's greatest achievements, the individual personality remains central to man's self-image. Each person is unique, and society should be structured to permit and encourage the individual to develop his personality to the fullest. Liberalism recognizes that society itself places limitations on individualism, that man can be truly free only in a society in which all men recognize and accept the limitations of law. Chaos is antithetical to the freedom that is necessary for individual growth and development. Man, the liberal holds, is capable of "making himself" and of fashioning his environment for the greatest good of the greatest number.

The liberal image of man is rejected, however, by the two other contending schools of ideology, the Soviet and the Chinese. Man, according to the Soviet Marxists, is the product of his material environment and of his relationship to "the means of production"—that is, to the social and economic relationships characteristic of his society. An individual is not the unique personality understood by the liberals but rather a member of a class, and it is his class status that determines his consciousness and his view of the world. Unlike the liberal, who believes that men should voluntarily join together to solve their problems, the Soviet Marxist sees men pitted against each other in an inevitable to-the-death struggle between social classes, a struggle which history dictates will be won by the "proletariat," the working class. To change man, society must be changed, and the most "enlightened" among men, those who are members of the Communist party, will lead mankind in the class struggle and the process of social change that will end in the emergence of the "new" man.

The Chinese Communists, though deriving a great deal of inspiration from the Soviet Marxists, offer a third view of man. According to them, man makes the world in which he lives: the world is essentially the product of man's consciousness. Therefore, the world can be changed, and man's new consciousness must be forged in the revolutionary struggle. Less materialistic than the Soviets, and laying greater emphasis on the necessity for change within each individual, the Chinese believe that man changes only within the collective community. At the same time, the Chinese are less deterministic and thus paradoxically less optimistic about man than either the liberals or the Soviet Marxists. They lay greater emphasis on struggle as an inherent part of man's nature.

The degree to which these ideologies have crossed the boundaries of political conflict becomes more and more apparent. In the United States the "hippies" believe in a society based on "love," and it is not an accident that one of their heroes, the Cuban revolutionary Ernesto "Che" Guevera, believed that "the true revolutionary is guided by a great feeling of love." In eastern Europe, and even in the Soviet Union itself, western liberal concepts of freedom and the unique worth of the individual personality are fundamental elements in the growing protest against totalitarianism.

SUMMARY

Tremendous seismic changes took place following World War II. In little more than a decade after 1945, Great Britain was forced to relinquish its big-power role, while the United States and the Soviet Union, each the chief exponent of rival ideologies, emerged as superpowers. Empires disappeared from the map, freeing hundreds of millions from colonial tutelage. For its part, Nationalist China was superseded by the world's most populous Communist regime, except for an ineffectual remnant stranded on Formosa.

Such transformations took place in the midst of a bipolar confrontation of rival power blocs led by the superpowers. Each of these strongly coordinated alliance systems possessed a distinctive value system whose interests it sought to protect and whose influence it endeavored to expand. This rivalry was summed up in the term cold war, which dominated international affairs for at least fifteen years following World War II.

The 1960's, however, saw some of the hitherto unquestioned assumptions of the postwar world called into question. Bipolarity gave way to polycentrism as new relationships among nations developed—with former allies often becoming less friendly, and former foes more so. Concomitantly, the value systems traditionally underpinning western liberalism and Marxist socialism alike came to be severely challenged by domestic critics, especially among the younger generation. Technology had been a source of historical optimism for both the Communist and capitalistic nations. The superpowers derived their status from their advanced technological and economic levels, and each tried to build power blocs and rebuild mankind in its particular image by exporting technology in the form of military equipment and the means for economic development. But in the 1960's, it became progressively apparent that technological and economic development did not necessarily resolve basic human problems such as alien-

ation and conflict that derived from racial, social, and cultural diversity. Soviet and east European Communist publications had to pay more attention to the problem of alienation, which Marx had thought would be solved by communism. Racial fears played motivating roles in the Sino-Soviet conflict as they did in the Sino-American tensions. In the United States, despite its possessing the world's highest living standards and most advanced technology, racial violence increased and poverty persisted among significant portions of the population.

The Sino-American, Sino-Soviet, Arab-Israeli, and Vietnam conflicts suggest that there is no one "reason" or "rationality" or "logic" that is characteristic of all enlightened men. Rather, there are many kinds of logic, many different definitions of rationality, and perhaps even different "scientific methods." There are often men of good will on both sides of many conflicts, but they oppose each other passionately, bitterly, and even with force of arms.

SUGGESTIONS FOR READING

J. Lukacs, **A New History of the Cold War,*** Anchor; D. Rees, **The Age of Containment,*** St. Martin's; N. Graebner, **Cold War Diplomacy,*** Anvil. Broad treatments of postwar international tensions. Appraisals of the United Nations are found in N. Padelford and L. Goodrich, eds., **United Nations in the Balance,*** Praeger; A. Boyd, **United Nations: Piety, Myth and Truth,*** Penguin; and H. G. Nicholas, **The United Nations as a Political Institution,*** Galaxy.

Dean Acheson, **Present at the Creation,** Norton, 1969; H. Cleveland, **The Obligations of Power,** Harper & Row, 1966; D. Brandon, **American Foreign Policy: Beyond Utopianism and Realism,*** Appleton. Analyses of U.S. foreign policy.

The resurgence of western Europe is dealt with in M. Salvadori, **NATO: A Twentieth-Century Community of Nations,*** Anvil; J. Freymond, **Western Europe Since the War,** Praeger, 1964; and W. Feld, **The European Common Market and the World,*** Prentice-Hall. For specific countries see F. Boyd **British Politics in Transition, 1945–1963,*** Praeger; R. C. Macridis, ed., **De Gaulle: Implacable Ally,*** Harper & Row; A. Grosser, **The Federal Republic of Germany,*** Praeger; and N. Kogan, **A Political History of Postwar Italy,*** Praeger. For Latin America see A. P. Whitaker and D. C. Jordan, **Nationalism in Contemporary Latin America,** Free Press, 1966; K. H. Silvert, **The Conflict Society,*** Harper & Row; and D. B. Jackson, **Castro: The Kremlin and Communism in Latin America,*** Johns Hopkins. H. Feis, **Contest Over Japan,*** Norton, examines the situation resulting from Japan's defeat and occupation, while D. and E. T. Riesman, **Conversations in Japan,** Basic Books, 1967, analyzes contemporary Japanese society.

I. Deutscher, **The Unfinished Revolution,** Oxford, 1967. An assessment of the first fifty years of Soviet history. For postwar developments see E. Crankshaw, **Khrushchev's Russia,*** Penguin; A. Dallin and T. B. Larson, **Soviet Politics Since Khrushchev,*** Spectrum; and H. Schwartz, **The Soviet Economy Since Stalin,*** Lippincott. The fragmentation of the Communist world is discussed in A. Dallin, ed., **Diversity in International Communism, A Documentary Record, 1961–1963,*** Columbia; A. Gyorgy, ed., **Issues of World Communism,*** Van Nostrand; and E. Crankshaw, **New Cold War: Moscow versus Peking,*** Penguin. On the Communist bloc in eastern Europe see Z. Brzezinski, **The Soviet Bloc: Unity and Conflict,** rev. ed., Harvard, 1967; and G. H. Skilling, **Communism, National and International,*** Oxford.

A. D. Barnett, **Communist China, The Early Years, 1949–1955.*** Praeger; J. Ch'en, **Mao and the Chinese Revolution,*** Galaxy; Claude A. Buss, **People's Republic of China,*** Van Nostrand. Examinations of the rise of Mao's regime. **The Great Cultural Revolution in China,** Tuttle, 1968, is a compilation of reference materials assembled by the Asia Research Center of Hong Kong.

On the prospects for improved relations between the western and Communist worlds see K. E. Boulding, **Conflict and Defense,*** Harper & Row; T. C. Schelling, **Arms and Influence,*** Yale; L. Bloomfield, ed., **Outer Space: Prospects for Man and Society,*** Praeger; and A. M. Taylor et al., **Peacekeeping: International Challenge and Canadian Response,*** Canadian Institute of International Affairs.

*Indicates an inexpensive paperbound edition.

Chapter 32

Nation-Building in the Third World

Africa, Asia, and the Middle East Since 1945

INTRODUCTION. One of the basic characteristics of the twentieth century has been its capacity for cosmic change involving all aspects of man's life. It has witnessed two vast world wars, the decline and fall of great monarchies, such as the Ottoman, the Hohenzollern, and the Romanov, the emergence of giant antidemocratic totalitarian systems, and amazing scientific and technological progress. Another basic transformation has been the eclipse of colonial systems. Imperial rule, at its height in Africa and Asia following World War I, molded and governed the lives of millions of subjects. This global grid of control gave a certain static stability in large areas of the world; but it could not continue. It had, by the 1940's, outlived its dynamism and usefulness. Stability imposed by alien rule, despite some positive consequences, was an inadequate substitute for self-rule and with it the opportunity for people to try to solve their own problems.

World War II had a shattering effect upon colonialism. Such imperial powers as Britain and France no longer had the strength, nor indeed the moral will, to hold down their colonial wards. Equally important, the conflict generated and spread the ideology of self-determination and nationalism. These aspirations could not be denied. Within a period of two decades some five dozen African and Asian colonial areas became independent. Constituting what is usually referred to as the Third World—in contrast to the western and Communist worlds—its members are newly independent, generally economically underdeveloped, and diplomatically nonaligned; and they have sedulously sought to avoid entanglements in big-power rivalry.

This tripartite distinction is not completely clear-cut, however. There are marginal states, such as Afghanistan, Thailand, Iran, and Ethiopia, which are underdeveloped but not newly independent, and which have never been under colonial control—except for a very brief period in two instances. Latin America is usually included as part of the western world. Although most of its nations have been independent for much more than a century and have at least the forms of democracy if not the reality, they can be classified as underdeveloped.

Undoubtedly the problems facing the nations of the Third World on the morrow of their independence were minimized. It is unnecessary, however, to ask whether the new nations would exchange their current condition, with all its problems, for their former colonial subjugation. A feeling of pride, of national manliness, suffuses the leaders of the Third World and grows among its peoples. Colonialism was essentially a dead-end street. Independence, on the other hand, with its freedom of choice, gives people the opportunity to make their own destiny rather than having it imposed upon them.

This chapter outlines the untenable position of colonialism following World War II, describes the rapid process of decolonization, and discusses the basic problems of nation-making following independence. Attention is then given to the impact of the new Africa upon the United States. Finally, in the international arena, the role and activities of Third World states in the United Nations and the problem of big-power intrusion into vacuum areas, notably in Vietnam and the Middle East, are described.

THE ECLIPSE OF EMPIRE

War's impact on imperialism. In 1945, European colonies, controlling more than one billion people, dotted the globe. Within the colonial powers there was a grudging realization that the days of Kipling and the domination by white men in Africa and Asia were drawing to a close. It was believed, however, that this liquidation would be a slow process. Actually it took just about two decades.

The war accelerated forces already in existence; in competition with these influences, imperialism could not endure. In areas once remote and untouched by modern change, westernized elites grew rapidly. The process of urbanization created professional and merchant classes imbued with western political ideology. The presence of European troops had a disturbing effect. It sometimes exposed the vices of the white man, and not infrequently some anticolonial European liberals made secret contact with native leaders. Allied propaganda, with its emphasis upon a better postwar world and the crusade for democracy, tended to encourage Afro-Asian peoples to expect a "new deal" following the war.

One of the most important anticolonial forces emanated from the United States. Various private organizations published programs for the postwar period, most of them calling for some reform or even abolition of the colonial system. Journals, such as *Life* and *Time*, continually attacked the idea of empire in the modern world. Influential figures in American life added their support to anticolonialism. Wendell Wilkie, the Republican candidate for president in 1940, declared:

I found the dread of imperialism everywhere. . . . In Africa, in the Middle East, as well as in China and the whole Far East, freedom means the orderly but scheduled abolition of the colonial system.[1]

Even more forthright were the words of Sumner Welles, American Undersecretary of State:

Our victory must bring in its train the liberation of all peoples. The age of imperialism is ended. The right of a people to their freedom must be recognized. The principles of the Atlantic Charter must be guaranteed to the world as a whole—in all oceans and in all continents.[2]

In the colonies the claim of European invincibility had been swept away by the shattering victories of Japanese arms at Pearl Harbor, Hong Kong, Singapore, and in Burma. These conquests led to the startling growth of nationalist movements in Asia—especially in Indonesia, French Indochina, Malaya, and Burma. Japanese occupation authorities carefully nourished anti-European sentiment. In India the western thrust of Japanese armies toward Bengal had caused the British government to make substantial concessions to Indian nationalist leaders. In 1942 the famous Cripps' Mission offered India independence within or without the British Commonwealth following the war.

During World War II Africa remained generally tranquil. But the lessons of Allied defeats and echoes of anti-imperialism reached educated African circles. In 1942 an African students' organization in London presented the government with a memorandum asking for "Internal Self-Government Now, with a definite guarantee of complete self-government within five years after the war."[3]

New colonial policies. The various colonial powers were sensitive both to the demands of nationalism in the colonies and to the censure of world opinion against imperialism. In England, especially, a tired and perhaps more realistic younger generation no longer had any heart for empire. In fact,

the British Labour party, which came into power in 1945, had always been anti-imperialistic. Toward the end of the war, however, the Labour party, supported by strong public opinion, realized the problems that would inevitably emerge with colonial independence and shifted its ground somewhat. It announced a policy of gradual advances toward self-government in many of the colonies, notably those in Africa, in the form of a partnership with Britain, which would provide substantial financial and technical aid. A Labour member in the House of Commons declared:

Britain today is in the colonies and she cannot withdraw; nor do I think it desirable that she should. We are pledged, in these colonial territories, to the pursuit of a policy of constructive trusteeship, a policy which is to lead, we hope, to partnership inside the British Commonwealth. . . . It would be undesirable, I think, that we should give up the job of developing these underdeveloped areas, not merely on grounds of humanism, but also on grounds of enlightened self-interest.[4]

For a decade following World War II Britain sought to pursue this policy of enlightened colonial partnership in its dependencies mainly in Africa and the West Indies. Its objectives were subsidized economic development, long-needed social reforms in education and health, and experience in self-government. The ultimate political aim was independence within a cooperative Commonwealth. Large sums, totaling $360 million by the end of 1956, were immediately granted for colonial development.

During the war France also formulated a new program for its colonies. In 1944 a significant conference held in French Equatorial Africa stated:

The chief aim of the colonial policy of the new France will be to ensure the material and moral development of the natives . . . while respecting their culture and civilization and having them participate, within the framework of a French Federation, in the evolution of Metropolitan France.[5]

After 1945 large sums were earmarked for colonial development. In sub-Saharan Africa,

As the colonial structure crumbled, the newly independent nations faced the future with buoyant optimism and pride. The Federation of Malaysia celebrated its independence on September 1, 1957, with a military parade in the capital city of Kuala Lumpur.

for example, $700 million had been granted by 1955, plus large loans on very generous terms. France envisaged eventual self-government for its colonies but, unlike the British idea of Commonwealth, within a political structure dominated by Paris.

Belgium badly underestimated the drive of nationalism in its huge African colony. Self-government in the Congo was ruled out as chimerical within the foreseeable future. What mattered was its economic development and the paternal treatment of Belgium's colonial wards. Portugal, on the other hand, had neither the resources nor the will to initiate a forward colonial policy. It denied that Angola and Mozambique were colonies, maintaining, as it still does, that they were integral units of the homeland and that all civilized Africans were therefore entitled to the same rights as citizens of Portugal. (Very few, however, had the opportunity to become educated and "civilized.") During the war the government of the Netherlands, an exile regime in England, issued statements indicating that following the reestablishment of peace, its empire would form a commonwealth, each part—especially the East Indies—having "complete self-reliance and freedom of conduct."

The chronicle of decolonization. These new colonial policies, based generally on programs of partnership between the imperial powers and their colonies, came too late. Nationalism would not be denied. Too much had happened during the war to undermine the traditional relationship of imperial overlordship and colonial subordination. The rapidity with which empires disappeared constitutes one of the great historic happenings of modern times. Their passing ended some four hundred years of what might be called the European phase of world history.

For a decade after 1945 it seemed possible that the new colonial policies might succeed, that independence might be gradually achieved. One of the first indications that the whole edifice of imperialism would quickly collapse came in the late 1940's when Indonesian nationalists demanded a complete break with the Netherlands. An ugly war ensued, and finally, in 1949, through UN mediation, the Dutch East Indies became Indonesia—a new nation. Largely with the help of the same international body, Libya, a former Italian colony, was tendered its freedom in 1951. Meanwhile, keeping its prewar promises, the United States had granted the Philippines independence in 1946. In the same part of the world France became embroiled in a tragically costly war while trying to restore some semblance of its authority in Indochina (see p. 787).

While not renouncing its program of enlightened guidance for the colonies, Britain realized that an exception would have to be made in the case of India which, during the war, had been given an unequivocal pledge of independence after the conflict. In 1947 this huge dependency gained its complete freedom as two nations: India and Pakistan. The following year the same status was granted to Burma and Ceylon. In the Middle East, Britain recognized the independence of Jordan in 1946 and two years later terminated its mandate of Palestine, an action that led to the creation of the state of Israel and a bitter war between this new nation and the Arab world.

Notwithstanding these cracks in the colonial structure, the new colonial programs appeared relatively successful, particularly in Africa. Appearances were deceptive, however, and mounting unrest in the West African colony of the Gold Coast forced Britain to give this colony independence as Ghana in 1957. In this same year Malaya became a sovereign state as Malaysia. Singapore, Malaya's major city and almost entirely Chinese in population, eventually broke away from the federation to become an independent member of the Commonwealth. It was now evident that nothing short of complete sovereignty could satisfy colonial nationalists. While on a tour of British Africa, Prime Minister Harold Macmillan acknowledged this fact when he declared:

The wind of change is blowing through this continent, and whether we like it or not this growth of national consciousness is a political fact, and our national policies must take account of it.[6]

Africans rightly think of 1960 as their year. Eighteen new nations emerged, the most important being Nigeria and the Congo. France had enacted various reforms seeking to keep its African territories as autonomous republics under the jurisdiction of the French-directed Community. (Guinea, however, had elected to become completely independent in 1958.) This ingenious compromise, however, could not satisfy African aspirations. In 1960, therefore, all thirteen African republics within the French Community proclaimed their independence. While the old assimilationist dream of a great French imperial structure had ended, France did retain a unique status in its former colonies. Its culture persists in what can be called French-speaking Africa; and the new republics rely upon France for financial and technical aid.

During the decade after 1960 further additions were made to the roster of new African nations, for example, Lesotho, Gambia, Algeria, and Zambia. By 1970 forty-three sovereign states could be identified, whereas in 1945 there had been only four. And in other parts of the world, colonies had practically disappeared from the map, with the exception of a few small oddments such as Gibralter, Hong Kong, and various French islands in the South Pacific.

While not so spectacular as the triumphs of freedom in Africa or in South Asia, independence was achieved by various islands in the British West Indies, notably Jamaica, Trinidad and Tobago, and Barbados. The South American mainland colony of British Guiana also gained the same status as Guyana.

In retrospect, the eclipse of empires was an amazingly peaceful phenomenon. The British left India with warm words from Prime Minister Nehru: "It is rare in history that such a parting takes place not only peacefully but also with goodwill."[7] There had been bloodshed in the Dutch East Indies, postindependence riots between Hindus and Muslims in India and Pakistan, a tribal uprising of the Mau Mau in Kenya, and tragic hostilities in the Congo. But considering the many territories and the millions of people involved, the transition from colonialism to statehood had been remarkably tranquil.

THE POLITICS OF INDEPENDENCE

In search of national unity. Many colonial peoples believed that the attainment of independence would usher in a golden age characterized by economic plenty, smooth-functioning governments, and proud national unity and purpose. There was euphoric optimism about what the future was to be following the exit of alien imperialists. Unfortunately, these hopes proved to be illusory. Nearly all the new nations were confronted by serious problems, some challenging their very existence.

At the outset the new nations were confronted with the heavy costs of creating a diplomatic service as well as a military establishment. Economic and social development were urgently needed. In addition, there existed a psychological drive for national prestige symbols, leading, in some instances, to showy nonproductive facilities such as uneconomic air lines and costly government buildings and hotels. The initial imperative task was how to build and maintain national unity, how to weld disparate and sometimes antagonistic religious, cultural, and ethnic groups into one.

In many instances the new political entities in Africa and Asia are not the end result of a long historical process such as took place in medieval Europe, when small feudal principalities were hammered into homogeneous nation-states. Numerous Third World states never existed in their present dimensions and boundaries until they were created by the action of the imperial power that ruled them until independence. Nigeria, for example, encompassing so many diverse and often hostile ethnic and tribal segments, was created by the force of British arms. It has been pointed out that the notoriously polyglot Hapsburg empire was more homogeneous than the present Congo—formerly administered by Belgium—or the Sudan.

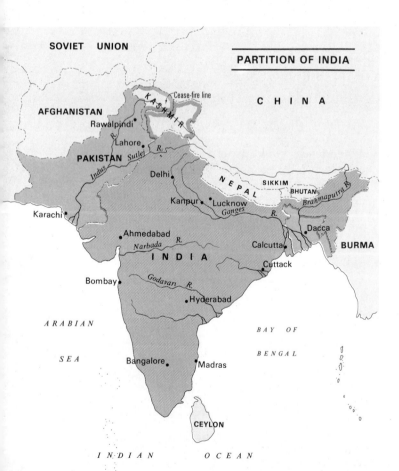

Regional tensions in India and Pakistan. During the heyday of western imperialism the largest mass of colonial people ruled by a single government was India. During its long history this subcontinent had only been partially united by the Mauryan emperor Ashoka and by the Mughul emperors. During the nineteenth century, however, its many linguistic and racial groups had been brought under a single British administration. Following World War II Britain stood ready to grant independence to India in accord with promises made during the conflict. Unfortunately, the chasm of suspicion between Hindus and Muslims had now widened to a menacing degree. Muhammad Ali Jinnah, leader of the Muslim League, demanded that India be partitioned, that Muslims not be included in an independent India dominated by its Hindu majority. Jinnah's position was clearly defined when he stated:

How can you even dream of Hindu-Moslem unity? Everything pulls us apart: we have no intermarriages. We have not the same calendar. The Moslems believe in a single God, and the Hindus are idolatrous. Like the Christians, the Moslems believe in an equalitarian society, whereas the Hindus maintain the iniquitous system of castes and leave heartlessly fifty million Untouchables to their tragic fate, at the bottom of the social ladder. Now again, the Hindus worship animals. They consider cows sacred. . . . We want to eat them. Another thing: no Hindu will take food from a Moslem. No orthodox Hindu will even touch food if the shadow of a Moslem or the shadow of a Hindu of a lower caste has polluted the bowl.[8]

Confronted by the intransigence of the Muslim League and Gandhi's and Nehru's predominantly Hindu National Congress, Britain, fearful of civil war, persuaded both parties that partition was inevitable. Thus in 1947 the economic and geographical unity of the subcontinent was sundered. Pakistan, especially, was an artificial creation, consisting of two provinces separated by some one thousand miles of intervening Indian territory.

The immediate aftermath of partition was a rash of bloody riots between Hindus and Muslims that resulted in the murder of thousands. One of the victims was Mahatma

Gandhi, who, because of his tolerance toward Muslims, was assassinated by a Hindu in 1948. Another tragic sequel was the quarrel over the status of Kashmir. Predominantly Muslim in population, much of this territory came under the control of India, and a full-scale war with Pakistan was narrowly averted by the intervention of the United Nations in 1948. An uneasy truce and a cease-fire line were arranged, but in 1965 a short but inconclusive war broke out over the disputed territory. Tension over Kashmir still continues to poison Indo-Pakistan relations.

Partition has not guaranteed the unity of these two nations. India is not a single nation but consists of numerous different racial, linguistic, and cultural groups. "Nowhere do so many linguistically differentiated peoples, all of them so self-aware, all numbered in millions and tens of millions, confront each other within a single national body politic."[9] Without the binding force of British alien rule, ancient cultural and regional loyalties have emerged to challenge national unity. The Dravidian-speaking south is vehemently opposed to the expansion of northern Hindi as the official language, labeling it as Hindi imperialism. This southern nationalism has gone so far as to speak of the creation of a separate Dravidian state. Meanwhile, riots between the Muslim minority and the Hindu majority occur from time to time in various parts of India. It is understandable that one scholar has referred to the Indian republic as possessing a "facade of union, perilously uncemented."

Pakistan, too, is threatened by this problem of regionalism. While its population is predominantly Muslim, its two main territorial segments, or provinces, differ widely in race, economic interests, and language. The Urdu-speaking western Pakistanis are better educated, have a higher standard of living, and are the dominant element in the civil service and the armed forces. Their fellow countrymen in eastern Pakistan speak Bengali, are generally backward economically and educationally, and complain of being exploited. On several occasions they have expressed their discontent in riots and threats of secession.

Racial problems in Malaysia. Other parts of former colonial Asia lack the national unity that is made possible only by a pervading sentiment of common patriotism. The Federation of Malaysia, for example, created in 1957, consisted of the Malay peninsula, Singapore, and various small states on the island of Borneo. Its population was very heterogeneous, consisting of 41 percent Malays, 30 percent Chinese, with the remainder being East Indians and aboriginal tribes. In this mixed society the Chinese, originally immigrants, came to exercise a virtual monopoly of economic wealth and power. The Malays, mainly farmers, were easygoing and resented the better educated and aggressive Chinese. This rivalry led to the dramatic secession from the Federation of Singapore, with its one and three-quarter million people, mainly Chinese. The island became a minuscule republic. Tension, however, still continued in Malaysia, and in 1969 serious riots exploded between Malays and Chinese in the capital city of Kuala Lumpur. Order was restored only after serious loss of life and property. The very future of Malaysia hinges on the restoration of multiracial harmony and leadership by moderates of both races.

Restless Indonesia. The huge archipelago of Indonesia, consisting of 3000 islands with a population of 110 million, has enjoyed little tranquillity since 1949, the year of its independence (see p. 766). A multi-ethnic state, it consists of a melange of many cultures, ranging from stone age to urban businessmen and sophisticated intellectuals. While some three hundred distinct ethnic groups have been identified, a major basic division exists between the Javanese and the non-Javanese in the Outer Islands. The two differ widely in economic interests, ways of life, and political outlook. Complicating the plural aspects of Indonesian society is the existence of a Chinese minority of some three million. Nearly all retail trading and moneylending is in its hands. As in Malaya, the native population resents this situation. There have been anti-Chinese outbursts and governmental attempts to restrict Chinese commercial activity.

The geographic and racial diversity of Indonesia would seem to call for a generous degree of decentralization in government and local autonomy. The central government at Jakarta, however, has been bureaucratic and highly centralized. The Outer Islands have opposed this Java centralism, demanding fewer Javenese officials, a larger share of revenues, and more regional self-government within the framework of the republic. From 1953 to 1958 there was a series of coups and revolts against central authority. The demand for a lessening of controls by Jakarta has been partially met, but suspicion and resentment still remain in the Outer Islands.

POLITICAL DIVISIVENESS IN AFRICA

Tribalism and national unity. While the plural society (see p. 691) is found in various new nations of the Third World, it is almost universal in sub-Saharan Africa in the form of hundreds of tribes. The term *tribe* has been used extensively in the past but without precise definition. It can refer to a group of a few hundred people or one numbering several million. This term came into current use in the nineteenth century and generally referred to non-Europeans who were thought of as inferior and primitive, especially in their material and technological culture. In recent times anthropologists and especially African intellectuals have criticized the use of the term as unnecessarily degrading and disparaging. Until a more widely acceptable term is introduced, however, *tribe*, rather than multi-ethnic societies, would seem to describe best the prevailing sociopolitical unit in Africa.

Tribalism is one of Africa's paramount problems. It originated in the partition of this continent in the 1880's and after, when numerous tribes were placed in colonies willy-nilly, surrounded by com-pletely artificial boundaries which had never existed before. On occasion tribes were arbitrarily divided, with one portion placed in one colony and the remainder in another. Such was the case of the Bakongo people who were located in the former Belgian Congo and in two neighboring colonies. The Somali were divided between Ethiopia, Kenya, and Somalia; and the famous lion-hunting Masai of East Africa found themselves in both former Tanganyika (now Tanzania) and Kenya.

African nationalists often deplore such tribal fragmentation. In general, however, the European-made colonies were larger and more economically viable than the hundreds of African tribal units they superseded. While there may ultimately be some rectification of these tribal separations, the urgent need in Africa is for the various tribes *within* the new nations to sublimate their traditional loyalties into a wider national allegiance. European colonialism has been referred to as "the glue that stuck these human [tribal] units together into a shape recognizable on an atlas and under a name like the Belgian Congo, Nigeria, Tanganyika, and so on."[10] Now that this foreign cohesive cement has gone, old tribal loyalties and rivalries are emerging to weaken national unity. The new elites and leaders think of themselves as Kenyans, Congolese, Ugandans, and Sierra Leonians, but the mass of people still continue to describe themselves as Kikuyu, Ibos, Hausa, or Masai. In too many instances African political parties base themselves on a tribe. This is an inducement to tribal rivalry and even civil war.

The reconciliation of tribal loyalties within the broader context of a national consciousness is a basic challenge in contemporary Africa. In the fairly stable and prosperous new nation of Zambia, its progressive president Kenneth Kaunda, commenting on a national election in 1967, declared:

We have canvassed so strongly and indeed viciously, along tribal, racial, and provincial lines, that one wonders whether we really have national or tribal and provincial leadership. I must admit publicly that I have never experienced, in the life of this young nation, such a spate of hate, based entirely on tribe, province, race, color and religion, which is the negation of all we stand for in this party and government.[11]

Tribal tensions in Kenya. The newly independent nation of Kenya has been torn by multitribal tensions. Its freedom had to be delayed because of tribal rivalries—especially between its two main tribes, the Kikuyu and Luo—and their jockeying for power. Following independence, however, a single political party supported by both of these tribes became dominant and controlled the government. One of the members of its cabinet, Tom Mboya from the Luo tribe, became known internationally as a brilliant and promising statesman. It was thought he might ultimately assume the leadership upon the retirement of the venerable president Jomo Kenyatta. In 1969 this possibility was removed by the tragic assassination of Mboya by a disgruntled Kikuyu. The motive for this act was unclear, but it exacerbated tribal tensions. Luos suspected Kikuyu ambitions of dominating the country; and at the funeral rites for Mboya disturbances broke out against the Kikuyu president, Kenyatta, and some Luo tribesmen threatened "to sharpen their spears."

West African tribalism. Other instances of tribal rivalries can be referred to in Ghana and Sierra Leone. In the first state, the martial and aristocratic Ashanti in the north, traditionally hostile to the more sophisticated people along the coast, are restless. Similarly, in Sierra Leone there is rivalry between the tribal and backward peoples of the north and the more westernized descendants of liberated slaves who think of themselves as superior to their neighbors in the interior.

Tribalism versus Congolese nationhood. Much world-wide publicity was given to the chaotic events following Belgium's grant of independence to the Congo in 1960 and the subsequent intervention of the United Nations. Possessing no ethnic or economic unity, this huge dependency, as large as western Europe, was carved out by the Belgian imperialist King Leopold I. Composed of some seventy major ethnic groups and divided into hundreds of tribes, the Congolese had been given practically no training in the art of self-government.

In 1959, however, confronted by general unrest and serious rioting, the Belgians precipitously promised independence. Meanwhile, the Congolese formed political parties that were primarily tribal associations. As the date for independence approached in 1960, tribal war broke out, accompanied by looting and massacres. Following independence in the summer of 1960, workers' strikes, the mutiny of the native army, and attacks on Europeans brought virtual anarchy to the Congo. The crisis was intensified by the secession of the rich mining province of Katanga. Its leader, Moise Tshombe, apparently had no intention of providing revenues to support the rest of the Congo, now wracked by violence. This action was also supported by foreign mining interests which controlled the Katanga mines. At the request of the central government, United Nations forces intervened to restore order and ultimately to end the Katanga secession. Following severe fighting this objective was achieved, and the UN forces were withdrawn during the summer of 1964. Peace and stability did not follow, however. Terrorism and rebellion again broke out in various parts of the Congo. The central government at Leopoldville (now renamed Kinshasa) was unable to restore order. During the emergency a rescue mission was organized to evacuate European hostages— but not before eighty of the prisoners had been massacred by the rebels. During 1965 a semblance of order was gained as the army took control of the civilian government in the person of its commander, Joseph Mobutu. Tribalism, regional revolts, and inexperience in self-government continued to harass the country; and as one authority observed, "It will be a miracle if the Congo at long last finds the stability it sorely needs."[12]

Arab versus African in the Sudan. Any discussion of the problem of national unity in sub-Saharan Africa must describe the postindependence situation in the Sudan. This huge area of 967,000 square miles is the largest in Africa. Ethnically and culturally it consists of two distinctive regions: the North populated mainly by Muslim Arabs and the South inhabited by pagan and Christian Africans. The latter, with memories of slave raids from the North, regard the Arabs as their traditional enemy. During British rule of the Sudan, the South was kept isolated from Arab penetration, and English was maintained as the lingua franca.

When the Sudan gained independence in 1956, no provision was made for the South's separation or its regional autonomy. Revolts against control by the government in Khartoum followed. In this so-called "Unknown War" perhaps half a million were killed, with some 200,000 refugees fleeing to nearby countries. The central government's small, well-equipped army gained control of much of the country, especially the main roads and towns. The southern armed forces were mainly guerrillas who attacked government convoys and ambushed its forces. During 1969 it appeared that while Khartoum had made no substantial concessions to the South, the central government still faced intermittent guerrilla outbreaks. Undoubtedly the forced union of the major regions of the Sudan had its supporters, but there would seem to be much credence to the view that "Putting them together into one state was less justified than would be to make one state of Germany and Poland."[13]

Nigeria at war with itself. Nigeria has been called Africa's giant, its most populous country with some 57 million people. Nigeria's progress toward modernization has been rapid since World War II. Endowed with a variety of important natural resources, especially oil, it promised to be one of Africa's richest nations. When Nigeria became independent in 1960, it had several thousand well-trained civil servants, more than five hundred doctors, an equal number of lawyers, and a substantial body of engineers and other professional men. And, unlike the Belgian Congo, it had some forty years of training in self-government. Its constitution was the end result of a decade of constitutional experiment and continuous discussions with British officials.

Nigeria, however, is similar to the Congo in its ethnic and tribal complexity. It has more than two hundred tribes and a dozen important languages. The three most important groups are the Yoruba, the Ibo, and the Hausa, each concentrated in one region. Living in western Nigeria, the Yoruba are a prosperous, sophisticated, urban people. One of their cities, Ibadan, has a population of more than a half a million. The eastern region is the home of the Ibo. Crowded on poor soil, they have taken eagerly to western education, migrating in large numbers to other parts of the country to seek their fortune. These two groups, totaling at least sixteen million, are large enough to be called nations rather than tribes. The northern part of Nigeria is populated by the Hausa, a proud people numbering twenty million, who are Muslim in religion and way of life. Under British protection the four dozen Hausa rulers, the emirs, lived in palaces and followed the feudal traditions of their forefathers. Western education was disdained, and Arabic rather than English was taught in the schools.

While some tension and rivalry existed between the Ibo and the Yoruba, the main antipathy was between them and the northern Hausa. The latter were contemptuous of these non-Muslims, mainly Christian or pagan, who were aggressive in business and assertive in politics. Especially irritating to the Hausa were the more than one million Ibo in their midst. Outside their cities were the Strangers Settlements, inhabited by non-Muslim southerners, who filled such skilled positions as telegraph clerks, mechanics, station masters, and office employees. This situation led to ill-feeling, and in 1953 there were severe riots between the migrant community and the Hausa in one of the emirates.

Notwithstanding regional tensions and those stemming from the rivalry between progressive and traditional forces, Nigeria gained its independence in 1960 as a single national entity. This accomplishment was regarded as a model experiment in national integration. With its representative institutions based on British models, Nigeria was held up as democracy's best hope in Africa.

Military coups and civil war in Nigeria. This hope for Nigeria was shown to be tragically unrealistic. Danger signals began to flash only two years after independence. Each of the three main regions had its own political party, and none had a broad national base of support. Electioneering, therefore, took on the form of intense rivalry between the three regional peoples: the Hausa, Yoruba, and Ibo. The north, because of its population majority, enjoyed a dominant position in the central federal government. Between 1962 and 1965 a series of crises—disputed elections, quarrels over census figures, rampant corruption, and lawlessness—threatened to tear the new nation apart. In 1966 a group of young army officers, all Ibo, seized control of the federal government and in the process murdered prominent leaders, especially in the north. Apparently the coup had mixed motives, such as ending corruption and pushing modernization; but it also had implications of Ibo nationalism.

Power was given to an Ibo officer, General Ironsi, who at the outset had a good chance to reconcile factions and clean up the government. Unfortunately his regime completely alienated the Muslim north. It did nothing to punish the perpetrators of the coup; it proceeded to strip the emirs in the north of their traditional functions; and, most important, it abolished the federation in favor of a unitary government in which the well-educated and enterprising Ibo might become dominant. The northerners now became fearful of the rising influence of the southerners.

In the spring and fall of 1966 rampaging mobs in the north, joined by soldiers, fell upon the hapless Ibos. Thousands were massacred and more than a million fled to their homeland in the eastern region. Meanwhile, a second coup had taken place; control over the central government was turned over to General Gowan and Ironsi was murdered.

The war for Biafran independence. After witnessing these events, the leader of the Ibos, Colonel Ojukwu in May 1967

Weary Biafran soldiers rest between battles during the recent Biafran war. Although the war ended in January 1970 when the Ibos surrendered their arms and their plans to secede, Nigeria still faces the problem of reconciling tribal loyalties within a wider sense of national unity.

proclaimed the secession of the Ibo from the federation as the state of Biafra. Hostilities between Biafra and the central government at Lagos began in July 1967. Outmanned and outgunned, the Ibo were encircled and driven into an area little more than sixty by forty miles by the summer of 1968. The conflict became a deadly siege in which six million civilians faced the prospect of starvation. Several thousand died daily, mainly young children. Public opinion in much of the world was shocked by the sufferings of Biafrans. Mercy flights carrying food to the starving Ibos were organized under great difficulty. By 1969, notwithstanding desperate resistance, the Biafran cause appeared hopeless. In January 1970 the secessionists laid down their arms, and thirty months of bitter fighting came to an end.

The political prospect in Nigeria, however, is not encouraging. National unity—except in the legal sense—has not been achieved. Numerous questions remain to be answered: can reconciliation of the Ibos be achieved with adequate guarantees for their safety, can the old tribal rivalries be assuaged, and what is to be the role of the military in the future? Nigeria is a crucial test case for national unity in Africa. If it disintegrates, other plural states may follow its example. "The Nigerian conflict may prove in retrospect, like the American Civil War, to have been a bitter prelude to a new national vision: but the obstacles to the realization of such a vision are formidable."[14]

Tribalism in retrospect. It can be seen that tribalism, conflicting regional cultures and loyalties, is a serious impediment to national unity in Africa. There is the rivalry between one tribe and another, as in the case of the Luo and Kikuyu in Kenya, and the conflict between progressive, modernist groups who seek to create a single national unity and traditional, aristocratic elements, as in the case of the Congo. In Nigeria the Ibos aroused the resentment of the traditional and less westernized northern population. This tribal rivalry, largely fed by economic competition, led to tragic civil war. A special variety of tribalism has also led to civil war in the Sudan, where African tribes have opposed domination by the ethnically and culturally different Arab ruling class.

Perspective on African nation-making. It is difficult to assess the prospects of nation-building in the Third World; too little time has elapsed to provide the necessary perspective. In attempting a balanced evaluation, one should keep in mind that numerous long-established western nations still have to contend with their "tribal tensions." One only has to refer to the smoldering antipathy between the Ulster Catholics and Protestants in northern Ireland which verged on civil war in 1969, the rancor between French and English Canadians in Quebec, and the rivalry in Belgium between the French-speaking Walloons and the Flemings speaking Dutch dialects. While the United States has been traditionally proud of its "melting pot," the plural basis of its society has been painfully manifest in recent demands of its Afro-American and Spanish-American (Chicano) subcultures.

THE SEARCH FOR NEW POLITICAL FORMS

Requisites for western democracy. The colonial peoples' drive for freedom following World War II generally included democratic and equalitarian ideals. Educated to admire western liberal thought, their leaders felt they could make a stronger case for independence if this goal were based on imitation of the democratic philosophy of the colonial powers. Both the national leaders and the western imperial powers thought that, following the attainment of independence, most of the new states would enjoy the blessings of stable government, procured by efficient executives, responsible legislatures, free elections, and incorruptible courts—all in the western classical manner. It was not understood that successful democracies are not created full grown but develop, in some instances over hundreds of years.

It is generally conceded that for reasonable success democracy requires a high degree of the following requisites: (1) a literate electorate, (2) a high standard of living, (3) a substantial middle class, (4) a reasonable degree of social mobility, and (5) traditions of tolerance by which the majority in power will respect the rights of the minority. In general, only a few of the new nations possessed some of these requirements, none had all of them, and some were lacking in virtually all five criteria.

Repudiation of western models. Practically all the new nations began with parliamentary governments patterned after western models. But these soon gave way to military dictators or authoritarian one-party systems. In one year, 1958, generals took over in six countries: Iraq, Lebanon, the Sudan, Pakistan, Burma, and Thailand; Indonesia retained only the remnants of parliamentary government, while Egypt and Syria were already under authoritarian rule.

Within the first several years of Africa's experience with independence, twenty-seven states experienced forceful takeovers; and in four months in 1967 there were four military coups. Witnessing these events, an Africanist observed:

Coups, counter-coups, plots and conspiracies, assassination attempts, communal violence, and even armed rebellions now seem almost commonplace in Africa; in fact, the march of recent events on the continent has raised serious doubts about the viability of many of the new African states.[15]

Following most of these changes, the outward forms of parliamentary government have often been retained, but these have only camouflaged centralized control. In most of the new states, a charismatic leader—a magnetic, forceful personality with mass appeal and support—has become the head of the state, either as a dictator or as the representative and voice of the dominant, and usually unopposed, political party. Thus Gamal Abdel Nasser came to dominate affairs in Egypt, Julius Nyerere in Tanzania, Kwame Nkrumah in Ghana, Ayub Khan in Pakistan, Achmed Sukarno in Indonesia, and Sekou Toure in Guinea.

In essence these political transformations demonstrate that what was tried was a graft of alien forms of government upon people whose institutions, traditions, and present conditions were utterly different from those in the West. Indonesia, Ghana, and Pakistan are cases in point, while India is a notable exception.

Sukarno's Indonesia. The biggest and richest nation in Southeast Asia is Indonesia. Yet for fifteen years after independence it was to experience declining exports, inflation, and food shortages. Its population problem had grown more acute and its economy more stagnant. The main responsibility for this debacle was Indonesia's flamboyant president, Achmed Sukarno (1901-1970). Following ruinous economic policies, he contracted huge Russian loans for arms, fought a costly guerrilla campaign against Malaysia, confiscated foreign businesses, and lavished money on costly, showy enterprises. At the same time he gathered all power into his own hands. Sukarno's only solution for his country's ills was to keep the masses in a continuous

state of emotional nationalism. For a number of years he mesmerized huge audiences with a torrent of slogans. In 1965 a Communist plot to take over the country—partly made possible by his leftist policies—was unsuccessful, but thousands of Communist sympathizers were butchered. In 1967, appalled by the direction of national affairs, a military regime under General Suharto removed the discredited Sukarno and took command of the government. The new regime has set about diligently to undo Sukarno's blunders but has not promised an early return to parliamentary institutions.

Nkrumah's Ghana. Ghana was the first nation south of the Sahara to rise out of subservience to the white man in 1957. Khame Nkrumah, its first prime minister, was the idol of all African nationalists; and his newly freed nation was the symbol of liberalism and democracy in emergent Africa. But almost immediately Nkrumah began to muzzle the press and imprison the opposition. Quickly an outright dicta-

The cult of personality, an important factor in the rise of many Third World leaders, often proves an unstable basis for leadership. Suffering the fate of other charismatic leaders, Prime Minister Nkrumah of Ghana was ousted in 1966, his toppled statue reduced to a plaything for children.

tor developed in the classic mold. At the same time he embarked on ruinous economic policies, such as showy projects and a large military establishment. Evidently enjoying his power, Nkrumah was presented as the Great Redeemer and His Messianic Majesty by his controlled press. Ghana progressively slid downhill economically, saddled by a huge national debt and aided by much corruption on the part of Nkrumah's colleagues. In 1966 a group of army officers, embittered by Ghana's plight, seized control of the government. Anxious to speed economic recovery and to restore some semblance of political freedom, the army leaders permitted the return of parliamentary institutions in 1969. Ghana thus became the first African country to return to multi-party government after being a one-party state.

Oligarchic democracy in Pakistan. Pakistan, as already noted, was plagued by feuds between its eastern and western wings. At the same time, chronic corruption and the whole tenor of politics demonstrated the people's inability to operate parliamentary democracy. Shortly after independence the prime minister was assassinated; a number of short-lived governments followed, accompanied by intermittent rioting and states of emergency.

Finally, in 1958, General Ayub Khan seized power. At this time the country seemed to be falling apart. Parliament was dissolved, the constitution abrogated, the new regime moved against black marketers, and corrupt politicians were barred from political activity. General Ayub had nothing but contempt for the politicians who had manipulated the votes of the masses and brought the country to the edge of ruin.

In line with this view, Ayub introduced a new plan of government, called Basic Democracy, which has been referred to as "the most impressive political innovation in the new states of Asia."[16] In essence this scheme was designed to give the common man experience in self-government at the local level. In 1962 martial law was ended and a new constitution adopted in which the president, General Ayub, held the reins of government firmly in his hands. While the peasants were given limited political responsibilities, in general the voice of the urban middle class in government was closely limited.

For ten years Ayub's system of enlightened despotism gave Pakistanis reasonable stability and relief from irresponsible politicking. It also registered substantial economic progress. In 1966 the national income increased 30 percent. In 1965 Ayub's popularity and the success of his Basic Democracy program seemed assured when he scored a decisive victory in the presidential election. But from this high point the strength of his government rapidly declined. Multiple factors explain this trend. The impoverished and overcrowded eastern province became increasingly irked at its economic stagnation compared with a veritable boom in the west. Demands for eastern autonomy, accompanied by ominous demonstrations, rapidly increased. The middle class had also never taken kindly to their virtual exclusion from politics. The most significant criticism of Ayub was that he had permitted a system of privilege to develop. Corruption and concentration of wealth were widespread—and nowhere greater than in the president's own family.

Pent-up dissatisfaction burst during the closing weeks of 1968. In the early months of the following year the country was convulsed by riots with demands for Ayub's resignation. Faced by what appeared to be a national revolt, the president resigned his office in March, turning it over to the leader of the armed forces, who proclaimed martial law. The new regime, however, pledged a return to parliamentary government, with elections scheduled for the fall of 1970.

India: the exception. In the long list of newly independent states few have retained genuine, liberal regimes. The only outstanding success in working a western-oriented political system is found in India, which—with its electorate of well over two hundred million—has been called the world's largest democracy. Since independence its parliamentary government has functioned with relatively little friction or upheaval. Three factors have been responsible for this achievement: (1) the valuable training in self-government given by the British; (2) the unusual leadership provided by the country's first prime minister; and (3) the prestige enjoyed by India's Congress party, which had gathered all shades of opinion under its mantle in the campaign against British rule.

Following the death of Nehru in 1964, however, various factions, without the binding force of common antagonism against British imperialism, began to disagree over domestic and foreign issues. In addition, the divisive force of regional linguistic nationalism became disquieting. In 1969 a serious schism in Congress, still the ruling party, threatened to break the party asunder. Mrs. Indira Gandhi, the prime minister and a quasi-socialist, clashed violently with conservative old-guard members of Congress. Whether a new political alignment will develop from the debris of this party, should it disintegrate, whether its demise will be followed by a multiparty structure leading to unstable coalitions, constituted India's most crucial problem at the beginning of the 1970's.

Third World variants of western democracy. On the surface what has happened politically in the new nations might seem to add up to a discouraging record. But perhaps the process should be viewed rather as a search for a governmental system that is best designed to solve urgent problems—a system that is not merely derivative but is rooted in indigenous institutions, influenced somewhat by western ideas. During this experimental period many new nations have generally discarded what is regarded as too costly and time-consuming—the institutionalized western two-party system. Only a single political organization, therefore, exists to carry on an undivided attack on national problems. It is believed that basic decisions can be reached by consensus within the ruling party. While these new regimes present some authoritarian features, it is important to note that they generally make a significant commitment to the general ideology of democracy. Thus various leaders refer to their governments as Guided Democracy, Basic Democracy, or One-Party Democracy.

In Egypt, where Nasser claimed that his military rule was democratic, it has been argued that the key to his concept of democracy was not so much the element of choice between candidates in elections as it was popular satisfaction with the individuals running the government and mass participation in implementing its progress.

Sub-Saharan Africa is *par excellence* the area of the one-party state. A distinctive ideology has been developed to explain and defend what is still termed democracy. Protagonists of this point of view argue that democracy can exist without western parliamentary institutions, especially without an institutionalized opposition. They believe that the basic characteristic of democracy is *discussion* and that this quality operates in their one-party systems. The essence of democracy (if not its western forms) has always existed in tribal Africa, they contend. Within this indigenous unit, policy has traditionally been arrived at by full and continuous discussion until a consensus has been reached. All members of the tribe then accepted the agreement. This traditional practice, it is argued, has now been made part of the African one-party state, which rests upon the consent of the people and dispenses with an organized opposition.

One-party states in retrospect. What will be the likely course of politics in the new nations? It is evident that, in most instances, western political theory and governmental forms are alien to the basic traditions of these lands and are considered inappropriate to meet the urgent needs of socioeconomic development. The task of reconciling one-party systems with some elements of what might be thought of as "universal democracy" will be difficult. Some political scientists have suggested that these governments, while not western in form or function, should endeavor to provide a political climate "in which dissent and opposition are not only tolerated but are provided a legitimate functional role in the political process."[17] It is likely that politics in the Third World will continue to be experimental during the foreseeable future.

The economics of politics. Political stability and dynamism in the new nations is influenced by economic factors. It is impossible to separate economics from politics. Throughout the Third World there is a prevalent belief among the masses that their depressed economic condition can be improved. This "revolution of rising expectations" comes at a time when economic productivity is still insufficient to satisfy these aspirations. Mistakes and failures in economic development can lead to frustrations, unrest, and social conflict.

Two thirds of the world's population currently lives in areas classified as underdeveloped, producing only one sixth of the world's income. The table at right depicts the gravity of the problem. The figures show that more than 60 percent of all people in the world have an annual income of less than $250, in contrast to $1400 in the European Common Market countries and more than $3000 in the United States.

The economic backwardness of Third World countries stems from such factors as undue dependence upon a single export commodity; the dominance of a peasant subsistence agricultural economy which is often inefficient; and lack of capital to

Economic Status of the World's Peoples

Number in millions	Classification	Per capita annual income
990	very poor	Less than $100
1150	poor	$100 to 250
390	middle income	$250 to 750
800	high income	More than $750

Adapted from George D. Woods, "The Development Decade in the Balance," *Foreign Affairs,* Vol. 44, January 1966, p. 207.

provide funds for economic modernization and for educational facilities. Governmental revenues, especially in the African states, are often quite inadequate to provide for the needs of a modern nation. Miniscule Gambia, for example, has an annual budget of little more than $5 million.

Above all there is the appalling incubus of population pressure (see p. 822). Although India's national income increased 70 percent since 1950, two thirds of this growth was needed to take care of additional population, running more than one million annually. The eastern wing of Pakistan has a population of seventy-two million jammed into an area not much larger than Arkansas. This area now has twice the population density of Japan and Holland with nothing remotely approaching their economic productivity. Until very recently Africa was thought to be a continent with reasonably good economic prospects, largely because of the absence of population pressure. The latest demographic studies, however, are disturbing. While Africa overall has a low average density, there are numerous pockets, as in Kenya and Tanzania, where the population pressure is acute. A distinguished Africanist observes: "Thus the entire continent is now, or soon will be, experiencing a population explosion of major proportions."[18]

At the beginning of the 1970's the nations of the Third World presented a spotty economic picture. In Southeast Asia there have been substantial advances in Thailand, Singapore, Malaysia, and the Philippines, and Indonesia after incredibly inept leader-

As part of India's "Green Revolution," workers prepare a field for the planting of wheat and barley on an experimental farm near Delhi. The program, started in 1965 on a budget of $13 million, aims at stopping India's chronic food shortages by employing modern farming techniques.

ship under Sukarno, seemed to be turning the economic corner. India and Pakistan, long plagued by serious food shortages, were experiencing the "Green Revolution." This program, utilizing improved seeds, better chemical fertilizer, and improved irrigation, seemed to promise a breakthrough in food yields for these and other deficit countries. In Africa there was the possibility that rich mineral resources could make possible substantial development in Mauretania, Liberia, Algeria, the Congo, and Libya. Economic gains have also been notable in Kenya and the Ivory Coast. In the valley of the Nile living conditions worsen as population mounts, and Egypt's energies are concentrated upon the tasks of war rather than those of peace. Meanwhile nearby Middle Eastern countries dissipate their energies and resources upon the confrontation with Israel. This nation, however, politically stable and technologically efficient, seems to be able to afford both guns and butter.

It is difficult to assess the economic prospects of the new nations. Two elements are crucial: the maintenance of political stability with reasonable governmental efficiency and a reduction in population pressures. In this struggle for economic development foreign aid is a critical factor, and it has been substantial. In 1967 the underdeveloped nations received grants and loans totaling nearly $12 billion. Ideally this aid should be even more massive, but it can only be a palliative unless the two elements mentioned above are realized.

AMERICA
AND THE NEW AFRICA

American interest before World War II . During the nineteenth century American official interest in African affairs was minimal. The shaky independence of Liberia, which was founded in 1821 as a haven for freed slaves, was supported by the United States, but generally Washington assumed no additional political responsibilities. While the slave trade was outlawed in 1807, the African squadron of the American navy accomplished little in intercepting slave ships. The main responsibility was assumed by Britain's permanent naval patrol along the west coast of Africa. With the abolition of slavery in 1863 by President Lincoln, and the same prohibition in Brazil, Cuba, and Puerto Rico in the 1870's and 1880's, the slave trade to the Americas dwindled to extinction.

In the closing decades of the nineteenth century American interest in Africa quickened somewhat. The government participated in the Berlin Conference (1884) which laid down the general rules regulating the colonial partition of Africa. Increasing humanitarian and scientific interest in the "Dark Continent" was sparked in the 1870's by the *New York Tribune*'s commission of H. M. Stanley to find David Livingstone in equatorial Africa. After the 1870's American missionary activity increased considerably, and the brutal exploitation of African labor in the Congo led the American public and governmental officials to insist upon reform in the early 1900's. At the peace settlement in Paris ending World War I the United States became briefly involved in African affairs. Its representatives were instrumental in drafting provisions for the League of Nations mandate system which internationalized the administration of the conquered German colonies. In the late nineteenth and early twentieth century black Americans periodically expressed interest in Africa as a refuge for their disadvantaged race; one of the most notable was Marcus Garvey in the 1920's.

During the 1920's and 1930's, a high point in American isolationism, little thought was given to Africa. The State Department could deal only on an official level with the various European colonial powers. No direct contact was possible with the African people. American diplomatic representation in the area was not of a high order. "It is not too much of an exaggeration to say that in 1948 our few posts in Africa were still a dumping ground for senior Foreign Service Officers who weren't good enough for promotion before retirement."[19] While missionary endeavor was substantial in these interwar years, American economic interests, in comparison with those in other world areas, were relatively minor.

World War II and Africa. World War II centered attention on Africa's strategic importance when lines of communication in the Mediterranean became precarious. The sea route around the Cape became vital for the supply of Allied forces in North Africa and the Middle East, and air transport routes to Egypt and surrounding areas were developed from South America to the western bulge of Africa.

World War II also demonstrated the wealth of Africa's raw materials. Africa produced immense quantities of uranium, copper, diamonds, gold, and cobalt. From 1945 to 1959 its mineral production increased 300 percent, and the 1960's witnessed the development of enormous petroleum production in Libya and Algeria. The United States became increasingly concerned about the access to these raw materials and conscious of Africa's strategic importance. For at least a decade, however, during the hectic initial years of the East-West cold war, its chief preoccupation was with problems and crises in western Europe, the Middle East, and Asia.

The impact of African nationalism. These diplomatic concerns presented themselves at a time when nationalism was increasingly challenging colonial rule in Africa. Thus American policy-makers found themselves in a dilemma. In accordance with its traditional support of self-determination, the United States had subscribed to provisions in the United Nations Charter pledging ultimate freedom for all colonial people; but its strategy of containing communism regarded colonial rule—at least in the short run—as the best way to maintain stability in Africa. While the United States wanted a friendly Africa, at the same time it did not wish to offend the colonial powers, such as Britain and France, who were NATO allies. Moreover, the United States thought well of the new postwar colonial policies, especially of France and Britain, which sought time to build solid economic and political foundations for independence. Such considerations

led American policy to stress the dangers of premature independence. In the United Nations the United States abstained from voting on numerous resolutions, supported by Afro-Asian members, criticizing various facets of colonialism. Such lukewarm opposition to decolonization, together with hazy adherence to self-determination as an abstract and desirable principle, led many Afro-Asian leaders to consider the United States a supporter of colonialism.

The challenge of the new Africa. The posture of Africa began to change rapidly in the late 1950's as African countries began to achieve independence. By 1960, therefore, the United States, without embarrassing its allies, could take a less equivocal stance on African self-determination. Internal pressure by black Americans and liberals also demanded new diplomacy. A State Department official in 1960 could assert: " 'as to their readiness,' I believe history has shown that this is almost an academic question. Peoples tend to acquire independence, ready or not, according to a timetable of their own choosing."[20]

Following 1957 independence came with a rush to many African states. American relations were no longer with colonial powers but with African governments. With western control gone, the United States set about establishing new and independent avenues of communication. In 1958 a separate Bureau for African Affairs was created, staffed by some one hundred professional officers. Foreign service personnel in Africa increased rapidly. In 1958 the foreign service had 256 officers in West Germany; in all of Africa 248. By the early 1960's the latter figure was some 3000. There were also 1500 Peace Corps volunteers. With this expansion, the United States sought to implement its policy objectives in the new Africa. High on the list of priorities was technical and economic aid. In 1952 funds totaling $4 million were given; in 1962 the figure had increased to $233 million, not including large contributions to the Congo plus other developmental loans. By 1968 the total United States foreign assistance to Africa had reached $407 million.

United States race relations become international relations. Another objective of

American policy, to cultivate friendship and understanding with the African people, was seriously jeopardized by racial problems in the United States. Examples of racial discrimination, such as occurred at Little Rock and the University of Mississippi, were given wide publicity in the new African states. It is interesting that when the Russians sent Sputnik I aloft, they derisively included Little Rock on its daily itinerary. Particularly embarrassing to the American image in Africa was the occasional rebuffing of African diplomats at restaurants as they were driven from Washington to attend UN meetings in New York. There is no doubt that the federal government's mounting offensive against discrimination can be explained not only by a sincere concern for civil rights for all but also by the competition of the cold war. In its brief in the famous school desegregation case of 1954 the Justice Department explained that racial discrimination in the United States must be viewed in the context of the world struggle between freedom and Communist tyranny. Thus "By focussing world publicity on American racial difficulties, the rise of Africa and Asia stimulated federal intervention to help American negroes in their long fight against discrimination."[21]

Issues of human rights continue to involve the United States in Africa as well as at home. In the UN the United States has taken forthright positions opposing the white regime in Rhodesia, the policies of Portugal in Angola and Mozambique, and *apartheid* in the Republic of South Africa. Nevertheless, notwithstanding African and some American criticism, the United States opposes the use of force against such regimes, and American business interests continue to be active.

The successful drive for freedom in Africa also gave strong impetus to black Americans in their campaign for civil rights. They were no longer a small minority but part of a great movement for human dignity that was ending imperialism overseas and segregation in the United States. Before the 1950's many black Americans looked at Africa as a primitive land. The emergence of respected African statesmen and their nations in world affairs, however, did much to transform this attitude of indifference and rejection to one of pride in the African heritage. In the words of one Afro-American:

Africa provides me today with a proud identification with ancestors. It can cause you to swell with pride to see an African on the podium of the UN, Africans who have to be consulted in the decision-making process in the world. The kind of pride other peoples have had, of being recognized.[22]

American interest in Africa's future. In the 1960's there were some six hundred African-oriented private organizations and foundations in the United States, signifying the rapid growth of interest in Africa. The largest group of American civilians in Africa were missionary workers, numbering several thousand. Business operations, while still small compared with other areas in the world, were growing significantly. Various educational and philanthropic organizations were rendering important service in acquiring knowledge about and providing assistance to the new Africa. Among the very active institutions were the Foreign Policy Association, the African Studies Association, and the African American Institute. Since its establishment in 1951, the Ford Foundation has been outstanding in providing large sums for the training of Africanists, for development programs in the new states, and for aiding the establishment of Africa studies programs in the United States. Undoubtedly American interest in Africa will continue to increase. This continent, with both its promise and problems, is destined to play an important role in world affairs.

THE AFRO-ASIAN PRESENCE IN WORLD AFFAIRS

Into an uncertain world. As colonial empires disappeared, newly independent states entered the family of nations during one of the most unstable and troubled periods in world history. New nations such as Canada, Australia, and the United States had in their infancy been generally isolated from the tensions of big-power rivalry. The conclusion of global hostilities in 1945, however, brought neither peace nor actual war but almost continuous international crises as East and West probed and jockeyed for advantage in the so-called cold war.

Seeking to protect and insulate their newly found freedom, most of the new nations adopted a number of similar objectives. There was the universal desire to secure a voice in the councils of nations, especially the UN, and to receive recognition of their new sovereign status. Representatives of these new states were also extremely sensitive to slights and discriminations, particularly if they were based on color. In all the nations of the Third World living conditions are, as we have seen, unbelievably low. And while some, such as India, Nigeria, and Indonesia, are potentially great powers by reason of size and population, others are so diminutive and poor as to promise little hope for eventual economic viability. The Republic of the Maldive Islands (see Reference Map 11), for example, a member of the United Nations, has an area of 115 square miles and a population of only 100,000.

To support ambitious development projects, governments have sought loans and technical assistance from the great powers. While seeking such aid, the emerging nations have sought to avoid domination by the major industrialized nations. The economic needs of the Third World states, however, make them vulnerable to foreign influences and pressures. Africans and Asians are especially sensitive to the dangers of "neocolonialism" made possible, if not always actual, by the necessary importation of business managers and technicians, dependence upon imported military supplies, and reliance upon set patterns of trade and outside sources of investment. Such factors can relegate a new nation to the status of a "client state."

Closely tied in with fear of "neocolonialism" has been the determination of Third World nations to avoid any involvement in superpower rivalry. Their diplomatic policy of nonalignment or neutralism regarded the cold war as a tragic and frustrating facet of international affairs, obstructing the overriding task of consolidating fledgling regimes and their all-out attack on economic backwardness, poverty, and disease. Nonalignment holds that peaceful coexistence with all the great powers is both mandatory and possible.

Confronted with the same hopes and fears, the nations of the Third World have sought to cooperate with each other in various conferences and regional associations. The first such effort, the Asian Relations Conference, held in New Delhi in 1947, pledged support for all national movements against colonial rule and explored the basic problems of Asian peoples. Perhaps the most famous Third World conclave was the Afro-Asian conference at Bandung in 1955, attended by twenty-nine countries representing more than half the population of the world. As at New Delhi, anticolonialism, economic development, and cultural cooperation were the dominant topics. In the Middle East the new states established the Arab League in 1945, with a permanent secretariat in Cairo. While the League has pursued various objectives, its dominant posture has been its implacable opposition to the state of Israel. Africa has witnessed the establishment of various regional organizations, the most promising being the Organization of African Unity, created at Addis Ababa in 1963. Based on the full sovereignty of its members, it was in no sense a real African political union. The OAU was designed

to promote the unity and solidarity of the African states; to coordinate and intensify the cooperation and efforts to achieve a better life for the peoples of Africa; to defend their sovereignty; to eradicate all forms of colonialism in Africa; and to promote international cooperation. . . .

These attempts by Third World nations to achieve a semblance of solidarity have not fulfilled expectations. There has been little agreement on many important issues. The Arab League has been torn by dissension between socialist-republican regimes, such as Egypt, and traditionalist-monarchist states, such as Saudi Arabia. While the OAU has witnessed some gains in African cooperation, its members have seemed primarily interested in pursuing their own national interests rather than those of continental dimensions.

Little else could be expected. After several centuries of intense nationalism, western nations have recently been moving toward various forms of regional interdependence in common markets, joint defense efforts, and monetary funds. It is unrealistic to expect the Third World nations, in little more than two decades, to proceed from colonial dependence to effective forms of international cooperation without experiencing a substantial period of nationalism with its profound sense of identity and political independence.

Afro-Asians in the United Nations. The most spectacular impact of the new nations has been in the United Nations, where they have been instrumental in transforming its membership and to some extent its tone and purpose. Initially with a roster of 51 members, the General Assembly had increased to 126 by 1970. The dominance of western members has decreased to 40 percent of the membership, with Afro-Asian states holding the balance of power. In 1961 about half the issues raised in the Assembly dealt with Africa; seldom has a UN bloc seized the limelight so quickly.

The overriding Afro-Asian preoccupation in the United Nations has been with anticolonialism and racial discrimination. While representatives of the Third World disagree on various issues, opposition to colonialism is an ideology they can all passionately support. Their constant pressure against the colonial powers, increasingly a minority in the Assembly, accelerated the rapid liquidation of colonies. Representatives of the new nations have also been vociferous in urging nuclear disarmament and supporting technical and economic assistance for underdeveloped areas.

Unfinished business in Africa. Meanwhile, southern Africa remains a potentially explosive area. The Zambesi has been called the frontier between black and white Africa. To the north lie the newly independent African states, but to the south are European-dominated Rhodesia, and white-ruled South Africa. Bordering these states are the Portuguese territories of Angola and Mozambique.

South Africa is the most economically advanced country on the continent. Booming cities, such as Johannesburg, rapidly growing industries, rich mining enterprises—especially gold—make South Africa a modern state except in its race relations. Observers the world over have been aware of the mounting strains within this republic, where the European minority has denied basic political and economic rights to the African majority by means of *apartheid*, a drastic policy of segregation and racial

Representatives of the thirty-two member nations of the Organization of African Unity meet for a conference in Addis Ababa in 1968. The mural on the wall depicts the new leaders of the independent African nations.

Under the policy of *apartheid* in South Africa, there are no shades of gray. Racially mixed groups are not allowed in public, and Africans may not attend the movies, theater, or opera in a white district without a special permit. Even footbridges are not free from segregation.

discrimination. How long the white community could hold down the lid of this African boiler was problematical.

It was felt that a new approach should be tried. The South African government inaugurated a program of territorial segregation. Eight distinct and partially self-governing African states known as Bantustans were planned, each to be aided by substantial economic grants. The first to be established was the Transkei, with a Bantu population of 3.5 million. South Africa, however, still continued to depend upon a large African labor force domiciled and employed in European areas.

While revolt has been smoldering for several years in the Portuguese territories, the most acute situation has arisen in Rhodesia. In 1965 this British colony, controlled by a small white minority, declared its independence from Great Britain, which insisted that such action could not be countenanced without the prior grant of full political rights to the African majority. Despite a crippling trade embargo imposed by Britain and economic sanctions levied by the United Nations, Rhodesia refused to accept Britain's

conditions, labeled as NIBMAR (no independence before majority rule).

If the European regime is ended in Rhodesia, Portuguese holdings would then likely succumb to the same pressure. White South Africa believes it would then be the ultimate objective. Rhodesia is thus regarded as a kind of bastion against black nationalism, and South African troops have actively joined local forces in seek-and-destroy missions against the guerrillas. In the fall of 1968 the British and Rhodesian prime ministers held a conference seeking some compromise solution perhaps on a promise of "unimpeded progress toward majority rule." No settlement was reached, however, and in the spring of 1970 the final ties with Britain were severed when Rhodesia assumed the status of a republic.

While some form of agreement might reduce tensions and the possibility of serious escalation, southern Africa will remain a troubled area in the foreseeable future. The South African prime minister has declared that if ever the African states use violence against his country, "We will hit them so hard that they will never forget it."

Big-power intrusion in the Third World.
Internal conflicts, political instability, and
dependence on outside sources for economic
aid and military supplies invited major-
power influence, and even interference, in
the affairs of emerging nations. During his
first state visit to independent Africa, Chou
En-lai, premier of Communist China, announced that the "area was ripe for revolution." Several African states have complained
of Chinese support of plots to overthrow
their governments. In the Nigerian civil
war over the secession of Biafra, both Russia
and Britain supplied the central government
with arms, while France responded in kind
for Biafra. All three powers were interested
in strengthening their political and economic influence in Nigeria.

Big-power rivalry and intervention was
also illustrated in the Congo following its
independence from Belgium in 1960. The
immediate aftermath was widespread chaos.
This problem was referred to the United
Nations, mainly on the initiative of the
United States. The Soviet Union, however,
sought to act independently by trying to
circumvent the UN operation in the Congo.
In effect this effort constituted a major cold
war crisis. Supported by the great majority
of its members, however, the United Nations
successfully insulated the problem from big-
power intervention.

Major-power rivalries have also been a
factor in Indo-Pakistan relations. During
the 1950's the United States supplied massive arms aid to Pakistan as a counterpoise
to potential Russian expansion. Such aid
from any source was denounced and ob-
durately refused by India's prime minister,
Nehru, who supported the neutralist policy
of nonalignment. Following the Chinese invasion of north India in 1962, however,
Nehru's government eagerly accepted
American military aid. Simultaneously,
Russia, increasingly disenchanted and fearful of China's growing power and mounting
enmity, also sent arms to India. Nonalignment had obviously become bi-alignment.
This case study of major-power diplomacy in
the Third World became increasingly complex when Pakistan, miffed over American arms aid to India, modified its diplo-

matic posture of a strong partner of the West
and turned to Communist China as a new
friend and ally.

The Middle East: after a third round. During the mid-1960's world peace was ominously threatened by the Arab-Israeli conflict. In 1948 and again in 1956 Israel and
the Arab countries had gone to war over
their respective claims, including Israel's
right to survival and free access to the Suez
Canal. Continuous Arab terrorist attacks
along Israel's borders, Arab refusal to recognize the existence of the state of Israel,
and the refusal of both nations to provide
some meaningful solution to the problem of
Arab refugees from the wars of 1948 and 1956
were constant threats to the status quo.

Throughout late 1966 and the first half of
1967 tension, never really below the surface, began to rise rapidly. Finally, the
Arabs mobilized their troops, requested the
withdrawal of the United Nations peacekeeping forces, and blockaded the Gulf of
Aqaba. In this situation of rapidly increasing tension, war broke out on June 5. In
seventy-two hours Israeli aircraft and tanks,
with lightning speed, completely overwhelmed the combined Arab forces, and by
the time a cease-fire was accepted on
June 10, Israel occupied the entire Sinai
peninsula including the east bank of the
Suez Canal, the whole west bank of the Jordan River, Old Jerusalem, and border areas
inside Syria commanding tactically important heights. Nothing, however, had been
settled by the conflict. For the moment Israel felt secure, but the Arab states refused
to enter into any direct negotiations aimed
at removing the causes of hostility.

An uneasy peace. The superpowers have
been deeply involved in the course of events
in the Middle East. This area not only has
the world's largest reserves of oil but strategically is a land bridge connecting three
continents. Definitely pro-Arab, Russia
hopes to become the major influence in the
area, while United States policy is to prevent this domination. As the major sup-
plier of arms and technicians to the Arab
states, especially Egypt, Russia can pose as
their benefactor and in turn expect to be the
recipient of important favors. Heavily com-

Although Israel and the Arab nations have continued a running battle for the past twenty years, their uncompromising positions have not softened. Young Israeli men and women are subject to military training, and Arab guerrilla organizations train children for the ultimate effort to destroy Israel or at least compel it to give up all territory gained in the 1967 war.

mitted to the continued existence of Israel, the United States tried to discourage any substantial imbalance in the armed strength of Israel and its Arab neighbors, thus attempting to secure a stable Middle East in which all states could live in peace and not become the puppet of a single great power.

During the opening months of 1970 intermittent attacks by Arab guerrillas and regular army detachments across the Israeli border were countered by Israeli commando raids. Realizing the danger of Russo-American confrontation should a new round of war explode, Britain, France, the United States, and Russia carried on four-power talks to explore the possibilities of an overall settlement between the contending parties. The issues discussed related to the possibility of some retrocession of captured Arab territory, a solution of the long-festering Arab refugee problem, and the internationalization of Jerusalem. Above all,

the Jews insist upon the Arabs' unequivocal recognition of Israel as a sovereign state and its right to exist. While some hope of a settlement arose in the summer of 1970 when a cease-fire was accepted, the situation became charged with uncertainty a few months later with Israel's charge of cease-fire violations by Egypt and the sudden death of Nasser, the Arab leader.

While big-power rivalry has exacerbated the situation, any solution to the problem depends on the Arabs and Israelis. The former have been deeply aroused by what they consider another alien and imperialistic intrusion into their midst, and they are reluctant to allow the humiliation of three defeats to remain unassuaged. On the other hand, the Israelis, after centuries of mistreatment of Jews in various lands and the recent memory of Hitler's unspeakable savagery, are determined to protect Israel. As one observer sees this confrontation:

The essence of the tragedy is a struggle of right against right. Its catharsis is the cleansing pity of seeing how good men do evil despite themselves out of unavoidable circumstance and irresistible compulsion. When evil men do evil, their deeds belong to the realm of pathology. But when good men do evil, we confront the essence of human tragedy.[23]

WAR IN VIETNAM

The First Indochinese War. Following the end of hostilities in Indochina after World War II and the ejection of the Japanese forces, France sought to restore a semblance of its colonial authority. In 1946, however, it was forced to grant a measure of autonomy to Cambodia and Laos. The crucial problem remained—the status of Vietnam. In Hanoi, in 1945, a nationalist and pro-Communist movement sparked by Ho Chi Minh had established the independent Republic of Vietnam, usually referred to as the Vietminh regime. The French countered with the vague offer of "self-government within the French Union." Following inconclusive negotiations, the First Indochinese War began in December 1946. Large armed forces were committed by the French, who were aided by some local native troops.

As the conflict got under way, the United States recognized a French puppet regime in Saigon in 1950; it also provided massive aid, both military and economic, as well as political support for the French military effort. The struggle was both anticolonial and confused by ideological differences between pro- and anti-Communist factions. The conflict lasted for nearly eight years and was characterized by cruel and violent tactics on both sides. Unequal to the guerrilla and jungle fighting, the French forces were gradually worn down. As French resistance waned, there was some thought in Washington of military intervention. Such a step at this time, however, had little support. The Vietminh, assisted by military aid from China, progressively went on the offensive. The end came dramatically at Dien Bien

Phu in 1954, when the French surrendered this massive stronghold, together with ten thousand troops. The French were compelled to accept a new political settlement later that year at the Geneva Conference, and agreements were reached regarding the future status of Laos, Cambodia, and Vietnam.

The accord ending hostilities in Vietnam, signed by representatives of France and the nationalist movement—that is, the Vietminh led by Ho Chi Minh—established a truce line at the 17th parallel, with the further agreement that the Vietminh forces were to withdraw to the north and the French-supported forces to the south. An International Control Commission, made up of India, Canada, and Poland, was to supervise the truce. A separate declaration regarded the truce line as temporary pending the holding of free nation-wide elections in July 1956 under international supervision—elections that never were held. Later a referendum was held in the area south of the 17th parallel on the form and leadership of a new government. Subsequently that region was proclaimed the Republic of South Vietnam, and in 1956 the Constituent Assembly promulgated a constitution. Meanwhile the split between the two geographical segments of Vietnam had increased with the movement of about one million people across the truce line to the south and with the progressive violation of the Geneva agreements by the introduction of military personnel and materials into South Vietnam by the Communists on one hand and South Vietnam's allies on the other.

For its part, Washington had refused to sign the Geneva agreements; instead, it sponsored the establishment of SEATO (Southeast Asia Treaty Organization) as a barrier against the further spread of communism into Cambodia, Laos, and South Vietnam. Having replaced France as the major western power in the region, the United States sought to create in South Vietnam a regime capable of holding its own against the Democratic Republic of Veitnam (Vietminh). American assistance was initially political and economic, with economic aid growing from $.1 million in 1954 to $278.5 million in 1965.

America's involvement grows. At first the United States gave full support to Ngo Dinh Diem, the leading figure of the non-Communist regime in the south. He rejected Ho Chi Minh's requests for holding elections throughout all Vietnam under the Geneva agreements because he feared that the Saigon government would lose to the Hanoi regime. There was doubt about the ability of international supervision to guarantee a truly free election. The north was more populous, and its totalitarian government was expected to exercise complete control of the vote in its own area, insuring an election majority over the divided vote in South Vietnam.

Unfortunately, despite Washington's urgings, the Diem government refused to carry out comprehensive land reforms, choosing instead to rely for support on the landlord class and the urban middle class. In addition, a very high proportion of officials was recruited from among Catholic refugees from the north. Diem, himself a Catholic in a predominately non-Catholic country, considered the northerners more reliable than the southerners, who in turn regarded the newcomers as carpetbaggers. Moreover, Diem suppressed opposition groups and dismantled the traditional village government system of elected elders, substituting Saigon-appointed officials, most of whom were not even from the provinces whose villages they ruled.

At the same time, the Communists, thwarted in their aim of having North and South Vietnam united by a general election, began guerrilla operations against the Diem regime. This so-called Second Vietnamese War began in 1957. Disillusioned by Diem's failure to initiate urgently needed land reforms, many peasants tacitly or actively supported the local Communist guerrilla activity in the rural areas. In December 1960 the National Liberation Front (NLF)—popularly known as the Viet Cong—was established in the south and thenceforth received support from the Communist regime at Hanoi in its mounting guerrilla operations. Diem, in the face of a rising crisis, became

more autocratic and less inclined to launch agrarian and other reforms. A coup and his assassination in 1963 did little to improve the situation as the NFL threatened to take over the entire country by force.

In 1960 there were only 800 American military advisers in the country; four years later this figure had risen to 23,000. In August 1964, North Vietnamese torpedo boats were accused of attacking United States destroyers in international waters in the Gulf of Tonkin. Following President Johnson's request, Congress adopted, by a Senate vote of 88-2 and a House vote of 416-0, a joint resolution which approved the taking of "all necessary measures . . . to prevent further aggression" and authorized the President, at his discretion, to assist South Vietnam in its defense—using armed force if required. Thereafter the war became increasingly Americanized, until by 1968 there were more than 500,000 American troops in the country. During these years the United States assumed a progressively larger share of the burden of actual combat and in 1965 initiated an intensive air war against North Vietnam. This air war failed to produce the desired results and became a subject of bitter controversy on the American domestic front.

Why this massive military commitment by the United States on Asian soil? Notwithstanding official references to moral obligation, pledged word in various defense agreements, and the protection of a small and "democratic" nation against aggression, the basic reason for intervention—no matter how incorrectly construed—was the protection of the national interests of the United States. The "Domino theory" held that the fall of the South Vietnam regime would ". . . whet the Communists' appetite for aggression and widen the scope of their subversion. It would probably lead in the long run to a Communist takeover of . . . Laos and Cambodia, as well as Thailand, and trigger guerrilla explosions in Asia and throughout the underdeveloped world. It would strengthen the extreme Chinese "line" throughout the Communist world, and perhaps undermine the more moderate trends seen in the Soviet Union and Eastern Europe."[24]

The American dilemma in Vietnam. By the latter half of 1968 the Vietnamese conflict had cost the United States more casualties than the Korean War and the money expended ran to more than $100 billion. A Communist "Tet"—or New Year's—offensive demonstrated the NFL's capability to penetrate the innermost defenses of major South Vietnamese cities. During the final months of President Johnson's administration nonpartisan efforts were made to find an honorable solution to the conflict. All bombing of North Vietnam was ended in October, and meanwhile peace talks between American and North Vietnamese representatives had begun in Paris; toward the end of the year they were joined by delegations from South Vietnam and the NLF.

When President Nixon assumed office, his administration had an unmistakable mandate to bring the conflict to as speedy an end as national commitments and interests permitted. Such an objective was fraught with hazards. At Paris the North Vietnamese maintained a hard line, insisting there could be no peace settlement until U.S. forces had left the country. At the same time the antiwar ranks in the United States increased their strength and their denunciations: the country had assumed an intolerable burden; vast sums expended in Asia were desperately needed for domestic reforms; the government of South Vietnam was corrupt and in no sense democratic, and no foreign power could make this regime acceptable to the people; and, finally, a Communist takeover of Southeast Asia would not threaten the national security. Utilizing these argu-

A wounded child is carried from the battle area; members of an American airborne division mourn their dead. After twenty years of protracted conflict, there is as yet little to show for the Vietnam War but a growing list of casualties and yet another generation of Vietnamese who know nothing of peace.

ments, and others branding the war as both immoral and illegal, some of the antiwar forces demanded immediate withdrawal, a unilateral pull-out; others a cease-fire; and some a fixed timetable for the return of all combat troops from Vietnam.

The problem of American disengagement. Confronted by massive opposition to the war and realizing that a military victory was impossible, President Nixon in the summer of 1969 initiated a policy of deescalation of the conflict, progressive withdrawal of U.S. troops coupled with accelerated Vietnamization of the armed forces. The president sought some form of negotiated settlement achieved by general agreement by all parties of perhaps a broader based Saigon regime or general elections to ascertain the free will of the South Vietnamese people. Such a program, however, necessitated time, and little was left for the White House. At Paris, Hanoi remained inflexible, merely following the antiwar campaign in the United States and the degree of success of Vietnamization. Hanoi, apparently, had all the time it needed.

The prospect of any unconditional U.S. withdrawal from Vietnam, resulting perhaps in a settlement "by massacre" and an uncertain future for other neighboring nations, caused some uneasiness in Southeast Asia and even Australia. The dilemma seemed to be that there could be no easy way out for Americans in Vietnam. The aftermath was bound to be traumatic. "Peace when it comes may be no less bloody than the war, and our crisis of conscience will persist long after the last American soldier has left South Vietnam."[25]

SUMMARY

The explosion of anti-imperialism and with it the collapse of colonial systems apparently came suddenly and unexpectedly in two short decades. This successful offensive of Afro-Asians, however, was not the sudden movement it appeared to be. Unobtrusively and gradually anti-imperialism had been developing for more than half a century. India—the forerunner—had witnessed the founding of the nationalist Congress party in 1885; and Gandhi's mass campaigns against British rule throughout the 1920's and 1930's were closely followed in other colonial areas. Emphasis upon Wilsonian self-determination during World War I and similar ideology during World War II kindled strong hopes and heady expectations among the world's colonial peoples. After 1945 they were sure not only that freedom would soon be won but that this new status would usher in a new and happier age of plenty and contentment for them.

Unfortunately, independence did not automatically solve age-old problems; indeed, in many instances, it added new ones. The consolidation of national unity proved especially precarious. India broke apart into two unfriendly states, and ethnic rivalries agitated both Malaysia and Indonesia. Tribalism proved to be a major weakness in many African states, erupting tragically into civil war in Nigeria.

In addition to attacks on national unity, Third World nations have experienced difficulty in maintaining the traditional elements of western democracy. Within a few years one-party states and military regimes became the prevailing political modes. In international affairs the new states have made a substantial impression. By 1970 they came to dominate the UN General Assembly. The overriding objective of this Afro-Asian majority was to end the last vestiges of racism and colonialism where they lingered in southern Africa. An interesting example of Third World influence in the international arena has been the new Africa's impact upon the United States. Its enhanced status caused the United States to give thought and action to strengthening its image and lines of communication in Africa. At the same time, black Americans tended to identify their struggle for civil rights and new dignity with the successful accomplishment of freedom in Africa.

The new nations have tried to present a united front in world affairs by the formation of such groups as the Arab League, the Bandung Conference, and the Organization of African Unity. Such endeavors championed the principles of nonalignment in the cold war and opposition to any form of neo-colonialism. Rivalries and instability in various areas of the Third World, however, notably in the Middle East and Vietnam, have invited big-power intrusion.

It is difficult to arrive at a balanced evaluation of the present and future of the emerging Afro-Asian states. Undoubtedly too much was expected from the winning of independence. It is likely, indeed inevitable, that in the immediate future there will be numerous instances of domestic turmoil; and in international affairs such confusion in "vacuum areas" may lead to big-power interference and ominous East-West confrontation. If the Third World can surmount these immediate dangers, it may, in the long-term future, gradually succeed in building stable nation-states administered by governments that are adequate for the tasks at hand and reasonably responsive to the will of the people.

Since their independence, the new nations have experienced reverses, some serious, and enjoyed achievements, some noteworthy. But generally their leaders are undaunted, facing the future with fortitude and hope. As one African statesman expressed his faith:

The problems of a nation, even a small one, cannot all be solved in the life span of any one man, or even in any one generation. The problems of Africa belong to many generations. The mountains that loom so formidably today will be distant hillocks behind the generations of tomorrow.[26]

SUGGESTIONS FOR READING

The political transformation of Asia is treated in T. W. Wallbank, **The Partition of India,** Heath; M. Brecher, **The New States of Asia,*** Oxford; A. M. Taylor, **Indonesian Independence and the United Nations,** Cornell, 1952; and G. McT. Kahin, ed., **Major Governments of Asia,** 2nd ed., Cornell, 1963. R. B. Morris, **The Emerging Nations and the American Revolution,** Harper & Row, 1970, appraises the influence of the first successful war of decolonization.

P. J. Griffiths, **Modern India,** Praeger, 1965. A study of post-independence India. See also S. S. Harrison, **India: The Most Dangerous Decades,** Princeton, 1960; G. Patterson, **Peking Versus Delhi,** Praeger, 1964; D. Wilbur, **Pakistan: Yesterday and Today,*** Holt, Rinehart & Winston; and Ved Mehta, **Portrait of India,** Farrar, Straus, 1969.

For studies of Southeast Asia see R. C. Bone's concise **Contemporary Southeast Asia,*** Random House; R. Butwell, **Southeast Asia Today and Tomorrow,*** Praeger; and B. Crozier, **Southeast Asia in Turmoil,*** Penguin. For specific countries see B. H. M. Vlekke, **Musantara: A History of Indonesia,** Quadrangle, 1959; C. M. Parkinson, **A Short History of Malaya,** Donald Moore, 1954; R. A. Smith, **Philippine Freedom, 1946–1958,** Columbia, 1958.

E. Hammer, **Vietnam Yesterday and Today,** Holt, Rinehart & Winston, 1966; B. Newman, **Background to Viet Nam,*** Signet. Concise treatments of Vietnamese history. On the Vietnam War see M. E. Gettleman, ed., **Viet Nam: History, Documents, and Opinions on a Major World Crisis,*** Crest. For an official American view see Department of State, **Aggression from the North,** Publication 7839, Washington, D.C. For personal assessments see C. Bain, **Vietnam: The Roots of Conflict,*** Spectrum; B. Fall, **The Two Vietnams,** 2nd rev. ed., Praeger, 1967; and A. M. Schlesinger, Jr., **The Bitter Heritage,** Houghton Mifflin, 1965. An excellent comparative background of the Vietnam War is S. E. Morison, *et al.,* **Dissent in Three American Wars,** Harvard, 1970.

M. Halpern, **The Politics of Social Change in the Middle East and North Africa,*** Princeton. A survey of the problems in-volved. Nasser's role is discussed in P. Mansfield, **Nasser's Egypt,*** Penguin. J. Morris, **Islam Inflamed,** Pantheon, 1957; and H. Finer, **Dulles Over Suez,** Quadrangle, 1964, analyze the Suez Canal problem. Arab-Israeli conflict is studied in W. Laquer, **The Road to Jerusalem,** Macmillan, 1968; and R. and W. Churchill, **The Six Day War,** Houghton Mifflin, 1967. W. Laquer, **The Struggle for the Middle East,** Macmillan, 1970, is the story of Soviet intrusion.

L. H. Gann and P. Duignan, **Burden of Empire,** Praeger, 1967. A reevaluation of African history and colonialism. The difficulties facing the newly emergent nations are analyzed in B. Crozier, **The Morning After,** Oxford, 1963; J. Hatch, **A History of Postwar Africa,*** Praeger; L. Gray Cowan, **The Dilemmas of African Independence,** Walker, 1964; and A. Rivkin, **Nation Building in Africa,** Rutgers, 1969. Ideological problems are the subject of Z. Brzezinski, ed., **Africa and the Communist World,*** Stanford. See also T. W. Wallbank, **Contemporary Africa,*** Anvil. On specific regions or countries see K. Post, **New States of West Africa,*** Penguin; D. Austin, **Politics in Ghana,** Oxford, 1964; C. Young, **Politics in the Congo,*** Princeton; J. A. Davis and J. K. Baker, eds., **Southern Africa in Transition,** Praeger, 1966; and Okoi Arikpo, **The Development of Modern Nigeria,*** Penguin.

V. McKay, **Africa in World Politics,** Harper & Row, 1963. Especially useful for Pan-Africanism and United States policy in Africa. Also recommended are W. Goldschmidt, **The United States and Africa,*** rev. ed., Praeger; and H. R. Isaacs, **The New World of Negro Americans,** John Day, 1963.

G. Myrdal, **Asian Drama, An Inquiry into the Poverty of Nations,*** 3 vols., Pantheon. Recent reevaluation of contemporary attitudes toward the problems of newly emergent nations. Less detailed are V. M. Dean, **The Nature of the Non-Western World,*** Mentor; and E. Staley, **The Future of Underdeveloped Countries,*** Praeger. W. A. Hance, **The Geography of Modern Africa,** Columbia, 1964, contributes to an understanding of the African economic scene.

*Indicates an inexpensive paperbound edition.

Chapter 33

Toward a New Life Style

**Intellectual and Cultural Ferment
in the Twentieth Century**

INTRODUCTION. In one sense human history is a continuum. On any given day occur innumerable births and deaths throughout the world, each birth a quantum of new life that merges into the pattern of the present like a thread woven into a tapestry or a dot of light on a television screen. In this sense, there are no breaks in history but only a gradual process of change in the planetary human pattern. And yet, if we are to try to understand this changing pattern, we must look for points of reference to which we can attach more than usual significance.

Bearing in mind that even during periods of massive innovation and rapid change, everyday life often proceeds with little disturbance for great masses of the population and that the effects of change may not become fully apparent for many years, it is nevertheless obvious that our own century has witnessed profound changes in the historical pattern. In particular, two global wars have provided significant watersheds in the course of events. As a consequence, after each holocaust men have acquired new perspectives in viewing both the world which they inhabit and their own role and status as individuals. Those who grew up after the First World War were bound to have a different outlook on life than those whose values and attitudes had been shaped before 1914. Similarly, today we are seeing the differences—and feeling the tensions—between those who grew up in the interwar years and those whose life styles have been shaped by the decades following World War I. Although these differences are commonly referred to as "generation gaps," it should be recognized that they are not based simply on the tensions that have always arisen between parents and their children in the family unit. The divisions are more deeply rooted. Our century has spawned different sets of values and life styles, and the resulting conflicts might be more accurately described as "culture gaps."

The First World War brought to an end a century of relative stability in world affairs. The previous hundred years had been characterized by an orderly if mechanistic view of the universe, coupled with a general belief in man's ability to master his environment. The prevailing mood was one of optimism that science and representative government together would usher in a new age when, in Tennyson's words, "the war drum throbbed no longer, and the battle-flags were furled / In the Parliament of man, the Federation of the world." This comfortable assumption that progress was an almost inevitable process was shattered by a war intercontinental in its dimensions and unprecedented in its carnage. After 1918, politics, art, and social attitudes reflected widespread disillusionment with the old ways. A world-wide economic depression and a second global conflict even more destructive than its predecessor not only shaped the values of those who had grown up during this period but also bequeathed a legacy—including the atomic bomb—to the billions who have been born since 1945 in the greatest population explosion in history. The postwar years brought new possibilities for constructive and destructive purposes alike. Consequently, if this chapter places a special emphasis upon developments during the past quarter of a century, it is because these years have set the stage for the convulsions that are presently rocking contemporary society to its innermost foundations. And always the search goes on: for new values, new modes of expression, and new insights into the nature of man himself.

THE INTERWAR YEARS: 1919-1939

Symbol for the present age. In his *Education* the American historian Henry Adams describes how in 1900 he passed the summer in Paris, spending long days at the Exposition, where the dynamos in Machinery Hall stirred his imagination deeply. Here was a new force, he thought, capable perhaps of transforming civilization, even as he believed that the worship of the Virgin had represented a unique force in the Middle Ages, one which had motivated society and fashioned the magnificent cathedrals of France.

Without doubt, the dynamo helped transform twentieth-century civilization into the most technologically advanced in history. Yet were he alive today, Henry Adams might ponder the implications of yet another machine capable of unleashing energy on an unprecedented scale—the synchrotron, a gigantic magnet that accelerates atomic particles to hundreds of millions of electron volts. The magnetic field of this atom-smashing machine can bring about the transmutation of elements. In this respect, the synchrotron is as much a symbol for our age as the dynamo was for Henry Adams. It is not only the physical elements that are being transmuted; today the interplay of technological, economic, political, and social forces has created a global field in which our human institutions and relationships are being constantly bombarded by these interacting forces—and rapidly transformed.

Actually, there is nothing new about this concept of change—Heraclitus proclaimed it in ancient Greece. What is unique in our century is the way in which the tempo of change has accelerated to unprecedented speeds, until by the close of the interwar years scientists had discovered how to bombard atomic nuclei so as to create a "chain reaction," thereby ushering in the Atomic Age. Already we possess thermonuclear power—and weapons—so that the problem of retaining equilibrium has become critical for man and society alike. Perhaps we have to emulate the lumberjack rolling a log in the river: he retains his balance only by moving in synchronization with that whirling log.

Science points the way. As we saw in Chapter 25, at the beginning of this century certain major scientific achievements occurred which were to lay the basis for a new interpretation of the universe. At this juncture we wish to recall certain of these developments because of their collective impact upon the course of thought for succeeding decades.

In 1900 Max Planck discovered new properties of atomic matter and the behavior of energy, thereby laying the basis of what is now called the quantum theory (see p. 586). Since he found that energy is transmitted in discontinuous "packages," or *quanta*, Planck strengthened the view that the atom itself was not a solid piece of matter but a unit of energy. Moreover, the quantum theory "indicates that precise location of small objects, such as electrons, is no longer possible, at least not by methods now at hand."[1] The physicist has to be content with mathematical probabilities; there is a factor of unpredictability in the phenomenal world. This aspect of quantum mechanics was further advanced by Werner Heisenberg with his "uncertainty principle" (1927); he showed that in atomic physics, while the behavior of groups of particles can be confidently predicted, no such prediction can be made for any one particle. This factor of indeterminacy has given rise to philosophical speculation beyond the

bounds of physics. The universe seems to be governed by statistical regularities, yet it does not preclude elements of freedom of movement or choice for the individual. (It is on this dual basis of group predictability and individual unforeseeability that insurance companies operate—profitably.)

The second revolutionary scientific development occurred in 1905 when Einstein published his Special Theory of Relativity which showed the interrelationships existing between mass, energy, and velocity (see p. 586). Of particular interest to us at this point, it represented a new way of thinking about the world of moving objects, involving the use of non-Euclidean geometry. While Newton's mechanics still continue to be of satisfactory use in everyday science and engineering, Einstein's more advanced concepts have completely reoriented men's attitudes toward the structure and mechanics of the universe. Moreover, as in the case of the quantum theory, these new concepts have had an important "spillover" effect. Not only was the Newtonian model of the cosmos, based upon *absolute* space, time, and gravitation, replaced by a relativistic space-time continuum, but henceforth other thinkers began to ask whether absolutes necessarily existed in their own disciplines. Consequently, religion, philosophy, morals, and ethics have been subjected to relativism. In addition, Einstein's conceptual approach helped shape our century's intellectual concern to search for "relationships," to stress "interdependence," and to analyze phenomena in terms of "systems."

Atomic structure and energy. The achievements of Planck and Einstein were especially important for atomic physics, probably the most revolutionary area of scientific development during the first half of this century. In 1897 Sir J. J. Thomson had disclosed that atoms contain particles carrying a negative electric charge—particles which he named electrons. In 1911 Ernest Rutherford discovered that the atom had a positively charged nucleus. His pupil, Niels Bohr, developed the theory that the atom is like a miniature solar system: most of the weight is concentrated in the nucleus around which the electrons revolve. Einstein's Special

Theory suggested that the atomic nucleus must contain enormous energy, because mass and energy are convertible and the amount of energy is equal to the mass multiplied by the square of the velocity of light. (This means that one pound of coal, if converted entirely into energy, would release as much energy as the combustion of one and a third million tons of coal.) However, this knowledge seemed to promise no practical application because the atoms of radioactive elements, such as radium and uranium, disintegrated at their own speed, and scientists did not know how to speed up this process in order to release enough energy capable of being harnessed.

The interwar years changed the situation. In 1919 Rutherford succeeded in transmuting one element into another by bombarding its nucleus with positively charged particles, but to do so he had to use more energy than was thereby released. During the next two decades physicists constructed atom-smashing machines (such as the cyclotron and, later, the synchrotron) for bombarding the atomic nucleus. In 1932 the neutron in the nucleus was discovered, and this proved ideal for the purpose since it carried no electric charge and was not repulsed by the positive charge. Enrico Fermi and other physicists were now able to produce nuclear reactions; however, more energy still had to be expended than was thereby released from the bombarded nuclei. They realized that just as a fire can continue to burn only because the combustion of each portion of fuel raises adjoining portions to the temperature of combustion, so an atomic "chain reaction" was required to split atoms in such a way as to produce more neutrons, which might then hit other atoms and cause them in turn to split and emit neutrons—and so on in a continuous fashion. In January 1939, eight months before the outbreak of World War II, two German physicists found that the splitting of a uranium atom caused its nucleus to produce barium and also emit large amounts of energy. Subsequent studies in the United States and elsewhere confirmed that the neutrons released during such fission made a chain reaction possible. Thus was

born the Atomic Age, with all its promise and peril implanted in the positively charged nucleus.

Biological advances. Meanwhile, by 1900 the experimental work upon heredity in plants as pioneered by Gregor Mendel (see p. 583) had been rediscovered, and its implications began to be vigorously pursued. As a result, the earlier concept that chance variations in the forms and processes of living creatures are alone responsible for evolution was supplanted by an understanding of ordered systems of genes and chromosomes. The life process itself was thus found to act in obedience to fundamental laws, and this conceptual breakthrough was dramatically corroborated by subsequent discoveries. Between World Wars I and II scientists isolated the enzyme (an organic catalyst, usually a protein, which controls a cell's chemical reactions) and discovered its relationship to genes. The next step was to find out the exact chemical nature of the gene itself, which proved to be composed of deoxyribo-

Henry Moore's sculpture "Nuclear Energy" stands near the spot at the University of Chicago where on December 2, 1942, Enrico Fermi and other physicists produced the first self-sustaining nuclear chain reaction, an event marking the beginning of the Atomic Age.

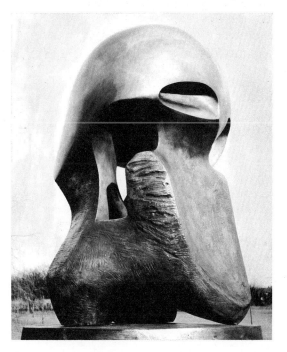

nucleic acid, or DNA for short. Then, in 1953, James D. Watson and Francis H. C. Crick provided a model of the structure of the DNA molecule. It is built "like a spiral staircase" in a double helix—and is mathematically "programmed" so that "one molecule of DNA in a human cell contains as much information as several encyclopedia sets."[2] Since DNA is the fundamental genetic material, analysis of its structure is expected to provide us with far-reaching insights into the processes of heredity—and with knowledge capable of shaping mankind's future as a species. Consequently, biology and related disciplines may well become the most revolutionary area of scientific development during the second half of our century.

The achievements of biologists and biochemists have also proved invaluable to medical research and treatment. During the interwar years a series of synthetic drugs based on sulfanilamide was developed which succeeded in curing a number of diseases due to streptococcus and pneumococcus infections. Similar success occurred in developing bacterial products derived from molds. In 1928 a Scottish biochemist, Alexander Fleming, discovered that a species of fungus known as *Penicillium notatum* destroyed colonies of staphylococcus. From his discovery came the development of the first antibiotic, penicillin, which with related drugs has proved the most effective means of treating syphilis, gonorrhea, certain types of pneumonia, and other infections. The result of such medical advances has been to lengthen our life span and to increase global population—the implications of which have become progressively apparent in the second half of the century.

A new scientific world view. By 1940 the physical and biological sciences had largely restructured the fundamental bases of the phenomenal world. They pointed the way toward a unified concept of the structure and processes of the universe in which matter, energy, space, and time may be found to be different manifestations of a single, universal field. Scientific reasoning coupled with technology enabled men to reach new levels of understanding about

atomic entities, the nonvisible but universally permeating force fields of gravitation and electromagnetism, and to construct meaningful models of both the macrocosmic universe and the microcosmic cell.

The significance of the new scientific world view would become progressively apparent in the postwar years as men realized how interrelated are all phenomenal systems, including man himself. He not only is part of a planetary ecology but possesses the intellectual capacity and tools to explore an extraterrestrial environment which is in turn regulated by laws that can be mathematically formulated and utilized. Thanks to quantum mechanics and the uncertainty principle, moreover, science has abandoned the clockwork determinism of previous centuries for a view of the universe that describes phenomena in terms of mass behavior, utilizing statistics and the laws of probability. In doing so, it has also recognized the subjective nature of human perception and understanding and has lent new credence to the argument that the evolutionary process remains open-ended and that the uncertainty principle may have some relationship to the concept of free will.

The "Wasteland Era" in literature. Literature, no less than science, was transformed after 1919 by new techniques and subject matter. Until the First World War men of letters for the most part had contented themselves with themes and values familiar to the previous century. The majority continued to write as though theirs was the best of all possible worlds, because it was one in which "progress" seemed assured. This complacency was shattered by the holocaust of 1914-1918. The standards of western society, which had been guilty of the worst bloodbath in history, were inevitably challenged. The youths who had been promised that the war was to save the world for democracy emerged from the trenches bitterly disillusioned—as attested by the verse of Wilfred Owen (see quotation, p. 568) and Erich Maria Remarque's *All Quiet on the Western Front*, one of many novels inveighing against mass slaughter and the apparent futility of modern war.

The latest theories of physics and psychology were seized upon as starting points for literary vogues. Since according to the Relativity Theory nothing was "fixed" in the universe and the once "indivisible" atom could have its nucleus transformed, why should not all customs, laws, and moral standards be considered equally relative? Meanwhile, man's dignity as a rational being had been dealt a rude shock by the psychologists. The behaviorists pictured him as a set of conditioned reflexes, while the psychoanalysts explained his conduct in terms of emotional drives and subconscious urgings, not of reason and free will. Man now appeared as an irrational, puny bundle of viscera governed by forces outside his control, and whose society was a thinly veneered savagery.

The postwar social milieu did little to counteract such views. The 1920's in the United States have been described as an era of "tremendous trivia"—flagpole sitting, "red-hot mamas," speakeasies, Broadway tickertape parades for celebrities, the Charleston, and a national craze for speculating in stocks and Florida real estate. Many Americans looked to Wall Street rather than to the White House for leadership (did not President Coolidge himself declare in 1925 that "The business of America is Business"?), and the country as a whole enjoyed unprecedented prosperity up to 1929 and appeared little interested in what transpired outside the three-mile limit—or rather the twelve-mile limit when it came to rumrunning. But if Americans had rejected President Wilson's plea to espouse the League of Nations rather than isolationism, in parts of western Europe the era was marked by "tremendous"—but scarcely "trivial"—developments. In Italy, Mussolini and his Fascist followers had overthrown democratic government and instituted a totalitarian society, while in Germany, Hitler and his Nazi associates were bending every effort to destroy the Weimar Republic (see Chapter 28).

In 1922 the Anglo-American poet T. S. Eliot published *The Waste Land*, a long poem which expressed weariness with the ugliness and sterility of industrialized civilization. It began:

April is the cruellest month, breeding
Lilacs out of the dead land, mixing
Memory and desire, stirring
Dull roots with spring rain.
. . . .
What are the roots that clutch, what branches
   grow
Out of this stony rubbish? Son of man,
You cannot say, or guess, for you know only
A heap of broken images, where the sun beats,
And the dead tree gives no shelter, the cricket
   no relief,
And the dry stone no sound of water.[3]

This work epitomized the atmosphere of skepticism and negation which largely pervaded the intellectual world in both England and the United States. Thus Aldous Huxley in verse, essays, and novels displayed a deep-seated skepticism regarding society's ability to act rationally, while Sinclair Lewis in a series of novels satirized the materialism and shallowness that he saw in much of American life during the twenties. Some Americans expatriated themselves to Paris. The novels of F. Scott Fitzgerald, which are associated with the term "jazz age," look at the problems of wealth and violence in the American scene. Another expatriate, Ernest Hemingway, rocketed to fame with vivid stories glorifying virility and action for its own sake. In Germany, Oswald Spengler evinced a brooding pessimism in his massive historical work, *The Decline of the West*.

The era also saw the appearance of a number of psychological studies. One American dramatist who probed into the psychological abnormalities of human nature was Eugene O'Neill. For his part, the English novelist D. H. Lawrence emphasized the significance of the sexual drive. In the multivolumed *Remembrance of Things Past* the French writer Marcel Proust explored psychological time, human relationships, and his own perceptions and mental processes by means of the stream-of-consciousness technique. This influential work recognized no lasting significance in the external world; one's own consciousness alone remains real. Also employing stream-of-consciousness, the Irish-born James Joyce underscored the complexity and disorder of contemporary civili-

In "Violin and Palette" (1909-1910) the only recognizable objects are fragmented, because, as Braque later said, "Fragmentation helped me to establish space and movement in space." This simultaneous representation of different views of the same object freed painters from the traditional interpretation of space in which an illusion of distance was created by means of geometric perspective.

zation in *Ulysses*, a report on the experiences of a group of people during a single day in Dublin. German literature was meanwhile being enriched by Thomas Mann, whose fame had been established in 1903 with *Buddenbrooks*, a masterly analysis of character extending over several generations.

In *The Magic Mountain*, an evocative novel about life in a tuberculosis sanitarium in the Alps, Mann shows how completely relative both time and human values can become in such an environment.

Impact of the depression. In the 1930's, marked by the depression and the triumph of totalitarianism in Germany and Italy, literature reflected a new emphasis upon social problems and the plight of the individual. Europe produced a number of eloquent spokesmen in this field. The Hungarian-born Arthur Koestler, a one-time member of the Communist party who also fought in the Spanish Civil War, found himself increasingly disillusioned with the intellectual enslavement inherent in totalitarian ideologies and became a champion of political freedom, as his *Darkness at Noon* and other works attest. In France, André Malraux emphasized the heroic qualities which revolutionary struggle can arouse in men—a theme found in his novel *Man's Fate*—and in Italy, Ignazio Silone analyzed the problems of his poor compatriots with a mixture of compassion and democratic socialism.

One of the most trenchant critics of social injustice was the English writer George Orwell, who in the thirties directed his attack against capitalistic exploitation and subsequently against totalitarianism of both the right and left, as shown in *Animal Farm* (1945) as well as in his postwar novel *1984*. In the United States the poverty, ignorance, and decadence of some parts of the South were portrayed by William Faulkner, while the plight of the "Okies" who trekked to California in the depression in search of economic survival was recounted by John Steinbeck in his moving novel, *Grapes of Wrath*.

Although there were other writers who did not set forth specific social views, a shift in their viewpoint indicated that the experience of the thirties had left a permanent impress. In more than one instance this meant renewed interest in religion or mysticism. T. S. Eliot himself replaced his former sophisticated weariness with an appeal for a return to Christian values, as the following lines from *Choruses from "The Rock"* (1934) attest:

Where is the Life we have lost in living?
Where is the wisdom we have lost in knowledge?
Where is the knowledge we have lost in infor-
mation?
The cycles of Heaven in twenty centuries
Bring us farther from God and nearer to the
Dust.[4]

The surge of social awareness and interdependence which marked the depression
years of the 1930's encouraged various segments of American society to take a new
look at one another, with some gratifying
results. Americans became aware that they
possessed rich and virtually untapped
sources of folk poetry and music. While
scholars recorded ballads from different
regions, Woody Guthrie and other folk
singers recaptured the kaleidoscopic moods
of a national heritage. It had required a
depression to take inventory of the country's
almost inexhaustible human resources.

Developments in painting. As we saw in
Chapter 25, the decades prior to World
War I had witnessed both a reaction against
academic painting and experimentation
with new concepts and forms. Among the
most prominent Expressionists were the
Frenchman Matisse and the Russian Wassily
Kandinsky (1866-1944), who by 1913 devoted

his talents entirely to abstract art, allowing
each viewer to derive his own interpretation and significance from the artist's
arrangement of colors and form. Meanwhile,
Cézanne's explorations in geometrizing
nature had been further developed by the
Cubists, notably Georges Braque (1882-1963)
and Picasso. In their experiments with
depicting an object from more than one
vantage point, the Cubists were making
use of concepts that were just becoming
understood by science. Thus Braque's representation of a violin from several points
of view, thereby emphasizing the concept
of simultaneity, has been described as an
esthetic counterpart to Einstein's Special
Theory of Relativity (which appeared about
the same time as the painting).

In the years after World War I the Expressionists and Cubists continued to expand
their influence. Abstract, nonrepresentational painting was taken up by young
artists all over the world—except in the
Soviet Union where initial attempts at experimentation were aborted by ideological
insistence upon "socialist realism." Among
the newer Expressionists was the American
Jackson Pollock (1912-1956) who became well
known after World War II for a new abstract

Picasso's "Guernica," named for a city destroyed in the Spanish civil war, expresses not only the
agony and brutality of that conflict but the horror of war itself. As shocking as a scream of pain, it
is one of his most famous works.

Advances in the physical sciences made Kandinsky, an avowed mystic, even more convinced that painting should be concerned with the spiritual rather than the physical world. In "Autumn" (1914) Kandinsky eliminated all resemblance to tangible objects, attempting to suggest the nature of the season by wholly abstract means. The content of the painting thus becomes what the person viewing it experiences.

style in which traditional structure gave way to a freer, more spontaneous use of pictorial space (see Color Plate 34). Meanwhile, the older Kandinsky continued to delight the artistic world with his seemingly inexhaustible reservoir of abstract configurations.

The interwar years saw Picasso modify his Cubist approach. One of his claims to permanent recognition, like that of the poet Eliot, lies in his continuous search after new standards and new forms of expression. He became the greatest artistic experimenter in an age full of experiments. Thus the 1920's found Picasso developing a neoclassical style, as seen in his "Woman in White," while in the following decade he painted his famous "Guernica" mural, vividly depicting the destruction of a small Spanish town by Fascist air forces in that country's civil war. Acknowledged a masterpiece, this painting combines artistic autonomy with a direct relationship to contemporary world events (see illustration, p. 799).

The Surrealists. Freud's emphasis upon the unconscious and irrational states of the human mind made a strong impact upon writers and artists alike. In the 1920's there emerged in Europe the Surrealists, who saw the subconscious mind as the vehicle which could free man from the shackles of modern society and lead him to freedom. They felt an affinity with "primitive" art and its close associations with magical and mythological themes, and they exalted the irrational and violent in human experience. The Surrealists found much of their inspiration in the imagery of dreams, as illustrated so vividly in the paintings of one of the movement's most brilliant exponents, Salvador Dali. Various Surrealists saw themselves allied with the industrial proletariat in its struggle against existing societal injustices. But an inherent contradiction existed between the requirements of revolutionary discipline and the freedom of artistic expression that was so characteristic of the movement. Consequently, it was in renewing linkages between the artist and the intuitive, as opposed to rational, lines of thinking that the Surrealists enjoyed their greatest success (see illustration, p. 677).

Photography comes of age. The revolt against traditional ways of thinking could also be discerned in the photographic arts. Still photography and motion pictures, whose basic principles had been developed in the last century, became major vehicles of expression in the years following World War One. Photographers and film producers began to explore the unique qualities of their media, in pursuit of new and vivid ways of *seeing*. In photography the classic rules of composition which had guided painters were cast aside in a deliberate attempt to avoid sentimentality and flattery. The brilliant use of film editing by the

The twentieth century saw the photographic arts attain not only popularity but full stature among the arts. Although early photographers used the traditional rules of painting as their standard, the realization that photography had a vitality of its own forced them to discover new modes of expression. Edward Steichen, one of America's most experimental and interpretative photographers, introduced entirely new concepts of realism and artistry to still photography. Exploring every nuance of an object's shape and form, Steichen photographed everything from fashion models to the graceful spiral of a snail's shell (top left). Dorothea Lange, who helped stir public opinion during the depression era, was one of the leading proponents of photojournalism. Viewing her subjects unflinchingly, she was a master of photographic social commentary, as is evident in "White Angel Breadline" (top right). The cinema also rose to artistic prominence, influenced by such great early directors as Sergei Eisenstein. His revolutionary use of montage, nonprofessional actors, and brutal close-ups makes the impact of his film *Potemkin* felt even today (bottom).

Russian producer Sergei Eisenstein helped point the way to motion pictures that were more than just recorded theater plays. Stylistically, the break with old values and the growth of a new social consciousness produced trends both to abstract expressionism and to documentary realism (see illustration, p. 801).

The documentary became an important way of arousing public opinion. True photo-reportage began in the mid-twenties, by which time improved equipment and technical facilities had made it possible to catch fleeting expressions and movements under varying lighting conditions. As books and mass-circulation magazines replaced art exhibits in acting as galleries for talented photographers, they also helped spur a preoccupation with everyday people and situations. During the depression Dorothea Lange and other photographers working for federal agencies, notably the Farm Security Administration, were using their art as a powerful weapon in awakening Americans to the plight of their fellow countrymen (see p. 801).

Movies were also used for social commentary in many countries. The Russian filmmakers, who had been inspired to social consciousness by the revolution, were forced to curtail their experimentation and channel their social commentary to the demands of "socialist realism" under Stalin, who insisted that art be subordinated to the interests of the state. In Germany a greater perversion of the cinema was accomplished under Hitler, as the power of film was harnessed to the purposes of Nazi propaganda.

Architecture and sculpture. In Chapter 25 we saw how Louis Sullivan helped revolutionize architectural concepts and techniques alike by his functional approach. In the interwar years functionalism developed into an internationally accepted style, with its most influential center located in Germany in the Bauhaus school, founded in 1918 by Walter Gropius. The center's teaching staff included architects such as Ludwig Mies van der Rohe (1886-1969) and artists Paul Klee (1879-1940) and Kandinsky. Teachers and students worked together in programs that aimed at joining artistic expression and industry in order to reconcile contemporary

Growing out of a new technological culture which made new forms and new functions possible through the use of such materials as steel, concrete, and glass, contemporary architecture may eventually be remembered as the most revolutionary of the visual arts in the twentieth century. Two architectural giants during the period were Mies van der Rohe and Le Corbusier, and the ongoing vitality of their individual approaches is evident in their continuing influence on other twentieth-century architects, who in turn are attempting to find their own particular style. The clean classical lines of Mies' 1921 project for a glass tower (top left) are reflected in many of the distinguished buildings being constructed today, such as Lake Point Tower (bottom left), a Chicago apartment building designed by Schipporeit-Heinrich, Inc. Similarly, the massive, sculptural grace of the entrance portico of the Assembly Building at Chandigarh (top right), one of three major government buildings Le Corbusier designed for the new capital of the Punjab in India, is echoed in the National Gymnasium in Tokyo by the Japanese architect Kenzo Tange (bottom right).

man with his technologically altered environment. From architecture to pottery, from typography to home furnishings, the Bauhaus design for living reflected its members' belief that art and function should be synthesized. After Hitler closed down the school in 1933, many of its prominent members fled to other countries to carry on their work and spread the Bauhaus philosophy. Among those who came to the United States and subsequently played a central role in developing architectural design and urban planning was Mies van der Rohe. The period also produced other major architects espousing the functional approach. These included the Swiss-born Le Corbusier (1887-1965), whose creative employment of geometric forms has influenced architectural design not only in Europe and Brazil but later in India, where he designed Chandigarh, the new provincial capital of the Punjab.

During our century sculpture has once more become a major art form, as it was in Egypt, in Greece, and during the Renaissance. Whereas it remained relatively static throughout the nineteenth century except for the efforts of Rodin (see p. 592), sculpture has again entered upon a dynamic phase. In keeping with the functionalist approach, the interwar years saw architecture and sculpture being integrated in terms of larger environmental planning. Consequently sculpture ceased to be bound by the academic tradition of mere realistic depiction of the model, becoming instead more abstract, geometrical, and symbolic than heretofore. This fundamental change is seen clearly in the monumental figures of the British sculptor Henry Moore (1898-   ) which are largely abstract and show affinity with "primitive" forms (see illustration, p. 795). The Rumanian sculptor Constantin Brancusi (1876-1957) exemplifies the tendency to employ the medium in order to maximize the concept of motion, whether it be in his abstract depiction of a "Bird in Space" or his marble portrait of "Mlle. Pogany" (see Color Plate 33).

Developments in music. Earlier in the century, as we saw in Chapter 25, composers had rebelled against traditional romanticism. They experimented with impressionism, as in the works of Debussy, with polytonality, as with Stravinski, or again with atonality, as in the case of Schönberg. During the interwar years Stravinski and other composers continued to experiment in terms of polytonality, dissonant harmonies, and percussive rhythms. This period was also marked by a rediscovery of folk music, with the rhythms of Balkan folk songs finding their way into the music of the Hungarian composer Béla Bartók (1881-1945). The major development in popular music during the 1920's was jazz, an American form that originated with Negro musicians in New Orleans and which after the war spread over the continent.

Jazz in its original form stressed improvisation, so that the arranger or performer tended to be more important than the composer. Small bands of musicians played for parades and river boats, night clubs and dance halls. They made use of both western and African music, drawing from brass band marches, French and Spanish songs and dances, and Negro spirituals and work songs. Later, as bands grew in size

By the mid-fifties jazz had attained world-wide recognition, and groups of all sizes toured abroad, sometimes teaming up with musicians from other countries for recording sessions. In 1957 the most famous of all jazz men, Louis Armstrong, who began his career in New Orleans during the 1920's, visited Ghana with his group.

and became more professional, more of their music was written down, so that free improvisation decreased as it became integrated with written music. Radio and the phonograph helped popularize jazz and indeed became important media for propagating all kinds of music, both "classical" and "popular."

THE AFTERMATH
OF WORLD WAR TWO

The temper of the times. The power discovered by physics in the atom had been unlocked under the pressure of war. The atomic bomb not only came to symbolize the strength of the postwar giants—the United States and the Soviet Union—but also brought home to men everywhere the precarious nature of existence upon this planet. Power realities found the United States and the Soviet Union dominating the global scene in a state of ideological, military, and geographical confrontation. The term "cold war" described this postwar state of international relations and also an attendant intellectual climate which tended to abort the ideals for which the "Grand Alliance" had fought and defeated the Axis.

As cold war tensions increased, anti-Communist feelings in the United States took on aspects of a crusade in the late 1940's and reached unexpected proportions. A widespread view that the government, labor unions, and universities were infested with Communists and their sympathizers was reinforced by the attacks of Senator Joseph McCarthy and his followers.

McCarthyism proved to be a virulent form of the populism that is deeply rooted in various parts of North America and has periodically manifested itself in both right- and left-wing forms. In linking the liberal forces and the Washington "establishment" to a subversive left-wing movement, McCarthy appealed to many people who felt frustrated by their lot in life. "Egghead" was a pejorative term likely to be applied to any socially conscious intellectual or "do-gooder."

This attitude, however, altered appreciably as a result of the launching of the Soviet Sputnik in 1957. This triumph stirred a national concern in the United States over the quality and need of American education, particularly in the physical sciences, so that the academic community came to be seen as a national resource rather than as a breeding ground for dangerous and subversive ideas.

"The Silent Generation." The cold war spirit could not fail to make its impact upon the students of the fifties who, by the standards of the next decade, seemed to conform to the prevailing social philosophy. In the United States, for example, what dissatisfaction there was tended to manifest itself in cynicism and the kind of personal retreat typified in the writings of J. D. Salinger. The "cool" jazz of Dave Brubeck found much appeal among this generation of students, who became known as "The Silent Generation." Their basically apolitical attitude has been interpreted as reflecting an America preponderantly intent upon personal interests and goals.

The most visible expression of dissent found form in the Beat movement, whose members believed that man's alienation from his world was the root cause of a contemporary social malaise. However, the Beats—or beatniks, as they were popularly known—lacked the direction or anger to be activists. Their subculture was artistic rather than political, their principal spokesmen being writers like the novelist Jack Kerouac and the poet Allen Ginsberg. Despite their retreat from involvement, the beatniks provided a refuge for alternative values and a portent of the more widespread rejection of the dominant value system which was to mark the next decade.

Affluence and the seeds of change. In many ways the fifties resembled the twenties, but with an added dash of paranoia to make up what they lacked in gaiety. In both decades the western nations were preoccupied with economic rebuilding and expansion, and their people with trying to return to the "good life" after the hardships of war. After World War II western Europe and America were busy building the consumer society: automobiles, highways, supermarkets, television sets. Mass production brought new levels of economic prosperity but also raised new questions about the quality of life in industrial society. For many, suburbia came to symbolize conformity and homogenization of taste. On the other hand, many Americans today recall the "Eisenhower years" as an interlude of peace and prosperity between years of war and confusion.

Yet despite surface appearances, even the material affluence of the postwar West had become a vehicle for change. Mass prosperity was breaking up old status structures and enabling more people from all strata of society to pursue pastimes from stock-car racing to ballet. Television and universal education were giving children new horizons on the world. Young people could afford to buy records and attend concerts featuring new forms of popular music. One such innovation was rock and roll, a mixture of black rhythm-and-blues and white country-and-western music. Ray Charles brought together the joyous sounds of gospel and the melancholy of the blues, while Elvis Presley turned white youth on to the new sounds, thereby helping destroy the segregation in musical taste which had existed between the races.

Portents of change. Meanwhile, certain profound changes in American life were in the making. The Supreme Court's ruling in 1954 on school integration marked the beginning of the end of legal segregation in this country. A bus boycott in Montgomery, Alabama, brought to prominence a young Baptist minister named Martin Luther King, Jr. (1929-1968), and demonstrated the effectiveness of mass action as a tactic in the civil rights struggle. In 1956 C. Wright Mills published *The Power Elite,* a harsh analysis of contemporary American society which implied a pessimistic assessment of the prospects for democracy. In spite of the cold war atmosphere—the "better dead than Red" philosophy, the air-raid drills and shelters—a reaction was emerging in the latter years of the decade that set the stage for the widespread questioning of national priorities and the antimilitarism of the sixties.

In *The Affluent Society* (1958) John Kenneth Galbraith attacked the concept that production was the central economic problem of the times. He contended that the value system which emphasizes the ability of a society to produce invariably evaluates persons by the products they possess and artificially stimulates consumer demand. Galbraith questioned the kind of thinking that makes public expenditure for educational and other social needs seem an intrusion into the private accumulation of goods, and he called for a reassessment of society's goals. In the criticisms he raised, Galbraith anticipated the principal issues of the 1960's and 1970's, for it was above all the implications and assumptions of affluence that were to occupy the national spotlight in the succeeding years.

THE KNOWLEDGE AND CULTURE EXPLOSION: 1960's-1970's

A critical mass. The 1960's were something different. A decade that began with the Twist and "The New Frontier" in America ended with men on the moon and riots in the streets. In the process many governments, values, and whole cultures in various parts of the world were thrown into turmoil; none seemed to escape completely unscathed. Even in Africa, Kenya's university students in Nairobi rebelled against their "establishment." It was as if all the fissionable elements of twentieth-century society had reached critical mass and exploded, bombarding the world with unexpected forces and mutant ideas. And in 1970 there seemed to be no letup in the storm.

The sixties seemed to be dominated by the young—and their cultural and spiritual "mentors," such as the philosopher Herbert Marcuse, the psychoanalyst Erich Fromm, and the communications specialist Marshall McLuhan. Fashion, politics, and art felt the impact of the postwar baby boom. The excesses of the young horrified many of their elders. Not unexpectedly, some have laid the blame at the door of Dr. Spock's permissive child-care program and the indulgences of a generation too intimidated by the hardships of depression and war to assert proper parental authority. But the real causes undoubtedly go much deeper than a child-care manual or a different set of parental attitudes. The world in which we live today has altered markedly from the way it used to be, in terms not of age-old drives and aspirations but of the environment which man confronts and shapes in pursuit of his goals.

The communications revolution. A transformation in communications has provided a new perspective of the world. Air travel and the automobile have given great masses of people unprecedented mobility. Whole nations have become economically interdependent as a result of technological advances and the multinational corporations. In such a world the values that were sustained by parochial uniqueness are rapidly disintegrating. Little wonder that children raised from birth in this new world often surprise their parents.

Marshall McLuhan, the much publicized Canadian prophet of the communications revolution, argues that there is an inherent relationship between technology and the way in which man perceives the world. Consequently the nature of any medium through which he is made aware of his environment becomes more important in determining the nature of that awareness than the content of the medium—hence the catchphrase "The medium is the message." According to McLuhan, the communications revolution occurring today signals a profound change in man's relation to his environment. The dominant western cultures which rose to prominence during the Renaissance, and which stressed specialized roles and the visual bias inherent in the printed word, are giving way to a world-wide "tribal echo chamber" that stresses empathy with the electronic environment and the interdependence of peoples. The transition from one type of culture to another is a time of great upheaval and pain as men strive desperately after roles that will enable them to regain a sense of identity. Whatever may be the merits of McLuhan's thesis

—and they are hotly debated—his is an example of the self-analysis of an era that has been undergoing profound changes and trying to make sense of them.

"After affluence, what?" Economic security and the prolongation of the individual's education have enabled him as seldom before to examine himself and his society. In so doing, a substantial number among the young have accused modern industrial society of being deficient on two major counts. First, it has failed to distribute the economic product equitably among all sectors of the population. Second, it has failed to improve significantly the quality of life even in the midst of material abundance. Societal values which measure success in terms of material achievement no longer seem to provide meaningful direction for the life of the individual, and he feels alienated from the consumer society.

Yet these criticisms of a "consumer society" are in turn open to counterattack. It is scarcely logical to decry the materialistic values of an automobile culture while at the same time owning a new sports model provided by one's "square" father. Moreover, for most of the world's masses, better housing, roads, transportation, and the much decried "gadgets" which lighten housekeeping chores would provide a welcome substitute for the traditional poverty and drudgery prevalent in technologically retarded societies.

Whatever the verdict, it would appear that the traditional work ethic is losing much of its moral imperative in societies like America which are being forced increasingly to concern themselves with leisure in its broadest sense, as the pursuit of quality replaces the pursuit of quantity. A corollary is the refusal of many to accept a life of postponed gratification in which the realization of dreams is subordinated to the necessity of functioning as a productive unit of the economy. In the lyrics of Bob Dylan:

Ah, get born, keep warm
Shorts pants, romance, learn to dance
Get dressed, get blessed
Try to be a success
Please her, please him, buy gifts
Don't steal, don't lift

Twenty years of schoolin'
And they put you on the day shift.*

The counterculture. Instead, there is developing what has been called a "counterculture." The individual is urged to develop his unique potential through an increased awareness of experiences afforded by the present. Imagination, spontaneity, and a heightened sense of feeling are stressed. Above all, the counterculture appeals for freer, more sensitive human relationships to replace a social structure which many think has alienated man both from his fellow man and from the world he inhabits.

The counterculture calls for a "new morality" whose fundamental tenets reject the concept of original sin. Instead, it sees human nature as basically good but thwarted by oppressive institutions. In its emphasis on liberating the human spirit, it recalls in different degrees both Rousseau's "noble savage" and nineteenth-century Marxism, as well as the "life, liberty, and pursuit of happiness" of the Declaration of Independence. There is thus a strong tendency to reject authority and what is regarded as institutional manipulation. This rejection is accompanied by an insistence to follow personal modes of conduct, as expressed in the cliché "Do your own thing."

The counterculture has been exemplified in its most extreme forms by the "hippies" and "yippies." Both groups have rejected traditional values and a whole way of life formerly unquestioned in its assumptions and have in turn aroused animosities, extending from billboards that urge "Beautify America—Get a Haircut" to the type of overt hostility depicted in the movie *Easy Rider.* In general, hippies tend to be cultural rather than political revolutionaries. For their part, the yippies (supposedly members of the Youth International Party) who appeared at the 1968 Democratic party convention in Chicago represent a movement toward mass action and the confrontation politics of the New Left.

Countering the counterculture. Critics of the counterculture have disputed the concept of a generation gap. Recent studies show that the popular notion of a massive struggle

between the forces of parental authority and youthful rebellion has been exaggerated. Some three fourths of the young vote for the same party as their parents; hence political cleavages also split the younger generation itself. Research indicates that attitudes toward sexual conduct have been liberalized, yet only gradually—a trend which probably began in the 1920's. In regard to taking drugs, on the other hand, more of a gap exists, especially in the use of marijuana.

The counterculturalists have been accused of psychological and intellectual deficiencies. It has been suggested that because the postwar environment in which they were raised tended to be bland, uniform, and monotonous "like a modern housing development," they were conditioned to think in broad generalizations and to be preoccupied with collectivities and abstractions—rather than getting down to the specifics of surviving as individuals, in contrast to their parents who had personally to overcome the crises of the depression and World War ii. Confrontation against the "system" with its large, impersonal government and corporate structures provides a substitute that enables these dissidents to release their frustrations and to mount their own crusade against new villains.

Finally, critics charge that the emphasis which the activists place upon mass action runs counter to the achievement of their professed humanistic goals. They have been accused of displaying the very technocratic philosophy which they claim to oppose. And in continually talking of such collectivities as "establishment" and "power structures," they may be displaying an inability to think of the realities that comprise today's complex institutions.

The Movement. The Civil Rights Acts of the sixties represented a victory for the nonviolent civil rights movement under Martin Luther King's leadership and for the liberal forces which had responded to it. At the same time, American society witnessed the rise to prominence of the radical

*"Subterranean Homesick Blues" by Bob Dylan. © 1965 by M. Witmark & Sons. Used by permission of Warner Bros. Music. All rights reserved.

In the sixties massive student demonstrations became a world-wide phenomenon. A protest in May 1968 by French students against university living conditions developed into full-scale rebellion when they joined the workers in expressing their dissatisfaction with de Gaulle's domestic policies.

student politics which had been nurtured by the civil rights movement—and also of the more traditional forces of conservatism which had always represented a substantial segment of the nation. In short, the stage was being set for what has been described as "politics of confrontation."

In the United States the sense of social outrage that had affected so many during the civil rights movement became focused on problems of poverty and other ills. In eastern Europe there was a growing revolt against the stifling bureaucracies which had subverted the promise of Marxist revolution. Throughout the industrialized world a generation coming to maturity was taking seriously the old ideals on which their nations had been founded.

From Tokyo to Chicago, university students challenged the right to rule of those in power. Demonstrations sometimes met with violent reaction from authorities, with each side accusing the other of provoking the confrontation. The colonial status of

much of eastern Europe was confirmed when a widespread reform movement in Czechoslovakia was crushed by the Russian-led invasion of August 1968. Although there was no international conspiracy of radicals, the world-wide communications network which had permitted youth to develop a supranational world outlook encouraged a feedback of ideas. Thus an uprising at Columbia University in April 1968 could be followed the next month by a worker-student rebellion in Paris which almost toppled the French government, both revolts sparked by local issues but involving certain shared assumptions about the nature of the political order.

The very nature of New Left radicalism makes it hard to define with accuracy. In its passion for "participatory democracy," it is marked by factionalism and lack of any stable organizational structure on a large scale. Socialism, pacifism, and anarchism exist together in varying degrees. The heterogeneous conglomeration of groups and

During a decade of ferment various groups in the United States challenged the traditional view of their place in society, demanding an end to injustices and the right to take part in decisions affecting their lives. Encouraged by the gains of the black civil rights movement, American women, Indians, and Chicanos called not only for legal rights but for the breakdown of social and cultural barriers to equality. If their protests and demonstrations were not always successful in effecting change, they at least provided a means for communicating their views to the public.

individuals which propounds these philosophies is known collectively as "The Movement"—a term which aptly suggests the amorphous quality of the new radicalism. With its emphasis on decentralization, humanism, and cultural diversity, it differs from the more purely economic bias of the traditional Left. Today's radicals tend to feel that an individual can play a part in changing the world he lives in and therefore must assume the responsibility of striving to see his ideals realized. For many, participation in The Movement provides a sense of identity and direction that they fail to find in the "straight" world.

Liberals versus radicals. With the great expansion of higher education and with so many of those seeking change attending universities, it was inevitable that college campuses should become arenas of confrontation between liberals and radicals. Liberals and university administrators have accused the New Left of using fascist tactics in disrupting the traditional democratic procedures of free speech and compromise. At the same time, radicals have accused liberals of fascism in maintaining authoritarian and oppressive institutions. These charges and countercharges stem from fundamentally different assumptions about the nature of political institutions in the so-called "democracies."

Liberals believe that the institutions which order the political processes of these nations are in fact democratic—responsive to public demand—and can act as vehicles for effecting social changes desired by the public. From this it follows that those who refuse to be bound by the established political processes endanger the rights of all citizens and threaten to replace them with anarchy or totalitarianism. The radicals, on the other hand, through an analysis of society which ironically is claimed to be basically Marxist, have come to the conclusion that present institutions are inherently authoritarian and deny the opportunity for fundamental social change. They argue that in order to establish a truly democratic society in which the hierarchical nature of human relations is abolished, one cannot be bound by procedures which permit only

a semblance of change while in reality perpetuating the status quo.

Beyond the legal. A growing number of people are questioning traditional assumptions about man and his institutions. Social scientists today are less interested than heretofore in describing the formal structures by which societies regulate themselves and more interested in exploring the behavior patterns that explain man's interaction with his fellow man and physical environment.

Dissatisfaction with older viewpoints is a recurring theme in history, but today it is spurred by the communications revolution that spotlights and broadcasts overt acts of social injustice and by a technology that has the capability to end poverty. Consequently, in the United States blacks have become more militant in their demands for an attack on the root causes of injustice. Nor are they alone in demanding change. A growing number of women are protesting that the acquisition of the ballot has not ended discrimination in job opportunities and salary scales. The necessity of distinct male and female roles in a division of labor based on physical characteristics is breaking down because of a technology that increasingly enables brain to replace brawn. Such a development leads inevitably to the attempt to redefine the roles of the sexes based on an understanding of how much of an individual's makeup is biologically determined and how much is culturally conditioned. The very name of the Women's Liberation Movement, for example, suggests the abandonment of a purely legalistic analysis of social relations.

A new concept of art. Each age develops its own esthetic philosophy and relevant art forms. Today's world is marked by a breakdown of the traditional barrier separating "formal" and "popular" art. As we increasingly perceive our lives as part of an all-enveloping social and ecological system, we come to see the art through which we express our inner selves as inseparable from our environment. The elements of our technology are woven into our art forms, from pop art to electronic music. Total environment experiments have aimed at immersing

their audiences in the media of their milieu and obliterating the distinction between spectator and performer.

For the theater it has been a time for experimenting with new ideas and techniques —including theaters-in-the-round and the emergence of street companies, bringing the theater to the people and involving them in dialogues about the issues of the day. Writers like Norman Mailer and Tom Wolfe have spearheaded the New Journalism, a type of reporting in which the author dispenses with any attempt to remain an aloof observer and instead plunges in to convey the color and emotional atmosphere of the event he is recording. "Involvement" is the key word.

The desire to experience and comprehend all facets of our civilization has spurred new interest in all the tools which mankind employs in coming to terms with nature. The boundaries of art expand accordingly. Pop artists like Andy Warhol help give us a new awareness of everyday objects and the media which permeate our lives (see illustration, p. 814). Understandably, both academics and laymen are fascinated by the

"Involvement" was the key word in the art world of the sixties as the traditional barriers between audiences and art forms came tumbling down. Sculpture became something for a person to touch, sit on, walk through, and lose himself in for a while. New art forms were developed, such as multimedia light shows (right); employing sophisticated electrical equipment, sound systems, and a wide range of materials, they sometimes totally engulfed the observer and could only function with his help. In the theater, whether on the stage or in the street, the audience was often asked to join in the performance. Designed to instruct or fire up the audience, street companies performed for free in the neighborhoods, trying to involve the viewers in the issues of the day. The Bread and Puppet Theatre in New York City is shown above, presenting an antiwar protest.

implications of television, movies, and comic books.

Rock: a contemporary folk art. "Forms and rhythms in music are never changed without producing changes in the most important political forms and ways. . . . The new style quietly insinuates itself into manners and customs and from there it . . . goes on to attack laws and constitutions, displaying the utmost impudence, until it ends by overthrowing everything, both in public and in private."[5] Thus Plato recognized the relation between music and society. No one would suggest that rock music is the root cause of changes taking place in all walks of life. But as a major force in the matrix of the counterculture, rock both reflects the modern world and acts as a pervasive medium through which youth perceives and interprets that world.

The folk music revival of the early sixties was inextricably tied to the civil rights movement. Pete Seeger, Joan Baez, and others appeared regularly at civil rights rallies, none of which was complete without its quota of inspirational songs. In partic-

Pop art takes its subject matter from the everyday world, particularly the blatant commercialized environment surrounding modern urban man—billboards, comic strips, supermarket items, contemporary popular idols. "Elvis" by Andy Warhol is of course Elvis Presley, the rock and roll hero of the fifties.

ular, Bob Dylan brought a new freedom to lyrics, whether his songs dealt with social problems or with personal visions. More than anyone else, he is credited with making the influence of poetry felt in modern popular song.

The Beatles and other British groups led the rock and roll resurgence. The dynamic mixture of rhythm and blues appealed strongly to a postwar generation of British youth frustrated by social stratification. Quickly the "Mersey beat" struck an internationally responsive chord in young people discovering the possibilities open to their generation and restless to initiate change. Rock is a genuinely popular art in the sense that it is music by and for the people, stressing both audience involvement and

encouraging free-form dancing that reflects the individuality and participation idealized by the counterculture. It is also eclectic, assimilating and transmuting elements of other fields of popular and "serious" music, from country-and-western and jazz to baroque and Indian classical, and even to opera. That rock acts as a focus for a sense of community was illustrated in the pop festivals which became a marked phenomenon in 1969.

New identities in the Third World. The turmoil and change accompanying the search for new directions and identities has not been confined to the industrially advanced societies. This search has become a crucial issue in the division between the developed and underdeveloped worlds. Industrially advanced societies, including the Soviet Union, see themselves as models for emulation by the emergent nations. But among the latter, efforts are being made to find or define unique national and social identities that grow out of each society's own cultural traditions. "One of the most significant features of the contemporary age is the stimulus which the revolutions of the twentieth century, liberating them from their bonds to the past, to sterile forms and traditional themes, have given to the artistic and cultural life of other continents."[6]

In much of the Third World this awakening process has been relatively recent, being connected with political emancipation since World War II. But the process began much earlier in countries such as China and India. In the former, scholars like Chen Tu-hsiu and Hu Shih broke with classical traditions, substituting vernacular for literary Chinese in their own writings, whose contents stressed relevance and realism in contrast to the stereotyped and stilted subject matter of traditionalism. Vernacular literature spread rapidly during the interwar years and acquired a strongly social character.

These developments have been augmented in turn by Mao Tse-tung during the last two decades. According to Chinese communism, man makes the world in which he lives; therefore the world is essentially the product of man's consciousness. Since the world can be changed, man's new consciousness must be forged in the revolutionary struggle. Literature and the other arts are consequently regarded as vehicles of revolutionary change. In the sixties Mao initiated the "Cultural Revolution" in order to fortify Chinese communism against any lessening of ardor and enrolled the young Chinese in his campaign to purge their society of all "revisionist" tendencies. In this way Mao hoped to radicalize a new generation and so preserve his own version of true communism.

Perhaps the most famous Indian writer of this century has been Rabindranath Tagore (1846-1941), poet, author, painter, and dramatist. Steeped in India's ancient literary and philosophical traditions, Tagore described the *Vedas* as "the poetic testament of a people's collective reaction to the wonder and awe of existence." In his own works he sought in turn to interpret afresh the teachings of the *Vedas* and *Upanishads*, employing both English and Bengali as literary media, and to reawaken in his fellow countrymen a new understanding and appreciation of their cultural heritage. Though primarily a nationalist leader and politician, Jawaharlal Nehru also encouraged the Indian cultural revival by his own rediscovery of the subcontinent's variegated past.

Developments in Latin America. During the interwar years Spanish American literature became progressively concerned with indigenous themes and problems: the environmental challenge and the social dilemmas confronting the Indian and Negro uprooted from their indigenous culture patterns and seemingly condemned to alien subordination in a white man's world and value system. Since World War II this search for new cultural roots and an identity that differs from both Spanish and North American culture has accelerated. Thus we find the growth of a Negro style of art in Brazil, which has a large African population, as well as the emergence of *Indianismo* with its rediscovery of pre-Columbian America. The novels of Miguel Angel Asturias, the Guatemalan winner of the Nobel prize for literature, and the famous National Museum of

Rock festivals, like the one at Woodstock in the summer of 1969, are an intrinsic part of what has come to be known as the rock culture. Replete with popular recording artists and elaborate sound equipment, they have provided a convenient meeting ground for young people, giving them a sense of community.

Over the past twenty years the cinema has been employed by many Third World nations in an effort to bring attention to their cultural origins. One such film is Satyajit Ray's *Apu* trilogy (1956-1959). A comprehensive study of a young man's coming of age in an underdeveloped country, it gained world-wide notice for India's film industry when the first part took top honors at the 1956 Cannes Film Festival.

Anthropology in Mexico City are monuments to this search, as are the vivid frescoes of a brilliant coterie of Mexican painters, including José Clemente Orozco and Diego Rivera (see illustration, p. 611).

African "black culture." The rediscovery and reassertion of African values are epitomized in the term *Négritude* (see p. 359). It constitutes a rejection of western history and cultural standards and seeks to describe a uniquely African personality and culture on which new African societies can develop. The poetry of this cultural revolution was largely stimulated by two West Indians, Léon Damas and Aimé Césaire, and has perhaps reached its richest expression in the verse of the African Leopold Senghor. This mixture of rejected western technological standards and rediscovered African values is found in Césaire's lines:

Listen to the white world
how it resents its great efforts
how their protest is broken under the rigid stars
how their steel blue is paralysed in the mystery
    of the flesh.

Listen how their defeats sound from their victories.
Listen to the lamentable stumbling in the great alibis.
Mercy! mercy for our omniscient naïve conquerors.
Hurrah for those who never invented anything
hurrah for those who never explored anything
hurrah for those who never conquered anything
hurrah for joy
hurrah for love
hurrah for the pain of incarnate tears.[7]

As a part of this search for a sense of identity and viable culture, the African novel discloses an emphasis upon the following themes: reactions to the initial stages of colonization (such as Chinua Achebe's *Things Fall Apart* and *Arrow of God*); education and, in particular, the difficulties of adjusting to western education; the movement of Africans from rural areas to the cities; problems of nation-building both before and after independence (such as Peter Abrahams' *A Wreath for Udomo* or Achebe's *A Man of the People*); and problems of a more universal nature, including those of personality and psychology (examined in Ezekiel Mphahlele's *The Wanderers*).

Of course it can be argued—even as the critics of the western counterculture contend—that the poets, novelists, and painters of the Third World are only a small, though highly articulate, minority and cannot claim to represent entire populations. This is obviously true, but the writers and artists rejoin that they seek both to rediscover long-buried indigenous values and to interpret the contemporary scene in order to give their people at once a sense of new identity and a direction for future social development.

In short, an intellectual and artistic ferment is occurring everywhere. According to the English historian, Geoffrey Barraclough, "the literary and artistic evidence is unequivocal. The European age—the age which extended from 1498 to 1947—is over, and with it the predominance of the old European scale of values. Literature, like politics, has broken through its European bonds, and the civilization of the future . . . is taking shape as a world civilization in which all the continents will play their part."[8]

The new romanticism. Every age has had its dreamers as well as its "realists." Just as the elements of our environment are assimilated to the uses of art, so our inner visions are projected onto our environment. The last few years have seen the growth of a distinctly romantic conception of life that is world-wide in its sweep. We have just noted how this romantic perception of their social milieu has gripped the "dreamers" of the Third World—in terms of their national struggles, their rediscovery of the past, and the aspirations which they hold for their people. Among the artists and youth of western societies, in turn, passion, involvement, and idealism have replaced the cool and cynical detachment so typical of the immediate postwar years. In the midst of a society built by the rationale of science and dominated by "techno-

crats," the young once more see a universe filled with mystery and wonder.

Their behavior has assumed many forms. Some have plunged into astrology and the occult, while the young political radicals have been fascinated by revolutionary guerrilla leaders like Che Guevara and Ho Chih Minh. Psychedelic art abounds. In everything the imagination is exalted. The prevalent use of drugs reflects a wish not only to escape "reality" but also to find new ways of viewing the world and for experiences that lie beyond the boundaries of the ordinary and the rational.

The emphasis on experience and feeling today is undoubtedly accentuated by the threat of nuclear annihilation which has hung over the world since the end of World War II. The realization that the human race may be wiped out at any time has undermined the traditional sense of biological and cultural continuity in history and inten-

In their search for a national identity many emerging countries are rediscovering their rich and distinctive cultural heritage. Mexico City's National Museum of Anthropology not only expresses Mexican architectural history in modern materials and methods but is a monument linking the extinct indigenous civilizations with the people today.

sified anxiety about life and death. In seeking to restore to their lives a sense of continuity, many have turned to the religious philosophies of the East. Like his nineteenth-century predecessor, the modern-day romantic sees himself as part of an infinite whole.

The importance of self-determination is stressed, whether for individuals or nations. "All power to the people" is the cry of the militants and radicals. Cultural and ethnic groups all over the world demand the right to determine their own futures. The romantic seeks the independence which is a necessary precondition for a planetary interdependence that combines unity with diversity. In his life style he seeks to join inner fantasy and outer appearance into a new reality which transcends mere affectation.

Contemporary ferment and the historian. We began this chapter by suggesting the relevance of the synchrotron as a symbol for our century because of the central role played by science and technology in altering the physical environment and the unprecedented manner in which the processes of change have accelerated. Yet we must keep in mind that the phenomenal world is always undergoing change, and the historian can point to numerous seismic eras of flux and uncertainty in the past. In our own time of upheaval it is salutary—even reassuring—to maintain this historical perspective.

When change occurs gradually, so that new concepts, inventions, or values modify rather than destroy existing social institutions, it can be described as "evolutionary" in character. When, on the other hand, change occurs so rapidly or radically that the conceptual or institutional framework is destroyed, the historian may describe that phenomenon as "revolutionary." In the text we have examined a number of "revolutions," such as the Neolithic, Urban, Glorious, American, French, Russian, and Industrial. Whether these "revolutions" have been "good" or "bad" involves a value judgment: the first term is applied by their beneficiaries, the second by those who lost out in terms of ideology, fortune, or freedom. Therefore, if in fact we live in "revolutionary" times today, we cannot predict at this

juncture—if indeed ever—whether the consequences will prove simply good or bad. As in most human affairs, the results may well turn out to be a mixed bag.

Instead, our interest assumes a different viewpoint. It does not call for value judgments but rather for perspective. We included in our above list of revolutions the "Industrial." Actually, economic historians disagree among themselves whether any such upheaval occurred to overturn the existing economic and social order and thereby create "overnight" a modern urban-industrial Britain. (See p. 837 for the Historical Critique on this subject.) There is little doubt that the massive use of steam and iron supplanted existing production techniques and created a large-scale factory system. Yet a machine technology and incipient factory system had emerged as far back as the Middle Ages, while inventions in the past hundred years have created what is sometimes termed the "Second Industrial Revolution." In other words, we are suggesting that what may appear to be "sudden" and "revolutionary" in a brief time span becomes part of a larger, ongoing evolutionary process when viewed from a broader historical perspective. For example, when the civil rights legislation enacted in the United States during the past two decades is viewed from a limited perspective, it acquires a dimension of suddenness and innovation which can be described as "revolutionary." But when we consider these reforms within a historical continuum some rather "evolutionary" trends become evident: the reforms took place within an institutional structure that was sufficiently malleable to adjust to them; overall societal continuity was not only left intact but undoubtedly strengthened; and these changes represented an implementation, however belatedly, of the philosophical premises upon which American society had been founded.

Thus, while youth has always called for immediate, i.e., revolutionary, social reforms to end existing abuses, societal transformations are likely to be most enduring when they involve a synthesis of the new with the old. This calls not only for the abandonment of the obsolescent and spurious but for the retention of what is still relevant and worthwhile. To effect such syntheses has always been the historical challenge and creative opportunity for each succeeding generation. Hence the significance of the French proverb: *plus ça change, plus c'est la même chose* (the more things change, the more they remain the same). The cultural function of the historian in a rapidly changing world is discussed in the final Historical Critique, p. 843.

SUMMARY

The twentieth century has been marked by spectacular upheavals—on the battlefield, in the physics laboratory, in the painter's studio, and on our city streets. Traditional institutions and values have been challenged, so that every facet of the universal culture pattern has felt the impact.

Science and art have been indicators of new directions in society. Thus physics and biology broke with traditional concepts of certainty in favor of new principles of relativity and indeterminacy and replaced an earlier emphasis upon classification with one stressing integration and dynamics, such as are required to cope with the behavior of systems. The conceptual revolution in science was given primary impetus in the first two decades of the century with the announcement of Planck's quantum theory and Einstein's Special and General Theories of Relativity. During the interwar years quantum mechanics continued to make significant advances, while research on the structure and behavior of the atom led to an irreversible stage in planetary development: the advent of the Atomic Age. The second half of the century promises proportionately spectacular results in biology and other life sciences.

Meanwhile, the arts have been no less experimental and revolutionary in turn. The traditional emphasis upon representational forms, depicted from a fixed point of perspective and striving to convey an absolute standard of "beauty," had been challenged both immediately before and after the turn of the century. The Expressionists and Cubists sought with their nonrepresentational forms and abstract patterns to convey new "unfixed" perspectives and values that proved to be logically compatible with the implications of the quantum and relativity theories. With their discovery of so-called primitive art forms in Africa and Asia, painters and sculptors helped liberate western society from its long self-imposed ethnocentric bondage and to universalize esthetic and cultural values. This ecumenical trend continued during the interwar years, as attested by the Bauhaus school of architects, painters, and interior decorators who developed a cosmopolitan style of design. During these years, too, a typically twentieth-century art form came to maturity: photography which, augmented by motion so as to result in the movies, not only caught the actualities and dynamic movement of our times but became part of a communications network that has revolutionized the mass media on a global scale.

The military, economic, and social upheavals of our century could not but affect each new generation—sometimes with traumatic results. Having repulsed the totalitarian challenge in World War II, societies in the West turned to the tasks of reconstructing their war-dislocated economies and of fashioning the "good life" for themselves and their children. As a result, prewar depression and insecurity were replaced by postwar affluence, which was lavished on the next generation, in turn protected by a welfare structure. But affluence and security produced some unexpected by-products. Affluence did not breed contentment; permissiveness and self-reliance did not necessarily lead to maturity and self-discipline. While most offspring accepted the traditional value system and norms of conduct, a substantial and highly articulate minority challenged the basic societal assumptions and life style. Some advocated nonviolent change and championed civil rights causes to help disadvantaged groups to become part of the social mainstream; some called for violent destruction of the "establishment" and all its works; while still others "copped out" to become hippies or experiment in communal living outside organized society. As might be expected, these sociological developments have been accompanied by variegated experiments in the arts as well. Nor have these movements and confrontations affected only western societies; the Communist and Third Worlds are also undergoing profound conceptual dislocations, challenges, and forms of experimentation.

Because of our current "knowledge explosion" and technological capabilities, for the first time in history there is a real prospect that a substantial proportion of mankind can be freed from the need of having to work full-time to obtain the basic necessities of life. As a consequence, leisure is not only a goal but a problem to be progressively reckoned with. If individuals are to find a sense of direction in their lives, they must learn how to deal with their newfound freedom. Abundance in itself does not guarantee a decent quality of life. Our present age is witnessing the erosion of many of the traditional values which gave meaning and direction to the lives of people in other times. In their search for new standards by which to order their lives, those living today will play a large role in shaping the values of the future.

SUGGESTIONS FOR READING

W. W. Wagar, ed., **Science, Faith and Man in the Twentieth Century,*** Torchbooks; C. R. Walker, **Modern Technology and Civilization,*** McGraw-Hill; L. V. Berkner, **The Scientific Age: the Impact of Science on Society,** Yale, 1964. Useful overviews of scientific and intellectual developments since 1914.

For the contributions of some of the outstanding architects, see W. Gropius, **New Architecture and the Bauhaus,*** M.I.T.; and P. Blake's two studies, **Frank Lloyd Wright: Architecture and Space*** and **Mies van der Rohe: Architecture and Structure,*** Penguin. On the experimentation in art see A. Neumeyer, **Search for Meaning in Modern Art,*** Spectrum; Herbert Read, **Philosophy of Modern Art,*** Premier; and B. Rose, **American Art Since 1900,*** Praeger. See also P. Klee, **On Modern Art,*** Heinman; and P. Waldberg, **Surrealism,*** McGraw-Hill. The contributions of one of the century's most influential sculptors, Henry Moore, are found in his **Works,*** Fontana. On photography's rapid advance as an art form, see H. and A. Gernsheim, **Concise History of Photography,*** Grosset and Dunlap.

On the innovations in music see R. H. Myers, **Twentieth Century Music,*** Orion; and H. Hartog, ed., **European Music in the Twentieth Century,*** Pelican. The influence of jazz in the first half of the century is the subject of W. Sargeant, **Jazz: A History,*** McGraw-Hill; while the impact of rock and electronic forms in recent decades is discussed in Nik Cohn, **Rock from the Beginning,** Stein and Day, 1969; and J. Marks, **Rock and Other Four Letter Words: Music of the Electric Generation,*** Bantam.

A. Schlesinger, **Violence: America in the Sixties,*** Signet, analyzes the social upheavals of the last decade. Racial tensions in the United States are examined in G. Osofsky, **The Burden of Race: A Documentary History of Negro-White Relations in America,*** Harper & Row; M. L. King, **Where Do We Go From Here: Chaos or Community?*** Beacon; J. Baldwin, **Nobody Knows My Name,*** Dell; L. E. Lomax, **The Negro Revolt,*** Signet; and R. L. Scott and W. E. Brockreide, eds., **The Rhetoric of Black Power,** Harper & Row. The problems of the "ghetto" in American cities are examined in **Report of the National Advisory Commission on Civil Disorders,*** Bantam; while problems of educational opportunity and discrimination are analyzed in the United States Civil Rights Commission, **Racial Isolation in the Public Schools,** Washington, D.C., 1967. Youth's criticism of contemporary technocratic society is the subject of T. Roszak, **The Making of a Counter Culture,*** Anchor. World-wide campus unrest is assessed in H. Bourges, ed., **The French Student Revolt: The Leaders Speak,** Hill and Wang, 1968; and J. H. Califano, Jr., **The Student Revolution,*** Norton.

The "population explosion" is examined in P. M. Hauser, ed., **The Population Dilemma,*** Spectrum. See also S. Mudd, ed., **The Population and the Use of World Resources,** Humanities, 1964; and W. S. Thompson, **Population and Progress in the Far East,** Univ. of Chicago, 1959. The demographic factor is closely related to the availability and use of natural resources. See H. Boyko, ed., **Science and the Future of Mankind,** Indiana, 1964; and H. H. Landsberg, **Natural Resources for U.S. Growth: A Look Ahead to the Year 2000,*** Johns Hopkins. Our traditional cities are in transition—and trouble. What are the processes responsible, and what should be our goals for change? These are questions asked in L. Mumford, **The City in History,*** Harbinger; J. Gottman, **Megalopolis,*** M.I.T.; E. Saarinen, **The City: Its Growth, Its Decay, Its Future,*** M.I.T.; and F. L. Wright, **The Living City,*** Mentor.

To encourage informed discussion by the American public, President Eisenhower's Commission on National Goals issued a report, **Goals for Americans,** Spectrum, dealing with objectives attainable both at home and abroad. Such goals will have to take account of the impact of technology upon traditional social behavior and values, such as are discussed in J. T. Dunlop, ed., **Automation and Technological Change,*** Spectrum; and N. Wiener, **The Human Use of Human Beings: Cybernetics and Society,*** Discus. Science's impact upon western humanistic values must also be considered thoughtfully, as found in F. W. Matson, **The Broken Image: Man, Science and Society,*** Anchor; M. Polanyi, **Science, Faith and Society,*** Phoenix; and Z. Brzezinski, **Between Two Ages: America's Role in the Technetronic Era,** Viking, 1970.

*Indicates an inexpensive paperbound edition.

Epilogue

The Challenges Ahead

INTRODUCTION. Historians are understandably reluctant about predicting the future because of all the unknown variables involved. For example, a third world war—employing thermonuclear weapons—could conceivably destroy life on this planet. Assuming, however, that mankind can avoid this holocaust, it is possible, on the basis of available data, to make meaningful projections about feasible developments in man's physical and societal environments for the year 2000, and even beyond.

Our attempts to extrapolate from today to tomorrow are based upon a fundamental guideline—man's perennial search for meaning and order in his relationship to the planet and his fellow beings. That relationship is dynamic because his technology continually alters the landscape and man's capacity to control the environment; it is also open-ended because the process evolves from simple to more complex stages of organization and interaction, thereby challenging man at every step with new problems but also holding out the promise of discovering new levels of meaning and order. Our Paleolithic ancestors sought both to discover purpose in their existence and to set their mark upon the firmament. In tomorrow's world we can expect man to continue with unflagging zeal the quest initiated some two million years ago.

Man is not only a tool-maker; he is also a problem-solver (which helps explain why he not only makes tools but also has to solve new problems created by the use of those tools). If the solution of problems provides man with excite-ment and a sense of accomplishment, we need not fear that the decades ahead will find him bored, because they promise to confront him with some of the most massive problems in his varie-gated planetary existence. He will be challenged simultaneously in four interlocking environments: the physical, the political, the social, and the cultural—all of them global in their dimensions.

OUR PLANET

The population explosion. It is the application of technology to physical resources that sustains human life and ultimately sets the limits on the number of people who can be fed. But technology also provides the tools and techniques for lengthening life spans and reducing mortality rates. As a result, high birth rates are no longer closely matched by high death rates as they were until modern times; epidemics are much less frequent in most parts of the world, due largely to public health measures; and physical vitality has been increased by improved nutrition. These changes have brought about what is today familiarly called the "population explosion"— which, unless checked, could conceivably become the most catastrophic problem of the next half century.

In 1000 A.D. the estimated population of the world was 275 million, a figure which had approx-imately doubled by 1650. But whereas it took some 650 years for this increase to occur, the following 300 years brought a sixfold increase to over three billion people in 1962. In those three centuries some 23 billion people had been born—or more than half as many as in the pre-ceding 76 centuries. And the factor of acceleration continues: for example, the estimated increase in the population of Asia during the second half of this century will roughly equal the population of the entire world as of 1958, while Latin America will triple its numbers.

Also, it would appear that the western percent-age of world population probably reached its zenith around 1900 or shortly thereafter. Subse-quently, Asia, Africa, and Latin America have been growing more rapidly than Europe, Russia, and North America. In other words, the regions possessing the most advanced technology and highest living standards are likely to be a progres-sively diminishing portion of the global popu-lation. Since economic production is outstripping biological reproduction in the advanced countries of the West while the reverse situation threatens to occur in the rest of the world during the decades ahead, the resulting demographic-economic disequilibrium is almost certain to generate massive political and social tensions.

The scope and urgency of the questions raised by the population explosion are unprecedented. On the other hand, it is heartening to note that the interacting relationship between population growth, technological change, and the use of resources has at last been recognized as an inter-national challenge by the member states of the United Nations. It remains to be seen what ef-fective concerted action can—or will—be taken.

Natural resources: plenty or penury ahead? Can the planet's natural resources be allocated and developed to meet the growing needs of our accelerating population while still being con-served in amounts adequate for the unborn generations? Or are we exploiting them so quickly and wastefully that the decades ahead will find mankind impoverished? Earlier predictions of the inevitable total depletion of physical resources have proved premature. We have been able to discover new mineral deposits and mine others once considered inaccessible and to pro-cess ores and related sources hitherto discarded as being too low-grade to be economical. Also, synthetic substitutes for such raw materials as rubber have been developed, while in agri-culture, land once considered lost to erosion has in many cases been reclaimed, and new tech-niques in plant breeding have raised crop yields spectacularly.

Yet a fundamental problem confronts us: the planet and its resources are finite, and demands on those resources are multiplying even faster than the population increase. The United States itself has become a resource-deficit country. In March 1970 the Assistant Secretary of the Interior for mineral resources warned that the outlook for the country to obtain the mineral and energy resources required over the next three decades was bleak. At a time when international competition for these resources would increase enormously, the richer domestic deposits had already been skimmed off, and the country's environment had deteriorated so far that the rising costs of preserving it must be added to the costs of resource exploitation.

Faced with these prospects, the Nixon administration undertook to persuade the Canadian government to join in a continental program to exploit and market energy and mineral resources, particularly oil and water, of which Canada is one of the world's major suppliers. Figuring increasingly in this continental approach are the newly discovered oil fields in both Alaska and the Canadian Arctic. In Washington and Wall Street alike, a continental strategy of access to energy and fuel resources appeared to be imperative. In Canadian eyes, however, the problem was much more complex. Obvious short-term financial gains would have to be balanced against a massive depletion of nonrenewable resources on a scale that could endanger not only any remaining Canadian economic autonomy but also all long-term conservation measures to meet Canada's industrial and demographic requirements in the next century.

We have singled out the North American resource situation because it illustrates a contemporary phenomenon. Peoples everywhere are caught up in the "revolution of rising expectations" so that in underdeveloped countries men look forward to owning at least a few modern western appliances. But this psychological phenomenon of our times poses the question: will the earth's resources last long enough to enable the entire world—a world not of 3 billion but say 6 billion people—to approach the living standards of some 200 million Americans? Or will the oil fields of the Near East be depleted and the region revert to desert before the inhabitants can exchange their camels for family automobiles, if not for their ruler's cadillacs?

Our environment—pleasant or polluted? Not only is man the only creature capable of significantly altering the physical environment; he is also unique in his capacity to pollute and destroy it. As a litterbug he throws beer cans into the Grand Canyon while his children festoon the highways with discarded candy wrappers. His coal-fed generating plants fill the skies over metropolitan areas with hundreds of thousands of tons of soot and other impurities every year. His factories discharge a never-ending stream of industrial waste and toxicants into the Ohio and Mississippi and are presently creating patches of "dead water" in Lake Erie and elsewhere. Automobiles are the chief culprits in creating smog in Los Angeles and virtually every other North American city, while offshore oil-drilling and oil-tanker sinkings have been guilty of spillage which has polluted shorelines in California, the Gulf of Mexico, Nova Scotia, England, and France and has destroyed untold numbers of wildlife.

Some ecologists warn that the wastes being released by our technology into the atmosphere in the form of carbon dioxide could raise temperatures to the point where, unless checked, a "hothouse" effect could completely alter the biosphere, that is, the zone in which all organic life exists. Meanwhile, how shall we get rid of millions of

As the pollution of the environment increased alarmingly, the fear that the balance of nature might be overturned became a distinct possibility. Ecology teach-ins were held in universities across the United States, and some students dramatized the need for ending pollution by burying the engine of an automobile, a major pollutant.

tons of garbage which annually pile up in the United States? By burning or burying it, or by dumping it into already polluted lakes and oceans? Most hazardous of all potential dangers to health, how and where shall our nuclear age dispose of radioactive materials without destroying the air, earth, or water resources of this planet?

Americans comprise only 6 percent of the world's population, yet their advanced technology and unparalleled living standards consume at least 35 percent of current exploitation of global resources. It should be cause for sober reflection that they are also responsible for contributing about half of all planetary pollution. In 1970 President Nixon called for spending $10 billion over a five-year period to improve the quality of the national environment. While this initiative was commended, numerous scientists warned that three to five times that amount might have to be spent annually in order to save the environment and restore the quality of life known to earlier generations. Their concern has been reinforced by student demonstrations across the country. Environmental improvement and resource conservation will make heavy demands, calling as they must for a drastic reallocation of political, military, and social priorities, accompanied by large-scale financial expenditures in the civilian sector of the economy.

OUR POLITICAL ENVIRONMENT

War or peace, or war and peace? Men have always sought to control their environment, including their fellow human beings, often by use of physical force. Recourse to violence, whether on American city streets or along disputed frontiers of newly created states in Africa or Asia, is not likely to end in the foreseeable future. But the fundamental nature of conflict has been altered in our century. Twice warfare has escalated from its original locus of conflict to engulf the world, and now several nations are armed with nuclear, and even thermonuclear, weapons, coupled with an intercontinental delivery capability. For the first time in two million years man has acquired the dubious distinction of being able to destroy his own species and perhaps even immolate the planet.

What are the options available in the years ahead? The first accepts the continuation of the most lethal, and expensive, arms race in history —on the "realistic" basis that the dynamics of technological invention require a continuous updating of national armaments because to lag behind could be fatal. This line of reasoning has resulted, in 1970, in the expansion of the new "Safeguard" anti-ballistic-missile system (ABM) —with initial expenditures of many billion dollars—to be deployed against possible Soviet or Chinese penetration of American air space by means of MIRV's (multiple independently targeted reentry vehicles) with thermonuclear warheads. Continuation with this unprecedentedly sophisticated weapons system would of course carry the arms race to a new plateau of potential mass destruction.

Yet this plateau would not necessarily be the final one, according to military forecasts. The 1940's and 1950's possessed what has been described as a Model-T technology, relying upon "primitive" nuclear weapons, the use of airplanes for offense and defense, and some relatively simple ground-to-air and air-to-air missiles. In contrast, the last two decades of our century may possibly witness the mass production and spread of nuclear weapons and intercontinental delivery systems. Some analysts regard as distinct possibilities the invention of various types of death rays, techniques for effective chemical and biological warfare, earth scorchers, climate changers, various forms of psychological or even directly mental warfare, and a capability of developing Doomsday (or near-Doomsday) machines.

Confronted with these grisly prospects resulting from an unchecked arms race, many people have canvassed other options. Some advocate total disarmament. Unfortunately, more than a general consensus to outlaw war is required because the presence of even one dissenter in the international community can abort the entire process. Moreover, total disarmament among nations logically calls for a supranational agency entrusted with the authority and physical power to keep the peace, and states have not yet demonstrated their willingness to accept any such international authority.

A third option advocates a more limited objective, namely, to reduce armaments and prohibit the proliferation of nuclear weapons. In the 1960's the capacity of each superpower to destroy the other had resulted in a "balance of terror." Partial disarmament would at least reverse the continuing trend toward further arms escalation, with all the risks that such a race entails. But to deescalate also requires a rigorous maintenance of balance, since any unilateral act of reduction by one superpower would upset the balance in favor of the other camp. Even partial disarmament, then, calls for some form of international arms inspection scheme, but no acceptable formula has yet been devised.

The United States and the Soviet Union, however, have agreed on the folly of permitting an unchecked proliferation of nuclear-armed states. In 1968 they presented a draft treaty on nonproliferation which the United Nations adopted. While generally hailed as a sign of progress, this treaty has been rejected by Communist China, which contends that it is designed to ensure an atomic monopoly for the treaty's authors. Other nations, including France, have also objected to its provisions. Meanwhile, the United States and the Soviet Union have engaged in bilateral discussions at Helsinki and Vienna on limiting the use of strategic weapons. They understand the awesome destructive potential of their respective arsenals and are perhaps better able than any other state to judge the limits beyond which a conflict must not be allowed to escalate. The "hot line" linking Washington and Moscow is a tangible expression of sophisticated understanding between the superpowers on the war-and-peace equation.

The danger of uncontrollable violence exists rather at the other end of the power spectrum, among newly created states which all too often are both politically unstable and economically unviable yet share a common infection of nationalistic ambitions. Furthermore, a number of these small nations are linked by treaty with one or other of the superpowers so that, as client states, they are in a position to force the superpower into taking action that may go beyond the point which the latter's own interests or global commitments would counsel. This postwar proliferation of newly emergent countries and of client states could present the greatest risk of international tension and conflict in the years ahead.

International peacekeeping. To cope with this area of political instability requires a new technique in conflict-control. This has been developing in the form of international peacekeeping, in which "middle powers"—such as Canada, the Scandinavian countries, Brazil, and India—provide the United Nations with forces to cope with brush-fire conflicts before they get out of hand. United Nations peacekeeping has been able to contain conflicts in Indonesia, Kashmir, the Congo, Gaza, and Cyprus. That many of these crises remain localized rather than being resolved underscores a phenomenon with which we must learn to live in the years ahead: when ideological or national differences are too great to permit the pacific settlement of a dispute, the world community must act to quarantine it—in other words, to ensure its *pacific perpetuation* pending an ultimate resolution. Tomorrow's world is likely to be too complex to exist in terms of either war

or peace; it is more likely to have to cope with war *and* peace together.

The changing international environment. Neither individuals nor nations can insulate themselves from the unremitting play of forces that generate change in the contemporary international environment. Each year forges new links that cut across national boundaries: in trade, economic assistance, highway networks, transmission lines, pipelines, air lines, and lines of tourists waiting to have their passports stamped. Postal services and telecommunication systems transmit millions of messages hourly across national borders, and their volume will increase spectacularly between now and the year 2000.

During the past century there has emerged a transnational network of communications and institutions comprising international congresses and meetings, intergovernmental agencies and nongovernmental organizations. Their numbers and importance will progressively alter basic attitudes. In today's world, for example, a heart specialist leads a dual existence. He is a product and citizen of, say, South Africa or the United States and, at the same time, part of an international professional network whose members are linked by mutual interests. Our campus populations are continuously exposed to information from all over the world, which in turn both augments their knowledge and enables them to make more accurate assessments of cultural and behavioral patterns not found in the United States. One may ask what will be the long-term impact of this transnational communication upon traditional attitudes of loyalty and patriotism? Can the latter remain compartmentalized within politically imposed geographic boundaries?

The United Nations role. How will these changes affect the chief international organization? At the outset it should be pointed out that the United Nations is composed of member governments, each of which possesses sovereign status. Consequently the organization is primarily the agent of its sovereign masters, who have been responsible in the last analysis for the successes and failures of this world body since its inception in 1945.

The organization's future role will depend largely upon the attitude that prevails regarding its character and purpose and the resulting support of peoples and governments. According to the late secretary-general, Dag Hammarskjöld, the member states can choose between two basic concepts. The first regards the United Nations as a static conference machinery for resolving conflicts of interests and accommodating ideologies with a view to peaceful coexistence, and served by a Secretariat which represents in its ranks those same interests and ideologies. The second concept regards the organization rather as a dynamic instrument through which governments should seek both to reconcile differences and to develop forms of executive action in order to further the purposes of the Charter, and served by a truly international Secretariat.

The Soviet Union and other Communist nations have insisted upon the first concept, while western and nonaligned countries look more favorably upon the second. Moscow's attitude has been based upon the Marxist view that the United Nations is a forum of competing ideologies and the Communist members must use their entrenched position (including the Soviet veto power in the Security Council) to prevent the non-Communist majority from giving the organization executive powers capable of taking action in ways deemed inimical to Soviet or Communist interests.

Notwithstanding valuable activities in non-political areas, such as economic development, there was a general consensus that the United Nations on its twenty-fifth anniversary had reached a critical stage. Reflecting on the organization's inability to cope with such ominous problems as the Arab-Israeli confrontation, Secretary-General U Thant declared that the UN "has ten years to become effective or disappear."

OUR SOCIAL ENVIRONMENT

Technology in a space age. We can be certain that technology will continue to alter both our physical environment and many of our social values and goals. Space exploration promises to be among the most spectacular of these environment- and mind-expanding experiences. It is a measure of the accelerating pace of technological change that astronauts Armstrong and Aldrin set foot on the moon only two thirds of a century after the Wright brothers' first twelve-second flight at Kitty Hawk. Yet the exploration of space is more than simply an extension of air flight; it represents a new dimension in man's control of his environment. Physically and intellectually, it has created a new frontier. When the crew of Apollo 8 looked homeward to "that good earth," they saw a blue-green oasis of life in the barren wilderness of space. It has long been a fond hope that this view of the planet would enable mankind to see itself in a truer perspective and speed the end of the rivalries which divide men from one another. Moreover, in the challenge it provides, space

exploration may help provide a meaningful alternative to war, as men pit their courage and energies against the hostile forces that lie beyond the earth's atmosphere. And ultimately, the space age offers the hope of establishing contact with extraterrestrial intelligence elsewhere in the universe, and in all that such contact implies, even though this event may not be realized for centuries, if ever.

Technology's impact on our lives. On earth, meanwhile, technology promises to alter our lives progressively. Tomorrow's world will be much more automated than today's. Its mechanized and computerized economy will require much less physical effort, as well as fewer man-hours on the assembly line. Conversely, however, it will make greater demands upon the technicians employed, since in this complex system a small failure can swiftly mushroom to serious proportions unless the worker takes precise remedial action. Abundance will replace the scarcities which plagued past ages. Automation offers the opportunity to free man from drudgery and, by creating more leisure time, enables him to engage in creative, satisfying activity. In that sense, the new technology can assist people to develop their emotional and intellectual natures and thus come to more meaningful terms with their world. Such, at least, is the apparent promise of technology for the economically advanced countries, if not for the underdeveloped regions with their exploding populations having to compete for available resources and developmental capital.

Is the promise accompanied by a price tag? In the Industrial Revolution the means of production were mechanized, thus encouraging unrestricted production and the development of an economy that encouraged large-scale organization. Capital formation, machines, production schedules, and distribution outlets have called for operations on a scale possible only for huge corporations; and in today's world we now find not only conglomerates that own and operate a variety of enterprises, ranging from, say, making soap to publishing books, but also multinational corporations which operate throughout the western world. Big business is matched in turn by big trade unions, and big government. But in such a world of gigantism, decisions all too often tend to be based on economies of scale rather than on social needs and values.

An economic structure based upon economies of scale can also exert massive pressures in the direction of societal conformity. In a mass society decisions affecting the life of each individual are often made by a small number of public or business administrators. Their choices may be dictated by what they hope to be the greatest amount of good for the greatest number of people, but they feel that their decisions, to be "scientific," first require that John Smith and Mary Jones be "processed" as digits in a computer system. Already each of us has become aware of the extent to which our daily lives are being subjected to the computer, in terms of social security numbers, bank checks, bills, credit cards, and zip codes. Yet what happens to the individual in this complex process of data-processing and decision-making—since presumably they are the ultimate subjects of all this effort? Some economists, including John Galbraith, argue that the citizen, as a consumer, is today treated less as a subject than as the object of big business and big government. Not only do they largely decide the priorities and prices for the citizen-consumer, but they can also employ advertising and make use of the mass media to help create the desired demand.

Tomorrow's urban society. The exploding urban complexes of today will—in their future form—almost certainly dominate the physical environment of twenty-first-century man. Time and space, rather than production, will become the critical economic values in what has been described as a "postindustrial" society. Retaining the sense of spatial freedom which is so important to an individual's mental well-being is already a problem for substantial segments of humanity today, and the problem will assume even greater proportions in an urbanized world community unless effective countermeasures are taken. Today leading architects and urban planners are grappling with this problem of shaping the space man inhabits in order to make his environment livable. There is growing recognition of the need to think in terms of the totality of the environment and the interrelatedness of forms in space. "Today all development moves in the direction of making the aspect of major cities more rural and smaller rural agglomerations more urban. We now see the way before us, though it still has to be implemented: the reconquering of intimate life, the human scale, the planning for growth."[1]

Automation and cybernation can give man a new relationship with his environment. The centralization of the means of production that has hitherto been required by industry may no longer be necessary. It should prove possible to separate man and machine in space, thus alleviating much of the pollution and noise that afflicts the urban dweller today. Advances in electronic communication—such as the three-dimensional television foreshadowed by holography and personal transceivers that provide instantaneous person-to-person contact anywhere on earth —will permit greater physical mobility while at the same time shrinking the world to what Marshall McLuhan has called a "global village."

Unity and diversity. Science in our century has moved steadily in the direction of the integration of concepts and disciplines. In the political world we find a more complicated, and indeed paradoxical, situation. On the one hand, the process of decolonization has resulted in the creation of scores of new nation-states, each jealously maintaining its sovereign rights. At the same time, the technologically advanced countries have been progressively integrating their resources and placing less importance upon traditional political boundaries in order to create new forms of regional defense and economic development. The concept of the nation-state as the most important unit of the international political order no longer seems to satisfy the requirements of the new age. Technological developments and societal complexities are bringing men closer together and altering their consciousness of the world. Evidence of this new consciousness can be seen most clearly in the attitudes of today's youth, who tend to reject the idea of "my country right or wrong" and instead seek to confront the issues which are common to all men.

Barring a nuclear holocaust, the way ahead seems to lie in the direction of some kind of international community. The question then arises: what is to become of the individual in such a world, and what is to become of individual thought and life styles? Even in the small city-states of ancient Greece, men worried about the "tyranny of the majority," the subjugation of the individual to the mass. Are we to abolish war and poverty, only to replace them with mind-numbing uniformity? Will every African village have its piped-in musak, every polar community the same neon-lit supermarkets to be found in Dallas or Bangkok? Will the great masses of mankind, freed at last from backbreaking toil, spend their endless vacations in front of wall-to-wall television screens, popping down pep—or tranquilizing—pills like candy? If we are to avoid an Orwellian world order with its self-perpetuating equilibrium based upon a warfare totalitarianism, can we avoid in turn the pleasant meaninglessness of a *Brave New World*?

It would appear that despite unprecedented affluence, many people today suffer from anxiety and a sense of alienation. Failure to resolve conflict between international value systems (as demonstrated by the continuation of the most costly arms race in history) adds to the individual's inner tensions, as does the agglomeration of impersonal forces over which he feels unable to exercise any real control. Hence we find a paradox of physical security mated to psychological insecurity in those societies with the world's highest standards of living. Moreover, there is little reason to suppose that the high incidence of inner tensions and nervous disorders—accompanied by an increasing reliance upon barbiturates, alcohol, LSD, and "pot"—is a transitory phenomenon. Ours will probably continue to be an age of anxiety for the foreseeable future, for nations and individuals alike.

How efficacious is science? Looking ahead, some thinkers—including scientists themselves—have raised questions regarding the contributions which science and technology can make. Expenditures on national space programs can become so heavy as to delay the solution of domestic problems requiring massive investments. Again, as we saw earlier, medical triumphs have contributed to soaring population growth in underdeveloped countries, but when the economy does not keep pace, the net result can be an actual decline in living standards—paving the way in turn for domestic violence.

Another dilemma is the close relationship between science and war. Only a hair's-breadth divides the constructive from the destructive capacities of science—as the unleashing of atomic energy attests. After World War II physicists progressively came to realize that the optimistic concept of a "value-free" science was no longer valid. No longer is it possible for the scientist to pursue the "truth" in his laboratory unencumbered by the social and moral implications of his work. Henceforth, scientists will have to confront ethical considerations in determining the course of their work in the same way that policy-makers must confront them in determining political, social, and economic change.

OUR CULTURAL ENVIRONMENT

This is the dawning of the Age of Aquarius . . .
Harmony and understanding
Sympathy and trust abounding
No more falsehoods or derisions
Golden living dreams of visions
Mystic crystal revelation
And the mind's true liberation.*

*©1966, 1967, 1968 James Rado, Gerome Ragni, Galt MacDermot, Nat Shapiro, and United Artists Music Co., Inc. All rights administered by United Artists Music Co., Inc., New York, New York 10019. Used by permission.

The debate over progress. These lines from *Hair*, the internationally successful "American Tribal-Love Rock Musical," speak of a belief in the possibility of a more perfect society emerging in the future. Is this optimism justified? Or does it indicate an unwillingness, or inability, to face the hard facts of life? Progress means many things to many people, and one man's crosstown freeway is another man's shattered neighborhood. To some, the Woodstock Music and Art Fair can symbolize everything that is wrong with the postwar generation; to others, the world's best hope for the future.

It is only in relatively recent times that man has become obsessed with the idea of progress. The Industrial Revolution accelerated the pace of change and made economic productivity seem a natural yardstick by which to measure progress. Capitalism's spectacular industrial growth in the nineteenth century contributed to the predominant belief that progress in human affairs was inevitable. And Marxist theory, while forecasting the obsolescence of capitalist society, raised the concept of progress to the status of a historical law in the minds of its followers.

In the twentieth century, as we have seen, war and scientific concepts of relativity and uncertainty (indeterminacy) did much to shatter the idea of inevitable progress, especially in the West. Communist nations have tended to retain the Marxist ideas of evolution and progress in society, ideas which help explain Marxism's appeal among many of the world's destitute and oppressed peoples. As we would expect, the debate over progress has also affected the contemporary cultural environment.

This debate is nowhere better illustrated than in science fiction, a branch of literature that has tended to concern itself with the societal implications of science. H. G. Wells and other western writers have exhibited a marked ambivalence toward the notion that science and the intellect can lead the way to a more civilized existence. The fear that science can, like fire, be a splendid servant but a terrible master, is evidenced in such "anti-utopias" as Orwell's *1984*. In marked contrast, Soviet authors tend to reflect the official view that technological change never poses a threat to man. Consequently they have criticized their western counterparts for preaching "relativism, the helplessness of the mind against the mysterious and unknowable universe, and the illusory nature of social progress."[2]

Changing moral and ethical standards. In the past, when societies had to endure "times that try men's souls," they were sustained by traditional religious, ethical, and moral values. But tomorrow's world will have to evolve new values to give meaning and direction to the challenges posed by science and technology. In 1968, for example, a biological breakthrough provided evidence of man's capability to create in a test tube what has been described as a primitive form of life. What are the implications here—or in transplanting the heart from a dead person to prolong the life of its recipient—for man's relationship to the overarching question of life and death: is he now attempting to play God? The same question applies to such issues as abortion and birth control. If to take human life can be murder, what shall we deem the act that denies life in the first place—as meritorious when viewed in a planetary context with its specter of an uncontrollable population explosion, or as reprehensible when a personal decision? Furthermore, who or what shall decide how much life would be good for the planet, and have we succeeded in resolving the important question of the inherent worth, or sanctity, of the individual?

We do not mean to imply that there are simple, or satisfactory, answers to these questions, only that the present generation is confronted with fundamental moral issues for which there is often no historical precedent. Consequently, the decades ahead will have to search for new answers to new as well as to old questions. For example, our schools and churches have traditionally taught that we must work hard, be thrifty and save, and avoid self-indulgence and idleness. Generations of young Americans have been brought up on Benjamin Franklin's advice and what is sometimes called the "Puritan ethic." But today, to work hard may deprive another American of his job, especially if the Puritan ethic is carried to the point of moonlighting, whereas featherbedding can perhaps enable two families to be supported instead of just one. To be thrifty and save implied that one should pay with cash and not on time. But the North American economy is based upon credit rather than cash, and only installment purchasing enables today's production lines to keep in high gear. Again, while we appreciate products that are solid and durable, those very qualities can act as a brake upon the replenishing process to which the production lines are geared and thereby throw men out of work. Should obsolescence therefore be built into the product, even though it adds seriously to the waste of global natural resources? Perhaps our economic structure must assign a higher moral standard to quantity than to quality, but to what extent should such a priority apply to each of us as individuals? Were the older

values wrong? To what extent will they prove irrelevant in tomorrow's world?

Religious faith in transition. Coming to terms with the new forces that have been unleashed in the contemporary world means seeking new identities—new views of man's relationship to his universe. Today the search for meaning and direction is evident in the changes that are taking place in religious life. On the one hand the Christian churches have been suffering from a general apathy. Many persons, especially among the young, feel that the church has lost its relevance; it seems unable to confront the issues of the times.

And yet there is also occurring a reawakening of religious sensitivity that goes beyond any institutional structure to express itself in a commitment to personal integrity and the quest for greater empathy with all other humans. It is marked by a reverence for life and the joys that may be found therein: "Life is holy—celebrate it!"

Many today find it difficult to accept the idea of a stern God remote from the joys and sorrows of the world or that either Judaism or Christianity has a monopoly on truth or can claim to be the exclusive vehicle for human salvation. In turning to mysticism and eastern religious philosophies, many westerners, especially among the young, are affirming their concept of a God who manifests Himself in all life, while their search for a relevant religious philosophy has encouraged the comparative study of all major religions. Just as the science of ecology has made us conscious as never before of our planetary interdependence, and that as earthlings we must survive or perish together, so an ecumenical spirit permeates the religious sphere.

This ecumenical movement seeks not only to cut across the centuries-old barriers that schismatized the Christian community into rival denominations but also to create a new relationship between Christian institutions and the secular world. More and more clergy are committing themselves to living their beliefs by espousing far-reaching social reform and taking their renewed faith among the people.

A towering figure in the ecumenical movement was Pope John XXIII. During his brief pontificate (1958-1963) he sought to heal ancient divisions within Christendom and to find ethical, moral, and spiritual denominators common to all the world's major religions. And in his mission, John XXIII emphasized the "dignity of the human person" whose "rights and obligations are universal and inviolable so they cannot in any way be surrendered." From such portents, it is possible to infer that the decades ahead will see the world's religions playing a more vital role in daily life, but in forms that may well differ from today's.

Education in tomorrow's world. What should be the role of education in preparing young people to cope with the fast-changing final third of this century? To meet the technological challenge, it will be necessary to update the citizen's understanding of the information explosion and to provide for his periodic retraining, since automation will render numerous traditional occupations obsolete, while calling for the acquisition of new skills, such as in computer programming and cybernetics. Tomorrow's society will be much more learning-oriented, and education will come increasingly to be regarded as a lifelong process of adjustment, self-understanding, and growth.

A further problem arises in determining the appropriate curriculum to meet the changing needs of both society and the individual. The accelerative process quickens the tendency for data to become obsolete. As a result, the accumulation of facts can become self-defeating—unless the educational process can stimulate in the student what has been termed purposeful self-direction. In other words, there must be greater emphasis upon the recognition of problems and relationships arising from the corpus of factual information, a process that activates meaningful problem-solving responses. Consequently both the curriculum and the teaching process must be more strongly oriented toward the student himself as an active participant in the continuous reshaping of our social environment. Here data-retrieval banks and visual aid devices can be of service, by assisting the student to embark upon problems and lines of inquiry of specific concern to his own needs and objectives—with the teacher providing guidance and engaging in what could become a mutually rewarding intellectual dialogue.

Another problem at the center of our contemporary educational system is the lack of integration between our natural and social sciences and between theory and behavior. Today's students attend "multiversities," whose disciplines tend to be highly specialized and compartmentalized, lacking comparable terminologies and employing different methodological techniques. Perhaps this is the inevitable price which we must pay for the bewildering amounts of knowledge obtained in modern times, which in some disciplines doubles every ten to twenty years. To some critics of the contemporary academic environment, however, interdisciplinary activi-

ties disclose that important integrative principles do underly the physical, mathematical, and social sciences and that they should be analyzed and applied. If such an analysis proves valid, we can expect a concerted effort to find and utilize conceptual principles and methods common to all the main branches of human learning.

Toward a new Renaissance? Times of great change are often times of great creativity. Upheavals in the social order, ferment in the arts, new ideas in science—all are bound together. Today is such a time of great change. Perhaps not since the Renaissance has there been such far-reaching change in society, and future centuries may well rank the transitional age in which we live as one of the principal watersheds in human history. Even today we are aware that we live in an exceptional age, and some would argue that what we are witnessing is in fact the beginning of a new Renaissance.

Men have often looked back longingly to an imagined Golden Age, especially in times when the idea of progress lacked credibility. Today, with the limitations of unrestricted technological advance becoming increasingly obvious, many long for a simpler life. If a new Renaissance is to eventuate, it would seem clear that we must strive to recapture the human scale in all things. Otherwise, the alternatives would appear to be ecological destruction, war, and totalitarianism. There must be a new set of priorities on the societal level. In particular, the enormous wealth that nations waste in war preparations must be diverted to alleviating social ills. Only in this way can technology's true promise be realized, and enable us to build a society that combines the gifts of science with a new social sanity. The dangers ahead are many, but with the decline of the old parochialisms and the rigid ideologies which accompanied them, a new wealth of ideas is becoming available with which to build the future.

Fundamental change will only become possible when there is a new scale of values permeating society, so that people refuse to tolerate the brutality and ugliness that has been an inherent part of human activity in past and present ages. In this there may lie an admonition to those in whom recent years have instilled a romantic idealism. A romanticism that looks only to the past must lead inevitably to a blind alley, but one that is intelligently rooted in the possibilities of the future can open the way to a new Renaissance in human creativity. Who knows—we might even succeed in establishing the world's first *humane* civilization.

Historical Critique 1

THE BIRTH OF HISTORY IN THE WEST
by Thomas W. Africa

Thomas W. Africa, currently Professor of History at the University of Southern California, is the author of *Phylarchus and the Spartan Revolution* (1961), *Rome of the Caesars* (1965), and *Science and the State in Greece and Rome* (1968).

Although Herodotus is called the father of history, the label is not accurate even for Greek history. The writing of history seems to have begun in the ancient Near East with official reports to the gods. Kings boasted of military victories and the construction of temples and often inscribed their letters to Heaven in inaccessible places where only the gods would see them. Successful rulers also made public reports of their deeds to awe posterity; but, of course, these brief annals did not explore the problems of causation. Priestly scribes, however, saw men and events in a broader perspective and sought lessons in history. The author of the Sumerian King List claimed that "universal kingship" (control over Mesopotamia) had been "lowered from Heaven" and bestowed in turn on various cities in the primeval past. Nonetheless, in dealing with more recent events "after the flood," the Sumerian historian dispensed with the Mandate of Heaven and attributed shifts in imperial fortune to warfare. In Mesopotamian historiography religious and realistic concepts existed side by side, and the scholars of Babylon carefully recorded the sins (usually impiety) which brought about the fall of great kingdoms. The Hittites, too, were concerned with sin and retribution as causal factors in history, and Hittite kings confessed their own errors in remarkably frank autobiographies. The realism of the Hittites was in sharp contrast to the boastful annals of the Egyptians, who were unable to raise history above the level of propaganda for the reigning dynasty. Yet all Near Eastern peoples agreed that the gods would not tolerate undue wickedness.

The most impressive remains of Near Eastern historiography are the historical books of the Old Testament. Like their neighbors, the Hebrews drew upon legends and sagas for their notions of prehistory and antiquity. However, an anonymous contemporary wrote a vivid account of David's career, filled with admiration for the king but forthrightly depicting his crimes and follies as well. This historical masterpiece (the "Early Source") may be found in parts of the Books of Samuel and Kings. Later Hebrew historians idealized the image of David; but they had little sympathy with most of the kings of Israel and Judah, and the general tone of the Old Testament is hostile to monarchy. The authors of the Book of Kings explained the successes and failures of the Hebrew states as rewards or punishments dealt out by the national god, Yahweh, who made his servants prosper and handed sinners over to their enemies. When the Jews returned to Palestine after the Babylonian Captivity, Jerusalem became a temple state ruled by priests, who assembled the body of literature which is the Old Testament. In their pious hands, even secular history was edited to follow the religious theme of a constantly unfolding covenant between Yahweh and Israel. Accordingly, the post-exilic historians of the Book of Chronicles revised the national past from a theocratic point of view with great emphasis on priests and ritual. Later, the Hellenistic Book of Daniel added a scheme of history which was probably borrowed from Iranian sources. According to Daniel, a series of four great monarchies would be followed by a universal empire, the Messianic kingdom. In every era history was to Hebrew historians a record of Yahweh's acts, usually in the interest of Israel.

In contrast to the Near Eastern traditions, there was no Hellenic point of view on history—only the views of individual Greeks. About 700 B.C. the poet Hesiod saw history as a grim pattern of decline, in which mankind degenerated from a utopian primal age of gold through eras of silver and bronze into the warlike present, an age of iron. At best, Hesiod's notions were poetic insights. Two centuries later Ionian intellectuals replaced imagery with facts and wrote history in prose. Unlike poets who relied on intuition, historians wrote only after investigation (*historia* in Greek), and some, like Hecataeus, were openly skeptical of the legends of the past. Herodotus, too, was a rationalist and enjoyed debunking pious tales, but he also believed that man was morally accountable for his sins and that the gods particularly punished the sin of arrogance. His great history of the Persian invasions of Greece centered on the theme: Pride goes before a fall. Like other Asian Greeks, Herodotus was interested in foreign peoples and wrote sympathetic accounts of their folkways. For the most part, he was broad-minded and freely conceded the merits of Persians, the enemies of Hellas. With his wide interests and general fairness, Herodotus was the first universal historian.

The Athenian historian Thucydides had narrower notions of men and history. He was contemptuous of the past and exaggerated the importance of the war between Athens and Sparta in which he had participated. Exiled from Athens because of his failure as a military commander, Thucydides filled his account of the war with bitter criticism of his political enemies, the democratic leaders of the city. In general, he was a pessimist and believed that most men were motivated by a lust for power. Unlike Herodotus, Thucydides did not view the gods as active agents in history, but he was a fervent moralist and felt that Attic arrogance brought about the war and Athens' ultimate defeat. A keen student of international relations, Thucydides distinguished between the immediate causes of the conflict and the underlying psychological conditions which made men willing to fight. Though scrupulous in collecting and assessing evidence, Thucydides had no qualms about putting appropriate speeches in the mouths of historical figures. This practice set a disastrous precedent for succeeding historians in Greece and Rome, who filled their works with pompous artificial speeches. Both Herodotus and Thucydides display the moralistic tendencies of Greek historiography, and both consciously composed works of literature.

In the fourth century lesser authors followed the examples of the two great historians. Like Thucydides, Xenophon wrote about contemporary events, but Ephorus saw history on a broader scale and wrote a general history of Hellas beginning with the Dorian invasions. Many Greek historians inflated their works with rhetoric, and the exploits of Alexander the Great soon gave such writers an opportunity to describe sensational events. There was also a growing concern over the role of the unpredictable in human affairs, and historians often personified the factor of chance as Fortune. In the Hellenistic Age some historians sought to recapture the vitality of the past by writing in a highly dramatic style, emphasizing emotion and pathos and even inventing episodes to enliven their narratives. Hellenistic historians also loved to moralize, particularly on the whims of Fortune and the corrupting effects of luxury. As a result of these tendencies, history became popular among general readers, but truth was often sacrificed for dramatic effect.

However, one major Greek historian, Polybius (c. 200-117 B.C.), protested against dramatic history in the name of science. He scoffed at sensationalism and demanded that historians be able to validate their accounts of the past. Yet Polybius was equally critical of scholars who never left their libraries. In his view, history should only be written by former politicians and ex-generals, who are familiar with public affairs. The historian should also travel and investigate the scenes where history took place, and he must consult original documents whenever possible. Above all, the historian must be impartial and overcome the biases of his sources and informants. In effect, Polybius expressed the ideal of scientific history which is often associated with the nineteenth century A.D. He was a diligent researcher and composed an impressive history of the Mediterranean world from 220 to 145 B.C. Characteristically, Polybius distinguished between the pretexts over which nations fought and the underlying causes of war (such as national rivalries and resentment over past injuries). However, like his contemporaries, Polybius retained the concept of Fortune as a major factor in history.

On most matters Polybius was more reliable than other Greeks or those Romans who wrote on the same topics, but he failed to attain his own ideal of scientific objectivity. In discussing Hellenic affairs Polybius was blindly prejudiced against opponents of his own city, and in regard to Roman politics he embraced the biases of his friends in the Roman aristocracy. He was also unscientific in employing the concept of historical cycles. Continual linear progress was too optimistic a notion for the pessimistic Greeks, and the spectacle of the rise, decline, and fall of both Persia and Macedon may have suggested the idea of fixed cycles. Some Greeks believed that decay and collapse were implicit in any society, however flourishing it might appear to be. Polybius was the most famous historian to embrace the concept of predictable patterns of growth and decline, but he modified the "laws of history" to account for the Roman experience. Thus Rome conquered the Mediterranean world because of the superiority of its "mixed constitution," and as long as Rome retained this constitutional balance in its political life, the cycle of decay would be arrested. (In reality, the "mixed constitution" was a thin veil for oligarchy, and Polybius was hostile to democracy.) Should the balance ever be upset—that is, if the senatorial nobles lost control and Rome became more democratic—the cycle would turn again, and the Roman state would soon decline and perish. Though he was sure that he was being scientific, Polybius' law of "cyclic arrest" was an expression of his own political conservatism. Nevertheless, Polybius was the greatest Hellenistic historian and a devoted exponent of the ideal of scientific history.

At Rome, the writings of Polybius were highly regarded, for he was an apologist for Roman dominion, but his pleas for science and objectivity had little effect. Among the Romans, history was a political weapon with which to attack enemies while glorifying one's own family and faction. Roman historians were hopelessly partisan and constantly revised the past to fit the preconceptions of their friends in the present. New nobles discovered previously unknown glories for their ancestors, and the constitutional evolution of the republic was freely rewritten to justify the political biases of historians. In addition, Roman writers aped the bad habits of Greek historians, inventing speeches and dramatizing episodes beyond recognition. A typical republican historian was the gloomy Sallust, who moralized about corruption, maligned his opponents, and often lapsed into melodrama. The most famous historian of the republic was Livy, who composed a long but highly dramatic epic history of Rome's divinely ordained and very manifest destiny. As a patriot, Livy defamed Hannibal and the enemies of Rome; as a moralist, he deplored "modern godlessness" and depicted the early republic as a golden age of simple virtue and rustic valor. According to Livy, the empire had brought luxury and laxity, and struggles for power among Roman leaders had led to the greatest of evils, civil war. Happily for Livy, his views of the Roman past coincided with the aims of his patron, the emperor Augustus, who planned to restore patriotism and piety. Propaganda is most effective when the author himself believes it, and Livy's history was a great literary success, still worth reading today.

Under the emperors, many Roman historians were mere apologists for the men in power; others were hostile to the regime but feared to speak openly. In the second century A.D. Tacitus recounted the crimes and follies of the rulers of the first century, but he failed to do justice to their merits. Tacitus had loyally served the despot Domitian, and he later relieved his guilt by portraying all emperors, except Vespasian, as tyrants. Obsessed with abuses of power, Tacitus dis-

torted the image of an entire era with his grim epigrams and sly innuendos. To the last days of the empire, Roman historiography remained warped by political partisanship. Accordingly, even accounts of able emperors were marred by sensational reports of vice and crime, which modern readers should view with suspicion.

Modern readers will search the classical historians in vain for more than passing comments on economic causation in history. Class conflict was a commonplace to them, but their orientation was political, not economic. The ancients were interested in individuals, their interactions in factions and groups, their personal virtues (e.g., courage) and failings (e.g., the lust for power), and the major roles played by great men for good or ill. Except for two centuries at Athens, history was made by the few, not the many, and the history of the Roman republic was essentially that of an oligarchy. Accordingly, history was written by the few for the few, and the illiterate masses could not even read it. Ancient historians made only brief mention of economic factors and sociological changes; instead, they concentrated on the intricacies of politics, the psychology of leaders, and the disturbing element of Fortune.

The distinguishing features of classical historiography, its overemphasis upon politics, personalities, and even melodrama, do not diminish its positive contributions to the discipline of history. The great historians of Greece and Rome—Herodotus, Thucydides, Polybius, Livy, and Tacitus—were men of intelligence and perception who rescued the past from oblivion and tried to enlighten their readers with pungent comments on human nature. Since they felt too strongly about men and events, objectivity was beyond their grasp; but this is a failing not confined to ancient writers.

SUGGESTED READINGS

Penguin Books has published excellent modern translations of Herodotus, Thucydides, Xenophon, Livy, Tacitus, and Plutarch. A. J. Toynbee's *Greek Historical Thought*, Mentor, 1952, is a very useful anthology. The scholarly literature on ancient historiography is vast, but interested students should sample J. L. Myres, *Herodotus: Father of History*, Oxford, 1953; F. E. Adcock, *Thucydides and His History*, Cambridge, 1963; or P. G. Walsh, *Livy: His Historical Aims and Methods*, Cambridge, 1961.

Historical Critique 2

CHINESE AND INDIAN HISTORIOGRAPHY
by James T. C. Liu
and Ainslie T. Embree

James T. C. Liu, educated mainly in pre-World War II China, is Professor of History and Oriental Studies at Princeton University. His works include *Reform in Sung China* (1959), *Ou-yang Hsiu: An Eleventh-century Neo-Confucianist* (1967), and *Change in Sung China, Innovation or Renovation* (1968) which he coedited with Peter J. Golas. Ainslie T. Embree is the author of *Charles Grant and British Rule in India* (1962) and the editor of *The Hindu Tradition* (1966). He has spent ten years teaching in India and is currently Associate Professor of Indian History at Columbia University.

Compared to the European tradition of historical writing, in which there is a considerable time gap from its Greek and Roman origins to the Renaissance, Asian historiography, like Asian civilization as a whole, has had a more continuous development. But Indian and Chinese historical writing, while offering a sharp contrast to the western tradition, also differ markedly from each other. The Chinese produced the most voluminous body of written records among all ancient societies; while India, to all appearances, had no historical chronicles until the Muslim histories in the thirteenth century A.D.

Two major characteristics of Chinese historiography distinguish it clearly from both European and Indian historical writing. The first is an essentially linear concept of time, reflecting the Chinese self-conscious awareness of their homogeneous, long, and continuous civilization. The second is an overriding humanism.

How did the Chinese develop such a strong emphasis on history? The first records were kept by diviners and ritualists in the classic period (the millennium before imperial unification under the Ch'in). When the practice of noting secular matters in these archaic records gradually evolved, Chinese historiography was born. This process of secularization included an urge to establish what may be called in modern terms *group identity*. Aristocratic families, for example, kept genealogical records, and individual feudal states kept political chronicles; both conceived history

to be the record of human rather than divine activity, and both recognized its role in defining and preserving group character.

From these early beginnings, Chinese history became a more and more important part of the culture and philosophy that produced it. The Chinese cultivated this historical-mindedness even more assiduously after political unification. The Han dynasty (206 B.C.-222 A.D.) saw great progress in historical scholarship, chiefly made by Ssu-ma Ch'ien (see Chapter 4). His monumental work, *Shih chi* (sometimes translated as *Historical Memoirs*), covers the entire time span from antiquity to his own era and was for the Chinese their universal history. Integrating the information he gathered from written sources, oral legend, and his own travels, Ssu-ma Ch'ien established the technique of quoting earlier records whenever he considered them reliable and setting different accounts side by side whenever reliability was in doubt. His history presents an unfolding panorama of successive events, forming an unbroken thread linking past and present.

Since Ssu-ma is known as the "Chinese Herodotus," the essential differences between these two great historians are particularly revealing. While Herodotus was more informative on such concrete details as climates, soils, tides, rivers, architecture, and military logistics, Ssu-ma confined much of his attention to the imperial reigns, treating various government functions as separate topics and devoting individual chapters to the biographies of a few important men while grouping a large number of minor characters under various categories—such as imperial favorites, famous outlaws, poets, and many other classifications. For Herodotus, the emphasis was on man reacting to his environment, hopefully in the direction of the individual freedom and local autonomy found, most notably, in Athens. For Ssu-ma, the emphasis was on man's realization of his moral ideals through the improvement of the imperial rule and social well-being. In fact, one may characterize the entire body of Chinese historical writing as Confucian, human-centered, morally oriented, and institutionally weighted. This social concern (the second principal mark of Chinese history as a discipline) is illustrated by the fact that the most decisive role in the early development of history belonged to the rising philosophers. In their hands historical records took on a solemn ethical function: they were held as persuasive precedents in arguments, as a source of moral lessons, and as a standard for pronouncing lasting judgment of "praise and blame" on men. Later these records served as guidebooks for bureaucrats and elite elements in society.

History was further institutionalized during the T'ang period (618-907 A.D.). From this time on historical compilations were no longer left to individuals. Instead, a government agency called the History Office entrusted the writing of history to a corps of scholars, consisting of dozens of editors, and hundreds of copyists and clerks. Remarkably, the Chinese awareness of linear continuity manifested itself in this uninterrupted institution. Successive dynasties regarded it as their duty to produce with considerable fairness the history of preceding dynasties, while in turn leaving the definitive account of their own time to their successors. The scope and detail of these dynastic histories is suggested by the account of the Ming, which was begun in 1679, took fifty-three scholars some forty-six years to complete, and contained one hundred volumes. More than mere chronicles, these official histories contain treatises on law, economics, government administration, anthropological accounts of primitive tribes, and records of astronomical and other scientific phenomena, and each is accompanied by a variety of private works such as annotations, summaries, commentaries, interpretations, and the like. This enormous body of information is unrivaled in any civilization.

Following a few T'ang forerunners, the scholars of the Sung period (960-1279) pushed Chinese historiography to full maturity, developing critical methods, sophisticated techniques in writing, and a great variety of other genres quite apart from the dynastic histories. Unfortunately, the Sung growth in historiography was followed in later centuries by a rather rigid, unimaginative pedantry.

How accurate and objective were the traditional Chinese historians? They often suffered from blind conformity to convention, lack of independent verification, personal partiality, and sometimes outside pressure or fear of retaliation. These shortcomings, however, are much the common lot of historians in any land. On the whole, Chinese historiography had high professional standards and applied them with vigor. Although some modern critics have condemned the technique established by Ssu-ma Ch'ien as a primitive patchwork of paraphrased primary sources, the Chinese historians in their days thought they were reproducing authentic records faithfully. The neglect of ordinary peasant life has also been criticized, but Confucian scholars believed that in the final analysis it was the elite leadership that mattered.

Indian historiography presents a sharp contrast to that of China. Except for the *Rajatarangini* (a poetical chronicle of the history of Kashmir written during the thirteenth-century Muslim invasions) the Indian literary tradition is almost wholly lacking in the kinds of historical works in which Chinese culture is so rich. It is not very fruitful, however, to ask why India failed to produce such historical literature. The only general answer possible is that the needs of Indian civilization did not demand or foster this form of intellectual expression. Nor should the lack of historical narratives be taken as any indication that records were not kept, for like rulers everywhere, Indian kings sought to immortalize their greatness and to provide information for their administrative structures. But the ravages of climate and political change have prevented the preservation of royal archives, and all we have from Indian antiquity are inscriptions in stone and other durable materials. From these it has been possible to work out a rough chronology of Indian history from about 500 B.C. to 1200 A.D., when the Muslim histories begin, but there are many gaps. The normal method of transmitting the tradition was oral, not written; this worked well for the preservation of religious works, but dynastic chronicles were likely to disappear with a dynasty.

It should be emphasized that the intellectual classes in India were the guardians of the past, and in almost all periods the Brahmins were the intellectuals. They were profoundly interested in such questions as man's social role and kingship and the state as institutions; thus the assertion that their metaphysical concerns made them indifferent to the human situation is erroneous. But their concern must be seen in the context of the unquestioned assumptions of Indian society, and these are radically different from those of China or Greece.

Three such assumptions are especially relevant to the understanding of history in traditional Indian society. One is the concept of time, not as linear, but as moving in cycles without beginning or end, and including not just the terrestrial world but the whole cosmic universe of the gods. Within each cycle there is a movement of birth, growth, decay, and dissolution, but the cycles are endlessly renewed. These cycles, or *yugas,* are of varying length, but always, in normal human terms, of immense duration. The shortest one, the Kali-Yuga in which present human history is set, lasts for 432,000 years. Each cycle is characterized by increasing decline in virtue until its dissolution comes at the nadir of degradation, when the process is renewed. There are no unique events, no personalities that alter the process of devouring time; even the incarnations of great gods like Vishnu occur repeatedly. This concept of time, which makes life a process of eternal duration and repetition, has obvious implications for historiography, and the human story is placed in a perspective wholly different from that provided by Chinese or Greek conceptions. (Although some Greeks had a cyclical concept of time, its influence on the writers of history seems to have been minimal.)

Closely connected with the Indian understanding of time was the belief in rebirth, the most pervasive of all Indian ideas. Everything that has sentient life, including the divine order of beings, dies and is born again through *karma*, a working of cosmic law as impartial and as impersonal as the law of gravity. The Indian ideas of time and rebirth place men and gods in a continuum in which, strictly speaking, there is no dividing line between human and divine history.

A third assumption that colors Indian historical thinking is the elusive concept of *dharma*, perhaps best understood as duties and obligations which are imposed by life but which, when consciously accepted, define the good man. Through the working of *karma* men are born into the social order at a particular time and place, but virtue consists in their willingness to preserve this social order. Since society is part of the cosmic process, maintaining the social fabric is the ultimate concern of Indian social and political thought. The institutional expression of this concern is the system of caste and class that looms so large in Indian social history. In theory caste and class are parts of the eternal order, and their preservation represents the attempt to maintain man's harmonious place in the universe. Thus the concern with royal genealogy in Indian literature does not spring from a desire to show an exalted pedigree or links with a former dynasty but rather from a desire to legitimize a ruler, who was frequently either a usurper from a low caste or a foreigner. *Dharma* means, both in fact and theory, that society is stronger than the state. Two of the grand themes of western

history, the conflict between church and state and of the individual against society, are lacking in the Indian tradition. The individual and the state find their meaning in their recognition of the relation of the social order to the cosmos.

Given these assumptions it can be argued that traditional India did not lack a concern with history but that the understanding of what constituted the human story was vastly different from western—and Chinese—perceptions. The needs met in Greece and China by narrative historical works were filled in Indian culture by such literary productions as the *Mahabharata* and the *Puranas*, the class of literature referred to within the tradition as "history."

In summary, it is essential to recognize that the Indian concept of time is cyclical, whereas the Chinese concept is linear. That is, the Indian historian tends to perceive in human events a recurring pattern, whereas the Chinese historian has "straightened out" time to emphasize how one phenomenon *succeeds* another—an attitude that favors both classification and chronology in organizing temporal data. As regards the character and purpose of human society, the Indian saw man and his works integrated in a cosmic process. Consequently, societal relationships were always seen within a universal framework. The Chinese Confucians, however, emphasized the *social* order and correct relationships between the individual and his fellow beings. In effect, the Indian saw no fixed division between human and divine history, while the Confucian preferred to lower his sights and to depict the realization of virtue in human society.

SUGGESTED READINGS

For students interested in Chinese historiography, the following commentaries will be useful: W. G. Beasley and E. G. Pulleyblank, eds., *Historians of China and Japan*, Cambridge Univ. Press, 1961; or C. S. Gardner, *Chinese Traditional Historiography*, Harvard, 1961. Additional analysis of Indian historical writing may be found in C. H. Philips, ed., *Historians of India, Pakistan, and Ceylon*, Oxford, 1961; and a good brief summary is Robert Crane, *The History of India, Its Study and Interpretation*, Washington, D. C.: Service Center for Teachers of History, 1958.

Historical Critique 3

WAS THERE AN "INDUSTRIAL REVOLUTION"?
by Peter d'A. Jones

Peter d'A. Jones is a British-born and trained economic historian whose main interest is the comparative history of modern industrial society. He emigrated to the United States in 1959 and has taught at various American colleges and universities including Tulane, Columbia, and Smith. Dr. Jones is now Professor of History at the University of Illinois at Chicago Circle. Among his many books are *The Consumer Society: A History of American Capitalism* (1965) and *The Christian Socialist Revival, 1877-1914* (1968).

The answers we receive from the study of history depend a great deal on the sort of questions we choose to ask. Economic history, from its earliest emergence as a self-conscious, separate discipline in late nineteenth-century Britain, tended to ask questions which seemed to take for granted that the flow of economic history was uneven, discontinuous, and subject to violent change and cataclysm. Such an attitude may be partly explained by the conditions under which the writers themselves lived—the recurring booms and slumps that plagued Victorian capitalism. But beyond this, economic historians were intellectually weaned on the concept of the "Industrial *Revolution*": the notion that in a relatively short space of time, "suddenly," an economic and social upheaval radically overturned the existing social order, destroyed rural, traditional society with its residual feudalism, and "overnight" created modern urban-industrial Britain. This was said to have taken place, give or take a decade, between about 1760 and about 1830.

The juxtaposition of the words *industry* and *revolution* goes back at least to 1806 and is found first in France, where the political revolution of 1789 was a very recent reality and parallel, and where, in the north, linen making in the home was being displaced by mechanized cotton textile manufacture. Thirty years later the process of industrialization was even more advanced and more socially evident, and the actual phrase *révolution industrielle* was adopted by the economist Blanqui. The idea was picked up rapidly and repeated down the years in the writings of Engels (1845), J. S. Mill (1848), Marx (1867), and Arnold Toynbee (1884).

Transplanted to Britain the phrase seemed felicitous enough. But its widespread adoption did tend to exaggerate the revolutionary and underplay the evolutionary aspects of Britain's economic and social transformation. History, after all, is concerned both with change and with continuity, with "structure" and with "process." The very language of most commentators on the Industrial Revolution precluded adequate consideration of the deeper origins of complex social changes. Popular opinion congealed and became fixed in an essentially pessimistic, romantic mold: for decades thereafter people regarded the Industrial Revolution as nothing less than "a cataclysm followed by a catastrophe" (to borrow Eric Lampard's telling phrase). Whether the pessimists are correct, and the Industrial Revolution was a "catastrophe" or not, is not the main theme of this essay. The social evils of industrial life are adequately described in Chapter 21. But let us ask here, was the Industrial Revolution a "cataclysm," in the sense of a sudden, violent overturning of the economic and social order (whether for good or for evil)? In a word, was it a revolution at all?

Blanqui's *révolution industrielle* was mainly technological. His *Histoire de l'économie politique* (1837) directly identified the revolutionary aspect of the process with the inventions of "two men of genius, Watt and Arkwright." The roots of the simplistic idea that inventions make an economic revolution go deep in time; a clear line is visible from Blanqui's men of genius to the schoolboy essay (real or fictitious) quoted by T. S. Ashton in 1948: "About 1760 a wave of gadgets swept over England." Arnold Toynbee took up the technical invention theme about fifty years after Blanqui; but the weight of Toynbee's interpretation seemed to fall less on technology than on the conditions of economic policy—on the concept of laissez faire. He more than anyone implanted in the minds of generations of later students a horror of "the evils of laissez faire." His famous lectures give us in classic simplicity the traditional picture of the Industrial Revolution: against a broad backdrop of trade expansion and population growth, sudden technical breakthroughs (made in response to the pressure of increasing demand for raw materials and for better transportation methods), produced an agricultural revolution in the countryside and an industrial revolution in the towns in the last decade of the eighteenth century; the factory system sprang to life. Workers were separated from ownership of the tools and means of production. Laissez faire policies quickly destroyed the vestiges of *noblesse oblige*, mutual respect between the social classes, and considerations of public welfare that Britain had inherited from the days of craft guilds and Tudor paternalism. "Free competition" reigned supreme, and the Devil take the hindmost. In three areas—technology, the organization of production, and public policy and morality—the Industrial Revolution is presented by Toynbee as a sharp and rude break with Britain's historic past: a cataclysm.

Historical portraits rarely go unchallenged for very long, though Toynbee's survived longer than most. From the 1920's on, and particularly since World War II, the patient work of research scholars has subtly altered the portrait, dissolved its color highlights, washed out its *chiaroscuro*. The present picture we have of the Industrial Revolution is less dramatic than Toynbee's, and much less romantic. Modern scholars find a deeper continuity in his three areas of sudden change: *technology*—the ingenious mechanical inventions by which industry was transformed are now seen to have histories going way back into antiquity; *organization*—not only were there individual factories long before 1760, but the factory system did not become typical of British industrial structure until long after 1830; *economic policy*—laissez faire did not appear from out of the blue in the late eighteenth century; it was not uniquely English, nor did it mean total government abstinence on the national or local level from economic activities, or total disregard for planning, or for the needs of labor. In brief, the pure, classical economic model of "free enterprise capitalism" has never existed in historical reality. There was no sudden break with the past after 1760, although some acceleration of age-old and well-established historical tendencies cannot be denied.

An interesting argument against the idea that there was a unique industrial breakthrough in the late eighteenth century has been the identification of *earlier* "industrial revolutions"—in the sixteenth century, for instance, or in the thirteenth century. It is not hard to discover such alleged economic revolutions even in the remote past: the late Bronze Age for example. But the student should beware of developing a spurious historical relativism in all this. The "industrial revolution" of the thirteenth century meant principally the introduction of the fulling mill into medieval English cloth manufacture and the subsequent relocation of the industry—a significant change, but perhaps something less than a "revolution."

The difficulty is that the term *Industrial Revolution* is often inadequately defined. If taken to mean the transformation of a single industry, the thirteenth century fits the model. But more usually it implies national, or at least regional, transformations affecting more than one basic industry.

In recent years economic historians have begun to adopt the more precise definitions and terminology of economists, where these are applicable, and as a result it is possible to take the earlier "revolutions" into account in one general statement. If we take *Industrial Revolution* to mean only that particular breakthrough or acceleration of economic change which leads to a condition of self-sustaining growth thereafter, then clearly the earlier revolutions do not fit easily. The revolutions of the thirteenth and the sixteenth centuries can thus be seen as partial or abortive movements, "false starts" in the industrialization process. Only the breakthrough of the late eighteenth century produced continuing economic growth thereafter. According to this view we live in an ongoing and incessant Industrial Revolution which really began in the late eighteenth century.

There were "false starts" not only in earlier time periods but also in other regions: the Netherlands in the seventeenth century for example. It was only in one place, Britain, and in one unique period, the late eighteenth century, that *the* Industrial Revolution, the first true such revolution, made the crucial breakthrough to a regime of continuous economic change. (In the initial stages the revolution was based technologically on the exploitation of coal and iron resources and on steam power. These essential elements the Netherlands lacked.)

Students will recognize in this approach the ideas of the economist W. W. Rostow, who coined the phrase "take-off" to describe the breakthrough. After Britain's initial "take-off" the economic revolution spread eastward over the European continent to Belgium, northern France, and central Europe, in successive stages. Various opinions exist as to the timing and pattern of these stages. The revolution also spread westward by cultural diffusion and migration and gained full strength in New England by the 1840's. The more rapid assimilation of the revolution in some nations than in others (e.g., the United States) was determined to a large degree by differential degrees of receptivity. This "receptivity" is itself a matter of great historical interest and is worthy of close investigation.

Where does this leave us as far as the original cataclysmic views of Arnold Toynbee and his followers are concerned? Clearly Rostow's "take-off" is in some ways close to Toynbee's concept of "Industrial Revolution." Yet the latest approach leads the student into areas of research and contemplation far removed from the simple verities of Toynbee's world. The idea of *receptivity*, for example, takes one deep into the study of comparative cultures and social structures. Here current sociology may prove helpful to the historian as much as economic science. The works of the Toynbee school were relatively insular and English. Moreover, the science of economics has not been standing still since the 1880's, and we now know a good deal more about the technical economics of industrialization.

Modern analysts talk of regional differentials and balances, capital-output ratios in specific economic sectors, social overhead capital, and so on. Beyond economic technicalities, students of "development" (as it is now called) investigate political and administrative determinants of growth. The enforcement of contracts, relative freedom from civil disorder, reliable legal principles consistently applied—all these are basic political preconditions for any "Industrial Revolution" in any nation. A further precondition is what the German sociologist Max Weber called the "institutionalization of rationality"—the embodiment in leading groups or elites of a problem-solving, rationalistic frame of mind, dedicated to the deliberate pursuit of social change. As for the "captain of industry," the entrepreneur (the "robber baron" as he was stigmatized in the United States of the Gilded Age), modern economic historians are less interested in describing swashbuckling, individualistic, heroic figures of capitalist history than in determining the social conditions which make possible the emergence of entrepreneurial groups and attitudes in some societies rather than in others. Students today want to know where the great capitalists and inventors and managers came from, which social strata, which ethnic and religious groups. For instance, do some minority groups, denied normal civil rights, therefore contribute more in the way of leadership in the relatively "open" economic sphere, where civil disabilities are minimal? What is the influence of family structure, religious observation, or educational structure on economic growth and the likelihood of "take-off"?

Not only are such questions very different from those asked by the Toynbee school, who were anxious above all to ascribe blame for the "evils" of industrialism, but they all have a decidedly practical slant. They have clearly been stimulated by the changed conditions of the mid-twentieth century, the breakup of former empires, and the nationalist aspirations of new nations. For a major

difference between the earlier cataclysmic writers on the Industrial Revolution and the protagonists of the "take-off" concept of today is that the former were deeply pessimistic and critical of industrialization, while the latter are optimistic and celebrate industrialization. Indeed, they study the "take-off" of Britain in order to learn how to induce similar "take-offs" in the undeveloped and underdeveloped nations.

But despite the greater sophistication and knowledge of the most recent school of interpretation of the Industrial Revolution, the fact remains that the new economic-sociological approach, with its heavy dramatization of the "take-off" as a very brief time period in which an economy is virtually transformed, is nothing less than a reversal to the original position of Arnold Toynbee in the 1880's. It is the cataclysmic view, restated in the technical language of development economics. Not all economists or historians accept Rostow's analysis; in fact, a controversy still rages over the whole question of "take-off," and not only its timing is at issue but the very definition of the phrase itself—as with the original phrase, *industrial revolution*. The student might well be tempted to murmur at this point, *plus ça change, plus c'est la même chose* (the more things change, the more they remain the same). The criticism would be unfair, however, for historical knowledge and understanding of the whole process of industrialization has advanced quite dramatically in recent years and the writing of economic history improves with each new generation of students.

Was there an Industrial *Revolution?* To this question most scholars today would probably answer a qualified Yes. The controversy goes on however, and the evolutionists have not yet had their last say.

SUGGESTED READINGS

A good, short synthesis is the revised version of H. L. Beales, *The Industrial Revolution,* Cass, 1958. For the "take-off," see W. W. Rostow, *The Stages of Economic Growth,* Cambridge, 1960. Arnold Toynbee's classic lectures are now reprinted in paperback: *The Industrial Revolution,* Beacon, 1956. An excellent short historiographical treatment is Eric Lampard's *Industrial Revolution: Interpretations and Perspectives,* A.H.A. Service Center for Teachers of History, Pubn. No. 4, Washington, D.C., 1957. On the entrepreneurs, see Peter d'A. Jones, ed., *The Robber Barons Revisited,* Heath, 1968.

Historical Critique 4

VARIETIES OF SOCIAL DARWINISM
by Gertrude Himmelfarb

A distinguished scholar of Victorian social and intellectual history, Gertrude Himmelfarb has written several books on this period, including *Lord Acton: A Study in Conscience and Politics* (1952), *Darwin and the Darwinian Revolution* (1959), and *Victorian Minds* (1968). She is currently Professor of History at Brooklyn College of the City University of New York.

"Ideas," a great historian has said, "have a radiation and development, an ancestry and posterity of their own, in which men play the part of godfathers and godmothers more than that of legitimate parents."[1] While few would challenge Darwin's paternity in regard to the theory of natural selection itself, with respect to the variety of theories going by the name of Social Darwinism, one can charge him with no more than godfatherhood. Darwin may be likened to the old friend of the family who had amiably agreed to take part in the baptismal ceremonies and years later was dismayed to find himself responsible for an ill-assorted, erratic, and not particularly congenial set of godchildren. And yet, like the typical godfather, Darwin did have some responsibility, intellectually and spiritually, for the offspring of his friends.

Apart from the various social theories to which Darwin stood in *loco parentis,* there are others commonly ascribed to him which cannot claim even this tenuous relationship. Walter Bagehot's *Physics and Politics,* for example, which professed to be "the application of the principles of 'Natural Selection' and 'Inheritance' to political society," was in fact not only non-Darwinian but anti-Darwinian in its main thesis: that the progress of society takes place when competition and natural selection are suppressed by a single dominant authority.

Similarly, historiographical works frequently pay tribute to Darwin, and works on Darwinism almost invariably include some reference to his supposed influence on the writing of history. Typical is the statement of one historian: "Among the various intellectual and scientific influences which have revolutionized the perspective, orientation, and ideals of dynamic historical writing there is little doubt that the evolutionary hypothesis must be assigned the foremost place."[2] Yet it hardly took Darwinism to impress historians either with the fact or the dynamics of change.

There are, to be sure, social and historical theories that can more legitimately claim descent from Darwin. But first one must pay respect to the only true and lawfully begotten theory of Darwin: the theory conceived in the *Origin of Species* and brought to maturity in the *Descent of Man.* The essential features of that theory were clearly visible at birth, and lest anyone mistake them, Darwin formally incorporated them into the title of his famous book: *The Origin of Species by Means of Natural Selection, or the Preservation of Favored Races in the Struggle for Life.* From one or another part of this multibarreled title may be traced most of the theories seeking legitimacy in the name of Social Darwinism. This process of legitimization may be demonstrated in the case of the most common variety of Social Darwinism: the doctrine of laissez faire.

As an economic theory, laissez faire—the free, unrestrained competition of individuals—was born at least three quarters of a century before the *Origin,* and indeed the *Origin* itself owed its very existence to one of the classics of this doctrine, Malthus' *Essay on Population.* By a curious inversion, however, Darwin was made to legitimize laissez fairism.

The laissez fairists derived their sanction from that part of Darwinism which envisaged the individual members of any given species competing against each other for the available resources—out of which competition the fittest individuals survived, perpetuated their kind, and thus contributed to the betterment and evolution of their species. But there was also going on, according to Darwin, a struggle *among* the species—an *inter*-species competition as well as an *intra*-species competition. And while the first, the intra-species competition, seemed to validate the ideology of laissez faire, the second, the inter-species competition, suggested a very different and, as it sometimes appeared, contrary ideology—the ideology of nationalism, imperialism, and militarism.

Darwin sometimes professed to find this second deduction from his theory as ludicrous as the first. Yet he himself wrote, in a letter shortly before his death: "I could show fight on natural selection having done and doing more for the progress of civilization than you seem inclined to admit. . . . The more civilized so-called Caucasian races have beaten the Turkish hollow in the struggle for existence. Looking to the world at no very distant date, what an endless number of the lower races will have been eliminated by the higher civilized races throughout the world."[3]

One can make out a strong case for Social Darwinism in this sense. Just as the hero, superman, or führer may be assumed to have established his preëminence as a result of the struggle for existence within the state, so the state itself, under his leadership, will engage in a struggle with other states to establish its preëminence in the world.

When Darwin and his followers spoke of the triumph of the "higher civilized races" in this international struggle for existence, they generally identified races with nations. But there were more precise biological racial implications that might be extracted from Darwin's theory. Again Darwin himself may be quoted on both sides of this issue. On the one hand, by denying the separateness of species, by showing how species evolved from each other and ultimately how all derived from a single primordial form, the theory of natural selection implicitly challenged the racial purity that has been an important ingredient in most racist creeds, and affirmed the brotherhood of man that has been the classical refutation of racism. This brotherhood of man was, indeed, the message which many contemporaries extracted from the *Origin*.

Still others, however, managed to reconcile the *Origin* and racism and even use the *Origin* to legitimize racism. For although Darwin did derive all races, like all species, from a single ancestor, he by no means denied the present reality of distinctive races, any more than he denied the present reality of distinctive species. Indeed a primary purpose of the theory of natural selection was precisely to account for the reality of species and races, to show not only how they evolved but also how they became stabilized and fixed in form, sometimes over very long periods of time.

Similarly, advocates of both racial segregation and desegregation could appeal for support to different aspects of Darwinism. The desegregationists could, and did, quote the *Origin* to the effect that crosses between varieties tend to increase the number, size, and vigor of the offspring; while segregationists cited passages demonstrating that in many circumstances such a cross would prove fatal to both varieties.

Even if Darwinism canceled itself out, so to speak, in respect to the reality of races, or the desirability of a mixture of races, it told heavily in favor of a struggle of races and the inevitable and proper domination of the weak by the strong. Karl Pearson, the eugenicist, regarded this racial struggle as a necessary appendage to the imperialist struggle.

Pearson's particular variety of Social Darwinism is especially intriguing, because he took Darwinism to be a legitimization not only of im-

perialism and racism but also of what he thought of as socialism. Pearson, in fact, read in Darwin's theory a refutation of laissez fairism. Since he regarded the inter-species, the international struggle, as paramount, he argued that that struggle could only be effectively fought if the intra-species struggle, the struggle within the nation, was suppressed. Wide social and economic distinctions, he maintained, undermined the sense of a national, common purpose.

Marxian socialism also found an ally in Darwinism. Marx himself was so taken with the *Origin* that he proposed to dedicate *Das Kapital* to Darwin. Darwin politely declined the honor, candidly writing to a German scientist: "What a foolish idea seems to prevail in Germany on the connection between Socialism and Evolution through Natural Selection."[4] But Marx saw nothing foolish in the idea. Indeed he looked upon the *Origin* as a basis for his own views, the struggle of species in nature being paralleled by the struggle of classes in history, with nature and history evolving in the same natural, inevitable fashion.

Still other socialists—anti-imperialist and anti-Marxist—used the *Origin* to different effect. They argued that since the social and economic struggle for existence could result in the survival of those with the least desirable, the least worthy human characteristics, the lesson of Darwinism was to encourage the cooperative rather than competitive instincts of men. The evolution of society was thus made to depend on the growth of cooperative institutions and the lessening of the class struggle.

Another school of thought—not socialist now, but eugenicist—proposed to intervene even more directly and dramatically in the evolutionary process. Francis Galton, Darwin's cousin, said that his aim was to "further the ends of evolution more rapidly and with less distress than if events were left to their own course," to "discover and expedite the changes that are necessary to adapt circumstance to race and race to circumstance."[5] Darwin approved in theory of Galton's proposal for a registry of superior and inferior families, so that society would know who should be encouraged to breed and who discouraged or prevented from breeding.

At this point the entire edifice of Social Darwinism threatens to collapse under the weight of contradiction, complication, and paradox. Laissez fairism and socialism, racism and anti-racism, segregationism and desegregationism, imperialism and anti-imperialism, Marxism and evolutionary socialism—surely they cannot all legitimately claim descent from the same ancestor. Yet, like the evolutionary tree itself, with its many branches and off-shoots, they are all related—not directly to each other but to the parent doctrine, each deriving from a different part of that doctrine, each with a lineage and legitimacy of its own.

A final antithesis is conveniently epitomized by two members of the distinguished Huxley family, speaking under the same auspices exactly fifty years apart. In 1893 T. H. Huxley, one of Darwin's most loyal disciples, defined evolution as that "cosmic process" by which man and nature, proceeding by struggle, selection, and survival, had arrived at their present state. Ethics, on the other hand, was the very opposite of that cosmic process. So far from being a guide to morality, evolution was a lesson in immorality. It put a premium on those qualities that moralists could only deplore: cunning, brute force, ruthlessness, ferocity. Civilized man could learn from it only what to avoid and condemn.

Fifty years later T. H. Huxley's grandson, the eminent scientist Julian Huxley, argued the opposite thesis: that evolution provided an objective basis for human values and social progress. "The facts of nature," he observed in flat contrast to his grandfather, "as demonstrated in evolution, give us assurance that knowledge, love, beauty, selfless morality, and firm purpose are ethically good."[6]

More recently, Julian Huxley put the case for evolutionary ethics on a different plane. Comparing man's present state with that of our amphibian ancestors 300 million years ago, when they were evolving from a life confined to the sea to the vastly extended opportunities of a life upon land, Huxley has come to see man in a similar state of transition—from the biological area of evolution into the psychosocial area. Our evolution, he believes, will proceed by "breakthroughs to new dominant patterns of mental organization, of knowledge, ideas and beliefs—ideological instead of physiological or biological organization."[7] This is not to say that we are assured of a boundless evolutionary progress; for Huxley warns us of the pitfalls in our way—such fatal pitfalls as nuclear warfare, overpopulation, and the like. But it does suggest that all the means for overcoming these pitfalls are in our hands and that evolution is the foremost of these means.

Thus the debate over Social Darwinism concludes with a still more fundamental disagreement: whether evolution is, as Julian Huxley suggests, the source and guide of social morality or whether, as his grandfather maintained, evolution is at best irrelevant to and at worst opposed to the very idea of social morality.

FOOTNOTES

1. Lord Acton, *Letters to Mary Gladstone*, 1st ed. (New York; 1905), p. 99.
2. Harry Elmer Barnes, *A History of Historical Writing*, 2nd ed., Dover, 1962, p. 331.
3. *Life and Letters of Charles Darwin*, I, ed. by Francis Darwin, Appleton, 1887, p. 316 (July 3, 1881).
4. *Life and Letters of Darwin*, III, p. 237 (December 26, 1879).
5. Francis Galton, *Inquiries into Human Faculty and Its Development*, I, J. M. Dent, Everyman, n.d., p. 218.
6. Julian Huxley, *Evolutionary Ethics*, Oxford, 1943, p. 41.
7. Julian Huxley, "The Evolutionary Vision," *Evolution After Darwin*, III, ed. by Sol Tax and Charles Callender, Univ. of Chicago, 1960, p. 251.

SUGGESTED READINGS

For a more detailed analysis of Darwin's impact, read Richard Hofstadter, *Social Darwinism in American Thought*, rev. ed., Beacon, 1955; or Gertrude Himmelfarb, *Darwin and the Darwinian Revolution*, Doubleday, 1959.

Historical Critique 5

TWENTIETH-CENTURY REINTERPRETATIONS OF HISTORY AND SOCIETY
by Hayden V. White

Hayden V. White, Professor of History at the University of California, Los Angeles, is the author (with Willson H. Coates) of *The Emergence of Liberal Humanism* (1966), editor of *The Uses of History* (1968), and author of many articles on the philosophy of history.

At the beginning of the twentieth century philosophers of history and social theorists tended to be either humanistic or deterministic in their basic outlook. Humanists viewed the historical process as a product of free human choices and wrote history as a record of the creative acts of the human spirit. Determinists, by contrast, regarded the historical process as a product of more basic, impersonal forces over which man had no control.

On the whole, however, professional historians did not accept either of these views. They purported to tell *how* things had happened in the past without prejudging the deeper philosophical question of *why*. They tended to concentrate on those situations in which individuals and groups had had immediate and easily perceived effects on their worlds, as in politics, diplomacy, and economics. This was a great age of biography, and when historians did not write about such commanding figures as Bismarck, Gladstone, and Rockefeller, they wrote about nations, classes, and peoples as if they were human individuals, with distinct physiognomies, character traits, and personalities of their own. Moreover, historians tended to view relations among the nations as essentially similar to relations among individuals. That is, they assumed that on the whole nations would cooperate with one another, and that when they did not, they would be able to work out compromises with one another which would, in the long run, benefit everyone.

During the two decades before World War I the dominant assumptions of the professional historians were subjected to repeated criticism by philosophers and social theorists. Sociologists, psychologists, political theorists, and philosophers all stressed the complexities of the social process and the difficulties both of understanding and of controlling it. They called for new scientific approaches which would take account of the ir-rational factors in human behavior and the unconscious motivations which underlay, and often determined, the course of the social process. They criticized historians for fostering the "illusion" of inevitable progress and the "delusions" that competition necessarily ended in cooperation, that violence bred peace in the long run, and that individual selfishness eventuated in the greatest good for the greatest number.

World War I confirmed the need for a new social science and a new historical vision. Prior to the war, history had stood at the very center of all human and social studies. But historical training had not enabled men to foresee the outbreak of the war, to encompass its magnitude, or, once it had ended, to explain convincingly why it had erupted and who was responsible for it. Apparently no one had wanted such a war; certainly no one had wanted it to continue for as long as it had or to cause such wide destruction. Was society in the grip of "dark" forces after all? Were men nothing but pawns of some greater fatality? Had the self-confidence and material security of the nineteenth century been purchased at the cost of human self-knowledge? None of the conventional conceptions of history seemed able to comprehend, much less answer, such questions. And everywhere men began to lose faith in the power of reason to comprehend the historical process and the power of human will to control it. This loss of faith in reason bred relativism; the feeling of loss of social control promoted pessimism. And these two attitudes—relativism and pessimism—dominated much of the best historical theory during the 1920's and 1930's.

Relativism permeated historical thinking in both Europe and America. It was characterized by the belief that men were essentially products of the cultures into which they had been born, that the kinds of questions they could ask of history were dictated by their immediate interests, and that their answers to those questions would be meaningful only as they related to current needs. Such notions discouraged belief in the progress, and even in the continuity, of historical knowledge. Historians were urged to rewrite the entire history of the world anew for each generation; they were encouraged to cultivate their personal biases, to give vent to their prejudices, and to judge both the past and present ruthlessly, in order to make a virtue out of an inevitability, their own time-boundedness. This was a period of debunking of once honored pieties, religious, political, social; of sensational revelations about the private lives of the once revered culture-heroes; of cynical unmasking of the presumed base motives underlying every supposedly idealistic endeavor. Marxism and Freudism became popular instruments of historical analysis, since they purported to be able to distinguish between true and apparent motives in all human acts.

Relativism was often, though not inevitably, accompanied by pessimism. Many literary artists, taking their cues from the philosopher Nietzsche, the novelist Gide, and the poet Valéry, denied that history had any "meaning" whatsoever. The study of the past, it was held, was a flight from the present and a denial of the future. The historian thus appeared as the servant of the dead and the enemy of the living. And writers like André Malraux, James Joyce, D. H. Lawrence, Ernst Jünger, Franz Kafka, and many others taught that men must be relieved of the burden of history, of the weight of the past, if the vital impulses within them were not to be frustrated completely. Most of these thinkers foresaw the destruction of civilization itself, and they counseled immersion in the thrills of the moment, in war, love, revolution, or sport, as the sole effective antidote to a deadening reverence for the past.

This mood of desolation was deepened by the onset of the Great Depression in 1929 and the advent of totalitarian political systems all over the world shortly thereafter. Like World War I, the depression was an event of world-wide scope and effect; few had been able to foresee it; and it seemingly did not respond to human manipulation or control. Like the war, the depression reinforced the conviction that men and society were merely instrumentalities of vast, impersonal forces which it would be folly to oppose. And many thinkers preached dumb submission to these forces as the only choice open to the "realist."

The outstanding representative of the relativist and pessimist position in historical thinking was Oswald Spengler. His *Decline of the West,* which appeared during the war, captured perfectly the mood of despair which had seized intellectuals everywhere during the war's late stages. Civilizations, Spengler argued, were closed systems, like plants; they lived through regular cycles which were analogous to the plant's responses to the changing seasons. Springtime burgeoning and summer flowering were followed ineluctably by autumnal decline and wintery desolation. Nothing could be done to avoid the onset of each succeeding stage in a civilization's growth and death cycle. Youthful strength was followed by mature reflection, mature reflection by the melancholy of old age, and old age by disintegration. The last stages of a civilization's life were marked by vast internecine wars, the rise of military conquerors, and the dominance of the engineer and

technician over the artist and moralist. History provided no formulas for avoiding destruction; men did not learn anything from the study of the past except the inevitability of their own degradation. They could lessen the pain of such degradation, however, by submitting to the inevitable instead of opposing it.

On the whole, professional historians did not accept Spengler's ideas. They were especially offended by his inclination to play the prophet. Most of them believed that although the writing of history required objectivity and precision, historical thought itself could never aspire to the status of a full-blown science. The fragmentary character of the historical record plus the impossibility of reproducing past events precluded any scientific reconstruction of the evidence. Hence, history was to be studied "for its own sake," an an occasion for artistic representation or at best as an introduction into the difficulties of ever arriving at complete knowledge in human affairs.

During the interwar period, however, such thinkers as the Positivists and the Marxists rejected the idea that history was essentially an art. They claimed to possess instruments for surveying the historical process as a whole, for discerning its true "meaning," and for prescribing the uses to which historical knowledge could be put.

The Positivists offered the most pressing challenge to conventional historical thinking, and their position has grown in authority since World War II. Briefly, they maintain that the only valid explanations are the kind found in the physical sciences, explanations which subsume individual events under general causal laws. Every proper explanation, they insist, is ultimately syllogistic: with major premises consisting of general social laws, minor premises of the "facts" obtaining at a given time and place, and conclusions which are logically deducible from the premises. Actually, Positivists maintain, historians *always* assume or invoke some general principle of human comportment or social process which has the force of law in their explanations. Hence, historical explanations differ from explanations in the physical sciences only in the *direction* of the inquiry. Whereas physical scientists are interested in prediction of future events, historians are interested preëminently in retrodiction of past events. That is to say, the historian knows the *outcome* of a series of events, such as the rise to power of Napoleon at the end of the French Revolution. His problem is to discover the specific conditions anterior to Napoleon's rise and the general laws that explain the degeneration of an originally democratic movement into a dictatorship. And this means, Positivists conclude, that historiography converges with sociology: both are properly concerned with establishing the general laws of social process by which known events can be gathered under the appropriate general laws.

Marxists, today as well as in the interwar period, resemble Positivists in their demand for a scientific historiography but differ in their conviction that the teachings of Marx, Engels, and Lenin constitute such a science. Their basic presupposition is that all changes in culture and society can be traced to transformations occurring in the substructure of society, what they call "the modes of production." More important than this conviction, however, is their belief that historical science can and ought to serve the needs of the class struggle. Thus, Marxists all over the world have not shrunk from writing history with what non-Marxists regard as indefensible biases. But, as a dispassionate reading of historians committed to the "free enterprise" system will plainly show, the writing of biased history is not a monopoly of Marxists.

At present, historians and social theorists are coping with the impact of the electronics revolution on their work. The computerization of information storage and retrieval seems to foreshadow a time when historians will have to do very little searching of the historical record. In the near future, libraries may be able to serve up in an instant all of the relevant data on any problem. Then the historian's principal problem will be theoretical rather than manual; his principal challenge will be to frame hypotheses by which the data can be molded into an interesting and comprehensible form. Thus, far from deadening the imagination, as once was feared, the mechanization of historical learning may well free the fancy of the historian for imaginative flights never before contemplated.

Of course, the computerization of knowledge is a two-edged sword. The categories of storage may themselves be based upon value judgments about the nature of the knowledge available; an element of preselection may enter into the cataloguing just as it does now in conventional libraries. Moreover, the centralization of knowledge offers massive opportunities for information control by governments and groups whose interests lie in propaganda rather than in dissemination of information, or education.

The main questions facing the historian today, then, are: What is the cultural *function* of historical knowledge? To serve the purposes of science, art, moral edification, or ideology? What is the proper *form* of historical explanation? Ought it be structural and schematic, like sociology, or narrative and discursive, like a novel? Increasingly, it is felt that in an age of world conflict, historians ought to relate their learning more directly to the efforts of men of goodwill everywhere who are seeking to resolve, instead of increase, such conflict. In short, the view is growing that history may be able to serve as a basis for an enlightened, humanistic ethics, if historians work more closely with moralists, psychologists, and anthropologists. Historians do not necessarily agree on what the study of history will provide—apart from systematized evidence of past events—in the way of guidelines for social or personal behavior. Yet increasingly philosophers are contending that historical knowledge is a necessary prerequisite to responsible and sophisticated philosophizing. And for their part, historians are recognizing that the way to a more creative future society lies in crossing the barriers that have hitherto separated the disciplines.

SUGGESTED READINGS

For a general outline of philosophy of history, see Bruce Mazlish, *The Riddle of History*, Harper & Row, 1966; and Page Smith, *The Historian and History*, Vintage, 1966. The best defense of an "idealistic" conception of historical knowledge will be found in R. G. Collingwood, *The Idea of History*, Oxford, 1956, while the Positivists' position can be found in K. R. Popper, *The Poverty of Historicism*, Routledge, 1961. The best introduction to the logical analysis of history and social science is Morton White, *The Foundations of Historical Knowledge*, Harper & Row, 1965, while the most perceptive study of the literary side of historical writing, especially in respect to the structure of historical narrative, is W. B. Gallie's *Philosophy and the Historical Understanding*, Chatto and Windus, 1964. The beginning student will find a good introduction to all the major positions on the problem of history and the social sciences in W. H. Dray, *Philosophy of History*, Prentice-Hall, 1966, which can be supplemented with a reading of the essays collected in W. H. Dray, ed., *Philosophical Analysis and History*, Harper & Row, 1966. Further readings in the literature can be found in Patrick Gardiner, ed., *Theories of History*, Free Press, 1959.

Chronological Table 1

NEAR EAST AND EGYPT	INDIA AND CHINA

Neolithic revolution c. 7000

Sumerian city-states emerge c. 3500

B.C. 3000 Menes unites Egypt c. 3100

Old Sumerian period c. 2800-2370
Old Kingdom in Egypt c. 2700-2200

Akkadian empire c. 2370-2230
Neo-Sumerian period c. 2113-2006
Middle Kingdom in Egypt c. 2050-1800
2000 Hittites enter Asia Minor c. 2000

Indus valley civilization c. 2300-1800—capitals at Mohenjo-Daro and Harappa

Hammurabi rules lower Mesopotamia 1760
Hittites sack Babylon 1595
New Kingdom or Empire in Egypt c. 1570-1090
1500 Thutmose III c. 1490-1436—the "Napoleon of Egypt"

Hittite empire c. 1450-1200
Akhenaton c. 1369-1353
Era of small states 1200-700
Phoenician and Aramean traders; the alphabet

Invasion of India by Aryans from Black and Caspian seas c. 1500
Vedic Age c. 1500-900—beginning of three pillars of Indian society; autonomous village, caste system, joint-family
Vedas—oldest Sanskrit literature
Shang dynasty 1500-1027—China's first civilization

Chou dynasty 1027-256—China's "classical age"—Mandate of Heaven promulgated

Period of Decadence in Egypt c. 1090-332
1000 United Hebrew kingdom (1020-922): Saul, David, Solomon
Divided Hebrew kingdom: Israel (922-721); Judah (922-586)
The great Hebrew prophets 750-550
Assyrian empire 745-612
Lydians and Medes
Chaldean empire (604-539): Nebuchadnezzar
Zoroaster, early 6th century
Persian empire (550-330): Cyrus; Darius (522-486)
End of the Babylonian Exile of the Jews 538
500

Later Vedic Age in India c. 900-500—caste system becomes more complex: priest, warrior, merchant, serf, "untouchable"

Upanishads 800-600—foundation of Hinduism

Guatama Buddha 563?-483—founder of Buddhism
Confucius 551-479—most famous and influential Chinese philosopher

400

Chinese poetry collected in *Shih Ching*, or *Book of Odes*
Two greatest Indian epics composed: the *Mahabharata* (including the *Bhagavad-Gita*) and the *Ramayama*

Lao-tzu and Taoism—aim: intuitive approach to life; *Tao te Ching*
Mencius c. 372-289 links theory of Mandate of Heaven to democratic concept of the will of the people in government
Alexander the Great crosses Indus valley 326
Chandragupta Maurya founds Mauryan dynasty in India 322-c. 185

Conquests of Alexander the Great 334-331
300 Death of Alexander (323); Ptolemy siezes Egypt; Seleucus rules Asia

Ashoka 273-232—"the first great royal patron of Buddhism"
Period of Warring States in China—Ch'in defeat Chou 221
China reunited under First Emperor, Shih Huang-ti 221-210
Han dynasty of China 202 B.C.-220 A.D.
Tamil kindgoms—Hindu states, chief trading area with the West
200 Mauryan empire falls 185; Bactrian rule extends to India and Punjab; Graeco-Bactrian kingdom created
Han emperor Wu Ti 141-87

Maccabean revolt wins independence for Judea 142 (see Chapter 5)
100

Kushan empire in India (first century B.C.-220 A.D.)
Kanishka, Kushan ruler c. 78-128, sponsors *Mahayana*
("Great Vehicle") school of Buddhism, which spreads north and east;
Hinayana ("Lesser Vehicle") Buddhism spreads south and east

Dead Sea Scrolls
Pompey annexes Syria and Palestine 63
Herod the Great, king of Judea 37-4
Jesus Christ c. 4 B.C.-30 A.D.
Paul (d. c. 65)
A.D. 100 Jews revolt from Rome (66-70)—end of the ancient Hebrew state

GREECE

ROME

3000 B.C.

Aegean civilization c. 2000-1200
Achaean Greeks invade Peloponnesus c. 2000

Indo-Europeans invade Italian peninsula 2000-1000; Latins settle in lower Tiber valley (Latium)

2000

Zenith of Minoan culture 1700-1450

Mycenaean Age 1450-1200

1500

Dorian invasion c. 1200

Greek Dark Ages c. 1150-750 and Homeric Age

Etruscans settle on Italy's west coast
Carthage founded in North Africa by Phoenicians c. 800
Rome founded 753
Greeks colonize southern Italy and Sicily

1000

Hellenic Age c. 750-338
Age of Oligarchy (c. 750-500): Hesiod; colonization
Athens—growth of democracy: Solon (594), Pisistratus (560), Cleisthenes (508)
Sparta—militaristic totalitarian state, Spartan League

Etruscans conquer Rome c. 600

Roman Republic established 509

500

Persian Wars (490-479): Marathon, Thermopylae
Delian League (478) and Athenian imperialism
Athen's Golden Age under Pericles (461-429)
Peloponnesian War (431-404)—Athens vs. Sparta

Plebeians vs. patricians (509-287)—tribunes and *Concilium Plebis*

Laws of the Twelve Tables c. 450

400

Philip II of Macedonia conquers Greece 338
Hellenic culture: Thales, Pythagoras, Democritus, Hippocrates, Socrates, Plato, Aristotle, Herodotus, Thycydides, Sappho, Aeschylus, Sophocles, Euripides, Aristophanes, Phidias, Praxiteles
Alexander the Great conquers Persia 331
Hellenistic Age 323-31—Ptolemaic Egypt, Seleucid Asia, Macedonia; Greek federal leagues

Hellenistic culture: Epicurus, Zeno, Eratosthenes, Aristarchus, Euclid, Archimedes, Hipparchus, Polybius, Theocritus

Roman expansion in Italy (338-270): Latins, Etruscans, Samnites, Greeks

300

Roman expansion in western Mediterranean 270-146—Punic wars: Hannibal

Roman expansion in eastern Mediterranean 200-133—wars with Macedonia and the Seleucids; Macedon and Greece annexed (146); first Roman province in Asia (133)
Reform movement of the Gracchi 133-121

200

Civil wars 88-30
Marius vs. Sulla (88-82): dictatorship of Sulla (82-79)
Pompey vs. Caesar (49-46): dictatorship of Julius Caesar (46-44)
Antony vs. Octavian (32-30)
Augustus' reconstruction—the Principate 30 B.C.-180 A.D.
Golden Age of literature: Cicero, Catullus, Lucretius, Virgil, Horace
Julio-Claudian and Flavian emperors 14 A.D.-96 A.D.
Antonine emperors (96-180): Hadrian, Marcus Aurelius
Silver Age of literature: Juvenal, Tacitus, Seneca, Plutarch

100

100 A.D.

Chronological Table 2

EUROPE

B.C. **100**

A.D. **1**

100 End of the *Pax Romana* 180-285—civil wars, economic decline, invasions
Reconstruction by Diocletian (285-305)—the Dominate
300 Constantine (306-337)—Edict of Milan (313), Council of Nicaea (325), founding of Constantinople (330)
Ulfilas (d. 383), missionary to the Goths
Theodosius divides Roman Empire 395
Battle of Adrianople (378)—German invasions begin
400 Alaric sacks Rome 410
Western Church Fathers: Jerome, Ambrose, Augustine
St. Patrick in Ireland c. 450
Attila crosses the Rhine—battle near Troyes 451
Pope Leo the Great (440-461)
Odovacar deposes last western emperor 476
Clovis (481-511) unites Franks, and rules Gaul
500 Theodoric (493-526) rules Italy; Cassiodorus and Boethius
St. Benedict establishes Benedictine Order 529
Lombards invade Italy 568
Merovingian decline, sixth-seventh centuries
600 Pope Gregory the Great (590-604)
Isidore of Seville (d. 636)—the *Etymologies*

700 Charles Martel (714-741) rules the Franks; defeats Muslims at Tours 732
Bede (d. 735)
St. Boniface (d. 755), "the apostle to the Germans"
Pepin the Short (741-768) ends rule of Merovingian kings; "Donation of Pepin" to pope
Charlemagne (768-814) revives Roman Empire in the West (800); fosters Carolingian Renaissance

800 Treaty of Verdun divides Carolingian empire into West Frankland, East Frankland, and Lorraine 843
Magyar, Muslim, and Viking invasions terrorize Europe (ninth-tenth centuries)
Alfred the Great (871-899) establishes strong Anglo-Saxon kingdom in England
Kievan Russia emerges
900 Feudalism well established in France c. 900
Henry I, the Fowler (919-936), founds Saxon dynasty in Germany
Otto I, the Great (936-973)—alliance of crown and Church; routs Magyars at battle of Lechfeld 955; crowned emperor by pope 962
Ethelred the Unready 978-1016—power of English government lags; invasion by Canute, Viking king
Hugh Capet (987) founds Capetian dynasty
1000 Peace and Truce of God (eleventh century)
Normans arrive in Italy 1016
Yaroslav the Wise 1019–1054—peak of Kievan Russia; Byzantine influences in art and literature
Salian House succeeds Saxon kings in Germany 1024
College of Cardinals formed to elect pope 1059
Pope Gregory VII (1073-1085) supports Cluniac religious reform; Investiture Struggle
Norman Conquest of England 1066
Fall of Bari to Normans 1071—last Byzantine stronghold in Italy
The *Reconquista* gains Toledo from Muslims 1085
First Crusade—Jerusalem captured; Latin kingdom of Jerusalem established 1099
1100 Renaissance of the twelfth century; revival of trade and towns
Welf-Hohenstaufen rivalry (1106-1152) wrecks structure for a strong German State
Louis the Fat 1108—first strong Capetian ruler in France
Concordat of Worms 1122
Second Crusade 1147
Frederick Barbarossa (1152-1190)—centralized feudal monarchy; struggle with popes and Lombard League
Henry II (1154-1189) reforms English judicial system; Thomas à Becket
St. Dominic (1170-1221); St. Francis of Assisi (1182?-1226)
Philip II Augustus (1180-1223) extends royal power
Third Crusade 1189—the "Crusade of Kings"
Frederick II 1194-1250—end of the medieval German empire
1200 Pope Innocent III 1198-1216—zenith of the medieval papacy
Fourth Crusade 1202-1204—crusaders sack Constantinople
King John of England signs Magna Carta 1215
Kiev destroyed by Mongols 1240
St. Thomas Aquinas (1225?-1274) reconciles faith and reason in *Summa Theologica*; zenith of scholasticism
Louis IX (1226–1270) brings dignity to the French crown
Edward I (1272–1307)—rise of Parliament; power of nobility curtailed
Philip IV, the Fair (1285-1314), centralizes French government; humiliates Pope Boniface VIII
Acre, last Christian stronghold in Holy Land, conquered by Muslims 1291
1300 Dante (d. 1321)
Hundred Years' War between France and England 1337-1453
1400 Chaucer (d. 1400)

NEAR EAST AND BYZANTINE EMPIRE	INDIA, CHINA, AND JAPAN	
	Rule by Yamato clan in Japan	**100** B.C.
(See also Chronological Table 1)	Kanishka ruler in India (c. 78-128)	**1** A.D.
Christian missionaries	Expansion of Indian culture into Southeast Asia begins (second century) Fall of Han dynasty in China 220	**100**
Eastern Church Fathers: Clement of Alexandria Council of Nicaea 325—Nicene Creed Constantine establishes New Rome (Constantinople) 330 St. Basil (330-379) establishes Rule of St. Basil	Buddhism gains popularity in China (third century) Chandragupta I founds Gupta dynasty in India 320	**300**
	Chandragupta II (c. 380-c. 413)—zenith of Gupta power Kalidasa (c. 400-450), lyric poet, the "Indian Shakespeare"	**400**
	Buddhism enters Japan (sixth century)	**500**
Justinian (527-565)—reconquests; *Corpus Juris Civilis*; Hagia Sophia		
Muhammad 570-632—the Hijra Heraclius (610-641)—regains Syria, Palestine, Egypt from Persians First four caliphs (632-661)—conquest of Syria, Iraq, most of Egypt and Persia Rise of the Shia	Harsha (606-647) rules northern India T'ang dynasty founded 618; golden era of China T'ai Tsung (627-650)—first great T'ang ruler Taika reform in Japan 646; ruler considered divine	**600**
Umayyad dynasty 661-750—expands in North Africa, Turkestan, Indus valley, Spain; defeated by Franks at Tours 732 Leo III (717-741) repulses Muslims 718; administrative and military reforms; iconoclastic controversy Abbasid dynasty 750-1258—end of Arab predominance; peak of Islamic power, civilization, and prosperity Harun-al-Rashid 768-809—relations with Charlemagne Cyril and Methodius—missionaries to the Slavs	T'ang poets: Li Po and Tu Fu Japanese court established at Nara 710	**700**
	Fujiwara period in Japan (857-1160); capital at Kyoto *Diamond Sutra* printed 868	**800**
Golden age of Muslim learning 900-1100—advances in medicine, mathematics, literature, philosophy, architecture, decorative arts; geniuses of this period and later: Al-Razi, Avicenna, Alhazen, Al-Khwarizmi, Omar Khayyám, Averroës, ibn-Khaldun	T'ang dynasty falls 906 Expansion of Indian culture into Southeast Asia ends (tenth century) Sung dynasty founded in China 960	**900**
Basil II (976-1025) defeats Bulgars	Gunpowder used by Sung c. 1000	**1000**
Final separation of the churches 1054 Seljuk Turks seize Persia and Iraq, conquer Baghdad (1055)	Wang An-shih (1021 1086), Chinese socialist reformer Muslims invade India; Turks and Afghans annex Punjab 1022	
Battle of Manzikert 1071—loss of Asia Minor to Seljuks		
Alexius Comnenus and the First Crusade 1096 Kingdom of Jerusalem (1099-1291) and crusader states	Angkor Wat built c. 1100	**1100**
	China divided between empires of Sung (south) and Chin (north) 1127	
	Yoritomo (1147-1199) rules Japan as *shogun* from Kamakura 1192	
	Genghis Khan (1162-1227) unites Mongols	
Saladin regains Jerusalem 1187		
Fourth Crusade 1202-1204—Constantinople sacked Latin Empire 1204-1261	Hojo period in Japan 1199-1333 Delhi sultanate established 1206; Indian culture divided into Hindu and Muslim	**1200**
Fall of Abbasid dynasty—Baghdad conquered by Mongols 1258 Michael Palaeologus regains Constantinople 1261	Mongols conquer China 1234; *Pax Tatarica* links East and West via trade routes Kublai Khan (1260-1294), Yüan emperor of China Marco Polo arrives at Kublai Khan's court c. 1275 "The Divine Wind" 1281	
Ottoman Turks invade Europe 1356	Kamakura destroyed 1333; Ashikaga shogunate founded in Japan 1338	**1300**
Constantinople falls to Ottoman Turks 1453	Ming dynasty established in China 1368 Tamerlane (Timur the Lame) destroys Delhi 1398	**1400**

Chronological Table 3

THE EUROPEAN SCENE

300

900

1000

1100

1200   Mongols conquer Kiev 1240
Transitional period in Italian art c. 1250-c. 1400—Giotto d. 1336
Rudolf of Hapsburg becomes Holy Roman emperor 1291
Pope Boniface VIII (1294-1303) feuds with Philip IV

1300   Avignon papacy 1309-1376
Hundred Years' War (1337-1453) begins
Golden Bull 1356
Petrarch 1304-1374
Great Schism 1378-1417
John Wycliffe d. 1384
Grand Prince of Moscow defeats Mongols at Kulikovo 1380

1400   The *quattrocento* (fifteenth century) of Italian Renaissance
Council of Constance 1414
Commercial Revolution 1450-1650
Gutenberg used movable type to print Bible 1454
Early Renaissance masters in Italy—Brunelleschi, Ghiberti, Donatello, Masaccio, Montegna, Botticelli
Wars of the Roses 1455-1485
Louis XI (the "universal spider") of France (1461-1483)
Ivan III (the Great) of Russia (1462-1505)
Ferdinand and Isabella begin joint rule in Spain 1479
Henry VII (1485-1509) founds Tudor dynasty in England
Reconquista ends with conquest of Granada 1492; unification of Spain completed
Maximilian I (1493-1519), Holy Roman emperor
Italian Wars (1494-1513) begin
Leonardo da Vinci 1452-1519

1500   Northern Renaissance (sixteenth century)—painters Jan van Eyck, Albrecht Dürer, Hans Holbein the Younger, Brueghel the Elder
Late Renaissance in Italy c. 1500-1530—Bramante, Michelangelo, Da Vinci, Raphael, Giogione, Titian, Castiglione, Cellini
Henry VIII of England 1509-1547
Luther posts ninety-five theses 1517; excommunicated, declared heretic at Diet of Worms 1521
Charles V elected Holy Roman emperor 1519
Suleiman rules the Turks 1520-1566
Peace of Augsburg 1555 ends Schmalkaldic Wars (1546-1555)
The Prince (1532) by Machiavelli
Henry VIII founds Anglican Church 1534
Loyola establishes Jesuit order 1534
John Calvin published *Institutes of the Christian Religion* 1536
Erasmus d. 1536
Council of Trent 1545-1563
Ivan IV (the Terrible) of Russia 1547-1584

1550   Mary Tudor reinstates Catholicism in England 1553-1558
Philip II of Spain 1556-1598
Era of Religious Wars (1556-1650) begins
Elizabeth of England 1558-1603
St. Bartholomew's Day Massacre 1572
Shakespeare 1564-1616
Battle of Lepanto 1571
Dutch United Provinces declare independence 1581
Time of Trouble in Russia 1584-1613
Spanish Armada 1588
Henry IV (1589-1610) founds Bourbon dynasty in France
Edict of Nantes 1598

1600   James I (1603-1625) founds Stuart dynasty in England
Bank of Amsterdam founded 1609
Thirty Years' War (1618-1648)—Peace of Westphalia 1648
De Jure Belli ac Pacis (1625) by Grotius
Colbert d. 1683
Lloyd's of London founded c. 1688
Bank of England chartered 1694

FAR EAST

AMERICAS AND AFRICA

	Ghana empire in Africa c. 300-1200	**300**
	Mayan city-states in Yucatan peninsula 980-1200	**900**
	Eric the Red discovers Greenland c. 982	
Muslims invade India; Turks and Afghans annex Punjab 1022	Mali empire in Africa c. 1000-c. 1400	**1000**
	Zenj empire in Africa c. 1000-1497	
China divided into two empires: Sung and Chin 1127	Incas settle Cuzco valley in Andes (eleventh century)	**1100**
Yoritomo (1147-1199) rules Japan as *shogun* from Kamakura 1192	Ghana captured by Berbers 1076	
Hojo period in Japan 1199-1333	Toltecs dominate Mexican plateau (twelfth century)	
Delhi sultanate established 1206		**1200**
Mongols conquer China 1234	Fall of Ghana state 1240	
Kublai Khan 1260-1294—Marco Polo arrives at his court c. 1275		
	Aztec confederacy in Mexico (fourteenth century)	**1300**
Kamakura destroyed 1333; Ashikaga shogunate founded in Japan 1338		
Fall of Mongol China; Ming dynasty founded 1368		
Timur the Lame (Tamerlane) destroys Delhi 1398	Songhai empire in the African Sudan c. 1400-c. 1600	**1400**
Chinese naval expeditions to India, Near East, Africa (fifteenth century)	Atlantic slave trade begins (fifteenth century)	
	Zenith of Inca empire 1438-1532	
	Prince Henry the Navigator (1394-1460)	
	Diaz rounds Cape of Good Hope 1488	
	Columbus discovers New World 1492	
	Bull of Demarcation 1493; Treaty of Tordesillas 1494	
	North America claimed by Cabot for England 1497	
	Da Gama reaches India 1498	
Portuguese trade monopoly in Far East (sixteenth century)		**1500**
	Albuquerque captures Goa (1510) and Malacca (1511)	
Chinese edict bans foreign merchants in Chinese waters 1522	Balboa sights Pacific Ocean 1513	
Babur (the Tiger) defeats Delhi sultanate and Rajputs 1526-1527; founds Mughul empire in India	Cortés arrives in Mexico 1519; Aztec empire falls	
	Magellan rounds South America 1520	
Akbar (1556-1605) expands Mughul empire; promotes religious tolerance	*Conquistadores* in New World	**1550**
Portuguese granted right to trade with Chinese at Macao 1557	Jacques Cartier explores St. Lawrence River 1534	
Spanish use Philippines as trading stop c. 1565	Bartolomé de Las Casas c. 1560	
Japanese attempt invasion of China and Korea 1592		
Hideyoshi persecutes Christians in Japan 1592		
English East India Company incorporated 1600	Jamestown founded 1607; Quebec 1608	**1600**
Dutch East India Company formed 1602	Henry Hudson attempts to find shorter route to Far East 1609	
Tokugawa period begins in Japan 1603		
Foundations for Dutch East Indies laid by Coen 1618	Plymouth founded 1620	
Shah Jahan (1628-1658) promotes Muslim faith; height of Mughul empire in India	Dutch West India Company founds Manhattan 1624	
Europeans forbidden entry to Japan 1639	René La Salle takes possession of Louisiana territory for France 1681	
Manchu invade Ming China; establish Manchu dynasty 1644		
Aurangzeb (1658-1707); decline of Mughul power		

Chronological Table 4

SCIENCE AND TECHNOLOGY, THOUGHT AND ART

1500 Revolution in astronomy—Copernicus proposes heliocentric theory of universe, publishes *Concerning the Revolutions of Heavenly Spheres* 1543; Brahe attempts compromise between geocentric and heliocentric theories; Kepler coordinates Brahe's data; Galileo confirms Copernican theory

1550 Pioneers in medicine: Paracelsus experiments with new drugs; Vesalius, founder of modern anatomy; Harvey describes circulation of blood in *Anatomical Exercise on the Motion of the Heart and Blood* 1628
El Greco (1541?–1614), master of Mannerist style in painting

Francis Bacon (1561–1626) champions deductive method of philosophical inquiry; *Novum Organum* 1620; *New Atlantis* 1627

Descartes (1590–1650) proposes deductive method of philosophical inquiry; develops analytical geometry; proposes theory of philosophical dualism
1600 Gilbert's *De Magnete* 1600

Neoclassical dramatists in France—Corneille, Racine, Moliere
Inventions of seventeenth century: telescope, microscope, thermometer, pendulum clock, micrometer, barometer, air pump
Baroque style: Rubens, Velázquez, Vermeer, Hals, Rembrandt, Bernini; opera originates in Italy

1650 Defenders of absolutism—Hobbes of England, author of *Leviathan* 1651, and Bossuet of France

Scientific societies founded: Academy of Experiments at Florence 1657; Royal Society of London 1662; French Academy of Science at Paris 1666
Boyle's law is formulated 1660
Spinoza expresses his pantheistic philosophy; publishes *Ethics* 1663

Newton expounds theory of gravitation in *Philosophiae Naturalis Principia Mathematica* 1687

Locke, publishes *An Essay Concerning Human Understanding* 1690; advances doctrine of popular sovereignty as argument against absolutism in "Of Civil Government" 1690
Rococo style exemplified in works of Watteau; English portrait painting by Reynolds, Gainsborough

1700

Novel appears: Defoe's *Robinson Crusoe* 1719; Swift's *Gulliver's Travels* 1726; Richardson's *Pamela* 1740–1741; Fielding's *Tom Jones* 1749
Pope, foremost Neoclassical English poet, publishes *An Essay on Man* 1733
Hogarth's "The Rake's Progress" 1735;

Intellectuals adopt Deism, belief that God is creator of universe but cannot change laws of nature; Pietism develops to restore emotion and faith to religion, is later called Methodist movement under Wesley brothers in England 1738; Quietism is crushed in Catholic countries

Further experiments with electricity: Leyden Jar 1745; Franklin's experiment with kite 1752
Intellectual assault on absolutism led by *philosophes* Montesquieu (*The Spirit of Laws*, 1748) and Rousseau (*Social Contract*, 1762)
1750 Reaction on the Continent against Baroque and Rococo styles of architecture is manifested in Neoclassical style c. 1750
Formalism in music—Handel, Bach, Mozart, Haydn
Voltaire, prince of *philosophes*, publishes *Candide* 1759; Diderot spreads doctrines of rationalism and Deism, edits *Encyclopedie*
Great works of social sciences: Rousseau's *Emile* 1762; Beccaria's *Essay on Crimes and Punishments* 1764; Gibbon's *Decline and Fall of the Roman Empire* 1776–1788; Condorcet's *Progress of the Human Mind* 1794

Priestley isolates ammonia; discovers oxygen 1774; produces carbon monoxide gas 1799
Adam Smith's *An Inquiry into the Nature and Causes of the Wealth of Nations* defends laissez-faire economics 1776
Lavoisier discovers the law of the conservation of matter and formulates his combustion theory 1777
Kant's *Critique of Pure Reason* (1781)

Edmund Burke defends conservatism in *Reflections on the Revolution in France* 1790

Hutton's *Theory of the Earth* 1795—pioneer work in geology
Edward Jenner develops safe vaccination against smallpox c. 1798
1800 Volta discovers method for generating continuous flow of electricity 1800
Goya's "The Disasters of War" 1810

POLITICS

James of England (1603–1625) and successor Charles I antagonize Parliament; Petition of Right denies king's right of taxation with parliamentary consent 1628
Richelieu 1624–1642 becomes real authority behind French throne

Frederick William, the Great Elector (1640–1688), makes Brandenburg the most important Protestant state in Germany
English Civil War (1642–1648); the Commonwealth and the Protectorate (1649–1660)
Mazarin (1643–1661) governs France during minority of Louis XIV; triumphs over enemies during civil war 1648–1653

Restoration of Stuart kings in England—controversy between Charles II and Parliament 1660–1685; secret Treaty of Dover with Louis XIV 1670; Whig and Tory parties organized; Habeas Corpus Act 1679
Louis XIV (1661–1715) transforms French state into an absolute monarchy; invades Spanish Netherlands and German border districts 1667–1697; halted by William of Orange and allied nations
Peter the Great 1682–1725, absolutist tsar of Russia, attempts to westernize realm
James II of England (1685–1688) attempts to impose absolute rule
Louis XIV revokes Edict of Nantes 1685
Glorious Revolution—Whigs and Tories invite William of Orange to rule England; Bill of Rights passed; Parliament becomes dominant agency in government 1688

Great Northern War 1700–1721—Charles XII of Sweden defeated by Peter the Great and allies
War of the Spanish Succession—English and allies renew struggle against French 1701; Treaty of Utrecht 1713
Frederick William I of Prussia (1713–1740) creates all-powerful central government; builds up army
George I initiates Hanoverian dynasty in England; beginning of creative cabinet government 1714
Robert Walpole becomes first prime minister of England 1721–1742

Frederick II, the Great (1740–1786), makes Prussia important power in European politics
War of the Austrian Succession 1740–1749—Frederick the Great invades Silesia 1740; France and England enter first stage of duel for world empire; Peace of Aix-la-Chapelle 1748

Seven Years' War 1756–1763—Diplomatic Revolution aligns Austria and France against England and Prussia; struggle on Continent and in colonies; William Pitt's "system" brings English victories, such as battle of Plassey (1757) and battle of Quebec (1759); Treaty of Paris 1763
Catherine the Great (1762–1796) makes Russia major European power
George III of England (1770–1782) strives to destroy cabinet system; secures control of Parliament
Poland partitioned in three stages among Russia, Prussia, and Austria 1772–1795
American Revolution 1775–1783—Declaration of Independence 1776

American Articles of Confederation 1781; Constitutional Convention 1787; American Constitution adopted 1789
Pitt the Younger becomes prime minister 1783; restores cabinet government
French Revolution (first phase)—storming of Bastille; National Constituent Assembly draws up Declaration of the Rights of Man; formulates new constitution and government (Legislative Assembly) 1789–1791
French Revolution (second phase)—agitation by Jacobin movement led by Marat, Danton, and Robespierre; radical insurrection in Paris; National Convention proclaims the Republic; France repels invasion by Austria and Prussia 1792
Louis XVI executed 1793; Reign of Terror begins under Robespierre 1793; Robespierre executed; Directory assumes power 1795; Directory smashes First Coalition, except for England 1797
Napoleon establishes Consulate 1799; scatters Second Coalition forces 1799–1802; climaxes reforms with Civil Code, proclaims himself emperor 1804; destroys armies of Third Coalition; is defeated by British at Trafalgar, defeats Prussia 1805–1806; his invasion of Russia fails 1812

English and allies defeat Napoleon at Leipzig 1813; Napoleon abdicates throne, goes to Elba 1814; returns to France and is defeated by Britain and Prussia at Waterloo; exiled to St. Helena 1815
Revolution in Latin America—Bolivar and San Martin gain independence for Spanish colonies in South America 1817–1825; Iturbide proclaims Mexican independence 1821; Pedro is crowned emperor of independent Brazil 1822

Chronological Table 5

POLITICS

1800

Congress of Vienna 1814–1815—Russia, Britain, France, Austria attempt to restore Old Regime; Quadruple (later Quintuple) Alliance formed
Louis XVIII of France establishes constitutional monarchy 1814–1824

Carlsbad Decrees temporarily discourage German nationalist youth movement 1819
Revolutions in Spain and Italy 1820–1821
Greeks rise against Turkish rule 1821–1827; Greek independence attained at Treaty of Adrianople 1829

Charles X, exponent of divine right, ascends French throne 1824
Tsar Nicholas I crushes Decembrist Revolt 1825; imposes reactionary repressive system
Catholic Emancipation Act in England 1829
Revolutions of 1830—July Revolution in Paris enthrones Louis Philippe; Belgians throw off Dutch rule; revolt unsuccessful in Poland
Mazzini initiates Italian *Risorgimento* c. 1830
Whigs end reactionary Tory rule 1830; Reform Bill 1832; slavery abolished 1833
Turkey becomes a protectorate of Russia 1831

Chartist movement for reform in England fails (1839, 1842, 1848)

Repeal of Corn Laws 1846
Revolution of 1848 in France—Louis Napoleon becomes president of Second Republic 1848
Revolution of 1848 in Germany—Frederick William IV of Prussia grants constitutional government; Frankfurt Assembly fails to establish new union; German Confederation restored at Olmütz 1850

1850

Cavour becomes prime minister of Italy 1852
Louis Napoleon proclaims himself Emperor Napoleon III 1852
Crimean War—Russia invades Turkey 1853; defeated at Sevastopol 1854–1855; Treaty of Paris 1856
Italy unified under Cavour—Austro-Italian War 1859; first Italian parliament 1861; Rome capital of united Italy 1871
Tsar Alexander II issues Emancipation Proclamation 1861; introduces reform 1864–1874
Bismarck appointed Prussian prime minister 1862
Polish insurrection crushed; policy of repression reimposed by Alexander II 1863
Germany unified under Bismarck—Prussia defeats Denmark (1864) and Austria (1866); wins Franco-Prussian War; William of Prussia proclaimed emperor of united Germany 1871
Ausgleich establishes Dual Monarchy of Austria-Hungary 1867
Gladstone and Disraeli alternate as English prime minister 1867–1880; Reform Bill of 1867 extends vote; Gladstone's Glorious Ministry 1868–1874
Parnell leads Irish Home Rulers; Gladstone introduces unsuccessful home rule bills 1886, 1893; third home rule bill passed 1919
Third Republic proclaimed in France 1870
Revolutionary Paris Commune 1871
Bismarck begins *Kulturkampf* 1872; forms Three Emperors' League with Russia and Austria-Hungary 1873; Triple Alliance with Austria and Italy 1882; Reinsurance Treaty with Russia 1887
Turkey crushes Bosnian and Bulgarian revolts, defeats Serbia, Montenegro 1875; Russia defeats Turkey 1877-1878; Treaty of San Stefano 1878
Congress of Berlin 1878
Abdul Hamid II imposes absolute rule over Ottoman empire 1878
Alexander II assassinated 1881; Alexander II revives system of repression, attempts policy of Russification 1881–1894
England approaches universal manhood suffrage 1884
Spirit of internationalism—annual Universal Peace Congresses begin 1889; first Pan-American Conference 1889; Hague Tribunal 1899
Emperor William II dismisses Birmarck 1890; allows Reinsurance Treaty to lapse; France forms Dual Alliance with Russia 1894
Dreyfus case 1894–1906
Nicholas II becomes tsar of Russia 1894
Herzl introduces Zionism; first Zionist congress meets 1897

1900

Social Democrats divide into moderate Mensheviks and radical Bolsheviks 1903; massacre of Bloody Sunday 1905; October Manifesto calls national Duma 1905
Britain forms alliance with Japan 1902; proclaims Entente Cordiale with France 1904; establishes Triple Entente with Russia and France 1907
Young Turks rebel 1908
Parliament Bill of 1911 curtails power of House of Lords
Diplomatic crises lead to World War I 1905–1914
Balkan Wars 1912–1913
Archduke Francis Ferdinand is assassinated 1914
World War I begins 1914

ECONOMICS AND SCIENCE

ARTS

Inventions revolutionize textile industry 1700's

Modern canal building in England begins 1759

Industrial use of Watt's steam engine 1785

Laissez-faire theory popularized—Malthus, Ricardo, Bantham, John Stuart Mill

First voyage of Fulton's steamship *Clermont* 1807

Atomic theory c. 1808

Industrial Revolution 1815–1870

Utopian socialists Saint-Simon, Fourier, Owen propose cooperative societies (early 1800's)

Lyell's *Principles of Geology* 1830–1833

Faraday's electric dynamo 1831

English social and economic reforms such as Factory Act of 1833 diminish doctrine of laissez faire

Penny post introduced in England 1840

Zollverein stimulates industry in German states

Morse perfects telegraph 1844

First law of thermodynamics stated 1847

Marx and Engels publish *Communist Manifesto* 1848

Proudhon founds anarchism

Christian socialist emphasize social aspects of Christ's teachings

Comte initiates science of sociology; Ranke founds school of scientific history

Bessemer improves smelting, refining of iron ore 1850's

Great Exhibition in London 1851

Darwin publishes *Origin of Species* 1859

Internal combustion engine 1860

Lister uses asepsis and antisepsis in surgery c. 1860

First International fails, anarchists under Bakunin oppose Marxist majority 1864–1873

Marx's scientific socialism expounded in *Das Kapital* 1867–1894

Mendelyeev classifies all known elements in periodic table 1869

Railroads cross North American 1869; Suez Canal 1869

New industrialism c. 1870–1914

Darwin's *Descent of Man* (1871)

Clerk-Maxwell advances electromagnetic theory of light 1873

Bell invents telephone 1876

Weismann distinguishes somatic and germ cells; Mendel formulates laws of heredity; Galton pioneers in eugenics

Pasteur and Koch prove germ theory of disease 1881

Hertz proves existence of electromagnetic waves 1886

Second International founded 1889; revisionism grows on Continent 1890's

Freud pioneers in psychoanalysis 1890's

Syndicalists emerge in France 1890's

Marconi devises wireless telegraphy 1895

X-ray discovered 1895

Electron theory formulated c. 1897

Pierre and Marie Curie discover radium 1898

Planck formulates quantum theory 1900

Pavlov advances study of conditioned reflexes 1900

Mendel's laws of heredity gain recognition c. 1900

Wright brothers' airplane 1903

Einstein produces equation $E=mc^2$, theory of relativity

Ford's Model T 1909

Rutherford's theory of positively charged atomic nucleus 1911

Einstein's general theory 1912

Preromantic writers—Rosseau, Schiller, Goethe **1800**

Goethe's *Faust*, Part I 1808

Romantic writers—Wordsworth, Coleridge, Shelley, Byron, Keats, Scott

Romanticist painters revel against classical rules—Delacroix, Constable, Turner

Romanticism in music—Beethoven, Brahms, Tschaikovsky, Chopin; operas by Wagner and Verdi

Romantic nationalist writers—Hugo, Pushkin, Hegel; Michelet, Bancroft, Macaulay write national histories

Period of Gothic revival in architecture c. 1830

Goethe's *Faust*, Part II 1832

Victorian novelists—Thackeray, Dickens

Victorian poets—Tennyson, Browning **1850**

Social criticism—Arnold, Carlyle, Ruskin

Realistic painters Courbet and Daumier

Free and compulsory education becomes almost universal in western Europe 1870–1914

Impressionist painters Monet, Degas, Renoir; sculptor Rodin

Post-Impressionistic painters Cézanne, Van Gogh

Realist writers Tolstoy, Hardy, James, Clemens; naturalist Zola; Ibsen and Shaw write "problem plays"; symbolists represent reactions against extreme realism

Darwinian theory influences philosophers James (pragmatism) and Bergson (vitalism) **1900**

Music—Richard Strauss (post-Wagnerian), Debussy (impressionism), Stravinski (polytonality), Schönberg (twelve-tone system)

Architecture—Sullivan, Wright, Gropius

Expressionism and Cubism

Chronological Table 6

U. S. AND LATIN AMERICA	BRITISH DOMINIONS
1750	Peace of Paris—Canada becomes British possession 1763
American Revolution 1775-1783	Canada's formative period 1763-1867—Quebec Act guarantees French custom and Catholicism in Canada 1774; division into Upper and Lower Canada 1791
Adoption of the United States Constitution 1789	Sydney, first English colony in Australia, established 1788
1800	
Louisiana Purchase 1803	
War of 1812—United States vs. Britain and Canada 1812-1814	
Missouri Compromise establishes boundaries of slave territory in United States 1820	
Brazil independence achieved 1822	
Monroe Doctrine 1823	
Andrew Jackson's presidency 1829-1837	British government assumes protection of New Zealand 1840
Pedro II brings political liberty and economic and cultural progress to Brazil 1840-1889	
United States land area doubled by annexation of California, Texas, Oregon, the Southwest 1845-1860	Australian colonies achieve near self-government c. 1850; secret ballot in Australia 1855
1850	Provinces of Canada form a federal union under British North America Act, and Canada becomes a Confederation 1867
Mexican dictator Santa Anna overthrown 1855; Juárez institutes anti-clerical *Reforma*; civil war ensues	
American Civil War—the Federal Union preserved, slavery abolished 1861-1865	
Argentina becomes united republic 1862	
Napoleon III invades Mexico, establishes brief empire under Maximilian 1863-1867	
United States occupies Midway Islands 1867	
Russia sells Alaska to United States 1867	
1870	
Porfirio Diaz, dictator, brings order without liberty to Mexico 1877-1880, 1884-1911	Treaty of Washington—Canada and United States arbitrate major differences 1871
First Pan-American Conference 1889	
Progressive movement in the United States initiates economic reform c. 1890-1914—trust-busting and regulation of transportation, foods, drugs under Theodore Roosevelt 1901-1909; Wilson's militant reform campaign, "New Freedom," initiates Federal Reserve Act 1913, Clayton Anti-Trust Act and Federal Trade Commission 1914	
"Dollar diplomacy"—United States exercises indirect controls in Latin America to protect investments 1890-1920's	Woman suffrage introduced in New Zealand 1893
Spanish-American War 1898; United States gains the Philippines, Guam, and Puerto Rico; Cuba becomes protectorate 1901	
United States annexes Hawaii 1898	
1900 Open Door Policy is declared 1900	
United States emerges as most powerful nation in the Western Hemisphere c. 1900	
Panama Canal begun under Theordore Roosevelt (1901-1909)	Commonwealth of Australia formed 1901
Era of Big Stick policy begins with the Roosevelt Corollary to the Monroe Doctrine 1904	
Madero defeats Diaz, rules Mexico 1911-1913	
Panama Canal opened 1914	

ASIA

AFRICA

1750

Battle of Plassey (1757) begins domination of India by British East India Company and England; Parliament takes control of East India Company 1773, appoints its highest official, the governor general of India 1784

1800

English acquire Ceylon 1796
Dutch government takes over East Indies; abolishes East India Company 1798

Cape Colony incorporated into British empire 1815

Boers establish Orange Free State and the Transvaal 1830's

China wars with England over opium and western exploitation 1839-1842; new ports opened to trade

1850

Taiping Rebellion—revolt against the Manchu 1850-1864; Manchu empress Tzu Hsi establishes national stability and furthers Chinese hatred of the West 1861-1908

Japan opens first ports to the West after Perry's visit 1854
English crush Indian Mutiny 1857, relieve East India Company of political responsibilities 1858
Russia penetrates land of the Caucasus, Turkestan c. 1860-1870

Livingstone begins explorations in Central Africa 1853
Britain makes treaties with Boers acknowledging their independence 1852, 1854; increased friction between Britons and Boers 1860-1885

Suez Canal completed 1869

The Meiji period—emperor made supreme authority; Japan modernized 1868-1912
Russia pushes south to Afghanistan and India c. 1870-1880

1870

Europe's golden age of imperialism 1870-1914: Belgium—Leopold II acquires Congo region 1876-1882; Leopold forced to turn over Congo Free State to Belgian government 1908. France—Egypt under joint financial control of Britain and France 1879; French obtain Tunisia 1881; Morocco made a French protectorate 1912. Britain—gains practical control of Suez Canal 1875; joint control of Egypt by British and French 1879; Lord Cromer assumes administration in Egypt 1883-1907; Somaliland is taken 1884; protectorate over Bechuanaland declared 1885; area developed for Britain by Rhodes' British South Africa Company named Rhodesia 1890; Anglo-Egyptian Sudan conquered 1898; Gambia, Sierra Leone, Gold Coast, and Nigeria gained through Royal Niger Company 1900. Germany—acquires Togoland, the Cameroons, German East Africa, German Southwest Africa 1880's; British and Germans settle dispute over territories in East Africa 1886, 1890. Italy—fails in attempted capture of Abyssinia 1896

Indian National Congress is formed 1885
Burma conquered by British c. 1885
French gain control over Indochina c. 1885
New constitution promulgated in Japan 1889

Gold discovered in Transvaal 1885

Japan defeats China in Sino-Japanese War 1894-1895
Filipinos rebel against American forces 1899-1902

Boer War 1899-1902—British defeat Dutch

1900

Boxer Rebellion—Chinese attack Europeans and are finally defeated by an international army 1900-1901
Open Door Policy calls for equal commercial rights in China for all nations 1900
Russo-Japanese War 1904-1905—Japan victorious
Anglo-Russian entente—Persia is put under dual control of Britain and Russia 1907

Boers and Britons join states and form Union of South Africa 1909

Japan annexes Korea 1910; accepted as first-class power
Republic of China proclaimed with Sun Yat-sen as president 1912

Italy wrests Tripoli from the Turks 1912

Chronological Table 7

INTERNATIONAL POLITICS	WESTERN DEMOCRACIES
1914 World War I 1914-1918	
Armistice is signed 1918 Wilson presents Fourteen Points 1918	Czech republic established 1918
Paris Peace Conference; League of Nations established 1919; Treaty of Versailles signed with Germany, Treaty of St. Germain with Austria, Treaty of Neuilly with Bulgaria 1919; Treaty of Sèvres with Ottoman empire, Treaty of Trianon with Hungary 1920 Little Entente formed 1920-1921; French allies include Belgium, Poland, Czechoslovakia, Rumania, Yugoslavia 1920-1927	U.S. rejects membership in League of Nations 1919
Washington Conference—limited naval disarmament 1921-1922 Nine-Power Treaty—signatories agree to respect sovereignty of China 1922 Mussolini defies League of Nations in Corfu incident 1923 France invades German Ruhr, 1923 Dawes Plan eases German reparations, France evacuates Ruhr 1924 Locarno Pact 1925	Unstable coalition governments in France 1920's Irish Free State created in southern Ireland 1921 Conservative Republican era in U.S. politics—Harding 1921-1923; Coolidge 1923-1929; Hoover 1929-1933 U.S. levies high tariffs, jeopardize war-debt payments, reparations MacDonald, Britain's first Labourite prime minister 1924; Conservatives in power 1924-1929
Kellogg-Briand Pact renounces war 1928	
1929	Stock market crash in U.S. leads to world depression 1929 Labour party regains power in England 1929-1931 Revolutions in six South American nations 1930
Young Plan scales down reparations payments 1930	
	Spain becomes republic 1931 National Coalition government in Britain begins 1931 Statute of Westminster creates constitution for British Commonwealth of Nations 1931
	U.S. inaugurates Good Neighbor Policy 1933 Franklin D. Roosevelt becomes president of U.S. 1933; inaugurates New Deal
Mussolini conquers Abyssinia 1936	Popular Front gains power in France 1936
Rome-Berlin Axis formed, Japan and Germany form Anti-Comintern Pact 1936; Italy joins the Pact 1937 Spanish civil war 1936-1939	Conservatives regain control in France 1937 Neville Chamberlain, advocate of appeasement, becomes prime minister of England 1937
Hitler engineers coup in Austria 1938 Surrender of Sudetenland to Germany at Munich 1938; Hitler seizes Czechoslovakia, Mussolini seizes Albania 1939	
1939 Russia, Germany sign nonaggression pact 1939 World War II—Germany invades Poland; France, Britain declare war 1939. *Sitzkrieg;* Russia defeats Finland 1939-1940. Hitler seizes Denmark, Norway, Low Countries, France 1940. Battle of Britain; Italian invasion of Greece and Africa fails; Hitler seizes Hungary, Balkans 1940-1941. Germany attacks Russia; Atlantic Charter signed; Pearl Harbor attack brings U.S. into war 1941. Japanese victories in Pacific 1941-1942. Battles of Midway and Coral Sea; Rommel victorious in Libya 1942. Soviets seize offensive in Russia; Axis surrender in Africa; Italy invaded; Allies launch second front; Normandy invasion, battle of Leyte 1944. Yalta agreements; Germany surrenders; A-bomb dropped on Japan; Japanese surrender 1945.	Churchill becomes prime minister of England 1940 U.S. passes Lend-Lease Act 1941
1945	

RISE OF TOTALITARIANISM

ASIA AND AFRICA

Revolution in China 1911-1912; Manchu emperor abdicates, Yüan Shih-kai heads republic 1912-1916   **1914**
Japan presents China with the Twenty-one Demands 1915
Arabs revolt against Ottoman rule 1916-1918
Balfour Declaration 1917

Russian Revolution—Duma names provisional government, tsar abdicates, Bolsheviks under Lenin seize government 1917; Bolsheviks destroy White Russian resistance 1918-1920
Period of war communism 1918-1921
German revolution 1918; Weimar Republic set up 1919
Third Communist International (Comintern) formed 1919

Government of India Act of 1919 and Rowlatt Act passed, Gandhi begins campaign for independence 1919
French repress Arab nationalism in Morocco, Tunisia, Algeria, Syria-Lebanon 1919-1939
San Remo Conference—Allies overrule Arab nationalism, create mandates from Arab territories 1920
Communist party (1920), Indonesian Nationalist party (1927) oppose Dutch rule in East Indies
Sun Yat-sen controls Canton government in China 1921-1925
Riza Shah Pahlavi seizes Iran government 1921-1925

War between Russia, Poland 1920
NEP—Lenin restores some capitalistic practices 1921-1928
Mussolini establishes National Fascist party 1921; seizes Italian government in march on Rome 1922; divides Italian economy into government-controlled syndicates
Union of Soviet Socialist Republics established 1922
Hitler stages unsuccessful *Putsch* in Munich 1923; begins *Mein Kampf* 1925

Egypt becomes sovereign, with British restrictions 1923
Republic of Turkey set up with Mustafa Kemal Pasha as president, Treaty of Lausanne signed 1923
Ibn-Saud gains control of Arabian peninsula 1924-1925

Election of Hindenburg as president underlines rising German ultra-nationalism 1925
Trotsky loses bid for power to Stalin 1927
Stalin purges rivals 1928-1931, 1935-1938
Stalin inaugurates first Five Year Plan 1928

Universal Manhood Suffrage Bill passed in Japan 1925

Chiang Kai-shek purges Communists 1927; conquers Peking, unites China 1928

Hamaguchi's ministry peak of liberalism in Japan 1929; his assassination   **1929**
causes permanent liberal setback 1930
Iraq gains full independence from Britain 1930
Round-table conferences on India 1930-1932
Arab violence in British mandate of Palestine 1930's
Segregation, unrest grow in Union of South Africa 1930's
Communists oppose French rule in Indochina 1930's
Japan invades Manchuria 1931
Chinese Communists proclaim Chinese Soviet Republic 1931; Chiang launches campaigns against Communists 1931-1934
Ibn-Saud's holdings renamed Saudi Arabia 1932

Republic in Portugal replaced by dictatorship of Salazar 1932
Russia begins second Five-Year Plan 1933
Hitler becomes dictator of Germany, Germany withdraws from League of Nations 1933; first Four-Year Plan established 1933, second 1936

Coup d'état in Siam (Thailand) 1932, new constitution promulgated
Japan withdraws from League of Nations, pushes into China 1933; T'ang-ku Truce 1933

Dictatorships formed in Albania, Bulgaria by 1935; in Greece 1936
Germans march into Rhineland 1936

Commonwealth of Philippines formed 1935
Government of India Act of 1935 goes into effect in British India 1937-1939; is rejected by native princes 1939

Italy withdraws from League of Nations 1937

British grant Burma restricted home rule 1937
War breaks out again between Japan and China 1937; Japan proclaims New Order in Asia 1938

Russia initiates third Five-Year Plan 1938

Fascist dictator Franco gains power, ends republic after Spanish civil war 1939

1939

Tojo becomes premier of Japan 1941

1945

Chronological Table 8

1945

Yalta Conference (Feb. 4-11)

Death of Roosevelt; Truman becomes president (Apr. 12)

Mussolini shot Italian partisans (Apr. 28)

Hitler commits suicide (Apr. 30?)

V-E Day; surrender of Nazi Germany (May 8)

UN Charter signed at San Francisco (June 26)

Potsdam Conference (July 17-Aug. 2)

Atomic bomb dropped on Hiroshima (Aug. 6)

Unconditional surrender of Japan (Aug. 14)

1946

First General Assembly of the UN in London (Jan. 10)

Independence of the Philippines proclaimed (July 4)

New constitution establishes Fourth French Republic (Oct. 13)

Germany divided into Soviet, British, American, and French zones (Oct. 29)

1947

Truman requests aid for Greece and Turkey; the Truman Doctrine (Mar. 12)

Secretary of State Marshall introduces idea of aid to Europe; the European Recovery Plan or the Marshall Plan (June 5)

British rule in India ended: dominions of India and Pakistan formed (Aug. 15)

1948

Gandhi assassinated (Jan. 30)

Communist coup in Czechoslovakia (Feb. 25)

Organization of American States (OAS) established (Apr. 30)

Israel proclaimed state (May 14)

Berlin blockade (June 18, 1948-Sept. 30, 1949)

Defection of Tito from Cominform (June 28)

Republic of Korea proclaimed in Seoul (Aug. 15)

1949

North Atlantic Treaty (NATO) signed (Apr. 4)

German Federal Republic born in West Germany (May 23)

Soviets found German Democratic Republic (May 30)

Adenauer's Christian Democrats sweep West German elections (Aug. 14)

People's Republic of China established (Sept. 21)

Explosion of first Soviet atomic bomb announced (Sept. 23)

Chinese nationalists abandon mainland for Formosa (Dec. 8)

Indonesia granted independence (Dec. 27)

1950

India becomes republic within British Commonwealth (Jan. 26)

U.S.S.R. and Red China sign thirty-year alliance (Feb. 14)

North Korean forces cross 38th parallel (June 25)

UN endorses Truman's request to send troops to South Korea (June 27)

Red Chinese forces move into Tibet (Oct. 25)

1951

Chinese Communists attack UN forces in Korea (Jan. 1)

ANZUS Pacific Security Pact signed (Sept. 1)

Japan signs peace treaty and agreement permitting U.S. troops to remain in Japan (Sept. 8)

Turkey and Greece join NATO (Sept. 20)

1952

Batista's coup d'état in Cuba (Mar. 10)

First U.S. H-bomb tested at Eniwetok (Nov. 1)

1953

Stalin dies, succeeded by Malenkov (Mar. 5)

Workers riot in East Berlin, proclaim general strike (June 17)

Egypt declared a republic (June 18)

Korean armistice signed at Panmunjon (July 27)

1954

Nasser becomes premier of Egypt (Feb. 25)

U.S. Supreme Court outlaws racial segregation in public schools (May 17)

French defeated at Dien Bien Phu (May 7); armistice concluded and Vietnam divided (July 21)

Southeast Asia Treaty Organization (SEATO) formed (Sept. 8)

1955

Malenkov resigns; replaced by Bulganin and Khrushchev (Feb. 8)

Baghdad Pact signed between Turkey and Iraq (Feb. 24); Britain, Pakistan, and Iran join (Oct.); Iraq withdraws from Bagdad Pact, which is renamed Central Treaty Organization (CENTO) (Aug. 21, 1959)

Afro-Asian Conference at Bandung, Indonesia (Apr. 18-24)

West Germany admitted to NATO (May 9)

U.S.S.R. and eastern European satellites sign Warsaw Pact (May 14)

1956

Anglo-Egyptian Sudan becomes independent republic of Sudan (Jan. 1)

U.S. promises to support Middle Eastern nations if attacked; the Eisenhower Doctrine (Apr. 9)

Egypt seizes Suez Canal; Nasser announces its nationalization (July 26)

Revolution in Hungary; crushed by Soviet army (Oct. 23-Nov. 30)

Israelis invade Sinai Peninsula, drive toward Suez Canal (Oct. 29)

1957

Gomulka's National Unity front wins Polish elections (Jan. 20)

Ghana becomes sovereign state in British Commonwealth (Mar. 6)

Inner Six nations agree to creation of European Economic Community (Common Market) and Euratom (Mar. 25)

Malaya becomes independent state with British Commonwealth (Aug. 31)

Soviet Sputnik fired into orbit; space age begins (Oct. 4)

1958

Khrushchev becomes Soviet premier (Mar. 27)

First conference of independent African states opens in Accra, Ghana (Apr. 15)

De Gaulle becomes premier of France (June 1)

New constitution for Fifth Republic approved in France (Sept. 28)

Guinea granted independence from France (Sept. 29)

Ayub Khan seizes power in Pakistan (Oct. 7)

1959

Cuban rebels under Castro overthrow Batista (Jan. 1)

Lunik I launched; first artificial planet to orbit the sun (Jan. 3)

Big Four foreign ministers meet in Geneva, discuss reunification of Germany (May 11-June 20; July 13-Aug. 5)

Sukarno dissolves Indonesian parliament, assumes dictatorial power (July 5)

Outer Seven nations complete agreements to set up European Free Trade Association (Nov. 20)

1960

U.S. and Japan renew mutual security pact (Jan. 19)

First French atomic bomb tested in Sahara (Feb. 13)

Big Four Paris summit meeting collapses (May 16)

Belgian Congo declared independent republic of the Congo (June 30)

Nigeria granted independence (Oct. 1)

1961

UN Security Council authorizes peace-keeping force in Congo (Feb. 21).

U.S. supported Cuban expedition defeated at Bay of Pigs (Apr. 17)

Beginning of Berlin Wall (Aug. 13)

1962

New U.S. military command established in South Vietnam (Feb. 8)

Chinese Communists attack Indian Himalayan frontier (Oct. 20)

U.S.-Soviet crisis over missile bases in Cuba (Oct. 22-28)

1963

Official surrender to UN of Katangese secession forces in Congo (Jan. 17)

France vetoes British entry to Common Market (Jan. 29)

Signing of nuclear test ban treaty by U.S., Britain, and U.S.S.R. (Aug. 5)

West German chancellor Adenauer resigns (Oct. 16)

Diem ousted and assassinated by South Vietnamese forces (Nov. 2)

U.S. president John F. Kennedy assassinated (Nov. 22)

1964

Rift between China and Soviet Union splits leadership in Communist world

France recognizes Communist China (Jan. 27)

Nehru dies; succeeded by Shastri (May 27)

U.S. adopts comprehensive Civil Rights Bill (July 2)

Khrushchev ousted; replaced by Brezhnev and Kosygin (Oct. 14)

Communist China explodes its first atomic bomb (Oct. 16)

1965

U.S. begins bombing North Vietnam (Feb. 7)

Dominican Republic Revolt overthrows U.S.-supported Cabral government (April 24-25)

Rhodesia declares independence from Britain (Nov. 11)

1966

Shastri dies (Jan. 10); Indira Gandhi becomes prime minister of India (Jan. 19)

Army officers seize control of Ghana, ousting Nkrumah (Feb. 24)

French government announces withdrawal of its troops from NATO and requires removal of all NATO bases from France (Mar. 9)

Sukarno surrenders power to Suharto (Mar. 12)

1967

Civil war begins between Nigerian federation and Biafra (May 30)

Six-day Arab-Israeli war (June 5-10)

1968

American and North Vietnamese representatives meet in Paris (May 13)

Nuclear nonproliferation treaty accepted by UN (June 10)

Soviet invasion of Czechoslovakia (Aug. 20)

President Johnson announces halt in bombing of North Vietnam (Oct. 31)

Nixon elected U.S. president (Nov. 5)

Apollo 8 orbits the moon (Dec. 21-27)

1969

Ayub Khan resigns; armed forces take control of Pakistan (Mar. 25)

De Gaulle resigns (Apr. 28); Pompidou elected premier of France (June 16)

Nixon announces policy of deescalation of Vietnam conflict (June 9)

Ho Chi Minh dies (Sept. 4)

Willy Brandt elected chancellor of West Germany (Oct. 22)

1970

Biafran war ends (Jan. 13)

Rhodesia becomes a republic (Mar. 2)

Arabs and Israelis accept cease-fire (July 31)

Nasser dies (Sept. 28); Anwar Sabat becomes premier of Egypt (Oct. 15)

De Gaulle dies (Nov. 9)

The Historian's Workshop: A List of Readings

An asterisk after a title indicates an inexpensive paperbound edition.

TOOLS OF THE TRADE

Some of the historians' most important tools are the bibliographies which provide compilations of the literature available in many areas. **The American Historical Association's Guide to Historical Literature,** rev. ed., Macmillan, 1961, is indispensable for world history. For the general student the inexpensive pamphlets published by the Service Center for Teachers of History, sponsored by the American Historical Association, cannot be recommended too highly. Trends in historical research, the status of scholarship, important archives, and schools of interpretation—all are touched upon in these booklets. Also useful is John Roach, ed., **A Bibliography of Modern History,** Cambridge, 1968.

General reference works include W. Bridgwater and E. J. Sherwood, eds., **The Columbia Encyclopedia,** Columbia, 1950; W. L. Langer, ed., **An Encyclopedia of World History,** Houghton Mifflin, 1968; R. B. Morris, ed., **Encyclopedia of American History,** Harper & Row, 1965; Van Nostrand's **Scientific Encyclopedia,** 1958; **The Worldmark Encyclopedia of the Nations,** Harper & Row, 1960; A. W. Palmer, **A Dictionary of Modern History,*** Penguin; S. H. Steinberg, ed., **New Dictionary of British History,** St. Martin's, 1963. For biographies, the **Dictionary of National Biography,** a multivolumed series, is indispensable for information concerning British personalities; for American notables, see the **Dictionary of American Biography.**

The following atlases are most helpful: A. Boyd, **An Atlas of World Affairs,*** Praeger; J. D. Fage, **An Outline Atlas of African History,** Arnold, 1958; E. W. Fox and H. S. Deighton, eds., **Atlas of European History,*** Oxford; G. Goodall and R. F. Treharne, eds., **Muir's Historical Atlas—Ancient, Medieval and Modern,** Barnes and Noble, 1956; C. L. Lord and E. H. Lord, **Historical Atlas of the United States,** Holt, 1953; R. R. Palmer, ed., **Atlas of World History,** Rand McNally, 1957; W. R. Shepherd, **Historical Atlas,** Barnes and Noble, 1956.

Invaluable for reference purposes are a number of well-known multivolumed works written by specialists: **The Cambridge Ancient History,** 12 vols., 1923–1939 (Vols. I-II are being revised); **The Cambridge Medieval History,** 8 vols., 1911–1936; **The Cambridge Modern History,** 14 vols., 1902–1912. **A New Cambridge Modern History** is now appearing, and numerous volumes are available. One of the most notable series on European history, profusely illustrated and strong in intellectual and cultural history, is W. L. Langer, ed., **The Rise of Modern Europe,*** 13 vols., Torchbooks. A. Nevins and H. Ehrmann, eds., **The University of Michigan History of the Modern World,** is a series which will interest not only the scholar of history but the amateur and the beginning student as well. For American history, the following sets are recommended: H. S. Commager and R. B. Morris, eds., **The New American Nation Series,*** Torchbooks; A. M. Schlesinger and D. R. Fox, eds., **A History of American Life,** 13 vols., Macmillan (this series is strong in social and intellectual history); **Chicago History of American Civilization,** Univ. of Chicago.

MEANING AND METHOD IN HISTORY

To obtain a general idea of what history is all about, one could not do better than to read the short volume by A. L. Rowse, **The Use of History,*** Collier, in which a British historian examines the content, use, and pleasures of history and its relation to life and culture. Other helpful studies on the philosophy and meaning of history are R. Aron, **Introduction to the Philosophy of History,*** Beacon; E. H. Carr, **What Is History?,** Knopf, 1962; B. Mazlish, **The Riddle of History: The Great Speculators from Vico to Freud,** Harper & Row, 1966; J. Burckhardt, **Judgments on History and Historians,** Beacon, 1958; H. Butterfield, **Man on His Past,*** Beacon; R. G. Collingwood, **The Idea of History,*** Oxford; D. H. Fischer, **Historians' Fallacies,** Harper & Row, 1970; Martin Duberman, **The Uncompleted Past,** Random House, 1970. Different approaches to the writing of history are described in H. E. Barnes, **A History of Historical Writing,*** Dover; F. Stern, ed., **The Varieties of History,*** Meridian.

The most ambitious treatment of history on a grand philosophical scale is Arnold J. Toynbee's multivolumed work, **A Study of History,** which was published between 1934 and 1954 by Oxford. (There exists a two-volume abridgment of the ten-volume work by D. C. Somervell, Oxford, 1947, 1957). Toynbee's views and interpretations have been challenged and even castigated by a number of important historians, yet in its grand sweep and its immense erudition his work is one of the greatest achievements in historical writing by a single historian since the days of Herodotus. For critiques on Toynbee's work see E. Gargan, ed., **The Intent of Toynbee's History,** Loyola, 1961; Pieter Geyl, **Debates with Historians,*** Meridian; Ashley Montagu, ed., **Toynbee and History,** Porter Sargent, 1956. William McNeill, **The Rise of the West,** Univ. of Chicago, 1963, is a provocative interpretation of world history.

THE RAW STUFF OF HISTORY

In each major field of study there are literally tens of thousands of government documents, newspapers, periodicals, diaries, and memoirs that speak for the past. In the last few decades a feature of the teaching of the history of civilization has been the publication of excellent collections of source material. For the development of western civilization, the following are most useful: F. Le Van Baumer, ed., **Main Currents of Western Thought,** Knopf, 1964; Norman Cantor, ed., **Ideas and Institutions in Western Civilization,*** 5 vols. Macmillan, 1963; H. J. Carroll, Jr., *et al.,* eds., **The Development of Civilization,*** 2 vols., Scott, Foresman; G. H. Knoles and R. K. Snyder, **Readings in Western Civilization,** Lippincott, 1960. For United States history, see H. S. Commager, ed., **Documents of American History,** Appleton, 1958; A. Craven *et al.,* **A Documentary History of the American People,** Ginn, 1951; M. Meyers *et al.,*

Sources of the American Republic,* 2 vols., Scott, Foresman, 1960–1961. There are numerous collections of source material in the field of European history, such as A. Baltzly and A. W. Salomone, eds., **Readings in Twentieth Century Europe,** Appleton, 1950; L. Bernard and T. Hodges, eds., **Readings in European History,** Macmillan, 1958; K. M. Setton and H. Winkler, **Great Problems in European Civilization,** Prentice-Hall, 1965; L. L. Snyder, ed., **Documents of German History,** Rutgers, 1958; W. Walsh, ed., **Readings in Russian History,** Syracuse, 1958. Source collections in other fields are W. T. DeBary, Jr., *et al.,* **Sources of Japanese Tradition, Sources of Indian Tradition, Sources of Chinese Tradition,** Columbia, 1958–1960; H. J. Bender and J. A. Larkin, **The World of Southeast Asia,** * Harper & Row; J. Duffy and R. Manners, eds., **Africa Speaks,** Van Nostrand, 1961; B. Keen, ed., **Readings in Latin-American Civilization,** Houghton Mifflin, 1955; Theodore McNelly, ed., **Sources in Modern East Asian History and Politics,** * Appleton; Lin Yutang, ed., **The Wisdom of China and India,** Random House, 1942.

PREHISTORY

M. Burkitt, **The Old Stone Age,** * Atheneum; R. J. Braidwood, **The Near East and the Foundations for Civilization,** Oregon, 1952; Bernard Campbell, **Human Evolution: An Introduction to Man's Adaptations,** Aldine, 1966; V. G. Childe, **Man Makes Himself,** * Mentor; S. Cole, **The Prehistory of East Africa,** * Mentor; H. Hays, **From Ape to Angel,** * Capricorn; L. S. Leakey, **Adam's Ancestors: The Evolution of Man and His Culture,** * Torchbooks; K. Macgowan and J. Hester, **Early Man in the New World,** * Anchor; B. Malinowski, **Crime and Custom in Primitive Society,** * Littlefield; R. Redfield, **The Primitive World and Its Transformations,** * Cornell; F. Zeuner, **Dating the Past: An Introduction to Geochronology,** 4th ed., Hafner, 1962.

ANCIENT NEAR EAST, GREECE, AND ROME

T. Africa, **The Ancient World,** Houghton Mifflin, 1969; N. Bailkey, **Readings in Ancient History: From Gilgamesh to Diocletian,** * Heath; W. Caldwell and M. Giles, **The Ancient World,** 3rd ed., Holt, Rinehart & Winston, 1966; M. Finley, ed., **Slavery in Classical Antiquity,** Barnes and Noble, 1968; E. Gardiner, **Athletics in the Ancient World,** Oxford, 1955; M. Grant, **The Ancient Mediterranean,** Scribner, 1969; Tom Jones, **From the Tigris to the Tiber: An Introduction to Ancient History,** * Dorsey; H. Marrou, **A History of Education in Antiquity,** * Mentor; H. J. Muller, **Freedom in the Ancient World,** Harper & Row, 1961; C. Roebuck, **The World of Ancient Times,** Scribner, 1966; C. Seltman, **Women in Antiquity,** * Collier; F. Snowden, Jr., **Blacks in Antiquity: Ethiopians in the Greco-Roman Experience,** Harvard, 1970; C. Starr, **A History of the Ancient World,** Oxford, 1965 (includes India and China); J. Swain, **The Ancient World,** 2 vols., Harper & Row, 1950.

J. Bottero, ed., **The Near East: The Early Civilizations,** Delacorte, 1967; J. Finegan, **Light from the Ancient Past,** * 2 vols., Princeton.

F. Adcock, **The Greek and Macedonian Art of War,** * California; A. R. Burn, **Greece and Rome,** * Scott, Foresman, 1969; M. Grant, ed., **The Birth of Western Civilization: Greece and Rome,** McGraw-Hill, 1964 (contains over 700 illustrations); N. Hammond, **A History of Greece to 322 B.C.,** 2nd ed., Oxford, 1967; C. E. Robinson, **Hellas: A Short History of Ancient Greece,** * Beacon, and **Everyday Life in Ancient Greece,** * Oxford.

P. Arnott, **The Romans and Their World,** * St. Martin's; F. Bourne, **A History of the Romans,** Heath, 1966; M. Cary, **A History of Rome,** 2nd ed., St. Martin's, 1963; D. Dudley, **The Romans 850 B.C.–A.D. 337,** Knopf, 1970; J. Vogt, **The Decline of Rome,** Praeger, 1969.

MEDIEVAL EUROPE

C. Brooke, **Europe in the Central Middle Ages, 962–1154,** Holt, Rinehart & Winston, 1964; N. Cantor, **Medieval History: The Life and Death of a Civilization,** 2nd ed., Macmillan, 1968; M. Keen, **The Pelican History of Medieval Europe,** * Penguin; R. Lopez, **The Birth of Europe,** Lippincott, 1967; J. Morall, **The Medieval Imprint: The Founding of the Western European Tradition,** * Penguin; H. B. Parkes, **The Divine Order: Western Culture in the Middle Ages and the Renaissance,** Knopf, 1969; J. Strayer and D. Munro, **The Middle Ages: 395–1500,** 5th ed., Appleton-Century-Crofts, 1970; B. Tierney and S. Painter, **Western Europe in the Middle Ages, 300–1475,** Knopf, 1970; D. Waley, **The Italian City-Republics,** * McGraw-Hill, 1969; N. Zacour, **An Introduction to Medieval Institutions,** * St. Martin's, 1969.

MODERN EUROPE TO 1945

General: C. E. Black, **Twentieth Century Europe: A History,** Knopf, 1966; E. H. Carr, **The Twenty Years' Crisis, 1919–1939,** * Torchbooks; S. B. Clough *et al.,* eds., **The European Past: Reappraisals in History,** * 2 vols., 2nd ed., Macmillan, 1970; G. Craig, **Europe Since 1815,** 2nd ed., Holt, Rinehart & Winston, 1966; H. Gollwitzer, **Europe in the Age of Imperialism: 1880–1914,** * Harcourt, Brace & World; B. Gooch, **Europe in the Nineteenth Century,** Macmillan, 1970; E. Gulick, **Europe's Classical Balance of Power,** * Norton; H. Holborn, **The Political Collapse of Europe** [1914–1945], Knopf, 1951; J. McManners, **European History, 1789–1914: Men, Machines and Freedom,** * Torchbooks; E. Nolte, **Three Faces of Fascism,** * Mentor; J. M. Roberts, **Europe, 1880–1945,** Holt, Rinehart & Winston, 1967; P. Stearns, **Modern Europe,** * Scott, Foresman; A. J. P. Taylor, **From Sarajevo to Potsdam,** * Harcourt, Brace & World; S. H. Thomson, **Europe in Renaissance and Reformation,** Harcourt, Brace & World, 1963; Barbara W. Tuchman, **The Proud Tower,** Macmillan, 1966; J. Wheeler-Bennett, **Munich: Prologue to Tragedy,** * Compass; R. S. White, **Europe in the Eighteenth Century,** * St. Martin's; E. Wiskemann, **Europe of the Dictators, 1919–1945,** * Torchbooks.

England: D. Beales, **From Castlereagh to Gladstone, 1815–1885,** * Norton; W. L. Burn, **The Age of Equipoise: A Study of the Mid-Victorian Generation,** * Norton; Winston S. Churchill, **History of the English-Speaking Peoples: Arranged for One Volume,** * Pocket Books; A. B. Erickson and M. Havran, **England: Prehistory to the Present,** * Anchor; G. Finlayson, **Decade of Reform: England in the 1830's,** * Norton; R. Graves and A. Hodge, **The Long Weekend: A Social History of Great Britain, 1918 to 1939,** * Norton; E. Hobsbawm, **Industry and Empire,** * Penguin; A. Havighurst, **Twentieth-Century Britain,** * Harper & Row; W. Lunt, **History of England,** 4th ed., Harper & Row, 1957; D. Keir, **Constitutional History of Modern England since 1485,** * Norton; M. Naidis, **The Second British Empire, 1783 to 1965,** Addison-Wesley, 1970; G. M. Trevelyan, **A Shortened History of England,** * Penguin; A. J. P. Taylor, **English History, 1914 to 1945,** * Galaxy; R. K. Webb, **Modern England: From the Eighteenth Century to the Present,** Dodd Mead, 1968.

France: A. Cobban, **History of Modern France,** * 3 vols., Penguin; A. De Tocqueville, **The Old Regime and the French Revolution,** * Anchor; B. Ehrlich, **Resistance: France 1940–1945,** * Mentor; J. Friguglietti and E. Kennedy, **The Shaping** of Modern France: Writings on French History Since 1715, Macmillan, 1969; A. Guérard, **France: A Modern History,** Michigan, 1959; Gordon Wright, **France in Modern Times: 1760 to the Present,** Rand McNally, 1960.

Germany: A. Bullock, **Hitler, A Study in Tyranny,*** Torchbooks; W. Carr, **A History of Germany, 1815–1945,** St. Martin's, 1969; G. Craig, **From Bismarck to Adenauer: Aspects of German State- craft,*** Torchbooks; R. Dahrendorf, **Society and Democracy in Germany,*** Anchor; J. Marriott and C. Robertson, **The Evolu- tion of Prussia: The Making of an Empire,** Oxford, 1946; K. Pinson, **Modern Germany,** 2nd ed., Macmillan, 1966; A. Ramm, **Germany 1789–1919: A Political History,** Methuen, 1967; H. Vogt, **The Burden of Guilt: A Short History of Germany, 1914– 1945,*** Oxford.

Italy: R. Albrecht-Carrié, **Italy from Napoleon to Mussolini,*** Columbia; H. Hearder and D. Waley, eds., **A Short History of Italy from Classical Times to the Present,*** Cambridge; C. Seton-Watson, **Italy from Liberalism to Fascism, 1870–1925,** Barnes and Noble, 1967.

Russia: J. D. Clarkson, **A History of Russia,** 2nd ed., Random House, 1969; M. Florinsky, **Russia: A History and an Interpreta- tion,** 2 vols., Macmillan, 1954; S. Harcave, **Years of the Golden Cockerel: The Last Romanov Tsars, 1814–1917,** Macmillan, 1968; R. Hingley, **The Tsars: From Ivan the Terrible to Nicholas II,** Macmillan, 1968; L. Kochan, **The Making of Modern Russia,*** Penguin; J. Lawrence, **A History of Russia,*** Mentor.

Other European States: M. Mitchison, **A History of Scotland,*** Barnes & Noble, 1970; W. Atkinson, **A History of Spain and Portugal,*** Penguin; R. Carr, **Modern Spain, 1808–1939,** Oxford, 1966; A. Barnouw, **The Pageant of Netherlands History,** Long- mans, 1952; I. Andersson, **A History of Sweden,** Praeger, 1968; W. Mead, **Finland,** Praeger, 1968; C. Macartney and A. Palmer, **Independent Eastern Europe,*** St. Martin's, 1962; N. Pounds, **Eastern Europe,** Aldine, 1969; D. Sinor, **History of Hungary,** Praeger, 1959; E. Forster, **A Short History of Modern Greece, 1821–1956,** Praeger, 1958.

THE POSTWAR WORLD

Dean Acheson, **Present at the Creation,** Norton, 1969; René Albrecht-Carrié, **One Europe: The Historical Background of European Unity,** Doubleday, 1965; John Ardagh, **The New French Revolution,*** Colophon; M. Balfour, **West Germany,** Praeger, 1968; G. Barraclough, **An Introduction to Contemporary History,*** Penguin; J. F. Brown, **The New Eastern Europe,*** Praeger; E. Crankshaw, **Khrushchev, A Career,*** Discus; A. Dallin ed., **Diversity in International Communism, A Docu- mentary Record, 1961–1963,*** Columbia; M. M. Drachkovitch, ed., **Marxism in the Modern World,*** Stanford; C. Eichelberger, **UN: The First Twenty Years,** Harper & Row, 1965; Kent Forster, **Recent Europe,** Ronald Press, 1965; J. Freymond, **Western Europe Since the War,** Praeger, 1964; F. Hartmann, **Germany Between East and West: The Reunification Problem,*** Spectrum; F. H. Hinsley, **Power and the Pursuit of Peace,*** Cambridge; J. Lukacs, **A New History of the Cold War,*** Anchor; W. H. McNeill, **The Contemporary World,*** Scott, Foresman; A. Marwick, **Britain in the Century of Total War,** Little, Brown, 1968; H. J. Morgenthau, **Politics Among Nations: The Struggle for Power and Peace,** Knopf, 1967; N. Padelford and L. Good- wich, eds., **United Nations in the Balance,*** Praeger; D. Pickles, **The Fifth French Republic,*** Praeger; H. E. Salisbury, ed., **The Soviet Union, The Fifty Years,** Harcourt, Brace & World, 1967; A. Sampson, **Anatomy of Britain,*** rev. ed., Colophon; Paul Seaburg, **The Rise and Decline of the Cold War,** Basic

Books, 1967; H. Seton-Watson, **The East European Revolution,*** Praeger; H. G. Shaffer, **The Soviet System in Theory and Practice,*** Appleton; E. Stillman and W. Pfaff, **The Politics of Hysteria; The Sources of Twentieth Century Conflict,*** Colo- phon; J. G. Stoessinger, **The United Nations and the Super- powers,*** Random House; A. B. Ulam, **The New Face of Soviet Totalitarianism,*** Praeger; A. Werth, **De Gaulle, A Political Biography,** Simon and Schuster, 1966; F. O. Wilcox and H. F. Haviland, Jr., eds., **The Atlantic Community: Progress and Prospects,*** Praeger; F. Roy Willis, **France, Germany and the New Europe 1945–1963,*** Stanford.

ASIA THROUGH THE AGES

Two general reference works in this area are Guy Wint, **Asia: A Handbook,** Praeger, 1966; and S. Bahattacharya, **A Dictionary of Indian History,** Braziller, 1967.

India and Pakistan: The best general introduction to the history and culture of India is J. Nehru, **The Discovery of India,*** Anchor. The following are excellent basic histories: **The Cam- bridge Shorter History of India,** Macmillan, 1934; **A History of India,*** Penguin, Vol. I by Romila Thapar and Vol. II by Percival Spear; R. C. Majumdar *et al.,* **An Advanced History of India,** 2 vols., St. Martin's, 1951; W. H. Moreland and A. C. Chatterjee, **A Short History of India,** McKay, 1957; J. C. Powell-Price, **A History of India,** Nelson, 1955; C. G. Rawlinson, **India: A Short Cultural History,*** Praeger; Percival Spear, ed., **The Oxford History of India,*** Oxford; T. W. Wallbank, **A Short History of India and Pakistan,*** Mentor; W. N. Brown, **The United States and India and Pakistan,** rev. ed., Harvard, 1963, is an excellent survey by an American scholar—only one chapter is devoted to Indo-American relations. Other aspects of Indian history are covered in S. Gopal, **The Viceroyal- ty of Lord Irwin,** Oxford, 1957; K. A. N. Sastri, **A History of South India,** 3rd ed., Oxford, 1966; Percival Spear, **India: A Modern History,** Michigan, 1961; Philip Woodruff, **The Men Who Ruled India,*** 2 vols., Schocken.

Recent events and problems of the Indian subcontinent are discussed in K. Callard, **Pakistan: A Political Study,** Verry, 1958; S. S. Harrison, **India: The Most Dangerous Decades,** Princeton, 1960; H. R. Isaacs, **India's Ex-Untouchables,** John Day, 1965; Josef Korbel, **Danger in Kashmir,*** Princeton; V. P. Menon, **The Transfer of Power in India,** Princeton, 1957; Frank Moraes, **India Today,*** Macmillan; Khalid B. Sayeed, **Pakistan, The Formative Phase, 1857–1948,** 2nd ed., Oxford, 1968; R. Symonds, **The Making of Pakistan,** Faber, 1951; Phillips Talbot and S. L. Poplai, **India and America,** Harper & Row, 1958; Robert Trumbull, **As I See India,** Sloane, 1956.

China, Japan, and South Asia: Histories covering all the historic cultures of this area are scant: K. S. Latourette, **A Short History of the Far East,** 4th ed., Macmillan, 1964, covers China, India, Japan, and some of the lesser areas; the same general treatment is found in P. H. Clyde and B. F. Beers, **The Far East,** 4th ed., Prentice-Hall, 1966. Other useful general histories include F. H. Michael and G. E. Taylor, **The Far East in the Modern World,** rev. ed., Holt, Rinehart & Winston, 1964; H. Vinacke, **A History of the Far East in Modern Times,** 6th ed., Appleton, 1959. For a useful contemporary political analysis of the region, see G. McT. Kahin, ed., **Major Governments of Asia,** Cornell, 1959. The best general survey of Chinese, Korean, and Japanese culture and history is E. O. Reischauer and J. K. Fairbank, **A History of East Asian Civilization,** 2 vols., Houghton Mifflin, 1960, 1965. Also highly recommended is E. O. Reischauer, **Japan, The Story of a Nation,** Knopf, 1970. As for China, useful general surveys are D. J. Li, **The Ageless Chinese,*** Scribner; C. P.

Fitzgerald, **China: A Short Cultural History**, Praeger, 1954; L. C. Goodrich, **A Short History of the Chinese People,*** Torchbooks; R. Grousset, **The Rise and Splendour of the Chinese Empire,*** California; K. S. Latourette, **The Chinese, Their History and Culture,** 4th ed., Macmillan, 1964. For Japan, G. B. Sansom, **Japan: A Short Cultural History**, rev. ed., Appleton, 1962, is a scholarly survey; the same author's **The Western World and Japan**, Knopf, 1950, is a valuable study of western impacts not only on Japan but on Asia in general. Also recommended are H. Borton, **Japan's Modern Century**, Ronald, 1955; and C. Yanaga, **Japan Since Perry**, Shoe String, 1966. For Southeast Asia, see John F. Cady, **Southeast Asia: Its Historical Development**, McGraw-Hill, 1964.

China and Japan in recent times are treated in Gerald Clark, **Impatient Giant: Red China Today**, McKay, 1959; O. W. Clubb, **Twentieth-Century China**, Columbia, 1963; John Fairbank, **The United States and China**, Harvard, 1958 (the best short interpretive study); C. P. Fitzgerald, **A Concise History of East Asia,*** Praeger; F. C. Jones, **Japan's New Order in East Asia: The Story of Its Rise and Fall**, Oxford, 1954; K. Kawai, **Japan's American Interlude**, Univ. of Chicago, 1960; Li Chien-Nung, **The Political History of China, 1840–1928,*** Stanford; Immanuel C. Y. Hsu, **The Rise of Modern China**, Oxford, 1970; George N. Patterson, **Peking Versus Delhi**, Praeger, 1964; Harold Quigley and J. E. Turner, **The New Japan**, Minnesota, 1956; Peter Tang, **Communist China Today**, Praeger, 1957; R. L. Walker, **China Under Communism**, Verry, 1956. For recent developments in southern Asia, see Amry Vandenbosch and Richard A. Butwell, **Southeast Asia Among the World Powers**, Kentucky, 1957; for Indochina, see Ellen J. Hammer, **The Struggle for Indochina,*** Stanford; and for Indonesia, J. D. Legge, **Indonesia,*** Spectrum, 1964, and Alastair M. Taylor, **Indonesian Independence and the United Nations**, Cornell, 1960.

AFRICA AND THE MIDDLE EAST IN HISTORY

Africa: There is no single comprehensive account of African history from the earliest times to the present. One can obtain only an incomplete picture of ancient and medieval Africa from the following: E. W. Bovill and R. Hallett, **The Golden Trade of the Moors**, 2nd ed., Oxford, 1968; Basil Davidson, **The Lost Cities of Africa,*** Little Brown, 1959; John De Graft-Johnson, **African Glory**, Praeger, 1955; W. E. B. Du Bois, **The World and Africa**, Viking, 1947.

There are a few general accounts of African history. J. D. Fage, **History of West Africa: An Introductory Survey,*** Cambridge; and Zoe Marsh and G. Kingsnorth, **An Introduction to the History of East Africa**, 3rd ed., Cambridge, 1965, are two valuable surveys. T. W. Wallbank, **Contemporary Africa: Continent in Transition,*** Anvil, is a brief account with emphasis on recent times. See also F. Oliver and J. D. Fage, **A Short History of Africa,*** Penguin; and R. Oliver and A. Atmore, **Africa Since 1800,*** Cambridge; R. I. Rotberg, **A Political History of Tropical Africa**, Harcourt, Brace & World, 1965. For the opening and partition of Africa, the following are recommended: Norman D. Harris, **Europe and Africa**, Houghton Mifflin, 1927; Robin Hallett, **Africa to 1875**, Michigan, 1970; Parker T. Moon, **Imperialism and World Politics**, Macmillan, 1926; Alan Moorehead, **The White Nile,*** Dell; Margery Perham and J. Simmons, eds., **African Discovery**, Northwestern, 1963 (a good historical anthology). For the various colonial areas, see James Coleman, **Nigeria: Background to Nationalism**, California, 1958; R. Coupland, **East Africa and Its Invaders**, Russell, 1938; C. W. De Kiweiet, **A History of South Africa,***

Oxford; James Duffy, **Portuguese Africa,** Harvard, 1959; Thomas Hodgkin, **Nigerian Perspectives**, Oxford, 1960 (an anthology); Kenneth Ingham, **The Making of Modern Uganda**, Macmillan, 1958; Eric Walker, **A History of Southern Africa**, 3rd., 1964, Barnes and Noble; W. E. F. Ward, **A History of Ghana**, Macmillan, 1959. Indispensable anthologies by P. J. M. McEwan, are **Africa from Early Times to 1800, Nineteenth-Century Africa,** and **Twentieth-Century Africa**, Oxford, 1968.

The most comprehensive and up-to-date survey of the African scene—social, economic, and political—is George T. Kimble, **Tropical Africa**, 2 vols., The Twentieth Century Fund, 1960. Other interesting works dealing with trends and issues in contemporary Africa include Gwendolen Carter, **Independence for Africa,*** Praeger, and **The Politics of Inequality: South Africa Since 1948**, Praeger, 1959; T. R. M. Creighton, **Anatomy of Partnership: Southern Rhodesia and the Central African Federation**, Faber, 1960; John A. Davis and James K. Baker, eds., **Southern Africa in Transition,*** Praeger; Maurice Hennessy, **The Congo: A Brief History and Appraisal**, Praeger, 1961; A. P. Merriam, **Congo: Background of Conflict**, Northwestern, 1961; R. A. Reeves, **Shooting at Sharpeville**, Houghton Mifflin, 1961; Virginia Thompson and Richard Adloff, **French West Africa**, Stanford, 1958, and **The Emerging States of French Equatorial Africa**, Stanford, 1960.

The Middle East: The most useful histories of a general nature are Sydney N. Fisher, **The Middle East**, 2nd ed., Knopf, 1968; Philip K. Hitti, **The Near East in History**, Van Nostrand, 1961, and **History of the Arabs,*** St. Martin's; A. Hourani, **Syria and Lebanon,*** Oxford; George E. Kirk, **A Short History of the Middle East,*** Praeger. Recommended special studies include George Antonius, **The Arab Awakening,*** Capricorn; Clare Hollingworth, **The Arabs and the West**, Methuen, 1952; Harry Hopkins, **Egypt, the Crucible**, Macmillan, 1969; J. C. Hurewitz, **The Struggle for Palestine**, Norton, 1950; Nejla Izzeddin, **The Arab World**, Regnery, 1953; George Kirk, **Contemporary Arab Politics,*** Praeger; Walter Laquer, ed., **The Middle East in Transition**, Praeger, 1958; James Parker, **Whose Land? A History of the Peoples of Palestine**, Penguin, 1970; Keith Wheelock, **Nasser's New Egypt**, Praeger, 1960.

THOUGHT, ART, AND RELIGION

Science and Technology: H. Butterfield *et al.,* **A Short History of Science: Origins and Results of the Scientific Revolution,*** Anchor; W. C. Dampier, **A Shorter History of Science,*** Meridian; B. Farrington, **Greek Science,*** Penguin; R. J. Forbes, **Man the Maker: A History of Technology and Engineering**, Abelard-Schuman, 1958; M. Kranzberg and C. Pursell, **Technology in Western Civilization**, 2 vols., Oxford, 1967; G. de Santillana, **The Origins of Scientific Thought: From Anaximander to Proclus, 600 B.C. to 300 A.D.,*** New American Library; C. J. Singer *et al.,* **A History of Technology**, 5 vols., Oxford, 1954–1958; W. Wagar, ed., **Science, Faith, and Man: European Thought Since 1914,*** Torchbooks.

Fine Arts: A. Bowness, **Modern Sculpture,*** Dutton; J. Burchard and A. Bush-Brown, **The Architecture of America,*** Little, Brown; D. Grout, **A History of Western Music**, Norton, 1960; H. W. Janson, **History of Art**, Abrams, 1962; S. Kramrisch, **The Art of India**, 3rd ed., Phaidon, 1969; P. Lang, **Music in Western Civilization**, Norton, 1941; M. Levey, **History of Western Art,*** Praeger; H. Munsterberg, **Arts of Japan: An Illustrated History,*** Tuttle; N. Pevsner, **An Outline of European Architecture,*** Penguin; N. Ponente, **Modern Painting: Contemporary Trends**, Skira, 1960; B. Rose, **American Art Since 1900,*** Praeger; L. Sickman and A. Soper, **The Art and**

Architecture of China, Penguin; M. Sullivan, **A Short History of Chinese Art**,* California; J. Sweeney, ed., **African Sculpture**,* Princeton; E. M. Upjohn, **History of World Art**, Oxford, 1958.

Religion: A. Bouquet, **Sacred Books of the World**,* Penguin; C. Braden, **The World's Religions**,* Apex; H. Butterfield, **Christianity and History**,* Scribner; E. Conze, **Buddhism: Its Essence and Development**,* Torchbooks; G. Cragg, **From Puritanism to the Age of Reason**,* Cambridge; H. Creel, **Confucius and the Chinese Way**,* Torchbooks; J. Duchesne-Guillemin, **Zoroastrianism**,* Torchbooks; I. Epstein, **Judaism**,* Penguin; J. Ferguson, **The Religions of the Roman Empire**, Cornell, 1970; C. Humphreys, **Buddhism**,* Penguin; E. O. James, **Ancient Gods**,* Capricorn; B. Landis, **World Religions**,* Dutton; K. Latourette, **Christianity Through the Ages**,* Harper & Row; M. Nilsson, **History of Greek Religion**,* Norton; F. Norwood, **The Development of Modern Christianity Since 1500**,* Apex; G. Parrinder, **Religion in Africa**,* Penguin; F. Rahman, **Islam**,* Anchor; Huston Smith, **The Religions of Man**,* Harper & Row.

Philosophy: C. Brinton, **Ideas and Men: The Story of Western Thought**, Prentice-Hall, 1963; F. Copleston, **History of Philosophy**,* 8 vols., Image; H. Creel, **Chinese Thought from Confucius to Mao Tse-tung**,* Mentor; W. Durant, **The Story of Philosophy**,* Washington Square; F. Heer, **The Intellectual History of Europe**,* 2 vols., Anchor; W. T. Jones, **History of Philosophy**,* 4 vols., Harcourt, Brace & World; J. W. Krutch, **The Modern Temper**,* Harcourt, Brace & World; G. Mosse, **The Culture of Western Europe: The Nineteenth and Twentieth Centuries**, Rand McNally, 1961; Robert Olson, **A Short History of Philosophy**,* Harcourt, Brace & World; J. H. Randall, **The Making of the Modern Mind**, Houghton Mifflin, 1940; B. Russell, **A History of Western Philosophy**, Simon and Schuster, 1945; R. Stromberg, **An Intellectual History of Modern Europe**, Appleton-Century-Crofts, 1966; A. Waley, **Three Ways of Thought in Ancient China**,* Anchor.

Footnotes

PROLOGUE: PERSPECTIVE ON MAN

1. P. Gardiner, *The Nature of Historical Explanation* (London: Oxford University Press, 1952), p. 98.
2. H. Butterfield, *Christianity and History* (London: G. Bell & Sons, Ltd., 1949), p. 132.
3. See A. J. Toynbee, *Civilization on Trial* (New York: Oxford University Press, 1948).
4. H. A. L. Fisher, *A History of Europe*, I (Boston: Houghton Mifflin Co., 1935), p. vii.
5. Toynbee, p. 11.
6. W. D. Howells, *Mankind So Far* (New York: Doubleday & Co., Inc., 1952), p. 312.

CHAPTER 1: ALONG THE BANKS OF RIVERS

1. Melville J. Herskovits, *The Human Factor in Changing Africa* (New York: Alfred A. Knopf, Inc., 1962), p. 38.
2. Robert I. Rotberg, *A Political History of Tropical Africa* (New York: Harcourt, Brace & World, Inc., 1965), p. 3.
3. Jacquetta Hawkes and Sir Leonard Woolley, *Prehistory and the Beginning of Civilization* (New York: Harper & Row, 1963), p. 351.
4. V. Gordon Childe, *New Light on the Most Ancient East* (London: Routledge & Kegan Paul Ltd., 1954), p. 114.
5. Tom B. Jones, *Ancient Civilization* (Chicago: Rand McNally & Co., 1960), p. 10.
6. V. Gordon Childe, *What Happened in History* (New York: Pelican Books, 1946), p. 74.
7. The ancient Mesopotamian chronology followed here is that presented in *The Cambridge Ancient History,* rev. ed. (1962), Vol. I, Ch. 6.
8. H. Frankfort, *The Birth of Civilization in the Near East* (London: Williams and Norgate, Ltd., 1951), p. 60.
9. "Les reformes d'Urukagina," trans. by M. Lambert in *Revue d'Assyriologie*, L (Paris, 1956), p. 183.
10. James B. Pritchard, ed., *Ancient Near Eastern Texts Relating to the Old Testament*, 2nd ed., trans. by E. A. Speiser (Princeton: Princeton University Press, 1955), p. 119.
11. *Sumerische und Akkadische Hymnen und Gebete*, trans. by A. Falkenstein and W. von Soden (Zurich: Artemis-Verlag, 1953), p. 188. For a partial translation and full discussion of this text, see S. N. Kramer, *From the Tablets of Sumer* (Indian Hills, Col.: The Falcon's Wing Press, 1956), pp. 267-271.
12. H. de Genouillac, trans., in *Revue d'Assyriologie, XXV* (Paris, 1928), p. 148.
13. Quoted in Kramer, p. 50.
14. R. F. Harper, *The Code of Hammurabi* (Chicago: University of Chicago Press, 1904), p. 3.
15. *Ibid.*, p. 49.
16. *Ibid.*, p. 101.
17. From *Epic of Gilgamesh*, trans. by E. A. Speiser, in Pritchard, p. 90.
18. Quoted in Sabatino Moscati, *The Face of the Ancient Orient* (Chicago: Quadrangle Books, Inc., 1960), p. 84.
19. Quoted in *City Invincible: A Symposium on Urbanization and Cultural Development in the Ancient Near East*, ed. by Carl H. Kraeling and Robert McC. Adams (Chicago: University of Chicago Press, 1960), p. 163.
20. Quoted in M. A. Murray, *The Splendour That Was Egypt* (London: Sidgwick & Jackson, Ltd., 1949), p. 67.
21. Trans. by John A. Wilson, *The Burden of Egypt* (Chicago: University of Chicago Press, 1951), p. 117.
22. *Ibid.*, p. 164.
23. Adolf Erman, *The Literature of the Ancient Egyptians*, trans. by Aylward M. Blackman (London: Methuen & Co., Ltd., 1927), pp. 190, 196, 197.
24. From "The Instruction of Meri-ka-Re," trans. by John A. Wilson, *The Burden of Egypt*, p. 120.
25. *Ibid.*, p. 119.
26. Quoted in George Steindorff and George Hoyningen-Huene, *Egypt* (Locust Valley, N.Y.: J. J. Augustin Inc., 1943), p. 23.
27. Trans. by George Steindorff and Keith E. Seele, *When Egypt Ruled the East* (Chicago: University of Chicago Press, 1942), p. 125.
28. Quoted in J. H. Breasted, *The Dawn of Conscience* (New York: Charles Scribner's Sons, 1939), p. 284.
29. Ezekiel 27:33-34. Revised Standard Version of the Bible.
30. B. W. Anderson, *Understanding the Old Testament* (Englewood Cliffs, N.J.: Prentice-Hall, Inc., 1957), p. 537.
31. I Samuel 8:6, 20. Revised Standard Version of the Bible.
32. I Kings 4:20 ff.; 10:14 ff. Revised Standard Version of the Bible.
33. II Kings 25:14. Revised Standard Version of the Bible.
34. Micah 6:8. Revised Standard Version of the Bible.
35. D. D. Luckenbill, *Ancient Records of Assyria and Babylonia*, I (Chicago: University of Chicago Press, 1926), p. 147.
36. Quoted in Georges Roux, *Ancient Iraq* (Baltimore: Penguin Books, Inc., 1966), p. 278.
37. Nahum 3:8. Revised Standard Version of the Bible.
38. Herodotus, *History*, I, 181; trans. by George Rawlinson.
39. Daniel 5:27. Revised Standard Version of the Bible.
40. Herodotus, IX, 122; trans. by A. R. Burn, *Persia and the West* (New York: St. Martin's Press, 1962), p. 61.
41. Herodotus, VIII, 98; trans. by Rawlinson.

CHAPTER 2: THE GLORY THAT WAS GREECE

1. Plutarch's *Lives*, II, trans. by Sir T. North (London: J. M. Dent & Sons Ltd., 1898), p. 144.
2. See Leonard R. Palmer, *Mycenaeans and Minoans: Aegean Prehistory in the Light of the Linear B Tablets* (New York: Alfred A. Knopf, Inc., and London: Faber and Faber, Ltd., 1961), Chapter 5, "The Last Days of Pylos."
3. Quoted in Werner Jaeger, *Paideia: The Ideals of Greek Culture*, I (New York: Oxford University Press, 1939), p. 70.
4. "Laws," V, 735; in *The Dialogues of Plato*, II, trans. by B. Jowett (New York: Random House, 1937), p. 503.
5. Plutarch's *Lives*, trans. by J. Dryden, rev. by A. H. Clough (New York: Modern Library, 1932), p. 107.
6. Trans. by A. R. Burn, *The Pelican History of Greece* (Baltimore: Penguin Books, Inc., 1966), p. 186.
7. C. E. Robinson, *Hellas: A Short History of Ancient Greece* (New York: Pantheon Books, 1948), p. 68.
8. Thucydides, *The History of the Peloponnesian War*, II, 65, ed. in trans. by Sir R. W. Livingstone, The World's Classics (New York: Oxford University Press, 1963), p. 130.
9. *Ibid.*, II, 37, 40, pp. 111, 113.
10. Thucydides, II, 40-41, trans. by Sir R. W. Livingstone.
11. *Ibid.*, I, 23, p. 46.
12. *Ibid.*, II, 65, p. 130.
13. *Ibid.*, V, 105, p. 270.
14. *Ibid.*, VI, 90, p. 325.
15. Herodotus, *History of the Persian Wars*, VII, 10.
16. Quoted in M. Cary and T. J. Haarhoff, *Life and Thought in the Greek and Roman World* (London: Methuen & Co., Ltd., 1951), p. 200.
17. "Apology," in *The Four Socratic Dialogues of Plato*, trans. by B. Jowett (Oxford: Clarendon Press, 1924), pp. 91-92.
18. "Phaedrus," 247; quoted in *The Greek World*, ed. by Hugh Lloyd-Jones (Baltimore: Penguin Books, Inc., 1965), pp. 137-138.
19. Quoted in Cary and Haarhoff, p. 192.
20. Thucydides, I, 22, trans. by Sir R. W. Livingstone, pp. 44-45.
21. Trans. by Andrew Robert Burn, *The Lyric Age of Greece* (London: Edward Arnold Ltd. and New York: St. Martin's Press, 1960), p. 166. Copyright 1960. Reprinted by permission of Edward Arnold Publishers Ltd.
22. *Ibid.*, p. 236.
23. From *Agamemnon*, trans. by Gilbert Murray in *Ten Greek Plays*, ed. by Lane Cooper (New York: Oxford University Press, 1929), p. 96.
24. Quoted in *The Cambridge Ancient History*, XI (Cambridge: The University Press, 1936), p. 696.
25. Moschus, *Idyl IX*, trans. by Ernest Myers in A. Lang, *Theocritus, Bion and Moschus* (London: Macmillan & Co. Ltd., 1911), p. 210. Reprinted by permission of the publisher.
26. G. Murray, *Hellenism and the Modern World* (Boston: Beacon Press, 1953), pp. 56-57.

CHAPTER 3: THE GRANDEUR THAT WAS ROME

1. Polybius, *Histories*, I, 10, trans. by Evelyn S. Shuckburgh (Bloomington: Indiana University Press, 1962), Vol. I, p. 10.
2. Livy, *Roman History*, XXXIII, 33, trans. by E. T. Sage in The Loeb Classical Library (Cambridge: Harvard University Press, 1945), Vol. IX, p. 367.
3. Plutarch's *Lives*, "Tiberius Gracchus," IX, 5, trans. by Bernadotte Perrin in The Loeb Classical Library (Cambridge: Harvard University Press, 1945), Vol. X, pp. 165, 167.
4. M. Hammond, *City-State and World State in Greek and Roman Political Theory Until Augustus* (Cambridge: Harvard University Press, 1951), p. 153.
5. Tacitus, *Annals*, XV, 44; trans. by Michael Grant (Baltimore: Penguin Books, Inc., 1959), p. 354.
6. Tertullian, *Concerning the Soul*, quoted in S. Katz, *The Decline of Rome and the Rise of Medieval Europe* (Ithaca, N.Y.: Cornell University Press, 1955), p. 7.
7. Virgil, *Aeneid*, VI, 847-853, in *Roman Civilization: Selected Readings*, II, ed. by Naphtali Lewis and Meyer Reinhold (New York: Columbia University Press, 1955), p. 23.
8. Aelius Aristides, *To Rome* (Oration XXVI), trans. by S. Levin (Glencoe, Ill.: The Free Press, 1950), p. 126.
9. R. C. Trevelyan, *Translations from Horace, Juvenal and Montaigne* (New York: Cambridge University Press, 1941), p. 129.
10. Quoted in Grant Showerman, *Century Readings in Ancient Classical Literature* (New York: The Century Co., 1925), p. 386.
11. Lucretius, *On the Nature of the Universe*, Book III, line 70, trans. by Ronald Latham (Baltimore: Penguin Books, Inc., 1951), p. 98.
12. Horace, *Odes*, III, 29 (in part), trans. by John Dryden.
13. *Juvenal's Satires*, trans. by William Gifford, rev. by John Warrington, Everyman's Library Edition (New York: E. P. Dutton & Co., Inc., 1954), p. 5.
14. Lucretius, *On the Nature of Things*, Book III, lines 830 ff., trans. by John Dryden.
15. Pliny, *Natural History*, II, xlv, 117-118; trans. by H. Rackham, The Loeb Classical Library (Cambridge: Harvard University Press, 1938), Vol. I, pp. 259, 261.
16. Quoted in W. Durant, *Caesar and Christ* (New York: Simon & Schuster, Inc., 1944), p. 506.

CHAPTER 4: THE ASIAN WAY OF LIFE

1. A. Coomaraswamy, *The Dance of Shiva* (Bombay: Asia Publishing House, 1948), p. 22.
2. W. T. de Bary, Jr., *et al.*, eds., *Sources of Indian Tradition* (New York: Columbia University Press, 1958), pp. 284-285.
3. R. K. Mookerji, *Hindu Civilization* (London: Longmans, Green & Co., Ltd., 1936), p. 249.
4. N. Dutt, "Religion and Philosophy," in *The Age of Imperial Unity*, Vol. II of *The History and Culture of the Indian People*, ed. by R. C. Majumdar and A. D. Pusalker (Bombay: Bharatiya Vidya Bhavan, 1951), p. 371.

5. Cited in H. G. Rawlinson, *India: A Short Cultural History* (New York: D. Appleton-Century Co., Inc., 1938), pp. 51-52.

6. Quoted in H. G. Rawlinson, *Intercourse Between India and the Western World from the Earliest Times to the Fall of Rome* (New York: Cambridge University Press, 1926), p. 39.

7. R. K. Mookerji, "Asoka the Great," in *The Age of Imperial Unity*, Vol. II of *The History and Culture of the Indian People*, p. 92.

8. W. W. Tarn, *The Greeks in Bactria and India* (New York: Cambridge University Press, 1951), p. 181.

9. R. Grousset, *The Rise and Splendour of the Chinese Empire* (Berkeley and Los Angeles: University of California Press, 1953), p. 26.

10. W. T. de Bary, Jr., *et al.*, eds., *Sources of Chinese Tradition* (New York: Columbia University Press, 1960), pp. 63-64.

11. Quoted in Hu Shih, *Development of the Logical Method in Ancient China* (Shanghai: The Oriental Book Company, 1928), p. 4.

12. E. O. Reischauer and J. K. Fairbank, *East Asia: The Great Tradition* (Boston: Houghton Mifflin Co., 1958), p. 87.

13. See Hu Shih, "The Establishment of Confucianism As a State Religion During the Han Dynasty," *Journal of the North China Branch of the Royal Asiatic Society*, LX (Shanghai, 1929), pp. 34-35. See also J. K. Shryock, *The Origin and Development of the State Cult of Confucius* (New York: D. Appleton-Century Co., Inc., 1932).

14. Pliny, *Natural History*, trans. by H. Rackham (London: William Heinemann, Ltd., 1945), Book VI, I. 101, and Book XII, I. 84.

15. J. Needham, *Introductory Orientations*, Vol. I of *Science and Civilisation in China* (New York: Cambridge University Press, 1954), p. 239.

CHAPTER 5: THE CITY OF GOD

1. St. Jerome's *Commentary of Ezekiel*, I, Prologue.

2. E. Wilson, *The Scrolls from the Dead Sea* (New York: Oxford University Press, 1955), p. 60.

3. Frank M. Cross, Jr., *The Ancient Library of Qumran and Modern Biblical Studies*, rev. ed. (Garden City, N.Y.: Doubleday Anchor Books, 1961), p. 242.

4. John 18:33-38. *Good News for Modern Man: The New Testament in Today's English Version* (New York: American Bible Society, 1966), p. 258.

5. Acts 22:6-10. *Good News for Modern Man*, p. 324.

6. Galatians 2:16; 3:28. *Good News for Modern Man*, pp. 421, 424.

7. Tertullian, *Apology*, Ch. 50, trans. by A. Souter (Cambridge: Cambridge University Press, 1917), p. 145.

8. Quoted in Henry Bettenson, ed., *Documents of the Christian Church* (London: Oxford University Press, 1943), p. 28.

9. *Ibid.*, p. 9.

10. Naphtali Lewis and Meyer Reinhold, *Roman Civilization: Selected Readings*, II (New York: Columbia University Press, 1955), pp. 464-465.

11. Tacitus, *Germania*, Ch. 14, trans. by H. Mattingly, *Tacitus on Britain and Germany* (Harmondsworth: Penguin Books, Ltd., 1948), p. 112.

12. S. Katz, *The Decline of Rome and the Rise of Medieval Europe* (Ithaca, N.Y.: Cornell University Press, 1955), p. 7.

13. E. Gibbon, *The History of the Decline and Fall of the Roman Empire* (London: Methuen & Co., Ltd., 1896), Ch. XXXVIII, "General Observations on the Fall of the Roman Empire in the West."

14. A. E. R. Boak, *Manpower Shortage and the Fall of the Roman Empire in the West* (Ann Arbor: University of Michigan Press, 1955), p. 115.

15. Katz, p. 98.

CHAPTER 6: CITADEL AND CONQUEROR

1. Procopius, *History of the Wars*, Book I, trans. by H. B. Dewing (London: William Heinemann, Ltd., 1914), pp. 231, 233.

2. Geoffrey de Villehardouin, *The Conquest of Constantinople*, trans. by Sir Frank T. Marzials, *Memoirs of the Crusades* (New York: Everyman's Library, E. P. Dutton & Co., Inc., 1933), pp. 51, 65.

3. Quoted in J. F. C. Fuller, *A Military History of the Western World*, I (New York: Funk & Wagnalls, 1954), p. 522.

4. "The Book of the Prefect," trans. by A. E. R. Boak, *Journal of Economic and Business History*, I (1929), p. 600.

5. Quoted by C. Diehl, "Byzantine Art," in *Byzantium: Introduction to East Roman Civilization*, ed. by N. H. Baynes and H. St. L. B. Moss (New York: Oxford University Press, 1948), p. 166.

6. Procopius, *Buildings*, I, i, 33-34, trans. by H. B. Dewing (Cambridge: Harvard University Press, 1940), p. 17.

7. D. Talbot Rice, *Byzantine Art* (Harmondsworth: Penguin Books, Ltd., 1954), pp. 150-151.

8. Quoted in Alfred Guillaume, *Islam* (Harmondsworth: Penguin Books, Ltd., 1954), pp. 28-29.

9. See T. P. Hughes, *A Dictionary of Islam* (London: W. H. Allen and Co., 1885).

10. Quoted in E. H. Palmer, *Haroun Alraschid, Caliph of Bagdad* (London: Marcus Ward and Company, 1881), p. 76.

11. H. A. R. Gibb, "Literature," in *The Legacy of Islam*, ed. by T. W. Arnold and A. Guillaume (Oxford: Clarendon Press, 1931), p. 182.

12. *Rubáiyát of Omar Khayyám*, trans. by Edward Fitzgerald, Stanzas 12, 13, 71, 72.

13. Ibn Khaldun, *The Mugaddimah: An Introduction to History*, trans. by Franz Rosenthal, Vol. I (London: Routledge & Kegan Paul Ltd., 1958), p. 71.

CHAPTER 7: THE GUPTAS AND THE T'ANG: TWO GOLDEN AGES

1. Quoted in H. H. Gowen and J. W. Hall, *An Outline History of China* (New York: D. Appleton & Co., 1926), p. 117.

2. From *The Works of Li Po; The Chinese Poet Done into English Verse,* by Shigeyoshi Obata, with an introduction and biographical critical matter translated from the Chinese. Copyright, 1922, by E. P. Dutton & Co., Inc. Renewal copyright 1950 by E. P. Dutton & Co., Inc., and reprinted with their permission.
3. Quoted in Gowen and Hall, p. 127.
4. Obata, p. 39.
5. Quoted in Gowen and Hall, p. 142.
6. K. S. Latourette, *The Chinese: Their History and Culture,* II (New York: The Macmillan Company, 1934), p. 264.
7. Quoted in I. Nitobé, *Bushido, the Soul of Japan* (Tokyo: Maruzen, 1935), p. 592.

CHAPTER 8: EUROPE'S SEARCH FOR STABILITY

1. Gregory of Tours, *History of the Franks,* II, 30; quoted in Eleanor S. Duckett, *The Gateway to the Middle Ages* (New York: The Macmillan Company, 1938), p. 231.
2. Quoted in C. Dawson, *The Making of Europe* (London: Sheed & Ward Ltd., 1932), p. 76.
3. Quoted in M. L. W. Laistner, *Thought and Letters in Western Europe, A.D. 500 to 900* (Ithaca, N.Y.: Cornell University Press, 1931), pp. 196-197.
4. *Ibid.,* p. 390.
5. *Piers the Plowman,* quoted in G. B. Adams, *Civilization During the Middle Ages* (New York: Charles Scribner's Sons, 1914), p. 222.
6. Quoted in E. M. Hulme, *History of the British People* (New York: Century Co., 1929), pp. 121-122.
7. Quoted in Sidney Painter, *French Chivalry: Chivalric Ideas and Practices in Medieval France* (Baltimore: Johns Hopkins Press, 1940), p. 169.

CHAPTER 9: THE WEST TAKES THE OFFENSIVE

1. Trans. by D. C. Munro, *Translations and Reprints from the Original Sources of European History,* Vol. I, No. 2 (Philadelphia: University of Pennsylvania Press, 1897), pp. 6-7.
2. Quoted in A. C. Krey, *The First Crusade* (Princeton: Princeton University Press, 1921), p. 261.
3. Quoted in R. H. C. Davis, *A History of Medieval Europe: From Constantine to Saint Louis* (London: Longmans, Green & Co., Ltd., 1957), p. 290.
4. E. P. Cheyney, *The Dawn of a New Era, 1250-1453* (New York: Harper & Bros., 1936), p. 132.

CHAPTER 10: NATIONS IN THE MAKING

1. Quoted in Dorothy Whitelock, *The Beginning of English Society* (Baltimore: Penguin Books, Inc., 1952), p. 66.
2. Quoted in E. P. Cheyney, *Readings in English History Drawn from the Original Sources* (Boston: Ginn and Co., 1908), p. 112.
3. D. C. Douglas and G. Greenaway, *English Historical Documents, 1042-1189* (New York: Oxford University Press, 1953), p. 200.

4. W. S. Churchill, *The Birth of Britain,* Vol. I of *A History of the English-Speaking Peoples* (New York: Dodd, Mead & Co., 1965), pp. 222-223.
5. Quoted in Churchill, I, p. 210.
6. Quoted in Cheyney, pp. 157-158.
7. Quoted in *ibid.,* pp. 183, 185.
8. Quoted in J. H. Robinson, *Readings in European History,* I (Boston: Ginn and Co., 1904), p. 202.
9. *Ibid.,* p. 204.
10. Jonathon F. Scott *et al., Readings in Medieval History* (New York: F. S. Crofts and Company, 1933), pp. 464-465.
11. *The Poem of the Cid,* trans. by W. S. Merwin (London: J. M. Dent & Sons, 1959), pp. 79-80, 82. Reprinted by permission of David Higham Associates, Ltd.
12. R. H. C. Davis, *A History of Medieval Europe: From Constantine to Saint Louis* (London: Longmans, Green & Co., Ltd., 1957), p. 315.

CHAPTER 11: TO THE GLORY OF GOD

1. Quoted in R. H. C. Davis, *A History of Medieval Europe: From Constantine to Saint Louis* (London: Longmans, Green & Co., Ltd., 1957), p. 80.
2. Quoted in S. M. Brown, *Medieval Europe* (New York: Harcourt, Brace & Co., 1935), pp. 382-383.
3. Harry J. Carroll, Jr., *et al., The Development of Civilization: A Documentary History of Politics, Society, and Thought,* I (Chicago: Scott, Foresman and Co., 1961), p. 304.
4. Henry Bettenson, ed., *Documents of the Christian Church* (London: Oxford University Press, 1943), p. 144.
5. Quoted in J. H. Robinson, *Readings in European History,* I (Boston: Ginn and Co., 1904), p. 283.
6. Quoted in S. R. Packard, *Europe and the Church Under Innocent III* (New York: Henry Holt & Co., 1927), p. 15.
7. Summerfield Baldwin, *The Organization of Medieval Christianity* (New York: Henry Holt & Co., 1929), p. 35.
8. T. Morrison, ed. and trans., *The Portable Chaucer* (New York: Viking Press, 1949), p. 74. Copyright 1949 by Theodore Morrison. Reprinted by permission of The Viking Press, Inc.
9. Quoted in J. Evans, *Life in Medieval France* (New York: Oxford University Press, 1925), p. 87.
10. *A Catholic Dictionary,* ed. by Donald Attwater (New York: The Macmillan Company, 1949), p. 227.
11. Luke 9:1-6. *Good News for Modern Man: The New Testament in Today's English* (New York: American Bible Society, 1966), p. 158.
12. Morrison, pp. 80-81.
13. Robert S. Lopez, *The Tenth Century: How Dark the Dark Ages?* (New York: Rinehart and Co., 1959), p. 1.
14. Quoted in Urban T. Holmes, Jr., "Transitions in European Education," in *Twelfth-Century Europe and the Foundations of Modern Society,* ed. by Marshall Clagett, Gaines Post, and Robert Reynolds (Madison: University of Wisconsin Press, 1961), p. 17.

15. *The Story of My Misfortunes: The Autobiography of Peter Abélard,* trans. by Henry Adams Bellows (Glencoe, Ill.: The Free Press, 1958), pp. 3, 10.

16. Quoted in *Introduction to Contemporary Civilization in the West: A Source Book,* I (New York: Columbia University Press, 1946), p. 85.

17. *An Encyclopedist of the Dark Ages: Isidore of Seville,* trans. by E. Brehaut (New York: Columbia University Press, 1912), pp. 218-219.

18. *The Art of Falconry . . . of Frederick II of Hohenstaufen,* trans. by Casey A. Wood and F. Marjorie Fyfe (Boston: Charles T. Branford Co., 1943), pp. 3-4.

19. Quoted in H. O. Taylor, *The Mediaeval Mind,* II (London: Macmillan & Co. Ltd., 1938), p. 524.

20. J. A. Symonds, *Wine, Women and Song* (New York: Oxford University Press, and London: Chatto & Windus Ltd., 1931), pp. 67-69.

21. Quoted in F. B. Artz, *The Mind of the Middle Ages, A.D. 300-1500,* 2nd ed. (New York: Alfred A. Knopf, Inc., 1954), p. 332.

22. C. Warren Hollister, *Medieval Europe: A Short History* (New York: John Wiley & Sons, Inc., 1964), p. 230.

23. Amy Kelly, *Eleanor of Aquitaine and the Four Kings* (Cambridge: Harvard University Press, 1952), p. 86.

24. *L'Inferno,* Canto I, lines 1-3, trans. by Dorothy L. Sayers, *Dante, The Divine Comedy, I: Hell* (Harmondsworth: Penguin Books, Ltd., 1949), p. 71.

25. *Paradise,* Canto XXXIII, lines 121, 144, trans. by J. B. Fletcher.

26. Geoffrey Chaucer, *Canterbury Tales,* trans. by J. U. Nicolson (New York: Crown Publishers, Inc., 1936), pp. 3-5.

CHAPTER 12: EUROPE IN TRANSITION

1. A. C. Flick, *Decline of the Medieval Church,* I (London: Kegan Paul, Trench, Trubner and Co., Ltd., 1930), p. 293.

2. R. H. Bainton, *The Reformation of the Sixteenth Century* (Boston: Beacon Press, 1952), p. 15.

3. Quoted in M. Cherniavsky, "'Holy Russia': A Study in the History of an Idea," *The American Historical Review,* LXIII, No. 3 (April 1958), p. 625.

4. G. Barraclough, *History in a Changing World* (Oxford: Basil Blackwell, 1955), p. 134.

CHAPTER 13: MAN IS THE MEASURE

1. Quoted in J. Burckhardt, *The Civilization of the Renaissance in Italy,* trans. by S. G. C. Middlemore (London: George Allen & Unwin Ltd., 1921), p. 138.

2. William Shakespeare, *The Tempest,* Act V, Scene i.

3. Quoted in J. H. Randall, Jr., *The Making of the Modern Mind* (Boston: Houghton Mifflin Co., 1940), p. 213.

4. Quoted in F. B. Artz, *The Mind of the Middle Ages A.D. 200-1500,* 2nd ed. (New York: Alfred A. Knopf, Inc., 1954), p. 307.

5. *The Decameron of Giovanni Boccaccio,* trans. by Richard Aldington (New York: Garden City Publishing Co., 1949), p. 559.

6. F. B. Artz, *From the Renaissance to Romanticism: Trends in Style in Art, Literature, and Music, 1300-1830* (Chicago: University of Chicago Press, 1962), p. 102.

7. H. O. Taylor, *Thought and Expression in the Sixteenth Century,* I (New York: The Macmillan Company, 1920), p. 175.

8. Quoted in Randall, p. 118.

9. From the 1684 translation by Gilbert Burnet, in *Introduction to Contemporary Civilization in the West: A Source Book,* I (New York: Columbia University Press, 1946), p. 461.

10. *Ibid.,* p. 460.

11. Quoted in Taylor, pp. 328-329.

12. Montaigne, "Of the Education of Children," in *The Complete Works of Montaigne,* trans. by D. M. Frame (Stanford: Stanford University Press, 1957), p. 112.

13. *Ibid.,* p. 110.

14. J. van der Elst, *The Last Flowering of the Middle Ages* (New York: Doubleday & Co., Inc., 1946), p. 59.

CHAPTER 14: HERE I TAKE MY STAND

1. Quoted in R. H. Bainton, *Here I Stand: A Life of Martin Luther* (New York and Nashville: Abingdon-Cokesbury Press, 1950), p. 65. Copyright 1950.

2. *Ibid.,* pp. 66-67.

3. Quoted in R. H. Bainton, *The Reformation of the Sixteenth Century* (Boston: Beacon Press, 1952), p. 27.

4. Quoted in C. Hayes, *A Political and Cultural History of Modern Europe,* I (New York: The Macmillan Company, 1933), p. 154.

5. Quoted in H. Bettenson, ed., *Documents of the Christian Church* (London: Oxford University Press, 1943), p. 261 ff.

6. Quoted in P. Smith, *The Age of the Reformation* (New York: Henry Holt & Co., 1920), p. 69.

7. Quoted in George L. Mosse, *The Reformation,* 3rd ed. (New York: Holt, Rinehart and Winston, Inc., 1963), p. 31.

8. Quoted in Bainton, *The Reformation of the Sixteenth Century,* p. 58.

9. Quoted in Bettenson, pp. 282-283.

10. From *The Twelve Articles* in A. Schrier *et al., Modern European Civilization: A Documentary History of Politics, Society, and Thought from the Renaissance to the Present* (Chicago: Scott, Foresman and Co., 1963), pp. 105-106.

11. Quoted in H. J. Grimm, *The Reformation Era, 1500-1650* (New York: The Macmillan Company, 1956), p. 175.

12. R. Fife, *The Revolt of Martin Luther* (New York: Columbia University Press, 1957), p. 693.

13. Bainton, *The Reformation of the Sixteenth Century,* p. 114.

14. Bettenson, p. 365.

15. Quoted in F. Eby and C. F. Arrowood, *The Development of Modern Education* (New York: Prentice-Hall, Inc., 1936), p. 91.

16. *Concerning Heretics . . . . An anonymous work attributed to Sebastian Castellio,* ed. by R. H. Bainton (New York: Columbia University Press, 1935), pp. 122-123.
17. *Ibid.,* pp. 134-135.
18. Quoted in V. H. H. Green, *Luther and the Reformation* (New York: Capricorn Books, 1964), p. 141.
19. *Ibid.,* p. 142.
20. R. H. Tawney, *Religion and the Rise of Capitalism* (Baltimore: Penguin Books, Inc., 1947), p. 99.

CHAPTER 15: THE STRIFE OF STATES AND KINGS

1. Quoted in B. Reynolds, *Proponents of Limited Monarchy in Sixteenth Century France: Francis Holman and Jean Bodin* (New York: Columbia University Press, 1931), p. 182.
2. Quoted in G. Mattingly, *Renaissance Diplomacy* (London: Jonathan Cape, 1962), p. 239.
3. Quoted in M. Guizot, *The History of France from the Earliest Times to 1848,* II (New York: Thomas Y. Crowell & Co., n. d.), p. 428.
4. *Machiavelli: The Prince and Other Works,* trans. by A. H. Gilbert (Chicago: Packard and Co., 1941), p. 177 (Ch. 26).
5. *Ibid.,* p. 148 (Ch. 18).
6. *Ibid.,* p. 150 (Ch. 18).
7. *Ibid.,* p. 177 (Ch. 26).
8. Quoted in R. Ergang, *Europe from the Renaissance to Waterloo* (Boston: D. C. Heath & Co., 1954), p. 296.
9. *Ibid.,* p. 246.
10. Quoted in J. H. Elliott, *Imperial Spain, 1469-1716* (New York: St. Martin's Press, 1964), p. 282.
11. *Ibid.,* p. 283.
12. Quoted in P. Smith, *The Age of the Reformation* (New York: Henry Holt & Co., 1920), p. 215.
13. Quoted in Carl L. Becker, *Modern History* (Chicago: Silver Burdett Co., 1942), pp. 204, 205.
14. Carl J. Friedrich, *The Age of Baroque, 1610-1660* (New York: Harper & Bros., 1952), p. 129.
15. See "Grotius: *Law of War and Peace, Prolegomena,*" in *The American Journal of International Law,* XXXV, No. 2 (April 1941), pp. 206, 217.

CHAPTER 16: OLD WORLDS BEYOND THE HORIZON

1. This classification follows that of Melville Herskovits, *The Human Factor in Changing Africa* (New York: Alfred A. Knopf, Inc., 1962).
2. Cited from Roland Oliver and J. D. Fage, *A Short History of Africa* (Baltimore: Penguin Books, Inc., 1962), p. 90.
3. This classification is from George H. Kimble, *Tropical Africa,* II (New York: Twentieth Century Fund, 1960), p. 19.
4. Lord Hailey, *An African Survey* (New York: Oxford University Press, 1957), p. 68.
5. Colin M. Turnbull, *The Peoples of Africa* (Leicester,

England: Brockhampton Press, 1963), pp. 29-30.
6. Cited in Herskovits, p. 469.

CHAPTER 17: SEEK OUT, DISCOVER, AND FIND

1. See H. Ingstad, "Vinland Ruins Prove Vikings Found the New World," *National Geographic Magazine,* Vol. 126, No. 5 (November 1964), pp. 708-734.
2. Quoted in Sir Percy Sykes, *A History of Exploration,* Harper Torchbooks (New York: Harper & Row, 1961), p. 108.
3. Quoted in H. H. Gowen, *An Outline History of Japan* (New York: D. Appleton Co., 1927), p. 255.
4. Quoted in H. Herring, *A History of Latin America,* 3rd ed. (New York: Alfred A. Knopf, Inc., 1968), p. 173.
5. Quoted in H. Robinson, *The Development of the British Empire* (Boston: Houghton Mifflin Co., 1922), p. 38.
6. Quoted in Sir George Clark, *The Seventeenth Century* (New York: Oxford University Press, 1961), p. 24.
7. Quoted in H. Heaton, *Economic History of Europe* (New York: Harper & Bros., 1948), p. 315.
8. Quoted in *ibid.,* p. 238.
9. Quoted in J. B. Botsford, *English Society in the Eighteenth Century, As Influenced from Oversea* (New York: The Macmillan Company, 1924), p. 70.
10. Heaton, p. 239.
11. *Ibid.* (published in 1936), p. 363.

CHAPTER 18: NEW DIMENSIONS OF THE MIND

1. Quoted in *Introduction to Contemporary Civilization in the West,* I (New York: Columbia University Press, 1946), pp. 845-859.
2. F. Bacon, *The Works of Francis Bacon,* III, ed. by J. Spedding (London: Longman and Co., 1861), p. 156.
3. Quoted in J. H. Randall, Jr., *The Making of the Modern Mind,* rev. ed. (Boston: Houghton Mifflin Co., 1940), p. 221.
4. Quoted in *Introduction to Contemporary Civilization in the West,* I, p. 557.
5. Quoted in *Sir Isaac Newton's Mathematical Principles of Natural Philosphy and His System of the World,* ed. and trans. by F. Cajori (Berkeley: University of California Press, 1946).
6. H. Butterfield, *The Origins of Modern Science* (London: G. Bell and Sons, Ltd., 1949), p. 104.
7. See P. Hazard, *The European Mind: The Critical Years* (New Haven: Yale University Press, 1953).
8. A. Pope, "The Universal Prayer," in *The Poetical Works of Alexander Pope* (London: John James Chidley, 1846), p. 145.
9. W. L. Dorn, *Competition for Empire, 1740-1763* (New York: Harper and Bros., 1940), p. 181.
10. Quoted in F. E. Manuel, *The Age of Reason* (Ithaca, N.Y.: Cornell University Press, 1951), p. 39.
11. G. M. Trevelyan, *History of England* (London: Longmans, Green & Co., Ltd., 1937), p. 514.

12. Preserved Smith, *Origins of Modern Culture, 1543-1687* (New York: P. F. Collier, Inc., 1962), p. 484.
13. A. Pope, "Epistle to Dr. Arbuthnot," in *The Literature of England,* I, 5th ed., ed. by G. K. Anderson and W. E. Buckler (Glenview, Ill.: Scott, Foresman and Co., 1958), p. 1580.
14. A. Pope, "An Essay on Man," in *The Literature of England,* I, p. 1568.

CHAPTER 19: L'ÉTAT, C'EST MOI

1. Quoted in J. H. Robinson, *Readings in European History,* II (Boston: Ginn and Co., 1906), pp. 273-275.
2. Quoted in W. G. Crane *et al., Twelve Hundred Years: The Literature of England,* I (New York: Stackpole and Heck, Inc., 1948), p. 572.
3. Quoted in A. F. Tyler, *The Modern World* (New York: Farrar and Rinehart, 1939), p. 186.
4. *Encyclopaedia Britannica,* VII, 1947 ed., p. 16.
5. Sir Ernest Barker *et al., The European Inheritance,* II (London: Clarendon Press, 1954), p. 144.
6. Quoted in E. P. Cheyney, *Readings in English History Drawn from the Original Sources* (Boston: Ginn and Co., 1908), p. 426.
7. Quoted in *ibid.,* p. 503.
8. Quoted in P. Smith, *A History of Modern Culture,* I (London: George Routledge and Sons, Ltd., 1930), p. 226.
9. John Milton, "Areopagitica," in *The Literature of England,* I, 5th ed., ed. by G. K. Anderson and W. E. Buckler (Glenview, Ill.: Scott, Foresman and Co., 1966), p. 1182.
10. Quoted in G. B. Adams, *Constitutional History of England* (New York: Henry Holt & Co., 1934), p. 406.
11. Quoted in R. Ergang, *The Potsdam Führer, Frederick William I* (New York: Columbia University Press, 1941), p. 7.
12. W. L. Dorn, *Competition for Empire, 1740-1763* (New York: Harper & Bros., 1940), p. 9.
13. Quoted in *ibid.,* p. 139.
14. W. P. Hall and R. G. Albion, *A History of England and the British Empire, 1789-1914* (Boston: Ginn and Co., 1946), p. 453.
15. Quoted in Dorn, p. 314.
16. Quoted in P. Gaxotte, *Frederick the Great* (London: G. Bell & Sons, Ltd., 1941), p. 357.
17. Quoted in H. Robinson, *The Development of the British Empire* (Boston: Houghton Mifflin Co., 1922), p. 96.

CHAPTER 20: THE RIGHTS OF MAN

1. Thomas Mun, "England's Treasure by Foreign Trade" (1664), in *Introduction to Contemporary Civilization in the West: A Source Book,* I (New York: Columbia University Press, 1946), p. 641.
2. Adam Smith, *An Inquiry into the Nature and Causes of the Wealth of Nations,* Modern Library Edition (New York: The Macmillan Company, 1937), pp. 14, 421.

3. Quoted in G. R. Havens, *The Age of Ideas* (New York: Henry Holt & Co., 1955), pp. 105-106.
4. Quoted in J. E. Gillespie, *A History of Geographical Discovery, 1400-1800* (New York: Henry Holt & Co., 1933), p. 99.
5. J. J. Rousseau, *The Social Contract,* Book III, Chapter XVIII.
6. Quoted in J. H. Robinson and C. A. Beard, *Readings in Modern European History,* I (Boston: Ginn and Co., 1908), pp. 202-205.
7. Quoted in G. P. Gooch, *Frederick the Great; the Ruler, the Writer, the Man* (New York: Alfred A. Knopf, Inc., 1947), p. 109.
8. Quoted in C. Rossiter, *The First American Revolution* (New York: Harcourt, Brace & Co., 1956), prefatory note.
9. L. M. Larson, *History of England and the British Commonwealth* (New York: Henry Holt and Co., 1924), p. 529.
10. C. J. H. Hayes, *A Political and Cultural History of Modern Europe,* I (New York: The Macmillan Company, 1932), p. 614.
11. "The Declaration of the Rights of Man," in *The World in Literature,* III, rev. ed., ed. by R. Warnock and G. K. Anderson (Glenview, Ill.: Scott, Foresman and Co., 1967), pp. 288-289.
12. Quoted in J. E. Gillespie, *A History of Europe, 1500-1815* (New York: Alfred A. Knopf, Inc., 1928), p. 529.
13. Quoted in L. Madelin, *The French Revolution* (London: William Heinemann, Ltd., 1916), p. 323.
14. W. Wordsworth, "The Prelude; or, Growth of a Poet's Mind," Book XI, lines 108-112.
15. E. Burke, "Reflections on the Revolution in France," in *The Works of the Right Honorable Edmund Burke,* II (London: G. Bell & Sons, Ltd., 1886), p. 284.
16. Quoted in J. H. Randall, Jr., *The Making of the Modern Mind* (Boston: Houghton Mifflin Co., 1940), p. 433.
17. Quoted in Gillespie, p. 537.
18. Quoted in J. H. Rose, *The Life of Napoleon,* I (New York: The Macmillan Company, 1902), p. 264.
19. H. A. L. Fisher, *A History of Europe,* III (Boston: Houghton Mifflin Co., 1936; London: Eyre and Spottiswoode, Ltd.), p. 891.
20. George Rudé, *Revolutionary Europe, 1783-1815* (New York: Harper Torchbooks, 1966), p. 290.

CHAPTER 21: REVOLUTION: IN ART, THOUGHT, AND INDUSTRY

1. L. A. Willoughby, *The Romantic Movement in Germany* (London: Oxford University Press, 1930), p. 8.
2. W. Wordsworth, "Composed in the Valley near Dover, on the Day of Landing," in *English Poetry and Prose of the Romantic Movement,* ed. by G. B. Woods (Glenview, Ill.: Scott, Foresman and Co., 1950), p. 313.
3. C. A. and M. Beard, *The Industrial Era,* Vol. II of *The Rise of American Civilization* (New York: The Macmillan Company, 1927), p. 763.
4. C. Dickens, *Hard Times* (London: Thomas Nelson and Sons, Ltd., n.d.), p. 26.

5. T. R. Malthus, "An Essay on Population," in *Introduction to Contemporary Civilization in the West,* II (New York: Columbia University Press, 1955), p. 196.
6. Quoted in W. P. Hall and W. S. Davis, *The Course of Europe Since Waterloo* (New York: D. Appleton-Century Co., Inc., 1941), p. 262.
7. Quoted in *ibid.*, pp. 262-263.
8. David Thomson, *England in the Nineteenth Century, 1815-1914* (Harmondsworth: Penguin Books, Ltd., 1950), p. 101.
9. Quoted in B. Willey, *Nineteenth Century Studies* (London: Chatto and Windus, 1949), p. 262.
10. T. Carlyle, "The Present Time," quoted in E. D. Mackerness, "The Voice of Prophecy: Carlyle and Ruskin," in *From Dickens to Hardy,* ed. by B. Ford (New York: Penguin Books, Inc., 1958), p. 294.
11. The Earl of Beaconsfield, K.G., *Sybil; or, The Two Nations* (London: Longmans, Green & Co., Ltd., 1926), pp. 76-77.
12. W. Godwin, "Political Justice," in S. Hook, *Marx and the Marxists: The Ambiguous Legacy* (Princeton: D. Van Nostrand Co., Inc., 1955), p. 28.
13. Quoted in E. R. A. Seligman, ed., *Encyclopaedia of the Social Sciences,* XIII (New York: The Macmillan Company, 1935), p. 510a.
14. Quoted in H. J. Laski, *Communist Manifesto: Socialist Landmark* (London: George Allen & Unwin, Ltd., 1948), p. 168.
15. Quoted in *ibid.*, p. 141.
16. R. Browning, "Song from 'Pippa Passes,'" in *The Literature of England,* II, 5th ed., ed. by G. K. Anderson and W. E. Buckler (Glenview, Ill.: Scott, Foresman and Co., 1966), p. 657.

CHAPTER 22: TO THE BARRICADES

1. Lord Byron, "Don Juan," Canto III, in *The Literature of England,* II, 5th ed., ed. by G. K. Anderson and W. E. Buckler (Glenview, Ill.: Scott, Foresman and Co., 1966), p. 306.
2. G. M. Young, ed., *Selected Speeches by Lord Macaulay* (London: Oxford University Press, 1935), pp. 18-19.
3. Quoted in P. Robertson, *Revolutions of 1848* (Princeton: Princeton University Press, 1952), p. 14.
4. Quoted in C. D. Hazen, *Europe Since 1815* (New York: Henry Holt and Co., 1910), p. 129.
5. A. L. Fisher, *A History of Europe,* III (Boston: Houghton Mifflin Co., 1936; London: Eyre and Spottiswoode, Ltd., 1924), p. 956.

CHAPTER 23: NATIONALISM AND AUTHORITARIAN REGIMES

1. Quoted in J. S. Schapiro, *Modern and Contemporary European History, 1815-1940* (Boston: Houghton Mifflin Co., 1940), p. 222.
2. Quoted in K. S. Pinson, *Modern Germany* (New York: The Macmillan Company, 1954), p. 116.
3. Quoted in Schapiro, p. 237.
4. Sir J. A. R. Marriott, *A Short History of France* (New York: Oxford University Press, 1944), p. 233.
5. Quoted in F. A. Ogg and W. R. Sharp, *Economic Development of Europe* (New York: The Macmillan Company, 1926), p. 551.
6. Quoted in C. G. Robertson, *Bismarck* (London: Constable and Co., Ltd., 1918), p. 472.
7. Quoted in Schapiro, p. 425.
8. Quoted in *Encyclopaedia Britannica,* III, 1910 ed., p. 231.
9. Quoted in M. T. Florinsky, *Russia: A History and Interpretation,* II (New York: The Macmillan Company, 1953), pp. 809-810.
10. I. Turgenev, *Fathers and Children,* trans. by C. Garnett (New York: The Macmillan Company, 1924), p. 36.
11. Quoted in K. Zilliacus, *The Russian Revolutionary Movement* (London: Alston Rivers, 1905), p. 59.
12. Quoted in R. W. Postgate, *Revolution from 1789 to 1906* (Boston: Houghton Mifflin Co., 1921), pp. 363-364.
13. J. A. R. Marriott, *The Eastern Question* (London: Clarendon Press, 1924), p. 2.
14. A. J. P. Taylor, *The Struggle for Mastery in Europe, 1848-1918* (London: Clarendon Press, 1954), p. 231.
15. Quoted in J. F. C. Fuller, *A Military History of the Western World,* III (New York: Funk & Wagnalls, 1956), p. 104.

CHAPTER 24: HOPE AND HOLOCAUST

1. Quoted in J. E. Gillespie, *Europe in Perspective* (New York: Harcourt, Brace & Co., 1942), p. 253.
2. Quoted in F. Owen, *Tempestuous Journey: Lloyd George, His Life and Times* (London: Hutchinson & Co., Ltd., 1954), p. 186.
3. Quoted in J. V. Ducattillon, "The Church in the Third Republic," in *The Making of Modern Europe,* II, ed. by H. Ausubel (New York: Dryden Press, 1951), p. 861.
4. Quoted by C. J. H. Hayes, *A Political and Cultural History of Modern Europe,* II (New York: The Macmillan Company, 1939), p. 572.
5. Viscount Grey of Fallodon, *Twenty-Five Years,* II (New York: Frederick A. Stokes Co., 1925), p. 20.
6. *The New Cambridge Modern History,* XII, 1960, p. 373.
7. Quoted in F. P. Chambers, *The War Behind the War, 1914-1918* (New York: Harcourt, Brace & Co., 1939), p. 473.
8. From "The Soldier." Reprinted by permission of Dodd, Mead & Company, Inc., from *The Collected Poems of Rupert Brooke.* Copyright 1915 by Dodd, Mead & Company, Inc. Copyright 1943 by Edward Marsh.
9. From "Anthem for Doomed Youth" by Wilfred Owen in *Collected Poems.* Copyright Chatto & Windus, Ltd., 1946, © 1963. Reprinted by permission of New Directions Publishing Corporation, Mr. Harold Owen, and Chatto & Windus, Ltd.
10. Quoted in A. F. Tyler, *The Modern World* (New York: Farrar and Rinehart, 1939), p. 733.
11. S. E. Morison and H. S. Commager, *The Growth of*

the *American Republic,* II (New York: Oxford University Press, 1950), pp. 453-454.

12. E. M. Remarque, *The Road Back,* trans. by A. W. Wheen (Boston: Little, Brown and Co., 1931), p. 25.

CHAPTER 25: SURVIVAL OF THE FITTEST

1. R. Browning, "Song from 'Pippa Passes,' " in *Poetry of the Victorian Period,* 3rd ed., ed. by J. H. Buckley and G. B. Woods (Glenview, Ill.: Scott, Foresman and Co., 1965), p. 184.

2. F. Schevill, *A History of Europe* (New York: Harcourt, Brace & Co., 1938), p. 481.

3. Quoted in R. N. Carew Hunt, *The Theory and Practice of Communism* (London: Geoffrey Bles, 1950), p. 72.

4. C. Darwin, "The Origin of Species," in *Introduction to Contemporary Civilization in the West,* II (New York: Columbia University Press, 1955), pp. 453-454.

5. J. Huxley and J. Fisher, eds., *The Living Thoughts of Darwin* (New York: Longmans, Green & Co., Inc., 1939), pp. 150-151.

6. Quoted in J. Chapin, ed., *The Book of Catholic Quotations* (New York: Farrar, Straus and Cudahy, 1956), p. 706.

7. T. Veblen, *The Theory of the Leisure Class* (New York: The Macmillan Company, 1902), p. 188.

CHAPTER 26: NEW EUROPES OVERSEAS

1. Quoted in J. Quincy, *Speeches Delivered in the Congress of the United States* (Boston: Little, Brown and Co., 1874).

2. Quoted in C. G. Sellers, Jr., *Jacksonian Democracy* (Washington, D.C.: Service Center for Teachers of History, 1958), p. 1.

3. C. Van Doren, ed., *The Literary Works of Abraham Lincoln* (New York: The Limited Editions Club, Inc., 1942), p. 65.

4. Quoted in F. R. Dulles, *America's Rise to World Power* (New York: Harper & Bros., 1955), p. 4.

5. Quoted in *ibid.,* pp. 6-7.

6. H. S. Commager, *Documents of American History* (New York: Appleton-Century-Crofts, Inc., 1958), p. 170.

7. Quoted in H. C. Hockett and A. M. Schlesinger, *Land of the Free* (New York: The Macmillan Company, 1944), p. 482.

8. M. Ugarte, *The Destiny of a Continent* (New York: Alfred A. Knopf, Inc., 1925), p. 288.

9. Quoted in J. L. Mecham, "Conflicting Ideals of Pan-Americanism," *Current History,* XXXIII, No. 3 (December 1930), p. 402.

10. F. D. Scott, *Emigration and Immigration* (New York: The Macmillan Company, for the American Historical Association, 1963), p. 1.

11. S. E. Morison, *The Oxford History of the American People* (London: Oxford University Press, 1965), p. 793.

12. P. D. Curtin, *African History* (New York: The Macmillan Company, for the American Historical Association, 1964), p. 40.

13. Hubert Herring, *History of Latin America* (New York: Alfred A. Knopf, Inc.), p. 97.

14. L. M. Thompson in, Louis Hartz, *The Founding of New Societies* (New York: Harcourt, Brace & World, 1964), p. 207.

15. R. N. Rosecrance in *ibid.,* p. 285.

CHAPTER 27: THE APOGEE OF IMPERIALISM

1. R. Kipling, "The White Man's Burden," from *Rudyard Kipling's Verse: Definitive Edition.* Reprinted by permission of Mrs. George Bambridge, Doubleday & Company, Inc., and The Macmillan Company of Canada Limited.

2. J. Gallagher and R. Robinson, "The Imperialism of Free Trade," *The Economic Review,* Vol. VI, No. I, 1953, pp. 1-15.

3. M. Israel, "Great Britain, Europe and Empire," in *Pax Britannica,* ed. by M. Israel (Edinburgh and London: Oliver and Boyd, 1968), p. 7.

4. See especially R. Robinson and J. Gallagher, *Africa and the Victorians* (New York: St. Martin's Press, 1961).

5. See Hannah Arendt, *The Origins of Totalitarianism* (New York: Meridian Books, 1958), esp. Ch. 5.

6. J. Schumpeter, *Imperialism: Its Sociology* (New York: Meridian Books, 1955), p. 65.

7. P. D. Curtin, *African History* (New York: The Macmillan Company, for the American Historical Association, 1964), p. 48.

8. K. S. Latourette, *A Short History of the Far East* (New York: The Macmillan Company, 1947), p. 184.

9. Li Chien-nung, *The Political History of China, 1840-1928,* trans. by Sau-Yu-Teng and J. Ingalls (Princeton: D. Van Nostrand Co., Inc., 1956), p. 29.

10. Quoted in T. A. Bailey, *The American Pageant* (Lexington, Mass.: D. C. Heath & Co., 1956), p. 630. Copyright 1956.

11. Cited in Peter Fleming, *Bayonets to Lhasa* (New York: Harper & Bros, 1961), p. 21.

12. Quoted in N. D. Harris, *Europe and the East* (Boston: Houghton Mifflin Co., 1926), p. 285.

13. Quoted in M. E. Townsend, *European Colonial Expansion Since 1871* (New York: J. B. Lippincott Co., 1941), p. 367.

14. B. Davidson, *Africa: History of a Continent* (New York: The Macmillan Company, 1966), p. 293.

15. J. A. Hobson, *Imperialism: A Study* (London: Constable and Co., Ltd., 1905), p. 324.

16. W. L. Langer, "A Critique of Imperialism," in *The Making of Modern Europe,* II, ed. by H. Ausubel (New York: Dryden Press, 1951), p. 928.

CHAPTER 28: NEW VISTAS AND OMINOUS FEARS

1. Quoted in L. M. Hacker and B. B. Kendrick, *The United States Since 1865* (New York: F. S. Crofts and Co., 1939), p. 520.

2. Quoted in F. P. Walters, *A History of the League of Nations*, I (London: Oxford University Press, 1952), p. 48.

3. Quoted in R. J. Sontag, *European Diplomatic History, 1871-1932* (New York: The Century Co., 1933), p. 275.

4. Quoted by E. Achorn, *European Civilization and Politics Since 1815* (New York: Harcourt, Brace & Co., 1938), p. 470.

5. Quoted in Sontag, p. 392.

6. J. M. Keynes, *The Economic Consequences of the Peace* (London: Macmillan and Co. Ltd., 1924), p. 211.

7. G. F. Kennan, *The Decision to Intervene* (Princeton: Princeton University Press, 1958), p. 471.

8. Quoted in A. G. Mazour, *Russia Past and Present* (New York: D. Van Nostrand Co., Inc., 1951), p. 576.

9. Quoted in Walters, I, p. 213.

10. Sir Bernard Pares, "Rasputin and the Empress, Authors of the Russian Collapse," *Foreign Affairs*, VI, No. I (October 1927), p. 140.

11. W. H. Chamberlain, *The Russian Revolution, 1917-1921*, I (New York: The Macmillan Company, 1952), p. 73.

12. *The New Cambridge Modern History*, XII, 1960, p. 9.

13. E. Crankshaw, cited in "The Coup That Changed the World," *New York Times Magazine*, February 19, 1967, p. 96.

14. Karl Lowenstein, in *Governments of Continental Europe*, ed. by J. T. Shotwell (New York: The Macmillan Company, 1940), p. 473.

15. Keynes, pp. 278-279.

16. Quoted in W. C. Langsam, *The World Since 1914* (New York: The Macmillan Company, 1943), p. 685.

CHAPTER 29: AFRICA AND ASIA ASTIR

1. W. E. B. Du Bois, *The World and Africa* (New York: Viking Press, 1947), pp. 148-163.

2. J. S. Furnivall, *Netherlands India* (Cambridge University Press, 1939), p. 446.

3. *African Liberator* (c. 1935). By permission of T. Walter Wallbank.

4. Blanche E. C. Dugdale, *Arthur James Balfour* (New York: G. P. Putnam's Sons, 1937), p. 325.

5. Quoted in H. Kohn, *Nationalism and Imperialism in the Hither East* (London: G. Routledge and Sons, Ltd., 1932), pp. 132-133.

6. J. Nehru, *Toward Freedom* (New York: John Day Co., 1942), p. 353.

7. E. O. Reischauer, J. K. Fairbank, and A. M. Craig, *East Asia, the Modern Transformation* (Boston: Houghton Mifflin Co., 1965), p. 751.

8. Compare F. W. Price and C. P. Barry, eds., *Collier's Encyclopedia*, V (New York: P. F. Collier and Son Corp., 1950), p. 180.

CHAPTER 30: THE TRAGIC DECADE AND GLOBAL CONFLICT

1. Quoted in F. P. Chambers, C. P. Grant, C. C. Bayley, *This Age of Conflict* (New York: Harcourt, Brace & Co., 1943), p. 495.

2. J. K. Galbraith, *The Great Crash, 1929* (Boston: Houghton Mifflin Co., 1955), p. 104.

3. *Ibid,* Chapter X.

4. John H. Williams, "Economic Lessons of Two World Wars," in *An Age of Controversy*, ed. by G. Wright and A. Mejia, Jr. (New York: Dodd, Mead and Company, 1966), p. 239.

5. Quoted in A. Bullock, *Hitler: A Study in Tyranny* (London: Odhams Press, Ltd., 1952), pp. 642-643.

6. R. G. L. Waite, ed., *Hitler and Nazi Germany* (New York: Holt, Rinehart & Winston, Inc., 1965), p. 4.

7. Quoted in W. C. Langsam, *Major European and Asiatic Developments Since 1935* (New York: The Macmillan Company, 1938), p. 15.

8. W. C. Langsam, *The World Since 1914* (New York: The Macmillan Company, 1948), p. 214.

9. Rene Albrecht-Carrie, *France, Europe and the Two World Wars* (New York: Harper & Bros., 1961), p. 56.

10. W. S. Churchill, *Blood, Sweat and Tears* (New York: G. P. Putnam's Sons, 1941), p. 66.

11. F. D. Roosevelt, "Address at Chicago, October 5, 1937," in *The Literature of the United States*, II, ed. by W. Blair, T. Hornberger, and R. Stewart (Chicago: Scott, Foresman and Co., 1953), pp. 831-832.

12. Quoted in W. L. Langer and S. E. Gleason, *The Challenge to Isolation* (New York: Harper & Bros., 1952), p. 138.

13. Quoted in *ibid.*, p. 181.

14. Quoted in *ibid.*, p. 200.

15. S. E. Ayling, *Portraits of Power* (New York: Barnes & Noble, Inc., 1963), p. 159.

16. Churchill, p. 297.

CHAPTER 31: TWO WORLDS: CONFRONTATION AND DÉTENTE

1. Roberto de Oliveira Campos, "Gringos and Generals," *Interplay: The Magazine of International Affairs*, Vol. 3, No. 2 (August-September 1969), p. 5.

2. Lawrence Olson, *Japan Today and Tomorrow*, Headlines Series (New York: Foreign Policy Association, 1967), p. 37.

3. Hugh Seton-Watson, *From Lenin to Khrushchev: The History of World Communism* (New York: Frederick A. Praeger, Inc., 1960), p. 246.

4. Harry Schwartz, *China; An Introduction to China, Its Role in the Modern World and Its Importance for the Future* (New York: Atheneum Publishers, 1965), pp. 113-114.

5. *Ibid.*, p. 112.

6. "The Neurotic Trillionaire: Nixon's America—Present and Future," *The Economist*, reprinted in *Atlas* (July 1969), pp. 18-25.

7. John K. Fairbank, "China's Foreign Policy in Historical Perspective," *Foreign Affairs*, Vol. 47, No. 3 (April 1969), p. 461.

8. *Ibid.*, p. 463.

CHAPTER 32: NATION-BUILDING IN THE THIRD WORLD

1. Quoted in James S. Coleman, *Nigeria: Background to Nationalism* (Berkeley: University of California Press, 1958, from *New York Times*, Oct. 27, 1942), pp. 232-233.

2. Quoted in T. Walter Wallbank, "The Future of Colonies," *World Affairs Interpreter* (Los Angeles, Winter 1945), p. 375.
3. Quoted in Coleman, p. 240.
4. Cited in T. Walter Wallbank, "Britain's New Program for the Colonies," *Current History* (August 1948), p. 85.
5. Quoted in Wallbank, "The Future of Colonies," p. 379.
6. From Prime Minister Harold Macmillan's speech, February 3, 1960, *Vital Speeches* (March 1, 1960).
7. Quoted in Earl Louis Mountbatten, *Time Only to Look Forward* (London: Nicholas Kaye, 1949), p. 74.
8. Quoted in Eva Curie, *Journey Among Warriors* (New York: Doubleday, Doran, 1943), p. 462.
9. Selig Harrison, *India: The Most Dangerous Decades* (Princeton: Princeton University Press, 1960), p. 4.
10. Elspeth Huxley, "Africa's First Loyalty," *New York Times Magazine* (September 18, 1960), p. 14.
11. Quoted from address of Kaunda in *Africa Report* (December 1967) p. 33.
12. Harry R. Rudin, "Political Rivalry in the Congo" *Current History* (March 1966), p. 179.
13. Stanislav Andreski, *The African Predicament* (New York: Atherton Press, 1969), p. 61.
14. John D. Chick, "Nigeria at War," *Current History* (February 1968), p. 113.
15. Victor T. Le Vine, "Independent Africa in Trouble," *Africa Report* (December 1967), p. 19.
16. Quoted in Michael Brecher, *The New States of Asia* (London: Oxford University Press, 1963), p. 74.
17. James S. Coleman, "The Character and Viability of African Political Systems," in W. Goldschmidt, *The United States and Africa* (New York: Frederick A. Praeger, Inc., 1963), pp. 39-40.
18. William A. Hance, "The Race Between Population and Resources," *Africa Report* (January 1968), p. 11.
19. Vernon McKay, *Africa in World Politics* (New York: Harper & Row, 1963), p. 289.
20. *Ibid.*, p. 343.
21. *Ibid.*, p. 404.
22. Quoted in Harold R. Isaacs, *The New World of Negro Americans* (New York: The John Day Company, Inc., 1963), p. 292.
23. I. F. Stone, "Holy War," *The New York Review of Books,* IX (Aug. 3, 1967), pp. 12-13.
24. Denis Warner, "Vietnam," *Atlantic* (August 1969), p. 22.
25. *Ibid.*, p. 22.
26. K. A. Busia, *The Challenge of Africa* (New York: Frederick A. Praeger, Inc., 1962), p. 149.

CHAPTER 33: TOWARD A NEW LIFE STYLE

1. Henry Margenau, *The Nature of Physical Reality: A Philosophy of Modern Physics* (New York: McGraw-Hill, 1950), p. 39.
2. John Pfeiffer, *The Cell* (New York: Life Science Library, 1964), p. 61.
3. T. S. Eliot, *Collected Poems, 1909-1935* (London: Faber and Faber, Ltd., 1951), pp. 12-13. Reprinted by permission of Harcourt Brace Jovanovich, Inc., and Faber and Faber Ltd.
4. *Ibid.*, p. 157.
5. *The Republic,* Book IV.
6. Geoffrey Barraclough, *An Introduction to Contemporary History* (Baltimore: Penguin Books, Inc., 1964), p. 259.
7. Quoted by Colin Legum, *Pan-Africanism* (London, 1962), p. 93 from a translation of Césaire's *Cahier d'un retour au pays natal.*
8. Barraclough, p. 268.

EPILOGUE: THE CHALLENGES AHEAD

1. Siegfried Giedion, *Space, Time and Architecture* (Cambridge: Harvard University Press, 1967), p. 36.
2. E. Brandis and V. Dmitrevskiy, "The Future: Its Promoters and False Prophets," *The Magazine of Fantasy and Science Fiction* (October 1965), pp. 62-63.

List of Illustrations

LIST OF CHARTS AND DRAWINGS

LIST OF MAPS

Index

Abbreviations for special features—Reference Maps (*Ref. M.*), spot maps (*m.*), and illustrations (*ill.*)— are indicated in italics. Suggested pronunciations for difficult or unusual words are respelled according to the table below, which is repeated in simplified form at the bottom of each right-hand page of the INDEX. The local pronunciations of many foreign words are too unusual for persons untrained in linguistics, and pronunciations given here are those commonly acceptable in unaffected, educated American speech.

a	hat, cap	ô	order, all
ā	age, face	oi	oil, toy
ã	care, air	ou	out, now
ä	father, far		
		p	pet, cup
b	bad, rob	r	run, try
ch	child, much	s	say, yes
d	did, red	sh	she, rush
		t	tell, it
e	let, best	th	thin, both
ē	equal, see	ŦH	then, smooth
ėr	term, learn		
		u	cup, son
f	fat, if	ů	put, book
g	go, bag	ü	rule, move
h	he, how	ū	use, music
i	it, pin	v	very, save
ī	ice, five	w	will, woman
		y	you, yet
j	jam, enjoy	z	zero, breeze
k	kind, seek	zh	measure, seizure
l	land, coal		
m	me, am	ə	represents:
n	no, in	*a*	in *a*bout
ng	long, bring	*e*	in tak*e*n
		i	in penc*i*l
o	hot, rock	*o*	in lem*o*n
ō	open, go	*u*	in circ*u*s

FOREIGN SOUNDS

Y as in French *lune.* Pronounce ē with the lips rounded as for English ü in *rule.*

Œ as in French *deux.* Pronounce ā with the lips rounded as for ō.

N as in French *bon.* The N is not pronounced, but shows that the vowel before it is nasal.

H as in German *ach.* Pronounce k without closing the breath passage.

hat, āge, cāre, fär; let, ēqual, tėrm; it, īce; hot, ōpen, ôrder; oil, out; cup, půt, rüle, ūse; ch, child; ng, long; th, thin; ᴛн, then; zh, measure; ə represents *a* in *a*bout, *e* in tak*e*n, *i* in penc*i*l, *o* in lem*o*n, *u* in circ*u*s.

hat, āge, cãre, fär; let, ēqual, tėrm; it, īce; hot, ōpen, ôrder; oil, out; cup, pùt, rüle, ūse; ch, child; ng, long; th, thin; ᴛʜ, then; zh, measure; ə represents *a* in *a*bout, *e* in tak*e*n, *i* in penc*i*l, *o* in lem*o*n, *u* in circ*u*s.

hat, āge, cāre, fär; let, ēqual, tėrm; it, īce; hot, ōpen, ôrder; oil, out; cup, pùt, rüle, ūse; ch, child; ng, long; th, thin; ᴛʜ, then; zh, measure; ə represents *a* in *a*bout, *e* in tak*e*n, *i* in penc*i*l, *o* in lem*o*n, *u* in circ*u*s.

hat, āge, cãre, fär; let, ēqual, tėrm; it, īce; hot, ōpen, ôrder; oil, out; cup, pút, rüle, ūse; ch, child; ng, long; th, thin; ᴛʜ, then; zh, measure; ə represents *a* in *a*bout, *e* in tak*e*n, *i* in penc*i*l, *o* in lem*o*n, *u* in circ*u*s.

---

hat, āge, cãre, fär; let, ēqual, tėrm; it, īce; hot, ōpen, ôrder; oil, out; cup, pùt, rüle, ūse; ch, child; ng, long; th, thin; ᴛʜ, then; zh, measure; ə represents *a* in *about*, *e* in *taken*, *i* in *pencil*, *o* in *lemon*, *u* in *circus*.

hat, āge, cãre, fär; let, ēqual, tėrm; it, īce; hot, ōpen, ôrder; oil, out; cup, pùt, rüle, ūse; ch, child; ng, long;
th, thin; ᴛʜ, then; zh, measure; ə represents *a* in *a*bout, *e* in tak*e*n, *i* in penc*i*l, *o* in lem*o*n, *u* in circ*u*s.

hat, āge, cāre, fär; let, ēqual, tėrm; it, īce; hot, ōpen, ôrder; oil, out; cup, pu̇t, rüle, ūse; ch, child; ng, long; th, thin; ᴛʜ, then; zh, measure; ə represents *a* in *a*bout, *e* in tak*e*n, *i* in penc*i*l, *o* in lem*o*n, *u* in circ*u*s.

---

hat, āge, cāre, fär; let, ēqual, tėrm; it, īce; hot, ōpen, ôrder; oil, out; cup, pùt, rüle, ūse; ch, child; ng, long; th, thin; ŦH, then; zh, measure; ə represents *a* in *a*bout, *e* in tak*e*n, *i* in penc*i*l, *o* in lem*o*n, *u* in circ*u*s.

hat, āge, cāre, fär; let, ēqual, tėrm; it, īce; hot, ōpen, ôrder; oil, out; cup, pu̇t, rüle, ūse; ch, child; ng, long; th, thin; ᵺH, then; zh, measure; ə represents *a* in *a*bout, *e* in tak*e*n, *i* in penc*i*l, *o* in lem*o*n, *u* in circ*u*s.

---

hat, āge, cāre, fär; let, ēqual, tėrm; it, īce; hot, ōpen, ôrder; oil, out; cup, pùt, rüle, ūse; ch, child; ng, long; th, thin; ᴛʜ, then; zh, measure; ə represents *a* in *a*bout, *e* in tak*e*n, *i* in penc*i*l, *o* in lem*o*n, *u* in circ*u*s.

Ursulines, 317
Uruguay, 612, 625, 746, *Ref. M. 12*
Urukagina, 18
U.S.S.R. *See* Soviet Union
U Thant, 826
Utilitarianism, 489-490
Utopia, 298-299
Utopian socialism, 495
Utrecht, Treaty of, 425, 620

V

Vaisyas, 93
Valencia, *Ref. M. 2, 4*
Valois (vä lwä′) dynasty, 335
Vandals, 135, *m. 134*
Van Eyck (vän īk′), Jan, 303
Van Gogh (van gôн′), Vincent, 593
Varangians (ve ran′ji ənz), 152, *m. 153*
Vatican, 292, 462-463, 526, 677
Vatican Council, 588
Vedas (vā′dəz), 92, 94, 95
Vedic Age, 92-93
Velázquez (ve läth′keth), Diego, 409
Venetia, 502, 525, 526, *m. 526, Ref. M. 7*
Venezuela (ven e zwā′lə), 377, 467, 468, 608, 612, 613, 615, 684, 746, *Ref. M. 6, 12*
Venice, 144, 145, 207, 212, 274, 275, 295, 382, *m. 235, 276, 526, Ref. M. 4, 5, 7, 8, 14. See also* Venetia
Ventris, Michael, 41
Venus of Willendorf, *ill. 14*
Verrazzano, Giovanni da, 372
Verdi, Giuseppe, 478-479, 595
Verdun, 457, 566-567, *m. 192, 566, Ref. M. 4, 5:* Treaty of, 194, 233
Vermeer, Jan, 410
Verona, 505, *m. 505, Ref. M. 7*
Verrocchio, Andrea del (ver rök′kyô, än dre′ä del), 291
Versailles, 383, 453, 662, *Ref. M. 7:* palace of, 412, 422, 530; Treaty of, 564, 662, 680
Vesalius (vi sā′lē əs), Andreas, 405
Vespasian (ves pā′zhi ən), 76, 123
Vico (vē′kō), Giovanni Battista, 404
Victor Emmanuel ii, king of Italy, 520, 525, 526
Victor Emmanuel iii, king of Italy, 676
Victoria, Australia, 619
Victoria, Lake, 648, *Ref. M. 9, 10*
Victoria, queen of England, 511, 631
Victoria Falls, 647
Victorian Compromise, 549
Vienna, 329, *m. 327, 505, 563, 566, Ref. M. 5, 7, 8, 14:* Congress of, 501-504, 516
Viet Cong, 760, 788
Vietminh (Democratic Republic of Vietnam), 787
Vietnam (vē et′näm′), 350, 642, 702, 787-790, *Ref. M. 11*

Vietnam War, 743, 754, 755, 760, 787-790
Vikings, 194-195. *See also* Norsemen
Villa Rotunda, 408
Vindhya (vind′yä) Mountains, 343, *m. 91*
Vinland, 367
Virgil, 65, 78, 85, 86
Virtû, 286
Vishnu, 96
Visigoths, 135, 188, 190, 207, 208, *m. 134*
Vladimir (vlad′ə mir′), Prince, 143, 152
Volga River, *m. 434, Ref. M. 3, 7, 8, 11, 14*
Volksschule, 533
Volta, Alessandro, 407
Voltaire, 274, 401-402, 403, 404, 414, 450
Von Hutten, Ulrich, 299

W

Wagner (väg′ner), Richard, 478, 595
Wailing Wall, 123
Wake Island, 644
Walachia, 507, 544, *m. 506*
Waldensians, 248
Waldo, Peter, 248
Wales, 228, *Ref. M. 4, 14*
Wallace, William, 228
Walpole, Robert, 432-433
Wang An-shih (wäng′ än′shē′), 176-177
War communism, period of, 672
Warhol, Andy, 812
War of the Austrian Succession, 439
War of the Spanish Succession, 424-425, 437
Warsaw Pact, 741
Wars of the Roses, 271, 426
Washington, D.C., Conference, 668; Treaty of, 621
Washington, George, 450, 451
Waste Land, The, 797
Waterloo, *Ref. M. 7:* battle of, 465, *m. 462*
Watson, James D., 796
Watt, James, 482
Watteau, Jean Antoine, 412
Wealth of Nations, 445-446, 488
Weihaiwei (wā′hī′wā′), 636, 637, *m. 636*
Weimar (vī′mär), 475
Weimar Republic, 679-681, 715
Weismann (vīs′män), August, 583
Weizmann, Chaim, 693
Welfare state, 551, 579, 626
Welfs, 236
Welles, Sumner, 765
Wellington, Duke of, 465, 511
Weltpolitik, 560
Wesley, John and Charles, 402-403
Wessex, 220, *m. 192*
West Berlin, 740-741, 742

---

hat, āge, cãre, fär; let, ēqual, tėrm; it, īce; hot, ōpen, ôrder; oil, out; cup, pu̇t, rüle, ūse; ch, child; ng, long; th, thin; ŦH, then; zh, measure; ə represents *a* in *a*bout, *e* in tak*e*n, *i* in penc*i*l, *o* in lem*o*n, *u* in circ*u*s.

hat, āge, cāre, fär; let, ēqual, tėrm; it, īce; hot, ōpen, ôrder; oil, out; cup, pùt, rüle, ūse; ch, child; ng, long; th, thin; ᴛʜ, then; zh, measure; ə represents *a* in *a*bout, *e* in tak*e*n, *i* in penc*i*l, *o* in lem*o*n, *u* in circ*u*s.

The Reference Maps

History accounts for man's activities in time, and maps depict them in space. Therefore, to understand mankind's experiences, knowledge of the planetary environment is essential. These reference maps show key areas at significant periods; they include basic physical features which affect man's attempts to control his environment as well as his fellow man.

Map 1: The Ancient Near East and Greece. In the area displayed we can trace the progressive expansion of man's environmental control resulting from his invention of new tools and social institutions. Thus the transition from food collecting to farming occurred in well-watered sites bordering the Syrian, Arabian, and Iranian deserts—such as at Jericho in the Great Rift Valley of the Jordan and at Jarmo in uplands to the east of the Tigris. The breakthrough from Neolithic barbarism to civilization, i.e., to societies sufficiently complex to permit the emergence of urban centers, occurred in two important river basins, the Tigris-Euphrates and the Nile—linked by a Fertile Crescent with minimal natural obstacles to impede the movement of peoples and goods.

Employing primitive craft, Neolithic seafarers had hugged the Mediterranean coasts and slowly pushed westward—as attested by Neolithic sites in Cyprus, Rhodes, and Crete. Improvements in maritime technology permitted the emergence of a splendid Aegean civilization centering at Knossos in Crete, and Pylos on the Greek mainland, and Troy in northwest Asia Minor. Civilization's center of gravity shifted progressively northward across the eastern basin of the Mediterranean, culminating in Hellas with its sea-oriented city-states: Corinth, Thebes, and, above all, Athens. Continued advances in maritime technology enabled the Greeks to master the eastern Mediterranean and Black seas and establish colonies, while the Phoenicians carried their mercantile ventures from their port cities of Tyre and Sidon along the North African coast. What the Tigris-Euphrates had been to the Babylonians, and the Nile to the Egyptians, the Mediterranean became to the Greeks, the Phoenicians, and eventually to the Romans—the "middle of the earth."

Map 2: The Roman Empire c. 117 A.D. This map underscores the importance of physical features in the creation of the Roman world-state. From its east-west maritime axis, the Roman *imperium* stretched into the hinterland, which was linked by rivers and roads to strategically located ports that provided transshipment to other parts of the empire.

The expansion of the Roman world followed a logical sequence. It began with Rome's conquest of the Italian peninsula and Great Greece (including Sicily). The Punic Wars opened up the entire western basin of the Mediterranean, while subsequent intrusion into the eastern basin made Rome mistress of the Hellenistic world. The first century B.C. saw the consolidation of Roman control in Asia Minor, the conquest of transalpine Gaul by Julius Caesar, and the annexation of Egypt, Numidia, and Cyrenaica. The territorial domain was rounded out later by the acquisition of Mauretania, Dacia, Armenia, and Mesopotamia.

Here we see the Roman world at its broadest expanse, encompassing almost 100 million diverse peoples and linked by the greatest communications network then devised. However, the world-state soon entered its time of troubles, attended by decline of population, of administrative efficiency, and of military power. The empire then found itself overextended and had to reduce its territorial perimeter. Armenia, Mesopotamia, and Dacia were abandoned, and eventually the Roman legions were recalled from Britain.

In the fourth century the once majestic Roman empire was polarized into two unequal segments —the western section administered from Rome and having the weaker but spatially larger area; and the eastern section controlled from New Rome (Constantinople) and having a larger population, more compact territory, and a stronger economy. At last the two segments, each centering on one of the major basins of the Mediterranean, were split asunder by the barbarian invasions. The classical world then gave way to the medieval world.

Map 3: The Ancient East. Here we encounter the homelands of the two major fluvial civilizations (societies originating in river basins) centering on the Indus-Gangetic and the Huang Ho drainage basins. The remarkable longevity of Indian and Chinese societies owes much to physical factors which inhibited alien intrusion. The Indian triangle was protected by the Indian Ocean and the Himalayas, though invasion was possible through the western passes; as for China, the obstacles posed by the Pacific Ocean, the forbidding Taklamakan and Gobi deserts, and a series of mountain ranges effectively limited entrance into the Huang Ho valley.

The map also shows the boundaries of three empires: the Han in China, the Mauryan in India, and the Parthian in western Asia. Note that they are contemporary with the Roman world-state at its zenith. After centuries of feudal fragmentation, China was reunited, and under Shih Huang-ti, the Great Wall was rebuilt and lengthened to keep the nomadic tribes in the north and west from pillaging the sedentary farmers tilling the "good earth" to the south. The centuries marked by the Han dynasty were stable and prosperous. So too were the centuries of Mauryan rule in India. Under Ashoka, a single administration extended from the Himalayas across the Narbada River and included the Deccan—leaving only the southernmost part of the subcontinent outside its rule. Meanwhile, to the northwest lay Bactria, where Hellenistic and Indian culture interfused, producing the Gandharran art found in Taxila.

This is the era, too, when the western and eastern segments of the Eurasian land mass were in commercial and cultural contact. Ships plied the Indian Ocean, taking advantage of the recently discovered monsoon mechanism while a tenuous but profitable Silk Route stretched from Ch'ang-an through Kashgar, Samarkand, and across Parthian lands to Ecbatana, Ctesiphon, and Seleucia. In addition, the movement of goods from both China and India westward enriched the "caravan cities" such as Palmyra (see Map 2).

Map 4: Medieval France, Spain, and the British Isles 1328. We can perceive here the emerging outlines of the national state system in western Europe. For example, in 1328 Edward II had to officially recognize Scotland as independent, while across the Channel, the extinction of the Capetian line set the stage for a protracted struggle over the succession to the French throne. Known as the Hundred Years' War (1337–1453), it was marked by the loss of large English holdings obtained in Plantagenet days. Meanwhile, ambitious French kings enlarged their domain from the Ile de France around Paris southward to the Mediterranean and then sought to expand their territory eastward at the expense of the feudal-fragmented Holy Roman Empire. The Iberian peninsula was also fragmented, but here the Christian kingdoms were girding to clear the peninsula of those Moors still entrenched in Granada.

Certain areas are noteworthy for their economic importance at this juncture: the Low Countries, where the textile industry enriched such towns as Bruges, Lille, Ghent, Ypres, and Cambrai; Champagne in northeastern France, where the most famous medieval fairs in all Europe were held; and southern France, with its thriving commercial centers at Narbonne and Marseille.

Note, too, that whereas in classical times urban centers predominated on the coast, in medieval Europe a large number of river-oriented towns were founded or acquired increasing importance. Roads were poor, and river transport was both economical and efficient. Rivers such as the Thames, Meuse, Seine, Loire, Rhone, Garonne, Tagus, Guadalquivir, and Po were being constantly utilized, while the Rhine and Danube, important as political and military boundaries in Roman times, were vital waterways throughout medieval times.

Map 5: Europe 1648. The year 1648 is a crucial one, for the Thirty Years' War, started as a religious conflict, ended with the victory of the national state which acknowledged no authority higher than its own sovereignty and interests. The map indicates the further territorial consolidation of the national state system (as compared with Map 4). Thus Scotland and England are now one political entity; the Iberian peninsula is demarcated as Spain and Portugal (though neither is any longer a first-class power); France has acquired bishoprics in Lorraine and a foothold in Alsace. The map also shows the emergence of Switzerland, the three Scandinavian countries, Poland, and Russia.

Germany and Italy remain territorially fragmented and politically unstable, as the Holy Roman Empire has vanished in everything but name and pretensions. The situation in the flat north European plain remains fluid; the boundaries of Brandenburg, Poland, and Russia were always subject to change on that plain, reflecting the fluctuating power relations of those states. Meanwhile, the Ottoman Turks continue to threaten central Europe despite their defeat at sea at Lepanto in 1571.

Map 6: European Empires c. 1700. With the age of exploration, western Europeans set out to explore the unmapped portions of the globe, spreading their religion, cultures, and languages wherever their questing galleons made a new landfall. In the wake of the explorer went the missionary, merchant, and musketeer so that in time Europeans controlled most, or all, of the land surface of every other continent. The age of exploration both intensified and territorially expanded European national rivalries.

This map has much to tell us. The European states bordering the Atlantic attempted to explore and colonize lands in the New World in latitudes roughly comparable to their own. Thus the Danes proceeded northwestward to Iceland and Greenland, the English and French competed for lands north of the Gulf of Mexico, and Spain and Portugal laid their claims in more southerly latitudes. Following Portuguese initiative, other Europeans sought out—and fought over—islands, coastal strips, and spheres of interest around the African and Indian coasts and in the archipelagoes of Southeast Asia.

The contrasting depths of European penetration of the New and Old Worlds at this juncture are significant. In the Americas, Europeans encountered either Stone Age Amerinds or pre-Columbian civilizations incapable of assimilating, much less fighting off, the newcomers. Consequently, the European acquisition of North and South America—and later of Australia—was complete. This resulted in the establishment of colonial empires in which the language, laws, religion, and cultural values of the respective metropolitan nations were brought *in toto* to the New World. In contrast, in sub-Saharan Africa as well as South and East Asia, the Europeans were invariably outnumbered. Hence, though they managed to establish trading settlements along the coast, and eventually acquire political ascendency in most of these regions, they did not succeed in replacing the indigenous culture patterns.

Map 7: Europe 1815. This map can best be examined by comparing it with Map 5—the European landscape 167 years earlier. The fewest territorial-political changes have occurred in western Europe, though some further consolidation has taken place. Thus Ireland is now part of the United Kingdom; Sweden has been allowed by the major powers to annex Norway (in compensation for its loss of Finland to Russia); while what had formerly been Holland and the Spanish Netherlands are now included in the Kingdom of the Netherlands. France, though deprived of some of Napoleon's earlier territorial conquests, has by this time acquired Alsace and Lorraine, and Franche Comté (to the immediate west of Switzerland).

A comparison of Maps 4 and 7 would seem to point to greater fragmentation of the defunct Holy Roman Empire. Actually the German people have now to give their allegiances to only thirty-nine states, as compared with some three hundred in the old Empire, and are loosely organized in a confederation. Most striking is the growth of Prussia from its nucleus in Brandenburg, due to its superb army, to dynastic inheritances, and to astute diplomacy. Italy remains highly fragmented; in Metternich's disdainful phrase, it is only a "geographical expression."

Further east, the political and territorial changes that occurred between 1648 and 1815 are more dramatic. The Austrian empire has expanded into northern Italy and also includes parts of Poland and territory formerly conquered by the Ottoman empire. Meanwhile, due to the partitions of 1772, 1793, and 1795, Poland has ceased to exist, while the corruption-ridden Turks are being forced back toward their home base in Asia Minor.

The most spectacular of all territorial gains has been registered by Russia, advancing westward toward the heart of Europe and southward in the general direction of Constantinople. Moscow has acquired Finland, Estonia, the bulk of Poland, the Ukraine, and Bessarabia.

Map 8: Europe August 1939. This map can be profitably compared with the map on page 566. The most noticeable changes result from the defeat of the Central Powers in World War I and also from alterations in what had formerly been tsarist Russia. Germany was shorn of its overseas colonies, while in Europe it lost Alsace-Lorraine, half of Schleswig, three western districts to Belgium, the Polish Corridor, and a zone in the Rhineland, which was demilitarized. The Austrian empire was dismembered; the nationalist movements of the Czechs, Poles, and Slavs achieved formal territorial recognition; and the remnant of the empire was converted into the separate states of Austria and Hungary. The Ottoman empire was in turn dissected: Greece obtained nearly all of European Turkey, Syria was mandated to France, Palestine and Iraq to Great Britain. After the Bolshevik Revolution, Russia lost much of its western territory, resulting in the establishment of Finland, Estonia, Latvia, and Lithuania, as well as the major portion of reconstituted Poland, while Bessarabia was ceded to Rumania.

Important changes also took place during the interwar years. Under Hitler, Nazi Germany reoccupied the Rhineland in 1936, seized Austria and occupied Sudetenland in 1938, and the following year seized other Czech territory as well as Memel. In 1939, too, Hungary annexed part of Slovakia, while Mussolini's Italy defeated and annexed Albania. The stage was also set for Russia to reannex territory lost after the Bolshevik Revolution.

Map 9: Africa 1914. Four major cultural environments of Africa, each with its unique historical development, may be partially explained by two physical features of the continent—the Sahara Desert and the Great Rift Valley, which runs from the Jordan Valley in Palestine to Western Tanzania. Separated from the rest of the continent by more than 1000 miles of the Sahara, most of the peoples of northwest Africa live close to the Mediterranean, which connects them with Europe from which has long come a flow of people, goods, and ideas. Northeast Africa, partly cut off from the rest of the continent by the Sahara, has long been linked with southwest Asia. Moreover, the Red Sea has always facilitated movement between northeast Africa and Arabia. Africa east of the Great Rift Valley has long been oriented to the Indian Ocean, to the Arab trader, and, since, the last century, to the European who has farmed the plateaus of Kenya, Uganda, and Tanzania.

The lands in the southern section of the Great Rift Valley also form part of sub-Saharan Africa. In this huge area the Sudanese savanna lands, equatorial rain forest, and the steppes and deserts of southern Africa succeed each other from north to south. In these lands occurred Europe's great scramble for empire in the nineteenth century.

Map 10: Africa. Profound political and territorial changes have occurred in Africa since 1914—undoubtedly the most spectacular to be found in any continent during the past half century. From being a vast collection of colonial holdings, Africa has emerged as an agglomeration of national states, virtually all having minimal political stability or economic viability. During the interwar years some major changes took place on the political landscape. German Togoland and the Cameroons were mandated to Great Britain and France; German East Africa was divided into two mandates: Ruanda-Urundi (Belgium) and Tanganyika (Great Britain); and German Southwest Africa was mandated to South Africa. Egypt became an independent kingdom, but Italy's possessions in East Africa were enlarged by the conquest of Abyssinia. Since World War II, however, a spectacular alteration has occurred. The entire continent has passed into indigenous political control, save for Angola, Mozambique, Rhodesia, and South Africa, where European domination remains entrenched.

Map 11: U.S.S.R. and Asia. Dominating Eurasia, the greatest land mass on earth, is the enormous area of the Soviet Union (more than 8 million square miles), extending on a west-east axis for 5000 miles. European Russia, largely a continuation of the north European plain, is drained by the Dvina, Dnieper, Don, and Volga, the last three flowing southward. East of the Urals virtually all rivers flow north to the Arctic, save the Amur, which in its eastward journey also serves as a boundary with China. As the river pattern indicates, Soviet Asia tends to be separated from middle- and low-latitude Asia by physical obstacles, in this case steppes, deserts, mountains. The highest population and urban densities are found in Soviet Europe, while in Siberia, which is rapidly growing, the population is located along the major waterways or the Trans-Siberian Railroad.

As a result of their eastward expansion, the Russians had settled on the Pacific by 1649. In the next two centuries they penetrated east of the Caspian in what is now the Kazakh, Uzbek, and Turkmen Soviet Socialist Republics. In their expansion they collided with the Chinese in Sinkiang, Mongolia, and Manchuria. These border regions today constitute areas of tension and jockeying between the two major Communist powers.

For its part, China has continued to develop south of the Great Wall and Gobi Desert and east and north of such massive mountain ranges as the Tien Shan, Pamirs, and Himalayas. The vast majority of its estimated 750 million people live in the fertile Huang Ho and Yangtze basins or along the coast. Similarly, Indian society has continued to multiply within the confines of its triangular subcontinent, while influencing the culture patterns of neighboring lands to the east and south.

Southeast Asia has long been subject to recurrent cultural and military intrusions alike. Its highly indented coastline and physical terrain have contributed to a fragmentation of cultures and languages. Offshore in East and Southeast Asia are three archipelagoes: the Philippines; Japan, which is the most highly industrialized and prosperous of nonwestern countries; and Indonesia, whose estimated 110 million people make it the world's fifth largest country.

Map 12: Latin America. Latin America was first colonized by Southern Europeans, notably the Spaniards and Portuguese. Exploiting the mountain ranges, running the length of Central and South America, for their precious metals, the Spaniards increased their holdings until the close of the eighteenth century. They created several viceroyalties: New Spain, including Mexico and Central America; Peru, at first embracing all of Spanish South America; New Granada, in what is now Colombia and Venezuela; and La Plata, which subsequently became Bolivia, Paraguay, Uruguay, and Argentina. Brazil, discovered by the Portuguese Cabral in 1500, was made a viceroyalty in 1714.

In half a century (1776–1826) of colonial revolutions in the New World, Spanish and Portuguese

America became independent (except for Cuba and Puerto Rico which remained Spanish until 1898); but each of the Spanish viceroyalties split into more than one political entity.

The tropical regions of Latin America, including Mexico, Central America, and the lands drained by the Magdalena, Orinoco, and Amazon rivers, have predominantly Amerind populations. In contrast, temperate South America, comprising southern Brazil, Uruguay, Argentina, and Chile, finds Europeans in the majority. In 1960 Latin America had some 200 million people, roughly equivalent to the population of Anglo-America. But Latin America is the fastest-growing region in the world and within forty or fifty years may have a population of perhaps 600 million—or about double that of the United States and Canada.

Map 13: The Middle East. This region—segmented by deserts and seas, but with the latter providing interconnecting routes of travel—has long permitted maximal movement of peoples, goods, and ideas in virtually all directions. In this area, which is unique for the convergence of three continents, we find the birthplace of "civilization" and of three major religions, as well as a continuous succession of dynasties and empires. For centuries Islamic political authority and cultural vitality were bound up with the fortunes of the Ottoman empire, and when the latter was defeated by European powers, the Muslim peoples of this region were in turn subordinated in status and made to feel inferior. The twentieth century, however, has witnessed a resurgence of Islamic culture and political strength—attended by the creation of numerous independent states, including Morocco, Algeria, Libya, Egypt, Sudan, Syria, Lebanon, Jordan, Iraq, and Pakistan; and this resurgence has capitalized upon the strategic value of the region in the geopolitical programs of the superpowers, as well as upon its massive oil resources.

The region has also been in a state of continuous tension and intermittent conflict since the end of World War II, because of Arab-Israeli animosities. When the British mandate of Palestine was terminated in 1948, the area proclaimed itself the new state of Israel—a step sanctioned by the United Nations as well as both the United States and the Soviet Union. But the Arab states remained implacably opposed to any such recognition, and several campaigns were mounted in an effort to regain Palestine for the Muslim Arabs.

In 1967 the six-day war resulted in an Israeli victory and the occupation of the west bank of the Jordan River, the Sinai peninsula, and the east bank of the Suez Canal.

Map 14: Europe. This map can profitably be compared with Map 8 in order to obtain a clearer picture of territorial changes resulting from the outcome of World War II. As after World War I, defeated Germany and its allies were deprived of territory, with the Soviet Union emerging as the greatest single territorial beneficiary.

In 1945 Germany was stripped of East Prussia, while its eastern boundary was set at the Oder-Neisse rivers—the farthest line west achieved by the Slavs since the twelfth century. Moreover, postwar Germany was both ideologically and territorially split, its western segment associated in military and economic pacts with the western world, its eastern section integrated in the Communist world and a member of the Warsaw Pact. While faring better, defeated Italy lost its overseas colonies and Albania.

Conversely, the Soviet Union expanded westward, annexing part of Finland, all of Estonia, Latvia, and Lithuania, and the eastern portion of Poland, shifting that country's center of gravity westward at the expense of Germany. Stalinist policies and power also created a series of "people's democracies" from the Baltic to the Black seas, resulting in the iron curtain. Yet the region was to prove far from monolithic. Shortly after the war Tito declared Yugoslavia an independent Communist state, tiny Albania was later to ally itself with Peking in the great split within the Communist world, while the 1950's and 1960's also witnessed abortive attempts in Hungary and Czechoslovakia to gain greater freedom from Moscow's control.

The contemporary map of Europe differs markedly from earlier maps of the continent not only because of its ideological division but also because of the emergence of new economic groupings. To break down traditional trade barriers, the European Economic Community (the "Common Market") was formed. Another such community is the European Free Trade Association, or "Outer Seven." In an effort to keep pace, the Communist countries organized the Council of Mutual Economic Assistance. It will be interesting to watch the long-term effects of these economic groupings upon the traditional political forces—and boundaries—of Europe.

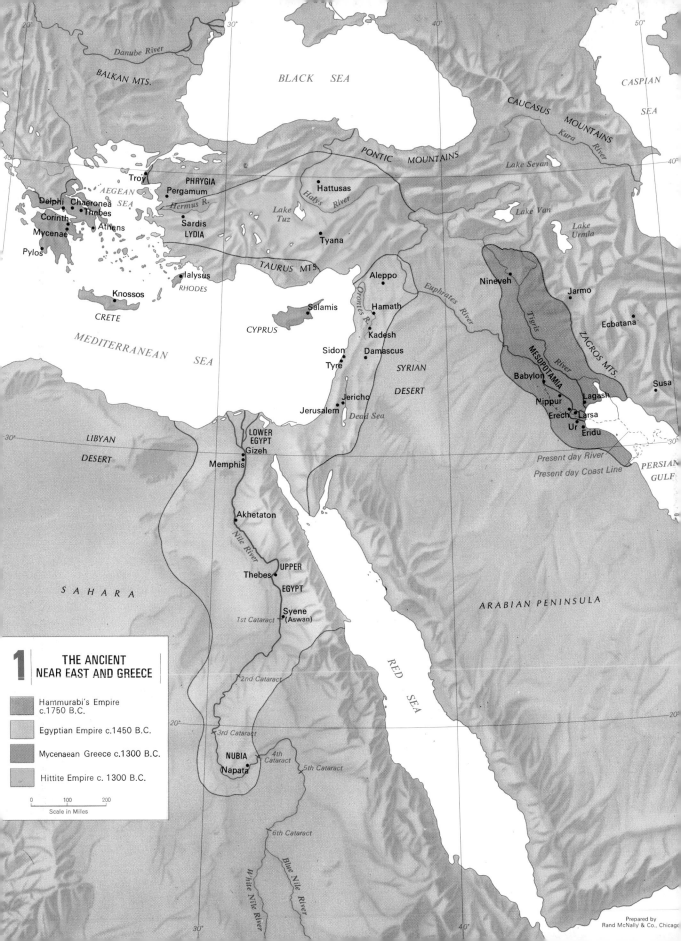

Danube River

BALKAN MTS.

BLACK SEA

CASPIAN SEA

PONTIC MOUNTAINS

CAUCASUS MOUNTAINS

Kura River

Lake Sevan

Troy

PHRYGIA
Pergamum

AEGEAN SEA

Hattusas

Lake Van

Lake Urmia

Delphi · Chaeronea
Corinth · Thebes
· Athens
Mycenae

Sardis
LYDIA

Lake Tuz

Halys River

Pylos

Tyana

Nineveh

Jarmo

Ecbatana

Ialysus

RHODES

TAURUS MTS.

Aleppo

Euphrates River

ZAGROS MTS.

Knossos

CRETE

Salamis

CYPRUS

Orontes R.

Hamath

Kadesh

Tigris River

MESOPOTAMIA

Susa

MEDITERRANEAN SEA

Sidon
Tyre

Damascus

SYRIAN DESERT

Babylon
Nippur
Erech
Ur

Lagash
Larsa
Eridu

Jericho

Jerusalem

Dead Sea

LIBYAN DESERT

LOWER EGYPT
Gizeh

Memphis

Present day River
Present day Coast Line

PERSIAN GULF

Akhetaton

Nile River

SAHARA

Thebes

UPPER EGYPT

ARABIAN PENINSULA

Syene
(Aswan)

1st Cataract

2nd Cataract

RED SEA

2 0°

3rd Cataract

NUBIA

4th Cataract

Napata

5th Cataract

6th Cataract

Blue Nile River

White Nile River

Prepared by
Rand McNally & Co., Chicago

1 THE ANCIENT
NEAR EAST AND GREECE

Hammurabi's Empire
c.1750 B.C.

Egyptian Empire c.1450 B.C.

Mycenaean Greece c.1300 B.C.

Hittite Empire c. 1300 B.C.

0   100   200
Scale in Miles

ATLANTIC

OCEAN

NORTH
SEA

IRELAND

IRISH
SEA

Antoninus' Wall
(C. 140 A.D.)

Hadrian's Wall
(C. 122 A.D.)

PENNINES

York

Chester

Lincoln

BRITAIN

Colchester

Bath

London

Thames R.

ENGLISH CHANNEL

GERMAN

Cologne

River

Elbe

Rhine River

Mainz

BELGICA

River

Seine River

Paris

Meuse

Loire River

Saône R.

Danube

GAUL

BAY OF
BISCAY

Bordeaux

Garonne R.

CENTRAL
MASSIF

Rhône R.

Lyons

ALPS

CISALPINE GAUL

Po River

CANTABRIAN MTS.

Douro River

Ebro River

PYRENEES

Segovia

Genoa

Ravenna

Marseilles

Pisa

ADRIAT

Tagus River

SPAIN

CORSICA

APENNINES

ITALY

Guadiana River

Toledo

Saguntum

Rome

SIERRA MORENA

Cordova

Valencia

SARDINIA

Naples

Pom

Guadalquivir R.

Cádiz

SIERRA NEVADA

BALEARIC
ISLANDS

TYRRHENIAN
SEA

Strait of Gibraltar

New
Carthage

Tangier

Pillars of Hercules

Messina

MADEIRA
ISLANDS

MAURETANIA

MOUNTAINS

Utica

SICILY

Syr

ATLAS

Moulouya R.

Chélif R.

Medjerda R.

Carthage

MALTA

CANARY
ISLANDS

Chott
Djerid

NUMIDIA

Oea

Leptis
Magna

GRAND ERG OCCIDENTAL

GRAND ERG ORIENTAL

2 | THE ROMAN EMPIRE
C. 117 A.D.

0   100   200   300
Scale in Miles

AHAGGAR

MOUNTAINS

SAHARA

GOTHS

HUNS

Western Dvina River

Bug River
...a R.

Dnieper River

Dniester River

SARMATIA

CARPATHIANS

TRANSYLVANIAN ALPS

• Apulum

DACIA

BALKAN MTS.

• Naissus

THRACE

EDONIA

Byzantium •

Sea of Marmara

AEGEAN SEA

• Pergamum

• Thebes

ASIA

MTS

orinth • • Athens

• Ephesus

• Sparta

RHODES

• Knossos

CRETE

SEA

• Cyrene

CYRENAICA

Alexandria •

Memphis •

EGYPT

LIBYAN

DESERT

Volga River

Kama River

URAL MOUNTAINS

Tobol R.

Ural River

Volga River

Don River

• Olbia

SEA OF AZOV

BLACK   SEA

• Sinope

• Trapezus

PONTIC MOUNTAINS

PONTUS

Kizil River

Lake Tuz

• Tarsus

CILICIA

CYPRUS

• Sidon

• Tyre

PALESTINE

• Palmyra

• Dura Europos

SYRIA

• Damascus

• Jerusalem

Dead Sea

Nile River

• Thebes

• Syene

• Berenice

RED   SEA

ARABIA

CAUCASUS MOUNTAINS

Kura River

Aras River

Lake Sevan

• Artaxata

ARMENIA

Lake Van

Lake Urmia

ASSYRIA

Tigris River

MESOPOTAMIA

Euphrates River

• Ctesiphon

Euphrates River

CASPIAN SEA

ELBURZ MTS.

Daryācheh-ye Namak

PLATEAU

• Ecbatana

ZAGROS

PARTHIAN EMPIRE   OF   IRAN

MTS.

PERSIAN GULF

ARAL SEA

Prepared by
Rand McNally & Co., Chicago

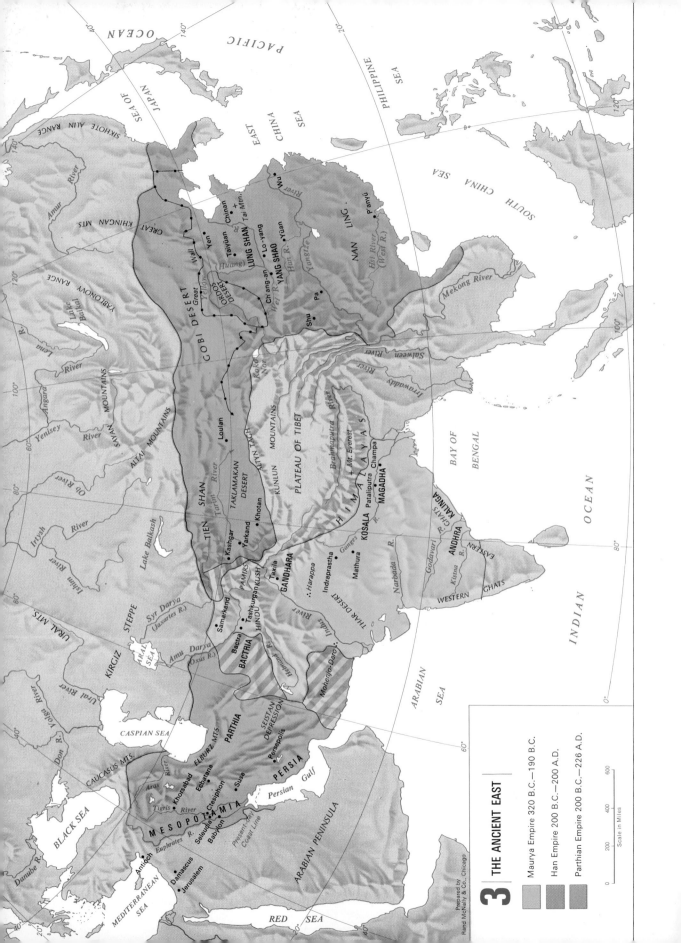

ARCTIC OCEAN

PACIFIC OCEAN

SEA OF JAPAN

EAST CHINA SEA

PHILIPPINE SEA

SOUTH CHINA SEA

SIKHOTE ALIN RANGE

Amur River

KHINGAN MTS

GREAT KHINGAN RANGE

YABLONOV RANGE

Lena River

Lake Baikal

SAYAN MOUNTAINS

Angara River

Yenisey River

Ob River

Irtysh River

Ishim River

URAL MTS

KIRGIZ STEPPE

Ural River

ALTAI MOUNTAINS

Lake Balkash

GOBI DESERT

Great Wall

Yellow River

Huang River

ORDOS DESERT

Yen

Taiyuan

Chinan

Chinan

LUNG SHAN

Tai Mtn.

Lo-yang

Ch'ang-an

YANG SHAO

Wei R.

Shu

Pa

NAN LING

Wu

Yangtze

Han R.

Yüan

Hsi River (West R.)

P'anyü

Mekong River

Salween River

Irrawaddy River

TIEN SHAN

Tarim River

Loulan

TAKLAMAKAN DESERT

ALTYN TAGH

KUNLUN MOUNTAINS

PLATEAU OF TIBET

Lob Nor

Kashgar

Yarkand

Khotan

PAMIRS

Samarkand

Tashkurgan

HINDU KUSH

Bactria

BACTRIA

Amu Darya (Oxus R.)

ARAL SEA

Syr Darya (Jaxartes R.)

Taxila

GANDHARA

Harappa

Indus River

THAR DESERT

Mohenjo-Daro

Helmand R.

SEISTAN DEPRESSION

PARTHIA

PERSIA

Persepolis

Susa

ELBURZ MTS

Ecbatana

Khorsabad

Ctesiphon

Seleucia

Babylon

MESOPOTAMIA

Euphrates R.

Tigris River

Aras River

CAUCASUS MTS

CASPIAN SEA

BLACK SEA

Antioch

Damascus

Jerusalem

MEDITERRANEAN SEA

RED SEA

ARABIAN PENINSULA

Persian Gulf

Present-day Coast Line

ARABIAN SEA

HIMALAYAS

Brahmaputra River

+ Mt. Everest

Champa

Pataliputra

MAGADHA

KOSALA

Ganges R.

Mathura

Indraprastha

Narbada R.

Godavari R.

Kistna R.

WESTERN GHATS

EASTERN GHATS

ANDHRA

KALINGA

BAY OF BENGAL

INDIAN OCEAN

Volga River

Don R.

Danube River

DAMASCUS

Prepared by
Rand McNally & Co., Chicago

3 | THE ANCIENT EAST

Maurya Empire 320 B.C.—190 B.C.

Han Empire 200 B.C.—200 A.D.

Parthian Empire 200 B.C.—226 A.D.

Scale in Miles

0   200   400   600

NORWAY

SWEDEN

DENMARK

Copenhagen

ATLANTIC

OCEAN

NORTH

SEA

SCOTLAND

Aberdeen

Glasgow

Edinburgh

Durham

IRELAND

Galway

Dublin

Limerick

Chester

Wexford

Cork

St. David's

WALES

York

Lincoln

ENGLAND

Shannon

Severn R.

Brandenburg

Elbe River

Weser River

Haarlem

Amsterdam

Rotterdam

Bath

Winchester

Hastings

Bruges

Ghent

Louvain

London

Thames River

Rhine River

FLANDERS

Ypres

Brussels

Agincourt

Lille

Cateau-

Cambrésis

LUXEMBOURG

ARDENNES

Crécy

Cambrai

Rocroy

Amiens

Vervins

Verdun

HOLY

Rouen

Soissons

LORRAINE

ENGLISH CHANNEL

Compiègne

Paris

Toul

ALSACE

Seine R.

CHAMPAGNE

NORMANDY

Chartres

Clairvaux

ROMAN

Brest

Mont St. Michel

Orléans

Molesme

Luxeuil

ALPS

BRITTANY

Champeaux

ANJOU

Vézelay

Danube River

Carnac

Loire R.

Tours

BURGUNDY

Saône R.

SWITZERLAND

EMPIRE

VENICE

FRANCE

Cluny

Po River

POITOU

Poitiers

Lyons

PAPAL

BAY

CENTRAL

STATES

OF

MASSIF

Cognac

BISCAY

AQUITAINE

Rhône R.

THE CORNICHE

CORSICA

Bordeaux

Dordogne

GASCONY

Garonne River

Nîmes

Marseilles

Toulon

Toulouse

Carcassonne

Narbonne

Santiago de

Compostela

ASTURIAS

Roncesvalles

Perpignan

SARDINIA

Oviedo

Cave of

Covadonga

KINGDOM

OF

NAVARRE

CANTABRIAN MTS.

PYRENEES

Miño R.

León

Ebro R.

Cagliari

Saragossa

Porto

Douro River

KINGDOM

Barcelona

Salamanca

OF

PORTUGAL

Segovia

ARAGON

KINGDOM OF

Madrid

Toledo

Lisbon

Tagus River

CASTILE AND

Valencia

Palma

BALEARIC ISLANDS

MEDITERRANEAN

Las Navas

de Tolosa

LEON

Segura R.

Guadiana River

Cordova

Guadalquivir River

SEA

Seville

Granada

KINGDOM OF GRANADA

Cádiz

Strait of Gibraltar

Pillars of Hercules

Tangier

MUSLIM

STATES

Prepared by
Rand McNally & Co., Chicago

Legend

4 MEDIEVAL FRANCE, SPAIN, AND THE BRITISH ISLES 1328

- England and possessions
- France
- Kingdom of Navarre
- Kingdom of Castile and Leon and dependencies
- Kingdom of Aragon and dependencies
- Kingdom of Granada
- Portugal

0   100   200

Scale in Miles

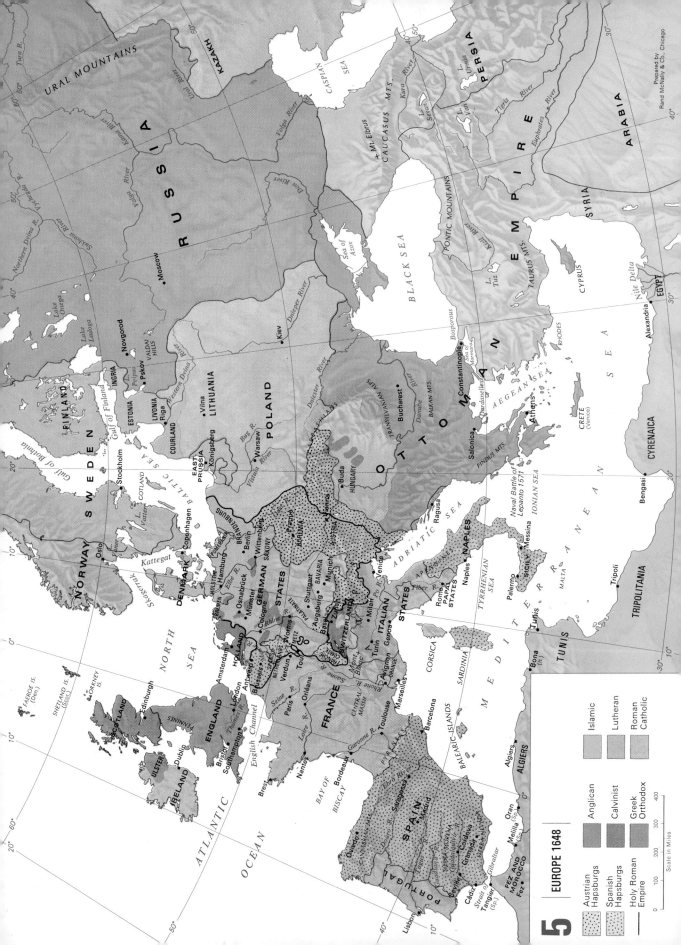

EUROPE 1648

5

Prepared by
Rand McNally & Co., Chicago

	Austrian Hapsburgs		Anglican		Islamic
	Spanish Hapsburgs		Calvinist		Lutheran
	Holy Roman Empire		Greek Orthodox		Roman Catholic

Scale in Miles
0   100   200   300   400

URAL MOUNTAINS

KAZAKH

RUSSIA

Tura R.
Vycbegda R.
Kama River
Ural River
Northern Dvina R.
Suchona River
Volga River
Western Dvina River
Don River

PERSIA

ARABIA

SYRIA

EGYPT

Kura River
Kizil River
Tigris River
Euphrates River
L. Van
L. Urmia
L. Sevan
Mt. Elbrus

CAUCASUS MTS.

PONTIC MOUNTAINS

TAURUS MTS.

CYPRUS

CASPIAN SEA

BLACK SEA

Sea of Azov

Moscow

Novgorod

Pskov

Kiev

CRIMEA

CRETE (Venice)

RHODES

CYRENAICA

Alexandria

Nile Delta

Bengasi

NORWAY

SWEDEN

FINLAND

INGRIA

ESTONIA

LIVONIA

COURLAND

LITHUANIA

POLAND

OTTOMAN EMPIRE

Lake Onega
Lake Ladoga
VALDAI HILLS
Gulf of Finland
Gulf of Bothnia
L. Vänern
L. Vättern
Dnieper River
Dniester River
Bug R.
Vistula River
Western Dvina River

Stockholm

Oslo

Copenhagen

Riga

Vilna

Königsberg

Warsaw

Buda

EAST PRUSSIA

TRANSYLVANIA

CARPATHIAN MTS.

Bucharest

Danube
Balkan Mts.

BALTIC SEA

GOTLAND

DENMARK

HOLSTEIN

BRANDENBURG

POMERANIA

GERMAN STATES

SAXONY

BOHEMIA

AUSTRIA

HUNGARY

SILESIA

Vienna

Prague

Wittenberg

Berlin

Hamburg

Bremen

Osnabrück

Münster

Cologne

Stuttgart

Augsburg

Munich

BAVARIA

Constantinople
Sea of Marmara
Dardanelles
Bosporus

Salonica

Athens

AEGEAN SEA

PINDUS MTS.

Naval Battle of Lepanto 1571

IONIAN SEA

ADRIATIC SEA

Ragusa

SWITZERLAND

PALATINATE

ALSACE

Rhine R.
Elbe R.
Main R.
Danube R.

Worms

Metz

Verdun

Basel

Zurich

Turin

Genoa

Milan

Venice

Po R.

SAVOY

Mont Blanc

ITALIAN STATES

PAPAL STATES

NAPLES

Rome

Naples

Palermo

Messina

SICILY

SARDINIA

CORSICA

TYRRHENIAN SEA

MALTA (It.)

Tiber R.
Apennines

HOLLAND

SP. NETHERLANDS

Amsterdam

London

Brussels

Antwerp

Toul

Orange

Avignon

Marseilles

FRANCE

CENTRAL MASSIF

Paris

Orléans

Nantes

Bordeaux

Toulouse

Brest

Seine R.
Loire R.
Rhône R.
Saône R.
Garonne R.

BAY OF BISCAY

PYRENEES

Barcelona

BALEARIC ISLANDS

SPAIN

Madrid

Oviedo

Saragossa

Córdova

Granada

Seville

Cádiz

Tangier (Sp.)

Gibraltar

Oran (Sp.)

Melilla (Sp.)

FEZ AND MOROCCO

Fez

Strait of Gibraltar

Lisbon

PORTUGAL

Duero R.
Douro River
Ebro River
Tagus River
Guadiana R.
Guadalquivir R.
SIERRA MORENA
SIERRA NEVADA

Algiers

ALGIERS

TUNIS

Tunis

Bona

Bona (It.)

Tripoli

TRIPOLITANIA

MEDITERRANEAN SEA

ATLANTIC OCEAN

NORTH SEA

Edinburgh

SCOTLAND

ENGLAND

IRELAND

ULSTER

Dublin

Bristol

Southampton

English Channel

PENNINES

FAEROE IS. (Den.)

SHETLAND IS. (Scot.)

ORKNEY IS.

Skagerrak

Kattegat

Thames R.

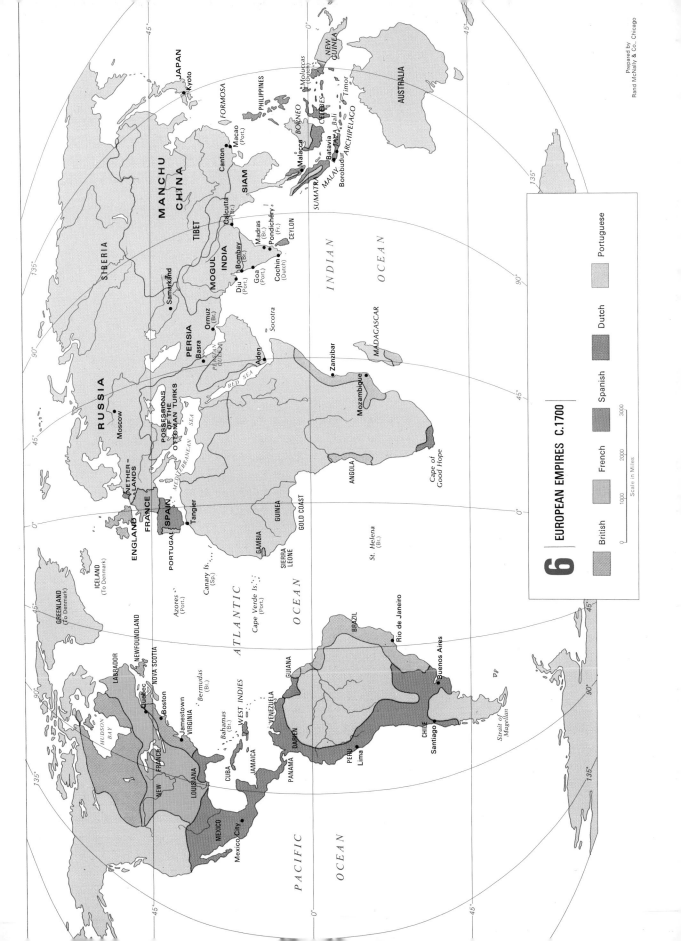

6 EUROPEAN EMPIRES C.1700

British · French · Spanish · Dutch · Portuguese

Scale in Miles
0 — 1000 — 2000 — 3000

Prepared by
Rand McNally & Co. Chicago

GREENLAND
(To Denmark)

ICELAND
(To Denmark)

LABRADOR

NEWFOUNDLAND

NOVA SCOTIA

Québec

Boston

Jamestown
VIRGINIA

HUDSON BAY

NEW FRANCE

LOUISIANA

MEXICO

Mexico City

CUBA

JAMAICA

Bahamas (Br.)

WEST INDIES

Bermudas (Br.)

PANAMA

DARIEN

VENEZUELA

GUIANA

BRAZIL

Rio de Janeiro

Buenos Aires

CHILE

Santiago

PERU

Lima

Strait of Magellan

PACIFIC OCEAN

ATLANTIC OCEAN

Azores (Port.)

Canary Is. (Sp.)

Cape Verde Is. (Port.)

St. Helena (Br.)

ENGLAND

NETHER-LANDS

FRANCE

PORTUGAL

SPAIN

Tangier

MEDITERRANEAN SEA

POSSESSIONS OF THE OTTOMAN TURKS

RUSSIA

Moscow

SIBERIA

GAMBIA

SIERRA LEONE

GUINEA

GOLD COAST

ANGOLA

Cape of Good Hope

Zanzibar

Mozambique

MADAGASCAR

Socotra

Aden

RED SEA

PERSIA

Basra

PERSIAN GULF

Ormuz (Br.)

Samarkand

MOGUL INDIA

Diu (Port.)

Goa (Port.)

Bombay (Br.)

Cochin (Dutch)

Madras (Br.)

Pondichéry (Fr.)

Calcutta (Br.)

CEYLON

TIBET

MANCHU CHINA

Canton

Macao (Port.)

FORMOSA

JAPAN

Kyoto

SIAM

PHILIPPINES

SUMATRA

Malacca

MALAY

BORNEO

CELEBES

Batavia

Borobudur

Bali

Timor

Moluccas (Dutch)

ARCHIPELAGO

NEW GUINEA

AUSTRALIA

INDIAN OCEAN

MOUNTAINS

URAL

Tunda R.

Tura R.

Tobol River

Ural River

CASPIAN SEA

PERSIA

Prepared by
Rand McNally & Co., Chicago

CAUCASUS

CIRCASSIA

PONTIC MOUNTAINS

SYRIA

Sukhona R.

Northern Dvina R.

White Sea

Arkhangelsk

L. Onega

R U S S I A N   E M P I R E

Moscow

Tsaritsyn

Volga River

Don River

Sea of Azov

BLACK SEA

Kura River

Aras River

Mt. Elbrus

CAUCASUS MTS.

TAURUS

L. Urmia

L. Van

Tigris River

Euphrates River

Beirut

Jerusalem

CYPRUS

L. Ladoga

St. Petersburg

Novgorod

L. Ilmen

VALDAI HILLS

Kharkov

Poltava

Kiev

UKRAINE

Dnieper River

Odessa

CRIMEA

Sevastopol

Sea of Marmara

Bosporus

Constantinople

Ankara

Smyrna

AEGEAN SEA

Alexandria

EGYPT

White Sea

FINLAND

Nystad

Helsinki

Narva

L. Peipus

Reval

Western Dvina R.

Niemen R.

Bug R.

Warsaw

POLAND

Vistula R.

LITHUANIA

Tilsit

BESSARABIA

MOLDAVIA

Dniester River

Pruth R.

WALLACHIA

Bucharest

TRANSYLVANIAN ALPS

Danube River

RUMANIA

BALKAN MTS.

BULGARIA

Adrianople

San Stefano

Dardanelles

GREECE

Athens

IONIAN ISLANDS (Br.)

CRETE

S E A

Gulf of Bothnia

Bergen

KINGDOM OF NORWAY AND SWEDEN

Oslo

Stockholm

Göteborg

Kattegat

Aland Is.

Gotland

Oland

BALTIC SEA

Riga

Königsberg

Danzig

PRUSSIA

KINGDOM OF PRUSSIA

Breslau

Oder

Sadowa

Troppau

CARPATHIANS

BOHEMIA

Austerlitz

EMPIRE OF AUSTRIA

Buda

Pest

KINGDOM OF HUNGARY

TRANSYLVANIA

Karlowitz

Belgrade

SERBIA

HERZEGOVINA

MONTENEGRO

ALBANIA

Ionian Sea

Adriatic Sea

IONIAN (Br.)

FAEROE IS. (Den.)

SHETLAND IS. (Br.)

ORKNEY IS. (Br.)

Edinburgh

THE UNITED KINGDOM OF GREAT BRITAIN AND IRELAND

Dublin

IRISH SEA

Liverpool

Manchester

Birmingham

London

ENGLISH CHANNEL

Dover

NORTH SEA

Copenhagen

KINGDOM OF DENMARK

HOLSTEIN

SCHLESWIG

Hamburg

Bremen

HANOVER

KINGDOM OF THE NETHERLANDS

Amsterdam

The Hague

Utrecht

Antwerp

Brussels

BELGIUM

Waterloo

Sedan

Valmy

Berlin

BRANDENBURG

SAXONY

Leipzig

Cologne

Aix-la-Chapelle

Frankfurt

BERG

NASSAU

HESSE

BADEN

WÜRTEMBERG

BAVARIA

Munich

Augsburg

Ulm

Prague

Carlsbad

SWITZERLAND

Neuchâtel

Geneva

Mt. Blanc

ALPS

TYROL

Vienna

Laibach

DALMATIA

CROATIA

SLAVONIA

BOSNIA

LIECHTENSTEIN

VENETIA

Venice

LOMBARDY

Verona

PIEDMONT

KINGDOM OF SARDINIA

Nice

MONACO

PARMA

MODENA

LUCCA

TUSCANY

Florence

SAN MARINO

PAPAL STATES

Rome

APENNINES

Corsica (Fr.)

ATLANTIC OCEAN

Le Havre

Paris

Versailles

Seine River

Loire River

Nantes

La Rochelle

FRANCE

CENTRAL MASSIF

Rhône R.

Saône R.

Bordeaux

BAY OF BISCAY

Garonne River

PYRENEES

ANDORRA

Barcelona

BALEARIC ISLANDS

Marseilles

MEDITERRANEAN SEA

Tyrrhenian Sea

Naples

KINGDOM OF NAPLES AND SICILY

Palermo

MALTA (Br.)

Douro River

PORTUGAL

Lisbon

SPAIN

Madrid

Tagus River

Guadiana River

SIERRA MORENA

SIERRA NEVADA

Guadalquivir River

CANTABRIAN MTS.

Ebro River

Cadiz

Cape Trafalgar

Gibraltar (Br.)

Strait of Gibraltar

Ceuta (Sp.)

Melilla (Sp.)

MOROCCO

Casablanca

ATLAS MOUNTAINS

Oran

Algiers

ALGERIA

Tunis

TUNIS

Tripoli

TRIPOLITANIA

Bengasi

7 | EUROPE 1815

Boundary of German Confederation

Small German States

Scale of Miles

0   100   200   300   400

EUROPE AUGUST 1939

ATLANTIC

OCEAN

London
Amsterdam • Berlin
Brussels • Warsaw
Paris
Danube R.
Vienna
Budapest
Belgrade
BLACK SEA
Rome
Constantinople
Madrid
Lisbon
Athens
Tehran
Tangier
SP. MOROCCO
Algiers
Tunis
Casablanca
MOROCCO
ATLAS MOUNTAINS
TUNISIA
Tripoli
Bengasi
Alexandria
Damascus
Baghdad
Jerusalem
IFNI
Cairo
ALGERIA
LIBYA
EGYPT
ARABIA
MADEIRA IS. (Port.)
CANARY IS. (Br.)
RIO DE ORO
AHAGGAR MTS.
LIBYAN DESERT
Aswan
Villa Cisneros
S A H A R A
TIBESTI MASSIF
NUBIAN DESERT
Mecca PENINSULA
FRENCH WEST AFRICA
ANGLO-
Dakar
Timbuktu
ERITREA
GAMBIA
SENEGAL R.
Omdurman
Khartoum
Asmara
Aden
Bissau
PORT. GUINEA
Bamako
L. Chad
CHAD
Ft. Lamy
EGYPTIAN
FR. SOM.
Djibouti
Berbera
FRENCH GUINEA
Kano
Shari R.
SUDAN
BR. SOM.
SIERRA LEONE
Freetown
NIGERIA
Benue R.
Addis Ababa
Monrovia
LIBERIA
IVORY COAST
GOLD COAST
TOGO
DAHOMEY
Lagos
CAMEROONS
EQUATORIAL AFRICA
UBANGI-SHARI
ABYSSINIA (ETHIOPIA)
Accra
Lome
Douala
Bomu R.
Uele R.
FERNANDO PO (Sp.)
GULF OF GUINEA
PRINCIPE (Port.)
RIO MUNI
Libreville
CONGO
Congo
L. Albert
Stanleyville
UGANDA
KENYA (BR. EAST AFR.)
Mogadishu
ITALIAN SOMALILAND
SAO TOME (Port.)
ANNOBÓN (Sp.)
GABON
FRENCH
BASIN
Entebbe
L. Rudolf
Brazzaville
BELGIAN
Lake Victoria
Nairobi
INDIAN
CABINDA
Léopoldville
CONGO
Mt. Kilimanjaro
Mombasa
OCEAN
Kasai R.
Tabora
ZANZIBAR (Br.)
ALDABRA (Br.)
Luanda
GERMAN EAST AFRICA
Dar-es-Salaam
Lake Tanganyika
9 AFRICA 1914
COMORO IS. (Fr.)
British
French
German
Belgian
Portuguese
Italian
Spanish
Benguela
ANGOLA (PORT. WEST AFR.)
Lake Nyasa
MADAGASCAR
Tama
Tananariv
NORTHERN RHODESIA
NYASALAND
Blantyre
Zambezi R.
0   400   800
Scale in Miles
Livingstone
Salisbury
SOUTHERN RHODESIA
Beira
MOZAMBIQUE (PORT. EAST AFR.)
GERMAN
Victoria Falls
SOUTHWEST
BECHUANALAND
AFRICA
Windhoek
KALAHARI DESERT
Mafeking
Pretoria
Lourenço Marques
Walvis Bay
Limpopo R.
Johannesburg
SWAZILAND
Lüderitz
Orange R.
BASUTOLAND
Durban
UNION OF
SOUTH AFRICA
East London
Cape Town
Port Elizabeth
Cape of Good Hope
Prepared by Udi-Map Inc. Palatine

ATLANTIC

OCEAN

Azores
(Port.)

Madeira Is.
(Port.)

Canary Is.
(Sp.)

NORTH
SEA

BALTIC
SEA

Dublin
London
Amsterdam • Berlin • Warsaw • Moscow
Brussels • Prague
Paris • E U R O P E
Bern • Vienna • Budapest
Belgrade • Bucharest
Rome • BLACK SEA • CAUCASUS MTS.
Madrid
Lisbon
MEDITERRANEAN
Algiers
Tunis • CRETE • SEA • CYPRUS
Strait of Gibraltar • Tangier
Rabat • ATLAS • MOUNTAINS • TUNISIA • Tripoli
Casablanca • MOROCCO
Agadir
IFNI • TUNISIA
Sidi Ifni
Aiún

ALPS
Rhine R.
Warsaw
Danube R.
Dnieper
Volga
Don R.
CASPIAN SEA
Aral Sea
Baku

Istanbul
Ankara
Athens
Beirut
Tel Aviv • Damascus • Amman
Jerusalem • ASIA
Israeli – occupied area
June, 1967
ARABIAN
Baghdad
Euphrates R. • Tigris R.
Tehran
PERSIAN GULF
Riyadh
Mecca
PENINSULA
Sana

SPANISH
SAHARA

ALGERIA

LIBYA

UNITED
ARAB
REPUBLIC
(EGYPT)

LIBYAN
DESERT

RED SEA

Bengasi
Alexandria
Cairo
Suez Canal
Nile R.

NUBIAN
DESERT

Aden
Gulf of Aden

MAURITANIA

S A H A R A

MALI

NIGER

TIBESTI
MASSIF

CHAD

Khartoum

SUDAN

Asmara
ERITREA
AFARS AND
ISSAS(F.) • Djibouti
AMHARA
L.
Tana

Nouakchott

S U D A N

Senegal R.
Niger R.

Dakar
GAMBIA
Bathurst
PORT
GUINEA
Bissau

SENEGAL
Bamako
Niamey
Kano
Fort-Lamy
L. Chad

Conakry
Freetown

GUINEA
UPPER VOLTA
Ouagadougou

NIGERIA

CENTRAL
AFRICAN REPUBLIC

SIERRA
LEONE
IVORY
COAST • GHANA
Lomé
DAHOMEY
TOGO
Accra

LIBERIA
Monrovia • Abidjan
Cape Palmas

Benue R.
Lagos
Porto-
Novo

CAMEROON

Bangui

Bomu R.

Addis Ababa
PLATEAU
ETHIOPIA

SOMALI
REPUBLIC

GULF OF GUINEA

Santa Isabel
EQUATORIAL
GUINEA
Príncipe
(Port.)
São Tomé
(Port.)
Annobón
(Sp.)

Yaoundé
Bata
Libreville

GABON

CONGO

CONGO
BASIN

CONGO

Ubangi R.
Uélé
Congo R.

L.
Albert

L. Rudolf

UGANDA
Kampala

KENYA
Mt. Kenya
Nairobi

Mogadiscio

ATLANTIC

OCEAN

Ascension
(Br.)

St. Helena
(Br.)

Brassaville
CABINDA
(Angola)

Kinshasa
(Léopoldville)

Luanda

Kasai R.

Kwango R.
Kasai R.

Kisangani
(Stanleyville)

THE
CONGO

RWANDA • Kigali
BURUNDI • Bujumbura

Lake
Victoria

Kilimanjaro

Dar es Salaam • Zanzibar

TANZANIA

INDIAN

OCEAN

Aldabra Is.
(Br.)

Benguela

ANGOLA
(Port.)

Cunene R.

L.
Tanganyika

ZAMBIA
Lusaka
Zambezi R. • Zumba

MALAWI
L.
Nyasa

Comoro Is.
(Fr.)

MADAGASCAR

SOUTH WEST

AFRICA
(S. Africa
Admin.)

Windhoek

Walvis Bay
(S. Africa)

KALAHARI
DESERT

BOTSWANA
Gaberones
Serowe

Victoria
Falls
Kuriba
Lake

RHODESIA
Salisbury
Zimbabwe

Ruvuma R.

MOZAMBIQUE
(Port.)

MOZAMBIQUE CHANNEL

Tananarive

MALAGASY
REPUBLIC

Mafeking
Johannesburg
Pretoria
SOUTH

Namib Desert
Orange R.

AFRICA
Mbabane
SWAZILAND
Maseru
LESOTHO
Durban

DRAKENSBERG
Lourenço Marques

Cape Town
Cape of Good Hope
Port Elizabeth

Prepared by
Rand McNally & Co., Chicago

OCEAN

NEW SIBERIAN ISLANDS

Wrangel I.

CHERSKIY MTS.

Lene River

VERKHOYANSK

Verkhoyansk

Zhigansk

MOUNTAINS

Vilyuy River

Yakutsk

LIST REPUBLIC

Aldan River

Seymchan

Kolyma R.

Markovo

ANADYR RANGE

60°

BERING SEA

Magadan

SEA OF OKHOTSK

KAMCHATKA PENINSULA

Petropavlovsk

Aleutian Islands

Amur River

PUBLICS

Irkutsk

Ulan-Ude

Lake Baikal

Chita

YABLONOVY RANGE

MONGOLIA

GOBI DESERT

GREAT KHINGAN MTS.

Aleksandrovsk

SAKHALIN

Korsakov

Kuril Islands

180°

Khabarovsk

Harbin

Kalgan

Paotow

Peking (Peiping)

Mukden

Port Arthur

Tientsin

Pyongyang

Vladivostok

NORTH KOREA

SOUTH KOREA

Seoul

KOREA

SEA OF JAPAN

HOKKAIDO

JAPAN

HONSHU

NAN SHAN

Koko Nor

Lanchow

Sian

Yellow River

(Huang)

YELLOW SEA

Pusan

Kitakyushu

KYUSHU

Osaka

Tokyo

SHIKOKU

PACIFIC

TIBET

Lhasa

Yangtze River

Wuhan

Shanghai

EAST CHINA SEA

Ryukyu Islands

30°

CHINA

MALAYAS

SIKKIM

BHUTAN

Chungking

Han R.

Foochow

NAN LING

Taipei

OCEAN

ras

Dacca

Brahmaputra R.

PAK.

Calcutta

BURMA

Irrawaddy R.

Kunming

Mekong River

Canton

Kowloon

Macao (Port.)

Victoria

HONG KONG (Br.)

TAIWAN (FORMOSA)

Hanoi

HAINAN

Rangoon

Vientiane

NORTH VIETNAM

LAOS

VIETNAM

SOUTH CHINA

LUZON

Quezon City

Manila

PHILIPPINES

PHILIPPINE

Guam I. (U.S.)

BAY OF BENGAL

as

THAILAND

Bangkok

SOUTH VIETNAM

CAMBODIA

Phnom Penh

Saigon

SEA

SEA

Celebes Sea

MINDANAO

EYLON

mbo

MALAYSIA

BRUNEI (Br.)

SABAH

MALAYA

Kuala Lumpur

SINGAPORE

SARAWAK

BORNEO

0°

SUMATRA

CELEBES

MOLUCCA ISLANDS

NEW IRELAND

OCEAN

Sukarnapura

NEW

TERRITORY OF NEW GUINEA (Austl.)

WEST IRIAN (Indo.)

GUINEA

PAPUA (Austl.)

NEW BRITAIN

Djakarta

Surabaja

JAVA

FLORES

Dili

PORT. TIMOR

TIMOR

INDONESIA

OCUSSI (Port. Timor)

Port Moresby

AUSTRALIA

90°

120°

150°

ATLANTIC

OCEAN

Bermuda Is.
(Br.)

Great
Salt Lake

ROCKY MOUNTAINS

Colorado R.

UNITED STATES

Chicago
Washington
• New York

Denver

St. Louis

Missouri River

Mississippi River

Dallas

New Orleans

GULF OF CALIFORNIA

SIERRA MADRE OCCIDENTAL

Laredo

Monterrey

SIERRA MADRE ORIENTAL

Tampico

M E X I C O

GULF OF MEXICO

Miami

Havana

BAHAMA ISLANDS (Br.)

WEST

C U B A

Guadalajara

Mexico City

Chapultepec

Acapulco

Mérida

Chichen Itza

Uxmal

Veracruz

Oaxaca

Tikal

BRITISH HONDURAS

Belize

GUATEMALA

Guatemala

HONDURAS

San Salvador

EL SALVADOR

NICARAGUA

Tegucigalpa

Managua

COSTA RICA

San José

CANAL ZONE (U.S.)

Colón

Panamá

PANAMA

Kingston

JAMAICA

Port-au-Prince

HAITI

DOMINICAN REPUBLIC

Santo Domingo

PUERTO RICO (U.S.)

Guadeloupe (Fr.)

Martinique (Fr.)

BARBADOS

I N D I E S

CARIBBEAN SEA

TRINIDAD AND TOBAGO

Port-of-Spain

Barranquilla

Lake Maracaibo

Caracas

Orinoco R.

VENEZUELA

Georgetown

GUYANA

Paramaribo

SURINAM

FRENCH GUIANA

Cayenne

Bogotá

COLOMBIA

Buenaventura

Magdalena

GUIANA HIGHLANDS

Rio Negro

Japurá R.

Quito

ECUADOR

Guayaquil

GALÁPAGOS IS. (Ec.)

Iquitos

Marañón R.

Amazon River

Manaus

Negro River

Belém

PERU

Ucayali R.

Purús R.

Madeira River

Tapajós R.

Xingu R.

Tocantins R.

B R A Z I L

Recife

Lima

Arequipa

Lake Titicaca

La Paz

Guaporé R.

Mamoré R.

PLATEAU OF MATO GROSSO

BRAZILIAN HIGHLANDS

São Francisco R.

Brasília

Salvador

BOLIVIA

Sucre

Rio Grande

Bello Horizonte

PACIFIC

OCEAN

Antofagasta

ATACAMA DESERT

GRAN CHACO

PARAGUAY

Pilcomayo R.

Asunción

São Paulo

Rio de Janeiro

Santos

Tucumán

Salado R.

Paraná River

Iguassú Falls

Uruguay R.

Córdoba

Mt. Aconcagua

Valparaíso

Santiago

Mendoza

A R G E N T I N A

C H I L E

Santa Fé

Rosario

URUGUAY

Montevideo

Buenos Aires

Rio de la Plata

PAMPAS

Colorado R.

Bahía Blanca

ATLANTIC

OCEAN

Valdivia

Chubut R.

P A T A G O N I A

ANDES MTS.

FALKLAND IS. (Br.)

Punta Arenas

TIERRA DEL FUEGO

SOUTH GEORGIA (Br.)

Cape Horn

Drake Passage

SOUTH ORKNEY IS. (Br.)

ANTARCTICA

12 | **LATIN AMERICA**

Map information based upon
data available August 1968

0   400   800

Scale in Miles

Prepared by
Rand McNally & Co., Chicago

SOVIET UNION

KYZYL KUM DESERT

KARA KUM DESERT

KOPET MTS.

Amu Darya R.

Chardzhou
Maimana
Kandahar
AFGHANISTAN
Herat
Helmand R.
PAKISTAN
Meshed
Ashkhabad
Krasnovodsk
Birjand
Kerman
I R A N
PLATEAU OF IRAN
DASHT-I-KAVIR (DESERT)
Yezd
Shiraz
Isfahan
Tehran
Hamadan
ELBURZ MTS.
Resht
Baku
CASPIAN SEA
Tabriz
L. Urmia
L. Sevan
MT. ARARAT
ZAGROS MOUNTAINS
Bushire
Abadan
Kermanshah
KURDISTAN
Kirkuk
Mosul

ARABIAN SEA
Masqat
Sur
MUSCAT AND OMAN
GULF OF OMAN
KURIA MURIA IS. (Br.)
TRUCIAL COAST
Sharja
Boundary
Sayhut
PERSIAN GULF
BAHREIN
Doha
QATAR
Dhahran
Hofuf
Mukalla
YEMEN
SOUTHERN
AL KHALI
R U B'
QUARTER
(E M P T Y)
Undefined
Riyadh
Buraida
S A U D I   A R A B I A
N E J D
Hail
AN NAFUD
Medina
Mecca
ASIR
San'a
YEMEN
Aden
Hodeida
Taima
Yanbú
Jiddah
HEJAZ
R E D   S E A
Port Sudan
Asmara
ETHIOPIA
Kassala
Atbara
Omdurman
Khartoum
Blue Nile
White Nile
S U D A N
El Obeid
Dongola
Wadi Halfa
Aswan
Kharga
Qena
Asyut
El Minya
El Faiyum
UNITED ARAB REPUBLIC (EGYPT)
Siwa
LIBYAN DESERT
L I B Y A
Tobruk
Bengasi
El Alamein
Alexandria
Cairo
Port Said
Suez
SINAI
Gulf of Suez
Gulf of Aqaba
Elath
Eilat
JORDAN
Amman
Jerusalem
Tel-Aviv
ISRAEL
Beirut
LEBANON
Damascus
Homs
Hama
SYRIA
Aleppo
SYRIAN DESERT
Euphrates
Baghdad
Karbala
An Najaf
I R A Q
Tigris
Basra
NEUTRAL ZONES
Kuwait
KUWAIT
Gaziantep
Adana
TAURUS MTS.
Konya
Ankara
Kayseri
Eskisehir
Bursa
Istanbul
Sea of Marmara
Uskudar
Izmir
AEGEAN SEA
GREECE
Athens
Thessaloniki
Samsun
Trabzon
Erzurum
Diyarbekir
T U R K E Y
Kura R.
Tiflis
MEDITERRANEAN SEA
CRETE
RHODES
CYPRUS
Nicosia